Karl A Sl[illegible]

# AMERICAN GOVERNMENT

## Freedom and Power

6TH EDITION

6TH EDITION

Theodore J. Lowi
CORNELL UNIVERSITY

and

Benjamin Ginsberg
THE JOHNS HOPKINS UNIVERSITY

# AMERICAN GOVERNMENT

## Freedom and Power

W • W • NORTON & COMPANY NEW YORK • LONDON

FOR OUR FAMILIES:

Angele, Anna, and Jason Lowi
Sandy, Cindy, and Alex Ginsberg


Printed in the United States of America

The text of this book is composed in ITC Galliard
with the display set in New Baskerville, Snell Bold, and Shelley Andante.
Composition by TSI Graphics
Manufacturing by The Courier Companies, Inc.
Book design by Jack Meserole and Mary McDonnell

Library of Congress Cataloging-in-Publication Data

Lowi, Theodore J.
American government : freedom and power / Theodore J. Lowi and Benjamin Ginsberg.—6th ed.
p. cm.
Includes bibliographical references and index.
**ISBN 0-393-97471-5 (pbk.)**
1. United States—Politics and government. I. Title.
JK271.L68 2000
320.473—dc21 99-37633

W. W. Norton & Company, Inc., 500 Fifth Avenue, New York, N.Y. 10110
www.wwnorton.com

W. W. Norton & Company Ltd., 10 Coptic Street, London WC1A 1PU
1 2 3 4 5 6 7 8 9 0

# Contents

# INSTITUTIONS

POLITICS

# PART 4
# GOVERNANCE

## APPENDIX

# Preface

In the years since the original publication of *American Government: Freedom and Power,* the world has changed in a number of surprising ways. Symbolized by the destruction of the Berlin Wall, the Soviet Union has collapsed, Russia has been compelled to seek economic aid from the West, and the cold war that once seemed to threaten the survival of civilization has come to an end. In the Middle East, the United States fought a short but decisive war against Iraq and is now leading a diplomatic initiative that may, after fifty years of violence, bring about some solution to the problems of the Middle East. In South Africa, the hated system of apartheid has disintegrated in the face of domestic opposition and international pressure. The nations of Western Europe have taken giant steps toward economic and political integration.

American domestic politics also seem to be undergoing dramatic change. After years of Democratic control, both the House and Senate were captured by the Republicans in the 1994 elections. With the once solidly Democratic South becoming solidly Republican, we may be witnessing a major electoral realignment that will leave the GOP in control of the nation's government. Of course, some elements of American politics never seem to change. Political participation in the United States is as low as ever.

In a changing world it is more important than ever to understand the politics of the United States. More than at any time since the Second World War, the world is looking to America for leadership and for an example of popular government in action. Throughout the world, America—despite its problems and faults—symbolizes the combination of freedom and power to which so many now aspire. This makes the task of our book all the more important.

The collaboration on this book began nearly ten years before its publication, and the book is in every way a product of collaboration in teaching, research, and writing. Each author has taught other courses—for forty-one and twenty-seven years, respectively—and has written other books; but we agree that no course has been more challenging than the introductory course, and no book has been more difficult to write. Someone once asked if it is difficult for scholars to "write down" to introductory students. No. It is difficult to "write up" to them. Introductory students, of whatever age or reading level, need more, require more, and expect more of a book.

A good teaching book, like a good novel or play, is written on two levels. One is the level of the narrative, the story line, the characters in action. The second is the level of character development, of the argument of the book or play. We would not be the first to assert that theater is an aspect of politics, but our book may be unusual to the extent that we took that assertion as a guide. We have packed it full of narrative—with characters and with the facts about the complex situations in which they find themselves. We have at the same time been determined not to lose sight of the second level, yet we have tried to avoid making the second level so prominent as to define us as preachers rather than teachers.

The book is only one product of our collaboration. The other important product is about 5,000 Cornell and Johns Hopkins students who took the courses out of which this book grew. There is no way to convey adequately our appreciation to those students. Their raw intelligence was not satisfied until the second level could provide a logic linking the disparate parts of what we were asserting was a single system of government. And these linkages had to be made in ordinary language. We hope we brought this to the book.

We hope also that we brought over from our teaching experience a full measure of sympathy for all who teach the introductory course, most particularly those who are obliged to teach the course from departmental necessity rather than voluntarily as a desired part of their career. And we hope our book will help them appreciate the course as we do—as an opportunity to make sense of a whole political system, one's own, and one of the largest, most durable, and most consequential ever. Much can be learned about the system from a re-examination of the innumerable familiar facts, under the still more challenging condition that the facts be somehow interesting, significant, and, above all, linked.

This points to what must be the most troublesome, sometimes the most embarrassing, problem for this course, for this book, and for political science in general: All Americans are to a great extent familiar with the politics and government of their own country. No fact is intrinsically difficult to grasp, and in such an open society, facts abound. In America, many facts are commonplace that are suppressed elsewhere. The ubiquity of political commonplaces is indeed a problem, but it can be turned into a virtue. These very commonplaces give us a vocabulary that is widely shared, and such a vocabulary enables us to communicate effectively at the first level of the book, avoiding abstract concepts and professional language (jargon). Reaching beyond the commonplaces to the second level also identifies what is to us the single most important task of the teacher of political science—to confront the million commonplaces and to choose from among them the small number of really significant concepts. Students give us proportion; we must in turn give the students priorities. Virtually everything we need to know about the institutions and processes of government and politics is readily at hand. But to choose a few commonplaces from the millions—there's the rub.

We have tried to provide a framework to help the teachers make choices among commonplaces and to help the students make some of the choices for themselves. This is good political science, and it is good citizenship, which means more than mere obedience and voting; it means participation through constructive criticism, being able to pierce through the periphery of the great information explosion to the core of lasting political reality.

Our framework is freedom and power. To most Americans that means freedom *versus* governmental power, because Americans have been raised to believe that every expansion of the government's power involves a contraction of personal freedom. Up to a point we agree with this traditional view. The institutions of American government are in fact built on a contradiction: Popular freedom and governmental power *are* contradictory, and it is the purpose of our Constitution to build a means of coping with that contradiction. But as Supreme Court justices sometimes say to their colleagues, "We concur, dissenting in part." For in truth, freedom and power are related to each other as husband and wife—each with some conflicting requirements, but neither able to produce, as a family, without the other.

Just as freedom and power are in conflict, so are they complementary. *There can be little freedom, if any, without governmental power.* Freedom of any one individual depends fundamentally on the restraints of everyone else in their vicinity. Most of these restraints are self-imposed. We call that *civility,* respect for others borne of our awareness that it is a condition of their respect for us. Other restraints vital to personal freedom are imposed spontaneously by society. Europeans call those restraints *civil society;* sociologists call them *institutions.* Institutions exist as society's means of maintaining order and predictability through routines, customs, shared values. But even in the most stable society, the restraints of civility and of civil society are incomplete and insufficient; there remains a sphere of deliberate restraint that calls for the exercise of public control (public power). Where society falls down, or where new events and new technologies produce new stresses, or where even the most civil of human beings find their basic needs in conflict with others, there will be an exercise of public control, or public power. Private property, that great bastion of personal freedom in the Western world, would disappear without elaborate government controls over trespass.

If freedom were only a matter of the absence of control, there would be no need for a book like ours. In fact, there would be little need for political science at all. But politics, however far away in the national or the state capital, is a matter of life and death. It can be as fascinating as any good novel or adventure film if the key political question is one's own survival or the survival of one's society. We have tried to write each chapter of this book in such a way that the reader is tempted to ask what that government institution, that agency, this committee or that election, this group or that amendment has to do with *me* and *us,* and how has it come to be that way. That's what freedom and power are all about—my freedom and your restraint, my restraint and your freedom.

Having chosen a framework for the book there was also a need for a method. The method must be loyal to the framework; it must facilitate the effort to choose which facts are essential, and it must assist in evaluating those facts in ways that not only enlighten students but enable them to engage in analysis and evaluation for themselves. Although we are not bound exclusively to a single method in any scientific or philosophic sense, the method most consistently employed is one of history, or history as development: First, we present the state of affairs, describing the legislature, the party, the agency, or policy, with as many of the facts as are necessary to tell the story and to enable us to reach the broader question of freedom versus governmental power. Next, we ask how we have gotten to where we are. By what series of steps, and when by choice, and when by accident? To what extent was the history of Congress or of the parties or the presidency a fulfillment of constitutional principle, and when were the developments a series of dogged responses to economic necessity? History is our method because it helps choose which facts are significant. History also helps those who would like to try to explain why we are where we are. But more important even than explanation, history helps us make judgments. In other words, we look less to causes and more to consequences. Political science cannot be satisfied with objective description, analysis, and explanation. Political science would be a failure if it did not have a vision about the ideal as well as the real. What is a good and proper balance between freedom and governmental power? What can a constitution do about it? What can enlightened people do about it?

Evaluation makes political science worth doing but also more difficult to do. Academics make a distinction between the hard sciences and the soft sciences, implying that hard science is the only real science: laboratory, people in white coats, precision instruments making measurements to several decimal points, testing hypotheses with "hard data." But as medical scientist Jared Diamond observes, that is a recent and narrow view, considering that science in Latin means knowledge and careful observation. Diamond suggests, and we agree, that a better distinction is between hard (i.e., difficult) science and easy science, with political science fitting into the hard category, precisely because many of the most significant phenomena in the world cannot be put in a test tube and measured to several decimal points. We must nevertheless be scientific about them. And more: Unlike physical scientists, social scientists have an obligation to judge whether the reality could be better. In trying to meet that obligation, we hope to demonstrate how interesting and challenging political science can be.

## THE DESIGN OF THE BOOK

The objective we have taken upon ourselves in writing this book is thus to advance our understanding of freedom and power by exploring in the fullest possible detail the way Americans have tried to balance the two through careful crafting of the rules, through constructing balanced institutions, and by maintaining moderate forms of organized politics. The book is divided into four parts, reflecting the historical process by which freedom and governmental power are (or are not) kept in balance. Part I, "Foundations," comprises the chapters concerned with the writing of the rules of the contract. The founding of 1787–1789 put it all together, but that was actually a second effort after a first failure. The original contract, the Articles of Confederation, did not achieve an acceptable balance—too much freedom, and not enough power. The second founding, the Constitution ratified in 1789, was itself an imperfect effort to establish the rules, and within two years new terms were added—the first ten amendments, called the Bill of Rights. And for the next century and a half following their ratification in 1791, the courts played umpire and translator in the struggle to interpret those terms. Chapter 1 introduces our theme. Chapter 2 concentrates on the founding itself. Chapters 3 and 4 chronicle the long struggle to establish what was meant by the three great principles of limited government, *federalism, separation of powers,* and *individual liberties and rights.*

Part II, "Institutions," includes the chapters sometimes referred to as the "nuts and bolts." But none of these particles of government mean anything except in the larger context of the goals governments must meet and the limits, especially of procedure, that have been imposed upon them. Chapter 5 is an introduction to the fundamental problem of *representative government* as this has been institutionalized in Congress. Congress, with all its problems, is the most creative legislative body in the world. But how well does Congress provide a meeting ground between consent and governing? How are society's demands taken into account in debates on the floor of Congress and deliberations by its committees? What interests turn out to be most effectively "represented" in Congress? What is the modern Congress's constituency?

Chapter 6 explores the same questions for the presidency. Although Article II of the Constitution provides that the president should see that the laws made by Congress are "faithfully executed," the presidency was always part of our theory of representative government, and the modern presidency has increasingly become a law *maker* rather than merely a law implementer. What, then, does the strong presidency do to the conduct and the consequences of representative government? Chapter 7 treats the executive branch as an entity separate from the presidency, but ultimately it has to be brought back into the general process of representative government. That, indeed, is the overwhelming problem of what we call "bureaucracy in a democracy." After spelling out the organization and workings of "the bureaucracy" in detail, we then turn to an evaluation of the role of Congress and the president in imposing some political accountability on an executive branch composed of roughly five million civilian and military personnel.

Chapter 8 on the judiciary should not be lost in the shuffle. Referred to by Hamilton as "the least dangerous branch," the judiciary truly has become a co-equal branch, to such an extent that if Hamilton were alive today he would probably eat his words.

Part III we entitle simply "Politics" because politics encompasses all the efforts by any and all individuals and groups inside as well as outside the government to determine what government will do and on whose behalf it will be done. Our chapters take the order of our conception of how politics developed since the Age of Revolution and how politics works today: Chapter 9, "Public Opinion"; Chapter 10, "Elections"; Chapter 11, "Political Parties"; Chapter 12, "Groups and Interests"; and Chapter 13, "The Media."

Part IV is entitled "Governance." These are chapters primarily about public policies, which are the most deliberate and goal-oriented aspects of the still-larger phenomenon of "government in action." We begin Chapter 14, "Government in Action: Public Policy and the Economy," by looking at policies that are concerned with the conduct of business, the obligations of employers, the rights and limits of workers to organize, and the general ability of the economy to operate without flying apart. We conclude with the "techniques of control" that any public policy goal must embody if the goal is even partially to be fulfilled. These "techniques of control" are the analytic units of the succeeding policy chapters. Chapter 15, "Government and Society," looks at similar "techniques of control" as these are utilized to affect conduct in the society at large, outside and beyond the economic marketplace. Since ours is a commercial society, many policies aimed at the society have direct economic consequences. For example, many aspects of what we call the welfare state are social policies, but they have a profound effect on the economy, because welfare, as we put it, changes the rules governing who shall be poor. Chapter 16, "Foreign Policy and Democracy," turns to the international realm and

America's place in it. Our concern here is to understand American foreign policies and why we have adopted the policies that we have. Given the traditional American fear of "the state" and the genuine danger of international involvements to domestic democracy, a chapter on foreign policies is essential to a book on American government and also reveals a great deal about America as a culture.

Chapter 17 is our analysis of the state of the American politics today. Much has been said and written about the state of American politics, but we believe that to fully understand the transformations occurring in American politics, one must assess the historical roots of these changes. However, we recognize that, although there may be a pattern to American politics, it is not readily predictable. One need only contemplate the year-long nomination of presidential candidates to recognize how much confusion and downright disorder there is in what we political scientists blithely call "political process." Chapter 17 is an evaluation of that process. We ask whether our contemporary political process is consistent with good government. Unfortunately, the answer is not entirely positive. We conclude by assessing America's role as both economic and political leader in the world. Is "America the Beacon?" the role for the United States in the twenty-first century?

## The Lowi and Ginsberg webBOOK

With this new Sixth Edition, the Lowi and Ginsberg webBOOK, an interactive Web site supporting the text and authored by Derek Reveron, has been dramatically rethought and revised to link material closely from the text to the Web site. Students and professors using the Lowi and Ginsberg webBOOK will find that the site "opens" the book in new and highly original ways. The webBOOK is organized into three separate units:

*Investigate* These features tie in to the "Debating the Issues" boxes and the "Globalization and Democracy" photo essays that appear throughout the text. On the Lowi and Ginsberg webBOOK, links are built into these features to direct the user to new sources on that topic, which can be found on the Web.

*Review* These features include more review of the central question of each chapter as well as a review of the "nuts and bolts" material contained in each chapter.

*Participate* These two types of Web-based exercises link to the analytical features of the text. "Analyzing Politics" exercises get students to assess arguments about the political process through more in-depth analysis of data found on the Web. "Current Politics" exercises challenge students to tie arguments or discussions from the text to stories of current political events provided by media organizations, such as the *Washington Post National Weekly Edition,* National Public Radio, or C-SPAN, that are linked to the Lowi and Ginsberg webBOOK.

The webBOOK also includes an interactive practice quiz for each chapter that immediately grades students' responses and directs them to the portions of the text they need to review.

The webBOOK is valuable not only for helping students prepare for exams, but also for keeping them up-to-date on current events and issues. In addition, the Lowi and Ginsberg webBOOK includes links to "e-2000," a Norton Web site devoted to the latest in election coverage, including weekly updates of the unfolding campaigns as well as analysis of election results. E-2000's analytical focus on the role of the Internet in the political process will also help students think critically about the changing face of today's politics. Finally, the e-2000 icon appears throughout our text of *American Government.* This marginal icon indicates an additional discussion of that topic on the e-2000 Web site.

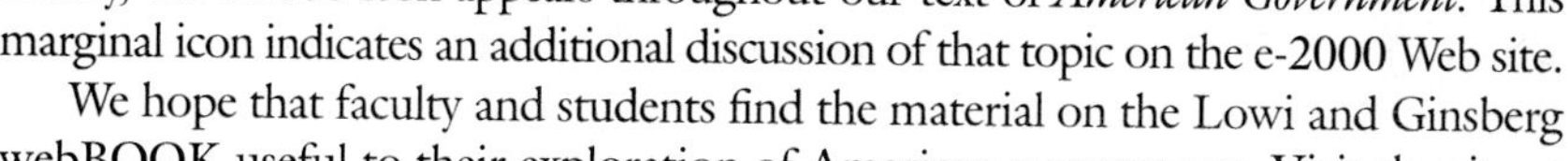

We hope that faculty and students find the material on the Lowi and Ginsberg webBOOK useful to their exploration of American government. Visit the site at **http://www.wwnorton.com/lowi6**

## ACKNOWLEDGMENTS

Our students at Cornell and Johns Hopkins have already been identified as an essential factor in the writing of this book. They have been our most immediate intellectual community, a hospitable one indeed. Another part of our community, perhaps a large suburb, is the discipline of political science itself. Our debt to the scholarship of our colleagues is scientifically measurable, probably to several decimal points, in the footnotes of each chapter. Despite many complaints that the field is too scientific or not scientific enough, political science is alive and well in the United States. It is an aspect of democracy itself, and it has grown and changed in response to the developments in government and politics that we have chronicled in our book. If we did a "time line" on the history of political science, as we have done in each chapter of the book, it would show a close association with developments in "the American state." Sometimes the discipline has been out of phase and critical; at other times, it has been in phase and perhaps apologetic. But political science has never been at a loss for relevant literature, and without it, our job would have been impossible.

There have, of course, been individuals on whom we have relied in particular. Of all writers, living and dead, we find ourselves most in debt to the writing of two—James Madison and Alexis de Tocqueville. Many other great authors have shaped us as they have shaped all political scientists. But Madison and Tocqueville have stood for us not only as the bridge to all timeless political problems; they represent the ideal of political science itself—that political science must be steadfastly scientific in the search for what is, yet must keep alive a strong sense of what ought to be, recognizing that democracy is neither natural nor invariably good, and must be fiercely dedicated to constant critical analysis of all political institutions in order to contribute to the maintenance of a favorable balance between individual freedom and public power.

We are pleased to acknowledge our debt to the many colleagues who had a direct and active role in criticism and preparation of the manuscript. The first edition was read and reviewed by Gary Bryner, Brigham Young University; James F. Herndon, Virginia Polytechnic Institute and State University; James W. Riddlesperger, Jr., Texas Christian University; John Schwarz, University of Arizona; Toni-Michelle Travis, George Mason University; and Lois Vietri, University of Maryland. Their comments were enormously helpful.

For subsequent editions, we relied heavily on the thoughtful manuscript reviews we received from David Canon, University of Wisconsin; Russell Hanson, Indiana University; William Keech, University of North Carolina; Donald Kettl, University of Wisconsin; Anne Khademian, University of Wisconsin; William McLauchlan, Purdue University; J. Roger Baker, Wittenburg University; James Lennertz, Lafayette College; Allan McBride, Grambling State University; Joseph Peek, Jr., Georgia State University; Grant Neeley, Texas Tech University; Mark Graber, University of Maryland; John Gilmour, College of William and Mary; Victoria Farrar-Myers, University of Texas at Arlington; Timothy Boylan, Winthrop University; Robert Huckfeldt, Indiana University; Mark Joslyn, University of Kansas; Beth Leech, Texas A&M University; and Charles Noble, California State University, Long Beach. Other colleagues who offered helpful comments based upon their own experience with the text include Douglas Costain, University of Colorado; Robert Hoffert, Colorado State University; David Marcum, University of Wyoming; Mark Silverstein, Boston University; and Norman Thomas, University of Cincinnati.

We also want to reiterate our thanks to the four colleagues who allowed us the privilege of testing a trial edition of our book by using it as the major text in their introductory American Government courses. Their reactions, and those of their students, played an important role in our first edition. We are grateful to Gary Bryner, Brigham Young University; Allan J. Cigler, University of Kansas; Burnet V. Davis, Albion College; and Erwin A. Jaffe, California State University-Stanislaus.

We are also extremely grateful to a number of colleagues who were kind enough to loan us their classrooms. During the past six years, we had the opportunity to lecture at a number of colleges and universities around the country and to benefit from discussing our book with those who know it best—colleagues and students who used it. We appreciate the gracious welcome we received at Austin Community College, Cal State–Fullerton, University of Central Oklahoma, Emory University, Gainesville College, Georgia Southern University, Georgia State University, Golden West College, Grambling State, University of Houston–University Park, University of Illinois–Chicago, University of Illinois–Urbana-Champaign, University of Maryland–College Park, University of Massachusetts–Amherst, Morgan State University, University of North Carolina–Chapel Hill, University of North Texas, University of Oklahoma, Oklahoma State University, Pasadena City College, University of Richmond, Sam Houston State, San Bernadino Valley College, Santa Barbara City College, Santa Monica College, University of Southern California, Temple University, University of Texas–Austin, Texas Tech University, Virginia Commonwealth University, and University of Wisconsin–Madison.

We owe a special debt to several individuals who helped us prepare the many special features in the book. Greg Wawro of Columbia University authored the "Analyzing American Politics" essays. Doug Harris of the University of Texas at Dallas prepared the "American Political Development" sidebars and "Then and Now: Changes in American Politics" boxes. Mark Hallerberg of the University of Pittsburg, Kirk Bowman of Georgia Tech, and Brian Woodall also of Georgia Tech co-authored the "Globalization and Democracy" essays. Finally, Robert J. Spitzer of State University of New York–College of Cortland prepared the "Debating the Issues" features.

One novel feature is a series of "Process Boxes" that illustrate the actual operation of a major political institution or procedure. Several individuals, all leading figures in their own fields, were generous enough to contribute their time and expertise to helping us develop these useful pedagogic tools. Our thanks to Thomas Edsall, the *Washington Post;* Kathleen Francovic, CBS News; Benjamin L. Ginsberg, Republican National Committee; and Ray Rist, U.S. General Accounting Office.

We also are grateful for the talents and hard work of several research assistants, whose contribution can never be adequately compensated: Douglas Dow, John Forren, Michael Harvey, Doug Harris, Brenda Holzinger, Steve McGovern, Melody Butler, Nancy Johnson, Noah Silverman, Rebecca Fisher, David Lytell, Dennis Merryfield, Rachel Reiss, Nandini Sathe, Rob Speel, Jennifer Waterston, and Daniel Wirls. For the Sixth Edition, Mingus Mapps devoted a great deal of time and energy.

Jacqueline Discenza not only typed several drafts of the manuscript, but also helped to hold the project together. We thank her for her hard work and dedication.

Theodore Lowi would like to express his gratitude to the French-American Foundation and the Gannett Foundation, whose timely invitations helped him prepare for his part of this enterprise.

Perhaps above all, we wish to thank those who kept the production and all the loose ends of the book coherent and in focus. Steve Dunn has been an extremely talented editor, continuing to offer numerous suggestions for each new edition. Scott McCord located the photos illustrating the book and has helped keep track of the many details. Lynn Cannon Menges has been an eagle-eyed proofreader. Kathy Talalay has been a superb manuscript and project editor, following in the great tradition of her predecessors. Through all our editions, Ruth Dworkin has been an efficient production manager. John Darger contributed many good ideas to the book and a great deal of time to its success. Steve Hoge brought a vision to the Web site and spent countless hours making it a reality. For their work on previous editions of the book, we want to thank Margaret Farley, Traci Nagle, Margie Brassil, Stephanie Larson, Sarah Caldwell, Nancy Yanchus, Jean Yelovich, Sandra Smith, Sandy Lifland, Amy Cherry, and especially Roby Harrington.

We are more than happy, however, to absolve all these contributors from any flaws, errors, and misjudgments that will inevitably be discovered. We wish the book could be free of all production errors, grammatical errors, misspellings, misquotes, missed citations, etc. From that standpoint, a book ought to try to be perfect. But substantively we have not tried to write a flawless book; we have not tried to write a book to please everyone. We have again tried to write an effective book, a book that cannot be taken lightly. Our goal was not to make every reader a political scientist. Our goal was to restore politics as a subject matter of vigorous and enjoyable discourse, recapturing it from the bondage of the thirty-second sound bite and the thirty-page technical briefing. Every person can be knowledgeable because everything about politics is accessible. One does not have to be a television anchorperson to profit from political events. One does not have to be a philosopher to argue about the requisites of democracy, a lawyer to dispute constitutional interpretations, an economist to debate a public policy. We would be very proud if our book contributes in a small way to the restoration of the ancient art of political controversy.

Theodore J. Lowi
Benjamin Ginsberg
*December 1999*

# PART 1
# FOUNDATIONS

# 1

# Freedom and Power: An Introduction to the Problem

A story often told by politicians concerns a voter from the Midwest who, upon returning home from military service in Korea, took advantage of his federal educational benefits under the G.I. Bill to complete college. After graduation, this individual was able to obtain a government loan from the Small Business Administration (SBA) to help him start a business, and a mortgage subsidized by the Federal Housing Administration (FHA) to purchase a home. Subsequently, he received medical care in a Veteran's Administration Hospital, including treatment with drugs developed by the National Institutes of Health. This voter drove to work every day on a four-lane highway built under the federal interstate highway program, frequently used Amtrak to travel to a nearby city, and, though he was somewhat nervous about air travel, relied on the Federal Aviation Administration (FAA) to make certain that the aircraft he depended on for business and vacation trips were safe. When this voter's children reached college age, they obtained federal student loans to help pay their expenses. At the same time, his aging parents were happy to be receiving monthly Social Security checks and, when his father unexpectedly required major surgery, financial disaster was averted because the federal government's Medicare program paid the bulk of the cost. What was our midwestern friend's response to all of this? Well, in both 1980 and 1984, he strongly supported Ronald Reagan's presidential candidacy because of Reagan's promise to get the federal government off people's backs. In 1988, our friend voted for George Bush because he believed that Bush would continue Reagan's efforts to hold the line on federal domestic spending. But in 1992, disgusted by Bush's failure to adhere to his pledge not to raise taxes, this midwesterner supported Ross Perot. In 1996, our midwestern friend voted for the re-election of Bill Clinton, though without much enthusiasm, because the economy was strong, his stock investments were performing extremely well, and he did not think Bob Dole was up to the job of running the country. Just to be on the safe side, however, he voted for the Republican's House and Senate candidates, calculating that as long as control of the government was divided, neither party would be able to get the country into too much trouble. In previous elections our friend had always voted for the re-election of his congressman, a staunch Democrat, who steadfastly opposed any cuts in the government's domestic programs. This is an example of the love-hate relationship between Americans and their government.

**CORE OF THE ARGUMENT**

- Government has become a powerful and pervasive force in the United States.
- American government is based on democratic electoral institutions and popular representative bodies.
- Once citizens perceive that government can respond to their demands, they become increasingly willing to support its expansion.
- The growth of governmental power can pose a threat because it reduces popular influence over policy making and diminishes the need for citizen cooperation.

## Freedom and Power: The Enduring Debate

*Striking the right balance between freedom and power is the essential paradox of governing. One could select any point in American history and find a vigorous debate between those who want a stronger government and those who believe that individual freedom is endangered by an encroaching state. This debate was a central feature of the early struggle to establish a permanent, stable, yet limited national government in America.*

*Thomas Jefferson was an eloquent spokesman for a government of sharply limited powers. He laid his trust in majority will and personal freedom. In fact, he considered regular revolts by the people to be healthy for a democracy, not unlike the way the physicians of his time viewed bloodletting. "The tree of liberty must be refreshed from time to time, with the blood of patriots and tyrants."*

*Opposing him was Alexander Hamilton, an avowed elitist, who recognized the failings of weak government (which the country had experienced under the Articles of Confederation). Hamilton argued that the national government had to possess the power to enforce its decisions in order to ensure the political and economic well-being of its citizenry.*

### JEFFERSON

I own, I am not a friend to a very energetic government. It is always oppressive. It places the governors indeed more at their ease, at the expense of the people. The late rebellion in Massachusetts [Shays's Rebellion] has given more alarm, than I think it should have done. Calculate that one rebellion in thirteen States in the course of eleven years, is but one for each State in a century and a half. No country should be so long without one. Nor will any degree of power in the hands of government, prevent insurrections. . . . And say . . . whether peace is best preserved by giving energy to the government, or information to the people. This last is the most certain, and the most legitimate engine of government. Educate and inform the whole mass of the people. Enable them to see that it is their interest to preserve peace and order, and they will preserve them. And it requires no very high degree of education to convince them of this. They are the only sure reliance for the preservation of our liberty. After all, it is my principle that the will of the majority should prevail.[1]

### HAMILTON

If it be possible at any rate to construct a federal government capable of regulating the common concerns, and preserving the general tranquillity, it must be founded . . . upon the reverse of the principle contended for by the opponents of the proposed Constitution [that is, a confederacy]. It must carry its agency to the persons of the citizens. It must stand in need of no intermediate legislations, but must itself be empowered to employ the arm of the ordinary magistrate to execute its own resolutions. The majesty of the national authority must be mani-

[1]Thomas Jefferson, Letter to James Madison, 20 December 1787, in *Jefferson's Letters,* arr. by Willson Whitman (Eau Claire, WI: E. M. Hale, 1950), p. 85.

fested through the medium of the courts of justice. The government of the Union, like that of each State, must be able to address itself immediately to the hopes and fears of individuals; and to attract to its support those passions which have the strongest influence upon the human heart. It must, in short, possess all the means, and have a right to resort to all the methods, of executing the powers with which it is entrusted, that are possessed and exercised by the governments of the particular States.[2]

[2]Clinton Rossiter, ed., *The Federalist Papers* (New York: New American Library, 1961), No. 16, p. 116.

Government has become a powerful and pervasive force in the United States. In 1789, 1889, and even in 1929, America's national government was limited in size, scope, and influence, and most of the important functions of government were provided by the states. By 1933, however, the influence of the government expanded to meet the crises created by the stock market crash of 1929, the Great Depression, and the run on banks of 1933. Congress passed legislation that brought the government into the business of home mortgages, farm mortgages, credit, and relief of personal distress. Whereas in 1933 people tried to withdraw their money from the banks only to find that their savings had been wiped out, sixty years later most are confident that although many savings and loan institutions may be insolvent, their money is still safe because it is guaranteed by the government. Today, the national government is an enormous institution with programs and policies reaching into every corner of American life. It oversees the nation's economy; it is the nation's largest employer; it provides citizens with a host of services; it controls a formidable military establishment; and it regulates a wide range of social and commercial activities in which Americans engage. The past few years have seen attempts to establish a national health care system, which would give the federal government a substantial measure of control over another enormous segment of America's economy. America's founders never dreamed the government could take on such obligations; we today can hardly dream of a time when the government was not so large a part of our lives.

The growth of government in the United States has been accompanied by a change in the way Americans perceive government. In the nineteenth century, Americans generally were wary of government, especially the national government. Government meant control, and control meant reduction in individual liberties. National government was a still greater threat because it was remote. The best government, as Thomas Jefferson put it, was the one that governed least. Many Americans today continue to pay lip service to this early view of government, but a new theory of democratic government has gradually come to dominate modern American perceptions. From the perspective of this new theory, if government could be made less of a threat and less remote by the development of elections, representative bodies, and other mechanisms of popular control and if government could be made to pay attention to its citizens' needs and wishes, then a more powerful government would be a government with a greater capacity to serve the people. In other words, government control of the people would be more acceptable if the people, in turn, controlled the government.[1]

Today, the consensus favoring a large and active government is so broad that even self-styled "conservatives" differ more with their "liberal" counterparts over the proper character of government than over its ultimate desirability. In his first inaugural address, Ronald Reagan, our most conservative president in more than half a century, pledged to curb the growth of the federal establishment but at the same time declared, "Now so there will be no misunderstanding, it is not my intention to do away with government. It is, rather, to make it work."[2] Reagan repeated this sentiment in his 1985 inaugural address. In 1992, in his speech accepting the Democratic presidential nomination, Bill Clinton noted correctly that "the Republicans have campaigned against big government for a generation. . . . But have you noticed? They've run this big government for a generation and they haven't changed a thing."[3]

According to the polls, Americans want to keep the political and economic benefits they believe they derive from government (see Table 1.1). A recent survey by the *Washington Post,* for example, revealed that nearly 75 percent of all Americans opposed making any cuts in Social Security and Medicare, although, in theory, most also favor the idea of balancing the federal budget.[4] Social Security and Medicare programs are, of course, major components of the federal government's domestic spending. Indeed, many Americans want the government not only to continue its present involvement but actually to do more in a variety of areas. According to the 1994 University of Michigan National Election Study, over half of all voters believe that it is important for the government to provide more services, even if it requires more spending.[5]

How did government come to play such an important role in our lives? How did Americans come to lose some of their fear of remote government and to perceive government as a valuable servant rather than a threat to freedom?

To answer these questions, this chapter will first assess the meaning and character of government as a phenomenon and will describe some of the alternative forms government can take and the key differences among them. Second, the chapter will examine the factors that led to one particular form of government—representative democracy—in western Europe and the United States. Finally, we will begin to address the question central not only to our book but also to the most fundamental and enduring problem of democratic politics—"What is the relationship between government and freedom?"

**THE CENTRAL QUESTION**

"What is the relationship between government and freedom?"

[1]For examples, see Richard Wollheim, "A Paradox in the Theory of Democracy," in *Philosophy, Politics and Society,* ed. Peter Laslett and W. G. Runciman (Oxford: Blackwell, 1962).

[2]"President Reagan's Inaugural Address," *New York Times,* 21 January 1981, p. B1.

[3]E. J. Dionne, "Beneath the Rhetoric, an Old Question," *Washington Post,* 31 August 1992, p. 1.

[4]Eric Pianin and Mario Brossard, "Social Security and Medicare: Sacred Cows," *Washington Post National Weekly Edition,* 7 April 1997, p. 35.

[5]1994 American National Election Study conducted by the Center for Political Studies at the University of Michigan. Data is provided by the Inter-University Consortium for Political and Social Research in Ann Arbor, Michigan.

## Table 1.1

### Some Activities of the U.S. Government in 1996

| BENEFICIARY AND PROGRAM | COST (IN $) | BENEFICIARY AND PROGRAM | COST (IN $) |
|---|---|---|---|
| **Homeowners** | | **Farmers** | |
| HUD, *Federal Housing Administration Fund* | 2,300,000,000 | USDA, *Farm Income Stabilization* | 5,000,000,000 |
| **Needy Children** | | USDA, *Research* | 2,700,000,000 |
| Department of Agriculture, Food & Nutrition Science, *Child Nutrition Program* | 6,200,000,000 | **Business** | |
| Department of Health & Human Services, *Health Resources & Human Services* | 2,100,000,000 | Department of Energy, *Energy Supply, Research & Development Activities* | 3,200,000,000 |
| **College and University Students** | | Export-Import Bank of U.S. | 3,200,000,000 |
| Department of Education, Office of Postsecondary Education, *Grants and Loans* | 11,400,000,000 | **Labor** | |
| **The Elderly** | | Department of Labor, *Unemployment Compensation* | 26,000,000,000 |
| HHS, *Medicare* | 177,600,000,000 | **The Sick and Disabled** | |
| HHS, *Federal Old-Age & Survivors Insurance* | 350,900,000,000 | Department of Health, *Consumer and Occupational Health* | 2,900,000,000 |
| **Law Enforcement** | | HHS, *Health Research* | 11,500,000,000 |
| Federal Agencies | 13,800,000,000 | HHS, Social Security, *Federal Disability Insurance* | 63,000,000,000 |
| Federal Prisons | 3,000,000,000 | **Veterans** | |
| | | Veterans Administration, *Compensation* | 18,100,000,000 |
| | | V.A., *Education & Rehabilitation* | 1,100,000,000 |
| | | V.A., *Medical Care* | 17,100,000,000 |

SOURCE: Executive Office of the President, Office of Management and Budget, *Budget of the United States, Fiscal Year 1996* (Washington, DC: Government Printing Office, 1997).

## Government and Control

***Government*** is the term generally used to describe the formal institutions through which a land and its people are ruled. To govern is to rule. *Government is composed of institutions and processes that rulers establish to strengthen and perpetuate their power or control over a territory and its inhabitants.* A government may be as simple as a tribal council that meets occasionally to advise the chief, or as complex as our own vast establishment with its forms, rules, and bureaucracies. This more complex government is sometimes referred to as "the state," an abstract concept referring to the source of all public authority.

Whatever their makeup, governments historically have included two basic components: a means of coercion, such as an army or police force, and a means of collecting revenue. These two components have been the essential foundations of government—the building blocks that all individuals and groups who ever sought to rule have been compelled to construct if they were to secure and maintain a measure of control over their territory and its people. Groups aspire to govern for a variety of reasons. Some have the most high-minded aims, while others are little more than ambitious robbers. But whatever their motives and character, those who aspire to rule must be able to secure obedience and fend off rivals as well as collect the revenues needed to accomplish these tasks.[6] Some governments, including many of those in the less developed nations today, have consisted of little more than an army and a tax-collecting agency. Other governments, especially those in the developed nations, have attempted to provide services as well as to collect taxes in order to secure popular consent and control. For some, power is an end in itself. For most, power is necessary for the maintenance of public order. For all, power is needed to permit governments to provide the collective goods and services that citizens want and need but cannot provide for themselves.[7]

**The Means of Coercion** Government must have the power to order people around, to get people to obey its laws, and to punish them if they do not. Coercion takes many different forms, and each year millions of Americans are subject to one form of government coercion or another. Table 1.2 is an outline of the uses of coercion by federal and state governments in America. Chapter 14 will bring these into the context of public policy in its discussion of "the techniques of control."

One aspect of coercion is ***conscription,*** whereby government requires certain involuntary services of citizens. The best-known example of conscription is military conscription, which is called "the draft." Although there has been no draft since 1974, there were drafts during the Civil War, World War I, World War II, and the wars in Korea and Vietnam. With these drafts, our government compelled millions of men to serve in the armed forces; one-half million of these soldiers made the ultimate contribution by giving their lives in their nation's service.

[6]For an excellent discussion, see Charles Tilly, "Reflections on the History of European State-Making," in *The Formation of National States of Western Europe,* ed. Charles Tilly (Princeton: Princeton University Press, 1975), pp. 3–83. See also Charles Tilly, "War Making and State Making as Organized Crime," in *Bringing the State Back In,* ed. Peter Evans, Dietrich Rueschemeyer, and Theda Skocpol (New York: Cambridge University Press, 1985), pp. 169–91.

[7]The question of "why do governments exist?" has been of special interest to social scientists in recent years. One general answer is that governments can help solve problems of collective action and can provide public goods that would be insufficiently provided in the absence of government. An example of a collective action problem is getting everyone to drive on the same side of the road. Governments can set up rules that help coordinate our activities so that we all benefit (by not crashing into each other). An example of a public good is national defense. For an excellent and accessible introduction to collective action problems and public goods, see Kenneth A. Shepsle and Mark S. Bonchek, *Analyzing Politics: Rationality, Behavior, and Institutions* (New York: W. W. Norton, 1997), pp. 197–296.

**TABLE 1.2**

**The Means of Coercion in 1996**

| FORMS | INSTANCES | LEVEL OF GOVERNMENT |
|---|---|---|
| Arrests | 11,912,000 | Federal, state, and local |
| Prison inmates | 1,016,760 | Federal and state |
| Jail inmates | 490,442 | County and municipal |
| Executions | 31 | State |

SOURCE: U.S. Bureau of the Census, *Statistical Abstract of the United States: 1996* (Washington, DC: U.S. Department of Commerce, 1996).

If the need arose, military conscription would undoubtedly be reinstituted. All eighteen-year-old males are required to register today, just in case.

Military conscription, however, is not the only form of involuntary service that government can compel Americans to perform. We can, by law, be compelled to serve on juries, to appear before legal tribunals when summoned, to file a great variety of official reports, including income tax returns, and to attend school or to send our children to school.

**The Means of Collecting Revenue** Each year American governments collect enormous sums from their citizens to support their institutions and programs. Taxation has grown steadily over the years. In 1989, the national government alone collected $516 billion in individual income taxes, $117 billion in corporate income taxes, $337 billion in social insurance taxes, $26 billion in excise taxes, and another $18 billion in miscellaneous revenue. The grand total amounted to more than $1 trillion, or more than $4,000 from every living soul in the United States. And of course, while some groups receive more in benefits from the government than they pay in taxes, others get less for their tax dollar. One of the perennial issues in American politics is the distribution of tax burdens versus the distribution of program benefits. Every group would like more of the benefits while passing more of the burdens of taxation onto others.

## Forms of Government

Governments vary in their institutional structure, in their size, and in their modes of operation. Two questions are of special importance in determining how governments differ from each other: Who governs? How much government control is permitted?

In some nations, governing is done by a single individual—a king or dictator, for example. This state of affairs is called ***autocracy.*** Where a small group of landowners, military officers, or wealthy merchants controls most of the governing decisions, that government is said to be an ***oligarchy.*** If more people participate, and if the populace is deemed to have some influence over decision making, that government is tending toward ***democracy.***

Governments also vary considerably in terms of how they govern. In the United States and a small number of other nations, governments are severely limited as to *what* they are permitted to control (substantive limits), as well as *how* they go about it (procedural limits). Governments that are so limited are called ***constitutional,*** or liberal governments. In other nations, including many in Europe as well as in South America, Asia, and Africa, though the law imposes few real limits, a government is nevertheless kept in check by other political and social institutions that the government is unable to control but must come to terms with—such as autonomous territories, an organized church, organized business groups, or organized labor unions. Such governments are generally called ***authoritarian.*** In a third group of nations, including the Soviet Union under Joseph Stalin, Nazi Germany, and perhaps prewar Japan and Italy, governments not only are free of legal limits but in addition seek to eliminate those organized social groupings that might challenge or limit their authority. These governments typically attempt to dominate or control every sphere of political, economic, and social life and, as a result, are called ***totalitarian*** (see Box 1.1).

## Why is Government Necessary?

As we have just seen, control is the basis for government. But what forms of government control are justifiable? To answer this question, we begin by examining the ways in which government makes it possible for people to live together in harmony.

**To Maintain Order** Human beings usually do not venture out of their caves (or the modern counterpart) unless there is a reasonable probability that they can return safely. But in order for people to live together peacefully, law and order are required, the institutionalization of which is called government. From the standpoint of this definition, the primary purpose of government is to maintain order. But order can only come about by controlling a territory and its people. This may sound like a threat to freedom, until you ponder the absence of government, or anarchy—the absence of rule. According to Thomas Hobbes (1588–1679), author of the first great masterpiece of political philosophy in the English language, anarchy is even worse than the potential tyranny of government, because anarchy, or life outside "the state," is one of "continual fear, and danger of violent death [where life is] solitary, poor, nasty, brutish and short."[8] Governmental power can be a threat to freedom, yet at the same time we need government to maintain order so that we can enjoy our freedom.

**To Protect Property** After safety of persons comes security of a person's labor, which we call property, or private property. Protection of property is almost universally recognized as a justifiable function of government. John Locke (1632–1704), the worthy successor to Thomas Hobbes, was first to assert clearly

[8]Thomas Hobbes, *Leviathan* (New York: MacMillan, 1947), p. 82.

**Box 1.1**

### Constitutional, Authoritarian, and Totalitarian Governments

Most Western democracies have constitutions that actually define the limits and scope of governmental power. But the mere existence of a constitution does not, by itself, define a regime as constitutional. Some governments have constitutions that they ignore. At least until recently, this was the case in such East European nations as Romania and Bulgaria. In the true constitutional setting, the actual processes of government follow the forms prescribed by the constitution, and groups in society have sufficient freedom and power to oppose efforts by the government to overstep these limits. The governments in the United States and Western Europe provide the best examples.

Authoritarian governments must sometimes be responsive to a small number of powerful social groups and institutions such as the army, but such governments recognize no formal obligations to consult their citizens or to respect limits on their actions. Examples of authoritarian governments in the recent past include Spain under the leadership of General Francisco Franco and Portugal under Prime Minister Antonio Salazar.

Totalitarian governments can be distinguished from both democratic and authoritarian governments by the lack of any distinction between the government and other important social institutions. Indeed, totalitarian governments generally seek to destroy all other social institutions—for example, churches, labor unions, and political parties—that may function as rival sources of power. Examples of totalitarian governments include the Third Reich in Germany under Adolf Hitler in the 1930s and 1940s and the government of the Soviet Union under Joseph Stalin between the 1930s and 1950s.

In recent years, a number of authoritarian regimes in Eastern Europe, including the Soviet Union and its satellite states, faced severe economic hardship and popular discontent. Most of these regimes, including those in Czechoslovakia, Poland, Hungary, East Germany, and the Soviet Union, itself, collapsed and were replaced by new governments.

that whatever we have removed from Nature and also mixed our labor with, is considered our property:

> For this "labour" being the unquestionable property of the laborer, no man but [the laborer] can have a right to what that [labour is joined to]. . . .

But even Locke recognized that although the right to the ownership of what we have produced by our own labor is absolute, it means nothing if someone with greater power than ours decides to take it or trespass on it. As Locke puts it,

> If man . . . be absolute Lord of his own person and possessions . . . why will he part with his freedom . . . ? To which, it is obvious to answer, that the enjoyment of it is very uncertain. . . . This makes him willing to quit this condition, which, however free, is full of fears and continual danger; and it is not without reason that he seeks out and

is willing to join in society with others . . . for the mutual preservation of their lives, liberties, and estates.[9]

So, something we call our own *is only ours as long as the laws against trespass* improve the probability that we can enjoy it, use it, consume it, trade it, and sell it. In reality, then, property can be defined as *all the laws against trespass* that not only permit us to call something our own but also to make sure that our claim sticks. In other words, property, that is, private property, is virtually meaningless without a government of laws and policies that makes trespass prohibitive.

**To Provide Public Goods** David Hume (1711–1776), another worthy successor to Thomas Hobbes, observed that although two neighbors may agree voluntarily to cooperate in draining a swampy meadow, the more neighbors there are, the more difficult it will be to cooperate in order to get the task done. A few neighbors might clear the swamp because they understand the benefits each of them will receive. But as you begin to expand the number of neighbors who might benefit from clearing the swamp, many neighbors will realize that all of them can get the same benefit if only a few clear the swamp and the rest do nothing. This is called the "free-rider" effect (see also Chapter 12). A public (or collective) good is therefore a benefit that neighbors or members of a group cannot be kept from enjoying once any individual or small minority of members have provided the benefit for themselves—the clearing of the swamp, for example, or national defense, for another example. Without government's coercive powers through a policy (backed by taxation) to build a bridge, produce an army, provide a swamp-free meadow, "legal tender," or uniform standards of weights and measures, there is no incentive, in fact very often there is a *dis*incentive, for even the richest, most concerned members to provide the benefit.[10]

Although public order, the protection of property, and the provision of public goods are justifications for government, they are not justifications for all its actions. A government's actions can only be justified by the people being governed. This is why government would be intolerable without politics. With politics, we have at least a faint hope that a government's actions can be influenced in some way.

## Influencing the Government: Politics

In its broadest sense, the term "politics" refers to conflicts over the character, membership, and policies of any organization to which people belong. As Harold Lasswell, a famous political scientist, once put it, politics is the struggle over "who gets what, when, how."[11] Although politics is a phenomenon that can be found in any organization, our concern in this book is more narrow. Here, politics will be used to refer only to conflicts and struggles over the leadership, struc-

[9]This quote and the previous one are from John Locke's masterpiece, *Two Treatises of Government* (London: Everyman, 1993), pp. 178 and 180.

[10]The most instructive treatment of the phenomenon of public goods and the "free rider" is Mancur Olson, *The Logic of Collective Action: Public Goods and the Theory of Groups* (Cambridge: Harvard University Press, 1965 and 1971), pp. 33–43, esp. footnote 53.

[11]Harold Lasswell, *Politics: Who Gets What, When, How* (New York: Meridian Books, 1958).

ture, and policies of *governments.* The goal of politics, as we define it, is to have a share or a say in the composition of the government's leadership, how the government is organized, or what its policies are going to be. Having a share is called *power* or *influence.* Most people are eager to have some "say" in matters affecting them; witness the willingness of so many individuals over the past two centuries to risk their lives for voting rights and representation. In recent years, of course, Americans have become more skeptical about their actual "say" in government, and many do not bother to vote. This increased skepticism, however, does not mean that Americans no longer want to have a share in the governmental process. Rising levels of skepticism mean, rather, that many Americans doubt the capacity of the political system to provide them with influence.

As we shall see throughout the book, not only does politics influence government, but the character and actions of government also influence a nation's politics. A constitutional government is actually an effort to gain more popular consent by opening channels for political expression. People are moved to accept these channels in the hope that they can make the government more responsive to their demands. These channels can be *democratic politics,* through election of candidates to fill the top governing positions; or they can be *mass politics,* through voting on proposed government actions one at a time, as in a ***referendum*** or a ***plebiscite.*** When the political channels are indirect, through methods of selecting representatives, that system is usually called *republican politics,* or ***representative democracy.*** When politics is provided or sought by competition among leaders or among powerful groups outside the government, we call this ***pluralist politics.*** Sometimes politics does not take place through formal channels but through direct action. ***Direct action politics*** can be either violent politics or ***civil disobedience***—both of which attempt to shock rulers into behaving more responsibly. Or direct action politics can be ***revolutionary politics,*** which rejects the system entirely and attempts to replace it with a new ruling group that has a new set of rules. But all of these are politics—some of it encouraged by the rulers themselves, some of it accepted begrudgingly by rulers, and some brutally suppressed by rulers.

Most democratic nations today practice representative democracy. At the national level, America is a representative democracy in which citizens select the major government officials but do not vote on government programs. Some states, however, have provisions for direct legislation through popular referendum. For example, California voters in 1996 decided to limit the state's affirmative action programs. As we shall see in Chapter 10, there are a variety of different ways in which democratic governments tally their citizens' votes and translate popular preferences into collective electoral decisions. The basic democratic practice of voting can lead to enormous complexities for both political leaders and students of politics.[12]

[12]An example of this potential complexity involves the principle of majority rule. Ninety-five percent of Americans agree that public officials should be chosen by majority vote. But social scientists have shown that under certain circumstances, majority rule does not produce outcome that reflects the preferences of the majority of individuals. For an explanation of these circumstances, see Shepsle and Bonchek, *Analyzing Politics,* pp. 39–48. Here, Shepsle and Bonchek emphatically remind us that institutions, "the rules of the game," matter; in this instance "the institutional features of the voting system will be absolutely essential in determining which alternative wins."

## From Coercion to Consent

Americans have the good fortune to live in a nation in which limits are placed on *what* governments can do and *how* governments can do it. But such constitutional democracies are relatively rare in today's world—it is estimated that only twenty or so of the world's nearly two hundred governments could be included in this category. And constitutional democracies were unheard of before the modern era. In many areas of the world today, governments have little interest in the views of their citizens and recognize few formal limits on the scope of their power.

### The Extraction-Coercion Cycle

Many Americans truly believe that governments originate from a general agreement entered into by individuals trying to address common problems. This is called the ***contract model*** of the origins of the state, and some governments actually come close to fitting that model. The Mayflower Compact is one of the few such efforts, and our Constitution may be considered another. But most governments begin with efforts by a small group to subdue all their rivals and to institutionalize their power and their privileges. Often, of course, such efforts fail. But, in general, those governments that survive and flourish do so because their leaders are able to set in motion a process that Samuel Finer, a famous British political scientist, called the ***extraction-coercion cycle.*** This means that rulers initially use what force they can muster to collect taxes and to compel military service. Whatever revenues and services they initially acquire increase their capacity to extract more revenues and services, which in turn makes possible larger armies and bureaucracies, which enable them to extract more revenues and services.

The cycle of extraction and coercion was at the heart of state-building in western Europe. In 1640, when Frederick William succeeded as the elector of Brandenburg-Prussia, he commanded a military force consisting of a mere 1,300 mercenary troops, his government had virtually no central administrative machinery, and he was at the mercy of the Estates, the assembly of provincial nobles, for tax revenues. In stages over the next forty years, Frederick William used his troops to acquire more funds, with which he in turn enforced the collection of more taxes. By the conclusion of Frederick William's reign in 1688, Brandenburg-Prussia boasted a standing army of 30,000 men and an elaborate administrative machinery. This cycle was continued by his successors, particularly by Frederick William I, King of Prussia, who was able to construct what, on a per capita basis, was the largest standing army in Europe in the early eighteenth century. This permanent force of 80,000 troops both supported and was supported by an extensive bureaucracy and tax collection apparatus.

For many centuries, even in nations such as Britain where constitutional democracy and democratic forms of rule eventually developed, rulers relied almost exclusively on force to maintain their power and to secure the compliance of their subjects. This style of rule can eventually bring on riots and insurrections, but civil disturbances usually posed no real challenge to these early governments. Indeed, given the local character of governmental administration, rioting and disorder also tended to be local and usually did not disrupt affairs elsewhere in that country.

## Limits and Democratization

Prior to the eighteenth and nineteenth centuries, governments seldom sought—and rarely received—the support of their ordinary subjects. The available evidence strongly suggests that the ordinary people had little love for the government or for the social order. After all, they had no stake in it. They equated government with the police officer, the bailiff, and the tax collector.[13]

Beginning in the seventeenth century, in a handful of Western nations, two important changes began to take place in the character and conduct of government. First, governments began to acknowledge formal limits upon their power. Second, a small number of governments began to provide the ordinary citizen with a formal voice in public affairs through the vote. Obviously, the desirability of limits on government and the expansion of popular influence on government were at the heart of the American Revolution of 1776. "No taxation without representation," as we shall see in Chapter 2, was hotly debated beginning with the American Revolution and through the founding in 1789. But even before the American Revolution, there was a tradition of limiting government and expanding participation in the political process all over western Europe. Thus, to understand how the relationship between rulers and the ruled was transformed, we must broaden our focus to take into account events in Europe as well as those in America. We will have to divide the transformation into its two separate parts. The first is the effort to put limits on government. The second is the effort to expand the influence of the people through politics.

**Limiting Government** The key force behind the imposition of limits on government power was a new social class, the "bourgeoisie." *Bourgeoisie* is French for freeman of the city, or *bourg*. Being part of the bourgeoisie later became associated with being "middle class" and with being in commerce or industry. In order to gain a share of control of government—to join the kings, aristocrats, and gentry who had dominated governments for centuries—the bourgeoisie sought to change existing institutions—especially parliaments—into instruments of real political participation. Parliaments had existed for centuries, controlling from the top and not allowing influence from below. The bourgeoisie embraced parliament as the means by which they could exert the weight of their superior numbers and growing economic advantage against their aristocratic rivals. At the same time, the bourgeoisie sought to place checks on the capacity of governments to threaten these economic and political interests by placing formal or constitutional limits on governmental power. The three bourgeois (also called liberal) philosophers with the strongest influence on American thinking were John Locke, Adam Smith, and John Stuart Mill (see Box 1.2).

Although motivated primarily by the need to protect and defend their own interests, the bourgeoisie advanced many of the principles that became the central

[13]See Eugen Weber, *Peasants into Frenchmen* (Stanford: Stanford University Press, 1976), Chapter 5.

BOX 1.2

### The Philosophical Basis of Limited Government

Three liberal philosophers had a particularly strong influence on American political thought: John Locke (1632–1704), Adam Smith (1723–1790), and John Stuart Mill (1806–1873). These three thinkers espoused the liberal philosophy that placed limits on government.

John Locke argued for limited government because of his belief that, just as a person had a right to his own body, he had a right to his own labor and the fruits of that labor. From that he argued that people formed a government to protect their property, lives, and liberty, and that this government could not properly act to harm or take away that which it had been created to protect. According to Locke in his *Second Treatise on Government* (1690), government could only properly function with the consent of the governed through their representatives; if the government acted improperly, it would have broken its contract with society and would no longer be a legitimate government. The people would have the right to revolt and the right to form a new government.

Adam Smith supported a severely limited government as a protection for the economic freedom of the individual. In his *Wealth of Nations* (1776), he argued for private enterprise as the most efficient means of production, leading to the growth of national wealth and income. He believed that freedom for individual economic and social advancement was only possible in a competitive free market, unhindered by government intervention. Nonetheless, he argued that government must protect the economic freedoms—free trade, free choice of individuals to do what they wanted, to live where they wished, and to invest and spend as they saw fit—by ensuring that the market remains competitive and honest through such governmental actions as the regulation of standard weights and measures, the prevention of the formation of monopolies, and the defense of the community.

John Stuart Mill believed that government should be limited so as not to interfere with the self-development of the individual. In order for individuals to fully develop their faculties, Mill believed that they need as large a sphere of freedom as possible, including freedom of thought and discussion. In *On Liberty* (1859), Mill argued that any restrictions on individuals ought to be based on recognized principles rather than on the preferences of the majority. He believed that social control should be exercised only to prevent harm to others. He maintained that when thoughts are suppressed, if they are right, individuals are deprived of truth; if the ideas are wrong, they are deprived of that better understanding of truth that comes out of conflict with error.

underpinnings of individual freedom for all citizens—freedom of speech, of assembly, of conscience, and freedom from arbitrary search and seizure. It is important to note here that the bourgeoisie generally did not favor democracy as such. They were advocates of electoral and representative institutions, but they favored property requirements and other restrictions so as to limit participation to the middle classes. Yet, once these institutions of politics and the protection of the right to engage in politics were established, it was difficult to limit them just to the bourgeoisie. We will see time after time that principles first advanced to justify a selfish interest tend to take on a life of their own and to be extended to those for whom the principles were not at first designed.

**The Expansion of Democratic Politics** Along with limits on government came an expansion of democratic government. Three factors explain why rulers were forced to give ordinary citizens a greater voice in public affairs: the first is internal conflict, the second is external threat, and the third is national unity and development.[14]

First, during the eighteenth and nineteenth centuries, every nation was faced with intense conflict among the landed gentry, the bourgeoisie, lower-middle-class shopkeepers and artisans, the urban working class, and farmers. Many governments came to the conclusion that if basic class and group conflicts were not dealt with in some constructive way, disorder and revolution might well result. One of the most effective ways of responding to such conflict was to extend the rights of political participation, especially voting rights, to each new group as it grew more powerful. Such a liberalization was sometimes followed by suppression, as rulers began to fear that their calculated risk was not paying off. This was true even in the United States. The Federalists, who were securely in control of the government after 1787, began to fear the emergence of an opposition party being led by Thomas Jefferson. Fearing Jefferson as leader of a vulgar and dangerous democratic party, the Federalist majority in Congress adopted an infamous law, the Alien and Sedition Acts of 1798, which, among other things, declared any opposition to or criticism of the government to be a crime. Hamilton and other Federalist leaders went so far as to urge that the opposition be eliminated by force, if necessary. The failure of the Federalists to suppress their Republican opposition was, in large measure, attributable to the fact that the Federalists lacked the military and political means of doing so. Their inability to crush the opposition eventually led to acceptance of the principle of the "Loyal Opposition."[15]

Another form of internal threat is social disorder. Thanks to the Industrial Revolution, societies had become much more interdependent and therefore much more vulnerable to disorder. As that occurred, and as more people moved from rural areas to cities, disorder had to be managed, and one important approach to that management was to give the masses a bigger stake in the system itself. As one supporter of electoral reform put it, the alternative to voting was "the spoliation of property and the dissolution of social order."[16] In the modern world, social disorder helped compel East European regimes to take steps toward democratic reform. The most notable example is the territory formerly called the German Democratic Republic (DDR or East Germany), which, in 1990, was absorbed into the Federal Republic of Germany.

[14]For a fuller account, see Benjamin Ginsberg, *The Captive Public* (New York: Basic Books, 1986), Chapter 1.

[15]See Richard Hofstadter, *The Idea of a Party System* (Berkeley: University of California Press, 1969).

[16]Quoted in John Cannon, *Parliamentary Reform 1640–1832* (Cambridge, England: Cambridge University Press, 1973), p. 216.

GLOBALIZATION AND DEMOCRACY

## *Has Globalization Changed American Politics?*

The focus of this book is on American politics, and the chapters you will read rightly focus on what is referred to as "domestic" politics. Yet the United States has not developed in a bubble, separated from the rest of the world. Influences from abroad have profoundly affected the way Americans think, act, and govern themselves.

Such influence has often been welcome. The framers of the Constitution relied upon the writings of French thinkers (like Montesquieu) and English thinkers (like John Locke). At the beginning of the nineteenth century, American textile producers eagerly copied techniques from their more technologically advanced English competitors. The United States actively encouraged people from Africa, Asia, and Europe to immigrate and to bring their skills and know-how to build a new economy in a new world. Today, Americans happily wear tennis shoes made in China and sweaters made in Italy.

But Americans have also had mixed feelings about how much "foreign" influence they wanted in their everyday affairs. Indeed, it was a revolt against too much foreign control of government in the American colonies that eventually led to the Revolutionary War.

America is part of a global community, and although this book focuses on domestic politics, it is also important to examine how "globalization" has affected American politics. Therefore, a section at the end of each chapter will look at today's globalization, a term that authors define in different ways. Some authors focus on the economic definition, identifying three essential elements:[1]

1. **Increasing levels of cross-border trade.** In the U.S. context, to what extent has the American economy become more dependent upon trade in world markets?

2. **Increasing levels of capital movements and the more general integration of world financial markets.** How easily can investors move their money across borders? It is fairly easy today, for example, to buy stocks abroad. Foreigners can also easily purchase American Treasury bonds.

[1]See Geoffrey Garrett, "Global Markets and National Politics: Collision Course or Virtuous Circle?" *International Organization* 52, 4 (Autumn 1998), pp. 787–824.

3. **The growth of truly multinational corporations.** How much growth is there? A corporation like the Coca-Cola Company, for example, has operations in almost two hundred countries around the world.

When discussing globalization, other authors stress the impact of cultural ideas, cultural norms, and cultural practices across borders. It is not uncommon for people living in Berlin, Buenos Aires, and Tokyo to listen to the same Madonna CD when they return home from work. The spread of such cultural ideas and norms can affect the way people conceive of values like democracy, freedom, and equality.[2]

The key question examined in these globalization boxes is the extent to which economic, cultural, and political forces outside the United States have influenced America's development. Answers to this question not only increase our understanding of why America's political system functions the way it does but also indicate what features of the system are unique in the world.

A second related question is the extent to which Americans can accelerate or retard globalization's impact on American politics. This question is related to the first one—if international forces have almost no effect upon American politics, then there is no need to encourage or regulate these forces.

Let us look at the debates about tariffs on imports into the United States as an illustration of globalization's effect. An important issue in American elections throughout the nineteenth and early twentieth centuries concerned the tariff rate on imports. A high tariff increased prices on foreign-produced goods and reduced competition for domestic producers of goods. At the same time, the high tariff also increased prices for domestic consumers, which could have led to retaliation from other countries against American exports. Openness to world markets was therefore a feature of globalization that the U.S. government could regulate, and it had aspects that helped some Americans while it hurt others.

[2]Benjamin Barber, *Jihad versus McWorld* (New York: Times Books, 1995).

The DDR had been created in the portion of Germany occupied by Soviet troops after World War II, and became one of the most ruthless authoritarian regimes in Eastern Europe. In the late 1980s, this regime was faced with massive popular demonstrations as well as the spectacle of hundreds of thousands of citizens fleeing across the border to the West. The government at first responded with force. However, the Soviet Union, which exercised considerable control over the DDR's military and security forces, was anxious to improve its relations with the West and to reduce its military commitments. As a result, the Soviets refused to permit the East German government to use its military and police forces to curb disorder. The government of the DDR was forced to introduce a variety of reforms and concessions including, of course, the dramatic opening of the Berlin Wall that had divided the two Germanys for two generations. In 1990, the citizens of the DDR voted to abolish their government and join the Federal Republic.

**External Threat** The main external threat to governments' power is the existence of other nation-states. During the past three centuries, more and more tribes and nations—people tied together by a common culture and language—have formed into separate principalities, or ***nation-states,*** in order to defend their populations more effectively. But as more nation-states formed, there was a vastly increased probability that external conflicts would take place. War and preparation for war became constant rather than intermittent facts of national life, and the size and expense of military forces increased dramatically with the size of the nation-state and the size and number of its adversaries.

The cost of defense against external threats forced rulers to seek popular support to maintain military power. Huge permanent armies of citizen-soldiers could be raised more easily and could be induced to fight more vigorously and to make greater sacrifices if imbued with enthusiasm for cause and country. The turning point was the French Revolution in 1789. The unprecedented size and commitment and the military success of the French citizen-army convinced the rulers of all European nations that military power was forevermore closely linked with mass support. The expansion of participation and representation were key tactics in the efforts of European regimes to convince citizens that they should be willing to contribute to the defense of the nation. Throughout the nineteenth century, war and the expansion of the suffrage went hand in hand.

**National Unity and Development** The expansion of popular participation often has been associated with efforts to promote national unity and development. In some instances, governments seek to subvert local or regional popular loyalties by linking citizens directly to the central government via the ballot box. America's founders saw direct popular election of members of the House of Representatives as a means through which the new federal government could compete with the states for popular allegiance.

In addition, many governments have conceived the expansion of popular participation to be a way of persuading citizens to be more willing to provide the taxes and services sometimes associated with large-scale economic development or political change, and to build popular support for attacks on entrenched elites or bureaucracies that are resistant to change. While he was the Soviet premier, Mikhail Gorbachev, for example, initiated more democratic forms of participation primarily to generate greater popular support for economic development and for his campaigns against opponents in the Communist party and the state bureaucracy. Gorbachev was able to win the support of many professionals and intellectuals, the nearest Eastern European equivalent of the eighteenth-century Western European bourgeoisie.

### The Great Transformation: Tying Democracy to Strong Government

The construction of democratic electoral institutions and popular representative bodies had two historic consequences. First, democratization opened up the possibility that citizens might now use government for their own benefit rather than simply watching government being used for the benefit of others. This consequence is widely understood. But the second is not so well understood: Once citizens perceived that governments could operate in response to their demands, citizens *became increasingly willing to support the expansion of government.* The public's belief in its capacity to control the government's actions is only one of the many factors responsible for the growth of government. But at the very least, this linkage of democracy and government set into motion a wave of governmental growth in the West that began in the middle of the nineteenth century and has continued to this day.

The U.S. government appears at first to be an exception to this pattern because the national government, as we observed at the outset, remained so weak and small throughout the nineteenth century, and well into the twentieth century. But as we shall see, particularly in Chapter 3, that is a misleading impression. There was in fact a great deal of governmental growth during the nineteenth century, but most of that growth took place in the state governments, as provided for by our federal Constitution. Thus, we have a very different system, but it does not exempt us from the general pattern in which democracy and the support of the people for stronger government are related.

## FREEDOM AND POWER: THE PROBLEM

Ultimately, the growth of governmental power poses the most fundamental threat to the liberties Americans have so long enjoyed. Because ours is a limited government subject to democratic control, we often see government as simply a powerful servant. However, the growth of governmental power continues to raise profound questions about the future.

First, expansion of governmental power can reduce popular influence over policy making. On the one hand, expanding the role of government has the effect of removing decisions from the private to the public sphere. This means that questions that might have been decided by, say, a small number of business executives can become issues to be decided by a popularly elected legislature or even the electorate itself. Environmental policy is an example. Questions about who is responsible for cleaning up pollution are, for better or worse, regulated by the U.S. Congress and are thus matters for public discussion rather than private decision-making alone.

At the same time, however, the enormous scope of national programs in the twentieth century has required the construction of a large and elaborate state apparatus and the transfer of considerable decision-making power from political bodies like Congress to administrative agencies. As a consequence, the development and implementation of today's public policies are increasingly dominated by bureaucratic institutions, rules, and procedures that are not so easily affected by the citizen in the voting booth. Can citizens use the power of the bureaucracies we have created, or are we doomed simply to become their subjects?

Second, as government has grown in size and power, the need for citizen cooperation has diminished. In the eighteenth and nineteenth centuries, rulers sought popular support and became responsive to mass opinion because of the fragility of state power. Rulers lacked the means to curb disorder, collect taxes, and maintain their military power without popular support. In an important sense, the eighteenth and nineteenth centuries in the West represented a "window of opportunity" for popular opinion. A conjunction of political and social circumstances compelled those in power to respond to public opinion to shore up their power. To the extent that they think about such matters at all, westerners tend to assume that this commitment on the part of the eighteenth- and nineteenth-century rulers forever binds their successors to serve public opinion. It is true that the institutional linkages—elections, representative bodies, and so on—between government and opinion developed during the eighteenth and nineteenth centuries and have flourished for nearly two hundred years. But what has generally gone unnoticed is that the underlying conditions—the window of opportunity—that produced these institutions have, in many respects, disappeared. Unlike their predecessors, many Western states today may now have sufficiently powerful administrative, military, and police agencies that they *could* curb disorder, collect taxes, and keep their foes in check without necessarily depending upon popular support and approval. Will government necessarily continue to bow to the will of the people even though favorable public opinion may not be as crucial as it once was?

Finally, because Americans view government as a servant, they believe that they can have both the blessings of freedom and the benefits of government. Even most self-proclaimed conservatives have learned to live with Big Brother. In today's America, agencies of the government have considerable control over who may enter occupations, what may be eaten, what may be seen and heard over the airwaves, what forms of education are socially desirable, what types of philanthropy serve the public interest, what sorts of business practices are acceptable, as well as citizens' marital plans, vacation plans, child-rearing practices, and medical care. Is this government still a servant? Of course, we continue to exert our influence through elections, representation, and referenda. But do even these processes mean that we can control the government? One hundred fifty years ago, Alexis de Tocqueville predicted that Americans would eventually permit their government to become so powerful that elections, representative processes, and so on would come to be ironic interludes providing citizens little more than the opportunity to wave the chains by which the government had bound them. Can we have both freedom and government? To what extent can we continue to depend upon and benefit from the state's power while still retaining our liberties? These are questions that every generation of Americans must ask.

## For Further Reading

Bendix, Reinhard. *Kings or People: Power and the Mandate to Rule.* Berkeley: University of California Press, 1978.

Bendix, Reinhard. *Nation-Building and Citizenship.* New York: Wiley, 1964.

Dahl, Robert A. *Polyarchy: Participation and Opposition.* New Haven: Yale University Press, 1971.

Grant, Ruth W. *John Locke's Liberalism.* Chicago: University of Chicago Press, 1987.

Hartz, Louis. *The Liberal Tradition in America.* New York: Harcourt, Brace, 1955.

Higgs, Robert. *Crisis and Leviathan: Critical Episodes in the Growth of American Government.* New York: Oxford University Press, 1987.

Huntington, Samuel P. *American Politics: The Promise of Disharmony.* Cambridge: Harvard University Press, 1981.

Keller, Morton. *Affairs of State: Public Life in Late Nineteenth Century America.* Cambridge: Harvard University Press, 1977.

Moore, Barrington. *Social Origins of Dictatorship and Democracy.* Boston: Beacon Press, 1966.

Putnam, Robert. *Making Democracy Work: Civic Traditions in Modern Italy.* Princeton: Princeton University Press, 1993.

Schumpeter, Joseph A. *Capitalism, Socialism and Democracy.* New York: Harper, 1942.

Skocpol, Theda. *States and Social Revolutions.* New York: Cambridge University Press, 1979.

Strayer, Joseph R. *On the Medieval Origins of the Modern State.* Princeton: Princeton University Press, 1970.

Tilly, Charles, ed. *The Formation of Nation-States in Western Europe.* Princeton: Princeton University Press, 1975.

Tocqueville, Alexis de. *Democracy in America.* Translated by Phillips Bradley. New York: Knopf, Vintage Books, 1945; orig. published 1835.

Weber, Max. *The Theory of Social and Economic Organization.* Translated by Talcott Parsons. New York: Oxford University Press, 1947.

# Constructing a Government: The Founding and the Constitution

We the People of the United States, in Order to form a more perfect Union, establish Justice,

Article I

## TIME LINE ON THE FOUNDING

| Events | | Institutional Developments |
|---|---|---|
| | 1750 | |
| | | Albany Congress calls for colonial unity (1754) |
| French defeated in North America (1760) | | |
| Stamp Act enacted (1765) | | Stamp Act Congress attended by delegates from all colonies (1765) |
| Townshend duties enacted (1767) | | |
| Boston Massacre (1770) | 1770 | |
| Tea Act; Boston Tea Party (1773) | | |
| British adopt Coercive Acts to punish colonies (1774) | | First Continental Congress rejects plan of union, but adopts Declaration of American Rights denying Parliament's authority over internal colonial affairs (1774) |
| Battles of Lexington and Concord (1775) | | Second Continental Congress assumes role of revolutionary government (1775); adopts Declaration of Independence (1776) |
| | | New state constitutions adopted after ties with Britain severed (1776–1784) |
| | | Congress adopts Articles of Confederation as constitution for new government (1777) |
| | 1780 | |
| British surrender at Yorktown (1781) | | |
| Shays's Rebellion (1787) | | Annapolis Convention calls for consideration of government revision (1786) |
| | | Constitutional Convention drafts blueprint for new government (1787) |
| *Federalist Papers* (1788) | | Constitution ratified by states (1788–1790) |
| | 1790 | |

"No taxation without representation" were words that stirred a generation of Americans long before they even dreamed of calling themselves Americans rather than Englishmen. Reacting to new English attempts to extract tax revenues to pay for the troops that were being sent to defend the colonial frontier, protests erupted throughout the colonies against the infamous Stamp Act of 1765. This act created revenue stamps and required that they be affixed to all printed and legal documents, including newspapers, pamphlets, advertisements, notes and bonds, leases, deeds, and licenses. To show their displeasure with the act, the colonists conducted mass meetings, parades, bonfires, and other demonstrations throughout the spring and summer of 1765. In Boston, for example, a stamp agent was hanged and burned in effigy. Later, the home of the lieutenant-governor was sacked, leading to his resignation and that of all of his colonial commission and stamp agents. By November 1765, business proceeded and newspapers were published without the stamp; in March 1766, Parliament repealed the detested law. Through their protest, the nonimportation agreements that the colonists subsequently adopted, and the Stamp Act Congress that met in October 1765, the colonists took the first steps that ultimately would lead to war and a new nation.

**CORE OF THE ARGUMENT**

- The American Revolution and the Constitution were expressions of competing interests.
- The framers of the Constitution married interest and principle by creating a government capable of defending national interests, promoting commerce, and protecting property.
- To secure popular consent for the government, the Constitution provides for the direct popular election of representatives and includes the Bill of Rights.
- To prevent the new government from abusing its power, the Constitution incorporates principles such as the separation of powers and federalism.
- The Constitution and its amendments establish a framework within which government and law making can take place.

The people of every nation tend to glorify their own history and especially their nation's creation. Americans are no exception. To most contemporary Americans, the revolutionary period represents a heroic struggle by a determined and united group of colonists against British oppression. The Boston Tea Party, the battles of Lexington and Concord, the winter at Valley Forge—these are the events that we emphasize in our history. Similarly, the American Constitution—the document establishing the system of government that ultimately emerged from this struggle—is often seen as an inspired, if not divine, work, expressing timeless principles of democratic government. These views are by no means false. During the founding era, Americans did struggle against misrule. Moreover, the American Constitution did establish the foundations for over two hundred years of democratic government.

**THE CENTRAL QUESTION**

"Was the Constitution based more on principle or interest?"

To really understand the character of the American founding and the meaning of the American Constitution, however, it is essential to look beyond the myths and rhetoric, and to explore the conflicting interests and forces at work during the revolutionary and constitutional periods. Thus, we will first assess the political backdrop of the American Revolution, and then we will examine the Constitution that ultimately emerged as the basis for America's government. We will conclude with a reflection upon the founding period by assessing the question that we believe is essential to understanding the meaning of the Constitution: "Was the Constitution based more on principle or interest?"

## THE FIRST FOUNDING: INTERESTS AND CONFLICTS

Competing ideals and principles often reflect competing interests, and so it was in revolutionary America. The American Revolution and the American Constitution were outgrowths and expressions of a struggle among economic and political forces within the colonies. Five sectors of society had interests that were important in colonial politics: (1) the New England merchants; (2) the Southern planters; (3) the "royalists"—holders of royal lands, offices, and patents (licenses to engage in a profession or business activity); (4) shopkeepers, artisans, and laborers; and (5) small farmers. Throughout the eighteenth century, these groups were in conflict over issues of taxation, trade, and commerce. For the most part, however, the Southern planters, the New England merchants, and the royal office and patent holders—groups that together made up the colonial elite—were able to maintain a political alliance that held in check the more radical forces representing shopkeepers, laborers, and small farmers. After 1750, however, by seriously threatening the interests of New England merchants and Southern planters, British tax and trade policies split the colonial elite, permitting radical forces to expand their political influence, and set into motion a chain of events that culminated in the American Revolution.[1]

### British Taxes and Colonial Interests

Beginning in the 1750s, the debts and other financial problems faced by the British government forced it to search for new revenue sources. This search rather quickly led to the Crown's North American colonies, which, on the whole, paid remarkably little in taxes to the mother country. The British government reasoned that a sizable fraction of its debt was, in fact, attributable to the expenses it had incurred in defense of the colonies during the recent French and Indian wars, as well as to the continuing protection that British forces were giving the colonists from Indian attacks and that the British navy was providing for colonial shipping. Thus, during the 1760s, England sought to impose new, though relatively modest, taxes upon the colonists.

[1]The social makeup of colonial America and some of the social conflicts that divided colonial society are discussed in Jackson Turner Main, *The Social Structure of Revolutionary America* (Princeton: Princeton University Press, 1965).

Like most governments of the period, the British regime had at its disposal only limited ways to collect revenues. The income tax, which in the twentieth century has become the single most important source of governmental revenues, had not yet been developed. For the most part, in the mid-eighteenth century, governments relied on tariffs, duties, and other taxes on commerce, and it was to such taxes, including the Stamp Act, that the British turned during the 1760s.

The Stamp Act and other taxes on commerce, such as the Sugar Act of 1764, which taxed sugar, molasses, and other commodities, most heavily affected the two groups in colonial society whose commercial interests and activities were most extensive—the New England merchants and Southern planters. Under the famous slogan "no taxation without representation," the merchants and planters together sought to organize opposition to the new taxes. In the course of the struggle against British tax measures, the planters and merchants broke with their royalist allies and turned to their former adversaries—the shopkeepers, small farmers, laborers, and artisans—for help. With the assistance of these groups, the merchants and planters organized demonstrations and a boycott of British goods that ultimately forced the Crown to rescind most of its new taxes. It was in the context of this unrest that a confrontation between colonists and British soldiers in front of the Boston customs house on the night of March 5, 1770, resulted in what came to be known as the Boston Massacre. Nervous British soldiers opened fire on the mob surrounding them, killing five colonists and wounding eight others. News of this event quickly spread throughout the colonies and was used by radicals to fan anti-British sentiment.

From the perspective of the merchants and planters, however, the British government's decision to eliminate most of the hated taxes represented a victorious end to their struggle with the mother country. They were anxious to end the unrest they had helped to arouse, and they supported the British government's efforts to restore order. Indeed, most respectable Bostonians supported the actions of the British soldiers involved in the Boston Massacre. In their subsequent trial, the soldiers were defended by John Adams, a pillar of Boston society and a future president of the United States. Adams asserted that the soldiers' actions were entirely justified, provoked by a "motley rabble of saucy boys, negroes and mulattoes, Irish teagues and outlandish Jack tars." All but two of the soldiers were acquitted.[2]

Despite the efforts of the British government and the better-to-do strata of colonial society, it proved difficult to bring an end to the political strife. The more radical forces representing shopkeepers, artisans, laborers, and small farmers, who had been mobilized and energized by the struggle over taxes, continued to agitate for political and social change within the colonies. These radicals, led by individuals like Samuel Adams, cousin of John Adams, began to assert that British power supported an unjust political and social structure within the colonies, and began to advocate an end to British rule.[3]

[2]George B. Tindall and David E. Shi, *America: A Narrative History,* 5th ed. (New York: W. W. Norton, 1999), p. 218.

[3]For a discussion of events leading up to the Revolution, see Charles M. Andrews, *The Colonial Background of the American Revolution* (New Haven: Yale University Press, 1924).

## Political Strife and the Radicalizing of the Colonists

The political strife within the colonies was the background for the events of 1773–1774. In 1773, the British government granted the politically powerful East India Company a monopoly on the export of tea from Britain, eliminating a lucrative form of trade for colonial merchants. To add to the injury, the East India Company sought to sell the tea directly in the colonies instead of working through the colonial merchants. Tea was an extremely important commodity in the 1770s, and these British actions posed a mortal threat to the New England merchants. Together with their Southern allies, the merchants once again called upon their radical adversaries for support. The most dramatic result was the Boston Tea Party of 1773, led by Samuel Adams.

This event was of decisive importance in American history. The merchants had hoped to force the British government to rescind the Tea Act, but they did not support any demands beyond this one. They certainly did not seek independence from Britain. Samuel Adams and the other radicals, however, hoped to provoke the British government to take actions that would alienate its colonial supporters and pave the way for a rebellion. This was precisely the purpose of the Boston Tea Party, and it succeeded. By dumping the East India Company's tea into Boston Harbor, Adams and his followers goaded the British into enacting a number of harsh reprisals. Within five months after the incident in Boston, the House of Commons passed a series of acts that closed the port of Boston to commerce, changed the provincial government of Massachusetts, provided for the removal of accused persons to England for trial, and most important, restricted movement to the West—further alienating the Southern planters who depended upon access to new western lands. These acts of retaliation confirmed the worst criticisms of England and helped radicalize Americans. Radicals like Samuel Adams and Christopher Gadsden of South Carolina had been agitating for more violent measures to deal with England. But ultimately they needed Britain's political repression to create widespread support for independence.

Thus, the Boston Tea Party set into motion a cycle of provocation and retaliation that in 1774 resulted in the convening of the First Continental Congress—an assembly consisting of delegates from all parts of the country—that called for a total boycott of British goods and, under the prodding of the radicals, began to consider the possibility of independence from British rule. The eventual result was the Declaration of Independence.

## The Declaration of Independence

In 1776, the Second Continental Congress appointed a committee consisting of Thomas Jefferson of Virginia, Benjamin Franklin of Pennsylvania, Roger Sherman of Connecticut, John Adams of Massachusetts, and Robert Livingston of New York to draft a statement of American independence from British rule. The Declaration of Independence, written by Jefferson and adopted by the Second Continental Congress, was an extraordinary document both in philosophical and political terms. Philosophically, the Declaration was remarkable for its assertion that certain rights, called "unalienable rights"—including life, liberty, and the pursuit of happiness—could not be abridged by governments. In the world of 1776, a world in which some kings still claimed to rule by divine right, this was a dramatic statement. Politically, the Declaration was remarkable because, despite the differences of interest that divided the colonists along economic, regional, and philosophical lines, the Declaration identified and focused on problems, grievances, aspirations, and principles that might unify the various colonial groups. The Declaration was an attempt to identify and articulate a history and set of principles that might help to forge national unity.[4]

## The Articles of Confederation

Having declared their independence, the colonies needed to establish a governmental structure. In November of 1777, the Continental Congress adopted the ***Articles of Confederation and Perpetual Union***—the United States's first written constitution. Although it was not ratified by all the states until 1781, it was the country's operative constitution for almost twelve years, until March 1789.

The Articles of Confederation was a constitution concerned primarily with limiting the powers of the central government. The central government, first of all, was based entirely in Congress. Since it was not intended to be a powerful government, it was given no executive branch. Execution of its laws was to be left to the individual states. Second, Congress had little power. Its members were not much more than delegates or messengers from the state legislatures. They were chosen by the state legislatures, their salaries were paid out of the state treasuries, and they were subject to immediate recall by state authorities. In addition, each state, regardless of its size, had only a single vote.

Congress was given the power to declare war and make peace, to make treaties and alliances, to coin or borrow money, and to regulate trade with the Native Americans. It could also appoint the senior officers of the United States Army. But it could not levy taxes or regulate commerce among the states. Moreover, the army officers it appointed had no army to serve in because the nation's armed forces were composed of the state militias. Probably the most unfortunate part of the Articles of Confederation was that the central government could not prevent one state from discriminating against other states in the quest for foreign commerce.

In brief, the relationship between Congress and the states under the Articles of Confederation was much like the contemporary relationship between the United Nations and its member states, a relationship in which virtually all governmental powers are retained by the states. It was properly called a "confederation" because, as provided under Article II, "each state retains its sovereignty, freedom and independence, and every Power, Jurisdiction and right, which is not by this confederation expressly delegated to the United States, in Congress assembled." Not only was there no executive, there was also no judicial authority and no other means of enforcing Congress's will. If there was to be any enforcement at all, it would be done for Congress by the states.[5]

[4]See Carl Becker, *The Declaration of Independence* (New York: Vintage, 1942).

[5]See Merrill Jensen, *The Articles of Confederation* (Madison: University of Wisconsin Press, 1963).

# THE SECOND FOUNDING: FROM COMPROMISE TO CONSTITUTION

The Declaration of Independence and the Articles of Confederation were not sufficient to hold the nation together as an independent and effective nation-state. From almost the moment of armistice with the British in 1783, moves were afoot to reform and strengthen the Articles of Confederation.

## International Standing and Balance of Power

There was a special concern for the country's international position. Competition among the states for foreign commerce allowed the European powers to play the states against each other, which created confusion on both sides of the Atlantic. At one point during the winter of 1786–1787, John Adams of Massachusetts, a leader in the independence struggle, was sent to negotiate a new treaty with the British, one that would cover disputes left over from the war. The British government responded that, since the United States under the Articles of Confederation was unable to enforce existing treaties, it would negotiate with each of the thirteen states separately.

At the same time, well-to-do Americans—in particular the New England merchants and Southern planters—were troubled by the influence that "radical" forces exercised in the Continental Congress and in the governments of several of the states. The colonists' victory in the Revolutionary War had not only meant the end of British rule, but it also significantly changed the balance of political power within the new states. As a result of the Revolution, one key segment of the colonial elite—the royal land, office, and patent holders—was stripped of its economic and political privileges. In fact, many of these individuals, along with tens of thousands of other colonists who considered themselves loyal British subjects, left for Canada after the British surrender. And while the pre-revolutionary elite was weakened, the pre-revolutionary radicals were now better organized than ever before, and were the controlling forces in such states as Pennsylvania and Rhode Island, where they pursued economic and political policies that struck terror into the hearts of the pre-revolutionary political establishment. In Rhode Island, for example, between 1783 and 1785, a legislature dominated by representatives of small farmers, artisans, and shopkeepers had instituted economic policies, including drastic currency inflation, that frightened businessmen and property owners throughout the country. Of course, the central government under the Articles of Confederation was powerless to intervene.

## The Annapolis Convention

The continuation of international weakness and domestic economic turmoil led many Americans to consider whether their newly adopted form of government might not already require revision. In the fall of 1786, many state leaders accepted an invitation from the Virginia legislature for a conference of representatives of all the states. Delegates from five states actually attended. This conference, held in Annapolis, Maryland, was the first step toward the second founding. The one positive thing that came out of the Annapolis Convention was a carefully worded resolution calling on Congress to send commissioners to Philadelphia at a later time "to devise such further provisions as shall appear to them necessary to render the Constitution of the Federal Government adequate to the exigencies of the Union."[6] This resolution was drafted by Alexander Hamilton, a thirty-four-year-old New York lawyer who had played a significant role in the Revolution as George Washington's secretary and who would play a still more significant role in framing the Constitution and forming the new government in the 1790s. But the resolution did not necessarily imply any desire to do more than improve and reform the Articles of Confederation.

## Shays's Rebellion

It is quite possible that the Constitutional Convention of 1787 in Philadelphia would never have taken place at all except for a single event that occurred during the winter following the Annapolis Convention: Shays's Rebellion.

Daniel Shays, a former army captain, led a mob of farmers in a rebellion against the government of Massachusetts. The purpose of the rebellion was to prevent foreclosures on their debt-ridden land by keeping the county courts of western Massachusetts from sitting until after the next election. The state militia dispersed the mob, but for several days, Shays and his followers terrified the state government by attempting to capture the federal arsenal at Springfield, provoking an appeal to Congress to help restore order. Within a few days, the state government regained control and captured fourteen of the rebels (all were eventually pardoned). In 1787, a newly elected Massachusetts legislature granted some of the farmers' demands.

Although the incident ended peacefully, its effects lingered and spread. Washington summed it up: "I am mortified beyond expression that in the moment of our acknowledged independence we should by our conduct verify the predictions of our transatlantic foe, and render ourselves ridiculous and contemptible in the eyes of all Europe."[7]

Congress under the Confederation had been unable to act decisively in a time of crisis. This provided critics of the Articles of Confederation with precisely the evidence they needed to push Hamilton's Annapolis resolution through the Congress. Thus, the states were asked to send representatives to Philadelphia to discuss constitutional revision. Delegates were eventually sent by every state except Rhode Island.

## The Constitutional Convention

Twenty-nine of a total of 73 delegates selected by the state governments convened in Philadelphia in May 1787, with political strife, international embarrassment, national weakness, and local rebellion fixed in their minds. Recognizing that these

[6]Reported in Samuel E. Morrison, Henry Steele Commager, and William Leuchtenberg, *The Growth of the American Republic,* vol. 1 (New York: Oxford University Press, 1969), p. 244.
[7]Ibid., p. 242.

DEBATING THE ISSUES

## The Constitution: Property versus Pragmatism

*Throughout the second half of the nineteenth century, the prevailing attitude toward the country's founders was increasingly that of veneration, even worship. Like Moses receiving the Ten Commandments, the founders came to be viewed as messengers from God who had received the Constitution intact and whole rather than creating it through a messy political process. Historian Charles Beard helped shatter this myth in the early twentieth century when he argued that the founders were members of the social and economic elite, little interested in democracy and more motivated by a desire to protect their property and wealth, and that the Constitution was their instrument to achieve this end.*

*Many have examined Beard's work and found fault with his arguments and facts. Notably, political scientist John P. Roche, writing in the 1960s, argued that the founders, even if they were elite, were excellent politicians who were simply trying to forge a government that would be more effective than the Articles of Confederation. Still, Beard's impact was great, in that he helped move constitutional analysis away from uncritical worship and much closer to viewing the political realities of the late eighteenth century.*

### Beard

The Constitution was essentially an economic document based upon the concept that the fundamental private rights of property are anterior to government and morally beyond the reach of popular majorities.

The major portion of the members of the [Constitutional] Convention are on record as recognizing the claim of property to a special and defensive position in the Constitution.

In the ratification of the Constitution, about three-fourths of the adult males failed to vote on the question, having abstained from the elections at which delegates to the state conventions were chosen, either on account of their indifference or their disfranchisement by property qualifications.

The Constitution was ratified by a vote of probably not more than one-sixth of the adult males.

It is questionable whether a majority of the voters participating in the elections for the state [ratifying] conventions in New York, Massachusetts, New Hampshire, Virginia, and South Carolina, actually approved the ratification of the Constitution. . . .

In the ratification, it became manifest that the line of cleavage for and against the Constitution was between substantial personalty interests on the one hand and the small farming and debtor interests on the other.

The Constitution was not created by "the whole people" as the jurists have said; neither was it created by "the states" as Southern nullifiers long contended; but it was the work of a consolidated group whose interests knew no state boundaries and were truly national in their scope.[1]

[1]Charles Beard, *An Economic Interpretation of the Constitution of the United States* (New York: Macmillan, 1913), pp. 324–25.

The Constitution . . . was not an apotheosis of "constitutionalism," a triumph of architectonic genius; it was a patch-work sewn together under the pressure of both time and events by a group of extremely talented democratic politicians. They refused to attempt the establishment of a strong, centralized sovereignty on the principle of legislative supremacy for the excellent reason that the people would not accept it. They risked their political fortunes by opposing the established doctrines of state sovereignty because they were convinced that the existing system was leading to national impotence and probably foreign domination. For two years, they worked to get a convention established. For over three months, in what must have seemed to the faithful participants an endless process of give-and-take, they reasoned, cajoled, threatened, and bargained amongst themselves. The result was a Constitution which the people, in fact, by democratic processes, did accept, and a new and far better national government was established.[2]

[2]John P. Roche, "The Founding Fathers: A Reform Caucus in Action," *American Political Science Review* 55 (December 1961), pp. 815–16.

issues were symptoms of fundamental flaws in the Articles of Confederation, the delegates soon abandoned the plan to revise the Articles and committed themselves to a second founding—a second, and ultimately successful, attempt to create a legitimate and effective national system. This effort occupied the convention for the next five months.

**A Marriage of Interest and Principle** Scholars have for years disagreed about the motives of the founders in Philadelphia (see "Debating the Issues," above). Among the most controversial views of the framers' motives is the "economic" interpretation put forward by historian Charles Beard and his disciples.[8] According to Beard's account, America's founders were a collection of securities speculators and property owners whose only aim was personal enrichment. From this perspective, the Constitution's lofty principles were little more than sophisticated masks behind which the most venal interests sought to enrich themselves.

Contrary to Beard's approach is the view that the framers of the Constitution *were* concerned with philosophical and ethical principles. Indeed, the framers sought to devise a system of government consistent with the dominant philosophical and moral principles of the day. But, in fact, these two views belong together; the founders' interests were reinforced by their principles. The convention that drafted the American Constitution was chiefly organized by the New England merchants and Southern planters. Though the delegates representing these groups

[8]Charles A. Beard, *An Economic Interpretation of the Constitution of the United States* (New York: Macmillan, 1913).

did not all hope to profit personally from an increase in the value of their securities, as Beard would have it, they did hope to benefit in the broadest political and economic sense by breaking the power of their radical foes and establishing a system of government more compatible with their long-term economic and political interests. Thus, the framers sought to create a new government capable of promoting commerce and protecting property from radical state legislatures. At the same time, they hoped to fashion a government less susceptible than the existing state and national regimes to populist forces hostile to the interests of the commercial and propertied classes.

**The Great Compromise** The proponents of a new government fired their opening shot on May 29, 1787, when Edmund Randolph of Virginia offered a resolution that proposed corrections and enlargements in the Articles of Confederation. The proposal, which showed the strong influence of James Madison, was not a simple motion. It provided for virtually every aspect of a new government. Randolph later admitted it was intended to be an alternative draft constitution, and it did in fact serve as the framework for what ultimately became the Constitution. (There is no verbatim record of the debates, but Madison was present during virtually all of the deliberations and kept full notes on them.[9])

The portion of Randolph's motion that became most controversial was the "Virginia Plan." This plan provided for a system of representation in the national legislature based upon the population of each state or the proportion of each state's revenue contribution, or both. (Randolph also proposed a second branch of the legislature, but it was to be elected by the members of the first branch.) Since the states varied enormously in size and wealth, the Virginia Plan was thought to be heavily biased in favor of the large states.

While the convention was debating the Virginia Plan, additional delegates were arriving in Philadelphia and were beginning to mount opposition to it. Their resolution, introduced by William Paterson of New Jersey and known as the "New Jersey Plan," did not oppose the Virginia Plan point for point. Instead, it concentrated on specific weaknesses in the Articles of Confederation, in the spirit of revision rather than radical replacement of that document. Supporters of the New Jersey Plan did not seriously question the convention's commitment to replacing the Articles. But their opposition to the Virginia Plan's scheme of representation was sufficient to send its proposals back to committee for reworking into a common document. In particular, delegates from the less populous states, which included Delaware, New Jersey, Connecticut, and New York, asserted that the more populous states, such as Virginia, Pennsylvania, North Carolina, Massachusetts, and Georgia, would dominate the new government if representation were to be determined by population. The smaller states argued that each state should be equally represented in the new regime regardless of its population.

The issue of representation was one that threatened to wreck the entire constitutional enterprise. Delegates conferred, factions maneuvered, and tempers flared.

[9]Madison's notes along with the somewhat less complete records kept by several other participants in the convention are available in a four-volume set. See Max Farrand, *The Records of the Federal Convention of 1787*, 4 vols., rev. ed. (New Haven: Yale University Press, 1966).

James Wilson of Pennsylvania told the small-state delegates that if they wanted to disrupt the union they should go ahead. The separation could, he said, "never happen on better grounds." Small-state delegates were equally blunt. Gunning Bedford of Delaware declared that the small states might look elsewhere for friends if they were forced. "The large states," he said, "dare not dissolve the confederation. If they do the small ones will find some foreign ally of more honor and good faith, who will take them by the hand and do them justice." These sentiments were widely shared. The union, as Oliver Ellsworth of Connecticut put it, was "on the verge of dissolution, scarcely held together by the strength of a hair."

The outcome of this debate was the Connecticut Compromise, also known as the ***Great Compromise.*** Under the terms of this compromise, in the first branch of Congress—the House of Representatives—the representatives would be apportioned according to the number of inhabitants in each state. This, of course, was what delegates from the large states had sought. But in the second branch—the Senate—each state would have an equal vote regardless of its size; this was to deal with the concerns of the small states. This compromise was not immediately satisfactory to all the delegates. Indeed, two of the most vocal members of the small-state faction, John Lansing and Robert Yates of New York, were so incensed by the concession that their colleagues had made to the large-state forces that they stormed out of the convention. In the end, however, both sets of forces preferred compromise to the breakup of the union, and the plan was accepted.

**The Question of Slavery: The "Three-fifths" Compromise** The story so far is too neat, too easy, and too anticlimactic. If it were left here, it would only contribute to American mythology. After all, the notion of a bicameral (two-chambered) legislature was very much in the air in 1787. Some of the states had had this for years. The Philadelphia delegates might well have gone straight to the adoption of two chambers based on two different principles of representation even without the dramatic interplay of conflict and compromise. But a far more fundamental issue had to be confronted before the Great Compromise could take place: the issue of slavery.

Many of the conflicts that emerged during the Constitutional Convention were reflections of the fundamental differences between the slave and the nonslave states—differences that pitted the Southern planters and New England merchants against one another. This was the first premonition of a conflict that was almost to destroy the Republic in later years. In the midst of debate over large versus small states, Madison observed:

> The great danger to our general government is the great southern and northern interests of the continent, being opposed to each other. Look to the votes in Congress, and most of them stand divided by the geography of the country, not according to the size of the states.[10]

Over 90 percent of all slaves resided in five states—Georgia, Maryland, North Carolina, South Carolina, and Virginia—where they accounted for 30 percent of

[10]Ibid., vol. 1, p. 476.

the total population. In some places, slaves outnumbered nonslaves by as much as ten to one. If the Constitution were to embody any principle of national supremacy, some basic decisions would have to be made about the place of slavery in the general scheme. Madison hit on this point on several occasions as different aspects of the Constitution were being discussed. For example, he observed:

> It seemed now to be pretty well understood that the real difference of interests lay, not between the large and small but between the northern and southern states. The institution of slavery and its consequences formed the line of discrimination. There were five states on the South, eight on the northern side of this line. Should a proportional representation take place it was true, the northern side would still outnumber the other: but not in the same degree, at this time; and every day would tend towards an equilibrium.[11]

**AMERICAN POLITICAL DEVELOPMENT**

Some delegates to the Constitutional Convention advocated that slaves should not be counted for the purposes of apportioning House seats; others thought they should be counted as equal to free men; and the compromise between these two positions suggested that five slaves would count as three free men. Had slaves not been counted at all in 1790, the South would still have garnered 41 percent of House seats; were slaves counted as equal to free men, the South would have 49.9 percent. Under the three-fifths rule, the South had 46.5 percent of House seats. Under any of these scenarios, it was expected that the South's representation would increase, since it was widely believed that the population was growing in a "southwestwardly" direction. This expectation also explains disproportionate Southern support for proportional representation under the Virginia plan.

SOURCE: Donald Robinson, *Slavery in the Structure of American Politics, 1765–1820* (New York: Harcourt Brace Jovanovich, 1971), pp. 178–81.

Northerners and Southerners eventually reached agreement through the ***Three-fifths Compromise.*** The seats in the House of Representatives would be apportioned according to a "population" in which five slaves would count as three persons. The slaves would not be allowed to vote, of course, but the number of representatives would be apportioned accordingly. This arrangement was supported by the slave states, which obviously included some of the biggest and some of the smallest states at that time. It was also accepted by many delegates from nonslave states who strongly supported the principle of property representation, whether that property was expressed in slaves or in land, money, or stocks. The concern exhibited by most delegates was over how much slaves would count toward a state's representation rather than whether the institution of slavery would continue. The Three-fifths Compromise, in the words of political scientist Donald Robinson, "gave Constitutional sanction to the fact that the United States was composed of some persons who were 'free' and others who were not, and it established the principle, new in republican theory, that a man who lives among slaves had a greater share in the election of representatives than the man who did not. Although the Three-fifths Compromise acknowledged slavery and rewarded slave owners, nonetheless, it probably kept the South from unanimously rejecting the Constitution."[12]

The issue of slavery was the most difficult one faced by the framers and nearly destroyed the Union. Although some delegates believed slavery to be morally

[11]Ibid., vol. 2, p. 10.

[12]Donald Robinson, *Slavery in the Structure of American Politics, 1765–1820* (New York: Harcourt Brace Jovanovich, 1971), p. 201.

wrong, an evil and oppressive institution that made a mockery of the ideals and values espoused in the Constitution, morality was not the issue that caused the framers to support or oppose the Three-fifths Compromise. Whatever they thought of the institution of slavery, most delegates from the Northern states opposed counting slaves in the distribution of congressional seats. Wilson of Pennsylvania, for example, argued that if slaves were citizens they should be treated and counted like other citizens. If on the other hand, they were property, then why should not other forms of property be counted toward the apportionment of Congress? But Southern delegates made it clear that if the Northerners refused to give in, they would never agree to the new government. William R. Davie of North Carolina heatedly said that it was time "to speak out." He asserted that the people of North Carolina would never enter the Union if slaves were not counted as part of the basis for representation. Without such agreement, he asserted ominously, "the business was at an end." Even Southerners like Edmund Randolph of Virginia, who conceded that slavery was immoral, insisted upon including slaves in the allocation of congressional seats. This conflict between the Southern and Northern delegates was so divisive that many came to question the possibility of creating and maintaining a union of the two. Pierce Butler of South Carolina declared that the North and South were as different as Russia and Turkey. Eventually, the North and South compromised on the issue of slavery and representation. Indeed, Northerners even agreed to permit a continuation of the odious slave trade to keep the South in the union. But, in due course, Butler proved to be correct, and a bloody war was fought when the disparate interests of the North and South could no longer be reconciled.

## THE CONSTITUTION

The political significance of the Great Compromise and Three-fifths Compromise was to reinforce the unity of the mercantile and planter forces that sought to create a new government. The Great Compromise reassured those who feared that the importance of their own local or regional influence would be reduced by the new governmental framework. The Three-fifths Compromise temporarily defused the rivalry between the merchants and planters. Their unity secured, members of the alliance supporting the establishment of a new government moved to fashion a constitutional framework consistent with their economic and political interests.

In particular, the framers sought a new government that, first, would be strong enough to promote commerce and protect property from radical state legislatures such as Rhode Island's. This became the constitutional basis for national control over commerce and finance, as well as the establishment of national judicial supremacy and the effort to construct a strong presidency. Second, the framers sought to prevent what they saw as the threat posed by the "excessive democracy" of the state and national governments under the Articles of Confederation. This led to such constitutional principles as ***bicameralism*** (division of the Congress into two chambers), checks and balances, staggered terms in office, and indirect election (selection of the president by an electoral college rather than by voters directly). Third, the framers, lacking the power to force the states or the public at large to accept the new form of government, sought to identify principles that would help to secure support. This became the basis of the constitutional provision for direct popular election of representatives and, subsequently, for the addition of the Bill of Rights to the Constitution. Finally, the framers wanted to be certain that the government they created did not use its power to pose even more of a threat to its citizens' liberties and property rights than did the radical state legislatures they feared and despised. To prevent the new government from abusing its power, the framers incorporated principles such as the separation of powers and federalism into the Constitution. Let us assess the major provisions of the Constitution's seven articles to see how each relates to these objectives.

## The Legislative Branch

The first seven sections of Article I of the Constitution provided for a Congress consisting of two chambers—a House of Representatives and a Senate. Members of the House of Representatives were given two-year terms in office and were to be elected directly by the people. Members of the Senate were to be appointed by the state legislatures (this was changed in 1913 by the Seventeenth Amendment, which instituted direct election of senators) for six-year terms. These terms, moreover, were staggered so that the appointments of one-third of the senators would expire every two years. The Constitution assigned somewhat different tasks to the House and Senate. Though the approval of each body was required for the enactment of a law, the Senate alone was given the power to ratify treaties and approve presidential appointments. The House, on the other hand, was given the sole power to originate revenue bills.

The character of the legislative branch was directly related to the framers' major goals. The House of Representatives was designed to be directly responsible to the people in order to encourage popular consent for the new Constitution and, as we saw in Chapter 1, to help enhance the power of the new government. At the same time, to guard against "excessive democracy," the power of the House of Representatives was checked by the Senate, whose members were to be appointed for long terms rather than be elected directly by the people. The purpose of this provision, according to Alexander Hamilton, was to avoid "an unqualified complaisance to every sudden breeze of passion, or to every transient impulse which the people may receive."[13] Staggered terms of service in the Senate, moreover, were intended to make that body even more resistant to popular pressure. Since

### AMERICAN POLITICAL DEVELOPMENT

There were checks on "excessive democracy" within the House itself. House terms were twice the generally accepted length, as suggested by the common refrain, "Where annual elections end, tyranny begins." Moreover, the constitutional provision that "the number of Representatives shall not exceed one for every 30,000" concerned Antifederalists, who thought the number was too high and therefore the common people would not be represented in the legislature.

SOURCE: Joseph M. Bessette, *The Mild Voice of Reason* (Chicago: University of Chicago Press, 1994), p. 23; John P. Kaminski and Richard Leffler, *Federalists and Antifederalists: The Debate over the Ratification of the Constitution* (Madison, WI: Madison House, 1998), pp. 42–44.

[13]E. M. Earle, ed., *The Federalist* (New York: Modern Library, 1937), No. 71.

only one-third of the senators would be selected at any given time, the composition of the institution would be protected from changes in popular preferences transmitted by the state legislatures. This would prevent what James Madison called "mutability in the public councils arising from a rapid succession of new members."[14] Thus, the structure of the legislative branch was designed to contribute to governmental power, to promote popular consent for the new government, and at the same time to place limits on the popular political currents that many of the framers saw as a radical threat to the economic and social order.

**The Powers of Congress and the States** The issues of power and consent were important throughout the Constitution. Section 8 of Article I specifically listed the powers of Congress, which include the authority to collect taxes, to borrow money, to regulate commerce, to declare war, and to maintain an army and navy. By granting it these powers, the framers indicated very clearly that they intended the new government to be far more influential than its predecessor. At the same time, by defining the new government's most important powers as belonging to Congress, the framers sought to promote popular acceptance of this critical change by reassuring citizens that their views would be fully represented whenever the government exercised its new powers.

As a further guarantee to the people that the new government would pose no threat to them, the Constitution implied that any powers not listed were not granted at all. This is the doctrine of ***expressed power.*** The Constitution grants only those powers specifically *expressed* in its text. But the framers intended to create an active and powerful government, and so they included the ***necessary and proper clause,*** sometimes known as the elastic clause, which signified that the enumerated powers were meant to be a source of strength to the national government, not a limitation on it. Each power could be used with the utmost vigor, but no new powers could be seized upon by the national government without a constitutional amendment. In the absence of such an amendment, any power not enumerated was conceived to be "reserved" to the states (or the people).

## The Executive Branch

The Constitution provided for the establishment of the presidency in Article II. As Alexander Hamilton commented, the presidential article aimed toward "energy in the Executive." It did so in an effort to overcome the natural stalemate that was built into the bicameral legislature as well as into the separation of powers among the legislative, executive, and judicial branches. The Constitution afforded the president a measure of independence from the people and from the other branches of government—particularly the Congress.

In line with the framers' goal of increased power to the national government, the president was granted the unconditional power to accept ambassadors from other countries; this amounted to the power to "recognize" other countries. He was also given the power to negotiate treaties, although their acceptance required

[14]Ibid., No. 62.

the approval of the Senate. The president was given the unconditional right to grant reprieves and pardons, except in cases of impeachment. And he was provided with the power to appoint major departmental personnel, to convene Congress in special session, and to veto congressional enactments. (The veto power is formidable, but it is not absolute, since Congress can override it by a two-thirds vote.)

The framers hoped to create a presidency that would make the federal government rather than the states the agency capable of timely and decisive action to deal with public issues and problems. This was the meaning of the "energy" that Hamilton hoped to impart to the executive branch.[15] At the same time, however, the framers sought to help the president withstand (excessively) democratic pressures by making him subject to indirect rather than direct election (through his selection by a separate electoral college). The extent to which the framers' hopes were actually realized will be the topic of Chapter 6.

## The Judicial Branch

In establishing the judicial branch in Article III, the Constitution reflected the framers' preoccupations with nationalizing governmental power and checking radical democratic impulses, while guarding against potential interference with liberty and property from the new national government itself.

Under the provisions of Article III, the framers created a court that was to be literally a supreme court of the United States, and not merely the highest court of the national government. The most important expression of this intention was granting the Supreme Court the power to resolve any conflicts that might emerge between federal and state laws. In particular, the Supreme Court was given the right to determine whether a power was exclusive to the federal government, concurrent with the states, or exclusive to the states. The significance of this was noted by Justice Oliver Wendell Holmes, who observed:

> I do not think the United States would come to an end if we lost our power to declare an act of Congress void. I do think the union would be imperilled if we could not make that declaration as to the laws of the several states.[16]

In addition, the Supreme Court was assigned jurisdiction over controversies between citizens of different states. The long-term significance of this was that as the country developed a national economy, it came to rely increasingly on the federal judiciary, rather than on the state courts, for resolution of disputes.

Judges were given lifetime appointments in order to

**AMERICAN POLITICAL DEVELOPMENT**

The design of the Court to check "radical democratic impulses" raised concerns among Antifederalists who thought that the mode of selecting judges (for life) kept these men too far removed from the people. Moreover, some Antifederalists were concerned about other provisions in Article III, which did not provide for the democratic check of jury trial in civil court cases.

SOURCE: John P. Kaminski and Richard Leffler, *Federalists and Antifederalists: The Debate over the Ratification of the Constitution* (Madison, WI: Madison House, 1998), pp. 120–35.

[15]*The Federalist,* No. 70.

[16]Oliver Wendell Holmes, *Collected Legal Papers* (New York: Harcourt Brace, 1920), pp. 295–96.

protect them from popular politics and from interference by the other branches. This, however, did not mean that the judiciary would actually remain totally impartial to political considerations, or to the other branches, for the president was to appoint the judges, and the Senate to approve the appointments. Congress would also have the power to create inferior (lower) courts, to change the jurisdiction of the federal courts, to add or subtract federal judges, even to change the size of the Supreme Court.

No direct mention is made in the Constitution of ***judicial review***—the power of the courts to render the final decision when there is a conflict of interpretation of the Constitution or of laws between the courts and Congress, the courts and the executive branch, or the courts and the states. Scholars generally feel that judicial review is implicit in the very existence of a written Constitution and in the power given directly to the federal courts over "all Cases . . . arising under this Constitution, the Laws of the United States, and Treaties made, or which shall be made, under their Authority" (Article III, Section 2). The Supreme Court eventually assumed the power of judicial review. Its assumption of this power, as we shall see in Chapter 8, was not based on the Constitution itself but on the politics of later decades and the membership of the Court.

## National Unity and Power

Various provisions in the Constitution addressed the framers' concern with national unity and power, including Article IV's provisions for comity (reciprocity) among states and among citizens of all states.

Each state was prohibited from discriminating against the citizens of other states in favor of its own citizens, with the Supreme Court charged with deciding in each case whether a state had discriminated against goods or people from another state. The Constitution restricted the power of the states in favor of ensuring enough power to the national government to give the country a free-flowing national economy.

The framers' concern with national supremacy was also expressed in Article VI, in the ***supremacy clause,*** which provided that national laws and treaties "shall be the supreme law of the land." This meant that all laws made under the "authority of the United States" would be superior to all laws adopted by any state or any other subdivision, and the states would be expected to respect all treaties made under that authority. This was a direct effort to keep the states from dealing separately with foreign nations or businesses. The supremacy clause also bound the officials of all state and local as well as federal governments to take an oath of office to support the national Constitution. This meant that every action taken by the United States Congress would have to be applied within each state as though the action were in fact state law.

**AMERICAN POLITICAL DEVELOPMENT**

The central government's control of "western lands" helped to establish the supremacy of the national government over the states. Not only could the national government use these land resources to provide land grants to states, but Congress's ability to create new states that would be equal in status and political power to existing states implied that the national government had power over both new and existing states.

SOURCE: Peter S. Onuf, *The Origins of the Federal Republic: Jurisdictional Controversies in the United States, 1775–1787* (Philadelphia: University of Pennsylvania Press, 1983), Chapter 2.

## Amending the Constitution

The Constitution established procedures for its own revision in Article V. Its provisions are so difficult that Americans have availed themselves of the amending process only seventeen times since 1791, when the first ten amendments were adopted. Many other amendments have been proposed in Congress, but fewer than forty of them have even come close to fulfilling the Constitution's requirement of a two-thirds vote in Congress, and only a fraction have gotten anywhere near adoption by three-fourths of the states. The Constitution could also be amended by a constitutional convention. Occasionally, proponents of particular measures, such as a balanced-budget amendment, have called for a constitutional convention to consider their proposals. Whatever the purpose for which it was called, however, such a convention would presumably have the authority to revise America's entire system of government.

## Ratifying the Constitution

The rules for the ratification of the Constitution of 1787 were set forth in Article VII of the Constitution. This provision actually violated the amendment provisions of the Articles of Confederation. For one thing, it adopted a nine-state rule in place of the unanimity among the states required by the Articles of Confederation. For another, it provided that ratification would occur in special state conventions called for that purpose rather than in the state legislatures. All the states except Rhode Island eventually did set up state conventions to ratify the Constitution, and none seemed to protest very loudly the extralegal character of the procedure.

## Constitutional Limits on the National Government's Power

As we have indicated, though the framers sought to create a powerful national government, they also wanted to guard against possible misuse of that power. To that end, the framers incorporated two key principles into the Constitution—the ***separation of powers*** and ***federalism*** (see Chapter 3). A third set of limitations, in the form of the ***Bill of Rights,*** was added to the Constitution to help secure its ratification when opponents of the document charged that it paid insufficient attention to citizens' rights.

**The Separation of Powers** No principle of politics was more widely shared at the time of the 1787 founding than the principle that power must be used to balance power. The French political theorist Montesquieu (1689–1755) believed that this balance was an indispensable defense against tyranny, and his writings, especially his major work, *The Spirit of the Laws,* "were taken as political gospel" at the Philadelphia Convention.[17] The principle of the separation of powers is

[17]Max Farrand, *The Framing of the Constitution of the United States* (New Haven: Yale University Press, 1962), p. 49.

nowhere to be found explicitly in the Constitution, but it is clearly built on Articles I, II, and III, which provide for the following:

1. Three separate and distinct branches of government.
2. Different methods of selecting the top personnel, so that each branch is responsible to a different constituency. This is supposed to produce a "mixed regime," in which the personnel of each department will develop very different interests and outlooks on how to govern, and different groups in society will be assured some access to governmental decision making.
3. ***Checks and balances***—a system under which each of the branches is given some power over the others. Familiar examples are the presidential veto power over legislation, the power of the Senate to approve presidential appointments, and judicial review of acts of Congress.

One clever formulation of the separation of powers is that of a system not of separated powers but of "separated institutions sharing power,"[18] and thus diminishing the chance that power will be misused.

**Federalism** Compared to the confederation principle of the Articles of Confederation, federalism was a step toward greater centralization of power. The delegates agreed that they needed to place more power at the national level, without completely undermining the power of the state governments. Thus, they devised a system of two sovereigns—the states and the nation—with the hope that competition between the two would be an effective limitation on the power of both.

**The Bill of Rights** Late in the Philadelphia Convention, a motion was made to include a bill of rights in the Constitution. After a brief debate in which hardly a word was said in its favor and only one speech was made against it, the motion to include it was almost unanimously turned down. Most delegates sincerely believed that since the federal government was already limited to its expressed powers, further protection of citizens was not needed. The delegates argued that the states should adopt bills of rights because their greater powers needed greater limitations. But almost immediately after the Constitution was ratified, there was a movement to adopt a national bill of rights. This is why the Bill of Rights, adopted in 1791, comprises the first ten amendments to the Constitution rather than being part of the body of it. We will have a good deal more to say about the Bill of Rights in Chapter 4.

## The Fight for Ratification

The first hurdle faced by the new Constitution was ratification by state conventions of delegates elected by the people of each state. This struggle for ratification was carried out in thirteen separate campaigns. Each involved different men,

[18]Richard E. Neustadt, *Presidential Power* (New York: Wiley, 1960), p. 33.

moved at a different pace, and was influenced by local as well as national considerations. Two sides faced off throughout all the states, however, calling themselves Federalists and Antifederalists. The Federalists (who more accurately should have called themselves "Nationalists," but who took their name to appear to follow in the revolutionary tradition) supported the Constitution and preferred a strong national government. The Antifederalists opposed the Constitution and preferred a federal system of government that was decentralized; they took on their name by default, in reaction to their better-organized opponents. The Federalists were united in their support of the Constitution, while the Antifederalists were divided as to what they believed the alternative to the Constitution should be.

During the struggle over ratification of the proposed Constitution, Americans argued about great political issues and principles. How much power should the national government be given? What safeguards were most likely to prevent the abuse of power? What institutional arrangements could best ensure adequate representation for all Americans? Was tyranny to be feared more from the many or from the few?

In political life, of course, principles—even great principles—are seldom completely divorced from some set of interests. In 1787, Americans were divided along economic, regional, and political lines. These divisions inevitably influenced their attitudes toward the profound political questions of the day. Many well-to-do merchants and planters, as we saw earlier, favored the creation of a stronger central government that would have the capacity to protect property, promote commerce, and keep some of the more radical state legislatures in check. At the same time, many powerful state leaders, like Governor George Clinton of New York, feared that strengthening the national government would reduce their own influence and status. Each of these interests, of course, justified its position with an appeal to principle.

Principles are often important weapons in political warfare, and seeing how and by whom they are wielded can illuminate their otherwise obscure implications. In our own time, dry academic discussions of topics such as "free trade" become easier to grasp once it is noted that free trade and open markets are generally favored by low-cost producers, while protectionism is the goal of firms whose costs of production are higher than the international norm.

Even if a principle is invented and initially brandished to serve an interest, however, once it has been articulated it can take on a life of its own and prove to have implications that transcend the narrow interests it was created to serve. Some opponents of the Constitution, for example, who criticized the absence of a bill of rights in the initial document, did so simply with the hope of blocking the document's ratification. Yet, the Bill of Rights that was later added to the Constitution has proven for two centuries to be a bulwark of civil liberty in the United States.

Similarly, closer to our own time, support for the extension of voting rights and for massive legislative redistricting under the rubric of "one man, one vote" during the 1960s came mainly from liberal Democrats who were hoping to strengthen their own political base, since the groups that would benefit most from these initiatives were overwhelmingly Democratic. The principles of equal access to the ballot and one man, one vote, however, have a moral and political validity that is independent of the political interests that propelled these ideas into the political arena.

These examples show us that truly great political principles surmount the interests that initially set them forth. The first step in understanding a political principle is understanding why and by whom it is espoused. The second step is understanding the full implications of the principle itself—implications that may go far beyond the interests that launched it. Thus, even though the great political principles about which Americans argued in 1787 *did* reflect competing interests, they also represented views of society, government, and politics that surmount interest, and so must be understood in their own terms. Whatever the underlying clash of interests that may have guided them, the Federalists and Antifederalists presented important alternative visions of America.

## Federalists versus Antifederalists

During the ratification struggle, thousands of essays, speeches, pamphlets, and letters were presented in support of and in opposition to the proposed Constitution. The best-known pieces supporting ratification of the Constitution were the eighty-five essays written, under the name of "Publius," by Alexander Hamilton, James Madison, and John Jay between the fall of 1787 and the spring of 1788. These *Federalist Papers,* as they are collectively known today, defended the principles of the Constitution and sought to dispel fears of a national authority. The Antifederalists published essays of their own, arguing that the new Constitution betrayed the Revolution and was a step toward monarchy. Among the best of the Antifederalist works were the essays, usually attributed to New York Supreme Court justice Robert Yates, that were written under the name of "Brutus" and published in the *New York Journal* at the same time *The Federalist Papers* appeared. The Antifederalist view was also ably presented in the pamphlets and letters written by a former delegate to the Continental Congress and future U.S. senator, Richard Henry Lee of Virginia, using the pen name "The Federal Farmer." These essays highlight the major differences of opinion between Federalists and Antifederalists. Federalists appealed to basic principles of government in support of their nationalist vision. Antifederalists cited equally fundamental precepts to support their vision of a looser confederacy of small republics.

**Representation** One major area of contention between the two sides was the question of representation. The Antifederalists asserted that representatives must be, "a true picture of the people, . . . [possessing] the knowledge of their circumstances and their wants."[19] This could only be achieved, argued the Antifederalists, in small, relatively homogeneous republics such as the existing states. In their view, the size and extent of the entire nation precluded the construction of a truly representative form of government.

The absence of true representation, moreover, would mean that the people would lack confidence in and attachment to the national government and would refuse to voluntarily obey its laws. As a result, according to the Antifederalists,

[19]Melancton Smith, quoted in Herbert Storing, *What the Antifederalists Were For: The Political Thought of the Opponents of the Constitution* (Chicago: University of Chicago Press, 1981), p. 17.

## "We Must Build a Kind of United States of Europe"[1]

Immediately following World War II, Western Europe had its own debate between federalists and Antifederalists. Unlike in the United States of America, however, the federalists did not immediately triumph.

There are several parallels between the United States during the post–Revolutionary period from 1781 to 1789 and Western Europe during the postwar period from 1945 to 1958. In both cases the individual states worried about their international standing and their ability to act together against a future enemy. While the states under the Articles of Confederation were concerned with Great Britain, Western Europe feared the growing influence of the Soviet Union. Indeed, even without a Soviet-inspired coup, in both postwar France and Italy there was a real possibility that communist parties would gain power by winning elections.

Western Europe also had experiences similar to Shays's Rebellion. Farmers throughout Europe had suffered from the ravages of war, and they were often the first to rebel against the government. As their support in Germany for the Nazis in the late 1920s and 1930s showed, they were also willing to support nondemocratic parties. There was a sense in Europe both that the farmers' concerns needed to be addressed and that a federal government might be the best way to satisfy this group.[2]

The most important reason to consider a federal Europe, however, had no parallel in what was to become the United States. The greatest fear was another World War begun by Western Europe states, and in particular another war between France and Germany. The hope of many European federalists was that a truly federalist

[1]Winston Churchill, "Speech in Zurich," September 1946.

[2]Alan Milward, while disagreeing with the argument that a federalist solution was necessary, stresses the importance of satisfying farmers. Alan Milward, *The European Rescue of the Nation-States* (Berkeley and Los Angeles: University of California Press, 1992).

system would prevent such wars. Resistance groups fighting the German occupation of their countries made their aspirations for a federalist system explicit at a meeting in May 1944. In a famous joint declaration, these groups called for the European states after the war to "surrender irrevocably their sovereign rights in the sphere of defense, relations with powers outside the Union, international exchange and communications." The practical steps they advocated included a joint army, a joint democratically elected parliament, and a Supreme Court.[3] Altiero Spinelli, one of the main leaders of the federalist movement, also called for a common European currency. While the European federalists did not call for a European president, the federalist system that they proposed was otherwise similar to the federalist structure embodied in the U.S. Constitution.

Although the move in the 1950s to establish European-level institutions was initially heartening, the results were ultimately disappointing. Six states formed the European Coal and Steel Community in 1951 with the intent to regulate the two industries most vital to fighting war, coal and steel. The Community did establish a type of Supreme Court—the European Court of Justice—as well as a parliament, but the parliament was not directly elected by the people. And the effort to create a common European army, known as the European Defense Community, collapsed after the French National Assembly voted against the body in 1954. Even after the Treaty of Rome in 1957 established the European Economic Community, which sought to integrate all aspects of the member states' economies, the states still did not have a common currency, a common democratically elected parliament, or a common army.

At the dawn of a new century, the federalist movement in Europe has revived. Today, there are fifteen members of a body that is now known as the European Union. As of 1999, eleven of these states have a common currency, the euro. Since 1979, citizens of these countries have been able to elect directly the members of the European Parliament, and, while that parliament has nowhere near the powers of the U.S. Congress, its powers are growing. There is even some movement again towards common European defense policies, although a common army still is many years away. Much like the growing power of the federal government mentioned in the following chapter, the power of the European Union institutions that are "federal" have been growing as well. There are indeed many parallels between the birth of the United States of America and a rapidly evolving United States of Europe. Winston Churchill's goal of a federal Europe may yet be realized.

[3]Some members of Resistance groups in Europe, "Draft Declaration II on European Federation," Geneva, May 1944. Partially reprinted in Trevor Salmon and Sir William Nicoll, *Building European Union* (Manchester, England and New York: Manchester University Press, 1997), pp. 24–26.

the national government described by the Constitution would be compelled to resort to force to secure popular compliance. The Federal Farmer averred that laws of the remote federal government could be "in many cases disregarded, unless a multitude of officers and military force be continually kept in view, and employed to enforce the execution of the laws, and to make the government feared and respected."[20]

Federalists, for their part, did not long for pure democracy and saw no reason that representatives should be precisely like those they represented. In their view, government must be representative *of* the people, but must also have a measure of autonomy *from* the people. Their ideal government was to be so constructed as to be capable of serving the long-term public interest even if this conflicted with the public's current preference.

Federalists also dismissed the Antifederalist claim that the distance between representatives and constituents in the proposed national government would lead to popular disaffection and compel the government to use force to secure obedience. Federalists replied that the system of representation they proposed was more likely to produce effective government. In Hamilton's words, there would be "a probability that the general government will be better administered than the particular governments."[21] Competent government, in turn, should inspire popular trust and confidence more effectively than simple social proximity between rulers and ruled.

**Tyranny of the Majority** A second important issue dividing Federalists and Antifederalists was the threat of ***tyranny***—unjust rule by the group in power. Both opponents and defenders of the Constitution frequently affirmed their fear of tyrannical rule. Each side, however, had a different view of the most likely source of tyranny and, hence, of the way in which the threat was to be forestalled.

From the Antifederalist perspective, the great danger was the tendency of all governments—including republican governments—to become gradually more and more "aristocratic" in character, where the small number of individuals in positions of authority would use their stations to gain more and more power over the general citizenry. In essence, the few would use their power to tyrannize the many. For this reason, Antifederalists were sharply critical of those features of the Constitution that divorced governmental institutions from direct responsibility to the people—institutions such as the Senate, the executive, and the federal judiciary. The latter, appointed for life, presented a particular threat: "I wonder if the world ever saw . . . a court of justice invested with such immense powers, and yet placed in a situation so little responsible," protested Brutus.[22]

The Federalists, too, recognized the threat of tyranny, but they believed that the danger particularly associated with republican governments was not aristocracy, but instead, majority tyranny. The Federalists were concerned that a popular majority, "united and actuated by some common impulse of passion, or of inter-

[20]"Letters from the Federal Farmer," No. 2, in Herbert Storing, ed., *The Complete Anti-Federalist* (Chicago: University of Chicago Press, 1981).

[21]*The Federalist,* No. 27.

[22]"Essays of Brutus," No. 15, in Storing (ed.), *The Complete Anti-Federalist.*

est, adverse to the rights of other citizens," would endeavor to "trample on the rules of justice."[23] From the Federalist perspective, it was precisely those features of the Constitution attacked as potential sources of tyranny by the Antifederalists that actually offered the best hope of averting the threat of oppression. The size and extent of the nation, for instance, was for the Federalists a bulwark against tyranny. In Madison's famous formulation,

> The smaller the society the fewer will probably be the distinct parties and interests, the more frequently will a majority be found of the same party; and the smaller the number of individuals composing a majority, and the smaller the compass within which they are placed, the more easily will they concert and execute their plans of oppression. Extend the sphere and you take in a greater variety of parties and interests; you make it less probable that a majority of the whole will have a common motive to invade the rights of other citizens; or if such a common motive exists, it will be more difficult for all who feel it to discover their own strength and to act in unison with each other.[24]

The Federalists understood that, in a democracy, temporary majorities could abuse their power. Their misgivings about majority rule were reflected in the constitutional structure. The indirect election of senators, the indirect election of the president, the judicial branch's insulation from the people, the separation of powers, the president's veto power, and the federal system were all means to curb majority tyranny. Except for the indirect election of senators (which was changed in 1913), these aspects of the constitutional structure remain in place today.[25]

**Governmental Power** A third major difference between Federalists and Antifederalists, and the one most central to this book, was the issue of governmental power. Both the opponents and proponents of the Constitution agreed on the principle of limited government. They differed, however, on the fundamentally important question of how to place limits on governmental action. Antifederalists favored limiting and enumerating the powers granted to the national government in relation both to the states and to the people at large. To them, the powers given the national government ought to be "confined to certain defined national objects."[26] Otherwise, the national government would "swallow up all the power of the state governments."[27] Antifederalists bitterly attacked the supremacy clause and the necessary and proper clause of the Constitution as unlimited and dangerous grants of power to the national government.[28]

[23]*The Federalist,* No. 10.

[24]Ibid.

[25]They also serve as a source of interest for political scientists who ponder how a different constitutional structure would produce different policy outcomes. Contemporary social theorists have also been interested in the ironies and paradoxes of majority rule. For a brief explanation, see the Analyzing American Politics box in this chapter, pp 54–55. For a more substantial review of the voting paradox and a case study of how it applies today, see Kenneth A. Shepsle and Mark S. Bonchek, *Analyzing Politics: Rationality, Behavior, and Institutions* (New York: W. W. Norton, 1997), pp. 49–81.

[26]"Essays of Brutus," No. 7.

[27]"Essays of Brutus," No. 6.

[28]Storing, *What the Anti-Federalists Were For,* p. 28.

ANALYZING AMERICAN POLITICS

## *The Instability of Majority Rule and the Strategic Design of the Constitution*

American democracy rests upon the principle of majority rule, that is, the wishes of the majority determine what government does. Ninety-five percent of Americans believe that public officials should be chosen by majority rule. The House of Representatives—a large body elected directly by the people—was designed in particular by the framers of the Constitution to ensure majority rule.

But the framers of the Constitution—James Madison in particular—were also concerned that, in a democracy, majority rule could lead to instability in governmental institutions. Madison was aware of the French political philosopher Marquis de Condorcet, who wrote about the theoretical underpinnings of the potential problems that majority rule can create. As Condorcet pointed out, under certain circumstances, a majority-rule vote can fail to produce an outcome that represents a unique majority view. How is this possible? Consider the following:

Let's say you and two friends are deciding where to go for dinner. You suggest Taco Bell, your friend Joe wants McDonald's, and your other friend Sue wants Pizza Hut. Since you cannot agree on where to go, you decide to take a vote and, through a process of elimination, let the majority decide. The initial step is for each of you to decide what your first, second, and third choices are, as represented below:

| | You | Joe | Sue |
|---|---|---|---|
| 1st choice | Taco Bell | McDonald's | Pizza Hut |
| 2nd choice | McDonald's | Pizza Hut | Taco Bell |
| 3rd choice | Pizza Hut | Taco Bell | McDonald's |

Antifederalists also demanded that a bill of rights be added to the Constitution to place limits upon the government's exercise of power over the citizenry. "There are certain things," wrote Brutus, "which rulers should be absolutely prohibited from doing, because if they should do them, they would work an injury, not a benefit to the people."[29] Similarly, the Federal Farmer maintained that "there are certain unalienable and fundamental rights, which in forming the social compact . . . ought to be explicitly ascertained and fixed."[30]

Federalists favored the construction of a government with broad powers. They wanted a government that had the capacity to defend the nation against for-

[29] "Essays of Brutus," No. 9.

[30] "Letters from the Federal Farmer," No. 2.

You start by asking your friends, "Would you rather go to Taco Bell or McDonald's?" (your top two choices). Joe votes for McDonald's, Sue votes for Taco Bell, and you vote for Taco Bell, so Taco Bell beats McDonald's 2 to 1. But since Sue isn't happy that her first choice, Pizza Hut, wasn't voted on, she asks, "Well, what about between Pizza Hut and Taco Bell?" She and Joe vote for Pizza Hut, and you vote for Taco Bell, so Pizza Hut beats Taco Bell 2 to 1. Joe is miffed that his two top choices haven't been put to a vote against each other, so he asks, "What about between McDonald's and Pizza Hut?" You and Joe vote for McDonald's, and Sue votes for Pizza Hut, so McDonald's beats Pizza Hut 2 to 1. Each of the three restaurants wins one of the votes. There is no overall winner. Following these procedures of majority rule, can any of these alternatives—Taco Bell, McDonald's, or Pizza Hut—be chosen as the majority preference? It depends on the order that alternatives are voted on and thus who constitutes the majority. If it's you and Joe, then McDonald's is the majority preference. But if Sue proposes a different majority, you and herself, then the majority preference is Taco Bell. Thus, in general, decisions reached by majority rule can be overturned by proposing a different alternative favored by a different majority. This is the kind of instability of majority rule that Condorcet identified.

Political scientists have argued that the framer's misgivings about majority rule were reflected in the design of the Constitution.[1] The separation of powers, the bicameral design of Congress, the presidential veto power, and the power of Congress to override a presidential veto are among the many features of the constitutional structure of American government that illustrate both the framers' sensitivities to the problems of the instability of democratic institutions as well as their genius in designing institutions that would ensure a viable republic.

[1]See Thomas H. Hammond and Gary J. Miller, "The Core of the Constitution," *American Political Science Review* 81 (1987), pp. 1155–74.

eign foes, guard against domestic strife and insurrection, promote commerce, and expand the nation's economy. Antifederalists shared some of these goals but still feared governmental power. Hamilton pointed out, however, that these goals could not be achieved without allowing the government to exercise the necessary power. Federalists acknowledged, of course, that every power could be abused but argued that the way to prevent misuse of power was not by depriving the government of the powers needed to achieve national goals. Instead, they argued that the threat of abuse of power would be mitigated by the Constitution's internal checks and controls. As Madison put it, "the power surrendered by the people is first divided between two distinct governments, and then the portion allotted to each subdivided among distinct and separate departments. Hence, a double security arises to the rights of the people. The different governments will control each other, at the same time that each will be controlled by itself."[31] The Federalists' concern with avoiding unwarranted limits on governmental power led them to oppose a bill of rights, which they saw as nothing more than a set of unnecessary restrictions on the government.

The Federalists acknowledged that abuse of power remained a possibility, but felt that the risk had to be taken because of the goals to be achieved. "The very idea of power included a possibility of doing harm," said the Federalist John Rutledge during the South Carolina ratification debates. "If the gentleman would show the power that could do no harm," Rutledge continued, "he would at once discover it to be a power that could do no good."[32]

## Changing the Framework: Constitutional Amendment

The Constitution has endured for two centuries as the framework of government. But is has not endured without change. Without change, the Constitution might have become merely a sacred text, stored under glass.

### Amendments: Many Are Called, Few Are Chosen

The need for change was recognized by the framers of the Constitution, and the provisions for amendment incorporated into Article V were thought to be "an easy, regular and Constitutional way" to make changes, which would occasionally be necessary because members of Congress "may abuse their power and refuse their consent on the very account . . . to admit to amendments to correct the source of the abuse."[33] Madison made a more balanced defense of the amendment procedure in Article V: "It guards equally against that extreme facility, which would render the Constitution too mutable; and that extreme difficulty, which might perpetuate its discovered faults."[34]

Experience since 1789 raises questions even about Madison's more modest claims. The Constitution has proven to be extremely difficult to amend. In the history of efforts to amend the Constitution, the most appropriate characterization is "many are called, few are chosen." Between 1789 and 1993, 9,746 amendments were formally offered in Congress. Of these, Congress officially proposed only 29, and 27 of these were eventually ratified by the states. But the record is even more severe than that. Since 1791, when the first 10 amendments, the Bill of Rights, were added, only 17 amendments have been adopted. And two of them—Prohibition and its repeal—cancel each other out, so that for all practical purposes, only 15 amendments have been added to the Constitution since 1791.

[31]*The Federalist,* No. 51.

[32]Quoted in Storing, *What the Anti-Federalists Were For,* p. 30.

[33]Observation by Colonel George Mason, delegate from Virginia, early during the convention period. Quoted in Farrand, *The Records of the Federal Convention of 1787,* vol. 1, pp. 202–3.

[34]Clinton Rossiter, ed. *The Federalist Papers* (New York: New American Library, 1961), No. 43, p. 278.

Despite vast changes in American society and its economy, only 12 amendments have been adopted since the Civil War amendments in 1868.

Four methods of amendment are provided for in Article V:

1. Passage in House and Senate by two-thirds vote; then ratification by majority vote of the legislatures of three-fourths (thirty-eight) of the states.
2. Passage in House and Senate by two-thirds vote; then ratification by conventions called for the purpose in three-fourths of the states.
3. Passage in a national convention called by Congress in response to petitions by two-thirds of the states; ratification by majority vote of the legislatures of three-fourths of the states.
4. Passage in a national convention, as in (3); then ratification by conventions called for the purpose in three-fourths of the states.

(Process Box 2.1 illustrates each of these possible methods.) Since no amendment has ever been proposed by national convention, however, methods (3) and (4) have never been employed. And method (2) has only been employed once (the Twenty-first Amendment, which repealed the Eighteenth, or Prohibition, Amendment). Thus, method (1) has been used for all the others.

**AMERICAN POLITICAL DEVELOPMENT**

Although there have been important changes in the Constitution with regard to the rights of individuals (especially the Bill of Rights and the Civil War–era amendments), only two amendments—the Seventeenth, which provided for the direct election of senators, and the Twenty-second, which limited presidents to two terms—"have affected in any way the character of the institutions that were bequeathed to the twentieth century by the eighteenth."

SOURCE: James L. Sundquist, *Constitutional Reform and Effective Government,* rev. ed. (Washington, DC: Brookings Institution, 1992), pp. 2–3.

Now we should be better able to explain why it has been so difficult to amend the Constitution. The main reason is the requirement of a two-thirds vote in the House and the Senate, which means that any proposal for an amendment in Congress can be killed by only 34 senators *or* 136 members of the House. What is more, if the necessary two-thirds vote is obtained, the amendment can still be killed by the refusal or inability of only thirteen state legislatures to ratify it. Since each state has an equal vote regardless of its population, the thirteen holdout states may represent a very small fraction of the total American population.

## The Case of the Equal Rights Amendment

The Equal Rights Amendment (ERA) is a good illustration of the amending process. Its failure despite strong popular support is indicative of the great difficulty of amending the Constitution.[35] ERA is all the more interesting because it

[35]The proposed Equal Rights Amendment (1972) is one of only six amendments proposed and adopted by Congress but not ratified by the states: (1) An amendment proposed in 1789 with the Bill of Rights providing that there would be one Representative for every 30,000 persons, until the number of the House grew to 100, after which the proportion would be regulated by Congress. (2) An amendment proposed in 1810 to strip any person of citizenship who accepted a title of nobility. (3) An amendment proposed in 1861 to permit any amendment to the Constitution or any Act of

PROCESS BOX 2.1

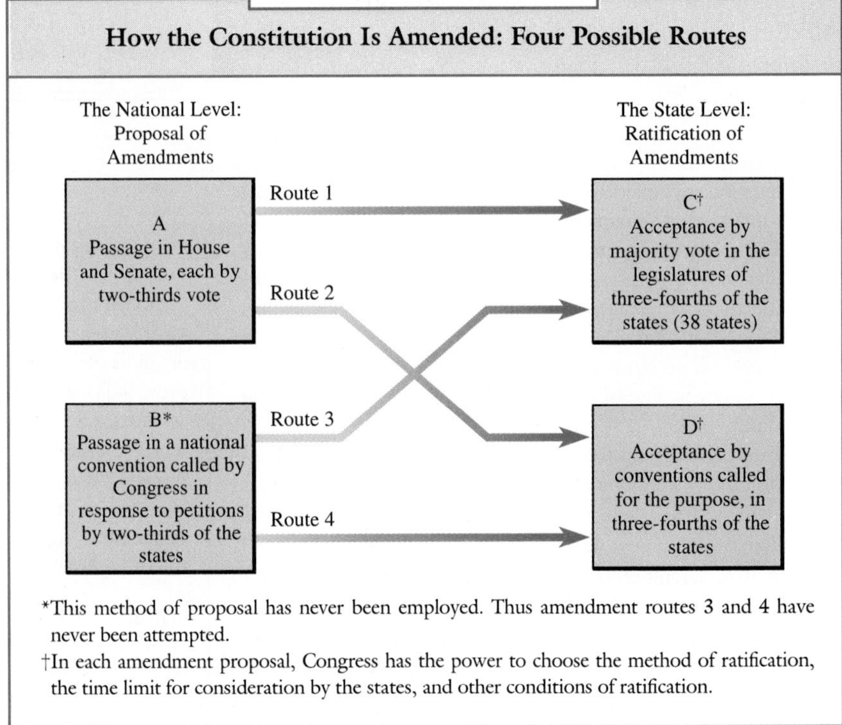


is one of the very few proposals that got the necessary two-thirds vote in Congress and then failed to obtain the ratification of the requisite thirty-eight states.

On October 12, 1971, the U.S. House of Representatives approved the Equal Rights Amendment by the required two-thirds majority; the Senate followed suit on March 22, 1972. The amendment was very simple:

> Sec. 1. Equality of rights under the law shall not be denied or abridged by the United States or by any State on account of sex.
> Sec. 2. The Congress shall have the power to enforce, by appropriate legislation, the provisions of this article.
> Sec. 3. This amendment shall take effect two years after the date of ratification.

The congressional resolution provided for the accustomed method of ratification through the state legislatures rather than by state conventions—method (1) rather than method (2) on Process Box 2.1—and that it had to be completed within seven years, by March 22, 1979.

---

Congress to abolish slavery. (4) An amendment offered for the first time in 1924 to prohibit the employment of persons under the age of 18. (5) An amendment offered for the first time in 1978 to provide statehood for the District of Columbia.

Since the amendment was the culmination of nearly a half-century of efforts, and since the women's movement had spread and intensified its struggle for several years prior to 1971, the amendment was ratified by twenty-eight state legislatures during the very first year. But opposition forces quickly organized into the "Stop ERA" movement. By the end of 1974, five more states had ratified the amendment, but three states that had ratified it in 1973—Idaho, Nebraska, and Tennessee—had afterwards voted to rescind their ratification. This posed an unprecedented problem: whether a state legislature had the right to rescind its approval. The Supreme Court steadfastly refused to deal with this question, insisting that it was a "political question" to be settled by Congress. If ERA had been ratified by the thirty-eight-state minimum, Congress would have had to decide whether to respect the rescissions or to count them as ratifications.

This point was rendered moot by events. By the end of 1978, thirty-five state legislatures had ratified ERA—counting the three rescinding legislatures as ratifiers. But even counting them, the three additional state ratifications necessary to reach thirty-eight became increasingly difficult to get. Among the remaining fifteen states, the amendment had already been rejected at least once. The only hope of the ERA forces was that the 1978 elections would change the composition of some of those state legislatures. Pinning their hopes on that, the ERA forces turned back to Congress and succeeded in getting an extension of the ratification deadline to June 30, 1982. This was an especially significant victory, because it was the first time Congress had extended the time limit since it began placing time restrictions on ratification in 1917. But this victory in Washington failed to impress any of the fifteen holdout legislatures. June 30, 1982, came and went, and the ERA was, for the time being at least, laid to rest. It was beaten by the efforts of the "Stop ERA" group and by the emergence of conservatism generally, which had culminated in Ronald Reagan's election as president.[36]

## Which Were Chosen? An Analysis of the Twenty-Seven

There is more to the amending difficulties than the politics of campaigning and voting. It would appear that only a limited number of changes needed by society can actually be made through the Constitution. Although we shall see that the ERA and the balanced-budget amendment fit the pattern of successful amendments, most efforts to amend the Constitution failed because they were simply attempts to use the Constitution as an alternative to legislation for dealing directly with a public problem. A review of the successful amendments will provide two insights: First, it will give us some understanding of the conditions underlying successful amendments; and second, it will reveal a great deal about what constitutionalism means.

The purpose of the ten amendments in the Bill of Rights was basically

[36]See Marcia Lee, "The Equal Rights Amendment—Public Policy by Means of a Constitutional Amendment," in *The Politics of Policy-Making in America,* ed. David Caputo (San Francisco: W. H. Freeman, 1977); Jane Mansbridge, *Why We Lost the ERA* (Chicago: University of Chicago Press, 1986); and Donald Mathews and Jane Sherron DeHart, *Sex, Gender, and the Politics of the ERA* (New York: Oxford University Press, 1990).

structural, *to give each of the three branches clearer and more restricted boundaries.* The First Amendment clarified the jurisdiction of Congress. Although the powers of Congress under Article I, Section 8, would not have justified laws regulating religion, speech, and the like, the First Amendment made this limitation explicit: "Congress shall make no law. . . ." The Second, Third, and Fourth Amendments similarly spelled out specific limits on the executive branch. This was seen as a necessity given the abuses of executive power Americans had endured under British rule.

The Fifth, Sixth, Seventh, and Eighth Amendments contain some of the most important safeguards for individual citizens against the arbitrary exercise of government power. And these amendments sought to accomplish their goal by defining the judicial branch more concretely and clearly than had been done in Article III of the Constitution. Table 2.1 analyzes the ten amendments included in the Bill of Rights.

Five of the seventeen amendments adopted since 1791 are directly concerned with expansion of the electorate (see Table 2.2). These occasional efforts to expand the electorate were made necessary by the fact that the founders were unable to establish a national electorate with uniform voting qualifications. Stalemated on that issue, the delegates decided to evade it by providing in the final draft of Article I, Section 2, that eligibility to vote in a national election would be the same as "the Qualification requisite for Elector of the most numerous branch of the state Legislature." Article I, Section 4, added that Congress could alter state regulations as to the "Times, Places, and Manner of holding Elections for

TABLE 2.1

**The Bill of Rights: Analysis of Its Provisions**

| AMENDMENT | PURPOSE |
|---|---|
| I | *Limits on Congress:* Congress is not to make any law establishing a religion or abridging the freedom of speech, press, assembly, or the right to petition freedoms. |
| II, III, IV | *Limits on Executive:* The executive branch is not to infringe on the right of people to keep arms (II), is not to arbitrarily take houses for a militia (III), and is not to engage in the search or seizure of evidence without a court warrant swearing to belief in the probable existence of a crime (IV). |
| V, VI, VII, VIII | *Limits on Courts:* The courts are not to hold trials for serious offenses without provision for a grand jury (V), a petit (trial) jury (VII), a speedy trial (VI), presentation of charges, confrontation of hostile witnesses (VI), immunity from testimony against oneself (V), and immunity from trial more than once for the same offense (V). Neither bail nor punishment can be excessive (VIII), and no property can be taken without just compensation (V). |
| IX, X | *Limits on National Government:* All rights not enumerated are reserved to the states or the people. |

TABLE 2.2

**Amending the Constitution to Expand the Electorate**

| AMENDMENT | PURPOSE | YEAR PROPOSED | YEAR ADOPTED |
|---|---|---|---|
| XIV | Section 1 provided national definition of citizenship* | 1866 | 1868 |
| XV | Extended voting rights to all races | 1869 | 1870 |
| XIX | Extended voting rights to women | 1919 | 1920 |
| XXIII | Extended voting rights to residents of the District of Columbia | 1960 | 1961 |
| XXIV | Extended voting rights to all classes by abolition of poll taxes | 1962 | 1964 |
| XXVI | Extended voting rights to citizens aged 18 and over | 1971 | 1971 |

*In defining *citizenship,* the Fourteenth Amendment actually provided the constitutional basis for expanding the electorate to include all races, women, and residents of the District of Columbia. Only the "eighteen-year-olds' amendment" should have been necessary, since it changed the definition of citizenship. The fact that additional amendments were required following the Fourteenth suggests that voting is not considered an inherent right of U.S. citizenship. Instead it is viewed as a privilege.

Senators and Representatives." Nevertheless, this meant that any important *expansion* of the American electorate would almost certainly require a constitutional amendment.

Six more amendments are also electoral in nature, although not concerned directly with voting rights and the expansion of the electorate (see Table 2.3).

TABLE 2.3

**Amending the Constitution to Change the Relationship between Elected Offices and the Electorate**

| AMENDMENT | PURPOSE | YEAR PROPOSED | YEAR ADOPTED |
|---|---|---|---|
| XII | Provided separate ballot for vice president in the electoral college | 1803 | 1804 |
| XIV | Section 2 eliminated counting of slaves as "three-fifths" citizens for apportionment of House seats | 1866 | 1868 |
| XVII | Provided direct election of senators | 1912 | 1913 |
| XX | Eliminated "lame duck" session of Congress | 1932 | 1933 |
| XXII | Limited presidential term | 1947 | 1951 |
| XXV | Provided presidential succession in case of disability | 1965 | 1967 |

TABLE 2.4

**Amending the Constitution to Expand or Limit the Power of Government**

| AMENDMENT | PURPOSE | YEAR PROPOSED | YEAR ADOPTED |
|---|---|---|---|
| XI | Limited jurisdiction of federal courts over suits involving the states | 1794 | 1798 |
| XIII | Eliminated slavery and eliminated the right of states to allow property in persons | 1865* | 1865 |
| XIV | (Part 2) Applied due process of Bill of Rights to the states | 1866 | 1868 |
| XVI | Established national power to tax incomes | 1909 | 1913 |
| XXVII | Limited Congress's power to raise its own salary | 1789 | 1992 |

*The Thirteenth Amendment was proposed January 31, 1865, and adopted less than a year later, on December 18, 1865.

These six amendments are concerned with the elective offices themselves (the Twentieth, Twenty-second, and Twenty-fifth) or with the relationship between elective offices and the electorate (the Twelfth, Fourteenth, and Seventeenth).

Another five amendments have sought to expand or to delimit the powers of the national and state governments (see Table 2.4).[37] The Eleventh Amendment protected the states from suits by private individuals and took away from the federal courts any power to take suits by private individuals of one state (or a foreign country) against another state. The other three amendments in Table 2.4 are obviously designed to reduce state power (Thirteenth), to reduce state power and expand national power (Fourteenth), and to expand national power (Sixteenth). The Twenty-seventh put a limit on Congress's ability to raise its own salary.

The two missing amendments underscore the meaning of the rest: the Eighteenth, or Prohibition, Amendment and the Twenty-first, its repeal. This is the only instance in which the country tried to *legislate* by constitutional amendment. In other words, the Eighteenth is the only amendment that was designed to deal directly with some substantive social problem. And it was the only amendment ever to have been repealed. Two other amendments—the Thirteenth, which abolished slavery, and the Sixteenth, which established the power to levy an income tax—can be said to have had the effect of legislation. But the purpose of the Thirteenth was to restrict the power of the states by forever forbidding them to treat any human being as property. As for the Sixteenth, it is certainly true that income tax legislation followed immediately; nevertheless, the amendment concerns itself strictly with establishing the power of Congress to enact such legislation. The

[37]The Fourteenth Amendment is included in this table as well as in Tables 2.2 and 2.3 because it seeks not only to define citizenship but *seems* to intend also that this definition of citizenship included, along with the right to vote, all the rights of the Bill of Rights, regardless of the state in which the citizen resided. A great deal more will be said about this in Chapter 4.

legislation came later; and if down the line a majority in Congress had wanted to abolish the income tax, they could also have done this by legislation rather than through the arduous path of a constitutional amendment repealing the income tax.

All of this points to the principle underlying the twenty-five existing amendments: All are concerned with the structure or composition of government. This is consistent with the dictionary, which defines *constitution* as the makeup or composition of a thing, anything. And it is consistent with the concept of a constitution as "higher law," because the whole point and purpose of a higher law is to establish *a framework within which government and the process of making ordinary law can take place.* Even those who would have preferred more changes in the Constitution would have to agree that there is great wisdom in this principle. A constitution ought to enable legislation and public policies to take place, but it should not determine what that legislation or those public policies ought to be.

For those whose hopes for change center on the Constitution, it must be emphasized that the amendment route to social change is, and always will be, extremely limited. Through a constitution it is possible to establish a working structure of government; and through a constitution it is possible to establish basic rights of citizens by placing limitations and obligations on the powers of that government. Once these things have been accomplished, the real problem is how to extend rights to those people who do not already enjoy them. Of course, the Constitution cannot enforce itself. But it can and does have a real influence on everyday life because a right or an obligation set forth in the Constitution can become a *cause of action* in the hands of an otherwise powerless person.

Private property is an excellent example. Property is one of the most fundamental and well-established rights in the United States; but it is well established not because it is recognized in so many words in the Constitution, but because legislatures and courts have made it a crime for anyone, including the government, to trespass or to take away property without compensation.

## Reflections on the Founding: Principles or Interests?

The final product of the Constitutional Convention would have to be considered an extraordinary victory for the groups that had most forcefully called for the creation of a new system of government to replace the Articles of Confederation. Antifederalist criticisms forced the Constitution's proponents to accept the addition of a bill of rights designed to limit the powers of the national government. In general, however, it was the Federalist vision of America that triumphed. The Constitution adopted in 1789 created the framework for a powerful national government that for more than two hundred years has defended the nation's interests, promoted its commerce, and maintained national unity. In one notable instance, the national government fought and won a bloody war to prevent the nation from breaking apart.

Though the Constitution was the product of a particular set of political forces, the principles of government it established have a significance that goes far beyond the interests of its authors. Two of these principles, federalism and civil liberties, will be discussed in Chapters 3 and 4. A third important constitutional principle that has affected America's government for the past two hundred years is the principle of *checks and balances.* As we saw earlier, the framers gave each of the three branches of government a means of intervening in and blocking the actions of the others. Often, checks and balances have seemed to prevent the government from getting much done. During the 1960s, for example, liberals were often infuriated as they watched Congress stall presidential initiatives in the area of civil rights. More recently, conservatives were outraged when President Clinton thwarted congressional efforts to enact legislation promised in the Republican "Contract with America." At various times, all sides have vilified the judiciary for invalidating legislation enacted by Congress and signed by the president.

Over time, checks and balances have acted as brakes on the governmental process. Groups hoping to bring about changes in policy or governmental institutions seldom have been able to bring about decisive and dramatic transformations in a short period of time. Instead, checks and balances have slowed the pace of change and increased the need for compromise and accommodation.

THEN AND NOW

## Changes in American Politics

Many of the things we take for granted in American politics are not due to the "natural" flow of government but are instead the result of institutional choices made at the time of the founding, as well as the result of government's development and expansion.

- The effects of the Three-fifths compromise on Southern representation in the House of Representatives were significant at the time of its adoption, and it was expected that these effects would only increase as the free and slave populations of the South and West continued to grow. The Three-fifths Compromise remained in effect until the ratification of the Fourteenth Amendment in 1868.
- The Constitution designed Congress with neither party leadership nor a committee system in mind. This early latitude enhanced Congress's capacity for action, however.
- The Constitution determined that there would be a unitary executive, independent of the Congress. At the Constitutional Convention, founders debated having a plural executive (for example, a three-person executive council). They also debated having an executive who would be selected by the legislature.
- The contours of the federal judiciary power were not outlined in the Constitution but rather in the first years of the republic. The structure of the federal judiciary was established in the Judiciary Act of 1789, and the power of "judicial review" was a product of the Court's 1803 *Marbury v. Madison* decision (see page 320).

Groups able to take control of the White House, for example, must negotiate with their rivals who remain entrenched on Capitol Hill. New forces in Congress must reckon with the influence of other forces in the executive branch and in the courts. Checks and balances inevitably frustrate those who desire change, but they also function as a safeguard against rash action. During the 1950s, for example, Congress was caught up in a quasi-hysterical effort to unmask subversive activities in the United States, which might have led to a serious erosion of American liberties if not for the checks and balances provided by the executive and the courts. Thus, a governmental principle that serves as a frustrating limitation one day may become a vitally important safeguard the next.

As we close our discussion of the founding, it is also worth reflecting on the Antifederalists. Although they were defeated in 1789, the Antifederalists present us with an important picture of a road not taken and of an America that might have been. Would we have been worse off as a people if we had been governed by a confederacy of small republics linked by a national administration with severely limited powers? Were the Antifederalists correct in predicting that a government given great power in the hope that it might do good would, through "insensible progress," inevitably turn to evil purposes? Two hundred years of government under the federal Constitution are not necessarily enough to definitively answer these questions. Time yet will tell.

## SUMMARY

Political conflicts between the colonies and England, and among competing groups within the colonies, led to the first founding as expressed by the Declaration of Independence. The first constitution, the Articles of Confederation, was adopted one year later (1777). Under this document, the states retained their sovereignty. The central government, composed solely of Congress, had few powers and no means of enforcing its will. The national government's weakness soon led to the Constitution of 1787, the second founding.

In this second founding the framers sought, first, to fashion a new government sufficiently powerful to promote commerce and protect property from radical state legislatures. Second, the framers sought to bring an end to the "excessive democracy" of the state and national governments under the Articles of Confederation. Third, the framers introduced mechanisms that helped secure popular consent for the new government. Finally, the framers made certain that their new government would not itself pose a threat to liberty and property.

The Constitution consists of seven articles. In part, Article I provides for a Congress of two chambers (Sections 1–7), defines the powers of the national government (Section 8), and interprets the national government's powers as a source of strength rather than a limitation (necessary and proper clause). Article II describes the presidency and establishes it as a separate branch of government. Article III is the judiciary article. While there is no direct mention of judicial review in this article, the Supreme Court eventually assumed that power. Article IV addresses reciprocity among states and their citizens. Article V describes the procedures for amending the Constitution. Hundreds of amendments have been offered but only twenty-seven have been adopted. With the exception of the two Prohibition amendments, all amendments were oriented toward some change in the framework or structure of government. Article VI establishes that national laws and treaties are "the supreme law of the land." And finally, Article VII specifies the procedure for ratifying the Constitution of 1787.

The struggle for the ratification of the Constitution pitted the Antifederalists against the Federalists. The Antifederalists thought the proposed new government would be too powerful, and they fought against the ratification of the Constitution. The Federalists supported the Constitution and were able to secure its ratification after a nationwide political debate.

## For Further Reading

Anderson, Thornton. *Creating the Constitution: The Convention of 1787 and the First Congress.* University Park: Pennsylvania State University Press, 1993.

Andrews, Charles M. *The Colonial Background of the American Revolution.* New Haven: Yale University Press, 1924.

Bailyn, Bernard. *The Ideological Origins of the American Revolution.* Cambridge: Harvard University Press, 1967.

Beard, Charles. *An Economic Interpretation of the Constitution of the United States.* New York: Macmillan, 1913.

Becker, Carl L. *The Declaration of Independence*. New York: Vintage, 1942.

Cohler, Anne M. *Montesquieu's Politics and the Spirit of American Constitutionalism.* Lawrence: University Press of Kansas, 1988.

Farrand, Max, ed. *The Records of the Federal Convention of 1787.* 4 vols. New Haven: Yale University Press, 1966.

Hamilton, Alexander, James Madison, and John Jay. *The Federalist Papers.* Edited by Isaac Kramnick. New York: Viking Press, 1987.

Jensen, Merrill. *The Articles of Confederation.* Madison: University of Wisconsin Press, 1963.

Lipset, Seymour M. *The First New Nation: The United States in Historical and Comparative Perspective.* New York: Basic Books, 1963.

McDonald, Forrest. *The Formation of the American Republic.* New York: Penguin, 1967.

Main, Jackson Turner. *The Social Structure of Revolutionary America.* Princeton: Princeton University Press, 1965.

Palmer, R. R. *The Age of the Democratic Revolution.* Princeton: Princeton University Press, 1964.

Rossiter, Clinton, ed. *The Federalist Papers.* New York: New American Library, 1961.

Storing, Herbert, ed. *The Complete Anti-Federalist.* 7 vols. Chicago: University of Chicago Press, 1981.

Wills, Gary. *Explaining America.* New York: Penguin, 1982.

Wood, Gordon S. *The Creation of the American Republic.* New York: W. W. Norton, 1982.

# The Constitutional Framework: Federalism and the Separation of Powers

## TIME LINE ON FEDERALISM

| Events | | Institutional Developments |
|---|---|---|
| | | Congress establishes national economic power, power to tax, power over foreign policy (1791–1795) |
| | | Bill of Rights ratified (1791) |
| | 1800 | Epoch of dual federalism: Congress promotes commerce; states possess unchallenged police power (1789–1937) |
| Hartford Convention—New England states threaten secession from Union (1814) | | *McCulloch v. Maryland* (1819) and *Gibbons v. Ogden* (1824) reaffirm national supremacy |
| President Andrew Jackson decisively deals with South Carolina's threat to secede (1833) | | |
| Attempt to use U.S. Bill of Rights to restrict state power (1830s) | | *Barron v. Baltimore*—State power not subject to the U.S. Bill of Rights (1833) |
| Territorial expansion; slaves taken into territories (1800s) | 1850 | *Dred Scott v. Sandford*—Congress may not regulate slavery in the territories (1857) |
| Secession of Southern states (1860–1861); Civil War (1861–1865) | | Union destroyed (1860–1861) |
| | | Union restored (1865) |
| | | Constitution amended: XIII (1865), XIV (1868), XV (1870) Amendments |
| Reconstruction of South (1867–1877) | 1870 | |
| Compromise of 1877—self-government restored to former Confederate states (1877) | | Reestablishment of South's full place in the Union (1877) |
| Consolidation of great national industrial corporations (U.S. Steel, AT&T, Standard Oil) (1880s and 1890s) | | Interstate Commerce Act (1887) and Sherman Antitrust Act (1890) provide first national regulation of monopoly practices |
| | 1930 | |
| Franklin D. Roosevelt's first New Deal programs for national economic recovery enacted by Congress (1933) | | Supreme Court upholds expanded powers of president in *U.S. v. Curtiss-Wright* (1936), and of Congress in *Steward Machine v. Davis* (1937) and *NLRB v. Jones & Laughlin Steel* (1937) |
| Blacks reject segregation after World War II (1950s) | 1950 | |
| Black protests against segregation in South (1950s and 1960s) | | Supreme Court holds that segregation is "inherently unequal" in *Brown v. Board of Ed.* (1954) |
| Drive to register Southern blacks to vote (1965) | | Voting Rights Act (1965) |
| | | National power expanded to reach discrimination, poverty, education, and poor health (1960s) |

| Events | | Institutional Developments |
|---|---|---|
| Republicans take control of the White House (1968) | | |
| | 1970 | |
| | | Revenue sharing under Nixon to strengthen state governments (1972) |
| Election of Ronald Reagan (1980) | | States' rights reaffirmed by Reagan and Bush administrations (1980–1990s) |
| Election of George Bush (1988) | | |
| | 1990 | |
| | | Americans with Disabilities Act (1990); Civil Rights Act (1991) |
| Election of Bill Clinton; Democrats control Congress and Executive (1992) | | |
| Republicans take control of Congress (1994) | | Contract with America pledges devolution and privatization (1995) |
| | | Supreme Court in *U.S. v. Lopez* recognizes a limit to Congress's power to regulate commerce (1995) |
| Clinton re-elected, but with Republican Congress and divided government (1996) | | Bipartisan adoption of welfare reform, terminating entitlements and delegating welfare power to the states (1996) |
| Democrats reverse midterm precedent and gain seats in the House (1998) | | |
| Clinton, despite high ratings, is impeached in the House (1998); acquitted in Senate (1999) | | Effect of impeachment on presidency and separation of powers a major unknown factor (1999) |

Replacement of the Articles of Confederation by the Constitution is a classic case study of political realism. As an instrument of government, the Articles of Confederation had many virtues. Many considered it the second greatest constitution ever drafted. But as a confederation it left too much power to the states, whose restrictions and boundaries interfered with national and international markets being sought by new economic interests. The Articles of

## CORE OF THE ARGUMENT

- Federalism limits national power by creating two sovereigns—the national government and the state governments.
- Under "dual federalism," which lasted from 1789–1937, the national government limited itself primarily to promoting commerce, while the state governments directly coerced citizens.
- After 1937, the national government began to expand, yet the states maintained most of their traditional powers.
- Under "cooperative federalism," the national government influences state and local governments through grants-in-aid to encourage the pursuit of national goals.
- Checks and balances ensure the sharing of power among separate institutions of government. Within the system of separated powers, the framers of the Constitution provided for legislative supremacy.

Confederation had to be replaced, and a stronger national power had to be provided for, if the barriers to economic progress were to be lowered.[1]

To a point, political realists are correct. Everything in politics revolves around interests; a constitution must satisfy those interests or it will not last long as a governing instrument. But just as pure force is an inadequate foundation for government, so is pure interest, despite its immediate importance. Interests must be translated into higher principles, and there will be no loyalty or support for any government unless most of the powerful as well as the powerless accept the principles as *legitimate*. Acceptance of the interests will follow.

Legitimacy can be defined as *the next best thing to being good*. Legitimacy is not synonymous with popularity. A government can be considered legitimate when its actions appear to be consistent with the highest principles that people already hold. In most countries, governments have attempted to derive their legitimacy from *religion* or from a common past of shared experiences and sacrifices that are called *tradition*. Some governments, or their rulers, have tried to derive their legitimacy from the *need for defense against a common enemy*. The American approach to legitimacy contained parts of all of these factors but with a unique addition: *contract*. A contract is an exchange, a deal. The contract we call the American Constitution was simply this: *The people would give their consent to a strong national government if that government would in turn accept certain strict limitations on its powers*. In other words, power in return for limits, or ***constitutionalism***.

## THE CENTRAL QUESTION

"How do federalism and the separation of powers limit the power of the national government?"

Three fundamental limitations were the principles involved in the contract between the American people and the framers of the Constitution: *federalism*, the *separation of powers*, and *individual rights*. Nowhere in

[1]For two important realist interpretations of the rejection of the Articles in favor of the Constitution, see John P. Roche, "The Founding Fathers: A Reform Caucus in Action," *American Political Science Review* 55 (December 1961), pp. 799–816, and the discussion of Charles Beard's economic interpretation in the text and "Debating the Issues," both in Chapter 2 of this book.

the Constitution were these mentioned by name, but we know from the debates and writings that they were the primary framework of the Constitution. We can call them the *framework* because they were to be the structure, the channel through which governmental power would flow.

The principle of *federalism* sought to limit government by dividing it into two levels—national and state—each with sufficient independence, or ***sovereignty,*** to compete with the other, thereby restraining the power of both.

The principle of the *separation of powers* sought to limit the power of the national government by dividing government against itself—by giving the legislative, executive, and judicial branches separate functions, thus forcing them to share power.

The principle of *individual rights* sought to limit government by defining the people as separate from it—granting to each individual an identity in opposition to the government itself. Individuals are given rights, which are claims to identity, to property, and to personal satisfaction or "the pursuit of happiness," that cannot be denied except by extraordinary procedures that demonstrate beyond doubt that the need of the government or the "public interest" is more compelling than the claim of the citizen. The principle of individual rights implies also the principle of *representation.* If there is to be a separate private sphere, there must be a set of procedures, separate from judicial review of individual rights, that somehow takes into account the preferences of citizens before the government acts.

Political realists treat these three great principles as a mere front for the economic interests that were dominant in Philadelphia in 1787 and in the state legislatures during ratification. But that would be only half the truth. The other half is that *principles themselves are an aspect of political realism.* Although a principle may first be stated to promote self-interests, once the principle has been expressed, it tends to take on a life of its own. Thus, a principle like federalism may serve one interest best at one point and work against that interest later. To be a source of legitimacy, principles in a constitution must be consistent with interests yet must transcend those interests and connect with higher, more universal values. This is why a constitution cannot last if it is written for the present only; it cannot last unless it is written with a keen sense of history and philosophy. Chief Justice John Marshall was being a political realist when in 1819 he observed that "a constitution [is] intended to endure for ages to come and, consequently, to be adapted to the various crises of Human Affairs."[2]

This chapter will be concerned with the first two principles—federalism and the separation of powers. The purpose here is to look at the evolution of each principle in order to understand how we got to where we are and what the significance of each principle in operation is. We will conclude by reviewing the central question of the chapter, "How do federalism and the separation of powers limit the power of the national government?" The third key principle, individual rights, will be the topic of the next chapter. But all of this is for introductory purposes only. All three principles form the background and the context for every chapter in this book.

[2]McCulloch v. Maryland, 4 Wheaton 316 (1819).

## THE FEDERAL FRAMEWORK

The Constitution has had its most fundamental influence on American life through federalism. ***Federalism*** can be defined with misleading ease and simplicity as the division of powers and functions between the national government and the state governments. Tracing out the influence of federalism is not so simple, but we can make the task easier by breaking it down into three distinctive forms.

First, federalism sought to limit national and state power by creating two sovereigns—the national government and the state governments, each to a large extent independent of the other. As we saw in Chapter 2, the states had already existed as former colonies before independence, and for nearly thirteen years they were virtually autonomous units under the Articles of Confederation. In effect, the states had retained too much power under the Articles, a problem that led directly to the Annapolis Convention in 1786 and to the Constitutional Convention in 1787. Under the Articles, disorder within states was beyond the reach of the national government (see Shays's Rebellion, Chapter 2), and conflicts of interest between states were not manageable. For example, states were making their own trade agreements with foreign countries and companies that might then play one state against another for special advantages. Some states adopted special trade tariffs and further barriers to foreign commerce that were contrary to the interests of another state.[3] Tax and other barriers were also being erected between the states.[4] But even after the ratification of the Constitution, the states continued to be more important than the national government. For nearly a century and a half, virtually all of the fundamental policies governing the lives of Americans were made by the state legislatures, not by Congress.

Second, that same federalism specifically restrained the power of the national government over the economy. The Supreme Court's definition of "interstate commerce" was so restrictive that Congress could only legislate as to the actual flow of goods across state lines; local conditions were protected from Congress by the contrary doctrine called "intrastate" commerce. As we shall see later in this chapter and again in Chapters 14 and 15, the federalism of strong states and weak national government was not changed until 1937, when the Supreme Court in *NLRB v. Jones & Laughlin Steel Corporation* reversed itself and redefined "interstate commerce" to permit the national government to regulate local economic conditions.

Third, since federalism freed the states to make so many important policies according to the wishes of their own citizens, states were therefore also free to be different from each other. Federalism allowed a great deal of variation from state to state in the rights enjoyed by citizens, in the roles played by governments, and in definitions of crime and its punishment. During the past half-century, we have

[3]For good treatment of these conflicts of interests between states, see Forrest McDonald, *E Pluribus Unum—The Formation of the American Republic, 1776–1790* (Boston: Houghton Mifflin, 1965), Chapter 7, especially pp. 319–38.

[4]See David O'Brien, *Constitutional Law and Politics,* vol. 1 (New York: W. W. Norton, 1997), pp. 602–3.

moved toward greater national uniformity in state laws and in the rights enjoyed by citizens. Nevertheless, as we shall see, federalism continues even today to permit significant differences among the states.

Each of these consequences of federalism will be considered in its turn. The first two—the creating of two sovereigns and the restraining of the economic power of the national government—will be treated in this chapter. The third, even though it is an aspect of federalism, will be an important part of the next chapter, because it is that part of federalism that relates to the framework of individual rights and liberties.

## Dividing National Power with Dual Federalism, 1789–1937

The Constitution created two layers of government: the national government and the state governments. This two-layer system can be called ***dual federalism*** or dual sovereignty. Even though there have been many changes since 1937, the consequences of dual sovereignty are fundamental to the American system of government in theory and in practice.

Table 3.1 is a listing of the major types of public policies by which Americans were governed for the first century and a half under the Constitution. We call it the "traditional system" because it prevailed for three-quarters of our history and because it closely approximates the intentions of the framers of the Constitution.

Under the traditional system, the federal government was quite small by comparison both to the state governments and to the governments of other Western nations. Not only was it smaller than most governments of that time, it was actually very narrowly specialized in the functions it performed. Our national government built or sponsored the construction of roads, canals, and bridges ("internal improvements"). It provided cash subsidies to shippers and ship builders, and free or low-priced public land to encourage western settlement and business ventures. It placed relatively heavy taxes on imported goods (tariffs), not only to raise revenues but to protect "infant industries" from competition from the more advanced European enterprises. It protected patents and provided for a common currency, also to encourage and facilitate enterprises and to expand markets.

These functions of the national government reveal at least two additional insights. First, virtually all the functions of the national government were limited to its ***commerce power***, and were aimed at assisting commerce. It is quite appropriate to refer to the traditional American system as a "commercial republic." Second, virtually none of the national government's policies directly coerced citizens. The emphasis of governmental programs was on assistance, promotion, and encouragement—the allocation of land or capital where they were insufficiently available for economic development.

Meanwhile, state legislatures were actively involved in economic regulation during the nineteenth century. In the United States, then and now, private property exists only in state laws and state court decisions regarding property, trespass, and real estate. American capitalism took its actual form from state property and trespass laws, as well as state laws and court decisions regarding contracts, markets, credit, banking, incorporation, and insurance. Laws concerning slavery were a subdivision of property law in states where slavery existed. State law regulated

TABLE 3.1

**The Federal System: Specialization of Governmental Functions in the Traditional System (1789–1937)**

| NATIONAL GOVERNMENT POLICIES (DOMESTIC) | STATE GOVERNMENT POLICIES | LOCAL GOVERNMENT POLICIES |
|---|---|---|
| Internal improvements | Property laws (including slavery) | Adaptation of state laws to local conditions ("variances") |
| Subsidies | Estate and inheritance laws | Public works |
| Tariffs | Commerce laws | Contracts for public works |
| Public lands disposal | Banking and credit laws | Licensing of public accommodations |
| Patents | Corporate laws | Assessable improvements |
| Currency | Insurance laws | Basic public services |
| | Family laws | |
| | Morality laws | |
| | Public health laws | |
| | Education laws | |
| | General penal laws | |
| | Eminent domain laws | |
| | Construction codes | |
| | Land-use laws | |
| | Water and mineral laws | |
| | Criminal procedure laws | |
| | Electoral and political parties laws | |
| | Local government laws | |
| | Civil service laws | |
| | Occupations and professions laws | |

the practice of important professions such as law and medicine. The birth or adoption of a child, marriage, and divorce have all been controlled by state law. To educate or not to educate a child has been a decision governed more by state laws than by parents, and not at all by national law. It is important to note also that virtually all the criminal laws—regarding everything from trespass to murder—have been state laws. Most of the criminal laws adopted by Congress are concerned with the District of Columbia and other federal territories.

All this (and more, as shown in column 2 of Table 3.1) demonstrates without any question that most of the fundamental governing in this country was done by the states. The contrast between national and state policies, as shown by the table, demonstrates the difference in the power vested in each. The list of items in column 2 could actually have been made much longer. Moreover, each item on the list is only a category made up of laws that fill many volumes of statutes and court decisions for each state.

This contrast between national and state governments is all the more impressive because it is basically what was intended by the framers of the Constitution. There is probably no better example in world history of consistency between formal intentions and political reality.[5] Since the 1930s, the national government has expanded into local and intrastate matters, far beyond what anyone would have foreseen in 1890 or even in 1914. But this significant expansion of the national government did not alter the basic framework. The national government has become much larger, but the states have continued to be central to the American system of government. Since the 1930s, the national government has had a wide range of laws and agencies dealing with corporations, capital investment, the value of money, the level of interest, and other such issues. But most people are not large corporations or interstate investors, and therefore most people still have their primary government experience with state government and state laws. The national government has expanded, *but only minimally at the expense of the states.* (The exceptions, where states have lost some powers, will be identified below, as will the place of local government.)

And here lies probably the most important point of all: The fundamental impact of federalism on the way the United States is governed comes not from any particular provision of the Constitution but from the framework itself, which has determined the flow of government functions and, through that, the political developments of the country. By allowing state governments to do most of the fundamental governing, the Constitution saved the national government from many policy decisions that might have proven too divisive for this large but very young country. There is no doubt that if the Constitution had provided for a unitary rather than a federal system, the war over slavery would have come in 1789 or 1809 rather than 1860; and if it had come that early, the South might very well have seceded and established a separate and permanent slaveholding nation. In helping the national government remain small and aloof from the most divisive issues of the day, federalism contributed significantly to the political stability of the nation even as the social, economic, and political systems of many of the states and regions of the country were undergoing tremendous and profound, and sometimes violent, change.[6] As we shall see, some important aspects of federalism have changed, but the federal framework has survived two centuries and a devastating civil war.

[5]Alexander Hamilton, the founder most famous for favoring a strong national government, came up with a list of extremely bold proposals for the national government when he was the first secretary of the treasury under President Washington; but when these are examined, they turn out to be nothing more than a detailed set of proposals very like the policies Congress ultimately adopted. Hamilton's proposals are contained in his *Report on Manufactures* (1791), one of the most important state papers ever written.

[6]For a good treatment of the contrast between national political stability and social instability, see Samuel P. Huntington, *Political Order in Changing Societies* (New Haven: Yale University Press, 1968), Chapter 2.

## Federalism as a Limitation on the National Government's Power

Having created the national government, and recognizing the potential for abuse of power, the states sought through federalism to constrain the national government. The "traditional system" of weak national government prevailed for over a century despite economic forces favoring its expansion and despite Supreme Court cases giving a pro-national interpretation to Article I, Section 8, of the Constitution.

That article delegates to Congress the power "to regulate commerce with foreign nations, and among the several States and with the Indian tribes," and this clause was consistently interpreted *in favor* of national power by the Supreme Court for most of the nineteenth century. The first and most important case favoring national power over the economy was *McCulloch v. Maryland*.[7] The case involved the Bank of the United States and the question of whether Congress had the power to charter a bank, since such an explicit grant of power was nowhere to be found in Article I, Section 8. Chief Justice John Marshall answered that the power could be "implied" from other powers that were expressly delegated to Congress, such as the "powers to lay and collect taxes; to borrow money; to regulate commerce; and to declare and conduct a war." The constitutional authority for the implied powers doctrine is a clause in Article I, Section 8, which enables Congress "to make all laws which shall be necessary and proper for carrying into Execution the foregoing powers." By allowing Congress to use the "necessary and proper" clause to interpret its delegated powers, the Supreme Court created the potential for an unprecedented increase in national government power.

A second historic question posed by *McCulloch* was whether a state had the power to tax the Baltimore branch of the U.S. Bank, since it was a national agency. Here Marshall again took the side of national supremacy, arguing that an agency created by a legislature representing all the people (Congress) could not be put out of business by a state legislature (Maryland) representing only a small portion of the people (since "the power to tax is the power to destroy"). Marshall concluded that whenever a state law conflicted with a federal law, the state law would be deemed invalid since "the laws of the United States . . . 'shall be the supreme law of the land.'" Both parts of this historic case were "pro-national," yet Congress did not immediately attempt to expand the policies of the national government.

This nationalistic interpretation of the Constitution was reinforced by another major case, that of *Gibbons v. Ogden* in 1824. The important but relatively narrow issue was whether the state of New York could grant a monopoly to Robert Fulton's steamboat company to operate an exclusive service between New York and New Jersey. Ogden had secured his license from Fulton's company, while Gibbons, a former partner, secured a competing license from the

[7] McCulloch v. Maryland, 4 Wheaton 316 (1819).

PROCESS BOX 3.1

**How the National Government Actually Governs—There Is More to American Government than Federalism**

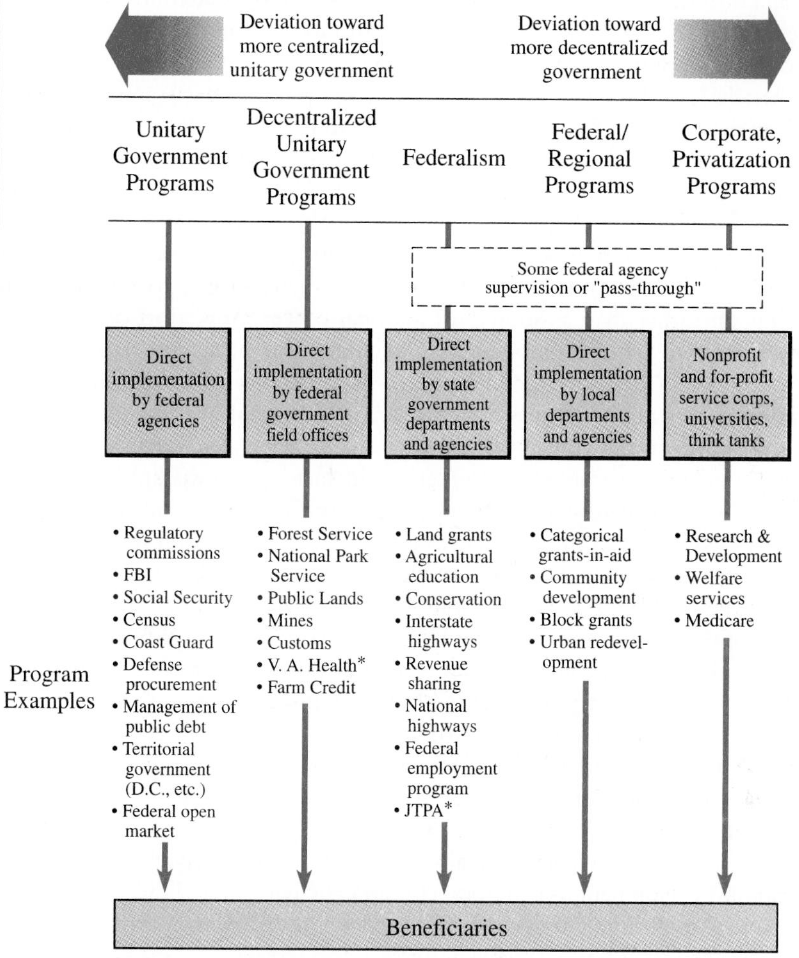

*V.A. = Veterans Administration; JTPA = Job Training Partnership Act

SOURCE: Thanks to Randall Ripley, Gary Bryner, and Donald Kettl for help in adapting a General Accounting Office diagram. See also Randall Ripley and Grace Franklin, *Policy Implementation and Bureaucracy* (Homewood, IL: Dorsey Press, 1986), p. 69.

U.S. government. Chief Justice Marshall argued that Gibbons could not be kept from competing because the state of New York did not have the power to grant this particular monopoly. In order to reach this decision, it was necessary for Chief Justice Marshall to define what Article I, Section 8, meant by "commerce among the several states." Marshall insisted that the definition was "comprehensive," extending to "every species of commercial intercourse." He did say that this comprehensiveness was limited "to that commerce which concerns more states than one," giving rise to what later came to be called "interstate commerce." *Gibbons* is important because it established the supremacy of the national government in all matters affecting interstate commerce.[8] What would remain uncertain during several decades of constitutional discourse was the precise meaning of interstate commerce, notwithstanding John Marshall's expansive reading of "commerce among the several states."

Article I, Section 8, backed by the "implied powers" decision in *McCulloch* and by the broad definition of "interstate commerce" in *Gibbons,* was a source of power for the national government as long as Congress sought to improve commerce through subsidies, services, and land grants. But later in the nineteenth century, when the national government sought to use those powers to *regulate* the economy rather than merely to promote economic development, federalism and the concept of interstate commerce began to operate as restraints on rather than as sources of national power. Any effort of the federal government to regulate commerce in such areas as fraud, the production of impure goods, the use of child labor, or the existence of dangerous working conditions or long hours was declared unconstitutional by the Supreme Court as a violation of the concept of interstate commerce. Such legislation meant that the federal government was entering the factory and workplace, and these areas were considered inherently local, because the goods produced there had not yet passed into commerce. Any effort to enter these local workplaces was an exercise of police power—the power reserved to the states for the protection of the health, safety, and morals of their citizens. No one questioned the power of the national government to regulate certain kinds of businesses, such as railroads, gas pipelines, and waterway transportation, because they intrinsically involved interstate commerce.[9] But well into the twentieth century, most other efforts by the national government to regulate commerce were blocked by the Supreme Court's interpretation of federalism, which used the concept of interstate commerce as a barrier against most efforts by Congress to regulate local conditions.

This aspect of federalism was alive and well during an epoch of tremendous economic development, the period between the Civil War and the 1930s. It gave the American economy a freedom from federal government control that closely approximated the ideal of "free enterprise." The economy was, of course, never entirely free; in fact, entrepreneurs themselves did not want complete freedom from government. They needed law and order. They needed a stable currency. They needed courts and police to enforce contracts and prevent trespass. They

[8]Gibbons v. Ogden, 9 Wheaton 1 (1824).

[9]In Wabash, St. Louis, and Pacific Railway Company v. Illinois, 118 U.S. 557 (1886), the Supreme Court struck down a state law prohibiting rate discrimination by a railroad; in response, Congress passed the Interstate Commerce Act of 1887 creating the Interstate Commerce Commission (ICC), which was the first federal administrative agency.

needed roads, canals, and railroads. But federalism, as interpreted by the Supreme Court for seventy years after the Civil War, made it possible for business to have its cake and eat it, too. Entrepreneurs enjoyed the benefits of national policies facilitating commerce and were protected by the courts from policies regulating commerce.[10]

All this changed after 1937, when the Supreme Court threw out the old distinction between interstate and intrastate commerce, converting the commerce clause from a source of limitations to a source of power. The Court began to refuse to review appeals challenging acts of Congress protecting the rights of employees to organize and engage in collective bargaining, regulating the amount of farmland in cultivation, extending low-interest credit to small businesses and farmers, and restricting the activities of corporations dealing in the stock market, and many other laws that contributed to the construction of the "welfare state." This has been referred to as the First Constitutional Revolution.[11] (A second Constitutional Revolution will be discussed in Chapter 4.)

**AMERICAN POLITICAL DEVELOPMENT**

The change that occurred in the traditional federalist system with the advent of the New Deal can be traced in two important cases decided by the Supreme Court in 1937, *NLRB* v. *Jones & Laughlin Steel Corp.* and *Stewart Machine Co.* v. *Davis*. The first case validated efforts by the national government to regulate the economy in a way traditionally regulated by the states, and the second validated the welfare state.

## The Changing Role of the States

As we have seen, the Constitution contained the seeds of a very expansive national government—in the commerce clause. For much of the nineteenth century, federal power remained limited. The Tenth Amendment was used to bolster arguments about ***states' rights,*** which in their extreme version claimed that the states did not have to submit to national laws when they believed the national government had exceeded its authority. These arguments in favor of states' rights were voiced less often after the Civil War. But the Supreme Court continued to

[10]The Sherman Antitrust Act, adopted in 1890, for example, was enacted not to restrict commerce but rather to protect it from monopolies, or trusts, so as to prevent unfair trade practices, and to enable the market again to become *self-regulating*. Moreover, the Supreme Court sought to uphold liberty of contract to protect businesses. For example, in Lochner v. New York, 198 U.S. 45 (1905), the Court invalidated a New York law regulating the sanitary conditions and hours of labor of bakers on the grounds that the law interfered with liberty of contract.

[11]The key case in the First Constitutional Revolution is generally considered to be NLRB v. Jones & Laughlin Steel Corporation, 301 U.S. 1 (1937), in which the Supreme Court approved federal regulation of the workplace and thereby virtually eliminated interstate commerce as a limit on national government power. Equally important was the Supreme Court's approval of the welfare state and of the national power of taxation to redistribute wealth, in Steward Machine Co. v. Davis, 301 U.S. 548 (1937). Since at least the 1960s, "interstate commerce" has become a source of congressional power rather than restraint, especially in national efforts to improve the status of blacks and other minorities. The Court held valid provisions of the Civil Rights Act of 1964 regulating racial discrimination in restaurants, motels, and other public accommodations even when these accommodations were not directly in the stream of interstate commerce. See, for example, Heart of Atlanta Motel v. U.S., 379 U.S. 241 (1964); and Katzenbach v. McClung, 379 U.S. 294 (1964). See also Chapter 4.

use the Tenth Amendment to strike down laws that it thought exceeded national power, including the Civil Rights Act passed in 1875.

In the early twentieth century, however, the Tenth Amendment appeared to lose its force. Reformers began to press for national regulations to limit the power of large corporations and to preserve the health and welfare of citizens. The Supreme Court approved of some of these laws but it struck others down, including a law combating child labor. The Court stated that the law violated the Tenth Amendment because only states should have the power to regulate conditions of employment. By the late 1930s, however, the Supreme Court had approved such an expansion of federal power that the Tenth Amendment appeared irrelevant. In fact, in 1941, Justice Harlan Fiske Stone declared that the Tenth Amendment was simply a "truism," that it had no real meaning.[12]

Yet the idea that some powers should be reserved to the states did not go away. Indeed, in the 1950s, southern opponents of the civil rights movement revived the idea of states' rights. In 1956, ninety-six southern members of Congress issued a "Southern Manifesto" in which they declared that southern states were not constitutionally bound by Supreme Court decisions outlawing racial segregation. They believed that states' rights should override individual rights to liberty and formal equality. With the triumph of the civil rights movement, the slogan of "states' rights" became tarnished by its association with racial inequality.

Recent years have seen a revival of interest in the Tenth Amendment and important Supreme Court decisions limiting federal power. Much of the interest in the Tenth Amendment stems from conservatives who believe that a strong federal government encroaches on individual liberties. They believe such freedoms are better protected by returning more power to the states through the process of ***devolution.*** In 1996, Republican presidential candidate Bob Dole carried a copy of the Tenth Amendment in his pocket as he campaigned, pulling it out to read at rallies.[13] The Supreme Court's ruling in *United States v. Lopez* in 1995 fueled further interest in the Tenth Amendment. In that case, the Court, stating that Congress had exceeded its authority under the commerce clause, struck down a federal law that barred handguns near schools. This was the first time since the New Deal that the Court had limited congressional powers in this way. The Court further limited the power of the federal government over the states in a 1996 ruling that prevented Native Americans from the Seminole tribe from suing the state of Florida in federal court. A 1988 law had given Indian tribes the right to sue a state in federal court if the state did not negotiate in good faith over issues related to gambling casinos on tribal land. The Supreme Court's ruling appeared to signal a much broader limitation on national power by raising new questions about whether individuals can sue a state if it fails to uphold federal law.[14]

Another significant decision involving the relationship between the federal government and state governments was the 1997 case *Printz v. United States* (joined with *Mack v. United States*), in which the Court struck down a key provision of the "Brady Bill," enacted by Congress in 1993 to regulate gun sales.

[12]U.S. v. Darby Lumber Co., 312 U.S. 100 (1941).

[13]W. John Moore, "Pleading the 10th," *National Journal,* 29 July 1995, p. 1940.

[14]Seminole Indian Tribe v. Florida, 116 S.Ct. 1114 (1996).

Under the terms of the act, state and local law enforcement officers were required to conduct background checks on prospective gun purchasers. The Court held that the federal government cannot require states to administer or enforce federal regulatory programs. Since the states bear administrative responsibility for a variety of other federal programs, this decision could have far-reaching consequences. Finally, in another major ruling from the 1996–1997 term, in *City of Boerne v. Flores,* the Court ruled that Congress had gone too far in restricting the power of the states to enact regulations they deemed necessary for the protection of the public health, safety, or welfare. It remains to be seen whether these rulings signal a move toward a much more restricted federal government in future Supreme Court decisions, or whether they will simply serve as a reminder that federal power is not infinite.[15]

**The Powers of State Government** Even if we remain in suspense over how restrictive the Constitution is going to be over the powers of the *national* government, there is no reason for suspense about the continuing health and strength of federalism as far as the integrity and the powers of the *state* governments are concerned. First, although the national government has expanded its activities far beyond what anyone would have foreseen before 1933, this significant expansion of national power did not alter the basic framework of federalism: *The national government has become much larger, but the states have continued to be central to the American system of government. The national government has expanded, but only minimally at the expense of the states.*

Second, as mentioned above, state governments have actually increased in power during the last decade because Congress has actually been choosing to devolve some of its recognized powers to the states and to delegate important responsibilities to state governments to implement federal programs. For example, a very large portion of the important programs that comprise welfare and public assistance in the United States are federally financed and federally authorized programs that are implemented in large part at the discretion of the states.

Although the national government is far larger today than it was in the 1930s, this growth did not come at the expense of the states. No better demonstration of the continuing significance of states in our federal system can be offered than column 2 of Table 3.1 (page 74). This is as accurate a portrayal of state government today as it was in the 1930s or the 1890s. To be sure, column 1 has grown much longer. But column 2 did not shrink in the process. Granted, some national policies constrain the states, and the Supreme Court has interpreted the Bill of Rights and the Fourteenth Amendment to take away the power of the states to make slaves of human beings, to segregate the races, to require religious observance in schools, or to outlaw all abortions. But in most areas of traditional government, the states still reign supreme.

In point of fact, state powers have been expanding. The Supreme Court's scrutiny of state actions has been measurably less strict in such areas as criminal justice, civil rights, and abortion regulation. Another important sign of the trend back toward expanding the powers of the states is Congress's own actions, which

[15]United States v. Lopez, 115 S.Ct. 1624 (1995).

GLOBALIZATION AND DEMOCRACY

## *Globalization's Impact on American Federalism*

Globalization adds a new twist to federalism in the United States. When global markets had little impact on the American economy, the debate about states' rights was fundamentally about where power should reside—at the state level or at the federal level. Today, however, globalization is reversing the trend of the ever-growing federal government described in this chapter and has in fact pushed the federal government toward obsolescence when dealing with the many pressing economic problems. As Michael Keating and John Loughlin write,

> [There] is the notion that with economic globalization, that is, the creation of world-wide markets and the internationalization of factors of production linked to new technological developments, new economic regions are emerging as the key territorial units of economic activity. Within this perspective, nation-states are no longer adequate units within which to frame economy activity. They are too small for the global aspects and too large for the regional dimension.[1]

In the American context, some international disputes in trade policy are now settled by the World Trade Organization (WTO), not directly by the United States government. This trend of delegating the resolution of trade disputes to a supranational body above the federal government like the WTO will likely continue as world

[1]Michael Keating and John Loughlin, "Introduction," in Michael Keating and John Loughlin, eds, *The Political Economy of Regionalism* (London: Frank Cass, 1997), p. 7.

markets grow and as national governments feel increasingly powerless in the face of global capital. Indeed, even an (in)famous currency trader like George Soros, who has made billions of dollars by exploiting the inability of governments to control their economies, now calls for an international body to regain the power over markets that individual governments have lost.[2]

Globalization also increases the strains on the federal government's capacity to act, which sometimes makes the government more willing to delegate power below it, to the states. This transfer removes potentially difficult responsibilities from the federal government, allowing it to concentrate on policy areas (such as national defense) in which it still can function well in a globalized world. This logic provides one explanation for the devolution to the states of many aspects of the welfare state, including most notably Aid to Families with Dependent Children, in the form of block grants. Similar devolutions of power in countries like Australia, Belgium, Canada, Spain, and the United Kingdom add impetus to the argument that globalization is forcing a rebalancing of the relationship between state and national governments around the world.

Increased globablization has also forced American states to compete more aggressively with one another for the attention of foreign businesses and foreign governments. This need to compete has made states more active in economic policy. The competition is especially acute among states trying to attract foreign investors. State delegates—often the governor—now travel abroad to attract investment and trade to their states. It is likely that your governor spends several weeks a year either preparing for or making these recruiting trips.

This competition can ultimately be harmful to the states themselves. Alabama, for example, in its successful bid to convince Mercedes to open a manufacturing plant there, put together a package of tax incentives that amounted to over $250 million. This figure translated into $168,000 per job.[3] One can argue that this money would have been better spent upgrading the state's lowly regarded public schools.

Regardless of whether one thinks that this competition is good or bad for state governments, it is clear that globalization has changed the relationship between the states and the federal government.

[2]George Soros, *The Crisis of Global Capitalism* (New York: Public Affairs, 1998).

[3]The Federal Reserve Bank of Minneapolis, "The Economic War among the States: An Overview," *The Region,* June 1996 (available at http://woodrow.mpls.frb.fed.us/sylloge/econwar/farrel.html).

often go beyond the Supreme Court. In April of 1996, for example, Congress adopted the Antiterrorism and Effective Death Penalty Act, which severely tightened the deadlines for appeals that prisoners can make for review of their capital punishment sentences. In 1996, Congress also killed funding for all nonprofit death-penalty resource centers that provide legal advice for filing capital punishment appeals. And, of course, the best indication of Congress's increasing confidence in the powers of the states is probably the Personal Responsibility and Work Opportunity Reconciliation Act of 1996, popularly known as welfare reform, which devolves to the discretion of the states the lion's share of power over public assistance to the poor. The decision in September 1996 to terminate national poverty entitlements under the most important welfare program, Aid to Families with Dependent Children (AFDC), and to turn over virtually all of the discretion for the implementation of these welfare activities to state governments—a bipartisan decision involving the dramatic public approval of Democratic President Clinton and the Republican 104th Congress—is indicative of the present and future of federalism in the United States.

**Cooperation and Competition among State Governments** "Horizontal" federalism refers to the cooperative and competitive relations that states have with each other. As we saw earlier, the Constitution sought to discourage destructive competition between the states, such as discriminatory taxes or trade barriers. But today there are many opportunities for competition as well as for cooperation. The most spectacular example of interstate cooperation is probably the Port Authority of New York and New Jersey, a public corporation operating ports, access highways, and other related public works in the vast New York–New Jersey port complex. The corporation was the result of a 1921 "interstate compact," which has become the model for both interstate and intrastate public authorities and public corporations that are set up to engage independently in constructing and operating highways, tunnels, and other public works.[16]

Lines of cooperation may become increasingly important as interstate *competition intensifies.* Professor Thomas Dye has coined the term "competitive federalism" to describe as well as encourage the rivalries between and among states wanting to attract new industry by offering tax and zoning advantages, improved local public works, and improved education accompanied by a low tax base. But there is a darker side to interstate competition, which many refer to as the "race to the bottom." In their push to compete, governors and mayors may seek to attract new companies by cutting welfare programs, discouraging unions, cracking down on tenement housing, and suppressing rather than expanding public works.

[16]Article I, Section 10, authorizes states to make contracts or compacts with each other, as along as Congress consents. Until 1900, there had been only 24 such interstate compacts. By 1955, there were 121, covering such matters as fisheries, oil extraction, stream pollution, and, especially, water—e.g., equitable access to the Colorado River from the several water-hungry states along its banks. By 1980, 169 interstate compacts were in operation. For a good treatment of this phenomenon, see Nicholas Henry, *Governing at the Grassroots: State and Local Politics* (Englewood Cliffs, NJ: Prentice Hall, 1980).

**State Obligations to One Another** The Constitution also creates obligations among the states. These obligations, spelled out in Article IV, were intended to promote national unity. By requiring the states to recognize actions and decisions taken in other states as legal and proper, the framers aimed to make the states less like independent countries and more like parts of a single nation.

Article IV, Section I, calls for "Full Faith and Credit" among states, meaning that each state is normally expected to honor the "public Acts, Records, and judicial Proceedings" that take place in any other state. So, for example, if a couple is married in Texas—marriage being regulated by state law—Missouri must also recognize that marriage, even though they were not married under Missouri state law.

This ***full faith and credit clause*** has recently become embroiled in the controversy over gay and lesbian marriage. In 1993, the Hawaii Supreme Court prohibited discrimination against gay and lesbian marriage except in very limited circumstances. Many observers believe that Hawaii will eventually fully legalize gay marriage. This possibility raises the question of whether other states will also have to recognize gay marriage as legal under the full faith and credit clause. Anxious to show its disapproval of gay marriage, Congress passed the Defense of Marriage Act in 1996, which declared that states will *not* have to recognize a same-sex marriage, even it if is legal in one state. The act also said that the federal government will not recognize gay marriage—even if it is legal under state law—and that gay marriage partners will not be eligible for the federal benefits, such as Medicare and Social Security, normally available to spouses.[17]

Because of this controversy, the extent and meaning of the full faith and credit clause is sure to be considered by the Supreme Court. In fact, it is not clear that the clause requires states to recognize gay marriage because the Court's interpretation of the clause in the past has provided exceptions for "public policy" reasons: if states have strong objections to a law they do not have to honor it. In 1997 the Supreme Court took up a case involving the full faith and credit clause. The case concerns a Michigan court order that prevented a former engineer for General Motors Corporation from testifying against the company. The engineer, who left the company on bad terms, later testified in a Missouri court about a car accident in which a woman died when her Chevrolet Blazer caught fire. General Motors challenged his right to testify, arguing that Missouri should give "full faith and credit" to the Michigan ruling. The Supreme Court ruled that the engineer could testify and that the court system in one state cannot hinder other state courts in their "search for the truth."[18]

Article IV, Section 2, known as the "comity clause," also seeks to promote national unity. It provides that citizens enjoying the ***Privileges and Immunities*** of one state should be entitled to similar treatment in other states. What this has come to mean is that a state cannot discriminate against someone from another

[17]Ken I. Kersch, "Full Faith and Credit for Same-Sex Marriages?" *Political Science Quarterly* 112 (Spring 1997), pp. 117–36; Joan Biskupic, "Once Unthinkable, Now Under Debate," *Washington Post,* 3 September 1996, p. A1.

[18]Linda Greenhouse, "Supreme Court Weaves Legal Principles from a Tangle of Legislation," *New York Times,* 30 June 1988, p. A20.

state or give special privileges to its own residents. For example, in the 1970s, when Alaska passed a law that gave residents preference over nonresidents in obtaining work on the state's oil and gas pipelines, the Supreme Court ruled the law illegal because it discriminated against citizens of other states.[19] This clause also regulates criminal justice among the states by requiring states to return fugitives to the states from which they have fled. Thus, in 1952, when an inmate escaped from an Alabama prison and sought to avoid being returned to Alabama on the grounds that he was being subjected to "cruel and unusual punishment" there, the Supreme Court ruled that he must be returned according to Article IV, Section 2.[20] This example highlights the difference between the obligations among states and those among different countries. Recently, France refused to return an American fugitive because he might be subject to the death penalty, which does not exist in France.[21] The Constitution clearly forbids states from doing something similar.

**Local Government and the Constitution** The continuing vitality of the federal framework and of state government can be seen in still another area: local government. Local government occupies a peculiar but very important place in the American system. In fact, the status of American local government is probably unique in world experience.

Americans must love local government, because there are so many of them. According to Table 3.2, there were 87,504 governments in the United States as of 1997, and all but 51 of those are local governments. The number of local governments is an important datum in itself, but the role of local government in the nurturing of democracy can be better understood when we add the fact that these 87,453 local governments are comprised of around 500,000 offices that are filled by election.[22] This makes for an enormous "electoral domain," whose contribution to American democracy can hardly be overestimated. This tremendous electoral domain has first of all provided an extraordinarily broad opportunity for political participation, for voters as well as for the politically ambitious. In addition, this electoral domain provided the spawning ground for political parties. The story of American democracy cannot be told without appreciation of the fact that political parties were a response to electoral opportunity and have little meaning outside this context.[23]

[19]Hicklin v. Orbeck, 437 U.S. 518 (1978).

[20]Sweeny v. Woodall, 344 U.S. 86 (1953).

[21]Marlise Simons, "France Won't Extradite American Convicted of Murder," *New York Times,* 5 December 1997, p. A9.

[22]Source for the number of elected officials: Department of Commerce, *Statistical Abstract of the United States, 1998* (Washington, DC: Government Printing Office, 1998), Tables No. 477 and No. 496.

[23]The role of local government in the development of democracy is now being recognized in the People's Republic of China. There are about 900,000 villages in China, housing as many as three-quarters of the country's 1.3 billion people. *The Economist* reports that since 1988, over 80 percent of these villages have elected, through universal suffrage and secret ballots, their own chiefs and village committees. By 1997, 95 percent of these villages will have held elections—some for their third election in a row. Village democratization has been flowering, despite the return to repressiveness at the national level after Tiananmen in 1989. "China's Grassroots Democracy," *The Economist,* 2 November 1996, pp. 33–35.

**TABLE 3.2**

**87,504 Governments in the United States**

| TYPE | NUMBER |
|---|---|
| National | 1 |
| State | 50 |
| County | 3,043 |
| Municipal | 19,372 |
| Township | 16,629 |
| School districts | 13,726 |
| Other special districts | 34,683 |
| TOTAL | 87,504 |

SOURCE: Department of Commerce, *Statistical Abstract of the United States, 1998* (Washington, DC: Government Printing Office, 1998), Table No. 496.

Local governments became administratively important in the early years of the Republic because the states possessed little administrative capability, and they relied on local governments to implement the laws of the state. Local government was an alternative to a statewide bureaucracy. The states created two forms of local government: territorial and corporate. The basic territorial unit is the county; every resident of the state is also a resident of a county (except in Rhode Island and Connecticut, which do not have county governments). Traditionally, counties existed only for handling state obligations, whether these were administrative, legislative, or judicial, whether the job was building roads, or collecting state taxes, or catching bootleggers.

The second, or corporate, unit is the city, town, or village. These are called corporate because each holds an actual corporate charter granted it by the state government; they are formed ("incorporated") by residents of an area as these residents discover that their close proximity and common problems can be more effectively and cheaply dealt with cooperatively. Not everyone lives in a city or town; many rural areas are "unincorporated."

Although cities, especially larger cities, develop their own unique political and government personalities, they are nevertheless like the counties in being units of state administration. We associate police forces, fire fighting companies, and public health and zoning agencies with the very essence of local government. But all of those functions and agencies are operating under state laws. The state legislatures and courts allow cities to adapt state laws to local needs, and out of that discretion cities can develop their own political personalities. But they remain under state authority, applying state laws to local conditions.[24]

[24]A good discussion of the constitutional position of local governments is in York Willbern, *The Withering Away of the City* (Bloomington: Indiana University Press, 1971). For more on the structure and theory of federalism, see Thomas R. Dye, *American Federalism: Competition among the States* (Lexington, MA: Lexington Books, 1990), Chapter 1; and Martha Derthick, "Up-to-Date in Kansas City:

Changes in the traditional place of local government began to take place in the latter part of the nineteenth century with the adoption of ***home rule.*** Beginning in Missouri in 1875, the states one after another changed their constitutions to permit cities (and eventually a few counties) of a certain size and urban density to frame and adopt local charters. By the beginning of the twentieth century, home rule was adopted in many of the states, and the provisions were extended until home rule came to mean giving cities the right of ordinary corporations to change their government structures, to hold property, to sue and be sued, and most importantly, to be guaranteed that state legislatures would not pass legislation concerning the "local affairs, property, and government" of cities except by laws of statewide application. This was a guarantee within the state constitution that no city would be subjected to special legislation imposed on that city alone by the state legislature. As part of this movement, many states began to allow cities to make the basic laws for themselves rather than administering laws passed by the state legislature. Cities were given the power to make their own laws ***(ordinances)*** to regulate slaughterhouses, to regulate and establish public transportation services and facilities, to regulate local markets and trade centers, to set quality and safety standards for the construction of apartments and other private buildings, and to control properties for administering fire prevention.

As local government responsibilities expanded, they often exceeded established government boundaries. Many local programs and services had become too expensive, unless they were carried out on a scale larger than the corporate city, town, or village where the need was first recognized and where the initiative might first have been taken. The way the proponents put it, if they could expand their area of service, they could reduce the "unit cost" of those services. Since all local governments (except the counties, as observed above) are corporate and voluntary and therefore organized for the convenience and efficiency of the residents, it was only natural to organize another unit of local government within a large city, or to create a unit of local government that actually cut across the boundaries of several contiguous towns or cities. This new unit was called the *special district.* If we include school districts as special districts—as we surely should, because they are the most numerous and most prized of all special districts—there were in 1997 just under 48,500 special district governments in the United States, comprising 55 percent of all local governments.[25] The other special districts have been formed to provide, among others, fire protection (the largest type of special district after school districts), water supply, sewerage services, electric power, and air pollution control. Beyond the need to reduce the unit cost of services, another important justification frequently offered in favor of creating a special district is "to take the politics out of government." Wherever there are public services or proposals for public services, there will be politics. But the special district does create its own type of politics, and that, of course, can be a blessing or a curse. In that context it is interesting to offer one particularly significant example of a spe-

Reflections on American Federalism" (the 1992 John Gaus Lecture), *PS: Political Science & Politics* (December 1992), pp. 671–75.

[25]*Statistical Abstract of the United States 1998* (Washington, DC: Government Printing Office, 1998), Table No. 496.

cial district: Walt Disney World. The Reedy Creek Improvement District in Orlando, Florida, was formed in 1967 after lengthy and elaborate negotiations between Walt Disney and the state of Florida. Disney's first legal request was for the creation of the Reedy Creek Drainage District, which would have the power to regulate land use, provide police and fire service, build roads and sewer lines, and construct an airport, as well as carry out the initial plan for flood control and drainage. The deal included an agreement stating that surrounding local governments could not impose any growth control or other fees on highway approaches or other relations to Disney World. What a special district indeed![26]

Finally, there is another kind of local government that has no geographic identity but still looms relatively large in the modern history of local government: government by contract.

Nowadays, many cities, especially in the western states, do not have any public garbage collecting system because it is all done by private companies. As privatization has become more popular over the past twenty years, there has been a parallel expansion of contractual approaches to local government provision for local services, not only an expansion of conventional uses of the contract approach but also less conventional ones—for example, the "charter schools" and private, for-profit prisons. "Charter" is simply another name for contract, one implying closer public regulation and supervision than with a normal contract but still using contracts with private companies to meet compulsory schooling requirements. This movement of charter schooling is slowly but surely taking off nationwide. The contractual, for-profit prison is an even bolder venture in the use of contracts for services, yet it has spread faster and wider than the charter school. Largely done through state contracts, the for-profit prison is an important illustration of the expanding private/contractual approach to local as well as to state government. Thirty states now permit privatized, contract, for-profit prisons, and it is only a matter of time before we see private, for-profit county and city jails as well as state and federal for-profit penitentiaries.[27]

With all of this power already residing in local governments to provide so many services in so many different ways, and with continued expansion of local government responsibilities, it is inevitable that people occasionally come to the conclusion that cities constitute a third level of sovereignty. But such a conclusion is distinctly false. However large some cities become, and however strong the support grows for keeping government at the local level, there are still only two levels of sovereignty in the federal system of the United States—the national government and the state governments. Local governments, as important as they have become or may become in this urban nation, remain exactly as they always have been—creatures of state government.

[26]For a good treatment of this and other special districts, see Nancy Burns, *The Formation of American Local Governments: Private Values in Public Institutions* (New York: Oxford University Press, 1994), pp. 31–35. See also an important source for her treatment, Richard E. Foglesong, "Do Politics Matter in the Formulation of Local Development Policies? The Orlando–Disney World Relationship," paper presented at 1989 American Political Science Association Annual Meeting, Atlanta, GA, August 31–September 3, 1989.

[27]For good treatment of the for-profit prison movement, see Vince Beiser, "Jailing for Dollars: The New Growth Industry," *The New Leader,* 5 May 1997, pp. 10–11.

## Who Does What? The Changing Federal Framework

Questions about how to divide responsibilities between the states and the national government first arose more than two hundred years ago, when the framers wrote the Constitution to create a stronger union. But they did not solve the issue of who should do what. There is no "right" answer to that question; each generation of Americans has provided its own answer. In recent years, Americans have grown distrustful of the federal government and have supported giving more responsibility to the states.[28] Even so, they still want the federal government to set standards and promote equality.

Political debates about the division of responsibility often take sides: some people argue for a strong federal role to set national standards, while others say the states should do more. These two goals are not necessarily at odds. The key is to find the right balance. During the first 150 years of American history, that balance favored state power. But the balance began to shift toward Washington in the 1930s. In this section, we will look at how the balance shifted, and then we will consider current efforts to reshape the relationship between the national government and the states.

**Cooperative Federalism and Grants-in-Aid:** So far we have talked about "vertical" federalism, relations between national government and the state; "horizontal" federalism, cooperative relations between states; and "competitive" federalism, antagonistic and sometimes destructive relations between states and cities. Now there is another—***cooperative federalism***—which generally refers to supportive relations, sometimes partnerships, between national government and the state and local governments. It comes in the form of federal subsidization of special state and local activities; these subsidies are called ***grants-in-aid.*** But make no mistake about it: Although many of these state and local programs would not exist without the federal grant-in-aid, the grant-in-aid is also an important form of federal influence. (Another form of federal influence, the mandate, will be covered in the next section.)

A grant-in-aid is really a kind of bribe, or inducement, whereby Congress appropriates money for state and local governments with the condition that the money be spent for a particular purpose as defined by Congress. Congress uses grants-in-aid because it does not have the political or constitutional power to command cities to do its bidding. When you can't command, a monetary inducement becomes a viable alternative.

The principle of the grant-in-aid goes back to the nineteenth-century land grants to states for the improvement of agriculture and farm-related education. Since farms were not in "interstate commerce," it was unclear whether the Constitution would permit the national government to provide direct assistance to agriculture. Grants-in-aid to the states, earmarked to go to farmers, presented a

[28]See the poll reported in Guy Gugliotta, "Scaling Down the American Dream," *Washington Post,* 19 April 1995, p. A21.

way of avoiding the constitutional problem while pursuing what was recognized in Congress as a national goal.



Beginning in the late 1930s, this same approach was applied to cities. Congress set national goals such as public housing and assistance to the unemployed and provided grants-in-aid to meet these goals. World War II temporarily stopped the distribution of these grants. But after the war, Congress resumed providing grants for urban development and lunches in the schools. The value of such ***categorical grants-in-aid*** increased from \$2.3 billion in 1950, to \$7 billion in 1960, \$24 billion in 1970, \$91 billion in 1980, to \$234 billion in 1997 (see Table 3.3). Sometimes Congress requires the state or local government to match the national contribution dollar for dollar, but for some programs, such as the interstate highway system, the congressional grant-in-aid provides 90 percent of the cost of the program. The nationwide speed limit of 55 mph was not imposed on individual drivers by an act of Congress. Instead, Congress bribed the state legislatures by threatening to withdraw the federal highway grants-in-aid if the states did not set a 55 mph speed limit. In the early 1990s, Congress began to ease up on the states, permitting them, under certain conditions, to go back to the 65 mph speed limit (or higher) without losing their highway grants.

TABLE 3.3

**Historical Trend of Federal Grants-in-Aid**

| | | GRANTS-IN-AID AS A PERCENTAGE OF | | | |
|---|---|---|---|---|---|
| FISCAL YEAR | AMOUNT OF GRANTS-IN-AID (IN BILLIONS) | TOTAL FEDERAL OUTLAYS | FEDERAL DOMESTIC PROGRAMS[1] | STATE AND LOCAL EXPENDITURES | GROSS DOMESTIC PRODUCT |
| **Five-year intervals** | | | | | |
| 1950 | \$2.3 | 5.3% | 11.6% | 8.2% | 0.8% |
| 1955 | 3.2 | 4.7 | 17.2 | 9.7 | 0.8 |
| 1960 | 7.0 | 8.0 | 18.0 | 19.0 | 1.0 |
| 1965 | 10.9 | 9.0 | 18.0 | 20.0 | 2.0 |
| 1970 | 24.1 | 12.0 | 23.0 | 24.0 | 2.0 |
| 1975 | 49.8 | 15.0 | 22.0 | 27.0 | 3.0 |
| **Annually** | | | | | |
| 1980 | 91.4 | 15.0 | 22.0 | 31.0 | 3.0 |
| 1985 | 105.9 | 11.0 | 18.0 | 25.0 | 3.0 |
| 1990 | 135.3 | 11.0 | 17.0 | 21.0 | 2.0 |
| 1995 | 225.0 | 15.0 | 22.0 | 25.0 | 3.0 |
| 1996 | 227.8 | 15.0 | 21.0 | 24.0 | 3.0 |
| 1997 | 234.2 | 15.0 | 21.0 | 24.0 | 3.0 |

[1]Excludes outlays for national defense, international affairs, and net interest.

SOURCE: Office of Management and Budget, *Budget of the United States Government, Fiscal Year 1999, Analytical Perspectives* (Washington, DC: Government Printing Office, 1998), Table 9-2, p. 216.

## AMERICAN POLITICAL DEVELOPMENT

The basis for cooperative federalism dates to the founding period. In the early years of the Republic (1787–1800), the national government provided aid to the states in the form of land grants and by assuming state debts incurred during the Revolutionary War. During the nineteenth century, despite differences over the balance of power between the national government and the states—most notably during the Civil War—the relationship between the national government and the states was fairly cooperative, especially after the national government began providing federal grants to states. Over time (and particularly after the New Deal), this cooperative relationship became more routine and institutionalized.

SOURCE: Daniel J. Elazar, *The American Partnership: Intergovernmental Cooperation in the Nineteenth-Century United States* (Chicago: University of Chicago Press, 1962); and Morton Grodzins, *The American System: A New View of Government in the United States* (Chicago: Rand McNally, 1966).

For the most part, the categorical grants created before the 1960s simply helped the states perform their traditional functions.[29] In the 1960s, however, the national role expanded and the number of categorical grants increased dramatically. For example, during the Eighty-ninth Congress (1965–1966) alone, the number of categorical grant-in-aid programs grew from 221 to 379.[30] The grants authorized during the 1960s announced national purposes much more strongly than did earlier grants. Central to that national purpose was the need to provide opportunities to the poor.

Many of the categorical grants enacted during the 1960s were ***project grants,*** which require state and local governments to submit proposals to federal agencies. In contrast to the older ***formula grants,*** which used a formula (composed of such elements as need and state and local capacities) to distribute funds, the new project grants made funding available on a competitive basis. Federal agencies would give grants to the proposals they judged to be the best. In this way, the national government acquired substantial control over which state and local governments got money, how much they got, and how they spent it.

On more than one occasion, the number of such specific categorical grants-in-aid and the amount of money involved in them have come under criticism, by Democrats as well as Republicans, ultra-liberals as well as ultraconservatives. But there is general agreement that grants-in-aid help to reduce disparities of wealth between rich states and poor states. And although some critics have asserted that grants encouraged state and local governments to initiate programs merely because "free money from Washington" was available, the fact is that when federal grants were reduced by the Reagan administration, most states and localities continued funding the same programs with their own revenues. Daniel Elazar, an authority on federalism, has observed that "Despite many protestations to the contrary, only in rare situations have federal grant programs served to alter state administrative patterns in ways that did not coincide with already established state policies."[31]

Federalism has not stood still. If the traditional system of two separate sovereigns performing highly different functions (as shown in Table 3.1) is considered dual federalism, historians of federalism suggest that the system since the era of

[29]Kenneth T. Palmer, "The Evolution of Grant Policies," in *The Changing Politics of Federal Grants,* by Lawrence D. Brown, James W. Fossett, and Kenneth T. Palmer (Washington, DC: Brookings Institution, 1984), p. 15.

[30]Ibid., p. 6.

[31]Daniel Elazar, *American Federalism: A View from the States,* 3rd ed. (New York: Harper & Row, 1984), p. 110. For a view from the cities, see Paul Kantor, *The Dependent City: The Changing Political Economy of Urban America* (Glencoe, IL: Scott Foresman, 1988).

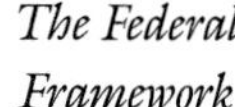

FIGURE 3.1

The Rise and Decline of Federal Aid

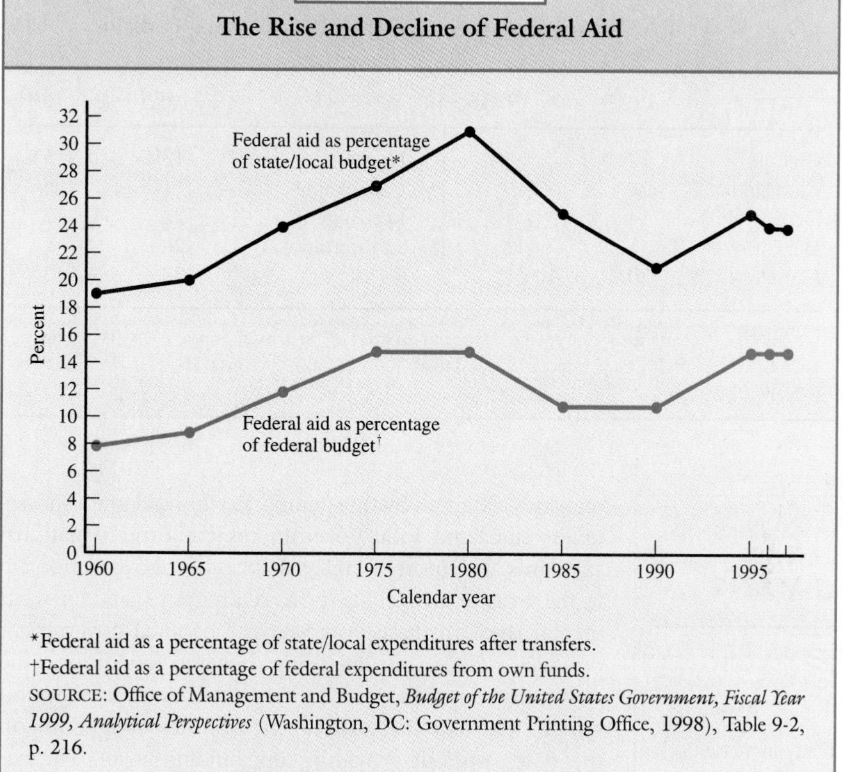


*Federal aid as a percentage of state/local expenditures after transfers.
†Federal aid as a percentage of federal expenditures from own funds.
SOURCE: Office of Management and Budget, *Budget of the United States Government, Fiscal Year 1999, Analytical Perspectives* (Washington, DC: Government Printing Office, 1998), Table 9-2, p. 216.

the New Deal is cooperative federalism. The most important student of the history of federalism, Morton Grodzins, characterized this as a move from "layer cake federalism" to "marble cake federalism,"[32] in which intergovernmental cooperation and sharing have blurred the distinguishing line, making it difficult to say where the national government ends and the state and local governments begin. Figure 3.1 demonstrates the financial basis of the marble cake idea. At the high point of grant-in-aid policies in the late 1970s federal aid contributed about 25–30 percent of the operating budgets of all the state and local governments in the country. The numbers in Table 3.4 present some of the more extreme examples from 1977 and the severe drop since that time.

**Regulated Federalism and National Standards** Developments in the past twenty-five years have moved well beyond marble cake federalism to what might be called "regulated federalism."[33] In some areas the national government actually

[32]Morton Grodzins, "The Federal System," in *Goals for Americans* (Englewood Cliffs, NJ: Prentice-Hall, 1960), p. 265. In a marble cake, the white cake is distinguishable from the chocolate cake, but the two are streaked rather than in distinct layers.

[33]The concept and the best discussion of this modern phenomenon will be found in Donald F. Kettl, *The Regulation of American Federalism* (Baltimore: Johns Hopkins University Press, 1983 and 1987), especially pp. 33–41.

TABLE 3.4

**Federal Aid as a Percentage of General Annual Expenditure**

| CITY | 1977 | 1995 | CITY | 1977 | 1995 |
|---|---|---|---|---|---|
| Chicago | 20% | 8% | Houston | 13% | 5% |
| Cleveland | 29 | 10 | Indianapolis | 21 | 6 |
| Denver | 14 | 1 | Los Angeles | 22 | 12 |
| Detroit | 31 | 12 | San Antonio | 28 | 4 |
| Honolulu | 30 | 8 | Seattle | 23 | 3 |

SOURCE: Department of Commerce, *Statistical Abstract of the United States, 1999* (Washington, DC: Government Printing Office, 1999), Tables 504 and 506; *Statistical Abstract,* 1998, Tables 525 and 526.

**AMERICAN POLITICAL DEVELOPMENT**

There has been a steady increase each decade since the 1960s in both the volume and power of "regulatory federalism" or unfunded mandates. Whereas only two such programs existed from 1931 to 1960, there were over ten from 1961 to 1970, more than twenty from 1971 to 1980, and more than twenty-five from 1981 to 1990. Timothy Conlan argues not only that there were more mandates in the 1980s, but that they "tended to be the most coercive varieties."

SOURCE: Timothy Conlan, *From New Federalism to Devolution: Twenty-Five Years of Intergovernmental Reform* (Washington, DC: Brookings Institution, 1998), p. 205.

regulates the states by threatening to withhold grant money unless state and local governments conform to national standards. The most notable instances of this regulation are in the areas of civil rights, poverty programs, and environmental laws. In these instances, the national government provides grant-in-aid financing but sets conditions the states must meet in order to keep the grants. In other instances, the national government imposes obligations on the states without providing any funding at all. The national government refers to these policies as "setting national standards." Important cases of such efforts are in interstate highway use, in social services, and in education. The net effect of these national standards is that state and local policies are more uniform from coast to coast. However, there are a number of other programs in which the national government engages in regulated federalism by imposing obligations on the states *without providing any funding at all.* These have come to be called ***"unfunded mandates."*** States complained that mandates took up so much of their budgets that they were not able to set their own priorities.[34]

These burdens became a major part of the rallying cry that produced the famous Republican Congress elected in 1994, with its Contract with America. One of the first measures adopted by the 104th Republican Congress was an act to

[34]John DiIulio and Don Kettl report that in 1980 there were 36 laws that could be categorized as unfunded mandates. And despite the concerted opposition of the Reagan and Bush administrations, another 27 laws qualifying as unfunded mandates were adopted between 1982 and 1991. See John DiIulio, Jr., and Donald F. Kettl, *Fine Print: The Contract with America, Devolution, and the Administrative Realities of American Federalism* (Washington, DC: Brookings Institution, 1995), p. 41.

limit unfunded mandates—the Unfunded Mandates Reform Act (UMRA). This was considered a triumph of lobbying efforts by state and local governments, and it was "hailed as both symbol and substance of a renewed congressional commitment to federalism."[35] Under this law, any mandate with an uncompensated state and local cost estimated at greater than $50 million a year, as determined by the Congressional Budget Office (CBO), can be stopped by a point of order raised on the House or Senate floor. This was called a "stop, look and listen" requirement, forcing Congress to take positive action to own up to the mandate and its potential costs. During 1996, its first full year of operation (and the only year available at this time), only eleven bills included mandates that exceeded the $50 million threshold—from a total of sixty-nine estimates of actions in which mandates were included. Examples included minimum wage increase, parity for mental health and health insurance, mandated use of Social Security numbers on driver's licenses, and extension of Federal Occupation Safety and Health to state and local employees. Most of them were modified in the House, to reduce their costs. However, as one expert put it, "The primary impact of UMRA came not from the affirmative blockage of [mandate] legislation, but rather from its effect as a deterrent to mandates in the drafting and early consideration of legislation."[36]

As indicated by the first year of its operation, the effect of UMRA will not be revolutionary. UMRA does not prevent congressional members from passing unfunded mandates; it only makes them think twice before they do. Moreover, the act exempts several areas from coverage by UMRA. And states must still enforce antidiscrimination laws and meet other requirements to receive federal assistance. But on the other hand, UMRA does represent a serious effort to move the national/state relationship a bit further toward the state side.

**New Federalism and the National-State Tug-of-War** Federalism in the United States can best be understood today as a tug-of-war between those seeking more uniform national standards and those seeking more room for variability from state to state. Presidents Nixon and Reagan called their efforts to reverse this trend toward national standards and reestablish traditional policy making and implementation the "new federalism," by which national policies attempted to return more discretion to the states. This was the purpose of Nixon's revenue sharing and the goal of Reagan's block grants, which consolidated a number of categorical grants into one larger category, leaving the state (or local) government to decide how to use the grant. Presidents Nixon and Reagan, as well as President Bush, were sincere in wanting to return somewhat to a traditional notion of freedom of action for the states. They called it new federalism, but their concept and their goal were really much closer to the older, traditional federalism that predated Franklin Roosevelt.

Although Reagan succeeded in reducing national appropriations for grants-in-aid during his first term, he could not prevent increases during his

[35]Paul Posner, "Unfunded Mandate Reform: How Is It Working?" *Rockefeller Institute Bulletin* (Albany: Nelson A. Rockefeller Institute of Government, 1998), p. 35.

[36]Ibid., p. 36.

DEBATING THE ISSUES

## Can the States Do It Better?

*For the last two decades, the hallowed principle of federalism has come under intense focus, as a rising chorus of critics have argued on behalf of turning over more powers and responsibilities to the states. Few have defended a stronger role for the federal government; rather, arguments have centered on how far this process of "devolution" of powers to the states should go. In 1994, Republican governors issued the "Williamsburg Resolves," constituting a blueprint for devolution of powers to the states. Clinton administration official Alice Rivlin argues for a more cautious approach, urging a "dividing the job" approach between the federal government and the states.*

### Republican Governors' Conference

Concerns about the condition of federal-state relations have been voiced throughout our nation's history. But, today, there is a unique need—and a unique opportunity—for reform.

Never has there been a broader consensus among the states—and among the elected officials and voters in the states, regardless of party—that the federal government has pervasively exceeded its constitutional bounds and must be restrained. . . .

Recognizing the urgency of the need and the uniqueness of the opportunity for reform, we declare our common resolve to restore balance to the federal-state relationship and renew the framers' vision. An agreed agenda for concerted action to achieve this objective is essential. Among the principal elements of this common agenda of reform are these:

*I. Mobilizing the People to Reclaim Their Freedom. . . .*

Too few of our citizens appreciate the central role that the erosion of state and local prerogatives, and the emergence of the federal bureaucratic, judicial and legislative leviathan, have played in their loss of political liberty.

We are resolved to bring these developments and consequences urgently to the attention of the people of our states, and all Americans. Only when our citizens fully appreciate the practical and pervasive impact on their daily lives of federalism's decline will they demand change.

*II. Litigation to Enforce the Tenth Amendment. . . .*

We are . . . resolved to pursue energetically in the federal courts Tenth Amendment challenges to federal encroachments in the domain of the states.

*III. Restriction on Federal Mandates and Other Legislative Initiatives*

Across the country, governors, mayors, county officials, and state legislators of both parties are working together to obtain relief from burdensome federal mandates. . . . we are resolved to promote prompt and dramatic mandate relief during the next Congress.

*IV. A Conference of the States to Forge Consensus on Structural Reforms. . . .*

A Conference of the States would enable state representatives to consider, refine, and adopt proposals for structural change in our federal system. The proposals so adopted would comprise the States' Petition, which would be a powerful instrument for arousing popular support and promoting change in Congress and state legislatures. . . . [1]



## RIVLIN

"Dividing the job" would involve five major changes in policy. First, the federal government would take charge of reforming the nation's health care financing system to accomplish two objectives: firm control of medical costs and universal health insurance. . . . Second, the states, not the federal government, would take charge of accomplishing a "productivity agenda" of reforms designed to revitalize the economy and raise incomes. These reforms would address needs such as education and skills training, child care, housing, infrastructure, and economic development. . . .

Third, the following federal programs would be devolved to the states or gradually wither away: elementary and secondary education, job training, economic and community development, housing, most highways and other transportation, social services, and some pollution control programs. Some specific programs where federal action is needed would be retained, even expanded; for example, higher education scholarships for low-income students and federal support for scientific research. . . .

Fourth, the federal government would bring its budget from deficit into surplus (including social security). . . . Fifth, the states, with the blessing or the assistance of the federal government, would strengthen their tax systems and increase revenue by adopting one or more common taxes (same base, same rate) and sharing proceeds. . . .

Despite its name, the "dividing the job" scenario does not involve a return to dual federalism. There are important areas in which cooperative federalism is necessary and desirable. One of those is environmental protection. Many hazards to the environment cross state lines and cannot be satisfactorily dealt with by states and localities acting alone. Others are of largely local concern.

Welfare for families with children (AFDC) also remains a shared state and federal responsibility in this scenario. Some would argue for making AFDC federal or at least for a basic federal program that the state could supplement. Joint responsibility, however, would give both levels of government incentives to try hard to reduce welfare dependency. To this end, the states should improve education, training, and child care for welfare mothers, and the federal government should adjust the income tax to increase the after-tax rewards for low-wage work.[2]

[1]"The Williamsburg Resolves," *Rockefeller Institute Bulletin 1996: The Devolution Revolution* (Albany: The Rockefeller Institute, 1996), pp. 17–19.

[2]Alice M. Rivlin, "Rethinking Federalism," in *Readings in State and Local Government,* ed. by David C. Saffell and Harry Basehart (New York: McGraw-Hill, 1994), pp. 27–36.

second term. Both he and Bush were able to hold the line only enough to keep these outlays from increasing faster than the overall increase in the national budget.

Grants-in-aid began to grow slowly toward the end of the Bush administration and through Clinton's first term; however, the growth has been modest and almost entirely through block grants that give states and localities considerable flexibility. In effect, President Clinton has adopted the "new federalism" of Nixon and Reagan even while expanding federal grant activity. Clinton also signed the Unfunded Mandates Reform Act of 1995. Although Clinton signed the new act with misgivings and promised to "fix it" in 1997, he signed into law the Personal Responsibility and Work Opportunity Reconciliation Act of 1996, which goes farther than any other act of Congress in the past sixty years to relieve the states from national mandates, funded or unfunded. The new law replaces the sixty-one-year-old program of Aid to Families with Dependent Children (AFDC) and its education, work, and training program, with block grants to states for Temporary Assistance to Needy Families (TANF). Although some national standards remain (see Chapter 15), the place of the states in the national welfare system has been virtually revolutionized.

By changing welfare from a combined federal-state program into a block grant to the states, Congress gave the states more responsibility for programs that serve the poor. One argument in favor of this decision is that states can act as "laboratories of democracy," by experimenting with many different approaches to find one that best meets the needs of their citizens.[37] As states have altered their welfare programs in the wake of the new law, they have indeed designed diverse approaches. For example, Minnesota has adopted an incentive-based approach that offers extra assistance to families that take low-wage jobs. Other states, such as California, have more "sticks" than "carrots" in their new welfare programs. It is still too early to say whether giving the states more responsibility for welfare has been a success. The new programs have been in place for only a short time and they were launched in a time of unusually low unemployment. Advocates of more federal responsibility for welfare fear that when a recession occurs, serious problems will emerge. When state budgets grow tighter, there will be considerable pressure to reduce social spending at the same time that unemployment is growing.

As the case of welfare shows, assessments about "the right way" to divide responsibility in the federal system change over time. The case of speed limits, discussed earlier in this chapter, provides another example. Speed limits have traditionally been a state and local responsibility. But in 1973, at the height of the oil shortage, Congress passed legislation to withhold federal highway funds from states that did not adopt a maximum speed limit of 55 miles per hour (mph). The lower speed limit, it was argued, would reduce energy consumption by cars. Although Congress had not formally taken over the authority to set speed limits, the power of its purse was so important that every state adopted the new speed limit. As the energy crisis faded, the national speed limit lost much of its support, even though it was found to have reduced the number of traffic deaths. In 1995, Congress repealed the penalties for higher speed limits, and states once again became free to set their own speed limits. Many states with large rural areas raised their maximum to 75 mph; Montana set unlimited speeds in the rural areas during daylight hours. Early

[37]The phrase "laboratories of democracy" was coined by Supreme Court Justice Louis Brandeis in his dissenting opinion in New State Ice Co. v. Liebman, 285 U.S. 262 (1932).

**Box 3.1**

### Other Federal Systems

In contrast to unitary systems, the key feature of federal systems of government is that their powers are constitutionally divided between a central government and regional governments. Each of these levels of government typically has constitutionally allocated legislative, executive, and judicial powers, and each level has sovereignty within its sphere of responsibility.

The United States, which owes its federalism largely to the fact that separate states existed as politically distinct entities long before any unitary national government, is by no means unique in possessing a federal system. Switzerland, for instance, has a history of federalism that goes back as far as the thirteenth century. If one defines federalism broadly to mean any system that permits some degree of regional internal autonomy from a central government, nearly two dozen countries, possessing in total about half of the world's territory and a third of its population, may be seen as having federal systems. Even if one defines federalism more narrowly to mean those countries in which neither the central nor the regional governments have constitutional or political supremacy, the list includes Switzerland, Australia, Brazil, India, and Canada.

The "marble cake" image of American federalism derives in part from the incorporation of the principle of the separation of powers into both levels of government in the United States. With power and authority widely diffused at both the national and the state levels of government, there are many points of contact between the two levels. In federal systems that have not incorporated the principle of the separation of powers to such a great degree, the two levels of government have far fewer points of contact, and most of the interactions and relations between levels occur at the parliamentary or cabinet level. Such a pattern of "parliamentary" or "executive" federalism typifies states like Canada and Australia.

research indicates that numbers of highway deaths have indeed risen in the states that increased the limits.[38] As new evidence becomes available, it will surely provide fuel for the ongoing debate about what are properly the states' responsibilities and what the federal government should do.

For the moment, the balance seems to be tipped toward the states, though the tug-of-war between the states and national government will certainly continue. As a result of this ongoing struggle for power, federalism remains a vital part of the American system of government. States and cities may clamor (and lobby) for a larger share of the national budget, and state and local leaders have shown a willingness to cooperate with the national standards embodied in environmental protection laws and civil rights laws. But states continue to hold on jealously to the maximum freedom of action that is embodied in the historic concept of federalism.

[38]"Motor Vehicle Fatalities in 1996 Were 12 Percent Higher on Interstates, Freeways in 12 States That Raised Speed Limits," press release of the Insurance Institute for Highway Safety, 10 October 1997.

# THE SECOND PRINCIPLE: THE SEPARATION OF POWERS

James Madison is best qualified to speak to Americans about the separation of powers:

> There can be no liberty where the legislative and executive powers are united in the same person . . . [or] if the power of judging be not separated from the legislative and executive powers.[39]

Using this same reasoning, many of Madison's contemporaries argued that there was not *enough* separation among the three branches, and Madison had to backtrack to insist that the principle did not require complete separation:

> . . . unless these departments [branches] be so far connected and blended as to give each a constitutional control over the others, the degree of separation which the maxim requires, as essential to a free government, can never in practice be duly maintained.[40]

This is the secret of how we have made the separation of powers effective: We made the principle self-enforcing by giving each branch of government the means to participate in, and partially or temporarily to obstruct, the workings of the other branches.

## Checks and Balances

The means by which each branch of government interacts is known informally as ***checks and balances.*** The best-known examples are the presidential power to veto legislation passed by Congress; the power of Congress to override the veto by a two-thirds majority vote, to impeach the president, and (of the Senate) to approve presidential appointments; the power of the president to appoint the members of the Supreme Court and the other federal judges with Senate approval; and the power of the Supreme Court to engage in judicial review (to be discussed below). These and other examples are shown in Table 3.5. The framers sought to guarantee that the three branches would in fact use the checks and balances as weapons against each other by giving each branch a different political constituency: direct, popular election of the members of the House; indirect election of senators (until the Seventeenth Amendment, adopted in 1913); indirect election of the president (which still exists, at least formally, today); and appointment

[39]Clinton Rossiter, ed., *The Federalist Papers* (New York: New American Library, 1961), No. 47, p. 302.

[40]Ibid., No. 48, p. 308.

TABLE 3.5

**Checks and Balances**

| | LEGISLATIVE BRANCH CAN BE CHECKED BY: | EXECUTIVE BRANCH CAN BE CHECKED BY: | JUDICIAL BRANCH CAN BE CHECKED BY: |
|---|---|---|---|
| Legislative branch can check: | NA | Can overrule veto (2/3 vote)<br>Controls appropriations<br>Controls by statute<br>Impeachment of president<br>Senate approval of appointments and treaties<br>Committee oversight | Controls appropriations<br>Can create inferior courts<br>Can add new judges<br>Senate approval of appointments<br>Impeachment of judges |
| Executive branch can check: | Can veto legislation<br>Can convene special session<br>Can adjourn Congress when chambers disagree<br>Vice president presides over Senate and votes to break ties | NA | President appoints judges |
| Judicial branch can check: | Judicial review of legislation<br>Chief justice presides over Senate during proceedings to impeach president | Judicial review over presidential actions<br>Power to issue warrants<br>Chief justice presides over impeachment of president | NA |

NA = Not applicable.

of federal judges for life. All things considered, the best characterization of the separation of powers principle in action is, as we said in Chapter 2, "separated institutions sharing power."[41]

## Legislative Supremacy

Although each branch was to be given adequate means to compete with the other branches, it is also clear that within the system of separated powers the framers provided for ***legislative supremacy*** by making Congress the preeminent branch. It may appear to be paradoxical or downright illogical to combine "co-equal branches" with legislative supremacy, but that is the case. And legislative supremacy made the provision of checks and balances in the other two branches all the more important.

The most important indication of the intention of legislative supremacy was made by the framers when they decided to place the provisions for national powers in Article I, the legislative article, and to treat the powers of the national government as powers of Congress. In a system based on the "rule of law," the power to make the laws is the supreme power. Section 8 provides in part that "*Congress* shall have Power . . . to lay and collect taxes . . . to borrow money . . . to regulate commerce . . ." [emphasis added]. The founders also provided for legislative supremacy in their decision to give Congress the sole power over appropriations and to give the House of Representatives the power to initiate all revenue bills. Madison recognized legislative supremacy as part and parcel of the separation of powers:

> . . . It is not possible to give each department equal power of self defense. In republican government, the legislative authority necessarily predominates. The remedy for this inconvenience is to divide the legislature into different branches; and to render them, by different modes of election and different principles of action, as little connected with each other as the nature of their common functions and their common dependence on the society will admit.[42]

In other words, Congress was so likely to dominate the other branches that it would have to be divided against itself, into House and Senate. One could say that the Constitution provided for four branches, not three.

Legislative supremacy became a fact soon after the founding decade was over. National politics centered on Congress. Undistinguished presidents followed one another in a dreary succession. Even Madison—so brilliant as a constitutional theorist, so loyal as a constitutional record keeper, and so effective in the struggle for the founding—was a weak president. Jackson and Lincoln are the only two who stand out in the entire nineteenth century, and their successors dropped back out of sight; except for these two, the other presidents operated within the accepted framework of legislative supremacy (see Chapter 6).

The development of political parties, and in particular the emergence in 1832 of the national convention method of nominating presidential candidates (which

[41]Richard E. Neustadt, *Presidential Power: The Politics of Leadership from Roosevelt to Reagan*, rev. ed. (New York: Free Press, 1990; orig. published 1960), p. 33.

[42]*The Federalist Papers*, No. 51, p. 322.

replaced the congressional "King Caucus" method discussed in Chapters 6 and 11), saved the presidency from complete absorption into the orbit of legislative power by giving the presidency a base of power independent of Congress. But although this preserved the presidency and salvaged the separation of powers, it did so only in a negative sense. That is to say, presidents were more likely (after 1832 when the national conventions were established) to veto congressional enactments than before, or to engage in a military action, but they were not more likely to present programs for positive legislation or to attempt to lead Congress in the enactment of legislation.[43] This fact underscored the significance of the shift to presidential supremacy when it came after 1937 (see also Chapter 6).

The role of the judicial branch in the separation of powers has depended upon the power of judicial review (see also Chapter 8), a power not provided for in the Constitution but asserted by Chief Justice Marshall in 1803:

> If a law be in opposition to the Constitution; if both the law and the Constitution apply to a particular case, so that the Court must either decide that case conformable to the law, disregarding the Constitution, or conformable to the Constitution, disregarding the law; the Court must determine which of these conflicting rules governs the case: This is of the very essence of judicial duty.[44]

The Supreme Court has exercised the power of judicial review with caution, as though to protect its power by using it sparingly.

Review of the constitutionality of acts of the president or Congress is in fact very rare.[45] In the sixty years since the rise of big government and strong presidents, only a handful of important congressional enactments have been invalidated on constitutional grounds.[46] During the same time, there have been only

[43]For a good review of the uses of the veto, see Raymond Tatalovich and Byron Daynes, *Presidential Power in the United States* (Monterey, CA: Brooks/Cole, 1984), pp. 148–51; and Robert Spitzer, *The Presidential Veto: Touchstone of the American Presidency* (Albany: State University of New York Press, 1988).

[44]Marbury v. Madison, 1 Cranch 137 (1803).

[45]In response to New Deal legislation, the Supreme Court struck down eight out of ten New Deal statutes. For example, in Panama Refining Co. v. Ryan, 293 U.S. 388 (1935), the Court ruled that a section of the National Industrial Recovery Act was an invalid delegation of legislative power to the executive branch. And in Schechter Poultry Co. v. U.S., 295 U.S. 495 (1935), the Court found the National Industrial Recovery Act itself to be invalid for the same reason. But since 1935, the Supreme Court has rarely confronted the president or Congress on constitutional questions.

[46]Since 1937, only a handful of cases of any significance whatsoever can be identified where the Court actually invalidated an act of Congress on constitutional grounds. The first of these was INS v. Chadha, 462 U.S. 919 (1983), in which the Supreme Court declared unconstitutional the so-called legislative veto, whereby Congress had required certain regulatory agencies to submit proposed regulations to Congress for approval prior to implementation. The second case, Bowsher v. Synar, 92 L.Ed. 583 (1986), struck down the Gramm-Rudman Act mandating a balanced federal budget. Only one part of the act was declared unconstitutional: the part delegating to the comptroller general the power to direct the president to reduce the budget by a specified amount if the budget deficit provided by Congress exceeded a certain set amount. The Court argued that since the comptroller general could be removed only by Congress, it was unconstitutional for Congress to give the comptroller general "executive" powers. Another case, U.S. v. Lopez, 115 S.Ct. 1624 (1995), validated the Gun-Free School Zones Act of 1990, making it a federal crime to carry firearms within a radius of a thou-

three important judicial confrontations with the president. One was the so-called *Steel Seizure* case of 1952. The second case was *U.S. v. Nixon* in 1974, where the Court declared unconstitutional President Nixon's refusal to respond to a subpoena to make available the infamous White House tapes as evidence in a criminal prosecution. The Court argued that although ***executive privilege*** did protect the confidentiality of communications to and from the president, this did not extend to data in presidential files or tapes bearing upon criminal prosecutions.[47] And, most recently, the Supreme Court rejected President Clinton's claim that the pressures and obligations of the office were so demanding that "in all but the most exceptional cases the Constitution requires federal courts to defer such litigation until his term end. . . ."[48]

All in all, the separation of powers has had an uneven history. Although "presidential government" seemed to supplant legislative supremacy after 1937, the relative power position of the three branches has not been static. The degree of conflict between the president and Congress has varied with the rise and fall of political parties, and it has been especially intense during periods of ***divided government,*** when one party controls the White House and another controls the Congress, as has been the case almost solidly since 1969 (see Table 3.6).

Since Watergate, Congress has tried to get back some of the power it had delegated to the president (see Chapter 6). One of the methods it seized upon was the Ethics in Government Act of 1978, which established a "special prosecutor" (later called ***independent counsel***) with the authority to investigate allegations of wrongdoing by executive branch officials. Independent counsel Kenneth Starr's investigation of President Clinton's affair with Monica Lewinsky and Clinton's subsequent impeachment in the House of Representatives are indications that the give and take between Congress and president is more contested than ever (see also Chapters 5 and 17).

The very effort of Congress to provide by law for competition with the executive branch suggests that the separation of powers is still very much alive. And

---

sand feet around a public or private school. This case was followed two years later by judicial review and invalidation of an important provision of the Brady Handgun Violence Prevention Act by imposing unconstitutional "unfunded mandates" to state and local officials to implement the federal law requiring background checks, and the like, on gun customers (Printz v. U.S. and Mack v. U.S., 117 S.Ct. 2365 [1997]). Finally, the case of City of Boerne v. Flores, 117 S.Ct. 73 F. 3d 1352 (1997) struck down the federal Religious Freedom Restoration Act of 1993 (RFRA) on the grounds that Congress had exceeded its constitutional authority by forbidding the local government from obeying the state historic landmarks laws. A local Catholic church had been refused a permit to build an expansion of its church because the building had been set aside as a landmark. The church sued the city on the grounds that they had violated First Amendment "free exercise" rights by making them obey the state historic landmark laws. RFRA was invalidated as a consequence. It is thus interesting and probably quite significant that the only cases where congressional enactments were declared unconstitutional by the Supreme Court were cases where the Court was actually defending the principles of federalism and the separation of powers.

[47]Youngstown Sheet & Tube Co. v. Sawyer, 343 U.S. 579 (1952) (the official name of the *Steel Seizure* case); U.S. v. Nixon, 418 U.S. 683 (1974); and Clinton v. Jones, 117 S.Ct. 1636 (1997). See also Raoul Berger, *Executive Privilege: A Constitutional Myth* (Cambridge: Harvard University Press, 1974).

[48]Clinton v. Jones, 117 S.Ct. 1636 (1997).

**TABLE 3.6**

**The Record of Divided Government**

| DATE | PARTY CONTROLLING: PRESIDENT | CONGRESS | GOVERNMENT: YEARS DIVIDED |
|---|---|---|---|
| 1946–48 | Truman, Democratic | Republican | Divided 2 |
| 1948–52 | Truman, Democratic | Democratic | |
| 1952–54 | Eisenhower, Republican | Republican | |
| 1954–60 | Eisenhower, Republican | Democratic | Divided 6 |
| 1960–64 | Kennedy/Johnson, Democratic | Democratic | |
| 1964–68 | Johnson, Democratic | Democratic | |
| 1968–72 | Nixon, Republican | Democratic | Divided 4 |
| 1972–76 | Nixon/Ford, Republican | Democratic | Divided 4 |
| 1976–80 | Carter, Democratic | Democratic | |
| 1980–86 | Reagan, Republican | Republican Senate<br>Democratic House | Divided/mixed 6 |
| 1986–88 | Reagan, Republican | Democratic | Divided 2 |
| 1988–92 | Bush, Republican | Democratic | Divided 4 |
| 1992–94 | Clinton, Democratic | Democratic | |
| 1994–2000 | Clinton, Democratic | Republican | Divided 6 |
| | TOTAL YEARS 54 | TOTAL YEARS DIVIDED 34 | |

the judiciary is very much a part of the continuing vitality of the separation of powers. Although they rarely question the constitutionality of a statute, the federal courts are constantly involved in judicial review of statutes and administrative orders because agencies have to get court orders to enforce their decisions. This gives the judiciary a regular opportunity to influence executive as well as legislative actions, as was shown in Table 3.5 (page 101). In other words, in order to apply a statute, the court has to first interpret it; and to interpret a statute is to have the power to change it (see also Chapter 8). This offers more evidence of the continuing vitality of the separation of powers.

## THE CONSTITUTION AND LIMITED GOVERNMENT

Federalism and the separation of powers are two of the three most important constitutional principles upon which the United States' system of limited government is based (the third is the principle of individual rights). As we have seen, federalism limits the power of the national government in numerous ways. By its very existence, federalism recognizes the principle of two sovereigns, the national government and the state government (hence the term "dual federalism"). In addition, the Constitution specifically restrained the power of the national government to regulate the economy. As a result, the states were free to do most of the fundamental governing for the first century and a half of American government. This began to change during and following the New Deal, as the national government began to exert more influence over the states through grants-in-aid and mandates. But even as the powers of the national government grew, so did the powers of the states. In the last decade, as well, we have noticed a countertrend to the growth of national power as Congress has opted to devolve some of its powers to the states. The most recent notable instance of devolution was the welfare reform plan of 1996. Federalism has also been strengthened by a revival of state governments over the last two decades. When all is said and done, one can confidently conclude that federalism remains a vital part of American government.

The second principle of limited government, separation of powers, is manifested in our system of checks and balances, whereby separate institutions of government share power with each other. Even though the Constitution clearly provided for legislative supremacy, checks and balances have functioned well. Some would say they have worked too well. The last fifty years has witnessed long periods of divided government, when one party has controlled the White House and the other party controlled Congress. During these periods, the level of conflict between the executive and legislative branches has been particularly divisive, resulting in what some analysts derisively call gridlock. Nevertheless,

THEN AND NOW

## Changes in American Politics

- Under "dual federalism," which lasted from 1789–1937, the national government limited itself primarily to promoting commerce, while the states did most of the fundamental governing for the country.
- After 1937, the national government expanded its power, but not at the expense of the powers of the states.
- From the 1960s to the 1990s, the national government sought to "regulate" the states by withholding grant money unless state governments conformed to national standards. Today, "new" federalism involves a tug-of-war between those continuing to seek uniform national standards and those seeking more room for variability from state to state.
- Within the system of separated powers, the framers of the Constitution provided for legislative supremacy by making Congress the preeminent branch. After 1937, presidential government seemed to supplant legislative supremacy. Today, the two branches continue to compete for power.

this is a genuine separation of powers, not so far removed from the intent of the framers. With the rise of political parties, Americans developed a parliamentary theory that "responsible party government" requires that the same party control both branches, including both chambers of the legislature. But that kind of parliamentary/party government is a "fusion of powers," not a separation of powers. Although it may not make for good government, having an opposition party in majority control of the legislature reinforces the separation and the competition that was built into the Constitution. We can complain at length about the inability of divided government to make decisions, and we can criticize it as stalemate or gridlock,[49] but even that is in accord with the theory of the framers of the *American* Constitution that public policy is supposed to be difficult to make.

The purpose of a constitution is to provide a framework. A constitution is good if it produces the *cause of action* that leads to good legislation, good case law, and appropriate police behavior. A constitution cannot eliminate power. But its principles can be a citizen's dependable defense against the abuse of power.

## SUMMARY

In this chapter we have traced the development of two of the three basic principles of the U.S. Constitution—federalism and the separation of powers. Federalism involves a division between two layers of government: national and state. The separation of powers involves the division of the national government into three branches. These principles are limitations on the powers of government; Americans made these compromises as a condition of giving their consent to be governed. And these principles became the framework within which the government operates. The persistence of local government and of reliance of the national government on grants-in-aid to coerce local governments into following national goals was used as a case study to demonstrate the continuing vitality of the federal framework. Examples were also given of the intense competition between the president, Congress, and the courts to dramatize the continuing vitality of the separation of powers.

The purpose of a constitution is to organize the makeup or the composition of the government, the *framework within which* government and politics, including actual legislation, can take place. A country does not require federalism and the separation of powers to have a real constitutional government. And the country does not have to approach individual rights in the same manner as the American Constitution. But to be a true constitutional government,

[49]Not everybody will agree that divided government is all that less productive than government in which both branches are controlled by the same party. See David Mayhew, *Divided We Govern: Party Control, Law Making and Investigations, 1946–1990* (New Haven: Yale University Press, 1991). For another good evaluation of divided government, see Charles O. Jones, *Separate But Equal Branches—Congress and the Presidency* (Chatham, NJ: Chatham House, 1995).

a government must have a few principles that cannot be manipulated by people in power merely for their own convenience. This is the essence of constitutionalism—principles that are above the reach of everyday legislatures, executives, bureaucrats, and politicians, yet that are not so far above their reach that these principles cannot under some conditions be adapted to changing times.

## FOR FURTHER READING

Anton, Thomas. *American Federalism and Public Policy.* Philadelphia: Temple University Press, 1989.

Bensel, Richard. *Sectionalism and American Political Development: 1880–1980.* Madison: University of Wisconsin Press, 1984.

Bernstein, Richard B., with Jerome Agel. *Amending America—If We Love the Constitution So Much, Why Do We Keep Trying to Change It?* (Lawrence: University Press of Kansas, 1993).

Black, Charles Jr. *Impeachment: A Handbook.* New Haven: Yale University Press, 1974, 1998.

Caraley, Demetrios. "Dismantling the Federal Safety Net: Fictions versus Realities," *Political Science Quarterly,* Summer 1996, Vol. 111, No. 2, pp. 225–58.

Corwin, Edward, and J. W. Peltason. *Corwin & Peltason's Understanding the Constitution,* 13th ed. Fort Worth: Harcourt Brace, 1994.

Crovitz, L. Gordon, and Jeremy Rabkin, eds. *The Fettered Presidency: Legal Constraints on the Executive Branch.* Washington, DC: American Enterprise Institute, 1989.

Elazar, Daniel. *American Federalism: A View from the States,* 3rd ed. New York: Harper & Row, 1984.

Grodzins, Morton. *The American System.* Chicago: Rand McNally, 1974.

Kettl, Donald. *The Regulation of American Federalism.* Baltimore: Johns Hopkins University Press, 1987.

Palley, Marian Lief, and Howard Palley. *Urban America and Public Policies.* Lexington, MA: D. C. Heath, 1981.

Peterson, Paul, Barry Rabe, and Kenneth K. Wong. *When Federalism Works.* Washington, DC: Brookings Institution, 1986.

Smith, Rogers. *Civic Ideals: Conflicting Visions of Citizenship in U.S. History.* New Haven: Yale University Press, 1997.

# 4

# The Constitutional Framework and the Individual: Civil Liberties and Civil Rights

## TIME LINE ON CIVIL LIBERTIES AND CIVIL RIGHTS

| Events | | Institutional Developments |
|---|---|---|
| Bill of Rights sent to states for ratification (1789) | | States ratify U.S. Bill of Rights (1791) |
| Undeclared naval war with France (1798–1800); passage of Alien and Sedition Acts (1798) | 1800 | Alien and Sedition Acts disregarded and not renewed (1801) |
| Maine admitted to Union as free state (1820); Missouri admitted as slave state (1821) | | Missouri Compromise regulates expansion of slavery into territories (1820) |
| | | *Barron v. Baltimore* confirms dual citizenship (1833) |
| Slaves taken into territories (1800s) | | *Dred Scott v. Sandford* invalidates Missouri Compromise, perpetuates slavery (1857) |
| | 1860 | |
| Civil War (1861–1865) | | Emancipation Proclamation (1863); Thirteenth Amendment prohibits slavery (1865) |
| Southern blacks now vote but Black Codes in South impose special restraints (1865) | | Civil Rights Act (1866) |
| Reconstruction (1867–1877) | | Fourteenth Amendment ratified (1868) |
| "Jim Crow" laws spread throughout the South (1890s) | | *Plessy v. Ferguson* upholds doctrine of "separate but equal" (1896) |
| World War I (1914–1918) | | |
| Postwar pacifist and anarchist agitation and suppression (1920s and 1930s) | 1920 | *Gitlow v. N.Y.* (1925) and *Near v. Minnesota* (1931) apply First Amendment to states |
| U.S. in World War II (1941–1945); pressures to desegregate in the Army; revelations of Nazi genocide | | President's commission on civil rights (1946) |
| | 1950 | |
| Civil Rights Movement: Montgomery bus boycott (1955); lunch counter sit-ins (1960); freedom riders (1961) | | *Brown v. Board of Education* overturns *Plessy*, invalidates segregation (1954); federal use of troops to enforce court order to integrate schools (1957) |
| March on Washington—largest civil rights demonstration in American history (1963) | | Civil Rights Act outlaws segregation (1964) |
| | | *Katzenbach v. McClung* upholds use of commerce clause to bar segregation (1964) |
| Spread of movement politics—students, women, environment, right to life (1970s) | 1970 | *Roe v. Wade* prohibits states from outlawing abortion (1973) |

| Events | Institutional Developments |
|---|---|
| Affirmative action plans enacted in universities and corporations (1970s and 1980s) | Court orders to end malapportionment and segregation (1970s and 1980s) |
| | *Bowers v. Hardwick* upholds state regulation of homosexual activity (1986) |
| Challenges to affirmative action plans (1980s–1990s) | Court accepts affirmative action on a limited basis—*Regents of Univ. of Calif. v. Bakke* (1978), *Wards Cove v. Atonio* (1989), *Martin v. Wilks* (1989) |
| | Missouri law restricting abortion upheld in *Webster v. Reproductive Health Services* (1989) |
| 1990 | |
| States adopt restrictive abortion laws (1990–1991) | |
| Bush signs civil rights bill favoring suits against employment discrimination (1991) | Court permits school boards to terminate busing (1991) |
| Right to abortion established in *Roe v. Wade* upheld in *Planned Parenthood of SE Penn. v. Casey* (1992) | Clinton positions on abortion and gay rights revive civil rights activity and controversy (1993) |
| Clinton appoints Ginsburg (1993) and Breyer (1994) to Supreme Court | President and Congress limit death penalty appeals; quick Court approval in *Felker v. Turpin* (1996) suggests continuing conservative direction on criminal rights; but Court protection of abortion clinics with a "buffer zone" in *Madsen v. Women's Health Center* (1994) suggests a more moderate direction on abortion |

When the First Congress under the new Constitution met in late April of 1789 (having been delayed since March 4 by lack of a quorum because of bad winter roads), the most important item of business was consideration of a proposal to add a bill of rights to the Constitution. Such a proposal by Virginia delegate George Mason had been turned down with little debate in the waning days of the Philadelphia Constitutional Convention in September 1787, not because the delegates were too tired or too hot or against rights, but because of arguments by Hamilton and other Federalists that a bill of rights was irrelevant in a constitution providing the national government with only delegated powers. How could the national government abuse powers not given to it in the first place? But when the

### CORE OF THE ARGUMENT

- The rights in the Bill of Rights are called "civil liberties" because they protect citizens' freedom from arbitrary government action.
- Although the Fourteenth Amendment was ratified in 1868, it was not until the 1960s that it was interpreted to incorporate all of the civil liberties established by the Bill of Rights and to apply to the states as well as to the national government.
- Civil rights are obligations, imposed on government by the "equal protection" clause of the Fourteenth Amendment, to take positive action to protect citizens from the illegal actions of other citizens and government agencies.
- The "equal protection" clause was not enforced consistently until after World War II and the breakthrough case of *Brown v. Board of Education.*
- Since the passage of major civil rights legislation in 1964, the civil rights struggle has been expanded and universalized to include women and the disabled, gays, lesbians, and other minority groups.

Constitution was submitted to the states for ratification, Antifederalists, most of whom had *not* been delegates in Philadelphia, picked up on the argument of Thomas Jefferson (who also had not been a delegate) that the omission of a bill of rights was a major imperfection of the new Constitution. Whatever the merits of Hamilton's or Jefferson's positions, in order to gain ratification, the Federalists in Massachusetts, South Carolina, New Hampshire, Virginia, and New York made an "unwritten but unequivocal pledge" to add a bill of rights and a promise to confirm (in what became the Tenth Amendment) the understanding that all powers not delegated to the national government or explicitly prohibited to the states were reserved to the states.[1]

James Madison, who had been a delegate at the Philadelphia Convention and later became a member of Congress, may still have agreed privately that a bill of rights was not needed. But in 1789, recognizing the urgency of obtaining the support of the Antifederalists for the Constitution and the new government, he fought for the bill of rights, arguing that the principle it embodied would acquire "the character of fundamental maxims of free Government, and as they become incorporated with the national sentiment, counteract the impulses of interest and passion."[2]

"After much discussion and manipulation . . . at the delicate prompting of Washington and under the masterful prodding of Madison," the House adopted seventeen amendments; the Senate adopted twelve of these. Ten of the amendments were ratified by the states on December 15, 1791—from the start these ten were called the Bill of Rights.[3]

The Bill of Rights—its history and the controversy of interpretation surrounding it—can be usefully subdivided into two categories: civil liberties and civil rights. This chapter will be divided accordingly. ***Civil liberties*** are defined as *protections of citizens from improper government action.* When adopted in 1791, the

[1]Clinton Rossiter, *1787: The Grand Convention,* Norton Library Edition (New York: W. W. Norton, 1987), p. 302.

[2]Quoted in Milton Konvitz, "The Bill of Rights: Amendments I–X," in *An American Primer,* ed. Daniel J. Boorstin (Chicago: University of Chicago Press, 1966), p. 159.

[3]Rossiter, *1787: The Grand Convention,* p. 303, where he also reports that "in 1941 the States of Connecticut, Massachusetts, and Georgia celebrated the sesquicentennial of the Bill of Rights by giving their hitherto withheld and unneeded assent."

Bill of Rights was seen as guaranteeing a private sphere of personal liberty free of governmental restrictions.[4] As Jefferson had put it, a bill of rights "is what people are entitled to *against every government on earth. . . .*" Note the emphasis—citizen *against* government. In this sense, we could call the Bill of Rights a "bill of liberties" because the amendments focus on what government must *not* do. For example (with emphasis added),

1. "Congress shall make *no* law . . . " (I)
2. "The right to . . . bear Arms, shall *not* be infringed," (II)
3. "*No* soldier shall . . . be quartered . . ." (III)
4. "*No* warrants shall issue, but upon probable cause . . ." (IV)
5. "*No* person shall be held to answer . . . unless on presentment or indictment of a Grand Jury . . ." (V)
6. "Excessive bail shall *not* be required . . . *nor* cruel and unusual punishments inflicted." (VIII)

Thus, the Bill of Rights is a series of "thou shalt nots"—restraints addressed to government. Some of these restraints are *substantive,* putting limits on *what* the government shall and shall not have power to do—such as establishing a religion, quartering troops in private homes without consent, or seizing private property without just compensation. Other restraints are *procedural,* dealing with *how* the government is supposed to act. For example, even though the government has the substantive power to declare certain acts to be crimes and to arrest and imprison persons who violate its criminal laws, it may not do so except by fairly meticulous observation of procedures designed to protect the accused person. The best-known procedural rule is that "a person is presumed innocent until proven guilty." This rule does not question the government's power to punish someone for committing a crime; it questions only the way the government determines *who* committed the crime. Substantive and procedural restraints together identify the realm of civil liberties.

We define ***civil rights*** as obligations imposed on government to *guarantee equal citizenship and to protect citizens from discrimination by other private citizens and other government agencies.* Civil rights did not become part of the Constitution until 1868 with the adoption of the Fourteenth Amendment, which addressed the issue of who was a citizen and provided for each citizen "the equal protection of the laws." From that point on, we can see more clearly the distinction between civil liberties and civil rights, because civil liberties issues arise under the "due process of law" clause, and civil rights issues arise under the "equal protection of the laws" clause.

We turn first to civil liberties and to the long history of the effort to make personal liberty a reality for every citizen in America. The struggle for freedom against arbitrary and discriminatory actions by governments has continued to this day. And inevitably it is tied to the continuing struggle for civil rights, to persuade those same governments to take positive actions. We shall deal with

[4]Lest there be confusion in our interchangeable use of the words "liberty" and "freedom," treat them as synonyms. "Freedom" is from the German, *Freiheit.* "Liberty" is from the French, *liberté.* Both have to do with the absence of restraints on individual choices of action.

that in the second section of this chapter, but we should not lose sight of the connection in the real world between civil liberties and civil rights. We should also not lose sight of the connection between this principle and the constitutional framework established in Chapter 3. Although the principle of individual liberties and rights was identified in Chapter 3 as comprising the third of the three most important principles in the Constitution, the third cannot be understood except in the context of the other two, especially federalism. Americans are forever fearful about their individual autonomy, and American history is filled with discourse about how to protect and expand individual freedom. This has given Americans a love/hate relationship with government, because the individual recognizes the need to be protected *from* government and at the same time recognizes that an active government is needed to protect and to advance the individual's opportunity to enjoy liberty.[5] We believe that there is an important lesson to be learned here, and we hope that readers of this book will always keep this important question in mind: "How are Americans protected both from and by the national government?"

**THE CENTRAL QUESTION**

"How are Americans protected both from and by the national government?"

## Civil Liberties: Nationalizing the Bill of Rights

The First Amendment provides that "Congress shall make no law respecting an establishment of religion . . . or abridging freedom of speech, or of the press; or the right of [assembly and petition]." But this is the only amendment in the Bill of Rights that addresses itself exclusively to the national government. For example, the Second Amendment provides that "the right of the people to keep and bear Arms shall not be infringed." The Fifth Amendment says, among other things, that "*no person* shall . . . be twice put in jeopardy of life or limb" for the same crime; that *no person* "shall be compelled in any Criminal Case to be a witness against himself"; that *no person* shall "be deprived of life, liberty, or property, without due process of law"; and that private property cannot be taken "without just compensation."[6] Since the First Amendment is the only

[5]For some recent scholarship on the Bill of Rights and its development, see Geoffrey Stone, Richard Epstein, and Cass Sunstein, eds., *The Bill of Rights and the Modern State* (Chicago: University of Chicago Press, 1992); and Michael J. Meyer and William A. Parent, eds., *The Constitution of Rights* (Ithaca, NY: Cornell University Press, 1992).

[6]It would be useful at this point to review all the provisions of the Bill of Rights (in the Appendix) to confirm this distinction between the wording of the First Amendment and the rest. Emphasis in the example quotations was not in the original. For a spirited and enlightening essay on the extent to which the entire Bill of Rights was about equality, see Martha Minow, "Equality and the Bill of Rights," in Meyer and Parent, *The Constitution of Rights,* pp. 118–28.

PROCESS BOX 4.1

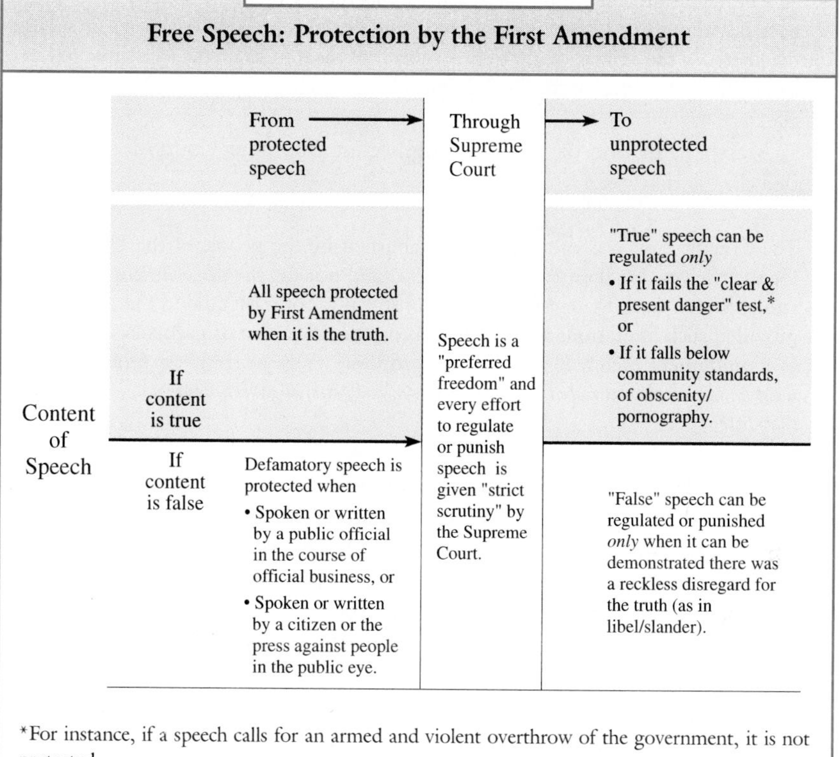


part of the Bill of Rights that is explicit in its intention to put limits on the national government, a fundamental question inevitably arises: *Do the remaining amendments of the Bill of Rights put limits on state governments or only on the national government?*

## Dual Citizenship

The question concerning whether the Bill of Rights also limits state governments was settled in 1833 in a way that seems odd to Americans today. The 1833 case was *Barron v. Baltimore,* and the facts were simple. In paving its streets, the city of Baltimore had disposed of so much sand and gravel in the water near Barron's wharf that the value of the wharf for commercial purposes was virtually destroyed. Barron brought the city into court on the grounds that it had, under the Fifth Amendment, unconstitutionally deprived him of his property. Barron had to take his case all the way to the Supreme Court, despite the fact that the argument made by his attorney seemed airtight. The following is Chief Justice Marshall's characterization of Barron's argument:

> The plaintiff [Barron] . . . contends that it comes within that clause of the Fifth Amendment of the Constitution which inhibits the taking of private property for public use without just compensation. He insists that this amendment, being in favor of the liberty of the citizen, ought to be so construed as to restrain the legislative power of a State, as well as that of the United States.[7]

Then Marshall, in one of the most significant Supreme Court decisions ever handed down, disagreed:

> The Constitution was ordained and established by the people of the United States for themselves, for their own government, and not for the government of the individual States. Each State established a constitution for itself, and in that constitution provided such limitations and restrictions on the powers of its particular government as its judgment dictated. . . . If these propositions be correct, *the fifth amendment must be understood as restraining the power of the general government, not as applicable to the States.*[8]

In other words, if an agency of the *national* government had deprived Barron of his property, there would have been little doubt about Barron's winning his case. But if the constitution of the state of Maryland contained no such provision protecting citizens of Maryland from such action, then Barron had no legal leg to stand on against Baltimore, an agency of the state of Maryland.

*Barron v. Baltimore* confirmed "dual citizenship," that is, that each American was a citizen of the national government and *separately* a citizen of one of the states. This meant that the Bill of Rights did not apply to decisions or to procedures of state (or local) governments. Even slavery could continue, because the Bill of Rights could not protect anyone from state laws treating people as property. In fact, the Bill of Rights did not become a vital instrument for the extension of civil liberties for anyone until after a bloody Civil War and a revolutionary Fourteenth Amendment intervened. And even so, as we shall see, nearly a second century would pass before the Bill of Rights would truly come into its own.

## The Fourteenth Amendment

From a constitutional standpoint, the defeat of the South in the Civil War settled one question and raised another. It probably settled forever the question of whether secession was an option for any state. After 1865 there was to be more "united" than "states" to the United States. But this left unanswered just how much the states were obliged to obey the Constitution and, in particular, the Bill of Rights. Just reading the words of the Fourteenth Amendment, anyone might think it was almost perfectly designed to impose the Bill of Rights on the states and thereby to reverse *Barron v. Baltimore*. The very first words of the Fourteenth Amendment point in that direction:

> All persons born or naturalized in the United States, and subject to the jurisdiction thereof, are citizens of the United States and of the State wherein they reside.

[7]Barron v. Baltimore, 7 Peters 243 (1833).
[8]Ibid. [Emphasis added.]

This provides for a *single national citizenship,* and at a minimum that means that civil liberties should not vary drastically from state to state. That would seem to be the spirit of the Fourteenth Amendment: *to nationalize the Bill of Rights by nationalizing the definition of citizenship.*

This interpretation of the Fourteenth Amendment is reinforced by the next clause of the Amendment:

> *No state* shall make or enforce any law which shall abridge the privileges or immunities of citizens of the United States; nor shall any state deprive any person of life, liberty, or property without due process of law. [Emphasis added.]

All of this sounds like an effort to extend the Bill of Rights in its *entirety* to citizens *wherever* they might reside.[9] But this was not to be the Supreme Court's interpretation for nearly a hundred years. Within five years of ratification of the Fourteenth Amendment, the Court was making decisions as though it had never been adopted. The shadow of *Barron* grew longer and longer. In an important 1873 decision known as the *Slaughter-House Cases,* the Supreme Court determined that the federal government was under no obligation to protect the "privileges and immunities" of citizens of a particular state against arbitrary actions by that state's government. The case had its origins in 1867, when a corrupt Louisiana legislature conferred upon a single corporation a monopoly of all the slaughterhouse business in the city of New Orleans. The other slaughterhouses, facing bankruptcy, all brought suits claiming, like Mr. Barron, that this was a taking of their property in violation of Fifth Amendment rights. But unlike Mr. Barron, they believed that they were protected now because, they argued, the Fourteenth Amendment incorporated the Fifth Amendment, applying it to the states. The suits were all rejected. The Supreme Court argued, first, that the primary purpose of the Fourteenth Amendment was to protect "Negroes as a class." Second, and more to the point here, the Court argued, without trying to prove it, that the framers of the Fourteenth Amendment could not have intended to incorporate the entire Bill of Rights.[10] Yet, when the Civil Rights Act of 1875 attempted to protect blacks from discriminatory treatment by proprietors of hotels, theaters, and other public accommodations, the Supreme Court disregarded its own primary argument in the previous case and held the act unconstitutional, declaring that the Fourteenth Amendment applied only to discriminatory actions by state officials, "operating under cover of law," and not to discrimination against blacks by private individuals, even though these private individuals were companies offering services to the public.[11] Such narrow interpretations raised the inevitable question of whether the Fourteenth Amendment had incorporated *any* of the Bill of Rights. The Fourteenth Amendment remained shadowy until

[9]The Fourteenth Amendment also seems designed to introduce civil rights. The final clause of the all-important Section 1 provides that no state can "deny to any person within its jurisdiction the equal protection of the laws." It is not unreasonable to conclude that the purpose of this provision was to obligate the state governments as well as the national government to take *positive* actions to protect citizens from arbitrary and discriminatory actions, at least those based on race. This will be explored in the second half of this chapter.

[10]The Slaughter-House Cases, 16 Wallace 36 (1873).

[11]The Civil Rights Cases, 109 U.S. 3 (1883).

TABLE 4.1

**Incorporation of the Bill of Rights into the Fourteenth Amendment**

| SELECTED PROVISIONS AND AMENDMENTS | NOT "INCORPORATED" UNTIL | KEY CASE |
|---|---|---|
| Eminent domain (V) | 1897 | *Chicago, Burlington, and Quincy R.R. v. Chicago* |
| Freedom of speech (I) | 1925 | *Gitlow v. New York* |
| Freedom of press (I) | 1931 | *Near v. Minnesota* |
| Freedom of assembly (I) | 1939 | *Hague v. CIO* |
| Freedom from warrantless search and seizure (IV) ("exclusionary rule") | 1961 | *Mapp v. Ohio* |
| Right to counsel in any criminal trial (VI) | 1963 | *Gideon v. Wainwright* |
| Right against self-incrimination and forced confessions (V) | 1964 | *Malloy v. Hogan*<br>*Escobedo v. Illinois* |
| Right to counsel and to remain silent (VI) | 1966 | *Miranda v. Arizona* |
| Right against double jeopardy (V) | 1969 | *Benton v. Maryland* |
| Right to privacy (III, IV, & V) | 1973 | *Roe v. Wade*<br>*Doe v. Bolton* |

the mid-twentieth century. The shadow was *Barron v. Baltimore* and the Court's unwillingness to "nationalize" civil liberties—that is, to interpret the civil liberties expressed in the Bill of Rights as imposing limitations not only on the federal government but also on the states.

It was not until the very end of the nineteenth century that the Supreme Court began to nationalize the Bill of Rights by incorporating its civil liberties provisions into the Fourteenth Amendment. Table 4.1 outlines the major steps in this process. The only change in civil liberties during the first sixty years following the adoption of the Fourteenth Amendment came in 1897, when the Supreme Court held that the due process clause of the Fourteenth Amendment did in fact prohibit states from taking property for a public use without just compensation.[12] This effectively overruled *Barron,* because it meant that the citizen of Maryland or any state was henceforth protected from a "public taking" of property (eminent domain) even if the state constitution did not provide such protection. However, in a broader sense, *Barron* still cast a shadow, because the Supreme Court had "incorporated" into the Fourteenth Amendment only the property protection provision of the Fifth Amendment and no other clause, let alone the other amendments of the Bill of Rights. In other words, although "due process" applied to the taking of life and liberty as well as property, only property was incorporated into the Fourteenth Amendment as a limitation on state power.

No further expansion of civil liberties through incorporation occurred until 1925, when the Supreme Court held that freedom of speech is "among the

[12]Chicago, Burlington, and Quincy Railroad Company v. Chicago, 166 U.S. 226 (1897).

fundamental personal rights and 'liberties' protected by the due process clause of the Fourteenth Amendment from impairment by the states."[13] In 1931, the Court added freedom of the press to that short list of civil rights protected by the Bill of Rights from state action; in 1939, it added freedom of assembly.[14] But that was as far as the Court was willing to go. As late as 1937, the Supreme Court was still loathe to nationalize civil liberties beyond the First Amendment. In fact, the Court in that year took one of its most extreme turns backward toward *Barron v. Baltimore.* The state of Connecticut had indicted a man named Palko for first-degree murder, but a lower court had found him guilty of only second-degree murder and sentenced him to life in prison. Unhappy with the verdict, the state of Connecticut appealed the conviction to its highest court, won the appeal, got a new trial, and then succeeded in getting Palko convicted of first-degree murder. Palko appealed to the Supreme Court on what seemed an open and shut case of ***double jeopardy***—being tried twice for the same crime. Yet, though the majority of the Court agreed that this could indeed be considered a case of double jeopardy, they decided that double jeopardy was *not* one of the provisions of the Bill of Rights incorporated in the Fourteenth Amendment as a restriction on the powers of the states. Justice Benjamin Cardozo, considered one of the most able Supreme Court justices of this century, rejected the argument made by Palko's lawyer that "whatever is forbidden by the Fifth Amendment is forbidden by the Fourteenth also." Cardozo responded tersely, "There is no such general rule." As far as Cardozo and the majority were concerned, the only rights from the Bill of Rights that ought to be incorporated into the Fourteenth Amendment as applying to the states as well as to the national government were those that were "implicit in the concept of ordered liberty." He asked the questions: Does double jeopardy subject Palko to a "hardship so acute and shocking that our polity will not endure it? Does it violate those 'fundamental principles of liberty and justice which lie at the base of all our civil and political institutions?' . . . The answer must surely be 'no.'"[15] Palko was eventually executed for the crime, because he lived in the state of Connecticut rather than in some state whose constitution included a guarantee against double jeopardy.

Cases like *Palko* extended the shadow of *Barron* into its second century, despite adoption of the Fourteenth Amendment. The Constitution, as interpreted by the Supreme Court, left standing the framework in which the states had the power to determine their own law on a number of fundamental issues. It left states with the power to pass laws segregating the races—and thirteen Southern states chose to exercise that power. The constitutional framework also left states with the power to engage in searches and seizures without a warrant, to indict accused persons without benefit of a grand jury, to deprive persons of trial by jury, to force persons to testify against themselves, to deprive accused persons of their right to confront adverse witnesses, and as we have seen, to prosecute accused persons more than once for the same crime.[16] Few states chose the option to use

[13]Gitlow v. New York, 268 U.S. 652 (1925).

[14]Near v. Minnesota, 283 U.S. 697 (1931); Hague v. C.I.O., 307 U.S. 496 (1939).

[15]Palko v. Connecticut, 302 U.S. 319 (1937).

[16]All of these were implicitly identified in the *Palko* case as "not incorporated" into the Fourteenth Amendment as limitations on the powers of the states.

that kind of power, but some states did, and the power to do so was there for any state whose legislative majority so chose.

## The Second Constitutional Revolution

For nearly thirty years following the *Palko* case,[17] the nineteenth-century framework was sustained, but signs of change came after 1954, in *Brown v. Board of Education,* when the Supreme Court overturned the infamous *Plessy v. Ferguson.*[18] *Plessy* was a civil rights case involving the "equal protection" clause of the Fourteenth Amendment and was not an issue of applying the Bill of Rights to the states. (It will be dealt with in the next section.) Nevertheless, even though *Brown* was not a civil liberties case, it indicated rather clearly that the Supreme Court was going to be expansive about civil liberties, because with *Brown* the Court had effectively promised that it was *actively* going to subject the states and all actions affecting civil rights and civil liberties to *strict scrutiny.* In retrospect, one could say that the Second Constitutional Revolution was given a "jump start" by the *Brown* decision,[19] even though the results were not apparent until after 1961, when the number of civil liberties incorporated increased (see Table 4.1).

**Nationalizing the Bill of Rights** As with the First, the Second Constitutional Revolution was a movement toward nationalization. But the two revolutions required opposite motions on the part of the Supreme Court. In the area of commerce (the first revolution), the Court had to decide to assume a *passive* role by not interfering as Congress expanded the meaning of the commerce clause of Article I, Section 8. This expansion has been so extensive that the national government can now constitutionally reach a single farmer growing twenty acres of wheat or a small neighborhood restaurant selling barbecues to local "whites only" without being anywhere near interstate commerce routes. In the second revolution—involving the Bill of Rights through the Fourteenth Amendment rather than the commerce clause—the Court had to assume an *active* role, which required close review not of Congress but of the laws of state legislatures and decisions of state courts, in order to apply a single national Fourteenth Amendment standard to the rights and liberties of all citizens.

Table 4.1 shows that until 1961, only the First Amendment had been fully and clearly incorporated into the Fourteenth Amendment.[20] After 1961, several

[17]*Palko* was explicitly reversed in Benton v. Maryland, 395 U.S. 784 (1969), in which the Court said that double jeopardy was in fact incorporated in the Fourteenth Amendment as a restriction on the states.

[18]Plessy v. Ferguson, 163 U.S. 537 (1896).

[19]The First Constitutional Revolution, beginning with NLRB v. Jones & Laughlin Steel Corp. (1937), was discussed in Chapter 3.

[20]The one exception was the right to public trial (the Sixth Amendment), but the 1948 case did not actually mention the right to public trial as such; it was cited in a 1968 case as a case establishing the right to public trial as part of the Fourteenth Amendment. The 1948 case was in re Oliver, 33 U.S. 257, where the issue was put more generally as "due process" and public trial itself was not actually mentioned. Later opinions, such as Duncan v. Louisiana, 391 U.S. 145 (1968), cited the *Oliver* case as the precedent for incorporating public trials as part of the Fourteenth Amendment.

other important provisions of the Bill of Rights were incorporated. Of the cases that expanded the Fourteenth Amendment's reach, the most famous was *Gideon v. Wainwright,* which established the right to counsel in a criminal trial, because it became the subject of a best-selling book and a popular movie.[21] In *Mapp v. Ohio,* the Court held that evidence obtained in violation of the Fourth Amendment ban on unreasonable searches and seizures would be excluded from trial.[22] This "exclusionary rule" was particularly irksome to the police and prosecutors because it meant that patently guilty defendants sometimes go free because the evidence that clearly damned them could not be used. In *Miranda,*[23] the Court's ruling required that arrested persons be informed of the right to remain silent and to have counsel present during interrogation. This is the basis of the ***Miranda rule*** of reading persons their rights, which has been made famous by TV police shows.

By 1969, in *Benton v. Maryland,* the Supreme Court had come full circle regarding the rights of the criminally accused, explicitly reversing the *Palko* ruling and thereby incorporating double jeopardy. During the 1960s and early 1970s, the Court also expanded another important area of civil liberties: rights to privacy. When the Court began to take a more activist role in the mid-1950s and 1960s, the idea of a "right to privacy" was revived. In 1958, the Supreme Court recognized "privacy in one's association" in its decision to prevent the state of Alabama from using the membership list of the National Association for the Advancement of Colored People in the state's investigations.[24]

The sphere of privacy was drawn in earnest in 1965, when the Court ruled that a Connecticut statute forbidding the use of contraceptives violated the right of marital privacy. Estelle Griswold, the executive director of the Planned Parenthood League of Connecticut, was arrested by the state of Connecticut for providing information, instruction, and medical advice about contraception to married couples. She and her associates were found guilty as accessories to the crime and fined $100 each. The Supreme Court reversed the lower court decisions and declared the Connecticut law unconstitutional because it violated "a right of privacy older than the Bill of Rights—older than our political parties, older than our school system."[25] Justice William O. Douglas, author of the majority decision in the *Griswold* case, argued that this right of privacy is also grounded in the Constitution, because it fits into a "zone of privacy" created by a combination of the Third, Fourth, and Fifth Amendments. A concurring opinion, written by Justice Arthur Goldberg, attempted to strengthen Douglas's argument by adding that "the concept of liberty . . . embraces the right of marital privacy though that right is not mentioned explicitly in the Constitution [and] is supported by numerous decisions of this Court . . . and *by the language and history of the Ninth Amendment* [emphasis added]."[26]

[21]Gideon v. Wainwright, 372 U.S. 335 (1963); Anthony Lewis, *Gideon's Trumpet* (New York: Random House, 1964).

[22]Mapp v. Ohio, 367 U.S. 643 (1961).

[23]Miranda v. Arizona, 384 U.S. 436 (1966).

[24]NAACP v. Alabama ex rel. Patterson, 357 U.S. 449 (1958).

[25]Griswold v. Connecticut, 381 U.S. 479 (1965).

[26]Griswold v. Connecticut, concurring opinion. In 1972, the Court extended the privacy right to unmarried women: Eisenstadt v. Baird, 405 U.S. 438 (1972).

**AMERICAN POLITICAL DEVELOPMENT**

The expansion of Court activity, which facilitates both the nationalization of the Bill of Rights and the expansion of civil rights in general, is, in part, a product of structural changes in the Courts, which have made them increasingly tied to and responsive to interests in society.

SOURCE: Mark Silverstein and Benjamin Ginsberg, "The Supreme Court and the New Politics of Judicial Power," *Political Science Quarterly* 102 (Fall 1987), pp. 371–88.

The right to privacy was confirmed—and extended—in 1973 in the most important of all privacy decisions, and one of the most important Supreme Court decisions in American history: *Roe v. Wade*.[27] This decision established a woman's right to have an abortion and prohibited states from making abortion a criminal act. The basis for the Supreme Court's decision in *Roe* was the evolving right to privacy. But it is important to realize that the preference for privacy rights and for their extension to include the rights of women to control their own bodies was not something invented by the Supreme Court in a political vacuum. Most states did not begin to regulate abortions in any fashion until the 1840s (by 1839 only six of the twenty-six existing states had any regulations governing abortion). In addition, many states began to ease their abortion restrictions well before the 1973 Supreme Court decision (see Process Box 4.2). In recent years, however, a number of states have reinstated restrictions on abortion, testing the limits of *Roe*.

Like any important principle, once privacy was established as an aspect of civil liberties protected by the Bill of Rights through the Fourteenth Amendment, it took on a life all its own. In a number of important decisions, the Supreme Court and the lower federal courts sought to protect rights that could not be found in the text of the Constitution but could be discovered through the study of the philosophic sources of fundamental rights. Through this line of reasoning, the federal courts sought to protect sexual autonomy, lifestyle choices, sexual preferences, procreational choice, and various forms of intimate association.

Criticism mounted with every extension of this line of reasoning. The federal courts were accused of creating an uncontrollable expansion of rights demands. The Supreme Court, the critics argued, had displaced the judgments of legislatures and state courts with its own judgment of what is reasonable, without regard to local popular majorities and without regard to specific constitutional provisions. This is virtually the definition of what came to be called "judicial activism" in the 1980s, and it was the basis for a more strongly critical label, "the imperial judiciary."[28]

## Rehnquist: A De-Nationalizing Trend?

Controversy over judicial power has not diminished. In fact it is intensifying under Chief Justice William Rehnquist, an avowed critic of "judicial activism" as it relates to privacy, criminal procedure, and other new liberties, such as the right

[27]Roe v. Wade, 410 U.S. 113 (1973).

[28]A good discussion will be found in Paul Brest and Sanford Levinson, *Processes of Constitutional Decision-Making: Cases and Materials,* 2nd ed. (Boston: Little, Brown, 1983), p. 660. See also Chapter 8.

**PROCESS BOX 4.2**

## Abortion Regulation and Deregulation

| Federal or Supreme Court action | State action |
|---|---|
| | States adopt anti-abortion laws: 6 before 1940; 29 from 1840–1869; 15 after 1869 |
| | States permit therapeutic abortions: MS, CO, CA, NC, GA, MD (1966–1968); AR, DE, KS, NM, OR (1969); SC, VA, FL (1970–1972) |
| | States repeal anti-abortion laws: AL, HI, NY, WA (1970) |
| Supreme Court rules all state abortion laws invalid: *Roe v. Wade* (1973) | |
| | States adopt new anti-abortion laws: MO, OH, IL, MN (1980) |
| Court re-opens way for state regulation of abortion: *Webster v. Reproductive Health Services* (1989); *Rust v. Sullivan* (1991); *Planned Parenthood of SE Penn. v. Casey* (1992) | States adopt new laws restricting abortions: PA (1989); SC, OH, MN, Guam, LA, MI (1990); UT, MS, KS (1991) |
| Congress requires use of Medicaid funds to pay for abortions in cases of rape or incest, not just when mother's life is in danger (1993) | States announce that they will defy the new Medicaid rule: AR, SD, PA, MI, LA, KY, UT, OK, AL, CO, NE (1994) |
| Court continues to review cases involving the 15-foot buffer protecting abortion clinics, which began in 1991 with *Madsen* (1996–1997) | |

SOURCE: Raymond Tatalovich and Byron Daynes, *The Politics of Abortion* (New York: Praeger, 1981), p. 18. Copyright © 1981 by Praeger Publishers. Used with permission. Updated with data from the *New York Times*, 4–6 July 1989, and the *Los Angeles Times*, 31 March 1994.

not to be required to participate in prayers in school.[29] Although it is difficult to determine just how much influence Rehnquist has had as Chief Justice, the Court has in fact been moving in a less activist and more conservative, de-nationalizing direction.

[29]Engel v. Vitale, 370 U.S. 421 (1962), in which the Court struck down a state-composed prayer for recitation in the schools. Of course, a whole line of cases followed *Engel*, as states and cities tried various ways of getting around the Court's principle that any organized prayer in the public schools violates the First Amendment rights of the individual.

The best measure of the decline of activism is the decline in the Court's annual case load from 150 to 75, which Court watchers call the "incredible shrinking docket."[30] One of the most eminent Court watchers agrees that this is a momentous trend, which must be attributed in large part to Rehnquist's personal influence. Granted, there was a diminishing supply of new statutory activity during the 1980s and early 1990s, and granted also, there was far less civil rights litigation than there had been. As Justice Souter observed in a very frank appraisal of the recent history of the Supreme Court, "There hasn't been an awful lot for us to take."[31] However, this did not "just happen." An activist court can virtually always find cases if it is seeking them. Meanwhile, year by year during the Rehnquist tenure, the case load shrank from the average of 150 cases during the years prior to his appointment in 1986 to 132 cases in 1988–1989, to 129 in 1989–1990, to 112 in 1990–1991, to 108 in 1991–1992, to 107 in 1992–1993. There was a sharp drop to 84 in 1993–1994, to 82 in 1994–1995 and finally a small increase to 90 in 1996–1997.[32]

A good measure of the Court's growing conservatism is the following comparison made by constitutional scholar David M. O'Brien: Between 1961 and 1969, more than 76 percent of the Warren Court's rulings from term to term tended to be liberal—that is, tending toward nationalizing the Bill of Rights to protect individuals and minorities mainly against the actions of state government. During the Burger years, 1969–1986, the liberal tendency dropped on the average below 50 percent. During the first four years of the Rehnquist Court (the extent of O'Brien's research), the average liberal "score" dropped to less than 35 percent.[33] For example, he reports that in the 1990 term, the Court ruled against prisoners' claims in twenty-three out of thirty-one cases, leaving more power over prisoners in state and local hands. Deference to state power over prisoners was extended most significantly in one particular area, capital punishment. In 1991, Rehnquist achieved his first victory in a 6-to-3 ruling severely limiting repeated prisoner *habeas corpus* petitions, stressing in the 1991 opinion that "perpetual disrespect for the finality of convictions disparages the entire criminal justice system."[34] But he achieved closer to complete victory in 1996 in *Felker v. Turpin*. Writing for a *unanimous* Court, Rehnquist upheld provisions of the Antiterrorism and Effective Death Penalty Act of 1996 that sought to limit state prisoners' filing second or successive applications for writs of *habeas corpus* if no new claim is presented.[35]

Another area in which the Supreme Court has moved in a conservative direction in recent years involves the First Amendment's "establishment clause," which estab-

[30]Quoted in David Garrow, "The Rehnquist Reins," *New York Times Magazine,* 6 October 1996, p. 82.

[31]Quoted in ibid., p. 71.

[32]Cited in ibid., p. 71.

[33]David M. O'Brien, *Supreme Court Watch—1991,* Annual Supplement to *Constitutional Law and Politics* (New York: W. W. Norton, 1991), p. 6 and Chapter 4.

[34]McCleskey v. Zant, 111 S.Ct. 1454 (1991).

[35]*Felkner v. Turpin,* 116 S.Ct. 2333 (1996). A "writ of *habeas corpus*" is an order by a judge to produce the prisoner so that the court can determine if the prisoner was lawfully arrested and imprisoned. The "privilege of the Writ of *Habeas Corpus*" is not in the Bill of Rights but is in Article I, Section 9, of the original Constitution. And its presence there was a major point in Alexander Hamilton's argument in *The Federalist Paper,* No. 84, that rights were so well taken care of in the original document that there was no need for a Bill of Rights.

lished a "wall of separation" between church and state. In the 1995 case of *Rosenberger v. University of Virginia,* the Court seemed to open a new breach in the wall between church and state when it ruled that the university had violated the free speech rights of a Christian student group by refusing to provide student activity funds to the group's magazine, although other student groups had been given funds for their publications. In the 1997 case of *Agostini v. Felton,* the Court again breached the wall between church and state, ruling that states could pay public school teachers to offer remedial courses at religious schools.[36]

The conservative trend has also extended to the burning question of abortion rights. In *Webster v. Reproductive Health Services,* the Court narrowly upheld by a 5-to-4 majority the constitutionality of restrictions on the use of public medical facilities for abortion.[37] And in 1992, in the most recent major decision on abortion, *Planned Parenthood v. Casey,* another 5-to-4 majority of the Court barely upheld *Roe* but narrowed its scope, refusing to invalidate a Pennsylvania law that significantly restricts freedom of choice. The decision defined the right to an abortion as a "limited or qualified" right subject to regulation by the states as long as the regulation does not impose an "undue burden."[38] As one constitutional authority concluded from the decision in *Casey,* "Until there is a Freedom of Choice Act, and/or a U.S. Supreme Court able to wean *Roe* from its respirator, state legislatures will have significant discretion over the access women will have to legalized abortions."[39]

One area in which Chief Justice Rehnquist seems determined to expand rather than shrink the Court's protection of privacy rights is in the constitutional protection of property rights. But this is itself a conservative direction and the Court's conservative justices, led by Chief Justice Rehnquist, have pushed for a broader interpretation of the Fifth Amendment's takings clause to put limits on the degree to which local, state, and federal governments can impose restrictions on land use. In an important case from 1994, the Court overturned a Tigard, Oregon, law that had required any person seeking a building permit to give the city ten percent of his or her property. In a 5-to-4 decision, the Court ruled that such a requirement fell into the Fifth Amendment's prohibition against taking of property "without just compensation." In his opinion, Chief Justice Rehnquist wrote, "We see no reason why the takings clause of the Fifth Amendment, as much a part of the Bill of Rights as the First Amendment or Fourth Amendment, should be relegated to the status of a poor relation in those comparable circumstances."[40]

[36]Rosenberger v. University of Virginia, 94-329 (1995); Agostini v. Felton, 96-522 (1997).

[37]In Webster v. Reproductive Health Services, 109 S.Ct. 3040 (1989), Chief Justice Rehnquist's decision upheld a Missouri law that restricted the use of public medical facilities for abortion. The decision opened the way for other states to limit the availability of abortion. The first to act was the Pennsylvania legislature, which adopted in late 1989 a law banning all abortions after pregnancy had passed twenty-four weeks, except to save the life of the pregnant woman or to prevent irreversible impairment of her health. In 1990, the pace of state legislative action increased, with new statutes passed in South Carolina, Ohio, Minnesota, and Guam. In 1991, the Louisiana legislature adopted, over the governor's veto, the strictest law yet. The Louisiana law prohibits all abortions except when the mother's life is threatened or when rape or incest victims report these crimes immediately.

[38]Planned Parenthood of Southeastern Pennsylvania v. Casey, 112 S.Ct. 2791 (1992).

[39]Gayle Binion, "Undue Burden? Government Now Has Wide Latitude to Restrict Abortions," *Santa Barbara News-Press,* 5 July 1992, p. A13.

[40]Dolan v. City of Tigard, 93-518 (1994).

In recent years, the Court has also expanded the protection of free speech. In the Court's most important recent free speech case, *Reno v. American Civil Liberties Union,* the Communication Decency Act, a federal law restricting indecent material on the Internet, was struck down as a violation of free speech. In another important free speech case, the Court in 1999 ruled that a Colorado statute regulating ballot petitions was a violation of the First Amendment.[41] The state had required that individuals circulating petitions on behalf of ballot initiatives be registered Colorado voters, that they wear name tags, and that their names and occupations be matters of public record. The Court ruled that these requirements constituted an impermissible infringement upon "political conversation and the exchange of ideas."

Still the question remains: Will a Supreme Court, even with a majority of conservatives, reverse the nationalization of the Bill of Rights? Possibly, but not necessarily. First of all, the Rehnquist Court has not actually reversed any of the decisions made during the 1960s by the Warren or Burger Courts nationalizing most of the clauses of the Bill of Rights. As we have seen, the Rehnquist Court has given narrower and more restrictive interpretations of the earlier decisions, but it has not reversed any, not even *Roe v. Wade.* Second, President Clinton's appointments to the Court, Ruth Bader Ginsburg and Stephen Breyer, have helped form a centrist majority that seems unwilling, for the time being at least, to sanction any major steps to turn back the nationalization of the Bill of Rights. But with any future Clinton nominations to the Court now having to be approved by a Republican-controlled Senate, the question of the expansion or contraction of the Bill of Rights and the Fourteenth Amendment is certain to be in the forefront of political debate for a long time to come.

Thus we end about where we began. The spirit of *Barron v. Baltimore* has not been entirely put to rest, and its shadow over the Bill of Rights still hovers. We hear less of the plea for the Supreme Court to take the final step they didn't quite take in the 1960s, to declare as a matter of constitutional law that the *entire* Bill of Rights is incorporated into the Fourteenth Amendment. If that more liberal Court was not willing to do so, the more conservative Court of today is all the less willing. We are thus still in suspense, because a Court with the power to expand the Bill of Rights also has the power to contract it.[42]

## Civil Rights

The very simplicity of the "civil rights clause" of the Fourteenth Amendment left it open to interpretation:

> No State shall make or enforce any law which shall . . . deny to any person within its jurisdiction the equal protection of the laws.

[41]Buckley v. American Constitutional Law Foundation, 97-930 (1999).

[42]For a lively and readable treatment of the possibilities of restricting provisions of the Bill of Rights, without actually reversing Warren Court decisions, see David G. Savage, *Turning Right: The Making of the Rehnquist Supreme Court* (New York: Wiley, 1992).

But in the very first Fourteenth Amendment case to come before the Supreme Court, the majority gave it a distinct meaning:

> . . . it is not difficult to give meaning to this clause ["the equal protection of the laws"]. The existence of laws in the States . . . which discriminated with gross injustice and hardship against [Negroes] as a class, was the evil to be remedied by this clause, and by it such laws are forbidden.[43]

Beyond that, contemporaries of the Fourteenth Amendment understood well that private persons offering conveyances, accommodations, or places of amusement to the public incurred certain public obligations to offer them to one and all—in other words, these are *public* accommodations, such that arbitrary discrimination in their use would amount to denial of equal protection of the laws—unless a government took action to overcome the discrimination.[44] This puts governments under obligation to take positive actions to equalize the opportunity for each citizen to enjoy his or her freedom. A skeptic once observed that "the law, in its majestic equality, forbids the rich as well as the poor to sleep under bridges, to beg in the streets, and to steal bread."[45] The purpose of civil rights principles and laws is to use government in such a way as to give equality a more substantive meaning than that.

Discrimination refers to the use of any unreasonable and unjust criterion of exclusion. Of course, all laws discriminate, including some people while excluding others; but some discrimination is considered unreasonable. Now, for example, it is considered reasonable to use age as a criterion for legal drinking, excluding all persons younger than twenty-one. But is age a reasonable distinction when seventy (or sixty-five or sixty) is selected as the age for compulsory retirement? In the mid-1970s, Congress answered this question by making old age a new civil right; compulsory retirement at seventy is now an unlawful, unreasonable, discriminatory use of age.

## *Plessy v. Ferguson:* "Separate but Equal"

Following its initial decisions making "equal protection" a civil rights clause, the Supreme Court turned conservative, no more ready to enforce the civil rights aspects of the Fourteenth Amendment than it was to enforce the civil liberties provisions. As we have seen, the Court declared the Civil Rights Act of 1875 unconstitutional on the ground that the act sought to protect blacks against discrimination by *private* businesses, while the Fourteenth Amendment, according to the Court's interpretation, was intended to protect individuals from discrimination only against actions by *public* officials of state and local governments.

In 1896, the Court went still further, in the infamous case of *Plessy v. Ferguson,* by upholding a Louisiana statute that *required* segregation of the races on trolleys and other public carriers (and by implication in all public facilities, including schools). Plessy, a man defined as "one-eighth black," had violated a Louisiana

[43]The Slaughter-House Cases, 16 Wallace 36 (1873).
[44]See Civil Rights Cases, 109 U.S. 3 (1883).
[45]Anatole France, *Le lys rouge* (1894), Chapter 7.

law that provided for "equal but separate accommodations" on trains and a $25 fine for any white passenger who sat in a car reserved for blacks or any black passenger who sat in a car reserved for whites. The Supreme Court held that the Fourteenth Amendment's "equal protection of the laws" was not violated by racial distinction as long as the facilities were equal. People generally pretended they were equal as long as some accommodation existed. The Court said that although "the object of the [Fourteenth] Amendment was undoubtedly to enforce the absolute equality of the two races before the law, . . . it could not have intended to abolish distinctions based on color, or to enforce social, as distinguished from political, equality, or a commingling of the two races upon terms unsatisfactory to either."[46] What the Court was saying in effect was that the use of race as a criterion of exclusion in public matters was not unreasonable. This was the origin of the ***"separate but equal" rule,*** which was not reversed until 1954.

## Racial Discrimination after World War II

The shame of discrimination against black military personnel during World War II, plus revelation of Nazi racial atrocities, moved President Harry S. Truman finally to bring the problem to the White House and national attention, with the appointment in 1946 of a President's Commission on Civil Rights. In 1948, the committee submitted its report, *To Secure These Rights,* which laid bare the extent of the problem of racial discrimination and its consequences. The report also revealed the success of experiments with racial integration in the armed forces during World War II to demonstrate to Southern society that it had nothing to fear. But the committee recognized that the national government had no clear constitutional authority to pass and implement civil rights legislation. The committee proposed tying civil rights legislation to the commerce power, although it was clear that discrimination was not itself part of the flow of interstate commerce.[47] The committee even suggested using the treaty power as a source of constitutional authority for civil rights legislation.[48]

As for the Supreme Court, it had begun to change its position on racial discrimination before World War II by being stricter about the criterion of equal facilities in the "separate but equal" rule. In 1938, the Court rejected Missouri's policy of paying the tuition of qualified blacks to out-of-state law schools rather than admitting them to the University of Missouri Law School.[49]

[46]Plessy v. Ferguson, 163 U.S. 537 (1896).

[47]The prospect of a Fair Employment Practices law tied to the commerce power produced the Dixiecrat break with the Democratic party in 1948. The Democratic party organization of the States of the Old Confederacy seceded from the national party and nominated its own candidate, the then-Democratic governor of South Carolina, Strom Thurmond, who is now a Republican senator. This almost cost President Truman the election.

[48]This was based on the provision in Article VI of the Constitution that "all treaties made, . . . under the authority of the United States," shall be the "supreme law of the land." The committee recognized that if the U.S. Senate ratified the Human Rights Covenant of the United Nations—a treaty—then that power could be used as the constitutional umbrella for effective civil rights legislation. The Supreme Court had recognized in Missouri v. Holland, 252 U.S. 416 (1920), that a treaty could enlarge federal power at the expense of the states.

[49]Missouri ex rel. Gaines v. Canada, 305 U.S. 337 (1938).

After the war, modest progress resumed. In 1950, the Court rejected Texas's claim that its new "law school for Negroes" afforded education equal to that of the all-white University of Texas Law School; without confronting the "separate but equal" principle itself, the Court's decision anticipated *Brown v. Board* by opening the question of whether *any* segregated facility could be truly equal.[50]

But the Supreme Court, in ordering the admission of blacks to all-white state law schools, did not directly confront the principle of the "separate but equal" rule of *Plessy* because the Court needed only to recognize the absence of any equal law school for blacks. The same was true in 1944, when the Supreme Court struck down the Southern practice of "white primaries," which legally excluded blacks from participation in the nominating process. Here the Court simply recognized that primaries could no longer be regarded as the private affairs of the parties but were an integral aspect of the electoral process. This made parties "an agency of the State," and therefore any practice of discrimination against blacks was "state action within the meaning of the Fifteenth Amendment."[51] The most important pre-1954 decision was probably *Shelley v. Kraemer*,[52] in which the Court ruled against the widespread practice of "restrictive covenants," whereby the seller of a home added a clause to the sales contract requiring the buyers to agree not to sell their home to any non-Caucasian, non-Christian, etc. The Court ruled that although private persons could sign such restrictive covenants, they could not be judicially enforced since the Fourteenth Amendment prohibits any organ of the state, including the courts, from denying equal protection of its laws.

However, none of these pre-1954 cases had yet confronted head-on the principle of "separate but equal" as such and its legal and constitutional support for racial discrimination. Each victory by the Legal Defense Fund of the National Association for the Advancement of Colored People (NAACP) was celebrated for itself and was seen, hopefully, as a trend; but each was still a small victory, not a leading case. After *Shelley v. Kraemer*, Thurgood Marshall, the leading litigator for the Legal Defense Fund, "would no longer try to shoehorn his cases into the often cramped and distorting logic of straight legal precedent."[53] And, all along, both the friends and the foes of segregation were recognizing that

> The bitter fight would be waged on the level of the elementary and secondary schools . . . [and] the segregationists hoped that they would be able to prevent or forestall indefinitely the admission of blacks . . . by moving toward the equalization of Negro schools. . . . Southern states spent funds, almost desparately, on Negro schools . . . to equalize white and black schools as rapidly as possible.[54]

This massive effort by the Southern states to resist direct desegregation and to prevent further legal actions against it by making a show of equalizing the quality of white and black schools, kept Marshall pessimistic about the readiness of the

[50]Sweatt v. Painter, 339 U.S. 629 (1950).

[51]Smith v. Allwright, 321 U.S. 649 (1944).

[52]Shelley v. Kraemer, 334 U.S. 1 (1948).

[53]Richard Kluger, *Simple Justice* (New York: Vintage, 1977), p. 254.

[54]John Hope Franklin, *From Slavery to Freedom: A History of Negro Americans,* 4th ed. (New York: Knopf, 1974), pp. 420–21.

Supreme Court for a full confrontation with the constitutional principle sustaining segregation. But the publication of the extraordinary Truman Commission Report on Civil Rights and President Truman's election for a full term, both in 1948, coupled with the continued unwillingness of Congress after 1948 to consider fair employment legislation, seemed to have convinced Marshall and the NAACP that the courts were their only hope. Thus, by 1951, the NAACP finally decided to attack the principle of segregation itself as unconstitutional and, in 1952, instituted cases in South Carolina, Virginia, Kansas, Delaware, and the District of Columbia. The obvious strategy was that by simultaneously filing suits in different federal districts, inconsistent results between any two states would more quickly lead to Supreme Court acceptance of at least one appeal.[55]

**AMERICAN POLITICAL DEVELOPMENT**

Social changes and, specifically, attitudinal changes helped support certain legal and political revisions that expanded protection of civil rights. For example, the percentage of whites approving public school integration more than doubled, from 30 percent to 62 percent, from 1942 to 1963.

SOURCE: Herbert H. Hyman and Paul B. Sheatsley, "Attitudes Toward Desegregation," *Scientific American* 211 (July 1964), pp. 20–21, cited in Richard P. Young and Jerome S. Burstein, "Federalism and the Demise of Prescriptive Racism in the United States," *Studies in American Political Development* 9 (1995), pp. 1–54, esp. p. 13.

All through 1951 and 1952, as cases like *Brown v. Board* and *Bolling v. Sharpe* were winding slowly through the lower-court litigation maze, intense discussions and disagreements continued among NAACP lawyers as to whether the full-scale assault on *Plessy* was good strategy.[56] But for lawyers like Marshall, small victories and further delays could amount to defeat. South Carolina, for example, under the leadership of Governor James F. Byrnes, who had left the Supreme Court and Roosevelt's cabinet in order to lead the pro-segregation fight as governor of South Carolina, was making considerable headway to render moot any further litigation against the principle of separate but equal by making the Negro schools in South Carolina virtually equal in all physical matters to the all-white schools.

In the fall of 1952, the Court had on its docket cases from Kansas, South Carolina, Virginia, Delaware, and the District of Columbia challenging the constitutionality of school segregation. Of these, the Kansas case became the chosen one. It seemed to be ahead of the pack in its district court, and it had the special advantage of being located in a state outside the Deep South.[57]

Oliver Brown, the father of three girls, lived "across the tracks" in a low-income, racially mixed Topeka neighborhood. Every school-day morning, Linda Brown took the school bus to the Monroe School for black children about a mile away. In September

[55]The best reviews of strategies, tactics, and goals is found in John Hope Franklin, op cit., Chapter 22; and Kluger, op cit., Chapters 21 and 22.

[56]Kermit L. Hall, *The Magic Mirror: Law in American History* (New York: Oxford University Press, 1989), pp. 322–24. See also Kluger, op cit., pp. 530–37.

[57]The District of Columbia case came up too, but since the District of Columbia is not a state, this case did not directly involve the Fourteenth Amendment and its "equal protection" clause. It confronted the Court on the same grounds, however—that segregation is inherently unequal. Its victory in effect was "incorporation in reverse," with equal protection moving from the Fourteenth Amendment to become part of the Bill of Rights. See Bolling v. Sharpe, 347 U.S. 497 (1954).

1950, Oliver Brown took Linda to the all-white Sumner School, which was actually closer to home, to enter her into the third grade in defiance of state law and local segregation rules. When they were refused, Brown took his case to the NAACP, and soon thereafter *Brown v. Board of Education* was born. In mid-1953, the Court announced that the several cases on their way up would be re-argued within a set of questions having to do with the intent of the Fourteenth Amendment. Almost exactly a year later, the Court responded to those questions in one of the most important decisions in its history.

In deciding the case, the Court, to the surprise of many, basically rejected as inconclusive all the learned arguments about the intent and the history of the Fourteenth Amendment and committed itself to considering only the consequences of segregation:

> Does segregation of children in public schools solely on the basis of race, even though the physical facilities and other "tangible" factors may be equal, deprive the children of the minority group of equal educational opportunities? We believe that it does. . . . We conclude that in the field of public education the doctrine of "separate but equal" has no place. Separate educational facilities are inherently unequal.[58]

The *Brown* decision altered the constitutional framework in two fundamental respects. First, after *Brown,* the states would no longer have the power to use race as a criterion of discrimination in law. Second, the national government would from then on have the constitutional basis for extending its power (hitherto in doubt, as we saw earlier) to intervene with strict regulatory policies against the discriminatory actions of state or local governments, school boards, employers, and many others in the private sector.

## *Simple Justice:* The Courts, the Constitution, and Civil Rights after *Brown v. Board of Education*

Although *Brown v. Board of Education* withdrew all constitutional authority to use race as a criterion of exclusion, this historic decision was merely a small opening move.[59] First, the Court ruling "to admit to public schools on a racially nondiscriminatory basis with all delibrate speed," which came a year later,[60] was directly binding only on the five school boards that had been defendants in the cases appealed to the Supreme Court. Rather than fall into line, as most parties do when a new judicial principle is handed down, most states refused to cooperate until sued, and many ingenious schemes were employed to delay obedience (such as paying the tuition for white students to attend newly created "private" academies). Second, even as Southern school boards began to cooperate by eliminating their legally enforced (***de jure***) school segregation, there remained extensive actual (***de facto***) school segregation in the North as well as in the South, as a

[58]Brown v. Board of Education of Topeka, Kansas, 347 U.S. 483 (1954).

[59]The heading for this section is drawn from the title of Richard Kluger's important book, *Simple Justice.*

[60]Board of Education of Topeka, Kansas, 349 U.S. 294 (1955), often referred to as *Brown II.*

**AMERICAN POLITICAL DEVELOPMENT**

Arguing that separate facilities for African Americans and white Americans were "inherently unequal," *Brown v. Board of Education* (1954) overturned the previous ruling of *Plessy v. Ferguson.* Despite this ruling, substantial integration of Southern schools did not occur until the late 1960s: The percentage of Southern black children attending school with white children was less than 1 percent in 1961; by 1968, that percentage had jumped to over 30 percent.

SOURCE: Gerald N. Rosenberg, *The Hollow Hope: Can Courts Bring About Social Change?* (Chicago: University of Chicago Press, 1991), p. 51.

consequence of racially segregated housing that could not be reached by the 1954–1955 *Brown* principles. Third, discrimination in employment, public accommodations, juries, voting, and other areas of social and economic activity were not directly touched by *Brown*.

A decade of frustration following *Brown* made it fairly obvious to all that adjudication alone would not succeed. The goal of "equal protection" required positive, or affirmative, action by Congress and by administrative agencies. And given massive Southern resistance and a generally negative national public opinion toward racial integration, progress would not be made through courts, Congress, *or* agencies without intense, well-organized support. Table 4.2 shows the increase in civil rights demonstrations for voting rights and public accommodations during the fourteen years following Brown.

It shows that there were very few organized civil rights demonstrations prior to *Brown v. Board* and that the frequency of these demonstrations took a sudden jump in 1960 and continued to mount during the 1960s. It is quite evident that this direct-movement action contributed mightily to the congressional majorities that produced a series of historic new civil rights laws in in 1964 and 1965. It would appear from the data on Table 4.2 that the constitutional decisions made by the Supreme Court in 1954–1955 had either produced or triggered the civil rights movement, as it came to be known. This was substantially confirmed in a systematic study of all "movement-initiated events" from 1948 through 1970.[61]

Adding Table 4.3 to Table 4.2 brings forth still another insight into the political relationships among the three branches of the national government: Just as *political* agitation to expand rights followed the Court's formal recognition of their existence, so did greatly expanded *judicial* action follow the success of political action in Congress. Table 4.3 confirms this with the enormous jump in NAACP-sponsored civil rights cases brought in the federal courts, from 107 in 1963 to 145 in 1964 and 225 in 1965, continuing to move upward thereafter. The number of actual cases brought by the Legal Defense Fund of the NAACP actually continued to go up at a significant rate even as the number of individuals defended by these cases dropped. This suggests how strongly the NAACP was interested in using the cases to advance the principles of civil rights rather than to improve the prospects of individual black litigants.

[61]The data on civil rights movements are from Jonathan D. Casper, *The Politics of Civil Liberties* (New York: Harper & Row, 1972), p. 90; the broader study of social movements providing the confirming data was conducted by Doug McAdam, *Political Process and the Development of Black Insurgency, 1930–1970* (Chicago: University of Chicago Press, 1982), p. 123. For an alternative view, see Gerald N. Rosenberg, The Hollow Hope (Chicago: University of Chicago Press, 1991).

TABLE 4.2

**Peaceful Civil Rights Demonstrations, 1954–1968***

| YEAR | TOTAL | FOR PUBLIC ACCOMMODATIONS | FOR VOTING |
|---|---|---|---|
| 1954 | 0 | 0 | 0 |
| 1955 | 0 | 0 | 0 |
| 1956 | 18 | 6 | 0 |
| 1957 | 44 | 9 | 0 |
| 1958 | 19 | 8 | 0 |
| 1959 | 7 | 11 | 0 |
| 1960 | 173 | 127 | 0 |
| 1961 | 198 | 122 | 0 |
| 1962 | 77 | 44 | 0 |
| 1963 | 272 | 140 | 1 |
| 1964 | 271 | 93 | 12 |
| 1965 | 387 | 21 | 128 |
| 1966 | 171 | 15 | 32 |
| 1967 | 93 | 3 | 3 |
| 1968 | 97 | 2 | 0 |

*This table is drawn from a search of the *New York Times Index* for all references to civil rights demonstrations during the years the table covers. The table should be taken simply as indicative, for the data—news stories in a single paper—are very crude. The classification of the incident as peaceful or violent and the subject area of the demonstration are inferred from the entry in the *Index,* usually the headline from the story. The two subcategories reported here—public accommodations and voting—do not sum to the total because demonstrations dealing with a variety of other issues (e.g., education, employment, police brutality) are included in the total.

SOURCE: Jonathan D. Casper, *The Politics of Civil Liberties* (New York: Harper & Row, 1972), p. 90.

TABLE 4.3

**Activity of NAACP Legal Defense and Educational Fund (LDF), 1963–1967**

| YEAR | INDIVIDUALS DEFENDED BY THE LDF | CASES ON LDF DOCKET |
|---|---|---|
| 1963 | 4,200 | 107 |
| 1964 | 10,400 | 145 |
| 1965 | 17,000 | 225 |
| 1966 | 14,000 | 375 |
| 1967 | 13,000 | 420 |

SOURCE: Data from *Report 66,* published in 1967 by the NAACP Legal Defense and Educational Fund. Reprinted from Jonathan D. Casper, *The Politics of Civil Liberties* (New York: Harper & Row, 1972), p. 91. Reprinted by permission of the NAACP Legal Defense and Educational Fund, Inc.

**School Desegregation, Phase One** Although the District of Columbia and some of the school districts in the border states began to respond almost immediately to court-ordered desegregation, the states of the Deep South responded with a carefully planned delaying tactic commonly called "massive resistance" by the more demagogic Southern leaders and "nullification" and "interposition" by the centrists. Either way, Southern politicians stood shoulder to shoulder to declare that the Supreme Court's decisions and orders were without effect. The legislatures in these states enacted statutes ordering school districts to maintain segregated schools and state superintendents to terminate state funding wherever there was racial mixing in the classroom. Some Southern states violated their own long traditions of local school autonomy by centralizing public school authority under the governor or the state board of education and by giving states the power to close the schools and to provide alternative private schooling wherever local school boards might be tending to obey the Supreme Court.

Most of these plans of "massive resistance" were tested in the federal courts and were struck down as unconstitutional.[62] But Southern resistance was not confined to legislation. For example, in Arkansas in 1957, Governor Orval Faubus mobilized the National Guard to intercede against enforcement of a federal court order to integrate Central High School of Little Rock, and President Eisenhower was forced to deploy U.S. troops and literally place the city under martial law. The Supreme Court considered the Little Rock confrontation so historically important that the opinion it rendered in that case was not only agreed to unanimously but was, unprecedentedly, signed personally by each and every one of the justices.[63] The end of massive resistance, however, became simply the beginning of still another Southern strategy, "pupil placement" laws, which authorized school districts to place each pupil in a school according to a whole variety of academic, personal, and psychological considerations, never mentioning race at all. This put the burden of transferring to an all-white school on the non-white children and their parents, making it almost impossible for a single court order to cover a whole district, let alone a whole state. This delayed desegregation a while longer.[64]

As new devices were invented by the Southern states to avoid desegregation, the federal courts followed with cases and decisions quashing them. Ten years after *Brown,* less than 1 percent of black school-age children in the Deep South

[62]The two most important cases were Cooper v. Aaron, 358 U.S. 1 (1958), which required Little Rock, Arkansas, to desegregate; and Griffin v. Prince Edward County School Board, 377 U.S. 218 (1964), which forced all the schools of that Virginia county to reopen after five years of closing to avoid desegregation.

[63]In *Cooper,* the Supreme Court ordered immediate compliance with the lower court's desegregation order and went beyond that with a stern warning that it is "emphatically the province and duty of the judicial department to say what the law is."

[64]Shuttlesworth v. Birmingham Board of Education, 358 U.S. 101 (1958), upheld a "pupil placement" plan purporting to assign pupils on various bases, with no mention of race. This case interpreted *Brown* to mean that school districts must stop explicit racial discrimination but were under no obligation to take positive steps to desegregate. For a while black parents were doomed to case-by-case approaches.

were attending schools with whites.[65] It had become unmistakably clear well before that time that the federal courts could not do the job alone. The first modern effort to legislate in the field of civil rights was made in 1957, but the law contained only a federal guarantee of voting rights, without any powers of enforcement, although it did create the Civil Rights Commission to study abuses. Much more important legislation for civil rights followed, especially the Civil Rights Act of 1964. It is important to observe here the mutual dependence of the courts and legislatures—not only do the legislatures need constitutional authority to act, but the courts need legislative and political assistance, through the power of the purse and the power to organize administrative agencies to implement court orders, and through the focusing of political support. Consequently, even as the U.S. Congress finally moved into the field of school desegregation (and other areas of "equal protection"), the courts continued to exercise their powers, not only by placing court orders against recalcitrant school districts, but also by extending and reinterpreting aspects of the "equal protection" clause to support legislative and administrative actions.

**School Desegregation: Busing and Beyond** The most important judicial extension of civil rights in education after 1954 was probably the *Swann* decision (1971), which held that state-imposed desegregation could be brought about by busing children across school districts even where relatively long distances were involved:

> If school authorities fail in their affirmative obligations judicial authority may be invoked. Once a right and a violation have been shown, the scope of a district court's equitable powers to remedy past wrongs is broad. . . . *Bus transportation [is] a normal and accepted tool of educational policy.*[66]

But the decision went beyond that, adding that under certain limited circumstances even racial quotas could be used as the "starting point in shaping a remedy to correct past constitutional violations," and that pairing or grouping of schools and reorganizing school attendance zones would also be acceptable.

Three years later, however, the *Swann* case was severely restricted when the Supreme Court determined that only cities found guilty of deliberate and *de jure* racial segregation (segregation in law) would have to desegregate their schools.[67] This decision was handed down in the 1974 case of *Milliken v. Bradley* involving the city of Detroit and its suburbs. The *Milliken* ruling had the effect of exempting most Northern states and cities from busing because school segregation in Northern cities is generally *de facto* segregation (segregation in fact) that follows from segregated housing and from thousands of acts of private discrimination against blacks and other minorities.

[65]For good treatments of that long stretch of the struggle of the federal courts to integrate the schools, see Brest and Levinson, *Processes of Constitutional Decision-Making,* pp. 471–80; and Kelly et al., *The American Constitution,* pp. 610–16.

[66]Swann v. Charlotte-Mecklenberg Board of Education, 402 U.S. 1 (1971). [Emphasis added.]

[67]Milliken v. Bradley, 418 U.S. 717 (1974).

PROCESS BOX 4.3

## Cause and Effect in the Civil Rights Movement: Which Came First—Government Action or Political Action?

| Judicial and Legal Action | Political Action |
|---|---|
| **1954** *Brown v. Board of Education* | |
| **1955** *Brown* II—Implementation of *Brown* I | **1955** Montgomery Bus Boycott |
| **1956** Federal courts order school integration, especially one ordering Autherine Lucy admitted to University of Alabama, with Governor Wallace officially protesting | |
| **1957** Civil Rights Act creating Civil Rights Commission; President Eisenhower sends paratroops to Little Rock, Arkansas, to enforce integration of Central High School | **1957** Southern Christian Leadership Conference (SCLC) formed, with King as president |
| **1960** First substantive Civil Rights Act, primarily voting rights | **1960** Student Nonviolent Coordinating Committee (SNCC) formed to organize protests, sit-ins, freedom rides |
| **1961** Interstate Commerce Commission orders desegregation on all buses, trains, and in terminals | |
| **1961** JFK favors executive action over civil rights legislation | |
| **1963** JFK shifts, supports strong civil rights law; assassination; LBJ asserts strong support for civil rights | **1963** Nonviolent demonstrations in Birmingham, Alabama, lead to King's arrest and his "Letter from the Birmingham Jail" |
| | **1963** March on Washington |
| **1964** Congress passes historic Civil Rights Act covering voting, employment, public accommodations, education | |
| **1965** Voting Rights Act | **1965** King announces drive to register 3 million blacks in the South |
| **1966** War on Poverty in full swing | **1966** Movement dissipates: part toward litigation, part toward Community Action Programs, part toward war protest, part toward more militant "Black Power" actions |

Detroit and Boston provide the best illustrations of the agonizing problem of making further progress in civil rights in the schools under the constitutional framework established by the *Swann* and *Milliken* cases. Following *Swann,* the federal district court and the court of appeals had found that Detroit had engaged in deliberate segregation and that, since Detroit schools were overwhelmingly black, the only way to provide a remedy was to bus students between Detroit and the white suburbs beyond the Detroit city boundaries. The Supreme Court in *Swann* had approved a similar "interdistrict" integration plan for Charlotte, North Carolina, but in *Milliken* it refused to do so for Detroit. Although Detroit's segregation had been deliberate, the city and suburban boundary lines had not been drawn deliberately to separate the races. Therefore, the remedy had to take place within Detroit. That same year, and no doubt influenced by the Detroit decision as well as by President Nixon, Congress amended Title VI of the 1964 Civil Rights Act, reducing the authority of the federal government to withhold monetary assistance only in instances of proven *de jure,* state-government-imposed segregation. This action was extremely significant in taking the heat off most Northern school districts.

In Boston, school authorities were found guilty of deliberately building school facilities and drawing school districts "to increase racial segregation." After vain efforts by Boston school authorities to draw up an acceptable plan, federal Judge W. Arthur Garrity ordered an elaborate desegregation plan of his own involving busing between the all-black ghetto of Roxbury and the nearby white, working-class community of South Boston. Opponents of this plan were organized and eventually took the case to the Supreme Court, where *certiorari* (the Court's device for accepting appeals) was denied; this had the effect of approving Judge Garrity's order (see Chapter 8). The facts were that the city's schools were so segregated and uncooperative that even the conservative Nixon administration had already initiated a punitive cutoff of funds. But many liberals also criticized Judge Garrity's plan as being badly conceived, because it involved two neighboring communities with a history of tension and mutual resentment. The plan worked well at the elementary school level but proved so explosive at the high school level that it generated a continuing crisis for the city of Boston and for the whole nation over court-ordered, federally directed desegregation in the North.[68]

Additional progress in the desegregation of schools is likely to be extremely slow unless the Supreme Court decides to permit federal action against *de facto* segregation and against the varieties of private schools and academies that have sprung up for the purpose of avoiding integration. The prospects for further school integration diminished with the Supreme Court decision handed down on January 15, 1991. The opinion, written for the Court by Chief Justice Rehnquist, held that lower federal courts could end supervision of local school boards if those boards could show compliance "in good faith" with court orders to desegregate and could show that "vestiges of past discrimination" had been elimi-

[68]For a good evaluation of the Boston effort, see Gary Orfield, *Must We Bus? Segregated Schools and National Policy* (Washington: Brookings Institution, 1978), pp. 144–46. See also Bob Woodward and Scott Armstrong, *The Brethren: Inside the Supreme Court* (New York: Simon and Schuster, 1979), pp. 426–27; and J. Anthony Lukas, *Common Ground* (New York: Random House, 1986).

nated "to the extent practicable." It is not necessarily easy for a school board to prove that the new standard has been met, but this is the first time since *Brown* and the 1964 Civil Rights Act that the Court opened the door at all to retreat.[69] This door was opened wider in *Freeman v. Pitts* (1992) when the Court gave lower courts still greater leeway to withdraw judicial supervision of desegregation efforts; this cast a very deep and dark shadow over the historic ruling in *Brown v. Board of Education* of 1954.[70] And if there was any doubt that the door might close, this was put to rest in 1995 in *Missouri v. Jenkins,* in which the Court signaled to the lower courts that they should "disengage from desegregation efforts."[71] This is a direct and explicit threat to the main basis of the holding in the original 1954 *Brown v. Board.*

## The Rise of the Politics of Rights

**Outlawing Discrimination in Employment** Despite the agonizingly slow progress of school desegregation, there was some progress in other areas of civil rights during the 1960s and 1970s. Voting rights were established and fairly quickly began to revolutionize Southern politics. Service on juries was no longer denied to minorities. But progress in the right to participate in politics and government dramatized the relative lack of progress in the economic domain, and it was in this area that battles over civil rights were increasingly fought.

The federal courts and the Justice Department entered this area through Title VII of the Civil Rights Act of 1964, which outlawed job discrimination by all private and public employers, including governmental agencies (such as fire and police departments), that employed more than fifteen workers. We have already seen that the Supreme Court gave "interstate commerce" such a broad definition that Congress had the constitutional authority to cover discrimination by virtually any local employers.[72] Title VII makes it unlawful to discriminate in employment on the basis of color, religion, sex, or national origin, as well as race.

The first problem with Title VII was that the complaining party had to show that deliberate discrimination was the cause of the failure to get a job or a training opportunity. Rarely does an employer explicitly admit discrimination on the basis of race, sex, or any other illegal reason. Recognizing the rarity of such an admis-

[69]Board of Education of Oklahoma City public Schools v. Dowell, 111 S. Ct. 630 (1991).

[70]Freeman v. Pitts, 503 U.S. 467 (1992).

[71]Missouri v. Jenkins, 115 S.Ct. 2038 (1995). The quote is from O'Brien, *Supreme Court Watch 1996,* op cit., p. 220.

[72]See especially Katzenbach v. McClung, 379 U.S. 294 (1964). Almost immediately after passage of the Civil Rights Act of 1964, a case was brought challenging the validity of Title II, which covered discrimination in public accommodations. Ollie's Barbecue was a neighborhood restaurant in Birmingham, Alabama. It was located eleven blocks away from an interstate highway and even farther from railroad and bus stations. Its table service was for whites only; there was only a take-out service for blacks. The Supreme Court agreed that Ollie's was strictly an intrastate restaurant, but since a substantial proportion of its food and other supplies were bought from companies outside the state of Alabama, there was a sufficient connection to interstate commerce; therefore, racial discrimination at such restaurants would "impose commercial burdens of national magnitude upon interstate commerce." Although this case involved Title II, it had direct bearing on the constitutionality of Title VII.

sion, the courts have allowed aggrieved parties (the plaintiffs) to make their case if they can show that an employer's hiring practices had the *effect* of exclusion. A leading case in 1971 involved a "class action" by several black employees in North Carolina attempting to show with statistical evidence that blacks had been relegated to only one department in the Duke Power Company, which involved the least desirable, manual-labor jobs, and that they had been kept out of contention for the better jobs because the employer had added high school education and the passing of specially prepared aptitude tests as qualifications for higher jobs. The Supreme Court held that although the statistical evidence did not prove intentional discrimination, and although the requirements were race-neutral in appearance, their effects were sufficient to shift the burden of justification to the employer to show that the requirements were a "business necessity" that bore "a demonstrable relationship to successful performance."[73] The ruling in this case was subsequently applied to other hiring, promotion, and training programs.[74]

**Gender Discrimination** Even before equal employment laws began to have a positive effect on the economic situation of blacks, something far more dramatic began happening—the universalization of civil rights. The right not to be discriminated against was being successfully claimed by the other groups listed in Title VII—those defined by sex, religion, or national origin—and eventually by still other groups defined by age or sexual preference. This universalization of civil rights has become the new frontier of the civil rights struggle, and women have emerged with the greatest prominence in this new struggle. The effort to define and end gender discrimination in employment has led to the historic joining of women's rights to the civil rights cause.

Despite its interest in fighting discrimination, the Supreme Court during the 1950s and 1960s paid little attention to gender discrimination. Ironically, it was left to the more conservative Burger Court (1969–1986) to establish gender discrimination as a major and highly visible civil rights issue. Although the Burger Court refused to treat gender discrimination as the equivalent of racial discrimination,[75] it did make it easier for plaintiffs to file and win suits on the basis of gender discrimination by applying an "intermediate" level of review to these cases.[76] This intermediate level of scrutiny is midway between traditional rules of evidence, which put the burden of proof on the plaintiff, and the doctrine of "strict scrutiny," which requires the defendant to show not only that a particular

**AMERICAN POLITICAL DEVELOPMENT**

Early antecedents of today's women's movement are found in the mid-nineteenth-century Seneca Falls Convention. The convention was primarily concerned with women's suffrage. Although Seneca Falls is a pivotal event, women's efforts to gain the vote date back at least to the time of the American Revolution.

[73]Griggs v. Duke Power Company, 401 U.S. 24 (1971). See also Allan Sindler, *Bakke, DeFunis, and Minority Admissions* (New York: Longman, 1978), pp. 180–89.

[74]For a good treatment of these issues, see Charles O. Gregory and Harold A. Katz, *Labor and the Law* (New York: W. W. Norton, 1979), Chapter 17.

[75]See Frontiero v. Richardson, 411 U.S. 677 (1973).

[76]See Craig v. Boren, 423 U.S. 1047 (1976).

classification is reasonable but also that there is a need or compelling interest for it. "Intermediate" scrutiny, therefore, shifts the burden of proof partially onto the defendant, rather than leaving it entirely on the plaintiff.

One major step was taken in 1992, when the Court decided in *Franklin v. Gwinnett County Public Schools* that violations of Title IX of the 1972 Education Act could be remedied with monetary damages.[77] Title IX forbade gender discrimination in education, but it intially sparked little litigation because of its weak enforcement provisions. The Court's 1992 ruling that monetary damages could be awarded for gender discrimination opened the door for more legal action in the area of education. The greatest impact has been in the areas of sexual harassment—the subject of the *Franklin* case—and in equal treatment of women's athletic programs. The potential for monetary damages has made universities and public schools take the problem of sexual harassment more seriously. Colleges and universities have also started to pay more attention to women's athletic programs. In the two years after the *Franklin* case, complaints to the Education Department's Office for Civil Rights about unequal treatment of women's athletic programs nearly tripled. In several high-profile legal cases, some prominent universities have been ordered to create more women's sports programs; many other colleges and universities have begun to add more women's programs in order to avoid potential litigation.[78] In 1997, the Supreme Court refused to hear a petition by Brown University challenging a lower court ruling that the university establish strict sex equity in its athletic programs. The Court's decision meant that in colleges and universities across the country, varsity athletic positions for men and women must now reflect their overall enrollment numbers.[79]

In 1996, the Supreme Court made another important decision about gender and education by putting an end to all-male schools supported by public funds. It ruled that the policy of the Virginia Military Institute not to admit women was unconstitutional.[80] Along with the Citadel, another all-male military college in South Carolina, VMI had never admitted women in its 157-year history. VMI argued that the unique educational experience it offered—including intense physical training and the harsh treatment of freshmen—would be destroyed if women students were admitted. The Court, however, ruled that the male-only policy denied "substantial equality" to women. Two days after the Court's ruling, the Citadel announced that it would accept women. VMI considered becoming a private institution in order to remain all-male, but in September 1996, the school board finally voted to admit women. The legal decisions may have removed formal barriers to entry, but the experience of the new female cadets at these schools has not been easy. The first female cadet at the Citadel, Shannon Faulkner, won admission in 1995 under a federal court order but quit after four days. Although four women were admitted to the Citadel after the Supreme Court decision, two

[77]New York Times v. Sullivan, 376 U.S. 254 (1964).

[78]Masson v. New Yorker Magazine, 111 S.Ct. 2419 (1991).

[79]Hustler Magazine v. Falwell, 108 S.Ct. 876 (1988).

[80]Roth v. US, 354 U.S. 476 (1957).

of the four quit several months later. They charged harassment from male students, including attempts to set the female cadets on fire.[81]

Ever since sexual harassment was first declared a form of employment discrimination, employers and many employees have worried about the ambiguity of the issue. When can an employee bring charges and when is the employer liable? In 1998, the Court clarified these questions in an important ruling. It said that if a company has an effective antiharassment policy in place, which the employee fails to use, the company cannot be held liable for sexual harassment. If no policy is in place, the company may be held legally responsible for harassment. In addition, the Court ruled that to pursue a suit on the grounds of sexual harassment, the employee does not have to show that she or he suffered a tangible loss, such as loss of promotion. Most important is whether an effective policy is in place and available to employees.[82]

The development of gender discrimination as an important part of the civil rights struggle has coincided with the rise of women's politics as a discrete movement in American politics. As with the struggle for racial equality, the relationship between changes in government policies and political action suggests a two-way pattern of causation, where changes in government policies can produce political action and vice versa. Today, the existence of a powerful women's movement derives in large measure from the enactment of Title VII of the Civil Rights Act of 1964 and from the Burger Court's vital steps in applying that law to protect women. The recognition of women's civil rights has become an issue that in many ways transcends the usual distinctions of American political debate. In the heavily partisan debate over the federal crime bill enacted in 1994, for instance, the section of the bill that enjoyed the widest support was the Violence Against Women Act, whose most important feature is that it defines gender-biased violent crimes as a matter of civil rights, and creates a civil rights remedy for women who have been the victims of such crimes. Women may now file civil as well as criminal suits against their assailants, which means that they are no longer solely dependent on prosecutors to defend them against violent crime.

**Discrimination against Other Groups** As gender discrimination began to be seen as an important civil rights issue, other groups arose demanding recognition and active protection of their civil rights. Under Title VII of the 1964 Civil Rights Act, any group or individual can try, and in fact is encouraged to try, to convert goals and grievances into questions of rights and the deprivation of those rights. A plaintiff must only establish that his or her membership in a group is an unreasonable basis for discrimination unless it can be proven to be a "job-related" or otherwise clearly reasonable and relevant decision. In America today, the list of individuals and groups claiming illegal discrimination is lengthy. The disabled, for instance, increasingly press their claim to equal treatment as a civil rights

[81]Concurring opinion in Jacobellis v. Ohio, 378 U.S. 184 (1964).
[82]Miller v. California, 413 U.S. 15 (1973).

# *Globalization and Rights*

The 1948 Universal Declaration of Human Rights globalized civil liberties and civil rights. The Declaration was championed by Eleanor Roosevelt and drew heavily on U.S. constitutional law and practice, including the Bill of Rights and subsequent interpretive jurisprudence that had greatly expanded notions of basic rights in the United States. The Declaration's thirty articles have been accepted by every country in the world, save Saudi Arabia. The first five articles enumerate basic individual rights, while Articles 6 through 21 specify political and civil rights. While the U.S. Constitution was the model for the entire document, the last twenty-one articles enhance the civil liberties and rights guaranteed by U.S. law. For example, Article 5 forbids torture; Article 14 provides that "Everyone has the right to seek and enjoy in other countries asylum from persecutions." Articles 22 through 27 go far beyond what the U.S. Constitution requires, demanding that countries provide an array of social and welfare rights, including the right to social security, the right to work, the right to an adequate standard of living, the right to education, the right to enjoy the arts, the right to periodic holidays with pay, and even the right to intellectual property.

The Universal Declaration has had a major impact around the world, with its principles embodied in nearly every new or heavily revised constitution in the past half-century. In contrast, the impact on U.S. law has been very limited, with no new rights or liberties transferred directly from the Declaration to U.S. constitutional jurisprudence. This is not surprising, since the United States already had a well-established constitutional framework, a set of amendments and interpretations defining rights and liberties, and a resistance to external influences on national politics. But the impact (on the United States) of the

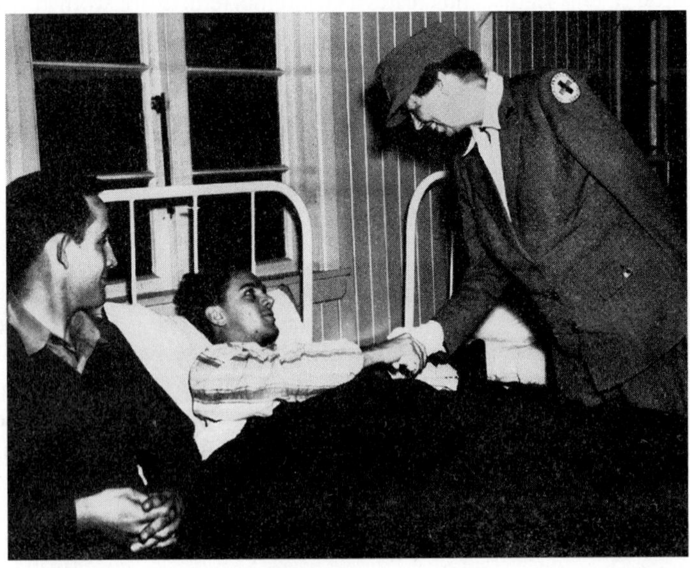

social and welfare rights enumerated in Articles 22 through 27, which were included in the Declaration largely through the influence of Eleanor Roosevelt, is significant. Some scholars trace a boomerang effect from Mrs. Roosevelt to the Declaration and then back to the Great Society policies of the 1960s, when health care, minimum wages, education, welfare, and other Universal Human Rights became American "entitlements."[1]

The Declaration has been used extensively as a foreign policy tool. Since the rights and liberties enumerated have been almost universally accepted, the United States and other countries—without being accused of imposing American values—can point a finger at countries that grossly abuse "universal" human rights. Since 1961, the Senate has prohibited economic assistance to countries that show a pattern of violating internationally accepted human rights. President Jimmy Carter withheld U.S. military assistance from Latin American military governments such as Guatemala because of their human rights violations. Likewise, many countries banned economic activity with apartheid-era South Africa, an activity that eventually contributed to historic changes for that country. And in 1998, President Clinton used the Universal Declaration of Human Rights to scold and prod the Chinese government during his visit to that country.

Nongovernmental organizations (NGOs) such as Amnesty International have emerged in our interdependent world as major international proponents of human rights. Ironically, at about the same time that President Clinton was lecturing the Chinese on their human rights shortcomings, Amnesty International was unleashing its first worldwide campaign for human rights in the United States. More than a million Amnesty International members worlwide actively joined in the "Rights for All" campaign, which charged that the United States failed to meet the internationally accepted human rights standards agreed to in the Universal Declaration. The U.S. record on the death penalty—only China, Iran, and Saudi Arabia execute more people—is listed along with prison conditions, the inhumane treatment of asylum seekers, and the correlation between race and punishment as areas where U.S. practices constitute human rights violations.

[1] See for example Louis Henkin, "The Universal Declaration and the U.S. Constitution," *PS: Political Science & Politics* (September 1998), pp. 512–15.

matter, a stance encouraged by the Americans with Disabilities Act of 1990.[83] Deaf Americans increasingly demand social and legal recognition of deafness as a separate culture, not simply as a disability.[84] One of the most familiar of these groups has been the gay and lesbian movement, which in less than thirty years has emerged from invisibility to become one of the largest civil rights movements in contemporary America. The place of gays and lesbians in American society is now the subject of a highly charged debate, but it is a debate that was not even heard before the rise of the politics of rights in the last thirty years. The debate is out of the closet and the movement's progress is also producing equal and opposite reactions, to say the least. What appeared at first to be a most important breakthrough was the promise made by President Clinton, during the 1992 campaign, to end discrimination against gays in the military. But soon after his inauguration in 1993, President Clinton was unable to handle the heat of opposition, and he settled for a compromise that could only have been treated as a dismal disappointment by the gay and lesbian movement: "Don't ask, don't tell," meaning that a gay or lesbian member of the armed forces would be protected against discrimination only as long as they remain silent and inactive with regard to the observances of their own lifestyle. But despite their disappointment, homosexuals can claim some progress along legal lines, especially in *Romer v. Evans* (1996). In November 1992, a Colorado referendum approved an amendment to the state constitution forbidding localities from enacting any ordinance that outlaws discrimination against homosexuals. The amendment denied to any municipality the power to adopt a law that gives homosexuals "minority status" that protects them from discrimination. In a 6-to-3 decision, the Court held that the Colorado amendment actually classifies homosexuality not as a status equal to everyone else but as a status that "make[s] them unequal to everyone else. This Colorado cannot do. A State cannot so deem a class of persons a stranger to its laws. Amendment 2 violated the Equal Protection Clause. . . ."[85]

## Affirmative Action

The politics of rights not only spread to increasing numbers of groups in the society, it also expanded its goal. The relatively narrow goal of equalizing opportunity by eliminating discriminatory barriers had been developing toward the far broader goal of ***affirmative action***—compensatory action to overcome the consequences of past discrimination and to encourage greater diversity. An affirmative action policy tends to involve two novel approaches: (1) positive or benign discrimination in which race or some other status is actually taken into account, but

[83]In 1994, for instance, after pressure from the Justice Department under the terms of the Americans with Disabilities Act, one of the nation's largest rental-car companies agreed to make special hand-controls available to any customer requesting them. See "Avis Agrees to Equip Cars for Disabled," *Los Angeles Times,* 2 September 1994, p. D1.

[84]Thus a distinction has come to be made between "deaf," the pathology, and "Deaf," the culture. See Andrew Solomon, "Defiantly Deaf," *New York Times Magazine,* 28 August 1994, pp. 40ff.

[85]Romer v. Evans, 116 S.Ct. 1620 (1996).

for compensatory action rather than mistreatment; and (2) compensatory action to favor members of the disadvantaged group who themselves may never have been the victims of discrimination. Quotas may be but are not necessarily involved in affirmative action policies.

In 1965, President Johnson attempted to inaugurate affirmative action by executive orders directing agency heads and personnel officers to pursue vigorously a policy of minority employment in the federal civil service and in companies doing business with the national government. But affirmative action did not become a prominent goal until the 1970s.

As this movement spread, it also began to divide civil rights activists and their supporters. The whole issue of qualification versus minority preference was addressed formally in the case of Allan Bakke. Bakke, a white male with no minority affiliation, brought suit against the University of California at Davis Medical School on the grounds that in denying him admission the school had discriminated against him on the basis of his race (that year the school had reserved 16 of 100 available slots for minority applicants). He argued that his grades and test scores had ranked him well above many students who had been accepted at the school and that the only possible explanation for his rejection was that those others accepted were black or Hispanic while he was white. In 1978, Bakke won his case before the Supreme Court and was admitted to the medical school, but he did not succeed in getting affirmative action declared unconstitutional. The Court rejected the procedures at the University of California because its medical school had used both a quota *and* a separate admissions system for minorities. The Court agreed with Bakke's argument that racial categorizations are suspect categories that place a severe burden of proof on those using them to show a "compelling public purpose." The Court went on to say that achieving "a diverse student body" was such a public purpose, but the method of a rigid quota of student slots assigned on the basis of race was incompatible with the equal protection clause. Thus, the Court permitted universities (and presumably other schools, training programs, and hiring authorities) to continue to take minority status into consideration, but limited severely the use of quotas to situations in which (1) previous discrimination had been shown, and (2) it was used more as a *guideline* for social diversity than as a mathematically defined ratio.[86]

For nearly a decade after *Bakke,* the Supreme Court was tentative and permissive about efforts by corporations and governments to experiment with affirmative

### AMERICAN POLITICAL DEVELOPMENT

The origins of the concept of "affirmative action" have been traced to a number of actions undertaken in the Kennedy and Johnson presidential administrations. In 1961, President Kennedy issued an executive order that "called for 'affirmative action' to counter the effects of discrimination." By the mid-1960s, the Johnson administration sought to encourage the hiring of minorities by government contractors and, through the Small Business Act of 1965, mandated that some government contracts be reserved as "minority set-asides." This relatively recent policy is under both political and legal attack.

SOURCE: W. Avon Drake and Robert D. Holsworth, *Affirmative Action and the Stalled Quest for Black Progress* (Urbana: University of Illinois Press, 1996), p. 12.

[86]Regents of the University of California v. Bakke, 438 U.S. 265 (1978).

DEBATING THE ISSUES

# Affirmative Action

*The principle of equality has long been a bedrock value of the American political system. Yet the devotion to equality has contrasted sharply with the fact that Americans have not all been treated equally. Women, African Americans, Latinos, Native Americans, and other groups rightly claim that they have suffered historical patterns of discrimination that have deprived them of basic rights. Many African Americans in particular believe that hundreds of years of slavery and savage treatment cannot simply be wiped away by the proclamation that all are now equal.*

*This belief has prompted the government to promote affirmative action programs designed to provide an added advantage for minorities in areas such as college admissions and employment, based on the principle that past discrimination against African Americans and others can be rectified only by tilting the scales more in their favor now. Advocates of affirmative action, such as Supreme Court Justice Thurgood Marshall, have argued that equal treatment of unequals merely perpetuates inequality. Opponents of such programs, such as law professor Stephen L. Carter, contend that such preferential treatment is inconsistent with American values and may actually harm those it tries to help.*

## MARSHALL

Three hundred and fifty years ago, the Negro was dragged to this country in chains to be sold into slavery. Uprooted from his homeland and thrust into bondage for forced labor, the slave was deprived of all legal rights. It was unlawful to teach him to read; he could be sold away from his family and friends at the whim of his master; and killing or maiming him was not a crime. The system of slavery brutalized and dehumanized both master and slave.

The denial of human rights was etched into the American colonies' first attempts at establishing self-government. . . . The self-evident truths and the unalienable rights were intended . . . only to apply to white men. . . . The implicit protection of slavery embodied in the Declaration of Independence was made explicit in the Constitution. . . . The status of the Negro as property was officially erased by his emancipation at the end of the Civil War. But the long awaited emancipation, while freeing the Negro from slavery, did not bring him citizenship or equality in any meaningful way. Despite the passage of the Thirteenth, Fourteenth, and Fifteenth Amendments, the Negro was systematically denied the rights those amendments were supposed to secure. . . . In light of the sorry history of discrimination and its devastating impact on the lives of Negroes, bringing the Negro into the mainstream of American life should be a state interest of the highest order. To fail to do so is to ensure that America will forever remain a divided society. . . . We now must permit the institutions of this society to give consideration to race in making decisions about who will hold the positions of influence, affluence and prestige in America. For far too long, the doors to those positions have been shut to Negroes.[1]

[1]Regents of the University of California v. Bakke, 438 U.S. 265, 387 (1978).

If we as a people were not defeated by slavery and Jim Crow, we will not be defeated by the demise of affirmative action. Before there were any racial preferences, before there was a federal antidiscrimination law with any teeth, our achievements were already on the rise: our middle class was growing, as was our rate of college matriculation—both of them at higher rates than in the years since. Black professionals, in short, should not do much worse without affirmative action than we are doing with it, and thrown on our own resources and knowing that we have no choice but to meet the same tests as everybody else, we may do better.

We must be about the business of defining a future in which we can be fair to ourselves and demand opportunities without falling into the trap of letting others tell us that our horizons are limited, that we cannot make it without assistance. . . . The likely demise, or severe restriction, of racial preferences will also present for us a new stage of struggle, and we should treat it as an opportunity, not a burden. It is our chance to make ourselves free of the assumptions that too often underlie affirmative action, assumptions about our intellectual incapacity and other competitive deficiencies. It is our chance to prove to a doubting, indifferent world that our future as a people is in our hands.[2]

[2]Stephen L. Carter, *Reflections of an Affirmative Action Baby* (New York: Basic Books, 1991), as excerpted in George McKenna and Stanley Feingold, eds., *Taking Sides: Clashing Views on Controversial Political Issues,* 8th ed. (Guilford, CT: Dushkin, 1993), pp. 192–93.

action programs in employment.[87] But in 1989, the Court returned to the *Bakke* position that any "rigid numerical quota" is suspect. In *Wards Cove v. Atonio,* the Court further weakened affirmative action by easing the way for employers to prefer white males, holding that the burden of proof of unlawful discrimination should be shifted from the defendant (the employer) to the plaintiff (the person claiming to be the victim of discrimination).[88] This decision virtually overruled the Court's prior holding.[89] That same year, the Court ruled that any affirmative action program already approved by federal courts could be subsequently challenged by white males who alleged that the program discriminated against them.[90]

[87]United Steelworkers v. Weber, 443 U.S. 193 (1979); and Fullilove v. Klutznick, 100 S.Ct. 2758 (1980).

[88]Wards Cove v. Atonio, 109 S.Ct. 2115 (1989).

[89]Griggs v. Duke Power Company, 401 U.S. 24 (1971).

[90]Martin v. Wilks, 109 S.Ct. 2180 (1989). In this case, some white firefighters in Birmingham challenged a consent decree mandating goals for hiring and promoting blacks. This was an affirmative action plan that had been worked out between the employer and aggrieved black employees and had been accepted by a federal court. Such agreements become "consent decrees" and are subject to enforcement. Chief Justice Rehnquist held that the white firefighters could challenge the legality of such programs, even though they had not been parties to the original litigation.

In 1991, after a lengthy battle with the White House, Congress enacted a piece of legislation designed to undo the effects of these decisions. Under the terms of the Civil Rights Acts of 1991, the burden of proof in employment discrimination cases was shifted back to employers, overturning the *Wards Cove* decision. In addition, the act made it more difficult to mount later challenges to consent decrees in affirmative action cases, reversing the *Martin v. Wilks* decision. Despite Congress's actions, however, the federal judiciary will have the last word when cases under the new law reach the courts. In a 5-to-4 decision in 1993, the Court ruled that employees had to prove their employers intended discrimination, thus again placing the burden of proof on employees.[91]

In 1995, the Supreme Court's ruling in *Adarand Constructors v. Pena* further weakened affirmative action. This decision stated that race-based policies, such as preferences given by the government to minority contractors, must survive strict scrutiny, placing the burden on the government to show that such affirmative action programs serve a compelling government interest and are narrowly tailored to address identifiable past discrimination.[92] President Clinton responded to the *Adarand* decision by ordering a review of all government affirmative action policies and practices. Although many observers suspected that the president would use the review as an opportunity to back away from affirmative action, the conclusions of the task force largely defended existing policies. Reflecting the influence of the Supreme Court's decision in *Adarand,* President Clinton acknowledged that some government policies would need to change. But on the whole, the review found that most affirmative action policies were fair and did not "unduly burden nonbeneficiaries."[93]

Although Clinton sought to "mend, not end" affirmative action, developments in the courts and the states continued to restrict affirmative action in important ways. One of the most significant was the *Hopwood* case, in which white students challenged admissions practices in the University of Texas Law School, charging that the school's affirmative action program discriminated against whites. In 1996, a federal court (the U.S. Court of Appeals for the Fifth Circuit) ruling on the case stated that race could never be considered in granting admissions and scholarships at state colleges and universities.[94] This decision effectively rolled back the use of affirmative action permitted by the 1978 *Bakke* case. In *Bakke,* as discussed earlier, the Supreme Court had outlawed quotas but said that race could be used as one factor among many in admissions decisions. Many universities and colleges have since justified affirmative action as a way of promoting racial diversity among their student bodies. What was new in the *Hopwood* decision was the ruling that race could *never* be used as a factor in admissions decisions, even to promote diversity.

In 1996, the Supreme Court refused to hear a challenge to the *Hopwood* case. This meant that its ruling remains in effect in the states covered by the Fifth Circuit—Texas, Louisiana, and Mississippi—but does not apply to the rest of the country. The impact of the *Hopwood* ruling is greatest in Texas because Louisiana

[91]St. Mary's Honor Center v. Hicks, 113 S.Ct. 2742 (1993).

[92]Adarand Constructors, Inc. v. Pena, 115 S.Ct. 2097 (1995).

[93]Ann Devroy, "Clinton Study Backs Affirmative Action," *Washington Post,* 19 July 1995, p. A1.

[94]Hopwood v. State of Texas, 78 F3d 932 (Fifth Circuit, 1996).

and Mississippi are under conflicting court orders to desegregate their universities. In Texas, in the year after the *Hopwood* case, minority applications to Texas universities declined. Concerned about the ability of Texas public universities to serve the state's minority students, the Texas legislature quickly passed a new law granting students who graduate in the top 10 percent of their classes automatic admission to the state's public universities. It is hoped that this measure will ensure a racially diverse student body.[95]

The weakening of affirmative action in the courts was underscored in a case the Supreme Court agreed to hear in 1998. A white schoolteacher in New Jersey who had lost her job had sued her school district, charging that her layoff was racially motivated: a black colleague hired on the same day was not laid off. Under President George Bush, the Justice Department had filed a brief on her behalf in 1989, but in 1994 the Clinton administration formally reversed course in a new brief supporting the school district's right to make distinctions based on race as long as it did not involve the use of quotas. Three years later, the administration, worried that the case was weak and could result in a broad decision against affirmative action, reversed course again. It filed a brief with the Court urging a narrow ruling in favor of the dismissed worker. Because the school board had justified its actions on the grounds of preserving diversity, the administration feared that a broad ruling by the Supreme Court could totally prohibit the use of race in employment decisions, even as one factor among many designed to achieve diversity. But before the Court could issue a ruling, a coalititon of civil rights groups brokered and arranged to pay for a settlement. This unusual move reflected the widespread fear of a sweeping negative decision. Cases involving dismissals, as the New Jersey case did, are generally viewed as much more difficult to defend than cases that concern hiring. In addition, the particular facts of the new Jersey case—two equally qualified teachers hired on the same day—were seen as unusual and unfavorable to affirmative action.[96]

The courts have not been the only center of action: challenges to affirmative action have also emerged in state and local politics. One of the most significant state actions was the passage of the California Civil Rights Initiative, also known as Proposition 209, in 1996. Proposition 209 outlawed affirmative action programs in the state and local governments of California, thus prohibiting state and local governments from using race or gender preferences in their decisions about hiring, contracting, or university admissions. The political battle over Proposition 209 was heated, and supporters and defenders took to the streets as well as the airwaves to make their cases. When the referendum was held, the measure passed with 54 percent of the vote, including 27 percent of the black vote, 30 percent of the Latino vote, and 45 percent of the Asian American vote.[97] In 1997, the Supreme Court refused to hear a challenge to the new law.

[95]See Lydia Lum, "Applications by Minorities Down Sharply," *Houston Chronicle,* 8 April 1997, p. A1; R. G. Ratcliffe, "Senate Approves Bill Designed to Boost Minority Enrollments," *Houston Chronicle,* 8 May 1997, p. A1.

[96]Linda Greenhouse, "Settlement Ends High Court Case on Preferences," *New York Times,* 22 November 1997, p. A1; Barry Bearak, "Rights Groups Ducked a Fight, Opponents Say," *New York Times,* 22 November 1997, p. A1.

[97]Michael A Fletcher, "Opponents of Affirmative Action Heartened by Court Decision," *Washington Post,* 13 April 1997, p. A21.

Many observers predicted that the success of California's ban on affirmative action would provoke similar movements in states and localities across the country. But the political factors that contributed to the success of Proposition 209 in California may not exist in many other states. In contrast to California Republican governor Pete Wilson, who strongly opposed affirmative action, other Republican governors, such as New Jersey's Christine Todd Whitman, are strong supporters. Moreover, because public opinion on the issue is very conflicted, the outcome of efforts to roll affirmative action back depends greatly on how the issue is posed to voters. California's Proposition 209 was framed as a civil rights initiative: "the state shall not discriminate against, or grant preferential treatment to, any individual or group on the basis of race, sex, color, ethnicity, or national origin." Different wording can produce quite different outcomes, as a 1997 vote on affirmative action in Houston revealed. There, the ballot initiative asked voters whether they wanted to ban affirmative action in city contracting and hiring, not whether they wanted to end preferential treatment. Fifty-five percent of Houston voters decided in favor of affirmative action.[98]

Affirmative action will continue to be a focus of controversy in coming years, as several other cases challenging affirmative action reach the Supreme Court. There are now several suits similar to the *Hopwood* case working their way through the lower courts, including one against the University of Michigan's affirmative action program. If the Supreme Court decides to hear these cases, the future of affirmative action in universities and colleges will be on the line. Affirmative action is also sure to remain prominent in state and local politics across the country. Efforts to ban affirmative action are under way in a number of states, including Washington, Colorado, Michigan, Massachusetts, Arizona, Arkansas, Ohio, North Dakota, and Oregon.

Affirmative action efforts have contributed to the polarization of the politics of civil rights. At the risk of grievous oversimplification, we can divide the sides by two labels: liberals and conservatives.[99] The conservatives' argument against affirmative action can be reduced to two major points. The first is that rights in the American tradition are innately individual, and affirmative action violates this concept by concerning itself with "group rights," an idea said to be alien to the American tradition. The second point has to do with quotas. Conservatives would argue that the Constitution is "color blind," and that any discrimination, even if it is called positive or benign discrimination, ultimately violates the equal protection clause and the American way.

The liberal side agrees that rights ultimately come down to individuals but argues that, since the essence of discrimination is the use of unreasonable and unjust criteria of exclusion to deprive *an entire group* of access to something valuable

[98]See Sam Howe Verhovek, "Houston Vote Underlined Complexity of Rights Issue," *New York Times,* 6 November 1997, p. A1.

[99]There are still many genuine racists in America, but with the exception of a lunatic fringe, made up of neo-Nazis and members of the Ku Klux Klan, most racists are too ashamed or embarrassed to take part in normal political discourse. They are not included in either category here.

**TABLE 4.4**

**Opinions on Affirmative Action Programs**

*Responses to the question "All in all, do you favor or oppose affirmative action programs for blacks and other minority groups?"*

| | WHITES | BLACKS |
|---|---|---|
| Favor | 36% | 76% |
| Oppose | 50 | 16 |
| Not sure | 14 | 8 |

SOURCE: NBC/Wall Street Journal Poll, October 1995, reported in *The Public Perspective,* February/March 1996, p. 26.

the society has to offer, then the phenomenon of discrimination itself has to be attacked on a group basis. Liberals can also use Court history to support their side, because the first definitive interpretation of the Fourteenth Amendment by the Supreme Court in 1873 gave a "color conscious" argument:

> The existence of laws in the state where the newly emancipated Negroes resided, which discriminated with gross injustice and hardship against them *as a class,* was the evil to be remedied by this clause.[100]

Although the problems of rights in America are agonizing, they can be looked at optimistically. The United States has a long way to go before it constructs a truly just, "equally protected" society. But it also has come very far in a relatively short time. All explicit *de jure* barriers to minorities have been dismantled. Many *de facto* barriers have also been dismantled, and thousands upon thousands of new opportunities have been opened. Perhaps the greatest promise, however, is in fact the rise of the "politics of rights." The American people are now accustomed to interest groups—conservative and liberal—who call themselves "public interest groups" and accept the efforts of such groups to translate their goals in vigorous and eloquent statements about their rights to their goals. Few people now fear that such a politics of rights will produce violence. Deep and fundamental differences have polarized many groups (see Table 4.4), but political and governmental institutions have proven themselves capable of maintaining balances between them. This kind of balancing can be done without violence so long as everyone recognizes that policy choices, even about rights, cannot be absolute.

Finally, the most important contribution to be made by the politics of rights is probably to the American conscience. Whatever compromises have to be made in order to govern without violence, Americans cannot afford to be satisfied. Injustices do exist. We cannot eliminate them all, but we must maintain our sense of

[100]Slaughter-House Cases, 16 Wallace 36 (1873). [Emphasis added.]

ANALYZING AMERICAN POLITICS

# *The Rational-Choice Approach, Collective Action, and the Civil Rights Movement*

In the past several decades, a new approach to studying politics—the *rational-choice* approach—has emerged and taken its place among other ways of studying politics. This new approach, which grew out of the field of economics, borrows the ideas that economists assume about economic actors and applies them to political actors. One of the key differences between the rational-choice approach and other approaches is that the former assumes that individuals are self-interested, rational actors.

People often object to this approach because the words "self-interested" and "rational" are too loaded. How can one claim that a prominent political actor such as Martin Luther King, Jr. was self-interested? Is it reasonable to assume that in the realm of politics, where fundamental questions over heated topics such as racism, freedom of speech, and abortion are debated and resolved, that people behave rationally—at least in the traditional sense of the word? However, those who adopt the rational-choice approach to politics have a very narrow definition for the terms "self-interested" and "rational." By "self-interested" they mean that individuals have their own goals. Thus Martin Luther King's behavior was motivated by self-interest, not in the sense that he was out for material gain, but in that he had personal goals for protecting and guaranteeing the civil rights of African Americans. The term "rational" means that for a given set of choices, individuals will opt for the alternative that they think will offer them the best terms for achieving their goals.

From those basic assumptions, scholars in the rational-choice tradition attempt to explain political processes and outcomes. The three key questions in a rational-choice analysis are 1) Who are the important actors (e.g., members of a congressional committee, party leaders, bureaucrats, leaders of interest groups); 2) What are their goals/interests (do they want to get re-elected, do they want to get a tax break for their industry, do they want to save old-growth forests from development); and 3) How can they attain those goals (should they try to get a law passed, should they lobby a committee chair to pressure a federal agency, should they donate soft money to a political party, should they pursue legal action through the courts)?

Although this approach has become widely accepted in the study of political science, it still remains controversial.[1] How does it explain, for example, why people

[1]Theodore Lowi, "The State in Politial Science: How We Become What We Study," *American Political Science Review* 86 (March 1992), pp. 1–7; Donald P. Green and Ian Shapiro, *Pathologies of Rational Choice Theory* (New Haven: Yale University Press, 1994).

participated in civil rights marches during the 1950s and 1960s? As we will see in later chapters, one of the tenets of the rational-choice perspective is that individuals have little incentive to participate in mass action politics. After all, what possible difference could one person make by taking part in a civil rights protest? Participation was costly in terms of time and, in the case of civil rights marchers, even health or one's life. The risks outweighed the potential benefits, yet hundreds of thousands of people *did* participate. Why?

Though little scholarly attention has been paid by those who apply the rational-choice perspective to the civil rights movements,[2] a general answer is available. As Kenneth A. Shepsle and Mark S. Bonchek explain in their book *Analyzing Politics: Rationality, Behavior, and Institutions,*

> Most rational analysis takes behavior to be *instrumental*—to be motivated by and directed toward some purpose or objective. But behavior may also be *experiential.* People do things, on this account, because they like doing them—they feel good inside, they feel free of guilt, they take pleasure in the activity for its own sake. We maintain that this second view of behavior is entirely compatible with rational accounts. Instrumental behavior may be thought of as *investment activity,* whereas experiential behavior may be thought of as *consumption activity.* . . . [I]t is the behavior itself that generates utility, rather than the consequences produced by the behavior. To take a specific illustration of collective action, many people certainly attended the 1964 march on Washington because they cared about civil rights. But it is unlikely that many deluded themselves into thinking their individual participation made a large difference to the fate of the civil rights legislation in support of which the march was organized. Rather, they attended because they wanted to be a part of a social movement, to hear Martin Luther King speak, and to identify with the hundreds of thousands of others who felt the same way. Also, and this should not be minimized, they participated because they anticipated that the march would be fun—an adventure of sorts.

So, experiential behavior is consumption-oriented activity predicated on the belief that the activity in question is fulfilling apart from its consequences. Individuals, complicated things that they are, are bound to be animated both by the consumption value of a particular behavior that we just described *and* its instrumental value, the rational (investment) explanation that we have used throughout this book. To insist on only one of these complementary forms of rationality, and to exclude the other, is to provide but a partial explanation.[3]

[2]One notable exception is Dennis Chong, *Collective Action and the Civil Rights Movement* (Chicago: University of Chicago Press, 1991).
[3]Kenneth A. Shepsle and Mark S. Bonchek, *Analyzing Politics: Rationality, Behavior, and Insitutions* (New York: W. W. Norton, 1997), pp. 247–48.

shame for the injustices that persist. This is precisely why the constitutional framework is so important in the real world and not just in theory. It establishes a context of rights, defined both as limits on the power of the government (civil liberties) and as rightful claims to particular opportunities or benefits (civil rights). Without that framework, rights would remain in the world of abstract philosophy; with that framework, in the United States, they remain now as they did two hundred years ago, as real *causes of action.*

## Reflections on Government, Liberties, and Rights

This chapter, properly understood, can provide the best possible insight into the nature of government, not only in the United States but everywhere and for all time: Government is a contradictory beast, possessing all the best and many of the worst features of the people who created it. The first great masterpiece of political thought in the English language is *Leviathan* (1651) by Thomas Hobbes. Leviathan, an aquatic monster with origins traceable back to the Old Testament, is a symbol of evil ultimately defeated by the power of good. Hobbes chose this symbol because of the great power of the beast, like government, to do good as well as evil. Forty years later, his successor John Locke would, in the same spirit, ask: "If man in the state of nature be so free . . . , why will he part with his freedom . . . ? To which, it is obvious to answer, that though in the state of nature he hath such [freedom], yet the enjoyment of it is very uncertain . . . and it is not without reason that he seeks out and is willing to join in society with others . . . for the mutual preservation of their lives. . . ." A century later, James Madison wrote in the same spirit,

> . . . what is government itself but the greatest of all reflections on human nature? If men were angels, no government would be necessary. If angels were to govern men, neither external nor internal controls on government would be necessary. In framing a government which is to be administered by men over men, the great difficulty lies in this: you must first enable the government to control the governed; and in the next place oblige it to control itself.[101]

Our property is hardly worth the map the land title is printed on, nor the contract worth more than the paper containing the agreement, unless there is a government strong enough to ward off trespassers and to enforce contracts. Speech is no freer than the dedication of the local police and courts to defend the most unpopular speaker or reporter. And although expanding markets provide most of the economic opportunity a society can have, it may take law, courts, and administrators to control conduct based on prejudices that build brick walls and glass ceilings against the access of individuals because of their race, gender, or other so-

[101]*The Federalist,* No. 51.

cial categories held in contempt. In other words, the very conception of rights and liberties requires the imagination of great thinkers and constitution writers, but the hopes their teachings instill in us require a government strong enough to help us realize them. Thus, is it any surprise that a government of sufficient strength to thwart unjust private force and to defend all individuals against external adversaries will be strong enough to be a threat to the same liberties, rights, and protections?

We can deal with this contradiction, but it is not easy. No solution is perfect or lasts for long. And there is no foolproof way and no one-best-way. To "enable the government to control the governed," we gave the national government its powers in Article I. As we saw in Chapter 3, to "oblige it to control itself," we took back part of its power to act with the federal principle—reserving the bulk of governmental powers to the states—and we took back another part of its power to act with the separation of powers, or, as Madison put it, building competition within the government so that "ambition must be made to counteract ambition." The procedural restraints were put largely in the Bill of Rights, providing an independent judiciary with the power to hold the legislature and the executive to some fairly high standard of "due process of law." But due process itself implies a government with power to act—so long as it respects some limit on how it acts.

Thus, the question "How are individuals protected from the national government as well as by the national government?" becomes "How *well* can we do *both*?" A balance must be maintained between strong government and restrained government, and it is a balance that cannot be set once and for all but must be constantly adjusted. Maintaining such a balance would be a lot simpler if it were merely a matter of fine-tuning any expansion of government as popular reactions against such expansions begin to mount. But the question of "How can individuals be protected from and by the national government?" is complicated by the fact that different *kinds* of government power and different *kinds* of individual freedom are involved. Liberals seek more political and social freedom and opportunity, and they seek more governmental power, especially at the national level, to expand and protect these even at the expense of economic freedoms. The older Libertarians (sometimes erroneously called conservatives) take a fairly opposite view that government always has too much power because, as it seeks to protect political and social freedoms, it acts in such a manner as to restrain economic freedoms and therefore can interfere with economic progress that is to everyone's advantage. They tend to see virtually *all* government—national, state, and local—as a threat to freedom. Conservatives favor more government power to reduce political, social, *and* economic freedoms in the name of defending community and family values and religiously generated moralities. Since state governments have most of the governmental power to regulate matters of value and morality, conservatives tend to oppose the national government while favoring very strong *state* government.

Thus, along with "How do we maintain a balance between governmental power and individual freedom?" we have to ask who wants what kind of balance. This chapter is but a first step, albeit a fundamental step, in the whole inquiry into power and freedom, when they are consonant and when they are at odds.

## SUMMARY

Although freedom and power are inextricably intertwined, they had to be separated for purposes of analysis. *Civil liberties* and *civil rights* are two quite different phenomena and have to be treated legally and constitutionally in two quite different ways. We have defined *civil liberties* as that sphere of individual freedom of choice created by restraints on governmental power. When the Constitution was ratified, it was already seen as inadequate in the provision of protections of individual freedom and required the addition of the Bill of Rights. The Bill of Rights explicitly placed a whole series of restraints on government. Some of these were *substantive,* regarding *what* government could do; and some of these restraints were *procedural,* regarding *how* the government was permitted to act. We call the rights in the Bill of Rights civil liberties because they are rights to be free from arbitrary government interference.

But *which* government? This was settled in the *Barron* case in 1833 when the Supreme Court held that the restraints in the Bill of Rights were applicable only to the national government, and not to the states. The Court was recognizing "dual citizenship." At the time of its adoption in 1868, the Fourteenth Amendment was considered by many as a deliberate effort to reverse *Barron,* to put an end to dual citizenship, and to nationalize the Bill of Rights, applying its restrictions to state governments as well as to the national government. But the post–Civil War Supreme Court interpreted the Fourteenth Amendment otherwise. Dual citizenship remained almost as it had been before the Civil War, and the shadow of *Barron* extended across the rest of the nineteenth century and well into the twentieth century. The slow process of nationalizing the Bill of Rights began in the 1920s, when the Supreme Court recognized that at least the restraints of the First Amendment had been "incorporated" into the Fourteenth Amendment as restraints on the state governments. But it was not until the 1960s that most of the civil liberties in the Bill of Rights were incorporated into the Fourteenth Amendment. Almost exactly a century after the adoption of the Fourteenth Amendment, the Bill of Rights was nationalized. Citizens now enjoy close to the same civil liberties regardless of the state in which they reside.

As for the second aspect of protection of the individual, *civil rights,* stress has been put upon the expansion of governmental power rather than restraints upon it. If the constitutional base of civil liberties is the "due process" clause of the Fourteenth Amendment, the constitutional base of civil rights is the "equal protection" clause. This clause imposes a positive obligation on government to advance civil rights, and its original motivation seems to have been to eliminate the gross injustices suffered by "the newly emancipated Negroes . . . as a class." But as with civil liberties, there was little advancement in the interpretation or application of the "equal protection" clause until after World War II. The major breakthrough came in 1954 with *Brown v. Board of Education,* and advancements came in fits and starts during the succeeding ten years.

After 1964, Congress finally supported the federal courts with effective civil rights legislation that outlawed a number of discriminatory practices in the private

THEN AND NOW

## Changes in American Politics

The relationship between U.S. citizens and their government has changed dramatically from the nineteenth century to the present.

- In the case of *Barron v. Baltimore,* the Court decided that the Bill of Rights did not apply to state actions. Even though the Fourteenth Amendment seemed to have protected citizens' rights from state action, it was not until the twentieth century that many rights were "selectively incorporated" into the Fourteenth Amendment and thus protected from state action. Speech, press, and assembly rights were incorporated as late as the 1920s and 1930s, while it was not until the 1960s that various rights in criminal proceedings were selectively incorporated.
- The principle set forth in the Declaration of Independence that "all men are created equal" has lived beyond its proponents and been used for the expansion of rights to various groups. The language of the Declaration was used in support of the women's movement in the Seneca Falls Convention in 1848, where the declaration read that "all men *and women* are created equal." The principle was also invoked during the civil rights movement, most notably by Martin Luther King, Jr., in his "I Have a Dream" speech.
- The government's treatment of African Americans has undergone several transformations. At the founding, the Constitution not only condoned but rewarded slavery by providing disproportionate House representation to states with large slave populations. In the twentieth century, the national government has (with some success) protected African Americans by expanding civil rights and affirmative action.
- National government policies that address racial inequities in the United States are both very recent and still controversial. The implementation of "affirmative action" policies only began in the 1960s. The implementation of school desegregation met much resistance during the 1960s and 1970s.

sector and provided for the withholding of federal grants-in-aid to any local government, school, or private employer as a sanction to help enforce the civil rights laws. From that point, civil rights developed in two ways. First, the definition of civil rights was expanded to include victims of discrimination other than blacks. Second, the definition of civil rights became increasingly positive; affirmative action has become an official term. Judicial decisions, congressional statutes, and administrative agency actions all have moved beyond the original goal of eliminating discrimination toward creating new opportunities for minorities and, in some areas, compensating today's minorities for the consequences of discriminatory actions not directly against them but against members of their group in the past.

Because compensatory civil rights action has sometimes relied upon quotas, there has been intense debate over the constitutionality as well as the desirability of affirmative action.

The story has not ended and is not likely to end. The politics of rights will remain an important part of American political discourse.

## For Further Reading

Abraham, Henry. *Freedom and the Court: Civil Rights and Liberties in the United States.* 5th ed. New York: Oxford University Press, 1994.

Baer, Judith A. *Equality under the Constitution: Reclaiming the Fourteenth Amendment.* Ithaca, NY: Cornell University Press, 1983.

Drake, W. Avon, and Robert D. Holsworth. *Affirmative Action and the Stalled Quest for Black Progress.* Urbana: University of Illinois Press, 1996.

Eisenstein, Zillah. *The Female Body and the Law.* Berkeley: University of California Press, 1988.

Friendly, Fred W. *Minnesota Rag: The Dramatic Story of the Landmark Supreme Court Case that Gave New Meaning to Freedom of the Press.* New York: Vintage, 1982.

Garrow, David J. *Bearing the Cross: Martin Luther King and the Southern Christian Leadership Conference: A Personal Portrait.* New York: William Morrow, 1986.

Glendon, Mary Ann. *Rights Talk: The Impoverishment of Political Discourse.* New York: Free Press, 1991.

Greenberg, Jack. *Crusaders in the Courts: How a Dedicated Band of Lawyers Fought for the Civil Rights Revolution.* New York: Basic Books, 1994.

Hentoff, Nat. *The First Freedom: The Tumultuous History of Free Speech in America.* New York: Delacorte, 1980.

Kelly, Alfred, Winfred A. Harbison, and Herman Beltz. *The American Constitution: Its Origins and Development.* 7th ed. New York: W. W. Norton, 1991.

Levy, Leonard. *Freedom of Speech and Press in Early America: Legacy of Suppression.* New York: Harper, 1963.

Lewis, Anthony. *Gideon's Trumpet.* New York: Random House, 1964.

Minow, Martha. *Making All the Difference—Inclusion, Exclusion, and American Law.* Ithaca, NY: Cornell University Press, 1990.

Nava, Michael. *Created Equal: Why Gay Rights Matter to America.* New York: St. Martin's Press, 1994.

Rosenberg, Gerald N. *The Hollow Hope: Can Courts Bring About Social Change?* Chicago: University of Chicago Press, 1991.

Silberman, Charles. *Criminal Violence, Criminal Justice.* New York: Random House, 1978.

Silverstein, Mark. *Constitutional Faiths.* Ithaca, NY: Cornell University Press, 1984.

Thernstrom, Abigail M. *Whose Votes Count? Affirmative Action and Minority Voting Rights.* Cambridge: Harvard University Press, 1987.

PART 2

# INSTITUTIONS

# 5

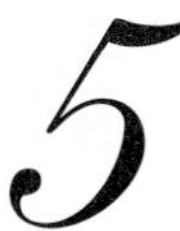

# Congress: The First Branch

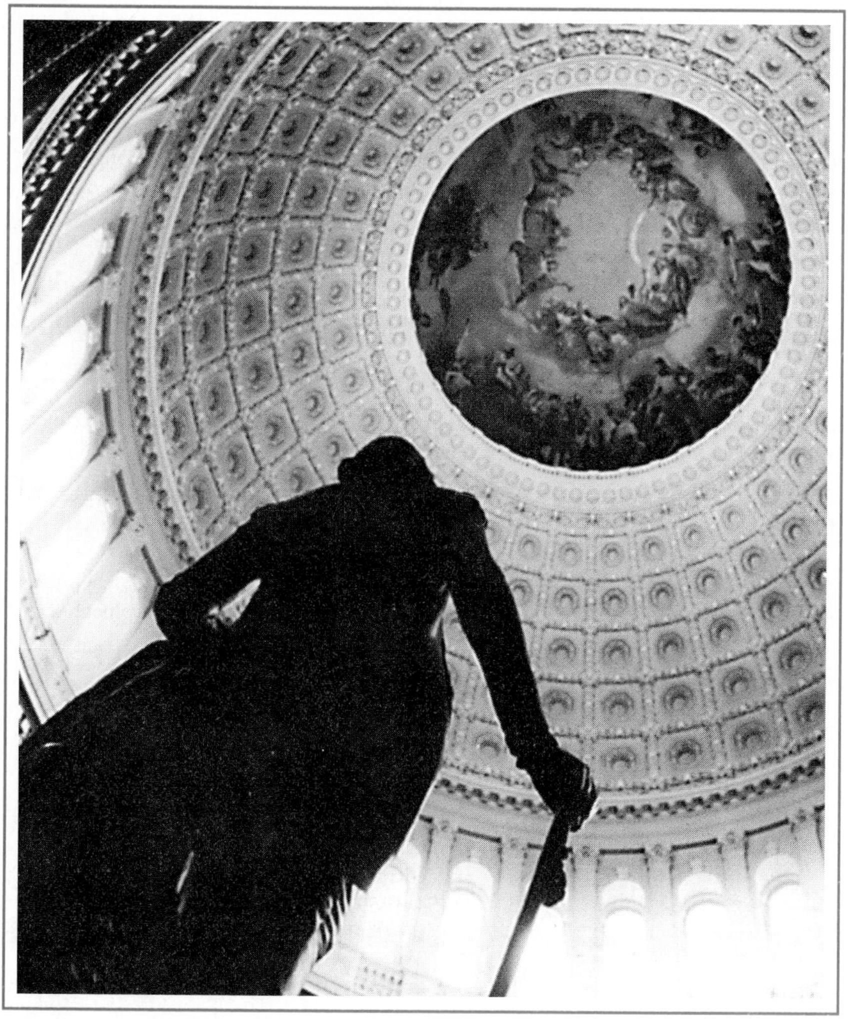

## TIME LINE ON CONGRESS

| Events | | Institutional Developments |
|---|---|---|
| New Congress of U.S. meets for first time (1789) | | Creation of House Ways and Means Committee (1789) |
| Jeffersonian party born in Congress (1792) | | House committees develop. First procedural rules adopted—Jefferson's Rules (1790s) |
| | 1800 | |
| | | Congressional party caucuses control presidential nominations (1804–1828) |
| | | Congressional committees take control of legislative process. Rise of congressional government (1820s) |
| Andrew Jackson renominated for president by Democratic party convention (1832) | | Presidential nominating conventions replace caucuses (1831–1832) |
| Abraham Lincoln elected president (1860) | 1860 | |
| South secedes. Its delegation leaves Washington (1860–1861); period of Republican leadership (1860s) | | No longer blocked by Southerners, Congress adopts protective tariff, transcontinental railroad, Homestead Act, National Banking Act, Contract Labor Act (1861–1864) |
| Congress impeaches but does not convict Andrew Johnson (1868) | | Filibuster developed as a tactic in the Senate (1880s) |
| Era of Republican ascendancy begins (1897) | | |
| | 1900 | |
| Theodore Roosevelt makes U.S. a world power (1901–1909) | | House revolt against power of Speaker; rise of seniority system in House (1910) |
| Democratic interlude with election of Woodrow Wilson (1912) | | Seventeenth Amendment ratified; authorizes direct election of senators (1913) |
| | | Senate cloture rule (1917) |
| | | Budget and Accounting Act—development of presidential budget (1921) |
| | 1930 | Rise of presidential government as Congress passes FDR's New Deal legislation (1930s) |
| Democrats take charge; Franklin Delano Roosevelt elected president (1932) | | Legislative Reorganization Act (1946) |
| | | Regulation of lobbyists (1949) |
| | | Democratic Congresses expand Social Security and federal expenditures for public health (1954–1959) |

| Events | | Institutional Developments |
|---|---|---|
| McCarthy hearings (1950s) | 1950 | Use of legislative investigations as congressional weapon against executive (1950s–1980s) |
| | | Growing importance of incumbency (1960s–1980s) |
| | | Code of ethics adopted (1971) |
| Watergate hearings (1973–1974) | | Campaign Finance Act (1974) |
| Richard Nixon resigns presidency (1974) | | Filibuster reform (1975) |
| | | Enactment of statutory limits on presidential power—War Powers Resolution (1973), Budget and Impoundment Control Act (1974), amendments to Freedom of Information Act (1974), Ethics in Government Act (1978) |
| | | Revival of party caucus and weakening of seniority rules (1970s–1980s) |
| Ronald Reagan elected president (1980) | 1980 | Large deficits impose budgetary limits on Congress; period of intense conflict between legislative and executive branches (1980s and 1990s) |
| Republicans temporarily take control of Senate (1980–1986) | | |
| George Bush elected president (1988) | | |
| | 1990 | |
| Democrats control Congress and White House for first time in 12 years; Republicans use Senate filibuster threat to influence Clinton program (1993) | | Congress enacts new tax and deficit reduction programs (1993) |
| Republicans win control of Congress (1994) | | |
| Clinton defeats Republicans in budget battle (1995) | | Republicans in Congress fight to enact "Contract with America" (1995) |
| Republicans retain control of Congress (1996) | | Republicans lose public support after government shutdown (1995–1996) |
| Republicans lose seats in midterm election but hold onto slim margin (1998) | | 105th Congress historically unproductive (1997–1998) |
| House impeaches Clinton for obstruction of justice and perjury charges in Monica Lewinsky investigation (1998) | | House speaker Newt Gingrich resigns; Denny Hastert elected as Speaker (1998–1999) |
| Senate acquits Clinton (1999) | | |

## CORE OF THE ARGUMENT

- The struggle for power between Congress and the president results from the Constitution's system of checks and balances.
- The power of Congress is a function of its capacity to effectively represent important groups and forces in society.
- During the first hundred years of American government, Congress was the dominant institution; with the beginning of the New Deal, the presidency became the more accessible and dominant branch of American government.
- Before a bill can become a law, it must pass through the legislative process, a complex set of organizations and procedures in Congress.
- The legislative process is driven by six sets of political forces: political parties, committees, staffs, caucuses, rules of lawmaking, and the president.

The U.S. Congress is the "first branch" of government under Article I of our Constitution and is also among the world's most important representative bodies. Throughout American history, the Congress has initiated, fashioned, and implemented programs in all areas of American domestic and foreign policy. Prior to the twentieth century, the Congress, not the executive, was the central policy-making institution in the United States. Congressional leaders like Henry Clay, Daniel Webster, and John C. Calhoun were the dominant political figures of their time and often treated mere presidents with disdain. But during the twentieth century, although Congress continues to be important, its influence has waned relative to that of the executive branch. The presidency has become the central institution of American government. Members of Congress may support or oppose, but they are seldom free to ignore presidential leadership. Moreover, the bureaucracies of the executive branch have—often with the encouragement of Congress—usurped a good deal of legislative power.

Despite this decline in influence, however, the U.S. Congress is still the only national representative assembly that can actually be said to govern. Many of the world's representative bodies only represent, that is, their governmental functions consist mainly of affirming and legitimating the national leadership's decisions, tying local activists more firmly to the central government by allowing them to take part in national political affairs, and giving all citizens the impression that popular views actually play a role in the decision-making process. For example, before the collapse of the U.S.S.R., its national representative body, the Supreme Soviet, included deputies representing every locality, as well as every ethnic, religious, and occupational group in Soviet society. The Supreme Soviet, however, possessed only the power to say "yes" to leadership proposals. Its visible approval of policies and programs was seen by the Communist party hierarchy as a useful way of convincing citizens that their interests were taken into account at some point in the national decision-making process.

Although many of the world's representative bodies possess only the right to say "yes," a second, smaller group of representative institutions—most notably West European parliaments—also have the power to say "no" to the proposals of executive agencies. Such institutions as the British Parliament have the power to reject programs and laws sought by the government, although the use of this power is constrained by the fact that the rejection of an important governmental proposal can lead to Parliament's dissolution and the need for new elections. While they can and sometimes do say "no," West European parliaments generally do not have the power to modify governmental proposals or, more important, to initiate major programs. The only national representative body that actually possesses such powers is the U.S. Congress. For example, while the U.S. Congress never accedes to the president's budget proposals without making major changes, both the British House of Commons and the Japanese Diet always accept the budget exactly as proposed by the government.

In this chapter, we shall try to understand how the U.S. Congress is able to serve simultaneously as a representative assembly and a powerful agency of government. Unlike most of its counterparts around the world, Congress controls a formidable battery of powers that it uses to shape policies and, when necessary, defend its prerogatives against the executive branch. We shall examine each of these powers in its turn.

As we shall see, however, congressional power cannot be separated from congressional representation. Indeed, there is a reciprocal relationship between the two. Without its important governmental powers, Congress would be a very different sort of representative body. Americans might feel some sense of symbolic representation if they found that Congress contained members of their own race, religion, ethnic background, or social class. They might feel some sense of gratification if members of Congress tried to help them with their problems. But without its array of powers, Congress could do little to represent effectively the views and interests of its constituents. Power is necessary for effective congressional representation. At the same time, the power of Congress is ultimately a function of its capacity to effectively represent important groups and forces in American society.

We shall return to this central question—"What is the relationship between congressional power and representation?"—at the conclusion of this chapter. Before we do this, however, let us look more carefully at each individual part of the equation. First, let us examine some of the ways in which Congress can be said to "represent" the American people. Second, let us examine the institutional structure of Congress and how congressional powers are organized and used. Finally, we will assess the contemporary connection between congressional power and congressional representation.

**THE CENTRAL QUESTION**

"What is the relationship between congressional power and representation?"

## REPRESENTATION

Assemblies and the idea of representation have been around in one form or another for centuries. But until the eighteenth century—with the American and French revolutions—assemblies were usually means used by monarchs to gain or regain the support of local leaders. According to political theorist Carl Friedrich, the calling of assemblies "was necessary because the undeveloped state of central administrative systems and the absence of effective means of coercion rendered the collection of . . . war taxes impossible without local cooperation."[1]

Eventually, the regional lords and lesser barons, joined by the rising merchant classes, began to see the assembly as a place where they could state their case against the monarch, rather than merely receive his messages to take back to their regions. Through their efforts, the assembly was slowly converted from part of the monarch's regime to an institution that could be used against the monarchy and, later, used by the middle classes against the aristocracy. But the original function of the assembly—getting obedience through consent—never disappeared. It was simply joined by new functions. Once the assembly had evolved into a place where demands could be made, it became a "parliament"—a place where people could come together to talk. ("Parliament" is derived from the French *parler*—to talk.) The French and many other Europeans gave their national assemblies the name "parliament" because they felt that talk was the essential feature of these bodies. Although the U.S. Congress does not share that name, talk is still one of its essential ingredients, built into its very structure. Talk is facilitated by the fact that each member of the House and Senate is, in principle, equal to all the other members. Although the committee structure of Congress gives some members more power than others, a measure of equality in Congress exists by virtue of the fact that membership is determined entirely by election from districts defined as absolutely equal. Each member's primary responsibility is to the district, to his or her ***constituency,*** not to the congressional leadership, a party, or even the institution. Another important support for the parliamentary aspect of Congress is a provision in the Constitution that exempts members of Congress from arrest for any except the most serious crimes while conducting congressional business. Article I, Section 6, has generally freed members of Congress from the fear of libel and slander suits and therefore from the fear of any negative consequences from things said in the heat of debate or elsewhere. Supreme Court decisions have extended this immunity to their activities as members of committees.

## Sociological versus Agency Representation

We have become so accustomed to the idea of representative government that we tend to forget what a peculiar concept representation really is. A representative claims to act or speak for some other person or group. But how can one person be trusted to speak for another? How do we know that those who call themselves our representatives are actually speaking on our behalf, rather than simply pursuing their own interests?

There are two circumstances under which one person reasonably might be trusted to speak for another. The first of these occurs if the two individuals are so similar in background, character, interests, and perspectives that anything said by one would very likely reflect the views of the other as well. This principle is at the heart of what is sometimes called ***sociological representation***—the sort of representation that takes place when representatives have the same racial, ethnic, religious, or educa-

[1]Carl Friedrich, *Constitutional Government and Democracy,* 4th ed. (Boston: Ginn, 1968), p. 274.

tional backgrounds as their constituents. The assumption is that sociological similarity helps to promote good representation, and thus, the composition of a properly constituted representative assembly should mirror the composition of society.[2]

The second circumstance under which one person might be trusted to speak for another occurs if the two are formally bound together so that the representative is in some way accountable to those he or she purports to represent. If representatives can somehow be punished or held to account for failing to speak properly for their constituents, then we know they have an incentive to provide good representation even if their own personal backgrounds, views, and interests differ from those they represent. This principle is called ***agency representation***—the sort of representation that takes place when constituents have the power to hire and fire their representatives.

Both sociological and agency representation play a role in the relationship between members of Congress and their constituencies.

**The Social Composition of the U.S. Congress** The extent to which the U.S. Congress is representative of the American people in a sociological sense can be seen by examining the distribution of important social characteristics in the House and Senate today. It comes as no surprise that the religious affiliations of members of both the House and Senate are overwhelmingly Protestant—the distribution is very close to the proportion in the population at large—although the Protestant category is composed of more than fifteen denominations. Catholics continue to comprise the second largest category of religious affiliation, and Jews a much smaller third category. Nonetheless, since most policies that cut along religious lines are dealt with by state legislatures, the religious affiliations of members of Congress are almost entirely symbolic.

African Americans, women, Hispanic Americans, and Asian Americans have increased their congressional representation somewhat in the past two decades. In 1998, fifty-eight women were elected to the House of Representatives (up from only twenty-nine in 1990). Nine women now serve in the Senate.

Even now, however, representation of women and minorities in Congress is still not comparable to their proportions in the general population. Since many important contemporary national issues do cut along racial and gender lines, a considerable amount of clamor for reform in the representative process is likely to continue until these groups are fully represented.

The occupational backgrounds of members of Congress have always been a matter of interest because so many issues cut along economic lines that are relevant to occupations and industries. The legal profession is the dominant career of most members of Congress prior to their election to Congress. Public service or politics is also a significant background. In addition, many members of Congress also have important ties to business and industry. One composite portrait of a typical member of Congress has been that of "a middle-aged male lawyer whose father was of the professional or managerial class; a native-born 'white,' or—if he cannot avoid being an immigrant—a product of northwestern or central Europe or Canada, rather than of eastern or southern Europe, Latin America, Africa or

[2]See Carol Swain, *Black Faces, Black Interests: The Representation of African Americans in Congress* (Cambridge: Harvard University Press, 1993).

Asia."[3] This is not a portrait of the U.S. population. Congress is not a sociological microcosm of our society, and it probably can never become one. One obvious reason is that the skills and resources needed to achieve political success in the United States are much more likely to be found among well-educated and relatively well-to-do Americans than among members of minority groups and the poor. Take money, for example. As we shall see in Chapter 10, successful congressional candidates must be able to raise hundreds of thousands of dollars to finance their campaigns. Poor people from the inner city are much less likely to be able to convince corporate political action committees to provide them with these funds.

Is Congress still able to legislate fairly or to take account of a diversity of views and interests if it is not a sociologically representative assembly? The task is certainly much more difficult. Yet there is reason to believe it can. Representatives, as we shall see shortly, can serve as the agents of their constituents, even if they do not precisely mirror their sociological attributes. Yet, sociological representation is a matter of some importance, even if it is not an absolute prerequisite for fair legislation on the part of members of the House and Senate. At the least, the social composition of a representative assembly is important for symbolic purposes—to demonstrate to groups in the population that they are taken seriously by the government. For this very reason, acting under authority of the 1982 Voting Rights Act, the Justice Department has sought to intervene in the legislative districting process to assure greater minority representation in Congress and the state legislatures. Concern about the proportion of women, African Americans, and ethnic minorities in Congress and elsewhere in government would exist whether or not these social characteristics influenced the outcomes of laws and policies. It is rare to find a social group whose members do not feel shortchanged if someone like themselves is not a member of the assembly. Thus, the symbolic composition of Congress is ultimately important for the political stability of the United States. If Congress is not representative symbolically, then its own authority and indeed that of the entire government would be reduced.[4]

**Representatives as Agents** A good deal of evidence indicates that whether or not members of Congress share their constituents' sociological characteristics, they *do* work very hard to speak for their constituents' views and serve their constituents' interests in the governmental process. The idea of representative as agent is similar to the relationship of lawyer and client. True, the relationship between the member of Congress and as many as 550,000 "clients" in the district, or the senator and millions of clients in the state, is very different from that of the lawyer and client. But the criteria of performance are comparable. One expects at the very least that each representative will constantly be seeking to discover the interests of the constituency and will be speaking for those interests in Congress and in other centers of government.[5]

[3]Marian D. Irish and James Prothro, *The Politics of American Democracy,* 5th ed. (Englewood Cliffs, NJ: Prentice-Hall, 1971), p. 352.

[4]For a discussion, see Benjamin Ginsberg, *The Consequences of Consent* (New York: Random House, 1982), Chapter 1.

[5]For some interesting empirical evidence, see Angus Campbell, Philip Converse, Warren Miller, and Donald Stokes, *Elections and the Political Order* (New York: Wiley, 1966), Chapter 11.

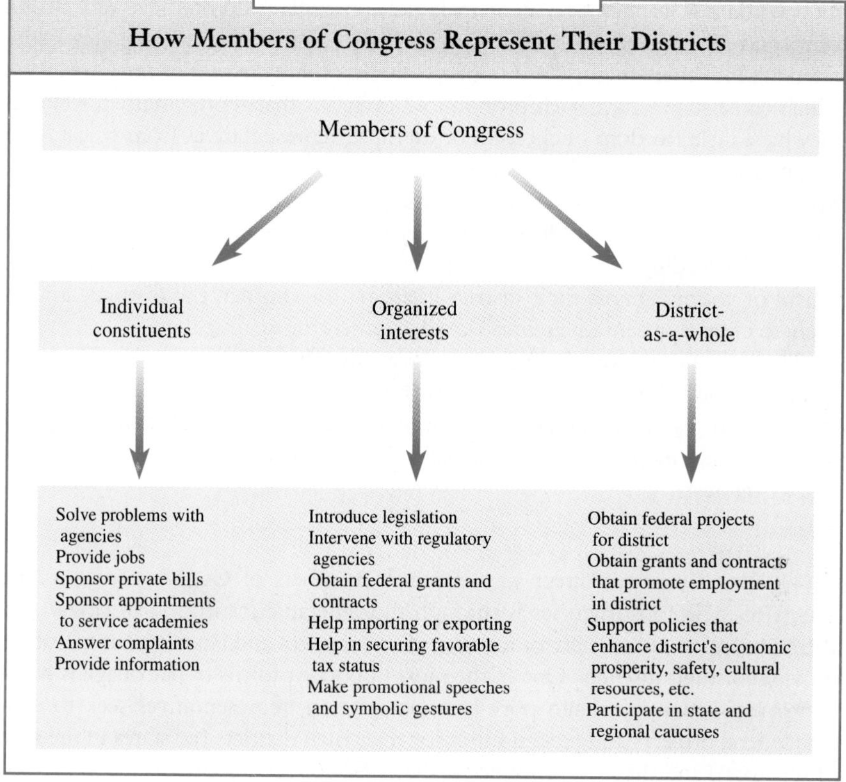


There is constant communication between constituents and congressional offices. For example, each year the House and Senate post offices handle nearly 100 million pieces of incoming mail, and in recent years, members of Congress have sent out nearly 400 million pieces of mail.[6]

The seriousness with which members of the House attempt to behave as representatives can be seen in the amount of time spent on behalf of their constituents. Well over a quarter of their time and nearly two-thirds of the time of their staff members is devoted to constituency service (termed "case work"). This service is not merely a matter of writing and mailing letters. It includes talking to constituents, providing them with minor services, presenting special bills for them, and attempting to influence decisions by regulatory commissions on their behalf.[7]

[6]Congressional Quarterly, *Guide to the Congress of the United States,* 2nd ed. (Washington, DC: Congressional Quarterly Press, 1976), p. 588.

[7]John S. Saloma, *Congress and the New Politics* (Boston: Little, Brown, 1969), pp. 184–85. A 1977 official report using less detailed categories came up with almost the same impression of Congress's workload. Commission on Administrative Review, *Administrative Reorganization and Legislative Management,* House Doc. #95-232 (28 September 1977), vol. 2, especially pp. 17–19.

Although no members of Congress are above constituency pressures (and they would not want to be), on many issues constituents do not have very strong views and representatives are free to act as they think best. Foreign policy issues often fall into this category. But in many districts there are two or three issues on which constituents have such pronounced opinions that representatives feel that they have little freedom of choice. For example, representatives from wheat, cotton, or tobacco districts probably will not want to exercise a great deal of independence on relevant agricultural legislation. In the oil-rich states (such as Oklahoma, Texas, and California), the senators and members of the House are likely to be leading advocates of oil interests. For one thing, they are probably fearful of voting against their district interests; for another, the districts are unlikely to elect representatives who would *want* to vote against them.

The influence of constituencies is so pervasive that both parties have strongly embraced the informal rule that nothing should be done to endanger the re-election chances of any member. Party leaders obey this rule fairly consistently by not asking any member to vote the party line whenever it might conflict with a district interest.

**Patronage** One very direct way in which members of Congress serve as the agents of their constituencies is through the venerable institution of ***patronage.*** Patronage refers to a variety of forms of direct services and benefits that members provide for their districts. One of the most important forms of patronage is ***pork-barrel legislation.*** Through pork-barrel legislation, representatives seek to capture federal projects and federal funds for their own districts (or states in the case of senators), and thus to "bring home the pork" for their constituents. Many observers of Congress argue that pork-barrel bills are the only ones that some members are serious about moving toward actual passage because they are seen as so important to members' re-election bids.

A common form of pork barreling is the "earmark," the practice through which members of Congress insert into otherwise pork-free bills language that provides special benefits for their own constituents.[8] For instance, the massive transportation bill enacted in 1998 contained billions of dollars in earmarks. One senator, Ted Kennedy (D-Mass.), claimed that he was able to obtain nearly $200 million in earmarks. In addition to $100 million for highway construction in Boston, these included a myriad of small items such as $1.6 million for the Longfellow National Historic Site and $3.17 million for the Silvio Conte National Fish and Wildlife Refuge.[9]

Often, congressional leaders will use pork-barrel projects in exchange for votes on other matters. For example, while serving as Senate majority leader in 1957, Lyndon Johnson won crucial support for civil rights legislation by awarding water projects to Senators Margaret Chase Smith of Maine and Frank Church of Idaho. The most important rule of pork-barreling is that any member of Con-

[8]For an excellent study of academic earmarking, see James Savage, *Funding Science in America* (New York: Cambridge University Press, 1999).

[9]*Congressional Quarterly Weekly Report,* 17 October 1998, p. 2792.

gress whose district receives a project as part of a bill must support all the other projects on the bill. This cuts across party and ideological lines. Thus, the same 1984 appropriations bill that was supported by conservative Republican senator Ted Stevens of Alaska because it provided funds for Blackhawk helicopters for the Alaska National Guard was also supported by liberal Democrat Ted Kennedy, who had won a provision for $2 million for a lighthouse at Nantucket.

The pork-barrel tradition in Congress is so strong that some members insist on providing their districts with special benefits whether their constituents want them or not. In 1994, for example, members of the House Public Works Committee managed to channel millions of dollars in federal highway funds to their own states and districts. California, which has eight representatives on the Public Works Committee, received fifty-one special federal highway projects worth nearly $300 million. The problem is that under federal law, these special funds are charged against the state's annual grant from the Highway Trust Fund. States rely heavily upon their Highway Trust Fund grants to fund high-priority road work. One exasperated state official declared, "For years our members have tried to explain that to the members of Congress . . . 'No, you did not bring me any new money. All you did was reprogram money from here to there.'"[10]

In 1996, fulfilling a promise made in their "Contract with America," congressional Republicans pushed through legislation giving the president a ***line-item veto,*** which allowed the president to eliminate such earmarks before signing a bill. In 1998, however, the Supreme Court declared the line-item veto to be unconstitutional (see Chapter 6). In retrospect, most members of Congress were not displeased by the Court's decision, having come to feel that they had made a mistake when they granted the president such an important new power.

A limited amount of other direct patronage also exists. One important form of this constituency service is intervention with federal administrative agencies on behalf of constituents. Members of the House and Senate and their staff members spend a great deal of time on the telephone and in administrative offices seeking to secure favorable treatment for constituents and supporters. A small but related form of patronage is getting an appointment to one of the military academies for the child of a constituent. Traditionally, these appointments are allocated one to a district.

A different form of patronage is the ***private bill***—a proposal to grant some kind of relief, special privilege, or exemption to the person named in the bill. The private bill is a type of legislation, but it is distinguished from a public bill, which is supposed to deal with general rules and categories of behavior, people, and institutions. As many as 75 percent of all private bills introduced (and one-third of the ones that pass) are concerned with providing relief for foreign nationals who cannot get permanent visas to the United States because the immigration quota for their country is filled or because of something unusual about their particular situation.[11]

[10]Jon Healey, "The Unspoken Expense of the Highway Bill," *Congressional Quarterly Weekly Report,* 28 May 1994, p. 1375.

[11]Congressional Quarterly, *Guide to the Congress of the United States,* pp. 229–310.

Private legislation is a congressional privilege that is often abused, but it is impossible to imagine members of Congress giving it up completely. It is one of the easiest, cheapest, and most effective forms of patronage available to each member. It can be defended as an indispensable part of the process by which members of Congress seek to fulfill their role as representatives. And obviously they like the privilege because it helps them win re-election.

## Representation and Elections

The sociological composition of Congress and the activities of representatives once they are in office are very much influenced by electoral considerations. Three factors related to the U.S. electoral system affect who gets elected and what they do once in office. The first set of issues concerns who decides to run for office and which candidates have an edge over others. The second issue is that of incumbency advantage. Finally, the way congressional district lines are drawn can greatly affect the outcome of an election. Let us examine more closely the impact that these considerations have on representation.

Voters' choices are restricted from the start by who decides to run for office. In the past, decisions about who would run for a particular elected office were made by local party officials. A person who had a record of service to the party, or who was owed a favor, or whose "turn" had come up might be nominated by party leaders for an office. Today, few party organizations have the power to slate candidates in that way. Instead, the decision to run for Congress is a more personal choice. One of the most important factors determining who runs for office is a candidate's individual ambition.[12] A potential candidate may also assess whether he or she can attract enough money to mount a credible campaign. The ability to raise money depends on connections with other politicians, interest groups, and national party organizations. In the past, the difficulty of raising campaign funds posed a disadvantage to female candidates. Since the 1980s, however, a number of political action committees (PACs) and other organizations (see Chapter 12) have emerged to recruit women and fund their campaigns. The largest of them, EMILY's List, has become one of the most powerful fundraisers in the nation. Recent research shows that money is no longer the barrier it once was to women running for office.[13]

Features distinctive to each congressional district also affect the field of candidates. Among them are the range of other political opportunities that may lure potential candidates away. In addition, the way the congressional district overlaps with state legislative boundaries may affect a candidate's decision to run. A state-level representative or senator who is considering running for the U.S. Congress is

[12]See Linda Fowler and Robert McClure, *Political Ambition: Who Decides to Run for Congress* (New Haven: Yale University Press, 1989); and Alan Erhenhalt, *The United States of Ambition* (New York: Times Books, 1991).

[13]See Barbara C. Burrell, *A Woman's Place Is in the House: Campaigning for Congress in the Feminist Era* (Ann Arbor: University of Michigan Press, 1994), Chapter 6; and the essays in Elizabeth Adell Cook, Sue Thomas, and Clyde Wilcox, eds., *The Year of the Woman: Myths and Realities* (Boulder, CO: Westview, 1994).

more likely to assess his or her prospects favorably if his or her state district coincides with the congressional district (because the voters will already know him or her). And for any candidate, decisions about running must be made early, because once money has been committed to already-declared candidates, it is harder for new candidates to break into a race. Thus, the outcome of a November election is partially determined many months earlier, when decisions to run are finalized.

Incumbency plays a very important role in the American electoral system and in the kind of representation citizens get in Washington. Once in office, members of Congress possess an array of tools that they can use to stack the deck in favor of their re-election. The most important of these is constituency service: taking care of the problems and requests of individual voters. Through such services and through regular newsletter mailings, the incumbent seeks to establish a "personal" relationship with his or her constituents. The success of this strategy is evident in the high rates of re-election for congressional incumbents: over 95 percent for House members and nearly 90 percent for members of the Senate in recent years (see Figure 5.1).[14] It is also evident in what is called sophomore surge—the tendency for candidates to win a higher percentage of the vote when seeking future terms in office.

**AMERICAN POLITICAL DEVELOPMENT**

Incumbents have generally enjoyed an advantage in House elections throughout much of American history. However, the electoral security of incumbents as measured by the "sophomore surge" (the average increase in vote percentage between a member's first election and his or her first re-election) increased dramatically in the mid-1960s.

SOURCE: John R. Alford and David W. Brady, "Personal and Partisan Advantage in U.S. Congressional Elections, 1846–1990," in *Congress Reconsidered,* 5th ed., ed. Lawrence C. Dodd and Bruce I. Oppenheimer (Washington, DC: Congressional Quarterly Press, 1993), pp. 141–57.

Incumbency can also help a candidate by scaring off potential challengers. In many races, potential candidates may decide not to run because they fear that the incumbent simply has too much money or is too well liked or too well known.[15] Potentially strong challengers may also decide that a district's partisan leanings are too unfavorable. The experience of Republican representative Dan Miller in Florida is instructive. When Miller first ran in 1992, he faced five opponents in the Republican primary and a bruising campaign against his Democratic opponent in the general election. In the 1994 election, by contrast, Miller faced only nominal opposition in the Republican primary, winning 81 percent of the vote. In the general election, the strongest potential challenger from the Democratic party decided not to run; the combination of the incumbency advantage coupled with the strongly Republican leanings of

[14]Norman J. Ornstein, Thomas E. Mann, and Michael J. Malbin, *Vital Statistics on Congress, 1995–1996* (Washington, DC: Congressional Quarterly Press 1996), pp. 60–61; Robert S. Erickson and Gerald C. Wright, "Voters, Candidates, and Issues in Congressional Elections," in *Congress Reconsidered,* 5th ed., ed. Lawrence C. Dodd and Bruce I. Oppenheimer (Washington, DC: Congressional Quarterly Press, 1993), p. 99; John R. Alford and David W. Brady, "Personal and Partisan Advantage in U.S. Congressional Elections, 1846–1990," in *Congress Reconsidered,* ed. Dodd and Oppenheimer, pp. 141–57.

[15]See Sara Fritz and Dwight Morris, *Gold-Plated Politics* (Washington, DC: Congressional Quarterly Press, 1992).

FIGURE 5.1

**The Power of Incumbency**

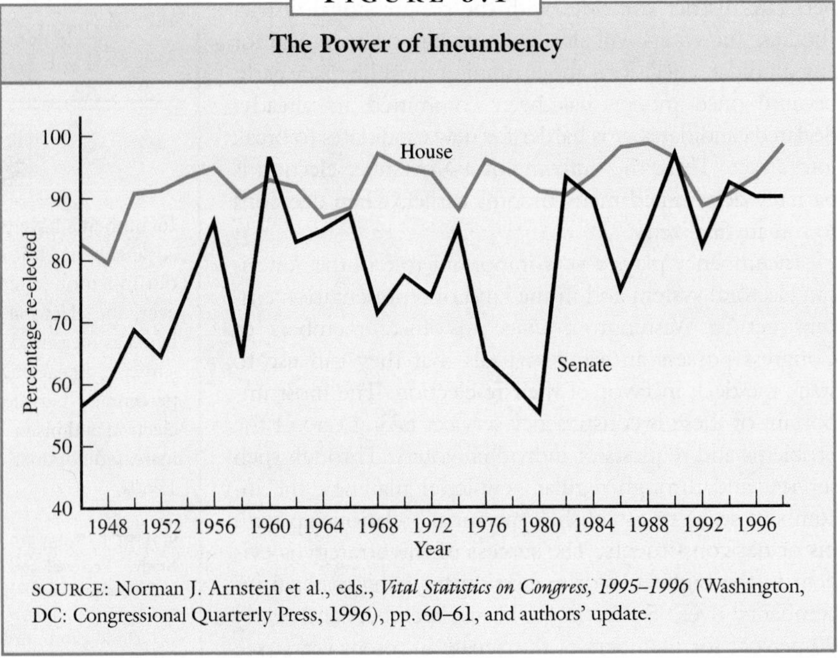


SOURCE: Norman J. Arnstein et al., eds., *Vital Statistics on Congress, 1995–1996* (Washington, DC: Congressional Quarterly Press, 1996), pp. 60–61, and authors' update.

the district gave the Democrats little chance of winning. Miller was re-elected without a challenge.[16]

The advantage of incumbency thus tends to preserve the status quo in Congress by discouraging potentially strong challengers from running. When incumbents do face strong challengers, they are often defeated.[17] For example, in 1998, New York Republican senator Al D'Amato was trounced by former representative Charles Schumer, a strong candidate who was able to raise nearly as much money as D'Amato. The role of incumbency has implications for the social composition of Congress. For example, incumbency advantage makes it harder for women to increase their numbers in Congress because most incumbents are men. Women who run for open seats (for which there are no incumbents) are just as likely to win as male candidates.[18] Supporters of term limits argue that such limits are the only way to get new faces into Congress. They believe that incumbency advantage and the tendency of many legislators to view politics as a career mean that very little turnover will occur in Congress unless limits are imposed on the number of terms a legislator can serve.

[16]Kevin Merida, "The 2nd Time Is Easy; Many House Freshmen Have Secured Seats," *Washington Post,* 18 October 1994, p. A1.

[17]Gary Jacobson, *The Politics of Congressional Elections* (Reading, MA: Addison-Wesley, 1996).

[18]See Burrell, *A Woman's Place Is in the House;* and David Broder, "Key to Women's Political Parity: Running," *Washington Post,* 8 September 1994, p. A17.

But the tendency toward the status quo is not absolute. In recent years, political observers have suggested that the incumbency advantage may be declining. In the 1992 and 1994 elections, for example, voters expressed considerable anger and dissatisfaction with incumbents, producing a 25 percent turnover in the House in 1992 and a 20 percent turnover in 1994. Yet the defeat of incumbents was not the main factor at work in either of these elections; 88.3 percent of House incumbents were re-elected in 1992, and 90.2 percent won re-election in 1994. In 1992, an exceptionally high retirement rate (20 percent, as opposed to the norm of 10 percent) among members of Congress created more open seats, which brought new faces into Congress. In 1994, a large number of open seats combined with an unprecedented mobilization of Republican voters to shift control of Congress to the Republican party. Incumbents fared better in 1996 and 1998, when approximately 95 percent of House and Senate incumbents were re-elected.[19]

The final factor that affects who wins a seat in Congress is the way congressional districts are drawn. Every ten years, state legislatures must redraw congressional districts to reflect population changes. This is a highly political process: districts are shaped to create an advantage for the majority party in the state legislature, which controls the redistricting process. In this complex process, those charged with drawing districts use sophisticated computer technologies to come up with the most favorable district boundaries. Redistricting can create open seats and may pit incumbents of the same party against one another, ensuring that one of them will lose. Redistricting can also give an advantage to one party by clustering voters with some ideological or sociological characteristics in a single district, or by separating those voters into two or more districts. Gerrymandering can have a major impact upon the outcomes of congressional elections. For example, prior to 1980, California House seats had been almost evenly divided between the two parties. After the 1980 census, a redistricting effort controlled by the Democrats, who held both houses of the state legislature as well as the governorship, resulted in Democrats taking control of two-thirds of the state's seats in the U.S. House of Representatives.[20] Examples like this explain why the two parties invest substantial resources in state legislative and gubernatorial contests during the electoral cycle prior to the year that congressional district boundaries will be redrawn.

As we shall see in Chapter 10, since the passage of the 1982 amendments to the 1964 Civil Rights Act, race has become a major—and controversial—consideration in drawing voting districts. These amendments, which encouraged the creation of districts in which members of racial minorities have decisive majorities, have greatly increased the number of minority representatives in Congress. After the 1991–1992 redistricting, the number of predominantly minority districts doubled, rising from twenty-six to fifty-two. Among the most fervent supporters of the new minority districts were white Republicans, who used the

[19]Based on authors' tabulations.

[20]David Butler and Bruce Cain, *Congressional Redistricting* (New York: MacMillan, 1992).

opportunity to create more districts dominated by white Republican voters. These developments raise thorny questions about representation. Some analysts argue that the system may grant minorities greater sociological representation, but it has made it more difficult for minorities to win substantive policy goals.

In 1995, the Supreme Court limited racial redistricting in *Miller v. Johnson,* in which the Court stated that race could not be the predominant factor in creating electoral districts. Yet concerns about redistricting and representation have not disappeared. The distinction between race being a "predominant" factor and its being one factor among many is very hazy. Because the drawing of district boundaries affects incumbents as well as the field of candidates who decide to run for office, it continues to be a key battleground on which political parties fight about the meaning of representation.

## House and Senate: Differences in Representation

The framers of the Constitution provided for a ***bicameral legislature***—that is, a legislative body consisting of two chambers. As we saw in Chapter 2, the framers intended each of these chambers, the House and Senate, to represent a different constituency. Members of the Senate, appointed by state legislatures for six-year terms, were to represent the elite members of society and to be more attuned to the interests of property than of population. Today, members of the House and Senate are elected directly by the people. The 435 members of the House are elected from districts apportioned according to population; the 100 members of the Senate are elected by state, with two senators from each. Senators continue to have much longer terms in office and usually represent much larger and more diverse constituencies than do their counterparts in the House of Representatives (see Table 5.1).

TABLE 5.1

**Differences between the House and the Senate**

| | HOUSE | SENATE |
|---|---|---|
| Minimum age of member | 25 years | 30 years |
| U.S. citizenship | at least 7 years | at least 9 years |
| Length of term | 2 years | 6 years |
| Number per state | Depends on population: 1 per 30,000 in 1789; now 1 per 550,000 | 2 per state |
| Constituency | Tends to be local | Both local and national |

The House and Senate play different roles in the legislative process. In essence, the Senate is the more deliberative of the two bodies—the forum in which any and all ideas can receive a thorough public airing. The House is the more centralized and organized of the two bodies—better equipped to play a routine role in the governmental process. In part, this difference stems from the different rules governing the two bodies. These rules give House leaders more control over the legislative process and provide for House members to specialize in certain legislative areas. The rules of the much-smaller Senate give its leadership relatively little power and discourage specialization.

**AMERICAN POLITICAL DEVELOPMENT**

The differences between the House and the Senate in regard to majority rule and minority rights have been traced to decisions made during the first two decades of the nineteenth century. In 1811, the House adopted a "previous question" rule—it allowed a majority to cut off debate—while the Senate specifically eliminated such a rule in 1806, leaving open the possibility for unlimited debate and the filibuster. These decisions affected subsequent procedural and policy decisions, thus helping to shape the House as a majoritarian institution and the Senate as an institution with greater deference to minority viewpoints.

SOURCE: Sarah A. Binder, *Minority Rights, Majority Rule* (Cambridge: Cambridge University Press, 1997).

Both formal and informal factors contribute to differences between the two chambers of Congress. Differences in the length of terms and requirements for holding office specified by the Constitution in turn generate differences in how members of each body develop their constituencies and exercise their powers of office. The result is that members of the House most effectively and frequently serve as the agents of well-organized local interests with specific legislative agendas—for instance, used-car dealers seeking relief from regulation, labor unions seeking more favorable legislation, or farmers looking for higher subsidies. The small size and relative homogeneity of their constituencies and the frequency with which they must seek re-election make House members more attuned to the legislative needs of local interest groups.

Senators, on the other hand, serve larger and more heterogeneous constituencies. As a result, they are somewhat better able than members of the House to serve as the agents for groups and interests organized on a statewide or national basis. Moreover, with longer terms in office, senators have the luxury of considering "new ideas" or seeking to bring together new coalitions of interests, rather than simply serving existing ones.

In recent years, the House has exhibited considerably more intense partisanship and ideological division than the Senate. Because of their diverse constituencies, senators are more inclined to seek compromise positions that will offend as few voters and interest groups as possible. Members of the House, in contrast, typically represent more homogeneous districts in which their own party is dominant. This situation has tended to make House members less inclined to seek compromises and more willing to stick to partisan and ideological guns than their counterparts in the Senate during the past several decades. For instance, the House divided almost exactly along partisan lines on the 1998 vote to impeach President Clinton. In the Senate, by contrast, ten Republicans joined Democrats to acquit Clinton of obstruction of

justice charges and, in a separate vote, five Republicans joined Democrats to acquit Clinton of perjury.[21]

## THE ORGANIZATION OF CONGRESS

The United States Congress is not only a representative assembly. It is also a legislative body. For Americans, representation and legislation go hand in hand. As we saw earlier, however, many parliamentary bodies are representative without the power to legislate. It is no small achievement that the U.S. Congress both represents *and* governs.

It is extraordinarily difficult for a large, representative assembly to formulate, enact, and implement laws. The internal complexities of conducting business within Congress—the legislative process—alone are daunting. In addition, there are many individuals and institutions that have the capacity to influence the legislative process. For example, legislation to raise the salaries of members of the House of Representatives received input from congressional leaders of both parties, special legislative task forces, the president, the national chairmen of the two major parties, public interest lobbyists, the news media, and the mass public before it became law in 1989. Since successful legislation requires the confluence of so many distinct factors, it is little wonder that most of the thousands of bills considered by Congress each year are defeated long before they reach the president.

Before an idea or proposal can become a law, it must pass through a complex set of organizations and procedures in Congress. Collectively, these are called the policy-making process, or the legislative process. Understanding this process is central to understanding why some ideas and proposals eventually become law while most do not. Although the supporters of legislative proposals often feel that the formal rules of the congressional process are deliberately designed to prevent their own deserving proposals from ever seeing the light of day, these rules allow Congress to play an important role in lawmaking. If it wants to be more than simply a rubber stamp for the executive branch, like so many other representative assemblies around the world, a national legislature like the Congress must develop a division of labor, set an agenda, maintain order through rules and procedures, and place limits on discussion. Equality among the members of Congress must give way to hierarchy—ranking people according to their function within the institution.[22]

[21]Eric Pianin and Guy Gugliotta, "The Bipartisan Challenge: Senate's Search for Accord Marks Contrast to House," *Washington Post,* 8 January 1999, p. 1.

[22]The organization of Congress also facilitates cooperation among its members. Since members of Congress represent diverse constituencies and possess different views and preferences, they have different policy agendas. The hierarchical nature of Congress, reflected in its organization and internal rules and procedures, is necessary to reach a consensus, and thus produce legislation. For more on how institutionalization facilitates cooperation, see Kenneth A. Shepsle and Mark S. Bonchek, *Analyzing Politics: Rationality, Behavior, and Institutions* (New York: W. W. Norton, 1997), pp. 312–16.

To exercise its power to make the law, Congress must first bring about something close to an organizational miracle. We will now examine the organization of Congress and the legislative process, particularly the basic building blocks of congressional organization: political parties, the committee system, congressional staff, the caucuses, and the parliamentary rules of the House and Senate. Each of these factors plays a key role in the organization of Congress and in the process through which Congress formulates and enacts laws. We will then look at other powers Congress has in addition to lawmaking and explore the future role of Congress in relation to the powers of the executive. Once we review the organization and powers of Congress, we can reconnect them to congressional representation to understand the role of Congress in modern America.

## Party Leadership in the House and the Senate

Every two years, at the beginning of a new Congress, the members of each party gather to elect their House leaders. This gathering is traditionally called the ***caucus,*** or conference (by the Republicans). The elected leader of the majority party is later proposed to the whole House and is automatically elected to the position of ***Speaker of the House,*** with voting along straight party lines. The House majority caucus (or conference) then also elects a ***majority leader.*** The minority party goes through the same process and selects the ***minority leader.*** Both parties also elect whips to line up party members on important votes and relay voting information to the leaders.

In December 1998, prior to the opening of the 106th Congress, House Republicans elected Dennis Hastert, a little-known representative from Illinois, to replace Newt Gingrich as Speaker. Gingrich announced he would not be a candidate for the Speakership and would, indeed, resign from Congress in the wake of the GOP's disappointing showing in the 1998 congressional elections (see Chapter 10). Initially it appeared that Gingrich would be succeeded by Appropriations Committee Chairman Robert Livingston of Louisiana. In a surprising turn of events, however, Livingston announced his own resignation after it was revealed that he had engaged in a number of extramarital affairs. After a battle, Richard Armey of Texas was re-elected majority leader. Tom DeLay, also of Texas, was unopposed for re-election as whip. On the Democratic side, Dick Gephardt of Missouri was unopposed for re-election as minority leader, and David Bonior of Michigan won re-election as minority whip without facing any challenge.

Next in order of importance for each party after the Speaker and majority or minority leader are the majority and minority whip, followed by the caucus (Democrats) or conference (Republicans) chairs. Next comes the Committee on Committees (called the Steering and Policy Committee by the Democrats), whose tasks are to assign new legislators to committees and to deal with the requests of incumbent members for transfers from one committee to another. The Speaker serves as chair of the Republican Committee on Committees, while the minority leader chairs the Democratic Steering and Policy Committee. (The Republicans have a sep-

arate Policy Committee.) At one time, party leaders strictly controlled committee assignments, using them to enforce party discipline. Today, representatives expect to receive the assignments they want and resent leadership efforts to control committee assignments. For example, during the 104th Congress (1995–1996) the then-Chairman of the powerful Appropriations Committee, Robert Livingston (R-La.), sought to remove freshman Mark Neumann (R-Wisc.) from the committee because of his lack of party loyalty. The entire Republican freshman class angrily opposed this move and forced the leadership to back down. Not only did Neumann keep his seat on the Appropriations Committee, but he was given a seat on the Budget Committee, as well, to placate the freshmen.[23] The leadership's best opportunities to use committee assignments as rewards and punishments come when a seat on the same committee is sought by more than one member.

Generally, representatives seek assignments that will allow them to influence decisions of special importance to their districts. Representatives from farm districts, for example, may request seats on the Agriculture Committee.[24] Seats on powerful committees such as Ways and Means, which is responsible for tax legislation, and Appropriations are especially popular.

Within the Senate, the president pro tempore exercises mainly ceremonial leadership. Usually, the majority party designates a member with the greatest seniority to serve in this capacity. Real power is in the hands of the majority leader and minority leader, each elected by party caucus. Currently, Trent Lott of Mississippi is majority leader and Tom Daschle of South Dakota serves as minority leader. Together they control the Senate's calendar, or agenda for legislation. In addition, the senators from each party elect a whip. Each party also selects a Policy Committee, which advises the leadership on legislative priorities. The structure of majority party leadership in the House and Senate is shown in Figures 5.2 and 5.3.

In recent years, party leaders have sought to augment their formal powers by reaching outside Congress for resources that might enhance their influence within Congress. One aspect of this external strategy is the increased use of national communications media, including televised speeches and talk show appearances by party leaders. Former Republican House Speaker Newt Gingrich, for example, used television extensively to generate support for his programs among Republican loyalists.[25] As long as it lasted, Gingrich's support among

**AMERICAN POLITICAL DEVELOPMENT**

From the first Congress until the revolt against Speaker Cannon in 1910, the Speaker of the House wielded the greatest influence in making committee assignments. In 1911, that power was transferred to the Committee on Ways and Means for Democrats, where it resided until House reforms of the early 1970s, when it was transferred to the party-dominated Steering and Policy Committee.

SOURCE: Forrest Maltzman, *Competing Principals: Committees, Parties, and the Organization of Congress* (Ann Arbor: University of Michigan Press, 1997), pp. 41–44.

[23]Linda Killian, *The Freshman: What Happened to the Republican Revolution* (Boulder, CO: Westview, 1998).

[24]Richard Fenno, Jr., *Home Style: House Members in Their Districts* (Boston: Little, Brown, 1978).

[25]Douglas Harris, *The Public Speaker* (Ph.D. diss., Johns Hopkins University, 1998).

FIGURE 5.2

**Majority Party Structure in the House of Representatives**

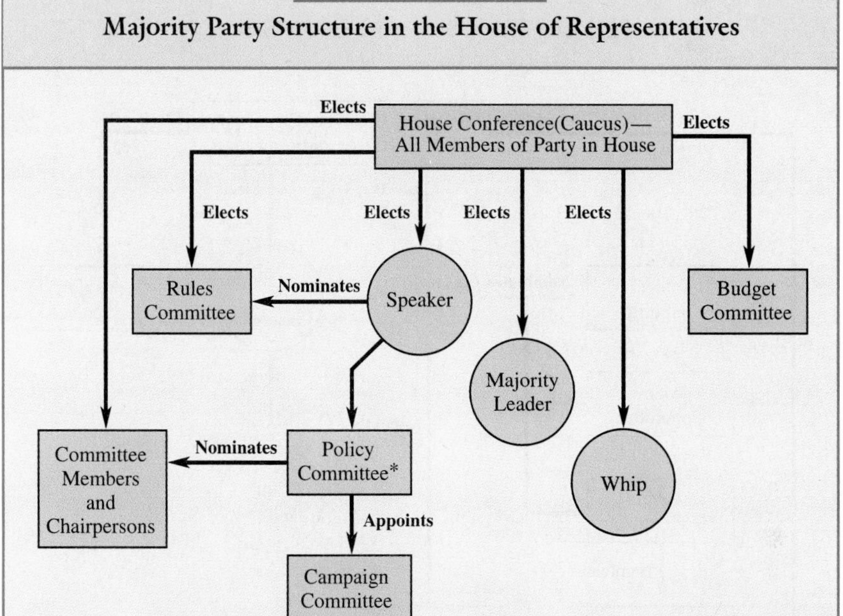


*Incudes Speaker (chair), majority leader, chief and deputy whips, caucus chair, four members appointed by the Speaker, and twelve members elected by regional caucuses.

the Republican rank-and-file gave him an added measure of influence over Republican members of Congress.

A second external strategy involves fund-raising. In recent years, congressional leaders have frequently established their own political action committees. Interest groups are usually eager to contribute to these "leadership PACs" to curry favor with powerful members of Congress. The leaders, in turn, use these funds to support the various campaigns of their party's candidates in order to create a sense of obligation. For example, in the 1998 congressional election, Majority Leader Dick Armey, who was running unopposed, raised more than $6 million, which he distributed to less well-heeled Republican candidates. Armey's generosity served him well in the leadership struggle that erupted after the election.

In addition to the tasks of organizing Congress, congressional party leaders may also seek to establish a legislative agenda. Since the New Deal, presidents have taken the lead in creating legislative agendas (this trend will be discussed in the next chapter). But in recent years congressional leaders, especially when facing a White House controlled by the opposing party, have attempted to devise their own agendas. Democratic leaders of Congress sought to create a common Democratic perspective in

FIGURE 5.3

**Majority Party Structure in the Senate**

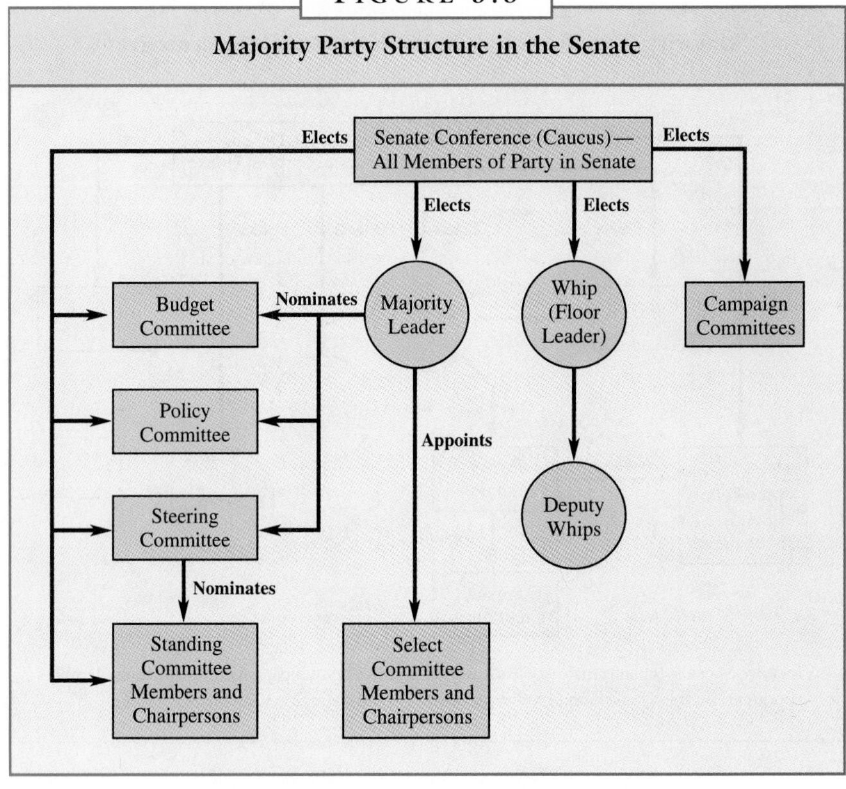


1981 when Ronald Reagan became president. The Republican Congress elected in 1994 expanded on this idea with its "Contract with America." In both cases, the majority party leadership has sought to create a consensus among its congressional members around an overall vision to guide legislative activity and to make individual pieces of legislation part of a bigger picture that is distinct from the agenda of the president.[26]

## The Committee System: The Core of Congress

The committee system provides Congress with its second organizational structure, but it is more a division of labor than a hierarchy of power. Committee and subcommittee chairs have a number of important powers, but their capacity to discipline committee members is limited. Ultimately, committee members are hired and fired by the electorate, not by the leadership.

[26]For a more complete discussion of agenda setting, see Shepsle and Bonchek, *Analyzing Politics,* pp. 386–92, especially pp. 390–91 for an analysis of the agenda-setting power of the Speaker of the House.

Congress had only a few standing committees during the first twenty-five years of its existence. As the national government expanded, however, Congress expanded these committees. The committee system has been reformed, reorganized, and streamlined on several occasions.

Six fundamental characteristics define the congressional committee system:

1. *Each **standing committee** is given a permanent status by the official rules, with a fixed membership, officers, rules, staff, offices, and, above all, a jurisdiction that is recognized by all other committees and usually the leadership as well* (see Table 5.2).
2. *The jurisdiction of each standing committee is defined by the subject matter of legislation.* Except for the House Rules Committee, all the important committees receive proposals for legislation and process them into official bills. The House Rules Committee decides the order in which bills come up for a vote and determines the specific rules that govern the length of debate and opportunity for amendments.
3. *Standing committees' jurisdictions usually parallel those of the major departments or agencies in the executive branch.* There are important exceptions—Appropriations (House and Senate) and Rules (House), for example—but by and large, the division of labor is self-consciously designed to parallel executive branch organization.

TABLE 5.2

**Permanent Committees of Congress**

| HOUSE COMMITTEES | |
|---|---|
| Agriculture | Judiciary |
| Appropriations | National Security |
| Banking and Financial Services | Resources |
| Budget | Rules |
| Commerce | Science |
| Economic and Educational Opportunities | Small Business |
| Government Reform and Oversight | Standards of Official Conduct |
| House Oversight | Transportation and Infrastructure |
| International Relations | Veterans Affairs |
| | Ways and Means |
| **SENATE COMMITTEES** | |
| Agriculture, Nutrition, and Forestry | Finance |
| Appropriations | Foreign Relations |
| Armed Services | Governmental Affairs |
| Banking, Housing, and Urban Affairs | Judiciary |
| Budget | Labor and Human Resources |
| Commerce, Science, and Transportation | Rules and Administration |
| Energy and Natural Resources | Small Business |
| Environment and Public Works | Veterans Affairs |

## AMERICAN POLITICAL DEVELOPMENT

Initially, congressional committee work was done by select rather than standing committees. These early groups would consider one piece of legislation and then disband. The use of standing committees increased during the first half of the nineteenth century: In the first session of the 10th Congress (1807), only 47 percent of bills were referred to standing committees, but by the 18th Congress (1823), 89 percent were referred there.

SOURCE: Gerald Gamm and Kenneth Shepsle, "Emergence of Legislative Institutions: Standing Committees in the House and Senate, 1810–1825," *Legislative Studies Quarterly* 14 (1989), pp. 39–66, esp. p. 51.

4. *Bills are assigned to standing committees on the basis of subject matter, but the Speaker of the House and the Senate's presiding officer have some discretion in the allocation of bills to committees.* Most bills "die in committee"—that is, they are not reported out favorably. Ordinarily this ends a bill's life. There is only one way for a legislative proposal to escape committee processing: A bill passed in one chamber may be permitted to go directly onto the calendar of the other chamber. Even here, however, the bill has received the full committee treatment before passage in the first chamber.
5. *Each standing committee is unique.* No effort is made to compose the membership of any committee to be representative of the total House or Senate membership. In both the House and the Senate, each party has established a Committee on Committees, which determines the committee assignments of new members and of established members who wish to change committees. Ordinarily, members can keep their committee assignments as long as they like.
6. *Each standing committee's hierarchy is based on seniority.* ***Seniority*** is determined by years of continuous service on a particular committee, not years of service in the House or Senate. In general, each committee is chaired by the most senior member of the majority party. Although the power of committee chairs is limited, they help determine hearing schedules, select subcommittee members, and appoint committee staff. Because Congress has a large number of subcommittees and has given each representative a larger staff, the power of committee chairs has been diluted.[27]

Over the years, Congress has reformed its organizational structure and operating procedures. Most changes have been made to improve efficiency, but some reforms have also represented a response to political considerations. In the 1970s, for example, a series of reforms substantially altered the organization of power in Congress. Among the most important changes put into place at that time were an increase in the number of subcommittees; greater autonomy for subcommittee chairs; the opening of most committee deliberations to the public; and a system of multiple referral of bills, which allowed several committees to consider one bill at the same time. One of the driving impulses behind these reforms was an effort to reduce the power of committee chairs. In the past, committee chairs exercised considerable power; they determined hearing schedules, selected subcommittee members, and appointed committee staff. Some chairs used their power to block consideration of bills they opposed. Because of the seniority system, many of the

[27]For a formal analysis of the division of labor among congressional committees and the powers that result, see Shepsle and Bonchek, *Analyzing Politics,* pp. 323–43. In addition to committees' proposal power and after-the-fact authority to bargain with the other chamber and overseeing agencies in the executive branch, Shepsle and Bonchek identify another important component of committee power: the gatekeeping authority to set its own agenda.

key committees were chaired by Southern Democrats who stymied liberal legislation throughout the 1960s and early 1970s. By enhancing subcommittee power and allowing more members to chair subcommittees and appoint subcommittee staff, the reforms undercut the power of committee chairs.

Yet the reforms of the 1970s created new problems for Congress. One of these reforms, the opening of most committee hearings to the public—sometimes called a "sunshine" rule—is frequently criticized by members of Congress. Most members believe that "sunshine" makes deliberation difficult—because members "grandstand" for the TV camera—and renders compromise impossible because rival constituency groups often view any compromise as a betrayal of principle.[28] As a consequence of the reforms, power became more fragmented, making it harder to reach agreement on legislation. With power dissipated over a large number of committees and subcommittees, members spent more time in unproductive "turf battles."[29] In addition, as committees expanded in size, members found they had so many committee meetings that they had to run from meeting to meeting. Thus their ability to specialize in a particular policy area diminished as their responsibilities increased.[30] The Republican leadership of the 104th Congress sought to reverse the fragmentation of congressional power and concentrate more authority in the party leadership. One of the ways the House achieved this was by violating the principle of seniority in the selection of a number of committee chairs. This move tied committee chairs more closely to the leadership. In addition, the Republican leadership eliminated 25 of the House's 115 subcommittees and gave committee chairs more power over their subcommittees. The result was an unusually cohesive congressional majority, which pushed forward a common agenda.

**AMERICAN POLITICAL DEVELOPMENT**

In the 1880s, seniority was more likely to be ignored than followed while selecting committee chairs. By 1897, seniority was a generally accepted principle in selecting a committee chair, and by the 1950s it had become nearly inviolable. It was not until the 1970s' committee reforms that the seniority principle would be weakened.

SOURCE: Nelson W. Polsby, Miriam Gallaher, and Barry Spencer Rundquist, "The Growth of the Seniority System in the U.S. House of Representatives," *American Political Science Review* 63 (1969), pp. 787–807, esp. pp. 792–93.

## The Staff System: Staffers and Agencies

A congressional institution second in importance only to the committee system is the staff system. Every member of Congress employs a large number of staff

[28]See, for example, Dale Bumpers, "How the Sunshine Harmed Congress," *New York Times,* 3 January 1999, p. 9.

[29]See David C. King, *Turf Wars: How Congressional Committees Claim Jurisdiction* (Chicago: University of Chicago Press, 1997).

[30]See Thomas E. Mann and Norman J. Ornstein, *Renewing Congress: A First Report of the Renewing Congress Project* (Washington, DC: American Enterprise Institute and Brookings Institution, 1992). See also the essays in Roger H. Davidson, ed., *The Postreform Congress* (New York: St. Martin's, 1992).

members, whose tasks include handling constituency requests and, to a large and growing extent, dealing with legislative details and the activities of administrative agencies. Increasingly, staffers bear the primary responsibility for formulating and drafting proposals, organizing hearings, dealing with administrative agencies, and negotiating with lobbyists. Indeed, legislators typically deal with one another through staff, rather than through direct, personal contact. Representatives and senators together employ nearly eleven thousand staffers in their Washington and home offices. Today, staffers even develop policy ideas, draft legislation, and in some instances, have a good deal of influence over the legislative process.

In addition to the personal staffs of individual senators and representatives, Congress also employs roughly two thousand committee staffers. These individuals comprise the permanent staff, who stay regardless of turnover in Congress and are attached to every House and Senate committee. They are responsible for organizing and administering the committee's work, including research, scheduling, organizing hearings, and drafting legislation. Congressional staffers can come to play key roles in the legislative process. One example of the importance of congressional staffers is the so-called Gephardt health care reform bill, named for the then-House majority leader, Richard Gephardt of Missouri, and introduced in August 1994. Though the bill bore Gephardt's name, it was actually crafted by a small group of staff members of the House Ways and Means Committee. These aides, under the direction of David Abernathy, the staff's leading health care specialist, debated methods of cost control, service delivery, the role of the insurance industry, and the needs of patients, and listened to hundreds of lobbyists before drafting the complex Gephardt bill.[31]

**AMERICAN POLITICAL DEVELOPMENT**

In 1930, the House employed 870 staff members while the Senate employed 280. In 1993, the House employed 7,400 and the Senate employed 4,138.

SOURCE: Norman J. Ornstein, Thomas E. Mann, and Michael J. Malbin, *Vital Statistics of Congress, 1995–1996* (Washington, DC: Congressional Quarterly Press 1996), p. 133.

The number of congressional staff members grew rapidly during the 1960s and 1970s, leveled off in the 1980s, and decreased dramatically in 1995. This sudden drop fulfilled the Republican congressional candidates' 1994 campaign promise to reduce the size of committee staffs.

Not only does Congress employ personal and committee staff, but it has also established three ***staff agencies*** designed to provide the legislative branch with resources and expertise independent of the executive branch. These agencies enhance Congress's capacity to oversee administrative agencies and to evaluate presidential programs and proposals. They are the Congressional Research Service, which performs research for legislators who wish to know the facts and competing arguments relevant to policy proposals or other legislative business; the General Accounting Office, through which Congress can investigate the financial and administrative affairs of any government agency or pro-

[31]Robert Pear, "With Long Hours and Little Fanfare, Staff Members Crafted a Health Bill," *New York Times,* 6 August 1994, p. 7.

gram; and the Congressional Budget Office, which assesses the economic implications and likely costs of proposed federal programs, such as health care reform proposals. A fourth agency, the Office of Technology Assessment, which provided Congress with analyses of scientific or technical issues, was abolished in 1995.

## Informal Organization: The Caucuses

In addition to the official organization of Congress, there also exists an unofficial organizational structure—the caucuses, formally known as legislative service organizations (LSOs). ***Caucuses*** are groups of senators or representatives who share certain opinions, interests, or social characteristics. They include ideological caucuses such as the liberal Democratic Study Group, the conservative Democratic Forum (popularly known as the "boll weevils"), and the moderate Republican Wednesday Group. At the same time, there are a large number of caucuses composed of legislators representing particular economic or policy interests, such as the Travel and Tourism Caucus, the Steel Caucus, the Mushroom Caucus, and the Concerned Senators for the Arts. Legislators who share common backgrounds or social characteristics have organized caucuses such as the Congressional Black Caucus, the Congressional Caucus for Women's Issues, and the Hispanic Caucus. All these caucuses seek to advance the interests of the groups they represent by promoting legislation, encouraging Congress to hold hearings, and pressing administrative agencies for favorable treatment. The Congressional Black Caucus, for example, which included forty representatives and one senator in 1996, has played an active role in Congress since 1970.

Before 1995, many of the largest and most effective caucuses were registered as Legislative Service Organizations (LSOs). LSOs were allotted office space in congressional buildings and congressional members were allowed to transfer some of their own budgets to the LSO. Several of the most effective LSOs, including the Black Caucus, the Hispanic Caucus, and the Women's Caucus, were closely tied to the Democratic party. One LSO, the Democratic Study Group, once employed eighteen full-time analysts to help congressional Democrats evaluate proposed and pending legislation. The Republican leadership of the 104th Congress (1995–1996) took away the budgets, staff, and offices of all LSOs, in part because of these large LSOs' links to the Democrats.[32] But most caucuses continued their activities, and new ones were created after this change. Of course, some of the larger caucuses found it harder to coordinate their activities and provide information to their members after they lost their status as LSOs, but caucuses continue to be an important part of congressional organization.[33]

[32]Kenneth Cooper, "GOP Moves to Restrict Office Funds," *Washington Post,* 7 December 1994, p. 1.

[33]Susan Webb Hammond, "Congressional Caucuses in the 104th Congress," in *Congress Reconsidered,* 6th ed., ed. Lawrence C. Dodd and Bruce I. Oppenheimer (Washington, DC: Congressional Quarterly Press, 1997).

ANALYZING AMERICAN POLITICS

## *Congressional Committees and Their Sources of Power*

Among political scientists, one of the most important debates on Congress concerns the roles of committees and the issue of committee power. Though there seems to be widespread agreement that committees play important roles and have substantial influence over the legislative process, there has also been considerable debate over what exactly the roles of committees are and what their source of power is. Two seemingly conflicting viewpoints have emerged: the ***distributive perspective*** and the ***informational perspective***.[1] Both deal with committees as institutions for collective decision-making. And both perspectives argue that committees are designed to solve problems that allow members to profit from cooperation.

The distributive perspective argues that the committee system serves as a mechanism for apportioning benefits to members' districts, which then helps the member get reelected. Yet members may want to deliver different types of benefits to their constituents. For example, members from agricultural districts may want to deliver farm subsidies to their constituents, while members from urban districts want to deliver subsidies for public transportation. But in order to deliver these services, members must pass legislation that provides these benefits. As a bargaining chip, legislators can exchange votes, or *logroll:* Urban representatives agree to vote for legislation that provides agricultural subsidies (even though their constituents do not benefit and may even be marginally hurt by such subsidies) in exchange for agricultural representatives' votes on public transportation subsidies. Thus both types of legislators realize gains from exchanging votes. But what is to prevent urban representatives from trying to renege on this logrolling deal and revoke the subsidies that benefit agricultural areas after new subways are built and new buses are bought?

The committee system helps prevent this. Committees have well-defined and exclusive jurisdictions over particular policies—e.g., the House Agriculture

---

[1]A third perspective known as the partisan perspective will not be discussed here due to space limitations. See Gary Cox and Mathew McCubbins, Legislative Leviathan (Berkeley: University of California Press, 1993).

Committee has exclusive jurisdiction over farm subsidies. This means that all farm policy legislation introduced in the House will be referred to the Agriculture Committee first, before it goes to the whole chamber. Committees also have gatekeeping power—i.e., by refusing to let legislation come up for vote in the chamber, they can prevent it from passing. Distributive models assume that members select themselves to committees in order to have jurisdictions over the policies their constituents care most about. These members can then effectively block others from passing legislation that might hurt their interests. For example, legislation introduced that proposed to revoke agricultural subsidies would be referred to the Agricultural Committee, and presumably the pro-farmer members of the committee would kill that legislation. Thus committee power comes from the authority that committees have to protect their own interests.

The informational perspective takes a different view of the role of committees and committee power. Rather than seeing committees as mechanisms for the distribution of legislative goodies, they see committees as mechanisms for producing policy-relevant information. Informational models assume that legislators benefit when they are provided with facts that will reduce their uncertainty about what effects particular policies might have on their constituents. The function of committees is first to acquire this kind of information and then to share it with the rest of the chamber.

But in order for committees to perform this function, their members must be sure that gathering and sharing information will not hurt their interests. Because committee members are often reluctant to share information, noncommittee members—collectively referred to as "the floor" in these models—may be dubious about the information the committee communicates. Let us continue with the agriculture policy example: If members of the Agriculture Committee argue that Congress should pass higher subsidies because otherwise there will be grave food shortages, should the floor believe them because the committee has superior information, or should the floor be concerned that the committee is just trying to deceive them to get more benefits for their constituents?

Informational models show how institutional arrangements solve these problems and promote informative communication between committees and the rest of the chamber. One of the main institutional arrangements for considering legislation are *committee assignments*. In order to promote informative communication, members should make assignments to a committee so that it becomes a microcosm of the larger chamber's policy preferences. The floor will be more willing to trust the committee's information if the committee has the same preferences as the floor. This stands in stark contrast to the way the distributive perspective contends committee assignments should be made. If members were allowed to self-select, committees' preferences would be dramatically different from those of the floor, which would inhibit informative communication.

## Rules of Lawmaking: How a Bill Becomes a Law

The institutional structure of Congress is one key factor that helps to shape the legislative process. A second and equally important set of factors are the rules of congressional procedures. These rules govern everything from the introduction of a bill through its submission to the president for signing. Not only do these regulations influence the fate of each and every bill, they also help to determine the distribution of power in the Congress.

### Committee Deliberation

Even if a member of Congress, the White House, or a federal agency has spent months developing and drafting a piece of legislation, it does not become a bill until it is submitted officially by a senator or representative to the clerk of the House or Senate and referred to the appropriate committee for deliberation. No floor action on any bill can take place until the committee with jurisdiction over it has taken all the time it needs to deliberate. During the course of its deliberations, the committee typically refers the bill to one of its subcommittees, which may hold hearings, listen to expert testimony, and amend the proposed legislation before referring it to the full committee for its consideration. The full committee may accept the recommendation of the subcommittee or hold its own hearings and prepare its own amendments. Or, even more frequently, the committee and subcommittee may do little or nothing with a bill that has been submitted to them. Many bills are simply allowed to "die in committee" with little or no serious consideration given to them. Often, members of Congress introduce legislation that they neither expect nor desire to see enacted into law, merely to please a constituency group. These bills die a quick and painless death. Other pieces of legislation have ardent supporters and die in committee only after a long battle. But, in either case, most bills are never reported out of the committees to which they are assigned. In a typical congressional session, 95 percent of the roughly eight thousand bills introduced die in committee—an indication of the power of the congressional committee system.

The relative handful of bills that are reported out of the committee to which they were originally referred must, in the House, pass one additional hurdle within the committee system—the Rules Committee. This powerful committee determines the rules that will govern action on the bill on the House floor. In particular, the Rules Committee allots the time for debate and decides to what extent amendments to the bill can be proposed from the floor. A bill's supporters generally prefer what is called a ***closed rule,*** which puts severe limits on floor debate and amendments. Opponents of a bill usually prefer an "open rule," which permits potentially damaging floor debate and makes it easier to add amendments that may cripple the bill or weaken its chances for passage. Thus, the outcome of the Rules Committee's deliberations can be extremely important, and the committee's hearings can be an occasion for sharp conflicts.

## Debate

Party control of the agenda is reinforced by the rule giving the Speaker of the House and the majority leader of the Senate the power of recognition during debate on a bill. Usually the chair knows the purpose for which a member intends to speak well in advance of the occasion. Spontaneous efforts to gain recognition are often foiled. For example, the Speaker may ask, "For what purpose does the member rise?" before deciding whether to grant recognition. In general, the party leadership in the House has total control over debate. In the Senate, each member has substantial power to block debate. This is one reason that the Senate tends to be a less partisan body than the House. A House majority can override opposition, while a majority in the Senate must still accommodate the views of other members.

In the House, virtually all of the time allotted by the Rules Committee for debate on a given bill is controlled by the bill's sponsor and by its leading opponent. In almost every case, these two people are the committee chair and the ranking minority member of the committee that processed the bill—or those they designate. These two participants are, by rule and tradition, granted the power to allocate most of the debate time in small amounts to members who are seeking to speak for or against the measure. Preference in the allocation of time goes to the members of the committee whose jurisdiction covers the bill.

In the Senate, other than the power of recognition, the leadership has much less control over floor debate. Indeed, the Senate is unique among the world's legislative bodies for its commitment to unlimited debate. Once given the floor, a senator may speak as long as he or she wishes. On a number of memorable occasions, senators have used this right to prevent action on legislation that they opposed. Through this tactic, called the ***filibuster***, small minorities or even one individual in the Senate can force the majority to give in to their demands. During the 1950s and 1960s, for example, opponents of civil rights legislation often sought to block its passage by adopting the tactic of filibuster. The votes of three-fifths of the Senate, or sixty votes, are needed to end a filibuster. This procedure is called ***cloture.***

Whereas the filibuster was once an extraordinary tactic used only on rare occasions, in recent years it has been used increasingly often. In 1994, the filibuster was used by Republicans and some Democrats to defeat legislation that would have prohibited employers from permanently replacing striking workers. Later, Republicans threatened to filibuster health care reform legislation. Some Democrats argued that Senate Republicans had begun to use the filibuster as a routine instrument of legislative obstructionism to make up for their minority status in Congress, and proposed rule changes that would make filibustering more difficult. One of the most senior Democrats in the Senate, however, former majority leader Robert Byrd of West Virginia, warned against limiting the filibuster,

### AMERICAN POLITICAL DEVELOPMENT

From 1919 to 1971, there were never more than seven attempts at cloture in a Congress. In only one Congress was there more than one successful attempt. From 1973 through 1994, however, clotures were attempted an average of 28.3 times per Congress, and there was an average of 11.1 successful clotures per Congress.

SOURCE: Norman J. Ornstein, Thomas E. Mann, and Michael J. Malbin, *Vital Statistics of Congress, 1995–1996* (Washington, DC: Congressional Quarterly Press, 1996), p. 169.

saying, "The minority can be right, and on many occasions in this country's history, the minority was right."[34] After the GOP won control of the Senate in 1994, many Democrats began to agree with Senator Byrd. Democrats employed the filibuster to block Republican initiatives on environmental and social policy. Similarly, a Republican-led filibuster in 1998 killed campaign finance reform legislation.

Although it is the best known, the filibuster is not the only technique used to block Senate debate. Under Senate rules, members have a virtually unlimited ability to propose amendments to a pending bill. Each amendment must be voted on before the bill can come to a final vote. The introduction of new amendments can only be stopped by unanimous consent. This, in effect, can permit a determined minority to filibuster-by-amendment, indefinitely delaying the passage of a bill.

In 1996, for example, an anti-stalking bill sponsored by Senator Kay Bailey Hutchison (R-Tex.) was delayed by Senator Frank Lautenberg's (D-N.J.) effort to attach an amendment prohibiting individuals convicted of domestic violence from purchasing or possessing a handgun. Lautenberg's proposal had been opposed by the powerful National Rifle Association and had little chance of reaching the floor on its own. By offering his proposal as an amendment, Lautenberg was effectively holding the popular anti-stalking bill hostage to obtain a vote on his proposal.[35]

Senators can also place "holds," or stalling devices, on bills to delay debate. Senators place holds on bills when they fear that openly opposing them will be unpopular. Because holds are kept secret, the senators placing the holds do not have to take public responsibility for their actions. For example, Senator John Chafee (R-R.I.) was widely believed to be responsible for a 1996 hold on a bill imposing sanctions against foreign companies that engaged in business with Iran and Libya. Chafee's office refused to confirm or deny the speculation.[36]

Once a bill is debated on the floor of the House and the Senate, the leaders schedule it for a vote on the floor of each chamber. By this time, congressional leaders know what the vote will be; leaders do not bring legislation to the floor unless they are fairly certain it is going to pass. As a consequence, it is unusual for the leadership to lose a bill on the floor. On rare occasions, the last moments of the floor vote can be very dramatic, as each party's leadership puts its whip organization into action to make sure that wavering members vote with the party.

## Conference Committee: Reconciling House and Senate Versions of a Bill

Getting a bill out of committee and through one of the houses of Congress is no guarantee that a bill will be enacted into law. Frequently, bills that began with similar provisions in both chambers emerge with little resemblance to each other.

[34]Richard Sammon, "Panel Backs Senate Changes, But Fights Loom for Floor," *Congressional Quarterly Weekly Report,* 18 June 1994, pp. 1575–76.

[35]Stephen Green, "Anti-Stalking Bill Falls Victim to Gun Control Politics," *San Diego Union-Tribune,* 24 July 1996, p. A2.

[36]Kimberley Music, "Iran/Libya Bill Remains Stalled in Senate," *Oil Daily,* vol. 46, no. 131, 12 July 1996, p. 1.

PROCESS BOX 5.2

## How a Bill Becomes a Law

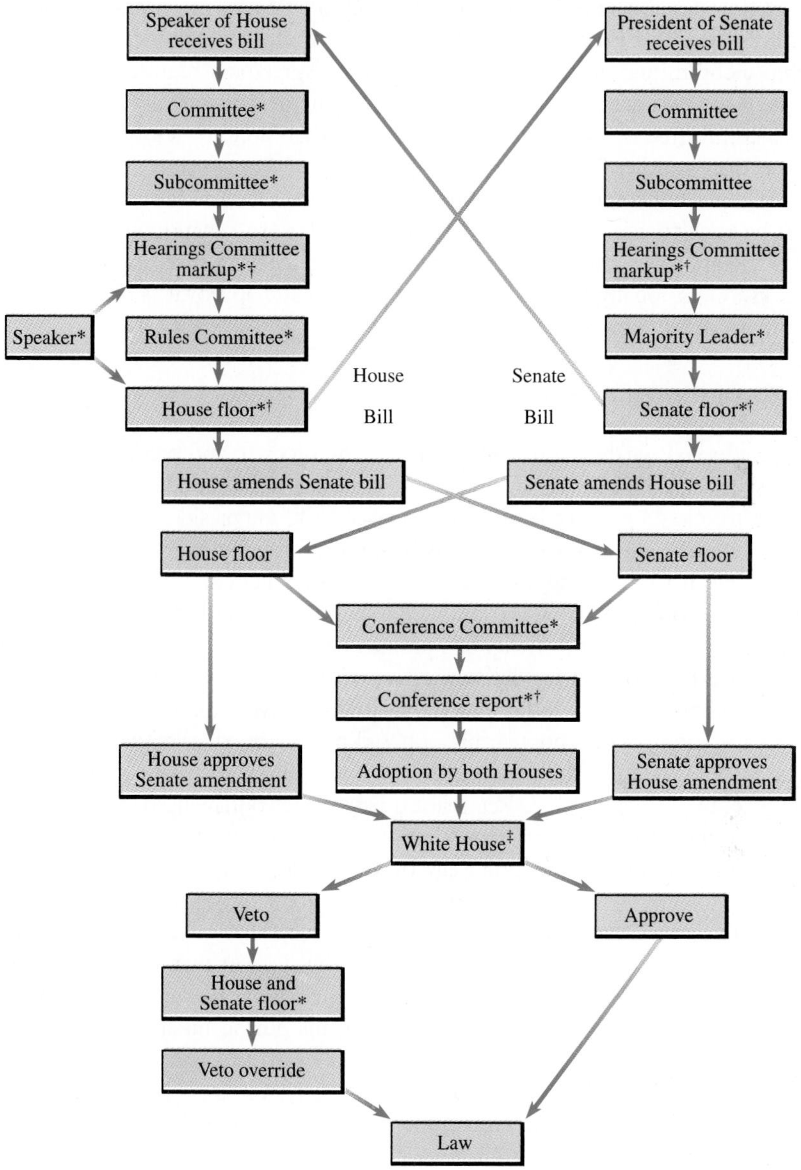

Speaker of House receives bill
Committee*
Subcommittee*
Hearings Committee markup*†
Speaker*
Rules Committee*
House floor*†

President of Senate receives bill
Committee
Subcommittee
Hearings Committee markup*†
Majority Leader*
Senate floor*†

House Bill
Senate Bill

House amends Senate bill
Senate amends House bill
House floor
Senate floor
Conference Committee*
Conference report*†
House approves Senate amendment
Adoption by both Houses
Senate approves House amendment
White House‡
Veto
Approve
House and Senate floor*
Veto override
Law

*Points at which bill can be amended.
†Points at which bill can die.
‡If the president neither signs nor vetoes the bill within ten days, it automatically becomes law.

Alternatively, a bill may be passed by one chamber but undergo substantial revision in the other chamber. In such cases, a conference committee composed of the senior members of the committees or subcommittees that initiated the bills may be required to iron out differences between the two pieces of legislation. Sometimes members or leaders will let objectionable provisions pass on the floor with the idea that they will get the change they want in conference. Usually, conference committees meet behind closed doors. Agreement requires a majority of each of the two delegations. Legislation that emerges successfully from a conference committee is more often a compromise than a clear victory of one set of forces over another.

When a bill comes out of conference, it faces one more hurdle. Before a bill can be sent to the president for signing, the House-Senate conference report must be approved on the floor of each chamber. Usually such approval is given quickly. Occasionally, however, a bill's opponents use approval as one last opportunity to defeat a piece of legislation.

## Presidential Action

Once adopted by the House and Senate, a bill goes to the president, who may choose to sign the bill into law or ***veto*** it. The veto is the president's constitutional power to reject a piece of legislation. To veto a bill, the president returns it within ten days to the house of Congress in which it originated, along with his objections to the bill. If Congress adjourns during the ten-day period, and the president has taken no action, the bill is also considered to be vetoed. This latter method is known as the ***pocket veto.*** The possibility of a presidential veto affects how willing members of Congress are to push for different pieces of legislation at different times. If they think a proposal is likely to be vetoed they might shelve it for a later time. Alternatively, the sponsors of a popular bill opposed by the president might push for passage in order to force the president to pay the political costs of vetoing it.[37] For example, in 1996 and 1997, Republicans passed bills outlawing partial-birth abortions though they knew President Clinton would veto them. The GOP calculated that Clinton would be hurt politically by vetoing legislation that most Americans favored.

A presidential veto may be overridden by a two-thirds vote in both the House and Senate. A veto override says much about the support that a president can expect from Congress, and it can deliver a stinging blow to the executive branch. Bush used his veto power on forty-six occasions during his four years in office and, in all but one instance, was able to defeat or avoid a congressional override of his action. Bush's frequent resort to the veto power was one indicator of the struggle between the White House and the Congress over domestic and foreign policy that took place during his term. Similarly, President Clinton used the veto to block Republican programs in 1995 and 1996. For example, in May 1996, President Clinton vetoed a Republican bill that would have placed limits on the punitive damages that could be awarded in product liability suits. The bill was supported by business groups and opposed by consumer groups and trial

[37]John Gilmour, *Strategic Disagreement* (Pittsburgh: University of Pittsburgh Press, 1995).

lawyers. Republicans charged that Clinton's veto was a pay-off to the trial lawyers, who are major contributors to the Democratic party.

The president's veto power is provided in Article I, Section 7 of the Constitution. In 1996, as part of the Republicans' "Contract with America," Congress granted the president a line-item veto, which allows the president to eliminate such earmarks from bills presented to the White House for signature. Republican leaders were willing to risk giving such a powerful tool to a Democratic president because they calculated that, over the decades of Democratic congresses, the GOP had learned to live without much pork, while Democrats had become dependent upon pork to solidify their electoral support. Republican leaders also hoped that a future Republican president, wielding the line-item veto, would be able to further undermine Democratic political strength. President Clinton used the line-item veto eleven times, eliminating eighty-two individual spending items. But in 1998 the Supreme Court struck down the line-item veto on the grounds that the Constitution does not give the president the power to amend or repeal parts of statutes.[38]

## How Congress Decides

What determines the kinds of legislation that Congress ultimately produces? According to the most simple theories of representation, members of Congress would respond to the views of their constituents. In fact, the process of creating a legislative agenda, drawing up a list of possible measures, and deciding among them is a very complex process, in which a variety of influences from inside and outside government play important roles. External influences include a legislator's constituency and various interest groups. Influences from inside government include party leadership, congressional colleagues, and the president. Let us examine each of these influences individually and then consider how they interact to produce congressional policy decisions.

### Constituency

Because members of Congress, for the most part, want to be re-elected, we would expect the views of their constituents to have a key influence on the decisions that legislators make. Yet constituency influence is not so straightforward. In fact, most constituents do not even know what policies their representatives support. The number of citizens who *do* pay attention to such matters—the attentive public—is usually very small. Nonetheless, members of Congress spend a lot of time worrying about what their constituents think, because these representatives realize that the choices they make may be scrutinized in a future election and used as ammunition by an opposing candidate. Because of this possibility, members of Congress will try to anticipate their constituents' policy views.[39]

[38]Clinton v. City of New York, 118 S.Ct. 2091 (1998).

[39]See John W. Kingdon, *Congressmen's Voting Decisions* (New York: Harper Row, 1973), Chapter 3; and R. Douglas Arnold, *The Logic of Congressional Action* (New Haven: Yale University Press, 1990).

DEBATING THE ISSUES

## The Pork Barrel: Government Waste or Good Politics?

*Many Americans consider the pork barrel a symbol of government's wasteful spending. The term "pork" implies a fat, slothful beast that consumes prodigiously and wallows in the muck. Over the past ten years, hundreds of newspaper and magazine articles have criticized the government's economic indulgence and inefficiency. The editorial below from the* Christian Science Monitor *is just one example of a common refrain that seems to be shared by the public at large: Is pork barrel really necessary? Before answering this question, one must remember that there is another side to the issue—that one person's pork is another person' s bacon. In fact, "bringing home the bacon" has been the aim of members of Congress since 1789. According to political scientist R. Douglas Arnold, pork barrel spending has relatively little effect on the government's overall budget. But it is politically important because gratitude by the constituents turns into votes for their members of Congress. The pork barrel has another important political benefit, as the political scientists John W. Ellwood and Eric M. Patashnik argue below: It makes governing possible.*

### CHRISTIAN SCIENCE MONITOR

. . . beneath the surface, some things never change. Take, for example, legislators' desire to earmark a little federal funding for the folks back home.

The pork barrel's still full, as those most determined to empty it, such as Sen. John McCain (R) of Arizona, point out. The senator is one Republican who's trying to remain true to his party's call for less federal spending. But many GOP loyalists see the garnering of projects for their districts as part of the job description. No different from Democrats in that regard.

One of the few bulwarks of bipartisanship is the readiness on all sides to make room for that special item that will bring a smile to constituents.

But there are a few who try to sniff out the pork and, at the least, expose it to public view. McCain's staff, for example, found $607 million worth of earmarked projects in the 1999 Veterans Affairs and Housing and Urban Development appropriations bill—hospitals, waste disposal plants, and other items.

What makes these items suspect, says the senator, quoted in *Congressional Quarterly Weekly,* is their distance from any "merit-based prioritization process." They are products of legislative opportunism, not deliberation. Overall, earmarked special projects account for about 2 percent of federal discretionary spending, as much as $15 billion a year.

Some of these projects may be worthwhile. If so, why not use the normal legislative process? The answer to that, sadly, is that pork-barrel add-ons are the norm. A cheer for those who want to change that.[1]

### ELLWOOD AND PATASHNIK

We believe in pork not because every new dam or overpass deserves to be funded, nor because we consider pork an appropriate instrument of fiscal policy (there are more efficient ways of stimulating a $5 trillion economy). Rather, we think that pork, doled out strategically, can help to sweeten an otherwise unpalatable piece of legislation.

No bill tastes so bitter to the average member of Congress as one that raises taxes or cuts popular programs. Any credible deficit-reduction package will almost certainly have to do both. In exchange for an increase in pork barrel spending, however, members of Congress just might be willing to bite the bullet and make the politically difficult decisions that will be required if the federal deficit is ever to be brought under control.

In a perfect world it would not be necessary to bribe elected officials to perform their jobs well. But, as James Madison pointed out two centuries ago in *Federalist* 51, men are not angels and we do not live in a perfect world. The object of government is therefore not to suppress the imperfections of human nature, which would be futile, but rather to harness the pursuit of self-interest to public ends.

Unfortunately, in the debate over how to reduce the deficit, Madison's advice has all too often gone ignored. Indeed, if there is anything the major budget-reform proposals of the last decade (Gramm-Rudman, the balanced-budget amendment, and entitlement cap) have in common, it is that in seeking to impose artificial limits on government spending without offering anything in return, they work against the electoral interests of congressmen instead of with them—which is why these reforms have been so vigorously resisted.

No reasonable observer would argue that pork barrel spending has always been employed as a force for good or that there are no pork projects that would have been better left unbuilt. But singling out pork as the culprit for our fiscal troubles directs attention away from the largest sources of budgetary growth and contributes to the illusion that the budget can be balanced simply by eliminating waste and abuse. While proposals to achieve a pork-free budget are not without superficial appeal, they risk depriving leaders trying to enact real deficit-reduction measures of one of the most effective coalition-building tools at their disposal.[2]

[1]*Christian Science Monitor*, "Perennial Pork," 4 September 1998.

[2]John W. Ellwood and Eric M. Patashnik, "In Praise of Pork," *Public Interest* (Winter 1993), pp. 19–33.

Legislators are more likely to act in accordance with those views if they think that voters will take them into account during elections. In this way, constituents may affect congressional policy choices even when there is little direct evidence of their influence.

## Interest Groups

Interest groups are another important external influence on the policies that Congress produces. When members of Congress are making voting decisions, those interest groups that have some connection to constituents in particular members' districts are most likely to be influential. For this reason, interest groups with the ability to mobilize followers in many congressional districts may be especially influential in Congress. The small-business lobby, for example, played an important role in defeating President Clinton's proposal for comprehensive health care reform in 1993–1994. The mobilization of networks of small businesses across the country meant that virtually every member of Congress had to take their views into account. In recent years, Washington-based interest groups with little grassroots strength have recognized the importance of such locally generated activity. They have, accordingly, sought to simulate grassroots pressure, using a strategy that has been nicknamed "Astroturf lobbying." Such campaigns encourage constituents to sign form letters or postcards, which are then sent to congressional representatives. Sophisticated "grassroots" campaigns set up toll-free telephone numbers for a system in which simply reporting your name and address to the listening computer will generate a letter to your congressional representative. One Senate office estimated that such organized campaigns to demonstrate "grassroots" support account for two-thirds of the mail the office received. As such campaigns increase, however, they may become less influential, because members of Congress are aware of how rare actual constituent interest actually is.[40]

Interest groups also have substantial influence in setting the legislative agenda and in helping to craft specific language in legislation. Today, sophisticated lobbyists win influence by providing information about policies to busy members of Congress. As one lobbyist noted, "You can't get access without knowledge. . . . I can go in to see [former Energy and Commerce Committee chair] John Dingell, but if I have nothing to offer or nothing to say, he's not going to want to see me."[41] In recent years, interest groups have also begun to build broader coalitions and comprehensive campaigns around particular policy issues. These coalitions do not rise from the grassroots, but instead are put together by Washington lobbyists who launch comprehensive lobbying campaigns that combine stimulated grassroots activity with information and campaign funding for members of Congress. In recent years, the Republican leadership worked so closely with lobbyists that critics charged that the boundaries between lobbyists and legislators had been erased, and that lobbyists had become "adjunct staff to the Republican leadership."[42]

## Party Discipline

In both the House and Senate, party leaders have a good deal of influence over the behavior of their party members. This influence, sometimes called "party discipline," was once so powerful that it dominated the lawmaking process. At the turn of the century, party leaders could often command the allegiance of more than 90 percent of their members. A vote on which 50 percent or more of the members of one party take one position while at least 50 percent of the members of the other party take the opposing position is called a ***party vote.*** At the beginning of the twentieth century, most ***roll-call votes*** in the House of Representatives were party votes. Today, this type of party-line voting is less common in Congress.

[40] Jane Fritsch, "The Grass Roots, Just a Free Phone Call Away," *New York Times,* 23 June 1995, p. A1.

[41] Daniel Franklin, "Tommy Boggs and the Death of Health Care Reform," *Washington Monthly,* April 1995, p. 36.

[42] Peter H. Stone, "Follow the Leaders," *National Journal,* 24 June 1995, p. 1641.

Typically, party unity is greater in the House than in the Senate. House rules grant greater procedural control of business to the majority party leaders, which gives them more influence over House members. In the Senate, however, the leadership has few sanctions over its members. Senate Minority Leader Tom Daschle once observed that a Senate leader seeking to influence other senators has as incentives "a bushel full of carrots and a few twigs."[43]

Party unity increased somewhat in recent sessions of Congress as a result of the intense partisan struggles that began during the Reagan and Bush years (see Figure 5.4). Straight party-line voting was seen briefly in the 103rd Congress (1993–1994) following Bill Clinton's election in 1992. The situation, however, soon gave way to the many long-term factors working against party discipline in the United States.[44]

After being named Speaker of the House, Gingrich sought to maintain Republican party unity behind a series of legislative proposals dubbed the "Contract with America." Among other things, this contract called for tax and spending cuts, a balanced budget amendment, civil litigation reforms, and congressional term limits. In 1995, at the beginning of the first session of the 104th Congress, Gingrich was able to secure the support of virtually all House Republicans for elements of the GOP "Contract." As the session wore on, party unity diminished, particularly on the issue of tax cuts, which divided Republican "deficit hawks" from "supply siders" seeking tax cuts.

The GOP's offensive against social programs initially produced high levels of Democratic party unity in both the House and Senate. By March 1995, however, some conservative Democrats had begun to break ranks. On the whole, there was more party unity in the House during 1995 than in any year since 1954 (see Figure 5.4). By 1996, the level of party unity was back to average. The Republicans who were newly elected in 1994 voted in near lock-step during 1995, but in 1996 they faced re-election and an electorate angry about the partisan gridlock that had produced a partial shutdown of the federal government at the end of 1995. The Republicans' caution resulted in a decline in party unity, which persisted into the 105th Congress in 1997. Party voting was back up in 1998. The differences between the two parties were perhaps best reflected by the intense partisanship shown during President Clinton's impeachment.

To some extent, party unity is based on ideology and background. Republican

**AMERICAN POLITICAL DEVELOPMENT**

Party discipline (when 90 percent of one party votes against 90 percent of the other) has generally declined throughout the twentieth century. In the fifteen Congresses between 1887 and 1917, there were twelve Congresses in which over one in five votes had 90 percent of Republicans voting against 90 percent of Democrats. In only one Congress from 1917 to 1969 has this level of partisanship been met—the first two years of Franklin Roosevelt's New Deal. Indeed, after 1950, the level of 90 percent versus 90 percent party voting never reached 10 percent.

SOURCE: Joseph Cooper, David W. Brady, and Patricia Hurley, "The Electoral Basis of Party Voting: Patterns and Trends in the U.S. House of Representatives, 1887–1969," in *The Impact of the Electoral Process,* ed. Louis Maisel and Joseph Cooper (Beverly Hills, CA: Sage, 1977), pp. 133–65.

[43]Holly Idelson, "Signs Point to Greater Loyalty on Both Sides of the Aisle," *Congressional Quarterly Weekly Report,* 19 December 1992, p. 3849.

[44]David Broder, "Hill Democrats Vote as One: New Era of Unity or Short-term Honeymoon?" *Washington Post,* 14 March 1993, p. A1. See also Adam Clymer, "All Aboard: Clinton's Plan Gets Moving," *New York Times,* 21 March 1993, sec. 4, p. 1.

**FIGURE 5.4**

**Party Unity Scores by Chamber***

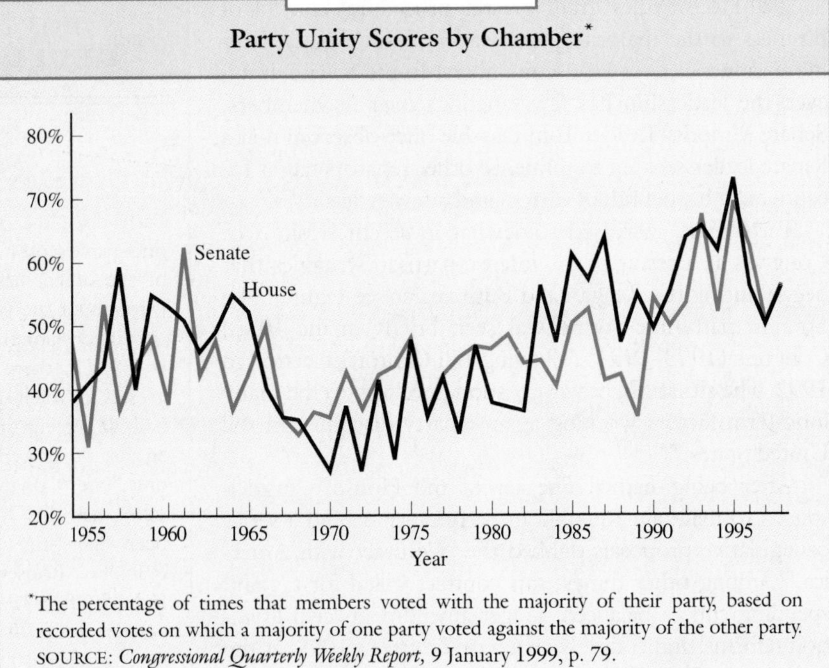


*The percentage of times that members voted with the majority of their party, based on recorded votes on which a majority of one party voted against the majority of the other party.
SOURCE: *Congressional Quarterly Weekly Report,* 9 January 1999, p. 79.

members of Congress are more likely than Democrats to be drawn from rural or suburban areas. Democrats are likely to be more liberal on economic and social questions than their Republican colleagues. These differences certainly help to explain roll-call divisions between the two parties. Ideology and background, however, are only part of the explanation of party unity. The other part has to do with party organization and leadership. Although party organization has weakened since the turn of the century, today's party leaders still have some resources at their disposal: (1) committee assignments, (2) access to the floor, (3) the whip system, (4) logrolling, and (5) the presidency. These resources are regularly used and are often effective in securing the support of party members.[45]

**Committee Assignments** Leaders can create debts among members by helping them get favorable committee assignments. These assignments are made early in the congressional careers of most members and cannot be taken from them if they later balk at party discipline. Nevertheless, if the leadership goes out of its way to get the right assignment for a member, this effort is likely to create a bond of obligation that can be called upon without any other payments or favors. This

[45]Legislative leaders also can possess a reputation for punishing uncooperative party members. For an analysis of Randall Calvert's argument on this topic, see Shepsle and Bonchek, *Analyzing Politics,* pp. 397–403. Calvert's argument appeared as "Reputation and Legislative Leadership," *Public Choice* 55 (1987): 81–120.

is one reason the leadership worked so hard to give freshmen favorable assignments in the 104th Congress.

**Access to the Floor** The most important everyday resource available to the parties is control over access to the floor. With thousands of bills awaiting passage and most members clamoring for access in order to influence a bill or to publicize themselves, floor time is precious. In the Senate, the leadership allows ranking committee members to influence the allocation of floor time—who will speak for how long; in the House, the Speaker, as head of the majority party (in consultation with the minority leader), allocates large blocks of floor time. Thus, floor time is allocated in both houses of Congress by the majority and minority leaders. More importantly, the Speaker of the House and the majority leader in the Senate possess the power of recognition. Although this power may not appear to be substantial, it is a formidable authority and can be used to stymie a piece of legislation completely or to frustrate a member's attempts to speak on a particular issue. Because the power is significant, members of Congress usually attempt to stay on good terms with the Speaker and the majority leader in order to ensure that they will continue to be recognized.

Some House members, Republicans in particular, have also taken advantage of "special orders," under which members can address the floor after the close of business. These addresses are typically made to an empty chamber, but are usually carried live by C-SPAN, a cable television channel. Before 1995, when Democrats controlled the House floor, Republicans often were forced to use special orders to present their views effectively to national audiences. Representative Newt Gingrich, for example, launched a televised after-hours attack on Democratic House Speaker Jim Wright in 1988 that ultimately led to Wright's resignation.[46]

**The Whip System** Some influence accrues to party leaders through the ***whip system,*** which is primarily a communications network. Between twelve and twenty assistant and regional whips are selected by zones to operate at the direction of the majority or minority leader and the whip. They take polls of all the members in order to learn their intentions on specific bills. This enables the leaders to know if they have enough support to allow a vote, as well as whether the vote is so close that they need to put pressure on a few swing votes. Leaders also use the whip system to convey their wishes and plans to the members, but only in very close votes do they actually exert pressure on a member. In those instances, the Speaker or a lieutenant will go to a few party members who have indicated they will switch if their vote is essential. The whip system helps the leaders limit pressuring members to a few times per session.

The whip system helps maintain party unity in both houses of Congress, but it is particularly critical in the House of Representatives because of the large number of legislators whose positions and votes must always be accounted for. The majority and minority whips and their assistants must be adept at

[46]See Beth Donovan, "Busy Democrats Skirt Fights to Get House in Order," *Congressional Quarterly Weekly Report,* 12 December 1992, p. 3778.

inducing compromise among legislators who hold widely differing viewpoints. The whips' personal styles and their perception of their function significantly affect the development of legislative coalitions and influence the compromises that emerge.

**Logrolling** An agreement between two or more members of Congress who have nothing in common except the need for support is called ***logrolling.*** The agreement states, in effect, "You support me on bill X and I'll support you on another bill of your choice." Since party leaders are the center of the communications networks in the two chambers, they can help members create large logrolling coalitions. Hundreds of logrolling deals are made each year, and while there are no official record-keeping books, it would be a poor party leader whose whips did not know who owed what to whom.[47] In some instances, logrolling produces strange alliances. A seemingly unlikely alliance emerged in Congress in June 1994, when 119 mainly conservative senators and representatives from oil-producing states met with President Clinton to suggest that they might be willing to support the president's health care proposals in exchange for his support for a number of tax breaks for the oil industry. Senator J. Bennett Johnson of Louisiana, a leader of the oil-state representatives, contended that the issues of health care and oil production were closely related since both "affected the long-term economic security of the nation." Ironically, the oil-producing groups that promoted this alliance are generally among the most conservative forces in the nation. When asked what he personally thought of the president's health care proposal, George Alcorn, a leading industry lobbyist involved in the logrolling effort, dismissed Clinton's plan as "socialized medicine." Another logrolling alliance of strange bedfellows was the 1994 "corn for porn" logroll, in which liberal urbanites supported farm programs in exchange for rural support for National Endowment for the Arts funding. Good logrolling, it would seem, is not hampered by minor ideological concerns.[48]

**The Presidency** Of all the influences that maintain the clarity of party lines in Congress, the influence of the presidency is probably the most important. Indeed, it is a touchstone of party discipline in Congress. Since the late 1940s, under President Truman, presidents each year have identified a number of bills to be considered part of their administration's program. By the mid-1950s, both parties in Congress began to look to the president for these proposals, which became the most significant part of Congress's agenda. The president's support is a criterion for party loyalty, and party leaders are able to use it to rally some members.

## Weighing Diverse Influences

Clearly, many different factors affect congressional decisions. But at various points in the decision-making process, some factors are likely to be more influen-

[47]For an analysis of the formal problems that logrolling (or vote trading) both solves and creates, see Shepsle and Bonchek, *Analyzing Politics,* pp. 317–19.

[48]Allen R. Meyerson, "Oil-Patch Congressmen Seek Deal With Clinton," *New York Times,* 14 June 1994, p. D2.

tial than others. For example, interest groups may be more effective at the committee stage, when their expertise is especially valued and their visibility is less obvious. Because committees play a key role in deciding what legislation actually reaches the floor of the House or Senate, interest groups can often put a halt to bills they dislike, or they can ensure that the options that do reach the floor are those that the group's members support.

Once legislation reaches the floor, and members of Congress are deciding among alternatives, constituent opinion will become more important. Legislators are also influenced very much by other legislators: many of their assessments about the substance and politics of legislation come from fellow members of Congress.

The influence of the external and internal forces described in the preceding section also varies according to the kind of issue being considered. On policies of great importance to powerful interest groups—farm subsidies, for example—those groups are likely to have considerable influence. On other issues, members of Congress may be less attentive to narrow interest groups and more willing to consider what they see as the general interest.

Finally, the mix of influences varies according to the historical moment. The 1994 electoral victory of Republicans allowed their party to control both houses of Congress for the first time in forty years. That fact, combined with an unusually assertive Republican leadership, meant that party leaders became especially important in decision making. The willingness of moderate Republicans to support measures they had once opposed indicated the unusual importance of party leadership in this period. As House Minority Leader Richard Gephardt put it, "When you've been in the desert 40 years, your instinct is to help Moses."[49]

## Beyond Legislation: Additional Congressional Powers

In addition to the power to make the law, Congress has at its disposal an array of other instruments through which to influence the process of government. The Constitution gives the Senate the power to approve treaties and appointments. And Congress has drawn to itself a number of other powers through which it can share with the other branches the capacity to administer the laws. The powers of Congress can be called "weapons of control" to emphasize the fact of Congress's power to govern and to call attention to what government power means.

[49]David Broder, "At 6 Months, House GOP Juggernaut Still Cohesive," *Washington Post*, 17 July 1995, p. A1.

## Oversight

***Oversight,*** as applied to Congress, refers not to something neglected but to the effort to oversee or to supervise how legislation is carried out by the executive branch. Oversight is carried out by committees or subcommittees of the Senate or House, which conduct hearings and investigations in order to analyze and evaluate bureaucratic agencies and the effectiveness of their programs. The purpose may be to locate inefficiencies or abuses of power, to explore the relationship between what an agency does and what a law intended, or to change or abolish a program. Most programs and agencies are subject to some oversight every year during the course of hearings on ***appropriations,*** that is, the funding of agencies and government programs.

Committees or subcommittees have the power to subpoena witnesses, take oaths, cross-examine, compel testimony, and bring criminal charges for contempt (refusing to cooperate) and perjury (lying). Hearings and investigations resemble each other in many ways, but they differ on one fundamental point. A hearing is usually held on a specific bill, and the questions asked there are usually intended to build a record with regard to that bill. In an investigation, the committee or subcommittee does not begin with a particular bill, but examines a broad area or problem and then concludes its investigation with one or more proposed bills. One example of an investigation is the congressional inquiry into the Clinton administration's acquisition of the FBI files of prominent Republicans.

## Advice and Consent: Special Senate Powers

The Constitution has given the Senate a special power, one that is not based on lawmaking. The president has the power to make treaties and to appoint top executive officers, ambassadors, and federal judges—but only "with the Advice and Consent of the Senate" (Article II, Section 2). For treaties, two-thirds of those present must concur; for appointments, a majority is required.

The power to approve or reject presidential requests also involves the power to set conditions. The Senate only occasionally exercises its power to reject treaties and appointments, and usually that is when opposite parties control the Senate and the White House. During the final two years of President Reagan's term, Senate Democrats rejected Judge Robert Bork's Supreme Court nomination and gave clear indications that they would reject a second Reagan nominee, Judge Douglas Ginsburg, who withdrew his nomination before the Senate could act. These instances, however, actually underscore the restraint with which the Senate usually uses its power to reject presidential requests. For example, only nine judicial nominees have been rejected by the Senate during the past century, while hundreds have been approved.

More common than Senate rejection of presidential appointees is a senatorial "hold" on an appointment. By Senate tradition, any member may place an indefinite hold on the confirmation of a mid- or lower-level presidential appointment. The hold is typically used by senators trying to wring concessions from the White House on matters having nothing to do with the appointment in question. In

1994, for example, Senator Max Baucus (D-Mont.) placed a hold on the confirmation of Mary Shapiro, President Clinton's choice to head the Commodity Futures Trading Commission, as well as those of four other Clinton nominees for federal regulatory posts. His aim was to win concessions from the administration for farmers in his state.

Most presidents make every effort to take potential Senate opposition into account in treaty negotiations and will frequently resort to ***executive agreements*** with foreign powers instead of treaties. The Supreme Court has held that such agreements are equivalent to treaties, but they do not need Senate approval.[50] In the past, presidents sometimes concluded secret agreements without informing Congress of the agreements' contents, or even their existence. For example, American involvement in the Vietnam War grew in part out of a series of secret arrangements made between American presidents and the South Vietnamese during the 1950s and 1960s. Congress did not even learn of the existence of these agreements until 1969. In 1972, Congress passed the Case Act, which requires that the president inform Congress of any executive agreement within sixty days of its having been reached. This provides Congress with the opportunity to cancel agreements that it opposes. In addition, Congress can limit the president's ability to conduct foreign policy through executive agreement by refusing to appropriate the funds needed to implement an agreement. In this way, for example, executive agreements to provide American economic or military assistance to foreign governments can be modified or even canceled by Congress.

## Impeachment

The Constitution also grants Congress the power of ***impeachment*** over the president, vice president, and other executive officials. Impeachment means to charge a government official (president or otherwise) with "Treason, Bribery, or other high Crimes and Misdemeanors" and bring him or her before Congress to determine guilt. Impeachment is thus like a criminal indictment in which the House of Representatives acts like a grand jury, voting (by simple majority) on whether the accused ought to be impeached. If a majority of the House votes to impeach, the impeachment trial moves to the Senate, which acts like a trial jury by voting whether to convict and forcibly remove the person from office (this vote requires a two-thirds majority of the Senate).

Controversy over Congress's impeachment power has arisen over the grounds for impeachment, especially the meaning of "high Crimes and Misdemeanors." A strict reading of the Constitution suggests that the only impeachable offense is an actual crime. But a more commonly agreed upon definition is that "an impeachable offense is whatever the majority of the House of Representatives considers it to be at a given moment in history."[51] In other words, impeachment, especially impeachment of a president, is a political decision.

[50]U.S. v. Pink, 315 U.S. 203 (1942). For a good discussion of the problem, see James W. Davis, *The American Presidency* (New York: Harper & Row, 1987), Chapter 8.

[51]Carroll J. Doherty, "Impeachment: How It Would Work," *Congressional Quarterly Weekly Report,* 31 January 1998, p. 222.

The closest that the United States has come to impeaching and convicting a president came in 1867. President Andrew Johnson, a southern Democrat who had battled a congressional Republican majority over Reconstruction, was impeached by the House but saved from conviction by one vote in the Senate. At the height of the Watergate scandal in 1974, the House started impeachment proceedings against President Richard M. Nixon, but Nixon resigned before the House could proceed. The possibility of impeachment arose again in 1998 when President Clinton was accused of lying under oath and obstructing justice in the investigation into his sexual affair with White House intern Monica Lewinsky. In October 1998, the House voted to open an impeachment inquiry against President Clinton. At the conclusion of the Senate trial in 1999, Democrats, joined by a handful of Republicans, acquited the president of both charges.

The impeachment power is a considerable one; its very existence in the hands of Congress is a highly effective safeguard against the executive tyranny so greatly feared by the framers of the Constitution.

## POWER AND REPRESENTATION

Because they feared both executive and legislative tyranny, the framers of the Constitution pitted Congress and the president against one another. But for more than one hundred years, the contest was unequal. During the first century of American government, Congress was the dominant institution. American foreign and domestic policy was formulated and implemented by Congress and generally, the most powerful figures in American government were the Speaker of the House and the leaders of the Senate—not the president. The War of 1812 was planned and fought by Congress. The great sectional compromises prior to the Civil War were formulated in Congress, without much intervention from the executive branch. Even during the Civil War, a period of extraordinary presidential leadership, a joint congressional committee on the conduct of the war played a role in formulating war plans and campaign tactics, and even had a hand in the promotion of officers. After the Civil War, when President Andrew Johnson sought to interfere with congressional plans for Reconstruction, he was summarily impeached, saved from conviction by only one vote. Subsequent presidents understood the moral and did not attempt to thwart Congress.

### AMERICAN POLITICAL DEVELOPMENT

During the nineteenth century, Congress—not the president—dominated press coverage on "the affairs of government." Today, it is reversed, and most observers suggest that presidential dominance of media politics has led to greater presidential power throughout the twentieth century.

SOURCE: Samuel Kernell and Gary C. Jacobson, "Congress and the Presidency as News in the Nineteenth Century," *Journal of Politics* 49 (1987), pp. 1016–35.

This congressional preeminence began to diminish after the turn of the century, so that by the 1960s, the executive had become, at least temporarily, the dominant branch of American government. The major domestic policy initiatives of the twentieth century—Franklin Roosevelt's "New Deal," Harry Truman's "Fair Deal," John F. Kennedy's "New Frontier," and Lyndon Johnson's "Great Society"—all included some congressional involvement but were essentially developed, introduced, and implemented by the executive. In the area of foreign policy, though Congress continued to be influential during the twentieth century, the focus of decision-making power clearly moved into the executive branch. The War of 1812 may have been a congressional war, but in the twentieth century, American entry into World War I, World War II, Korea, Vietnam, and a host of lesser conflicts was essentially a presidential—not a congressional—decision. In the last thirty years, there has been a good deal of resurgence of congressional power vis-à-vis the executive. This has occurred mainly because Congress has sought to represent many important political forces, such as the civil rights, feminist, environmental, consumer, and peace movements, which in turn became constituencies for congressional power. During the mid-1990s, Congress became more receptive to a variety of new conservative political forces, including groups on the social and religious right as well as more traditional economic conservatives. After Republicans won control of both houses in the 1994 elections, Congress took the lead in developing programs and policies supported by these groups. These efforts won Congress the support of conservative forces in its battles for power against a Democratic White House.

To herald the new accessibility of Congress, Republican leaders instituted a number of reforms designed to eliminate many of the practices they had criticized as examples of Democratic arrogance during their long years in opposition. Republican leaders imposed term limits on committee chairmen, eliminated the practice of proxy voting, reduced committee staffs by one-third, ended Congress's exemption from the labor health and civil rights laws it imposed on the rest of the nation, and prohibited members from receiving most gifts. The Republicans also introduced a budget resolution that would lead to a balanced budget within seven years. Fearing that he would be marginalized in the legislative process, President Clinton announced his own proposals for cuts in taxes and spending under the rubric of a "middle-class bill of rights." In June 1995, Clinton introduced his own balanced budget plan. Congressional Republicans dismissed the president's proposals as a crass effort to copy the GOP's successful campaign pledges. Even many Democrats felt that the president was in no position to compete with Gingrich and his resurgent party. Instead they hoped that Gingrich and congressional Republicans would make damaging errors.

The Democrats' hopes were realized when the GOP's congressional leadership suffered a crushing defeat in the climactic 1995–1996 battle over the federal budget. After the White House and congressional Republicans failed to reach agreement on a new budget, the federal government was shut down twice—once in November 1995, and again for a twenty-one-day period in December 1995 and into January, 1996. Nearly 800,000 federal workers were furloughed, though with a promise of back pay after the crisis ended. Hundreds of thousands of individuals working for private firms under federal government contracts were also furloughed, but with little chance of ever collecting back pay. The media and public response to the budget crisis shocked Republicans. Instead of leading to a realization that the nation could get along with a smaller government, as Republicans had anticipated, the budget crisis seemed to turn the public against the GOP.

The GOP's budget debacle discredited the Republican congressional leadership and, especially, the then-House Speaker Newt Gingrich. Republicans were unable to regain the legislative momentum demonstrated during the first

## GLOBALIZATION AND DEMOCRACY

### *Can Congress Protect America's Interests?*

As we pointed out earlier in this chapter, a part of Congress's power comes from its capacity to represent important groups and forces in society effectively. Globalization and the increased flow of investment capital have created strong new groups that, naturally, want to have their voices heard by Congress.

Beginning in earnest during the mid-1980s, more and more foreign-owned firms established factories and subsidiaries on American soil. In some cases, this rising tide of foreign investment was driven by the desire of these manufacturers to avoid the possibility of losing sales in the United States because of the threat of "local content laws." These laws require that a prescribed percentage of the components used in a finished product, such as a passenger car, must be manufactured domestically. Indeed, "sell here, build here" became a slogan of the United Auto Workers and other labor unions. As a result, for example, Honda automobiles are manufactured in Ohio, and BMW cars are assembled in a factory in South Carolina.

Because foreign investment holds the potential of creating new jobs and generating economic growth, localities compete to attract investors. As we mentioned earlier, members of Congress sometimes get involved in trying to lure investors to their districts. A former high-ranking Commerce Department official recounts a 1986 incident in which he briefed a group of Kentucky congressmen. They were on their way

months after the 1994 election. Gingrich became one of the most unpopular political figures in America and kept a low profile to avoid hurting his party. Democrats launched a series of ethics complaints against the Speaker in order to harass and humiliate him and preempt any efforts by him to repair his public image.

A second consequence of the GOP's budget debacle was the political rehabilitation of President Bill Clinton. Prior to the crisis, Clinton's standing in the polls had been abysmal and many analysts were comparing Clinton to Jimmy Carter and predicting that he would be a one-term president. Clinton had been widely blamed for the Democrats' loss of both houses of Congress in 1994, and he appeared to be a bystander as the GOP legislative juggernaut pushed forward in 1995.[52] After the budget crisis, however, Clinton's popularity began to improve, and he was able to win the 1996 presidential election by a landslide.

[52]Jon Healey, "Declining Fortunes: President's Leadership Role Eclipsed by Vigor and Unity of GOP Majority," *Congressional Quarterly Weekly Report,* 27 January 1996, pp. 193–98.

to Japan to plead their state's case for why a Toyota assembly plant slated to be built in the United States should come to Kentucky. "At one point I asked whether they realized that for every Japanese plant that opened in Kentucky, an American one in Michigan was likely to close. Their response was, 'We're not the congressmen from Michigan.'"[1]

Today, millions of American workers are employed by subsidiaries of companies that are headquartered overseas. These American workers, who are eager to keep their jobs, embody at least a latent "anti-protectionist" constituency in the event of economic conflict between the United States and their parent company. An example of this occurred in 1987 when a subsidiary of Japan's Toshiba Corporation was found to have sold sophisticated machine tools to the Soviet Union in violation of the Coordinating Committee on Export Controls. When Congress began considering the imposition of trade sanctions, Toshiba immediately directed its four thousand American workers to contact their representatives in Congress to plead for leniency for their parent company. Anxious to avoid increased costs that would have been passed along to consumers, American firms that relied on components manufactured by Toshiba found it expedient to join the chorus pressing for moderation in trade sanctions. In the end, the sanctions meted out by Congress were fraught with so many exemptions that Toshiba is estimated to have lost only a few million dollars of its then $3 billion in sales in the American market.[2]

In this way, globalization and increased interdependence create new sets of interests that demand representation in the corridors of Congress. Specifically, globalization creates important new groups and forces in society, and these groups and forces seek to press their views on Congress.

[1]Clyde V. Prestowitz, Jr., *Trading Places: How We Are Giving Our Future to Japan and How to Reclaim It* (New York: Basic Books, 1989), p. 369.

[2]This and many other cases are discussed in Pat Choate, *Agents of Influence* (New York: Knopf, 1990).

During Clinton's second term, however, House Republicans were able to impeach the president and force him to stand trial before the Senate in 1999 on charges of perjury and obstruction of justice. Though he escaped conviction, Clinton became only the second president in American history to face the humiliation of a Senate trial. The danger posed by this turn of events was that not only Clinton but that the institution of the presidency might be undermined.

The struggle between Congress and the White House is one more illustration of the dilemma that lies at the heart of the American system of government. The framers of the Constitution checked and balanced a powerful Congress with a powerful executive. This was seen as a way of limiting the potential for abuse of governmental power and of protecting freedom. No doubt, it has this effect. Certainly, a vigilant Congress was able to curb presidential abuse of power during the Nixon era. Similarly, the executive branch under the leadership of President Eisenhower played a role in curbing the congressional witch hunts, ostensibly aimed at uncovering communist agents in the federal government, that were conducted by Senator Joseph McCarthy (R–Wis.) during the 1950s.

At the same time, however, the constant struggle between Congress and the president can hinder stable, effective governance. Over the past quarter-century, in particular, presidents and Congresses have often seemed to be more interested in undermining one another than in promoting the larger public interest. On issues of social policy, economic policy, and foreign policy, Congress and the president have been at each other's throats while the nation suffered.

For example, during its first months in session, the 105th Congress (1997–1998) was able to pass a number of important pieces of legislation, including a major budget bill and legislation designed to protect taxpayers from abuse by the Internal Revenue Service. As the session continued, however, Congress became fully involved in its battle with President Clinton, culminating in the president's impeachment in December 1998. As a result, the Congress failed to act on most of the major pieces of legislation on its agenda (see Table 5.3). An even more striking example of the disruptive consequences of all-out struggle between the Congress and the president came in December 1998. While American forces were involved in military action against Iraq, Congress was so engrossed in the conflict over Republican efforts to impeach President Clinton that lawmakers regarded the Iraqi crisis as a diversion from the "real" political issue. Some even suggested that Clinton had manufactured the crisis to save his presidency.

Thus, we face a fundamental dilemma: A political arrangement designed to preserve freedom can undermine the government's power. Indeed, it can undermine the government's very capacity to govern. Must we always choose between freedom and power? Can we not have both? Let us turn next to the second branch of American government, the presidency, to view this dilemma from a somewhat different angle.

## SUMMARY

The U.S. Congress is one of the few national representative assemblies that actually governs. Members of Congress take their representative function seriously. They devote a significant portion of their time to constituent contact and service. Representation and power go hand in hand in congressional history.

The legislative process must provide the order necessary for legislation to take place amid competing interests. It is dependent on a hierarchical organizational structure within Congress. Six basic dimensions of Congress affect the legislative process: (1) the parties, (2) the committees, (3) the staff, (4) the caucuses (or conferences), (5) the rules, and (6) the presidency.

Since the Constitution provides only for a presiding officer in each house, some method had to be devised for conducting business. Parties quickly assumed the responsibility for this. In the House, the majority party elects a leader every two years. This individual becomes Speaker. In addition, a majority leader and a minority leader (from the minority party) and party whips are elected. Each party has a committee whose job it is to make committee assignments. Party structure

**Table 5.3**

**The Record of the 105th Congress**

| During 1997–1998, the 105th Congress . . . | |
|---|---|
| **. . . passed legislation to:** | **. . . considered but did not pass legislation to:** |
| • **Balance the budget** and **cut taxes,** including a $500-per-child credit and a reduction in the capital gains levy.<br>• Protect taxpayers from abuses by the **Internal Revenue Service.**<br>• Finance $216 billion of **highway,** bridge and transit construction over six years.<br>• Approve President Clinton's $1.1 billion proposal to **hire more teachers** (but rejected his school construction initiative); reauthorize higher education programs, including lower interest rates for student loans; expand the Head Start program for preschoolers and create a new literacy initiative.<br>• Revamp and expand **subsidized housing** to include more low- to moderate-income families in public housing.<br>• Pump $18 billion into the **International Monetary Fund** to help it cope with the global financial crisis.<br>• Strengthen pressure on foreign countries that engage in **religious persecution.**<br>• Expedite **Food and Drug Administration** consideration of prescription drugs and medical devices.<br>• Help the **high-tech industry** by restricting taxation of Internet commerce, protecting copyrights in cyberspace and providing more visas for highly skilled immigrants.<br>• Reorganize **foreign policy** agencies.<br>• Pay back dues to the **United Nations,** although Clinton vetoed the bill because of an unrelated antiabortion provision.<br><br>(The Senate also approved a treaty to ban **chemical weapons** and treaty changes to **expand NATO** to include Poland, Hungary and the Czech Republic.) | • Strengthen **campaign finance** laws by banning "soft money" contributions, controlling latebreaking issue ads and tightening disclosure rules.<br>• Regulate **health maintenance organizations** (HMOs) and other managed-care organizations.<br>• Enact the proposed national **tobacco settlement** and raise cigarette taxes to finance health programs and help curb teenage smoking.<br>• **Cut taxes by $80 billion** over five years for mostly middle-income families.<br>• Provide a tax break for private as well as public **school expenses.** Congress approved the measure but failed to override a veto.<br>• Ban certain **late-term abortions** and make it more difficult for minors to cross state lines to evade state laws requiring parental notification or consent for abortions. Congress approved the late-term abortion restrictions but failed to override Clinton's veto.<br>• Give the president **"fast-track"** authority to negotiate trade agreements that Congress could accept or reject but not amend.<br>• Initiate procedures for closing more obsolete **military bases.**<br>• Raise the **minimum wage** by $1 an hour to $6.15 over the next two years, as Democrats wanted.<br>• Streamline **regulatory procedures** and **curb lawsuits** over defective products, as Republicans wanted.<br>• Overhaul **financial services** laws to allow banks, insurance companies and securities firms to compete for each other's business. |

SOURCE: Helen Dewar, "The Record of the 105th Congress," *Washington Post,* 23 October, 1998, p. A16.

THEN AND NOW

## Changes in American Politics

The United States Congress continues to evolve institutionally. Some of its changes have been significant, others less so. But any understanding of Congress's evolution requires a protracted view of its institutions and practices.

- Congress has become more representative of the nation's sociological makeup only in the last decades of the twentieth century. From 1971 to 1997, the number of women in the House more than quadrupled, and the number of African Americans more than tripled.
- During the nineteenth century and early decades of the twentieth century, members of Congress were more likely to be selected and supported on the basis of their political parties than is currently the case. The decline of local party organizations and the changing modes of selecting candidates has made today's members of Congress more likely to be "free agents" than loyal party followers.
- Great changes in the institutionalization of party leaders within Congress took place at the end of the nineteenth century and the beginning of the twentieth. Key party leaders like the House majority whip or the Senate floor leaders were not created until 1897 and 1910 respectively.
- Prior to the ratification of the Seventeenth Amendment in 1913—which allowed senators to be chosen by popular vote—senators were elected by state legislatures.
- The selection of committee chairs by the seniority principle is a product of certain institutional conditions rather than of a general rule in congressional history. Seniority did not become a principle generally followed—much less the nearly inviolable rule it was in the 1950s—until the late 1800s. By the 1970s, congressional reforms weakened but did not eliminate the seniority principle.
- A revolt against the House Speaker in 1910 and a general decline in the organization of political parties thereafter led to a period of committee rather than party dominance of Congress in the middle decades of the twentieth century. Partisanship and party strength increased again by the 1980s and 1990s.
- Senate filibusters and clotures (efforts to stop filibusters) were much more frequent after the 1970s than they were in the earlier part of the twentieth century.
- The measure of partisanship most commonly used in the nineteenth century was the number of times 90 percent of one party voted against 90 percent of the other. Because of the decline of party strength in Congress, this threshold is infrequently met in the twentieth century. Instead, a common measure now of party voting is when 50 percent of one party votes against 50 percent of the other.
- During the nineteenth century, Congress dominated both media coverage and the presidency in politics. This changed in the twentieth century, when the ascendance of presidential power made for an "imperial presidency" that rivaled (if not dominated) Congress in policy making, administration, and the media.

in the Senate is similar, except that the vice president of the United States is the Senate president.

The committee system surpasses the party system in its importance in Congress. In the early nineteenth century, standing committees became a fundamental aspect of Congress. They have, for the most part, evolved to correspond to executive branch departments or programs and thus reflect and maintain the separation of powers.

The Senate has a tradition of unlimited debate, on which the various cloture rules it has passed have had little effect. Filibusters still occur. The rules of the House, on the other hand, restrict talk and support committees; deliberation is recognized as committee business. The House Rules Committee has the power to control debate and floor amendments. The rules prescribe the formal procedure through which bills become law. Generally, the parties control scheduling and agenda, but the committees determine action on the floor. Committees, seniority, and rules all limit the ability of members to represent their constituents. Yet, these factors enable Congress to maintain its role as a major participant in government.

While voting along party lines remains strong, party discipline has declined. Still, parties do have several means of maintaining discipline: (1) Favorable committee assignments create obligations; (2) Floor time in the debate on one bill can be allocated in exchange for a specific vote on another; (3) The whip system allows party leaders to assess support for a bill and convey their wishes to members; (4) Party leaders can help members create large logrolling coalitions; and (5) The president, by identifying pieces of legislation as his own, can muster support along party lines. In most cases, party leaders accept constituency obligations as a valid reason for voting against the party position.

The power of the post–New Deal presidency does not necessarily signify the decline of Congress and representative government. During the 1970s, Congress again became the "first branch" of government. During the early years of the Reagan administration, some of the congressional gains of the previous decade were diminished, but in the last two years of Reagan's second term, and in President Bush's term, Congress reasserted its role. At the start of the Clinton administration, congressional leaders promised to cooperate with the White House rather than confront it. But only two years later, confrontation was once again the order of the day.

## For Further Reading

Arnold, R. Douglas. *The Logic of Congressional Action.* New Haven: Yale University Press, 1990.

Baker, Ross K. *House and Senate,* 2nd ed. New York: W. W. Norton, 1995.

Burnham, James. *Congress and the American Tradition.* Chicago: Henry Regnery, 1965.

Congressional Quarterly, Inc. *Origins and Development of Congress,* 2nd ed. Washington, DC: Congressional Quarterly Press, 1982.

Davidson, Roger, H., ed. *The Postreform Congress.* New York: St. Martin's Press, 1991.

Dodd, Lawrence, and Bruce I. Oppenheimer, eds. *Congress Reconsidered,* 6th ed. Washington, DC: Congressional Quarterly Press, 1997.

Fenno, Richard F. *Congressmen in Committees.* Boston: Little, Brown, 1973.

Fenno, Richard F. *Homestyle: House Members in Their Districts.* Boston: Little, Brown, 1978.

Fiorina, Morris. *Congress: Keystone of the Washington Establishment,* 2nd ed. New Haven: Yale University Press, 1989.

Fisher, Louis. *The Politics of Shared Power: Congress and the Executive,* 3rd ed. Washington, DC: Congressional Quarterly Press, 1993.

Foreman, Christopher. *Signals from the Hill: Congressional Oversight and the Challenge of Social Regulation.* New Haven: Yale University Press, 1988.

Fowler, Linda, and Robert McClure. *Political Ambition: Who Decides to Run for Congress?* New Haven: Yale University Press, 1989.

Hinckley, Barbara. *Less than Meets the Eye: Foreign Policy Making and the Myth of the Assertive Congress.* Chicago: University of Chicago Press, 1994.

Leloup, Lance T. *Budgetary Politics.* Brunswick, OH: King's Court, 1986.

Light, Paul. *Forging Legislation.* New York: W. W. Norton, 1991.

Malbin, Michael. *Unelected Representatives: Congressional Staff and the Future of Representative Government.* New York: Basic Books, 1980.

Mayhew, David R. *Congress: The Electoral Connection.* New Haven: Yale University Press, 1974.

Oleszek, Walter J. *Congressional Procedures and the Policy Process,* 3rd ed. Washington, DC: Congressional Quarterly Press, 1989.

Rieselbach, Leroy. *Congressional Reform.* Washington, DC: Congressional Quarterly Press, 1986.

Ripley, Randall. *Congress: Process and Policy,* 4th ed. New York: W. W. Norton, 1988.

Schroedel, Jean Reith. *Congress, the President, and Policymaking: A Historical Analysis.* Armonk, NY: M. E. Sharpe, 1994.

Sinclair, Barbara. *The Transformation of the U.S. Senate.* Baltimore: Johns Hopkins University Press, 1989.

Smith, Steven S., and Christopher Deering. *Committees in Congress,* 2nd ed. Washington, DC: Congressional Quarterly Press, 1990.

Strahan, Randall. *New Ways and Means: Reform and Change in a Congressional Committee.* Chapel Hill: University of North Carolina Press, 1990.

Sundquist, James L. *The Decline and Resurgence of Congress.* Washington, DC: Brookings Institution, 1981.

Uslaner, Eric. *The Decline of Comity in Congress.* Ann Arbor: University of Michigan Press, 1994.

# The President: From Chief Clerk to Chief Executive

## TIME LINE ON THE PRESIDENCY

| Events | | Institutional Developments |
|---|---|---|
| George Washington elected first president (1789) | | President establishes powers in relation to Congress (1789) |
| Thomas Jefferson elected president (1800) | 1800 | |
| | | Orderly transfer of power from Federalists to Jeffersonian Republicans (1801) |
| "Midnight" judicial appointments by John Adams before he leaves office (1801) | | *Marbury v. Madison* holds that Congress and the president are subject to judicial review (1803) |
| Republican caucus nominates James Madison, who is elected president (1808) | | Congress dominates presidential nominations through "King Caucus" (1804–1831) |
| Andrew Jackson elected president (1828) | | Strengthening of presidency; nominating conventions introduced, broaden president's base of support (1830s) |
| Period of weak presidents (Martin Van Buren, William Harrison, James Polk, Zachary Taylor, Franklin Pierce, James Buchanan) (1836–1860) | | |
| Abraham Lincoln elected president (1860) | 1860 | "Constitutional dictatorship" during Civil War and after (1861–1865) |
| Impeachment of President Andrew Johnson (1868) | | Congress takes back initiative for action (1868–1933) |
| Industrialization, big railroads, big corporations (1860s–1890s) | | *In re Neagle*—Court holds to expansive inference from Constitution on rights, duties, and obligations of president (1890) |
| World War I (1914–1918) | | |
| Congress fails to approve Wilson's League of Nations (1919–1920) | 1920 | |
| | | Budget and Accounting Act; Congress provides for an executive budget (1921) |
| FDR proposes New Deal programs to achieve economic recovery from the Depression (1933) | | Congress adopts first New Deal programs; epoch of presidential government (1930s) |
| U.S. in World War II (1941–1945) | | *U.S. v. Pink*—Court confirms legality of executive agreements in foreign relations (1942) |
| Korean War without declaration (1950–1953) | 1950 | |
| | | *Steel Seizure* case holds that president's power must be authorized by statute and is not inherent in the presidency (1952) |
| Gulf of Tonkin Resolution (1964); U.S. troop buildup begins in Vietnam (1965) | | Great Society program enacted; president sends troops to Vietnam without consulting Congress (1965) |

| Events | | Institutional Developments |
|---|---|---|
| | 1970 | |
| Watergate affair (1972); Watergate cover-up revealed (1973–1974) | | Congressional resurgence begins—War Powers Act (1973); Budget and Impoundment Act (1974) |
| Nixon becomes first president to resign; Gerald Ford succeeds after Nixon's resignation (1974) | | |
| Reagan's election begins new Republican era of "supply side" economics, deregulation, and military buildup (1980–1988) | | *INS v. Chadha*—Court holds legislative veto to be unconstitutional (1983) |
| Iran-Contra affair revealed (1986–1987) | | Gramm-Rudman Act seeks to contain deficit spending (1985) |
| Bush elected on "no new taxes" pledge (1988) | | End of cold war puts new emphasis on foreign policy (1989) |
| | 1990 | |
| | | Desert Storm defines post–cold war conduct of foreign policy (1991) |
| Clinton election ends "divided government" (1992) | | Clinton pulls Democrats to the right with first deficit-reduction budget (1993) |
| Republican takeover of both houses of Congress renews "divided government" (1994) | | Clinton fails on health care and tax reform (1994) |
| Clinton re-elected, but divided government continued (1996) | | Congress gives president limited line-item veto power over appropriations (1997) |
| | | Court refuses to give president immunity from civil suit in *Clinton v. Jones* (1997) |
| Democrats reverse midterm precedent and gain seats in House (1998) | | Impeachment does not deter president, especially on foreign affairs (1997–1998) |
| Impeachment proceeds, despite election and high job ratings for Clinton (1998–1999) | | Supreme Court rules that limited line-item veto power is unconstitutional (1998) |
| | | Kosovo dominates U.S. foreign policy (1999) |

**CORE OF THE ARGUMENT**

- In the twentieth century, the president has been transformed from "chief clerk," the executor of Congress's wishes, into "chief executive," the leader and shaper of the national government.
- The institutional growth of the presidency since the 1930s has vastly increased its power, but the constitutional basis for presidential action means that the president is constantly vulnerable to congressional or judicial challenges.
- The critical resource of the modern presidency is mass public opinion.
- Because of their ultimate reliance on mass support rather than other resources such as party, patronage, or the cabinet, presidents tend to govern using the resource they control most firmly—the White House staff.

Throughout 1998, the presidency appeared to be in crisis. In January of that year, President Bill Clinton had just been cleared of accusations that he was involved with illegal fundraising during the 1996 campaign, but he was still defending himself against two sets of charges. The first involved a sexual harassment suit by Paula Jones, a former employee of the state of Arkansas (of which Clinton was governor before his election to the presidency). The second charge, being investigated by independent counsel Kenneth Starr, focused on Clinton's alleged involvement with illegal real-estate speculation as part of the Whitewater Development Corporation. In seeking to prove that Clinton made a practice of seeking sexual favors from employees, Paula Jones's lawyers issued a subpoena to a former White House intern, Monica Lewinsky. It was alleged that Clinton and Lewinsky had had a sexual affair and that Clinton had urged Lewinsky to perjure herself by denying the accusation in a sworn deposition. Although sexual misconduct of this kind has no legal significance, the charges against Clinton involved serious criminal charges of obstruction of justice. In December 1998, he was impeached by the House of Representatives on two articles—perjury and obstruction of justice—and was put before the Senate for possible conviction and removal from office, the first such action since President Andrew Johnson's impeachment in 1868. President Clinton was in trouble. What about the office of the presidency?

Public opinion about the President's affair with Lewinsky sheds light on the nature of the presidency today. When asked if they thought Clinton was engaged in a cover-up, 51 percent of respondents said yes. When asked if Clinton should be removed from office if he lied under oath about the affair, 55 percent said yes. When asked if he should be removed from office if he had encouraged Lewinsky to lie while under oath, 63 percent said yes. But when asked whether they approved or disapproved of the way President Clinton was handling his job, a whopping 68 percent said they approved, giving Clinton his highest approval rating up to that time.[1] Although the results of these polls may appear confusing at first glance, they confirm one important fact: the presidency has a dual nature, which Americans sense and act upon. The power that President Clinton exercises and the approval he seemed to gain following this setback are based more in the institution of the presidency than in the person of the president. In other words,

[1]CNN/*Times* polls, 23 and 30 January 1998.

Americans respect the presidency as an institution and all of its capabilities for governance, even if they don't approve of the individual in the office. It's the office that wields great power, not necessarily the person.

This duality has been the source of consternation and dispute since the founding itself, kept alive by an army of scholars puzzling out the intent of the framers. The framers, wanting "energy in the Executive," provided for a single-headed office with an electoral base independent of Congress. But by giving the presidency no explicit powers independent of Congress, each president would have to provide that energy by asserting powers beyond the Constitution itself. As Theodore Roosevelt so eloquently expressed it, "My belief was that it was not only [the president's] right but his duty to do anything that the needs of the nation demanded unless such action was forbidden by the Constitution or by the law."[2] John F. Kennedy echoed Roosevelt decades later:

> The Constitution is a very wise document. It permits the president to assume just about as much power as he is capable of handling. . . . I believe that the president should use whatever power is necessary to do the job unless it is expressly forbidden by the Constitution.[3]

A tug of war between formal constitutional provisions for a president who is little more than chief clerk and a theory of necessity favoring a real chief executive has persisted for over two centuries. President Jefferson's acquisition of the Louisiana Territory in virtual defiance of the Constitution seemed to establish the chief executive presidency; yet he was followed by three chief clerks, James Madison, James Monroe, and John Quincy Adams. Presidents Andrew Jackson and Abraham Lincoln believed in and acted on the theory of the strong president with power transcending the formal Constitution, but neither of them institutionalized the role, and both were followed by a series of chief clerks. Theodore Roosevelt and Woodrow Wilson were also considered genuine chief executives. But it was not until Franklin Roosevelt's election in 1932 that the tug of war seems to have been won for the chief executive presidency, because after FDR, as we shall see, every president has been strong, whether he was committed to the strong presidency or not.

Thus, a strong executive, a genuine chief executive, has been institutionalized in the twentieth century. But it continues to operate in a schizoid environment: As the power of the presidency has increased, popular expectations of presidential performance have increased at an even faster rate, requiring more leadership than was ever exercised by any but the greatest presidents in the past. The growth of the presidency has created a "dilemma of power":[4] How can we provide enough presidential power without providing too much? This dilemma of power is part of our past and will no doubt continue to be part of our future.

[2]Theodore Roosevelt, *An Autobiography* (New York: Charles Scribner's Sons, 1931), p. 388.

[3]Quoted in James MacGregor Burns, *John Kennedy—A Political Profile* (New York: Harcourt, Brace, 1959), p. 275. It is interesting that Kennedy made these remarks nearly two years prior to his election to the presidency.

[4]The idea of a "dilemma of power" comes from Barrington Moore, *Soviet Politics: The Dilemma of Power* (Cambridge: Harvard University Press, 1951).

Our focus in this chapter will be on the development of the institutional character of the presidency, the power of the presidency, and the relationship between the two. The chapter is divided into four sections. First, we shall review the constitutional origins of the presidency. In particular, this will involve an examination of the constitutional basis for the president's foreign and domestic roles. Second, we shall review the history of the American presidency to see how the office has evolved from its original status under the Constitution. We will look particularly at the ways in which Congress has augmented the president's constitutional powers by deliberately delegating to the presidency many of Congress's own responsibilities. Third, we shall assess both the formal and informal means by which presidents can enhance their own ability to govern. We will conclude by reviewing presidential power and evaluating the question "Does the president have too much or too little power?"

**THE CENTRAL QUESTION**

"Does the president have too much or too little power?"

## THE CONSTITUTIONAL BASIS OF THE PRESIDENCY

Article II of the Constitution, which establishes the presidency, does not solve the dilemma of power. Although Article II has been called "the most loosely drawn chapter of the Constitution,"[5] the framers were neither indecisive nor confused. They held profoundly conflicting views of the executive branch, and Article II was probably the best compromise they could make. The formulation the framers agreed upon is magnificent in its ambiguity: "The executive Power shall be vested in a President of the United States of America" (Article II, Section 1, first sentence). The meaning of "executive power," however, is not defined except indirectly in the very last sentence of Section 3, which provides that the president "shall take Care that the Laws be faithfully executed."[6]

One very important conclusion can be drawn from these two provisions: The office of the president was to be an office of ***delegated powers.*** Since, as we have already seen, all of the powers of the national government are defined as powers of Congress and are incorporated into Article I, Section 8, then the "executive power" of Article II, Section 3, must be understood to be defined as the power to execute faithfully the laws *as they are adopted* by Congress. This does not doom the presidency to weakness. Presumably, Congress can pass laws delegating almost any of its powers to the president. But presidents are not free to discover sources of executive power completely independent of the laws as passed by Congress. In the 1890 case of *In re Neagle,* the Supreme Court did hold that the president could be bold and expansive in the inferences he drew from the

[5]E. S. Corwin, *The President: Office and Powers,* 3rd rev. ed. (New York: New York University Press, 1957), p. 2.

[6]Article II, Section 3. There is a Section 4, but all it does is define impeachment.

Constitution as to "the rights, duties and obligations" of the presidency; but the ***inherent powers*** of the president would have to be inferred from that Constitution and laws, not from some independent or absolute idea of executive power.[7]

Immediately following the first sentence of Section 1, Article II defines the manner in which the president is to be chosen. This is a very odd sequence, but it does say something about the struggle the delegates were having over how to provide great power of action or energy to the executive and at the same time to balance that power with limitations. The struggle was between those delegates who wanted the president to be selected by, and thus responsible to, Congress and those delegates who preferred that the president be elected directly by the people. Direct popular election would create a more independent and more powerful presidency. With the adoption of a scheme of indirect election through an electoral college in which the electors would be selected by the state legislatures (and close elections would be resolved in the House of Representatives), the framers hoped to achieve a "republican" solution: a strong president responsible to state and national legislators rather than directly to the electorate.

The heart of presidential power as defined by the Constitution, however, is found in Sections 2 and 3, where the several clauses define the presidency in two dimensions: the president as head of state and the president as head of government. Although these will be given separate treatment here, the presidency can be understood only by the combination of the two.

## The President as Head of State: Some Imperial Qualities

The constitutional position of the president as head of state is defined by three constitutional provisions, which are the source of some of the most important powers on which presidents can draw. The areas can be classified as follows:

1. *Military.* Article II, Section 2, provides for the power as "Commander in Chief of the Army and Navy of the United States, and of the Militia of the several States, when called in to the actual Service of the United States."
2. *Judicial.* Article II, Section 2, also provides the power to "grant Reprieves and Pardons for Offenses against the United States, except in Cases of Impeachment."
3. *Diplomatic.* Article II, Section 3, provides the power to "receive Ambassadors and other public Ministers."

**Military** First, the position of commander in chief makes the president the highest military authority in the United States, with control of the entire defense establishment. No American president, however, would dare put on a military uniform for a state function—not even a former general like

[7]In re Neagle, 135 U.S. 1 (1890). Neagle, a deputy U.S. marshal, had been authorized by the president to protect a Supreme Court justice whose life had been threatened by an angry litigant. When the litigant attempted to carry out his threat, Neagle shot and killed him. Neagle was then arrested by the local authorities and tried for murder. His defense was that his act was "done in pursuance of a law of the United States." Although the law was not an act of Congress, the Supreme Court declared that it was an executive order of the president, and the protection of a federal judge was a reasonable extension of the president's power to "take care that the laws be faithfully executed."

Eisenhower—even though the president is the highest military officer in war and in peace. The president is also the head of the secret intelligence hierarchy, which includes not only the Central Intelligence Agency (CIA) but also the National Security Council (NSC), the National Security Agency (NSA), the Federal Bureau of Investigation (FBI), and a host of less well-known but very powerful international and domestic security agencies. But of course, care must be taken not to conclude too much from this—as some presidents have done. Although Article II, Section 1, does state that all the executive power is vested in the president, and Section 2 does provide that the president shall be commander in chief of all armed forces, including state militias, these impressive provisions must be read in the context of Article I, wherein seven of the eighteen clauses of Section 8 provide particular military and foreign policy powers to Congress, including the power to declare wars that presidents are responsible for. Presidents have tried to evade this at their peril. In full awareness of the woe visited upon President Lyndon Johnson for evading and misleading Congress at the outset of the Vietnam War, President Bush sought congressional authorization for the Gulf War in January 1991.

**Judicial** The presidential power to grant reprieves, pardons, and amnesties involves the power of life and death over all individuals who may be a threat to the security of the United States. Presidents may use this power on behalf of a particular individual, as did Gerald Ford when he pardoned Richard Nixon in 1974 "for all offenses against the United States which he . . . has committed or may have committed." Or they may use it on a large scale, as did President Andrew Johnson in 1868, when he gave full amnesty to all Southerners who had participated in the "Late Rebellion," and President Carter in 1977, when he declared an amnesty for all the draft evaders of the Vietnam War. This power of life and death over others helped elevate the president to the level of earlier conquerors and kings by establishing him as the person before whom supplicants might come to make their pleas for mercy.

**Diplomatic** When President Washington received Edmond Genêt ("Citizen Genêt") as the formal emissary of the revolutionary government of France in 1793 and had his cabinet officers and Congress back his decision, he established a greatly expanded interpretation of the power to "receive Ambassadors and other public Ministers," extending it to the power to "recognize" other countries. That power gives the president the almost unconditional authority to review the claims of any new ruling groups to determine if they indeed control the territory and population of their country, so that they can commit it to treaties and other agreements. Critics questioned the wisdom of President Nixon's recognition of the People's Republic of China and of President Carter's recognition of the Sandinista government in Nicaragua. But they did not question the president's authority to make such decisions. Because the breakup of the Soviet bloc was generally perceived as a positive event, no one criticized President Bush for his quick recognition of the several former Soviet and Yugoslav republics as soon as they declared themselves independent states.

**The Imperial Presidency?** Have presidents used these three constitutional powers—military, judicial, and diplomatic—to make the presidency too powerful, indeed "imperial?"[8] Debate over the answer to this question has produced an unusual lineup, with presidents and the Supreme Court on one side and Congress on the other. The Supreme Court supported the expansive view of the presidency in three historically significant cases. The first was *In re Neagle,* discussed above. The second was the 1936 *Curtiss-Wright* case, in which the Court held that Congress may delegate a degree of discretion to the president in foreign affairs that might violate the separation of powers if it were in a domestic arena.[9] In the third case, *U.S. v. Pink,* the Supreme Court upheld the president's power to use executive agreements to conduct foreign policy.[10] An ***executive agreement*** is exactly like a treaty because it is a contract between two countries; but an executive agreement does not require a two-thirds vote of approval by the Senate. Ordinarily, executive agreements are used to carry out commitments already made in treaties, or to arrange for matters well below the level of policy. But when presidents have found it expedient to use an executive agreement in place of a treaty, the Court has gone along. This verges on an imperial power.

Many recent presidents have even gone beyond formal executive agreements to engage in what amounts to unilateral action. They may seek formal congressional authorization, as in 1965 when President Lyndon Johnson convinced Congress to adopt the Gulf of Tonkin Resolution authorizing him to expand the American military presence in Vietnam. Johnson interpreted the resolution as a delegation of discretion to use any and all national resources according to his own judgment. Others may not even bother with the authorization but merely assume it, as President Nixon did when he claimed to need no congressional authorization at all to continue or to expand the Vietnam War.

These presidential claims and actions led to a congressional reaction, however. In 1973, Congress passed the War Powers Resolution over President Nixon's veto. This resolution asserted that the president could send American troops into action abroad only in the event of a declaration of war or other statutory authorization by Congress, or if American troops were attacked or directly endangered. This was an obvious effort to revive the principle that the presidency is an office

[8]Arthur Schlesinger, Jr., *The Imperial Presidency* (Boston: Houghton Mifflin, 1973).

[9]U.S. v. Curtiss-Wright Corp., 299 U.S. 304 (1936). In 1934, Congress passed a joint resolution authorizing the president to prohibit the sale of military supplies to Bolivia and Paraguay, who were at war, if the president determined that the prohibition would contribute to peace between the two countries. When prosecuted for violating the embargo order by President Roosevelt, the defendants argued that Congress could not constitutionally delegate such broad discretion to the president. The Supreme Court disagreed. Previously, however, the Court had rejected the National Industrial Recovery Act precisely because Congress had delegated too much discretion to the president in a domestic policy. See Schechter Poultry Corp. v. U.S., 295 U.S. 495 (1935).

[10]In United States v. Pink, 315 U.S. 203 (1942), the Supreme Court confirmed that an executive agreement is the legal equivalent of a treaty, despite the absence of Senate approval. This case approved the executive agreement that was used to establish diplomatic relations with the Soviet Union in 1933. An executive agreement, not a treaty, was used in 1940 to exchange "fifty over-age destroyers" for ninety-nine-year leases on some important military bases.

of *delegated* powers—that is, powers granted by Congress—and that there is no blanket prerogative—that is, no inherent presidential power.

Nevertheless, this resolution has not prevented presidents from using force when they deemed it necessary. President Reagan took at least four military actions that could be seen as violations of the War Powers Resolution. President Bush disregarded Congress in the 1989 invasion of Panama but was fortunate in bringing the affair to a successful conclusion quite quickly. In contrast, once he saw that the situation in Kuwait was tending toward protracted military involvement, he submitted the issue to Congress.

Although President Clinton had appeared at first to be reluctant to take bold international initiatives, he did not hesitate to use direct action when events seemed to threaten his own position or his view of the national interest. For example, Clinton did not seek congressional approval for ordering a missile launch against Iraqi intelligence headquarters in mid-1993, justifying it as a retaliation for an attack against the United States itself—Iraqi intelligence agents had allegedly plotted to assassinate former president George Bush. Clinton's ordering of military intervention in Haiti in September 1994 to overthrow Haiti's military regime would surely have brought loud calls in Congress for invocation of the War Powers Resolution if a single shot had been fired during the intervention. Fortunately for Clinton, his emissaries were able to persuade Haiti's military rulers to step down and to allow the restoration of civilian rule before any military action occurred.

Clinton's series of unilateral actions in Bosnia provided another demonstration of his view of his independence from Congress. First, Clinton unilaterally approved the use of American planes to bomb Serbian strategic positions in the late summer of 1995 (which pressured the Serbs to participate in peace negotiations with Croats and Bosnian Muslims). Second, to make the peace negotiation succeed, Clinton unilaterally pledged that American troops would be made available to monitor the implementation of the agreement; and he unilaterally committed 20,000 U.S. troops to fulfill his pledge once the agreement got underway. Then, with U.S. forces already in Bosnia, all Congress could do was pass a resolution in December 1995, after a long debate, to authorize financial support for the troops but to disapprove of Clinton's actions and to demand further reporting to Congress in the future. In December 1998, Clinton ordered the bombing of Iraqi military installations, without warning and without prior notice to Congress. What emerges from all these cases is a clear sense that no piece of legislation can end, once and for all, the struggle over questions of presidential power that is virtually lodged in our Constitution.

## The Domestic Presidency: The President as Head of Government

The constitutional basis of the domestic presidency also has three parts. And here again, although real power grows out of the combination of the parts, the analysis is greatly aided by examining the parts separately:

1. *Executive.* The "executive power" is vested in the president by Article II, Section 1, to see that all the laws are faithfully executed (Section 3), and to appoint, remove, and supervise all executive officers and to appoint all federal judges (Article II, Section 2).
2. *Military.* This power is derived from Article IV, Section 4, which stipulates that the president has the power to protect every state "against Invasion; . . . and . . . against domestic Violence."
3. *Legislative.* The president is given the power under various provisions to participate effectively and authoritatively in the legislative process.

**Executive Power** The most important basis of the president's power as chief executive is to be found in Article II, Section 3, which stipulates that the president must see that all the laws are faithfully executed, and Section 2, which provides that the president will appoint, remove, and supervise all executive officers, and appoint all federal judges. The *Neagle* case has already demonstrated the degree to which Article II, Section 1, is a source of executive power. Further powers do indeed come from this appointing power, although at first this may not seem to be very impressive. But the power to appoint the "principal executive officers" and to require each of them to report to the president on subjects relating to the duties of their departments makes the president the true chief executive officer (CEO) of the nation. In this manner, the Constitution focuses executive power and legal responsibility upon the president. The famous sign on President Truman's desk, "The buck stops here," was not merely an assertion of Truman's personal sense of responsibility but was in fact recognition by him of the legal and constitutional responsibility of the president. The president is subject to some limitations, because the appointment of all such officers, including ambassadors, ministers, and federal judges, is subject to a majority approval by the Senate. But these appointments are at the discretion of the president, and the loyalty and the responsibility of each appointment are presumed to be directed toward the president. Although the Constitution is silent on the power of the president to remove such officers, the federal courts have filled this silence with a series of decisions that grant the president this power.[11] Although the United States has no cabinet in the parliamentary sense of a collective decision-making body or board of directors with collective responsibilities (discussed later in this chapter), the Constitution nevertheless recognizes departments with department heads, and that recognition establishes the lines of legal responsibility up and down the executive hierarchy, culminating in the presidency (see Figure 6.1).

[11]The Supreme Court defined the president's removal power very broadly in Myers v. U.S., 272 U.S. 52 (1926). Later, in Humphrey's Executor v. U.S., 295 U.S. 62 (1935), the Court accepted Congress's effort to restrict presidential removal powers as they applied to heads of independent regulatory commissions. In those instances, the president can remove officers only "for cause." Two later cases restricted presidential power a bit further by providing that he could not remove at his pleasure certain other officers whose tasks require independence from the executive. See Wiener v. U.S., 357 U.S. 349 (1958); and Bowsher v. Synar, 478 U.S. 714 (1986). In another, more tricky case, the Court held that the attorney general, not the president, could remove a special prosecutor because of the power and obligation of the prosecutor to investigate the president. See Morrison v. Olson, 108 S.Ct. 2597 (1988).

FIGURE 6.1

**The Institutional Presidency***

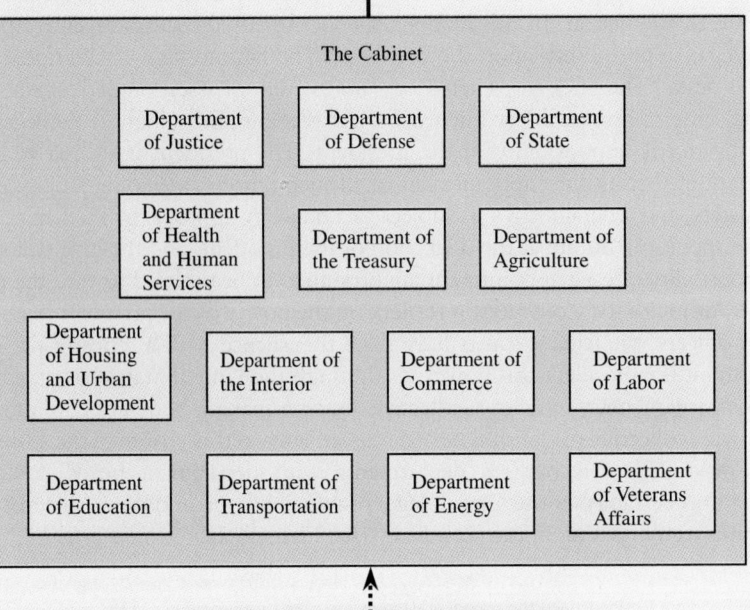


*Note: Arrows are used to indicate lines of legal responsibility.
Office of the Federal Register, National Archives and Records Administration, *The United States Government Manual, 1995–1996* (Washington, DC: Government Printing Office, 1995), p. 22.

DEBATING THE ISSUES

## Presidential Power: Broad or Narrow?

*Presidents and pundits have debated the proper scope of presidential power since the founding of the Republic. Some have argued that the Constitution provides broad latitude for presidents to act as they think best; others have asserted that presidents must be mindful of constitutional and political limitations in a three-branch system of government. In the twentieth century, the argument for a strong presidency has carried more weight. Yet in the face of such abuses of presidential power as Watergate and Iran-Contra, some have argued for a return to a more limited view of the presidency.*

*The first elected president of this century, Theodore Roosevelt, described in his autobiography his support for expansive presidential authority. Roosevelt's successor, William Howard Taft, summarized the arguments for presidential restraint. Their views are as timely today as a century ago.*

### ROOSEVELT

My view was that every executive officer, and above all every executive officer in high position, was a steward of the people bound actively and affirmatively to do all he could for the people, and not to content himself with the negative merit of keeping his talents undamaged in a napkin. . . . My belief was that it was not only his right but his duty to do anything that the needs of the nation demanded unless such action was forbidden by the Constitution or by the laws. Under this interpretation of executive power I did and caused to be done many things not previously done by the president and the heads of the departments. I did not usurp power, but I did greatly broaden the use of executive power. In other words, I acted for the public welfare, I acted for the common well-being of all our people, whenever and in whatever manner was necessary, unless prevented by direct constitutional or legislative prohibition.[1]

### TAFT

The true view of the executive functions is, as I conceive it, that the president can exercise no power which cannot be fairly and reasonably traced to some specific grant of power or justly implied and included within such express grant as proper and necessary to its exercise. Such specific grant must be either in the federal Constitution or in an act of Congress passed in pursuance thereof. There is no undefined residuum of power which he can exercise because it seems to him to be in the public interest, and there is nothing in the . . . law of the United States, or in other precedents, warranting such an inference. . . . [His] jurisdiction must be justified and vindicated by affirmative constitutional or statutory provision, or it does not exist.[2]

[1]Theodore Roosevelt, *An Autobiography* (New York: Scribners, 1958), pp. 197–200.
[2]William Howard Taft, *Our Chief Magistrate and His Powers* (New York: Columbia University Press, 1916), pp. 138–45.

**Military Sources of Domestic Presidential Power** Although Article IV, Section 4, provides that the "United States shall [protect] every . . . State . . . against Invasion . . . and . . . domestic Violence," Congress has made this an explicit presidential power through statutes directing the president as commander in chief to discharge these obligations.[12] The Constitution restrains the president's use of domestic force by providing that a state legislature (or governor when the legislature is not in session) must request federal troops before the president can send them into the state to provide public order. Yet, this proviso is not absolute. First, presidents are not obligated to deploy national troops merely because the state legislature or governor makes such a request. And more important, the president may deploy troops in a state or city without a specific request from the state legislature or governor if he considers it necessary in order to maintain an essential national service, in order to enforce a federal judicial order, or in order to protect federally guaranteed civil rights.

One historic example of the unilateral use of presidential power to protect the states against domestic disorder, even when the states don't request it, was the decision by President Eisenhower in 1957 to send troops into Little Rock, Arkansas, literally against the wishes of the state of Arkansas, to enforce court orders to integrate Little Rock's Central High School (see Chapter 4). Arkansas Governor Orval Faubus had actually posted the Arkansas National Guard at the entrance of the Central High School to prevent the court-ordered admission of nine black students. After an effort to negotiate with Governor Faubus failed, President Eisenhower reluctantly sent a thousand paratroopers to Little Rock, who stood watch while the black students took their places in the all-white classrooms. These cases make quite clear that the president does not have to wait for a request by a state legislature or governor before acting as a domestic commander in chief.[13]

However, in most instances of domestic disorder—whether from human or from natural causes—presidents tend to exercise unilateral power by declaring a "state of emergency," thereby making available federal grants, insurance, and direct assistance. In 1992, in the aftermath of the devastating riots in Los Angeles and the hurricanes in Florida, American troops were very much in evidence, sent in by the president, but in the role more of Good Samaritans than of military police.

**The President's Legislative Power** The president plays a role not only in the administration of government but also in the legislative process. Two constitutional provisions are the primary sources of the president's power in the legislative arena. The first of these is the provision in Article II, Section 3, providing that the president "shall from time to time give to the Congress Information of the State of the Union, and recommend to their Consideration such Measures as

[12]These statutes are contained mainly in Title 10 of the United States Code, Sections 331, 332, and 333.

[13]The best study covering all aspects of the domestic use of the military is that of Adam Yarmolinsky, *The Military Establishment* (New York: Harper & Row, 1971).

he shall judge necessary and expedient." The second of the president's legislative powers is of course the "veto power" assigned by Article I, Section 7.[14]

The first of these powers does not at first appear to be of any great import. It is a mere obligation on the part of the president to make recommendations for Congress's consideration. But as political and social conditions began to favor an increasingly prominent role for presidents, each president, especially since Franklin Delano Roosevelt, began to rely upon this provision to become the primary initiator of proposals for legislative action in Congress and the principal source for public awareness of national issues, as well as the most important single individual participant in legislative decisions. Few today doubt that the president and the executive branch together are the primary source for many important congressional actions.[15]

The ***veto*** power is the president's constitutional power to turn down acts of Congress. This power alone makes the president the most important single legislative leader.[16] No bill vetoed by the president can become law unless both the house and Senate override the veto by a two-thirds vote. In the case of a ***pocket veto,*** Congress does not even have the option of overriding the veto, but must reintroduce the bill in the next session. A pocket veto can occur when the president is presented with a bill during the last ten days of a legislative session. Usually, if a

**AMERICAN POLITICAL DEVELOPMENT**

In the nineteenth century, many presidents believed that the veto power should be used primarily (and, for some, exclusively) to protect the executive branch from congressional encroachment. Today's use of the veto for policy purposes only, greatly expands its use.

SOURCE: Louis Fisher, *Constitutional Conflicts between Congress and the President,* 4th rev. ed. (Lawrence: University Press of Kansas, 1997), pp. 119–32.

[14]There is a third source of presidential power implied from the provision for "faithful execution of the laws." This is the president's power to impound funds—that is, to refuse to spend money Congress has appropriated for certain purposes. One author referred to this as a "retroactive veto power" (Robert E. Goosetree, "The Power of the President to Impound Appropriated Funds," *American University Law Review,* January 1962). This impoundment power was used freely and to considerable effect by many modern presidents, and Congress occasionally delegated such power to the president by statute. But in reaction to the Watergate scandal, Congress adopted the Budget and Impoundment Control Act of 1974 and designed this act to circumscribe the president's ability to impound funds by requiring that the president must spend all appropriated funds unless both houses of Congress consent to an impoundment within forty-five days of a presidential request. Therefore, since 1974, the use of impoundment has declined significantly. Presidents have either had to bite their tongues and accept unwanted appropriations or had to revert to the older and more dependable but politically limited method of vetoing the entire bill. The line-item veto enacted by Congress in 1996 greatly increases the president's ability to use the veto to shape legislation.

[15]For a different perspective, see William F. Grover, *The President as Prisoner: A Structural Critique of the Carter and Reagan Years* (Albany: State University of New York Press, 1989).

[16]Although the veto power is the most important legislative resource in the hands of the president, it can often end in frustration, especially when the presidency and Congress are held by opposing parties. George Bush vetoed forty-six congressional enactments during his four years, and only one was overridden. Ronald Reagan vetoed thirty-nine in his eight years, and nine were overridden. This compares to thirty-one during Jimmy Carter's four years, with two overridden. In 1994, Bill Clinton did not veto a single bill, a record unmatched since the days of President Millard Fillmore in 1853; both, of course, were working with Congresses controlled by their own political party. For more on the veto, see Chapter 5 and Robert J. Spitzer, *The Presidential Veto—Touchstone of the American Presidency* (Albany: State University of New York Press, 1988).

ANALYZING AMERICAN POLITICS

## *Rational-Choice Perspectives on the Presidential Veto*

The role of the presidency vis-à-vis the separation of powers has changed dramatically since the dawn of the republic. One of the most important constitutional resources that presidents have used to equalize or perhaps upset the balance of power with Congress is the veto. While the simple power to reject or accept legislation in its entirety might seem like a crude tool for making sure that legislation adheres to a president's preferences, the politics surrounding the veto are quite complicated, and it is rare that vetoes are used simply as bullets to kill legislation dead. Instead, vetoes are usually part of an intricate bargaining process between the president and Congress, involving threats of vetoes, vetoes, repassing legislation, and re-vetoes. This process is the focus of Charles Cameron's recent book *Veto Bargaining*, the first book-length study to address the presidency from a rational-choice perspective.[1] This innovative work also synthesizes case studies and sophisticated statistical methods that test the rational-choice models.

Although presidents rarely veto legislation, Cameron argues that this does not mean vetoes and veto bargaining have an insignificant influence over the policy process. The fact that presidents vetoed only 434 of the 17,000 public bills that Congress sent to them between 1945 and 1992 belies the centrality of the veto to presidential power. Many of these bills were insignificant and not worth the veto effort. Thus it is important to separate "significant" legislation, for which vetoes frequently occur, from insignificant legislation.[2] Vetoes can also be effective—even though they are rarely employed—because of a concept known as "the second face of power," that is, individuals will condition their actions based on how they think others will respond.[3] With respect to vetoes, this means that members of Congress will alter the content of a bill to make it more to a president's liking in order to preempt a veto. Thus the veto power can be influential even when the veto pen rests in its inkwell. Cameron shows how the concept of "the second face of power" works to influence the content of legislation.

Rhetoric and reputation, he argues, take on particular importance when vetoes become part of a bargaining process. The key to veto bargaining is uncertainty. Members of Congress are often unsure about the

---

[1]Charles Cameron, *Veto Bargaining: Presidents and the Politics of Negative Power* (Cambridge: Cambridge University Press, 2000).

[2]David R. Mayhew, *Divided We Govern: Party Control, Lawmaking, and Investigations, 1946–1990* (New Haven: Yale University Press, 1991).

[3]Jack H. Nagel, *The Descriptive Analysis of Power* (New Haven: Yale University Press, 1975).

president's policy preferences and therefore don't know which bills the president would be willing to sign. When the policy preferences of the president and Congress diverge, as they typically do under divided government, the president tries to convince Congress that his preferences are more extreme than they really are in order to get Congress to enact something that is closer to what he really wants. If members of Congress knew the president's preferences ahead of time, they would pass a bill that was closest to what *they* wanted, minimally satisfying the president. Through strategic use of the veto and veto threats, a president tries to shape Congress's beliefs about his policy preferences to gain greater concessions from Congress. As in other contemporary studies, Cameron's work sees reputation as central to presidential effectiveness.[4] By influencing congressional beliefs, the president is building a policy reputation that will affect future congressional behavior.

Cameron develops rational-choice theories to explain veto bargaining and then tests these theories using data on significant legislation considered between 1945 and 1992. The theories focus on the ideological differences between the president and key members of Congress, in particular on the fact that members needed to form a two-thirds majority for overriding a veto. Cameron finds that the rational-choice theories do an extremely good job of explaining the data on vetoes. Some of his key findings are that veto threats occur more frequently under divided government than under unified government, and that veto threats are also more frequent under divided government when legislation is more significant. In addition, veto threats usually bring concessions, which in turn deter future vetoes.

Missing from Cameron's study is the relationship between mass public support for the president and the use of the veto. At least for the modern presidency, a crucial resource for the president in negotiating with Congress has been his public approval as measured by opinion polls.[5] This idea has been analyzed by political scientists Timothy Groseclose and Nolan McCarty. They examine situations where members of Congress pass a bill, not because they want to change policy but because they want to force the president to veto a popular bill that he disagrees with in order to make the president appear extreme and therefore to hurt his approval ratings.[6] The key to Groseclose and McCarty's theory is that the public, uncertain of the president's policy preferences, uses information conveyed by vetoes to update what they know about his preferences. In some cases, the president is willing to take a hit in his approval ratings if the bill is drastically inconsistent with his policies. Groseclose and McCarty found that a president's approval rating on average drops 2 percentage points when he vetoes a major piece of legislation. Thus vetoes can be very costly for presidents who may be reluctant to use vetoes to misrepresent their preferences to Congress (in order to gain concessions), if such vetoes will hurt them in the polls.

---

[4]Richard E. Neustadt, *Presidential Power* (New York: Wiley, 1960).

[5]Theodore J. Lowi, *The Personal President: Power Invested, Promise Unfulfilled* (Ithaca, NY: Cornell University Press, 1985).

[6]Timothy Groseclose and Nolan McCarty, "Partisanship, Vetoes, and the Politics of Blame." Paper presented at the 1995 Annual Meeting of the American Political Science Association.

president does not sign a bill within ten days, it automatically becomes law. But this is true only while Congress is in session. If a president chooses not to sign a bill within the last ten days that Congress is in session, then the ten-day limit does not expire until Congress is out of session, and instead of becoming law, the bill is vetoed. Process Box 6.1 illustrates the president's veto options. In 1996 a new power was added—the line-item veto—giving the president power to strike spe-

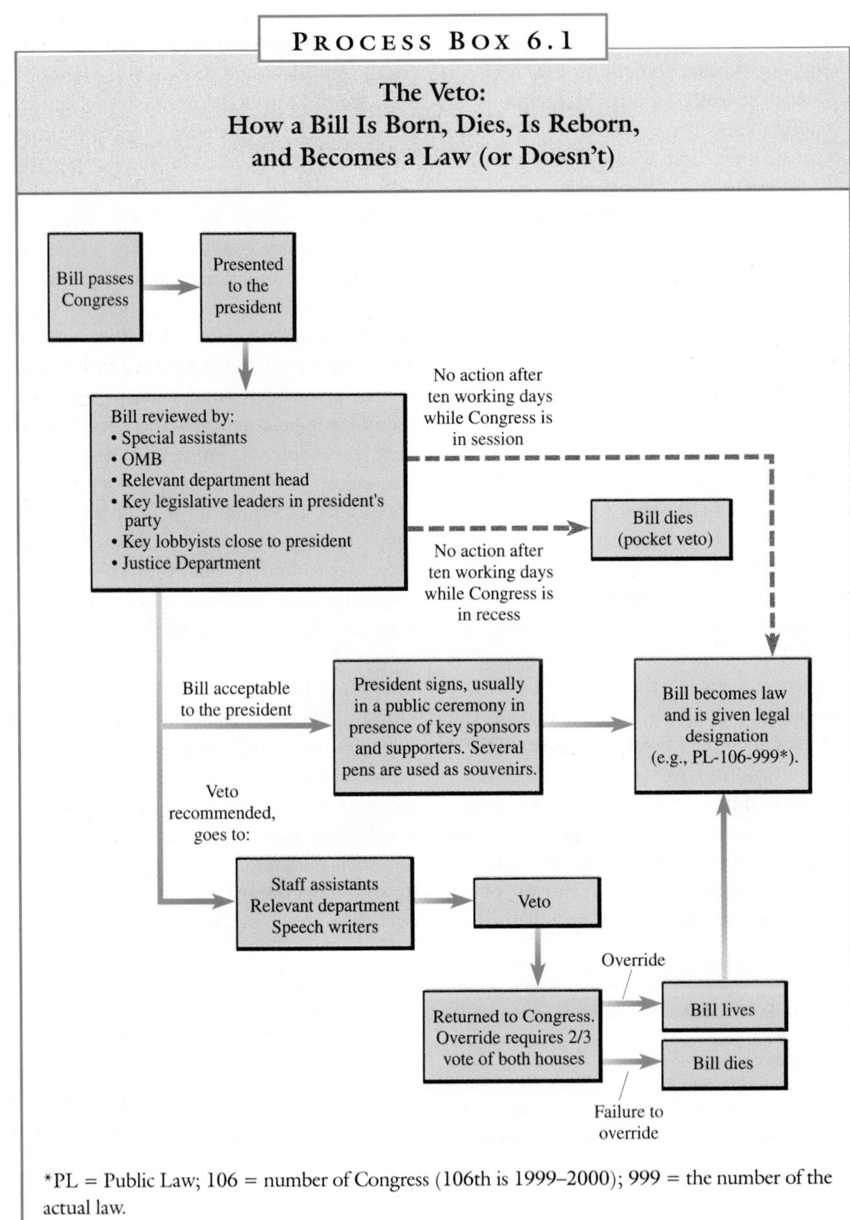

cific spending items from appropriations bills passed by Congress, unless re-enacted by a two-thirds vote of both House and Senate. In 1997, President Clinton used this power eleven times to strike eighty-two items from the federal budget. But, as we saw in Chapter 5, in 1998 the Supreme Court ruled that the Constitution does not authorize the line-item veto power. Only a constitutional amendment would restore this power to the president.

When these two sources of power are taken together—the president's constitutional duty to address Congress on the state of the union and the president's veto power—it is remarkable that it took so long—well over a century—for these constitutional powers to be fully realized. Let us see how this happened as well as why it took so long.

## THE RISE OF PRESIDENTIAL GOVERNMENT

Most of the real power of the modern presidency comes from the powers granted by the Constitution and the laws made by Congress.[17] Thus, any person properly elected and sworn in as president will possess almost all of the power held by the strongest presidents in American history. Even when they are "lame ducks," presidents still possess all the power of the office. For example, during the weeks after his electoral defeat in 1992, President Bush committed troops to Somalia and conducted a series of air strikes against Iraq.

This case illustrates an extremely important fact about the presidency: *The popular base of the presidency is important less because it gives the president power than because it gives him consent to use all the powers already vested by the Constitution in the office.* Anyone installed in the office could exercise most of its powers.

The presidency is a democratic institution. Although the office is not free from the powerful interests in society, neither is it a product or a captive of any one set of interests. Its broad popular base is a great resource for presidential power. *But resources are not power.* They must be converted to power, and as in physics, energy is expended in the conversion. It took more than a century, perhaps as much as a century and a half, before presidential government came to replace congressional government. A bit of historical review will be helpful in understanding how presidential government arose.

### The Legislative Epoch, 1800–1933

In 1885, an obscure political science professor named Woodrow Wilson entitled his general textbook *Congressional Government* because American government was just that, "congressional government." This characterization seemed to fly in the face of the separation of powers principle that the three separate branches

[17]This very useful distinction between pow*er* and pow*ers* is inspired by Richard Neustadt, *Presidential Power* (New York: Wiley, 1960), p. 28.

were and ought to be equal. Nevertheless, there is ample evidence that Wilson's description of the national government was not only consistent with nineteenth-century reality but also with the intentions of the framers. Within the system of three separate and competing powers, the clear intent of the Constitution was for *legislative supremacy.*

The strongest evidence of original intent is the fact that the powers of the national government were not placed in a separate article of the Constitution, but were instead listed in Article I, the legislative article. Madison had laid it out explicitly in *The Federalist* No. 51: "In republican government, the legislative authority necessarily predominates." President Washington echoed this in his first inaugural address in 1789:

> By the article establishing the Executive Department, it is made the duty of the President "to recommend to your consideration, such measures as he shall judge necessary and expedient."—The circumstances under which I now meet you, will acquit me from entering into that subject, farther than to refer to the Great Constitutional Charter . . . which, in defining your powers, designates the objects to which your attention is to be given.—It will be more consistent with those circumstances . . . to substitute, in place of a recommendation of particular measures, the tribute that is due . . . the characters selected to devise and adopt them.

The first decade was of course unique precisely because it was first; everything was precedent making, and nothing was secure. It was a state-building decade in which relations between president and Congress were more cooperative than they would be at any time thereafter. The First Congress of 1789–1791 accomplished an incredible amount. In seven short months following Washington's inauguration, Congress provided for the organization of the executive and judicial branches, established a first system of national revenue, and worked through the first seventeen amendments proposed to the Constitution, ten of which were to be ratified to become the Bill of Rights.[18]

One of the last actions of the First Congress, First Session, was to authorize the secretary of the treasury, Alexander Hamilton, to develop a policy to establish a system for national credit. In January 1790, during the Second Session, Hamilton submitted to Congress such a proposal; his *Report on Public Credit* is one of the great state papers in the history of American public policy. In 1791, Hamilton presented the second of the reports ordered by Congress, the *Report on Manufactures,* probably of even greater significance than the first, because its proposals for internal improvements and industrial policies influenced Congress's agenda for years to come. Thus, it was Congress that ordered that a policy agenda be prepared by the president or his agent. In creating the executive departments, however, Congress (in particular the House) was so fearful of the powers to be lodged in the Treasury Department that it came close to adopting a three-man board, which many Antifederalists favored. The compromise tried to make the Treasury Department an agent of Congress rather than simply a member of the

[18]See Richard Buel, Jr., *Securing the Revolution: Ideology in American Politics, 1789–1815* (Ithaca, NY: Cornell University Press, 1972), Part I; also see Chapter 4 of this book.

independent executive branch.[19] This kind of cooperation resembles the British parliamentary system, but it was not to last.

Before the Republic was a decade old, Congress began to develop a strong organization, including its own elected leadership, the first standing committees, and the party hierarchies. By President Jefferson's second term (1805), the executive branch was beginning to play the secondary role anticipated by the Constitution. The quality of presidential performance and then of presidential personality and character declined accordingly. The president during this era was seen by some observers as little more than America's "chief clerk." It was said of President James Madison, who had been principal author of the Constitution, that he knew everything about government except how to govern. Indeed, after Jefferson and until the beginning of this century, most historians agree that Presidents Jackson and Lincoln were the only exceptions to what had been a dreary succession of weak presidents. And those two exceptions can be explained. Jackson was a war hero and founder of the Democratic party. Lincoln was also a founder of his party, the Republican party, and although not a war hero, he was a wartime president who exercised the extraordinary powers that are available to any president during war, because during war the Constitution is put on hold. Both Jackson and Lincoln are considered great presidents because they used their great power wisely. But it is important in the history of the presidency that neither of these great presidents left their own powers as a new institutional legacy to their successors. That is to say, once Jackson and Lincoln left office, the presidency went back to the subordinate role it played during the nineteenth century.

One of the reasons that so few great men became presidents in the nineteenth century is that there was only occasional room for greatness in such a weak office.[20] As Chapter 3 indicated, the national government of that period was not a particularly powerful entity. Moreover, most of the policies adopted by the national government were designed mainly to promote the expansion of commerce. These could be directed and administered by the congressional committees and political parties without much reliance on an executive bureaucracy.

Another reason for the weak presidency of the nineteenth century is that during this period the presidency was not closely linked to major national political and social forces. Indeed, there were few important *national* political or social forces to which presidents could have linked themselves even if they had wanted to. Federalism had taken very good care of this by fragmenting political interests and diverting the energies of interest groups toward the state and local levels of government, where most key decisions were being made.

The presidency was strengthened somewhat in the 1830s with the introduction of the national convention system of nominating presidential candidates.

[19]See, for example, Forrest McDonald, *The Presidency of George Washington* (Lawrence: University Press of Kansas, 1974), pp. 36–42.

[20]For related appraisals, see Jeffrey Tulis, *The Rhetorical Presidency* (Princeton: Princeton University Press, 1987); Stephen Skowronek, *The Politics Presidents Make: Leadership from John Adams to George Bush* (Cambridge: Harvard University Press, 1993); and Robert Spitzer, *President and Congress: Executive Hegemony at the Crossroads of American Government* (New York: McGraw-Hill, 1993).

Until then, presidential candidates had been nominated by their party's congressional delegates. This was the *caucus* system of nominating candidates, and it was derisively called "King Caucus" because any candidate for president had to be beholden to the party's leaders in Congress in order to get the party's nomination and the support of the party's congressional delegation in the election. The national nominating convention arose outside Congress in order to provide some representation for a party's voters who lived in districts where they weren't numerous enough to elect a member of Congress. The political party in each state made its own provisions for selecting delegates to attend the presidential nominating convention, and in virtually all states the selection was dominated by the party leaders (called "bosses" by the opposition party). It is only in recent decades that state laws have intervened to regularize the selection process and to provide (in all but a few instances) for open election of delegates. The convention system quickly became the most popular method of nominating candidates for all elective offices and remained so until well into the twentieth century, when it succumbed to the criticism that it was a nondemocratic method dominated by a few leaders in a "smoke-filled room." But in the nineteenth century, it was seen as a victory for democracy against the congressional elite. And the national convention gave the presidency a base of power independent of Congress.

This additional independence did not immediately transform the presidency into the office we recognize today because the parties disappeared back into their states and Congress once the national election was over. But the national convention did begin to open the presidency to larger social forces and newly organized interests in society. In other words, it gave the presidency a constituency base that would eventually support and demand increased presidential power. Improvements in telephone, telegraph, and other forms of mass communication allowed individuals to share their complaints and allowed national leaders—especially presidents and presidential candidates—to reach out directly to people to ally themselves with, and even sometimes to create, popular groups and forces. Eventually, though more slowly, the presidential selection process began to be further democratized, with the adoption of primary elections through which millions of ordinary citizens were given an opportunity to take part in the presidential nominating process by popular selection of convention delegates.

Despite political and social conditions favoring the enhancement of presidential power, however, the development of presidential government as we know it today did not mature until the middle of our own century. For a long period, even as the national government began to grow, Congress was careful to keep tight reins on the president's power. For example, when Congress began to make its first efforts to exert power over the economy (beginning in 1887 with the

**AMERICAN POLITICAL DEVELOPMENT**

From the beginning of the republic until 1900, presidential leaders had to deal with powerful political elites who directly affected their reputations and their political parties. In the twentieth century, however, the ability to connect to various groups has led to a more "pluralist" or even a "plebiscitary" presidency, which has, in turn, mobilized some of these groups *against* the Washington elites.

SOURCE: Sidney M. Milkis, *The President and the Parties* (New York: Oxford University Press, 1993).

adoption of the Interstate Commerce Act and in 1890 with the adoption of the Sherman Antitrust Act), it sought to keep this power away from the president and the executive branch by placing these new regulatory policies in "independent regulatory commissions" responsible to Congress rather than to the president (see also Chapter 7).

The real turning point in the history of American national government came during the administration of Franklin Delano Roosevelt. The New Deal was a response to political forces that had been gathering national strength and focus for fifty years. What is remarkable is not that they gathered but that they were so long gaining influence in Washington—and even then it took the Great Depression to bring about the new national government.

## The New Deal and the Presidency

The "First Hundred Days" of the Roosevelt administration in 1933 had no parallel in U.S. history. But this period was only the beginning. The policies proposed by President Roosevelt and adopted by Congress during the first thousand days of his administration so changed the size and character of the national government that they constitute a moment in American history equivalent to the founding or to the Civil War. The president's constitutional obligation to see "that the laws be faithfully executed" became, during Roosevelt's presidency, virtually a responsibility to shape the laws before executing them.

**New Programs Expand the Role of National Government** Many of the New Deal programs were extensions of the traditional national government approach, which was described already in Chapter 3 (see especially Table 3.1). But the New Deal went well beyond the traditional approach, adopting types of policies never before tried on a large scale by the national government; it began intervening into economic life in ways that had hitherto been reserved to the states. In other words, the national government discovered that it, too, had "police power" and could directly regulate individuals as well as provide roads and other services.

The new programs were such dramatic departures from the traditional policies of the national government that their constitutionality was in doubt. The Supreme Court in fact declared several of them unconstitutional, mainly on the grounds that in regulating the conduct of individuals or their employers, the national government was reaching beyond "*inter*state" into "*intra*state," essentially local, matters. Most of the New Deal remained in constitutional limbo until 1937, five years after Roosevelt was first elected and one year after his landslide 1936 re-election.

The turning point came with *National Labor Relations Board v. Jones & Laughlin Steel Corporation.* At issue was the National Labor Relations Act, or Wagner Act, which prohibited corporations from interfering with the efforts of employees to organize into unions, to bargain collectively over wages and working conditions, and under certain conditions, to go on strike and engage in picketing. The newly formed National Labor Relations Board (NLRB) had ordered Jones & Laughlin to reinstate workers fired because of their union activities. The appeal reached the Supreme Court because Jones & Laughlin had made a constitutional issue over the fact that its manufacturing activities were local and therefore beyond the national government's reach. The Supreme Court rejected this argument with the response that a big company with subsidiaries and suppliers in many states was innately in interstate commerce:

> When industries organize themselves on a national scale, making their relation to interstate commerce the dominant factor in their activities, how can it be maintained that their industrial labor relations constitute a forbidden field into which Congress may not enter when it is necessary to protect interstate commerce from the paralyzing consequences of industrial war?[21]

Since the end of the New Deal, the Supreme Court has never again seriously questioned the constitutionality of an important act of Congress broadly authorizing the executive branch to intervene into the economy or society.[22]

**Delegation of Power** The most important constitutional effect of Congress's actions and the Supreme Court's approval of those actions during the New Deal was the enhancement of *presidential power.* Most major acts of Congress in this period involved significant exercises of control over the economy. But few programs specified the actual controls to be used. Instead, Congress authorized the president or, in some cases, a new agency to determine what the controls would be. Some of the new agencies were independent commissions responsible to Congress. But most of the new agencies and programs of the New Deal were placed in the executive branch directly under presidential authority.

Technically, this form of congressional act is called the "delegation of power." In theory, the delegation of power works as follows: (1) Congress recognizes a problem; (2) Congress acknowledges that it has neither the time nor expertise to deal with the problem; and (3) Congress therefore sets the basic policies and then delegates to an agency the power to "fill in the details." But in practice, Congress was delegating not merely the power to "fill in the details," but actual and real *policy-making powers,* that is, real legislative powers, to the executive branch. For example, the president through the secretary of agriculture was authorized by the 1938 Agricultural Adjustment Act to determine the amount of acreage each and

[21]NLRB v. Jones & Laughlin Steel Corporation, 301 U.S. 1 (1937). Congress had attempted to regulate the economy before 1933, as with the Interstate Commerce Act and Sherman Antitrust Act of the late nineteenth century and with the Federal Trade Act and the Federal Reserve in the Wilson period. But these were rare attempts, and each was restricted very carefully to a narrow and acceptable definition of "interstate commerce." The big break did not come until after 1933.

[22]Some will argue that there are some exceptions to this statement. One was the 1976 case declaring unconstitutional Congress's effort to supply national minimum wage standards to state and local government employees (National League of Cities v. Usery, 426 U.S. 833 [1976]). But the Court reversed itself on this nine years later, in 1985 (Garcia v. San Antonio Metropolitan Transit Authority, 469 U.S. 528 [1985]). Another was the 1986 case declaring unconstitutional the part of the Gramm-Rudman law authorizing the comptroller general to make "across the board" budget cuts when total appropriations exceeded legally established ceilings (Bowsher v. Synar, 478 U.S. 714 [1986]). In 1999, executive authority was compromised somewhat by the Court's decision to question the Federal Communication Commission's authority to supervise telephone deregulation under the Telecommunications Act of 1996. But cases such as these are few and far between, and they only touch on part of a law, not the constitutionality of an entire program.

every farmer could devote to crops that had been determined to be surplus commodities, in order to keep prices up and surpluses down. This new authority extended from growers of thousands of acres of wheat for market to farmers cultivating twenty-five acres of feed for their own livestock.[23]

This authority continues today in virtually the same form, covering many commodities and millions of acres. Lest this is thought to be a power delegated to the president only during emergencies like the 1930s, take the example of environmental protection laws passed by Congress in the 1960s and 1970s. Under the president, the Environmental Protection Agency was given the authority to "monitor the conditions of the environment," "establish quantitative base lines for pollution levels," and "set and enforce standards of air and water quality and for individual pollutants."[24]

No modern government can avoid the delegation of significant legislative powers to the executive branch. But the fact remains that this delegation produced a fundamental shift in the American constitutional framework. *During the 1930s, the growth of the national government through acts delegating legislative power tilted the American national structure away from a Congress-centered government toward a president-centered government.*[25] Congress continues to be the constitutional source of policy, and Congress can rescind these delegations of power or can restrict them with later amendments, committee oversight, or budget cuts. But we can say that presidential government has become an established fact of American life.

**AMERICAN POLITICAL DEVELOPMENT**

The growth of national executive agencies and departments under the New Deal provided a new resource for presidential leadership: administrative leadership. Coupled with presidential frustration in leading a sometime recalcitrant Congress, this new capacity has provided potent opportunities for nonlegislative presidential policy making in the post–New Deal era. Unlike the nineteenth century, when there wasn't much to administer, today's presidential leadership is often administrative leadership.

SOURCE: Stephen Skowronek, *The Politics Presidents Make: Leadership from John Adams to Bill Clinton* (Cambridge: Harvard University Press), 1997, pp. 52–58.

## PRESIDENTIAL GOVERNMENT

There was no great mystery in the shift from Congress-centered government to president-centered government. As observed above, Congress simply delegated

[23]See Wickard v. Filburn, 317 U.S. 111 (1942).

[24]Environmental Reorganization Plan of July 9, 1970, reprinted in *Congressional Quarterly Almanac*, 1970, pp. 119a–120a. Other examples of broad delegations of power to the president will be found in Theodore J. Lowi, *The End of Liberalism* (New York: W. W. Norton, 1979), Chapter 5. See also Sotirios Barber, *The Constitution and the Delegation of Congressional Power* (Chicago: University of Chicago Press, 1975).

[25]The Supreme Court did in fact *dis*approve broad delegations of legislative power by declaring the National Industrial Recovery Act of 1933 unconstitutional on the grounds that Congress did not accompany the broad delegations with sufficient standards or guidelines for presidential discretion (Panama Refining Co. v. Ryan, 293 U.S. 388 [1935], and Schechter Poultry Corp. v. United States, 295 U.S. 495 [1935]). The Supreme Court has never reversed those two decisions, but it has also never really followed them. Thus, broad delegations of legislative power from Congress to the executive branch can be presumed to be constitutional.

its own powers to the executive branch. Congress committed legiscide—or at least partial legiscide. These delegated powers were the link from congressional dominance to presidential dominance, and they became the main resources for presidential government.

Congressional delegations of power, however, are not the only resources available to the president. Presidents have at their disposal a variety of other formal and informal resources that have important implications for their ability to govern. Indeed, without these other resources, presidents would lack the ability—the tools of management and public mobilization—to make much use of the power and responsibility given to them by Congress. Let us first consider the president's formal or official resources and then, in the section following, turn to the more informal resources that affect a president's capacity to govern, in particular the president's base of popular support.

## Formal Resources of Presidential Power

**Patronage as a Tool of Management** The first tool of management available to most presidents is a form of ***patronage***—the choice of high-level political appointees. These appointments allow the president to fill top management positions with individuals who will attempt to carry out his agenda. But he must appoint individuals who have experience and interest in the programs that they are to administer and who share the president's goals with respect to these programs. At the same time, presidents use the appointment process to build links to powerful political and economic constituencies by giving representation to important state political party organizations, the business community, organized labor, the scientific and university communities, organized agriculture, and certain large and well-organized religious groups.

**The Cabinet** In the American system of government, the ***cabinet*** is the traditional but informal designation for the heads of all the major federal government departments. The cabinet has no constitutional status. Unlike in England and many other parliamentary countries, where the cabinet *is* the government, the American cabinet is not a collective body. It meets but makes no decisions as a group. Each appointment must be approved by the Senate but cabinet members are not responsible to the Senate or to Congress at large. Cabinet appointments help build party and popular support, but the cabinet is not a party organ. The cabinet is made up of directors, but is not a board of directors.

Aware of this fact, the president tends to develop a burning impatience with and a mild distrust of cabinet members; to make the cabinet a rubber stamp for actions already decided on; and to demand results, or the appearance of results, more immediately and more frequently than most department heads can provide. Since cabinet appointees generally have not shared political careers with the president or with each other, and since they may meet literally for the first time after their selection, the formation of an effective governing group out of this motley collection of appointments is unlikely. While President Clinton's insistence on a cabinet diverse enough to resemble American society could be considered an act of political wisdom, it virtually guaranteed that few of his appointees would ever have spent much time working together or would even know the policy positions or beliefs of the other appointees.[26]

Some presidents have relied more heavily on an "inner cabinet," the National Security Council (NSC). The NSC, established by law in 1947, is composed of the president, the vice president, the secretaries of state, defense, and the treasury, the attorney general, and other officials invited by the president. It has its own staff of foreign-policy specialists run by the special assistant to the president for national security affairs. For these highest appointments, presidents turn to people from outside Washington, usually long-time associates. A counterpart, the Domestic Council, was created by law in 1970, but no specific members were designated for it. President Clinton hit upon his own version of the Domestic Council, called the National Economic Council, which shares competing functions with the Council of Economic Advisers.

Presidents have obviously been uneven and unpredictable in their reliance on the NSC and other subcabinet bodies, because executive management is inherently a personal matter. Despite all the personal variations, however, one generalization can be made: Presidents have increasingly preferred the White House staff instead of the cabinet as their means of managing the gigantic executive branch.

**AMERICAN POLITICAL DEVELOPMENT**

The cabinet as a collective has its origins in President George Washington's second term. He did not consult executive officers as a group during his first term, but when he perceived a need for assistance in 1793, he turned to the Supreme Court, which, because of an earlier refusal of executive duty (ostensibly on constitutional grounds), had to decline counsel. It was then that Washington turned to the heads of his executive departments for advice.

SOURCE: Forrest McDonald, *The American Presidency: An Intellectual History* (Lawrence: University Press of Kansas, 1994), pp. 227–28.

**The White House Staff**[27] It is not accidental that journalists have come to popularize the staff of most recent presidents with such names as the "Irish Mafia" (Kennedy), the "Georgia Mafia" (Carter), and the "California Mafia" (Reagan). President Bush's inner staff was characterized less as a "mafia" and more as a "club," composed of "camaraderie, humor, and male bonding."[28] Like every modern president, Bush gathered around him people who fought most of the battles with him during his long struggle for ultimate political success. President Clinton's early appointments indicated that his White House staff would be even more traditional than that of President Bush. His first chief of staff, Thomas "Mack" McLarty, was a close friend from Clinton's childhood, deeply familiar with and loyal to the president. The rest of the White House staff was, especially in the early phase of the Clinton presidency, much the same—lacking in independent political stature but long on familiarity and loyalty.

But after what seemed a promising beginning, Clinton's White House staff emerged as one of the chief failures in his efforts to develop a strong, cohesive

[26]*New York Times,* 23 December 1992, p. 1.

[27]A substantial portion of this section is taken from Theodore J. Lowi, *The Personal President* (Ithaca, NY: Cornell University Press, 1985), pp. 141–50.

[28]Ann Reilly Dowd, "How Bush Manages the Presidency," *Fortune,* 27 August 1990, p. 74.

**AMERICAN POLITICAL DEVELOPMENT**

The importance of a presidential staff is exemplified in the pre–New Deal era. President Theodore Roosevelt's atypical success in constructing naval policy in an otherwise Congress-dominated policy arena is attributed to his willingness and ability to assemble a protostaff of apolitical experts to assist him in developing naval policy.

SOURCE: Peri E. Arnold, "Policy Leadership in the Progressive Presidency: The Case of Theodore Roosevelt's Naval Policy and His Search for Strategic Resources," *Studies in American Political Development* 12 (1996), pp. 333–59.

presidency. Clinton's staff, to his misfortune, became one of the most ineffective and error-plagued in recent presidential memory.

The White House staff is composed mainly of analysts and advisers. Although many of the top White House staffers are given the title "special assistant" for a particular task or sector, the types of judgments they are expected to make and the kinds of advice they are supposed to give are a good deal broader and more generally political than those which come from the Executive Office of the President or from the cabinet departments.

From an informal group of fewer than a dozen people (at one time popularly called the ***Kitchen Cabinet***), and no more than four dozen at the height of the domestic Roosevelt presidency in 1937, the White House staff has grown substantially (see Table 6.1).[29] President Clinton promised during the 1992 campaign to reduce the White House staff by 25 percent, and by 1996 had trimmed it by about 15 percent. Nevertheless, a large White House staff has become essential.

The biggest variation among presidential management practices lies not in the size of the White House staff but in its organization. President Reagan went to the extreme in delegating important management powers to his chief of staff, and he elevated his budget director to an unprecedented level of power in *policy* making rather than merely *budget* making. President Bush centralized his staff even more under chief of staff John Sununu. At the same time, Bush continued to deal directly with his cabinet heads, the press, and key members of Congress. President Clinton showed a definite preference for competition among equals in his cabinet and among senior White House officials, obviously liking competition and conflict among staff members, for which FDR's staff was also famous. But the troubles Clinton has had in turning this conflict and competition into coherent policies and well-articulated messages suggests that he might have done better to emulate his immediate predecessors in their preference for hierarchy and centralization.[30]

**The Executive Office of the President** The development of the White House staff can be appreciated only in its relation to the still larger Executive Office of the President (EOP). Created in 1939, the EOP is what is often called the "institutional presidency"—the permanent agencies that perform defined management tasks for the president. The most important and the largest EOP agency is the Office of Management and Budget (OMB). Its roles in preparing the national

[29]All the figures since 1967, and probably 1957, are understated, because additional White House staff members were on "detailed" service from the military and other departments (some secretly assigned) and are not counted here because they were not on the White House payroll.

[30]See Donna K. H. Walter, "The Disarray at the White House Proves Clinton Wouldn't Last as a Fortune 500 CEO," *The Plain Dealer,* 10 July 1994, p. JC; and Paul Richeter, "The Battle for Washington: Leon Panetta's Burden," *Los Angeles Times Sunday Magazine,* 8 January 1995, p. 16.

TABLE 6.1

**The Expanding White House Staff**

| YEAR | PRESIDENT | FULL-TIME EMPLOYEES* |
|---|---|---|
| 1937 | Franklin D. Roosevelt | 45 |
| 1947 | Harry S Truman | 190 |
| 1957 | Dwight D. Eisenhower | 364 |
| 1967 | Lyndon B. Johnson | 251 |
| 1972 | Richard M. Nixon | 550 |
| 1975 | Gerald R. Ford | 533 |
| 1980 | Jimmy Carter | 488 |
| 1984 | Ronald Reagan | 575 |
| 1992 | George Bush | 605** |
| 1996 | Bill Clinton | 511** |

*The vice president employs over 20 staffers, and there are at least 100 on the staff of the National Security Council. These people work in and around the White House and Executive Office but are not included in the above totals.

**These figures include the staffs of the Office of the President, the Executive Residence, and the Office of the Vice President. None of the figures include the employees temporarily detailed to the White House from outside agencies (approximately 50 to 75 in 1992 and 1996). While not precisely comparable, these figures convey a sense of scale.

SOURCE: Thomas E. Cronin, "The Swelling of the Presidency: Can Anyone Reverse the Tide?" in *American Government: Readings and Cases,* 8th ed., ed. Peter Woll (Boston: Little Brown, 1984), p. 347. Copyright © 1984 by Thomas E. Cronin. Reproduced with the permission of the author. Figures for 1992 and 1996 provided by the Office of Management and Budget and the White House.

budget, designing the president's program, reporting on agency activities, and overseeing regulatory proposals make OMB personnel part of virtually every conceivable presidential responsibility. The status and power of the OMB has grown in importance with each successive president. The process of budgeting at one time was a "bottom-up" procedure, with expenditure and program requests passing from the lowest bureaus through the departments to "clearance" in OMB and hence to Congress, where each agency could be called in to reveal what its "original request" had been before OMB revised it. Now the budgeting process is a "top-down"; OMB sets the terms of discourse for agencies as well as for Congress. The director of OMB is now one of the most powerful officials in Washington. The staff of the Council of Economic Advisers (CEA) constantly analyzes the economy and economic trends and attempts to give the president the ability to anticipate events rather than to wait and react to events. The Council on Environmental Quality was designed to do the same for environmental issues as the CEA does for economic issues. The National Security Council (NSC) is composed of designated cabinet officials who meet regularly with the president to advise him on the large national security picture. The staff of the NSC both assimilates and

FIGURE 6.2

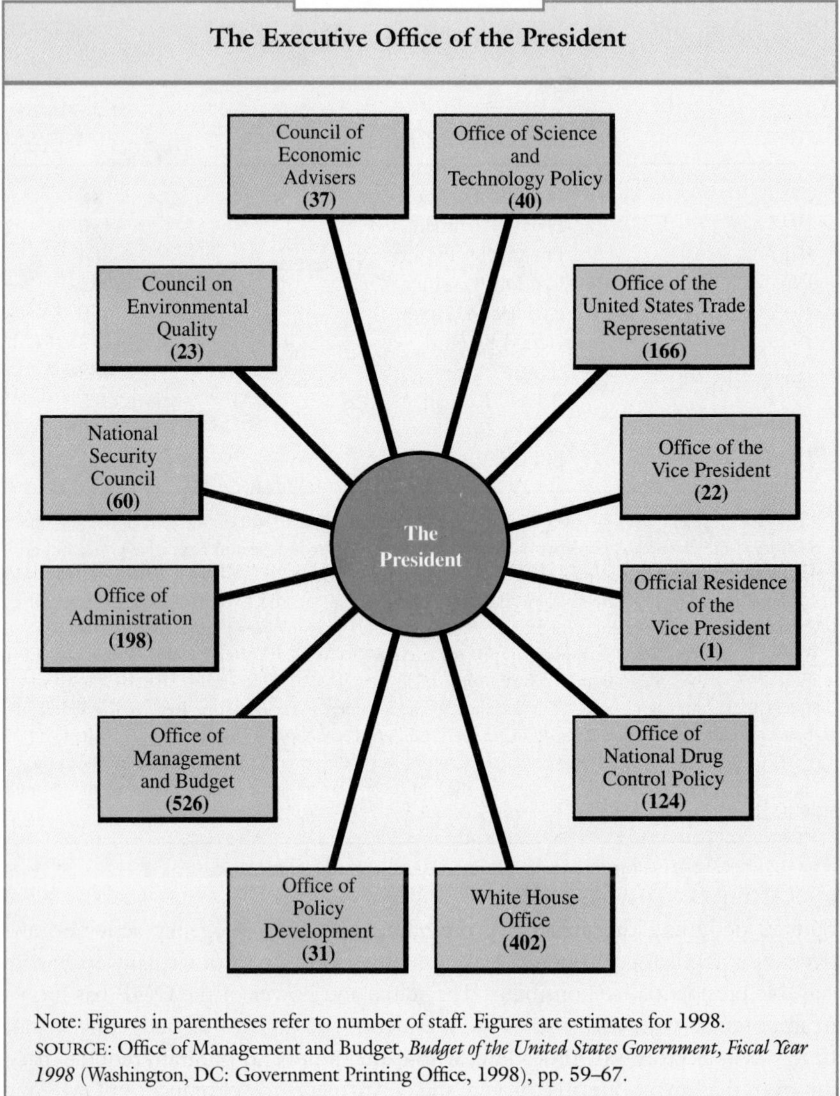


Note: Figures in parentheses refer to number of staff. Figures are estimates for 1998.
SOURCE: Office of Management and Budget, *Budget of the United States Government, Fiscal Year 1998* (Washington, DC: Government Printing Office, 1998), pp. 59–67.

analyzes data from all intelligence-gathering agencies (CIA, etc.). Other EOP agencies perform more specialized tasks for the president.

Somewhere between fifteen hundred and two thousand highly specialized people work for the EOP agencies.[31] Figure 6.2 shows the official numbers of

[31]The actual number is difficult to estimate because, as with White House staff, some EOP personnel, especially in national security work, are detailed to EOP from outside agencies.

employees in each agency of the EOP. However, these numbers do not include a substantial but variable number of key specialists detailed to EOP agencies from outside agencies, especially from the Pentagon to the staff of the NSC. The importance of each agency in EOP varies according to the personal orientations of each president. For example, the NSC staff was of immense importance under President Nixon, especially because it served essentially as the personal staff of presidential assistant Henry Kissinger. But it was of less importance to President Bush, who looked outside the EOP altogether for military policy matters, much more to the Joint Chiefs of Staff and its chair, General Colin Powell.

**AMERICAN POLITICAL DEVELOPMENT**

Prior to the ratification of the Twelfth Amendment in 1804, the vice president was the runner-up—rather than the running mate—to the president. The vice president's role as a campaign resource was enhanced, if not pioneered, by Theodore Roosevelt who, as a candidate for the vice presidency in 1900, was the first "vice presidential candidate . . . to campaign vigorously across the country. . . . Roosevelt gave 673 speeches to three million listeners in twenty-four states."

SOURCE: Michael Nelson, "Background Paper," in *A Heartbeat Away.* Report of the Twentieth Century Fund Task Force on the Vice Presidency (New York: Priority Press, 1988), p. 31.

**The Vice Presidency** The vice presidency is a constitutional anomaly even though the office was created along with the presidency by the Constitution. The vice president exists for two purposes only: to succeed the president in case of death, resignation, or incapacitation and to preside over the Senate casting the tie-breaking vote when necessary.[32]

The main value of the vice presidency as a political resource for the president is electoral. Traditionally, a presidential candidate's most important rule for the choice of a running mate is that he or she bring the support of at least one state (preferably a large one) not otherwise likely to support the ticket. Another rule holds that the vice presidential nominee should provide some regional balance and, wherever possible, some balance among various ideological or ethnic subsections of the party. It is very doubtful that John Kennedy would have won in 1960 without his vice presidential candidate, Lyndon Johnson, and the contribution Johnson made to carrying Texas. The emphasis, however, has recently shifted away from geographical to ideological balance. Bill Clinton combined considerations of region and ideology in his selection of a vice presidential running mate. The choice of Al Gore signaled that Bill Clinton was solidly in the right wing of the Democratic party and would also remain steadfastly a Southerner. Democratic strategists had become convinced that Clinton could not win without carrying a substantial number of Southern states.

Presidents have constantly promised to give their vice presidents more responsibility, but they almost always break their promise, indicating that they are unable to utilize the vice presidency as a management or political resource after the election. No one can explain exactly why. Perhaps it is just too much trouble

[32]Article I, Section 3, provides that "The Vice-President . . . shall be President of the Senate, but shall have no Vote, unless they be equally divided." This is the only vote the vice president is allowed.

to share responsibility. Perhaps the president as head of state feels unable to share any part of that status. Perhaps, like many adult Americans who do not draw up their wills, presidents may simply dread contemplating their own death. But management style is certainly a factor. President Clinton has relied greatly on his vice president, Al Gore, and Gore has emerged as one of the most trusted and effective figures in the Clinton White House.

Vice President Gore's enhanced status was signalled early on, when President Clinton kept him ostentatiously present at all public appearances during the transition and during the vital public and private efforts to present and campaign for the president's program early in 1993. Since then, he has remained one of the consistently praised members of the administration. Gore's most important task has been to oversee the National Performance Review (NPR), an ambitious program to "reinvent" the way the federal government conducts its affairs. The NPR was initially dismissed as show rather than substance, but even the administration's toughest critics have had to admit that Gore has led the drive to streamline the federal government with energy and effectiveness. With President Clinton's re-election, Gore's stature and role increased as a key advisor on new cabinet appointments. This took on all the greater significance because it gave Gore an ideal opportunity to build his Washington base and his national reputation toward a run for the presidency in 2000.

## Informal Resources of Presidential Power

**Elections as a Resource** What do we mean by the "democratization" of the presidency? We have already observed that an ordinary citizen placed legitimately in the presidency would be very powerful, regardless of any other consideration, because the Constitution and Congress have delegated to that office the legal powers and resources—in money and personnel—to carry out the duties of that office. But presidential power also comes from resources other than the formal, legal ones—and the greatest of these is the democratic base of the presidency. Obviously, presidents vary in their real power according to the size of their electoral victory. With a landslide (decisive) national electoral victory, a president may claim a "mandate," which is interpreted to mean that the electorate approved the victorious candidate's promised programs, and Congress must therefore go along. But even short of a mandate, a decisive election does increase the effectiveness of presidential leadership in Congress. Presidents Johnson and Reagan were much more effective in Congress during the "honeymoon" year following their landslide elections of 1964 and 1980, respectively, than were Kennedy after 1960, Nixon after 1968, and Carter after 1976. All three were hampered by their narrow victory margins. This was also true of President Clinton, who was an action-oriented president seriously hampered by having been elected in 1992 by a mere 43 percent of the popular vote. In 1993, President Clinton, accompanied by Vice President Gore and most of the members of his cabinet, traveled around the country campaigning to build the base of public support that had not been captured in the November 1992 election.

But the electoral base of presidential power goes deeper than the size of the margin during an election. Presidential power also comes from the selection process prior to the election. In the United States this is called the nominating process. Nomination means to name, and naming is what each party does when its members select the person they want to support as their candidate for a particular elective office. We will deal with this in detail in Chapter 11, but it is important to place the nominating process in the context of the presidency.

As we mentioned earlier, the original method for nominating presidential candidates was called "King Caucus"—the selection of a party's candidate for president by members of Congress who were declared affiliates of that party. But King Caucus was actually undermining both the independence of the presidency and the viability of the separation of powers by making all candidates for president, including the one eventually elected, beholden to Congress. America was becoming a parliamentary, "fusion-of-powers" system. The rise of the national presidential nominating convention in the 1830s gave the presidency a popular power base, which allowed enough independence from Congress to restore the separation of powers. Although the national convention method fell into disrepute during the twentieth century for being too much under the control of party bosses in "smoke-filled rooms," it was, relative to King Caucus, an extremely significant democratizing force in the nineteenth century: The method broadened the base of the parties by permitting all districts in the country to send delegates to a national convention for president, even if that district was not represented in Congress by a member of its party. Thus the national convention provided a channel for popular loyalty to the president that was separate from any loyalty that individuals might hold for their member of Congress.

**AMERICAN POLITICAL DEVELOPMENT**

The idea that presidents have a mandate for legislative action is a product of the slowly evolving concept of "a presidential mandate," which occurred from the 1820s to the 1860s. After his election in 1928, President Andrew Jackson laid claim to a popular mandate when faced with congressional opposition to his program. By the turn of the century, the concept of a presidential mandate had enjoyed a long and (for presidents) useful history.

SOURCE: Richard J. Ellis and Stephen Kirk, "Presidential Mandate in the Nineteenth Century: Conceptual Change and Institutional Development," *Studies in American Political Development* 9 (1995), pp. 117–86.

Nomination by primary elections has become the more popular method, but primaries did not destroy the national convention system, because primaries *elect* the delegates who go to the national conventions (rather than letting the state bosses appoint their own personal choices). It has now become an absolute prerequisite that presidential candidates prove themselves by having a significant number of delegates pledge their support in the primaries. This has made presidential candidacies much more expensive, but has also given the victor a far wider public base. The evolution of presidential selection, from caucus to convention to primary, is an example of what we mean by "democratization" of the presidency.

**Initiative as a Presidential Resource** "To initiate" means to originate, and in government that can mean power. The framers of the Constitution clearly saw this as one of the keys to executive power. The president as an individual is able to initiate decisive action, while Congress as a relatively large assembly must deliberate and debate before it can act. Initiative also means ability to formulate proposals for important policies. There is power in this too.

GLOBALIZATION AND DEMOCRACY

## *The President and the Global Economy*

The globalization of financial markets and the strong growth of international trade have strongly influenced American politics. The effect on the executive branch has been enormous, resulting in major new roles and responsibilities for the president and other cabinet officials. These changes have been swift and dramatic.

The end of the cold war contributed to a boom in international economic transactions. Economic liberalization—the opening of financial markets and the reduction of tariffs—has been the cornerstone of U.S. foreign economic policy in the 1990s. President Clinton and officials in the Treasury and Commerce Departments have been tireless (and successful) advocates for financial openings and freer capital mobility in emerging markets such as South Korea and Brazil. On a typical day in 1999, $1.5 trillion dollars changes hands in the world's foreign exchange markets. This is equivalent to total world trade for four months. Trade in derivatives, complex financial instruments that leverage borrowed money, amounted to $360 trillion in 1997, which is a dozen times the size of the world's annual economy.[1]

Americans' wealth is more and more tied to the stock market, and stock markets are more and more stateless. A steelworker in Pittsburgh may unknowingly have pension or mutual funds invested in Thai real estate, Russian banks, or even Brazilian steel. Capital mobility has contributed to the stock-market boom in recent years. Globalization has generated tremendous wealth while at the same time flirting with global economic chaos, where exchange-rate woes in a relatively small country (such as Thailand in 1997) can set off ripples that throw much of the world into recession. While the United States appears to be more immune than other countries to the effect of recession in emerging markets, an economic collapse in areas such as Latin America would have a serious negative impact on the U.S. economy.

Just as U.S. global leadership was crucial to the Western world during the cold war, the U.S. presidency has assumed unprecedented responsibility for steering the global economy through financial crisis and avoiding international economic meltdowns. This position was solidified in 1995 during the Mexican peso crisis. President Clinton attempted to get congressional authority to lend Mexico $40 billion, arguing that without a massive infusion of capital, the Mexican economy would collapse. The Mexican crisis came on the heels of the North American

[1]Nicholas D. Kristof and Edward Wyatt, "Who Sank, or Swam, in Choppy Currents of a World Cash Ocean," *New York Times,* 15 February 1999, p. A1.

Free Trade Agreement (NAFTA), and U.S. exporters and banks were exposed to more risk, since currency devaluations in Mexico would make U.S. exports more expensive and bank loans to Mexican companies more difficult to pay back. For example, imagine that a company in Mexico borrows $10 million from an American bank. The monthly payments are made in dollars and are $10 thousand per month. If the Mexican peso is devalued and loses 50 percent of its value against the dollar, then this company suddenly has its loan payments effectively doubled. Likewise, if a U.S. company is exporting widgets to Mexico for $1 a pound, and the peso is devalued by 50 percent, then Mexicans have to pay twice as much for the pound of widgets and, as a result, the demand will decline. Clinton claimed that a prolonged economic crisis in Mexico would lead to an explosion of illegal immigration and that the entire world economy would be adversely affected (the so-called Tequilla effect).[2] Congress refused to approve the assistance package, asserting that it set bad precedence for the United States to become the lender of last resort and that the money would mainly go to elite Wall Street banks and investment firms that had lent money to Mexico.

Clinton and Treasury Secretary Robert Ruben were undeterred, and they put together a $52 billion bail-out package that did not require congressional approval. Twelve billion dollars came from the Treasury Department's Exchange Stabilization Fund, which is ostensibly used to influence currency exchange rates, while the rest came from the International Monetary Fund (IMF). The United States taxpayer provides 18 percent of all IMF funds and U.S. Treasury officials largely determine IMF policy. Suddenly, the U.S. presidency had been thrust into a position of new global economic responsibility. When the Asian financial crisis erupted in the second half of 1997, President Clinton and treasury department officials Rubin and Lawrence Summers believed that the entire global economy was at risk. Following precedence from the Mexican experience, the president's team put together some $175 billion in public money to stem the crisis, again without congressional approval. The largest portion went to South Korea, a record $55 billion IMF package with $5 billion coming directly from the U.S. Treasury. With the stakes so high, many are calling for new international institutions to regulate global capital. Whether or not new institutions are created, globalization results in greatly expanded economic responsibilities for U.S. presidents.

[2]See Jorge Castañeda, *The Mexican Shock: Its Meaning for the United States* (New York: New Press, 1995).

Over the years, Congress has sometimes deliberately and sometimes inadvertently enhanced the president's power to seize the initiative. Curiously, the most important congressional gift to the president seems the most mundane, namely, the Office of Management and Budget, known until 1974 as the Bureau of the Budget.

In 1921, Congress provided for an "executive budget," and turned over to a new Bureau of the Budget in the executive branch the responsibility for maintaining the nation's accounts. In 1939, this bureau was moved from the Treasury Department to the newly created Executive Office of the President. The purpose of this move was to permit the president to make use of the budgeting process as a management tool. Through the new budgeting process, the president could keep better track of what was going on among all of the executive branch's hundreds of agencies and hundreds of thousands of civil servants. In this respect, the budget is simply a good investigative and informational tool for management. But in addition to that, Congress provided for a process called ***legislative clearance,*** defined as the power given to the president to require all agencies of the executive branch to submit through the budget director all requests for new legislation along with estimates of their budgetary needs. Thus, heads of agencies must submit budget requests to the White House so that the requests of all the competing agencies can be balanced. Although there are many violations of this rule, it is usually observed.

At first, legislative clearance was a defensive weapon, used mainly to allow the president to avoid the embarrassment of having to oppose or veto legislation originating in his own administration. But eventually, legislative clearance became far more important. It became the starting point for the development of comprehensive presidential programs.[33] As noted earlier, recent presidents have also used the budget process as a method of gaining tighter "top down" management control.

Presidential proposals fill the congressional agenda and tend to dominate congressional hearings and floor debates, not to speak of the newspapers. Everyone recognizes this, but few appreciate how much of this ability to maintain the initiative is directly and formally attributable to legislative clearance. Through this seemingly routine process, the president is able to review the activities of his administrators, to obtain a comprehensive view of all legislative proposals, and to identify those that are in accord with his own preferences and priorities. This is why the whole process of choice has come to be called "planning the president's program." Professed anti-government Republicans, such as Reagan and Bush, as well as allegedly pro-government Democrats, such as Clinton, are alike in their commitment to central management, control, and program planning. This is precisely why all three presidents have given the budget director cabinet status.

**Presidential Use of the Media** Although a more adequate treatment will have to await our chapter on the media (Chapter 13), let it be said here that the presi-

[33]Although dated in some respects, the best description and evaluations of budgeting as a management tool and as a tool of program planning is still found in Richard E. Neustadt's two classic articles, "Presidency and Legislation: Planning the President's Program," and "Presidency and Legislation: The Growth of Central Clearance," in *American Political Science Review*, September 1954 and December 1955.

dent is able to take full advantage of access to the communications media mainly because of the legal and constitutional bases of initiative. In the media, reporting on what is new sells newspapers. The president has at his command the thousands of policy proposals that come up to him through the administrative agencies; he can feed these to the media as being newsworthy initiatives. Consequently, virtually all newspapers and television networks habitually look to the White House as the chief source of news about public policy. They tend to assign one of their most skillful reporters to the White House "beat." And since news is money, they need the president as much as he needs them in order to meet their mutual need to make news. Presidents have successfully gotten from Congress significant additions to their staff to take care of press releases and other forms of communications. In this manner, the formal and the informal aspects of initiative tend to reinforce each other: The formal resources put the president at the center of policy formulation; this becomes the center of gravity for all buyers and sellers of news, which in turn requires the president to provide easy access to this news. Members of Congress, especially senators, are also key sources of news. But Congress is an anarchy of sources. The White House has more control over what and when. That's what initiative is all about.

Presidential personalities make a difference in how these informal factors are used. Different presidents use the media in quite different ways. For example, the press conference as an institution probably got its start in the 1930s, when Franklin Roosevelt gave several a month. But his press conferences were not recorded or broadcast "live"; direct quotes were not permitted. The model we know today got its start with Eisenhower and was put into final form by Kennedy. Since 1961, the presidential press conference has been a distinctive institution, available whenever the president wants to dominate the news. Between 300 and 400 certified reporters attend and file their accounts within minutes of the concluding words, "Thank you, Mr. President." But despite the importance of the press conference, its value to each president has varied. Although the average from Kennedy through Carter was about two press conferences a month, Johnson dropped virtually out of sight for almost half of 1965 when Vietnam was warming up, and so did Nixon for over five months in 1973 during the Watergate hearings. Moreover, Johnson and Ford preferred to call impromptu press conferences with only a few minutes' notice. President Reagan single-handedly brought the average down by holding only seven press conferences during his entire first year in office and only sporadically thereafter. In great contrast, President Bush held more conferences during his first seventeen months than Reagan held in eight years. Bush also shifted them from elaborate prime-time affairs in the ornate East Room to less formal gatherings in the

**AMERICAN POLITICAL DEVELOPMENT**

Although today's presidents frequently "go public" in order to help secure passage of preferred legislation, this was not the case during the nineteenth century. In part because the national media was not yet fully developed and because elite bargaining precluded such activity, nineteenth-century presidents (particularly prior to the Civil War) rarely gave public speeches, and only four presidents from Washington to McKinley used speeches to support or oppose specific legislation.

SOURCE: Samuel Kernell, *Going Public: New Strategies of Presidential Leadership*, 3rd ed. (Washington, DC: Congressional Quarterly Press, 1997); Jeffrey K. Tulis, *The Rhetorical Presidency* (Princeton: Princeton University Press, 1987), pp. 64–67.

White House briefing room. Fewer reporters and more time for follow-up questions permitted media representatives to "concentrate on information for their stories, rather than getting attention for themselves."[34] President Clinton has tended to take both Reagan and Bush approaches, combining Reagan's high profile—elaborate press conferences and prime-time broadcasts—with the more personal one-on-one approach generally preferred by Bush. But thanks to Ross Perot, there is now a third approach, for which President Clinton has shown a certain aptitude—the informal and basically nonpolitical talk shows, such as those of Larry King, MTV, and Oprah Winfrey. Such an informal approach has its risks, however: President Clinton is widely perceived as lacking the gravity a president is expected to possess. It is hard to argue with this conclusion when one considers that he is the first president to answer a question (on MTV) about what kind of underwear he wears.

Of course, in addition to the presidential press conference there are other routes from the White House to news prominence.[35] For example, President Nixon preferred direct television addresses, and President Carter tried to make the initiatives more homey with a television adaptation of President Roosevelt's "fireside chats." President Reagan made unusually good use of prime-time television addresses and also instituted more informal but regular Saturday afternoon radio broadcasts, a tradition that President Clinton has continued. Clinton has also added various kinds of impromptu press conferences and town meetings.

Walter Mondale, while vice president in 1980, may have summed up the entire media matter with his observation that if he had to choose between the power to get on the nightly news and veto power, he would keep the former and jettison the latter.[36] Of course, substance also counts. If you aren't good in front of reporters, or if you say inane or inappropriate things, getting media coverage can be a disaster. As a result, presidents (and all other important public figures) go to great lengths to prepare well in advance in order to *appear* spontaneous.

This is why one of the greatest technological advances for presidents in the past fifty years is the "see-through" lectern, a transparent monitor that the speaker can see through and the audience can see back through as if it weren't there, but on the speaker's side is the text of the speech, which is scrolled. The speaker reads the text word for word while the unsuspecting audience sees an exceptionally well-prepared public figure.

**Party as a Presidential Resource** Although on the decline, the president's party is far from insignificant as a political resource (see also Chapter 11). Figure 6.3 dramatically demonstrates the point with a forty-three-year history of the

[34]David Broder, "Some Newsworthy Presidential CPR," *Washington Post National Weekly Edition,* 4–10 June 1990, p. 4.

[35]See George Edwards III, *At the Margins—Presidential Leadership of Congress* (New Haven: Yale University Press, 1989), Chapter 7; and Robert Locander, "The President and the News Media," in *Dimensions of the Modern Presidency,* ed. Edward Kearney (St. Louis: Forum Press, 1981), pp. 49–52.

[36]Reported in Timothy E. Cook, *Governing with the News—The News Media as a Political Institution* (Chicago: University of Chicago Press, 1998), p. 133.

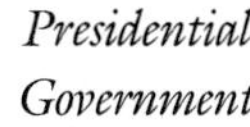

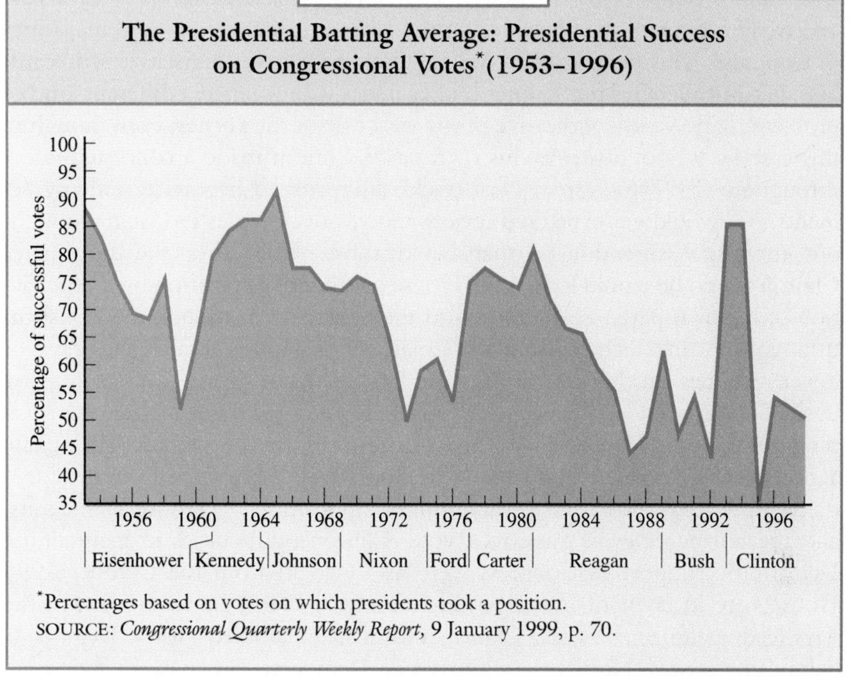


*Percentages based on votes on which presidents took a position.
SOURCE: *Congressional Quarterly Weekly Report,* 9 January 1999, p. 70.

"presidential batting average" in Congress—the percentage of winning roll-call votes in Congress on bills publicly supported by the president.

Bill Clinton, in his first two years in office, enjoyed very high legislative success rates—86 percent in both 1993 and 1994. But these dropped drastically to 35.1 percent in 1995 and have hovered just above 50 percent in the years since. Clinton's pattern of congressional success demonstrates the *importance of the political party as a presidential resource.* Democratic control of Congress was a regular pattern between 1954 and 1994, and therefore presidential batting averages were very high, with a Democratic president and a Democratic House and Senate. President Eisenhower's averages were also very high for his first two years, when his own party controlled Congress; but they quickly dropped when Republicans lost control of Congress, as did President Clinton's success rate when Republicans took over Congress in 1995 following the 1994 election (see Figure 6.3).

At the same time, party has its limitations as a resource. The more unified the president's party is behind his legislative requests, the more unified the opposition party is also likely to be. Unless the president's party majority is very large, he must also appeal to the opposition to make up for the inevitable defectors within the ranks of his own party. Consequently, the president often poses as being above partisanship in order to win "bipartisan" support in Congress. But to the extent he pursues a bipartisan strategy, he cannot throw himself fully into building the party loyalty and party discipline that would maximize the value of his own party's support in Congress. This is a dilemma for every president, particularly those faced with an opposition-controlled Congress.

Partisan opposition in Congress proved so strong that President Clinton was unable even to bring the centerpieces of his legislative agenda—health care and welfare reform—to votes during the years in which he enjoyed majorities in Congress. This helps explain the paradox of Clinton's legislative scorecard: high batting averages but failures on key issues. Clinton had a different kind of problem in 1997, one indicative of the vital role of the parties, even though in this case he was opposed by his own party. Clinton made a concerted effort throughout 1997 to restore "fast-track" authority to negotiate trade agreements that would get expedited review and yes-or-no votes in Congress, without the usual amendments that could substantially alter the agreement. Clinton feared he would lose in the House because of opposition by a large faction of his own party. So he turned to the Senate, even though the Constitution requires that such bills must originate in the House because they raise or lower revenues (in this case tariffs). He figured that a strong show of support in the Senate would influence the House. He even got the cooperation of Republican majority leader Senator Trent Lott in this flanking attack. The Senate action was not enough, however. The House leadership tabled the presidentially supported bill because of continued opposition by House Democrats, and the bill never even came to a vote. Clinton's difficulties in maintaining Democratic support in Congress were also evident from the October 1998 House vote in favor of investigating Clinton's possible impeachment. In the days leading up to the vote, Clinton and his staff lobbied House Democrats behind the scenes. Nonetheless, thirty-one Democrats broke ranks and voted in favor of the investigation. House Republicans, for their part, were united in favor of the impeachment inquiry. Fortunately for Clinton, Republicans failed to convince any Senate Democrats to convict him in his impeachment trial in early 1999.

**Groups as a Presidential Resource** The classic case in modern times of groups as a resource for the presidency is the Roosevelt or New Deal coalition.[37] The New Deal coalition was composed of an inconsistent, indeed contradictory, set of interests. Some of these interests were not organized interest groups, but were regional interests, such as Southern whites, or residents of large cities in the industrial Northeast and Midwest, or blacks who later succeeded in organizing as an interest group. In addition to these sectional interests that were drawn to the New Deal, there were several large, self-consciously organized interest groups. The most important in the New Deal coalition were organized labor, agriculture, and the financial community.[38] All of the parts were held together by a judicious

[37]A wider range of group phenomena will be covered in Chapter 12. In that chapter the focus is on the influence of groups *upon* the government and its policy-making processes. Here our concern is more with the relationship of groups to the presidency and the extent to which groups and coalitions of groups become a dependable resource for presidential government.

[38]For a more detailed review of the New Deal coalition in comparison with later coalitions, see Thomas Ferguson and Joel Rogers, *Right Turn: The Decline of the Democrats and the Future of American Politics* (New York: Hill & Wang, 1986), Chapter 2. For updates on the group basis of presidential politics, see Thomas Ferguson, "Money and Politics," in *Handbooks to the Modern World—The United States,* vol. 2, ed. Godfrey Hodgson (New York: Facts on File, 1992), pp. 1060–84; and Lucius J. Barker, ed., "Black Electoral Politics," *National Political Science Review,* vol. 2 (New Brunswick, NJ: Transaction Publishers, 1990).

use of patronage—not merely patronage in jobs but patronage in policies. Many of the groups were permitted virtually to write their own legislation. In exchange, the groups supported President Roosevelt and his successors in their battles with opposing politicians.

Republican presidents have had their group coalition base also. The most important segments of organized business, especially the large, "labor intensive" industries that deal with unions affiliated with the CIO, have tended to support Republican presidents. Organized business has been joined by upper-income interests, not set up as a single upper-class group but usually organized around their respective areas of wealth. Republicans also have their share of ethnic groups, including staunch Republican organizations whose members hail from Eastern European countries. An important and recent sectionally based ethnic group is the white South. Once a solid-Democratic South, whites in most of the Southern states have become virtually a solid-Republican group; and not far behind in importance within the Republican coalition is the so-called Sun Belt. Except for the white South, most of these groups have been Republicans for a long time. A newer presence within the white South is the Christian Right; although heavily Southern, its membership extends far beyond the South. The two best organized groups within the Christian Right—the Christian Coalition and the Focus on the Family—have strong and effective presence in many states in the West, the Northwest, and the border states. Although the Christian Right failed to get a Republican president in 1992—and some would say that the group actually hurt Bush's chances of re-election in 1992—it played a vital role in the Republican capture of the House and Senate in the 1994 midterm elections and would have played a much stronger role in 1996 if its members had been happier with a Republican presidential candidate other than Robert Dole.

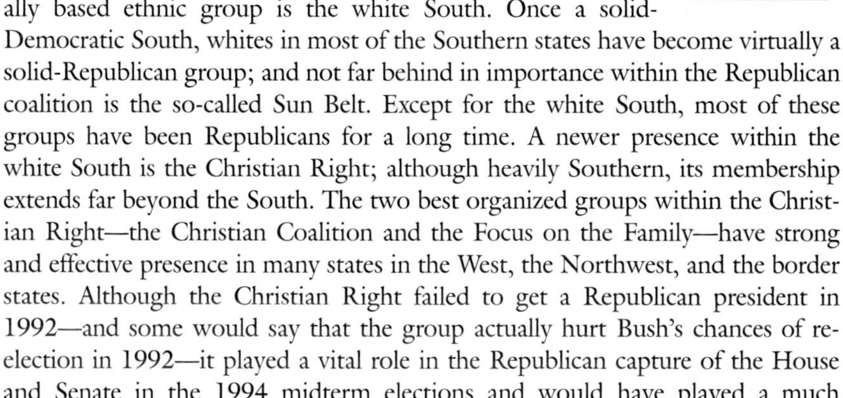


Clinton's chance for the Democratic nomination improved because he was a moderate Democrat from the New South. Although this got him the nomination, he did not succeed, despite valiant efforts, in bringing back together the original elements of the New Deal coalition. He captured only five of the thirteen formerly Democratic Deep South states in 1992 (Georgia, Louisiana, Arkansas, Tennessee, and Kentucky) and a slightly different set of five in 1996 (Florida, Louisiana, Arkansas, Tennessee, and Kentucky). Clinton was able to compensate for what appeared to be a permanent loss of constituents from the white South not only by keeping the Northeast, Midwest, and Far West within the Democratic column, but also by making advances among corporate interests, despite the revival of Democratic support from the trade unions.[39] He did this by ingeniously moving the Democratic party away from its traditional pro-welfare state liberal wing toward a center that was on the right-hand side of the Democratic spectrum and well into Republican policy territory. Beating the Republicans at their own game may end up being the most important part of the Clinton political legacy.

[39]For more up-to-date figures on the corporate members of the Clinton coalition, see Thomas Ferguson, *Golden Rule—The Investment Theory of Party Competition and the Logic of Money-Driven Political Systems* (Chicago: University of Chicago Press, 1995).

**Public Opinion and Mass Popularity: Resource or Liability** As presidential government grew, a presidency developed whose power is directly linked to the people. Successful presidents have to be able to mobilize mass opinion. But presidents tend to follow public opinion rather than lead it.

Presidents who devote too much of their time to the vicissitudes of public opinion polls often discover that they are several steps behind shifts in opinion, for polls tell politicians what the public wanted yesterday, not what it will think tomorrow. This was certainly President Clinton's experience in 1993–1994 with the issue of health care reform. Administration polls continually showed public support for the president's policy initiatives—until opponents of his efforts began getting their own message through. Using several highly effective media campaigns, Clinton's opponents convinced millions of Americans that the president's program was too complex and that it would reduce access to health care. The president was left promoting an unpopular program.

Bill Clinton relied heavily on public opinion in formulating and presenting many of his administration's programs. Several members of his staff were hired specifically to shape and influence public opinion. Clinton was heavily criticized for hiring David Gergen, who had previously worked for Ronald Reagan. This crossover raised important questions about the integrity of "spinmeisters" such as Gergen, who seem to care more about the influence they have with the public than about the policies they are hired to promote.

Politicians are generally better off if they try to do what they believe is best and then hope that the public will come to agree with them. Most politicians, however, are afraid to use such a simple approach.

In addition to utilizing the media and public opinion polls, recent presidents, particularly Bill Clinton, have reached out directly to the American public to gain its approval. President Clinton's enormously high public profile, as is indicated by the number of public appearances he makes (see Figure 6.4), is only the most recent dramatic expression of the presidency as a permanent campaign for reelection. A study by political scientist Charles O. Jones shows that President Clinton engaged in campaignlike activity throughout his presidency and is proving to be the most-traveled American president in history. In his first twenty months in office, he made 203 appearances outside of Washington, compared with 178 for George Bush and 58 for Ronald Reagan. Clinton's tendency to go around rather than through party organizations is reflected in the fact that while Presidents Bush and Reagan devoted about 25 percent of their appearances to party functions, Clinton's comparable figure is only 8 percent.[40] Throughout the controversy over campaign-finance abuses during 1997, President Clinton attended numerous fund-raising events to raise enough money to pay off the $30 million or more of debt from the 1996 presidential campaign. In fact, during the most intense moments of the Monica Lewinsky scandal of early 1998, Clinton continued his fund-raising, and the Democratic National Committee had to add staff to answer all the telephone calls and mail

[40]Study cited in Ann Devroy, "Despite Panetta Pep Talk, White House Aides See Daunting Task," *Washington Post*, 8 January 1995, p. A4.

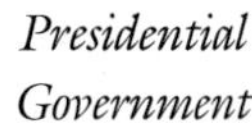

**FIGURE 6.4**

**Public Appearances by Presidents, 1929–95**

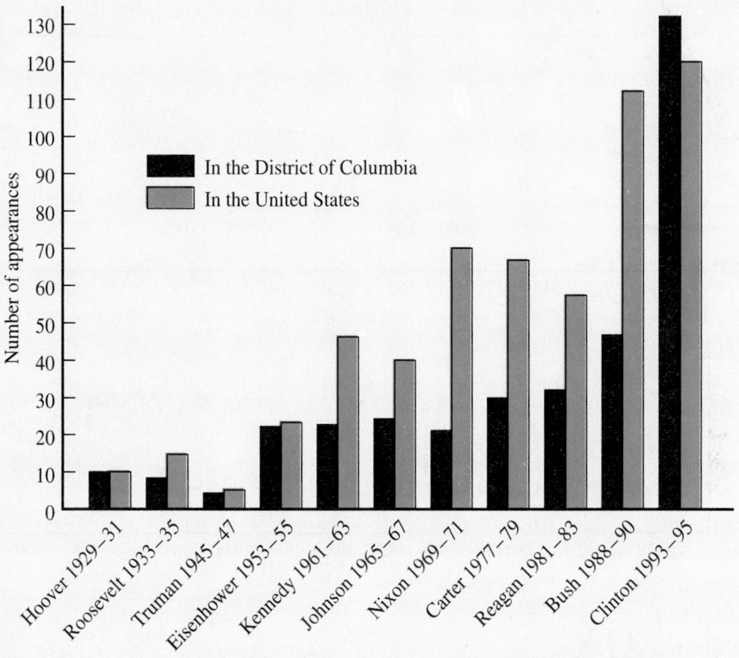

SOURCE: Samuel Kernell, *Going Public,* 3rd ed. (Washington, DC: Congressional Quarterly Press, 1998), p. 118.

that were responding positively to President Clinton's appeals. This is the essence of the permanent campaign.

Even with the help of all other institutional and political resources, successful presidents have to be able to mobilize mass opinion in their favor in order to keep Congress in line. But as we shall see, each president tends to *use up* mass resources. Virtually everyone is aware that presidents are constantly making appeals to the public over the heads of Congress and the Washington community. But the mass public is not made up of fools. The American people react to presidential actions rather than to mere speeches or other image-making devices.

The public's sensitivity to presidential actions can be seen in the tendency of all presidents to lose popular support. Despite the twists and turns shown on Figure 6.5, the percentage of positive responses to "Do you approve of the way the president is handling his job?" starts out at a level significantly higher than the percentage of votes the president got in the previous national election and then declines over the next four years. Though the shape of the line differs, the destination is the same. This general downward tendency is to be expected if American voters are rational, inasmuch as almost any action taken by the president can

**FIGURE 6.5**

**Presidential Performance Ratings from Kennedy to Clinton**

*Nationwide responses to the question: "Do you approve of the way the president is doing his job?"*

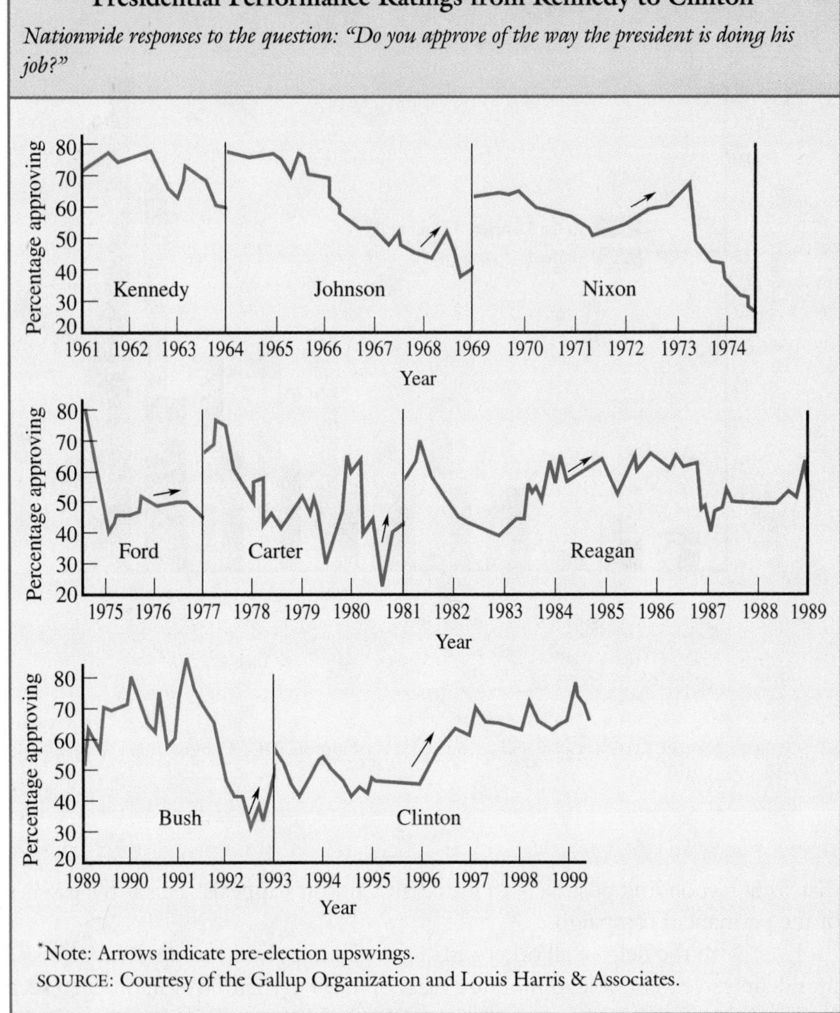


*Note: Arrows indicate pre-election upswings.

SOURCE: Courtesy of the Gallup Organization and Louis Harris & Associates.

be divisive, with some voters approving and other voters disapproving. Public disapproval of specific actions has a cumulative effect on the president's overall performance rating. Thus all presidents are faced with the problem of boosting their approval ratings. And the public generally reacts favorably to presidential actions in foreign policy or, more precisely, to international events associated with the president. Analysts call this the ***rallying effect.*** Nevertheless the rallying effect turns out to be only a momentary reversal of the more general tendency of presidents to lose popular support.

Looking again at Figure 6.5, the one notable exception to this general downward trend of presidential approval was during Clinton's second term. As expected, Clinton's approval rating surged before and after his re-election and then dropped over the course of 1997. But Clinton experienced two important upward blips, one early in 1998 and the other early in 1999, that were both related to the impeachment controversy, not to an international crisis. In both of these cases, the American people, while disapproving of Clinton's behavior in the Lewinsky scandal, were nonetheless rallying behind the institution of the presidency. In fact, it is probable that this rallying effect around the presidency kept Clinton in office. The powers of the office also remained intact, and Clinton was able to use them to lead a coalition of NATO allies in a war against Serbia. Despite successes like the war against Serbia, public expectations for the presidency are always high. As Clinton prepares to leave office, it is likely that he, like his predecessors, will go out as a disappointment, while the institution of the presidency will be stronger than ever.

## Reflections on Presidential Power

This chapter provides ample evidence that the president has great power. Harry Truman constantly referred to the presidency as "the most powerful office in the history of the world." We doubt he was very far off the mark, and this chapter validates his assertion with strong evidence, which actually continued to mount after he left office and was continuing to confirm his observation long after his death in 1972. The cold war impelled Congress to continue presidential war powers long after the hot war was over. Post–cold war military powers have escaped most of the budgetary belt tightening that seriously affect domestic activities, and occasional acts of terrorism keep the CIA as strong as ever, not only as a secret information-gathering agency but also as an agency capable of altering the regimes in countries likely to be our adversaries. In fact, such embarrassments as the Vietnam War and President Nixon's resignation fed America's sense of need for a powerful and unassailable presidency as Head of State. Domestic developments fed the power of the office as well, because Congress continued to commit "legiscide" by delegating its legislative powers to the executive branch through broadly drafted laws, which left great discretion to the president and his agencies—so much discretion that it amounted to actual policy making rather than "faithful execution of the law" as made in Congress. As we saw, Congress even tried to give the president more of its powers with the line-item veto.

Is the office *too* powerful? The answer would seem to be "yes." But the answer is also "no," because the president is not powerful enough to accomplish all the goals imposed on him through delegation of power from Congress. In fact, there is not enough power on earth or in anyone's imagination to accomplish what is expected of the president. This is why presidential approval ratings always tend to

THEN AND NOW

## Changes in American Politics

Perhaps no other institution in American politics has changed as dramatically as the presidency. In its structure, importance, and political strategies, the twentieth-century presidency is a remarkably more potent office than its nineteenth-century counterpart.

- Congress dominated American national politics in the nineteenth century. The increased importance of mass media, the immediacy of foreign policy, and the growth of a direct link between presidents and the people have led to an invigoration of the presidency in the twentieth century (particularly since the 1930s).
- The presidency was a very personal (and even singular) office throughout most of the nineteenth century. But the growth of a presidential staff and a proliferation of subunits and organizational divisions within that office have led to an institutionalization of the presidency as an organization that, in many respects, is separate and distinct from the president himself.
- The cabinet, as conceived by the founders, was not necessarily an advisory body to the president. In George Washington's second term, after having been denied the services of the Supreme Court, he turned to the heads of executive departments as an advisory body.
- The use of the veto power was much more common after the Civil War. Before the war, it was widely believed that the proper use of the veto was to protect the constitutional prerogatives of the presidency rather than for the president to assert his policy positions in legislative debates.
- Because of the decline of party powers and the particular problems of leading the deeply divided Democratic party during the 1930s, Franklin Roosevelt emphasized the importance of providing executive presidential leadership as a supplement to his legislative leadership. Although there wasn't much to administer during the nineteenth century, today a president's duties center around administrative leadership.
- Whereas nineteenth-century presidential leadership involved working with political and party elites, twentieth-century presidential leadership has come to rely upon connecting to the people. Today, presidents invoke electoral mandate, establish and maintain relationships with interest groups, monitor public opinion, and use mass media to "go public."

go downward! Americans are not fools. If the law says "clean the air" or "make medicine safe and effective," people are disappointed when those mandates are not met.

On the other hand, yes, the president *is* too powerful, or we should say, too powerful for his own good or for the good of the country. We cannot repeat too often that *with power goes vulnerability.* Since the president cannot possibly fulfill his oath of office by meeting all the mandates from Congress, he must turn to the next best strategy, *to control appearances.* In other words, to deceive. Ever since Teddy Roosevelt, the presidency has been called a "bully pulpit." And so it is. On many occasions this pulpit has been used magnificently to rally Americans to a good cause, to comfort Americans in their grief, to mobilize Americans for a worthy public policy goal, to inspire Americans to set aside their private interests for the greater good. But that same pulpit is subject to abuse, and many feel that the abuses have become the norm.

President Clinton has been criticized for subjecting every planned public appearance, every vacation, and virtually every phrase in his speeches to test marketing, tracking polls, and focus groups. These criticisms are appropriate, but what makes them more damning is that President Clinton was simply extending the practices of his predecessors. The distinction between campaigning and governing has been getting fuzzier and fuzzier. Many people are getting accustomed to referring to presidential conduct as "the permanent campaign."

However, Americans must break themselves of the habit of thinking in dichotomies such as: The president is too powerful versus the president is not powerful enough. Is government too big or not big enough? Issues just don't naturally come with two sides. We hope that our discussion leads the reader toward a more sober analysis of the multiple dimensions and contradictions that abound in the politics of freedom and power.

## SUMMARY

The foundations for presidential government were laid in the Constitution by providing for a unitary executive who is head of state as well as head of government. The first section of the chapter reviewed the powers of each: The head of state with its military, judicial, and diplomatic powers; the head of government with its executive, military, and legislative powers. But this section noted that the presidency was subordinated to congressional government during the nineteenth century and part of the twentieth, when the national government was small for domestic functions and inactive or sporadic in foreign affairs.

The second section of the chapter traced out the rise of modern presidential government after the much longer period of congressional dominance. There is no mystery in the shift to government centered on the presidency. Congress built the modern presidency by delegating to it not only the power to implement the vast new programs of the 1930s but also by delegating its own legislative power to make the policies themselves. The cabinet, the other top appointments, the White House staff, and the Executive Office of the President are some of the impressive formal resources of presidential power.

The chapter then focused on the president's informal resources, in particular his political party, the supportive group coalitions, and his access to the media and, through that, his access to the millions of Americans who make up the general public. But it was noted that these resources are not cost- or risk-free. The chapter concluded on a special problem: The president's direct relation with the mass public is his most potent modern resource, but also the most problematic.

## For Further Reading

Barber, James D. *The Presidential Character.* Englewood Cliffs, NJ: Prentice-Hall, 1985.

Corwin, Edward S. *The President: Office and Powers.* New York: New York University Press, 1957.

Drew, Elizabeth. *On the Edge: The Clinton Presidency.* New York: Simon and Schuster, 1994.

Hart, John. *The Presidential Branch: From Washington to Clinton.* Chatham, NJ: Chatham House, 1995.

Hinckley, Barbara, and Paul Brace. *Follow the Leader: Opinion Polls and Modern Presidents.* New York: Basic Books, 1992.

Kernell, Samuel. *Going Public: New Strategies of Presidential Leadership.* Washington, DC: Congressional Quarterly Press, 1986.

Lowi, Theodore J. *The Personal President: Power Invested, Promise Unfulfilled.* Ithaca, NY: Cornell University Press, 1985.

Mann, Thomas E., ed. *A Question of Balance: The President, Congress, and Foreign Policy.* Washington, DC: Brookings Institution, 1991.

Milkis, Sidney M. *The President and the Parties: The Transformation of the American Party System Since the New Deal.* New York: Oxford University Press, 1993.

Nelson, Michael, ed. *The Presidency and the Political System,* 4th ed. Washington, DC: Congressional Quarterly Press, 1994.

Neustadt, Richard E. *Presidential Power: The Politics of Leadership from Roosevelt to Reagan,* rev. ed. New York: Free Press, 1990.

Pfiffner, James P. *The Modern Presidency.* New York: St. Martin's Press, 1994.

Polsby, Nelson, and Aaron Wildavsky. *Presidential Elections: Contemporary Strategies of American Electoral Politics,* 8th ed. New York: Free Press, 1991.

Skowronek, Stephen. *The Politics Presidents Make: Leadership from John Adams to George Bush.* Cambridge: Harvard University Press, 1993.

Spitzer, Robert. *The Presidential Veto: Touchstone of the American Presidency.* Albany: State University of New York Press, 1988.

Tulis, Jeffrey. *The Rhetorical Presidency.* Princeton: Princeton University Press, 1987.

Watson, Richard A., and Norman Thomas. *The Politics of the Presidency.* Washington, DC: Congressional Quarterly Press, 1988.

# The Executive Branch: Bureaucracy in a Democracy

## TIME LINE ON THE BUREAUCRACY

| Events | | Institutional Developments |
|---|---|---|
| Washington appoints Jefferson (State), Knox (War), Hamilton (Treasury) to the first cabinet (1789) | 1789 | Congress creates first executive departments (State, War, Treasury) (1789) |
| Jackson elected president; "rule of the common man" (1828) | | Jackson supports "party rotation in office" and "spoils system" (1829–1836) |
| | 1880 | |
| President Garfield assassinated by disappointed office-seeker; President Arthur allies himself with civil service reformers (1881) | | Pendleton Act sets up Civil Service Commission and merit system for filling "classified services" jobs (1883) |
| Conflict between railroads and farmers over freight rates (1880s) | | Interstate Commerce Commission (ICC) created to regulate railroads; first independent regulatory commission (1887) |
| | 1900 | |
| Progressive attack parties and advance civil service reforms (1901–1908) | | Department of Commerce and Labor created (1903) |
| World War I (1914–1918) | | Federal Reserve Board (1913); Federal Trade Commission (1914) |
| Postwar labor unrest, race riots, Red Scare (1919–1920) | | General Accounting Office and Budget Bureau created; Congress turns over budget to the executive branch (1921) |
| Teapot Dome scandal (1924) | | Classification Act (1923); Corrupt Practices Act (1925) |
| Franklin Roosevelt and the New Deal (1930s) | 1930 | New Deal "alphabetocracy" created (1930s) |
| | | Administrative Reorganization Act creates Executive Office of the President (EOP) (1939) |
| | | Hatch Act restricts political activity of executive-branch employees (1939) |
| U.S. in World War II (1941–1945) | | Veterans' preference begun for civil service jobs (1944) |
| Cold war (1945–1989)<br>Red Scare (late 1940s–mid-1950s) | | National Security Act creates Department of Defense, National Security Council (NSC), CIA (1947); Truman and Eisenhower loyalty programs (1947–1954) |
| | 1950 | |
| Civil rights movement (1950s and 1960s) | | Equal Employment Opportunity Commission (EEOC) created (1964) |

| Events | | Institutional Developments |
|---|---|---|
| Growth of government (1962–1974) | | New welfare and social regulatory agencies (1965); Department of Housing and Urban Development, Dept. of Transportation (1966) |
| President Nixon enlarges the managerial presidency (1969–1974) | | |
| | 1970 | EOP reorganized; Office of Management and Budget (OMB) created (1970) |
| Watergate cover-up revealed (1973–1974) | | |
| President Carter attempts to make bureaucracy more accountable (1977–1980) | | Civil Service Reform Act (1978); creation of new departments: Energy (1977); Education (1980); Health and Human Services (1980) |
| President Reagan fires over 10,000 air traffic controllers; centralizes presidential management (1981–1988) | | OMB given power to review all proposed agency rules and regulations (1984) |
| Reagan and Bush tighten presidential control of all top political appointees (1982–92) | | |
| | 1990 | Supreme Court declares political patronage unconstitutional except for top political positions (1990) |
| Clinton decentralizes somewhat by appointing cabinet first and giving them share of subcabinet selection (1993) | | Federal civilian employment up from 2.8 million (1982) to 3.1 million (1992) |
| "Reinventing government" plan launched by Clinton to overhaul the federal government and reduce number of federal employees by more than 200,000 (1993) | | National Performance Review, headed by Vice President Gore, streamlines procurement, rules, and procedures; job reduction occurs (1993–1996) |
| Clinton campaign continues to tackle bureaucracy with promises of more cuts of employees and pages of regulations (1996) | | Clinton signs GOP welfare law replacing six decades of federal programs with devolution to state agencies (1996) |

During his 1980 campaign, Ronald Reagan promised to dismantle the Departments of Energy and Education as part of the "Reagan Revolution" commitment to "get the government off our backs." Reagan claimed that abolishing the Department of Energy (DOE) not only would save $250 million over a three-year period, but also would permit the free market to develop a much better system of energy production and distribution. At the same time, Republicans criticized President Carter for having created

## CORE OF THE ARGUMENT

- Despite its problems, the bureaucracy is necessary for the maintenance of order in a large society.
- The size of the federal bureaucracy is large, but it has not been growing any faster than the economy or the population as a whole.
- Government agencies vary in their levels of responsiveness to the president and his political appointees, congressional members and committees, and commercial and private interests.
- Responsible bureaucracy requires more than presidential power and management control.
- Congress has delegated much of its legislative power to the president and the bureaucracy; congressional committees use oversight to make the bureaucracy accountable.

the Department of Education (ED) mainly to repay a debt he owed the powerful National Education Association for its political support. After his election, in keeping with his campaign promises, President Reagan appointed as the new heads of these two departments individuals publicly committed to eliminating their departments and therefore their own jobs.

Even though the Departments of Energy and Education had only been established in 1977 and 1980 respectively, they had powerful allies. Strong support for both agencies developed in Congress, including support from some members who were otherwise supportive of the Reagan program of tax cuts, domestic budget cuts, and defense budget increases. By 1984, President Reagan seemed to have changed his mind, indicating he had "no intention of recommending abolition of the Department of Education at this time." Plans for abolishing the Energy Department and turning over its functions to other departments were relegated to the dead end of "further discussion." President Reagan actually did cut some employees after his inauguration and tried strenuously to continue cutting, but despite his commitment to this, the number of federal employees actually grew by about 18,000 during his first year in office. Although he continued to denounce "big government," by 1984, President Reagan had retreated from this arena in defeat. Eleven years later, in January 1995, one of the first commitments of the Republican 104th Congress was to abolish these same two departments along with a third, the Department of Commerce. Yet by 1997, all three departments were still very much alive. The Energy budget was cut barely, from the 1995 authorization of $15 billion to the 1997 authorization of $14.2 billion, while the Education budget was cut a bit more, from $32.3 billion to $30.2 billion. The authorization for the Department of Commerce fell from $4 billion to $3.7 billion. The campaign to abolish the three departments had virtually disappeared.[1]

What is this bureaucratic phenomenon that seems to expand despite policies to keep it in check? What is this structure that is the frustration of every president? Why does it seem to have a life of its own despite every presidential effort to make it respond to voters and public opinion? How is it possible for agencies that are composed of highly dependent employees to resist pointed efforts to reorganize or abolish their positions?

[1]For a very good case study on the politics (and the problem) of terminating agencies, see "Pressure to Curtail EPA Boomeranged . . . But GOP Can Claim Some Influence," *Congressional Quarterly,* 7 September 1996, pp. 2518–19.

In this chapter, we will focus on the federal bureaucracy—the administrative structure that on a day-to-day basis *is* the American government. We will first seek to answer these questions by defining and describing bureaucracy as a social and political phenomenon. Second, we will look in detail at American bureaucracy in action by examining the government's major administrative agencies, their role in the governmental process, and their political behavior. These details of administration are the very heart and soul of modern government and will provoke the question of the third and final sections of the chapter: "Can bureaucracy be made accountable to the president and Congress? Can bureaucracy and democracy co-exist?"

**THE CENTRAL QUESTION**

"Can bureaucracy and democracy co-exist?"

# THE BUREAUCRATIC PHENOMENON

Despite widespread and consistent complaints about "bureaucracy," most Americans recognize that the maintenance of order in a large society is impossible without a large governmental apparatus of some sort. When we approve of what a government agency is doing, we give the phenomenon a positive name, *administration;* when we disapprove, we call the phenomenon *bureaucracy.*[2]

Although the terms "administration" and "bureaucracy" are often used interchangeably, it is useful to distinguish between the two. Administration is the more general of the two terms; it refers to all the ways human beings might rationally coordinate their efforts to achieve a common goal. This applies to private as well as public organizations. ***Bureaucracy*** refers to the actual offices, tasks, and principles of organization that are employed in the most formal and sustained administration. Table 7.1 defines bureaucracy by identifying its basic characteristics.

## Bureaucratic Organization

The core of bureaucracy is the *division of labor.* The key to bureaucratic effectiveness is the coordination of experts performing complex tasks. If each job is specialized in order to gain efficiencies, then each worker must depend upon the output of other workers, and that requires careful *allocation* of jobs and resources. Inevitably, bureaucracies become hierarchical, often approximating a pyramid in form. At the base of the organization are workers with the fewest skills and specializations; one supervisor can deal with a relatively large number of these workers. At the next level of the organization, where there are more highly specialized workers, the supervision and coordination of work involves fewer workers per supervisor. Toward the top of the organization, a very small number of high-level executives engages in the "management" of the organization, meaning the orga-

[2]The title of this section is drawn from an important sociological work by Michel Crozier, *The Bureaucratic Phenomenon* (Chicago: University of Chicago Press, 1964).

TABLE 7.1

**The Six Primary Characteristics of Bureaucracy**

| CHARACTERISTIC | EXPLANATION |
|---|---|
| Division of labor | Workers are specialized. Each worker develops a skill in a particular job and performs the job routinely and repetitively, thereby increasing productivity. |
| Allocation of functions | Each task is assigned. No one makes a whole product; each worker depends on the output of other workers. |
| Allocation of responsibility | Each task becomes a personal responsibility—a contractual obligation. No task can be changed without permission. |
| Supervision | Some workers are assigned the special task of watching over other workers rather than contributing directly to the creation of the product. Each supervisor watches over a few workers (a situation known as span of control), and communications between workers or between levels move in a prescribed fashion (known as chain of command). |
| Purchase of full-time employment | The organization controls all the time the worker is on the job, so each worker can be assigned and held to a task. Some part-time and contracted work is tolerated, but it is held to a minimum. |
| Identification of career within the organization | Workers come to identify with the organization as a way of life. Seniority, pension rights, and promotions are geared to this relationship. |

nization and reorganization of all the tasks and functions, plus the allocation of the appropriate supplies, and the distribution of the outputs of the organization to the market (if it is a "private sector" organization) or to the public.

## The Size of the Federal Service

Americans like to complain about bureaucracy. Americans don't like Big Government because Big Government means Big Bureaucracy, and bureaucracy means *the federal service*—about 2.78 million civilian and 1.47 million military employees.[3] Promises to cut the bureaucracy are popular campaign appeals; "cutting out the fat" with big reductions in the number of federal employees is held out as a sure-fire way of cutting the deficit. President Bill Clinton has made it a

[3]This is just under 99 percent of all national government employees. About 1.4 percent work for the legislative branch and for the federal judiciary. See Office of Management and Budget, *Historical Tables, Budget of the United States Government, Fiscal Year 1999* (Washington, DC: Government Printing Office, 1998), p. 279.

priority, even though the Democratic party has traditionally been the pro-growth party. One of President Clinton's most successful efforts has been his National Performance Review, which has cut more than a quarter of a million jobs from the federal labor force (the total force reductions for most of his first term amounted actually to 293,000, although only 163,000 of those were from the civilian agencies that were subject to the NPR)[4]—although most Americans, according to polls, believe that the federal bureaucracy under Clinton is bigger than ever, and still growing.[5]

Despite fears of bureaucratic growth getting out of hand, however, the federal service has hardly grown at all during the past thirty years; it reached its peak postwar level in 1968 with 2.9 million civilian employees plus an additional 3.6 million military personnel (a figure swollen by Vietnam). The number of civilian federal employees has since remained close to that figure. (In 1997, it was about 2,725,000.[6]) The growth of the federal service is even less imposing when placed in the context of the total workforce and when compared to the size of state and local public employment. Figure 7.1 indicates that, since 1950, the ratio of federal service employment to the total workforce has been steady and in fact has declined slightly in the past twenty-five years. Another useful comparison is to be found in Figure 7.2. Although the dollar increase in federal spending shown by the bars looks very impressive, the horizontal line indicates that even here the national government has simply kept pace with the growth of the economy.

In 1950, there were 4.3 million state and local civil service employees (about 6.5 percent of the country's workforce). In 1978, there were 12.7 million (nearly 15 percent of the workforce), and the ratio remained about the same for the ensuing two decades. By 1997, state and local governments employed around 17 million workers, or about 12 percent of the workforce. Federal employment, in contrast, exceeded 5 percent of the workforce only during World War II (not shown), and almost all of that momentary growth was military. After the demo-

## AMERICAN POLITICAL DEVELOPMENT

Although the size of the federal service has not grown much in the last thirty years, the early twentieth century did see a substantial increase in the number of civilians employed by the federal government. From 1900 to 1909, the size of the federal service grew by a third. And from 1916 to 1920, the number of civilian employees in the federal government doubled, from slightly over 399,000 to 845,500.

SOURCE: Peri E. Arnold, *Making the Managerial Presidency: Comprehensive Reorganization Planning, 1905–1996,* 2nd ed. (Lawrence: University Press of Kansas, 1998), pp. 22–23, 53.

[4]Data source, *Historical Tables, Budget of the United States Government, Fiscal Year 1997* (Washington, DC: Government Printing Office, 1996), pp. 263–64.

[5]Average Americans are not the only ones who think the bureaucracy has grown too large. The neoclassical economist William Niskanen argued that rational bureaucrats will seek to increase the budgets for their bureaus to their maximum. As a result, Niskanen concluded that government bureaucracies are too big, their budgets too large, and their activities too extensive. For more details on Niskanen's argument see Kenneth A. Shepsle and Mark S. Bonchek, *Analyzing Politics: Rationality, Behavior, and Institutions* (New York: W. W. Norton, 1997), pp. 346–53. Throughout this chapter, we present arguments to counter Niskanen. Shepsle and Bonchek also review some of the more formal alternatives to Niskanen's model.

[6]*Historical Tables, Budget of the United States Government, Fiscal Year 1999* (Washington, DC: Government Printing Office, 1998), Table 17.5, p. 279.

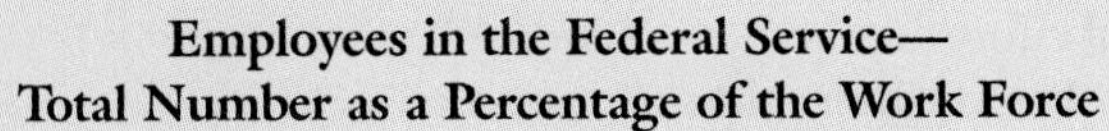
FIGURE 7.1

**Employees in the Federal Service—Total Number as a Percentage of the Work Force**

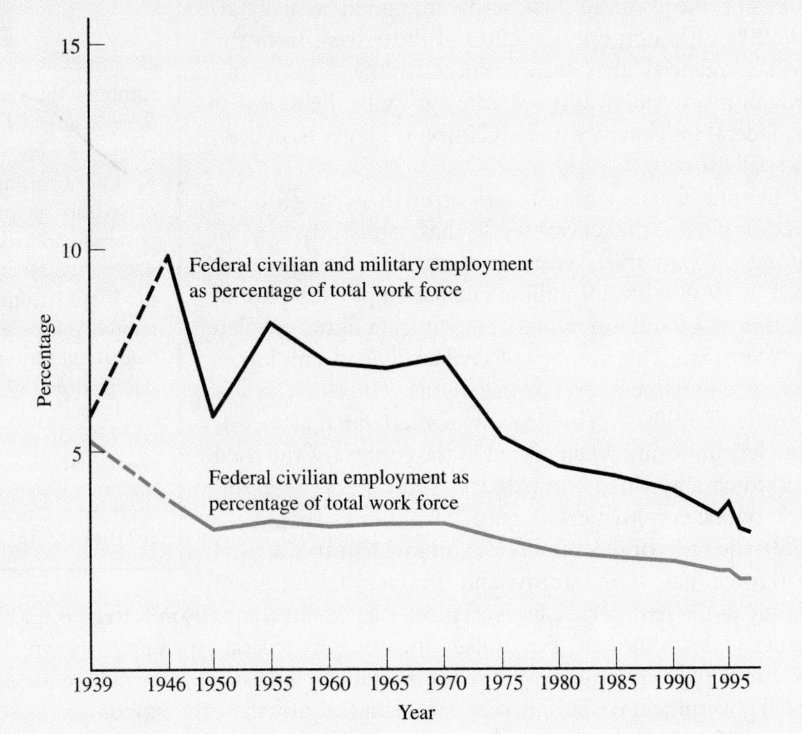


SOURCES: Tax Foundation, *Facts & Figures on Government Finance*, 1990 Edition. (Baltimore: Johns Hopkins University Press, 1990), pp. 22 and 44; Office of Management and Budget, *Historical Tables, Budget of the United States Government, Fiscal Year 1999* (Washington, DC: Government Printing Office, 1998), p. 279; and U.S. Department of Labor, Bureau of Labor Statistics, *Employment and Earnings* (monthly). Lines between 1939 and 1946 are broken for the obvious reason that they connect the last prewar year with the first postwar year, disregarding the temporary ballooning of federal employees, especially military, during the war years.

bilization, which continued until 1950 (as shown in Figure 7.1), the federal service has tended to grow at a rate that keeps pace with the economy and society. That is demonstrated by the lower line on Figure 7.1, which shows a constant relation between federal civilian employment and the size of the workforce. Variations in federal employment since 1946 have been in the military and directly related to war and the cold war (as shown by the top line on Figure 7.1). The same has been roughly true of state and local government personnel, but that may be changing because state and local government employment continued to grow while federal civil service personnel actually shrank. Thanks in part to the

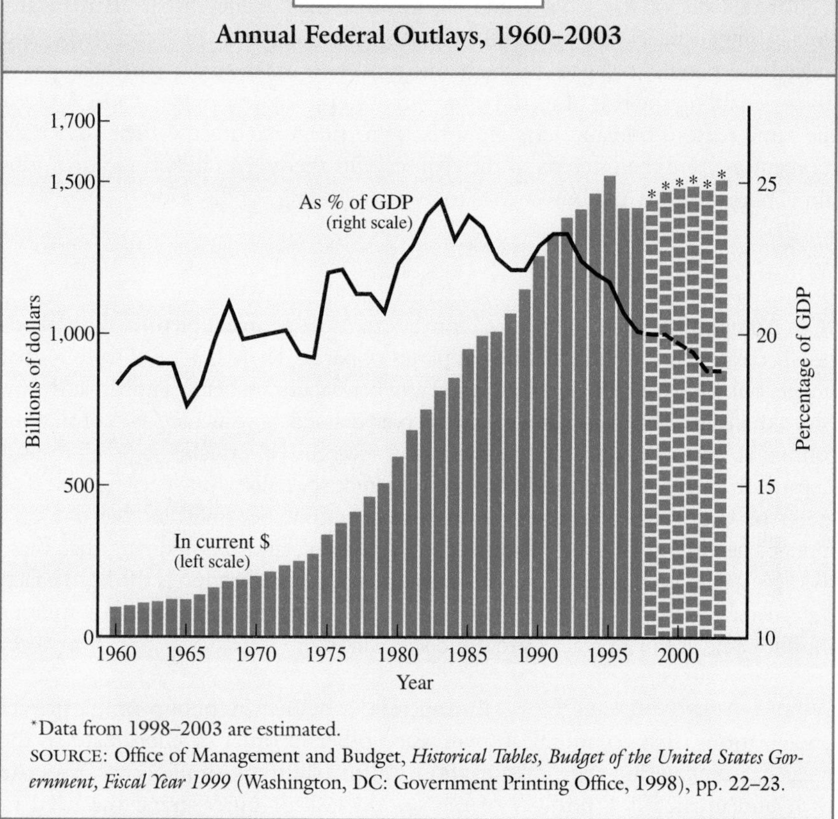


FIGURE 7.2

**Annual Federal Outlays, 1960–2003**

*Data from 1998–2003 are estimated.

SOURCE: Office of Management and Budget, *Historical Tables, Budget of the United States Government, Fiscal Year 1999* (Washington, DC: Government Printing Office, 1998), pp. 22–23.

vigor of many contemporary governors and in part to the bipartisan support in Washington for devolving more and more federal programs to the state and local governments, the number of civil service employees of state government, local government, county government, and special district government had grown to 16.9 million by 1997, and was still growing.[7] In sum, the national government is indeed "very large," but the federal service has not been growing any faster than the economy or the society. The same is roughly true of the growth pattern of state and local public personnel. Bureaucracy keeps pace with our society, despite our seeming dislike for it, because we can't operate the control towers, the prisons, the Social Security system, and other essential elements without bureaucracy. And we certainly could not have conducted a successful war in the Persian Gulf without a gigantic military bureaucracy.

Although the federal executive branch is large and complex, everything about it is commonplace. Bureaucracies are commonplace because they touch so many aspects of daily life. Government bureaucracies implement the decisions made by

[7]Ibid.

the political process. Bureaucracies are full of routine because that assures the regular delivery of the services and ensures that each agency fulfills its mandate. Public bureaucracies are powerful because legislatures and chief executives, and indeed the people, delegate to them vast power to make sure a particular job is done—enabling the rest of us to be more free to pursue our private ends. And for the same reason, bureaucracies are a threat to freedom, because their size, their momentum, and the interests of the civil servants themselves in keeping their jobs impel bureaucracies and bureaucrats to resist any change of direction.

## Bureaucrats

"Government by offices and desks" conveys to most people a picture of hundreds of office workers shuffling millions of pieces of paper. There is a lot of truth in that image, but we have to look more closely at what papers are being shuffled and why. More than fifty years ago, an astute observer defined bureaucracy as "continuous routine business."[8] Almost any organization succeeds by reducing its work to routines, with each routine being given to a different specialist. But specialization separates people from each other; one worker's output becomes another worker's input. The timing of such relationships is essential, and this requires that these workers stay in communication with each other. Communication is the key. In fact, bureaucracy was the first information network. Routine came first; voluminous routine came as bureaucracies grew and specialized.

**What Do Bureaucrats Do?** Bureaucrats, whether in public or in private organizations, first communicate with each other in order to coordinate all the specializations within their organization. All the shuffling of paper we associate with bureaucracy is a product of the second task of bureaucrats: the need to maintain a "paper trail," which is a routinized means of ensuring that individuals' responsibilities are met. If a process breaks down, if there is a failure, if there is a loss of profit in a private company or a rising dissatisfaction among clients of public agencies, the paper trail provides a means of determining who was responsible, who was at fault, and where routines ought to be improved.

One of the major reasons why there may be more paper shuffling in public agencies than in private agencies is the need to establish responsibility. As long as Americans want the agencies in the government bureaucracy to be maximally accountable to the people—directly and through Congress and the chief executive—there must be dependable and thorough means of determining responsibility and blame. "Red tape" is the almost universal cry of citizens against all the numbered forms and required signatures that bureaucracies generate.[9] Yet many of the same people who complain about red tape are the first to demand subpoenas requiring delivery of every conceivable document that may have some bearing on an alleged error of an agency or of individuals in an

[8]Arnold Brecht and Comstock Glaser, *The Art and Techniques of Administration in German Ministries* (Cambridge: Harvard University Press, 1940), p. 6.

[9]"Red tape" actually refers to the traditional practice of tying up bundles of bureaucratic records with red tape before storing them.

agency. What if the issue is the tragic explosion of the *Challenger* space shuttle or a gigantic overrun of expenditures for a new missile system for the Air Force? The bureaucrats in the National Aeronautics and Space Administration (NASA) or in the Air Force are required to create the record by which their own performances will later be judged.[10] And since Americans are more fearful of public bureaucracies and are therefore more likely to demand their accountability, public bureaucracies are likely to produce a great deal more paper than private bureaucracies.

Those first two activities of bureaucrats—communicating with each other and keeping copies of all those communications to maintain a paper trail—add up to a third: implementation, that is, implementing the objectives of the organization as laid down by its board of directors (if a private company) or by law (if a public agency). In government, the "bosses" are ultimately the legislature and the elected chief executive.

When the bosses—Congress, in particular, when it is making the law—are clear in their instructions to bureaucrats, implementation is a fairly straightforward process. Bureaucrats translate the law into specific routines for each of the employees of an agency. But what happens to routine administrative implementation when there are several bosses who disagree as to what the instructions ought to be? This requires yet a fourth job for bureaucrats: interpretation. Interpretation is a form of implementation, in that the bureaucrats still have to carry out what they believe to be the intentions of their superiors. But when bureaucrats have to interpret a law before implementing it, they are in effect engaging in *law making*.[11] Congress often deliberately delegates to an administrative agency the responsibility of lawmaking. Members of Congress often conclude that some area of industry needs regulating or some area of the environment needs protection, but they are unwilling or unable to specify just how that should be done.

**AMERICAN POLITICAL DEVELOPMENT**

The federal service was a political tool during much of the nineteenth century. Although partisanship was used as a criterion for appointments in the Jefferson administration, it was not until Andrew Jackson's administration that the "spoils system" made the executive branch more democratically responsive. Perceived abuses of the spoils system led to civil service reforms (most notably the 1883 Pendleton Act), which aimed for a more "politically neutral, independent, and competent" federal service.

SOURCE: Robert Maranto and David Schultz, *A Short History of the United States Civil Service* (Lanham, MD: University Press of America, 1991), p. 59.

[10]The presidential commission that investigated the *Challenger* tragedy was able to pinpoint a single technical failure on the basis of the evidence—the paper trail—assembled. Analysts of the tragedy concluded that "the decision to launch the *Challenger* was flawed. Those who made the decision were unaware of the recent history of [technical] problems . . . . If the decision-makers had known all the facts it is highly unlikely that they would have decided to launch [the shuttle] on January 28, 1986." See Barbara S. Romzek and Melvin Dubnick, "Accountability in the Public Sector: Lessons from the *Challenger* Tragedy," in *Current Issues in Public Administration,* 5th ed., ed. Frederick S. Lane (New York: St. Martin's, 1994), pp. 158–59.

[11]When bureaucrats engage in interpretation, the result is what political scientists call bureaucratic drift. Bureaucratic drift occurs because, as we've suggested, the "bosses" (in Congress) and the agents (within the bureaucracy) don't always share the same purposes. Bureaucrats also have their own agendas to fulfill. There exists a vast political science literature on the relationship between Congress and the bureaucracy. For a review, see Shepsle and Bonchek, *Analyzing Politics,* pp. 355–68. We'll also return to this point at the end of this chapter.

In such situations, Congress delegates to the appropriate agency a broad authority within which the bureaucrats have to make law, through the procedures of ***rule-making*** and ***administrative adjudication.*** Rulemaking is exactly the same as legislation; in fact it is often referred to as "quasi-legislation." Administrative adjudication is very similar to what the judiciary ordinarily does: applying rules and precedents to specific cases in order to settle disputes. Equally often, agencies engage in a combination of the two.

In sum, government bureaucrats do essentially the same things that bureaucrats in large private organizations do, and neither type deserves the disrespect embodied in the term "bureaucrat." But because of the authoritative, coercive nature of government, far more constraints are imposed on public bureaucrats than on private bureaucrats, even when their jobs are the same. Public bureaucrats are required to maintain a far more thorough paper trail. Public bureaucrats are also subject to a great deal more access from the public. Newspaper reporters, for example, have access to public bureaucrats. Public access has been vastly facilitated in the past thirty years; the adoption of the Freedom of Information Act (FOIA) in 1966 gave ordinary citizens the right of access to agency files and agency data to determine whether derogatory information exists in the file about citizens themselves and to learn about what the agency is doing in general.

And finally, citizens are given far more opportunities to participate in the decision-making processes of public agencies. There are limits of time, money, and expertise to this kind of access, but it does exist, and it occupies a great deal of the time of mid-level and senior public bureaucrats. This public exposure and access serves a purpose, but it also cuts down significantly on the efficiency of public bureaucrats. Thus, much of the lower efficiency of public agencies can be attributed to the political, judicial, legal, and publicity restraints put on public bureaucrats.

## Agencies and Their Politics

Cabinet departments, agencies, and bureaus are the operating parts of the bureaucratic whole. These parts can be separated into four general types: 1) cabinet departments, 2) independent agencies, 3) government corporations, and 4) independent regulatory commissions.

Although Figure 7.3 is an "organizational chart" of the Department of Agriculture, any other department could have been used as an illustration. At the top is the head of the department, who in the United States is called the "secretary" of the department. Below the department head are several top administrators, such as the general counsel and the judicial officer, whose responsibilities cut across the various departmental functions and provide the secretary with the ability to manage the entire organization. Of equal status are the assistant and under secretaries, each of whom has management responsibilities for a group of operating agencies, which are arranged vertically below each of the assistant secretaries.

The next tier, generally called the "bureau level," is the highest level of responsibility for specialized programs. The names of these "bureau-level agencies" are often very well known to the public: the Forest Service and the Food Safety and

FIGURE 7.3

**Organizational Chart of the Department of Agriculture**

Secretary
Deputy Secretary

Under Secretary for Natural Resources and Environment
- Forest Service
- Natural Resources Conservation Service

Under Secretary for Farm and Foreign Agricultural Services
- Farm Services Agency
- Foreign Agricultural Service

Under Secretary for Rural Economic and Community Development
- Rural Utilities Service
- Rural Housing and Community Development Service
- Rural Business and Cooperative Development Service

Under Secretary for Food, Nutrition, and Consumer Services
- Food and Consumer Service

Under Secretary for Food Safety
- Food Safety and Inspection Service

Under Secretary for Research, Education, and Economics
- Agricultural Research Service
- Cooperative State Research, Education, and Extension Service
- Economic Research Service
- National Agricultural Statistics Service

Assistant Secretary for Congressional Relations
- Office of Congressional and Intergovernmental Relations

Assistant Secretary for Marketing and Regulatory Services
- Agricultural Marketing Service
- Animal and Plant Health Inspection Service
- Grain Inspection, Packers and Stockyards Administration

Assistant Secretary for Administration
- Civil Rights Enforcement
- Information Resources Management
- Operations
- Personnel
- Administrative Law Judges
- Board of Contract Appeals

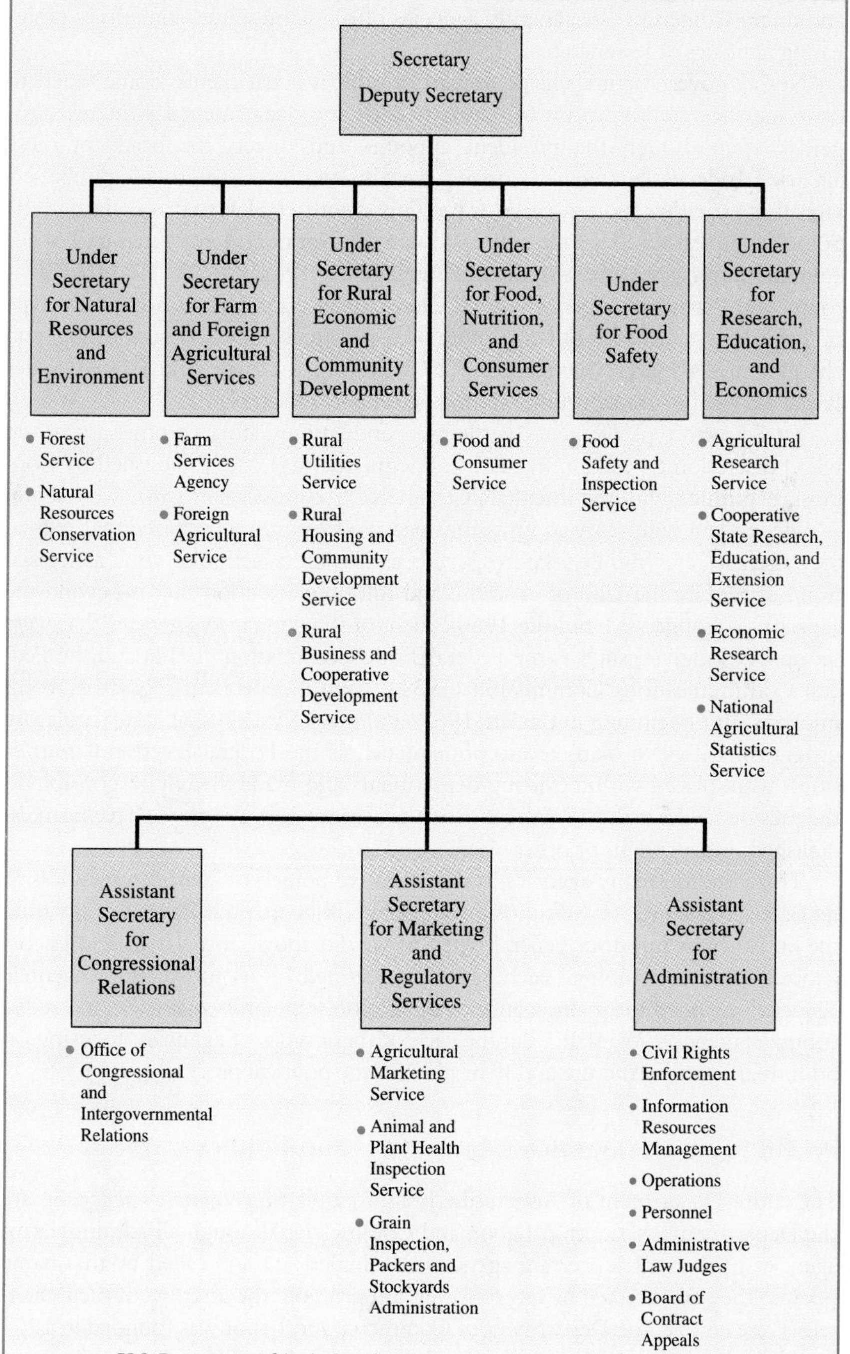

SOURCE: U.S. Department of Agriculture home page, http://www.usda.gov/agencies/agchart.htm

Inspection Service are two examples. Sometimes they are officially called bureaus, as in the Federal Bureau of Investigation (FBI), which is a bureau in the Department of Justice. Nevertheless, "bureau" is also the generic term for this level of administrative agency. Within the bureaus, there are divisions, offices, services, and units—sometimes designating agencies of the same status, sometimes designating agencies of lesser status.

Not all government agencies are part of cabinet departments. Some independent agencies are set up by Congress outside the departmental structure altogether, even though the president appoints and directs the heads of these agencies. Independent agencies usually have broad powers to provide public services that are either too expensive or too important to be left to private initiatives. Some examples of independent agencies are the National Aeronautics and Space Administration (NASA), the Central Intelligence Agency (CIA), and the Environmental Protection Agency (EPA). Government corporations are a third type of government agency, but are more like private businesses performing and charging for a market service, such as delivering the mail (the United States Postal Service) or transporting railroad passengers (Amtrak).

Yet a fourth type of agency is the independent regulatory commission, given broad discretion to make rules. The first regulatory agencies established by Congress, beginning with the Interstate Commerce Commission in 1887, were set up as independent regulatory commissions because Congress recognized that regulatory agencies are "minilegislatures," whose rules are exactly the same as legislation but require the kind of expertise and full-time attention that is beyond the capacity of Congress. Until the 1960s, most of the regulatory agencies that were set up by Congress, such as the Federal Trade Commission (1914) and the Federal Communications Commission (1934), were independent regulatory commissions. But beginning in the late 1960s and the early 1970s, all new regulatory programs, with two or three exceptions (such as the Federal Election Commission), were placed within existing departments and made directly responsible to the president. Since the 1970s, no major new regulatory programs have been established, independent or otherwise.

There are too many agencies in the executive branch to identify, much less to describe, so a simple classification of agencies will be helpful. Instead of dividing the bureaucracy into four general types, as we did above, this classification is organized by the mission of each agency, as defined by its jurisdiction: clientele agencies, agencies for maintenance of the Union, regulatory agencies, and redistributive agencies. We shall examine each of these types of agencies, focusing on both their formal structure and their place in the political process.

## The Clientele Agencies: Structures and Politics

The entire Department of Agriculture is an example of a ***clientele agency.*** So are the Departments of Interior, Labor, and Commerce. Although all administrative agencies have clientele, certain agencies are singled out and called by that name because they are directed by law to foster and promote the interests of their clientele. For example, the Department of Commerce and Labor was founded in 1903 as a single department "to foster, promote, and develop the foreign and domestic commerce, the mining, the manufacturing, the shipping, and fishing industries, and the transportation facilities of the United States."[12] It remained a single department until 1913, when the law created the two separate departments of Commerce and Labor, with each statute providing for the same obligation—to support and foster their respective clienteles.[13] The Department of Agriculture serves the many farming interests that, taken together, are the United States' largest economic sector (agriculture accounts for one-fifth of the U.S. total domestic output).

Most clientele agencies locate a relatively large proportion of their total personnel in field offices dealing directly with the clientele. The Extension Service of the Department of Agriculture is among the most familiar, with its numerous local "extension agents" who consult with farmers on farm productivity. These same agencies also seek to foster the interests of their clientele by providing "functional representation"; that is, they try to learn what their clients' interests and needs are and then operate almost as a lobby in Washington on their behalf. In addition to the Department of Agriculture, other clientele agencies include the Department of Interior and the five newest cabinet departments: Housing and Urban Development (HUD), created in 1966; Transportation (DOT), created in 1966; Energy (DOE), created in 1977; and Education (ED) and Health and Human Services (HHS), both created in 1979.[14]

Since clientele agencies exist to foster the interests of clients, it is no wonder that clients support the agency when it is in jeopardy of being abolished, reorganized, or cut back. Thus, it is not surprising to learn that client-supported agency resistance finally wore down President Reagan's resolve to abolish the Department of Energy, an entire clientele department. When created by President Carter, the Department of Energy had 18,000 employees and a $10 billion budget. The agencies in the new department were mainly pre-existing agencies drawn from other departments on the theory that agencies with related programs can be better managed within a common department. But each brought its own supportive clientele along. Imagine the resistance to abolition that arose from all the universities and corporations whose research labs depended on a piece of the DOE's multi-billion-dollar energy research budget.

The Department of Education is another case in point. Although President Reagan failed in his effort to abolish the department, he did manage to cut its budget. Yet, by 1987, the Office of Education and the entire Department of Education was back up to its pre-Reagan size. As reported earlier, the 1997 budget authorization for the Department of Education was barely cut, despite the strenuous efforts of the Republican 104th Congress. President Clinton's Goals 2000 renewed support for education with a $34 billion package for the Department of Education in the fiscal 1999 budget and $35 billion in the fiscal 2000 budget, giving the department a

[12]32 Stat. 825; 15 USC 1501.

[13]For a detailed account of the creation of the Department of Commerce and Labor and its split into two separate departments, see Theodore J. Lowi, *The End of Liberalism* (New York: W. W. Norton, 1979), pp. 78–84.

[14]The Departments of Education and of Health and Human Services until 1979 were joined in a single department, the Department of Health, Education, and Welfare (HEW), which had been established by Congress in 1953.

46-percent appropriations' increase since fiscal 1996. And the boldest proposal was yet to come. On February 16, Secretary of Education Riley presented a major proposal that the Department of Education regulate national teacher quality with a system of national testing and licensing. This would involve a quantum leap in the size of his department. Even conservative Elizabeth Dole jumped in with support for a larger education budget in her first speech on the 2000 presidential circuit.[15] The prime reason for the recovery of the Department of Education goes back to the nature of clientele agencies: Unless a president wants to drop everything else and concentrate on a single department, its constituency is just too much for a president to handle on a part-time basis. For example, the constituency of the Department of Education includes the departments of education in all the fifty states, and all the boards and school systems in thousands of counties and cities; there are also the teachers' colleges, and the major unions of secondary school teachers. One of the most formidable lobbies in the United States is the National Education Association (NEA), and there is a chapter of the NEA in every state in the country. It was the NEA's access to Carter that led to the creation of the Department of Education, and it is their continuing support of the department that frustrates efforts to change it, much less to abolish it.

These examples and those shown in Figure 7.4 point to what is known as an ***iron triangle,*** a pattern of stable relationships between an agency in the executive branch, a congressional committee or subcommittee, and one or more organized groups of agency clientele. Other configurations are of course possible. One of those might be called an iron rectangle or a network, because in recent years the federal courts have entered the process, sometimes on the side of clientele groups against an agency. But even so, the result reinforces the program against drastic change or abolition by a hostile president.[16]

These iron triangles, rectangles, and complexes make the clientele agencies the most difficult to change or to coordinate. Generally, these agencies are able to resist external demands or pressures for change and vigorously defend their own prerogatives and institutional integrity. Congress, in fact, felt compelled to adopt the Whistleblower Act in 1989, to encourage civil servants to report abuses of trust and to protect them from retaliations from within their own agencies. Because of their power of resistance, Congress and the president have frequently discovered that it is far easier to create new clientele agencies than to compel an existing agency to implement programs that it opposes. This has produced a strong tendency in the United States toward duplication, waste, and collusion.

## Agencies for Maintenance of the Union

These agencies could be called public order agencies were it not for the fact that the Constitution entrusts so many of the vital functions of public order, such as

[15]For details on President Clinton's Department of Education Program, see *Congressional Quarterly Weekly,* 6 February 1999, pp. 308–9.

[16]Martin Shapiro, "The Presidency and the Federal Courts," in *Politics and the Oval Office,* ed. Arnold Meltsner (San Francisco: Institute for Contemporary Studies, 1981), Chapter 8; and Hugh Heclo, "Issue Networks and the Executive Establishment," in *The New American Political System,* ed. A. King (Washington, DC: American Enterprise Institute, 1978), Chapter 3.

FIGURE 7.4

**Iron Triangles, Complexes, and Networks**

*These diagrams are classic uses of "iron triangles"; in fact, these are three of the cases observers had in mind when they invented the concept of "iron triangles."*

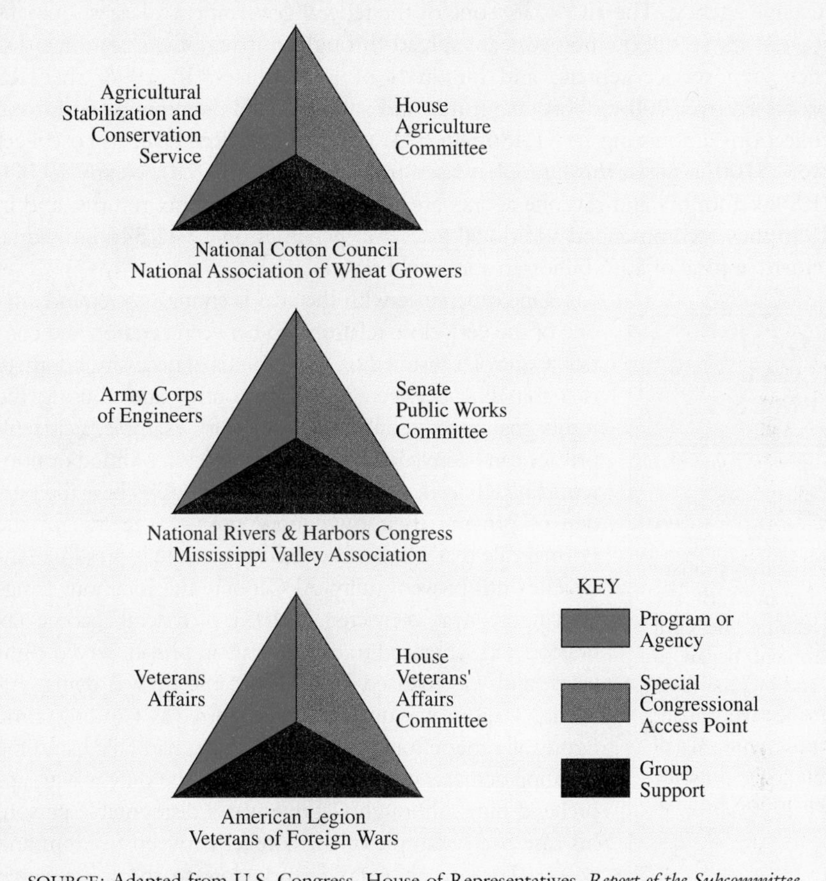


SOURCE: Adapted from U.S. Congress, House of Representatives, *Report of the Subcommittee for Special Investigations of the Committee on Armed Services,* 86th Congress, 1st session (Washington, DC: Government Printing Office, 1960), p. 7. Reprinted from Theodore J. Lowi, *Incomplete Conquest: Governing America,* 2nd ed. (New York: Holt, Rinehart and Winston, 1981), p. 139.

the police, to the state governments. This is indeed a remarkable feature of the American system, the more so because it is taken for granted that the United States has no national police force and little national criminal law. But some agencies vital to maintaining *national* bonds do exist in the national government, and they can be grouped for convenience into three categories: (1) agencies for control of the sources of government revenue, (2) agencies for control of conduct defined as a threat to internal national security, and (3) agencies for control of conduct threatening to external security. Most revenue control is housed in the Treasury

Department. Agencies for defending internal national security are housed mainly in the Department of Justice. Some such agencies are also found in the Departments of Defense and State, but the law is careful to limit their jurisdictions to external threats to security.

**Revenue Agencies** The Internal Revenue Service (IRS) is the most important revenue agency. The IRS is also one of the federal government's largest bureaucracies. Its 102,000 employees are spread through four regions, sixty-three districts, ten service centers, and hundreds of local offices. In 1996, the IRS processed over 200 million tax returns and supplemental documents, with total collections amounting to $1,486,546,674. (It costs the IRS 49 cents to collect every $100 in taxes; this figure has risen from 45 cents in 1970). Nearly 19,000 IRS tax auditors and revenue agents are engaged in auditing tax returns, and in 1996 they recommended additional taxes and penalties on 1,941,546 individual returns, a total of $7.6 billion in additional revenues.[17]

One experience with the IRS is enough to remind anyone of the very close relationship between taxation and control. Control is justified on the grounds of necessity, but there is a thin line between necessary control and abusing the rights guaranteed to all citizens since, for example, a citizen's privacy can be invaded if there is a suspicion of fraud or nonreporting. Indeed, persons accused in tax cases bear the burden of proving their own innocence—the reverse of the normal rule that a person accused of a crime is presumed innocent until proven guilty. Al Capone, the infamous gangland figure, was convicted in 1931 of federal income tax evasion and sentenced to eleven years in prison, served eight years, and was released in 1939 because he was dying. Although Capone was universally recognized as a leading crime figure, all other efforts to convict Capone had failed, and the tax approach was utilized because it was the only way to apprehend him. Although Capone was a disreputable person, his case is an example of the conflict between freedom and power. The power to tax is very close to the ***police power,*** since governments must rely on police power to collect taxes. But to use personal income tax records to imprison someone like Capone because the government lacked the evidence to convict him of his more serious crimes comes close to an improper linkage of the power to tax and the power to police. It can undermine the legitimacy of the tax system and instill fear in ordinary citizens that their privacy, if not their freedom, could be in danger.

The IRS is not unresponsive to political influences, given its close working relationship with Congress through the staffs as well as the members of the House

**AMERICAN POLITICAL DEVELOPMENT**

Although tariffs were the primary revenue producers for most of the nineteenth century, during the Civil War the U.S. government began to impose excise taxes and income taxes to defray some of the exhorbitant costs of the war. The Revenue Act of 1862 established a Bureau of Internal Revenue—a precursor to the Internal Revenue Service.

SOURCE: George Brown Tindall with David E. Shi, *America: A Narrative History,* 3rd ed. (New York: W. W. Norton, 1992), p. 672.

[17]These figures are from the *1998 Information Please Almanac* (Boston and New York: Houghton Mifflin, 1997), pp. 1000–1.

Ways and Means Committee and Senate Finance Committee. But the political patterns of the IRS are virtually opposite to those of a clientele agency; as one expert puts it, "probably no organization in the country, public or private, creates as much clientele *dis*favor as the Internal Revenue Service. The very nature of its work brings it into an adversary relationship with vast numbers of Americans every year."[18]

Back in the 1980s and early 1990s, when deficits were growing higher every year, Congress voted to stiffen penalties and to enforce the tax laws more stringently in order to collect a greater proportion of estimated tax revenues. But in the mid-1990s, as deficit pressures subsided and the budget began to balance and even show a surplus, Congress relented and began drawing up what came to be called a "taxpayer's bill of rights," which even included a reversal of the "burden of proof." Under the new provisions, the taxpayer would still have to cooperate, but proof of guilt would have to be provided by the IRS agents. This and other reforms would make tax collection a lot more difficult, but the hope was that the new bill would reduce animosities and improve voluntary cooperation in the payment of taxes. Whatever comes of the taxpayer bill of rights, it must be said that, despite many complaints, the IRS has maintained a reputation for being professional and evenhanded in its administration of the tax code; surprisingly few scandals have soiled its record.[19]

Most complaints against the IRS are against its needless complexity, its lack of sensitivity and responsiveness to individual taxpayers, and its overall lack of efficiency. As one of its critics put it, "Imagine a company that's owed $216 billion plus interest, a company with a 22-percent error rate. A company that spent $4 billion to update a computer system—with little success. It all describes the Internal Revenue Service."[20] Again leaving aside the issue of the income tax itself, all the other complaints amount to just one big complaint: the IRS is not bureaucratic enough; it needs more bureaucratization. It needs to succeed with its new computer processing system; it needs vast improvement in its "customer services"; it needs long-term budgeting and other management control; and it needs to borrow more management and technology expertise from the private sector.

**Agencies for Internal Security** As long as the country is not in a state of insurrection, most of the task of maintaining the Union takes the form of legal work, and the main responsibility for that lies in the Department of Justice. It is indeed a luxury, and rare in the world, when national unity can be maintained by routines of civil law instead of imposed by a real army with guns.

A strong connection exists between Justice and Treasury, because a major share of the responsibility for protecting national revenue sources is held by the Tax Division of the Justice Department. This agency handles the litigation arising out of actions taken by the IRS against delinquency, fraud, and dispute over interpretation of the Internal Revenue Code—the source of the tax laws and court interpretations.

[18]George E. Berkley, *The Craft of Public Administration* (Boston: Allyn & Bacon, 1975), p. 417.

[19]Good accounts of the efforts at reform of the IRS will be found in *Congressional Quarterly Weekly*, 9 May 1998, pp. 1224–27 and 6 June 1998, pp. 1505–6.

[20]Correspondent Kelli Arena, "Overhauling the IRS," CNN Financial Network, 7 March 1997.

In tax cases and in most other legal matters coming before agencies in the Justice Department, the United States itself is the sole party, as it is considered the legal representative of the American people as a whole and thus a legal individual (a legal fiction) that can sue and be sued. The Civil Division of the Justice Department (a bureau) deals with all litigation in which the United States is the ***defendant*** being sued by plaintiffs for injury and damage allegedly inflicted by the government or one of its officials. The agency also handles the occasional admiralty cases involving all disputes as to navigable waters or concerning shippers and shipworkers. The work of several other agencies in the Justice Department involves cases where the United States is the ***plaintiff.*** The largest and most important of these is the Criminal Division, which is responsible for enforcing all the federal criminal laws, except for a few specifically assigned to other divisions. Criminal litigation is actually done by the U.S. Attorneys. There is a presidentially appointed U.S. Attorney assigned to each federal judicial district, and he or she supervises the work of assistant U.S. Attorneys (see Chapter 8 for details). The work or jurisdiction of the Antitrust, Civil Rights, and Internal Security divisions is described by their official names.

Although it looms so very large in American folklore, the Federal Bureau of Investigation (FBI) is simply another bureau of the Department of Justice. The FBI handles no litigation, but instead serves as the information-gathering agency for all the other divisions. Established in 1908, the FBI expanded and advanced in stature during the 1920s and 1930s under the early direction of J. Edgar Hoover. Although it is only one of the fifteen bureaus and divisions in the department, and although it officially has no higher legal status than any of the others, its political importance is greater than that of the others. It is also the largest, taking over 40 percent of the appropriations allocated to the Department of Justice.

Despite its professionalism and its fierce pride in its autonomy, the FBI has not been unresponsive to the partisan commitments of Democratic and Republican administrations. Although the FBI has always achieved its best publicity from the spectacular apprehension of famous criminals, such as John Dillinger, George "Machine Gun" Kelly, and Bonnie and Clyde,[21] it has followed the president's direction in focusing on particular crime problems. Thus it has infiltrated Nazi and Mafia organizations; it operates the vast loyalty and security investigation programs covering all federal employees since the Truman presidency; it monitored and infiltrated the Ku Klux Klan and the civil rights movement in the 1950s and 1960s; and it has infiltrated radical political groups and extreme religious cults and survivalist militias in the 1980s and 1990s.

**AMERICAN POLITICAL DEVELOPMENT**

The expansion of FBI activities can be traced to presidential directives in 1936, 1939, 1943, 1950, and 1953. FBI director J. Edgar Hoover used these directives to justify new counterintelligence operations in the 1950s, which, on closer examination, proved unwarranted. Hoover's expansion was in part caused by inadequate supervision of the bureau by attorney generals and presidents.

SOURCE: Athan G. Theoharis, "The FBI's Stretching of Presidential Directives, 1936–1953," *Political Science Quarterly* 91 (1976–77), pp. 649–72.

[21]See William Keller, *The Liberals and J. Edgar Hoover* (Princeton: Princeton University Press, 1989). See also Victor Navasky, *Kennedy Justice* (New York: Atheneum, 1971), Chapter 2 and p. 8.

**Agencies for External National Security** Two departments occupy center stage here, State and Defense. There are a few key agencies outside State and Defense that have external national security functions. They will be treated in this chapter only as bureaucratic phenomena and as examples of the political problems relevant to administration. Although it is difficult to draw a clear line between policy and administration, the policy questions will be held over until Chapter 16.

Although diplomacy is generally considered the primary task of the State Department, diplomatic missions are only one of its organizational dimensions. As of 1996, the State Department comprised nineteen bureau-level units, each under the direction of an assistant secretary. Six of these are geographic or regional bureaus concerned with all problems within a defined region of the world; nine are "functional" bureaus, handling such things as economic and business affairs, intelligence and research, and international organizations. Four are bureaus of internal affairs, which handle such areas as security, finance and management, and legal issues.

These bureaus support the responsibilities of the elite of foreign affairs, the foreign service officers (FSOs), who staff U.S. embassies around the world and who hold almost all of the most powerful positions in the department below the rank of ambassador.[22] The ambassadorial positions, especially the plum positions in the major capitals of the world, are filled by presidential appointees, many of whom get their positions by having been important donors to the victorious political campaign.

Despite the importance of the State Department in foreign affairs, fewer than 20 percent of all U.S. government employees working abroad are directly under its authority. By far the largest number of career government professionals working abroad are under the authority of the Defense Department.

The creation of the Department of Defense by legislation from 1947 to 1949 was an effort to unify the two historic military departments, the War Department and the Navy Department, and to integrate with them a new department, the Air Force Department. Real unification, however, did not occur. Instead, the Defense Department adds more pluralism to national security.

The American military, following worldwide military tradition, is organized according to "chain of command," a tight hierarchy of clear responsibility and rank, made clearer by uniforms, special insignia, and detailed organizational charts and rules of order and etiquette (see Figure 7.5). The line agencies are the military commands, distributed geographically by divisions and fleets. ***Staff agencies,*** serving each military region, are logistics, intelligence, personnel, research and development (R&D), quartermaster, and engineering. At the top of the military chain of command is a chief of staff (called chief of naval operations in the navy, and commandant in the marines), of four-star rank. These chiefs of staff

[22]For more detail, consult John E. Harr, *The Professional Diplomat* (Princeton: Princeton University Press, 1972), p. 11; and Nicholas Horrock, "The CIA Has Neighbors in the 'Intelligence Community,'" *New York Times,* 29 June 1975, sec. 4, p. 2. See also Roger Hilsman, *The Politics of Policy Making in Defense and Foreign Affairs,* 3rd ed. (Englewood Cliffs, NJ: Prentice Hall, 1993).

**FIGURE 7.5**

## The Chain of Command in the Department of Defense

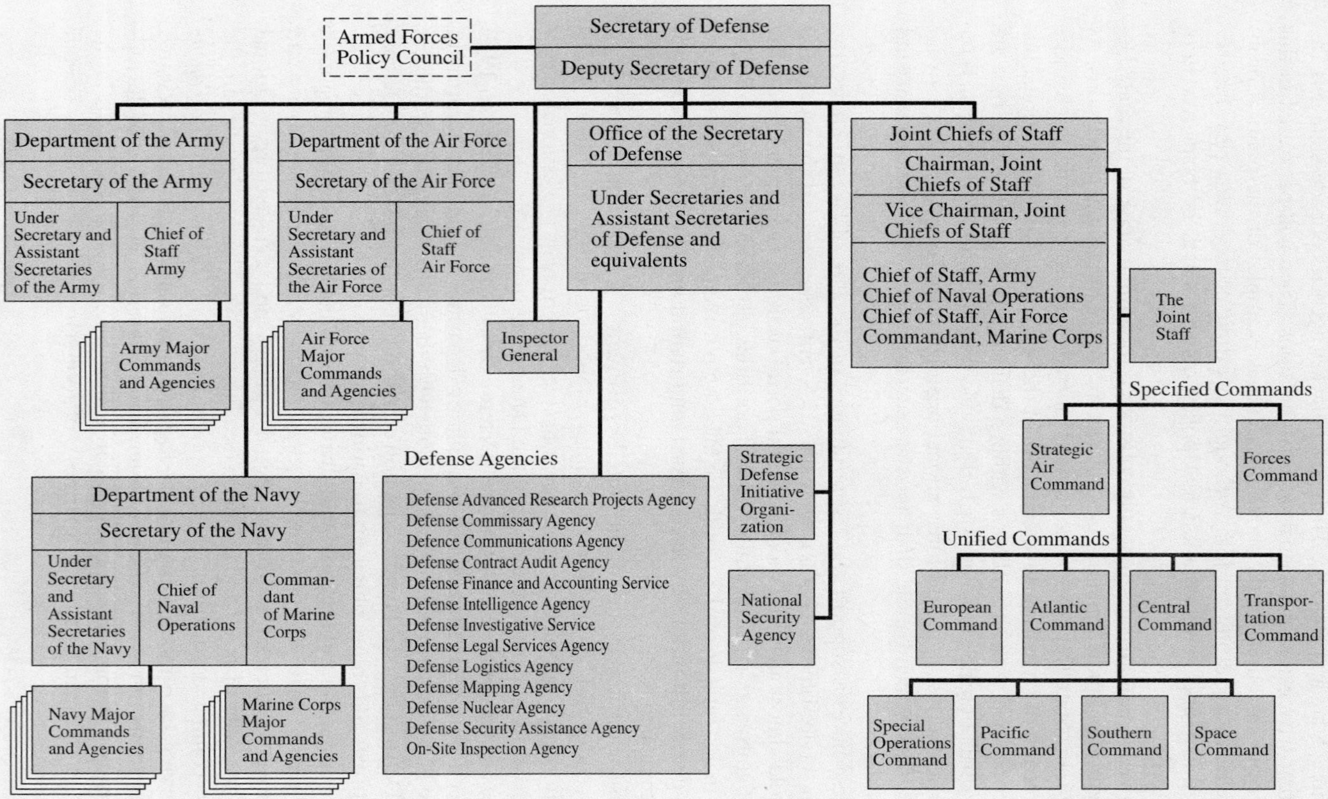

Armed Forces Policy Council

Secretary of Defense
Deputy Secretary of Defense

Department of the Army
Secretary of the Army
Under Secretary and Assistant Secretaries of the Army
Chief of Staff Army
Army Major Commands and Agencies

Department of the Air Force
Secretary of the Air Force
Under Secretary and Assistant Secretaries of the Air Force
Chief of Staff Air Force
Air Force Major Commands and Agencies

Inspector General

Office of the Secretary of Defense
Under Secretaries and Assistant Secretaries of Defense and equivalents

Joint Chiefs of Staff
Chairman, Joint Chiefs of Staff
Vice Chairman, Joint Chiefs of Staff
Chief of Staff, Army
Chief of Naval Operations
Chief of Staff, Air Force
Commandant, Marine Corps

The Joint Staff

Specified Commands
Strategic Air Command
Forces Command

Unified Commands
European Command
Atlantic Command
Central Command
Transportation Command
Special Operations Command
Pacific Command
Southern Command
Space Command

Department of the Navy
Secretary of the Navy
Under Secretary and Assistant Secretaries of the Navy
Chief of Naval Operations
Commandant of Marine Corps
Navy Major Commands and Agencies
Marine Corps Major Commands and Agencies

Defense Agencies
Defense Advanced Research Projects Agency
Defense Commissary Agency
Defence Communications Agency
Defense Contract Audit Agency
Defense Finance and Accounting Service
Defense Intelligence Agency
Defense Investigative Service
Defense Legal Services Agency
Defense Logistics Agency
Defense Mapping Agency
Defense Nuclear Agency
Defense Security Assistance Agency
On-Site Inspection Agency

Strategic Defense Initiative Organization

National Security Agency

SOURCE: Office of the Federal Register, *U.S. Government Manual, 1992–1993* (Washington, DC: Government Printing Office, 1992), p. 184.

serve as *ex officio* ("by virtue of their office") members of the Joint Chiefs of Staff—the center of military policy and management.

America's primary political problem with its military has not been the historic one of how to keep the military out of the politics of governing—a problem that has plagued so many countries in Europe and Latin America. The American military problem is one of the lower politics of the "pork barrel." President Clinton's long list of proposed military base closings, a major part of his budget-cutting drive for 1993, caused a firestorm of opposition even within his own party, including a number of members of Congress who were otherwise prominently in favor of significant reductions in the Pentagon budget. Emphasis on jobs rather than strategy and policy means pork barrel—use of the military for political purposes. The current Republican desire to increase the amount of defense spending, and President Clinton's willingness to cooperate in such increases by having proposed a $25 billion supplemental increase in the Pentagon budget for 1995, even in the face of tremendous fiscal pressures, have more to do with the domestic pressures of employment in defense and defense-related industries than with military necessity in a post–cold war era. This is why Congress had to create a Base Closing Commission in the late 1980s with authority independent of Congress and the president to decide which military bases could be closed and whether and how to compensate communities for job losses and other sacrifices.

The best way to understand the military in American politics is to study it within the same bureaucratic framework used to explain the domestic agencies. The everyday political efforts of American military personnel seem largely self-interested.

## The Regulatory Agencies

As we saw in Chapter 3, our national government did not even begin to get involved in the regulation of economic and social affairs until the late nineteenth century. Until then, regulation was strictly a state and local affair. The federal ***regulatory agencies*** are, as a result, relatively new, most dating from the 1930s. But they have come to be extensive and important. In this section, we will look at these regulatory agencies as an administrative phenomenon, with its attendant politics. We defer the policies to Chapter 14.

The United States has no Department of Regulation but has many regulatory agencies. Some of these are bureaus within departments, such as the Food and Drug Administration (FDA) in the Department of Health and Human Services, the Occupational Safety and Health Administration (OSHA) in the Department of Labor, and the Animal and Plant Health and Inspection Service (APHIS) in the Department of Agriculture. Other regulatory agencies are independent regulatory commissions.

**AMERICAN POLITICAL DEVELOPMENT**

Although most regulatory agencies date to the 1930s, there have been many new agencies since the 1960s. Congress created 42 "major regulatory agencies and programs" in the 1930s; that number increased to 53 in the 1960s and to 130 in the 1970s.

SOURCE: Gary C. Bryner, *Bureaucratic Discretion: Law and Policy in Federal Regulatory Agencies* (New York: Pergamon, 1987), p. 13.

An example is the Federal Trade Commission (FTC). But whether departmental or independent, an agency or commission is regulatory if Congress delegates to it relatively broad powers over a sector of the economy or a type of commercial activity and authorizes it to make rules governing the conduct of people and businesses within that jurisdiction. Rules made by regulatory agencies have the force and effect of legislation; indeed, the rules they make are referred to as ***administrative legislation.*** And when these agencies make decisions or orders settling disputes between parties or between the government and a party, they are really acting like courts.

Since regulatory agencies exercise a tremendous amount of influence over the economy, and since their rules are a form of legislation, Congress was at first loath to turn them over to the executive branch as ordinary agencies under the control of the president. Consequently, most of the important regulatory programs were delegated to independent commissions with direct responsibility to Congress rather than to the White House. This is the basis of the 1930s reference to them as the "headless fourth branch."[23] With the rise of presidential government, most recent presidents have supported more regulatory programs but have successfully opposed the expansion of regulatory independence. The 1960s and 1970s witnessed adoption of an unprecedented number of new regulatory programs but only four new independent commissions.

### AMERICAN POLITICAL DEVELOPMENT

Conflicts with the Environmental Protection Agency over environmental regulations led President Nixon to require "Quality of Life" reviews to accompany new regulations. President Ford required Inflation Impact Statements, and President Carter sought to have OMB (Office of Management and Budget) analyze new regulations and also evaluate existing rules. When President Reagan created OIRA (Office of Information and Regulatory Affairs) in 1981 to control regulations, he already had ample precedents.

SOURCE: William F. West and Joseph Cooper, "The Rise of Administrative Clearance," in *The Presidency and Public Policy Making*, ed. George C. Edwards III, Steven A. Shull, and Norman C. Thomas (Pittsburgh: University of Pittsburgh Press, 1985) pp. 192–214.

The political patterns of these agencies arise from their ability to play the president against the Congress. But this tends to throw the agencies into a more direct struggle with the interests they are regulating. And even though many of the regulatory programs were enacted over the opposition of the regulated groups, these groups often have succeeded in turning the programs to their advantage. Thus, for example, during the years when the airlines were being regulated by the Civil Aeronautics Board (CAB), they were able to protect themselves from competition from each other and to prevent new and more competitive transportation companies from entering the airlines market. Even organized labor found security within the CAB regulatory umbrella; regulation permitted the companies not only to charge exorbitant fares but to yield to pressure from airline unions for wage escalation far out of line with the rest of the work force. Consequently, in 1978, both airlines and organized labor within the airlines industry strongly opposed congressional efforts to deregulate the airlines by eliminating the CAB.[24]

[23]*Final Report of the President's Committee on Administrative Management* (Washington, DC: Government Printing Office, 1937). The term "headless fourth branch" was invented by a member of the committee staff, Cornell University government professor Robert Cushman.

[24]See Walter Adams and James Brock, *The Business Complex—Industry, Labor, and Government in the American Economy* (New York: Pantheon Books, 1986), pp. 229–31 and 322–23.

Three factors in particular have enabled regulated companies to turn the programs to their advantage. First, the top agency personnel are often drawn from the regulated industries themselves or from related law firms. Second, throughout its life, the regulatory agency has to depend on the regulated industries for important data about whether the industry is complying with the laws and rules. Third, regulated industries and their trade associations provide a preponderance of expert witnesses at agency hearings where new regulations are formulated. These factors encourage not only interdependence but interpenetration between regulators and regulated.[25]

During the 1970s there were two reactions. First, many citizens and members of Congress began to learn that regulatory agencies weren't necessarily regulating on behalf of what they considered to be the public interest. These people formed "public interest groups" or "public interest lobbies" and began to agitate to get regulatory agencies to maintain a more adversarial relation with the regulated companies. These groups even brought hundreds of lawsuits in federal courts to try to force agencies to be more zealous in regulating their part of the economy or society (see also Chapters 8 and 12). The second reaction was from many of the regulated interests themselves, who became convinced that they could do better without the safety of protective regulation; deregulation and the resulting more competitive market would, after a period of adjustment, be better for their entire industry. Moreover, the globalization of the economy provided new and vigorous international sources of competition in many industries, making the need for domestic regulation of these industries less compelling than when they had enjoyed virtual monopoly power within their domestic borders.[26]

Thus, the "new politics" movement and the ***deregulation*** movement started at about the same time, the first coming mainly from the liberal side of the political spectrum, and the second coming from some liberals as well as libertarians and conservatives. Nevertheless, all this pressure for both deregulation and for more regulation neither invigorated regulatory programs nor terminated them (see also Chapter 14).

## Redistributive Administration—Fiscal/Monetary and Welfare Agencies

Welfare agencies and fiscal/monetary agencies seem at first to be too far apart to belong to the same category, but they are related in a very special way. They are responsible for the transfer of literally hundreds of billions of dollars annually between the public and the private spheres, and through such transfers these agencies influence how people and corporations spend and invest trillions of dollars annually. We call them agencies of redistribution because they influence the amount of money in the economy and because they directly influence who has

[25]Lowi, *The End of Liberalism,* especially Chapters 5 and 11.

[26]Alfred C. Aman, Jr., *Administrative Law in a Global Era* (Ithaca, NY: Cornell University Press, 1992).

money, who has credit, and whether people will want to invest or save their money rather than spend it.

**Fiscal and Monetary Agencies** The best generic term for government activity affecting or relating to money is "fiscal" policy. The *fisc* was the Roman imperial treasury; fiscal can refer to anything and everything having to do with public finance. However, we in the United States choose to make a further distinction, reserving *fiscal* for taxing and spending policies and using *monetary* for policies having to do with banks, credit, and currency. And the third, *welfare,* deserves to be treated as an equal member of this redistributive category.

Administration of fiscal policy is primarily performed in the Treasury Department. It is no contradiction to include the Treasury here as well as with the agencies for maintenance of the Union. This indicates (1) that the Treasury is a complex department performing more than one function of government, and (2) that traditional controls have had to be adapted to modern economic conditions and new technologies.

Today, in addition to administering and policing income tax and other tax collections, the Treasury is also responsible for managing the enormous federal debt, which was close to $6 trillion in 1997. In 1998, interest payments on the debt amounted to 15 percent of the annual budget. This item alone is the fifth largest item in the entire annual budget, coming after Medicare and Medicaid (18 percent), Social Security (22 percent), national defense (16 percent), and all other domestic expenditures (16 percent). But debt is not something the country *has*; it is something a country has to *manage* and *administer.* Those thousands of billions of dollars of debt exist in the form of bonds, bank deposits, and obligations spelled out in contracts to purchase goods and services and research from the private sector. Even after we managed to balance the budget—a goal accomplished in 1998—and begin paying off the national debt, we still have to manage and administer the debt as one of the major functions of the national government. This requires a large and expert bureaucracy under any conditions.

The Treasury Department is also responsible for printing the currency that we use, but of course currency represents only a tiny proportion of the entire money economy. Most of the trillions of dollars used in the transactions that comprise the private and public sectors of the U.S. economy exist on printed accounts and computers, not in currency.

Another important fiscal agency (although for technical reasons it is called an agency of monetary policy) is the ***Federal Reserve System,*** headed by the Federal Reserve Board. The Federal Reserve System (the Fed) has authority over the credit rates and lending activities of the nation's most important banks. Established by Congress in 1913, the Fed is responsible for adjusting the supply of money to the needs of banks in the different regions and of the commerce and industry in each. The Fed helps shift money from where there is too much to where it is needed. It also ensures that the banks do not overextend themselves by too-liberal lending policies, out of fear that if there is a sudden economic scare, a run on a few banks might be contagious and cause another terrible crash like the one in 1929. The Federal Reserve Board sits at the top of the pyramid of twelve district Federal Reserve Banks, which are "bankers' banks," serving the monetary needs of the hundreds of member banks in the national bank system (see also Chapter 14).

**Welfare Agencies** Welfare agencies seem at first glance to be just another set of clientele agencies. But there is a big difference between the two categories. Access to clientele agencies is open to almost anyone who puts forward a claim. It may cost something to make one's way to a clientele agency or to write a proposal or to spend some time getting the agency's attention. But access is open to almost anyone. In contrast, welfare agencies operate under laws that discriminate between rich and poor, old and young, employed and unemployed. In other words, access to welfare agencies is restricted to those individuals who fall within some legally defined category. Those who fall outside the legal standards of that category would not be entitled to access even if they sought it.

The most important and expensive of the welfare programs are the Social Security programs. These are, roughly speaking, insurance programs, to which all employed persons contribute during their working years and from which those persons receive specified benefits as a matter of right when in need.[27] But there is an entirely separate category of programs that are popularly known as "welfare." The two most familiar examples are Temporary Assistance to Needy Families (TANF) and Supplemental Security Income (SSI)—both of which provide *cash benefits.* Eligible individuals receive actual cash payments. There is another category of public assistance or welfare called *in-kind benefits,* which include food stamps and Medicaid. In-kind benefits do involve expenditures of money, but not directly to the beneficiaries. For example, cash is involved in the Medicaid program, but the government acts as the "third party," guaranteeing payment to the doctor or hospital for the services rendered to the beneficiary.

No single government agency is responsible for all the programs comprising the "welfare state." The largest agency in this field is the Social Security Administration (SSA), which manages the social insurance aspects of Social Security and SSI. Other agencies in the Department of Health and Human Services administer TANF and Medicaid, and the Department of Agriculture is responsible for the food stamp program. With the exception of Social Security, these are *means-tested* programs, requiring applicants to demonstrate that their total annual cash earnings fall below an officially defined poverty line. These public assistance programs comprise a large administrative burden.

In August 1996, virtually all of the *means-tested* public assistance programs were legally abolished as national programs and were "devolved" to the states (see also Chapter 3). However, for the five years between fiscal 1996 and 2001, there will still be a great deal of national administrative responsibility, because federal funding of these programs will continue through large, discretionary block grants to each state. Other aspects of state welfare activity will have to be policed by federal agencies, and all of that requires about the same size of administrative capacity in welfare as existed before. Perhaps all this will begin to shrink at some later point, but not immediately. Those who expected some kind of revolution following adoption of the Personal Responsibility and Work Opportunity Reconciliation Act of 1996 are in for something of a disappointment.

Our concern in the first two sections of this chapter has been to present a

[27]These are called insurance because people pay premiums; however, the programs are not fully self-sustaining, and people do not receive benefits in proportion to the size of their premiums. For actual expenditures on these and other welfare programs, see Chapter 15.

## GLOBALIZATION AND DEMOCRACY

# *The Role of Bureaucracy in Regulating the Global Economy*

Until quite recently, a number of industries—such as telecommunications and public utilities—were granted absolute or virtual monopoly power within America's borders. Meanwhile, others, such as the transport, financial services, insurance, and broadcast industries, were heavily regulated. But rapid technological change and the globalization of the economy now create new and vigorous international sources of competition, making the need for government regulation and maintenance of monopoly privilege in these and other industries less compelling.

The changes in regulation can occur in two ways: (1) "liberalization" of markets through the introduction of new competition; and (2) "deregulation" of markets through the reduction or elimination of regulatory restraints on the conduct of individuals or private institutions.[1] The most celebrated example of market liberalization is the breakup of AT&T's monopoly—the dismantling of "Ma Bell" and the birth of a host of "Baby Bells" (e.g., Bell Atlantic, Pacific Bell, BellSouth)—and the emergence of new providers (e.g., MCI and Sprint), thus permitting competition in markets for long-distance and local telephone services. Meanwhile, efforts to deregulate the U.S. airline industry resulted in fewer government-imposed restrictions and increased competition. Liberalization and/or deregulation continues to be pressed in the banking and financial services, insurance, broadcast, trucking, and electric power and natural gas industries.

One of the most striking examples of the impact of globalization and technological change on government's ability to regulate industry is in the banking and financial services. As Richard B. McKenzie and Dwight W. Lee argue,

[1]The distinction between "liberalization" and "deregulation" is spelled out in Steven K. Vogel, *Freer Markets, More Rules: Regulatory Reform in Advanced Industrial Countries* (Ithaca, NY: Cornell University Press, 1996), p. 3.

picture of bureaucracy, its necessity as well as its scale, and the particular uses to which the bureaucracies are being put by the national government. But it is clearly impossible to present these bureaucracies merely as organizations when in fact they exist to implement actual public policies. We will have a great deal more to say directly about those public policies in later chapters (Chapters 14–16). What remains for this chapter is to explore how the American system of government has tried to accommodate this vast apparatus to the requirements of repre-

> . . . the recent revolution in computer and information technology has enabled firms to move assets around the world at the touch of a button. It has also caused an explosion of competition not only among businesses, but also among national governments seeking to attract new business and to keep existing business within their borders. This competition has forced governments to reduce tax rates, spending, and regulations to lower trade barriers. The resulting loss of fiscal and regulatory power has put a severe crimp in the very ability of these governments to govern.[2]

The fact that deregulation and liberalization became policy priorities not only in the United States but in every advanced industrialized country, attests to the impact of globalization on domestic politics.

While the advent of "footloose capital" (asset holders who are not bound by national borders) creates new concerns for policy makers, it would be foolish to assume that the government bureaucracy will surrender its regulatory powers without a protracted battle. For one thing, government regulators tend to become very protective of the interests of their client industries. In this regard, the most vocal opponents of change come from those well-organized interests that are unable to cope with the insecurities, instabilities, and inequalities that might follow in the wake of deregulation or increased competition. As German sociologist Max Weber noted, "Once it is fully established, bureaucracy is among those social structures which are the hardest to destroy."[3] In sum, even though the "downsizing" of government is likely to continue, it would be unwise to assume that the government bureaucracy will cease to perform a role.

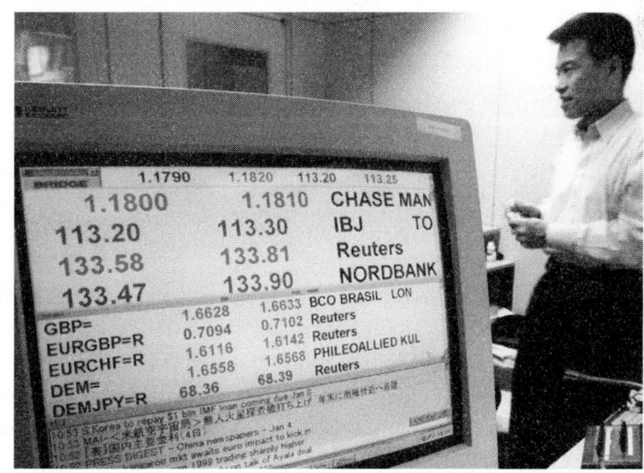


[2]Richard B. McKenzie and Dwight W. Lee, *Quicksilver Capital: How the Rapid Movement of Wealth Has Changed the World* (New York: Free Press, 1991), p. 1.

[3]H. H. Gerth and C. Wright Mills, eds. *From Max Weber: Essays in Sociology* (New York: Oxford University Press, 1958, p. 228.

sentative democracy. The title of the chapter, "Bureaucracy in a Democracy,"[28] was intended to convey the sense that the two are contradictory. We cannot live

[28]The title was inspired by an important book by Charles Hyneman, *Bureaucracy in a Democracy* (New York: Harper, 1950). For a more recent effort to describe the federal bureaucracy and to provide some guidelines for improvement, see Patricia W. Ingraham and Donald F. Kettl, *Agenda for Excellence: Public Service in America* (Chatham, NJ: Chatham House, 1992).

without bureaucracy, because it is the most efficient way to organize people and technology to get a large collective job done. But we can't live comfortably with bureaucracy either. Bureaucracy requires hierarchy, appointed authority, and professional expertise. Those requirements make bureaucracy the natural enemy of representation, which requires discussion among equals, reciprocity among equals, and a high degree of individualism. Yet, the task is not to retreat from bureaucracy but to try to take advantage of its strengths while trying to make it more *accountable* to the demands made upon it by democratic politics and representative government. That is the focus of the remainder of this chapter.

## CONTROLLING THE BUREAUCRACY

Two hundred years, millions of employees, and trillions of dollars after the founding, we must return to James Madison's observation that "You must first enable the government to control the governed; and in the next place oblige it to control itself."[29] Today the problem is the same, but the form has changed. Our problem today is bureaucracy and our inability to keep it accountable to elected political authorities. We conclude this chapter with a review of the presidency and Congress as institutions for keeping the bureaucracy accountable. Some of the facts from this and the preceding two chapters are repeated, but in this important context. We will then look at the special role of the federal courts in Chapter 8.

### President as Chief Executive

**Making the Managerial Presidency**[30] The rise of "presidential government" means above all that our system depends upon the president to establish and maintain a connection between popular aspirations and day-to-day administration. Congress and the American people have shown a consistent willingness to delegate to the president almost any powers he seeks, to enable him to meet this primary obligation. But there is no guarantee that the pow*ers* granted, no matter how many, will provide sufficient pow*er* to do the job. In 1937, President Roosevelt, through his President's Committee on Administrative Management, made the plea that "the president needs help." Each president since that time has found it necessary to make the same plea, because *presidents have great power to commit but much less power to guide*. In other words, the president can summon up popular opinion and congressional support to impose a new program and a new agency on the bureaucracy—even to impose an unwanted new responsibility on the FBI. But since the president can never have enough time and staff to watch over more than a few high-priority agencies, all the others can take advantage of their obscurity and go their merry way—until some scandal or dissatisfied client turns on the light.

[29]Clinton Rossiter, ed., *The Federalist Papers* (New York: New American Library, 1961), No. 51.

[30]Title inspired by Peri Arnold, *Making the Managerial Presidency* (Princeton: Princeton University Press, 1986).

The story of the modern presidency can be told largely as a series of responses to the rise of big government. *Each expansion of the national government in the twentieth century has been accompanied by a parallel expansion of presidential management authority,* that is, the expansion of the presidency as a real chief executive office. Table 7.2 provides a sketch of this pattern over most of the twentieth century. It shows, for example, that the first sustained expansion of the national government in the twentieth century, the Wilson period, was followed by one of the most important executive innovations in U.S. history, the Budget and Accounting Act of 1921. By this act, Congress turned over this prime legislative power, the budget, to the executive branch. Moving on to FDR, expansions of government during the 1930s were so large and were sustained over such a long period of time that reactions to control government growth occurred under the same president, producing some of the most important innovations in executive-branch management.

After World War II, the "managerial presidency" was an established fact, but its expansion continued, with each president trying to keep pace with the continually growing bureaucracy. And the purpose of the struggle remained the same: to react to every expansion with another mechanism of popular control. For example, as shown on Table 7.2, the two presidents most supportive of big government since Roosevelt were Kennedy and Johnson, but they were also equally committed to expanding the executive branch's managerial and oversight powers to control the expanded government. Management reform had become a regular and frequent activity.

President Nixon also greatly enlarged the managerial presidency. Nixon's approach to presidential reorganization can be attributed in part to his own boldness and confidence as president and in part to the great need of the Republicans at that time to impose their own brand of control on an executive branch that had been tremendously enlarged by the "pro-government" Democrats who had controlled the White House for twenty-eight of the previous thirty-six years.[31]

**AMERICAN POLITICAL DEVELOPMENT**

Presidents since FDR have enjoyed expanding resources to help them contain bureaucracy. Through increased use of the Executive Office of the President, they have been able to exercise greater control over political appointments, personnel management in the civil service, and centralized management. Still, these enhanced resources must be understood in the context of an increasingly large and complex bureaucracy, which by its very nature is more difficult to manage and control.

SOURCE: William F. West, *Controlling the Bureaucracy: Institutional Constraints in Theory and Practice* (Armonk, NY: M. E. Sharpe, 1995).

[31]For the story of Nixon's effort to transform the cabinet as a means of improving the management capacities of the chief executive, see Richard Nathan, *The Plot That Failed: Nixon and the Administrative Presidency* (New York: Wiley, 1975), pp. 68–76. To the secretary of state, there would be added three super secretaries, who were also to be appointed "counsellors to the president" and also to serve in the chair of each of three Domestic Council Committees, enabling them to supervise not only their own department but one or two other departments in their area. The secretary of agriculture would head a group called Natural Resources; the secretary of the then-Department of Health, Education, and Welfare would head a committee supervising other departments in the area of Human Resources, and the secretary of housing and urban development would head other departments in a general area called Community Development. This would have been a much more hierarchical approach to executive management, but it was a perfectly logical effort that failed largely because of the mounting distrust during the Watergate turmoil.

**TABLE 7.2**

**Government Expansions and Reform Responses to Them**

| PERIOD OF GOVERNMENT EXPANSION | RESPONSES OF THE PRESIDENCY TO EXPANSION |
|---|---|
| Wilson (1914–1918): World War I; budget up from average $800 million to over $18 billion in 1919; agencies expanded. | Budget and Accounting Act, 1921; (1) Bureau of the Budget in executive branch; (2) General Accounting Office (GAO) as agent of Congress. |
| Roosevelt (1933–1936): New Deal period; budget growth; addition of many new agencies, the "alphabetocracy." | Executive Office of the President, including Budget Bureau; reorganization powers, 1939. |
| Roosevelt (1940–1944): World War II; total mobilization. | Council of Economic Advisers, 1946; Secretary of Defense, National Security Council, Joint Chiefs of Staff, 1947. |
| Truman (1947–1951): Postwar, Korean War mobilization. | Emergence of "president's program," 1948+; emergence of White House staff, 1950+. |
| Eisenhower (1953–1960): Cold war; reaction against domestic government. | Formalizing of White House staff; enhancement of the National Security Council; effort to coordinate and control social agencies; Hoover Commission. |
| Kennedy (1961–1963): Comprehensive program; increased taxing power; direct pressure to control wages and prices. | Specialized White House staff; applied central budgeting (Planning Programming Budgeting System, PPBS) to Defense Department; upgraded Council of Economic Advisers. |
| Johnson (1964–1966): Great expansion of domestic social programs—Medicare and Medicaid, civil rights laws and agencies; expansion of war powers. | Applied PPBS to domestic agencies; created Organization for Economic Opportunity (OEO) to coordinate welfare programs: with "participatory democracy" established two departments (HUD and Transportation) to coordinate common activities. |
| Nixon (1969–1973): Increased Social Security benefits; expansion of diplomacy; price controls; many new regulatory programs. | Centralization and further specialization of White House staff; Office of Management and Budget (OMB) created; revenue sharing to decentralize urban and welfare programs; "indexing" of Social Security to eliminate annual legislative adjustments; cabinet-level coordinating councils on wages and prices and domestic policy; enhanced use of FBI surveillance of administrators. |
| Carter (1977–1980): Post-Watergate. | New Departments of Energy and Education; reform of U.S. civil service; zero-base budgeting; vast effort to reduce paperwork; first to impose cost-benefit analysis on regulation; first major effort to "deregulate." |
| Reagan (1981–1985): Dramatic expansion of defense budget; great expansion of national trade deficit. | Director of OMB promoted to cabinet status; expansion of OMB power of regulatory review; cabinet councils; expanded cost-benefit test for regulations. |
| Bush (1989–1993): Decision to put costs of Gulf War and S&L bail-out "off-budget," outside deficit-control calculations; deficits continue to mount. | More power given to OMB over total budget deficits, along with broad discretion to adjust agency budget targets to economic conditions. |
| Clinton (1993–2000): Continued deficit increases despite reduction efforts; health care reforms and welfare reforms involve expansion, not contraction, of budgets and bureaucracies. | National Performance Review to "reinvent government," under supervision of the vice president; Procurement Reform Act |

President Carter was probably more preoccupied with administrative reorganization than any other Democratic president in this century. Responding to Watergate, his 1976 campaign was filled with plans to make the bureaucracy more accountable as well as more efficient. His reorganization of the civil service will long be recognized as one of his more significant contributions. The Civil Service Reform Act of 1978 was the first major revamping of the civil service since its inception in 1883.

Although President Reagan gave the impression of being a "laid-back" president, he actually centralized management to an unprecedented degree. Reagan adopted a "top-down" approach whereby a White House budgetary decision would be made first and the agencies would be required to fit within it. The effect of this process was to convert OMB into an agency of policy determination and presidential management. As one expert put it, the Reagan management strategy was "centralization in the service of decentralization."[32] President Reagan brought the director of OMB into the cabinet and centralized the budget process as well as the process of regulatory review, as discussed earlier. President Bush went even further than President Reagan in using the White House staff instead of cabinet secretaries in management.

President Clinton has engaged in the most systematic and probably the most successful effort to "change the way the government does business," to borrow a phrase he has often used to describe the goal of his National Performance Review (NPR). The NPR is one of the more important administrative reforms of the twentieth century. All recent American presidents have decried the size and unmanageability of the federal bureaucracy, but Clinton actually managed to turn proposals for change into real reform. In September 1993, Clinton launched the NPR, based on a set of 384 proposals drafted by a panel headed by Vice President Gore. The avowed goal of the NPR is to "reinvent government"—to make the federal bureaucracy more efficient, accountable, and effective. Its goals include saving more than $100 billion over five years, in large part by cutting the federal workforce by 12 percent, or more than 270,000 jobs, by the end of fiscal year 1999. The NPR is also focused on cutting red tape, streamlining the way the government purchases goods and services, improving the coordination of federal management, and simplifying federal rules. Virtually all observers agree that the NPR has made substantial progress. For instance, the government's Office of Personnel Management has abolished the notorious 10,000-page Federal Personnel Manual and Standard Form 171, the government's arduous job application. Another example illustrates the nature of the NPR's work: The Defense Department's method for reimbursing its employees' travel expenses used to take seventeen steps and two months; an employee-designed reform encouraged by the NPR streamlined this to a four-step, computer-based procedure that takes less than fifteen minutes, with anticipated savings of $1 billion over five years.

One potential weakness of the NPR noted by its critics is that it has no strategy for dealing with congressional opposition to bureaucratic reform.

[32]Lester Salamon and Alan Abramson, "Governance: The Politics of Retrenchment," in *The Reagan Record,* ed. John Palmer and Isabel Sawhill (Cambridge, MA: Ballinger, 1984), p. 40.

DEBATING THE ISSUES

## The Federal Bureaucracy: Who Should Control It?

*Every modern president has entered office faced with the daunting task of developing meaningful and effective strategies for dealing with the federal government's sprawling bureaucracy. Presidents have alternately viewed the bureaucracy as a lion to be tamed or as a vast resource pool.*

*Political scientists Richard P. Nathan and Norton E. Long both recognize the role of politics in administrative actions. But Nathan argues that presidents should seek political control of the bureaucracy by pursuing an "administrative presidency" strategy. Long notes that the dispersal of power in government impels administrators to develop their own sources of power, including support from special interests outside of government, and that efforts by presidents to enforce administrative conformity are not only likely to fail but are undesirable as well.*

### NATHAN

. . . Such officials [as the president] should organize their office—appoint, assign, and motivate their principal appointees—in a way that *penetrates* the administrative process. The reason is that in a complex, technologically advanced society in which the role of government is pervasive, much of what we would define as policymaking is done through the execution of laws in the management process. . . .

. . . Ronald Reagan among recent presidents appears to have the best handle on the need for an administrative strategy. He avoided the pitfalls of Nixon's heavy-handedness, Johnson's grand design, and Carter's atomic-submarine approach to management. . . . The five main ingredients of an administrative presidency strategy . . . are: (1) selecting cabinet secretaries whose views are closely in line with those of the president; (2) selecting subcabinet officials who also share the president's values and objectives; (3) motivating cabinet and subcabinet officials to give attention to agency operations and administrative processes; (4) using the budget process as the central organizing framework for public policymaking; and, finally, (5) avoiding over-reliance on centralized White House clearance and control systems. . . .

I believe a managerial strategy is appropriate for the American presidency. Even if we assume that the president is successful in establishing a greater measure of managerial cohesion and control over the federal bureaucracy, there still exists an abundance of ways in which the president's power in this area and in others can be checked and balanced. . . . The exercise of a greater measure of . . . control over the executive branch of the American national government . . . is fully consistent with democratic values.[1]

### LONG

It is clear that the American political system of politics does not generate enough power at any focal point of leadership to provide the conditions for an even partially successful divorce of politics from administration. Subordinates [i.e., administrators] cannot depend on the formal chain of command to deliver enough political power to permit them to do their jobs. Accordingly they must supplement the resources available throughout the hierarchy with those they can muster on their own, or accept the consequences in frustration—a course itself not without danger. Administrative rationality demands that objectives be determined and sights set in conformity with a realistic appraisal of power position and potential. . . . The weakness in party structure both permits and makes necessary the . . . political activities of the administrative branch. . . . Agencies and bureaus . . . are in the business of building, maintaining, and increasing their political support. They lead and in large part are led by the diverse groups whose influence sustains them. . . . A major and most time-consuming aspect of administration consists of the wide range of activities designed to secure enough "customer" acceptance to survive and, if fortunate, develop a consensus adequate to program formulation and execution. . . .

The task of the Presidency lies in feeling out the alternatives of policy which are consistent with the retention and increase of the group support on which the Administration rests. . . . Like most judges, the Executive needs to hear argument for his own instruction. The alternatives presented by subordinates in large part determine the freedom and the creative opportunity of their superiors. . . . Reorganization of the executive branch to centralize administrative power in the Presidency . . . may effect improvement, but in a large sense it must fail.[2]

[1]Richard P. Nathan, *The Administrative Presidency* (New York: Wiley, 1983), pp. 82, 88, 93.
[2]Norton E. Long, "Power and Administration," *Public Administration Review* 9 (Autumn 1949), pp. 257–64.

Donald Kettl, a respected reform advocate, warns that "virtually no reform that really matters can be achieved without at least implicit congressional support. The NPR has not yet developed a full strategy for winning that support."[33] One consequence, for instance, was that in 1994 Congress voted to exempt the Department of Veterans Affairs from the personnel reductions imposed by the NPR, a development that could make attainment of its goals impossible. A good way to fight such congressional actions is with publicity, but a troubling sign for the NPR's long-term prospects (and for President Clinton's standing) is that in national polls two-thirds of Americans say either that they have never heard of it, or even that they believe the federal government is continuing to grow.

The overall accomplishment of President Clinton and the NPR has certainly been respectable, even in the eyes of Republican opposition (see Donald Kettl's Reinvention Report Card, Table 7.3). But despite the accomplishments so far and the optimism about further reform, a certain humility is in order when we think about "reforming" the federal bureaucracy and "reinventing" government.

[33]Quoted in Stephen Barr, "Midterm Exam for 'Reinvention': Study Cites 'Impressive Results' But Calls for Strategy to Win Congressional Support," *Washington Post,* 19 August 1994, p. A25.

TABLE 7.3

**The Reinventing Government Report Card for 1998**

| CATEGORY | GRADE | COMMENTS |
|---|---|---|
| Downsizing | B | Accomplished the goal, but planning to match downsized work force with agency missions was weak. |
| Identifying objectives of government | D | The NPR sought in 1995 to focus on what government *should* do—but the effort evaporated as the Republican threat faded. |
| Procurement reform | A | Fundamental transformation of procurement system. Some vendors complain, but the system is far more efficient than it was. |
| Customer service | B+ | Great progress in some agencies, but major failures in others—notably the IRS. |
| Disaster avoidance | B– | Substantial efforts in many agencies, notably FEMA. Spectacular failures in others, notably the IRS. The big test: the Y2K problem. |
| Political leadership | C+ | Consistently strong leadership from the top but inconsistent below. Federal workers have gotten mixed signals. |
| Performance improvements | C+ | Linkage of NPR with the Government Performance and Results Act is spotty. |
| Improved results in "high-impact" programs | INC | Good strategy—but likelihood of achieving goals is low. |
| Service coordination | INC | Efforts to improve the coordination of service delivery are embryonic. |
| Relations with Congress | D | Efforts to develop legislative support for NPR initiatives have, with the exception of procurement reform, been weak and ineffective. Support from Congress: poor. |
| Improvements in citizen confidence in government | C | The steady slide in public trust and confidence in government has ended, but that has more to do with a healthy economy than improved government performance. |
| Inspiration from other governments, private-sector reforms | B– | Wide survey of other ideas—but more a grab bag of options than a careful analysis of which ones fit federal problems. |
| Effort | A+ | No administration in history has invested such sustained, high-level attention to management reform efforts. |
| ***OVERALL GRADE*** | ***B*** | Substantial progress made over first five years, but much more work lies ahead. Successive administrations will have little chance but to continue the NPR in some form. |

SOURCE: Donald Kettl, "Reinventing Government: A Fifth-Year Report Card," CPM Report 98-1 (Washington, DC: Center for Public Management, Brookings Institution, 1998).

To make incremental changes, even dramatic ones, in bureaucracies is possible; to change the very nature of administration is not.

**The Problem of Management Control by the White House Staff** The cabinet's historic failure to perform as a board of directors, and the inability of any other agency to perform that function, has left a vacuum. OMB has met part of the need, and the management power of the director seems to go up with each president. But the need for executive management control goes far beyond what even the boldest of OMB directors can do. The White House staff has filled the vacuum to a certain extent precisely because in the past thirty years, the "special assistants to the president" have been given relatively specialized jurisdictions over one or more departments or strategic issues. These staffers have additional power and credibility beyond their access to the president because they also have access to confidential information. Since information is the most important bureaucratic resource, White House staff members gain management power by having access to the CIA for international intelligence and the FBI and the Treasury for knowledge about agencies, not only beyond what the agencies report but on matters that are likely to make agency personnel fearful and respectful. The FBI has exclusive knowledge about the personal life of every bureaucrat, since each one has to go through a rigorous FBI security clearance procedure prior to being appointed and promoted.

Responsible bureaucracy, however, is not going to come simply from more presidential power, more administrative staff, and more management control. All this was inadequate to the task of keeping the National Security Staff from seizing the initiative to run its own policies toward Iran and Nicaragua for at least two years (1985–1986) after Congress had restricted activities on Nicaragua and the president had forbidden negotiations with Iran. The Tower Commission, appointed to investigate the Iran-Contra affair, concluded that although there was nothing fundamentally wrong with the institutions involved in foreign policy making—State, Defense, the White House, and their relation to Congress—there had been a "flawed process" and "a failure of responsibility," and a thinness of the president's personal engagement in the issues. The Tower Commission found that "at no time did [President Reagan] insist upon accountability of performance review."[34]

No particular management style is guaranteed to work. Each White House management innovation, from one president to the next, shows only the inadequacy of the approaches of previous presidents. And as the White House and the EOP grow, the management bureaucracy itself becomes a management problem. Something more and different is obviously needed.

## Congress and Responsible Bureaucracy

Congress is constitutionally essential to responsible bureaucracy because the key to government responsibility is legislation. When a law is passed and its intent is clear, then the president knows what to "faithfully execute" and the responsible agency understands what is expected of it. In our modern age, legislatures rarely

[34]Quoted in I. M. Destler, "Reagan and the World: An 'Awesome Stubbornness,'" in *The Reagan Legacy—Promise and Performance*, ed. Charles O. Jones (Chatham, NJ: Chatham House, 1988), pp. 244, 257. The source of the quote is *Report of the President's Special Review Board,* 26 February 1987.

ANALYZING AMERICAN POLITICS

## *Congressional Oversight: Abdication or Strategic Delegation?*

The separation of powers requires that the legislative branch enact legislation while the executive branch implement that legislation. Congress often grants the executive-branch bureaucracies discretion in determining certain features of a policy during the implementation phase. Though the complexities of governing a modern industrialized democracy make the granting of discretion necessary, there are some who argue that Congress not only gives unelected bureaucrats too much discretion but also delegates too much policy-making authority to them. Congress, they say, has transferred so much power that it has created a "runaway bureaucracy" in which unelected officials accountable neither to the electorate nor to Congress make important policy decisions.[1] By enacting vague statutes that give bureaucrats broad discretion, members of Congress have effectively abdicated their constitutionally designated roles and effectively removed themselves from the policy-making process. The ultimate impact of this extreme delegation has left the legislative branch weak and ineffectual and has dire consequences for the health of our democracy.

Recently, scholars using the rational-choice approach have argued that delegation by Congress does not necessarily mean abdication, and that it is possible and sometimes even necessary for Congress to delegate in order to achieve desired policy outcomes.[2] This argument draws on "agency theory" from the discipline of economics: When a principal (in this case, Congress) assigns certain tasks to an agent (in this case, an executive branch agency), the principal can take certain steps to make sure that the agent performs the tasks to the principal's liking, even though there are numerous opportunities for the agent to do what he or she wants instead of what the principal wants. If tasks are delegated to those with a comparative advantage in

[1]Theodore Lowi, *The End of Liberalism,* 2nd ed. (New York: W. W. Norton, 1979); Lawrence C. Dodd and Richard L. Schott, *Congress and the Administrative State* (New York: Wiley, 1979).
[2]D. Roderick Kiewiet and Matthew D. McCubbins, *The Logic of Delegation: Congressional Parties and the Appropriations Process* (Chicago: University of Chicago Press, 1991).

make laws directly for citizens; most laws are really instructions to bureaucrats and their agencies. But when Congress enacts vague legislation, agencies are thrown back upon their own interpretations. The president and the federal courts step in to tell them what the legislation intended. And so do the intensely interested groups. But when everybody, from president to courts to interest groups, gets involved in the actual interpretation of legislative intent, to whom is the

performing them, then the results can be mutually beneficial. In order to be successful, certain principal/agent problems must be overcome. Proponents of the "congressional dominance" perspective of congressional-bureaucracy relations contend that Congress possesses various mechanisms, such as the power to appropriate funds for agencies and the confirmation of executive branch officials, to provide the necessary checks to overcome these problems.

Some claim that even though Congress may possess the tools to engage in effective oversight, it fails to do so, simply because we do not see Congress actively engaging in much oversight activity.[3] However, Matthew McCubbins and Thomas Schwartz argue that these critics have focused on the wrong type of oversight and have missed a type of oversight that benefits members of Congress in their bids for re-election.[4] McCubbins and Schwartz distinguish between two types of oversight: *police patrol* and *fire alarm*. Under the police patrol variety, Congress systematically initiates investigation into the activity of agencies. Under the fire alarm variety, members of Congress do not initiate investigations but wait for adversely affected citizens or interest groups to bring bureaucratic perversions of legislative intent to the attention of the relevant congressional committee. To make sure that individuals and groups will bring these violations to members' attention, Congress passes laws that help individuals and groups make claims against the bureaucracy, including granting them legal standing before administrative agencies and district courts.

McCubbins and Schwartz argue that this type of oversight is more efficient than the police patrol variety, given costs and the electoral incentives of members of Congress. Why should members spend the resources to initiate investigations without having any evidence that they will reap electoral rewards? Police patrol oversight can waste taxpayer dollars, since many investigations will not turn up any evidence on violations of legislative intent. It is much more cost-effective for members to conserve their resources and then claim credit for fixing the problem (and saving the day) after the fire alarms are pulled. McCubbins and Schwartz argue that given the incentives of elected officials, it makes sense that we would see Congress engaging more in fire alarm oversight than police patrol oversight. Thus the critics of Congress have incorrectly perceived a lack of oversight because they are looking in the wrong places.

[3]Morris Ogul, *Congress Oversees the Bureaucracy* (Pittsburgh: University of Pittsburgh Press, 1976); Peter Woll, *American Bureaucracy,* (New York: W. W. Norton, 1977).

[4]Matthew D. McCubbins and Thomas Schwartz, "Congressional Oversight Overlooked: Police Patrols versus Fire Alarms," *American Journal of Political Science* 28 (1984), pp. 165–79.

agency responsible? Even when it has the most sincere desire to behave responsibly, how shall this be accomplished?

The answer is ***oversight.*** The more legislative power Congress has delegated to the executive, the more it has sought to get back into the game through committee and subcommittee oversight of the agencies. The standing committee system in Congress is well-suited for oversight, inasmuch as most of the congressional committees and subcommittees are organized with jurisdictions roughly parallel to one or more executive departments or agencies. Appropriations committees as well as authorization committees have oversight powers—as do their respective subcommittees. In addition to these, there is a committee on government operations both in the House and in the Senate, each with oversight powers not limited by departmental jurisdiction.

The best indication of Congress's oversight efforts is the use of public hearings, before which bureaucrats and other witnesses are summoned to discuss and defend agency budgets and past decisions. The data drawn from systematic studies of congressional committee and subcommittee hearings and meetings show quite dramatically that Congress has tried through oversight to keep pace with the expansion of the executive branch. Between 1950 and 1980, the annual number of committee and subcommittee meetings in the House of Representatives rose steadily from 3,210 to 7,022 and in the Senate from 2,607 to 4,265 (in 1975–1976). Beginning in 1980 in the House and 1978 in the Senate, the number of committee and subcommittee hearings and meetings slowly began to decline, reaching 4,222 in the House and 2,597 in the Senate by the mid-1980s. This pattern of rise and decline in committee and subcommittee oversight activity strongly suggests that congressional vigilance toward the executive branch is responsive to long-term growth in government rather than to yearly activity or to partisan considerations.[35]

Oversight can also be carried out by individual members of Congress. Such inquiries addressed to bureaucrats are considered standard congressional "case work" and can turn up significant questions of public responsibility even when the motivation is only to meet the demand of an individual constituent. Oversight also takes place very often through communications between congressional staff and agency staff. Congressional staff has been enlarged tremendously since the Legislative Reorganization Act of 1946, and the legislative staff, especially the staff of the committees, is just as professionalized and specialized as the staff of an executive agency.[36] In addition, Congress has created for itself three quite large agencies whose obligations are to engage in constant research on problems taking place in the executive branch: the General Accounting Office, the Congressional Research Service, and the Congressional Budget Office. Each is designed to give

[35]Data from Norman Ornstein et al., *Vital Statistics on Congress, 1987–1988* (Washington, DC: Congressional Quarterly Press, 1987), pp. 161–62. Lawrence Dodd and Richard Schott, counting only hearings and not all meetings, report the same pattern for a shorter period. Between 1950 and 1970, the annual number of public hearings grew from about 300 in the Senate and 350 in the House to 700 in the Senate and 750 in the House. See *Congress and the Administrative State* (New York: Wiley, 1979), p. 169. For a valuable and skeptical assessment of legislative oversight of administrations, see James W. Fesler and Donald F. Kettl, *The Politics of the Administrative Process* (Chatham, NJ: Chatham House, 1991), Chapter 11.

[36]As illustrated here, oversight can take different forms. The political scientists Matthew McCubbins and Thomas Schwartz distinguished two forms: police-patrol and fire-alarm. "Police-patrol" oversight involves direct supervision from congressional committees and their staffs. "Fire-alarm" oversight occurs when a private citizen "pulls the lever" and reports misuse of bureaucratic authority. For more on this as well as on "fire-extinguisher" oversight, see Shepsle and Bonchek, *Analyzing Politics,* pp. 368–70.

Congress information independent of the information it can get through hearings and other communications directly from the executive branch.[37]

The better approach is for Congress to spend more of its time clarifying its legislative intent and less of its time on oversight activity. If its original intent in the law were clearer, Congress could then afford to defer to presidential management to maintain bureaucratic responsibility. Bureaucrats are more responsive to clear legislative guidance than to anything else. But when Congress and the president are at odds (or coalitions within Congress are at odds), bureaucrats have an opportunity to evade responsibility by playing one branch off against the other.[38]

## Bureaucracy in a Democracy

Bureaucracy is here to stay. The administration of a myriad of government functions and responsibilities in a large, complex society will always require "rule by desks and offices" (the literal meaning of "bureaucracy"). No "reinvention" of government, however well conceived or executed, can alter that basic fact, nor can it resolve the problem of reconciling bureaucracy in a democracy. President Clinton's National Performance Review has accomplished some impressive things: the national bureaucracy has become somewhat smaller, and in the next few years it will become smaller still; government procedures are being streamlined and are under tremendous pressure to become even more efficient. But these efforts are no guarantee that the bureaucracy itself will become more malleable. Congress will not suddenly change its practice of loose and vague legislative draftsmanship. Presidents will not suddenly discover new reserves of power or vision to draw more tightly the reins of responsible management. No deep solution can be found in quick fixes. As with all complex social and political problems, the solution to the problem of bureaucracy in a democracy lies mainly in a sober awareness of the nature of the problem. This awareness enables people to avoid fantasies about the abilities of a democratized presidency—or the potential of a reform effort, or the magical powers of the computer, or the populist rhetoric of a new Congress—to change the nature of governance by bureaucracy.

The problem of bureaucracy in a democracy is how to harness the bureaucracy to the service of democracy. Bureaucracy is like any powerful instrument, from a beast of burden to a supersonic jet; it must be subordinated to goals and

[37]Until 1983, there was still another official tool of legislative oversight, the legislative veto. Each executive agency was obliged to submit to Congress proposed decisions or rules. These were to lie before both houses for thirty to sixty days; then if Congress took no action by one-house or two-house resolution explicitly to veto a proposed measure, it became law. The legislative veto was declared unconstitutional by the Supreme Court in 1983 on the grounds that it violated the separation of powers because the resolutions Congress passed to exercise its veto were not subject to presidential veto, as required by the Constitution. See Immigration and Naturalization Service v. Chadha, 462 U.S. 919 (1983).

[38]Kenneth A. Shepsle has examined shifting coalitions within Congress as an explanation for bureaucratic drift. For a review of his argument as well as a concise review of the tensions between Congress and the bureaucracy, see Shepsle and Bonchek, *Analyzing Politics,* pp. 370–75.

services for which it is only imperfectly suited. Woodrow Wilson proclaimed that we were entering World War I to "make the world safe for democracy." Our job is to deal with bureaucracy in a similar but slightly different spirit, not to go to war against it but to make it safe for democracy.

Although making bureaucracy safe for democracy will never be easy, we have in fact made some progress. For example, while it is true that our civil servants (whom we irreverently call bureaucrats) may not be of Nobel Prize caliber (whose employees are?), they do in fact believe in democracy and are sincerely wedded to the professional ethic of subordination to law and to political authority. Americans take this for granted, not appreciating the fact that the historic attitude of bureaucrats is to call themselves "government officials" and to look with contempt upon citizens and, all too often, upon democracy itself. Thus, we have already succeeded in making bureaucracy safe for democracy, at least to the extent that we have democratized the bureaucrats. Important as that is, however, that is only part of the problem. The problem is to make each bureaucratic agency responsive to political direction while remaining professionally committed to that agency's mission. Members of Congress are even more democratized than bureaucrats, but they persist in abusing their democratic norms by the practice of poorly drafted legislation (forcing bureaucrats to make policy for them) followed by highly individualized and personal interference into agency business on behalf of constituents or interest group clients (called oversight and "case work"). All this deranges bureaucracy through no fault of the bureaucrats. And presidents, also monumentally committed to the democratic norm, lose sight of the difference between high-flown rhetoric, which creates unrealistically high public expectations, and responsible management through speeches and press conferences and bill drafting, which provides genuine leadership and guidance.

The bottom line (to use a bureaucratic cliché) is that bureaucracy can be put to the service of democracy if democracy and its political institutions can develop, express, and maintain a sense of direction that bureaucracies can use their professional abilities to pursue. Bureaucracy can be a good thing, as long as democracy is boss.

## SUMMARY

Most American citizens possess less information and more misinformation about bureaucracy than about any other feature of government. We therefore began the chapter with an elementary definition of bureaucracy, identifying its key characteristics and demonstrating the extent to which bureaucracy is not only a phenomenon but an American phenomenon. In the second section of the chapter we showed how all essential government services and controls are carried out by bureaucracies—or to be more objective, administrative agencies. Following a very general description of the different general types of bureaucratic agencies in the executive branch we divided up the agencies of the executive branch into four categories according to mission: the clientele agencies, the agencies for maintaining the Union, the regulatory agencies, and the agencies for redistribution. These illustrate the varieties of administrative experience in American government.

THEN AND NOW

## Changes in American Politics

The growth of the executive branch in the twentieth century raises important questions about democratic control in the United States. Because twentieth-century bureaucracy is both larger and more complex than it was in the nineteenth century, the ability of national institutions to control that bureaucracy has had to change as well.

- Although the federal service has not grown substantially over the last thirty years, its size today stands in sharp contrast to its size in the nineteenth century. Much of its growth occurred during the first four decades of the twentieth century.
- The federal service was a potent political tool in the nineteenth century, when presidents rewarded friends with jobs through the "spoils system." Civil service reforms during the late nineteenth and early twentieth centuries professionalized the federal service and decreased opportunities for both political control and political abuse.
- Political exigencies and structural developments have governed the expansion and development of the federal bureaucracy. The increased need to collect taxes during the Civil War led to the creation of a Bureau of Internal Revenue. And concerns over the activities of Communists and other potentially subversive organizations led to expansion in the powers of the FBI.
- Although regulatory agencies date to the establishment of the Interstate Commerce Commission in 1887 and grew significantly during the 1930s, their greatest expansion occurred during the last four decades, with the creation of new regulatory agencies and programs.
- The expansion of the executive branch has fueled expansion of presidential resources, which have in turn affected the increasingly complex federal bureaucracy. Moreover, congressional efforts to oversee the bureaucracy grew from the 1950s to the 1980s as well.

Although the bureaucratic phenomenon is universal, not all the bureaucracies are the same in the way they are organized, in the degree of their responsiveness, or in the way they participate in the political process.

Finally, the chapter concluded with a review of all three of the chapters on "representative government" (Chapters 5, 6, and 7) in order to assess how well the two political branches (the legislative and the executive) do the toughest job any government has to do: making the bureaucracy accountable to the people it serves and controls. "Bureaucracy in a Democracy" was the subtitle and theme of the chapter not because we have succeeded in democratizing bureaucracies but because it is the never-ending task of politics in a democracy.

## For Further Reading

Arnold, Peri E. *Making the Managerial Presidency: Comprehensive Organization Planning.* Princeton: Princeton University Press, 1986.

Bryner, Gary. *Bureaucratic Discretion.* New York: Pergamon Press, 1987.

Dodd, Lawrence C., and Richard L. Schott. *Congress and the Administrative State.* New York: Wiley, 1979.

Downs, Anthony. *Inside Bureaucracy.* Boston: Little, Brown, 1966.

Fesler, James W., and Donald F. Kettl. *The Politics of the Administrative Process.* Chatham, NJ: Chatham House, 1991.

Frederickson, H. George, ed. *Ethics and Public Administration.* Armonk, NY: M. E. Sharpe, 1993.

Fry, Bryan R. *Mastering Public Administration—From Max Weber to Dwight Waldo.* Chatham, NJ: Chatham House, 1989.

Heclo, Hugh. *A Government of Strangers.* Washington, DC: Brookings Institution, 1977.

Hill, Larry B., ed. *The State of Public Bureaucracy.* Armonk, NY: M. E. Sharpe, 1992.

Lynn, Naomi B., and Aaron Wildavsky. *Public Administration—The State of the Discipline.* Chatham, NJ: Chatham House, 1990.

Nachmias, David, and David H. Rosenbloom. *Bureaucratic Government USA.* New York: St. Martin's Press, 1980.

Nathan, Richard. *The Plot That Failed: Nixon's Administrative Presidency.* New York: Wiley, 1975.

Ripley, Randall B., and Grace A. Franklin. *Congress, the Bureaucracy and Public Policy,* 5th ed. Pacific Grove, CA: Brooks/Cole, 1991.

Rohr, John. *To Run a Constitution: The Legitimacy of the Administrative State.* Lawrence: University Press of Kansas, 1986.

Rourke, Francis E. *Bureaucracy, Politics and Public Policy.* Boston: Little, Brown, 1984.

Rubin, Irene S. *The Politics of Public Budgeting,* 2nd ed. Chatham, NJ: Chatham House, 1993.

Skowronek, Stephen. *Building a New American State: The Expansion of National Administrative Capacities, 1877–1920.* New York: Cambridge University Press, 1982.

Weaver, R. Kent. *Automatic Government: The Politics of Indexation.* Washington, DC: Brookings Institution, 1988.

Weiss, Carol H., and Allen H. Barton, eds. *Making Bureaucracies Work.* Beverly Hills, CA: Sage, 1980.

Wildavsky, Aaron. *The New Politics of the Budget Process,* 2nd ed. New York: HarperCollins, 1992.

Wilson, James Q. *Bureaucracy: What Government Agencies Do and Why They Do It.* New York: Basic Books, 1989.

Wood, Dan B. *Bureaucratic Dynamics: The Role of Bureaucracy in a Democracy*. Boulder, CO: Westview, 1994.

# The Federal Courts: Least Dangerous Branch or Imperial Judiciary?

## TIME LINE ON THE JUDICIARY

| Events | | Institutional Developments |
|---|---|---|
| George Washington appoints John Jay chief justice (1789–1795) | | Judiciary Act creates federal court system (1789) |
| | 1800 | |
| John Marshall appointed chief justice (1801) | | *Marbury v. Madison* provides for judicial review (1803) |
| States attempt to tax the second Bank of the U.S. (1818) | | *McCulloch v. Maryland*—Court upholds supremacy clause, broad construction of necessary and proper clause; denies right of states to tax federal agencies (1819) |
| Andrew Jackson appoints Roger Taney chief justice; Taney Court expands power of states (1835) | | *Barron v. Baltimore*—Court rules that only the federal government and not the states are limited by the U.S. Bill of Rights (1833) |
| | 1850 | |
| Period of westward expansion; continuing conflict and congressional compromises over slavery in the territories (1830s–1850s) | | *Dred Scott v. Sanford*—Court rules that federal government cannot exclude slavery from the territories (1857) |
| Civil War (1861–1865)<br>Reconstruction (1867–1877)<br>Self-government restored to former Confederate states (1877) | | *Slaughter-House Cases*—Court limits scope of Fourteenth Amendment to newly freed slaves; states retain right to regulate state businesses (1873) |
| "Jim Crow" laws spread throughout Southern states (1890s) | 1890 | *Plessy v. Ferguson*—Court upholds doctrine of "separate but equal" (1896) |
| World War I; wartime pacifist agitation in U.S. (1914–1919)<br>Red Scare; postwar anarchist agitation (1919–1920) | | *Abrams v. U.S.* (1919) and *Gitlow v. N.Y.* (1925) apply First Amendment to states and limit free speech by "clear and present danger" test |
| FDR's New Deal (1930s) | 1930 | Court invalidates many New Deal laws, e.g., *Schechter Poultry Co. v. U.S.* (1935) |
| Court-packing crisis—proposal to increase the number of Supreme Court justices defeated by Congress (1937) | | Court reverses position, upholds most of New Deal, e.g., *NLRB v. Jones & Laughlin Steel* (1937) |
| U.S. enters World War II (1941–1945) | | *Korematsu v. U.S.*—Court approves sending Japanese-Americans to internment camps (1944) |
| Korean War (1950–1953)<br>Earl Warren appointed chief justice (1953) | 1950 | *Youngstown Sheet & Tube Co. v. Sawyer*—Court rules that president's steel seizure must be authorized by statute (1952) |

| Events | | Institutional Developments |
|---|---|---|
| Civil rights movement (1950s and 1960s) | | *Brown v. Board of Ed.*—Court holds that school segregation is unconstitutional (1954) |
| | | Court begins nationalization of the Bill of Rights—*Gideon v. Wainwright* (1963); *Escobedo v. Ill.* (1964); *Miranda v. Arizona* (1966), etc. |
| Warren Burger appointed chief justice (1969) | | *Flast v. Cohen*—Court permits class action suits (1968) |
| Right-to-life movement (1970s–1990s) | 1970 | *Roe v. Wade*—Court strikes down state laws making abortion illegal (1973) |
| Affirmative action programs (1970s–1990s) | | *Univ. of Calif. v. Bakke*—Court holds that race may be taken into account but limits use of quotas (1978) |
| Court arbitrates conflicts between Congress and president (1970s and 1980s)<br>William Rehnquist appointed chief justice (1986) | | *U.S. v. Nixon*—Court limits executive privilege (1974); *Bowsher v. Synar*—Court invalidates portion of Gramm-Rudman Act (1986); *Morrison v. Olson*—Court upholds constitutionality of special prosecutor (1988) |
| | | *Webster v. Reproductive Health Services*—Court nearly overturns *Roe* (1989) |
| Bush appoints David Souter (1990), Clarence Thomas (1991) to the Supreme Court | 1990 | *Lucas v. South Carolina Coastal Council*—Court supports property owners against state land seizures (1992) |
| Clinton appoints Ruth Bader Ginsburg (1993), Stephen Breyer (1994) to the Supreme Court | | Court limits use of redistricting to help minorities—*Shaw v. Reno* (1993); *Holder v. Hall* and *Johnson v. DeGrandy* (1994) |
| | | Court rules 9-0 that a sitting president can be sued for his private conduct (*Clinton v. Jones,* 1997) |

Every year nearly 25 million cases are tried in American courts and one American in every nine is directly involved in litigation. Cases can arise from disputes between citizens, from efforts by government agencies to punish wrongdoing, or from citizens' efforts to prove that a right provided them by law has been infringed upon as a result of government action—or inaction. Many critics of

**CORE OF THE ARGUMENT**

- The Supreme Court's power of judicial review makes the Court a lawmaking body.
- The three dominant influences shaping Supreme Court decisions are the philosophies and attitudes of the members of the Court, the solicitor general's control over cases involving the government, and the pattern of cases that come before the Court.
- The role and power of the federal courts, particularly the Supreme Court, have been significantly strengthened and expanded in the last fifty years.

the American legal system assert that we have become much too litigious (ready to use the courts for all purposes), and perhaps we have. But the heavy use that Americans make of the courts is also an indication of the extent of conflict in American society. And given the existence of social conflict, it is far better that Americans seek to settle their differences through the courts rather than by fighting or feuding.

In this chapter, we will first examine the judicial process, including the types of cases that the federal courts consider and the types of law with which they deal. Second, we will assess the organization and structure of the federal court system as well as the flow of cases through the courts. Third, we will consider judicial review and how it makes the Supreme Court a "lawmaking body." Fourth, we will examine various influences on the Supreme Court. Finally, we will analyze the role and power of the federal courts in the American political process, looking in particular at the growth of judicial power in the United States.

The framers of the American Constitution called the Court the "least dangerous branch" of American government. Today, it is not unusual to hear friends and foes of the Court alike refer to it as the "imperial judiciary."[1] However, we must look in some detail at America's judicial process before we can understand this transformation and its consequences, and answer the question: "Is the Supreme Court the 'least dangerous branch' or an 'imperial judiciary'?"

**THE CENTRAL QUESTION**

"Is the Supreme Court the 'least dangerous branch' or an 'imperial judiciary'?"

## THE JUDICIAL PROCESS

Originally, a "court" was the place where a sovereign ruled—where the king and his entourage governed. Settling disputes between citizens was part of governing. According to the Bible, King Solomon had to settle the dispute between two women over which of them was the mother of the child both claimed. Judging is the settling of disputes, a function that was slowly separated from the king and

[1] See Richard Neely, *How Courts Govern America* (New Haven: Yale University Press, 1981).

the king's court and made into a separate institution of government. Courts have taken over from kings the power to settle controversies by hearing the facts on both sides and deciding which side possesses the greater merit. But since judges are not kings, they must have a basis for their authority. That basis in the United States is the Constitution and the law. Courts decide cases by hearing the facts on both sides of a dispute and applying the relevant law or principle to the facts.

## Cases and the Law

Court cases in the United States proceed under three broad categories of law: criminal law, civil law, and public law (see Table 8.1).

Cases of ***criminal law*** are those in which the government charges an individual with violating a statute that has been enacted to protect the public health,

TABLE 8.1

**Types of Laws and Disputes**

| TYPE OF LAW | TYPE OF CASE OR DISPUTE | FORM OF CASE |
|---|---|---|
| Criminal law | Cases arising out of actions that violate laws protecting the health, safety, and morals of the community. The government is always the plaintiff. | *U.S. (or state) v. Jones*<br>*Jones v. U.S. (or state),* if Jones lost and is appealing |
| Civil law | "Private law," involving disputes between citizens or between government and citizen where no crime is alleged. Two general types are contract and tort. *Contract cases* are disputes that arise over voluntary actions. *Tort cases* are disputes that arise out of obligations inherent in social life. Negligence and slander are examples of torts. | *Smith v. Jones*<br>*New York v. Jones*<br>*U.S. v. Jones*<br>*Jones v. New York* |
| Public law | All cases where the powers of government or the rights of citizens are involved. The government is the defendant. *Constitutional law* involves judicial review of the basis of a government's action in relation to specific clauses of the Constitution as interpreted in Supreme Court cases. *Administrative law* involves disputes over the statutory authority, jurisdiction, or procedures of administrative agencies. | *Jones v. U.S. (or state)*<br>*In re Jones*<br>*Smith v. Jones,* if a license or statute is at issue in their private dispute |

safety, morals, or welfare. In criminal cases, the government is always the ***plaintiff*** (the party that brings charges) and alleges that a criminal violation has been committed by a named ***defendant.*** Most criminal cases arise in state and municipal courts and involve matters ranging from traffic offenses to robbery and murder. However, a large and growing body of federal criminal law deals with such matters as tax evasion, mail fraud, and the sale of narcotics. Defendants found guilty of criminal violations may be fined or sent to prison.

Cases of ***civil law*** involve disputes among individuals or between individuals and the government where no criminal violation is charged. Unlike criminal cases, the losers in civil cases cannot be fined or sent to prison, although they may be required to pay monetary damages for their actions. In a civil case, the one who brings a complaint is the plaintiff and the one against whom the complaint is brought is the defendant. The two most common types of civil cases involve contracts and torts. In a typical contract case, an individual or corporation charges that it has suffered because of another's violation of a specific agreement between the two. For example, the Smith Manufacturing Corporation may charge that Jones Distributors failed to honor an agreement to deliver raw materials at a specified time, causing Smith to lose business. Smith asks the court to order Jones to compensate it for the damage allegedly suffered. In a typical tort case, one individual charges that he or she has been injured by another's negligence or malfeasance. Medical malpractice suits are one example of tort cases.

**AMERICAN POLITICAL DEVELOPMENT**

Although the number of criminal cases filed in U.S. district courts was only slightly higher in the 1980s and 1990s than in the 1950s, 1960s, and 1970s, the yearly number of civil cases since 1983 is regularly five times higher than in the 1950s.

SOURCE: Harold W. Stanley and Richard G. Niemi, *Vital Statistics on American Politics,* 5th ed. (Washington, DC: Congressional Quarterly Press, 1995), p. 284.

In deciding civil cases, courts apply statutes (laws) and legal ***precedents*** (prior decisions). State and federal statutes, for example, often govern the conditions under which contracts are and are not legally binding. Jones Distributors might argue that it was not obliged to fulfill its contract with the Smith Corporation because actions by Smith, such as the failure to make promised payments, constituted fraud under state law. Attorneys for a physician being sued for malpractice, on the other hand, may search for prior instances in which courts ruled that actions similar to those of their client did not constitute negligence. Such precedents are applied under the doctrine of ***stare decisis,*** a Latin phrase meaning "let the decision stand."

A case becomes a matter of the third category, ***public law,*** when a plaintiff or defendant in a civil or criminal case seeks to show that their case involves the powers of government or rights of citizens as defined under the Constitution or by statute. One major form of public law is constitutional law, under which a court will examine the government's actions to see if they conform to the Constitution as it has been interpreted by the judiciary. Thus, what began as an ordinary criminal case may enter the realm of public law if a defendant claims that his or her constitutional rights were violated by the police. Another important arena of public law is administrative law, which involves disputes over the jurisdiction, procedures, or authority of administrative agencies. Under this type of law, civil litigation between an individual and the government may become a matter of public law if the individual asserts that the government is violating a statute or abusing its power under the Constitution. For example, land owners have asserted that federal and state restrictions on land use constitute violations of the Fifth Amendment's restrictions on the government's ability to confiscate private property. Recently, the Supreme Court has been very sympathetic to such claims, which effectively transform an ordinary civil dispute into a major issue of public law.

Most of the important Supreme Court cases we will examine in this chapter involve judgments concerning the constitutional or statutory basis of the actions of government agencies. As we shall see, it is in this arena of public law that the Supreme Court's decisions can have significant consequences for American politics and society.

## Types of Courts

In the United States, systems of courts have been established both by the federal government and by the governments of the individual states. Both systems have several levels, as shown in Figure 8.1. More than 99 percent of all court cases in the United States are heard in state courts. The overwhelming majority of criminal cases, for example, involve violations of state laws prohibiting such actions as murder, robbery, fraud, theft, and assault. If such a case is brought to trial, it will be heard in a state ***trial court,*** in front of a judge and sometimes a jury, who will determine whether the defendant violated state law. If the defendant is convicted, he or she may appeal the conviction to a higher court, such as a state ***appellate court,***

FIGURE 8.1

**The U.S. Court System**

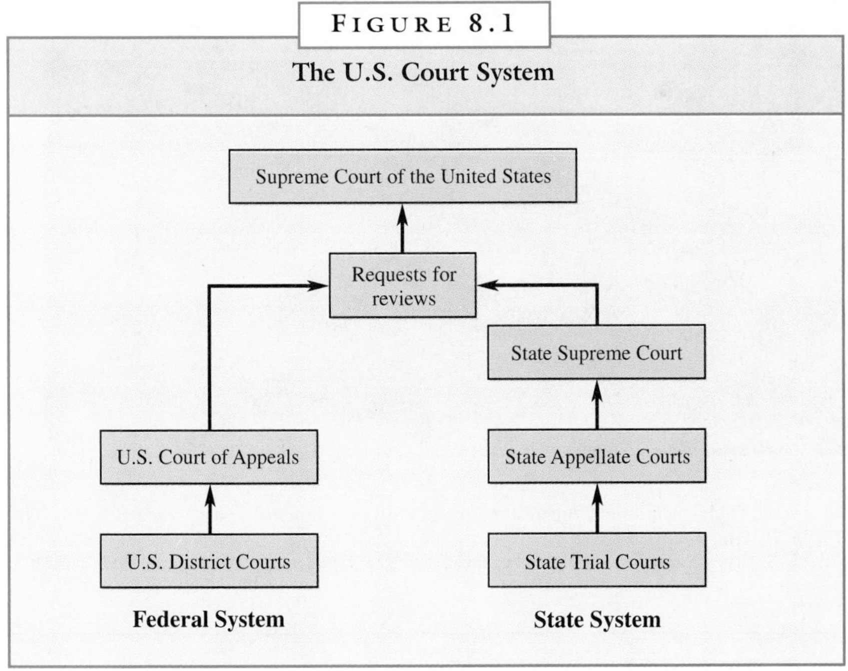

## *Enforcing International Trade Laws*

The United States has long been weary of supranational courts or tribunals that could mandate changes in U.S. policy laws. The most recent examples occurred in July 1998, when, along with six other countries, including Iraq, Libya, and Yemen, the United States voted against joining the International Criminal Court (ICC).[1] Other countries have been less reticent to cede sovereignty—120 countries voted to approve the ICC—and today many Latin American countries accept the jurisdiction of the Inter-American Court of Human Rights, while rulings by the European Court of Justice take precedence over the national laws of European Union countries. Until recently, the United States participated in international courts only if the rulings relied on voluntary compliance. For example, the International Court of Justice (ICJ) is the principal judicial organ of the United Nations, and the United States has often appeared before this court. However, there is no enforcement mechanism for the court outside of the United Nations Security Council, where the United States has veto power, and the United States has ignored those rulings that were unfavorable to them. In one instance, the ICJ ruled in favor of Nicaraguan charges against the United States for damages caused by CIA mining of Nicaraguan harbors in 1983–1984. The United States refused to pay the imposed fine that, with interest, had reached $17 billion by 1990.[2]

[1]See Ruth Wedgewood, "Fiddling in Rome: America and the International Criminal Court," *Foreign Affairs* (November 1998), pp. 20–24.

[2]Mark A. Uhlig, "U.S. Urges Nicaragua to Forgive Legal Claim," *New York Times,* 30 September 1990, p. A18.

One of the cornerstones of globalization (and one backed by the United States) is the growth in international trade of goods and services, and it is in this arena that the United States has bent the most to the jurisdiction of international tribunals. According to the World Trade Organization (WTO), world merchandise trade grew from $3.3 trillion in 1990 to over $5.3 trillion in 1997. Trade in goods and services has also mushroomed. To ensure a stable trading system and reduce the risk of trade wars, a new international organization—the WTO—was created. The WTO was formed in 1995, and by 1999 had 131 members, including all of the world's largest economies. The most important function of the WTO is to resolve trade disputes. The trade-dispute mechanism functions like a court and has supranational power. When the legislation for U.S. entry into the WTO came before Congress, many conservatives were opposed because they claimed it would be an unprecedented cessation of national sovereignty.

A brief examination of a case will illustrate how the WTO dispute mechanism functions and how it exerts supranational power. In 1995, Venezuela (later joined by Brazil) complained to the WTO's Dispute Settlement Body (DSD) that the United States was discriminating against gasoline imports. Under the Clean Air Act, the United States applied stricter environmental standards on imported gasoline than it did for domestically refined fuels. Venezuela and Brazil claimed that this violated the "national treatment" principle, and they initiated a claim. The United States countered that this was justifiable under health and environmental exceptions to WTO rules. The DSD formed a panel of trade experts to advise. After receiving the experts' report, the DSD ruled in favor of Venezuela and Brazil. The United States lodged an appeal, which was unsuccessful. At this point, the United States was forced either the negotiate with Venezuela and Brazil until they were satisfied or to face trade sanctions authorized by the WTO. The United States agreed to amend its regulations in order to comply with the WTO rulings, and in fact new U.S. gasoline regulations were enacted in August of 1997.

Is the Supreme Court still the highest law in the land? For issues that affect international trade, it is not. This is a transcendental change for the United States. Those Americans worried about the New World Order see this as a possible slippery slope towards further erosion of judicial sovereignty. Supporters to the WTO argue that it is the best way to create the stable international trade system required for continued growth of American exports.

and from there to a state's ***supreme court.*** Similarly, in civil cases, most litigation is brought in the courts established by the state in which the activity in question took place. For example, a patient bringing suit against a physician for malpractice would file the suit in the appropriate court in the state where the alleged malpractice occurred. The judge hearing the case would apply state law and state precedent to the matter at hand. (It should be noted that in both criminal and civil matters, most cases are settled before trial through negotiated agreements between the parties. In criminal cases these agreements are called ***plea bargains.***)

Although each state has its own set of laws, these laws have much in common from state to state. Murder and robbery, obviously, are illegal in all states, although the range of possible punishments for those crimes varies from state to state. Some states, for example, provide for capital punishment (the death penalty) for murder and other serious offenses; other states do not. As we saw in Chapter 4, however, some acts that are criminal offenses in one state may be legal in another state. Prostitution, for example, is legal in some Nevada counties, although it is outlawed in all other states. Considerable similarity among the states is also found in the realm of civil law. In the case of contract law, most states have adopted the ***Uniform Commercial Code*** in order to reduce interstate differences. In areas such as family law, however, which covers such matters as divorce and child custody arrangements, state laws vary greatly.

Cases are heard in the federal courts if they involve federal laws, treaties with other nations, or the U.S. Constitution; these areas are the official ***jurisdiction*** of the federal courts. In addition, any case in which the U.S. government is a party is heard in the federal courts. If, for example, an individual is charged with violating a federal criminal statute, such as evading the payment of income taxes, charges would be brought before a federal judge by a federal prosecutor. Civil cases involving the citizens of more than one state and in which more than fifty thousand dollars is at stake may be heard in either the federal or the state courts, usually depending upon the preference of the plaintiff.

Federal courts serve another purpose in addition to trying cases within their jurisdiction: that of hearing appeals from state-level courts. Individuals found guilty of breaking a state criminal law, for example, can appeal their convictions to a federal court by raising a constitutional issue and asking a federal court to determine whether the state's actions were consistent with the requirements of the U.S. Constitution. An appellant might assert, for example, that the state court denied him or her the right to counsel, imposed excessive bail, or otherwise denied the appellant ***due process.*** Under such circumstances, an appellant can ask the federal court to overturn his or her conviction. Federal courts are not obligated to accept such appeals and will do so only if they feel that the issues raised have considerable merit and if the appellant has exhausted all possible remedies within the state courts. (This procedure is discussed in more detail later in this chapter.) The decisions of state supreme courts may also be appealed to the U.S. Supreme Court if the state court's decision has conflicted with prior U.S. Supreme Court rulings or has raised some important question of federal law. Such appeals are accepted by the U.S. Supreme Court at its discretion.

Although the federal courts hear only a small fraction of all the civil and criminal cases decided each year in the United States, their decisions are extremely important. It is in the federal courts that the Constitution and federal laws that govern all Americans are interpreted and their meaning and significance established. Moreover, it is in the federal courts that the powers and limitations of the increasingly powerful national government are tested. Finally, through their power to review the decisions of the state courts, it is ultimately the federal courts that dominate the American judicial system.

## FEDERAL JURISDICTION

The overwhelming majority of court cases are tried not in federal courts but in state and local courts under state common law, state statutes, and local ordinances. Of all the cases heard in the United States in 1996, federal district courts (the lowest federal level) received 321,000. Although this number is up substantially from the 87,000 cases heard in 1961, it still constitutes under 1 percent of the judiciary's business. A major reason that the caseload of the federal courts has increased in recent years is that Congress has greatly expanded the number of federal crimes, particularly in the realm of drug possession and sale. Behavior that once was exclusively a state criminal question is now covered by federal law. Recently, Chief Justice Rehnquist criticized Congress for federalizing too many offenses and intruding unnecessarily into areas that should be handled by the state.[2] The federal courts of appeal listened to 51,524 cases in 1996, and the U.S. Supreme Court reviewed 4,613 in its 1996–1997 term. Only 90 cases were given full-dress Supreme Court review (the nine justices actually sitting *en banc*—in full court—and hearing the lawyers argue the case).[3]

### The Lower Federal Courts

Most of the cases of original federal jurisdiction are handled by the federal district courts. The federal district courts are trial courts of general jurisdiction and their cases are, in form, indistinguishable from cases in the state trial courts.

There are eighty-nine district courts in the fifty states, plus one in the District of Columbia and one in Puerto Rico, and three territorial courts. In an effort to deal with the greatly increased court workload of recent years, in 1978 Congress increased the number of district judgeships from 400 to 517. District judges are assigned to district courts according to the workload; the busiest of these courts may have as many as twenty-eight judges. Only one judge is assigned to each case, except where statutes provide for three-judge courts to deal with special issues. The routines and procedures of the federal district courts are essentially the same as those of the lower state courts, except that federal procedural requirements tend to be stricter. States, for example, do not have to provide a grand jury,

[2]Roberto Suro, "Rehnquist: Too Many Offenses are Becoming Federal Crimes," *Washington Post*, 1 January 1999, p. A2.

[3]U.S. Bureau of the Census, *Statistical Abstract of the United States, 1997* (Washington, DC: Government Printing Office, 1997).

a twelve-member trial jury, or a unanimous jury verdict. Federal courts must provide all these things.

## The Appellate Courts

Roughly 10 percent of all lower court and agency cases are accepted for review by the federal appeals courts and by the Supreme Court in its capacity as an appellate court. The country is divided into twelve judicial circuits, each of which has a U.S. Court of Appeals. Every state and the District of Columbia is assigned to the circuit in the continental United States that is closest to it.

Except for cases selected for review by the Supreme Court, decisions made by the appeals courts are final. Because of this finality, certain safeguards have been built into the system. The most important is the provision of more than one judge for every appeals case. Each court of appeals has from three to fifteen permanent judgeships, depending on the workload of the circuit. Although normally three judges hear appealed cases, in some instances a larger number of judges sit together *en banc*.

Another safeguard is provided by the assignment of a Supreme Court justice as the circuit justice for each of the eleven circuits. Since the creation of the appeals court in 1891, the circuit justice's primary duty has been to review appeals arising in the circuit in order to expedite Supreme Court action. The most frequent and best-known action of circuit justices is that of reviewing requests for stays of execution when the full Court is unable to do so—mainly during the summer, when the Court is in recess.

## The Supreme Court

The Supreme Court is America's highest court. Article III of the Constitution vests "the judicial power of the United States" in the Supreme Court, and this court is supreme in fact as well as form. The Supreme Court is made up of a chief justice and eight associate justices. The ***chief justice*** presides over the Court's public sessions and conferences. In the Court's actual deliberations and decisions, however, the chief justice has no more authority than his or her colleagues. Each justice casts one vote. To some extent, the influence of the chief justice is a function of his or her own leadership ability. Some chief justices, such as the late Earl Warren, have been able to lead the court in a new direction. In other instances, a forceful associate justice, such as the late Felix Frankfurter, are the dominant figures on the Court.

The Constitution does not specify the number of justices that should sit on the Supreme Court; Congress has the authority to change the Court's size. In the early nineteenth century, there were six Supreme Court justices; later there were seven. Congress set the number of justices at nine in 1869, and the Court has remained that size ever since. In 1937, President Franklin D. Roosevelt, infuriated by several Supreme Court decisions that struck down New Deal programs, asked Congress to enlarge the court so that he could add a few sympathetic justices to the bench. Although Congress balked at Roosevelt's "court packing" plan, the Court gave in to FDR's pressure and began to take a more favorable view of his policy initiatives. The president, in turn, dropped his efforts to enlarge the Court. The Court's surrender to FDR came to be known as "the switch in time that saved nine."



## Judicial Review

The Supreme Court has the power of ***judicial review***—the authority and the obligation to review any lower court decision where a substantial issue of public law is involved. The disputes can be over the constitutionality of federal or state laws, over the propriety or constitutionality of the court procedures followed, or over whether public officers are exceeding their authority. The Supreme Court's power of judicial review has come to mean review not only of lower court decisions but also of state legislation and acts of Congress. For this reason, if for no other, the Supreme Court is more than a judicial agency—it is also a major lawmaking body.

The Supreme Court's power of judicial review over lower court decisions has never been at issue. Nor has there been any serious quibble over the power of the federal courts to review administrative agencies in order to determine whether their actions and decisions are within the powers delegated to them by Congress. There has, however, been a great deal of controversy occasioned by the Supreme Court's efforts to review acts of Congress and the decisions of state courts and legislatures.

### Judicial Review of Acts of Congress

Since the Constitution does not give the Supreme Court the power of judicial review of congressional enactments, the Court's exercise of it is something of a usurpation. Various proposals were debated at the Constitutional Convention. Among them was the proposal to create a council composed of the president and the judiciary that would share the veto power over legislation. Another proposal would have routed all legislation through the Court as well as through the president; a veto by either one would have required an overruling by a two-thirds vote of the House and Senate. Each proposal was rejected by the delegates, and no further effort was made to give the Supreme Court review power over the other branches.

This does not prove that the framers of the Constitution opposed judicial review, but it does indicate that "if they intended to provide for it in the Constitution, they did so in a most obscure fashion."[4] Disputes over the intentions of the framers were settled in 1803 in the case of *Marbury v. Madison*.[5] Though Congress and the president have often been at odds with the Court, its legal power to review acts of Congress has not been seriously questioned since 1803 (see Box 8.1). One reason is that judicial power has been accepted as natural, if not intended. Another reason is that the Supreme Court has rarely

[4]C. Herman Pritchett, *The American Constitution* (New York: McGraw-Hill, 1959), p. 138.
[5]Marbury v. Madison, 1 Cr. 137 (1803).

**Box 8.1**

*Marbury v. Madison*

The 1803 Supreme Court decision handed down in *Marbury v. Madison* established the power of the Court to review acts of Congress. The case arose over a suit filed by William Marbury and seven other people against Secretary of State James Madison to require him to approve their appointments as justices of the peace. These had been last-minute ("midnight judges") appointments of outgoing President John Adams. Chief Justice John Marshall held that although Marbury and the others were entitled to their appointments, the Supreme Court had no power to order Madison to deliver them, because the relevant section of the first Judiciary Act of 1789 was unconstitutional—giving the Courts powers not intended by Article III of the Constitution.

Marshall reasoned that constitutions are framed to serve as the "fundamental and paramount law of the nation." Thus, he argued, with respect to the legislative action of Congress, the Constitution is a "superior . . . law, unchangeable by ordinary means." He concluded that an act of Congress that contradicts the Constitution must be judged void.

As to the question of whether the Court was empowered to rule on the constitutionality of legislative action, Marshall responded emphatically that it is "the province and duty of the judicial department to say what the law is." Since the Constitution is the supreme law of the land, he reasoned, it is clearly within the realm of the Court's responsibility to rule on the constitutionality of legislative acts and treaties. This principle has held sway ever since.

SOURCES: Gerald Gunther, *Constitutional Law* (Mineola, NY: Fountain Press, 1980), pp. 9–11; and Marbury v. Madison, 1 Cr. 137 (1803).

reviewed the constitutionality of the acts of Congress, especially in the past fifty years. When such acts do come up for review, the Court makes a self-conscious effort to give them an interpretation that will make them constitutional.

## Judicial Review of State Actions

The power of the Supreme Court to review state legislation or other state action and to determine its constitutionality is neither granted by the Constitution nor inherent in the federal system. But the logic of the ***supremacy clause*** of Article VI of the Constitution, which declares it and laws made under its authority to be the supreme law of the land, is very strong. Furthermore, in the Judiciary Act of 1789, Congress conferred on the Supreme Court the power to reverse state constitutions and laws whenever they are clearly in conflict with the U.S. Constitution, federal laws, or treaties.[6] This power gives the Supreme Court jurisdiction over all of the millions of cases handled by American courts each year.

[6]This review power was affirmed by the Supreme Court in Martin v. Hunter's Lessee, 1 Wheaton 304 (1816).

The supremacy clause of the Constitution not only established the federal Constitution, statutes, and treaties as the "supreme law of the land," but also provided that "the Judges in every State shall be bound thereby, any Thing in the Constitution or Laws of the State to the Contrary notwithstanding." Under this authority, the Supreme Court has frequently overturned state constitutional provisions or statutes and state court decisions it deems to contravene rights or privileges guaranteed under the federal Constitution or federal statutes.

The civil rights area abounds with examples of state laws that were overturned because the statutes violated guarantees of due process and equal protection contained in the Fourteenth Amendment to the Constitution. For example, in the 1954 case of *Brown v. Board of Education,* the Court overturned statutes from Kansas, South Carolina, Virginia, and Delaware that either required or permitted segregated public schools, on the basis that such statutes denied black school children equal protection of the law. In 1967, in *Loving v. Virginia,* the Court invalidated a Virginia statute prohibiting interracial marriages.[7]

AMERICAN POLITICAL DEVELOPMENT

In the first century of Court activity (1789–1888) the U.S. Supreme Court overturned only 21 acts of Congress and 79 state laws. In the next thirty-two years (1889–1921), it overturned 26 acts of Congress and 180 state laws. In fact, from 1889 to 1995, the Court overturned 125 acts of Congress and 852 state laws.

SOURCE: David M. O'Brien, *Storm Center: The Supreme Court in American Politics,* 4th ed. (New York: W. W. Norton, 1996), p. 54.

State statutes in other subject matter areas are equally subject to challenge. In *Griswold v. Connecticut,* the Court invalidated a Connecticut statute prohibiting the general distribution of contraceptives to married couples on the basis that the statute violated the couples' rights to marital privacy.[8] In *Brandenburg v. Ohio,* the Court overturned an Ohio statute forbidding any person from urging criminal acts as a means of inducing political reform or from joining any association that advocated such activities on the grounds that the statute punished "mere advocacy" and therefore violated the free speech provisions of the Constitution.[9]

## Judicial Review and Lawmaking

When courts of original jurisdiction apply existing statutes or past cases directly to citizens, the effect is the same as legislation. Lawyers study judicial decisions in order to discover underlying principles, and they advise their clients accordingly. Often the process is nothing more than reasoning by analogy; the facts in a particular case are so close to those in one or more previous cases that the same decision should be handed down. Such judge-made law is called common law.

The appellate courts are in another realm. Their rulings can be considered laws, but they are laws governing the behavior only of the judiciary. They influence citizens' conduct only because, in the words of Justice Oliver Wendell Holmes,

[7]Brown v. Board of Education, 347 U.S. 483 (1954); Loving v. Virginia, 388 U.S. 1 (1967).
[8]Griswold v. Connecticut, 381 U.S. 479 (1965).
[9]Brandenburg v. Ohio, 395 U.S. 444 (1969).

## AMERICAN POLITICAL DEVELOPMENT

Although the power of judicial review was not explicitly set forth in the Constitution, there is evidence that the founding fathers anticipated this role for the Court. During the colonial period, acts of colonial legislatures were subject to judicial review by the British Privy Council. And "at least 8" state-ratifying conventions "discussed *and* accepted" the principal of judicial review. Indeed, several state courts had exercised this power over state legislatures before 1789.

SOURCE: Henry J. Abraham and Barbara A. Perry, *Freedom and the Court: Civil Rights and Liberties in the United States* (New York: Oxford University Press, 1994), pp. 5–7.

who served on the Supreme Court from 1900–1932, lawyers make "prophecies of what the courts will do in fact."[10]

The written opinion of an appellate court is about halfway between common law and statutory law. It is judge-made and draws heavily on the precedents of previous cases. But it tries to articulate the rule of law controlling the case in question and future cases like it. In this respect, it is like a statute. But it differs from a statute in that a statute addresses itself to the future conduct of citizens, whereas a written opinion addresses itself mainly to the willingness or ability of courts in the future to take cases and render favorable opinions. Decisions by appellate courts affect citizens by giving them a cause of action or by taking it away from them. That is, they open or close access to the courts.

A specific case may help clarify the distinction. Before the Second World War, one of the most insidious forms of racial discrimination was the "restrictive covenant," a clause in a contract whereby the purchasers of a house agreed that if they later decided to sell it, they would sell only to a Caucasian. When a test case finally reached the Supreme Court in 1948, the Court ruled unanimously that citizens had a right to discriminate with restrictive covenants in their sales contracts but that the courts could not enforce these contracts. Its argument was that enforcement would constitute violation of the Fourteenth Amendment provision that no state shall "deny to any person within its jurisdiction equal protection under the law."[11] The Court was thereby predicting what it would and would not do in future cases of this sort. Most states have now forbidden homeowners to place such covenants in sales contracts.

*Gideon v. Wainwright* extends the point. When the Supreme Court ordered a new trial for Gideon because he had been denied the right to legal counsel,[12] it said to all trial judges and prosecutors that henceforth they would be wasting their time if they cut corners in trials of indigent defendants. It also invited thousands of prisoners to appeal their convictions.

Many areas of civil law have been constructed in the same way—by judicial messages to other judges, some of which are codified eventually into legislative enactments. An example of great concern to employees and employers is that of liability for injuries sustained at work. Courts have sided with employees so often that it has become virtually useless for employers to fight injury cases. It has become "the law" that employers are liable for such injuries, without regard to negligence. But the law in this instance is simply a series of messages to lawyers that they should advise their corporate clients not to appeal injury decisions.

[10]Oliver Wendell Holmes, Jr., "The Path of the Law," *Harvard Law Review* 10 (1897), p. 457.
[11]Shelley v. Kraemer, 334 U.S. 1 (1948).
[12]Gideon v. Wainwright, 372 U.S. 335 (1963).

The appellate courts cannot decide what behavior will henceforth be a crime. They cannot directly prevent the police from forcing confessions or intimidating witnesses. In other words, they cannot directly change the behavior of citizens or eliminate abuses of power. What they can do, however, is make it easier for mistreated persons to gain redress.

In redressing wrongs, the appellate courts—and even the Supreme Court itself—often call for a radical change in legal principle. Changes in race relations, for example, would probably have taken a great deal longer if the Supreme Court had not rendered the 1954 *Brown* decision that redefined the rights of African Americans.

Similarly, the Supreme Court interpreted the separation of church and state doctrine so as to alter significantly the practice of religion in public institutions. For example, in a 1962 case, *Engel v. Vitale,* the Court declared that a once widely observed ritual—the recitation of a prayer by students in a public school—was unconstitutional under the establishment clause of the First Amendment. Almost all the dramatic changes in the treatment of criminals and of persons accused of crimes have been made by the appellate courts, especially the Supreme Court. The Supreme Court brought about a veritable revolution in the criminal process with three cases over less than five years: *Gideon v. Wainwright,* in 1963, was discussed earlier in the chapter. *Escobedo v. Illinois,* in 1964, gave suspects the right to remain silent and the right to have counsel present during questioning. But the decision left confusions that allowed differing decisions to be made by lower courts. In *Miranda v. Arizona,* in 1966, the Supreme Court cleared up these confusions by setting forth what is known as the ***Miranda rule:*** Arrested people have the right to remain silent, the right to be informed that anything they say can be held against them, and the right to counsel before and during police interrogation.[13]

One of the most significant changes brought about by the Supreme Court was the revolution in legislative representation unleashed by the 1962 case of *Baker v. Carr.*[14] In this landmark case, the Supreme Court held that it could no longer avoid reviewing complaints about the apportionment of seats in state legislatures. Following that decision, the federal courts went on to force reapportionment of all state, county, and local legislatures in the country.

Many experts on court history and constitutional law criticize the federal appellate courts for being too willing to introduce radical change, even when these experts agree with the general direction of the changes. Often they are troubled by the courts' (especially the Supreme Court's) willingness to jump into such cases prematurely—before the constitutional issues are fully clarified by many

**AMERICAN POLITICAL DEVELOPMENT**

In the 1946 case *Colegrove v. Green,* the U.S. Supreme Court ruled that congressional "apportionment was a political question and thus non-justiciable." But as Court politics changed from "the dominant New Deal philosophy that a passive judiciary would best serve the needs of progressive politics" to a more liberal and activist Warren Court, the U.S. Supreme Court ruled in the 1962 *Baker v. Carr* case that it could no longer avoid reviewing complaints about apportionment.

SOURCE: Mark Silverstein, *Judicious Choices: The New Politics of Supreme Court Confirmations* (New York: W. W. Norton, 1994), pp. 53–54.

[13]Engel v. Vitale, 370 U.S. 421 (1962); Gideon v. Wainwright, 372 U.S. 335 (1963); Escobedo v. Illinois, 378 U.S. 478 (1964); and Miranda v. Arizona, 384 U.S. 436 (1966).

[14]Baker v. Carr, 369 U.S. 186 (1962).

related cases through decisions by district and appeals courts in various parts of the country.[15] But from the perspective of the appellate judiciary, and especially the Supreme Court, the situation is probably one of choosing between the lesser of two evils: They must take the cases as they come and then weigh the risks of opening new options against the risks of embracing the status quo.

## How Cases Reach the Supreme Court

Given the millions of disputes that arise every year, the job of the Supreme Court would be impossible if it were not able to control the flow of cases and its own case load. Its original jurisdiction is only a minor problem. The original jurisdiction includes (1) cases between the United States and one of the fifty states, (2) cases between two or more states, (3) cases involving foreign ambassadors or other ministers, and (4) cases brought by one state against citizens of another state or against a foreign country. The most important of these cases are disputes between states over land, water, or old debts. Generally, the Supreme Court deals with these cases by appointing a "special master," usually a retired judge, to actually hear the case and present a report. The Supreme Court then allows the states involved in the dispute to present arguments for or against the master's opinion.[16]

**Rules of Access** Over the years, the courts have developed specific rules that govern which cases within their jurisdiction they will and will not hear. In order to have access to the courts, cases must meet certain criteria. These rules of access can be broken down into three major categories: case or controversy, standing, and mootness.

Article III of the Constitution and Supreme Court decisions define judicial power as extending only to "cases and controversies." This means that the case before a court must be an actual controversy, not a hypothetical one, with two truly adversarial parties. The courts have interpreted this language to mean that they do not have the power to render advisory opinions to legislatures or agencies about the constitutionality of proposed laws or regulations. Furthermore, even after a law is enacted, the courts will generally refuse to consider its constitutionality until it is actually applied.

Parties to a case must also have ***standing,*** that is, they must show that they have a substantial stake in the outcome of the case. The traditional requirement for standing has been to show injury to oneself; that injury can be personal, economic, or even aesthetic, for example. In order for a group or class of people to have standing (as in class action suits), each member must show specific injury. This means that a general interest in the environment, for instance, does not provide a group with sufficient basis for standing.

The Supreme Court also uses a third criterion in determining whether it will

[15]See Philip Kurland, *Politics, the Constitution and the Warren Court* (Chicago: University of Chicago Press, 1970).

[16]Walter F. Murphy, "The Supreme Court of the United States," in *Encyclopedia of the American Judicial System,* ed. Robert J. Janosik (New York: Scribner's, 1987).

hear a case: that of ***mootness.*** In theory, this requirement disqualifies cases that are brought too late—after the relevant facts have changed or the problem has been resolved by other means. The criterion of mootness, however, is subject to the discretion of the courts, which have begun to relax the rules of mootness, particularly in cases where a situation that has been resolved is likely to come up again. In the abortion case *Roe v. Wade,* for example, the Supreme Court rejected the lower court's argument that because the pregnancy had already come to term, the case was moot. The Court agreed to hear the case because no pregnancy was likely to outlast the lengthy appeals process.

Putting aside the formal criteria, the Supreme Court is most likely to accept cases that involve conflicting decisions by the federal circuit courts, cases that present important questions of civil rights or civil liberties, and cases in which the federal government is the appellant. Ultimately, however, the question of which cases to accept can come down to the preferences and priorities of the justices. If a group of justices believes that the Court should intervene in a particular area of policy or politics, they are likely to look for a case or cases that will serve as vehicles for judicial intervention. For many years, for example, the Court was not interested in considering challenges to affirmative action or other programs designed to provide particular benefits to minorities. In recent years, however, several of the Court's more conservative justices have been eager to push back the limits of affirmative action and racial preference, and have therefore accepted a number of cases that would allow them to do so. In 1995, the Court's decisions in *Adarand Constructors v. Pena, Missouri v. Jenkins,* and *Miller v. Johnson* placed new restrictions on federal affirmative action programs, school desegregation efforts, and attempts to increase minority representation in Congress through the creation of "minority districts" (see Chapter 10).[17] Similarly, because some justices have felt that the Court had gone too far in the past in restricting public support for religious ideas, the Court accepted the case of *Rosenberger v. University of Virginia.* This case was brought by a Christian student group against the University of Virginia, which had refused to provide student activities fund support for the group's magazine, *Wide Awake.* Other student publications received subsidies from the activities fund, but university policy prohibited grants to religious groups. Lower courts supported the university, finding that support for the magazine would violate the Constitution's prohibition against government support for religion. The Supreme Court, however, ruled in favor of the students' assertion that the university's policies amounted to support for some ideas but not others. The Court said this violated the First Amendment.[18]

**Writs** Decisions handed down by lower courts can reach the Supreme Court in one of two ways: through a ***writ of certiorari,*** or, in the case of convicted state prisoners, through a ***writ of habeas corpus.*** A writ is a court document conveying an order of some sort. In recent years, an effort has been made to give the Court more discretion regarding the cases it chooses to hear. Before 1988, the Supreme

[17]Adarand Constructors v. Pena, 115 S.Ct. 2038 (1995); Missouri v. Jenkins, 115 S.Ct. 2573 (1995); Miller v. Johnson, 115 S.Ct. 2475 (1995).

[18]Rosenberger v. University of Virginia, 115 S.Ct. 2510 (1995).

PROCESS BOX 8.1

## How Cases Reach the Supreme Court

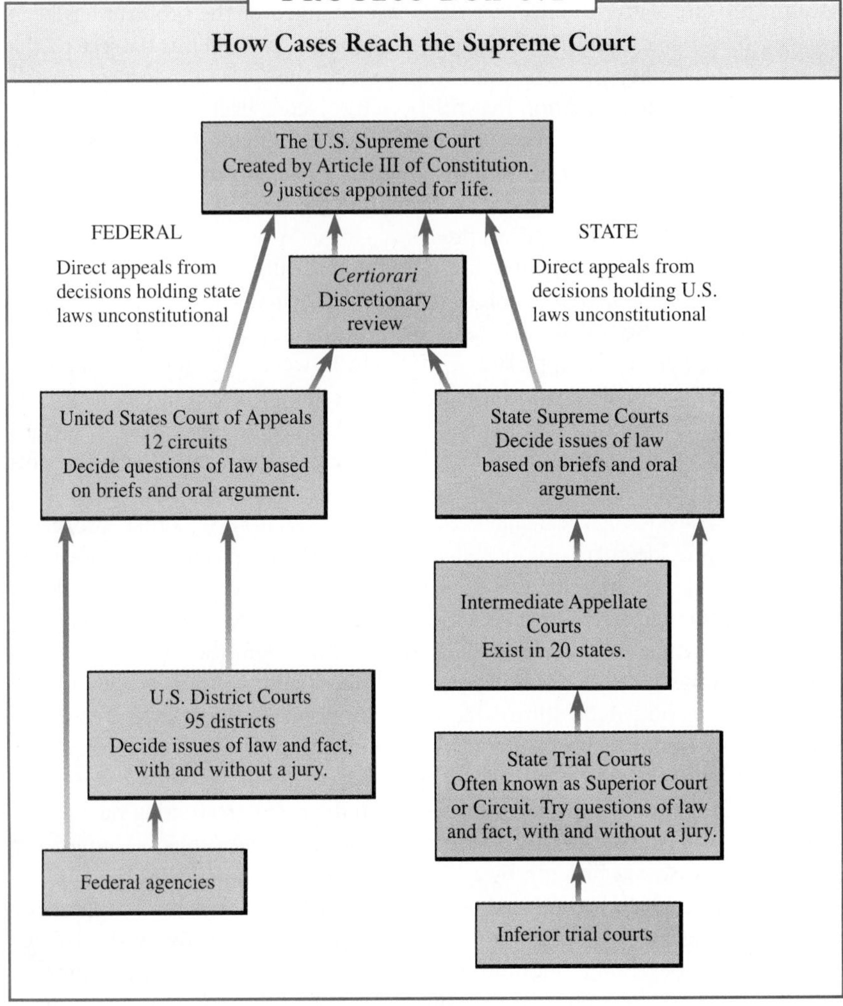


Court was obligated to review cases on what was called a writ of appeal. This has since been eliminated, and the Court now has virtually complete discretion over what cases it will hear.

Most cases reach the Supreme Court through the writ of *certiorari,* which is granted whenever four of the nine justices agree to review a case. The Supreme Court was once so inundated with appeals that in 1925 Congress enacted laws giving it some control over its case load with the power to issue writs of *certiorari.* Rule 10 of the Supreme Court's own rules of procedure defines *certiorari* as "not a matter of right, but of sound judicial discretion . . . granted only where there are special and important reasons therefor." The reasons provided for in Rule 10 are

1. Where a state has made a decision that conflicts with previous Supreme Court decisions;

2. Where a state court has come up with an entirely new federal question;
3. Where one court of appeals has rendered a decision in conflict with another;
4. Where there are other inconsistent rulings between two or more courts or states; and
5. Where a single court of appeals has sanctioned too great a departure by a lower court from normal judicial proceedings (a reason rarely given).

The writ of *habeas corpus* is a fundamental safeguard of individual rights. Its historical purpose is to enable an accused person to challenge arbitrary detention and to force an open trial before a judge. But in 1867, Congress's distrust of Southern courts led it to confer on federal courts the authority to issue writs of *habeas corpus* to prisoners already tried or being tried in state courts of proper jurisdiction, where the constitutional rights of the prisoner were possibly being violated. This writ gives state prisoners a second channel toward Supreme Court review in case their direct appeal from the highest state court fails. The writ of *habeas corpus* is discretionary; that is, the Court can decide which cases to review.

## Influences on Supreme Court Decisions

The judiciary is conservative in its procedures, but its impact on society can be radical. That impact depends on a variety of influences, three of which stand out above the rest. The first influence is the individual members of the Supreme Court, their attitudes, and their relationships with each other. The second is the Justice Department, especially the solicitor general, who regulates the flow of cases involving public law issues. The third is the pattern of cases.

### The Supreme Court Justices

If any individual judges in the country influence the federal judiciary, they are the Supreme Court justices. Many presidents have assumed that they can gain influence over the Court through the justices they appoint. That influence is usually overrated. Each justice is, after all, only one of nine, and each has the protection of lifetime tenure (see Table 8.2).

**Judicial Philosophy** From the 1950s to the 1980s, the Supreme Court took an activist role in such areas as civil rights, civil liberties, abortion, voting rights, and police procedures. For example, the Supreme Court was more responsible than any other governmental institution for breaking down America's system of racial segregation. The Supreme Court virtually prohibited states from interfering with the right of a woman to seek an abortion and sharply curtailed state restrictions on voting rights. And it was the Supreme Court that placed restrictions on the behavior of local police and prosecutors in criminal cases.

But since the early 1980s, resignations, deaths, and new judicial appointments have led to many shifts in the mix of philosophies and ideologies repre-

TABLE 8.2

**Supreme Court Justices, 1999 (in order of seniority)**

| NAME | YEAR OF BIRTH | PRIOR EXPERIENCE | APPOINTED BY | YEAR OF APPOINTMENT |
|---|---|---|---|---|
| William H. Rehnquist Chief Justice | 1924 | Assistant Attorney General | Nixon* | 1972 |
| John Paul Stevens | 1916 | Federal Judge | Ford | 1975 |
| Sandra Day O'Connor | 1930 | State Judge | Reagan | 1981 |
| Antonin Scalia | 1936 | Law Professor, Federal Judge | Reagan | 1986 |
| Anthony M. Kennedy | 1937 | Federal Judge | Reagan | 1988 |
| David H. Souter | 1940 | Federal Judge | Bush | 1990 |
| Clarence Thomas | 1948 | Federal Judge | Bush | 1991 |
| Ruth Bader Ginsburg | 1933 | Federal Judge | Clinton | 1993 |
| Stephen G. Breyer | 1938 | Federal Judge | Clinton | 1994 |

*Appointed chief justice by Reagan in 1986.

sented on the Court. Presidents have, of course, endeavored to appoint justices who shared their views on major issues, such as the role of government, civil liberties, affirmative action, and abortion.

Once on the Court, justices have sometimes confounded the presidents who appointed them. Over time, however, if one political party is able to control the White House for long periods, the character of the Supreme Court and other federal courts will inevitably be affected. During the long period between 1932 and 1968 when Democratic presidents generally resided at 1600 Pennsylvania Avenue, the federal judiciary gradually became a liberal bastion.

Similarly, between 1968 and Bill Clinton's victory in 1992, when the GOP generally controlled the White House, Republican presidents sought to use their appointments to transform the federal judiciary into a more conservative institution.

**The Rehnquist Court 1986–** Republican presidents Ronald Reagan and George Bush both assigned a high priority to the creation of a judiciary more sympathetic to conservative ideas and interests. Reagan made three significant appointments to the Supreme Court: Sandra Day O'Connor, the first woman to serve as a Supreme Court Justice; Antonin Scalia, a conservative who became an intellectual leader in the court; and Anthony Kennedy. Reagan also promoted Justice William Rehnquist to the position of chief justice following Warren Burger's resignation in 1986. George Bush appointed two more conservatives to the Court. In 1990, he appointed David Souter, a federal appeals judge from New Hampshire, and in 1991, he appointed Clarence Thomas, a prominent black conservative, to replace liberal Justice Thurgood Marshall. Thomas's nomination sparked one of the most bitter struggles in recent American political history. During his lengthy confirmation hearing, Anita Hill, a University of

Oklahoma law professor, testified that Thomas had sexually harassed her when she worked for him at the Equal Employment Opportunity Commission and, previously, at the Department of Education. At the end of the controversial hearing, Thomas was confirmed by the Senate by the narrow vote of 52 to 48. Reagan and Bush's appointments to the Supreme Court gave it a much more conservative cast than it had at any time since the New Deal.

In a series of 5-to-4 decisions in 1989, President Reagan's appointees were able to swing the Court to a more conservative position on civil rights and abortion. In the area of civil rights, the case of *Wards Cove v. Atonio* shifted the burden of proof from employers to employees in hiring and promotion discrimination suits. (This decision was subsequently reversed by Congress in the 1991 Civil Rights Act.)[19] In 1993, the Library of Congress made public the papers of the late Justice Thurgood Marshall, long a champion of the civil rights cause. Marshall's papers reveal not only his disappointment at the Court's change of direction, but also the key role played by President Reagan's appointees in bringing about this change.[20]

The Rehnquist Court's key abortion decision came in the case of *Webster v. Reproductive Health Services.* Justice Marshall's papers reveal that the Court actually came very close to overturning *Roe.* Rehnquist's early drafts of the decision would have effectively overturned *Roe.* He was able to win the support of only three other justices, Scalia, Kennedy, and White, for this course of action. A fourth justice, Sandra Day O'Connor, wavered for several weeks. Had O'Connor joined Rehnquist, of course, the Chief Justice would have had the five votes needed for a majority. Ultimately, O'Connor decided not to support overturning *Roe,* and Rehnquist was forced to write a narrower ruling, which nevertheless opened the way for new state regulation of abortion. Subsequently, the Court upheld state laws requiring parental notification before an abortion could be performed on a woman under the age of eighteen.[21]

In addition to these areas, the Rehnquist Court also eased restriction on the use of capital punishment, allowing states to execute mentally retarded murderers and murderers who were as young as sixteen at the time of their crimes.[22]

After 1990, the Court made a number of decisions in the areas of civil rights, abortion, property rights, and criminal procedure that indicated a shift to the political right under the influence of the Reagan and Bush appointees. For example, in the case of *Board of Education of Oklahoma City v. Dowell,* the Court restricted the use of judicially mandated busing plans to achieve school integration.[23] In the case of *Rust v. Sullivan,* the Court held that employees of federally financed family planning programs could be forbidden to discuss abortion with

[19]Wards Cove v. Atonio, 109 S.Ct. 2115 (1989).

[20]Joan Biskupic, "The Marshall Files: How an Era Ended in Civil Rights Law," *Washington Post,* 24 May 1993, p. 1.

[21]Benjamin Weiser and Bob Woodward, "Roe's Eleventh-Hour Reprieve: 89 Drafts Show Court Poised to Strike Abortion Ruling," *Washington Post,* 23 May 1993, p. 1. Webster v. Reproductive Health Services, 109 S.Ct. 3040 (1989); Hodgson v. Minnesota, 110 S.Ct. 2926 (1990); Ohio v. Akron Center for Reproductive Health, 110 S.Ct. 2972 (1990).

[22]Penry v. Lynaugh, 109 S.Ct. 2934 (1989); Stanford v. Kentucky, 109 S.Ct. 2969 (1989).

[23]Board of Education of Oklahoma City Public Schools v. Dowell, 111 S.Ct. 630 (1991).

ANALYZING AMERICAN POLITICS

## *Are Judges Strategic?*

The expanded policy-making role of the U.S. judiciary and especially the Supreme Court is one of the most important institutional changes of the twentieth century. One of the key questions that researchers are trying to answer concerns the degree to which Congress can constrain the judiciary. This question takes on particular importance in an era of judicial activism, when some are concerned about an "imperial judiciary" and that judges may be pursuing their own policy agendas within the separation of powers system.

Jeffrey Segal's recent article, which assesses two popular models of judicial decision-making, speaks to this question.[1] Segal examines the *attitudinal model* and the *separation of powers model (SOP)*. Both assume that judges are rational actors who seek to impose their policy preferences on society. The models diverge on the issue of whether or not judges vote *sincerely* or *strategically* when deciding cases. *Strategic voting* means voting in such a way that seems to contradict one's preferences so that a more preferred outcome can be obtained. According to the SOP model, judges will not always vote sincerely, because in certain situations, that may provoke Congress to enact new legislation that moves the policy further away from what the judges prefer. By voting for a lesser preference, the justices can get something they actually prefer (compared to the status quo) without provoking congressional action to overturn their decision. Thus

[1]"Separation-of-Powers Games in the Positive Political Theory of Congress and Courts," *American Political Science Review* 91 (March 1997), pp. 28–44.

their clients.[24] In *Arizona v. Fulminante,* the Court found that the use of a coerced confession in a trial did not automatically invalidate a conviction.[25] In *Lucas v. South Carolina Coastal Council,* the Court gave a sympathetic hearing to a property owner's claim that state restrictions on land development constituted a seizure of property without compensation in violation of the Constitution's Fifth Amendment.[26] In the 1993 case of *Shaw v. Reno,* the Court placed limits upon the "benign gerrymandering" of legislative district boundaries that is used to increase the representation of racial minorities.[27]

[24]Rust v. Sullivan, 111 S.Ct. 1759 (1991).
[25]Arizona v. Fulminante, 111 S.Ct. 1246 (1991).
[26]Lucas v. South Carolina Coastal Council, 112 S.Ct. 2886 (1992).
[27]Shaw v. Reno, 113 S.Ct. 2816 (1993).

concerns about a congressional response constrain the Supreme Court.

Though the SOP model is now accepted as accurate, Segal questions its validity. He takes issue with some of its key assumptions pointing out that if these assumptions do not hold, justices should not "fear" congressional reaction. For example, SOP models assume it is "costless" for members to pass new legislation. Yet the costs of enacting new legislation can be prohibitive, since multiple veto points (e.g., committee chairs, the president) mitigate against the passage of legislation. As a result, the need for justices to vote strategically decreases.

Segal assesses which of these models accurately represents judicial decision-making by examining how the policy preferences of relevant congressional actors affected the votes of justices in civil rights cases from 1975 to 1986. His statistical analysis produces little support for the argument that the policy preferences of key members of Congress affect the way justices vote. Thus, according to Segal, it appears that the attitudinal model is superior to the SOP model.

The jury is still out on what Segal's results imply for the expansion of the judiciary's role in the policy-making process. On the one hand, Segal's results should not come as a surprise, considering that the framers intended the judiciary to be independent of the other branches. On the other hand, those who are concerned about unfettered judicial activism will interpret these results as providing support for reining in the judicial branch. The latter group may take solace in recent research, which shows that Congress can constrain Supreme Court decision-making in other respects, for example, by expanding the number of lower courts.[2]

This area of research is currently one of the most important in political science, and the debate over the role of the judiciary continues. Judicial scholars have only recently begun to apply the tools of rational-choice and statistical analysis to this study, and our understanding of the courts now promises to be enhanced.

[2]Barry R. Weingast, Mathew D. McCubbins, and Roger Noll, "Politics and the Courts: A Positive Theory of Judicial Doctrine and the Rule of Law," *Southern California Law Journal* 68 (September 1995), pp. 1631–83.

Efforts by Reagan and Bush to reshape the federal judiciary, however, were not fully successful. Often in American history, judges have surprised and disappointed the presidents who named them to the bench, and the Reagan/Bush appointees were no exception. Justice Souter has been far less conservative than Republicans hoped. Justices O'Connor and Kennedy have disappointed conservatives by opposing limitations on abortion.

In the important 1992 case of *Planned Parenthood of Southeastern Pennsylvania v. Casey,* the Court upheld state regulations requiring that women seeking abortions wait twenty-four hours after being provided with the information about the process and also requiring parental consent for all minors.[28] Yet the Court

[28]Planned Parenthood of Southeastern Pennsylvania v. Casey, 112 S.Ct. 2791 (1992).

TABLE 8.3

**Presidential Impact on the Federal Courts**

| PRESIDENT | SUPREME COURT | DISTRICT AND APPEALS COURTS[1] | PERCENTAGE OF JUDGESHIPS FILLED BY PRESIDENT | TOTAL JUDGESHIPS[2] |
|---|---|---|---|---|
| Johnson (1963–69) | 2 | 162 | 37 | 449 |
| Nixon (1969–74) | 4 | 224 | 45 | 504 |
| Ford (1974–77) | 1 | 64 | 13 | 504 |
| Carter (1977–81) | 0 | 258 | 39 | 657 |
| Reagan (1981–89) | 3 | 368 | 50 | 740 |
| Bush (1989–93) | 2 | 185 | 22 | 825 |
| Clinton (1993–97) | 2 | 198 | 23 | 846 |

[1]Does not include the appeals court for the Federal Circuit; includes district courts in the territories.
[2]Total judgeships authorized in president's last year in office. Does not include Supreme Court.
SOURCE: Administrative Office of the U.S. Courts, reported in *Congressional Quarterly Weekly Report,* 19 January 1991, p. 173; ibid., 8 February 1997, p. 369.

reaffirmed the constitutional right to an abortion established by *Roe v. Wade.* Indeed, in their unusual joint opinion, Justices O'Connor, Kennedy, and Souter expressed irritation at the White House for its ceaseless pressure on the Court to strike down *Roe v. Wade.*[29] These three justices felt that this pressure represented a threat to the institutional integrity of the Supreme Court.

With a combined total of twelve years in office, Republican presidents Reagan and Bush were also able to exercise a good deal of influence on the composition of the federal district and appellate courts. By the end of Bush's term, he and Reagan together had appointed nearly half of all federal judges (see Table 8.3). Thus, whatever impact Reagan and Bush ultimately have on the Supreme Court, their appointments will continue to influence the temperament and behavior of the district and circuit courts for years to come. After his election in 1992, President Bill Clinton sought to appoint more liberal judges to these courts. Clinton named a number of women and minorities to the district and circuit benches. However, the president moved so slowly to fill vacancies that his impact on the lower federal courts has been less than liberals had hoped.[30] Clinton's efforts, of course, were hindered by the fact that the Judiciary Committee's Republican leadership made it clear that it would not approve nominees it deemed too liberal. This fact forced Clinton to be cautious in his nominations. The White House cancelled plans to nominate several liberals after determining that they had no chance of confirmation.

Republicans have been especially eager to prevent the appointment of liberal

[29]Joan Biskupic, "New Term Poses Test for Alliance at Center of Conservative Court," *Wall Street Journal,* 4 October 1992, p. A12.
[30]*Chicago Daily Law Bulletin,* 5 October 1994.

judges to the Ninth Circuit Court of Appeals, which covers California and eight other western states. Republicans consider the Ninth Circuit to be the most liberal in the nation and are determined to shift it back toward the center or right. As a result, the Judiciary Committee has refused to act on three Clinton nominees for vacancies on the Ninth Circuit. Law Professor William Fletcher has been waiting for hearings to be scheduled since his 1995 nomination. District Judge Richard Paez has been on hold since Clinton nominated him in 1996. More recently, the Judiciary Committee has failed to schedule hearings for labor lawyer Marsha Berzon, nominated in January 1998.[31]

In 1997 and 1998, the Republican tactic of delay coupled with Clinton's own distraction by his numerous legal problems, slowed the judicial appointment process to a crawl. At one point there were more than one hundred vacancies on the federal bench and, as of the beginning of 1999, seventy-three vacancies had not been filled.[32]

**Clinton's Supreme Court Appointments** Bill Clinton's election in 1992 and his re-election in 1996 seemed to reduce the possibility of much further rightward movement on the part of the Court. During Clinton's first year in office, Justice Byron White, the conservative bloc's lone Democrat, announced his desire to retire from the bench. After a long search, the president nominated a federal appeals court judge, Ruth Bader Ginsburg, a moderate liberal, to succeed White. She had a long record of support for abortion rights and women's rights. However, as a federal appeals court judge, she often sided with the government in criminal cases and did not hesitate to vote against affirmative action plans she deemed to be too broad.

During her first term on the Court, Ginsburg was most frequently aligned with Souter and generally strengthened the Court's moderate center,[33] especially cases dealing with the issues of religious exercise and abortion.

In 1994, President Clinton had another opportunity to alter the balance of the Court when he named Federal Appeals Court Judge Stephen Breyer to succeed retiring Justice Harry Blackmun. But Breyer was generally viewed as another judicial moderate, unlikely to change the Court's direction.

Since 1994, led by Chief Justice Rehnquist and Justices Scalia and Thomas, who were often joined by Justices O'Connor and Kennedy, the Court has continued on a conservative course in some areas, issuing rulings that placed limits on affirmative action, school desegregation, voting rights, the separation of church and state, and the power of the national government. As we saw in Chapter 4, in *Adarand Constructors v. Pena,* the Court ruled that federal programs that award preferences to people on the basis of race are presumed to be unconstitutional unless they are "narrowly tailored" to achieve a "compelling national interest." This

[31]Marsha Grunwald, "Coming Up Short on an Appeals Circuit," *Washington Post,* 6 October 1998, p. A21.

[32]Dan Carney, "Indicting the Courts: Congress's Feud with Judges," *Congressional Quarterly Weekly Report,* 20 June 1998, p. 1660.

[33]Joan Biskupic, "Justices Follow a Mostly Conservative Course," *Washington Post,* 4 July 1994, p. 1.

decision cast doubt on the constitutionality of all federal programs that classify people on the basis of race. As we also discussed in Chapter 4, in the case of *Missouri v. Jenkins,* the Court rescinded a school desegregation plan that it had earlier approved, indicating that it would no longer support ambitious efforts by lower courts to forcibly integrate public schools. And as we will discuss later in Chapter 10, the Court has continued to place limits upon efforts to use the Voting Rights Act to increase minority representation. Finally, we saw in Chapter 3 how several of the Court's recent decisions also unexpectedly reopened the question of the relationship between the federal government and the states, with the Court limiting the power of the national government vis-à-vis the states.

Two important recent decisions dealt with matters of congressional and presidential power. In 1998, as we saw in Chapter 5, the Supreme Court stripped the president of his newly won line-item veto authority.[34] Several months earlier, the Court had dealt President Clinton what turned out to be an even more serious blow when it ruled unanimously in *Clinton v. Jones* that the Constitution does not grant presidents immunity from civil suits stemming from their private unofficial conduct.[35] This decision freed Paula Jones, a former Arkansas state employee, to continue her sexual harassment suit against the president. Clinton's subsequent deposition in the *Jones* case, in which he denied having a sexual relationship with Monica Lewinsky, ultimately formed the basis for the perjury charge levied against the president in the articles of impeachment voted by the House in 1998.

During the struggle between Clinton and Special Counsel Kenneth Starr, which led to the impeachment inquiry, a number of other federal court decisions went against the president. In three separate cases, the U.S. Court of Appeals for the District of Columbia ruled that Secret Service officers can be compelled to give testimony before a federal grand jury, that the president's communication with government lawyers was not protected by attorney-client privilege, and that two senior White House aides could not refuse to testify before a grand jury by claiming executive privilege. The Supreme Court declined to hear the administration's appeals of the first two appellate court rulings.[36] Seen as precedents, these decisions potentially have long-term implications for the power of the presidency. Clinton's unsuccessful effort to protect himself from prosecution may have the consequence of leaving future presidents more vulnerable to prosecution and less well able to protect themselves and their office against congressional judicial inquiries.

The exception to the Court's conservative course has been in the areas of free speech, gay rights, and women's rights. In the civil rights decisions affecting women and gays, the Court appeared to be making a distinction between affirmative action—or positive governmental action on behalf of a minority group—and equal protection, meaning equality before the law. Liberals argue that equal protection is not enough to vindicate the rights of minorities that

[34]New York v. Clinton, 97-1374 (1998).

[35]Clinton v. Jones, 95-1853 (1997).

[36]Rubin v. U.S., 98-93 (1998), and Office of the President v. Office of Special Counsel, 98-316 (1998).

have long suffered from discriminatory treatment. The current Supreme Court majority, while supporting equal protection, does not appear to accept this broader view.

Thus, while the 1992 and 1996 elections had seemed to offer new possibilities for the expansion of judicial liberalism, by 1999 the Court's more conservative justices—Rehnquist, Scalia, and Thomas—appeared to have increased their influence. The political struggles of the 1980s and 1990s amply illustrate the importance of who sits on the Supreme Court. Is abortion a fundamental right or a criminal activity? How much separation must there be between church and state? Does the use of the Voting Rights Act to increase minority representation constitute a violation of the rights of whites? The answers to these and many other questions cannot be found in the words of the Constitution. They must be located, instead, in the hearts of the judges who interpret that text.

**Opinion Writing** The assignment to write the majority opinion in an important constitutional case is an opportunity for the chosen justice to exercise great influence on the Court. But in some ways it also severely limits that influence. The assignment is made by the chief justice or by the senior associate justice in the majority when the chief justice is a dissenter. But it is not a simple procedure. Serious thought has to be given to the impression the case will make on lawyers and on the public and to the probability that one justice's opinion will be more widely accepted than another's.

One of the more dramatic instances of this tactical consideration occurred in 1944, when Chief Justice Harlan F. Stone chose Justice Felix Frankfurter to write the opinion in the "white primary" case, *Smith v. Allwright.* The chief justice believed that this sensitive case, which overturned the Southern practice of prohibiting black participation in nominating primaries, required the efforts of the most brilliant and scholarly jurist on the Court. But the day after Stone made the assignment, Justice Robert H. Jackson wrote a letter to Stone urging a change of assignment. In it Jackson argued that Frankfurter, a foreign-born Jew from New England, would not win the South with his opinion, regardless of its brilliance. Stone accepted the advice and substituted Justice Stanley Reed, an American-born Protestant from Kentucky and a Southern Democrat in good standing.[37]

**Dissent** Ironically, the most dependable way an individual justice can exercise a direct and clear influence on the Court is to write a dissenting opinion. Because there is no need to please a majority, dissenting opinions can be more eloquent and less guarded than majority opinions. Some

[37]Smith v. Allwright, 321 U.S. 649 (1944).

**AMERICAN POLITICAL DEVELOPMENT**

Writing dissents in Supreme Court cases was much more commonplace in the second half of the twentieth century (particularly since the 1970s) than it was in earlier years. This does not necessarily reflect greater disagreement, however, as Court norms in the nineteenth century often led justices to stand by the decision of the Court despite disagreements.

SOURCE: David M. O'Brien, *Storm Center: The Supreme Court in American Politics,* 4th ed. (New York: W. W. Norton, 1996), p. 329–30.

of the greatest writing in the history of the Court is found in dissents, and some of the most famous justices, such as Oliver Wendell Holmes and Louis D. Brandeis earlier in this century, and liberal Justice William O. Douglas in more recent years, were notable dissenters. In the single 1952–1953 Court term, Douglas wrote thirty-five dissenting opinions. In the 1958–1959 term, he wrote eleven dissents. During the latter term, Justices Frankfurter and Harlan wrote thirteen and nine dissents, respectively.

Dissent plays a special role in the work and impact of the Court because it amounts to an appeal to lawyers all over the country to keep bringing cases of the sort at issue. Therefore, an effective dissent influences the flow of cases through the Court as well as the arguments that will be used by lawyers in later cases. Even more important, dissent emphasizes the fact that, although the Court speaks with a single opinion, it is the opinion only of the majority—and one day the majority might go the other way.

## Controlling the Flow of Cases

In addition to the judges themselves, three other agencies or groups play an important role in shaping the flow of cases through the federal courts: the solicitor general, the Federal Bureau of Investigation and other federal agencies, and federal law clerks.

**The Solicitor General** If any single person has greater influence than the individual justices over the work of the Supreme Court, it is the solicitor general of the United States. The solicitor general is third in status in the Justice Department (below the attorney general and the deputy attorney general) but is the top government lawyer in virtually all cases before the appellate courts where the government is a party. Although others can regulate the flow of cases, the solicitor general has the greatest control, with no review of his or her actions by any higher authority in the executive branch. More than half the Supreme Court's total work load consists of cases under the direct charge of the solicitor general.

The solicitor general exercises especially strong influence by screening cases long before they approach the Supreme Court; indeed, the justices rely on the solicitor general to "screen out undeserving litigation and furnish them with an agenda to government cases that deserve serious consideration."[38] Typically, more requests for appeals are rejected than are accepted by the solicitor general. Agency heads may lobby the president or otherwise try to circumvent the solicitor general, and a few of the independent agencies have a statutory right to make direct appeals, but these are almost inevitably doomed to ***per curiam*** rejection—rejection through a brief, unsigned opinion by the whole Court—if the solicitor general refuses to participate. Congress has given only the Interstate Commerce Commission, the Federal Communications Commission, the Federal Maritime Commission, and in some cases, the Department of Agriculture (even though it

[38]Robert Scigliano, *The Supreme Court and the Presidency* (New York: Free Press, 1971), p. 162. For an interesting critique of the solicitor general's role during the Reagan administration, see Lincoln Caplan, "Annals of the Law," *The New Yorker*, 17 August 1987, pp. 30–62.

is not an independent agency) the right to appeal directly to the Supreme Court without going through the solicitor general.

The solicitor general can enter a case even when the federal government is not a direct litigant by writing an ***amicus curiae*** ("friend of the court") brief. A "friend of the court" is not a direct party to a case but has a vital interest in its outcome. Thus, when the government has such an interest, the solicitor general can file as *amicus curiae,* or the Court can invite such a brief because it wants an opinion in writing. The solicitor general also has the power to invite others to enter cases as *amici curiae.*

In addition to exercising substantial control over the flow of cases, the solicitor general can shape the arguments used before the Court. Indeed, the Court tends to give special attention to the way the solicitor general characterizes the issues. The solicitor general is the person appearing most frequently before the Court and, theoretically at least, the most disinterested. The credibility of the solicitor general is not hurt when several times each year he or she comes to the Court to withdraw a case with the admission that the government has made an error.

The solicitor general's sway over the flow of cases does not, however, entirely overshadow the influence of the other agencies and divisions in the Department of Justice. The solicitor general is counsel for the major divisions in the department, including the Antitrust, Tax, Civil Rights, and Criminal Divisions. Their activities generate a great part of the solicitor general's agenda. This is particularly true of the Criminal Division, whose cases are appealed every day. These cases are generated by initiatives taken by the United States Attorneys and the district judges before whom they practice.

**AMERICAN POLITICAL DEVELOPMENT**

The United States did not have a solicitor general until the second half of the nineteenth century. Prior to the office's creation by the Judiciary Act of 1870, suits in which the United States was a party were argued by the attorney general (a position created by the Judiciary Act of 1789) or (between 1830 and 1869) by solicitors working for individual departments of the executive branch. The need for coordination of the various solicitors and an increase in government litigation after the Civil War led to the creation of the solicitor general's office.

SOURCE: Rebecca Mae Salokar, *The Solicitor General: The Politics of Law* (Philadelphia: Temple University Press, 1992), pp. 9–10.

**The FBI and Other Federal Agencies** Another important influence on the flow of cases through the appellate judiciary comes from the Federal Bureau of Investigation (FBI), one of the bureaus of the Department of Justice. Its work provides data for numerous government cases against businesses, individual citizens, and state and local government officials. Its data are the most vital source of material for cases in the areas of national security and organized crime.

The FBI also has the important function of linking the Justice Department very closely to cases being brought by state and local government officials. Since the FBI has a long history of cooperation with state and local police forces, the solicitor general often joins (as *amicus curiae*) appeals involving state criminal cases.

In recent years, other federal agencies have expanded their own law enforcement activities. The Treasury Department is responsible for the Bureau of Alcohol, Tobacco, and Firearms as well as the Secret Service. The Immigration and Naturalization Service employs thousands of Border Patrol agents. All told, more than 41,000 criminal investigators now work for thirty-two federal agencies.[39] All these agencies now join the FBI in providing material for federal cases.

**Law Clerks** Every federal judge employs law clerks to research legal issues and assist with the preparation of opinions. Each Supreme Court justice is assigned four clerks. The clerks are almost always honors graduates of the nation's most prestigious law schools. A clerkship with a Supreme Court justice is a great honor and generally indicates that the fortunate individual is likely to reach the very top of the legal profession. The work of the Supreme Court clerks is a closely guarded secret, but it is likely that some justices rely heavily upon their clerks for advice in writing opinions and in deciding whether an individual case ought to be heard by the Court. It is often rumored that certain opinions were actually written by a clerk rather than a justice.[40] Although such rumors are difficult to substantiate, it is clear that at the end of long judicial careers, justices such as William O. Douglas and Thurgood Marshall had become so infirm that they were compelled to rely on the judgments of their law clerks.

## The Case Pattern

The Supreme Court has discretion over which cases will be reviewed. The solicitor general can influence the Court's choice by giving advice and by encouraging particular cases and discouraging or suppressing others. But, neither the court nor the solicitor general can suppress altogether the kinds of cases that individuals bring to court. Each new technology, such as computers and communications satellites, produces new disputes and the need for new principles of law. Newly awakened interest groups, such as the black community after World War II or the women's and the environmental movements in the 1970s, produce new legislation, new disputes, and new cases. Lawyers are professionally obligated to appeal their clients' cases to the highest possible court if an issue of law or constitutionality is involved.

The litigation that breaks out with virtually every social change produces a pattern of cases that eventually is recognized by the state and federal appellate courts. Appellate judges may at first resist trying such cases by ordering them remanded (returned) to their court of original jurisdiction for further trial. They may reject some appeals without giving any reason at all *(certiorari* denied *per curiam)*. But eventually, one or more of the cases from the pattern may be reviewed and may indeed make new law.

Although some patterns of cases emerge spontaneously as new problems produce new litigation, many interest groups try to set a pattern as a strategy for expediting their cases through the appeals process. Lawyers representing these groups have to choose the proper client and the proper case, so that the issues in question are most dramatically and appropriately portrayed. They also have to

[39]Jim McGee, "At the Justice Department, Big Government Keeps Getting Bigger," *Washington Post,* 5 April 1996, p. A17.

[40]Edward P. Lazarus, *Closed Chambers* (New York: Times Books, 1998).

pick the right district or jurisdiction in which to bring the case. Sometimes they even have to wait for an appropriate political climate.

Group litigants have to plan carefully when to use and when to avoid publicity. They must also attempt to develop a proper record at the trial court level, one that includes some constitutional arguments and even, when possible, errors on the part of the trial court. One of the most effective litigation strategies used in getting cases accepted for review by the appellate courts is bringing the same type of suit in more than one circuit, in the hope that inconsistent treatment by two different courts will improve the chance of a Supreme Court review.

As we shall see more fully in Chapter 12, Congress will sometimes provide interest groups with legislation designed to facilitate their use of litigation. One important recent example is the 1990 Americans with Disabilities Act (ADA), enacted after intense lobbying by public interest and advocacy groups, which, in conjunction with the 1991 Civil Rights Act, opens the way for disabled individuals to make extremely effective use of the courts to press their interests. As the sponsors of ADA had hoped, over time the courts have expanded the rights of the disabled as well as the definition of disability. In 1998, for example, the Supreme Court ruled that individuals with HIV were covered by the act.[41]

**AMERICAN POLITICAL DEVELOPMENT**

Contemporary court workload problems are not unique to America today. In 1890, the Court had a "backlog of 1800 cases," and by "the end of World War I, the Court had fallen more than a year behind schedule." Prior to the Judges Bill of 1925, the court had less flexibility in refusing to hear cases. This act "established 'statutory certiorari' as the preponderant method of review in the U.S. Supreme Court." It set up the rule of four, which required four justices to agree that the Supreme Court should hear a case.

SOURCE: H. W. Perry, Jr., *Deciding to Decide: Agenda Setting in the United States Supreme Court* (Cambridge: Harvard University Press, 1991), pp. 299–301; Doris Marie Provine, *Case Selection in the United States Supreme Court* (Chicago: University of Chicago Press, 1980), p. 11.

The two most notable users of the pattern of cases strategy in recent years have been the National Association for the Advancement of Colored People (NAACP) and the American Civil Liberties Union (ACLU). For many years, the NAACP (and its Defense Fund organization—now a separate group) has worked through local chapters and with many individuals to encourage litigation on issues of racial discrimination and segregation. Sometimes it distributes petitions to be signed by parents and filed with local school boards and courts, deliberately sowing the seeds of future litigation. The NAACP and the ACLU often encourage private parties to bring suit and then join the suit as *amici curiae*.

One illustration of an interest group employing a carefully crafted litigation strategy to pursue its goals through the judiciary was the Texas-based effort to establish a right to free public school education for children of illegal aliens. The issue arose in 1977 when the Texas state legislature, responding to a sudden wave of fear about illegal immigration from Mexico, enacted a law permitting school districts to charge undocumented children a hefty tuition for the privilege of attending public school. A public interest law organization, the Mexican-American Legal Defense Fund, prepared to challenge the law in court after determining

[41]Bragdon v. Abbott, 118 S. Ct. 2186 (1998)

that public opposition precluded any chance of persuading the legislature to change its own law.

Part of the defense fund's litigation strategy was to bring a lawsuit in the northern section of Texas, far from the Mexican border, where illegal immigration would be at a minimum. Thus, in Tyler, Texas, where the complaint was initially filed, the trial court found only sixty undocumented alien students in a school district composed of 16,000. This strategy effectively contradicted the state's argument that the Texas law was necessary to reduce the burdens on educational resources created by masses of incoming aliens. Another useful litigation tactic was to select plaintiffs who, although illegal aliens, were nevertheless clearly planning to remain in Texas even without free public education for their children. Thus, all of the plaintiffs came from families that had already lived in Tyler for several years and included at least one child who was an American citizen by virtue of birth in the United States. By emphasizing the stability of such families, the defense fund argued convincingly that the Texas law would not motivate families to return to the poverty in Mexico from which they had fled, but would more likely result in the creation of a subclass of illiterate people who would add to the state's unemployment and crime rates. Five years after the lawsuit on behalf of the Tyler children began, the U.S. Supreme Court in the case of *Plyler v. Doe* held that the Texas law was unconstitutional under the equal protection clause of the Fourteenth Amendment.[42]

One area that will undoubtedly receive the scrutiny of the Supreme Court in the coming years is welfare. In 1996, welfare advocacy groups planned a broad legal assault on the new welfare reform bill that gave states more power over welfare programs, required welfare recipients to go to work after two years, and eliminated aid after five years. These groups planned suits in both federal and state courts charging that elements of the new law violated the rights of aid recipients. Some groups planned to challenge the portion of the new law that makes noncitizens ineligible for Supplementary Security Income and food stamp benefits. Other groups planned to argue that the states could not drop people from the welfare rolls even in the absence of a federal entitlement. Still others planned litigation challenging the new law's mandatory work requirements. A host of public interest and private attorneys indicated their interest in becoming involved in the dispute. "There is a field day for lawyers on this bill," said Ed Feaver, secretary of the Florida Department of Children and Family Services.[43] As this case illustrates, the enactment of legislation is often merely the beginning rather than the end of political struggle in contemporary America. The judicial arena has become every bit as important as the congressional arena of decision making, and contending political forces realize that victories won in Congress can be lost in the courts.

Thus, regardless of the wishes of the Justice Department or the Supreme Court, many pathbreaking cases are eventually granted *certiorari,* because continued refusal to review one or more of them would amount to a rule of law just as

[42]Plyler v. Doe, 457 U.S. 202 (1982).

[43]Judith Haveman and Barbara Vobejda, "Advocacy Groups Across U.S. Planning to Challenge Welfare Law," *Washington Post,* 30 September 1996, p. A6.

much as if the courts had handed down a written opinion. In this sense, the flow of cases, especially the pattern of significant cases, influences the behavior of the appellate judiciary.[44]

# Judicial Power and Politics

One of the most important institutional changes to occur in the United States during the past half-century has been the striking transformation of the role and power of the federal courts, those of the Supreme Court in particular. Understanding how this transformation came about is the key to understanding the contemporary role of the courts in America.

## Traditional Limitations on the Federal Courts

For much of American history, the power of the federal courts was subject to five limitations.[45] First, courts were constrained by judicial rules of standing that limited access to the bench. Claimants who simply disagreed with governmental action or inaction could not obtain access. Access to the courts was limited to individuals who could show that they were particularly affected by the government's behavior in some area. This limitation on access to the courts diminished the judiciary's capacity to forge links with important political and social forces. Second, courts were traditionally limited in the character of the relief they could provide. In general, courts acted only to offer relief or assistance to individuals and not to broad social classes, again inhibiting the formation of alliances between the courts and important social forces. Third, courts lacked enforcement powers of their own and were compelled to rely upon executive or state agencies to ensure compliance with their edicts. If the executive or state agencies were unwilling to assist the courts, judicial enactments could go unheeded, as when President Andrew Jackson declined to enforce Chief Justice John Marshall's 1832 order to the state of Georgia to release two missionaries it had arrested on Cherokee lands. Marshall asserted that the state had no right to enter the Cherokee's lands without their assent.[46] Jackson is reputed to have said, "John Marshall has made his decision, now let him enforce it."

Fourth, federal judges are, of course, appointed by the president (with the consent of the Senate). As a result, the president and Congress can shape the

[44]Some political scientists would argue that the pattern of cases also influences the behavior of bureaucrats. Recall from Chapter 7 that in implementing legislation passed by Congress, bureaucrats have the final word on how a law is shaped. Because courts have the authority to accept or reject these laws, bureaucrats must anticipate how the judiciary might react and interpret congressional intent accordingly. Bureaucrats learn how courts might respond by following the pattern of significant cases. For more on this line of argument, see Kenneth A. Shepsle and Mark S. Bonchek, *Analyzing Politics: Rationality, Behavior, and Institutions* (New York: W. W. Norton, 1997), pp. 422–28.

[45]For limits on judicial power, see Alexander Bickel, *The Least Dangerous Branch* (Indianapolis: Bobbs-Merrill, 1962).

[46]Worcester v. Georgia, 6 Peters 515 (1832).

## AMERICAN POLITICAL DEVELOPMENT

Many of the traditional limitations on federal courts were partially self-imposed. These limitations echoed the political alliances that had been implicitly struck during the late nineteenth century, when the courts "championed the cause of entrepreneurial liberty through a series of decisions that limited the reach of governmental power and directly linked the Court with the new forces of industrial and finance capitalism." Today, the courts are associated with more liberal forces, which are supportive of and nurtured by judicial activism.

SOURCE: Mark Silverstein, *Judicious Choices: The New Politics of Supreme Court Confirmations* (New York: W. W. Norton, 1994), p. 37.

composition of the federal courts and ultimately, perhaps, the character of judicial decisions. Finally, Congress has the power to change both the size and jurisdiction of the Supreme Court and other federal courts. For example, on one memorable occasion, presidential and congressional threats to expand the size of the Supreme Court—Franklin Roosevelt's "court packing" plan—encouraged the justices to drop their opposition to New Deal programs. In many areas, federal courts obtain their jurisdiction not from the Constitution but from congressional statutes. On a number of occasions, Congress has threatened to take matters out of the Court's hands when it was unhappy with the Court's policies.[47]

During the early 1980s, for example, Republicans introduced legislation designed to strip the lower federal courts of their jurisdiction in school prayer, busing, and abortion cases. If only the Supreme Court had jurisdiction in such matters, only a handful could ever be heard. This effort was blocked by the opposition of Democrats and even some Republicans like former Senator Barry Goldwater who denounced what he saw as a "frontal assault on the independence of the federal courts."[48] In 1996, a Republican Congress succeeded in enacting new limits on the jurisdiction of the federal courts. The Immigration Reform Act limited the ability of the courts to hear class action suits brought on behalf of immigrants seeking to fight deportation proceedings. The Prison Litigation Reform Act limited the ability of federal judges to place state and local prison systems in the hands of special masters. Finally, a provision of the 1996 Budget Act limited the ability of the federal courts to listen to class action suits brought by legal services lawyers.[49] These restrictions were designed to curb what conservatives viewed as the excessive power of the judiciary.

As a result of these five limitations on judicial power, through much of their history the chief function of the federal courts was to provide judicial support for executive agencies and to legitimate acts of Congress by declaring them to be consistent with constitutional principles. Only on rare occasions did the federal courts actually dare to challenge Congress or the executive.[50]

## Two Judicial Revolutions

Since the Second World War, however, the role of the federal judiciary has been strengthened and expanded. There have actually been two judicial revolutions in

[47]See Walter Murphy, *Congress and the Court* (Chicago: University of Chicago Press, 1962).

[48]Linda Greenhouse, "How Congress Curtailed the Courts' Jurisdiction," *New York Times,* 22 October 1996, p. E5.

[49]Ibid.

[50]Robert Dahl, "The Supreme Court and National Policy Making," *Journal of Public Law* 6 (1958), p. 279.

the United States since World War II. The first and most visible of these was the substantive revolution in judicial policy. As we saw earlier in this chapter and in Chapter 4, in policy areas, including school desegregation, legislative apportionment, and criminal procedure, as well as obscenity, abortion, and voting rights, the Supreme Court was at the forefront of a series of sweeping changes in the role of the U.S. government, and ultimately, in the character of American society.[51]

But at the same time that the courts were introducing important policy innovations, they were also bringing about a second, less visible revolution. During the 1960s and 1970s, the Supreme Court and other federal courts instituted a series of changes in judicial procedures that fundamentally expanded the power of the courts in the United States. First, the federal courts liberalized the concept of standing to permit almost any group that seeks to challenge the actions of an administrative agency to bring its case before the federal bench. In 1971, for example, the Supreme Court ruled that public interest groups could use the National Environmental Policy Act to challenge the actions of federal agencies by claiming that the agencies' activities might have adverse environmental consequences.[52] Congress helped to make it even easier for groups dissatisfied with government policies to bring their cases to the courts by adopting Section 1983 of the U.S. Code, which permits the practice of "fee shifting." Section 1983 allows citizens who successfully bring a suit against a public official for violating their constitutional rights to collect their attorneys' fees and costs from the government. Thus, Section 1983 encourages individuals and groups to bring their problems to the courts rather than to Congress or the executive branch. These changes have given the courts a far greater role in the administrative process than ever before. Many federal judges are concerned that federal legislation in areas such as health care reform would create new rights and entitlements that would give rise to a deluge of court cases. "Any time you create a new right, you create a host of disputes and claims," warned Barbara Rothstein, chief judge of the federal district court in Seattle, Washington.[53] Where issues of civil rights are in question, the 1976 Civil Rights Attorney Fees Act also provides for fee shifting. The act calls for the award of "reasonable attorneys fees," to a prevailing party in a civil rights law suit.

Second, the federal courts broadened the scope of relief to permit themselves to act on behalf of broad categories or classes of persons in "class action" cases, rather than just on behalf of individuals.[54] A ***class action suit*** is a procedural device that permits large numbers of persons with common interests to join together under a representative party to bring or defend a lawsuit. One example is the case of *In re Agent Orange Product Liability Litigation,* in which a federal judge in New York certified Vietnam War veterans as a class with standing to sue a manufacturer of herbicides for damages allegedly incurred from exposure to the defendants' product while in Vietnam.[55] The class potentially numbered in the tens of thousands. In a similar vein, in 1999, a consortium of several dozen law

[51]Martin Shapiro, "The Supreme Court: From Warren to Burger," in *The New American Political System,* ed. Anthony King (Washington, DC: American Enterprise Institute, 1978).

[52]Citizens to Preserve Overton Park v. Volpe, 401 U.S. 402 (1971).

[53]Toni Locy, "Bracing for Health Care's Caseload," *Washington Post,* 22 August 1994, p. A15.

[54]See "Developments in the Law—Class Actions," *Harvard Law Review* 89 (1976), p. 1318.

[55]In re Agent Orange Product Liability Litigation, 100 F.R.D. 718 (D.C.N.Y. 1983).

DEBATING THE ISSUES

## Interpreting the Constitution and Original Intent

*Judges bear the responsibility of interpreting the meaning and applicability of the Constitution, written over two hundred years ago, to modern society. The application of constitutional principles to modern problems is inherently difficult because of disagreements over what the founders intended and over how the Constitution's words ought to apply to issues and problems unimagined in the eighteenth century.*

*Former federal judge Robert H. Bork argues in favor of the "original intent" approach, urging judges to stick as closely to the Constitution's text and original meaning as possible. Constitutional scholar Leonard W. Levy counters that original intent, even if it could be divined, is an inadequate and inappropriate way to deal with constitutional interpretation.*

### BORK

What was once the dominant view of constitutional law—that a judge is to apply the Constitution according to the principles intended by those who ratified the document—is now very much out of favor among the theorists of the field. . . .

In truth, only the approach of original understanding meets the criteria that any theory of constitutional adjudication must meet in order to possess democratic legitimacy. Only that approach is consonant with the design of the American Republic. . . .

. . . The original understanding is . . . manifested in the words used and in secondary materials, such as debates at the conventions, public discussion, newspaper articles, dictionaries in use at the time, and the like.

The search for the intent of the lawmaker is the everyday procedure of lawyers and judges when they apply a statute, a contract, a will, or the opinion of a court. . . . Lawyers and judges should seek in the Constitution what they seek in other legal texts: the original meaning of the words. . . .

A judge, no matter on what court he sits, may never create new constitutional rights or destroy old ones. Any time he does so, he violates the limits of his own authority and, for that reason, also violates the rights of the legislature and the people. . . .

The role of a judge committed to the philosophy of original understanding is not to "choose a level of abstraction." Rather, it is to find the meaning of a text—a process which includes finding its degree of generality, which is part of its meaning—and to apply that text to a particular situation. . . . The equal-protection clause [for example] was adopted in order to protect freed slaves, but its language, being general, applies to all persons.[1]

### LEVY

James Madison, Father of the Constitution and of the Bill of Rights, rejected the doctrine that the original intent of those who framed the Constitution should be accepted as an authoritative guide to its meaning. "As a guide in expounding and applying the provisions of the Constitution . . . the debates and incidental decisions of the Convention can have no authoritative character.". . . We tend to forget the astounding fact that Madison's Notes were first published in 1840, fifty-three years after the Constitutional Convention had met. . . . What mattered to them [the founders] was the text of the Constitution, construed in the light of conventional rules of interpretation, the ratification debates, and other contemporary expositions. . . . Original intent is an unreliable concept because it assumes the existence of one intent. . . . The entity we call "the Framers" did not have a collective mind. . . . In fact, they disagreed on many crucial matters. . . .

Fifty years ago . . . Jacobus tenBroek asserted, rightly, that "the intent theory . . . inverts the judicial process." . . . Original intent . . . makes the judge "a mindless robot whose task is the utterly mechanical function" of using original intent as a measure of constitutionality. In the entire history of the Supreme Court . . . no Justice employing the intent theory has ever written a convincing and reliable study.

The Court has the responsibility of helping regenerate and fulfill the noblest aspirations for which the nation stands. It must keep constitutional law constantly rooted in the great ideals of the past yet in a state of evolution in order to realize them. . . . Chief Justice Earl Warren . . . declared, "We serve only the public interest as we see it, guided only by the Constitution and our own consciences." That, not the original intent of the Framers, is our reality.[2]

[1]Robert H. Bork, "The Case against Political Judging," *National Review,* 8 December 1989, pp. 23–28.

[2]Leonard W. Levy, *Original Intent and the Framers' Constitution* (New York: Macmillan, 1988), pp. 1–2, 294, 388, 396, 398.

firms prepared to file a class action suit against fire arms manufacturers on behalf of victims of gun violence. Claims could amount to billions of dollars. Some of the same law firms were involved earlier in the decade in a massive class action suit against cigarette manufacturers on behalf of the victims of tobacco-related illnesses. This suit eventually led to a settlement in which the tobacco companies agreed to pay out several billion dollars. The beneficiaries of the settlement included the treasuries of all fifty states, which received compensation for costs allegedly borne by the states in treating illnesses due to tobacco. Of course, the attorneys who brought the case also received an enormous settlement, splitting more than $1 billion.

Third, the federal courts began to employ so-called structural remedies, in effect retaining jurisdiction of cases until the court's mandate had actually been implemented to its satisfaction.[56] The best-known of these instances was Federal Judge W. Arthur Garrity's effort to operate the Boston school system from his bench in order to ensure its desegregation. Between 1974 and 1985, Judge Garrity issued fourteen decisions relating to different aspects of the Boston school desegregation plan that had been developed under his authority and put into effect under his supervision.[57] In another recent case, Federal Judge Leonard B. Sand imposed fines that would have forced the city of Yonkers, New York, into

[56]See Donald Horowitz, *The Courts and Social Policy* (Washington, DC: Brookings Institution, 1977).

[57]Moran v. McDonough, 540 F. 2nd 527 (1 Cir., 1976; *cert denied* 429 U.S. 1042 [1977]).

bankruptcy if it had refused to accept his plan to build public housing in white neighborhoods. After several days of fines, the city gave in to the judge's ruling.

Through these three judicial mechanisms, the federal courts paved the way for an unprecedented expansion of national judicial power. In essence, liberalization of the rules of standing and expansion of the scope of judicial relief drew the federal courts into linkages with important social interests and classes, while the introduction of structural remedies enhanced the courts' ability to serve these constituencies. Thus, during the 1960s and 1970s, the power of the federal courts expanded in the same way the power of the executive expanded during the 1930s—through links with constituencies, such as civil rights, consumer, environmental, and feminist groups, that staunchly defended the Supreme Court in its battles with Congress, the executive, or other interest groups.

During the 1980s and early 1990s, the Reagan and Bush administrations sought to end the relationship between the Court and liberal political forces. As we saw earlier, the conservative judges appointed by these Republican presidents modified the Court's position in areas such as abortion, affirmative action, and judicial procedure, though not as completely as some conservatives had hoped. Interestingly, however, the current Court has not been eager to surrender the expanded powers carved out by earlier, liberal Courts. In a number of decisions during the 1980s and 1990s, the Court was willing to make use of its expanded powers on behalf of interests it favored.[58]

In the 1992 case of *Lujan v. Defenders of Wildlife,* the Court seemed to retreat to a conception of standing more restrictive than that affirmed by liberal activist jurists.[59] Rather than representing an example of judicial restraint, however, the *Lujan* case was actually a direct judicial challenge to congressional power. The case involved an effort by an environmental group, the Defenders of Wildlife, to make use of the 1973 Endangered Species Act to block the expenditure of federal funds being used by the governments of Egypt and Sri Lanka for public works projects. Environmentalists charged that the projects threatened the habitats of several endangered species of birds and, therefore, that the expenditure of federal funds to support the projects violated the 1973 act. The Interior Department claimed that the act affected only domestic projects.[60]

The Endangered Species Act, like a number of other pieces of liberal environmental and consumer legislation enacted by Congress, encourages citizen suits—suits by activist groups not directly harmed by the action in question—to challenge government policies they deem to be inconsistent with the act. Justice Scalia, however, writing for the Court's majority in the *Lujan* decision, reasserted a more traditional conception of standing, requiring those bringing suit against a government policy to show that the policy is likely to cause *them* direct and imminent injury.

Had Scalia stopped at this point, the case might have been seen as an example of judicial restraint. Scalia, however, went on to question the validity of

[58]Mark Silverstein and Benjamin Ginsberg, "The Supreme Court and the New Politics of Judicial Power," *Political Science Quarterly* 102 (Fall 1987), pp. 371–88.

[59]Lujan v. Defenders of Wildlife, 112 S.Ct. 2130 (1992).

[60]Linda Greenhouse, "Court Limits Legal Standing in Suits," *New York Times,* 13 June 1992, p. 12.

any statutory provision for citizen suits. Such legislative provisions, according to Justice Scalia, violate Article III of the Constitution, which limits the federal courts to consideration of actual "cases" and "controversies." This interpretation would strip Congress of its capacity to promote the enforcement of regulatory statutes by encouraging activist groups not directly affected or injured to be on the lookout for violations that could provide the basis for lawsuits. This enforcement mechanism—which conservatives liken to bounty hunting—was an extremely important congressional instrument and played a prominent part in the enforcement of such pieces of legislation as the 1990 Americans with Disabilities Act (see Chapter 12). Thus, the *Lujan* case offers an example of judicial activism rather than of judicial restraint; even the most conservative justices are reluctant to surrender the powers now wielded by the Court.

## SUMMARY

Millions of cases come to trial every year in the United States. The great majority—nearly 99 percent—are tried in state and local courts. The types of law are civil law, criminal law, and public law. There are three types of courts that hear cases: trial court, appellate court, and (state) supreme court.

There are three kinds of federal cases: (1) civil cases involving diversity of citizenship, (2) civil cases where a federal agency is seeking to enforce federal laws that provide for civil penalties, and (3) cases involving federal criminal statutes or where state criminal cases have been made issues of public law. Judicial power extends only to cases and controversies. Litigants must have standing to sue, and courts neither hand down opinions on hypothetical issues nor take the initiative. Sometimes appellate courts even return cases to the lower courts for further trial. They may also decline to decide cases by invoking the doctrine of political questions, although this is seldom done today.

The organization of the federal judiciary provides for original jurisdiction in the federal district courts, the U.S. Court of Claims, the U.S. Tax Court, the Customs Court, and federal regulatory agencies.

Each district court is in one of the twelve appellate districts, called circuits, presided over by a court of appeals. Appellate courts admit no new evidence; their rulings are based solely on the records of the court proceedings or agency hearings that led to the original decision. Appeals court rulings are final unless the Supreme Court chooses to review them.

The Supreme Court has some original jurisdiction, but its major job is to review lower court decisions involving substantial issues of public law. Supreme Court decisions can be reversed by Congress and the state legislatures, but this seldom happens. There is no explicit constitutional authority for the Supreme Court to review acts of Congress. Nonetheless, the 1803 case of *Marbury v. Madison* established the Court's right to review congressional acts. The supremacy clause of Article VI and the Judiciary Act of 1789 give the Court the power to review state constitutions and laws. Cases reach the Court mainly

THEN AND NOW

## Changes in American Politics

Judicial politics have underdone significant changes in the twentieth century. Once seen as a protector of conservative interests, the federal judiciary came to be allied with liberal and progressive forces for much of the twentieth century. Moreover, significant institutional developments have altered the judiciary's role in policy making.

- The structure of the federal judiciary is subject to change by the U.S. Congress. There were six Supreme Court justices during the first half of the nineteenth century, expanding to nine in 1869. Congress created nine Courts of Appeals in 1891, alleviating the overburdened Supreme Court justices.

- During its first century, the Supreme Court overturned few acts of Congress and state laws. But by the late nineteenth century and throughout the twentieth century, this practice of overturning became much more common.

- The Court was much more activist during the second half of the twentieth century. For example, the Court was reluctant to rule on the issue of reapportionment of state and federal election districts in 1946, but by 1962 it was willing to rule.

- Court norms of the nineteenth century were such that relatively few dissenting opinions were issued by justices. This norm has waned in the twentieth century, and justices are much more willing to offer views that differ from the Court opinion.

- Although the solicitor general plays an important role in contemporary court politics, there was no such position in the United States until the Judiciary Act of 1870.

- Because the Court had less control over its own agenda prior to the Judges Bill of 1925, case backlogs were common during the nineteenth century.

- In an effort to enhance its political potency, the federal judiciary made it easier for groups dissatisfied with government policies to bring their cases before court, broadened the scope of relief it can provide to claimants, and enhanced its enforcement capabilities.

through the writ of *certiorari*. The Supreme Court controls its case load by issuing few writs and by handing down clear leading opinions that enable lower courts to resolve future cases without further review.

Both appellate and Supreme Court decisions, including the decision not to review a case, make law. The impact of such law usually favors the status quo. Yet, many revolutionary changes in the law have come about through appellate court and Supreme Court rulings—in the criminal process, in apportionment, and in civil rights.

The judiciary as a whole is subject to three major influences: (1) the individual members of the Supreme Court, who have lifetime tenure; (2) the Justice Department—particularly the solicitor general, who regulates the flow of cases; and (3) the pattern of cases.

The influence of the individual member of the Supreme Court is limited when the Court is polarized, and close votes in a polarized Court impair the value of the decision rendered. Writing the majority opinion for a case is an opportunity for a justice to influence the judiciary. But the need to frame an opinion in such a way as to develop majority support on the Court may limit such opportunities. Dissenting opinions can have more impact than the majority opinion; they stimulate a continued flow of cases around that issue. The solicitor general is the most important single influence outside the Court itself because he or she controls the flow of cases brought by the Justice Department and also shapes the argument in those cases. But the flow of cases is a force in itself, which the Department of Justice cannot entirely control. Social problems give rise to similar cases that ultimately must be adjudicated and appealed. Some interest groups try to develop such case patterns as a means of gaining power through the courts.

In recent years, the importance of the federal judiciary—the Supreme Court in particular—has increased substantially as the courts have developed new tools of judicial power and forged alliances with important forces in American society.

## For Further Reading

Abraham, Henry. *The Judicial Process,* 6th ed. New York: Oxford University Press, 1993.

Bickel, Alexander. *The Least Dangerous Branch.* Indianapolis: Bobbs-Merrill, 1962.

Bryner, Gary, and Dennis L. Thompson. *The Constitution and the Regulation of Society.* Provo, UT: Brigham Young University, 1988.

Davis, Sue. *Justice Rehnquist and the Constitution.* Princeton: Princeton University Press, 1989.

Faulkner, Robert K. *The Jurisprudence of John Marshall.* Princeton: Princeton University Press, 1968.

Graber, Mark A. *Transforming Free Speech: The Ambiguous Legacy of Civil Libertarianism.* Berkeley: University of California Press, 1991.

*History of the Supreme Court of the United States.* 9 vols. New York: Macmillan, 1981.

Kahn, Ronald. *The Supreme Court and Constitutional Theory, 1953–1993.* Lawrence: University Press of Kansas, 1994.

Maveety, Nancy. *Representation Rights and the Burger Years.* Ann Arbor: University of Michigan Press, 1991.

McCann, Michael W. *Rights at Work.* Chicago: University of Chicago Press, 1994.

Mezey, Susan G. *No Longer Disabled: The Federal Courts and the Politics of Social Security Disability.* New York: Greenwood, 1988.

Nardulli, Peter F., James Eisenstein, and Roy B. Fleming. *The Tenor of Justice: Criminal Courts and the Guilty Plea.* Urbana: University of Illinois Press, 1988.

O'Brien, David M. *Storm Center: The Supreme Court in American Politics,* 5th ed. New York: W. W. Norton, 1999.

Rosenberg, Gerald. *The Hollow Hope: Can Courts Bring about Social Change?* Chicago: University of Chicago Press, 1991.

Rubin, Eva. *Abortion, Politics and the Courts.* Westport, CT: Greenwood Press, 1982.

Silverstein, Mark. *Judicious Choices: The New Politics of Supreme Court Confirmations.* New York: W. W. Norton, 1994.

Stimson, Shannon C. *The American Revolution in the Law: Anglo-American Jurisprudence before John Marshall.* Princeton: Princeton University Press, 1990.

Tribe, Laurence. *Constitutional Choices.* Cambridge: Harvard University Press, 1985.

PART 3

# POLITICS

# Public Opinion

## TIME LINE ON PUBLIC OPINION

| Events | | Institutional Developments |
|---|---|---|
| Congressional investigation of Gen. St. Clair's conduct of war against Indians (1792) | | George Washington begins policy of executive secrecy in regard to congressional investigations (1792) |
| Territorial expansion (1800s) | 1800 | Straw polls and other impressionistic means of measuring opinion (1830s–1890s) |
| Civil War (1861–1865) | | Urban school systems—development of civic education programs (1880s) |
| Democrats denounce polling as a Republican plot; they instruct their voters not to answer questions (1896) | | Birth of advertising industry—scientific manipulation of public opinion (1880s) |
| | 1900 | |
| World War I (1914–1918) | | Creel Committee tries to "sell" WW I to American public (1917) |
| *Literary Digest* poll predicts Hoover will defeat Roosevelt (1932) | | Beginning of routine governmental efforts to manage opinion (1930s) |
| Media used to defeat Upton Sinclair in California campaign for governor (1934) | | Media experts manipulate public opinion through negative campaign using newspapers, leaflets, and radio (1934) |
| Gallup and Roper use sample surveys in national political polls (1936) | | Introduction of sample surveys to predict winners of national elections (1936) |
| *Chicago Tribune* poll shows Dewey victory over Truman (1948) | | Growth of national polls (1930s–1950s) |
| | 1950 | |
| Kennedy campaign uses computers to analyze polls and bellwether districts (1959–1960) | | Emergence of computer analysis of polls and bellwether districts (1959–1960) |
| CBS uses computer bellwether system to correctly forecast winner of California Republican primary (1964) | | Emergence of exit polls (1960s) |
| | | Media attack government opinion manipulation (1960s and 1970s) |
| | 1970 | |
| CBS airs "Selling of the Pentagon" (1971) | | |
| Exit polls used to predict presidential election outcome before polls close on West Coast (1976, 1980, 1984, 1988) | | Expansion of mass media; nationalization of public opinion (1960s–1980s) |
| | 1990 | |
| Daily polls on public support for Persian Gulf War (1991) | | Politicians create new media formats to pitch themselves and their programs; era of permanent campaign (1992) |

| Events | Institutional Developments |
|---|---|
| President Clinton uses town meetings and media appeals to bolster popular support for programs; lobbies Congress by mobilizing popular pressure (1993) | Members of presidential campaign staffs join White House staff to bolster public support for programs (1993) |
| Pre-election and exit polls unusually error-prone in 1996 elections (1996) | Push polling becomes campaign tool (1996) |

### CORE OF THE ARGUMENT

- Opinions are shaped by individuals' characteristics and also by institutional, political, and governmental forces.
- Government shapes citizens' beliefs about the political system through the promotion of nationalism, property ownership, education, and political participation.
- Various methods of polling are used to measure public opinion.
- The government and political leaders use measures of public opinion to shape their policy initiatives.

After his election to the presidency, Bill Clinton found that public opinion could be quite fickle. By May 1993, only one hundred days after his inauguration, Clinton's approval ratings had fallen sharply. For example, according to a May 4–6 *New York Times*/CBS News poll, 50 percent of Americans disapproved of the way President Clinton was handling the economy, while only 38 percent approved.[1] Only a month earlier, nearly half of all respondents to the same poll had said they approved of Clinton's economic performance, while only 37 percent had disapproved. Consistent with the pattern discussed in Chapter 6, Clinton's public approval rating briefly increased by 11 points in June 1993, after he ordered a cruise missile attack on Iraqi intelligence headquarters. The attack was in retaliation for an alleged Iraqi plot to assassinate former president George Bush. Clinton himself attributed his improved poll standing to what he termed better public understanding of his economic program. Within a few days, however, Clinton's approval rating had dropped back to 38 percent.

Clinton's approval rating continued to linger in this range during most of 1994. Indeed, despite the nation's strong economic performance during the first half of

[1]Gwen Ifill, "As Ratings Stall, Clinton Tries Tune-Up," *New York Times,* 10 May 1993, p. A16; Richard Morin and Ann Devroy, "President's Popularity Continues to Weaken," *Washington Post,* 30 June 1993, p. 1.

1994, the majority of those polled even disapproved of the president's handling of the economy.[2] By 1996, however, President Clinton's popular standing seemed to have been fully restored. In the weeks prior to the November 1996 presidential elections, Clinton's lead in the polls over his Republican challenger, Robert Dole, was as high as twenty-one points. Clinton continued to enjoy high levels of public approval throughout 1997 and 1998. This was remarkable, given the president's public acknowledgment that he had lied about having an extramarital relationship. Indeed, Clinton's poll standing remained high, even as he became only the second president in American history to be impeached by Congress!

Commentators and social scientists, of course, carefully plotted these massive changes in public opinion and pondered their causes. Significantly, no analyst charting these shifts in popular sentiment was so bold as to ask whether public opinion was right or wrong—whether it made sense or nonsense. Rather, opinion was viewed as some sort of natural force that, like the weather, affected everything but was itself impervious to intervention and immune to criticism.

Public opinion has become the ultimate standard against which the conduct of contemporary governments is measured. In the democracies, especially in the United States, both the value of government programs and the virtue of public officials are typically judged by the magnitude of their popularity. Most twentieth-century dictatorships, for their part, are careful at least to give lip service to the idea of popular sovereignty, if only to bolster public support at home and to maintain a favorable image abroad.

***Public opinion*** is the term used to denote the values and attitudes that people have about issues, events, and personalities. Although the terms are sometimes used interchangeably, it is useful to distinguish between values and beliefs on the one hand, and attitudes or opinions on the other. ***Values (or beliefs)*** are a person's basic orientations to politics. Values represent deep-rooted goals, aspirations, and ideals that shape an individual's perceptions of political issues and events. Liberty, equality, and democracy are basic political values that most Americans hold. Another useful term for understanding public opinion is *ideology*. ***Political ideology*** refers to a complex set of beliefs and values that, as a whole, form a general philosophy about government. As we shall see, liberalism and conservatism are important ideologies in America today.

The idea that governmental solutions to problems are inherently inferior to solutions offered by the private sector is a belief held by many Americans. This general belief, in turn, may lead individuals to have negative views of specific government programs even before they know much about them. An ***attitude (or opinion)*** is a specific view about a particular issue, personality, or event. An individual may have an opinion about the impeachment of President Clinton or an attitude toward American policy in Serbia. The attitude or opinion may have emerged from a broad belief about Democrats or military intervention, but an attitude itself is very specific. Some attitudes may be short-lived.

[2]Richard Morin, "Clinton Ratings Decline Despite Rising Economy," *Washington Post,* 9 August 1994, p. 1.

In this chapter, we will examine the role of public opinion in American politics. First, we will look at the institutions and processes that shape public opinion in the United States, most notably the "marketplace of ideas" in which opinions compete for acceptance. Second, we will assess the government's role in shaping public opinion. Third, we will address the problem of measuring opinion. Finally, we will consider the question: "Is government responsive to public opinion?"

**THE CENTRAL QUESTION**

"Is government responsive to public opinion?"

## THE MARKETPLACE OF IDEAS

Opinions are products of individuals' personalities, social characteristics, and interests. But opinions are also shaped by institutional, political, and governmental forces that make it more likely that citizens will hold some beliefs and less likely that they will hold others. In the United States and the other Western democracies, opinions and beliefs compete for acceptance in what is sometimes called the ***marketplace of ideas.*** In America, it is mainly the "hidden hand" of the market that determines which opinions and beliefs will flourish and which will fall to the wayside. Thus, to understand public opinion in the United States, it is important to understand the origins and operations of this "idea market."

### Origins of the Idea Market

Prior to the nineteenth century, each of the various regional, religious, ethnic, linguistic, and economic strata generally possessed their own ideas and beliefs based upon their own experiences and life circumstances. The members of different primary groups generally had little contact with one another, and they knew remarkably little about the history, customs, or character—much less the opinions—of their nominal countrymen.

In every European nation and in America, city was separated from countryside and region from region by the lack of usable roads, the unavailability of effective communications media, and, in many nations in Europe, by the absence of even a common national language. Language barriers could be formidable. For example, before the nineteenth century, Parisians traveling just a few days from the capital often reported that it was impossible to understand the patois of the local populace and that outside of the larger towns it was difficult to find anyone who spoke even a few words of French.[3] Equally significant was the matter of class. The members of the different social classes, even when living near each other, existed in very different worlds. Often, each class spoke its own language, adhered to its own religious beliefs, maintained its own cultural orientations, and manifested distinct conceptions of the political and social universe.

[3]Eugen Weber, *Peasants into Frenchmen* (Stanford: Stanford University Press, 1976).

The autonomy of the various regions, groups, and classes began to diminish in the nineteenth century. During this period, every European regime initiated the construction of what came to be called a "marketplace of ideas"—a national forum in which the views of all strata would be exchanged. Westerners often equate freedom of opinion and expression with the absence of state interference. Western freedom of opinion, however, is not unbridled freedom; rather, it is the structured freedom of a public forum constructed and maintained by the state. The creation and maintenance of this forum, this "marketplace of ideas," has required nearly two centuries of extensive governmental effort in the areas of education, communication, and jurisprudence.

First, in the nineteenth century, most Western nations engaged in intense efforts to impose a single national language upon their citizens. In the United States, massive waves of immigration during the nineteenth century meant that millions of residents spoke no English. In response, the American national government, as well as state and local governments, made vigorous efforts to impose the English language upon these newcomers. Schools were established to provide adults with language skills. At the same time, English was the only language of instruction permitted in the public elementary and secondary schools. Knowledge of English became a prerequisite for American citizenship. With some exceptions, the efforts of the United States and other Western nations to achieve linguistic unification succeeded by the twentieth century.

Second, and closely related to the effort to achieve linguistic unity was the matter of literacy. Prior to the nineteenth century, few ordinary people were able to read or write. Possession of these skills was, for the most part, limited to the upper strata. Widespread illiteracy in a pre-technological era meant that communication depended upon word of mouth, a situation hardly conducive to the spread of ideas across regional, class, or even village or neighborhood boundaries. During the nineteenth and twentieth centuries, however, all Western governments actively sought to expand popular literacy. With the advent of universal, compulsory education, children were taught to read and write the mother tongue. Together with literacy programs for adults, including extensive efforts by the various national military services to instruct uneducated recruits, this educational process led to the gradual reduction of illiteracy in the industrial West. Like the imposition of a common language, the elimination of illiteracy opened the way for the communication of ideas and information across primary group lines.[4]

A third facet of the construction of the marketplace of ideas was the development of various communications mechanisms. This process involved a number of elements. During the early nineteenth century, governments built hundreds of thousands of miles of roads, opening lines of communication among the various regions and between cities and the countryside. Road building was followed later in the century by governmental promotion of the construction of rail and telegraph lines, further facilitating the exchange of goods, persons, and, not least important, ideas and information among previously disparate and often isolated areas. Such "internal improvements" constituted the most important activity

[4]See Richard Hoggart, *The Uses of Literacy* (Oxford, England: Oxford University Press, 1970).

undertaken by the American central government both before and after the Civil War. During the twentieth century, all Western regimes promoted the development of radio, telephone, television, and the complex satellite-based communications networks that today link the world.

The final key component of the construction of a free market of ideas was, and is, legal protection for free expression of ideas. This last factor is, of course, what most clearly distinguished the construction of the West's idea market from the efforts of authoritarian regimes. Obviously, the development of communications networks, linguistic unification, and universal literacy were goals pursued just as avidly by autocratic nation-builders as by the more liberal regimes.

In most Western nations, at the present time, there are few physical or legal impediments to the transmission of ideas and information across municipal, regional, class, ethnic, or other primary group boundaries. All groups are, to a greater or lesser extent, linked by a common language, mass communications media, and transportation networks. In the United States, for example, the newspapers, wire services, radio, television, Internet Web sites, and news magazines present a common core of ideas and information to virtually the entire citizenry. Every region of the country can be reached by mail, phone, and broadcast and electronic media; virtually no area is inaccessible by road, rail, or air transport; and persons, ideas, and information can move freely across regions and between economic strata and ethnic groups. Similarly, the lifting of travel restrictions has been a major element in efforts to bring about European unification in recent years.

## The Idea Market Today

The operation of the idea market in the United States today has continually exposed individuals to concepts and information originating outside their own region, class, or ethnic community. It is this steady exposure that over time leads members of every social group to acquire at least some of the ideas and perspectives embraced by the others. Given continual exposure to the ideas of other strata, it is virtually impossible for any group to resist some modification of its own beliefs.

**Common Fundamental Values** Today most Americans share a common set of political beliefs and opinions. First, Americans generally believe in ***equality of opportunity.*** That is, they assume that all individuals should be allowed to seek personal and material success. Moreover, Americans generally believe that such success should be linked to personal effort and ability rather than family "connections" or other forms of special privilege. Second, Americans strongly believe in individual freedom. They typically support the notion that governmental interference with individuals' lives and property should be kept to the minimum consistent with the general welfare (although in recent years Americans have grown accustomed to greater levels of governmental intervention than would have been deemed appropriate by the founders of liberal theory). Third, most Americans believe in *democracy.* They presume that everyone should have the opportunity

FIGURE 9.1

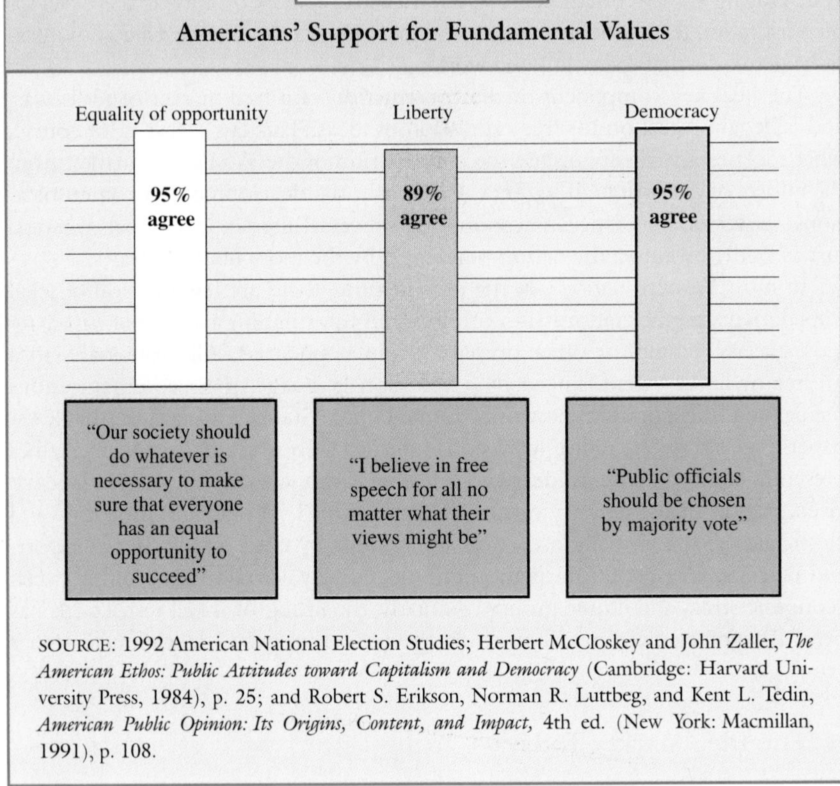


SOURCE: 1992 American National Election Studies; Herbert McCloskey and John Zaller, *The American Ethos: Public Attitudes toward Capitalism and Democracy* (Cambridge: Harvard University Press, 1984), p. 25; and Robert S. Erikson, Norman R. Luttbeg, and Kent L. Tedin, *American Public Opinion: Its Origins, Content, and Impact,* 4th ed. (New York: Macmillan, 1991), p. 108.

to take part in the nation's governmental and policy-making processes and to have some "say" in determining how they are governed (see Figure 9.1).[5]

One indication that Americans of all political stripes share these fundamental political values is the content of the acceptance speeches delivered by Bill Clinton and Bob Dole upon receiving their parties' presidential nominations in 1996. Clinton and Dole differed on many specific issues and policies. Yet the political visions they presented reveal an underlying similarity. A major emphasis of both candidates was equality of opportunity. Clinton referred frequently to opportunity in his speech, even beginning the speech with a poignant story about the importance of equality of opportunity in his own life.

> I never met my father. He was killed in a car wreck on a rainy road three months before I was born . . . After that my mother had to support us . . . My mother taught me. She

[5]For a discussion of the political beliefs of Americans, see Harry Holloway and John George, *Public Opinion* (New York: St. Martin's, 1986). See also Paul R. Abramson, *Political Attitudes in America* (San Francisco: W. H. Freeman, 1983).

taught me about family and hard work and sacrifice . . . We must have a government that expands opportunity . . . We offer our people a new choice based on old values. We offer opportunity . . . Old fashioned Americans for a new time. Opportunity. Responsibility. Community.

Dole, for his part, proclaimed,

And the guiding light of my administration will be that in this country we have no rank order by birth, no claim to favoritism by race, no expectation of judgment other than it be evenhanded. We cannot guarantee the outcome, but we shall guarantee the opportunity.

Thus, however much the two candidates differed on means and specifics, their understandings of the fundamental goals of government were quite similar.

Agreement on fundamental political values, though certainly not absolute, is probably more widespread in the United States than anywhere else in the Western world. During the course of Western political history, competing economic, social, and political groups put forward a variety of radically divergent views, opinions, and political philosophies. America was never socially or economically homogeneous. But two forces that were extremely powerful and important sources of ideas and beliefs elsewhere in the world were relatively weak or absent in the United States. First, the United States never had the feudal aristocracy that dominated so much of European history. Second, for reasons including America's prosperity and the early availability of political rights, no Socialist movements comparable to those that developed in nineteenth-century Europe were ever able to establish themselves in the United States. As a result, during the course of American history, there existed neither an aristocracy to assert the virtues of inequality, special privilege, and a rigid class structure, nor a powerful American Communist or Socialist party to seriously challenge the desirability of limited government and individualism.[6]

**Agreement and Disagreement on Issues** Agreement on fundamentals, however, by no means implies that Americans do not differ with one another on a wide variety of issues. American political life is characterized by vigorous debate on economic, foreign policy, and social policy issues; race relations; environmental affairs; and a host of other matters. At times, even in America, disagreement on issues becomes so sharp that the proponents of particular points of view have sought to stifle political debate by declaring their opponents' positions to be too repulsive to be legitimately discussed. During the 1950s, for example, some ultraconservatives sought to outlaw the expression of opinions they deemed to be "communistic." Often this label was applied to what were essentially liberal views as a way of discrediting them. In the 1990s, some groups have sought to discredit conservatives by accusing them of racism, sexism, and homophobia when their views have not agreed with prevailing liberal sentiments. On a number of university campuses, some African American and feminist groups have advocated the

[6]See Louis Hartz, *The Liberal Tradition in America* (New York: Harcourt, Brace, 1955).

adoption of speech codes outlawing expression seen as insulting to individuals on the basis of their race or gender. In general, however, efforts to regulate the expression of opinion in this way have not been very successful in the United States. Americans believe strongly in free speech and prefer the hidden regulatory hand of the market to the heavier regulatory hand of the law. Many of the universities that initially adopted speech codes have been forced to rescind them.[7]

Differences of political opinion are often associated with such variables as income, education, and occupation. Similarly, factors such as race, gender, ethnicity, age, religion, and region, which not only influence individuals' interests but also shape their experiences and upbringing, have enormous influence upon their beliefs and opinions. For example, individuals whose incomes differ substantially have rather different views on the desirability of a number of important economic and social programs. In general, the poor—who are the chief beneficiaries of these programs—support them more strongly than do those whose taxes pay for the programs. Similarly, blacks and whites have different views on questions of civil rights such as affirmative action—presumably reflecting differences of interest and historical experience. In recent years, many observers have begun to take note of a number of differences between the views expressed by men and those supported by women, especially on foreign policy questions, where women appear to be much more concerned with the dangers of war, and on social welfare issues, where women show more concern than men for the problems of the poor and unfortunate. Quite conceivably these differences—known collectively as the ***"gender gap"***—reflect the results of differences in the childhood experiences and socialization of men and women in America.

To say that individuals' opinions are related to their economic interests or social characteristics, however, is not to say that it is always easy or even possible to predict opinions from these factors. The views of "the rich," "women," or "young people" are hardly fixed and immutable attributes of these groups, but instead depend upon and often change as the interests and experiences of these groups interact with changing economic, social, and political realities.

**Liberalism and Conservatism** As we have seen, people's beliefs about government can vary widely. But for some individuals, this set of beliefs can fit together into a coherent philosophy about government. This set of underlying orientations, ideas, and beliefs through which we come to understand and interpret politics is called a political ideology. Ideologies take many different forms. Some people may view politics primarily in religious terms. During the course of European political history, for example, Protestantism and Catholicism were often political ideologies as much as they were religious creeds. Each set of beliefs not only included elements of religious practice but also involved ideas about secular authority and political action. Other people may see politics through racial lenses. Nazism was a political ideology that placed race at the center of political life and sought to interpret politics in terms of racial categories.

[7]Ben Gose, "Penn to Replace Controversial Speech Code; Will No Longer Punish Students for Insults," *Chronicle of Higher Education,* 29 June 1994, p. A30.

In America today, people often describe themselves as liberals or conservatives. Liberalism and conservatism are political ideologies that include beliefs about the role of the government, ideas about public policies, and notions about which groups in society should properly exercise power. Historically these terms were defined somewhat differently than they are today. As recently as the nineteenth century, a liberal was an individual who favored freedom from state control, while a conservative was someone who supported the use of governmental power and favored continuation of the influence of church and aristocracy in national life.

Today, the term ***liberal*** has come to imply support for political and social reform; support for extensive governmental intervention in the economy; the expansion of federal social services; more vigorous efforts on behalf of the poor, minorities, and women; and greater concern for consumers and the environment. In social and cultural areas, liberals generally support abortion rights, are concerned with the rights of persons accused of crimes, support decriminalization of drug use, and oppose state involvement with religious institutions and religious expression. In international affairs, liberal positions are usually seen as including support for arms control, opposition to the development and testing of nuclear weapons, support for aid to poor nations, opposition to the use of American troops to influence the domestic affairs of developing nations, and support for international organizations such as the United Nations.

By contrast, the term ***conservative*** today is used to describe those who generally support the social and economic status quo and are suspicious of efforts to introduce new political formulae and economic arrangements. Conservatives believe strongly that a large and powerful government poses a threat to citizens' freedom. Thus, in the domestic arena, conservatives generally oppose the expansion of governmental activity, asserting that solutions to social and economic problems can be developed in the private sector. Conservatives particularly oppose efforts to impose government regulation on business, pointing out that such regulation is frequently economically inefficient and costly and can ultimately lower the entire nation's standard of living. As to social and cultural positions, many conservatives oppose abortion, support school prayer, are more concerned for the victims than the perpetrators of crimes, and support traditional family arrangements. In international affairs, conservatism has come to mean support for the maintenance of American military power.

Often political observers search for logical connections among the various positions identified with liberalism or with conservatism, and they are disappointed or puzzled when they are unable to find a set of coherent philosophical principles that define and unite the several elements of either of these sets of beliefs. On the liberal side, for example, what is the logical connection between opposition to U.S. government intervention in the affairs of foreign nations and calls for greater intervention in America's economy and society? On the conservative side, what is the logical relationship between opposition to governmental regulation of business and support for a ban on abortion? Indeed, the latter would seem to be just the sort of regulation of private conduct that conservatives claim to abhor.

GLOBALIZATION AND DEMOCRACY

## *The International Marketplace of Ideas*

The world is rapidly shrinking and merging. A three-minute telephone call from New York to London that cost $30 in 1970 only costs 36 cents in 1999. Airfares have fallen nearly as dramatically, resulting in international travel rates never even imagined a generation ago. The Internet provides a global web of information and communication, allowing a person in Georgia to read same-day English- and Spanish-language newspapers for free and to communicate with a friend in Mali via e-mail. And the media is now transnational, with CNN beamed to much of the world. Our experiences and the information we receive help to shape public opinion. As those experiences and sources of information become more international, will public opinion become globalized?

Evidence suggests that Americans remain exceptionally provincial and immune to global influences on public opinion. Indeed, even as the world is shrinking, Americans care less and less about global events. According to Gallup poll reports, only 5 percent of U.S. citizens closely followed the debate on NATO enlargement,

[1]From a 1997 Pew Research Center for The People & The Press (available at http://www.peoplepress.org/nov97rpt.htm).

Frequently, the relationships among the various elements of liberalism or the several aspects of conservatism are *political* rather then *logical.* One underlying basis of liberal views is that all or most represent criticisms of or attacks on the foreign and domestic policies and cultural values of the business and commercial strata that have been prominent in the United States for the past century. In some measure, the tenets of contemporary conservatism represent this elite's de-

which is one of the most important international developments facing our world. The environment and global warming are major international issues, yet fewer Americans worry about the greenhouse effect today (25 percent) than they did in 1990 (30 percent ).[1] And poll numbers reveal that the vast majority of Americans are uninformed and indifferent when it comes to ethnic atrocities in East Timor, economic collapse in Russia, and U.S. trade issues in Latin America. The only international events that strongly shape American public opinion are those where U.S. citizens are adversely affected, such as the killing of American soldiers in Somalia in 1993 or major international conflicts such as Operation Desert Storm.

> Worry about foreign policy, international relations or war is almost totally missing from the forefront of American concerns today. This stands in sharp contrast to many other periods since World War II when foreign policy issues dominated the public's responses to this most important problems question.[2]

There are several reasons for a lack of interest in global issues. The end of the Communist threat has greatly reduced security concerns. An unprecedented expansion of the U.S. economy has led to both apathy for world economic crises and a declining interest in potentially explosive issues such as immigration, or the relocation of manufacturers such as Levi-Strauss from the United States to the Third World. International news stories are less frequently aired on the network news, and Americans, especially the young, watch less national news. The belief in U.S. exceptionalism makes Americans loathe to reassess their opinions on such issues as the death penalty or gun ownership just because the rest of the world holds different opinions.

While global events and opinion have not strongly altered U.S. public opinion, America shapes public opinion abroad in a variety of ways. Hollywood movies and popular television show such as *Baywatch* create fads and expectations in Tegucigalpa and Manila. CNN beams American news and opinion around the world. And American political operatives are exporting American-style political campaigns to much of the Western world. In 1999, former Clinton campaign manager James Carville advised presidential candidates in Argentina and Israel, and former Clinton advisor Dick Morris used modern polling and negative campaigning in the 1998 Honduran presidential elections. It appears that globalization is spreading U.S. values and opinions to the rest of the world much faster than it is bringing global opinion into the United States.

[2]Frank Newport, "No Single Problem Dominates Americans' Concerns Today," *Gallup Poll Archive* (2 May 1998).

fense of its positions against its enemies, who include organized labor, minority groups, and some intellectuals and professionals. Thus, liberals attack business and commercial elites by advocating more governmental regulation, including consumer protection and environmental regulation, opposition to military weapons programs, and support for expensive social programs. Conservatives counterattack by asserting that governmental regulation of the economy is ruinous, and that military weapons are needed in a changing world, and they seek to stigmatize their opponents for showing no concern for the rights of "unborn" Americans.

Of course, it is important to note that many people who call themselves liberals or conservatives accept only part of the liberal or conservative ideology. During the 1980s, many political commentators asserted that Americans were becoming increasingly conservative. Indeed, it was partly in response to this view that the Democrats in 1992 selected a presidential candidate (Bill Clinton) drawn from the party's moderate wing. Although it appears that Americans have adopted more conservative outlooks on some issues, their views in other areas have remained largely unchanged or even have become more liberal in recent years (see Table 9.1). Thus, many individuals who are liberal on social issues are conservative on economic issues. There is certainly nothing illogical about these mixed positions. They simply indicate the relatively open and fluid character of American political debate.

The idea market thus has created a common ground for Americans in which discussion of issues is encouraged and based on common understandings. Despite the many and often sharp divisions that exist—between liberals and conservatives, different income groups, different regional groups—most Americans see the world through similar lenses.

TABLE 9.1

**Have Americans Become More Conservative?**

| | 1972 | 1978 | 1980 | 1982 | 1984 | 1986 | 1988 | 1992 | 1996 |
|---|---|---|---|---|---|---|---|---|---|
| Percentage responding "yes" to the following questions: | | | | | | | | | |
| Should the government help minority groups? | 30% | 25% | 16% | 21% | 27% | 26% | 13% | 27% | 18% |
| Should the government see to it that everyone has a job and a guaranteed standard of living? | 27 | 17 | 22 | 25 | 28 | 25 | 24 | 30 | 24 |
| Should abortion never be permitted? | 9 | 10 | 8 | 13 | 13 | 13 | 12 | 12 | 13 |
| Should the government provide fewer services and reduce spending? | NA | NA | 27 | 32 | 28 | 24 | 25 | 33 | 31 |

NA = Not asked

SOURCE: Center for Political Studies of the Institute for Social Research, University of Michigan. Data were made available through the Inter-University Consortium for Political and Social Research.

## How Are Political Opinions Formed?

An individual's opinions on particular issues, events, and personalities emerge as he or she evaluates these phenomena through the lenses of the beliefs and orientations that, taken together, comprise his or her political ideology. Thus, if a conservative is confronted with a plan to expand federal social programs, he or she is likely to express opposition to the endeavor without spending too much time pondering the specific plan. Similarly, if a liberal is asked to comment on former president Ronald Reagan, he or she is not likely to hesitate long before offering a negative view. Underlying beliefs and ideologies tend to automatically color people's perceptions and opinions about politics.

Opinions on particular issues, however, are seldom fully shaped by underlying ideologies. Few individuals possess ideologies so cohesive and intensely held that they will automatically shape all their opinions. Indeed, when we occasionally encounter individuals with rigid worldviews, who see everything through a particular political lens, we tend to dismiss them as "ideologies," or lacking common sense.

Although ideologies color our political perspectives, they seldom fully determine our views. This is true for a variety of reasons. First, as noted earlier, most individuals' ideologies contain internal contradictions. Take, for example, a conservative view of the issue of abortion. Should conservatives favor outlawing abortion as an appropriate means of preserving public morality, or should they oppose restrictions on abortion because these represent government intrusions into private life? In this instance, as in many others, ideology can point in different directions.

Second, individuals may have difficulty linking particular issues or personalities to their own underlying beliefs. Some issues defy ideological characterizations. Should conservatives support or oppose the proposed elimination of the Department of Commerce? What should liberals think about America's 1999 bombing of Serbia? Each of these policies combines a mix of issues and is too complex to be viewed through simple ideological lenses.

Finally, most people have at least some conflicting underlying attitudes. Most conservatives support *some* federal programs—defense, or tax deductions for businesses, for example—and wish to see them, and hence the government, expanded. Many liberals favor American military intervention in other nations for what they deem to be humanitarian purposes, but generally oppose American military intervention in the affairs of other nations.

Thus, most individuals' attitudes on particular issues do not spring automatically from their ideological predispositions. It is true that most people have underlying beliefs that help to shape their opinions on particular issues, but two other factors are also important: a person's knowledge of political issues, and outside influences on that person's views.

**Political Knowledge** As we have seen, general political beliefs can guide the formation of opinions on specific issues, but an individual's beliefs and opinions are not always consistent with one another. Studies of political opinion have shown that most people don't hold specific and clearly defined opinions on every political issue. As a result, they are easily influenced by others. What best explains whether citizens are generally consistent in their political views or inconsistent and open to the influence of others? The key is knowledge and information about political issues. In general, knowledgeable citizens are better able to evaluate new information and determine whether it is relevant to and consistent with their beliefs and opinions. As a result, better-informed individuals can recognize their political interests and act consistently on behalf of them.

One of the most obvious and important examples of this proposition is voting. Despite the predisposition of voters to support their own party's candidates (see Chapter 11 for a discussion of party identification), millions of voters are affected by the information they receive about candidates during a campaign. During the 1996 presidential campaign, for instance, voters weighed the arguments of Bill Clinton against those of Bob Dole about who was better fit to run the U.S. economy based on what they (the voters) knew about the country's economic health. Many Republican voters actually supported Bill Clinton because they approved of the economic policies followed during his first term in office. Thus citizens can use information and judgment to overcome their predispositions. Without some political knowledge, citizens would have a difficult time making sense of the complex political world in which they live.

This point brings up two questions, however. First, how much political knowledge is necessary to act as an effective citizen? And second, how is political knowledge distributed throughout the population? In a recent study of political knowledge in the United States, political scientists Michael X. Delli Carpini and Scott Keeter found that the average American exhibits little knowledge of political institutions, processes, leaders, and policy debates. For example, in a 1996 poll, only about half of all Americans could correctly identify Newt Gingrich, who was then the Speaker of the House of Representatives.[8] Does this ignorance of key political facts matter?

Another important concern is the character of those who possess and act upon the political information that they acquire. Political knowledge is not evenly distributed throughout the population. Those with higher education, income, and occupational status and who are members of social or political organizations are more likely to know about and be active in politics. An interest in politics reinforces an individual's sense of political efficacy and provides more incentive to acquire additional knowledge and information about politics. Those who don't think they can have an effect on government tend not to be interested in learning about or participating in politics. As a result, individuals with a disproportionate share of income and education also have a disproportionate share of knowledge and influence and are better able to get what they want from government.

[8]Michael X. Delli Carpini and Scott Keeter, *What Americans Know about Politics and Why It Matters* (New Haven: Yale University Press, 1996).

**The Influence of Political Leaders, Private Groups, and the Media** When individuals attempt to form opinions about particular political issues, events, and personalities, they seldom do so in isolation. Typically, they are confronted—sometimes bombarded—by the efforts of a host of individuals and groups seeking to persuade them to adopt a particular point of view. Someone trying to decide what to think about Bill Clinton, Ken Starr, or Al Gore could hardly avoid an avalanche of opinions expressed through the media, in meetings, or in conversations with friends. Given constant exposure to the ideas of others, it is virtually impossible for most individuals to resist some modification of their own beliefs. For example, as we saw earlier, African Americans and white Americans disagree on a number of matters. Yet, as political scientists Paul Sniderman and Edward Carmines have shown, considerable cross-racial agreement has evolved on fundamental issues of race and civil rights.[9] Thus, to some extent, public opinion is subject to deliberate shaping and manipulation.

# Shaping Public Opinion

Public opinion is not some disembodied entity that stands alone and unalterable. Opinion can often be molded, shaped, or manipulated. In many areas of the world, governments determine which opinions their citizens may or may not express. People who assert views that their rulers do not approve of may be subject to imprisonment—or worse. Americans and the citizens of the other Western democracies are fortunate to live in nations where freedom of opinion and expression are generally taken for granted.

Even with freedom of opinion, however, not all ideas and opinions flourish. Both private groups and the government itself attempt to influence which opinions do take hold in the public imagination. We will first examine how government seeks to shape values that in turn influence public opinion. Then we will discuss the marketing of political issues, by the government, and by private groups, and by the media.

## Enlisting Public Support for Government

All governments attempt to shape or structure citizens' underlying beliefs about the regime, the social and economic structure, and the political process. Governments seek to imbue their citizens with positive feelings toward the established order through the creation of a national ethos, the promotion of property ownership, education, and the opportunity to participate in national politics. Nationalism, property ownership, education, and political participation can be labeled "deadly virtues." These may be forces for good if they help to create a unified and public-spirited citizenry, or forces for evil if they are merely used as instruments of control.

[9]Paul M. Sniderman and Edward G. Carmines, *Reaching Beyond Race* (Cambridge: Harvard University Press, 1997), Chapter 4.

AMERICAN POLITICAL DEVELOPMENT

At the time of the American founding, many people thought of America as "their nation," and some had a nationalist affinity to a "United States." Others, however, thought of their states as their nation. For example, Patrick Henry referred to Virginia as his "nation." Ultimately, the nationalist sentiments that the Antifederalists held posed challenges to centralization under the Constitution.

SOURCE: Herbert J. Storing, *What the Anti-Federalists Were For* (Chicago: University of Chicago Press, 1981), p. 86, n. 4.

**Nationalism** ***Nationalism*** is the belief that people who occupy the same territory have something important in common, making them separate from and superior to other people. It is based on myths about the origin and history of the people, their exploits and sufferings as a nation, their heroes, and their mission in the world. Such myths are not necessarily falsehoods. They are simply beliefs that are accepted whether they are true or false.

Nationalism takes root in family, community, and tribal loyalties, but it is strong enough to displace those local ties in favor of the nation. The great virtue of nationalism is precisely that it gives individuals something far larger than themselves with which to identify. It brings out nobility in people, calling on them to sacrifice something of themselves—perhaps even their lives—for their society. Nationalism helps weave the social fabric together with a minimum of coercion.

Nationalism also has a darker side, however. Since it encourages pride in one's own country, it can also produce distrust and hatred of others. This tendency is often encouraged by rulers as a means of whipping up support for a war or other international adventures. There will always be conflicts among nations, but these conflicts are much more likely to escalate toward full-scale war when each country is backed by strong national myths. The paramount example of the misuse of nationalism is the case of Nazi Germany, where nationalistic sentiment was perverted to justify aggression and murder on an unprecedented scale.

**Private Property** Property ownership is probably a less universal factor in the manipulation of belief than nationalism but that makes it no less important. Governments regard widespread property ownership to be a good, conservative force in society because it discourages disorder and revolution. The citizen who owns property has a stake in the existing order—a piece of the rock—which he or she will seek to protect.

Many important American leaders have dreamed of creating the ideal polity—political system—around property ownership. Thomas Jefferson, for example, believed that the American Republic ought to be composed of a population of farmers, each with enough property to appreciate social order and to oppose excessive wealth and power. Although the United States did not become a republic of farmers, this idea was certainly behind the federal government's nineteenth-century policy of giving millions of acres of land from the public treasury to persons who were willing to settle and improve it. ***Homesteading,*** or squatting, was the name for this method of gaining property ownership. It was justified—indeed encouraged—by the government in large part as a means of giving people a stake in their country.

Mass industrialization has expanded the meaning of property, but its value has not weakened. For most people, property is no longer a plot of land but instead is a mortgage on a house or a stock certificate that indicates ownership of a tiny proportion of some large corporation.

**Education** In the United States, education is a multi-billion-dollar investment. Few people question the need for the investment because it promises to yield people with high-level skills, problem-solving capacity, and high productivity, along with a significant amount of social mobility. This is not to say that a formal education has helped every American child realize the ideal of success. But it does mean that education has made it possible for most children in America to join the work force.

Formal schooling goes beyond skills and training, however. Schools shape values as well. Harry L. Gracey has described school as "academic boot camp." He meant that beginning as early as kindergarten students learn "to go through the routines and to follow orders with unquestioning obedience, even when these make no sense to them. They learn to tolerate and even to prosper in the bureaucratized environment of school, and this is preparation for their later life."[10]

French sociologist Émile Durkheim (1858–1917) said essentially the same thing when he observed matter-of-factly that education "consists of a methodical socialization of the younger generation" and that the education process "is above all the means by which society perpetually recreates the conditions of its very existence."[11] This is usually done at the state and local government levels, where most educational policies in the United States are formulated. The schools themselves are capable of adjusting their curricula to the occupational needs of their region.

**Participation and Cooptation** To participate is to share, or to take part in. It is an association with others, usually for the purpose of taking joint action and is essential for any kind of democratic government. Even representation is not enough unless there is widespread participation in the choice of representatives. Virtually all political leaders endorse some types of participation, particularly voting.

Participation is an instrument of governance because it encourages people to give their consent to being governed (see also Chapter 1). A broad and popularly based process of local consultation, discussion, town meetings, and secret ballots may actually produce a sense of the will of the people. But even when it does not produce a clear sense of that will, the purpose of participation is nonetheless fulfilled because the process itself produces consent. Deeply embedded in people's sense of fair play is the principle that those who play the game must accept the outcome. Those who participate in politics are similarly committed, even if they are consistently on the losing side. Why do politicians plead with everyone to get out and vote? Because voting is the simplest and easiest form of participation by masses of people. Even though it is minimal participation, it is sufficient to commit all

[10]Harry L. Gracey, "Learning the Student Role: Kindergarten as Academic Boot Camp," in *The Quality of Life in America,* ed. A. David Hill (New York: Holt, 1973), p. 261.

[11]Émile Durkheim, *Education and Sociology,* trans. Sherwood D. Fox (Glencoe, IL: Free Press, 1956), p. 71.

voters to being governed, regardless of who wins. (Voting will be discussed in more detail in Chapter 10.)

There are many examples in recent American history of the use of participation to generate more favorable popular beliefs about the government. It is no coincidence, for example, that youths between the ages of eighteen and twenty-one were given the right to vote in the late 1960s just at a time when they were already participating at almost historic levels. Young people were politically active, but they were not participating in the conventional forms, and they were protesting against established authority. Congress and the state legislatures, therefore, ratified the Twenty-sixth Amendment in 1971, giving eighteen-year-olds the right to vote. The vote was used to placate young Americans, to provide them with a conventional channel of participation, and to justify suppressing their disorderly activities. The following testimony by the late Senator Jacob Javits of New York is one example of the motivation behind the voting rights amendment:

> We all realize that only a tiny minority of college students on these campuses engaged in unlawful acts. But these deplorable incidents make a point. . . . I am convinced that self-styled student leaders who urged such acts of civil disobedience would find themselves with little or no support if students were given a more meaningful role in the political process. Passage of the [Twenty-sixth Amendment] . . . would give us the means, sort of the famous carrot and the stick, to channel this energy.[12]

The most familiar examples of cooptation through participation are the efforts of political leaders to balance their electoral tickets and their political appointments. Political party leaders in city, state, and national campaigns try their best to select candidates for public office who "represent" each of the important minorities in their constituency. This effort involves balancing ethnic, religious, and regional groups, as well as men and women and any other segments of the constituency. African American, Hispanic American, and women's movement leaders study presidential appointments with considerable interest. They do this not so much because an additional black or Hispanic or female representative would give them much more power but because such appointments are a measure of their current worth in national politics.

Nationalism, property ownership, education, and participation are used by all governments to bolster popular support for leaders and their policies. Through these four mechanisms, governments seek to give their citizens a more generally positive orientation toward the political and social order, regardless of their attitudes toward specific programs. Through these techniques, governments hope to convince their citizens voluntarily to obey laws, pay taxes, and serve in the armed forces. Many social scientists believe that if popular support falls below some minimum level, the result could be chaos or even some form of rebellion. This fear was especially manifest during the 1960s and 1970s when diminished levels of popular support did indeed coincide with increases in political violence and unrest. Trust in

[12]U.S. Senate, Committee on the Judiciary, *Hearings before the Subcommittee on Constitutional Amendments on S.J. Res. 8, S.J. Res. 14, and S.J. Res. 78 Relating to Lowering the Voting Age to 18,* 14, 15, and 16 May 1968 (Washington DC: Government Printing Office, 1968), p. 12.

FIGURE 9.2

**Trust in Government**

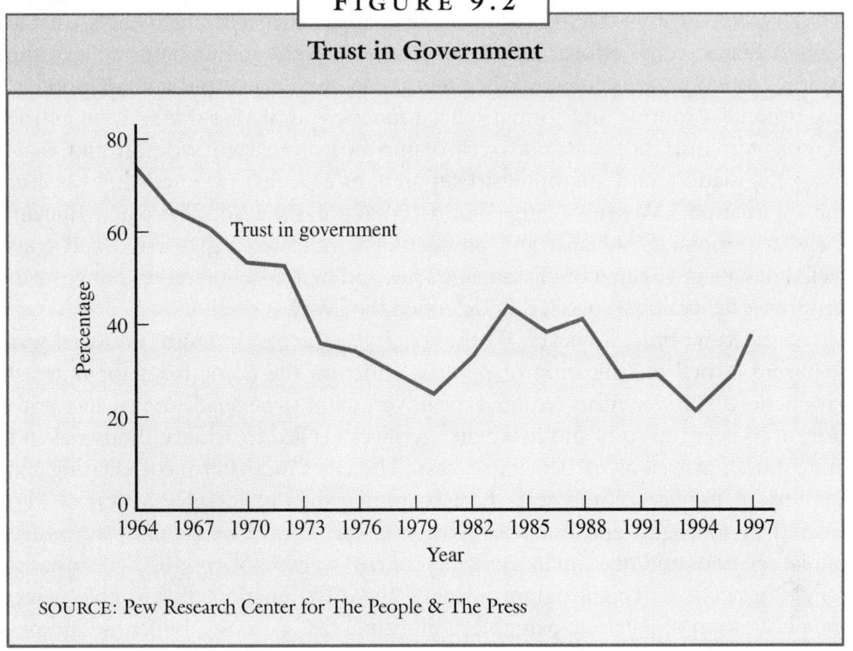


SOURCE: Pew Research Center for The People & The Press

government edged up slightly during the 1980s, dropped again in the early 1990s, and rose during the mid- and late 1990s (see Figure 9.2).

## Marketing Political Issues

Beyond these broad efforts by the government to shape popular attachments to the political regime, both the government and private groups attempt to muster support for different political ideas and programs. Both use public relations to enlist support and shape opinion.

Few ideas spread spontaneously. Usually, whether they are matters of fashion, science, or politics, ideas must be vigorously promoted to become widely known and accepted. For example, the clothing, sports, and entertainment fads that occasionally seem to appear from nowhere and sweep the country before being replaced by some other new trend are almost always the product of careful marketing campaigns by one or another commercial interest, rather than spontaneous phenomena. Even in the sciences, generally considered *the* bastions of objectivity, new theories, procedures, and findings are not always accepted simply and immediately on their own merit. Often, the proponents of a new scientific principle or practice must campaign within the scientific community on behalf of their views. Like their counterparts in fashion and science, successful—or at least widely held—political ideas are usually the products of carefully orchestrated campaigns by government or by organized groups and interests, rather than the results of spontaneous popular enthusiasm.

**Government Management of Issues** All governments attempt, to a greater or lesser extent, to influence, manipulate, or manage their citizens' beliefs. In the United States, some efforts have been made by every administration since the nation's founding to influence public sentiment. But efforts to shape opinion did not become a routine and formal official function until World War I, when the Wilson administration created a censorship board, enacted sedition and espionage legislation, and attempted to suppress groups that opposed the war, like the International Workers of the World (IWW) and the Socialist party. Eugene Debs, a prominent Socialist and presidential candidate, was arrested and convicted of having violated the Espionage Law, and he was sentenced to ten years in prison for delivering a speech that defended the IWW.

At the same time, however, World War I was the first modern industrial war requiring a total mobilization of popular effort on the home front for military production. The war effort required the government to persuade the civilian population to bear the costs and make the sacrifices needed to achieve industrial and agricultural, as well as battlefield, success. The chief mechanism for eliciting the support of public opinion was the Committee on Public Information (CPI), chaired by journalist and publicist George Creel. The CPI organized a massive public relations and news management program to promote popular enthusiasm for the war effort. This program included the dissemination of favorable news, the publication of patriotic pamphlets, films, photos, cartoons, bulletins, and periodicals, and the organization of "war expositions" and speakers' tours. Special labor programs were aimed at maintaining the loyalty and productivity of the workforce. Many of the CPI's staff were drawn from the major public relations firms of the time.[13]

The extent to which public opinion is actually affected by governmental public relations efforts is probably limited. The government—despite its size and power—is only one source of information and evaluation in the United States. Very often, governmental claims are disputed by the media, by interest groups, and at times, by opposing forces within the government itself. Often, too, governmental efforts to manipulate public opinion backfire when the public is made aware of the government's tactics. Thus, in 1971, the United States government's efforts to build popular support for the Vietnam War were hurt when CBS News aired its documentary "The Selling of the Pentagon," which purported to reveal the extent and character of governmental efforts to sway popular sentiment. In this documentary, CBS demonstrated the techniques, including planted news stories and faked film footage, that the government had used to misrepresent its activities in Vietnam. These revelations, of course, had the effect of undermining popular trust in all governmental claims. During the 1991 Persian Gulf War, the U.S. military was much more careful about the accuracy of its assertions.

**AMERICAN POLITICAL DEVELOPMENT**

Early examples of private groups shaping perceptions of public opinion occurred in the 1820s, when industrialists tried to demonstrate public support for increased tariffs by "turning out their work force for mass meetings."

SOURCE: Thomas Ferguson, *Golden Rule: The Investment Theory of Party Competition and the Logic of Money-Driven Political Systems* (Chicago: University of Chicago Press, 1995), p. 56.

[13]See George Creel, *How We Advertised America* (New York: Harper and Brothers, 1920).

A hallmark of the Clinton administration was the steady use of techniques like those used in election campaigns to bolster popular enthusiasm for White House initiatives. The president established a "political war room" in the Executive Office Building similar to the one that operated in his campaign headquarters. Representatives from all departments meet in the war room every day to discuss and coordinate the president's public relations efforts. Many of the same consultants and pollsters who directed the successful Clinton campaign were employed in the selling of the president's programs.[14]

Indeed, the Clinton White House has made more sustained and systematic use of public-opinion polling than any previous administration. For example, during his presidency Bill Clinton has relied heavily on the polling firm of Penn & Schoen to help him decide which issues to emphasize and what strategies to adopt. During the 1995–1996 budget battle with Congress, the White House commissioned polls almost every night to chart changes in public perceptions about the struggle. Poll data suggested to Clinton that he should present himself as struggling to save Medicare from Republican cuts. Clinton responded by launching a media attack against what he claimed were GOP efforts to hurt the elderly. This proved to be a successful strategy and helped Clinton defeat the Republican budget.[15] The administration, however, has asserted that it uses polls only as a check on its communications strategy.[16]

Evidence exists to back up the assertions of the Clinton White House. The political scientists Robert Shapiro and Lawrence Jacobs studied how polls are used by politicians and discovered that the ideology of political leaders, not public opinion, was the decisive influence on the formulation of a policy. They also found that the primary use of polling was to choose the language, rhetoric, and arguments for policy proposals in order to build the public's support.[17] However, according to former Clinton advisor Dick Morris, the president met every week with key aides to examine poll data and devise strategies to bolster his popularity.[18] For example, in April 1996, the administration's polls showed that an initiative to crack down on "deadbeat dads" who failed to pay child support would be popular. Several weeks later, the president announced new regulations requiring states to take more aggressive action to compel payment. Similarly, in July 1996, Clinton signed the Republican-sponsored welfare reform bill which he had previously opposed, when polls indicated that he would gain 8 points in the polls if he signed the bill.[19]

Of course, at the same time that the Clinton administration has worked diligently to mobilize popular support, its opponents have struggled equally hard to

[14]Gerald F. Seib and Michael K. Frisby, "Selling Sacrifice," *Wall Street Journal,* 5 February 1993, p. 1.

[15]Michael K. Frisby, "Clinton Seeks Strategic Edge with Opinion Polls," *Wall Street Journal,* 24 June 1996, p. A16.

[16]James Carney, "Playing by the Numbers," *Time,* 11 April 1994, p. 40.

[17]Reported in Richard Morin, "Which Comes First, the Politician or the Poll?" *Washington Post National Weekly Edition,* 10 February 1997, p. 31.

[18]John F. Harris, "New Morris Book Portrays How Polls, Clinton, Intersected," *Washington Post,* 22 December 1998, p. A18.

[19]Dick Morris, *Behind the Oval Office* (New York: Renaissance, 1998).

mobilize popular opinion against the White House. A host of public and private interest groups opposed to President Clinton's programs crafted public relations campaigns designed to generate opposition to the president. For example, in 1994, while Clinton campaigned to bolster popular support for his health care reform proposals, groups representing small business and segments of the insurance industry, among others, developed their own publicity campaigns that ultimately convinced many Americans that Clinton's initiative posed a threat to their own health care. These opposition campaigns played an important role in the eventual defeat of the president's proposal.

Often, claims and counterclaims by the government and its opponents are aimed chiefly at elites and opinion makers rather than directly at the public. For example, many of the television ads about the health care debate were aired primarily in and around Washington and New York City, where they were more likely to be seen by persons influential in politics, business, and the media. The presumption behind this strategy is that such individuals are likely to be the key decision makers on most issues. Political, business, and media elites are also seen as "opinion leaders" who have the capacity to sway the views of larger segments of the public. Thus both the president and his foes campaigned especially vigorously in Washington, New York, and a small number of other major metropolitan areas in their 1994 struggle over health care reform.[20]

**Private Groups and the Shaping of Public Opinion** Political issues and ideas seldom emerge spontaneously from the grass roots. We have already seen how the government tries to shape public opinion. But the ideas that become prominent in political life are also developed and spread by important economic and political groups searching for issues that will advance their causes. One example is the "right-to-life" issue that has inflamed American politics over the past twenty years.

The notion of right-to-life, whose proponents seek to outlaw abortion and overturn the Supreme Court's *Roe v. Wade* decision, was developed and heavily promoted by conservative politicians who saw the issue of abortion as a means of uniting Catholic and Protestant conservatives and linking both groups to the Republican coalition. These politicians convinced Catholic and evangelical Protestant leaders that they shared similar views on the question of abortion, and they worked with religious leaders to focus public attention on the negative issues in the abortion debate. To advance their cause, leaders of the movement sponsored well-publicized Senate hearings, where testimony, photographs, and other exhibits were presented to illustrate the violent effects of abortion procedures. At the same time, publicists for the movement produced leaflets, articles, books, and films such as *The Silent Scream*, to highlight the agony and pain ostensibly felt by the unborn when they were being aborted. All this underscored the movement's claim that abortion was nothing more or less than the murder of millions of innocent human beings. Finally, Catholic and evangelical Protestant religious leaders were organized to denounce abortion from their church pulpits and increasingly, from their electronic pulpits on the Christian Broadcasting Network

[20]David Broder, "White House Takes on Harry and Louise," *Washington Post,* 8 July 1994, p. A11.

(CBN) and the various other television forums available for religious programming. Religious leaders also organized demonstrations, pickets, and disruptions at abortion clinics throughout the nation.[21] Abortion rights remain a potent issue; it even influenced the health care reform debate.

Among President Clinton's most virulent critics have been leaders of the religious Right who were outraged by his support for abortion and gay rights. Conservative religious leaders like the Rev. Jerry Falwell and Pat Robertson, leader of the Christian Coalition, have used their television programs to attack the president's programs and to mount biting personal attacks on both Clinton and his wife, Hillary Rodham Clinton. Other conservative groups not associated with the religious Right have also launched sharp assaults against the president. The nationally syndicated talk-show host Rush Limbaugh, for one, is a constant critic of the administration. All these leaders and groups strongly supported President Clinton's impeachment in 1998 and 1999. Despite their efforts, however, they were unable to convince a majority of Americans that the president should be removed from office.

Typically, ideas are marketed most effectively by groups with access to financial resources, public or private institutional support, and sufficient skill or education to select, develop, and draft ideas that will attract interest and support. Thus, the development and promotion of conservative themes and ideas in recent years has been greatly facilitated by the millions of dollars that conservative corporations and business organizations such as the Chamber of Commerce and the Public Affairs Council spend each year on public information and what is now called in corporate circles "issues management." In addition, conservative businessmen have contributed millions of dollars to such conservative institutions as the Heritage Foundation, the Hoover Institution, and the American Enterprise Institute.[22] Many of the ideas that helped those on the right influence political debate were first developed and articulated by scholars associated with institutions such as these. For example, in 1997, scholars associated with the conservative Hudson Institute developed the idea of organizing conservative Christians to protest the alleged mistreatment of Christians in the Third World, China, and the former Soviet Union. This issue, which gave rise to congressional legislation aimed at limiting American trade with nations deemed to mistreat Christians, provided a useful focus for political mobilization on the political Right.

Although they do not usually have access to financial assets that match those available to their conservative opponents, liberal intellectuals and professionals have ample organizational skills, access to the media, and practice in creating, communicating, and using ideas. During the past three decades, the chief vehicle through which liberal intellectuals and professionals have advanced their ideas has been the "public interest group," an institution that relies heavily upon voluntary contributions of time, effort, and interest on the part of its members. Through groups like Common Cause, the National Organization for Women, the Sierra

[21]See Gillian Peele, *Revival and Reaction* (Oxford, England: Clarendon Press, 1985). Also see Connie Paige, *The Right to Lifers* (New York: Summit, 1983).

[22]See David Vogel, "The Power of Business in America: A Reappraisal," *British Journal of Political Science* 13 (January 1983), pp. 19–44.

Club, Friends of the Earth, and Physicians for Social Responsibility, intellectuals and professionals have been able to use their organizational skills and educational resources to develop and promote ideas.[23] Often, research conducted in universities and in liberal "think tanks" like the Brookings Institution provides the ideas upon which liberal politicians rely. For example, the welfare reform plan introduced by the Clinton administration in 1994 originated with the work of Harvard professor David Ellwood. Ellwood's academic research led him to the idea that the nation's welfare system would be improved if services to the poor were expanded in scope, but limited in duration. His idea was adopted by the 1992 Clinton campaign, which was searching for a position on welfare that would appeal to both liberal and conservative Democrats. The Ellwood plan seemed perfect: It promised liberals an immediate expansion of welfare benefits, yet it held out to conservatives the idea that welfare recipients would receive benefits only for a limited period of time. The Clinton welfare reform plan even borrowed phrases from Ellwood's book *Poor Support.*[24]

Journalist and author Joe Queenan has correctly observed that although political ideas can erupt spontaneously, they almost never do. Instead,

> issues are usually manufactured by tenured professors and obscure employees of think tanks. . . . It is inconceivable that the American people, all by themselves, could independently arrive at the conclusion that the depletion of the ozone layer poses a dire threat to our national well-being, or that an immediate, across-the-board cut in the capital-gains tax is the only thing that stands between us and the economic abyss. The American people do not have that kind of sophistication. *They have to have help.*[25]

Whatever their particular ideology or interest, those groups that can muster the most substantial financial, institutional, educational, and organizational resources—or, as we shall see later, access to government power—are also best able to promote their ideas in the marketplace. Obviously, these resources are most readily available to upper-middle- and upper-class groups. As a result, their ideas and concerns are most likely to be discussed and disseminated by books, films, newspapers, magazines, and the electronic media. As we shall see in Chapter 13, upper-income groups dominate the marketplace of ideas, not only as producers and promoters, but also as consumers of ideas. In general, and particularly in the political realm, the print and broadcast media and the publishing industry are most responsive to the tastes and views of the more "upscale" segments of the potential audience.

[23]See David Vogel, "The Public Interest Movement and the American Reform Tradition," *Political Science Quarterly* 96 (Winter 1980), pp. 607–27.

[24]Jason DeParle, "The Clinton Welfare Bill Begins Trek in Congress," *New York Times,* 15 July 1994, p. 1.

[25]Joe Queenan, "Birth of a Notion," *Washington Post,* 20 September 1992, p. C1.

# MEASURING PUBLIC OPINION

As recently as fifty years ago, American political leaders gauged public opinion by people's applause or cheers and by the presence of crowds in meeting places. This direct exposure to the people's views did not necessarily produce accurate knowledge of public opinion. It did, however, give political leaders confidence in their public support—and therefore confidence in their ability to govern by consent.

Abraham Lincoln and Stephen Douglas debated each other seven times in the summer and autumn of 1858, two years before they became presidential nominees. Their debates took place before audiences in parched cornfields and courthouse squares. A century later, the presidential debates, although seen by millions, take place before a few reporters and technicians in television studios that might as well be on the moon. The public's response cannot be experienced directly. This distance between leaders and followers is one of the agonizing problems of modern democracy. The communication media send information to millions of people, but they are not yet as efficient at getting information back to leaders. Is government by consent possible where the scale of communication is so large and impersonal? In order to compensate for the decline in their ability to experience public opinion for themselves, leaders have turned to science, in particular to the science of opinion polling.

It is no secret that politicians and public officials make extensive use of public opinion polls to help them decide whether to run for office, what policies to support, how to vote on important legislation, and what types of appeals to make in their campaigns. President Lyndon Johnson was famous for carrying the latest Gallup and Roper poll results in his hip pocket, and it is widely believed that he began to withdraw from politics because the polls reported losses in public support. All recent presidents and other major political figures have worked closely with polls and pollsters. Yet, even the most scientific measurements of public opinion do not necessarily lighten the burden of ignorance.

**AMERICAN POLITICAL DEVELOPMENT**

Although the *Harrisburg Pennsylvania* published a preference poll on the presidential candidates Andrew Jackson and John Quincy Adams in 1824, early applications of scientific public opinion polling to the art of politics date to the 1930s. This method represented a crossover of business and advertising techniques to politics, and it transformed the ways in which the public could be included in political decision-making.

SOURCE: Robert E. Denton, Jr. and Gary C. Woodward, *Political Communications in America,* 2nd ed. (New York: Praeger, 1990), p. 61.

## Getting Public Opinion Directly from People

American politicians want rapport with the people; they want to mingle, to shake hands, to get the feel of the crowd. And where crowds are too large to experience directly, the substitutes also have to be more direct than those described up to this point.

Approaches to the direct measurement of public opinion can be divided conveniently into two types—the impressionistic and the scientific. The impressionistic approach can be subdivided into at least three methods—person-to-person, selective polling, and the use of bellwether districts. The scientific approach may take on several different forms, but they all amount to an effort to use random sampling techniques and established and psychologically validated survey questions.

**Person-to-Person** Politicians traditionally acquire knowledge about opinions through direct exposure to a few people's personal impressions—the person-to-person approach. They attempt to convert these impressions into reliable knowledge by intuition. When they are in doubt about first impressions, they seek further impressions from other people; but the individuals they rely on the most heavily are their friends and acquaintances. Presidents have usually relied on associates for political impressions. These few friends occupy an inner circle, and they give political advice after the experts and special leaders have finished.

The advantage of the person-to-person approach is that it is quick, efficient, and inexpensive. Its major disadvantage is that it can close off unpleasant information or limit the awareness of new issues. Franklin Roosevelt, for example, was one of the best-informed presidents, and yet, when he attempted to influence the Supreme Court by increasing the number of justices on it and when he attempted to punish some of the opposition leaders in Congress by opposing their renomination in local primaries, he was shocked by the degree of negative public reaction. His inner circle had simply lost touch with the post-1936 electorate.

President Nixon's downfall from the Watergate scandal has been attributed in part to the fact that he isolated himself in the White House and relied too heavily on a few close personal advisers. Consequently, it is argued, he was unaware first of the strength of his own position as he approached the 1972 re-election campaign and then of the extent to which his political position had deteriorated because of the scandal.

**AMERICAN POLITICAL DEVELOPMENT**

Whereas today nationalization of politics and public opinion polling allow for "getting public opinion directly from the people," in the nineteenth century and before, opinion "was a property of . . . groups and classes." World War I represents a pivotal point, when government took on the role of a "manager" of public opinion.

SOURCE: Benjamin Ginsberg, *The Captive Public: How Mass Opinion Promotes State Power* (New York: Basic Books, 1986).

**Selective Polling** When politicians lack confidence in their own intuition or that of their immediate associates, and especially when they distrust the reports they get from group advocates, they turn to rudimentary forms of polling. They may informally interview a few ordinary citizens from each of the major religious faiths or from different occupations in an effort to construct a meaningful distribution of opinions in a constituency. Many politicians have been successful with such impressionistic methods (although skeptics attribute their success to luck). Moreover, these politicians have used more systematic approaches as soon as they could afford to.

Newspapers have followed suit. Not too long ago, the top journalists on major newspapers, such as the *New York Times,* based many of their political articles on selective, impressionistic polling. But in recent years, their newspapers have, at great expense, become clients of Gallup, Roper, and other large scientific polling organizations. Some media organizations have even joined forces to produce their own polls. The *New York Times*/CBS News Poll is one example.



**Bellwether Districts** The bellwether originally was the lead sheep of a flock, on whose neck a bell was hung. The term now refers generally to something that is used as an indicator of where a group is heading. A ***bellwether district*** or town is assumed to be a good predictor of the attitudes of large segments of the national population. Maine was once an important bellwether state for forecasting national elections (and therefore for plotting national campaign strategies). The old saying "As Maine goes, so goes the nation" was based on two facts. First, the distribution of Maine's votes for presidential candidates was often like that of the national popular two-party votes. Second, for many years, the wintry state of Maine held its general election in September rather than November, which provided a meaningful opportunity for forecasting. (Because Maine now holds its election in November like the rest of the states, it is no longer a good bellwether.)

The use of bellwether districts has been brought to greater and greater levels of precision in the past two decades because of advances in methods used by television networks. The three major networks have developed elaborate computerized techniques to predict the outcomes of elections within minutes after the polls close. The networks' news staffs spend months prior to election day selecting important districts—especially districts on the East Coast, where the polls close an hour to three hours earlier than in the rest of the country, thereby giving the forecasters a head start. They enter into a large computer the voting history of the selected districts, along with information about the opinions and the economic and social characteristics of the residents. As the voting results flow in from these districts on election night, the computer quickly compares them with prior elections and with other districts in the country in order to make fairly precise predictions about the outcome of the current election.

The commercial and political interests that rely on bellwether district methods closely guard the exact information they plug into the computer and the exact methods of weighing and comparing results in order to make their forecasts. It is nevertheless possible to evaluate the contributions this approach makes to political knowledge. First, the bellwether method is useful when there is an election involving a limited number of candidates. Second, it tends to work well only when the analysis takes place close to the actual day of the election. Third, the lasting knowledge to be gained from it is limited. No matter how accurately the bellwether district method forecasts elections, it is not particularly useful for stating what opinions people are holding, how consistently and with what intensity they hold opinions on various issues, why they hold these opinions, and how their opinions might be changing.

## Constructing Public Opinion from Surveys

The population in which pollsters are interested is usually quite large. To conduct their polls they choose a sample from the total population. The selection of this sample is important. Above all, it must be representative; the views of those in the sample must accurately and proportionately reflect the views of the whole. To a large extent, the validity of the poll's results depends on the sampling procedure used, several of which are described below.

***Quota sampling*** is the method used by most commercial polls. In this approach, respondents are selected whose characteristics closely match those of the general population along several significant dimensions, such as geographic region, sex, age, and race.

***Probability sampling*** is the most accurate polling technique. By definition, this method requires that every individual in the population must have a known (usually equal) probability of being chosen as a respondent so that the researcher can give equal weight to all segments of society. A requirement, then, is a complete list of the population or a breakdown of the total population by cities and counties. The simplest methods of obtaining a probability sample are ***systematic sampling,*** choosing every ninth name from a list, for instance, and ***random sampling,*** drawing from a container whose contents have been thoroughly mixed. This latter method, of course, can be simulated by computer-generated random numbers. Both quota sampling and probability sampling are best suited for polls of small populations.

For polls of large cities, states, or the whole nation, the method usually employed when a high level of accuracy is desired is ***area sampling.*** This technique breaks the population down into small, homogeneous units, such as counties. Several of these units are then randomly selected to serve as the sample. These units are, in turn, broken down into even smaller units. The process may extend even to individual dwellings on randomly selected blocks, for example. Area sampling is very costly and generally used only by academic survey researchers.

Some types of sampling do not yield representative samples and so have no scientific value. ***Haphazard sampling,*** for instance, is an unsystematic choice of respondents. A reporter who stands on a street corner and asks questions of convenient passersby is engaging in haphazard sampling. Systematically biased sampling occurs when an error in technique destroys the representative nature of the sample. A systematic error, for example, may cause a sample to include too many old people, too many college students, or too few minority group members.

Even with reliable sampling procedures, problems can occur. Validity can be adversely affected by poor question format, faulty ordering of questions, inappropriate vocabulary, ambiguity of questions, or questions with built-in biases. In some instances, bias may be intentional. Poll conducted on behalf of interest groups or political candidates are often designed to allow the sponsors of the poll to claim that they have the support of the American people.[26] Occasionally, respondents and pollsters may have very different conceptions of the meaning of the words used in a question. For example, an early Gallup poll that asked people if they owned any stock found that stock ownership in the Southwest was surprisingly high. It turned out that many of the respondents thought "stock" meant

[26]August Gribbin, "Two Key Questions in Assessing Polls: 'How?' and 'Why?'" *Washington Times,* 19 October 1998, p. A10.

cows and horses rather than securities.[27] Often, apparently minor differences in the wording of a question can convey vastly different meanings to respondents and, thus, produce quite different response patterns. For example, for many years the University of Chicago's National Opinion Research Center has asked respondents whether they think the federal government is spending too much, too little, or about the right amount of money on "assistance for the poor." Answering the question posed this way, about two-thirds of all respondents seem to believe that the government is spending too little. However, the same survey also asks whether the government spends too much, too little, or about the right amount for "welfare." When the word "welfare" is substituted for "assistance for the poor," about half of all respondents indicate that too much is being spent by the government.[28]

In a similar vein, what seemed to be a minor difference in wording in two December 1998 *New York Times* survey questions on presidential impeachment produced vastly different results. The first question asked respondents, "If the full House votes to send impeachment articles to the Senate for a trial, then do you think it would be better for the country if Bill Clinton resigned from office, or not?" The second version of the question asked, "If the full House votes to impeach Bill Clinton, then do you think it would better for the country if Bill Clinton resigned from office, or not?" Though the two questions seem almost identical, 43 percent of those responding to the first version said the president should resign, while 60 percent of those responding to the second version of the question said Clinton should resign.[29]

In recent years, a new form of bias has been introduced into surveys by the use of a technique called ***push polling.*** This technique involves asking a respondent a loaded question about a political candidate designed to elicit the response sought by the pollster and, simultaneously, to shape the respondent's perception of the candidate in question. For example, during the 1996 New Hampshire presidential primary, push pollsters employed by Lamar Alexander's rival campaign called thousands of voters to ask, "If you knew that Lamar Alexander had raised taxes six times in Tennessee, would you be less inclined or more inclined to support him?"[30] More than 100 consulting firms across the nation now specialize in push polling.[31] Calling push polling the "political equivalent of a drive-by shooting," Representative Joe Barton (R-Tex.) has launched a congressional investigation into the practice.[32] Push polls may be one reason that Americans are becoming increasingly skeptical about the practice of polling and increasingly unwilling to answer pollsters' questions.[33]

[27]Charles W. Roll and Albert H. Cantril, *Polls* (New York: Basic Books, 1972), p. 106.

[28]Michael Kagay and Janet Elder, "Numbers Are No Problem for Pollsters. Words Are," *New York Times,* 9 August 1992, p. E6.

[29]Richard Morin, "Choice Words," *Washington Post,* 10 January 1999, C1.

[30]Donn Tibbetts, "Draft Bill Requires Notice of Push Polling," *Manchester Union Leader,* 3 October 1996, p. A6.

[31]"Dial S for Smear," *Memphis Commercial Appeal,* 22 September 1996, p. 6B.

[32]Amy Keller, "Subcommittee Launches Investigation of Push Polls," *Roll Call,* 3 October 1996, p. 1.

[33]For a discussion of the growing difficulty of persuading people to respond to surveys, see John Brehm, *Phantom Respondents* (Ann Arbor: University of Michigan Press, 1993).

**Sample Size** The degree of precision in polling is a function of sample size, not population size. Just as large a sample is needed to represent a small population as to represent a large population. The typical size of a sample is from 450 to 1,500 respondents. This number, however, reflects a trade-off between cost and degree of precision desired. The degree of accuracy that can be achieved with a small sample can be seen from the polls' success in predicting election outcomes.

Table 9.2 shows how accurate two of the major national polling organizations have been in predicting the outcomes of presidential elections. In only three instances between 1952 and 1996 did the final October poll of a major pollster predict the wrong outcome, and in all three instances—Harris in 1968 and Gallup in 1976, as well as Roper in 1960—the actual election was extremely close and the prediction was off by no more than two percentage points. Even in 1948, when the pollsters were deeply embarrassed by their almost uniform prediction of a Dewey victory over Truman, they were not off by much. For example, Gallup predicted 44.5 percent for Truman, who actually received 49.6 percent. Although Gallup's failure to predict the winner was embarrassing, its actual percentage error would not be considered large by most statisticians.

Since 1948, Gallup has averaged a difference of less than 1 percent between what it predicts and the actual election outcome—and all its predictions have been made on the basis of random samples of not more than 2,500 respondents. In light of a national voting population of more than 60 million, these estimates are impressive.

This ability to predict elections by projecting estimates from small samples to enormous populations validates the methods used in sample survey studies of public opinion: the principles of random sampling, the methods of interviewing, and the statistical tests and computer programming used in data analysis. It also validates the model of behavior by which social scientists attempt to predict voting behavior on the basis of respondents' characteristics rather than on the basis of only their stated intentions. This model of behavior is built on the respondent's voting intention and includes data on (1) the influence of the respondent's place in the social structure, (2) the influence of habit and previous party loyalty, (3) the influence of particular issues for each election, (4) the direction and strength of the respondent's general ideology, and (5) the respondent's occupational and educational background, income level, and so on. Each of these characteristics is treated as a variable in an equation leading to a choice among the major candidates in the election. The influence of the variables, or correlates, is far greater than most respondents realize.

## Limits to Assessing Political Knowledge with Polls

The survey, or polling, approach to political knowledge has certain inherent problems. The most noted but least serious of them is the ***bandwagon effect,*** which occurs when polling results influence people to support the candidate marked as the

TABLE 9.2

## Two Pollsters and Their Records (1948–1996)

| | | HARRIS | GALLUP | ACTUAL OUTCOME |
|---|---|---|---|---|
| **1996** | Clinton | 51% | 52% | 49% |
| | Dole | 39 | 41 | 41 |
| | Perot | 9 | 7 | 8 |
| **1992** | Clinton | 44% | 44% | 43% |
| | Bush | 38 | 37 | 38 |
| | Perot | 17 | 14 | 19 |
| **1988** | Bush | 51% | 53% | 54% |
| | Dukakis | 47 | 42 | 46 |
| **1984** | Reagan | 56% | 59% | 59% |
| | Mondale | 44 | 41 | 41 |
| **1980** | Reagan | 48% | 47% | 51% |
| | Carter | 43 | 44 | 41 |
| | Anderson | | 8 | |
| **1976** | Carter | 48% | 48% | 51% |
| | Ford | 45 | 49 | 48 |
| **1972** | Nixon | 59% | 62% | 61% |
| | McGovern | 35 | 38 | 38 |
| **1968** | Nixon | 40% | 43% | 43% |
| | Humphrey | 43 | 42 | 43 |
| | G. Wallace | 13 | 15 | 14 |
| **1964** | Johnson | 62% | 64% | 61% |
| | Goldwater | 33 | 36 | 39 |
| **1960** | Kennedy | 49% | 51% | 50% |
| | Nixon | 41 | 49 | 49 |
| **1956** | Eisenhower | NA | 60% | 58% |
| | Stevenson | | 41 | 42 |
| **1952** | Eisenhower | 47% | 51% | 55% |
| | Stevenson | 42 | 49 | 44 |
| **1948** | Truman | NA | 44.5% | 49.6% |
| | Dewey | | 49.5 | 45.1 |

All figures except those for 1948 are rounded. NA = Not asked

SOURCES: Data from the Gallup Poll and the Harris Survey (New York: Chicago Tribune-New York News Syndicate, various press releases, 1964–1996). Courtesy of the Gallup Organization and Louis Harris Associates.

probable victor. Some scholars argue that this bandwagon effect can be offset by an "underdog effect" in favor of the candidate who is trailing in the polls.[34]

Other problems with polling are more substantial. One, of course, is human error—bad decisions based on poor interpretations of the data. That in itself is a problem of the users of the polls, not of polling itself. But the two most serious problems inherent in polling are the source of most of the human error. They are the illusion of central tendency and the illusion of saliency.

**The Illusion of Central Tendency** The assumption that attitudes tend toward the average or center is known as the ***illusion of central tendency.*** In any large statistical population, measurements tend to be distributed most heavily toward the middle, or average. Weights, heights, even aptitudes, tend so strongly toward the average that their graphic representation bulges high in the middle and low at each extreme, in the form of a bell-shaped curve. So many characteristics are distributed in the bell shape that it is called a "normal distribution." But are opinions normally distributed also? Some can be. Figure 9.3 shows the distribution for a hypothetical sample of individuals responding to the proposition that business in the United States has become too big. Respondents could agree or disagree, could agree strongly or disagree strongly, or could take a moderate to neutral position. The results shown by the figure indicate a bell-shaped curve.

But not all opinions in the United States are normally distributed. On at least a few issues, opinions are likely to be distributed bimodally, as shown in Figure 9.4. On a bimodal distribution of an issue, the population can be said to be polarized. For example, opinions about the right of women to have an abortion are highly polarized. Very few people are neutral; most are either strongly for or strongly against it.

Despite the variation in the actual distribution of opinions, politicians often assume that opinions are distributed more toward neutral and moderate than toward the extremes; and their assumption of (and wish for) a moderate electorate is reinforced by polling. A good poll can counteract this illusion. And, of course, people who come to the wrong conclusions on their own are not the responsibility of the pollsters. But the illusion of central tendency can be produced unintentionally by polls themselves. Respondents are usually required to express opinions in terms of five or six prescribed responses on a questionnaire. But this leaves out many of the issues' complexities. For example, during virtually the entire period of the Watergate affair between 1973 and 1974, the Gallup poll reported that most Americans were opposed when asked, "Should President Richard Nixon be impeached and compelled to leave the Presidency?" These findings strengthened the Nixon administration's view that the public supported the president. However, in mid-1974, the Gallup organization changed the wording of the question to ask if respondents "think there is enough evidence of possible wrongdoing in the case of President Nixon to bring him to trial before the Senate, or not?" With this new wording, as many as two-thirds of those surveyed answered that they

[34]See Michael Traugott in, "The Impact of Media Polls on the Public," in *Media Polls in American Politics,* ed. Thomas E. Mann and Gary R. Orren (Washington, DC: Brookings Institution, 1992), pp. 125–49.

FIGURE 9.3

**The Assumption of Centrality Visualized as a Bell-Shaped Curve**

*When asked to express their attitudes toward a moderately controversial proposition, members of a sample group might respond as illustrated by this bell-shaped distribution.*

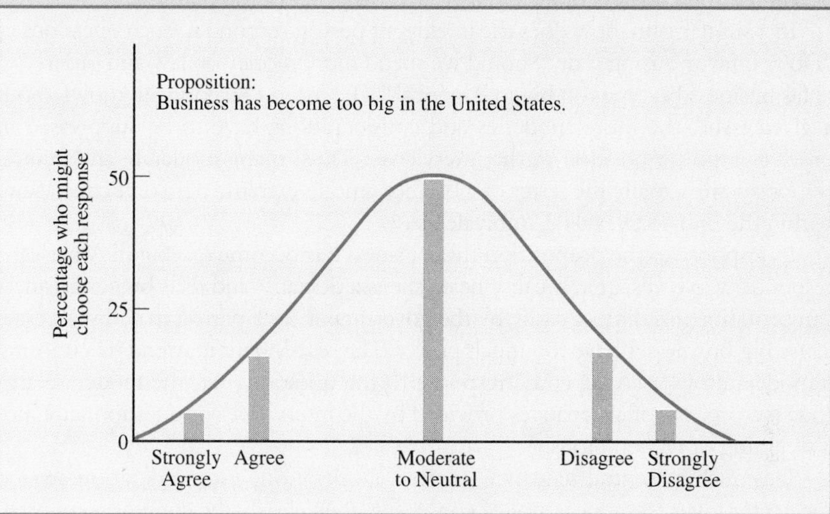


FIGURE 9.4

**A Polarized Population Visualized as a Bimodal Distribution**

*When asked to express their attitudes toward a highly controversial proposition, members of a sample group might respond as illustrated in this bimodal distribution.*

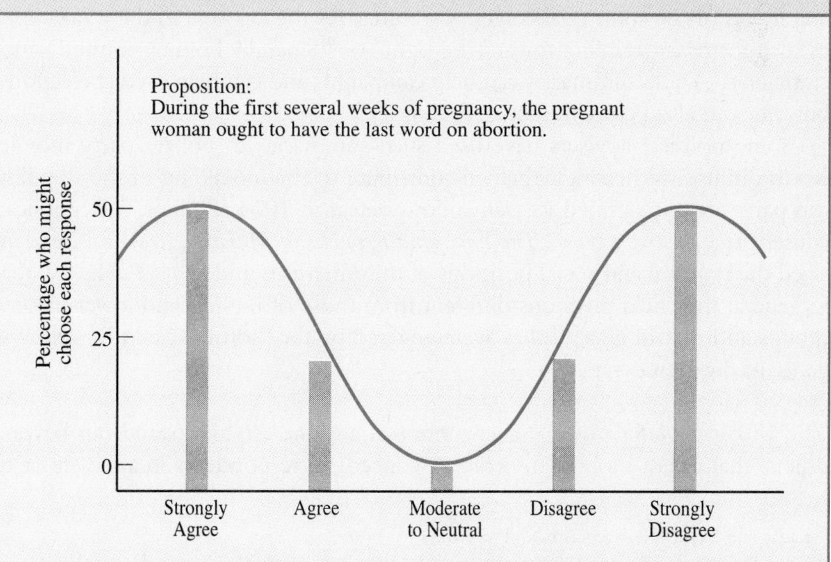

favored impeachment. Apparently, most Americans favored impeaching Nixon, as defined by the second question. However, they did not want to convict him without a trial, as implied by the original question. Thus, what had been seen by some as Americans' failure to respond to the serious charges made against the president, may have actually indicated that respondents' understanding of the impeachment process was more sophisticated than that of the pollsters.[35]

In a similar vein, how does the intelligent person respond to such questions as "Do you favor busing?" or "Should we spend more money on law and order?" or "Has business become too big in America?" The more a respondent knows about a given issue, the more subtleties and considerations have to be suppressed in order to report a position to the interviewer. Thus, many moderate and neutral responses are actually the result of a balance among extreme but conflicting views within the individual, called ambivalence.

In response to the proposition that business has become too big in America, a respondent may disagree because he or she is a Socialist and feels bigger business can be nationalized more easily by the government, or a person may disagree because big businesses have too much power. The respondent may end up choosing a moderate or "it all depends" response to the question. Yet, the moderate attitude is a product of alternatives provided by the interviewer or questionnaire, not a weighing of real opinions.

Inasmuch as central tendency suggests moderation, and moderation around the center gives the appearance of consensus, then clearly the consensus reported in opinion polls is often artificial. This does not mean that the data or the findings are false. Nor does it mean that they have been deliberately distorted by the pollsters. Rather, an artificial consensus is the result of mixing different opinions through the mechanical limits of questionnaires and multiple-choice responses.

Opinion polls can produce an artificial central tendency in still another way. Each survey asks respondents a whole series of questions about a variety of specific issues. But since the polling agency's clients are usually interested in the general mood of the country, the agency summarizes the answers to these questions in such forms as "tending toward the right" or "generally holding to the Democratic line." These summaries can help campaigns and can help predict elections, but they can also betray the actual findings.

Some political advisers have used such summaries to bolster party morale. Kevin Phillips, for example, helped contribute to the rebuilding of the Republican party after it suffered its tremendous defeat in 1964. Phillips, a Republican conservative, wrote a book, *The Emerging Republican Majority*, in which he identified the political and social positions of the American middle class. He saw that in general they held positions different from those of higher- and lower-income groups and that in general they were angered by the "softness" and the extravagance of the Democrats.[36]

**The Illusion of Saliency** Salient interests are interests that stand out beyond others, that are of more than ordinary concern to respondents in a survey or to

[35]Kagay and Elder, "Numbers Are No Problem."

[36]Kevin Phillips, *The Emerging Republican Majority* (New Rochelle, NY: Arlington House, 1969).

voters in the electorate. Politicians, social scientists, journalists, or pollsters who assume something is important to the public when in fact it is not are creating an ***illusion of saliency.*** This illusion can be created and fostered by polls despite careful controls over sampling, interviewing, and data analysis. In fact, the illusion is strengthened by the credibility that science gives survey results.

Thus, if a survey includes questions on twenty subjects—because the pollsters or their clients feel they might be important issues—that survey can actually produce twenty salient issues. Although the responses may be sincere, the cumulative impression is artificial, since a high proportion of the respondents may not have concerned themselves with many of the issues until actually confronted with questions by an interviewer. For example, usually not more than 10 percent (rarely more than 20 percent) of the respondents will report that they have no attitude on an issue. Yet, equally seldom will more than 30 percent of a sample spontaneously cite one or more issues as the main reason for their choices. It is nearly impossible to discover how many respondents feel obliged to respond to questions for which they never had any particular concern before the interview.

In a similar vein, an issue may become salient to the public *because* it is receiving a great deal of attention from political leaders and the mass media rather than because of a groundswell of public interest in the issue. For example, the issue of health care was frequently cited by poll respondents as one of their major concerns *after* it was introduced by President Clinton in 1993 and after it had been given a great deal of media coverage. Prior to the president's September 1993 speech to the nation on health care reform, the issue was seldom, if ever, mentioned by members of the public asked to cite what they believed to be important issues. In this instance, as in many others, an issue became salient to the public only after it was introduced by a significant political figure. As the famous Austrian-American economist, Joseph Schumpeter, once observed, public opinion is usually the product rather than the motivator of the political process. In other words, the public's concerns are often shaped by powerful political forces, rather than the other way around.

Similarly, when asked in the early days of a political campaign which candidates they do, or do not, support, the answers voters give often have little significance because the choice is not yet salient to them. Their preference may change many times before the actual election. This is part of the explanation for the phenomenon of the post-convention "bounce" in the popularity of presidential candidates, which was observed after the 1992 and 1996 Democratic and Republican national conventions. In general, presidential candidates can expect about a five-percentage-point bounce in their poll standings immediately after a national convention, though the effects of the bounce tend to disappear rapidly. In 1996, Bob Dole trailed Bill Clinton by as much as twenty-two points before the Republican convention but pulled to within seven points of Clinton afterward. This dramatic post-convention bounce, however, was completely erased a short month later. In the aftermath of the Democratic convention Clinton moved to a twenty-one-point lead, almost precisely where he had been before the Republican convention.[37]

[37]Michael X. Delli Carpini, "The Voter Bounce," *Memphis Commercial Appeal,* 15 September 1996, p. 4B.

# The Power of Public Opinion

*A central tenet of democratic nations holds that a government's rulers should be guided by the wishes of the people. Yet it is often difficult to discern what people want their government to do; moreover, leaders recognize that they are frequently in a position to shape or mold popular opinion.*

*Pollsters Charles W. Roll and Albert H. Cantril argue that public preferences ultimately prevail, even though most people are not well informed about the particulars of important public issues. Political scientist Benjamin Ginsberg argues that public opinion can indeed be shaped and molded by skillful leaders and that, ironically, the very method used to determine public preferences—public opinion polling—may also be the very device by which the public is molded and channeled.*

## ROLL AND CANTRIL

What is the competence of public opinion? . . . In our own view, the competence of public opinion is at the "feeling level." The public obviously cannot be expected to be informed and up-to-date in its understanding of complex issues, the implications of alternative courses of action, nor the advantages of specific instrumentalities by which a policy is effected. . . .

However, when it comes to generalized impressions, in two areas the public's judgment usually proves sound and prophetic. The public is quick to spot a phony—the disingenuous politician who is facile and whose transparency soon betrays itself. The public is also very sensitive to the direction and adequacy of policies being pursued by its leaders. While public opinion takes longer to jell with regard to policies, once it becomes clear a policy is unworkable or simply getting too costly, the public will desert its leaders. . . .

Thus, in political research the crucial dimension . . . is the public's sense of trust and confidence in its leaders. . . . What it judges its leaders on, then, is less the substance of policies and programs than the overall impression of whether its leaders "are on top of things." . . .

When events or actions by leaders bring an issue home to the public, public opinion can quickly catch up to events, and when it does, it becomes all powerful. To quote Woodrow Wilson: "Opinion ultimately governs the world."[1]

## GINSBERG

Polling fundamentally alters the character of the public agenda of opinion. . . . Opinions elicited by polls . . . mainly concern matters of interest to government, business, or other poll sponsors. Typically, poll questions have as their ultimate purpose some form of exhortation. Businesses poll to help persuade customers to purchase their wares. Candidates poll as part of the process of convincing voters to support them. Governments poll as part of the process of inducing citizens to obey. . . .

In essence, rather than offer governments the opinions that citizens want them to learn, polls tell governments—or other sponsors—what they would like to learn about citizens' opinions. The end result is to change the public expression of opinion from an assertion of demand to a step in the process of persuasion. . . .

Taken together, the changes produced by polling contribute to the transformation of public opinion from an unpredictable, extreme, and often dangerous force into a more docile expression of public sentiment. Opinion stated through polls imposes less pressure and makes fewer demands on government than would more spontaneous or natural assertions of popular sentiment. Though opinion may be expressed more democratically via polls than through alternative means, polling can give public opinion a plebiscitary character—robbing opinion of precisely those features that might maximize its impact on government and policy.[2]

[1]Charles W. Roll and Albert H. Cantril, *Polls: Their Use and Misuse in Politics* (Cabin John, MD: Seven Locks Press, 1972), pp. 143–45.
[2]Benjamin Ginsberg, *The Captive Public: How Mass Opinion Promotes State Power* (New York: Basic Books, 1986), pp. 82–83.

Analysis of focus group data suggests that Dole's temporary bounce was almost entirely the result of a positive voter reaction to his wife, Elizabeth, who made a major speech at the GOP convention. Faced with the reality of having to vote for Bob rather than Elizabeth Dole, many voters reconsidered their enthusiastic reaction.[38] Respondents' preferences reflected the amount of attention a candidate received during the convention rather than strongly held views.

The problem of saliency has become especially acute as a result of the proliferation of media polls. The television networks and major national newspapers all make heavy use of opinion polls. Increasingly, polls are being commissioned by local television stations and local and regional newspapers as well.[39] On the positive side, polls allow journalists to make independent assessments of political realities—assessments not influenced by the partisan claims of politicians.

At the same time, however, media polls can allow journalists to make news when none really exists. Polling diminishes journalists' dependence upon news makers. A poll commissioned by a news agency can provide the basis for a good story even when candidates, politicians, and other news makers refuse to cooperate by engaging in newsworthy activities. Thus, on days when little or nothing is actually taking place in a political campaign, poll results, especially apparent changes in candidate margins, can provide exciting news for voters. In 1996, hundreds of news stories focused on the magnitude of Clinton's lead over Dole and on the post-convention "bounce" in poll standings shown by the two candidates. As we saw above, the polls were inaccurate in their predictions, and the post-election bounce was, as always, a transient phenomenon. In

[38]Jamie Dettmer, "Focus Group Rates Conclaves," *Washington Times,* 23 September 1996, p. 6.
[39]See Mann and Orren, eds., *Media Polls in American Politics.*

effect, a huge percentage of pre-election news coverage was literally a waste of paper and ink.

Interestingly, because rapid and dramatic shifts in candidate margins tend to take place when voters' preferences are least fully formed, horse race news is most likely to make the headlines when it is actually least significant.[40] In other words, media interest in poll results is inversely related to the actual salience of voters' opinions and the significance of the polls' findings.

However, by influencing perceptions, especially those of major contributors, media polls can influence political realities. A candidate who demonstrates a lead in the polls usually finds it considerably easier to raise campaign funds than a candidate whose poll standing is poor. With additional funds, poll leaders can often afford to pay for television time and other campaign activities that will cement their advantage. For example, Bill Clinton's substantial lead in the polls during much of the summer of 1992 helped the Democrats raise far more money than in any previous campaign, primarily from interests hoping to buy access to a future President Clinton. For once, the Democrats were able to outspend the usually better-heeled Republicans. Thus, the appearance of a lead, according to the polls, helped make Clinton's lead a reality. Much the same effect was seen in 1996, when Clinton's lead in the polls caused many Republicans to write off the contest as hopeless weeks before the election.

**AMERICAN POLITICAL DEVELOPMENT**

Although tremendous advances in disseminating political information have occurred during the second half of the twentieth century, parallel increases in the public's knowledge of politics have not. A comparison of public knowledge surveys from the 1940s and 1950s to a survey from 1989 revealed slight increases in the percentage of those who could name the vice president or knew which party controlled the House of Representatives but decreases in the percentage of those who could name both of their U.S. senators and which party controlled the Senate.

SOURCE: Michael X. Delli Carpini and Scott Keeter, *What Americans Know about Politics and Why It Matters* (New Haven: Yale University Press, 1996), p. 117.

The two illusions engendered by polling often put politicians on the horns of a dilemma in which they must choose between a politics of no issues (due to the illusion of central tendency) and a politics of too many trivial issues (due to the illusion of saliency). This has to be at least part of the explanation for why many members of Congress can praise themselves at the end of the year for the hundreds of things they worked on during the past session while not perceiving that they have neglected the one or two overriding issues of the day. Similarly, politicians preparing for major state or national campaigns compose position papers on virtually every conceivable issue—either because they will not make a judgment as to which are the truly salient issues or because they feel that stressing all issues is a way of avoiding a choice among the truly salient ones.

## Public Opinion, Political Knowledge, and the Importance of Ignorance

Many people are distressed to find public opinion polls not only unable to discover public opinion, but unable to avoid producing unintentional distortions of

[40]For an excellent and reflective discussion by a journalist, see Richard Morin, "Clinton Slide in Survey Shows Perils of Polling," *Washington Post,* 29 August 1992, p. A6.

their own. No matter how hard pollsters try, no matter how mature the science of opinion polling becomes, politicians forever may remain largely ignorant of public opinion.

Although knowledge is good for its own sake, and knowledge of public opinion may sometimes produce better government, ignorance also has its uses. It can, for example, operate as a restraint on the use of power. Leaders who think they know what the public wants are often autocratic rulers. Leaders who realize that they are always partially in the dark about the public are likely to be more modest in their claims, less intense in their demands, and more uncertain in their uses of power. Their uncertainty may make them more accountable to their constituencies because they will be more likely to continue searching for consent.

One of the most valuable benefits of survey research is actually "negative knowledge"—knowledge that pierces through irresponsible claims about the breadth of opinion or the solidarity of group or mass support. Because this sort of knowledge reveals the complexity and uncertainty of public opinion, it can help make citizens less gullible, group leaders less strident, and politicians less deceitful. This alone gives public opinion research, despite its great limitations, an important place in the future of American politics.[41]

## Public Opinion and Government Policy

In democratic nations leaders should pay heed to public opinion, and most evidence suggests that indeed they do. There are many instances in which public policy and public opinion do not coincide, but in general the government's actions are consistent with citizens' preferences. One study, for example, found that between 1935 and 1979, in about two-thirds of all cases, significant changes in public opinion were followed within one year by changes in government policy consistent with the shift in the popular mood.[42] Other studies have come to similar conclusions about public opinion and government policy at the state level.[43] Some recent studies, however, have suggested the responsiveness of government to public opinion has been declining, reaching an all-time low during President Clinton's first term. These findings imply that, contrary to popular beliefs, elected leaders don't always pander to the results of public opinion polls, but instead use polling to sell their policy proposals and shape the public's views.[44]

[41]For a fuller discussion of the uses of polling and the role of public opinion in American politics, see Benjamin Ginsberg, *The Captive Public* (New York: Basic Books, 1986).

[42]Benjamin I. Page and Robert Y. Shapiro, "Effects of Public Opinion on Policy," *American Political Science Review* 77 (March 1983), pp. 175–90.

[43]Robert A. Erikson, Gerald Wright, and John McIver, *Statehouse Democracy: Public Opinion and Democracy in the American States* (New York: Cambridge University Press, 1994).

[44]The results of separate studies by the political scientists Lawrence Jacobs, Robert Shapiro, and Alan Monroe were reported by Richard Morin in "Which Comes First, the Politician or the Poll?" *Washington Post National Weekly Edition,* 10 February 1997, p. 35.

ANALYZING AMERICAN POLITICS

## *Public Opinion, Pandering, and Politics*

One of the fundamental notions on which the U.S. government was founded is that "the public" should not be trusted when it comes to governing. The framers designed institutions that, although democratic, insulated government decision-making from popular pressure. For example, the indirect elections of senators and presidents were supposed to prevent the government from being too dependent on the vagaries of public opinion.

Research from the 1950s and 1960s indicates that the framers' concerns were well founded. Individual-level survey analysis reveals that the respondents lacked fundamental political knowledge and had ill-formed opinions about government and public policy.[1] Their answers seemed nothing more than "doorstep opinions"—opinions given off the top of their heads. When an individual was asked the same questions at different times, he or she often gave different answers. The dramatic and unpredictable changes seemed to imply that the public was indeed unreliable as a guide for political decisions.

Benjamin Page and Robert Shapiro take issue with the notion that the public should not be trusted when it comes to policy making.[2] They contend that public opinion at the aggregate level is indeed "rational"—meaning that public opinion is coherent and stable, and that it moves in a predictable fashion in response to changing political, economic, and social circumstances.

How is this possible, given what previous studies have found? Page and Shapiro hypothesize that the individual-level re-

[1]Angus Campbell, Philip E. Converse, Warren E. Miller, and Donald E. Stokes, *The American Voter.* (New York: Wiley, 1960); Philip E. Converse, "The Nature of Belief Systems in Mass Publics" in *Ideology and Discontent,* ed. David E. Apter (New York: Free Press, 1964).

[2]Benjamin I. Page and Robert Y. Shapiro, *The Rational Public* (Chicago: University of Chicago Press, 1992).

In addition, there are always areas of disagreement between opinion and policy. For example, the majority of Americans favored stricter governmental control of handguns for years before Congress finally adopted the modest restrictions on firearms purchases embodied in the 1994 Brady Bill and the Omnibus Crime Control Act. Similarly, most Americans—blacks as well as whites—oppose school busing to achieve racial balance, yet such busing continues to be used in many parts of the nation. Most Americans are far less concerned with the rights of the accused

sponses are plagued with various types of errors that make the people's opinions seem incoherent and unstable. However, when a large number of individual-level responses to survey questions are added up to produce an aggregate public opinion, the errors or "noise" in the individual responses, if more or less random, will cancel each other out, revealing a collective opinion that is stable, coherent, and meaningful.

In order to test their hypothesis, Page and Shapiro amassed a vast amount of data, consisting of over a thousand survey questions covering a broad range of issues that were asked repeatedly over a fifty-year time period. One of the most important features of their research design is that the questions were asked in identical form so that any changes in opinion could not be chalked up to effects of the wording.

Using this data, Page and Shapiro reject much of the conventional wisdom about the problematic nature of public opinion. Public opinion does not change capriciously—in fact, in over half of the issues that they examined, Page and Shapiro found no substantively significant change. The changes that did occur were almost always in one direction or the other, contradicting the notion that public opinion fluctuates back and forth. In the few instances where they found dramatic change, the change occurred gradually over time and in a way that we would expect, given events and conditions.

From their results, Page and Shapiro conclude that the general public can indeed be trusted when it comes to governing. But how closely should elected officials follow public opinion? Politicians are often accused of following opinion polls too closely, pandering to the public, and failing to provide effective leadership.

A recent study on the role that public opinion played during the failed attempt to enact health care reform during 1993–1994 rejects the widely held belief that politicians pander to public opinion.[3] The study found that public opinion polls had very little influence on individual members of Congress, who used these polls first to justify positions they had already adopted and then to shape public thinking on the issue. However, the study also found that congressional party leaders designed their health care legislation strategies based on their concerns about the effects of public opinion on the electoral fortunes of individual members. Leaders' concerns about public opinion thus help explain why the congressional policy-making process follows public opinion, even though individual members of Congress do not.

[3]Lawrence R. Jacobs, Eric D. Lawrence, Robert Y. Shapiro, and Steven S. Smith, "Congressional Leadership of Public Opinion," *Political Science Quarterly* 113 (1998), pp. 21–41.

than the federal courts seem to be. Most Americans oppose U.S. military intervention in other nations' affairs, yet such interventions continue to take place and often win public approval after the fact.

Several factors can contribute to a lack of consistency between opinion and governmental policy. First, the nominal majority on a particular issue may not be as intensely committed to its preference as the adherents of the minority viewpoint. An intensely committed minority may often be more willing to commit its time, energy, efforts, and resources to the affirmation of its opinions than an apathetic, even if large, majority. In the case of firearms, for example, although the proponents of gun control are by a wide margin in the majority, most do not regard the issue as one of critical importance to themselves and are not willing to commit much effort to advancing their cause. The opponents of gun control, by contrast, are intensely committed, well organized, and well financed, and as a result are usually able to carry the day.

A second important reason that public policy and public opinion may not coincide has to do with the character and structure of the American system of government. The framers of the American Constitution, as we saw in Chapter 2, sought to create a system of government that was based upon popular consent but that did not invariably and automatically translate shifting popular sentiments into public policies. As a result, the American governmental process includes arrangements such as an appointed judiciary that can produce policy decisions that may run contrary to prevailing popular sentiment—at least for a time.

THEN AND NOW

## Changes in American Politics

Changes in both the technology and the nationalization of American politics have altered the measurement and importance of public opinion today.

- In most Western democracies, a nationalization of politics fostered by the expansion of national languages, literacy and communications media, and enhanced public interaction has increased the possibility of public conversations about politics and created the "marketplace of ideas."
- Prior to the use of scientific public opinion polls, "public opinion" was primarily discernible through political behavior (such as voting, riots and protests, and boycotts) and the intuition of politicians.
- During Woodrow Wilson's administration, officials of the national government became managers of public opinion, and the government's relationship to public opinion changed from reactive to proactive and manipulative.
- The application of public opinion surveys and polls to politics represented an innovation in which the technology of marketing and public relations were applied to politics. This development—with its roots in the 1910s and 1930s—continues to expand.
- Despite the growth of public information sources from the 1950s to the present, there is little evidence of enhanced public awareness about politics.

When all is said and done, however, there can be little doubt that in general the actions of the American government do not remain out of line with popular sentiment for very long. A major reason for this is, of course, the electoral process, to which we shall next turn. Lest we become too complacent, however, we should not forget that the close relationship between government and opinion in America may also partly be a result of the government's success in molding opinion.

## SUMMARY

All governments claim to obey public opinion, and in the democracies politicians and political leaders actually try to do so.

The American government does not directly regulate opinions and beliefs in the sense that dictatorial regimes often do. Opinion is regulated by an institution that the government constructed and that it maintains—the marketplace of ideas. In this marketplace, opinions and ideas compete for support. In general, opinions supported by upper-class groups have a better chance of succeeding than those views that are mainly advanced by the lower classes.

Americans share a number of values and viewpoints but often classify themselves as liberal or conservative in their basic orientations. The meaning of these terms has changed greatly over the past century. Once liberalism meant opposition to big government. Today liberals favor an expanded role for the government. Once conservatism meant support for state power and aristocratic rule. Today conservatives oppose government regulation, at least of business affairs.

Although the United States relies mainly on market mechanisms to regulate opinion, even our government intervenes to some extent, seeking to influence both particular opinions and, more important, the general climate of political opinion. Political leaders' increased distance from the public makes it difficult for them to gauge public opinion. Until recently, public opinion on some issues could be gauged better by studying mass behavior than by studying polls. Population characteristics are also useful in estimating public opinion on some subjects. Another approach is to go directly to the people. Two techniques are used: the impressionistic and the scientific. The impressionistic method relies on person-to-person communication, selective polling, or the use of bellwether districts. A person-to-person approach is quick, efficient, and inexpensive; but because it often depends on an immediate circle of associates, it can also limit awareness of new issues or unpleasant information. Selective polling usually involves interviewing a few people from different walks of life. Although risky, it has been used successfully to gauge public opinion. Bellwether districts are a popular means of predicting election outcomes. They are used by the media as well as by some candidates.

The scientific approach to learning public opinion is random sample polling. One advantage of random sample polling is that elections can be very accurately predicted; using a model of behavior, pollsters are often able to predict how voters will mark their ballots better than the voters themselves can predict. A second advantage is that polls provide information on the bases and conditions of voting decisions. They make it possible to assess trends in attitudes and the influence of ideology on attitudes.

There are also problems with polling, however. An illusion of central tendency can encourage politicians not to confront issues. The illusion of saliency, on the other hand, can encourage politicians to confront too many trivial issues. Even with scientific polling, politicians cannot be certain that they understand public opinion. Their recognition of this limitation, however, may function as a valuable restraint.

## For Further Reading

Bennett, W. Lance. *Public Opinion in American Politics.* New York: Harcourt Brace Jovanovich, 1980.

Elder, Charles D., and Roger W. Cobb. *The Political Uses of Symbols.* New York: Longman, 1983.

Erikson, Robert S., Norman Luttbeg, and Kent Tedin. *American Public Opinion: Its Origins, Content and Impact.* New York: Wiley, 1980.

Gallup, George. *The Pulse of Democracy.* New York: Simon and Schuster, 1940.

Ginsberg, Benjamin. *The Captive Public: How Mass Opinion Promotes State Power.* New York: Basic Books, 1986.

Herbst, Susan. *Numbered Voices: How Opinion Polling Has Shaped American Politics.* Chicago: University of Chicago Press, 1993.

Key, V. O. *Public Opinion and American Democracy.* New York: Alfred A. Knopf, 1961.

Lippmann, Walter. *Public Opinion.* New York: Harcourt, Brace and Co., 1922.

Margolis, Michael, and Gary A. Mauser. *Manipulating Public Opinion.* Pacific Grove, CA: Brooks/Cole, 1989.

Mueller, John. *Policy and Opinion in the Gulf War.* Chicago: University of Chicago Press, 1994.

Neuman, W. Russell. *The Paradox of Mass Politics: Knowledge and Opinion in the American Electorate.* Cambridge: Harvard University Press, 1986.

Roll, Charles W., and Albert H. Cantril. *Polls: Their Use and Misuse in Politics.* New York: Basic Books, 1972.

Smith, Craig A., and Cathy B. Smith. *The White House Speaks: Presidential Leadership as Persuasion.* Westport, CT: Greenwood Press, 1994.

Stimson, James. *Public Opinion in America: Moods, Cycles, and Swings.* Boulder, CO: Westview, 1991.

Sussman, Barry. *What Americans Really Think: And Why Our Politicians Pay No Attention.* New York: Pantheon, 1988.

Tanur, Judith, ed. *Questions about Questions: Inquiries into the Cognitive Bases of Surveys.* New York: Russell Sage, 1992.

Weissberg, Robert. *Public Opinion and Popular Government.* Englewood Cliffs, NJ: Prentice-Hall, 1976.

# 10

# Elections

## TIME LINE ON ELECTIONS

| Events | | Institutional Developments |
| --- | --- | --- |
| George Washington elected president (1789) | | Federalists in control of national government (1789–1800) |
| Thomas Jefferson elected president (1800) | 1800 | First electoral realignment—Jeffersonian Republicans defeat Federalists (1800) |
| Andrew Jackson elected president; beginning of party government (1828) | | Second realignment—Jacksonian Democrats take control of White House and Congress (1828) |
| | | Presidential nominating conventions introduced (1830s) |
| | | Whig party forms (1830s) |
| Whigs win; William Henry Harrison elected president (1840) | | |
| Lincoln elected president (1860); South secedes (1860–1861) | | Civil War realignment—Republican party founded (1856); Whig party destroyed (1860) |
| Civil War (1861–1865) | | |
| Reconstruction (1867–1877) | | Under Reconstruction Acts, blacks enfranchised in South (1867) |
| | 1870 | Fifteenth Amendment forbids states to deny voting rights based on race (1870) |
| Contested presidential election—Hayes v. Tilden (1876); Republican Rutherford Hayes elected by electoral vote of 185–184 (1876) | | Hayes's election leads to end of Reconstruction; voting rights of South restored (1877) |
| | | Southern blacks lose voting rights through poll taxes, literacy tests, grandfather clause (1870s–1890s) |
| | | Progressive reforms—direct primaries, civil service reform, Australian ballot, registration requirements; voter participation drops sharply (1890s–1910s) |
| Republican William McKinley elected president (1896) | | Realignment of 1896; Republican hegemony (1896–1932) |
| | 1900 | |
| | | Seventeenth Amendment authorizes direct election of senators (1913) |
| | | Nineteenth Amendment gives women right to vote (1920) |
| Democrat Franklin D. Roosevelt elected president (1932) | | Democratic realignment (1930s) |

| Events | | Institutional Developments |
|---|---|---|
| Democrat John F. Kennedy first Roman Catholic elected president (1960) | 1960 | |
| | | *Baker v. Carr*—Supreme Court declares doctrine of "one man, one vote" (1962); period of reapportionment (1960s) |
| | | Voting Rights Act (1965) |
| Republican Richard Nixon elected president (1968) | | Breakdown of Democratic New Deal coalition (1968) |
| Rise of black voting in the South (1970s) | | Twenty-sixth Amendment lowers voting age to eighteen (1971) |
| Era of new campaign technology and PACs (1970s–1980s) | | Federal Election Campaign Act (1971) |
| Republican Ronald Reagan elected president (1980) | 1980 | |
| Geraldine Ferraro first woman on major party national ticket (1984) | | Electoral stalemate; Democrats dominate Congress; Republicans control presidency (1986) |
| Jesse Jackson first black candidate to become important presidential contender (1988) | | |
| | 1990 | |
| Democrat Bill Clinton elected president (1992) | | New rules governing voter registration adopted (1993) |
| Republicans take control of Congress (1994) | | Congressional term limits enacted by several states, debated in Congress (1995) |
| Clinton re-elected president; Republicans maintain control of Congress (1996) | | Campaign finance reform fails on repeated occasions (1996–1998) |
| Republicans maintain slim advantage in both houses of Congress (1998) | | Rise of soft money spending by parties and use of issues advocacy increase to all-time high (1998) |

Over the past two centuries, elections have come to play a significant role in the political processes of most nations. The forms that elections take and the purposes they serve, however, vary greatly from nation to nation. The most important difference among national electoral systems is that some provide the opportunity for opposition while others do not. Democratic electoral systems, such as those that have

## CORE OF THE ARGUMENT

- Elections are important because they promote accountability in elected officials, they socialize political activity, they expand citizen involvement, and they prescribe conditions for acceptable participation in political life.
- The government exerts a measure of control over the electoral process by regulating the composition of the electorate, translating voters' choices into electoral decisions, and insulating day-to-day government from the impact of electoral decisions.
- The strongest influences on voters' decisions are partisan loyalty, issue and policy concerns, and candidate characteristics.
- The increasing importance of money in elections has profound consequences for American democracy.
- Ordinary voters have little influence on the political process today.

evolved in the United States and western Europe, allow opposing forces to compete against and even to replace current office holders. Authoritarian electoral systems, by contrast, do not allow the defeat of those in power. In the authoritarian context, elections are used primarily to mobilize popular enthusiasm for the government, to provide an outlet for popular discontent and to persuade foreigners that the regime is legitimate—i.e., that it has the support of the people. In the former Soviet Union, for example, citizens were required to vote even though no opposition to Communist party candidates was allowed.

In democracies, elections can also serve as institutions of legitimation and as safety valves for social discontent. But beyond these functions, democratic elections facilitate popular influence, promote leadership accountability, and offer groups in society a measure of protection from the abuse of governmental power. Citizens exercise influence through elections by determining who should control the government. The chance to decide who will govern serves as an opportunity for ordinary citizens to make choices about the policies, programs, and directions of government action. In the United States, for example, recent Democratic and Republican candidates have differed significantly on issues of taxing, social spending, and governmental regulation. As American voters have chosen between the two parties' candidates, they have also made choices about these issues.

Elections promote leadership accountability because the threat of defeat at the polls exerts pressure on those in power to conduct themselves in a responsible manner and to take account of popular interests and wishes when they make their decisions. As James Madison observed in the *Federalist Papers,* elected leaders are "compelled to anticipate the moment when their power is to cease, when their exercise of it is to be reviewed, and when they must descend to the level from which they were raised, there forever to remain unless a faithful discharge of their trust shall have established their title to a renewal of it."[1] It is because of this need to anticipate that elected officials constantly monitor public opinion polls as they decide what positions to take on policy issues.

Finally, the right to vote, or ***suffrage,*** can serve as an important source of protection for groups in American society. The passage of the 1965 Voting Rights Act, for example, enfranchised millions of African Americans in the South, paving the

[1]Clinton Rossiter, ed., *The Federalist Papers* (New York: New American Library, 1961), No. 57, p. 352.

way for the election of thousands of new black public officials at the local, state, and national levels and ensuring that white politicians could no longer ignore the views and needs of African Americans. The Voting Rights Act was one of the chief spurs for the elimination of many overt forms of racial discrimination as well as for the diminution of racist rhetoric in American public life.

Despite the potential importance of the suffrage, tens of millions of Americans routinely fail to exercise their right to vote. Turnout in recent presidential elections has barely reached 50 percent of those eligible, while congressional elections draw only about one-third of the potential electorate. As we shall see, low levels of voter participation have important implications for the American political process. While voting participation in the United States is low, the participation of wealthy and powerful interests in electoral politics appears to be at an all-time high. Campaign spending by candidates, parties, interest groups, and wealthy individuals achieved a new record, reaching the $2 billion mark in the 1996 election, just as voter turnout dropped to its lowest level since 1924. These two facts, taken together, should lead us to look carefully at the relationship between the *principles* and *practices* of American democratic politics.

In this chapter, we will look first at what distinguishes voting from other forms of political activity. Second, we will examine the formal structure and setting of American elections. Third, we will see how—and what—voters decide when they take part in elections. Fourth, we will focus on recent national elections, including the 1996 presidential race and the 1998 congressional contests. Fifth, we will discuss the role of money in the election process, particularly in recent elections. Finally, we will assess the place of elections in the American political process, raising the important question, "Do elections matter?"

**THE CENTRAL QUESTION**

"Do elections matter?"

## POLITICAL PARTICIPATION

In the twentieth century, voting is viewed as the normal form of mass political activity. Yet ordinary people took part in politics long before the introduction of the election or any other formal mechanism of popular involvement in political life. If there is any natural or spontaneous form of mass political participation, it is the riot rather than the election. Indeed, the urban riot and the rural uprising were a part of life in western Europe prior to the nineteenth century, and in eastern Europe until the twentieth. In eighteenth-century London, for example, one of the most notorious forms of popular political action was the "illumination." Mobs would march up and down the street demanding that householders express support for their cause by placing a candle or lantern in a front window. Those who refused to illuminate risked having their homes torched by the angry crowd. This eighteenth-century form of civil disorder may well be the origin of the expression "to shed light upon" an issue.

The fundamental difference between voting and rioting is that voting is a socialized and institutionalized form of mass political action.[2] When, where, how, and which individuals participate in elections are matters of public policy rather than questions of spontaneous individual choice. With the advent of the election, control over the agenda for political action passed at least in part from the citizen to the government.

In an important study of participation in the United States, Sidney Verba and Norman Nie define political participation as consisting of "activities 'within the system'—ways of influencing politics that are generally recognized as legal and legitimate."[3] This definition of participation is precisely in accord with most governments' desires. Governments try very hard to channel and limit political participation to actions "within the system." Even with that constraint, however, the right to political participation represents a tremendous advancement in the status of citizens on two levels. At one level, it improves the probability that they will regularly affect the decisions that governments make. On the other level, it reinforces the concept of the individual as independent from the state. It is on the basis of both dimensions that philosophers like John Stuart Mill argued that popular government was the ideal form of government.[4]

Those holding power are willing to concede the right to participate in the hope that it will encourage citizens to give their consent to being governed. This is a calculated risk for citizens. They give up their right to revolt in return for the right to participate regularly. They can participate, but only in ways prescribed by the government. Outside the established channels, their participation can be suppressed or disregarded. It is also a calculated risk for the politician, who may be forced into certain policy decisions or forced out of office altogether by citizens exercising their right to participate. This risk is usually worth taking, since in return, governments acquire consent, and through consent citizens become supporters of government action.[5]

## Encouraging Electoral Participation

Americans are free to assert whatever demands, views, and grievances they might have through a variety of different means. Citizens may, if they wish, lobby, petition, demonstrate, or file suit in court. Although there are some legal impediments to many of these forms of participation, relatively few modes of political expression are directly barred by law.

Despite the availability of an array of alternatives, in practice citizen participation in American politics is generally limited to voting and a small number of other electoral activities (for example, campaigning). It is true that voter turnout in the United States is relatively low. But when, for one reason or another, Americans do seek to participate, their participation generally takes the form of voting.

[2]For a fuller discussion, see Benjamin Ginsberg, *The Consequences of Consent* (New York: Random House, 1982).

[3]Sidney Verba and Norman Nie, *Participation in America* (New York: Harper & Row, 1972), pp. 2–3.

[4]John Stuart Mill, *Considerations on Representative Government* (London: Basil Blackwell, 1948; orig. published 1859), pp. 141–42.

[5]See Ginsberg, *Consequences of Consent.*

The preeminent position of voting in the American political process is not surprising. The American legal and political environment is overwhelmingly weighted in favor of electoral participation. Probably the most influential forces helping to channel people into the voting booth are law, civic education, and the party system. The availability of suffrage is, of course, a question of law. But in addition to simply making the ballot available, state legislation in the United States prescribes the creation of an elaborate and costly public machinery that makes voting a rather simple task for individuals. Civic education, to a large extent mandated by law, encourages citizens to believe that electoral participation is the appropriate way to express opinions and grievances. The major parties are legally charged with staffing and operating the normal machinery of elections and in a number of vital ways help directly to induce citizens to participate.

**Making It Easy to Vote** Despite complicating factors such as registration, the time, energy, and effort needed to vote are considerably less than are required for all but a few other political activities. The relatively low degree of individual effort required to vote, however, is somewhat deceptive. Voting is a simple way for large numbers of citizens to participate only because it is made simple by an elaborate and costly electoral system. The ease with which citizens can vote is a function of law and public policy. The costs of voting are paid mainly by the state.

In the United States, electoral contests are administered principally by states and localities. Although state law is sometimes conceived as only regulating and limiting suffrage, most states try to facilitate voting by as many citizens as possible. States and localities legally require themselves to invest considerable effort in the facilitation of voting. In every state, the steps needed to conduct an election fill hundreds of pages of statutes. At the state, county, and municipal levels, boards of elections must be established to supervise the electoral process. For every several hundred voters, in each state, special political units—precincts or election districts—are created and staffed exclusively for the administration of elections. During each electoral period, polling places must be set up, equipped with voting machines or ballots, and staffed by voting inspectors. Prior to an election, its date, the locations of polling places, and the names of candidates must be publicized. After each election, returns must be canvassed, tallied, reported, and often recounted.

Although every state makes voting easy by providing for the creation and funding of election machinery, states obviously vary in the precise extent to which they encourage electoral participation. Indeed, until the 1970s, states varied enormously in their voter residence requirements, registration procedures, absentee voting rules, and the hours that polls remained open. Until recent years, literacy tests and poll taxes, often employed in a deliberately discriminatory manner, were also important in producing interstate differences in the ease of voting.

**Civic Education** Laws, of course, cannot completely explain why most people vote rather than riot or lobby. If public attitudes were completely unfavorable to elections, it is doubtful that *legal* remedies alone would have much impact.

Positive public attitudes about voting do not come into being in a completely spontaneous manner. Americans are taught to equate citizenship with electoral

DEBATING THE ISSUES

## Do Elections and Voting Matter?

*Most Americans take pride in the country's annual election rituals, pointing out that few nations of the world have mechanisms for transferring power in such a smooth and peaceful fashion. Critics of American elections argue, however, that the differences between the candidates and political parties are marginal, if not nonexistent; that elections and campaigns are more spectacle and show than about real power; and that elections pacify the electorate more than they encourage true citizenship.*

*Political scientists Gerald M. Pomper and Susan S. Lederman argue that elections in fact do meet the criteria for meaningful political exercises. Political scientist Howard L. Reiter, on the other hand, argues that voting is at best a poor method for translating preferences into policies and, worse, that voting tends to channel citizens toward a relatively harmless political act and away from other more effective methods of political expression.*

### POMPER AND LEDERMAN

The first necessity for meaningful elections is an organized party system. . . . Without a choice between at least two competing parties, the electorate is powerless to exert its influence.

A related vital requirement is for free competition between the parties. The voters must be able to hear diverse opinions and be able to make an uncoerced choice. . . . Nomination and campaigning must be available to the full range of candidates, and the means provided for transmitting their appeals to the electorate. . . .

Elections in the United States do largely meet the standards of meaningful popular decisions; true voter influence exists. The two parties compete freely with one another, and the extent of their competition is spreading to virtually all states. Access to the voters is open to diverse candidates, and no party or administration can control the means of communication. Suffrage is virtually universal, and voters have fairly simple choices to make for regular offices. In the overwhelming number of cases, voting is conducted honestly. . . .

Whatever the future may hold, present conditions in the United States do enable the voters to influence, but not control, the government. The evidence . . . does not confirm the most extravagant expectations of popular sovereignty. Neither are elections demonstrably dangerous or meaningless. Most basically, we have found the ballot to be an effective means for the protection of citizen interests. Elections in America ultimately provide only one, but the most vital, mandate.[1]

### REITER

Most of the major issues in American history have been resolved not by elections but by other historical forces. . . . Elections are not very good ways of expressing the policy views of the people who actually vote. Elections are even less effective as a means of carrying out the policy views of all citizens. . . .

Politics, we are encouraged to believe, occurs once a year in November, and for most adults it occurs only once every four years. We are able to discharge our highest civic function by taking a few minutes to go into a booth and flip a few levers once every four years. Although we are all free to engage in other political activities, such as collective action, writing to officials or working on campaigns, most adults are quite content to limit their political activity to that once-in-a-quadrennium lever flip. And if we think of voting as the crown jewel of our liberties, we will not think that citizenship requires anything else.

All in all, the message that elections send us is to be passive about politics. Don't take action that involves any effort, don't unite with other citizens to achieve political goals, just respond to the choice that the ballot box gives us. In a strange way, then, elections condition us *away* from politics. A nation which defines its precious heritage in terms of political rights discourages its citizens from all but the *least* social, *least* public, and *least* political form of activity. This should raise the most profound questions for us. Why should we as a society discourage political activism? What is the real role that voting plays in our politics?[2]

[1]Gerald M. Pomper and Susan S. Lederman, *Elections in America: Control and Influence in Democratic Politics,* 2nd ed. (New York: Longman, 1980), pp. 223–25.
[2]Howard L. Reiter, *Parties and Elections in Corporate America* (New York: St. Martin's Press, 1987), pp. 1–3, 9.

participation. Civic training, designed to give students an appreciation for the American system of government, is a legally required part of the curriculum in every elementary and secondary school. Although it is not as often required by law, civic education usually manages to find its way into college curricula as well.

In the elementary and secondary schools, through formal instruction and, more subtly, through the frequent administration of class and school elections, students are taught the importance of the electoral process. By contrast, little attention is given to lawsuits, direct action, organizing, parliamentary procedures, lobbying, or other possible modes of participation. For example, the techniques involved in organizing a sit-in or protest march are seldom part of an official school course of study.[6]

The New York State first-grade social studies curriculum offers a fairly typical case study of the training in political participation given very young children. The state Education Department provides the following guidelines to teachers:

> To illustrate the voting process, present a situation such as: Chuck and John would both like to be the captain of the kickball team. How will we decide which boy will be the captain? Help the children to understand that the fairest way to choose a captain is by voting.

[6]See Fred Greenstein, *Children and Politics* (New Haven: Yale University Press, 1969). See also Robert Weissberg, *Political Learning, Political Choice and Democratic Citizenship* (Englewood Cliffs, NJ: Prentice-Hall, 1974).

Write both candidates' names on the chalk board. Pass out slips of paper. Explain to the children that they are to write the name of the boy they would like to have as their captain. Collect and tabulate the results on the chalk board.

Parallel this election to that of the election for the Presidency. Other situations which would illustrate the election procedure are voting for:

a game
an assignment choice
classroom helpers.[7]

**AMERICAN POLITICAL DEVELOPMENT**

Concern that "in the absence of republican virtue the American people would ultimately prove unable to sustain a free political life" led to education reform in Massachusetts during the mid-nineteenth century. This "common school reform" sought to shape the moral character of students because it considered "established institutions such as family and the churches no longer capable of teaching self-discipline and respect for law," two essential ingredients of republican government.

SOURCE: Mustafa Emirbayer, "The Shaping of a Virtuous Citizenry: Educational Reform in Massachusetts, 1830–1860," *Studies in American Political Development* 6 (1992), pp. 391–419, esp. pp. 399–400.

Although secondary-school students periodically elect student government representatives rather than classroom helpers and are given more sophisticated illustrations than kickball team elections, the same principle continues to be taught, in compliance with legal requirements. College students are also frequently given the opportunity to elect senators, representatives, and the like to serve on the largely ornamental representative bodies that are to be found at most institutions of higher learning. Obviously, civic education is not always completely successful. Rather than relying on the electoral process, people continue to demonstrate, sit in, and picket for various political causes.

Civic education, of course, does not end with formal schooling. Early training is supplemented by a variety of mechanisms, ranging from the official celebration of national holidays to the activities of private patriotic and political organizations. Election campaigns themselves are occasions for the reinforcement of training to vote. Campaigns and political conventions include a good deal of oratory designed to remind citizens of the importance of voting and the democratic significance of elections. Parties and candidates, even if for selfish reasons, emphasize the value of participation, of "being counted," and the virtues of elections as instruments of popular government. Exposure to such campaign stimuli appears generally to heighten citizens' interest in and awareness of the electoral process.

**The Party System** Law and civic education do not directly stimulate voting as much as they create a favorable climate for electoral participation. Within the context of this climate, the major parties, until recent years at least, have been the principal agents responsible for giving citizens the motivation and incentive to vote. By law, in most American states, party workers staff the electoral machinery. Indeed, at one time, the parties even printed the ballots used by voters. Although the parties have played a role in both civic education and legal facilitation of voting, their prin-

[7]The University of the State of New York, State Education Department, Bureau of Elementary Curriculum Development, *Social Studies—Grade 1, A Teaching System* (Albany, NY: 1971), p. 32.

cipal efforts have been aimed at the direct mobilization of voters. One of the most interesting pieces of testimony to the lengths to which parties have been willing to go to induce citizens to vote is a list of Chicago precinct captains' activities in the 1920s and 1930s. Among other matters, these party workers helped constituents obtain food, coal, and money for rent; gave advice in dealing with juvenile and domestic problems; helped constituents to obtain government and private jobs; adjusted taxes; aided with permits, zoning, and building-code problems; served as liaisons with social, relief, and medical agencies; provided legal assistance and help in dealing with government agencies; and in addition handed out Christmas baskets and attended weddings and funerals.[8] Obviously, all these services were provided in the hope of winning voters' support at election time.

Party competition has long been known to be a key factor in stimulating voting. As political scientists Stanley Kelley, Richard Ayres, and William Bowen note, competition gives citizens an incentive to vote and politicians an incentive to get them to vote.[9] The origins of the American national electorate can be traced to the competitive organizing activities of the Jeffersonian Republicans and the Federalists. According to historian David Fischer,

> During the 1790s the Jeffersonians revolutionized electioneering. . . . Their opponents complained bitterly of endless "dinings," "drinkings," and celebrations; of handbills "industriously posted along every road"; of convoys of vehicles which brought voters to the polls by the carload; of candidates "in perpetual motion."[10]

The Federalists, although initially reluctant, soon learned the techniques of mobilizing voters: "mass meetings, barbecues, stump-speaking, festivals of many kinds, processions and parades, runners and riders, door-to-door canvassing, the distribution of tickets and ballots, electioneering tours by candidates, free transportation to the polls, outright bribery and corruption of other kinds."[11]

The result of this competition for votes was described by historian Henry Jones Ford in his classic *Rise and Growth of American Politics.*[12] Ford examined the popular clamor against John Adams and Federalist policies in the 1790s that made government a "weak, shakey affair" and appeared to contemporary observers to mark the beginnings of a popular insurrection against the government.[13] Attempts by the Federalists initially to suppress mass discontent, Ford observed, might have "caused an explosion of force which would have blown up the government."[14] What intervened to prevent rebellion was Jefferson's "great unconscious achievement," the creation of an opposition party that served to

[8]Harold Gosnell, *Machine Politics, Chicago Model,* rev. ed. (Chicago: University of Chicago Press, 1968), Chapter 4.

[9]Stanley Kelley, Jr., Richard E. Ayres, and William G. Bowen, "Registration and Voting: Putting First Things First," *American Political Science Review* 61 (June 1967), pp. 359–70.

[10]David H. Fischer, *The Revolution of American Conservatism* (New York: Harper & Row, 1965), p. 93.

[11]Ibid., p. 109.

[12]Henry Jones Ford, *The Rise and Growth of American Politics* (New York: Da Capo Press, 1967 reprint of 1898 edition), Chapter 9.

[13]Ibid., p. 125.

[14]Ibid.

"open constitutional channels of political agitation."[15] The creation of the Jeffersonian party diverted opposition to the administration into electoral channels. Party competition gave citizens a sense that their votes were valuable and that it was thus not necessary to take to the streets to have an impact upon political affairs. Whether or not Ford was correct in crediting party competition with an ability to curb civil unrest, it is clear that competition between the parties promoted voting.

The parties' competitive efforts to attract citizens to the polls are not their only influence on voting. Individual voters tend to form psychological ties with parties. Although the strength of partisan ties in the United States has declined in recent years, a majority of Americans continue to identify with the Republican or Democratic party. Party loyalty gives citizens a stake in election outcomes that encourages them to take part with considerably greater regularity than those lacking partisan ties.[16] Even where both legal facilitation and competitiveness are weak, party loyalists vote with great regularity.

In recent decades, as we will see in Chapter 11, the importance of party as a political force in the United States has diminished considerably. The decline of party is undoubtedly one of the factors responsible for the relatively low rates of voter turnout that characterize American national elections. To an extent, the federal and state governments have directly assumed some of the burden of voter mobilization once assigned to the parties. Voter registration drives and public funding of electoral campaigns are two obvious ways in which government helps to induce citizens to go to the polls. Another more subtle public mechanism for voter mobilization is the primary election, which can increase voter interest and involvement in the electoral process. It remains to be seen, however, whether government mechanisms of voter mobilization can be as effective as party mechanisms. Of course, a number of private groups like the League of Women Voters, church groups, and civil rights groups have also actively participated in voter registration efforts, but none have been as effective as political parties.

## Regulating the Electoral Process

Elections allow citizens to participate in political life on a routine and peaceful basis. Indeed, American voters have the opportunity to select and, if they so desire, depose some of their most important leaders. In this way, Americans have a chance to intervene in and to influence the government's programs and policies. Yet, it is important to recall that elections are not spontaneous affairs. Instead, they are formal government institutions. While elections allow citizens a chance to participate in politics, they also allow the government a chance to exert a good deal of control over when, where, how, and which of its citizens will participate. Electoral processes are governed by a variety of rules and procedures that allow

[15]Ibid., p. 126.
[16]See Angus Campbell et al., *The American Voter* (New York: Wiley, 1960).

those in power a significant opportunity to regulate the character—and perhaps also the consequences—of mass political participation.

Thus, elections provide governments with an excellent opportunity to regulate and control popular involvement. Three general forms of regulation have played especially important roles in the electoral history of the Western democracies. First, governments often attempt to regulate the composition of the electorate in order to diminish the electoral weight of groups they deem to be undesirable. Second, governments frequently seek to manipulate the translation of voters' choices into electoral outcomes. Third, virtually all governments attempt to insulate policy-making processes from electoral intervention through regulation of the relationship between electoral decisions and the composition or organization of the government.

## Electoral Composition

Perhaps the oldest and most obvious device used to regulate voting and its consequences is manipulation of the electorate's composition. In the earliest elections in western Europe, for example, the suffrage was generally limited to property owners and others who could be trusted to vote in a manner acceptable to those in power. To cite just one illustration, property qualifications in France prior to 1848 limited the electorate to 240,000 of some 7 million men over the age of twenty-one.[17] Of course, no women were permitted to vote. During the same era, other nations manipulated the electorate's composition by assigning unequal electoral weights to different classes of voters. The 1831 Belgian constitution, for example, assigned individuals anywhere from one to three votes depending upon their property holdings, education, and position.[18] But even in the context of America's ostensibly universal and equal suffrage in the twentieth century, the composition of the electorate is still subject to manipulation. Until recent years, some states manipulated the vote by the discriminatory use of poll taxes and literacy tests or by such practices as the placement of polls and the scheduling of voting hours to depress participation by one or another group. Today the most important example of the regulation of the American electorate's composition is our unique personal registration requirements.

Levels of voter participation in twentieth-century American elections are quite low by comparison to those of the other western democracies (see Figure 10.1).[19] Indeed, voter participation in presidential elections in the United States has barely averaged 50 percent recently (see Figure 10.2). Turnout in the 1996 presidential election was 48.8 percent, the lowest turnout rate since 1924. During the nineteenth century, by contrast, voter turnout in the United States was extremely high. Records, in fact, indicate that in some counties as many as 105 percent of those eligible voted in presidential elections. Some proportion of this total obviously was artificial—a result

[17]Stein Rokkan, *Citizens, Elections, Parties* (New York: David McKay, 1970), p. 149.

[18]John A. Hawgood, *Modern Constitutions Since 1787* (New York: D. Van Nostrand, 1939), p. 148.

[19]See Walter Dean Burnham, "The Changing Shape of the American Political Universe," *American Political Science Review* 59 (1965), pp. 7–28.

FIGURE 10.1

**Voter Turnout Around the World**

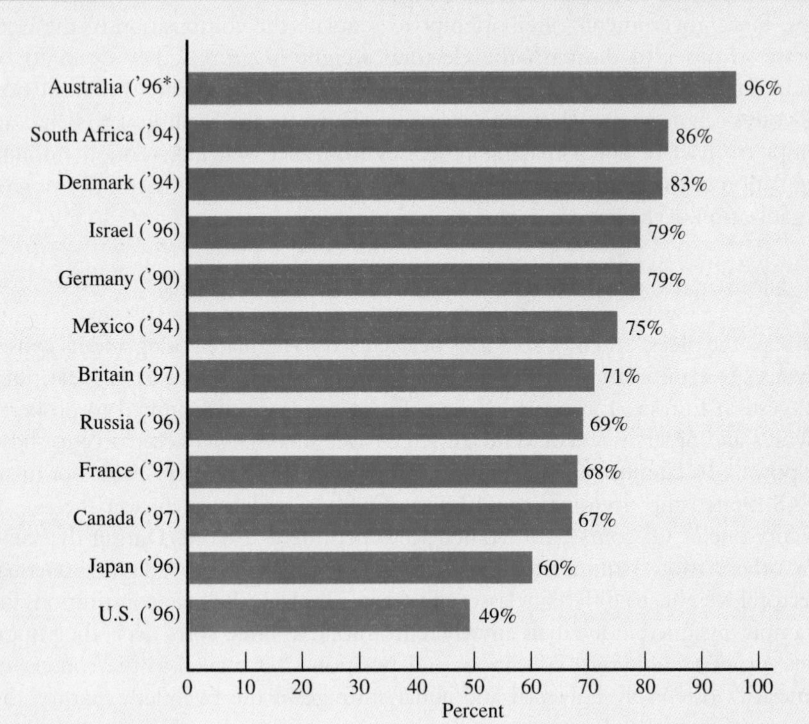


*Note: Year of the most recent national election.

SOURCES: "Diff'rent Votes," *Time,* 23 May 1994, p. 18; Israeli Ministry of Foreign Affairs home page, http://www.israel-mfa.gov.il/news/results.html; Folketingsvalg '94 home page, http://www.dknet.dk/valg94/landsresultat.html; Election Results Bundestagwahlen home page, http://www.jhu.edu/~aicgsdoc/wahlen/bundestag.html#Bundestag; Documents on Mexican Politics home page, http://daisy.uwaterloo.ca/~alopez-o/politics/resultados.html; Warren Hoge, "Blair Succeeds Major; Vows 'Practicable' Policies," *New York Times,* 3 May 1997, http://www.nytimes.com/library/world/050397britain-election.html; Russian Presidential Elections '96 home page, http://www.cs.indiana.edu/hyplan/dmiguse/Russian/elections.html; Canada Votes home page, http://www.votes.canada.com.html; Craig R. Whitney, "Routed in Voting, Premier of France Says He Will Quit," *New York Times,* 27 May 1997, http://www.nytimes.com/library/world/060397/france-election.html; Japan Center for Intercultural Communication, http://www.jinjapan.org/stat/data/03PLT11.html; and authors' update.

of the widespread corruption that characterized American voting practices during that period. Nevertheless, it seems clear that the proportion of eligible voters actually going to the polls was considerably larger in nineteenth-century America than it is today.

As Figure 10.2 indicates, the critical years during which voter turnout declined across the United States were between 1890 and 1910. These years coincide with the adoption of laws across much of the nation requiring eligible citizens to appear personally at a registrar's office to register to vote some time prior to the actual date of an election. Personal registration was one of several "Progressive" reforms of political practices initiated at the turn of the century. The ostensible purpose of registration was to discourage fraud and corruption. But to many Progressive reformers, "corruption" was a code word, referring to the type of politics practiced in the large cities where political parties had organized immigrant and ethnic populations. Reformers not only objected to the corruption that surely was a facet of party politics in this period, but they also opposed the growing political power of urban populations and their leaders.

Personal registration imposed a new burden upon potential voters and altered the format of American elections. Under the registration systems adopted after 1890, it became the duty of individual voters to secure their own eligibility. This duty could prove to be a significant burden for potential voters. During a personal appearance before the registrar, individuals seeking to vote were (and are) required to furnish proof of identity, residence, and citizenship. While the inconvenience of registration varied from state to state, usually voters could register only during business hours on weekdays. Many potential voters could not afford to lose a day's pay

FIGURE 10.2

**Voter Turnout in Presidential Elections (1860–1996)**

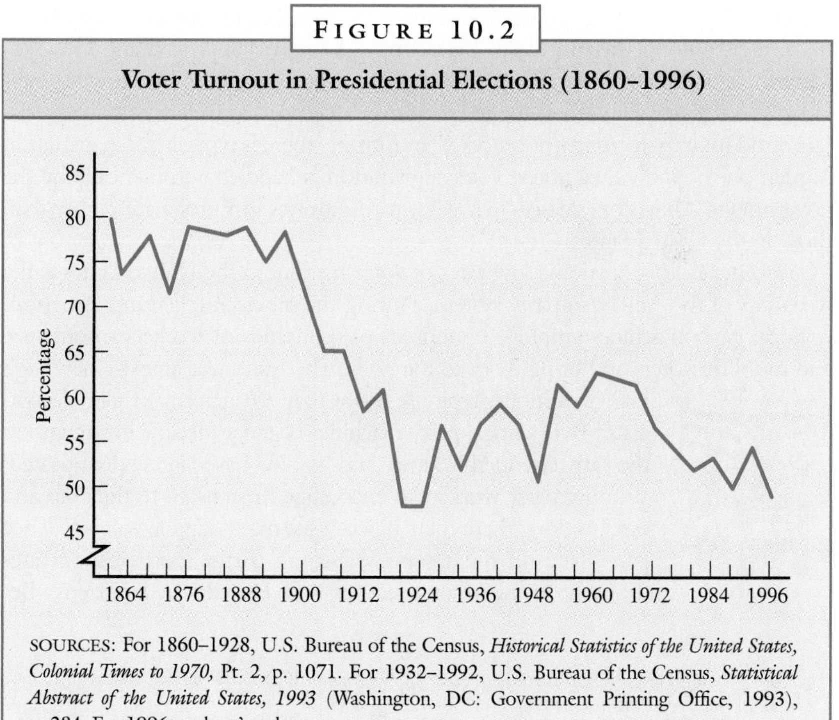


SOURCES: For 1860–1928, U.S. Bureau of the Census, *Historical Statistics of the United States, Colonial Times to 1970,* Pt. 2, p. 1071. For 1932–1992, U.S. Bureau of the Census, *Statistical Abstract of the United States, 1993* (Washington, DC: Government Printing Office, 1993), p. 284. For 1996, authors' update.

in order to register. Second, voters were usually required to register well before the next election, in some states up to several months earlier. Third, since most personal registration laws required a periodic purge of the election rolls, ostensibly to keep them up-to-date, voters often had to re-register to maintain their eligibility. Thus, although personal registration requirements helped to diminish the widespread electoral corruption that accompanied a completely open voting process, they also made it much more difficult for citizens to participate in the electoral process.

Registration requirements particularly depress the participation of those with little education and low incomes because registration requires a greater degree of political involvement and interest than does the act of voting itself. To vote, a person need only be concerned with the particular election campaign at hand. Yet, requiring individuals to register before the next election forces them to make a decision to participate on the basis of an abstract interest in the electoral process rather than a simple concern with a specific campaign. Such an abstract interest in electoral politics is largely a product of education. Those with relatively little education may become interested in political events once the stimuli of a particular campaign become salient, but by that time it may be too late to register. As a result, personal registration requirements not only diminish the size of the electorate but also tend to create an electorate that is, in the aggregate, better educated, higher in income and social status, and composed of fewer African Americans and other minorities than the citizenry as a whole. Presumably this is why the elimination of personal registration requirements has not always been viewed favorably by some conservatives.[20]

Over the years, voter registration restrictions have been modified somewhat to make registration easier. In 1993, for example, Congress approved and President Clinton signed the "Motor Voter" bill to ease voter registration by allowing individuals to register when they applied for driver's licenses, as well as in public assistance and military recruitment offices.[21] In Europe, there is typically no registration burden on the individual voter; voter registration is handled automatically by the government. This is one reason that voter turnout rates in Europe are higher than those in the United States.

Another factor explaining low rates of voter turnout in the United States is the weakness of the American party system. During the nineteenth century, American political party machines employed hundreds of thousands of workers to organize and mobilize voters and bring them to the polls. The result was an extremely high rate of turnout, typically more than 90 percent of eligible voters.[22] But political party machines began to decline in strength in the early twentieth century and by now have largely disappeared. Without party workers to encourage them to go to the polls and even to bring them there if necessary, many eligible voters will not participate. In the absence of strong parties, participation rates drop the most among poorer and less-educated citizens. Be-

[20]See Kevin Phillips and Paul H. Blackman, *Electoral Reform and Voter Participation* (Washington, DC: American Enterprise Institute, 1975).

[21]Helen Dewar, "'Motor Voter' Agreement Is Reached," *Washington Post,* 28 April 1993, p. A6.

[22]Eric Austin and Jerome Chubb, *Political Facts of the United States since 1789* (New York: Columbia University Press, 1986), pp. 378–79.

cause of the absence of strong political parties, the American electorate is smaller and skewed more toward the middle class than toward the population of all those potentially eligible to vote.

## Translating Voters' Choices into Electoral Outcomes

With the exception of America's personal registration requirements, contemporary governments generally do not try to limit the composition of their electorates. Instead, they prefer to allow everyone to vote, and then to manipulate the outcome of the election. This is possible because there is more than one way to decide the relationship between individual votes and electoral outcomes. There are any number of possible rules that can be used to determine how individual votes will be translated. Two types of regulations are especially important: the rules that set the criteria for victory and the rules that define electoral districts.

**The Criteria for Winning** In some nations, to win a seat in the parliament or other representative body, a candidate must receive a majority (50%+1) of all the votes cast in the relevant district. This type of electoral system is called a ***majority system*** and was used in the primary elections of most Southern states until recent years. Generally, majority systems have a provision for a second or "runoff" election among the two top candidates if the initial contest drew so many contestants that none received an absolute majority of the votes cast.

In other nations, candidates for office need not receive an absolute majority of the votes cast to win an election. Instead, victory is awarded to the candidate who receives the greatest number of votes in a given election regardless of the actual percentage of votes this represents. Thus, a candidate who received 40 percent or 30 percent of the votes cast may win the contest so long as no rival receives more votes. This type of electoral process is called a ***plurality system,*** and it is the system used in almost all general elections in the United States.[23]

Most European nations employ still a third form of electoral system, called ***proportional representation.*** Under proportional rules, competing political parties are awarded legislative seats roughly in proportion to the percentage of the popular vote that they receive. For example, a party that won 30 percent of the votes would receive roughly 30 percent of the seats in the parliament or other representative body. In the United States, proportional representation is used by many states in presidential primary elections. In these primaries, candidates for the Democratic and Republican nominations are awarded convention delegates in rough proportion to the percentage of the popular vote that they received in the primary.

Generally, systems of proportional representation work to the electoral advantage of smaller or weaker social groups, while majority and plurality systems tend to help larger and more powerful forces. This is so because in legislative elections,

[23]There are different types of plurality systems. The most famous and the one currently utilized in the United States in congressional and presidential elections is single-member districts and first-past-the-post. For an accessible analysis of the different types of plurality systems and a model for analyzing electoral systems, see Kenneth A. Shepsle and Mark S. Bonchek, *Analyzing Politics: Rationality, Behavior, and Institutions* (New York: W. W. Norton, 1997), pp. 178–87.

## AMERICAN POLITICAL DEVELOPMENT

In the early twentieth century, several cities, "including Boulder, Kalamazoo, Sacramento, Cambridge, Cleveland, Cincinnati, Toledo, New York, and Wheeling," employed proportional representation electoral systems. By the 1990s, "PR disappeared . . . [and] survives only in city council and school committee elections in Cambridge, Massachusetts, and in community school board elections in New York City."

SOURCE: Douglas J. Amy, *Real Choices/New Voices: The Case for Proportional Representation Elections in the United States* (New York: Columbia University Press, 1993), pp. 10–11.

proportional representation reduces, while majority and plurality rules increase, the number of votes that political parties must receive to win legislative seats. For instance, in European parliamentary elections, a minor party that wins 10 percent of the national vote will also receive 10 percent of the parliamentary seats. In American congressional elections, by contrast, a party winning only 10 percent of the popular vote would probably receive no congressional seats at all.[24] Obviously, choices among types of electoral systems can have important political consequences. Competing forces often seek to establish an electoral system they believe will serve their political interests while undermining the fortunes of their opponents. For example, in 1937, New York City Council seats were awarded on the basis of proportional representation. This led to the selection of several Communist party council members. During the 1940s, to prevent the election of Communists, the city adopted a plurality system. Under the new rule, the tiny Communist party was unable to muster enough votes to secure a council seat. In a similar vein, the introduction of proportional representation for the selection of delegates to the Democratic party's 1972 national convention was designed in part to maximize the voting strength of minority groups and, not entirely coincidentally, to improve the electoral chances of the candidates they were most likely to favor.[25]

**Electoral Districts** Despite the use of proportional representation and the occasional use of majority voting systems, most electoral contests in the United States are decided on the basis of plurality rules. Rather than seeking to manipulate the criteria for victory, American politicians have usually sought to influence electoral outcomes by manipulating the organization of electoral districts. Congressional district boundaries in the United States are redrawn by governors and state legislatures every ten years, after the decennial census determines the number of House seats to which each state is entitled. The manipulation of electoral districts to increase the likelihood of one or another outcome is called ***gerrymandering***, in honor of nineteenth-century Massachusetts governor Elbridge Gerry, who was alleged to have designed a district in the shape of a salamander to promote his party's interests. The principle is a simple one. Different distributions of voters among districts produce different electoral outcomes; those in a position to control the arrangements of districts are also in a position to manipulate the results. For example, until recent years, gerrymandering to

[24]Kenneth A. Shepsle has argued that plurality systems are governance-oriented while proportional representation (PR) systems are representation-oriented. For a brief overview of this argument, see Shepsle and Bonchek, *Analyzing Politics*, pp. 188–91.

[25]See Nelson Polsby and Aaron Wildavsky, *Presidential Elections* (New York: Scribners, 1980).

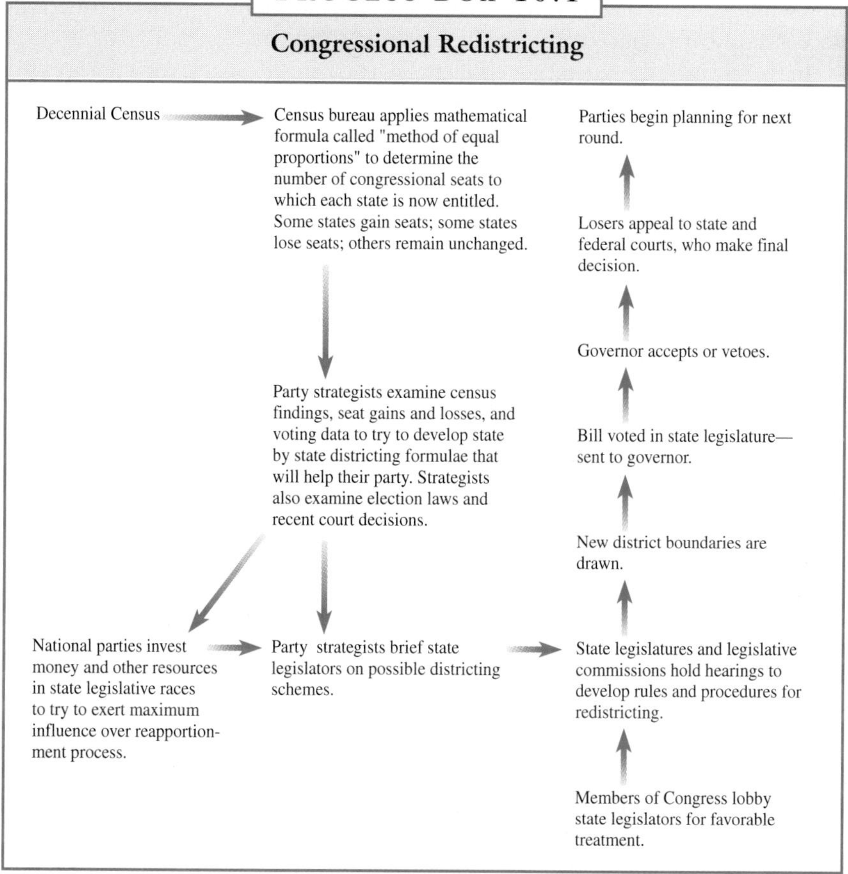


dilute the voting strength of racial minorities was employed by many state legislatures. One of the more common strategies involved redrawing congressional boundary lines in such a way as to divide and disperse a black population that would have otherwise constituted a majority within the original district.

This form of racial gerrymandering, sometimes called "cracking," was used in Mississippi during the 1960s and 1970s to prevent the election of a black congressman. Historically, the black population in Mississippi was clustered in the western half of the state, along the Mississippi Delta. From 1882 until 1966, the delta was one congressional district. Although blacks constituted a clear majority within the district (66 percent in 1960), the continuing election of white congressmen was assured simply because blacks were denied the right to register and vote. With Congress's passage of the Voting Rights Act of 1965, however, the Mississippi state legislature moved swiftly to minimize the potential voting power of blacks by redrawing congressional district lines in such a way as to fragment the black population in the delta into four of the state's five congressional districts. Mississippi's gerrymandering scheme was preserved in the state's redistricting plans in 1972 and 1981 and helped to prevent the election of any black representative until 1986, when Mike Espy became the first African American since Reconstruction to represent Mississippi in Congress.

In recent years, the federal government has encouraged what is sometimes called "benign gerrymandering," designed to increase minority representation in Congress. The 1982 amendments to the Voting Rights Act of 1965 encourage the creation of legislative districts with predominantly African American or Hispanic American populations by requiring states, when possible, to draw district lines that take account of concentrations of African American and Hispanic American voters. These amendments were initially supported by Democrats who assumed that minority-controlled districts would guarantee the election of Democratic members of Congress. However, Republicans have championed these efforts, reasoning that if minority voters were concentrated in their own districts, Republican prospects in other districts would be enhanced.[26] Moreover, Republicans hoped some Democratic incumbents might be forced from office to make way for minority representatives. In some cases, the Republicans' theory has proved correct. As a result of the creation of a number of new minority districts in 1991, several long-term white Democrats lost their congressional seats. The 1993 Supreme Court decision in *Shaw v. Reno,* however, opened the way for challenges by white voters to the drawing of these districts. In the 5-to-4 majority opinion, Justice O'Connor wrote that if district boundaries were so "bizarre" as to be inexplicable on any grounds other than an effort to ensure the election of minority group members to office, white voters would have reason to assert that they had been the victims of unconstitutional racial gerrymandering.[27] In its 1995 decision in *Miller v. Johnson,* the Court questioned the entire concept of benign racial gerrymandering by asserting that the use of race as a "predominant factor" in the drawing of district lines was presumptively unconstitutional. However, the Court held open the possibility that race could be *one* of the factors taken into account in legislative redistricting. Similarly, in *Bush v. Vera,* the Court ruled that three Texas congressional districts with black or Hispanic majorities were unconstitutional because state officials put too much emphasis on race in drawing boundaries. "Voters," said the Court, "are more than mere racial statistics." In *Shaw v. Hunt,* the Court struck down a North Carolina black majority voting district for similar reasons. Most recently, in the 1997 case of *Abrams v. Johnson,* the Court upheld a new Georgia congressional district map that eliminated two of the state's three majority-black districts.[28]

Although governments do have the capacity to manipulate electoral outcomes, this capacity is not absolute. Electoral arrangements conceived to be illegitimate may prompt some segments of the electorate to seek other ways of participating in

[26] Roberto Suro, "In Redistricting, New Rules and New Prizes," *New York Times,* 6 May 1990, sec. 4, p. 5.

[27] Shaw v. Reno, 113 S.Ct. 2816 (1993); Linda Greenhouse, "Court Questions Districts Drawn to Aid Minorities," *New York Times,* 29 June 1993, p. 1. See also Joan Biskupic, "Court's Conservatism Unlikely to Be Shifted by a New Justice," *Washington Post,* 30 June 1993, p. 1.

[28] Bush v. Vera, 116 S.Ct. 1941 (1996); Shaw v. Hunt, 64 USLW 4437 (1996); Abrams v. Johnson, 95-1425 (1997).

political life. Moreover, no electoral system that provides universal and equal suffrage can, by itself, long prevent an outcome favored by large popular majorities. Yet, faced with opposition short of an overwhelming majority, governments' ability to manipulate the translation of individual choices into collective decisions can be an important factor in preserving the established distribution of power.

## Insulating Decision-Making Processes

Virtually all governments attempt at least partially to insulate decision-making processes from electoral intervention. The most obvious forms of insulation are the confinement of popular election to only some governmental positions, various modes of indirect election, and lengthy tenure in office. In the United States, the framers of the Constitution intended that only members of the House of Representatives would be subject to direct popular selection. The president and members of the Senate were to be indirectly elected for rather long terms to allow them, as the *Federalist Papers* put it, to avoid "an unqualified complaisance to every sudden breeze of passion, or to every transient impulse which the people may receive."[29]

**The Electoral College** In the early history of popular voting, nations often made use of indirect elections. In these elections, voters would choose the members of an intermediate body. These members would, in turn, select public officials. The assumption underlying such processes was that ordinary citizens were not really qualified to choose their leaders and could not be trusted to do so directly. The last vestige of this procedure in America is the ***electoral college,*** the group of electors who formally select the president and vice president of the United States.

When Americans go to the polls on election day, they are technically not voting directly for presidential candidates. Instead, voters within each state are choosing among slates of electors who have either been elected or appointed to their positions some months earlier. The electors who are chosen in the presidential race are pledged to support their own party's presidential candidate. In each state (except for Maine and Nebraska), the slate that wins casts all the state's electoral votes for its party's candidate.[30] Each state is entitled to a number of electoral votes equal to the number of the state's senators and representatives combined, for a total of 538 electoral votes for the fifty states and the District of Columbia. Occasionally, an elector breaks his or her pledge and votes for the other party's candidate. For example, in 1976, when the Republicans carried the state of Washington, one Republican elector from that state refused to vote for Gerald Ford, the Republican presidential nominee. Many states have now enacted statutes formally binding electors to their pledges, but some constitutional authorities doubt whether such statutes are enforceable.

In each state, the electors whose slate has won proceed to the state's capital on the Monday following the second Wednesday in December and formally cast

[29]Rossiter, ed., *The Federalist Papers,* No. 71, p. 432.

[30]State legislatures determine the system by which electors are selected and almost all states use this "winner-take-all" system. Maine and Nebraska, however, provide that one electoral vote goes to the winner in each congressional district and two electoral votes go to the winner statewide.

**AMERICAN POLITICAL DEVELOPMENT**

The creation of the electoral college as a means of selecting the president was a compromise between supporters of direct popular election and those who wanted the president selected by the House of Representatives. Many opposed the direct election method because it relied too heavily on the people, represented a loss of Southern and small-state influence, and might empower the president too much. Opponents of House selection feared presidential subservience. Thus the electoral college was adopted as "the second choice of many delegates, though it was the first choice of few."

SOURCES: Neal R. Peirce and Lawrence D. Longley, *The People's President: The Electoral College in American History and the Direct Vote Alternative,* rev. ed. (New Haven: Yale University Press, 1981), p. 22; and Lawrence D. Longley and Neal R. Peirce, *The Electoral College Primer* (New Haven: Yale University Press, 1996), pp. 16–21.

their ballots. These are sent to Washington, tallied by the Congress in January, and the name of the winner is formally announced. If no candidate received a majority of all electoral votes, the names of the top three candidates would be submitted to the House, where each state would be able to cast one vote. Whether a state's vote would be decided by a majority, plurality, or some other fraction of the state's delegates would be determined under rules established by the House.

In 1800 and 1824, the electoral college failed to produce a majority for any candidate. In the election of 1800, Thomas Jefferson, the Jeffersonian Republican party's presidential candidate, and Aaron Burr, that party's vice presidential candidate, received an equal number of votes in the electoral college, throwing the election into the House of Representatives. (The Constitution at that time made no distinction between presidential and vice presidential candidates, specifying only that the individual receiving a majority of electoral votes would be named president.) Some members of the Federalist party in Congress suggested that they should seize the opportunity to damage the Republican cause by supporting Burr and denying Jefferson the presidency. Federalist leader Alexander Hamilton put a stop to this mischievous notion, however, and made certain that his party supported Jefferson. Hamilton's actions enraged Burr and helped lead to the infamous duel between the two men, in which Hamilton was killed. The Twelfth Amendment, ratified in 1804, was designed to prevent a repetition of such a situation by providing for separate electoral college votes for president and vice president.

In the 1824 election, four candidates—John Quincy Adams, Andrew Jackson, Henry Clay, and William H. Crawford—divided the electoral vote; no one of them received a majority. The House of Representatives eventually chose Adams over the others, even though Jackson won more electoral and popular votes. This choice resulted from the famous "corrupt bargain" between Adams and Henry Clay. After 1824, the two major political parties had begun to dominate presidential politics to such an extent that by December of each election year, only two candidates remained for the electors to choose between, thus ensuring that one would receive a majority. This freed the parties and the candidates from having to plan their campaigns to culminate in Congress, and Congress very quickly ceased to dominate the presidential selection process.

On all but two occasions since 1824, the electoral vote has simply ratified the nationwide popular vote. Since electoral votes are won on a state-by-state basis, it is mathematically possible for a candidate who receives a nationwide popular plurality to fail to carry states whose electoral votes would add up to a majority. Thus, in 1876, Rutherford B. Hayes received fewer popular votes than his rival, Samuel Tilden but was declared the winner by a specially appointed commission.

In 1888, Grover Cleveland received more popular votes than Benjamin Harrison, but received fewer electoral votes.

The possibility that in some future election the electoral college will, once again, produce an outcome that is inconsistent with the popular vote has led to many calls for the abolition of this institution and the introduction of some form of direct popular election of the president. In 1992, Ross Perot's candidacy, for example, at one point opened the possibility of a discrepancy between the popular and electoral totals, and even raised the specter of an election decided in the House of Representatives. Efforts to introduce such a reform, however, are usually blocked by political forces that believe they benefit from the present system. For example, minority groups that are influential in large urban states with many electoral votes feel that their voting strength would be diminished in a direct, nationwide, popular election. At the same time, some Republicans believe that their party's usual presidential strength in the South and the West gives them a distinct advantage in the electoral college. There is little doubt, however, that an election resulting in a discrepancy between the electoral and popular outcomes would create irresistible political pressure to eliminate the electoral college and introduce direct popular election of the president.

**Frequency of Elections** Somewhat less obvious are the insulating effects of electoral arrangements that permit direct, and even frequent, popular election of public officials, but tend to fragment the impact of elections upon the government's composition. In the United States, for example, the constitutional provision of staggered terms of service in the Senate was designed to diminish the impact of shifts in electoral sentiment upon the Senate as an institution. Since only one-third of its members were to be selected at any given point in time, the composition of the institution would be partially protected from changes in electoral preferences. This would prevent what the *Federalist Papers* called "mutability in the public councils arising from a rapid succession of new members."[31]

**Size of Electoral Districts** The division of the nation into relatively small, geographically based constituencies for the purpose of selecting members of the House of Representatives was, in part, designed to have a similar effect. Representatives were to be chosen frequently. And although not prescribed by the Constitution, the fact that each was to be selected by a discrete constituency was thought by Madison and others to diminish the government's vulnerability to mass popular movements.

In a sense, the House of Representatives was compartmentalized in the same way that a submarine is divided into watertight sections to confine the impact of any damage to the vessel. First, by dividing the national electorate into small districts, the importance of local issues would increase. Second, the salience of local issues would mean that a representative's electoral fortunes would be more closely tied to factors peculiar to his or her own district than to national responses to issues. Third, given a geographical principle of representation, national groups would be somewhat fragmented while the formation of local forces that might or

[31]Rossiter, ed., *The Federalist Papers,* No. 62.

might not share common underlying attitudes would be encouraged. No matter how well represented individual constituencies might be, the influence of voters on national policy questions would be fragmented. In Madison's terms, the influence of "faction" would thus become "less likely to pervade the whole body than some particular portion of it."[32]

**The Ballot** Another example of an American electoral arrangement that tends to fragment the impact of mass elections upon the government's composition is the Australian ballot (named for its country of origin). Prior to the introduction of this official ballot in the 1890s, voters cast ballots according to political parties. Each party printed its own ballots, listed only its own candidates for each office, and employed party workers to distribute its ballots at the polls. This ballot format had two important consequences. First, the party ballot precluded secrecy in voting. Because each party's ballot was distinctive in size and color, it was not difficult for party workers to determine how individuals intended to vote. This, of course, facilitated the intimidation and bribery of voters. Second, the format of the ballot prevented split-ticket voting. Because only one party's candidates appeared on any ballot, it was difficult for a voter to cast anything other than a straight party vote.

The official ***Australian ballot*** represented a significant change in electoral procedure. The new ballot was prepared and administered by the state rather than the parties. Each ballot was identical and included the names of all candidates for office. This reform, of course, increased the secrecy of voting and reduced the possibility for voter intimidation and bribery. Because all ballots were identical in appearance, even the voter who had been threatened or bribed might still vote as he or she wished, without the knowledge of party workers. But perhaps even more important, the Australian ballot reform made it possible for voters to make their choices on the basis of the individual rather than the collective merits of a party's candidates. Because all candidates for the same office now appeared on the same ballot, voters were no longer forced to choose a straight party ticket. It was indeed the introduction of the Australian ballot that gave rise to the phenomenon of split-ticket voting in American elections.[33] Ticket splitting is especially prevalent in states that use the "office-block" ballot format, which does not group candidates by their partisan affiliations. By contrast, the "party-column" format places all the candidates affiliated with a given party in the same row or column. The former facilitates straight-ticket voting while the latter encourages ticket splitting.

**AMERICAN POLITICAL DEVELOPMENT**

Despite its obvious negative impact on the strength of political parties, the Australian ballot, which facilitated split-ticket voting, "officially recognized political party nominations" by including party designations on ballots.

SOURCE: Leon D. Epstein, *Political Parties in the American Mold* (Madison: University of Wisconsin Press, 1986), p. 163.

It is this second consequence of the Australian ballot reform that tends to fragment the impact of American elections upon the government's composition. Prior

[32]Ibid., No. 10.

[33]Jerold G. Rusk, "The Effect of the Australian Ballot Reform on Split Ticket Voting: 1876–1908," *American Political Science Review* 64 (December 1970), pp. 1220–38.

to the reform of the ballot, it was not uncommon for an entire incumbent administration to be swept from office and replaced by an entirely new set of officials. In the absence of a real possibility of split-ticket voting, any desire on the part of the electorate for change could be expressed only as a vote against all candidates of the party in power. Because of this, there always existed the possibility, particularly at the state and local levels, that an insurgent slate committed to policy change could be swept into power. The party ballot thus increased the potential impact of elections upon the government's composition. Although this potential may not always have been realized, the party ballot at least increased the chance that electoral decisions could lead to policy changes. By contrast, because it permitted choice on the basis of candidates' individual appeals, the Australian ballot lessened the likelihood that the electorate would sweep an entirely new administration into power. Ticket splitting led to increasingly divided partisan control of government.

Taken together, regulation of the electorate's composition, regulation of the translation of voters' choices into electoral decisions, and regulation of the impact of those decisions upon the government's composition allow those in power a measure of control over mass participation in political life. These techniques do not necessarily have the effect of diminishing citizens' capacity to influence their rulers' conduct. Rather in the democracies, at least, these techniques are generally used to ***influence electoral influence.*** They permit governments a measure of control over what citizens will decide that governments should do.

## How Voters Decide

Thus far, we have focused on the election as an institution. But, of course, the election is also a process in which millions of individuals make decisions and choices that are beyond the government's control. Whatever the capacity of those in power to organize and structure the electoral process, it is these millions of individual decisions that ultimately determine electoral outcomes. Sooner or later the choices of voters weigh more heavily than the schemes of electoral engineers.

### The Bases of Electoral Choice

Three types of factors influence voters' decisions at the polls: partisan loyalty, issue and policy concerns, and candidate characteristics.

**Partisan Loyalty** Many studies have shown that most Americans identify more or less strongly with one or the other of the two major political parties. Partisan loyalty was considerably stronger during the 1940s and 1950s than it is today. But even now most voters feel a certain sense of identification or kinship with the Democratic or Republican party. This sense of identification is often handed down from parents to children and is reinforced by social and cultural ties. Partisan identification predisposes voters in favor of their party's candidates and against those of the opposing party. At the level of the presidential contest, issues and candidate personalities may become very important, although even here many Americans supported Bob Dole or Bill Clinton only because of partisan loyalty. But partisanship is more likely to assert itself in the less-visible races, where issues and the candidates are not as well known. State legislative races, for example, are often decided by voters' party ties. Once formed, voters' partisan loyalties seldom change. Voters tend to keep their party affiliations unless some crisis causes them to re-examine the bases of their loyalties and to conclude that they have not given their support to the appropriate party. During these relatively infrequent periods of electoral change, millions of voters can change their party ties. For example, at the beginning of the New Deal era between 1932 and 1936, millions of former Republicans transferred their allegiance to Franklin Roosevelt and the Democrats.

**Issues** Issues and policy preferences are a second factor influencing voters' choices at the polls. Voters may cast their ballots for the candidate whose position on economic issues they believe to be closest to their own. Similarly, they may select the candidate who has what they believe to be the best record on foreign policy. Issues are more important in some races than others. If candidates actually "take issue" with one another, that is, articulate and publicize very different positions on important public questions, then voters are more likely to be able to identify and act upon whatever policy preferences they may have. The 1992 election emphasized economic issues. Voters concerned with America's continuing economic recession and long-term economic prospects gave their support to Bill Clinton, who called for an end to "Reaganomics." Efforts by Bush to inject other issues, such as "family values," into the race proved generally unsuccessful. In 1996, Bob Dole's major issue was a pledge to cut federal income taxes. Bill Clinton called for a "middle-class bill of rights" and tough measures to deal with crime, and also advocated the "family values" that Bush had unsuccessfully championed in 1992.

The ability of voters to make choices on the bases of issue or policy preferences is diminished, however, if competing candidates do not differ substantially or do not focus their campaigns on policy matters. Very often, candidates deliberately take the safe course and emphasize topics that will not be offensive to any voters. Thus, candidates often trumpet their opposition to corruption, crime, and inflation. Presumably, few voters favor these things. While it may be perfectly reasonable for candidates to take the safe course and remain as inoffensive as possible, this candidate strategy makes it extremely difficult for voters to make their issue or policy preferences the bases for their choices at the polls.

Voters' issue choices usually involve a mix of their judgments about the past behavior of competing parties and candidates and their hopes and fears about candidates' future behavior. Political scientists call choices that focus on future behavior ***prospective voting,*** while those based on past performance are called ***retrospective voting.*** To some extent, whether prospective or retrospective evaluation is more important in a particular election depends on the

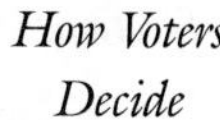

**PROCESS BOX 10.2**

## How a Presidential Campaign Is Conducted

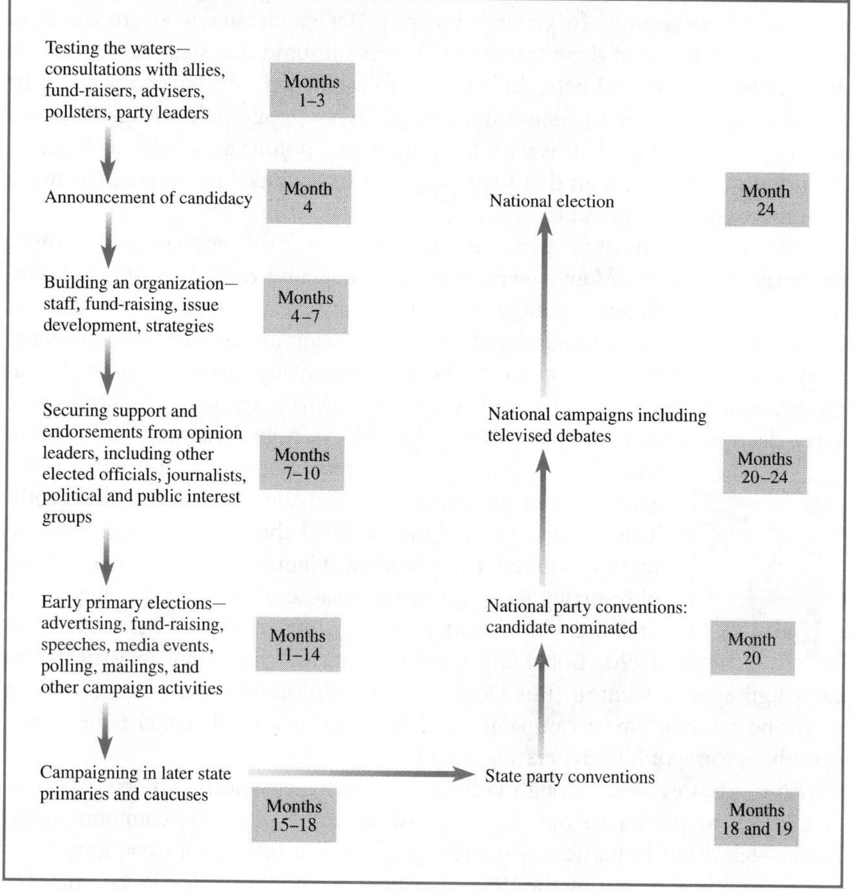

Testing the waters—consultations with allies, fund-raisers, advisers, pollsters, party leaders — Months 1–3

↓

Announcement of candidacy — Month 4

↓

Building an organization—staff, fund-raising, issue development, strategies — Months 4–7

↓

Securing support and endorsements from opinion leaders, including other elected officials, journalists, political and public interest groups — Months 7–10

↓

Early primary elections—advertising, fund-raising, speeches, media events, polling, mailings, and other campaign activities — Months 11–14

↓

Campaigning in later state primaries and caucuses — Months 15–18

→

State party conventions — Months 18 and 19

↑

National party conventions: candidate nominated — Month 20

↑

National campaigns including televised debates — Months 20–24

↑

National election — Month 24

strategies of competing candidates. Candidates always endeavor to define the issues of an election in terms that will serve their interests. Incumbents running during a period of prosperity will seek to take credit for the economy's happy state and define the election as revolving around their record of success. This strategy encourages voters to make retrospective judgments. By contrast, an insurgent running during a period of economic uncertainty will tell voters it is time for a change and ask them to make prospective judgments. Thus, Bill Clinton focused on change in 1992 and prosperity in 1996, and through well-crafted media campaigns was able to define voters' agenda of choices.

**Candidate Characteristics** Candidates' personal attributes always influence voters' decisions. Some analysts claim that voters prefer tall candidates to short ones, candidates with shorter names to candidates with longer names, and candidates with lighter hair to candidates with darker hair. Perhaps these rather frivolous criteria do play some role. But the more important candidate characteristics that affect voters' choices are race, ethnicity, religion, gender, geography, and social background. In general, voters prefer candidates who are closer to themselves in terms of these categories. Voters presume that such candidates are likely to have views and perspectives close to their own. Moreover, they may be proud to see someone of their ethnic, religious, or geographic background in a position of leadership. This is why, for many years, politicians sought to "balance the ticket," making certain that their party's ticket included members of as many important groups as possible.

Just as a candidate's personal characteristics may attract some voters, they may repel others. Many voters are prejudiced against candidates of certain ethnic, racial, or religious groups. And for many years voters were reluctant to support the political candidacies of women, although this appears to be changing.

Voters also pay attention to candidates' personality characteristics, such as their "decisiveness," "honesty," and "vigor." In recent years, integrity has become a key election issue. During the 1992 campaign, George Bush accused Bill Clinton of seeking to mislead voters about his anti–Vietnam War activities and his efforts to avoid the draft during the 1960s. This, according to Bush, revealed that Clinton lacked the integrity required of a president. Clinton, in turn, accused Bush of resorting to mudslinging because of his poor standing in the polls—an indication of Bush's own character deficiencies. In 1996, Bob Dole sought to make "character" an issue in his campaign against Clinton. But Dole was not comfortable with something that might be called a "smear campaign" and did not press the character issue as vigorously as some of his advisers suggested.

All candidates seek, through polling and other mechanisms, to determine the best image to project to the electorate. At the same time, the communications media—television in particular—exercise a good deal of control over how voters perceive candidates. During the 1992 campaign, the candidates developed a number of techniques designed to take control of the image-making process away from the media. Among the chief instruments of this "spin control" was the candidate talk-show appearance, used quite effectively by both Ross Perot and Bill Clinton. And in 1996, the Republican and Democratic parties sought to stage-manage their national conventions to control media coverage. As we will see in Chapter 13, however, no candidate was fully able to circumvent media scrutiny.

## THE 1996 AND 1998 ELECTIONS

President Clinton won a solid victory in the 1996 national presidential election to become the first Democratic president re-elected for a second term since Lyndon Johnson defeated Barry Goldwater in 1964, and the first to be re-elected for a second full term since Franklin Roosevelt's 1936 landslide victory.

FIGURE 10.3

**Distribution of Electoral Votes in the 1996 Election**

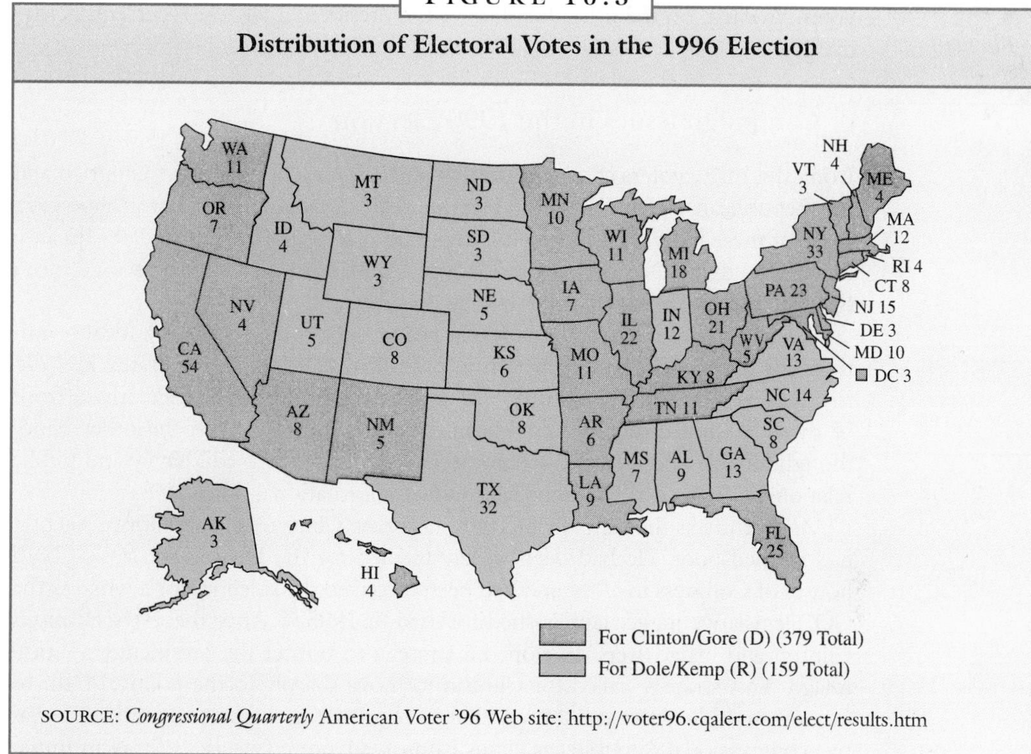


SOURCE: *Congressional Quarterly* American Voter '96 Web site: http://voter96.cqalert.com/elect/results.htm

Clinton won 49 percent of the popular vote and captured thirty-one states for a total of 379 electoral votes. Republican challenger Bob Dole won only 41 percent of the popular vote and carried nineteen states, almost entirely in the South and West, with 159 electoral votes (see Figure 10.3). Independent Ross Perot, who had won 19 percent of the popular vote in 1992, dropped to 8 percent in 1996. Voter turnout in the 1996 election fell to 48.8 percent of those eligible, the lowest percentage since 1924. The 1996 election year also set a record for campaign spending. Candidates, parties, and interest groups spent more than $1.6 billion in their campaigns. The combination of high spending and low turnout suggests that neither party devoted much energy to mobilizing new voters, preferring to work within the boundaries of the existing electorate.

Clinton ran well in traditionally Democratic constituencies. Voters with incomes below $30,000 supported Clinton by a margin of 56 to 33 percent. By contrast, those earning more than $75,000 gave Dole their support by a 50-to-42 percent margin. African Americans gave Clinton their overwhelming support, backing the president by a margin of 83 percent to only 12 percent for Dole. Those voters who call themselves liberals gave Clinton 78 percent of their votes. Those who said Medicare and Social Security were their major concerns gave Clinton 67 percent of their votes and Dole only 26 percent. Finally, as has been the case in recent elections, the 1996 results showed a significant "gender gap."

Men split evenly between the two candidates, giving each 44 percent of their votes. Women, on the other hand, gave the president a 54-to-37 percent victory margin.[34]

## Campaign Issues in the 1996 Election

Ironically, many voters chose Clinton, in part, as a reaction to Newt Gingrich and the Republican 104th Congress. Having decided to vote for Clinton, however, some of these individuals voted for Republican congressional candidates because they feared that a Democratic president plus a Democratic Congress would mean the enactment of expensive new federal programs.[35]

Against the backdrop of a nation at peace and a robust economy, ideal conditions for the re-election of any sitting president, Clinton demonstrated in 1996 that he was a polished, vigorous, and articulate campaigner, particularly in front of the television cameras. Republican nominee Bob Dole, on the other hand, though an able and effective senator, seemed to lack the media savvy and public relations skills needed by a modern candidate for national office.

As recently as the summer of 1995, however, Clinton's chances for re-election had seemed poor. He had been widely blamed for the Democrats' loss of both houses of Congress in 1994 and had been forced to the sidelines for a while as the GOP legislative juggernaut pushed forward in 1995.[36] After the 1994 elections Clinton and his advisers developed a strategy to bolster the president's political image. This strategy called for Clinton to move sharply to the political right to occupy a middle ground between liberal congressional Democrats and conservative congressional Republicans. Thus Clinton advocated a series of tax-cut initiatives (the "middle-class bill of rights"), called for tough anti-crime measures, embraced the idea of voluntary school prayer, spoke out against sex and violence on television, dropped much of his opposition to Republican welfare reform proposals, and advocated "family values" in a series of public addresses.

Clinton's shift to the right outraged many of his liberal advisers. However, his strategy successfully robbed the Republicans of their most potent issues in the 1996 elections.[37] The 1995–1996 budget battle in which congressional Republicans forced two partial shutdowns of federal agencies allowed Clinton to portray himself as a moderate, willing to compromise, while congressional Republicans were pilloried as militant radicals by the national media. "The most important event of 1995," said Democratic pollster Geoff Garin, "was that the Republicans vacated the center in a radical way, and President Clinton was very smart and very effective in filling the vacuum and occupying the center in American politics."[38]

[34]Data are drawn from exit poll results reported in the *Washington Post,* 6 November 1996, p. B7.

[35]See David Broder, "Parceling Out Power to Both Parties," *Washington Post,* 6 November 1996, p. B1.

[36]Jon Healey, "Declining Fortunes: President's Leadership Role Eclipsed by Vigor and Unity of GOP Majority," *Congressional Quarterly Weekly Report,* 27 January 1996, pp. 193–98.

[37]Elizabeth Drew, *Showdown: The Struggle between the Gingrich Congress and the Clinton White House* (New York: Simon and Schuster, 1996).

[38]John F. Harris, "Clinton Had Ingredients for Victory a Year Ago," *Washington Post,* 4 November 1996, p. 1.

Despite Clinton's solid victory, Democratic Senate and House candidates did not fare especially well in 1996. Republicans actually added two Senate seats to give the GOP a 55-to-45 majority in the upper chamber. In House races, Democrats gained eight seats, falling far short of the nineteen that would have been needed to recapture control of the House of Representatives. Republicans had a 227-to-205 House majority in the 105th Congress.

Because of the public's negative assessment of the accomplishments of the Republican 104th Congress in general and given the abysmal poll standing of Republican House Speaker Newt Gingrich in particular, Democrats had hoped to be able to make more substantial gains in House races. Members of the GOP freshman class of 1994 were seen as particularly vulnerable. Republican freshmen, however, proved adept at using the traditional advantages of incumbency to retain their seats. Of the sixty-nine who ran for re-election, fifty-six were able to retain their seats. At the same time, President Clinton devoted little time or energy to campaigning for a Democratic Congress. Clinton opted to concentrate on his own re-election, in essence choosing to wear a coat without tails. Nearly one in seven, or more than six million of the voters who supported Clinton, simultaneously gave their vote to a Republican congressional candidate.

## Campaign Issues in the 1998 Elections

Continuing Republican control of Congress after 1996 ensured that the work of the independent counsel investigating President Clinton's activities would continue. By 1997, independent counsel Kenneth Starr had acquired evidence indicating that Clinton had engaged in a sexual relationship with White House intern Monica Lewinsky and lied in a legal deposition about the matter. In September 1998, the president was compelled to admit publicly his affair with Lewinsky, sending shock waves through the nation. In response to Starr's findings, congressional Republicans launched an impeachment inquiry and eagerly looked forward to the 1998 elections. They assumed that voter disgust with Clinton's actions would give Republican candidates an edge in elections for House and Senate seats. Republican predictions were proven wrong, however. Most voters did not see Clinton's character as the central issue of the campaign. Moreover, as the GOP focused on Clinton's misdeeds, the party's leadership appeared to ignore other national issues. This provided Democratic candidates an opportunity to emphasize issues that voters cared about, such as education and Social Security. The results of the 1998 elections were a rebuke to the Republicans. In most midterm elections, the president's party loses seats in Congress; in 1998, however, the Democrats more than held their ground. In the House, Democrats posted a net gain of five seats, leaving the Republicans with a razor-thin 223-to-211 majority. In the Senate, the party balance remained unchanged at 55 to 45.

Initially, the 1998 results seemed to discourage the GOP from pursuing its effort to impeach Bill Clinton. The electorate was clearly weary of the relentless attack on the president, and many Republicans hoped that some compromise could be reached between Clinton and his opponents. Within a few days, however, the House GOP leadership resolved to resume the offensive against the president, and in December 1998, Clinton was impeached by the House of Representatives on an almost straight party-line vote. Two months later, after a relatively brief trial, Clinton was acquitted in the Senate.

The 1998 election also brought an end to the career of House Speaker Newt Gingrich. Many Republicans blamed Gingrich for the party's poor showing in the elections and demanded that he step down. Two days after the election, Gingrich became convinced that he could not be re-elected to the Speakership and announced that he would resign his House seat. Though Gingrich was the individual most responsible for leading the GOP to victory in 1994, many Republicans were now convinced that he had run out of ideas and lacked the skills needed for day-to-day management of the government. Gingrich's star had been fading since the politically disastrous 1995–1996 government shutdown. The 1998 election sealed his fate.

Gingrich was initially replaced by Bob Livingston (R-La.), chairman of the House Appropriations Committee. In a surprising turn of events, however, Livingston resigned from Congress after it was revealed that he had engaged in a number of extramarital affairs. Livingston urged President Clinton to follow his course. The president declined. The information about Livingston's transgressions had been released by Larry Flynt, publisher of *Hustler* magazine, who had made it his business to defend President Clinton by offering cash rewards to individuals who could prove that prominent Republicans were guilty of misdeeds similar to the president's. Such is the character of politics in America today that pornographers have been transformed into king makers. Livingston was replaced by Dennis Hastert of Illinois, an individual little-known outside the House who was, at least, able to assure his colleagues of his moral probity.

As the dust of the 1998 election settled, both parties lost no time in beginning their preparations for the 2000 national elections. On the Democratic side,

Vice President Al Gore seemed the clear front-runner for his party's presidential nomination, assuming that he was able to answer nagging questions about his 1996 fund-raising practices. Among Republican presidential contenders, Texas governor George Bush, Jr., son of the former president, seemed to be in a strong position after scoring an overwhelming re-election victory. In the Congress, the leaders of both parties promised to raise more money and to develop new issues that would carry their troops to victory.

## Money and Elections

Modern national political campaigns are fueled by enormous amounts of money. In a national race, millions of dollars are spent on media time, as well as on public opinion polls and media consultants. In 1996, political candidates spent a total of more than $2.2 billion on election campaigns. The average winning candidate in a campaign for a seat in the House of Representatives spent more than $500,000; the average winner in a senatorial campaign spent $4 million.[39]

In the 1998 congressional races, the single biggest spender was former New York senator Al D'Amato, who spent $22.6 million but lost to former New York congressman Charles Schumer. Among winning candidates, the individual who spent the least was Democratic congressman Gregory Meeks, who spent just $8,429 running unopposed for re-election from New York's 6th congressional district. The case of Al D'Amato not withstanding, in more than 90 percent of all contests the candidate who expended the most money won the race. In the relatively few elections where a candidate won despite being outspent, the dollar differences were relatively narrow.[40]

The 1996 Democratic and Republican presidential candidates each received $75 million in public funds to run their campaigns.[41] Each presidential candidate was also helped by tens of millions of dollars in so-called independent expenditures on the part of corporate and ideological "political action committees." As long as such political expenditures are not formally coordinated with a candidate's campaign, they are considered to be constitutionally protected free speech and are not subject to legal limitation or even reporting requirements. Likewise, independent ***soft money*** spending by political parties, that is, money contributed directly to political parties for voter registration and organization, is also considered to be an expression of free speech.[42]

## Sources of Campaign Funds

Federal Election Commission data suggest that approximately one-fourth of the private funds spent on political campaigns in the United States is raised through small, direct-mail contributions; about one-fourth is provided by large, individual gifts; and another fourth comes from contributions from PACs (political action committees). The remaining fourth is drawn from the political parties and from candidates' personal or family resources.[43]

**Direct Mail** Direct mail serves both as a vehicle for communicating with voters and as a mechanism for raising funds. Direct-mail fund-raising efforts begin with the purchase or rental of computerized mailing lists of voters deemed likely to support the candidate because of their partisan ties, interests, or ideology. Candidates send out pamphlets, letters, and brochures describing their views and appealing for funds. Tens of millions of dollars are raised by national, state,

[39]Jonathan Salant, "Million-Dollar Campaigns Proliferate in 105th," *Congressional Quarterly Weekly Report,* 21 December 1996, pp. 3448–51.

[40]Center for Responsive Politics, "Money and Incumbency Win Big on Election Day," 4 November 1998 press release.

[41]U.S. Federal Election Commission, "Financing the 1996 Presidential Campaign," Internet release, 28 April 1998.

[42]Buckley v. Valeo, 424 U.S. 1 (1976); Colorado Republican Party v. Federal Election Commission, 64 U.S.L.W. 4663 (1996).

[43]Federal Election Commission (FEC) reports.

GLOBALIZATION AND DEMOCRACY

## *Can Foreign Interests Influence American Elections?*

If globalization affects elections, it is most clearly reflected in campaign financing. As we noted in this chapter, the rate of voter participation is steadily dropping, while campaign spending is at an all-time high. The rising cost of political campaigns means an even more prominent role for wealthy and powerful interests, from whom parties and candidates eagerly solicit contributions. At the same time, globalization creates incentives for foreign governments, groups, corporations, and individuals (as well as American interests with a stake in international trade) to shape American policy through political donations. Although federal election law prohibits foreign contributions, it is conceivable that carefully targeted political donations from overseas could intentionally or inadvertently influence the outcome of U.S. elections.

Allegations of this sort arose in the wake of the 1996 presidential election. Soon after President Clinton was elected to a second term, questions emerged concerning large sums of money from Asian sources that had poured into the Democratic party's campaign war chest and into the Clinton's defense fund. Shortly after the story broke, the Senate Governmental Affairs Committee, under the chairmanship of Senator Fred Thompson (R-Ten.), launched an investigation of campaign financing during the 1996 election. The committee looked into the activities of a number of Asian and Asian American donors to the Democratic National Committee (DNC), including one Johnny Chung, a Taiwan-born entrepreneur living in California.[1] The Committee learned that Chung, as the DNC's chief fundraiser in the Asian American community, had raised and contributed $366,000 to the party in 1996. After receiving a grant of immunity from prosecution, Chung claimed that a high-ranking officer in China's People's Liberation Army

[1]Lena H. Sun and John Pomfret, "The Curious Cast of Asian Donors," *Washington Post,* 27 January 1997, p. AO1.

and local candidates through direct mail each year, usually in $25 and $50 contributions.[44]

**Political Action Committees** ***Political action committees (PACs)*** are organizations established by corporations, labor unions, or interest groups to channel the

[44]Ibid.

(PLA) paid him $300,000 to arrange access to U.S. government officials. Among other things, Chung admitted to setting up a "photo op" for the army officer with President Clinton at a Los Angeles fund-raiser. While the Chinese government categorically denies any attempt to manipulate U.S. elections, some believe that the money was intended to ensure renewal of China's most favored nation trading status and to bolster the Chinese satellite program by attracting customers and technology from the United States. Other questions were raised concerning a possible link between generous campaign contributions from the head of a U.S. satellite maker and a controversial decision by the Commerce Department to allow American satellites to be launched on Chinese rockets. In the end, the DNC returned millions of dollars in dubious campaign contributions.

It is important to emphasize that, until proven, allegations of foreign interests attempting to manipulate U.S. elections are merely allegations. Indeed, the Thompson Committee never managed to find the "smoking gun." But the essential point is that globalization, coupled with declining voter participation and the skyrocketing cost of campaigning, increases the incentives for overseas interests to use political donations to affect electoral outcomes and thereby shape policy. While these interests might use their financial contributions merely to obtain a photo opportunity with the leader of the free world or with the First Lady, they may also have the ulterior purpose of securing technology transfer or access to the American market. It is also well to bear in mind that American laws and attitudes toward political contributions are not universally embraced. In the words of a South Korean businessman whose company was linked to a $250,000 contribution to the DNC (the money was later returned), "This is a cultural question. In Korea and other Asian countries, we donate money to political parties without conditions, but we expect favors later. But [in the case of donating to the DNC] instead of getting favors, we just got trouble."[2]

[2]Ibid.

contributions of their members into political campaigns. Under the terms of the 1971 Federal Election Campaign Act, which governs campaign finance in the United States, PACs are permitted to make larger contributions to any given candidate than individuals are allowed to make. Individuals may donate a maximum of $1,000 to any single candidate, but a PAC may donate as much as $5,000 to each candidate. Moreover, allied or related PACs often coordinate their campaign contributions, greatly increasing the amount of money a candidate actually receives from the same interest group.

As a result, PACs have become important factors in campaign finance in the United States. Many critics assert that PACs corrupt the political process by allowing corporations and other interests to influence politicians with large contributions. It is by no means clear, however, that PACs corrupt the political process any more than large, individual contributions.

In recent years, candidates have learned to use several loopholes in the law governing PACs. For example, until a potential presidential candidate has actually declared his or her candidacy, expenditures by their political action committees generally do not count toward their presidential spending limits. A number of 2000 presidential hopefuls, including Dan Quayle, Jack Kemp, and John Kasich, began early to raise funds that were not subject to the nominal federal limits. Other candidates have discovered they can establish "issue advocacy" organizations rather than PACs and essentially circumvent all federal regulations. For example, in 1997 Steve Forbes created an organization called Americans for Hope, Growth and Opportunity (AHGO) to promote his presidential ambitions. AHGO, which quickly raised several million dollars, was nominally designed to promote issues such as school choice and the flat tax, and was not subject to federal funding rules. Finally, candidates have discovered that federal regulations govern federal PACs, but not state PACs. A number of national candidates have established state PACs, which then proceed to engage in political activities at the national level. For example, Republican presidential hopeful Lamar Alexander has established a national PAC and a Tennessee PAC in preparation for the 2000 presidential race. While his national PAC is subject to federal rules, Alexander's Tennessee PAC can accept unlimited contributions. Nothing prevents the Tennessee PAC from engaging in nationally helpful activities such as polling in Iowa or sponsoring a lobster-fest in New Hampshire.[45]

**The Candidates** On the basis of the Supreme Court's 1976 decision in *Buckley v. Valeo,* the right of individuals to spend their *own* money to campaign for office is a constitutionally protected matter of free speech and is not subject to limitation. Thus, extremely wealthy candidates often contribute millions of dollars to their own campaigns. Michael Huffington, for example, spent approximately $20 million of his own funds in an unsuccessful California Senate bid in 1994. In 1996, publisher Steve Forbes spent $37 million of his own money pursuing the Republican party presidential nomination.

**Independent Spending** As was noted above, "independent" spending is also free from regulation; private groups, political parties, and wealthy individuals

[45]Ruth Marcus, "Staying Ahead of the PACS: Would-Be Presidents Run Around Finance Rules," *New York Times,* 25 November 1997, p. 1.

may spend as much as they wish to help elect one candidate or defeat another, as long as these expenditures are not coordinated with any political campaign. Many business and ideological groups engage in such activities. For example, in 1998, a coalition of labor unions spent more than $1 million in the closing days of the Maryland gubernatorial race to air a series of radio and television ads supporting the re-election of incumbent Democratic governor Parris Glendening. So long as these ads were not formally coordinated with the Glendening campaign, they were considered constitutionally protected free speech and were not subject to federal regulation.

**Parties and Soft Money** State and local party organizations use soft money for get-out-the-vote drives and voter education and registration efforts. These are the party-building activities for which soft money contributions are nominally made. Most soft money dollars, however, are spent to assist candidates' re-election efforts in the form of "issue campaigns," campaigns on behalf of a particular candidate thinly disguised as mere advocacy of particular issues. For example, in 1996, issue advocacy commercials sponsored by state Democratic party organizations looked just like commercials for Clinton. The issue commercials praised the president's stand on major issues and criticized the GOP's positions. The only difference was that the issue ads did not specifically call for the re-election of President Clinton. Critics contend that soft money is less a vehicle for building parties than it is a mechanism for circumventing federal election laws. All told, the Republican party raised $138 million in soft money in 1996, while the Democrats brought in $123 million.[46] This soft money, much of it spent on television advertising in support of the Clinton and Dole campaigns, dwarfed the $60 million each candidate received in public funds, which nominally represented the total amount each was permitted to spend. Republican soft money generally came from corporate donors. Democrats received contributions from labor unions and liberal groups as well as from some foreign business interests. More than $3 million in questionable contributions from noncitizens eventually had to be returned. In 1998, the two parties received at least $220 million in soft money contributions.

In some instances, large donors to the Democratic and Republican parties do not want to be publicly identified. To accommodate these "stealth donors," both parties have created sham nonprofit groups to serve as the nominal recipients of the gifts. For example, the Democratic party established an organization called "Vote Now '96," which ostensibly worked to increase voter turnout. This organization received several million dollars in donations that were used on behalf of the Clinton-Gore re-election effort. For their part, Republicans created two nonprofit groups that took in more than $3 million.[47]

[46]Jill Abramson, "1996 Campaign Left Finance Laws in Shreds," *New York Times,* 2 November 1997, p. 1.

[47]Jill Abramson and Leslie Wayne, "Nonprofit Groups Were Partners to Both Parties in Last Election," *New York Times,* 24 October 1997, p. 1.

**Public Funding** The Federal Elections Campaign Act also provides for public funding of presidential campaigns. As they seek a major party presidential nomination, candidates become eligible for public funds by raising at least $5,000 in individual contributions of $250 or less in each of twenty states. Candidates who reach this threshold may apply for federal funds to match, on a dollar-for-dollar basis, all individual contributions of $250 or less they receive. The funds are drawn from the Presidential Election Campaign Fund. Taxpayers can contribute $1 to this fund, at no additional cost to themselves, by checking a box on the first page of their federal income tax returns. Major party presidential candidates receive a lump sum (currently nearly $75 million) during the summer prior to the general election. They must meet all their general expenses from this money. Third-party candidates are eligible for public funding only if they received at least 5 percent of the vote in the previous presidential race. This stipulation effectively blocks pre-election funding for third-party or independent candidates, although a third party that wins more than 5 percent of the vote can receive public funding after the election. In 1980, John Anderson convinced banks to loan him money for an independent candidacy on the strength of poll data showing that he would receive more than 5 percent of the vote and thus would obtain public funds with which to repay the loans. Under current law, no candidate is required to accept public funding for either the nominating races or general presidential election. Candidates who do not accept public funding are not affected by any expenditure limits. Thus, in 1992 Ross Perot financed his own presidential bid and was not bound by the $55 million limit to which the Democratic and Republican candidates were held that year. Perot accepted public funding in 1996.

## Campaign Finance Reform

The United States is one of the few advanced industrial nations that permit individual candidates to accept large private contributions from individual or corporate donors. Most mandate either public funding of campaigns or, as in the case of Britain, require that large private donations be made to political parties rather than to individual candidates. The logic of such a requirement is that a contribution that might seem very large to an individual candidate would weigh much less heavily if made to a national party. Thus, the chance that a donor could buy influence would be reduced.

Over the past several years, a number of pieces of legislation have proposed additional restrictions on the private funding of campaigns. Political reform has been blocked, however, because the two major parties disagree over the form it should take. The Republicans have developed a very efficient direct-mail apparatus and would be willing to place limits on the role of PACs. The Democrats, by contrast, depend more heavily on PACs and fear that limiting their role would hurt the party's electoral chances.

In the aftermath of the 1996 national elections, the role of soft money came under intense scrutiny. Both political parties raised and spent tens of millions of dollars in soft money to help their presidential candidates, congressional candidates, and candidates for state and local offices. The Democratic party, for example, conducted a $45 million advertising campaign in key states during the summer of 1996. The campaign, which promoted Clinton's record while attacking Bob Dole's, was nominally not coordinated with the Clinton campaign and was thus not subject to federal regulation. However, former Clinton staffers have acknowledged that the White House was effectively in control of the ads.[48] Indeed, many of the questionable fund-raising practices attributed to the president and vice president by congressional probers involved efforts to raise the money needed for this huge campaign effort.

In response to the success of Democratic television ads, the Republicans launched their own soft money advertising campaign on behalf of Bob Dole later in the summer of 1996. The GOP, however, reserved some of its soft money for use in congressional and local races. Some $30 million in national party funds helped Republicans to retain control of Congress and to strengthen their positions at the state and local levels.

In addition to the unregulated soft money spent by the two parties, political candidates in 1996 benefited from large expenditures by individuals and interest groups engaging in issues advocacy. We noted above that as a matter of constitutionally protected free speech, anyone may advocate any position during a political campaign without being subject to federal regulations, so long as they are not explicitly tied to or coordinated with any candidate's campaign organization. Some estimates suggest that groups and individuals spent as much as $150 million on issues advocacy—generally through television advertising—during the 1996 elections.[49]

Some groups are careful not to mention particular candidates in their issues ads to avoid any suggestion that they might merely be fronts for a candidate's campaign committee. Most issues ads, however, are attacks on the opposing candidate's record or character. Organized labor spent more than $35 million in 1996 to attack a number of Republican candidates for the House of Representatives. Business groups launched their own multimillion-dollar issues campaign to defend the GOP House members targeted by labor.[50]

In 1996, 1997, and 1998, Senators John McCain and Russell Feingold initiated an effort to pass legislation to restrict both soft money contributions and issues advocacy. A combination of partisan and constitutional concerns, however, repeatedly doomed the McCain-Feingold initiative to defeat.

In general, efforts to change the rules governing campaign expenditures are undermined by constitutional issues or by the fact that one political party fears that change would help its opponent. Thus, for example, Democrats are more dependent upon

[48]Fred Wertheimer, "Clinton's Subterfuge Is No Technicality," *Washington Post*, 9 November 1997, p. C1.

[49]David Broder and Ruth Marcus, "Wielding Third Force in Politics," *Washington Post*, 20 September 1997, p. 1.

[50]Ibid.

PACs than are Republicans and are, as a result, suspicious about efforts to diminish PAC spending. The GOP, on the other hand, is generally able to raise more money than the Democrats and is, as a result, dubious about calls for limits on soft money spending.

## Do Elections Matter?

What is the place of elections in the American political process? Unfortunately, recent political trends, such as the increasing importance of money, raise real questions about the continuing ability of ordinary Americans to influence their government through electoral politics.

### The Decline of Voting

Despite the sound and fury of contemporary American politics, one very important fact stands out: Participation in the American political process is abysmally low. Politicians in recent years have been locked in intense struggles. As we saw in Chapter 5, partisan division in Congress has reached its highest level of intensity since the nineteenth century. Nevertheless, millions of citizens have remained uninvolved. For every American who voted in the 1998 congressional races, for example, two stayed home.

This lack of popular involvement is sometimes attributed to the shortcomings of American citizens—many millions do not go to the trouble of registering and voting. In actuality, however, low levels of popular participation in American politics are as much (or more) the fault of politicians as of voters. Even with America's personal registration rules, higher levels of political participation could be achieved if competing political forces made a serious effort to mobilize voters. Unfortunately, however, contending political forces in the United States have found ways of attacking their opponents that do not require them to engage in voter mobilization, and many prefer to use these methods than to endeavor to bring more voters to the polls. The low levels of popular mobilization that are typical of contemporary American politics are very much a function of the way that politics is conducted in the United States today.

**AMERICAN POLITICAL DEVELOPMENT**

Much of the decline in voter turnout during the second half of the twentieth century can be attributed to generational changes in the electorate. "The gradual replacement of the habitual voters of the pre–New Deal generations with the nonvoting post–New Deal" generation explains much of the decline in turnout from the 1960s to the 1980s.

SOURCE: Warren E. Miller and J. Merrill Shanks, *The New American Voter* (Cambridge: Harvard University Press, 1996), pp. 40–42.

For most of U.S. history, elections were the main arenas of political combat. In recent years, however, elections have become less effective as ways of resolving political conflicts in the United States. Today's political struggles are frequently waged elsewhere, and crucial policy choices tend to be made outside the electoral realm. Rather than engage voters directly, contending political forces rely on such weapons of institutional combat as congressional investigations, media revelations, and judicial proceedings. In contemporary America, electoral success often fails to confer the capacity to govern, and political forces, even if they lose at the polls or do not even compete in the electoral arena, have been able to exercise considerable power (also see Chapter 17).

During the political struggles of the past decades, politicians sought to undermine the institution associated with their foes, disgrace one another on national television, force their competitors to resign from office, and in a number of cases, send their opponents to prison. Remarkably, one tactic that has not been so widely used is the mobilization of the electorate. Of course, Democrats and Republicans have contested each other and continue to contest each other in national elections. Voter turnout even inched up in 1992, before dropping again in 1996. However, neither side has made much effort to mobilize *new* voters, to create strong local party organizations, or in general, to make full use of the electoral arena to defeat its enemies.

The 1993 Motor Voter bill was, at best, a very hesitant step in the direction of expanded voter participation. This act requires all states to allow voters to register by mail when they renew their driver's licenses (twenty-eight states already had similar mail-in procedures) and provides for the placement of voter registration forms in motor vehicle, public assistance, and military recruitment offices. Motor Voter did result in some increases in voter registration. Thus far, however, few of these newly registered individuals have actually gone to the polls to cast their ballots. In 1996, the percentage of newly registered voters who appeared at the polls actually dropped.[51] Mobilization requires more than the distribution of forms.

It is certainly not true that politicians don't know how to mobilize new voters and expand electoral competition. Voter mobilization is hardly a mysterious process. It entails an investment of funds and organizational effort to register voters actively and bring them to the polls on election day. Occasionally, politicians demonstrate that they *do* know how to mobilize voters if they have a strong enough incentive. For example, a massive get-out-the-vote effort by Democrats to defeat neo-Nazi David Duke in the 1991 Louisiana gubernatorial election led to a voter turnout of over 80 percent of those eligible—twice the normal turnout level for a Louisiana election. And in the 1990s it was the GOP, through its alliance with conservative religious leaders, that made the more concerted effort to bring new voters into the electorate. This effort was limited in scope, but it played an important part in the Republican party's capture of both houses of Congress in 1994. The GOP's gains from this limited strategy of mobilization demonstrate what could be achieved from a fuller mobilization of the national electorate. Significantly, in 1996, while voter turnout dropped, campaign expenditures by parties, candidates, and interest groups rose sharply.

The 1996 national elections were the most expensive in American history, with many estimates placing total campaign spending on the part of candidates, parties, and interest groups at more than $2 billion. During the course of the presidential campaign, media accounts suggested that both parties had accepted

[51]Peter Baker, "Motor Voter Apparently Didn't Drive Up Turnout," *Washington Post,* 6 November 1996, p. B7.

ANALYZING AMERICAN POLITICS

## *Is It Rational to Vote?*

Compared to other democracies, voter turnout in national elections is extremely low in the United States. It is usually around 50 percent for presidential elections and between 30 percent and 40 percent for midterm elections. In other Western democracies, turnout regularly exceeds 80 percent. Though many scholars have tried to answer the question, "Why is turnout so low?" others have argued that the real question should be, "Why is turnout so high?" That is, why does anyone turn out to vote at all?

If we think of voter turnout in terms of cost-benefit analysis, then it isn't obvious why people vote. There are many costs to voting. People must take time out of their busy schedules, possibly incurring a loss in wages, in order to show up at the polls. In many states, voters have to overcome numerous hurdles just to register. If an individual wants to cast an informed vote, he or she must also spend time learning about the candidates and their positions.

Voters must bear these costs no matter what the outcome of the election, yet it is extremely unlikely that an individual's vote will actually affect the outcome, unless the vote makes or breaks a tie. It is almost certain that if an individual did not incur the costs of voting and stayed home instead, the election results would be the same. Gelman, King, and Boscardin estimate that the probability of a single vote being decisive in a presidential election is about one in ten million.[1] Given the tiny probability that an individual's vote will determine whether or not the candidate he or she

[1]Andrew Gelman, Gary King, and John Boscardin, "Estimating the Probability of Events That Have Never Occurred: When Is Your Vote Decisive?" *Journal of the American Statistical Association* 93, 441 (March 1998), pp. 1–9.

improper campaign contributions from foreign donors. Democratic National Committee official John Huang was compelled to resign in the wake of revelations connecting him with millions of dollars in contributions from Indonesian business interests. Obviously, neither party devoted much energy to mobilizing new voters, preferring, instead, to work within the boundaries of the established electorate.

Both sides give lip service to the idea of fuller popular participation in political life. Politicians and their upper-middle-class constituents in both camps, however, have access to a variety of different political resources—the news media, the courts, universities, and interest groups, to say nothing of substantial financial resources. As a result, neither side has much need for or interest in political tactics that might, in effect, stir up trouble from below. Both sides prefer to compete for

prefers is elected, it seems as if those who turn out to vote are behaving irrationally.

One possible solution to this puzzle is that people are motivated by more than just their preferences for electing a particular candidate—they are, in fact, satisfying their duty as citizens, and this benefit exceeds the costs of voting. Yet this hypothesis still does not provide an adequate answer to the rationality of voting—it only speaks to the fact that people value the *act of voting* itself. That is, people have a "taste" for voting. But rational-choice approach cannot say where tastes come from[2] and therefore can not say much about voter turnout.

John Aldrich offers another possible solution: He looks at the question from the politician's point of view.[3] Candidates calculate how much to invest in campaigns based on their probability of winning. In the unlikely event that an incumbent appears beatable, the challengers often invest heavily in their own campaigns because they believe the investment has a good chance of paying off. In response to these strong challenges, incumbents will not only work harder to raise campaign funds but also spend more of what they raise.[4] Parties seeking to maximize the number of positions in the government they control may also shift resources to help out the candidates in these close races.

More vigorous campaigns will generally lead to increased turnout. The increase is not necessarily due to citizens reacting to the closeness of the race (that is, the perception that their vote may affect the outcome) but to the greater effort and resources that candidates put into close races, which, in turn, reduce the costs of voting. Candidates share some of the costs of voting by helping citizens register and by getting them to the polls on election day. More heated advertising campaigns reduces the voters' costs of becoming informed (since candidates flood the public with information about themselves). This decrease in costs to individual voters in what strategic politicians perceive to be a close race, at least partially explains why rational individuals would turn out to vote.

---

[2]Brian Barry, *Sociologists, Economists, and Democracy* (London: Collier-Macmillan, 1970).
[3]John H. Aldrich, "Rational Choice and Turnout," *American Journal of Political Science* 37 (Feb. 1993), pp. 246–78.
[4]Gary C. Jacobson and Samuel Kernell, *Strategy and Choice in Congressional Elections,* 2nd ed. (New Haven: Yale University Press, 1983).

power without engaging in full-scale popular mobilization. Without mobilization drives that might encourage low-income citizens or minorities to register and to actually vote, the population that does vote tends to be wealthier, whiter, and better-educated than the population as a whole. There are marked differences in voter turnout linked to ethnic group, education level, and employment status. This trend has created a political process whose class bias is so obvious and egregious that, if it continues, may force Americans to begin adding a qualifier when they describe their politics as democratic. Perhaps the terms "semi-democratic," "quasi-democratic," or "neo-democratic" are in order to describe a political process in which ordinary voters have as little influence as they do in contemporary America.

## The Consequences of Consent

Voting choices and electoral outcomes can be extremely important in the United States. Yet, to observe that there can be relationships between voters' choices, leadership composition, and policy outputs is only to begin to understand the significance of democratic elections, rather than to exhaust the possibilities. Important as they are, voters' choices and electoral results may still be less consequential for government and politics than the simple fact of voting itself. The impact of electoral decisions upon the governmental process is, in some respects, analogous to the impact made upon organized religion by individuals being able to worship at the church of their choice. The fact of worship can be more important than the particular choice. Similarly, the fact of mass electoral participation can be more significant than what or how citizens decide once they participate. Thus, electoral participation has important consequences in that it socializes and institutionalizes political action.

First, democratic elections socialize political activity. Voting is not a natural or spontaneous phenomenon. It is an institutionalized form of mass political involvement. That individuals vote rather than engage in some other form of political behavior is a result of national policies that create the opportunity to vote and discourage other political activities relative to voting. Elections transform what might otherwise consist of sporadic, citizen-initiated acts into a routine public function. This transformation expands and democratizes mass political involvement. At the same time, however, elections help to preserve the government's stability by containing and channeling away potentially more disruptive or dangerous forms of mass political activity. By establishing formal avenues for mass participation and accustoming citizens to their use, government reduces the threat that volatile, unorganized political involvement can pose to the established order.

Second, elections bolster the government's power and authority. Elections help to increase popular support for political leaders and for the regime itself. The formal opportunity to participate in elections serves to convince citizens that the government is responsive to their needs and wishes. Moreover, elections help to persuade citizens to obey. Electoral participation increases popular acceptance of taxes and military service upon which the government depends. Even if popular voting can influence the behavior of those in power, voting serves simultaneously as a form of cooptation. Elections—particularly democratic elections—substitute consent for coercion as the foundation of governmental power.

Finally, elections institutionalize mass influence in politics. Democratic elections permit citizens to select and depose public officials routinely, and elections can serve to promote popular influence over officials' conduct. But however effective this electoral sanction may be, it is hardly the only means through which citizens can reward or punish public officials for their actions. Spontaneous or privately organized forms of political activity, or even the threat of their occurrence, can also induce those in power to heed the public's wishes. The behavior of even the most rigid autocrat, for example, can be influenced by the possibility that his policies may provoke popular disobedience, clandestine movements, or riot and insurrection. The alternative to democratic elections is not clearly and

THEN AND NOW

## Changes in American Politics

Developments in American politics such as ballot and election reforms, expansion of the suffrage, the decline of political parties, the rise of independent candidates, and technological innovations have all changed both the practice and importance of elections in America.

- Although elections are the obvious venues for political participation today, protests and riots were the dominant forms prior to the use of elections and the widespread expansion of suffrage.
- During the nineteenth and early twentieth centuries, much of the activities by political parties involved mobilizing the electorate to vote. Today, parties seem less willing to perform this role. Candidates and campaigns are now the more likely agents for enhancing electoral turnout.
- Voter turnout in presidential elections neared 80 percent during most of the second half of the nineteenth century. But political reforms between 1890 and 1910—aimed at reducing political corruption—actually decreased turnout in presidential elections. These reforms made it more difficult for voters to register and to remain registered.
- Prior to the 1890s, political parties prepared and distributed election ballots. But reforms adopted by the Australian (or secret) ballot decreased the role of parties in elections by allowing for secrecy in voting and for the possibility of split-ticket voting.

simply the absence of popular influence; it can instead be unregulated and unconstrained popular intervention into governmental processes. It is, indeed, often precisely because spontaneous forms of mass political activity can have too great an impact upon the actions of government that elections are introduced. Walter Lippman, a journalist who helped to pioneer the idea of public opinion voicing itself through the press via the "opinion-editorial," or op-ed, page, once observed that "new numbers were enfranchised because they had power, and giving them the vote was the least disturbing way of letting them exercise their power."[52] The vote can provide the "least disturbing way" of allowing ordinary people to exercise power. If the people had been powerless to begin with, elections would never have been introduced.

Thus, although citizens can secure enormous benefits from their right to vote, governments secure equally significant benefits from allowing them to do so.

[52]Walter Lippman, *The Essential Lippman,* ed. Clinton Rossiter and James Lare (New York: Random House, 1965), p. 12.

## Summary

Allowing citizens to vote represents a calculated risk on the part of power holders. On the one hand, popular participation can generate consent and support for the government. On the other hand, the right to vote may give ordinary citizens more influence in the governmental process than political elites would like.

Voting is only one of many possible types of political participation. The significance of voting is that it is an institutional and formal mode of political activity. Voting is organized and subsidized by the government. This makes voting both more limited and more democratic than other forms of participation.

All governments regulate voting in order to influence its effects. The most important forms of regulation include regulation of the electorate's composition, regulation of the translation of voters' choices into electoral outcomes, and insulation of policy-making processes from electoral intervention.

Voters' choices, themselves, are based on partisanship, issues, and candidates' personalities. Which of these criteria will be most important varies over time and depends upon the factors that opposing candidates choose to emphasize in their campaigns.

Campaign funds in the United States are provided by small, direct-mail contributions, large gifts, PACs, political parties, candidates' personal resources, and public funding. In 1996, some candidates also benefited from issues advocacy.

Campaign finance is regulated by the Federal Elections Campaign Act of 1971. Following the 1996 elections, the role of soft money was scrutinized. The McCain-Feingold bill, a bipartisan attempt to restrict soft money contributions and issues advocacy, failed in consecutive years to gain support in Congress.

Whatever voters decide, elections are important institutions because they socialize political activity, increase governmental authority, and institutionalize popular influence in political life.

## For Further Reading

Black, Earl, and Merle Black. *The Vital South: How Presidents Are Elected.* Cambridge: Harvard University Press, 1992.

Brady, David. *Critical Elections and Congressional Policymaking.* Stanford: Stanford University Press, 1988.

Carmines, Edward G., and James Stimson. *Issue Evolution: The Racial Transformation of American Politics.* Princeton: Princeton University Press, 1988.

Conway, M. Margaret. *Political Participation in the United States.* Washington, DC: Congressional Quarterly Press, 1985.

Fowler, Linda. *Candidates, Congress, and the American Democracy.* Ann Arbor: University of Michigan Press, 1994.

Fowler, Linda, and Robert D. McClure. *Political Ambition: Who Decides to Run for Congress.* New Haven: Yale University Press, 1989.

Ginsberg, Benjamin, and Martin Shefter. *Politics by Other Means: Institutional Conflict and the Declining Significance of Elections in America,* rev. and updated ed. New York: W. W. Norton, 1999.

Jackson, Brooks. *Honest Graft: Big Money and the American Political Process.* New York: Alfred A. Knopf, 1988.

Piven, Frances Fox, and Richard A. Cloward. *Why Americans Don't Vote.* New York: Pantheon, 1988.

Reed, Adolph. *The Jesse Jackson Phenomenon.* New Haven: Yale University Press, 1987.

Reichley, A. James, ed. *Elections American Style.* Washington, DC: Brookings Institution, 1987.

Sorauf, Frank. *Inside Campaign Finance: Myths and Realities.* New Haven: Yale University Press, 1992.

Tate, Katherine. *From Protest to Politics: The New Black Voters in American Elections.* Cambridge: Harvard University Press, 1994.

Witt, Linda, Karen Paget, and Glenna Matthews. *Running as a Woman: Gender and Power in American Politics.* New York: Free Press, 1994.

# 11

# Political Parties

## TIME LINE ON POLITICAL PARTIES

| Events | | Institutional Developments |
|---|---|---|
| Parties form in Congress (1790s) | | Washington peacefully assumes the presidency (1789) |
| Washington's farewell address warns against parties (1796) | | First party system: Federalists versus Jeffersonian Republicans (1790s) |
| Republican Thomas Jefferson elected president (1800) | 1800 | Federalists try to retain power by Alien and Sedition Acts (1798) and by appointing "midnight judges" (1801) |
| Jefferson renominated by congressional caucus; re-elected by a landslide (1804) | | Congressional caucuses nominate presidential candidates from each party (1804–1831) |
| Republican James Monroe re-elected president; no Federalist candidate; no caucuses called (1820) | | Destruction of Federalists; period of one partyism; "era of good feelings" (1810s–1830s) |
| | | Republican party splinters into National Republicans (Adams) and Democratic Republicans (Jackson) (1824) |
| Democrat Andrew Jackson elected president, ushering in "era of common man" (1828) | | Democrats use party rotation to replace National Republicans in government positions (1829) |
| | 1830 | National nominating conventions replace caucuses as method of selecting presidential candidates from each party (1830s) |
| National nominating conventions held by Democrats and National Republicans (1831) | | |
| Whig presidential candidates lose to Democratic candidate Martin Van Buren (1836) | | Second party system: Whig party forms in opposition to Jackson—Democrats versus Whigs (1830s–1850s) |
| Whig William Henry Harrison elected president (1840) | | Whigs gain presidency and majority in Congress; both parties organized down to the precinct level (1840) |
| | 1850 | Third party system: destruction of Whigs; creation of Republicans—Democrats versus Republicans (1850s–1890s) |
| Republican Abraham Lincoln elected president (1860) | | |
| Civil War (1861–1865) | | |
| Reconstruction (1867–1877) | | |
| Republican William McKinley elected president; Democrats decimated (1896) | | Fourth party system; both the Democratic and Republican parties are rebuilt along new lines (1890s–1930s) |
| Era of groups and movements; millions of southern and eastern European immigrants arrive in U.S. (1870s–1890s) | | Shrinking electorate; enactment of Progressive reforms, including registration laws, primary elections, the Australian ballot, and civil service reform; decline of party machines; emergence of many one-party states (1890s) |

| Events | | Institutional Developments |
|---|---|---|
| | 1900 | |
| Republican Theodore Roosevelt becomes president (1901) | | |
| Democrat Franklin D. Roosevelt elected president (1932) | | Fifth party system; period of New Deal Democratic dominance (1930s–1960s) |
| | 1960 | |
| Democratic convention—party badly damaged; Republican Richard Nixon elected president (1968) | | Disruption of New Deal coalition; decay of party organizations (1968) |
| Watergate scandal (1972–1974) | | Federal Election Campaign Act regulates campaign finance (1972) |
| Nixon resigns (1974) | | Introduction of new political techniques (1970s and 1980s) |
| Republican Ronald Reagan elected president (1980) | 1980 | Efforts by Republicans to build a national party structure (1980s) |
| Republican George Bush elected president; Democrats continue to control House and Senate (1988 and 1990) | 1990 | Continuation of divided government, with Democrats controlling Congress and Republicans the White House (1980s–1992) |
| Democrat Bill Clinton elected president; Democrats retain control of House and Senate (1992) | | |
| Republicans win control of House and Senate (1994) | | High levels of congressional party unity as Republicans seek to enact ambitious legislative program (1995) |
| Republicans retain control of Congress while Democrats hold White House (1996) | | Divided government continues (1994–2000) |
| Republicans maintain slim advantage in Congress; third-party candidate Jesse Ventura elected governor of Minnesota (1998) | | |

We often refer to the United States as a nation with a "two-party system." By this we mean that in the United States the Democratic and Republican parties compete for office and power. Most Americans believe that party competition contributes to the health of the democratic process. Certainly, we are more than just a bit suspicious of those nations that claim to be ruled by their people but do not tolerate the existence of opposing parties.

The idea of party competition was not always accepted in the United States.

**CORE OF THE ARGUMENT**

- Today the Democratic and Republican parties dominate the American two-party political system.
- The most important functions of American political parties are facilitating mass electoral choice and providing the organization and leadership of Congress.
- The role of parties in electoral politics has declined in the United States over the last thirty years.
- New political technology has strengthened the advantage of wealthier political groups.

In the early years of the Republic, parties were seen as threats to the social order. In his 1796 "Farewell Address," President George Washington warned his countrymen to shun partisan politics:

> Let me warn you in the most solemn manner against the baneful effects of the spirit of party generally. This spirit exists under different shapes in all government, more or less stifled, controlled, or repressed, but in those of the popular form it is seen in its greater rankness and is truly their worst enemy.

Often, those in power viewed the formation of political parties by their opponents as acts of treason that merited severe punishment. Thus, in 1798, the Federalist party, which controlled the national government, in effect sought to outlaw its Jeffersonian Republican opponents through the infamous Alien and Sedition Acts, which, among other things, made it a crime to publish or say anything that might tend to defame or bring into disrepute either the president or the Congress Under this law, twenty-five individuals—including several Republican newspaper editors—were arrested and convicted.[1]

These efforts to outlaw political parties obviously failed. By the nineteenth century American politics was dominated by powerful "machines" that inspired enormous voter loyalty, controlled electoral politics, and, through elections, exercised enormous influence over government and policy in the United States. In recent years, as we shall see, these party machines have all but disappeared. Electoral politics has become a "candidate-centered" affair in which individual candidates for office build their own campaign organizations, while voters make choices based more upon their reactions to the candidates than upon loyalty to the parties. Party organization, as we saw in Chapter 5, continues to be an important factor within the Congress. Even in the Congress, however, the influence of party leaders is based more upon ideological affinity than any real power over party members. The weakness of the party system is an important factor in understanding contemporary American political patterns.[2]

In this chapter, we will examine the realities underlying these changing conceptions. First, we will look at party organization and its place in the American political process. Second, we will evaluate America's two-party system. Third, we will

[1]See Richard Hofstadter, *The Idea of a Party System* (Berkeley: University of California Press, 1969).

[2]For an excellent discussion of the fluctuating role of political parties in the United States and the influence of government on that role, see John J. Coleman, *Party Decline in America: Policy, Politics, and the Fiscal State* (Princeton: Princeton University Press, 1996).

discuss the functions of the parties. Finally, we will address the significance and changing role of parties in American politics today and answer the question, "Is the party over?"

**THE CENTRAL QUESTION**

"Is the party over?"

## WHAT ARE POLITICAL PARTIES?

Political parties, like interest groups, are organizations seeking influence over government. Ordinarily, they can be distinguished from interest groups on the basis of their orientation. A party seeks to control the entire government by electing its members to office and thereby controlling the government's personnel. Interest groups usually accept government and its personnel as a given and try to influence government policies through them.

### Outgrowths of the Electoral Process

Political parties as they are known today developed along with the expansion of suffrage and can be understood only in the context of elections. The two are so intertwined that American parties actually take their structure from the electoral process. The shape of party organization in the United States has followed a simple rule: For every district where an election is held, there should be some kind of party unit. Republicans failed to maintain units in most of the Southern counties between 1900 and 1952; Democrats were similarly unsuccessful in many areas of New England. But for most of the history of the United States, two major parties have had enough of an organized presence to oppose each other in elections in most of the nation's towns, cities, and counties. This makes the American party system one of the oldest political institutions in the history of democracy.

Compared to political parties in Europe, parties in the United States have always seemed weak. They have no criteria for party membership—no cards for their members to carry, no obligatory participation in any activity, no notion of exclusiveness. Today, they seem weaker than ever; they inspire less loyalty and are less able to control nominations. Some people are even talking about a "crisis of political parties," as though party politics were being abandoned. But there continues to be at least some substance to party organizations in the United States.

### Outgrowths of the Policy-making Process

Political parties are also essential elements in the process of making policy. Within the government, parties are coalitions of individuals with shared or overlapping interests who, as a rule, will support one another's programs and initiatives. Even though there may be areas of disagreement within each party, a common party label in and of itself gives party members a reason to cooperate. Because they are permanent coalitions, parties greatly facilitate the policy-making process. If alliances had to be formed from scratch for each legislative proposal, the business of government would slow to a crawl or would halt altogether. Parties create a basis for coalition and thus sharply reduce the time, energy, and effort needed to advance a legislative proposal. For example, in January 1998 when President Bill Clinton considered a series of new policy initiatives, he met first with the House and Senate leaders of the Democratic party. Although some congressional Democrats disagreed with the president's approach to a number of issues, all felt they had a stake in cooperating with Clinton to burnish the party's image in preparation for the next round of national elections. Without the support of a party, the president would be compelled to undertake the daunting and probably impossible task of forming a completely new coalition for each and every policy proposal—a virtually impossible task.

## Party Organization: The Committees

In the United States, party organizations exist at virtually every level of government (see Figure 11.1). These organizations are usually committees made up of a number of active party members. State law and party rules prescribe how such committees are constituted. Usually, committee members are elected at local party meetings—called ***caucuses***—or as part of the regular primary election. The best-known examples of these committees are at the national level—the Democratic National Committee and the Republican National Committee.

**National Convention** At the national level, the party's most important institution is the quadrennial national convention. The convention is attended by delegates from each of the states; as a group, they nominate the party's presidential and vice presidential candidates, draft the party's campaign platform for the presidential race, and approve changes in the rules and regulations governing party procedures. Before World War II, presidential nominations occupied most of the time, energy, and effort expended at the national convention. The nomination process required days of negotiation and compromise among state party leaders and often required many ballots before a nominee was selected. In recent years, however, presidential candidates have essentially nominated themselves by winning enough delegate support in primary elections to win the official nomination on the first ballot. The actual convention has played little or no role in selecting the candidates.

The convention's other two tasks, determining the party's rules and its platform, remain important. Party rules can determine the relative influence of competing factions within the party and can also increase or decrease the party's chances for electoral success. In 1972, for example, the Democratic National Convention adopted a new set of rules favored by the party's liberal wing. Under these rules, state delegations to the Democratic convention were required to include women and members of minority groups in rough proportion to those groups' representation among the party's membership in that state. Liberals correctly calculated that women and African Americans would generally support liberal ideas and candidates. The rules also called for the use of proportional

FIGURE 11.1

**How American Parties Are Organized**

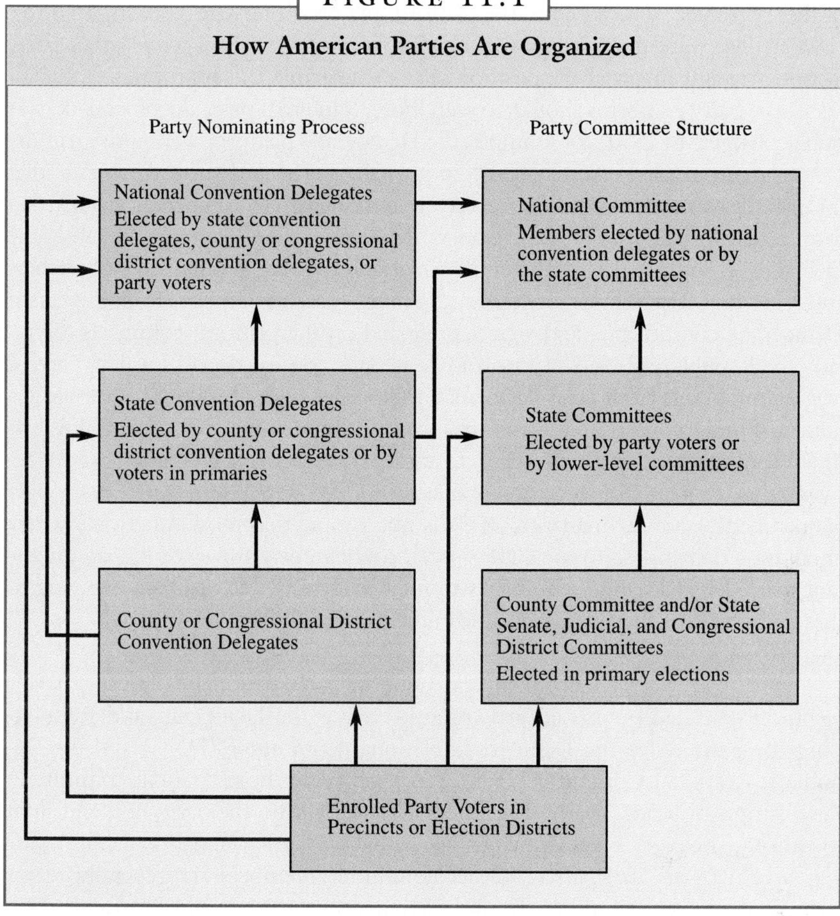


representation—a voting system liberals thought would give them an advantage by allowing the election of more women and minority delegates. (Although Republican rules do not require proportional representation, some state legislatures have moved to compel both parties to use this system in all their presidential primaries.)

The convention also approves the party platform. Platforms are often dismissed as documents filled with platitudes that are seldom read by voters. To some extent this criticism is well founded. Not one voter in a thousand so much as glances at the party platform, and even the news media pay little attention to the documents. Furthermore, the parties' presidential candidates make little use of the platforms in their campaigns; usually they prefer to develop and promote their own themes. Nonetheless, the platform can be an important document. The platform should be understood as a contract in which the various party factions attending the convention state their terms for supporting the ticket. For one faction, welfare reform may be a key issue. For another faction, tax reduction may be more important. For a third, the critical issue may be deficit reduction. When one of these "planks" is included in the platform, its promoters are asserting that this is what they want in exchange for their support of the ticket, while other party factions are agreeing that the position seems reasonable and appropriate.

Thus, party platforms should be seen more as internal party documents than as public pledges. In 1992, for example, the Democratic platform went into great detail on environmental issues such as "old-growth forests" and "critical habitats" that mean little to most voters but are very important to environmental groups that form an important part of the Democratic party's activist coalition. In 1996, the Democratic platform devoted an entire paragraph to praising public school teachers and criticizing Republicans for "teacher bashing." Teachers unions are an important Democratic constituency, and were represented on the platform committee. Similarly, the Republicans' 1992 platform advocated the construction of a wall to prevent illegal immigrants from crossing the nation's border with Mexico. This is hardly a matter of much concern to most of the country's Republicans. But to party loyalists in the southwestern states, as well as to some social conservatives among GOP activists, this is a matter of some significance. The 1996 Republican platform strongly condemned "same-sex marriage." This is not a topic that most Americans worry about on a daily basis. To the GOP's social conservatives, however, it is an important issue. By including these planks in their platforms, each party was saying to these activists that they were welcome in the party coalition.

**National Committee** Between conventions, each national political party is technically headed by its national committee. For the Democrats and Republicans, these are called the Democratic National Committee (DNC) and the Republican National Committee (RNC), respectively. These national committees raise campaign funds, head off factional disputes within the party, and endeavor to enhance the party's media image. The actual work of each national committee is overseen by its chairperson. Other committee members are generally major party contributors or fund raisers and serve in a largely ceremonial capacity.

For whichever party controls the White House, the party's national committee chair is appointed by the president. Typically, this means that that party's national committee becomes little more than an adjunct to the White House staff. For a first-term president, the committee devotes the bulk of its energy to the re-election campaign. The national committee chair of the party not in control of the White House is selected by the committee itself and usually takes a broader view of the party's needs, raising money and performing other activities on behalf of the party's members in Congress and in the state legislatures.

Senator Chris Dodd, who chaired the DNC during the 1996 national campaign, made President Clinton's re-election his top priority. RNC chair Haley Barbour not only worked to put a Republican in the White House, but also sought to strengthen the Republican party at the congressional and local levels by recruiting strong candidates and raising money for their campaigns. In 1996, Barbour was the master strategist behind the GOP congressional effort, deciding where to allocate funds and focus the party's efforts. Barbour's controversial decision to hold tens of millions of dollars in reserve for the closing days of the campaign is now credited with preserving the GOP's control over both houses of Congress.

**Congressional Campaign Committees** Each party forms House and Senate campaign committees to raise funds for House and Senate election campaigns. Their efforts may or may not be coordinated with the activities of the national committees. For the party that controls the White House, the national committee and the congressional campaign committees are often rivals, since both groups are seeking donations from the same people but for different candidates: The national committee seeks funds for the presidential race while the congressional campaign committees approach the same contributors for support for the congressional contests. In recent years, the Republican party has attempted to coordinate the fund-raising activities of all its committees. Republicans have sought to give the GOP's national institutions the capacity to invest funds in those close congressional, state, and local races where they can do the most good. The Democrats have been slower to coordinate their various committee activities, and this may have placed them at a disadvantage in recent congressional and local races.

In recent years, the various party committees have raised prodigious amounts of money for national elections. Through June 30, 1996, the Republican National Committee and the Republican congressional and senatorial campaign committees had, together, raised and spent more than $264 million to elect Republicans to national office. During the same period, the Democratic National Committee, along with the Democratic congressional and senatorial campaign committees, had raised $173 million.[3] On the basis of the Supreme Court's decision in the 1996 case of the Colorado Republican Federal Campaign Committee against the Federal Election Commission, the government may not limit the amount of money a political party may spend on any given race so long as its expenditures are not coordinated with those of the candidate.[4] In practice, of course, some measure of coordination is almost inevitable.

### AMERICAN POLITICAL DEVELOPMENT

Although there is evidence of earlier campaign coordination for House seats, one scholar dates the beginning of CCCs (Congressional Campaign Committees) to 1866. From then until 1920, CCCs for the House provided services such as arranging speakers for campaigns, providing press assistance, producing literature and issue books, and fund-raising. CCCs for the Senate began in 1920, after the Seventeenth Amendment provided for the direct election of senators. Campaign committees for both parties and in both chambers have expanded their services and fund-raising to meet growing demands of twentieth-century campaigning.

SOURCE: Robin Kolodny, *Pursuing Majorities: Congressional Campaign Committees in American Politics* (Norman: University of Oklahoma Press, 1998).

**State and Local Party Organizations** Each of the two major parties has a central committee in each state. The parties traditionally also have county committees and, in some instances, state senate district committees, judicial district committees, and in the case of larger cities, city-wide party committees and local assembly district "ward" committees as well. Congressional districts also may have party committees.

Some cities also have precinct committees. Precincts are not districts from which any representative is elected but instead are legally defined subdivisions of

[3]Jonathan Salant, "Finances Take Priority in This Year's Races," *Congressional Quarterly Weekly Report,* vol. 54, no. 43, 26 October 1996, pp. 3081–84.

[4]Colorado Republican Federal Campaign Committee v. Jones, 95-489 (1996).

BOX 11.1

## Boss Rule in Chicago

During the 1950s and 1960s, Mayor Richard J. Daley was the absolute ruler of the city of Chicago. Politicians, judges, the police and fire departments, and municipal agencies all were subservient to the Daley "machine." The source of machine power was its control of county and municipal elections. Those who supported Daley's political opponents often found that such heresy could be dangerous. Consider the case of one supporter of Republican Benjamin Adamowski, who opposed Daley in the 1957 mayoral election:

> The owner of a small restaurant at Division and Ashland, the heart of the city's Polish neighborhood, put up a big Adamowski sign. The day it went up the precinct captain came around and said, "How come the sign, Harry?" "Ben's a friend of mine," the restaurant owner said. "Ben's a nice guy, Harry, but that's a pretty big sign. I'd appreciate it if you'd take it down." "No, it's staying up."
>
> The next day the captain came back. "Look, I'm the precinct captain. Is there anything wrong, any problem, anything I can help you with?" Harry said no. "Then why don't you take it down. You know how this looks in my job." Harry wouldn't budge. The sign stayed up.
>
> On the third day, the city building inspectors came. The plumbing improvement alone cost Harry $2,100.

SOURCE: Mike Royko, *Boss: Richard J. Daley of Chicago* (New York: E. P. Dutton, Inc., 1971). 

wards that are used to register voters and set up ballot boxes or voting machines. A precinct is typically composed of three hundred to six hundred voters. Well-organized political parties—especially the famous old machines of New York, Chicago, and Boston—provide for "precinct captains" and a fairly tight group of party members around them (see Box 11.1). Precinct captains were usually members of long standing in neighborhood party clubhouses, which were important social centers as well as places for distributing favors to constituents.

In the nineteenth and early twentieth centuries, many cities and counties and even a few states upon occasion have had such well-organized parties that they were called machines and their leaders were called "bosses." Some of the great reform movements in American history were motivated by the excessive powers and abuses of these machines and their bosses. But few, if any, machines are left today. Traditional party machines depended heavily upon patronage, their power to control government jobs. With thousands of jobs to dispense, party bosses were able to recruit armies of political workers who, in turn, mobilized millions of voters. Today, because of civil service reform, party leaders no longer control many positions. Nevertheless, state and local party organizations are very active in recruiting candidates, conducting voter registration drives, and providing financial assistance to candidates. In many respects, federal election law has given state and local party organizations new life. Under current law, state and local party organizations can spend unlimited amounts of money on "party-building" activities such as voter registration and get-out-the-vote drives. As a result, the national party organizations, which have enormous fund-raising abilities but are limited by law in how much they can spend on candidates, each year transfer millions of dollars to the state and local organizations. The state and local parties, in turn, spend these funds, sometimes called soft money, to promote the candidacies of national, as well as state and local, candidates. In this process, as local organizations have become linked financially to the national parties, American political parties have become somewhat more integrated and nationalized than ever before. At the same time, the state and local party organizations have come to control large financial resources and play important roles in elections despite the collapse of the old patronage machines.[5]

## The Two-Party System in America

Although George Washington, and in fact many leaders of the time, deplored partisan politics, the two-party system emerged early in the history of the new Republic. Beginning with the Federalists and the Jeffersonian Republicans in the late 1780s, two major parties would dominate national politics, although which particular two parties they were would change with the times and issues. This two-party system has culminated in today's Democrats and Republicans.

### Historical Origins

Historically, parties form in one of two ways. The first, which could be called *internal mobilization,* occurs when political conflicts break out and government officials and competing factions seek to mobilize popular support. This is precisely what happened during the early years of the American Republic. Competition in the Congress between northeastern mercantile and southern agrarian factions led first the Southerners and then the Northeasterners to attempt to organize popular followings. The result was the foundation of America's first national parties—the Jeffersonians, whose primary base was in the South, and the Federalists, whose strength was greatest in the New England states.

The second common mode of party organization, which could be called *external mobilization,* takes place when a group of politicians outside the established governmental framework develops and organizes popular support to win governmental power. For example, during the 1850s, a group of state politicians who

[5]For a useful discussion, see John Bibby and Thomas Holbrook, "Parties and Elections," in *Politics in the American States,* ed. Virginia Gray and Herbert Jacob (Washington, DC: Congressional Quarterly Press, 1996), pp. 78–121.

opposed slavery, especially the expansion of slavery in America's territorial possessions, built what became the Republican party by constructing party organizations and mobilizing popular support in the Northeast and West. The evolution of American political parties is shown in Process Box 11.1.

America's two major parties are now, of course, the Democrats and Republicans. Each has had an important place in U.S. history.

**The Democrats** When the Jeffersonian party splintered in 1824, Andrew Jackson emerged as the leader of one of its four factions. In 1830, Jackson's group became the Democratic party. This new party had the strongest national organization of its time and presented itself as the party of the common man. Jacksonians supported reductions in the price of public lands and a policy of cheaper money and credit. Laborers, immigrants, and settlers west of the Alleghenies were quickly attracted to this new party.

From 1828, when Jackson was elected president, to 1860, the Democratic party was the dominant force in American politics. For all but eight of those years, the Democrats held the White House. In addition, a Democratic majority controlled the Senate for twenty-six years and the House for twenty-four years during the same time period. Nineteenth-century Democrats emphasized the importance of interpreting the Constitution literally, upholding states' rights, and limiting federal spending.

In 1860, the issue of slavery split the Democrats along geographic lines. In the South, many Democrats served in the Confederate government. In the North, one faction of the party (the Copperheads) opposed the war and advocated negotiating a peace with the South. Thus, for years after the war, Republicans denounced the Democrats as the "party of treason."

The Democratic party was not fully able to regain its political strength until the Great Depression. In 1933, Democrat Franklin D. Roosevelt entered the White House, and the Democrats won control of Congress as well. Roosevelt's New Deal coalition, composed of Catholics, Jews, blacks, farmers, intellectuals, and members of organized labor, dominated American politics until the 1970s and served as the basis for the party's expansion of federal power and efforts to remedy social problems.

The Democrats were never fully united. In Congress, Southern Democrats often aligned with Republicans in the "conservative coalition" rather than with members of their own party. But the Democratic party remained America's majority party, usually controlling both Congress and the White House, for nearly four decades after 1932. By the 1980s, the Democratic coalition faced serious problems. The once-Solid South often voted for the Republicans, along with many blue-collar Northern voters. On the other hand, the Democrats increased their strength among African American voters and women. The Democrats maintained a strong base in the bureaucracies of the federal government and the states, in labor unions, and in the not-for-profit sector of the economy. During the 1980s and 1990s, moderate Democrats were able to take control of the party nominating process and sought to broaden middle-class support for the party. This helped the Democrats elect a president in 1992. In 1994, however, the unpopularity of Democratic president Bill Clinton led to the loss of the Democrats' control over both houses of Congress for the first time since 1946. In 1996,

PROCESS BOX 11.1

## How the Party System Evolved

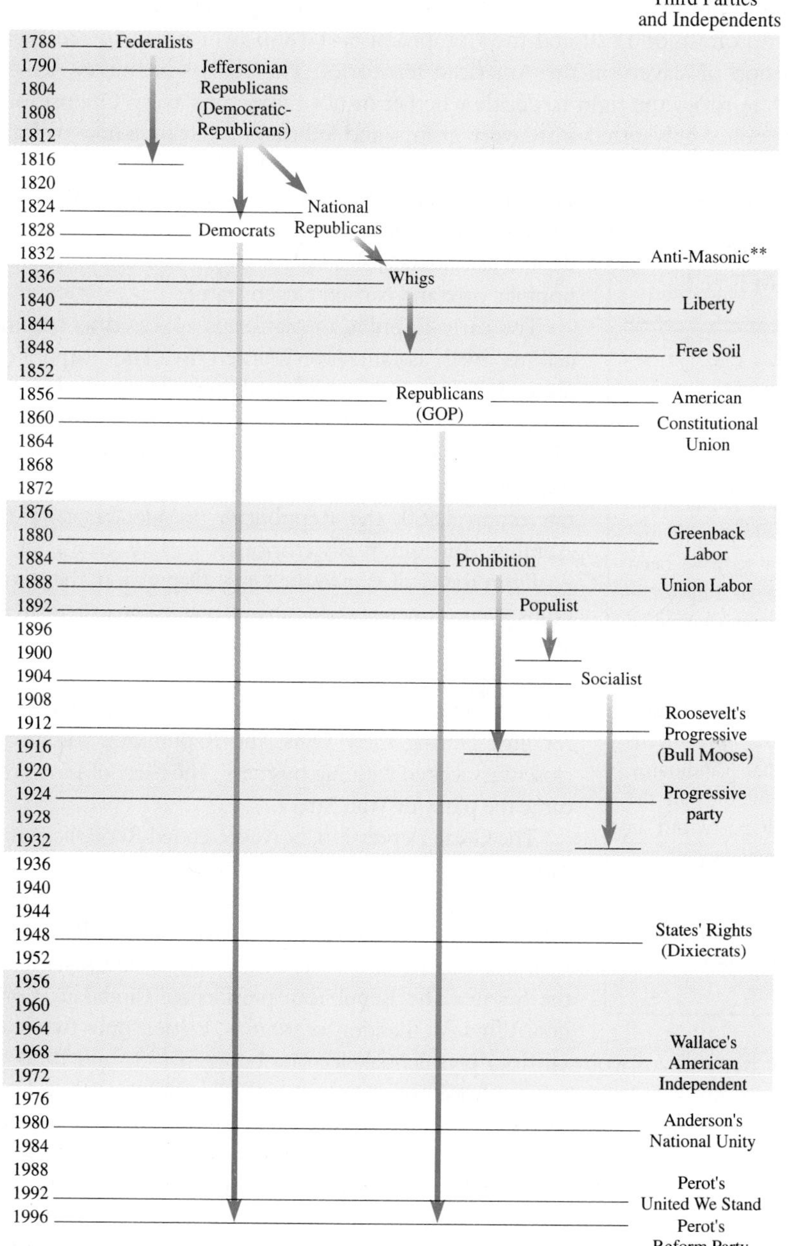


*Or in some cases, fourth party; most of these are one-term parties.

**The Anti-Masonics not only had the distinction of being the first third party, but they were also the first party to hold a national nominating convention and the first to announce a party platform.

Clinton was able to win re-election to a second term over the weak opposition of Republican candidate Robert Dole. Democrats were, however, unable to dislodge their GOP rivals from the leadership of either house of Congress in both 1996 and 1998.

**The Republicans** The 1854 Kansas-Nebraska Act overturned the Missouri Compromise of 1820 and the Compromise of 1850, which had barred the expansion of slavery in the American territories. The Kansas-Nebraska Act gave each territory the right to decide whether or not to permit slavery. Opposition to this policy galvanized antislavery groups and led them to create a new party, the Republicans. It drew its membership from existing political groups—former Whigs, Know-Nothings, Free Soilers, and antislavery Democrats. In 1856, the party's first presidential candidate, John C. Frémont, won one-third of the popular vote and carried eleven states.

The early Republican platforms appealed to commercial as well as antislavery interests. The Republicans favored homesteading, internal improvements, the construction of a transcontinental railroad, and protective tariffs, as well as the containment of slavery. In 1858, the Republican party won control of the House of Representatives; in 1860, the Republican presidential candidate, Abraham Lincoln, was victorious.

From the Civil War to the Great Depression, the Republicans were America's dominant political party, especially after 1896. In the seventy-two years between 1860 and 1932, Republicans occupied the White House for fifty-six years, controlled the Senate for sixty years, and the House for fifty. During these years, the Republicans came to be closely associated with big business. The party of Lincoln became the party of Wall Street.

The Great Depression, however, ended Republican hegemony. The voters held Republican president Herbert Hoover responsible for the economic catastrophe, and by 1936, the party's popularity was so low that Republicans won only eighty-nine seats in the House and seventeen in the Senate. The Republican presidential candidate, Governor Alfred M. Landon of Kansas, carried only two states. The Republicans won only four presidential elections between 1932 and 1980, and they controlled Congress for only four of those years (1947–1949 and 1953–1955).

The Republican party has widened its appeal over the last four decades. Groups previously associated with the Democratic party—particularly blue-collar workers and Southern Democrats—have been increasingly attracted to Republican presidential candidates (for example, Dwight D. Eisenhower, Richard Nixon, Ronald Reagan, and George Bush). Yet, Republicans generally did not do as well at the state and local levels and, until recently, had little chance of capturing a majority in either the House or Senate. Yet in 1994, the Republican party finally won a majority in both houses of Congress, in large part because of the party's growing strength in the South.

**AMERICAN POLITICAL DEVELOPMENT**

The organizational roots of contemporary parties began in the 1820s. After his defeat in the 1824 presidential election (the only presidential election in U.S. history to have been decided in the House of Representatives), Andrew Jackson started a decade-long process of party organization, which included popular mobilization of the electorate, the adoption of the convention system as a means of selecting presidential candidates, and democratization not only in the Jacksonian Democratic party but in the opposition Whig party as well.

SOURCE: Walter Dean Burnham, *The Current Crisis in American Politics* (New York: Oxford University Press, 1982), p. 104–6.

During the 1990s, conservative religious groups, who had been attracted to the Republican camp by its opposition to abortion and support for school prayer, made a concerted effort to expand their influence within the party. This effort led to conflict between these members of the "religious Right" and more traditional "country-club" Republicans, whose major concerns were matters such as taxes and federal regulation of business. This coalition swept the polls in 1994 and maintained its control of both houses of Congress in 1996. The GOP's 1996 presidential standard bearer, Senator Robert Dole, however, went down to defeat partly because Democrats were able to portray Republican social conservatives as dangerous "extremists."[6] In 1998, Democrats continued to portray Republicans as out of touch with the electorate during the investigation of Clinton's affair with Monica Lewinsky. Though Republicans maintained slim advantages in both houses of Congress following the 1998 elections, their poor showing forced House Speaker Newt Gingrich to resign from office immediately.

## Electoral Alignments and Realignments

In the United States, party politics has followed a fascinating pattern (see Figure 11.2). Typically, during the course of American political history, the national electoral arena has been dominated by one party for a period of roughly thirty years. At the conclusion of this period, the dominant party has been supplanted by a new party in what political scientists call an ***electoral realignment.*** The realignment is typically followed by a long period in which the new party is the dominant political force in the United States—not necessarily winning every election but generally maintaining control of the Congress and usually of the White House as well.[7]

Although there are some disputes among scholars about the precise timing of these critical realignments, there is general agreement that at least five have occurred since the founding of the American Republic. The first took place around 1800 when the Jeffersonian Republicans defeated the Federalists and became the dominant force in American politics. The second realignment occurred in about 1828, when the Jacksonian Democrats took control of the White House and the Congress. The third period of realignment centered on 1860. During this period, the newly founded Republican party led by Abraham Lincoln won power, in the process destroying the Whig party, which had been one of the nation's two major parties since the 1830s. During the fourth critical period, centered on the election of 1896, the Republicans reasserted their dominance of the national government, which had been weakening since the 1880s. The fifth realignment took place during the period 1932–1936 when the Democrats, led by Franklin Delano Roosevelt, took control of the White House and Congress and, despite sporadic interruptions, maintained control of both through the 1960s. Since that time, American party politics has been characterized primarily by ***divided***

[6]James Bennet, "Liberal Use of 'Extremist' is the Winning Strategy," *New York Times,* 7 November 1996, p. B1.

[7]See Walter Dean Burnham, *Critical Elections and the Mainsprings of American Electoral Politics* (New York: W. W. Norton, 1970). See also James L. Sundquist, *Dynamics of the Party System* (Washington, DC: Brookings Institution, 1983).

**Electoral Realignments**

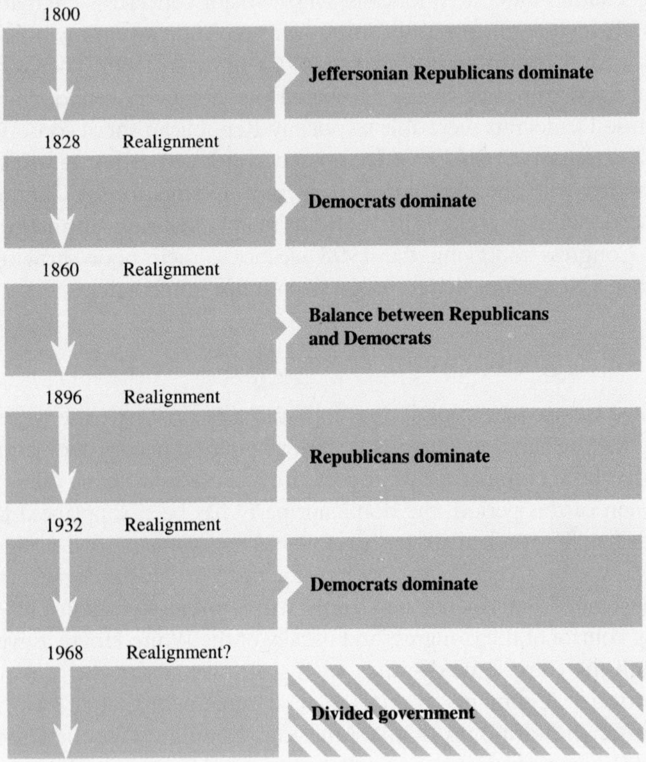

1800
Jeffersonian Republicans dominate
1828 Realignment
Democrats dominate
1860 Realignment
Balance between Republicans and Democrats
1896 Realignment
Republicans dominate
1932 Realignment
Democrats dominate
1968 Realignment?
Divided government

***government,*** wherein the presidency is controlled by one party while the other party controls one or both houses of Congress.

Historically, realignments occur when new issues combined with economic or political crises persuade large numbers of voters to re-examine their traditional partisan loyalties and permanently shift their support from one party to another. For example, during the 1850s, diverse regional, income, and business groups supported one of the two major parties, the Democrats or the Whigs, on the basis of their positions on various economic issues, such as internal improvements, the tariff, monetary policy, and banking. This economic alignment was shattered during the 1850s. The newly formed Republican party campaigned on the basis of opposition to slavery and, in particular, opposition to the expansion of slavery into the territories. The issues of slavery and sectionalism produced divisions within both the Democratic and the Whig parties, ultimately leading to the dissolution of the latter, and these issues compelled voters to re-examine their partisan allegiances. Many Northern voters who had supported the Whigs or the

Democrats on the basis of their economic stands shifted their support to the Republicans as slavery replaced tariffs and economic concerns as the central item on the nation's political agenda. Many Southern Whigs shifted their support to the Democrats. The new sectional alignment of forces that emerged was solidified by the trauma of the Civil War and persisted almost to the turn of the century.

In 1896, this sectional alignment was at least partially supplanted by an alignment of political forces based on economic and cultural factors. During the economic crises of the 1880s and 1890s, the Democrats forged a coalition consisting of economically hard-pressed Midwestern and Southern farmers, as well as small-town and rural economic interests. These groups tended to be descendants of British Isles, Dutch, and Hessian fundamentalist Protestants. The Republicans, on the other hand, put together a coalition comprising most of the business community, industrial workers, and city dwellers. In the election of 1896, Republican candidate William McKinley, emphasizing business, industry, and urban interests, decisively defeated Democrat William Jennings Bryan, who spoke for sectional interests, farmers, and fundamentalism. Republican dominance lasted until 1932.

**AMERICAN POLITICAL DEVELOPMENT**

Because, by definition, realignments require major shifts in the party identification of substantial portions of the electorate, many scholars have questioned whether or not realignments are possible today, given the weakness of political parties to mobilize the electorate. Although parties seem to play a significant role in elections, their connections to the electorate were weakened during the Progressive era and continued to wane throughout the twentieth century.

SOURCE: John H. Aldrich, *Why Parties?* (Chicago: University of Chicago Press, 1995).

Such periods of critical realignment in American politics have had extremely important institutional and policy results. Realignments occur when new issue concerns coupled with economic or political crises weaken the established political elite and permit new groups of politicians to create coalitions of forces capable of capturing and holding the reins of governmental power. The construction of new governing coalitions during these realigning periods has effected major changes in American governmental institutions and policies. Each period of realignment represents a turning point in American politics. The choices made by the national electorate during these periods have helped shape the course of American political history for generations.[8]

## American Third Parties

Although the United States is said to possess a two-party system, we have always had more than two parties. Typically, ***third parties*** in the United States have represented social and economic protests that, for one or another reason, were not given voice by the two major parties.[9] Such parties have had a good deal of influence on ideas and elections in the United States. The Populists, a party centered in the rural

[8]Benjamin Ginsberg, *The Consequences of Consent* (New York: Random House, 1982), Chap. 4.

[9]For a discussion of third parties in the United States, see Daniel Mazmanian, *Third Parties in Presidential Elections* (Washington, DC: Brookings Institution, 1974).

areas of the West and Midwest, and the Progressives, spokesmen for the urban middle classes in the late nineteenth and early twentieth centuries, are the most important examples in the past hundred years. More recently, Ross Perot, who ran in 1992 and 1996 as an independent, impressed some voters with his folksy style in the presidential debates and garnered almost 19 percent of the votes cast in the 1992 presidential election. In 1996, the Green Party nominated Ralph Nader as its presidential candidate in order to draw attention to its ideas on environmental policy and economic and political reform. The Greens had no expectation of winning the election, but hoped that Nader's visibility would encourage more people to take the party seriously. Table 11.1 shows a listing of all the parties that offered candidates in one or more states in 1996, as well as independent candidates who ran. With the exception of Ross Perot, the third-party and independent candidates together polled hardly more than one million votes. They gained no electoral votes for president, and most of them disappeared immediately after the presidential election. The significance of Table 11.1 is that it demonstrates the large number of third parties running candidates and appealing to voters. Although the Republican party was only the third American political party ever to make itself permanent (by replacing the Whigs), other third parties have enjoyed an influence far beyond their electoral size. This was because large parts of their programs were adopted by one or both of the major parties, who sought to appeal to the voters mobilized by the new party, and so to expand their own electoral strength. The Democratic party, for example, became a great deal more liberal when it adopted most of the Progressive program early in the twentieth century. Many Socialists felt that President Roosevelt's New Deal had adopted most of their party's program, including old-age pensions, unemployment compensation, an agricultural marketing program, and laws guaranteeing workers the right to organize into unions.

This kind of influence explains the short lives of third parties. Their causes are usually eliminated by the ability of the major parties to absorb their programs and to draw their supporters into the mainstream. There are, of course, additional reasons for the short duration of most third parties. One is the usual limitation of their electoral support to one or two regions. Populist support, for example, was primarily midwestern. The 1948 Progressive party, with Henry Wallace as its candidate, drew nearly half its votes from the state of New York. The American Independent party polled nearly ten million popular votes and forty-five electoral votes for George Wallace in 1968—the most electoral votes ever polled by a third-party candidate. But all of Wallace's electoral votes and the majority of his popular vote came from the states of the Deep South.

Americans usually assume that only the candidates nominated by one of the two major parties have any chance of winning an election. Thus, a vote cast for a

**AMERICAN POLITICAL DEVELOPMENT**

In the nineteenth century, there were more members of Congress not associated with the two major parties than there were in the twentieth century. In the 1850s, nearly 9 percent of Senate and House members did not belong to either major party. As late as the 1890s, this number was nearly 5 percent. In the twentieth century, this number never exceeded 2 percent and generally remained below 1 percent.

SOURCE: Joseph A. Schlesinger, "On the Theory of Party Organization," *Journal of Politics* 46 (1984), p. 370.

**TABLE 11.1**

**Parties and Candidates in 1996**

| CANDIDATE | PARTY | VOTE TOTAL* | % OF VOTE* |
|---|---|---|---|
| Bill Clinton | Democratic | 45,628,667 | 49.16% |
| Bob Dole | Republican | 37,869,435 | 40.80 |
| Ross Perot | Reform | 7,874,283 | 8.48 |
| Ralph Nader | Green | 580,627 | .63 |
| Harry Browne | Libertarian | 470,818 | .51 |
| Howard Phillips | U.S. Taxpayers | 178,779 | .19 |
| John Hagelin | Natural Law | 110,194 | .12 |
| Monica Moorehead | Workers World | 29,118 | .03 |
| Marsha Feinland | Peace and Freedom | 22,593 | .02 |
| James Harris | Socialist Workers | 11,513 | .01 |
| Charles Collins | Independent | 7,234 | .00 |
| Dennis Peron | Grassroots | 5,503 | .00 |
| Mary Hollis | Socialist | 3,376 | .00 |
| Jerry White | Socialist Equality | 2,752 | .00 |
| Diane Templin | Independent American | 1,875 | .00 |
| Earl Dodge | Independent | 1,198 | .00 |
| Peter Crane | Independent | 1,105 | .00 |
| Ralph Forbes | Independent | 861 | .00 |
| John Birrenbach | Independent Grassroots | 760 | .00 |
| Isabell Masters | Independent | 737 | .00 |
| Steve Michael | Independent | 407 | .00 |
| Other candidates | — | 5,575 | .00 |
| TOTAL | | 92,807,410 | 100.0% |

*With 99 percent of votes tallied.
SOURCE: *USA Today*, 8–10 November 1996, p. 8A.

third-party or independent candidate is often seen as a wasted vote. Voters who would prefer a third-party candidate may feel compelled to vote for the major-party candidate whom they regard as the "lesser of two evils," to avoid wasting their vote in a futile gesture. Third-party candidates must struggle—usually without success—to overcome the perception that they cannot win. Thus, in 1992, many voters who favored Ross Perot gave their votes to George Bush or Bill Clinton on the presumption that Perot was not really electable. In 1996, Perot sought to deal with this problem through a series of ads asserting that, in fact, votes for Clinton and Dole were "wasted" because neither of these candidates represented voters' true interests. Third-party candidacies also arise at the state and local levels. In New York, the Liberal and Conservative parties have been on the ballot for decades. In 1998, Minnesota elected a third-party governor, former professional wrestler Jesse Ventura.

As many scholars have pointed out, third-party prospects are also hampered by America's ***single-member-district*** plurality election system. In many other nations, several individuals can be elected to represent each legislative district. This is called a system of ***multiple-member districts.*** With this type of system, the candidates of weaker parties have a better chance of winning at least some seats. For their part, voters are less concerned about wasting ballots and usually more willing to support minor-party candidates.

Reinforcing the effects of the single-member district, plurality voting rules (as was noted in Chapter 10) generally have the effect of setting what could be called a high threshold for victory. To win a plurality race, candidates usually must secure many more votes than they would need under most European systems of proportional representation. For example, to win an American plurality election in a single-member district where there are only two candidates, a politician must win more than 50 percent of the votes cast. To win a seat from a European multimember district under proportional rules, a candidate may need to win only 15 or 20 percent of the votes cast. This high American threshold discourages minor parties and encourages the various political factions that might otherwise form minor parties to minimize their differences and remain within the major-party coalitions.[10]

It would nevertheless be incorrect to assert (as some scholars have maintained) that America's single-member plurality election system guarantees that only two parties will compete for power in all regions of the country. All that can be said is that American election law depresses the number of parties likely to survive over long periods of time in the United States. There is nothing magical about two. Indeed, the single-member plurality system of election can also discourage second parties. After all, if one party consistently receives a large plurality of the vote, people may eventually come to see their vote *even for the second party* as a wasted effort. This happened to the Republican party in the Deep South before World War II.

## FUNCTIONS OF THE PARTIES

Parties perform a wide variety of functions. They are mainly involved in nominations and elections—providing the candidates for office, getting out the vote, and facilitating mass electoral choice. They also influence the institutions of government—providing the leadership and organization of the various congressional committees.[11]

[10]See Maurice Duverger, *Political Parties* (New York: Wiley, 1954).

[11]Formal theorists of politics see political parties as institutions that help resolve the collective action problem, the difficulty in getting groups of individuals with shared interests to cooperate, of which there are two broad categories pertaining to parties. The first is the office-seeker's efforts to mobilize electoral support. The second is the office-holder's efforts to seek desirable public policy. Political parties can help facilitate both of these types of efforts. Although we will explore collective action in more detail in the following chapter, interested readers may now want to consult Kenneth A. Shepsle and Mark S. Bonchek, *Analyzing Politics: Rationality, Behavior, and Institutions* (New York: W. W. Norton, 1997), Chapters 8 and 9. For more details on parties, see the "Analyzing American Politics: Political Parties and Rational Politicians" box in this chapter and John H. Aldrich, *Why Parties?: The Origin and Transformation of Party Politics in America* (Chicago: University of Chicago Press, 1995).

## Recruiting Candidates

One of the most important but least noticed party activities is the recruitment of candidates for local, state, and national office. Each election year, candidates must be found for thousands of state and local offices as well as for congressional seats. Where they do not have an incumbent running for re-election, party leaders attempt to identify strong candidates and to interest them in entering the campaign.

An ideal candidate will have an unblemished record and the capacity to raise enough money to mount a serious campaign. Party leaders are usually not willing to provide financial backing to candidates who are unable to raise substantial funds on their own. For a House seat this can mean several hundred thousand dollars; for a Senate seat a serious candidate must be able to raise several million dollars. Often, party leaders have difficulty finding attractive candidates and persuading them to run. In 1998, for example, Democratic leaders in Kansas and Washington reported difficulties in recruiting congressional candidates. A number of potential candidates reportedly were reluctant to leave their homes and families for the hectic life of a member of Congress. GOP leaders in Washington and Massachusetts have had similar problems finding candidates to oppose popular Democratic incumbents.[12] Candidate recruitment has become particularly difficult in an era when political campaigns often involve mudslinging, and candidates must assume that their personal lives will be intensely scrutinized in the press.[13]

## Nominations

Article I, Section 4, of the Constitution makes only a few provisions for elections. It delegates to the states the power to set the "times, places, and manner" of holding elections, even for U.S. senators and representatives. It does, however, reserve to Congress the power to make such laws if it chooses to do so. The Constitution has been amended from time to time to expand the right to participate in elections. Congress has also occasionally passed laws about elections, congressional districting, and campaign practices. But the Constitution and the laws are almost completely silent on nominations, setting only citizenship and age requirements for candidates. The president must be at least thirty-five years of age, a natural-born citizen, and a resident of the United States for fourteen years. A senator must be at least thirty, a U.S. citizen for at least nine years, and a resident of the state he or she represents. A member of the House must be at least twenty-five, a U.S. citizen for seven years, and a resident of the state he or she represents.

[12]Alan Greenblatt, "With Major Issues Fading, Capitol Life Lures Fewer," *Congressional Quarterly Weekly Report,* 25 October 1997, p. 2625.

[13]For an excellent analysis of the parties' role in recruitment, see Paul Herrnson, *Congressional Elections: Campaigning at Home and in Washington* (Washington, DC: Congressional Quarterly Press, 1995).

DEBATING THE ISSUES

## The State of the Parties: Decaying or Revitalized?

*Many political observers have complained in recent years that America's political parties are dying. Both politicians and voters seem less concerned and less interested in party labels and party loyalty, a fact that, if true, means weaker and fewer links between citizens and the government. Yet not everyone agrees. Some argue that parties play a greater role in government than ever, as seen for example in recent sharp party clashes between the Republican-controlled Congress and the Democratic president. In the essays below, the political scientists William E. Hudson and Gerald M. Pomper summarize the arguments for and against decaying political parties.*

### HUDSON

Political parties have grown weaker organizationally in the past few decades, as have voter attachments to them. More voters, particularly among the higher educated and more affluent . . . are ticket splitters, voting for different political parties in a single election. With an electorate indifferent to party, those holding elective office are more apt to ignore party discipline and vote independently, behavior that only reinforces the electorate's perception that party labels do not matter. . . .

In the United States today, political parties have become increasingly marginalized as election vehicles. Because state election laws continue to make ballot access easier for party nominees and because enough voters retain party identification to give such nominees an automatic pool of support, candidates still seek the party label, but attaching the label tends to be all that parties contribute to the process. Modern campaigns have become candidate-centered rather than party centered. Individual candidates build their personal campaign organizations, using professional campaign managers and funds they have raised themselves. . . . Party attachments tend to be deemphasized, and party officials, as opposed to personal campaign advisers, are not involved in the process. Unfortunately for democracy, this new candidate-centered style of campaigning has undermined equal representation.[1]

### POMPER

I want to dispute [the] common assertion, that American parties have become weakened, irrelevant, and impotent. To the contrary, . . . parties are increasingly rooted in distinct voter coalitions, [are] stronger organizationally, and clearly relevant to the policy issues facing the nation. . . . the thesis of party decline fails because it rests on a flawed theoretical foundation. The thesis depends on a view of parties as collectivities of voters. In this view, parties are weaker because fewer voters are strongly indentified with the parties, and fewer are consistent supporters at the ballot box.

The problem with this argument is that parties are not properly considered as collections of voters. . . . Voters are not members of the party organization, but rather its clientele. . . . We do better to think of the parties as seekers of voters. . . .

We can point to a few indicators that the major parties . . . will be able to maintain themselves in the electoral marketplace. There are at least the following signs of party strengthening in the electorate:

—Party identification, the proportion of strong indentifiers, and affect toward the parties have all risen, after the decline of the 1970s.
—There is strong continuity in the electoral coalitions of the parties during the period of 1976–1992. . . .
—In the election of 1992, strong party loyalty is evident in individual-level data. Clinton won not only all states carried by Dukakis in 1988, but the overwhelming proportion of Dukakis's supporters (83 percent), and of self-identified Democrats (77 percent).
—In 1992, only 23.9 percent of the congressional districts voted for different parties for president and the U.S. House, the lowest proportion in four decades. . . .

We can see the emergence of stable voter coalitions and strengthened party organizations. Maybe, just maybe, and just in time, we can now observe an emerging "semi-responsible party government."[2]

[1]William E. Hudson, *American Democracy in Peril* (Chatham, NJ: Chatham House, 1995), pp. 41, 152.
[2]Gerald M. Pomper, "Alive! The Political Parties after the 1980–1992 Presidential Elections," *American Presidential Elections,* ed. Harvey L. Schantz (Albany, NY: SUNY Press, 1996), pp. 135, 140–41, 151–52.

***Nomination*** is the process by which a party selects a single candidate to run for each elective office. The nominating process can precede the election by many months, as it does when the many candidates for the presidency are eliminated from consideration through a grueling series of debates and state primaries until there is only one survivor in each party—the party's nominee.

Nomination is the parties' most serious and difficult business. When more than one person aspires to an office, the choice can divide friends and associates. In comparison to such an internal dispute, the electoral campaign against the opposition is almost fun, because there the fight is against the declared adversaries. In the course of American political history, the parties have used three modes of nomination—the caucus, the convention, and the primary election (see Process Box 11.2).

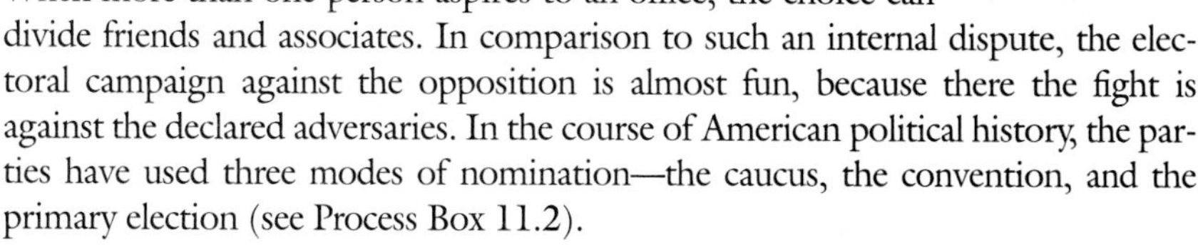

**The Caucus** In the eighteenth and early nineteenth centuries, nominations were informal, without rules or regulations. Local party leaders would simply gather all the party activists, and they would agree on the person, usually from among themselves, who would be the candidate. The meetings where candidates were nominated were generally called ***caucuses.*** Informal nomination by caucus

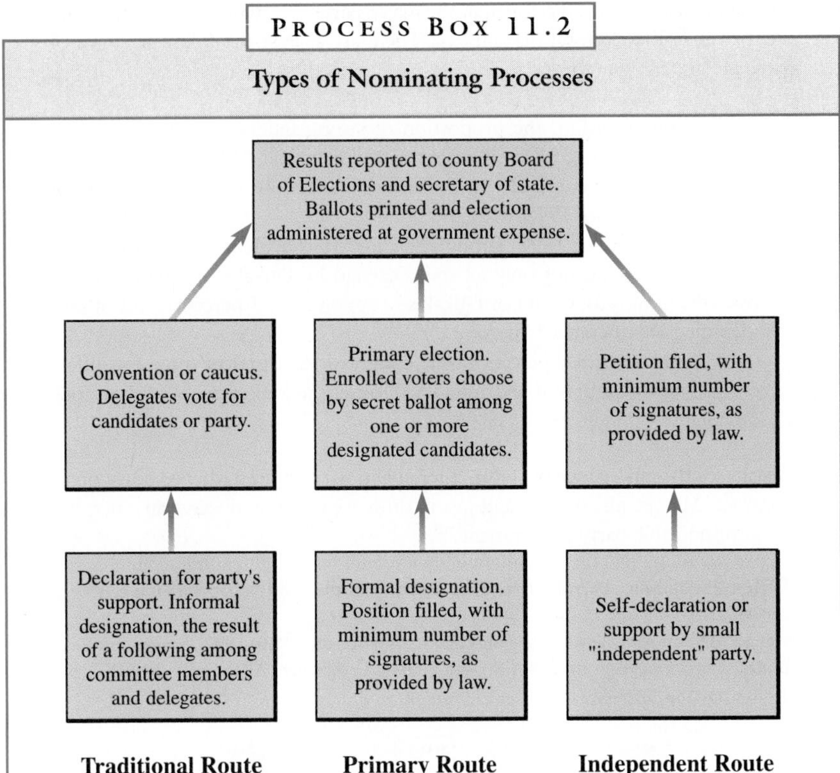


sufficed for the parties until widespread complaints were made about cliques of local leaders or state legislators dominating all the nominations and leaving no place for the other party members who wanted to participate. Beginning in the 1830s, nominating conventions were proposed as a reform that would enable the mass membership of a party to express its will.

**Nomination by Convention** A nominating convention is a formal caucus bound by a number of rules that govern participation and nominating procedures. Conventions are meetings of delegates elected by party members from the relevant county (county convention) or state (state convention). Delegates to each party's national convention (which nominates the party's presidential candidate) are chosen by party members on a state-by-state basis, for there is no single national delegate selection process.

Historically, the great significance of the convention mode of nomination was its effect on the presidential selection process and on the presidency itself. For more than fifty years after America's founding, the nomination of presidential candidates was dominated by meetings of each party's congressional delegations, meetings that critics called "King Caucus." In the early 1830s, when the major parties adopted the national nominating convention, they broke the power of King Caucus. This helped to give the presidency a mass popular base (see Chapter 6). Nevertheless, reformers in the early twentieth century regarded nominating conventions as instruments of "boss rule." They proposed replacing conventions with primaries, which provide for direct choice by the voters at an election some weeks or months before the general election.

**Nomination by Primary Election** In primary elections, party members select the party's nominees directly rather than selecting convention delegates who then select the nominees. Primaries are far from perfect replacements for conventions, since it is rare that more than 25 percent of the enrolled voters participate in them. Nevertheless, they are replacing conventions as the dominant method of nomination.[14] At the present time, only a small number of states, including Connecticut, Delaware, and Utah, provide for state conventions to nominate candidates for statewide offices, and even these states also use primaries whenever a substantial minority of delegates vote for one of the defeated aspirants.

Primary elections are of two types—closed and open. In a ***closed primary,*** participation is limited to individuals who have previously declared their affiliation by registering with the party. In an ***open primary,*** individuals declare their party affiliation on the actual day of the primary election. To do so, they simply go to the polling place and ask for the ballot of a particular party. The open primary allows each voter to consider candidates and issues before deciding whether to participate and in which party's contest to participate. Open primaries, therefore, are less conducive to strong political parties. But in either case, primaries are more open than conventions or caucuses to new issues and new types of candidates.

**AMERICAN POLITICAL DEVELOPMENT**

From 1912 to 1992, the number of presidential primaries has more than tripled. In 1912, the Democratic party had twelve primaries and the Republican party had thirteen. As late as 1968, that number remained as low as seventeen for each party. But in 1992, forty of fifty states had Democratic presidential primaries, and thirty-nine of fifty had Republican primaries.

SOURCE: Harold W. Stanley and Richard G. Niemi, *Vital Statistics on American Politics,* 5th ed. (Washington, DC: Congressional Quarterly Press, 1995), p. 138.

**Independent Candidates** Process Box 11.2 indicated that the convention and primary methods are not the only ways that candidates can get on the ballot. State laws extend the right of independent candidacy to individuals who do not wish to be nominated by political parties or who are unable to secure a party nomination.

Although nomination by a political party is complicated, the independent route to the ballot is even more difficult. For almost all offices in all states, the law requires more signatures for independent nomination than for party designation. For example, the candidate for a party's nomination to Congress in New York must get 1,250 valid signatures within the congressional district, while the independent candidate must get 3,500 signatures.

[14]For a discussion of some of the effects of primary elections see Peter F. Galderisi and Benjamin Ginsberg, "Primary Elections and the Evanescence of Third Party Activity in the United States," in *Do Elections Matter?* ed. Benjamin Ginsberg and Alan Stone (Armonk, NY: M. E. Sharpe Publishers, 1986), pp. 115–30.

**Contested Nominations** Even though state laws favor party nomination, the task of the parties is not an easy one. Party organizations have grown weaker over the years, and the number of contested primaries—primaries where two or more designated candidates compete for the party's nomination—has increased. At the same time, the ability of the "regular" party leaders to win in such primaries has diminished. Regardless of who wins, a contested nomination is costly. Money that is spent on campaigning in the primaries is no longer available to spend in the general election against the opponent nominated by the other party. Moreover, contested primaries can be particularly bitter and the feud long-lasting because the candidates are members of the same party, and often consider opposition a personal affront.

But although contested nominations deplete party resources and interfere with party campaign strategy, they can be a sign of healthy politics because they expose parties to new or underrepresented interests. Indeed, parties have often been a channel for resolving important social conflicts. Contested nominations, especially contested primaries, can speed the resolution of such conflicts. Civil rights became a national issue in 1948 through a struggle within the Democratic party over the antidiscrimination commitment in its platform. In 1968, the Vietnam War was debated more by Democratic president Lyndon Johnson and antiwar Democratic senator Eugene McCarthy than by Hubert Humphrey (who ultimately became the Democratic presidential candidate) and Republican Richard Nixon. Any number of important local political issues have been resolved between candidates fighting each other for the nomination for mayor or district attorney or governor.

Many important advances in the participation of ethnic and racial minorities have begun through victories in local primaries. Party leaders once considered the nominating process to be their own personal property. In fact, the Democratic party in many Southern states adopted rules excluding nonwhites from the primaries, on the grounds that political parties were the equivalent of private clubs. The Supreme Court did not invalidate all of these "white primaries" until 1944, when it held that primaries were an integral part of the electoral system and could not be left to private control.[15] The Court was recognizing a fact universally accepted well before 1944—that the nominating process is the first stage of the electoral process.

**AMERICAN POLITICAL DEVELOPMENT**

In an analysis of primary elections from 1956 to 1974, studies found that both party and incumbency are important factors in determining whether or not a primary contest for House seats will occur. Open seats are more likely to be contested than are seats with incumbents, and Democratic primaries are more likely to be contested than are Republican primaries.

SOURCE: Harvey L. Schantz, "Contested and Uncontested Primaries for the U.S. House," *Legislative Studies Quarterly* 4 (1980), pp. 545–62, esp. p. 548.

## The Role of the Parties in Getting Out the Vote

The actual election period begins immediately after the nominations. Historically, this has been a time of glory for the political parties, whose popular base of sup-

[15]Smith v. Allwright, 321 U.S. 649 (1944).

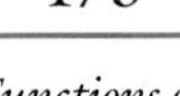

port is fully displayed. All the paraphernalia of party committees and all the committee members are activated into local party work forces.

The first step in the electoral process involves voter registration. This aspect of the process takes place all year round. There was a time when party workers were responsible for virtually all of this kind of electoral activity, but they have been supplemented (and in many states virtually displaced) by civic groups such as the League of Women Voters, unions, and chambers of commerce.

Those who have registered have to decide on election day whether to go to the polling place, stand in line, and actually vote for the various candidates and referenda on the ballot. Political parties, candidates, and campaigning can make a big difference in convincing the voters to vote.

On any general election ballot, there are likely to be only two or three candidacies where the nature of the office and the characteristics and positions of the candidates are well known to voters. But what about the choices for judges, the state comptroller, the state attorney general, and many other elective positions? And what about referenda? This method of making policy choices is being used more and more as a means of direct democracy. A referendum may ask: Should there be a new bond issue for financing the local schools? Should there be a constitutional amendment to increase the number of county judges? In 1996, Californians approved Proposition 201, a referendum that called for an end to most statewide affirmative action programs, including those employed for college admission. Another famous proposition on the 1978 California ballot was a referendum to reduce local property taxes. It started a taxpayer revolt that spread to many other states. By the time it had spread, most voters knew where they stood on the issue. But the typical referendum question is one on which few voters have clear and knowledgeable positions. Parties and campaigns help most by giving information when voters must choose among obscure candidates and vote on unclear referenda.

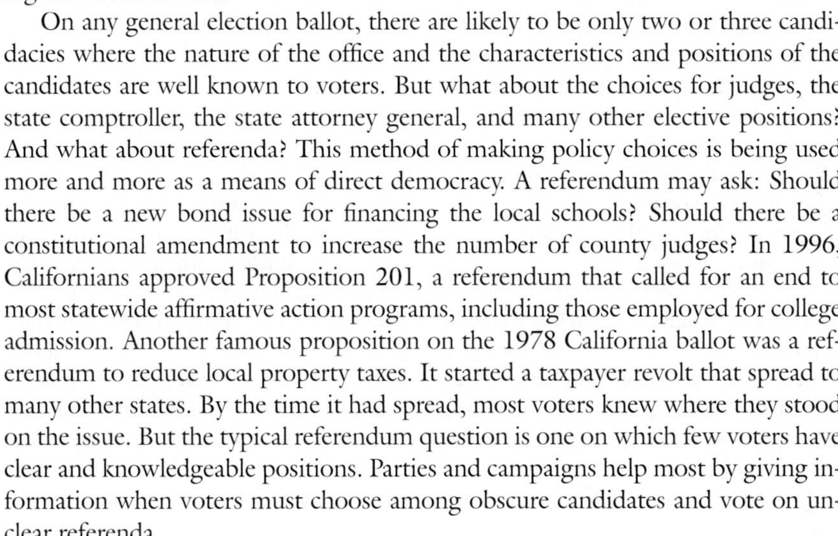

## Facilitation of Mass Electoral Choice

Parties facilitate mass electoral choice. As the late Harvard political scientist V. O. Key pointed out long ago, the persistence over time of competition between groups possessing a measure of identity and continuity is virtually a necessary condition for electoral control.[16] ***Party identification*** increases the electorate's capacity to recognize its options. Continuity of party division facilitates organization of the electorate on the long-term basis necessary to sustain any popular influence in the governmental process. In the absence of such identity and continuity of party division, the voter is, in Key's words, confronted constantly by "new faces, new choices."[17]

[16] V. O. Key, *Southern Politics* (New York: Random House, 1949), Chapter 14.
[17] Ibid.

ANALYZING AMERICAN POLITICS

## *Political Parties and Rational Politicians*

Even though political parties are not mentioned in the Constitution, they have become one of the central institutions of government in the United States. Why parties are so central is one of the questions that John Aldrich sets out to answer in *Why Parties?* Aldrich argues that parties are the creations of self-interested, rational actors who view parties as the best instrument for achieving their goals.

Aldrich discusses three roles of parties: *parties in government, parties in elections,* and *parties as organizations.* Parties in government mainly serve to organize the internal working of legislatures. They help to eliminate problems associated with collective decision-making[1] by organizing the institution and establishing rules that impose stability. For example, the leadership of the majority party sets the schedule for bringing legislation to the floor and presides over the deliberative process. This prevents certain legislative alternatives that would cause instability from being considered.

Because it is costly for voters to participate in elections and because many of the benefits that winning parties bestow are public goods (i.e., parties cannot exclude any individual from enjoying them), people will try to "free ride" or enjoy the benefits without incurring the costs of electing the party that provided the benefits. This is known as the *free rider problem,* and parties in the electorate (Aldrich's second role) are important because they help overcome this dilemma by mobilizing the voters to support the candidates. Parties also lower information costs of participating by providing a kind

[1]See William H. Riker's *The Art of Political Manipulation* (New Haven: Yale University Press, 1986) for an accessible presentation of the various problems with collective decision-making processes.

Even more significant, however, is the fact that party organization is generally an essential ingredient for effective electoral competition by groups lacking substantial economic or institutional resources. Party building has typically been the strategy pursued by groups that must organize the collective energies of large numbers of individuals to counter their opponents' superior material means or institutional standing. Historically, disciplined and coherent party organizations were generally developed first by groups representing the political aspirations of the working classes. Parties, French political scientist Maurice Duverger notes, "are always more developed on the Left than on the Right because they are always more necessary on the Left than on the Right."[18] In the United States, the first mass party was built by the Jeffersonians as a counterweight to the superior

[18]Duverger, *Political Parties,* p. 426.

of "brand name" recognizability, that is, voters know with a substantial degree of accuracy what kinds of positions a candidate will take just by identifying the candidate's party affiliation. In addition, parties give elections a kind of sporting-event atmosphere, with voters treating parties like teams that they can support and cheer on to victory. This enhances the entertainment value of participating in elections. Parties also direct the flow of government benefits, such as patronage jobs, to those who put the party in power. These and other activities encourage individuals to identify with and support one of the two parties, which is at the heart of the role that parties play in elections.

Aldrich presents a substantial amount of historical evidence to show how parties solved problems of instability in early Congresses and how they boosted turnout with the development of mass parties in the nineteenth century. But there is some question as to whether parties still serve these same functions today. Numerous political scientists and pundits have argued that parties are no longer relevant to American politics, that they no longer serve as the organizers of political campaigns or as purposive entities in Congress. One of the critics' key pieces of evidence is the decline of party identification in the electorate.

Aldrich takes issue with these critics and argues that parties continue to be important but that their roles have changed along with the dramatic transformations in the twentieth-century political environment. The critics have evaluated parties in terms of their *traditional* roles, Aldrich contends, and therefore have wrongly perceived the changing roles of parties as a decline. But these changes are perfectly consistent with Aldrich's argument that parties are institutions created by self-interested, rational actors.

One of the major changes that Aldrich focuses on has to do with technology. Technological advances such as television and direct mail have made it possible for candidates to create their own campaign organizations, which serve the same functions that parties once did. As a result, elections have become candidate-centered, contributing to a decline in partisan affiliation among voters. Yet parties-as-organizations are more professional, better-financed, and more organized than ever before. Aldrich argues that parties have evolved into "service organizations," which, though they no longer hold a monopoly over campaigns, still provide services to candidates, without which it would be extremely difficult for candidates to win and hold office. Parties have not declined but have simply adapted to serve the interests of political actors.

social, institutional, and economic resources that could be deployed by the incumbent Federalists. In a subsequent period of American history, the efforts of the Jacksonians to construct a coherent mass party organization were impelled by a similar set of circumstances. Only by organizing the power of numbers could the Jacksonian coalition hope to compete successfully against the superior resources that could be mobilized by its adversaries.

In the United States, the political success of party organizations forced their opponents to copy them in order to meet the challenge. It was, as Duverger points out, "contagion from the Left," that led politicians of the Center and Right to attempt to build strong party organizations.[19] These efforts were sometimes successful. In the United States during the 1830s, the Whig party, which

[19]Ibid., Chapter 1.

was led by northeastern business interests, carefully copied the effective organizational techniques devised by the Jacksonians. The Whigs won control of the national government in 1840. But even when groups nearer the top of the social scale responded in kind to organizational efforts by their inferiors, the net effect nonetheless was to give lower-class groups an opportunity to compete on a more equal footing. In the absence of coherent mass organization, middle- and upper-class factions almost inevitably have a substantial competitive edge over their lower-class rivals. Even when both sides organize, the net effect is still to erode the relative advantage of the well-off. Parties of the Right, moreover, were seldom actually able to equal the organizational coherence of the working-class opposition. As Duverger and others have observed, middle- and upper-class parties generally failed to construct organizations as effective as those built by their working-class foes, who typically commanded larger and more easily disciplined forces.

Although political parties continue to be significant in the United States, the role of party organizations in electoral politics has clearly declined over the past three decades. This decline, and the partial replacement of the party by new forms of electoral technology, is one of the most important developments in twentieth-century American politics.

## The Parties' Influence on National Government

The ultimate test of the party system is its relationship to and influence on the institutions of government and the policy-making process. Thus, it is important to examine the party system in relation to Congress and the president.

**Parties and Policy** One of the most familiar observations about American politics is that the two major parties try to be all things to all people and are therefore indistinguishable from each other. Data and experience give some support to this observation. Parties in the United States are not programmatic or ideological, as they have sometimes been in Britain or other parts of Europe. But this does not mean there are no differences between them. During the Reagan era, important differences emerged between the positions of Democratic and Republican party leaders on a number of key issues, and these differences are still apparent today. For example, the national leadership of the Republican party supports maintaining high levels of military spending, cuts in social programs, tax relief for middle- and upper-income voters, tax incentives to businesses, and the "social agenda" backed by members of conservative religious denominations. The national Democratic leadership, on the other hand, supports expanded social welfare spending, cuts in military spending, increased regulation of business, and a variety of consumer and environmental programs.

These differences reflect differences in philosophy as well as differences in the core constituencies to which the parties seek to appeal. The Democratic party at the national level seeks to unite organized labor, the poor, members of racial minorities, and liberal upper-middle-class professionals. The Republicans, by contrast, appeal to business, upper-middle- and upper-class groups in the private sector, and social conservatives. Often, party leaders will seek to develop issues they hope will add new groups to their party's constituent base. During the

1980s, for example, under the leadership of Ronald Reagan, the Republicans devised a series of "social issues," including support for school prayer, opposition to abortion, and opposition to affirmative action, designed to cultivate the support of white Southerners. This effort was extremely successful in increasing Republican strength in the once solidly Democratic South. In the 1990s, under the leadership of Bill Clinton, who called himself a "new Democrat," the Democratic party has sought to develop new social programs designed to solidify the party's base among working-class and poor voters, and new, somewhat more conservative economic programs aimed at attracting the votes of middle- and upper-middle-class voters.

As these examples suggest, parties do not always support policies because they are favored by their constituents. Instead, party leaders can play the role of policy entrepreneurs, seeking ideas and programs that will expand their party's base of support while eroding that of the opposition. It is one of the essential characteristics of party politics in America that a party's programs and policies often lead, rather than follow, public opinion. Like their counterparts in the business world, party leaders seek to identify and develop "products" (programs and policies) that will appeal to the public. The public, of course, has the ultimate voice. With its votes it decides whether or not to "buy" new policy offerings.

Through members elected to office, both parties have made efforts to translate their general goals into concrete policies. Republicans, for example, implemented tax cuts, increased defense spending, cut social spending, and enacted restrictions on abortion during the 1980s and 1990s. Democrats were able to defend consumer and environmental programs against GOP attacks and sought to expand domestic social programs in the late 1990s. Both parties, of course, have been hampered by internal divisions and the recurrent pattern of divided control of Congress and the executive branch that has characterized American politics for the past two decades.

**AMERICAN POLITICAL DEVELOPMENT**

The strength and centralization of congressional party leadership within the House is directly related to the strength of the party outside the legislature. When electoral parties are strong, as they were in the 1890s and early 1900s, the Speaker and other party leaders enjoy considerable influence and resources. But as party strength wanes, as was the case toward the middle of the twentieth century, even talented, influential Speakers and party leaders must resort to bargaining techniques rather than to strong, hierarchical leadership.

SOURCE: Joseph Cooper and David W. Brady, "Institutional Context and Leadership Style: The House from Cannon to Rayburn," *American Political Science Review* 75 (1981), pp. 411–25.

**The Parties and Congress** Congress, in particular, depends more on the party system than is generally recognized. First, the speakership of the House is essentially a party office. All the members of the House take part in the election of the Speaker. But the actual selection is made by the ***majority party***. When the majority party caucus presents a nominee to the entire House, its choice is then invariably ratified in a straight party-line vote.

The committee system of both houses of Congress is also a product of the two-party system. Although the rules organizing committees and the rules defining the jurisdiction of each are adopted like ordinary legislation by the whole membership, all other features of the committees are shaped by parties. For example, each party is assigned a quota of members for each committee, depending upon the percentage of total seats held by the party. On the rare occasions when an independent or third-party candidate is elected, the leaders of the two parties must agree against whose quota this member's committee assignments will count. Presumably the member will not be able to serve on any committee until the question of quota is settled.

As we saw in Chapter 5, the assignment of individual members to committees is a party decision. Each party has a "committee on committees" to make such decisions. Permission to transfer to another committee is also a party decision. Moreover, advancement up the committee ladder toward the chair is a party decision. Since the late nineteenth century, most advancements have been automatic—based upon the length of continual service on the committee. This seniority system has existed only because of the support of the two parties, and each party can depart from it by a simple vote. During the 1970s, both parties re-instituted the practice of reviewing each chairmanship—voting anew every two years on whether each chair would be continued. Few chairpersons actually have been removed, but notice has been served that the seniority system is no longer automatic and has thereby reminded everyone that all committee assignments are party decisions. Thus, although party leaders no longer can control the votes of many members, the party system itself remains an important factor.

## President and Party

As we saw earlier, the party that wins the White House is always led, in title anyway, by the president. The president normally depends upon fellow party members in Congress to support legislative initiatives. At the same time, members of the party in Congress hope that the president's programs and personal prestige will help them raise campaign funds and secure re-election. During his two terms in office, President Bill Clinton had a mixed record as party leader. In the realm of trade policy, Clinton sometimes found more support among Republicans than among Democrats. In addition, although Clinton proved to be an extremely successful fund-raiser, congressional Democrats often complained that he failed to share his largesse with them. At the same time, however, a number of Clinton's policy initiatives seemed calculated to strengthen the Democratic party as a whole. Clinton's early health care initiative would have linked millions of voters to the Democrats for years to come, much as FDR's Social Security program had done in a previous era. But by the middle of Clinton's second term, the president's acknowledgment of his sexual affair with a White House intern threatened his position as party leader. Initially, Democratic candidates nationwide feared that the scandal would undermine their own chances for election, and many moved to distance themselves from the president. The Democrats' surprisingly good showing in the 1998 elections,

however, strengthened Clinton's position and gave him another chance to shape the Democratic agenda.

## WEAKENING OF PARTY ORGANIZATION

George Washington's warning against the "baneful effects of the spirit of party" was echoed by the representatives of social, economic, and political elites in many nations who saw their right to rule challenged by groups able to organize the collective energies and resources of the mass public.

Opposition to party politics was the basis for a number of the institutional reforms of the American political process promulgated at the turn of the twentieth century during the so-called Progressive era. Many Progressive reformers were undoubtedly motivated by a sincere desire to rid politics of corruption and to improve the quality and efficiency of government in the United States. But simultaneously, from the perspective of middle- and upper-class Progressives and the financial, commercial, and industrial elites with which they were often associated, the weakening or elimination of party organization would also mean that power could more readily be acquired and retained by the "best men," that is, those with wealth, position, and education.

The list of anti-party reforms of the Progressive Era is a familiar one. The Australian ballot reform took away the parties' privilege of printing and distributing ballots and thus introduced the possibility of split-ticket voting. The introduction of nonpartisan local elections eroded grassroots party organization. The extension of "merit systems" for administrative appointments stripped party organizations of their vitally important access to patronage and thus reduced their ability to recruit workers. The development of the direct primary reduced party leaders' capacity to control candidate nominations. These reforms obviously did not destroy political parties as entities, but taken together they did substantially weaken party organizations in the United States. After the turn of the century, the strength of American political parties gradually diminished. Between the two world wars, organization remained the major tool available to contending electoral forces, but in most areas of the country the "reformed" state and local parties that survived the Progressive era gradually lost their organizational vitality and coherence, and they became less effective campaign tools. While most areas of the nation continued to boast Democratic and Republican party groupings, reform did mean the elimination of the permanent mass organizations that had been the parties' principal campaign weapons.

### High-Tech Politics

As a result of Progressive reform, American party organizations entered the twentieth century with rickety substructures. As the use of civil service, primary elections, and the other Progressive innovations spread during the period between

the two world wars, the strength of party organizations continued to be eroded. By the end of World War II, political scientists were already bemoaning the absence of party discipline and "party responsibility" in the United States. This erosion of the parties' organizational strength set the stage for the introduction of new political techniques. These new methods represented radical departures from the campaign practices perfected during the nineteenth century. In place of manpower and organization, contending forces began to employ intricate electronic communications techniques to attract electoral support. This new political technology includes six basic elements.

1. *Polling.* Surveys of voter opinion provide the information that candidates and their staffs use to craft campaign strategies. Candidates employ polls to select issues, to assess their own strengths and weaknesses (as well as those of the opposition), to check voter response to the campaign, and to determine the degree to which various constituent groups are susceptible to campaign appeals. Virtually all contemporary campaigns for national and statewide office as well as many local campaigns make extensive use of opinion surveys. As we saw in Chapter 9, President Clinton made extensive use of polling data both during and after the 1996 presidential election to shape his rhetoric and guide his policy initiatives.

2. *The broadcast media.* Extensive use of the electronic media, television in particular, has become the hallmark of the modern political campaign. One commonly used broadcast technique is the thirty- or sixty-second television spot advertisement—such as George Bush's "Willie Horton" ad in 1988 or Lyndon Johnson's famous "daisy girl" ad in 1964—which permits the candidate's message to be delivered to a target audience before uninterested or hostile viewers can psychologically, or physically, tune it out (see Box 11.2). Television spot ads and other media techniques are designed to establish candidate name recognition, to create a favorable image of the candidate and a negative image of the opponent, to link the candidate with desirable groups in the community, and to communicate the candidate's stands on selected issues. These spot ads can have an important electoral impact. Generally, media campaigns attempt to follow the guidelines indicated by a candidate's polls, emphasizing issues and personal characteristics that appear important in the poll data. The broadcast media are now so central to modern campaigns that most candidates' activities are tied to their media strategies.[20] Candidate activities are designed expressly to stimulate television news coverage. For instance, members of Congress running for re-election or for president almost always sponsor committee or subcommittee hearings to generate publicity.

3. *Phone banks.* Through the broadcast media, candidates communicate with voters *en masse* and impersonally. Phone banks, on the other hand, allow campaign workers to make personal contact with hundreds of thousands of voters. Personal contacts of this sort are thought to be extremely effective. Again, poll data serve to identify the groups that will be targeted for phone calls. Computers select phone numbers from areas in which members of these groups are concen-

[20]Larry J. Sabato, *The Rise of Political Consultants* (New York: Basic Books, 1981).

BOX 11.2

### The Daisy Girl

On September 7, 1964, NBC's *Monday Night at the Movies* was interrupted by what came to be one of the most famous and controversial political commercials ever shown on American television. In this ad, a little girl with long, light brown hair stood in a field picking daisy petals. As she pulled the petals, she counted, "1-2-3. . . ." At the same time, the voice of an announcer in the background counted backward, "10-9-8. . . ." As the counts continued, the announcer's voice became louder and the girl's voice more muted, until the girl reached 10 and the announcer counted down to 0. At that point, a blinding nuclear explosion destroyed everything, with President Johnson saying, "These are the stakes: To make a world in which all of God's children can live or go into the dark. We must either love each other or we must die." The announcer then urged viewers to vote for President Johnson on November 3. The ad was cut after one use, but the practice of short spots has continued.

Photo courtesy of the Lyndon Baines Johnson Presidential Library.

trated. Staffs of paid or volunteer callers, using computer-assisted dialing systems and prepared scripts, then place calls to deliver the candidate's message. The targeted groups are generally those identified by polls as either uncommitted or weakly committed, as well as strong supporters of the candidate who are contacted simply to encourage them to vote.

4. *Direct mail.* Direct mail serves both as a vehicle for communicating with voters and as a mechanism for raising funds. The first step in a direct mail campaign is the purchase or rental of a computerized mailing list of voters deemed to have some particular perspective or social characteristic. Often sets of magazine subscription lists or lists of donors to various causes are employed. For example, a candidate interested in reaching conservative voters might rent subscription lists from the *National Review;* a candidate interested in appealing to liberals might rent subscription lists from the *New York Review of Books* or from the *New Republic.*

Considerable fine-tuning is possible. After obtaining the appropriate mailing lists, candidates usually send pamphlets, letters, and brochures describing themselves and their views to voters believed to be sympathetic. Different types of mail appeals are made to different electoral subgroups. Often the letters sent to voters are personalized. The recipient is addressed by name in the text and the letter appears actually to have been signed by the candidate. Of course, these "personal" letters are written and even signed by a computer.

In addition to its use as a political advertising medium, direct mail has also become an important source of campaign funds. Computerized mailing lists permit campaign strategists to pinpoint individuals whose interests, background, and activities suggest that they may be potential donors to the campaign. Letters of solicitation are sent to these potential donors. Some of the money raised is then used to purchase additional mailing lists. Direct mail solicitation can be enormously effective.[21]

5. *Professional public relations.* Modern campaigns and the complex technology upon which they rely are typically directed by professional public relations consultants. Virtually all serious contenders for national and statewide office retain the services of professional campaign consultants. Increasingly, candidates for local office, too, have come to rely upon professional campaign managers. Consultants offer candidates the expertise necessary to conduct accurate opinion polls, produce television commercials, organize direct mail campaigns, and make use of sophisticated computer analyses.

6. *The Internet.* A more recent form of new technology has been the Internet. Most candidates for office set up a Web site as an inexpensive means to establish a public presence. The 1998 election saw increased use of the Internet by political candidates. Virtually all statewide candidates, as well as many candidates for Congress and local offices, developed Web sites providing contact information, press releases, speeches, photos, and information on how to volunteer, contact the candidate, or donate money to the campaign. During his campaign, Florida governor Jeb Bush sold "Jebware," articles of clothing emblazoned with his name, through his Web site. New Jersey's incumbent governor Christie Todd Whitman, re-elected in 1997, sponsored a site that included full-length commercials, downloadable posters and buttons, and campaign appeals in English and Spanish. Whitman printed her Web address (www.christie97.org.) on all her literature and touted it in radio and television appearances. Whitman's site had thousands of visitors and generated hundreds of campaign volunteers and contributors.[22]

Thus far, the political impact of the Internet has been limited by the fact that, unlike a TV commercial that comes to viewers without any action on their part, citizens must take the initiative to visit a Web site. In general, this means that only those already supporting a candidate are likely to visit the site, limiting its politi-

[21]Ibid., p. 250.

[22]John Martin, "Nationwide, Candidates Spin the Web," www.washingtonpost.com, 3 August 1998.

cal utility. However, as Whitman's strategy suggests, it may be possible to lure voters to Web sites through television advertising or, perhaps, through Internet links. California Republican gubernatorial hopeful Dan Lundgren, for example, linked his Web site to that of a burger chain. He still lost the race.

The number of technologically oriented campaigns increased greatly after 1971. The Federal Election Campaign Act of 1972 prompted the creation of large numbers of political action committees (PACs) by a host of corporate and ideological groups. This development increased the availability of funds to political candidates—conservative candidates in particular—which meant in turn that the new technology could be used more extensively. Initially, the new techniques were employed mainly by individual candidates who often made little or no effort to coordinate their campaigns with those of other political aspirants sharing the same party label. For this reason, campaigns employing new technology sometimes came to be called "candidate-centered" efforts, as distinguished from the traditional party-coordinated campaign. Nothing about the new technology, however, precluded its use by political party leaders seeking to coordinate a number of campaigns. In recent years, party leaders—Republicans in particular—have learned to make good use of modern campaign technology. The difference between the old and new political methods is not that the latter is inherently candidate-centered while the former is strictly a party tool. The difference is, rather, a matter of the types of political resources upon which each method depends.

## From Labor-Intensive to Capital-Intensive Politics

The displacement of organizational methods by the new political technology is, in essence, a shift from labor-intensive to capital-intensive competitive electoral practices. Campaign tasks were once performed by masses of party workers with some cash. These tasks now require fewer personnel but a great deal more money, for the new political style depends on polls, computers, and other electronic paraphernalia. Of course, even when workers and organization were the key electoral tools, money had considerable political significance. Nevertheless, during the nineteenth century, national political campaigns in the United States employed millions of people. Indeed, as many as 2.5 million individuals did political work during the 1880s.[23] The direct cost of campaigns, therefore, was relatively low. For example, in 1860, Abraham Lincoln spent only $100,000—which was approximately twice the amount spent by his chief opponent, Stephen Douglas.

Modern campaigns depend heavily on money. Each element of the new political technology is enormously expensive. A sixty-second spot announcement on prime-time network television costs hundreds of thousands of dollars each time it is aired. Opinion surveys can be quite expensive; polling costs in a statewide race can easily reach or exceed the six-figure mark. Campaign consultants can charge

[23] M. Ostrogorski, *Democracy and the Organization of Political Parties* (New York: Macmillan, 1902).

GLOBALIZATION AND DEMOCRACY

## *Will Globalization Reshape American Political Parties?*

Globalization is reflected in the increasing economic interdependence among nations, the expanding reach of multinational corporations (MNCs), and the swift and relatively unimpeded movement of capital across national borders. Some observers maintain that globalization has created an environment in which any government efforts to intervene in the economy are doomed to fail if they extend beyond minimal, efficiency-promoting measures.[1] This development means that traditional "left" policies that promote "big government" can no longer be used.

In the event that government should seek to promote redistributive policies at the expense of policies that enhance short-term corporate efficiency, it is assumed that MNCs and "footloose capital" (banks and financial institutions that are able to shift their assets electronically around the world) will simply move their money and operations to more hospitable climes in other countries. As Norman Macrae puts it, "In the future, we will vote more frequently with our feet. If politicians try to boss us, brainworkers will go away and telecommute from Tahiti. Countries that try to have too high a level of government expenditure or too fussy regulations will be residually inhabited mainly by dummies."[2]

If this view is correct, it would seem to dictate the extinction of the "welfare-state" policies that characterized the left side of the partisan continuum in U.S. politics from Franklin Roosevelt's

[1]The standard wisdom concerning the effects of globalization on partisan politics is explained—and refuted—in Geoffrey Garrett, *Partisan Politics in the Global Economy* (Cambridge, England: Cambridge University Press, 1998), esp. pp. 1–25.

[2]Norman Macrae, "New Jersey's Taxes: Why Don't They Love Them," *The Economist* 4 (August 1990), p. 23.

New Deal until the 1990s. But does the standard wisdom that globalization undermines big government reflect the realities of American politics? On the surface, at least, it would appear that the welfare state and many of its pillars of social support are being dismantled. For one thing, the percent of the total workforce that is unionized—this is potentially significant because unions are considered a loyal supporter of "big government" and a traditional stronghold of Democratic party activism—has declined markedly in recent decades. So, too, have the number of beneficiaries and the amount of benefits provided to a host of federally supported programs such as the Aid to Families with Dependent Children (AFDC) and Federal Food Assistance. In the case of the AFDC, for example, the number of beneficiaries and the total benefits paid grew steadily from 1970 (when there was a monthly average of 7.4 million recipients and total benefits exceeding $4 billion) until 1994 (14.2 million recipients and $22.8 billion in total benefits). Since that time, the AFDC program was abolished and replaced by the state-administered Temporary Aid to Needy Families (TANF) program. The number of individuals receiving TANF benefits decreased by 20 percent in the first year of the program's existence.

Although "big government" may be down, it may be a bit premature to predict its inevitable demise as a central issue in partisan politics. This is clear, for instance, in Bill Clinton's strategy of "Running 'Right' and Governing 'Left.'" Even as the Clinton administration presided over the deregulation of financial services and a reduction in social programs, it proposed a bailout of social security instead of a tax cut and pressed for creation of government-managed health care. Moreover, it is well to bear in mind that even though globalization grants "exit" options to footloose capital and some MNCs, it also creates a powerful incentive for less-mobile interests (e.g., American workers, welfare recipients, and, in fact, the majority of citizens) to "voice" their demands for government benefits. As Geoffrey Garrett observes,

> presiding over an expanding pie is not the only path to electoral success. Political parties can also attract support by distributing the social pie in ways that favor certain groups over others. Indeed, the short-term nature of democratic politics creates a bias in favor of distributional strategies: Governments cannot afford to do what is good for the economy in the long run if this immediately hurts their core electoral constituencies.[3]

In sum, while globalization has had an effect on partisan politics, it is likely that we have not heard the last of the welfare state.

[3]Geoffrey Garrett and Peter Lange, "Internationalization, Institutions, and Policy Change," in *Internationalization and Domestic Politics*, ed. Robert O. Keohane and Helen V. Milner (Ithaca, NY: Cornell University Press, 1996), pp. 48–75.

substantial fees. A direct mail campaign can eventually become an important source of funds but is very expensive to initiate. The inauguration of a serious national direct mail effort requires at least $1 million in "front end cash" to pay for mailing lists, brochures, letters, envelopes, and postage.[24] While the cost of televised debates is covered by the sponsoring organizations and the television stations and is therefore free to the candidates, even debate preparation requires substantial staff work and research, and, of course, money. It is the expense of the new technology that accounts for the enormous cost of recent American national elections.

Certainly "people power" is not irrelevant to modern political campaigns. Candidates continue to utilize the political services of tens of thousands of volunteer workers. Nevertheless, in the contemporary era, even the recruitment of campaign workers has become a matter of electronic technology. Employing a technique called "instant organization," paid telephone callers use phone banks to contact individuals in areas targeted by a computer (which they do when contacting potential voters, as we discussed before). Volunteer workers are recruited from among these individuals. A number of campaigns—Richard Nixon's 1968 presidential campaign was the first—have successfully used this technique.

The displacement of organizational methods by the new political technology has the most far-reaching implications for the balance of power among contending political groups. Labor-intensive organizational tactics allowed parties whose chief support came from groups nearer the bottom of the social scale to use the numerical superiority of their forces as a partial counterweight to the institutional and economic resources more readily available to the opposition. The capital-intensive technological format, by contrast, has given a major boost to the political fortunes of those forces whose sympathizers are better able to furnish the large sums now needed to compete effectively.[25] Indeed, the new technology permits financial resources to be more effectively harnessed and exploited than was ever before possible.

In a political process lacking strong party organizations, the likelihood that groups that do not possess substantial economic or institutional resources can ac-

**AMERICAN POLITICAL DEVELOPMENT**

The expenses of mass media are often cited as the reason campaign costs have increased. The Twentieth-Century Fund's Commission on Campaign Costs in the Electronic Era estimated that expenditures by national-level campaign committees more than tripled from 1956 to 1968. In fact, in 1968 expenditures were more than fifteen times those in 1912.

SOURCE: Robert L. Peabody, Jeffrey M. Berry, William G. Frasure, and Jerry Goldman, *To Enact a Law: Congress and Campaign Finance* (New York: Praeger, 1972), p. 11.

[24] Timothy Clark, "The RNC Prospers, the DNC Struggles as They Face the 1980 Election," *National Journal*, 27 October 1980, p. 1619.

[25] For discussions of the consequences, see Thomas Edsall, *The New Politics of Inequality* (New York: W. W. Norton, 1984). Also see Thomas Edsall, "Both Parties Get the Company's Money—But the Boss Backs the GOP," *Washington Post National Weekly Edition,* 16 September 1986, p. 14; and Benjamin Ginsberg, "Money and Power: The New Political Economy of American Elections," in *The Political Economy,* ed. Thomas Ferguson and Joel Rogers (Armonk, NY: M. E. Sharpe Publishers, 1984).

quire some measure of power is severely diminished. Dominated by the new technology, electoral politics becomes a contest in which the wealthy and powerful have a decided advantage.

## The Role of the Parties in Contemporary Politics

Political parties make democratic government possible. We often do not appreciate that democratic government is a contradiction in terms. Government implies policies, programs, and decisive action. Democracy, on the other hand, implies an opportunity for all citizens to participate fully in the governmental process. The contradiction is that full participation by everyone is often inconsistent with getting anything done. At what point should participation stop and governance begin? How can we make certain that popular participation will result in a government capable of making decisions and developing needed policies? The problem of democratic government is especially acute in the United States because of the system of separated powers bequeathed to us by the Constitution's framers. Our system of separated powers means that it is very difficult to link popular participation and effective decision making. Often, after the citizens have spoken and the dust has settled, no single set of political forces has been able to win control of enough of the scattered levers of power to actually do anything. Instead of government, we have a continual political struggle.

Strong political parties are a partial antidote to the inherent contradiction between participation and government. Strong parties can both encourage popular involvement and convert participation into effective government. More than fifty years ago, a committee of the academic American Political Science Association (APSA) called for the development of a more "responsible" party government. By responsible party government, the committee meant political parties that mobilized voters and were sufficiently well organized to develop and implement coherent programs and policies after the election. Strong parties can link democratic participation and government.

Although they are significant factors in politics and government, American political parties today are not as strong as the "responsible parties" advocated by the APSA. Many politicians are able to raise funds, attract volunteers, and win office without much help from local party organizations. Once in office, these politicians have no particular reason to submit to party discipline; instead they steer independent courses. They are often supported by voters who see independence as a virtue and party discipline as "boss rule." As we just saw, analysts refer to this pattern as a "candidate-centered" politics to distinguish it from a political process in which parties are the dominant forces. The problem with a candidate-centered politics is that it tends to be associated with low turnout, high levels of special-interest influence, and a lack of effective decision making. In short, many of the problems that have plagued American politics in recent years can be traced directly to the independence of American voters and politicians and the candidate-centered nature of American national politics.

The health of America's parties should be a source of concern to all citizens. Can political parties be strengthened? The answer is, in principle, yes. For example, political parties could be strengthened if the rules governing campaign finance were revised to make candidates more dependent financially upon state and local party organizations rather than on personal resources or private contributors. Such a reform, to be sure, would require more strict regulation of party fund-raising practices to prevent soft money abuses. The potential benefit, however, of a greater party role in political finance could be substantial. If parties controlled the bulk of the campaign funds, they would become more coherent and disciplined, and might come to resemble the responsible parties envisioned by the APSA. Political parties have been such important features of American democratic politics that we need to think long and hard about how to preserve and strengthen them.

### THEN AND NOW

## Changes in American Politics

Few institutions in America have undergone the radical changes that political parties have. In many ways, the parties of the nineteenth century were very different from the parties of today.

- By the 1840s, the national party nominating convention replaced the King Caucus as a means by which political parties nominated presidential candidates. Although both major parties still employ national nominating conventions, today's conventions generally ratify decisions that have already been made in presidential primaries and caucuses.
- The aspects of political parties that involve mobilizing voters and making connections between voters on the one hand, and candidates and incumbents on the other, have their roots in the 1820s. During this time, Andrew Jackson's Democratic party mobilized voters, employed national conventions, and created a general democratization of the political system.
- Third parties enjoyed more success in American national politics in the nineteenth century than they did in the twentieth century. In the 1850s, nearly 9 percent of Congress was composed of third-party members; this number never exceeded 2 percent in the twentieth century.
- The use of state presidential primaries for both parties has greatly expanded during the twentieth century.
- Election campaigning, which was labor intensive at the end of the nineteenth century, gave way to a system of capital intensive campaigning during the twentieth.
- The costs of political campaigns grew during the twentieth century, when party-centered elections shifted to candidate-centered elections and expensive mass media techniques of campaigning became more common.

## SUMMARY

Political parties seek to control government by controlling its personnel. Elections are one means to this end. Thus, parties take shape from the electoral process. The formal principle of party organization is this: For every district in which an election is held—from the entire nation to the local district, county, or precinct—there should be some kind of party unit.

The two-party system dominates U.S. politics. Today, on individual issues, the two parties differ little from each other. In general, however, Democrats lean more to the Left on issues and Republicans more to the Right. Even though party affiliation means less to Americans than it once did, partisanship remains important. What ticket-splitting there is occurs mainly at the presidential level.

Voters' choices have had particularly significant consequences during periods of critical electoral realignment. During these periods, which have occurred roughly every thirty years, new electoral coalitions have formed, new groups have come to power, and important institutional and policy changes have occurred. The last such critical period was associated with Franklin Roosevelt's New Deal.

Third parties are short-lived for several reasons. They have limited electoral support, the tradition of the two-party system is strong, and a major party often adopts their platforms. Single-member districts with two competing parties also discourage third parties.

Nominating and electing are the basic functions of parties. Originally nominations were made in party caucuses, and individuals who ran as independents had a difficult time getting on the ballot. In the 1830s, dissatisfaction with the cliquish caucuses led to nominating conventions. Although these ended the "King Caucus" that controlled the nomination of presidential candidates, and thereby gave the presidency a popular base, they too proved unsatisfactory. Primaries have now more or less replaced the conventions. There are both closed and open primaries. The former are more supportive of strong political parties than the latter. Contested primaries sap party strength and financial resources, but they nonetheless serve to resolve important social conflicts and recognize new interest groups. Winning at the top of a party ticket usually depends on the party regulars at the bottom getting out the vote. At all levels, the mass communications media are important. Mass mailings, too, are vital in campaigning. Thus, campaign funds are crucial to success.

Congress is organized around the two-party system. The House speakership is a party office. Parties determine the makeup of congressional committees, including their chairs, which are no longer based entirely on seniority.

In recent years, the role of parties in political campaigns has been partially supplanted by the use of new political technologies. These include polling, the broadcast media, phone banks, direct mail fund-raising and advertising, professional public relations, and the Internet. These techniques are enormously expensive and have led to a shift from labor-intensive to capital-intensive politics. This shift works to the advantage of political forces representing the well-to-do.

## For Further Reading

Aldrich, John H. *Why Parties?: The Origin and Transformation of Party Politics in America.* Chicago: University of Chicago Press, 1995.

Chambers, William N., and Walter Dean Burnham. *The American Party Systems: Stages of Political Development.* New York: Oxford University Press, 1975.

Coleman, John J. *Party Decline in America: Policy, Politics, and the Fiscal State*. Princeton: Princeton University Press, 1996.

Grimshaw, William J. *Bitter Fruit: Black Politics and the Chicago Machine, 1931–1991.* Chicago: University of Chicago Press, 1992.

Hofstadter, Richard. *The Idea of a Party System: The Rise of Legitimate Opposition in the United States, 1780–1840.* Berkeley: University of California Press, 1970.

Kayden, Xandra, and Eddie Mahe, Jr. *The Party Goes On: The Persistence of the Two-Party System in the United States.* New York: Basic Books, 1985.

Lawson, Kay, and Peter Merkl. *When Parties Fail: Emerging Alternative Organizations.* Princeton: Princeton University Press, 1988.

Milkis, Sidney. *The President and the Parties: The Transformation of the American Party System since the New Deal.* New York: Oxford University Press, 1993.

Polsby, Nelson W. *Consequences of Party Reform.* New York: Oxford University Press, 1983.

Shafer, Byron, ed. *Beyond Realignment? Interpreting American Electoral Eras.* Madison: University of Wisconsin Press, 1991.

Smith, Eric R. A. N. *The Unchanging American Voter.* Berkeley: University of California Press, 1989.

Sorauf, Frank J. *Party Politics in America.* Boston: Little, Brown, 1984.

Sundquist, James. *Dynamics of the Party System.* Washington, DC: Brookings Institution, 1983.

Wattenberg, Martin. *The Decline of American Political Parties, 1952–1988.* Cambridge: Harvard University Press, 1990.

# 12

# Groups and Interests

## TIME LINE ON INTEREST GROUPS

| Events | | Institutional Developments |
|---|---|---|
| Early trade associations and unions formed (1820s and 1830s) | | Term "lobbyist" is first used (1830) |
| Citizen groups and movements form—temperance (1820s), antislavery (1810–1830), women's (1848), abolition (1850s) | 1850 | Local regulations restricting or forbidding manufacture and sale of alcohol (1830–1860); several states pass laws granting women control over their property (1839–1860s) |
| Civil War (1861–1865) | | Lobbying is recognized in law and practice (1870s) |
| Development of agricultural groups, including the Grange (1860s–1870s) | | Grangers successfully lobby for passage of "Granger laws" to regulate rates charged by railroads and warehouses (1870s) |
| Farmers' Alliances and Populists (1880s–1890s) | 1880 | Beginnings of labor and unemployment laws (1880s) |
| American Federation of Labor (AFL) formed (1886) | | Election of candidates pledged to farmers (1890s) |
| Growth of movement for women's suffrage (1890s) | | Women's suffrage granted by Wyoming, Colorado, Utah, Idaho (1890s) |
| Middle-class Progressive movement and trade associations (1890s) | | Laws for direct primary, voter registration, regulation of business (1890s–1910s) |
| Strengthening of women's movements—temperance (1890s) and suffrage (1914) | 1900 | |
| World War I (1914–1918) | | Prohibition (Eighteenth) Amendment ratified (1919) |
| Growth of trade associations (1920s) | | Nineteenth Amendment gives women the vote (1920) |
| American Farm Bureau Federation (1920); farm bloc (1920s) | | Corrupt practices legislation passed; lobbying registration legislation (1920s) |
| Teapot Dome scandal (1924) | | Farm bloc lobbies for farmers (1921–1923) |
| CIO is formed (1938) | | Wagner National Labor Relations Act (1935) |
| | 1940 | |
| U.S. in W.W. II (1941–1945) | | Federal Regulation of Lobbying Act (1946) |
| Postwar wave of strikes in key industries (1945–1946) | | Taft-Hartley Act places limits on unions (1947) |
| | 1950 | |
| AFL and CIO merge (1955) | | |
| Senate hearings into labor racketeering (1950s) | | Landrum-Griffin Act to control union corruption (1959) |

| Events | | Institutional Developments |
|---|---|---|
| Civil rights movement—boycotts, sit-ins, vote drives (1957), March on Washington (1963) | | Passage of Civil Rights acts (1957, 1960, 1964), Voting Rights Act (1965) |
| National Organization for Women (NOW) formed (1966) | | |
| Vietnam War: antiwar movement (1965–1973) | | |
| | 1970 | |
| Watergate scandal (1972–1974) | | Campaign spending legislation leads to PACs (1970s) |
| Pro-life and pro-choice groups emerge (post-1973) | | *Roe v. Wade* (1973) |
| Public interest groups formed (1970s–1980s) | | Consumer, environmental, health, and safety legislation (1970s) |
| | | Ethics in Government Act (1978) |
| Moral Majority formed (late 1970s) | | PACs help to elect conservative candidates (1980s) |
| Pentagon procurement scandal (1988) | | Further regulation of lobbying (1980s) |
| Keating Five investigation (1990–1991) | 1990 | |
| Interest groups influence Clinton health care and economic proposals (1993) | | Proposals to restrict corporate lobbying activities (1993) |
| Expanded use of new technologies for grassroots lobby efforts (1993) | | |
| Growth in power of conservative groups such as Christian Coalition and National Federation of Independent Business (1994) | | Growth in influence of "soft money" in elections (1994–1998) |

In the spring of 1998, a seemingly unlikely meeting took place on Capitol Hill. Michael Eisner, Chairman of the Walt Disney Company, stopped to visit Republican senate majority leader Trent Lott to discuss issues of concern to the huge media and entertainment company. The meeting seemed unlikely because of Hollywood's well-known ties to the Democratic party. Yet with Republicans in control of Congress, Democrat Eisner had little choice but to turn to Republican Lott for help with a matter of great importance

## CORE OF THE ARGUMENT

- Interest groups have proliferated over the last thirty years as a result of the expansion of the federal government and the "new politics" movement.
- Interest groups use various strategies to promote their goals, including lobbying, gaining access to key decision makers, using the courts, going public, and influencing electoral politics.
- Though interest groups sometimes promote public concerns, they more often represent narrow interests.

to his company—the extension of Disney's copyright on the corporation's greatest asset, Mickey Mouse. Without help from Congress, Disney's ownership of the famed rodent, worth billions of dollars, will expire in 2003, seventy-five years after it was issued. To make matters worse, Disney's ownership of Pluto expires in 2006, and its exclusive right to Goofy ends in 2008. Rights to other characters, including Bambi, Donald Duck, Snow White and all the dwarfs, expire soon thereafter. Eisner needed congressional help to protect his company's most precious treasures, and working with the GOP was a small price to pay. After all, as a former Disney lobbyist put it, "Mickey Mouse is not a Republican or a Democrat."[1]

In actuality, despite the political liberalism of many well-known Hollywood personalities, the movie industry, like most of the nation's industries, is more concerned with the financial bottom line than with partisanship. The motion picture industry maintains an active lobbying arm in Washington, the Motion Picture Association of America, headed by Jack Valenti, once press secretary to President Lyndon Johnson. Under Valenti's leadership, the Hollywood studios have built strong ties to both parties and work vigorously to promote their political agenda, which includes strict protection for intellectual property, favorable tax treatment, and freedom from censorship. Valenti has encouraged the studios to adopt a bipartisan stance in dealing with lawmakers. Though the stars may be liberal Democrats, in recent years the film studios have contributed heavily to both political parties and have built bridges to members of Congress of all political stripes.

Though few other industries can boast a symbol as widely known as Mickey Mouse, the Hollywood studios are a fairly typical ***interest group,*** that is, a group of individuals and organizations that share a common set of goals and have joined together in an effort to persuade the government to adopt policies that will help them. There are thousands of interest groups in the United States. High-minded Americans have been complaining about the role of interest groups since the nation's founding. We should remember, however, that vigorous interest-group activity is a consequence and reflection of a free society. As James Madison put it so well in *The Federalist Papers,* No. 10, "liberty is to faction what air is to fire."[2]

As long as freedom exists, groups will organize and attempt to exert their influence over the political process. And groups will form wherever power exists. It should therefore be no surprise that even though interest groups have been part of the political landscape since the first days of the Republic, the most impressive

[1]Alan Ota, "Disney in Washington: The Mouse That Roars," *Congressional Quarterly Weekly Report,* 8 August 1998, p. 2167.

[2]Clinton Rossiter, ed., *The Federalist Papers* (New York: New American Library, 1961), No. 10, p. 78.

growth in the number and scale of interest groups has been at the national level since the 1930s. But even as the growth of the national government leveled off in the 1970s and 1980s, and actually declined in the late 1980s and 1990s, the spread of interest groups continued. It is no longer just the expansion of the national government that spawns interest groups, but the *existence* of that government with all the power it possesses. As long as there is a powerful government in the United States, there will be a large network of interest groups around it.

The framers of the American Constitution feared the power that could be wielded by organized interests. Yet, they believed that interest groups thrived because of freedom—the freedom that all Americans enjoyed to organize and express their views. To the framers, this problem presented a dilemma, indeed the dilemma of freedom versus power that is central to our text. If the government were given the power to regulate or in any way to forbid efforts by organized interests to interfere in the political process, the government would in effect have the power to suppress freedom. The solution to this dilemma was presented by James Madison:

> Take in a greater variety of parties and interest [and] you make it less probable that a majority of the whole will have a common motive to invade the rights of other citizens. . . . [Hence the advantage] enjoyed by a large over a small republic.[3]

According to the Madisonian theory, a good constitution encourages multitudes of interests so that no single interest can ever tyrannize the others. The basic assumption is that competition among interests will produce balance and compromise, with all the interests regulating each other.[4] Today, this Madisonian principle of regulation is called ***pluralism.*** According to pluralist theory, all interests are and should be free to compete for influence in the United States. Moreover, according to a pluralist doctrine, the outcome of this competition is compromise and moderation, since no group is likely to be able to achieve any of its goals without accommodating itself to some of the views of its many competitors.[5]

There are tens of thousands of organized groups in the United States, ranging from civic associations to huge nationwide groups like the National Rifle Association, whose chief cause is opposition to restrictions on gun ownership, or Common Cause, a public interest group that advocates a variety of liberal political reforms. The huge number of *interest groups* competing for influence in the U.S., however, does not mean that all *interests* are fully and equally represented in the American political process. As we shall see, the political deck is heavily stacked in favor of those interests able to organize and to wield substantial economic, social, and institutional resources on behalf of their cause. This means that within the universe of interest-group politics it is political power—not some abstract conception of the public good—that is likely to prevail. Moreover, this means that interest-group politics, taken as a whole, is a political format that works

[3]Rossiter, ed., *The Federalist Papers,* No. 10, p. 83.

[4]Ibid.

[5]The best statement of the pluralist view is in David Truman, *The Governmental Process* (New York: Knopf, 1951), Chapter 2.

more to the advantage of some types of interests than others. In general, a politics in which interest groups predominate is a politics with a distinctly upper-class bias.

In this chapter, we will examine some of the antecedents and consequences of interest-group politics in the United States. First, we will seek to understand the character of the interests promoted by interest groups. Second, we will assess the growth of interest-group activity in recent American political history, including the emergence of "public interest" groups. Third, we will review and evaluate the strategies that competing groups use in their struggle for influence. Finally, we will assess the question, "Are interest groups too influential in the political process?"

**THE CENTRAL QUESTION**

"Are interest groups too influential in the political process?"

## CHARACTER OF INTEREST GROUPS

Individuals form groups in order to increase the chance that their views will be heard and their interests treated favorably by the government.[6] Interest groups are organized to influence governmental decisions. There are an enormous number of interest groups in the United States, and millions of Americans are members of one or more groups, at least to the extent of paying dues or attending an occasional meeting.

### What Interests Are Represented

Interest groups come in as many shapes and sizes as the interests they represent. When most people think about interest groups, they immediately think of groups with a direct economic interest in governmental actions. These groups are generally supported by groups of producers or manufacturers in a particular economic sector. Examples of this type of group include the National Petroleum Refiners Association, the American Farm Bureau Federation, and the National Federation of Independent Business, which represents small business owners. At the same time that broadly representative groups like these are active in Washington, specific companies, like Disney, Shell Oil, International Business Machines, and General Motors, may be active on certain issues that are of particular concern to them.[7]

[6]For more explanatory detail on group formation and the problems of cooperation and coordination, see Kenneth A. Shepsle and Mark S. Bonchek, *Analyzing Politics: Rationality, Behavior, and Institutions* (New York: W. W. Norton, 1997), pp. 220–44, which includes an overview of Mancur Olson's classic, *The Logic of Collective Action* (Cambridge: Harvard University Press, 1965).

[7]See Case 9.1, "Who Is Represented?" in Shepsle and Bonchek, *Analyzing Politics,* pp. 224–25, for more details on the preponderance of business groups in Washington. This case study is taken from Kay Schlozman and John Tierney, *Organized Interests and American Democracy* (New York: Harper & Row, 1986).

Labor organizations are equally active lobbyists. The AFL-CIO, the United Mine Workers, and the Teamsters are all groups that lobby on behalf of organized labor. In recent years, lobbies have arisen to further the interests of public employees, the most significant among these being the American Federation of State, County, and Municipal Employees.

Professional lobbies like the American Bar Association and the American Medical Association have been particularly successful in furthering their own interests in state and federal legislatures. Financial institutions, represented by organizations like the American Bankers Association and the National Savings & Loan League, although often less visible than other lobbies, also play an important role in shaping legislative policy.

Recent years have witnessed the growth of a powerful "public interest" lobby purporting to represent interests whose concerns are not addressed by traditional lobbies. These groups have been most visible in the consumer protection and environmental policy areas, although public interest groups cover a broad range of issues. The National Resources Defense Council, the Union of Concerned Scientists, and Common Cause are all examples of public interest groups.

The perceived need for representation on Capitol Hill has generated a public sector lobby in the past several years, including the National League of Cities and the "research" lobby. The latter group comprises think tanks and universities that have an interest in obtaining government funds for research and support, and it includes institutions such as Harvard University, the Brookings Institution, and the American Enterprise Institute. Indeed, universities have expanded their lobbying efforts even as they have reduced faculty positions and course offerings and increased tuition.[8]

## Organizational Components

Although there are many interest groups, most share certain key organizational components. First, all groups must attract and keep members. Usually, groups appeal to members not only by promoting political goals or policies they favor but also by providing them with direct economic or social benefits. Thus, for example, the American Association of Retired Persons (AARP), which promotes the interests of senior citizens, at the same time offers members a variety of insurance benefits and commercial discounts. Similarly, many groups whose goals are chiefly economic or political also seek to attract members through social interaction and good fellowship. Thus, the local chapters of many national groups provide their members with a congenial social environment while collecting dues that finance the national office's political efforts.[9]

[8]Betsy Wagner and David Bowermaster, "B.S. Economics," *Washington Monthly* (November 1992), pp. 19–21.

[9]For a review of the theories of group formation and the incentives for joining, review pp. 241–48 in Shepsle and Bonchek, *Analyzing Politics.* Case 9.3, "What Does the Evidence Say?" (pp. 249–50) is a short summary of some of the notable political science literature. Also see "Analyzing American Politics: Cooperation in Groups" in this chapter.

AMERICAN POLITICAL DEVELOPMENT

The number of interest groups has grown dramatically since 1960. Then, the *Encyclopedia of Associations* listed eight thousand groups; by 1992, that number had more than tripled, to nearly 25,000. Interest groups have also become organizationally more complex. In 1961, only 23 out of 119 environmental groups had one staff member and 8 out of 119 had eleven staffers; by 1990, those numbers increased to 151 out of 448 and 50 out of 448 respectively. There was a similar increase in the staffs of health care associations during that time as well.

SOURCE: Frank Baumgartner and Jeffrey C. Talbert, "Interest Groups and Political Change," in *The New American Politics,* ed. Bryan D. Jones (Boulder, CO: Westview, 1995), pp. 93–108.

Second, every group must build a financial structure capable of sustaining an organization and funding the group's activities. Most interest groups rely on yearly membership dues and voluntary contributions from sympathizers. Many also sell some ancillary services, such as insurance and vacation tours, to members. Third, every group must have a leadership and decision-making structure. For some groups, this structure is very simple. For others, it can be quite elaborate and involve hundreds of local chapters that are melded into a national apparatus. Finally, most groups include an agency that actually carries out the group's tasks. This may be a research organization, a public relations office, or a lobbying office in Washington or a state capital.

One example of a successful interest group is the National Rifle Association (NRA). Founded in 1871, the NRA claims a membership of over three million. It employs a staff of 350 and manages an operating budget of $5.5 million. Organized ostensibly to "promote rifle, pistol and shotgun shooting, hunting, gun collecting, home firearm safety and wildlife conservation," the organization has been highly effective in mobilizing its members to block attempts to enact gun-control measures, even though such measures are supported by 80 percent of the Americans who are asked about them in opinion polls. The NRA provides numerous benefits to its members, like sporting magazines and discounts on various types of equipment, and it is therefore adept in keeping its members enrolled and active. Though the general public may support gun control, this support is neither organized nor very intense. This allows the highly organized NRA to prevail even though its views are those of a minority. Although the enactment of the federal "Brady bill," requiring a waiting period for firearms purchases, and the 1994 crime control act, which banned the sale of several types of assault weapons, were defeats of the NRA's agenda, the organization remains one of the most effective lobbies in the nation. In 1994, for example, after a bitter struggle against environmental groups, the NRA was able to secure passage by the House of Representatives of legislation allowing hunting to continue in California's Mojave Desert. In this particular legislative battle, the NRA defeated environmental groups, animal-rights groups, and the White House, all of which had sought to put an end to the hunting.[10]

## The Characteristics of Members

Membership in interest groups is not randomly distributed in the population. People with higher incomes, higher levels of education, and management or pro-

[10]Katherine Q. Seeyle, "In Victory for the NRA, House Backs Hunting in the Mojave," *New York Times,* 13 July 1994, p. D18.

fessional occupations are much more likely to become members of groups than those who occupy the lower rungs on the socioeconomic ladder.[11] Well-educated, upper-income business and professional people are more likely to have the time and the money, and to have acquired through the educational process the concerns and skills needed to play a role in a group or association. Moreover, for business and professional people, group membership may provide personal contacts and access to information that can help advance their careers. At the same time, of course, corporate entities—businesses and the like—usually have ample resources to form or participate in groups that seek to advance their causes.

The result is that interest-group politics in the United States tends to have a very pronounced upper-class bias. Certainly, there are many interest groups and political associations that have a working-class or lower-class membership—labor organizations or welfare-rights organizations, for example—but the great majority of interest groups and their members are drawn from the middle and upper-middle classes. In general, the "interests" served by interest groups are the interests of society's "haves." Even when interest groups take opposing positions on issues and policies, the conflicting positions they espouse usually reflect divisions among upper-income strata rather than conflicts between the upper and lower classes.

In general, to obtain adequate political representation, forces from the bottom rungs of the socioeconomic ladder must be organized on the massive scale associated with political parties. Parties can organize and mobilize the collective energies of large numbers of people who, as individuals, may have very limited resources. Interest groups, on the other hand, generally organize smaller numbers of the better-to-do. Thus, the relative importance of political parties and interest groups in American politics has far-ranging implications for the distribution of political power in the United States. As we saw in Chapter 11, political parties have declined in influence in recent years. Interest groups, on the other hand, as we shall see shortly, have become much more numerous, more active, and more influential in American politics.

## THE PROLIFERATION OF GROUPS

Over the past thirty years, there has been an enormous increase both in the number of interest groups seeking to play a role in the American political process and in the extent of their opportunity to influence that process. This explosion of interest-group activity has three basic origins—first, the expansion of the role of government during this period; second, the coming of age of a new and dynamic set of political forces in the United States—a set of forces that have relied heavily on "public interest" groups to advance their causes; and third, a revival of grassroots conservatism in American politics.

[11]Kay Lehman Schlozman and John T. Tierney, *Organized Interests and American Democracy* (New York: Harper & Row, 1986), p. 60.

ANALYZING AMERICAN POLITICS

## *Cooperation in Groups*

Cooperation is as essential to politics as it is to life. As we saw in Chapter 1, getting a few neighbors to cooperate in draining a swamp is a difficult task. Likewise, getting individuals to cooperate and to act collectively in achieving some political goal can be equally difficult. Situations like these are what political scientists refer to as *collective action problems.*

Collective action problems and how individuals solve them through *institutions* has become a main focus of the rational-choice approach to studying politics.[1] Researchers often rely on the *prisoners' dilemma game* when theorizing about social situations in which collective action problems occur. In the standard setup of this game, two individuals accused of jointly committing a crime are kept in separate rooms. Each is offered a plea bargain: to testify against the other prisoner in exchange for a reduced sentence. However, the amount of the reduction depends on whether or not the other accepts the plea bargain as well. If Prisoner A turns state's evidence and testi-fies against Prisoner B, then A will serve no jail time, provided that B does not "snitch" on A. However, Prisoner B is offered the same deal. The game gets interesting when we consider how the actions of the players affect each other's fates. If both prisoners snitch, the authorities will have enough evidence to put both of them away for three years. If neither of the prisoners snitch, the authorities only have flimsy evidence and can obtain sentences of just a year for each of the prisoners. If A snitches but B does not, then A serves no jail time, while B will receive a six-year sentence. If B snitches and A does not, B goes free and A gets put away for six years.

If we assume that A and B are self-interested, rational actors (that is, when given the choice between two alternatives, they will choose the one that offers them the best deal), and they want to serve as little jail time as possible, then both will choose to snitch and each will receive three years in prison. This may seem counterintuitive since if both of them refused to snitch, they would each serve only one year. The key to understanding this game is to focus on what happens when one snitches and the other does not. The player who does

[1]Much of this research is indebted to Mancur Olson, *The Logic of Collective Action* (Cambridge: Harvard University Press, 1965).

## The Expansion of Government

Modern governments' extensive economic and social programs have powerful politicizing effects, often sparking the organization of new groups and interests. The activities of organized groups are usually viewed in terms of their effects upon governmental action. But interest-group activity is often as much a consequence as

not snitch goes to prison for six years. If that player had snitched, at worst she would receive three years and at best, go free. It is therefore rational for that player to snitch. If she knows the other player is not going to snitch, then she has a choice between not snitching and serving one year, or snitching and serving no years. Since she wants to serve as little jail time as possible, she should always snitch. This protects her from getting the worst "payoff"—the six-year jail term—while making it possible for her to get the best payoff—being set free. But the other player faces the same choices and payoffs, and so will also always choose to snitch as well.

This game is a parallel of the swamp-clearing situation. Even though the individuals involved would be better off if they worked together and contributed to clearing the swamp (i.e., did not snitch on each other), as rational individuals they have incentives to "free-ride" (i.e., snitch) and try to enjoy the benefits of deswampification without incurring any of the costs. The individual who does not devote resources to clearing the swamp is just like the individual who snitches, hoping that she won't get a prison sentence. Although all individuals would be better off if they contributed to the swamp-clearing effort, just like the prisoners would be better off collectively if neither snitched, individual rationality leads to an outcome that is collectively worse. That is, individual rationality leads to less of the collective good.

Let's look at the swamp situation again. Since the number of concerned owners is small in this particular case, they might eventually be able to organize themselves to share the costs as well as enjoy the benefits of clearing the swamp. But suppose the numbers of interested people are increased. Suppose the common concern is not the neighborhood swamp but polluted air or groundwater involving thousands of residents in a region, or in fact millions of residents in a whole nation. National defense is the most obvious collective good whose benefits are shared by every resident, regardless of the taxes they pay or the support they provide. As the number of involved persons increases, or as the size of the group increases, the free-rider phenomenon may become more of a problem. Individuals do not have much incentive to become active members and supporters of a group that is already working more or less on their behalf. The group would no doubt be more influential if all concerned individuals were active members—if there were no free riders. But groups will not reduce their efforts just because free riders get the same benefits as dues-paying activists. In fact, groups may try even harder precisely because there are free riders, with the hope that the free riders will be encouraged to join in.

Despite the free rider problem, interest groups offer numerous incentives to join. Most important, they make various "selective benefits" available only to group members. These benefits include information provided through conferences, training programs, and newsletters and other periodicals sent automatically to those who have paid membership dues; services and goods such as discount purchasing, shared advertising, and health and retirement insurance; and the friendship and networking opportunities that membership provides.

an antecedent of governmental programs. Even when national policies are initially responses to the appeals of pressure groups, government involvement in any area can be a powerful stimulus for political organization and action by those whose interests are affected. A *New York Times* report, for example, noted that during the 1970s, expanded federal regulation of the automobile, oil, gas, education, and health care industries impelled each of these interests to increase substantially its efforts to influence the government's behavior. These efforts, in turn, had the effect of spurring the organization of other groups to augment or counter the activities of the first.[12] Similarly, federal social programs have occasionally sparked political organization and action on the part of clientele groups seeking to influence the distribution of benefits and, in turn, the organization of groups opposed to the programs or their cost. For example, federal programs and court decisions in such areas as abortion and school prayer were the stimuli for political action and organization by fundamentalist religious groups. Thus, the expansion of government in recent decades has also stimulated increased group activity and organization.

One contemporary example of a proposed government program that sparked intensive organization and political action by affected interests is the case of regulating the tobacco industry. In 1997, an enormous lobbying battle broke out in Washington, DC, over a proposed agreement regarding the liability of tobacco companies for tobacco-related illnesses. This agreement, reached between tobacco companies, state governments, trial lawyers (representing individuals and groups suing tobacco companies), and antismoking groups, called for the tobacco industry to pay the states and the trial lawyers nearly $400 billion over the next twenty-five years. In exchange the industry would receive protection from much of the litigation with which it is currently plagued. The settlement as negotiated would have required congressional and presidential approval.

After the settlement was proposed in June 1997, both the White House and some members of Congress began raising objections. Because of the enormous amounts of money involved, all the interested parties began intensive lobbying efforts aimed at both Congress and the executive branch. The tobacco industry retained nearly thirty lobbying firms at an initial cost of nearly $10 million to press its claims. During the first six months of 1997, the tobacco industry also contributed more than $2.5 million to political parties and candidates whom the industry thought could be helpful to its cause. One Washington lobbying firm, Verner, Liipfert, Bernhard, McPherson, and Hand, alone received nearly $5 million in fees from the four leading cigarette makers. The firm assigned a number of well-connected lobbyists, including former Texas governor Ann Richards, to press its clients' cause. Verner, Liipfert also hired pollsters, public relations firms, and economists to convince the public and the Washington establishment that the tobacco settlement made good sense.[13] Eventually a compromise settlement was reached between the tobacco companies and the state governments.

## The New Politics Movement and Public Interest Groups

The second factor accounting for the explosion of interest-group activity in recent years was the emergence of a new set of forces in American politics that can collectively be called the "New Politics" movement.

The New Politics movement is made up of upper-middle-class professionals and intellectuals for whom the civil rights and antiwar movements were forma-

[12]John Herbers, "Special Interests Gaining Power as Voter Disillusionment Grows," *New York Times*, 14 November 1978.

[13]Saundra Torry, "Army of Lobbyists Has Drawn $8 Million on Tobacco Fight," *Washington Post*, 11 September 1997, p. A4.

tive experiences, just as the Great Depression and World War II had been for their parents. The crusade against racial discrimination and the Vietnam War led these young men and women to see themselves as a political force in opposition to the public policies and politicians associated with the nation's postwar regime. In more recent years, the forces of New Politics have focused their attention on such issues as environmental protection, women's rights, and nuclear disarmament.

Members of the New Politics movement constructed or strengthened "public interest" groups such as Common Cause, the Sierra Club, the Environmental Defense Fund, Physicians for Social Responsibility, the National Organization for Women, and the various organizations formed by consumer activist Ralph Nader. Through these groups, New Politics forces were able to influence the media, Congress, and even the judiciary, and enjoyed a remarkable degree of success during the late 1960s and early 1970s in securing the enactment of policies they favored. New Politics activists also played a major role in securing the enactment of environmental, consumer, and occupational health and safety legislation.

New Politics groups sought to distinguish themselves from other interest groups—business groups, in particular—by styling themselves as "public interest" organizations to suggest that they served the general good rather than their own selfish interest. These groups' claims to represent *only* the public interest should be viewed with caution, however. Quite often, goals that are said to be in the general or public interest are also or indeed primarily in the particular interest of those who espouse them.

The term "public interest" has become so ubiquitous that it is not uncommon to find decidedly private interests seeking to hide under its cloak. For example, in 1996, the *Washington Post* looked into the finances of one public interest group, "Contributions Watch." The group, presenting itself as an independent and nonpartisan organization working for campaign finance reform, released a study purporting to detail millions of dollars in political contributions to Democratic candidates by trial lawyers. The implication was that the lawyers' groups had made the contributions as part of their effort to defeat Republican tort law reform proposals. The *Post*'s investigation revealed that Contributions Watch was created by a professional lobbying firm, State Affairs Co. The lobbying firm had been retained by a major Washington law firm, Covington and Burling, on behalf of its client, Philip Morris Tobacco. The giant tobacco company had sought the cover of public interest to mask an attack on its enemies, the trial lawyers, who in 1997 brought billions of dollars in damage suits against the tobacco companies.[14] Contributions Watch insisted that its report was accurate.

**AMERICAN POLITICAL DEVELOPMENT**

The late 1960s and early 1970s were conducive for the environmental movement. Although membership in environmental organizations continued to increase well into the 1980s, both in terms of new group creation and media coverage (as measured by inches in the *New York Times Index*), the environmental movement reached its apex from 1969 to 1972.

SOURCE: W. Douglas Costain and Anne N. Costain, "The Political Strategies of Social Movements: A Comparison of the Women's and Environmental Movements," *Congress and the Presidency* 19 (1992), pp. 1–27, esp. pp. 12–15.

[14]Ruth Marcus, "Tobacco Lobby Created Campaign 'Watchdog,'" *Washington Post,* 30 September 1996, p. 1.

## Conservative Interest Groups

The third factor associated with the expansion of interest-group politics in contemporary America has been an explosion of grassroots conservative activity. For example, the Christian Coalition, whose major focus is opposition to abortion, has nearly two million active members organized in local chapters in every state. Twenty of the state chapters have full-time staff and fifteen have annual budgets over $200,000.[15] The National Taxpayers Union has several hundred local chapters. The National Federation of Independent Business (NFIB) has hundreds of active local chapters throughout the nation, particularly in the Midwest and Southeast. Associations dedicated to defending "property rights" are organized at the local level throughout the West. Right-to-life groups are organized in virtually every U.S. congressional district. Even proponents of the rather exotic principle of "home schooling" are organized through the Home School Legal Defense Association (HSLDA), which has seventy-five regional chapters that, in turn, are linked to more than 3,000 local support groups.

These local conservative organizations were energized by the political struggles that marked Bill Clinton's two terms in office. For example, battles over the restrictions on gun ownership in the Clinton administration's 1993 crime bill helped the National Rifle Association (NRA) energize local gun owners' groups throughout the country. The struggle over a proposed amendment to the 1993 education bill, which would have placed additional restrictions on home schooling, helped the HSLDA enroll thousands of active new members in its regional and local chapters. After an intense campaign, HSLDA succeeded in both defeating the amendment and in enhancing the political awareness and activism of its formerly quiescent members. And, of course, the ongoing struggles over abortion and school prayer have helped the Christian Coalition, the Family Research Council, and other organizations comprising the Christian Right to expand the membership rolls of their state and local organizations. Anti-abortion forces, in particular, are organized at the local level throughout the United States and are prepared to participate in political campaigns and legislative battles.

This extensive organization has meant that conservatives not only have been able to bring pressure to bear upon the national government, but also have become a real presence in the corridors of state capitols, county seats, and city halls. For example, spurred by conservative groups and conservative radio programs, legislators in all fifty states have introduced property rights legislation. Eighteen states have already enacted laws requiring a "takings impact analysis" before any new government regulation affecting property can go into effect.[16] Such legislation is designed to diminish the ability of state and local governments to enact land use restrictions for environmental or planning purposes. In a similar vein, seventeen states, pressed by local conservative groups, have recently enacted legislation protecting or expanding the rights of gun owners.[17]

[15]Rich Lowry, "How the Right Rose," *National Review* 66, 11 December 1995, pp. 64–76.
[16]Neil Peirce, "Second Thoughts About Takings Measure," *Baltimore Sun,* 18 December 1995, p. 13A.
[17]Chris Warden, "A GOP Revolution That Wasn't," *Investor's Daily,* 2 January 1996, p. A1.

PROCESS BOX 12.1

**How Interest Groups Influence Congress**

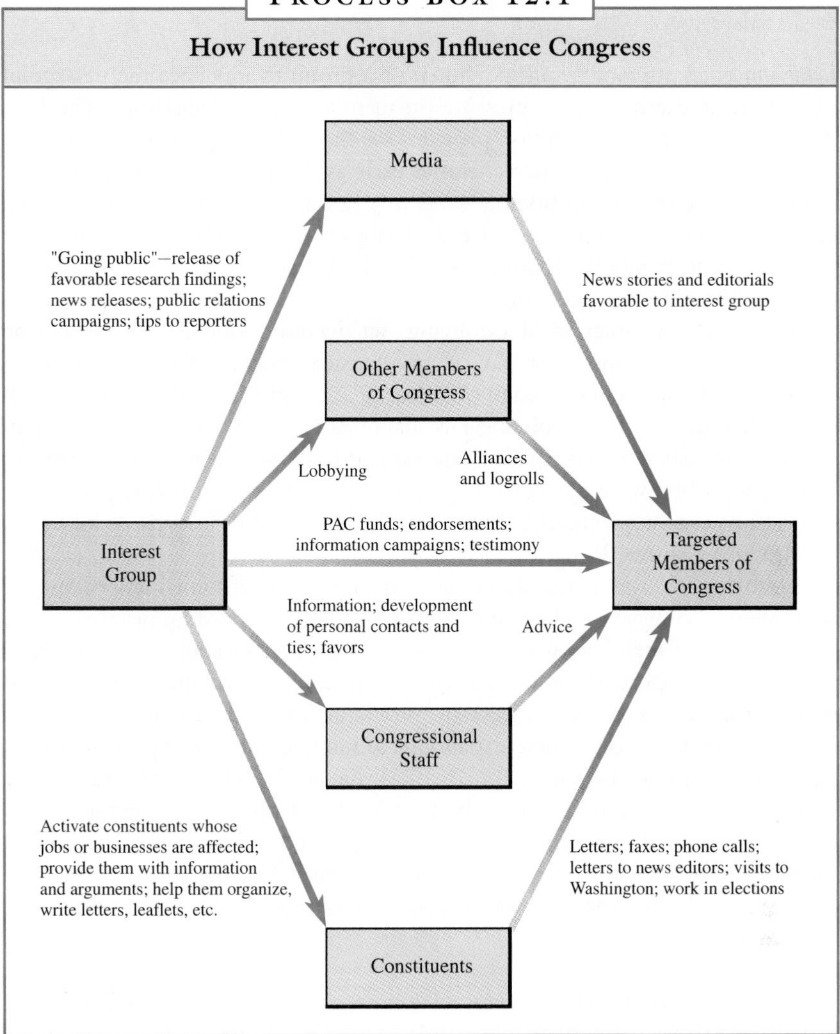


## STRATEGIES: THE QUEST FOR POLITICAL POWER

As we saw, people form interest groups in order to improve the probability that they and their policy interests will be heard and treated favorably by all branches and levels of the government. The quest for political influence or power takes many forms, but among the most frequently used strategies are lobbying, establishing access to key decision makers, using the courts, going public, and using electoral politics. These strategies do not exhaust all the possibilities, but they paint a broad picture of groups competing for power through the maximum utilization of their resources (see Process Box 12.1).

## Lobbying

***Lobbying*** is an attempt by an individual or a group to influence the passage of legislation by exerting direct pressure on members of the legislature. The First Amendment to the Constitution provides for the right to "petition the Government for a redress of grievances." But as early as the 1870s, "lobbying" became the common term for petitioning—and it is not an inaccurate one. Petitioning cannot take place on the floor of the House or Senate. Therefore, petitioners must confront members of Congress in the lobbies of the legislative chambers, giving rise to the term "lobbying."

The Federal Regulation of Lobbying Act defines a lobbyist as "any person who shall engage himself for pay or any consideration for the purpose of attempting to influence the passage or defeat of any legislation of the Congress of the United States." The Lobbying Disclosure Act requires all organizations employing lobbyists to register with Congress and to disclose whom they represent, whom they lobby, what they are lobbying for, and how much they are paid. More than 7,000 organizations, collectively employing many thousands of lobbyists, are currently registered.

Lobbying involves a great deal of activity on the part of someone speaking for an interest. Lobbyists badger and buttonhole legislators, administrators, and committee staff members with facts about pertinent issues and facts or claims about public support of them.[18] Lobbyists can serve a useful purpose in the legislative and administrative process by providing this kind of information. In 1978, during debate on a bill to expand the requirement for lobbying disclosures, Democratic senators Edward Kennedy of Massachusetts and Dick Clark of Iowa joined with Republican senator Robert Stafford of Vermont to issue the following statement: "Government without lobbying could not function. The flow of information to Congress and to every federal agency is a vital part of our democratic system."[19] But they also added that there is a darker side to lobbying—one that requires regulation.

**Types of Lobbyists** The business of lobbying is uneven and unstable. Some groups send their own loyal members to Washington to lobby for them. These representatives usually possess a lot of knowledge about a particular issue and the group's position on it, but they have little knowledge about or experience in Washington or national politics. They tend not to remain in Washington beyond the campaign for their issue.

Other groups select lobbyists with a considerable amount of Washington wisdom. During the battle over the 1996 federal budget, for example, medical specialists seeking favorable treatment under Medicare reimbursement rules retained a lobbying team that included former Minnesota Republican congressman Vin

[18]For discussions of lobbying, see Allan J. Cigler and Burdett A. Loomis, eds., *Interest Group Politics* (Washington, DC: Congressional Quarterly Press, 1983). See also Jeffrey M. Berry, *Lobbying for the People* (Princeton: Princeton University Press, 1977).

[19]"The Swarming Lobbyists," *Time,* 7 August 1978, p. 15.

Weber, former New York Democratic congressman Tom Downey, and former Clinton chief legislative aide Patrick Griffin. Former Senate Finance Committee chair Robert Packwood was retained by lumber mills and other small businesses to secure a cut in the estate tax. Similarly, in a fight between major airlines and regional carriers over airline taxes, the major airlines hired former transportation secretary James Burnley, former deputy Federal Aviation Administration administrator Linda Daschle (whose husband, Tom, is the Senate minority leader), former Reagan chief of staff Ken Duberstein, and former RNC chair Haley Barbour. The regional carriers retained former members of Congress Tom Downey and Rod Chandler, as well as a former top Senate Finance Committee staff member, Joseph O'Neil. In this battle of the titans, the major airlines ultimately prevailed.[20]

**The Lobbying Industry** The lobby industry in Washington is growing. New groups are moving in all the time, relocating from Los Angeles, Chicago, and other important cities. Local observers estimate that the actual number of people engaged in important lobbying (part-time or full-time) is closer to fifteen thousand. In addition to the various unions, commodity groups, and trade associations, the important business corporations keep their own representatives in Washington.

Many groups—even those with reputations for being powerful—are constantly forming and reforming lobby coalitions in order to improve their effectiveness with Congress and with government agencies. The AFL and the CIO, for example, merged in 1955, largely for political advantage, despite many economic disagreements between them. In the 1970s, the venerable National Association of Manufacturers (NAM) tried vainly to work out a merger with the Chamber of Commerce of the United States. During that same period, more than two hundred top executives of some of America's most important business corporations—including AT&T, Boeing, Du Pont, General Motors, Mobil Oil, and General Electric—joined in Washington to form a business roundtable, hoping to coordinate their lobbying efforts on certain issues. In subsequent years, the roundtable worked effectively to promote business interests on labor law reform, tax policy, and consumer protection.

On some occasions, lobbies lobby one another. What is called cross-lobbying came to play a major role in the struggle over health care reform. At one point, the tireless small-business lobbyists of the NFIB (discussed earlier) lobbied the American Medical Association (AMA) to drop its support for the employer mandate opposed by small business. The AMA did so in exchange for an NFIB agreement to oppose controls on physicians' fees. Similarly, the pharmaceutical industry has vigorously, but unsuccessfully, courted the American Association of Retired Persons to support its position on drug prices.[21]

Closely related to cross-lobbying is what might be called "reverse lobbying." This term refers to efforts by members of Congress to bring pressure to bear

[20]Ruth Marcus, "Lobbying's Big Hitters Go to Bat," *Washington Post,* 3 August 1997, p. 1.
[21]Michael Weisskopf, "Health Care Lobbies Lobby Each Other," *Washington Post,* 1 March 1994, p. A8.

## GLOBALIZATION AND DEMOCRACY

# *Foreign Interests in the United States*

Globalization is breaking down barriers to international trade and investment. This trend has led more and more foreign-owned enterprises and interests to establish a presence in the U.S.

Expanded trade and free-flowing investment capital have created an unprecedented number of interest groups that espouse a broad range of policy preferences. Today, more than ever before, foreign governments, corporations, and individuals, including the overseas parent firms of U.S. subsidiaries, are endeavoring to shape American policy to suit their wishes.

Not surprising, lobbying is a popular way for these interests to make their wishes known. Of course, lobbies representing foreign interests are an old and familiar fixture of the American political scene. For example, the "China Lobby" has long endeavored to ensure that the United States does not forget its "trusted old ally" Taiwan. Similarly, the American Israel Public Affairs Committee (AIPAC), part of the so-called Israeli Lobby, does its utmost to see that the United States pays heed to that country's interests in the volatile Middle East. These and other groups frequently employ the services of Washington lobbyists, many of whom are high-profile retired U.S. government officials or former politicians.[1] Even though the Foreign Agents Registration Act (1938) requires that these lobbyists report some of their client rela-

[1]In the controversial book *Agents of Influence* (New York: Alfred A Knopf, 1990), pp. 208–49, Pat Choate lists the names and affiliations of nearly two hundred former federal officials who represented foreign clients between 1980 and 1990.

tionship to the attorney general, there are many loopholes in the law. One effect of globalization, therefore, is to increase both the points of access to and the range of interests competing for access to policy makers. Because of different cultural attitudes, globalization increases the potential for corruption. What is viewed as legitimate gift-giving in South Korea may be clearcut bribery in the United States.

The expanded presence of foreign-owned American subsidiaries injects added complexity into interest-group politics. Take, for example, the 1994 case involving allegations of sexual harassment at a Mitsubishi Motors assembly plant near Chicago.[2] After investigating complaints by twenty-nine women who brought a federal lawsuit, the Equal Employment Opportunity Commission (EEOC) filed a class-action suit alleging that Mitsubishi management turned a blind eye to "gross and shocking sexual discrimination" at its subsidiary's plant. In response, Mitsubishi shut down two shifts of production at the plant and bused more than two thousand workers to Chicago to demonstrate outside the EEOC offices. The protesters, whose wages for the day and lunches reportedly were paid for by Mitsubishi, marched while chanting "Two, four, six, eight! We're here to set the record straight!" In addition, the company set up a telephone bank to enable employees to call the EEOC, their representatives in Congress, and the White House to dispute the allegations. On the one hand, the Mitsubishi case reveals the added pluralism that globalization has injected into interest-group politics. On the other hand, it is likely that one reason behind the complaints of sexual harassment at the Mitsubishi plant was because of the different cultural attitudes toward the role and treatment of female workers. The potential exists for similar misunderstandings with foreign owners and managers about the racial diversity and attitudes toward labor unions at their U.S. operations. In this sense, globalization may generate "culture clash."

[2]Details of the case are reported in "Mitsubishi Buses 2,000 Workers to Federal Office to Protest Sexual Harassment Claims," *The Detroit News,* 23 April 1996.

upon lobby groups to support particular courses of action. For example, in 1993 and 1994, the Conservative Opportunity Society (COS), an organization comprising the most conservative Republican members of the House of Representatives, brought intense pressure to bear upon the U.S. Chamber of Commerce to oppose the Clinton administration's policy initiatives. The Chamber of Commerce, one of the nation's leading business lobbies, has traditionally been aligned with the Republican party. In 1993, however, one of the organization's vice presidents, William Archey, decided that it might be worthwhile to cooperate with the Democratic administration. Outraged congressional Republicans mobilized the Chamber's members to oppose this apparent shift in the organization's stance. Republicans feared that any weakening of the Chamber's opposition to the Democrats would undermine their efforts to defeat President Clinton's major policy initiatives. After a struggle, Archey was compelled to resign and the Chamber returned to its traditional posture of support for the Republicans and opposition to the Democrats.[22] In a similar vein, Republican members of Congress sought to pressure the AMA to oppose President Clinton's health care initiatives.

In 1993, Clinton proposed that companies employing lobbyists be prohibited from deducting lobbying costs as business expenses from their federal taxes. This would, in effect, make it more difficult and costly for firms to employ lobbyists on behalf of their concerns. Not surprisingly, this proposal was bitterly resented by the lobbying industry, which saw it as a mortal threat to its own business interests. How did lobbying firms respond? By lobbying, of course. The American League of Lobbyists, a trade group representing the lobbying industry, quickly mobilized its members to conduct a vigorous campaign to defeat the proposal. One worried Washington lobbyist, however, observed, "This seems so self-serving, you wonder who is going to listen to us anyway."[23] Lobbyists turned out not to be so adept at lobbying for their own cause, and Clinton's proposal was enacted.

In 1994, Congress first passed and then rejected legislation requiring disclosure of lobbying activities and prohibiting lobbyists from giving gifts worth more than twenty dollars to members.[24] A gift ban was finally adopted by both houses of Congress in January 1996. Such lobbying-reform legislation could force interest groups to rely even more heavily upon grassroots campaigns and less heavily upon "buying access."

## Gaining Access

Lobbying is an effort by outsiders to exert influence on Congress or government agencies by providing them with information about issues, support, and even threats of retaliation. Access is actual involvement in the decision-making process. It may be the outcome of long years of lobbying, but it should not be confused

[22]Gregory B. Wilson, "A Congressional Lobbying Effort against the U.S. Chamber of Commerce," unpublished research paper, Johns Hopkins University, 1994.

[23]Michael Weisskopf, "Lobbyists Rally Around Their Own Cause: Clinton Move to Eliminate Tax Break Sparks Intense Hill Campaign," *Washington Post,* 14 May 1993, p. A16.

[24]Phil Kuntz, "Ticket to a Better Image?" *Congressional Quarterly Weekly Report,* 7 May 1994, p. 1105.

with lobbying. If lobbying has to do with "influence on" a government, access has to do with "influence within" it. Many interest groups resort to lobbying because they have insufficient access or insufficient time to develop it.

One interesting example of a group that had access but lost it, turned to lobbying, and later used a strategy of "going public" (see page 519) is the dairy farmers. Through the 1960s, dairy farmers were part of the powerful coalition of agricultural interests that had full access to the Congress and to the Department of Agriculture. During the 1960s, a series of disputes broke out between the dairy farmers and the producers of corn, grain, and other agricultural commodities over commodities prices. Dairy farmers, whose cows consume grain, prefer low commodities prices while grain producers obviously prefer to receive high prices. The commodities producers won the battle, and Congress raised commodities prices, in part at the expense of the dairy farmers. In the 1970s, the dairy farmers left the agriculture coalition, set up their own lobby and political action groups, and became heavily involved in public relations campaigns and both congressional and presidential elections. The dairy farmers encountered a number of difficulties in pursuing their new "outsider" strategies. Indeed, the political fortunes of the dairy operations were badly hurt when they were accused of making illegal contributions to President Nixon's re-election campaign in 1972.

**AMERICAN POLITICAL DEVELOPMENT**

Interest-group access to government has become increasingly institutionalized in the U.S. Congress since the 1970s' proliferation of congressional caucuses. Four caucuses were established from 1959 to 1970, fifty-eight from 1971 to 1980, and 114 from 1981 to 1990.

SOURCE: Susan Webb Hammond, *Congressional Caucuses in National Policy Making* (Baltimore, MD: Johns Hopkins University Press, 1998), p. 42.

Access is usually a result of time and effort spent cultivating a position within the inner councils of government. This method of gaining access often requires the sacrifice of short-run influence. For example, many of the most important organized interests in agriculture devote far more time and resources cultivating the staff and trustees of state agriculture schools and county agents back home than buttonholing members of Congress or bureaucrats in Washington.

Figure 12.1 is a sketch of one of the most important access patterns in recent American political history: that of the defense industry. Each such pattern is almost literally a triangular shape, with one point in an executive branch program, another point in a Senate or House legislative committee or subcommittee, and a third point in some highly stable and well-organized interest group. The points in the triangular relationship are mutually supporting; they count as access only if they last over a long period of time. For example, access to a legislative committee or subcommittee requires that at least one member of it support the interest group in question. This member also must have built up considerable seniority in Congress. An interest cannot feel comfortable about its access to Congress until it has one or more of its "own" people with ten or more years of continuous service on the relevant committee or subcommittee.

A number of important policy domains, such as the environmental and welfare arenas, are controlled, not by highly structured and unified iron triangles, but by rival ***issue networks.*** These networks consist of like-minded politicians, consul-

FIGURE 12.1

**The Iron Triangle in Defense**

*The emergence of an Iron Triangle was apparent very early in the relations of defense contractors and the federal government. Defense contractors are powerful actors in shaping defense policy, acting in concert with defense subcommittees in Congress and executive agencies concerned with defense.*

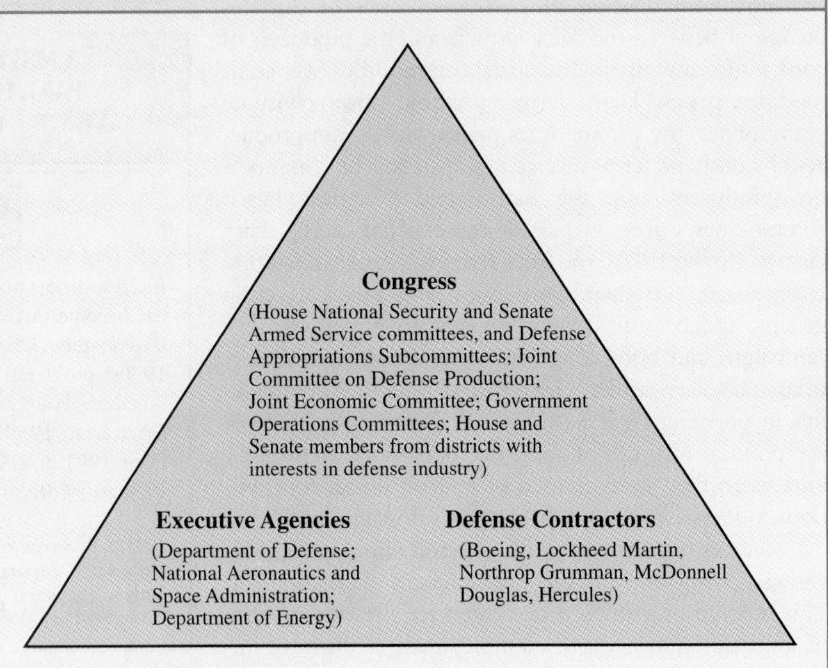


tants, public officials, political activists, and interest groups who have some concern with the issue in question. Activists and interest groups recognized as being involved in the area are sometimes called "stakeholders," and are customarily invited to testify before congressional committees or give their views to government agencies considering action in their domain.

**Corridoring: Gaining Access to the Bureaucracy** A bureaucratic agency is the third point in the iron triangle, and thus access to it is essential to the success of an interest group. Working to gain influence in an executive agency is sometimes called corridoring—the equivalent of lobbying in the executive branch. Even when an interest group is very successful at getting its bill passed by Congress and signed by the president, the prospect of full and faithful implementation of that law is not guaranteed. Often, a group and its allies do not pack up and go home as soon as the president turns their lobbied-for new law over to the appropriate agency. Agencies, too, can fall under the influence or be captured by an interest group or a coalition of well-organized groups.[25] Granted, agencies are not passive and can do a good bit of capturing themselves. The point is that those groups that ignore the role of the agency in implementing legislation are simply not going to have any role in the outcome of agency decisions.

It often used to be said that agriculture wrote its own ticket; this may be only a slight exaggeration of its political power until the 1980s. Agricultural interest groups often brought about great legislative successes without attracting much public attention. Their influence far exceeded their proportionate place in the American economy. Generally, agricultural interests managed to maintain high price supports even in inflationary periods. Tobacco farmers continued to get their special price supports even after tobacco was declared hazardous to people's health. After 1980, however, agriculture declined in political power (as the economic fortunes of the industry waned) and was deserted by some of its former political allies. In recent years, the agricultural lobby found itself unable to maintain a united and coherent stand. The farm lobby has had to contend with internal disputes among competing sectors as the pool of federal aid has shrunk. Disputes that would ordinarily have been kept as private matters now find themselves in the public eye: grain producers push for higher grain prices while poultry producers push for lower grain prices; cattle ranchers fight programs that allow dairy farmers to slaughter their cows and then dump the beef into the cattle ranchers' market. Relationships between interest group and agency can be so useful that some interest groups feel they are being shortchanged if the industries they represent do not have their own regulatory agency. "There is no doubt in my mind that we are at a competitive disadvantage in Washington, D.C.," said Robert Rusbuldt, a lobbyist for the Independent Insurance Agents of America, a group whose industry lacks a federal regulator.[26]

### AMERICAN POLITICAL DEVELOPMENT

The development of the iron triangle relationship in agricultural policy is explained by the creation and mobilization of farm organizations (such as the Grange and the American Farm Bureau Federation in the late 1910s), the institutionalization of their ties in Washington, and the decline of political parties in Congress, which caused legislators to turn to these groups for electoral and policy support because the parties no longer provided it.

SOURCE: John Mark Hansen, "Choosing Sides: The Creation of an Agriculture Policy Network in Congress, 1919–1932," *Studies in American Political Development* 2 (1987), pp. 183–229.

A very important example of access politics in action is the military-industrial complex—a notion put forth by President Eisenhower in his farewell address in January 1961. The military-industrial complex is a pattern of relationships among manufacturers, the Defense Department, and Congress that has emerged out of America's vast peacetime involvement in international military and economic affairs. More than four years before Eisenhower's farewell address, the House Armed Services Committee conducted a survey of the postmilitary careers of retired military officers above the rank of major. The survey disclosed that

[25] See especially Marver Bernstein, *Regulating Business by Independent Commission* (Princeton: Princeton University Press, 1955). See also George J. Stigler, "The Theory of Economic Regulation," *Bell Journal of Economics and Management Science* 2 (1971), pp. 3–21.

[26] David Hosansky, "Industries Get a Boost from Their Overseers," *Congressional Quarterly Weekly Report,* 18 April 1998, p. 968.

more than 1,400 officers, including 261 at the rank of general or its equivalent in the navy, had left the armed forces directly for employment by one of the hundred leading defense contractors.[27] This same pattern was at the heart of the military procurement scandal that rocked the Reagan administration in 1988, when the news media and congressional investigators revealed that some defense contractors had systematically and grossly overcharged the Pentagon for military hardware and supplies.

During the Reagan and Bush administrations, the military-industrial complex became more closely linked to the Republican White House than to the Democratic Congress. Indeed, Republicans in the executive branch saw the military-industrial complex as an institutional base that could serve the Republican party in much the same way that the welfare and regulatory agencies of the domestic state served the Democrats. Thus, military and defense agencies, linked to industries and regions of the country that benefited economically from high levels of defense spending, could enhance Republican political strength in the same way that domestic agencies, their clients in the public and not-for-profit sectors, and the beneficiaries of domestic spending programs strengthened the Democrats.

Between 1988 and 1990, the military-industrial complex was weakened by procurement scandals, budget cuts, and cost overruns that led to the cancellation of weapons projects such as the Navy's multi-billion-dollar A-12 bomber. In addition, the political and economic collapse of the Soviet Union seemed to weaken arguments for continuing high levels of spending on expensive new weapons systems. Yet despite the elimination of the major military threat to the United States—the threat that nominally justified enormous military outlays for nearly a half-century—the country continued to spend hundreds of billions of dollars on defense. It was a tribute, in large part, to the political skill of the military-industrial complex that the United States continued to support an enormous military force against a foe that no longer existed. But as the Clinton administration began to cut defense outlays to reduce the nation's budget deficit and free more funds for domestic programs, the military-industrial complex found itself losing influence. Some wondered whether it would survive the end of the cold war.[28]

Access politics through exchange of personnel is not limited to military industrial relationships, however. It has spread to other areas, too, where it has also created "complexes." The spectacular expansion in federally assisted research and development programs has fostered the development of a government-science or government-university complex. Changes in the manner in which federal aid is obtained for university research projects have generated a debate over the proper relationship between the federal government and institutions of higher education in recent years. Federal financing of research programs and facilities at public and private universities for several decades has contributed significantly to research efforts, reaching a high in the 1960s and early 1970s. Traditionally, funds

[27]U.S. Congress, House of Representatives, *Report of the Subcommittee for Special Investigations of the Committee on Armed Services,* 96th Congress, 1st session (Washington, DC: Government Printing Office, 1960), p. 7.

[28]Thomas Ricks, "With Cold War Over, the Military-Industrial Complex Is Dissolving," *Wall Street Journal,* 20 May 1993, p. 1.

for research and development were either meted out by Congress to various agencies such as the National Science Foundation and, particularly, the Department of Defense, or these agencies solicited projects, subjecting them to a peer review process to determine which proposals were worthy of funding.

Major research institutions had little quarrel with this system for many years, as it tended to reward them consistently for various types of basic research. As federal funding dried up in the mid-1970s, however, the nature of the fight for funding has changed, setting off intense competition and debate. Rather than competing for funds from agencies through a peer review process, many universities have hired lobbyists and attempted to obtain direct appropriations from Congress via pork-barrel legislation. Appealing to members of the House and Senate with promises that funding for research facilities will attract industry, universities have been able to persuade members of Congress to request funds for particular research projects without having to endure a peer review selection process.

**Influence Peddling** The grassroots approach of agriculture and the personnel interchange approach of many businesses are not the only ways to engage in access politics. It is possible, although not easy, to buy access by securing the services of certain important Washington lawyers and lobbyists. These people can, for proper consideration, provide real access; not merely the more impersonal representation of the lobbyist. "Influence peddling" is the negative term for this sale or rental of access that goes on openly in Washington. Former commerce secretary Ron Brown, for example, was an important Washington lawyer-lobbyist, earning nearly one million dollars annually for his services to corporate clients and foreign governments, before joining the government. Brown's ties to a variety of corporate interests raised many questions about President Clinton's wisdom in appointing him—questions that Brown and his supporters angrily rebutted.[29]

Many retired or defeated members of Congress join or form Washington law firms and spend all their time either lobbying or funneling access. An even larger number of former government officials and congressional staff members remain in Washington in order to make a living from their expertise and their access. (Laws that limit the freedom of former government employees to take jobs in directly related private companies do not apply to employees of congressional committees.) The senior partnerships of Washington's top law firms are heavily populated with these former officials and staffers, and they practice law before the very commissions and committees on which they once served. There's an old saying about members of Congress—"they never go back to Pocatello"—and it is as true today as when it was coined.

Influence can be expensive. In 1996, for example, wealthy donors, including representatives of foreign business interests, paid thousands of dollars each to have lunch or coffee with the president and vice president. Some of the most generous donors were invited to spend the night in the White House's Lincoln Bedroom. Despite the criticism engendered by these practices, President Clinton felt

[29]William Raspberry, "Why Did Ron Brown Become a Target?" *Washington Post,* 20 January 1993, p. A21.

compelled to resume this form of fund-raising in 1997 to help pay the Democratic party's enormous debt from the 1996 campaigns. Thus, in October 1997, the Democratic party invited donors to pay $50,000 each to participate in a Florida weekend retreat with the president, vice president, several members of Congress, and a number of administration officials. During the same month, while criticizing Clinton for his practices, Republicans invited donors to pay $10,000 apiece to have lunch with Senate Majority Leader Trent Lott. Donors are willing to contribute these large sums because they hope to benefit from rubbing shoulders with political leaders who are in a position to advance their economic interests or social concerns.[30]

## Using the Courts (Litigation)

Interest groups sometimes turn to litigation when they lack access or when they are dissatisfied with government in general or with a specific government program and feel they have insufficient influence to change the situation. They can use the courts to affect public policy in at least three ways: (1) by bringing suit directly on behalf of the group itself, (2) by financing suits brought by individuals, or (3) by filing a companion brief as *amicus curiae* (literally "friend of the court") to an existing court case.

Among the most significant modern illustrations of the use of the courts as a strategy for political influence are those that accompanied the "sexual revolution" of the 1960s and the emergence of the movement for women's rights. Beginning in the mid-sixties, a series of cases was brought into the federal courts in an effort to force definition of a right to privacy in sexual matters. The effort began with a challenge to state restrictions on obtaining contraceptives for nonmedical purposes, a challenge that was effectively made in *Griswold v. Connecticut,* where the Supreme Court held that states could neither prohibit the dissemination of information about nor prohibit the actual use of contraceptives by married couples. That case was soon followed by *Eisenstadt v. Baird,* in which the Court held that the states could not prohibit the use of contraceptives by single persons any more than it could prohibit their use by married couples. One year later, the Court held, in the 1973 case of *Roe v. Wade,* that states could not impose an absolute ban on voluntary abortions. Each of these cases, as well as others, were part of the Court's enunciation of a constitutional doctrine of privacy.[31]

**AMERICAN POLITICAL DEVELOPMENT**

Since the early 1970s, public interest and ideological groups have looked toward the courts to advance their policy goals. But in the late nineteenth century, interest groups such as business organizations and corporations had already used this strategy.

SOURCE: David M. O'Brien, *Storm Center: The Supreme Court in American Politics,* 4th ed. (New York: W. W. Norton, 1996), pp. 250–51.

The 1973 abortion case sparked a controversy that brought conservatives to the fore on a national level. These conservative groups made extensive use of the courts to whittle away the scope of the privacy doctrine. They obtained rulings,

[30]Ruth Marcus, "A $50,000 Weekend with Clinton, Gore," *Washington Post,* 22 October 1997, p. A4.

[31]Griswold v. Connecticut, 381 U.S. 479 (1965); Eisenstadt v. Baird, 405 U.S. 438 (1972); Roe v. Wade, 410 U.S. 113 (1973).

for example, that prohibit the use of federal funds to pay for voluntary abortions. And in 1989, right-to-life groups were able to use a strategy of litigation that significantly undermined the *Roe v. Wade* decision, namely in the case of *Webster v. Reproductive Health Services* (see Chapter 4), which restored the right of states to place restrictions on abortion.[32]

Another extremely significant set of contemporary illustrations of the use of the courts as a strategy for political influence are those found in the history of the NAACP. The most important of these court cases was, of course, *Brown v. Board of Education of Topeka,* in which the U.S. Supreme Court held that legal segregation of the schools was unconstitutional.[33]

Business groups are also frequent users of the courts because of the number of government programs applied to them. Litigation involving large businesses is most mountainous in such areas as taxation, antitrust, interstate transportation, patents, and product quality and standardization. Often a business is brought to litigation against its will by virtue of initiatives taken against it by other businesses or by government agencies. But many individual businesses bring suit themselves in order to influence government policy. Major corporations and their trade associations pay tremendous amounts of money each year in fees to the most prestigious Washington law firms. Some of this money is expended in gaining access. A great proportion of it, however, is used to keep the best and most experienced lawyers prepared to represent the corporations in court or before administrative agencies when necessary.

New Politics forces made significant use of the courts during the 1970s and 1980s, and judicial decisions were instrumental in advancing their goals. Facilitated by rules changes on access to the courts (the rules of standing are discussed in Chapter 8), the New Politics agenda was clearly visible in court decisions handed down in several key policy areas. In the environmental policy area, New Politics groups were able to force federal agencies to pay attention to environmental issues, even when the agency was not directly involved in activities related to environmental quality.

While the skirmishes continued on the environmental front, consumer activists were likewise realizing significant gains. Stung by harsh critiques in both the Nader Report and the Report of the American Bar Association in 1969, the Federal Trade Commission (FTC) became very responsive to the demands of New Politics activists. During the 1970s and 1980s, the FTC stepped up its activities considerably, litigating a series of claims arising under regulations prohibiting deceptive advertising in cases ranging from false claims for over-the-counter drugs to inflated claims about the nutritional value of children's cereal.

And while feminists and equal rights activists enjoyed enormous success in litigating discrimination claims under Title VII of the Civil Rights Act of 1964, anti-nuclear power activists succeeded in virtually shutting down the nuclear power industry. Despite significant defeats, most notably *Duke Power Company v. Carolina Environmental Study Group,* which upheld a federal statute limiting liability for damages accruing from nuclear power plant accidents, challenges to

[32]Webster v. Reproductive Health Services, 109 S.Ct. 3040 (1989).
[33]Brown v. Board of Education of Topeka, 347 U.S. 483 (1954).

power plant siting and licensing regulations were instrumental in discouraging energy companies from pursuing nuclear projects over the long term.[34]

Groups will also sometimes seek legislation designed to help them secure their aims through litigation. During the 1970s, for example, Congress fashioned legislation meant to make it easier for environmental and consumer groups to use the courts. Several regulatory statutes, such as the 1973 Endangered Species Act, contained "citizen suit" provisions that, in effect, gave environmental groups the right to bring suits challenging the decisions of executive agencies and the actions of business firms in environmental cases, even if the groups bringing suit were not being directly harmed by the governmental or private action in question. Such suits, moreover, could be financed by the expedient of "fee shifting"—that is, environmental or consumer groups could finance successful suits by collecting legal fees and expenses from their opponents.

In its decision in the 1992 case of *Lujan v. Defenders of Wildlife* (see Chapter 8), the Supreme Court seemed to question the constitutionality of citizen suit provisions. Justice Scalia indicated that such provisions violated Article III of the U.S. Constitution, which limits the jurisdiction of the federal courts to actual cases and controversies.[35] This means that only persons directly affected by a case can bring it before the courts. If the Court were to continue to take this position, the capacity of public interest groups to employ a strategy of litigation would be diminished.

An important recent product of this relationship between legislation and litigation is the 1990 Americans with Disabilities Act (ADA), which took full effect in July 1992. The act resulted from the lobbying efforts of a host of public interest and advocacy groups and is aimed at allowing individuals with hearing, sight, or mobility impairments to participate fully in American life. Under the terms of this significant piece of legislation, businesses, private organizations, and local governmental agencies were required to make certain that their administrative procedures and physical plants did not needlessly deprive individuals with physical or emotional disabilities of access to the use of their facilities, or of employment and other opportunities.

Subsequently, the 1991 Civil Rights Act granted disabled individuals who believed that their rights under the ADA had been violated the right to sue for compensatory and punitive damages, as well as the right to demand a jury trial. In other words, this *legislation* encouraged individuals with disabilities to make use of *litigation* to secure their new rights and press their interests.

Hundreds of legal complaints were immediately filed. To make use of the opportunity for litigation, an advocacy group, the Disability Rights Litigation and Defense Fund, trained five thousand "barrier busters" to look for violators of the act and file lawsuits. Federal officials estimated that the ADA would generate approximately fifteen thousand discrimination cases every year—an estimate the act's critics consider much too low.[36]

[34]Duke Power Co. v. Carolina Environmental Study Group, 438 U.S. 59 (1978).

[35]Lujan v. Defenders of Wildlife, 112 S.Ct. 2130 (1992); see also Linda Greenhouse, "Court Limits Legal Standing in Suits," *New York Times,* 13 June 1992, p. 12.

[36]See "Disabling America," *Wall Street Journal,* 24 July 1992, p. A10. See also Gary Becker, "How the Disabilities Act Will Cripple Business," *Business Week,* 14 September 1992, p. 14.

## Going Public

Going public is a strategy that attempts to mobilize the widest and most favorable climate of opinion. Many groups consider it imperative to maintain this climate at all times, even when they have no issue to fight about. An increased use of this kind of strategy is usually associated with modern advertising. As early as the 1930s, political analysts were distinguishing between the "old lobby" of direct group representation before Congress and the "new lobby" of public relations professionals addressing the public at large to reach Congress.[37]

One of the best-known ways of going public is the use of institutional advertising. A casual scanning of important mass circulation magazines and newspapers will provide numerous examples of expensive and well-designed ads by the major oil companies, automobile and steel companies, other large corporations, and trade associations. The ads show how much these organizations are doing for the country, for the protection of the environment, or for the defense of the American way of life. Their purpose is to create and maintain a strongly positive association between the organization and the community at large in the hope that these favorable feelings can be drawn on as needed for specific political campaigns later on.

Going public is not limited to businesses or to upper-income professional groups. Many groups resort to it because they lack the resources, the contacts, or the experience to use other political strategies. The sponsorship of boycotts, sit-ins, mass rallies, and marches by Martin Luther King's Southern Christian Leadership Conference (SCLC) and related organizations in the 1950s and 1960s is one of the most significant and successful cases of going public to create a more favorable climate of opinion by calling attention to abuses. The success of these events inspired similar efforts on the part of women. Organizations such as the National Organization for Women (NOW) used public strategies in their drive for legislation and in their efforts to gain ratification of the Equal Rights Amendment. In 1993, gay rights groups organized a mass rally in their effort to eliminate restrictions on military service and other forms of discrimination against individuals based on their sexual preference.

Another form of going public is the grassroots lobbying campaign. In such a campaign, a lobby group mobilizes ordinary citizens throughout the country to write to their representatives in support of the group's position. A grassroots campaign can cost anywhere from $40,000 to sway the votes of one or two crucial members of a committee or subcommittee, to millions of dollars to mount a national effort aimed at the Congress as a whole. In a recent year, interest groups spent nearly $1 billion on grassroots lobbying.[38] Grassroots lobbying has become more prevalent in Washington in the 1990s, because the adoption of congressional rules limiting gifts to members has made traditional lobbying more difficult.

[37]E. Pendleton Herring, *Group Representation before Congress* (New York: McGraw-Hill, 1936).

[38]Alison Mitchell, "A New Form of Lobbying Puts Public Face on Private Interest," *New York Times,* 30 September 1998, p. 1.

At the beginning of 1999, a number of grassroots campaigns were under way. For example, Leo Linbeck, a wealthy Houston construction executive, is directing a campaign to change radically the nation's tax system in ways that would generally benefit the wealthy. Linbeck's organization, "Americans for Fair Taxation," has already spent more than $15 million on a mass media campaign. In a similar vein, a coalition of business and labor interests that would suffer financially from the adoption of the Kyoto Global Climate Treaty negotiated in 1997, have formed the Global Climate Information Project, which sponsors television and radio ads warning Americans that they will lose their jobs and be forced to cut energy use if the treaty is adopted.

In a recent year, lobbyists for the Nissan Motor Company sought to organize a "grassroots" effort to prevent President Clinton from raising tariffs on imported minivans, including Nissan's Pathfinder model. Nissan's twelve hundred dealers across the nation, as well as their dealers' employees and family members, were urged to dial a toll-free number that would automatically generate a prepared mailgram opposing the tariff to be sent to the president and each dealer's senators. The mailgram warned that the proposed tariff increase would hurt middle-class auto purchasers and small businesses, such as the dealers'.[39] During his 1992 presidential campaign, Ross Perot showed how effectively television can be used to carry one's message to the grass roots.

Among the most effective users of the grassroots lobby effort in contemporary American politics is the religious Right. Networks of evangelical churches have the capacity to generate hundreds of thousands of letters and phone calls to Congress and the White House. For example, the religious Right was outraged when President Clinton announced soon after taking office that he planned to end the military's ban on gay and lesbian soldiers. The Reverend Jerry Falwell, an evangelist leader, called upon viewers of his television program to dial a telephone number that would add their names to a petition urging Clinton to retain the ban on gays in the military. Within a few hours, 24,000 persons had called to support the petition.[40]

Grassroots lobbying campaigns have been so effective in recent years that a number of Washington consulting firms have begun to specialize in this area. Firms such as Bonner and Associates, for example, will work to generate grassroots telephone campaigns on behalf of or in opposition to important legislative proposals. Such efforts can be very expensive. Reportedly, one trade association recently paid the Bonner firm three million dollars to generate and sustain a grassroots effort to defeat a bill on the Senate floor.[41]

Has grassroots campaigning been overutilized? One story in the *New York Times* forces us to ask that question. Ten giant companies in the financial services, manufacturing, and high-tech industries began a grassroots campaign in 1992 and spent millions of dollars over the next three years to influence a decision in

[39]Michael Weisskopf and Steven Mufson, "Lobbyists in Full Swing on Tax Plan," *Washington Post,* 17 February 1993, p. 1.

[40]Michael Weisskopf, "Energized by Pulpit or Passion, the Public Is Calling," *Washington Post,* 1 February 1993, p. 1.

[41]Stephen Engelberg, "A New Breed of Hired Hands Cultivates Grass-Roots Anger," *New York Times,* 17 March 1993, p. A1.

Congress to limit the ability of investors to sue for fraud. Retaining an expensive consulting firm, these corporations paid for the use of specialized computer software to persuade Congress that there was "an outpouring of popular support for the proposal." Thousands of letters from individuals flooded Capitol Hill. Many of those letters were written and sent by people who sincerely believed that investor lawsuits are often frivolous and should be curtailed. But much of the mail was phony, generated by the Washington-based campaign consultants; the letters came from people who had no strong feelings or even no opinion at all about the issue. More and more people, including leading members of Congress, are becoming quite skeptical of such methods, charging that these are not genuine grassroots campaigns but instead represent "Astroturf lobbying" (a play on the name of an artificial grass used on many sports fields). Such "Astroturf" campaigns have increased in frequency in recent years as members of Congress grow more and more skeptical of Washington lobbyists and far more concerned about demonstrations of support for a particular issue by their constituents. But after the firms mentioned above spent millions of dollars and generated thousands of letters to members of Congress, they came to the somber conclusion that "it's more effective to have 100 letters from your district where constituents took the time to write and understand the issue," because "Congress is sophisticated enough to know the difference."[42]

## Using Electoral Politics

Many interest groups decide that it is far more effective to elect the right legislators than to try to influence the incumbents through lobbying or through a changed or mobilized mass opinion. Interest groups can influence elections by two means: financial support funded through political action committees, and campaign activism.

**Political Action Committees** By far the most common electoral strategy employed by interest groups is that of giving financial support to the parties or to particular candidates. But such support can easily cross the threshold into outright bribery. Therefore, Congress has occasionally made an effort to regulate this strategy. Congress's most recent effort was the Federal Election Campaign Act of 1971 (amended in 1974), which we discussed in Chapter 10. This act limits campaign contributions and requires that each candidate or campaign committee itemize the full name and address, occupation, and principal business of each person who contributes more than $100. These provisions have been effective up to a point, considering the rather large number of embarrassments, indictments, resignations, and criminal convictions in the aftermath of the Watergate scandal.

The Watergate scandal, itself, was triggered by the illegal entry of Republican workers into the office of the Democratic National Committee in the Watergate apartment building. But an investigation quickly revealed numerous violations of

[42]Jane Fritsch, "The Grass Roots, Just a Free Phone Call Away," *New York Times,* 23 June 1995, pp. A1 and A22.

campaign finance laws, involving millions of dollars in unregistered cash from corporate executives to President Nixon's re-election committee. Many of these revelations were made by the famous Ervin Committee, whose official name and jurisdiction was the Senate Select Committee to Investigate the 1972 Presidential Campaign Activities.

Reaction to Watergate produced further legislation on campaign finance in 1974 and 1976, but the effect has been to restrict individual rather than interest-group campaign activity. Individuals may now contribute no more than $1,000 to any candidate for federal office in any primary or general election. A ***political action committee*** (PAC), however, can contribute $5,000, provided it contributes to at least five different federal candidates each year. Beyond this, the laws permit corporations, unions, and other interest groups to form PACs and to pay the costs of soliciting funds from private citizens for the PACs.

Electoral spending by interest groups has been increasing steadily despite the flurry of reform following Watergate. Table 12.1 presents a dramatic picture of the growth of PACs as the source of campaign contributions. The dollar amounts for each year indicate the growth in electoral spending. The number of PACs has also increased significantly—from 608 in 1974 to more than 4,000 in 1995 (see Figure 12.2). Although the reform legislation of the early and mid-1970s attempted to reduce the influence of special interests over elections, the effect has been almost the exact opposite. Opportunities for legally influencing campaigns are now widespread.

Indeed, PACs and campaign contributions provide organized interests with such a useful tool for gaining access to the political process that interests of all political stripes are now willing to suspend their conflicts and rally to the defense of political action committees when they come under attack. This support has

TABLE 12.1

**PAC Spending, 1977–1997**

| YEARS | CONTRIBUTIONS |
|---|---|
| 1977–1978 (est.) | $ 77,800,000 |
| 1979–1980 | 131,153,384 |
| 1981–1982 | 190,173,539 |
| 1983–1984 | 266,822,476 |
| 1985–1986 | 339,954,416 |
| 1987–1988 | 364,201,275 |
| 1989–1990 | 372,100,000 |
| 1991–1992 | 402,300,000 |
| 1993–1994 | 387,426,957 |
| 1995–1996 | 467,000,000 |
| 1996–1997 | 470,800,000 |

SOURCE: Federal Election Commission

FIGURE 12.2

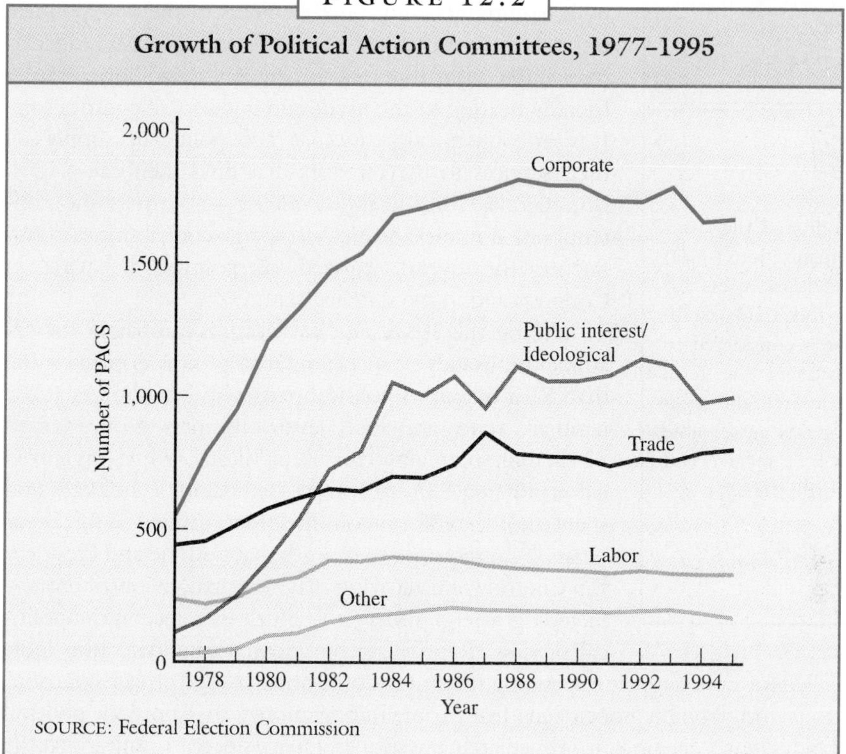


SOURCE: Federal Election Commission

helped to make the present campaign funding system highly resistant to reform. As we saw in Chapter 10, in May 1996, the Senate considered a bipartisan campaign finance bill sponsored by Senators John McCain (R-Ariz.), Russell Feingold (D-Wisc.), and Fred Thompson (R-Tenn.), which would have abolished political action committees. The bill was staunchly opposed by a coalition of business groups, labor unions, liberal groups like EMILY's List, and conservative groups like Americans for Tax Reform. Though these groups disagree on many substantive matters, they agreed on the principle that abolition of PACs would "diminish the ability of average citizens to join together to have their voices heard." A less positive interpretation was offered by Common Cause president Ann McBride, a proponent of abolishing PACs, who characterized the pro-PAC alliance as an example of "labor and business coming together and agreeing on the one thing that they can agree on, which is maintaining the status quo and their ability to use money to buy outcomes on Capitol Hill."[43]

[43]Ruth Marcus, "Campaign Finance Proposal Drawing Opposition from Diverse Groups," *Washington Post,* 1 May 1996, p. A12.

**AMERICAN POLITICAL DEVELOPMENT**

When Congress prohibited the Congress of Industrial Organizations (CIO) from using organizational assets for political purposes, the CIO established in 1943 what is considered to be the first PAC. Using the term Political Action Committee, the organization was designed as a "separate political fund set up to receive and spend voluntary contributions."

SOURCE: Frank J. Sorauf, *Money in American Elections* (Glencoe, IL: Scott Foresman, 1988), p. 73.

Given the enormous costs of television commercials, polls, computers, and other elements of the new political technology (see Chapter 11), most politicians are eager to receive PAC contributions and are at least willing to give a friendly hearing to the needs and interests of contributors. It is probably not the case that most politicians simply sell their services to the interests that fund their campaigns. But there is considerable evidence to support the contention that interest groups' campaign contributions do influence the overall pattern of political behavior in Congress and in the state legislatures.[44]

During the 1996 national election campaign, for example, thousands of special interest groups donated more than $1.5 billion to political parties and candidates at the national, state, and local levels. Business groups raised $242 million, mainly for Republicans, while organized labor donated $35 million to Democratic candidates and spent another $35 million directly to campaign for Democrats.[45] In response to charges that both he and President Bill Clinton were allowing major campaign contributors—including foreign firms—too much influence in the political process, Republican presidential candidate Bob Dole called for new campaign spending rules that would abolish large private contributions and prohibit noncitizens from contributing money to American political candidates.[46] Democrats immediately questioned Dole's sincerity, noting that the former Senate majority leader had personally raised some $100 million in campaign funds during the course of his long political career. While the two parties traded charges, Democratic fund-raiser John Huang was being forced to resign from the Democratic National Committee campaign staff amid allegations that he funneled millions of dollars in contributions from a wealthy Indonesian family into Democratic campaign coffers.[47]

In 1997, Vice President Al Gore was stung by charges that he had helped win federal contracts for a Massachusetts hazardous-waste disposal firm whose officers contributed heavily to the Clinton-Gore re-election effort. After officers of Molten Metal Technology, Inc., contributed generously to the Clinton-Gore campaign, the firm received millions of dollars in Department of Energy contracts. The firm's chief Washington lobbyist, Peter Knight, is also Gore's former chief of staff and a former chair of the Clinton-Gore re-election committee. Knight was

[44]In fact, a greater share of interest group campaign contributions is given to legislators who sit on powerful committees, especially those committees directly relevant to the group donating the money. For two short examples, see Case 12.1, "Campaign Contributions" (pp. 329–31) and Case 12.2, "Interest Group Influence" (pp. 338–39) in Shepsle and Bonchek, *Analyzing Politics*.

[45]Leslie Wayne, "Business Is Biggest Campaign Spender, Study Says," *New York Times*, 18 October 1996, p. 1.

[46]Thomas B. Edsall, "Dole Outlines Changes for Political Financing," *New York Times*, 21 October 1996, p. 1.

[47]David Sanger and James Sterngold, "Fund Raiser for Democrats Now Faces Harsh Spotlight," *New York Times*, 21 October 1996, p. 1.

able to arrange a visit by the vice president to Molten's plant to mark Earth Day. Gore, Knight, and Molten executives deny that there is any connection between the firm's campaign contributions and the contracts subsequently awarded to it by the federal government.[48]

PACs provide more than just the financial support that individual candidates receive. Under present federal law, there is no restriction on the amount that individuals and interests can contribute directly to the parties for voter registration, grassroots organizing, and other party activities not directly linked to a particular candidate's campaign. Such contributions, called ***soft money,*** allow individuals and interest groups to circumvent restrictions on campaign contributions. Critics argue that soft money contributions allow wealthy donors to have unfair influence in the political process. Perhaps this potential does exist. However, soft money also provides the national and state parties with the means to engage in voter registration and turnout drives. In 1996, the U.S. Supreme Court ruled in the case of *Colorado Republican Party v. Federal Election Commission* that the government could not restrict political parties' use of soft money.[49]

Often, the campaign spending of activist groups is carefully kept separate from party and candidate organizations in order to avoid the restrictions of federal campaign finance laws. So long as a group's campaign expenditures are not coordinated with those of a candidate's own campaign, the group is free to spend as much money as it wishes. Such expenditures are viewed as "issues advocacy" and are protected by the First Amendment and thus not subject to statutory limitation.[50]

In 1996, as mentioned in Chapter 10, organized labor budgeted $35 million for independent efforts to elect pro-union congressional candidates. At the same time, business groups sought to coordinate their activities through an alliance informally known as "the Coalition." Prominent members of the Coalition included the Chamber of Commerce, the National Federation of Independent Business, the National Association of Manufacturers, the National Association of Wholesale Distributors, and the National Restaurant Association. Coalition members spent tens of millions of dollars on radio and television advertising in support of conservative congressional candidates.

**Campaign Activism** Financial support is not the only way that organized groups seek influence through electoral politics. Sometimes, activism can be even more important than campaign contributions. Campaign activism on the part of conservative groups played a very important role in bringing about the Republican capture of both houses of Congress in the 1994 congressional elections. For example, Christian Coalition activists played a role in many races, including ones in which Republican candidates were not overly identified with the religious Right. One post-election study suggested that more than 60 percent of the over

[48]Guy Gugliotta and Edward Walsh, "House Fund-Raising Hearings Grow Stormy," *Washington Post,* 8 November 1997, p. A8.

[49]Filed as Colorado Republican Federal Campaign Committee v. Jones, 95-489 (1996).

[50]Ruth Marcus, "Outside Groups Pushing Election Laws into Irrelevance," *Washington Post,* 8 August 1996, p. A9.

DEBATING THE ISSUES

## PACs and Politics

*The attempt to reform campaign finance laws in the early 1970s had an unintended effect: It prompted an explosion in the number and influence of political action committees (PACs), organizations formed by corporations, unions, trade associations, and other entities to raise and distribute campaign contributions. Now numbering in the thousands, PACs are perfectly legal, yet are often condemned for corrupting the political process and providing incumbents with even more political advantages. (PACs rarely contribute to challengers since challengers have little chance of defeating incumbents.)*

*Campaign finance expert Herbert Alexander defends PACs, arguing that the case against them is exaggerated. Public interest activist Fred Wertheimer summarizes the objections to PACs.*

### ALEXANDER

Seen in historical perspective, political action committees represent a functional system for political fundraising that developed, albeit unintentionally, from efforts to reform the political process. PACs represent an expression of an issue politics that resulted from attempts to remedy a sometimes unresponsive political system. And they represent an institutionalization of the campaign fund solicitation process that developed from the enactment of reform legislation intended to increase the number of small contributors. . . . PAC supporters . . . should question the unarticulated assumptions at the basis of much anti-PAC criticism. Money is not simply a necessary evil in the political process. By itself money is neutral. . . . There is nothing inherently immoral or corrupting about corporate or labor contributions of money. . . . All campaign contributions are not attempts to gain special favors. . . . Money is not the sole, and often not even the most important, political resource. . . . Curbing interest group contributions will not free legislators of the dilemma of choosing between electoral necessity and legislative duty. . . . A direct dialogue between candidates and individual voters without interest group influence is not possible in a representative democracy. . . . The freedom to join in common cause with other citizens remains indispensable to our democratic system. The pursuit of self-interest is . . . a condition, not a problem.[1]

### WERTHEIMER

The growth of PACs and the increased importance of PAC money have had a negative effect on two different parts of the political process—congressional elections and congressional decision making. First, PAC money tends to make congressional campaigns less competitive because of the overwhelming advantage enjoyed by incumbents in PAC fund-raising. The ratio of PAC contributions to incumbents over challengers in 1984 House races was 4.6 to 1.0; in the Senate, incumbents in 1984 enjoyed a 3.0 to 1.0 advantage in PAC receipts [comparable ratios hold for subsequent elections]. . . . The advantage enjoyed by incumbents is true for all kinds of PAC giving—for contributions by labor groups, corporate PACs, and trade and membership PACs. . . .

Second, there is a growing awareness that PAC money makes a difference in the legislative process, a difference that is inimical to our democracy. PAC dollars are given by special interest groups to gain special access and special influence in Washington. Most often PAC contributions are made with a legislative purpose in mind. . . .

Common Cause and others have produced a number of studies that show a relationship between PAC contributions and legislative behavior. The examples run the gamut of legislative decisions. . . .

PAC gifts do not guarantee votes or support. PACs do not always win. But PAC contributions do provide donors with critical access and influence; they do affect legislative decisions and are increasingly dominating and paralyzing the legislative process.[2]

[1]Herbert Alexander, "The Case for PACs," Public Affairs Council monograph (Washington, DC, 1983).

[2]Fred Wertheimer, "Campaign Finance Reform: The Unfinished Agenda," *The Annals of the American Academy of Political and Social Science* 486 (July 1986), pp. 92–93.

600 candidates supported by the Christian Right were successful in state, local, and congressional races in 1994.[51] The efforts of conservative Republican activists to bring voters to the polls is one major reason that turnout among Republicans exceeded Democratic turnout in a midterm election for the first time since 1970. This increased turnout was especially marked in the South, where the Christian Coalition was most active. In many Congressional districts, Christian Coalition efforts on behalf of the Republicans were augmented by grassroots campaigns launched by the National Rifle Association (NRA) and the National Federation of Independent Business (NFIB). The NRA had been outraged by Democratic support for gun control legislation, while NFIB had been energized by its campaign against employer mandates in the failed Clinton health care reform initiative. Both groups are well organized at the local level and were able to mobilize their members across the country to participate in congressional races.

In 1996, by contrast, it was the Democrats who benefited from campaign activism. Organized labor made a major effort to mobilize its members for the campaign. Conservative activists, on the other hand, were not enthusiastic about GOP presidential candidate Bob Dole or his running mate Jack Kemp and failed to mobilize their forces for a maximum campaign effort. Dole belatedly recognized his need for the support of these activists, but was never able to energize them in sufficient numbers to affect the outcome of the election.[52] In 1998, organized labor redoubled its efforts and helped the Democrats achieve a gain in congressional seats.

[51]Richard L. Burke, "Religious-Right Candidates Gain as GOP Turnout Rises," *New York Times,* 12 November 1994, p. 10.

[52]John Harwood, "Dole Presses Hot-Button Issues to Try to Rouse GOP Activists Missing from Campaign So Far," *Wall Street Journal,* 16 October 1996, p. A22.

## Groups and Interests—The Dilemma

James Madison wrote that "liberty is to faction as air is to fire."[53] By this he meant that the organization and proliferation of interests was inevitable in a free society. To seek to place limits on the organization of interests, in Madison's view, would be to limit liberty itself. Madison believed that interests should be permitted to regulate themselves by competing with one another. So long as competition among interests was free, open, and vigorous there would be some balance of power among them and none would be able to dominate the political or governmental process.

There is considerable competition among organized groups in the United States. Nevertheless, interest-group politics is not as free of bias as Madisonian theory might suggest. Though the weak and poor do occasionally become organized to assert their rights, interest-group politics is generally a form of political competition in which the wealthy and powerful are best able to engage.

Moreover, though groups sometimes organize to promote broad public concerns, interest groups more often represent relatively narrow, selfish interests. Small, self-interested groups can be organized much more easily than large and more diffuse collectives. For one thing, the members of a relatively small group—say, bankers or hunting enthusiasts—are usually able to recognize their shared interests and the need to pursue them in the political arena. Members of large and more diffuse groups—say, consumers or potential victims of firearms—often find it difficult to recognize their shared interests or the need to engage in collective action to achieve them.[54] This is why causes presented as public interests by their proponents often turn out, upon examination, to be private interests wrapped in a public mantle.

Thus, we have a dilemma to which there is no ideal answer. To regulate interest-group politics is, as Madison warned, to limit freedom and to expand governmental power. Not to regulate interest-group politics, on the other hand, may be to ignore justice. Those who believe that there are simple solutions to the issues of political life would do well to ponder this problem.

## Summary

Efforts by organized groups to influence government and policy are becoming an increasingly important part of American politics. Such interest groups use a number of strategies to gain power.

Lobbying is the act of petitioning legislators. Lobbyists—individuals who receive some form of compensation for lobbying—are required to register with the

[53]*The Federalist Papers,* No. 10.

[54]Mancur Olson, *The Logic of Collective Action* (Cambridge: Harvard University Press, 1971).

THEN AND NOW

## Changes in American Politics

Because of the decline of political party importance, politicians and citizens now rely more on interest groups. Moreover, significant changes in the presidency, the courts, the Congress, elections, and media have altered the strategic landscape and thus the activities of interest groups in American politics.

- Although interest groups have always been a part of American politics, there has been an enormous increase in the number of groups since 1960.
- Public interest and environmental interest groups proliferated in the late 1960s and early 1970s.
- Traditional, internal interest-group lobbying is now used in tandem with interest-group strategies that involve grassroots, public relations, and media campaigns.
- Group representation has become more common in both the presidency and the Congress. Special organizational units within the office of the presidency now respond to and cultivate relationships with interest groups. In Congress, the interest-group explosion of the 1960s and 1970s was mirrored by the proliferation of special-interest oriented groups known as congressional caucuses.
- Interest groups' use of the courts reflects the ideological predispositions of the courts themselves. But long before the more liberal public interest groups turned to the courts, business organizations and corporations had already sought protection from them in the late nineteenth century.
- The first PAC was established in 1943. Since the mid-1980s, nearly four thousand PACs have been created, a result of organized campaign donations becoming a staple resource of contemporary interest groups.

House and Senate. In spite of an undeserved reputation for corruption, lobbyists serve a useful function, providing members of Congress with a vital flow of information.

Access is participation in government. Groups with access have less need for lobbying. Most groups build up access over time through great effort. They work years to get their members into positions of influence on congressional committees. Means of gaining access include the grassroots approach of agriculture, the personnel-interchange approach of many businesses, and the use of influence peddling.

Litigation sometimes serves interest groups when other strategies fail. Groups may bring suit on their own behalf, finance suits brought by individuals, or file *amicus curiae* briefs.

Going public is an effort to mobilize the widest and most favorable climate of opinion. Advertising is a common technique in this strategy. Others are boycotts, strikes, rallies, and marches.

Groups engage in electoral politics either by embracing one of the major parties, usually through financial support or through a nonpartisan strategy. Interest groups' campaign contributions now seem to be flowing into the coffers of candidates at a faster rate than ever before.

## For Further Reading

Cigler, Allan J., and Burdett A. Loomis, eds. *Interest Group Politics.* Washington, DC: Congressional Quarterly Press, 1983.

Clawson, Dan, Alan Neustadtl, and Denise Scott. *Money Talks: Corporate PACs and Political Influence.* New York: Basic Books, 1992.

Costain, Anne. *Inviting Women's Rebellion: A Political Process Interpretation of the Women's Movement.* Baltimore, MD: Johns Hopkins University Press, 1992.

Day, Christine. *What Older Americans Think: Interest Groups and Aging Policy.* Princeton: Princeton University Press, 1990.

Goldfield, Michael. *The Decline of Organized Labor in the United States.* Chicago: University of Chicago Press, 1987.

Hansen, John Mark. *Gaining Access: Congress and the Farm Lobby, 1919–1981.* Chicago: University of Chicago Press, 1991.

Heinz, John P., et al. *The Hollow Core: Private Interests in National Policy Making.* Cambridge: Harvard University Press, 1993.

Lowi, Theodore J. *The End of Liberalism.* New York: W. W. Norton, 1979.

Moe, Terry M. *The Organization of Interests.* Chicago: University of Chicago Press, 1980.

Olson, Mancur, Jr. *The Logic of Collective Action: Public Goods and the Theory of Groups.* Cambridge: Harvard University Press, 1971.

Olzak, Susan. *The Dynamics of Ethnic Competition and Conflict.* Stanford: Stanford University Press, 1992.

Paige, Connie. *The Right to Lifers.* New York: Summit, 1983.

Petracca, Mark, ed. *The Politics of Interests: Interest Groups Transformed.* Boulder, CO: Westview, 1992.

Pope, Jacqueline. *Biting the Hand That Feeds Them: Women on Welfare at the Grass Roots Level.* New York: Praeger, 1989.

Scholzman, Kay Lehman, and John T. Tierney. *Organized Interests and American Democracy.* New York: Harper & Row, 1986.

Staggenborg, Suzanne. *The Pro-Choice Movement: Organization and Activism in the Abortion Conflict.* New York: Oxford University Press, 1991.

Truman, David. *The Governmental Process: Political Interests and Public Opinion.* New York: Knopf, 1951.

Vogel, David. *Fluctuating Fortunes.* New York: Basic Books, 1989.

# 13

# The Media

## TIME LINE ON THE MEDIA

| Events | | Institutional Developments |
|---|---|---|
| Alien and Sedition Acts attempt to silence opposition press (1798) | | |
| | 1800 | Newspapers and pamphlets serve leaders (early 1800s) |
| New printing presses introduced, allowing cheaper printing of more newspapers (1820s–1840s) | | Expansion of popular press; circulation of more newspapers, magazines, and books (1840s) |
| First transmission of telegraph message, between Baltimore and Washington (1844) | | Nation begins to be linked by telegraph communications network (1840s) |
| Creation of Associated Press (AP) (1848) | | |
| | 1850 | |
| Completion of telegraph connections across country to San Francisco (1861) | | Advertising industry makes press financially free of parties; beginnings of an independent, nonpartisan press (1880s) |
| Rise of large corporations and municipal corruption spark Progressive reform efforts (1880s–1890s) | | Beginning of "muckraking"—exposure of social evils by journalists (1890s) |
| Publisher William R. Hearst sparks Spanish-American War (1898) | | Circulation war between Hearst's *N.Y. Journal* and Pulitzer's *N.Y. World* leads to "yellow journalism"—sensationalized reporting (1890s) |
| First news bulletins transmitted over radio; regular radio programs introduced (1920) | 1920 | Beginning of radio broadcasting (1920s) |
| NBC links radio stations into network (1926) | | Regulation of broadcast industry begins with Federal Radio Commission (1927) |
| Great Depression (1929–1933) | | *Near v. Minnesota*—Supreme Court holds that government cannot exercise prior restraint (1931) |
| Franklin D. Roosevelt uses radio "fireside chats" to assure the nation and restore confidence (1930s) | | Federal Communications Act creates Federal Communications Commission (FCC) (1934) |
| Televised Senate hearings (1950s) | 1950 | Television is introduced (late 1940s–1950s) |
| Televised Kennedy-Nixon debate (1960) | | Fairness doctrine governing TV coverage (1960s) |
| John F. Kennedy uses televised news conference to mobilize public support for his policies (1961–1963) | | Beginning of extended national television news coverage (1963) |
| "Daisy Girl" commercial helps defeat Goldwater and elect Lyndon Johnson president (1964) | | *N.Y. Times v. Sullivan* asserts "actual malice" standard in libel cases involving public officials (1964) |

| Events | | Institutional Developments |
|---|---|---|
| Vietnam War; American officials in Vietnam leak information to the press (1960s–early 1970s) | | Vietnam War first war to receive extended television coverage, which contributes to expansion of opposition to the war (1965–1973)<br>TV spot ads become candidates' major weapons (1960s–1990s)<br>*Red Lion Broadcasting v. U.S.* establishes "right of rebuttal" (1969) |
| | 1970 | |
| *Pentagon Papers* on Vietnam War published by *N.Y. Times* and *Washington Post* (1971)<br>Televised Watergate hearings (1973–1974) | | *N.Y. Times v. U.S.*—Supreme Court rules against prior restraint in *Pentagon Papers* case (1971) |
| | 1980 | |
| Unsuccessful libel suits by Israeli General Ariel Sharon against *Time* magazine (1984) and by General William Westmoreland against CBS News (1985)<br>Televised Iran-Contra hearings (1987) | | FCC stops enforcing fairness doctrine (1985)<br>Era of investigative reporting and critical journalistic coverage of government (1960s–1990s) |
| Live coverage of Persian Gulf War (1990) | 1990 | Military controls media access throughout Persian Gulf conflict (1990–1991) |
| Talk show appearances, "infomercials," televised town meetings used by candidates during campaign (1992)<br>Talk radio programs help Republicans defeat Democrats in congressional elections (1994)<br>Media frenzy during investigation of Clinton's affair with Monica Lewinsky (1998–1999) | | Politicians create new media formats to pitch themselves and their programs; era of permanent campaign (1992) |

The American news media are among the world's most free. Newspapers, news magazines, and the broadcast media regularly present information that is at odds with the government's claims, as well as editorial opinions sharply critical of the highest-ranking public officials. For example, even though Bill Clinton appeared to gain considerable media support during his first two months in office, the media's overall stance on Clinton has been critical. In June 1994, long before the Monica Lewinsky affair led to a storm of media criticism, Clinton lashed out at the media,

## CORE OF THE ARGUMENT

- Nationalization of the news has contributed greatly to the nationalization of politics and of political perspectives in the United States.
- The three major influences on the media's coverage are the producers of the news, the sources of the news, and the audience for the news.
- The media have tremendous power to shape the political agenda, to shape our images of politicians and policies, and to influence our images of ourselves and our society.
- Freedom of the press is critical to the maintenance of a democratic society.

averring that no previous president had ever "been subject to more violent personal attacks than I have, at least in modern history." Clinton charged that talk radio programs presented "a constant, unremitting drumbeat of negativism and criticism," and he particularly castigated two of his strongest critics, conservative radio host Rush Limbaugh and fundamentalist television preacher Rev. Jerry Falwell. The president went on to denounce the press for unfair coverage of his administration.[1] Clinton's remarks were ironic because, as we saw in Chapter 10, he had made such effective use of the media, particularly radio and television talk shows, during his 1992 presidential campaign. Andrea Mitchell of NBC News noted that Clinton had "had it so easy" on talk shows in 1992 that he was shocked by any criticism of his policies from that quarter.[2]

Other journalists declared that their attitude toward the White House had soured because of what they saw as the Clinton administration's repeated efforts to deceive the press and the public. One White House correspondent asserted that "nineteen months of repeated falsehoods and half-truths have corroded the relationship between this White House and the reporters who cover it,"[3] pointing particularly to deliberate administration efforts to deceive the press on aspects of the Whitewater affair, on First Lady Hillary Rodham Clinton's investments, and on the events surrounding the suicide of White House Deputy Counsel Vincent Foster.

By the end of August 1994, President Clinton and his advisers changed tactics and began to court rather than attack the news media. Clinton initiated a series of small, off-the-record gatherings with prominent journalists, including the correspondents for the major news networks; these events were designed to create a more positive image for the embattled president. According to some journalists who attended the gatherings, Clinton tried to flatter them by asking their advice on administration initiatives. Although Clinton's efforts appeared to have produced several sympathetic news stories, some journalists apparently were annoyed by the president's attempts to be nice to them. One responded to Clinton's request for advice by declaring that "advising presidents was not his province."[4]

[1]Douglas Jehl, "Clinton Calls Show to Assail Press, Falwell and Limbaugh," *New York Times,* 25 June 1994, p. 1.

[2]John H. Fund, "Why Clinton Shouldn't Be Steamed at Talk Radio," *Wall Street Journal,* 7 July 1994, p. A12.

[3]Ruth Marcus, "The White House Isn't Telling Us the Truth," *Washington Post,* 21 August 1994, p. C9.

[4]Howard Kurtz, "From Clinton, Schmooze Control," *Washington Post,* 26 August 1994, p. D1.

By 1996, editorial writers at least had forgiven Clinton for his earlier sins. Most of the leading daily newspapers, including the influential *New York Times* and *Washington Post,* endorsed the president for re-election.

The president's comments to the contrary notwithstanding, the media actually handled Clinton with kid gloves during his first term, compared to their treatment of other recent presidents. Until the emergence of Monica Lewinsky, critical media coverage of the White House reached its apex during the Nixon administration, when the three television networks frequently presented hostile assessments of presidential claims, actions, and speeches. Typically, a presidential address to the nation was followed by a half hour of network commentary purporting to correct inaccuracies and errors in the president's statements. These critical analyses led Nixon's vice president, Spiro T. Agnew, to characterize television broadcasters as "nattering nabobs of negativism."

In this chapter, we will examine the role and increasing power of the media in American politics. First, we will look at the media industry and government. Second, we will discuss the factors that help to determine "what's news," that is, the factors that shape media coverage of events and personalities. Third, we will examine the scope of media power in politics. Finally, we will address the question of responsibility: "In a democracy, to whom are the media accountable for the use of their formidable power?"

**THE CENTRAL QUESTION**

"In a democracy, to whom are the media accountable for the use of their formidable power?"

## The Media Industry and Government

The American news media are among the world's most vast and most free. Americans literally have thousands of available options to find political reporting. As we mentioned above, this wide variety of newspapers, news magazines, and broadcast media regularly present information that is at odds with the government's claims, as well as editorial opinions sharply critical of high-ranking officials. The freedom to speak one's mind is one of the most cherished of American political values—one that is jealously safeguarded by the media. Yet although thousands of media companies exist across the United States, surprisingly little variety appears in what is reported about national events and issues.

### Types of Media

Americans obtain their news from broadcast media (radio, television), print media (newspapers and magazines), and, increasingly, from the Internet. Each of these sources has distinctive characteristics. Television news reaches more Americans than any other single news source (see Figure 13.1). Tens of millions of indi-

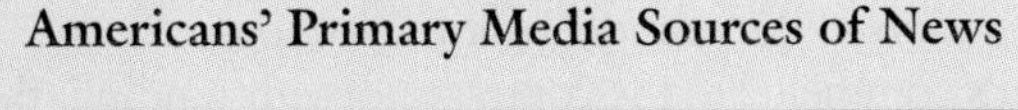

FIGURE 13.1

**Americans' Primary Media Sources of News**

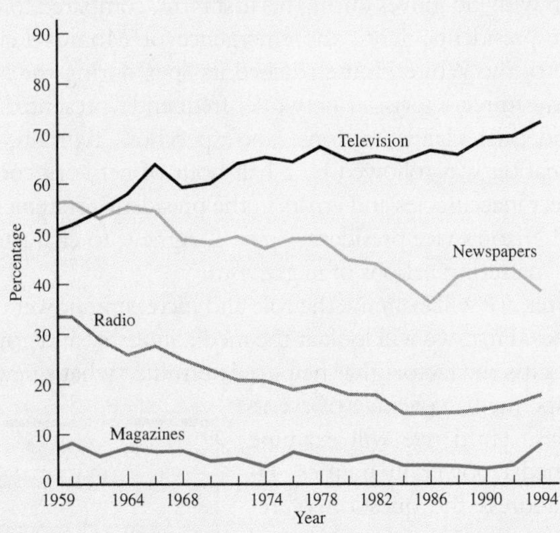


Note: (Multiple responses permitted)
SOURCE: *America's Watching: Public Attitudes toward Television* (New York: Roper Starch Worldwide, 1995), p. 17.

viduals watch national and local news programs every day. Television news, however, covers relatively few topics and provides little depth of coverage. Television news is more like a series of newspaper headlines connected to pictures. It serves the extremely important function of alerting viewers to issues and events, but provides little else.

Radio news is also essentially a headline service, but without pictures. In the short time—usually five minutes per hour—they devote to news, radio stations announce the day's major events without providing much detail. In major cities, all-news stations provide a bit more coverage of major stories, but for the most part these stations fill the day with repetition rather than detail. All-news stations like Washington, DC's WTOP or New York's WCBS assume that most listeners are in their cars and that, as a result, the people in the audience change markedly throughout the day as listeners reach their destinations. Thus, rather than use their time to flesh out a given set of stories, they repeat the same stories each hour to present them to new listeners. In recent years, radio talk shows have become important sources of commentary and opinion. A number of conservative radio

**AMERICAN POLITICAL DEVELOPMENT**

The twenty-four-hour news coverage on CNN is a significant development over early television news. Well into the 1960s, television's evening news programs were only fifteen minutes.

hosts such as Rush Limbaugh have huge audiences and have helped to mobilize support for conservative political causes and candidates. Liberals have been somewhat slower to recognize the potential impact of talk radio.

The most important source of news is the old-fashioned newspaper. Newspapers remain critically important even though they are not the primary news source for most Americans. The print media are important for two reasons. First, as we shall see later in this chapter, the broadcast media rely upon leading newspapers such as the *New York Times* and the *Washington Post* to set their news agenda. The broadcast media engage in very little actual reporting; they primarily cover stories that have been "broken," or initially reported, by the print media. For example, sensational charges that President Bill Clinton had an affair with a White House intern were reported first by the *Washington Post* and *Newsweek* before being trumpeted around the world by the broadcast media. It is only a slight exaggeration to observe that if an event is not covered in the *New York Times,* it is not likely to appear on the *CBS Evening News.* The print media are also important because they are the prime source of news for educated and influential individuals. The nation's economic, social, and political elites rely upon the detailed coverage provided by the print media to inform and influence their views about important public matters. The print media may have a smaller audience than their cousins in broadcasting, but they have an audience that matters.

A relatively new source of news is the Internet. Every day, several million Americans scan one of many news sites on the Internet for coverage of current events. For the most part, however, the Internet provides electronic versions of coverage offered by print sources. One great advantage of the Internet is that it allows frequent updating. It potentially can combine the depth of coverage of a newspaper with the timeliness of television and radio, and probably will become a major news source in the next decade. Already, most political candidates and many interest groups have created sites on the World Wide Web. Some of the more sensational aspects of President Clinton's relationship with Monica Lewinsky were first reported on a Web site maintained by Matt Drudge, an individual who specializes in posting sensational charges about public figures. Though many deny it, most reporters scan Drudge's site regularly hoping to pick up a bit of salacious gossip. As on-line access becomes simpler and faster, the Internet could give Americans access to unprecedented quantities of up-to-the-minute information. If only computers could also give Americans the ability to make good use of that information!

## Organization of the Media

The United States boasts more than one thousand television stations, approximately eighteen hundred daily newspapers, and more than nine thousand radio stations. The great majority of these enterprises are locally owned and operated and present a good deal of news and many features with a distinctly local flavor. For example, for many months, viewers of the Syracuse, New York, evening news were informed that the day's "top story" concerned the proposed construction of a local garbage-burning steam plant. Similarly, in Seattle, Washington, viewers

## AMERICAN POLITICAL DEVELOPMENT

Television news began in 1940, with NBC's *The Esso Television Reporter.* Throughout that decade, NBC experimented with the format of television news, which vacillated between earlier radio-news formats and motion-picture newsreel formats. These experiments would prove influential when other networks began their own television news programs. Today's "pressure for pictures" to accompany a story is one by-product of these early experiments.

SOURCE: Kristine Brunovska Karnick, "NBC and the Innovation of Television News, 1945–1953," *Journalism History* 15 (1988), pp. 26–34.

were treated to years of discussion about the construction of a domed athletic stadium, and audiences in Baltimore, Maryland, watched and read about struggles over downtown redevelopment. In all these cases, as in literally thousands of others, the local media focused heavily on a matter of particular local concern, providing local viewers, readers, and listeners with considerable information and viewpoints.

Yet, however much variation the American news media offer in terms of local coverage, there is far less diversity in the reporting of national events and issues. Most of the national news that is published by local newspapers is provided by the one wire service, the Associated Press. More than five hundred of the nation's TV stations are affiliated with one of the four networks and carry its evening news reports. Dozens of others carry PBS (Public Broadcasting System) news. Several hundred local radio stations also carry network news or National Public Radio news broadcasts. At the same time, although there are only three truly national newspapers, the *Wall Street Journal,* the *Christian Science Monitor,* and *USA Today,* two other papers, the *New York Times* and the *Washington Post,* are read by political leaders and other influential Americans throughout the nation. Such is the influence of these two "elite" newspapers that their news coverage sets the standard for virtually all other news outlets. Stories carried in the *New York Times* or the *Washington Post* influence the content of many other papers as well as the network news. Note how often this text, like most others, relies upon *New York Times* and *Washington Post* stories as sources for contemporary events.

National news is also carried to millions of Americans by the three major news magazines—*Time, Newsweek,* and *U.S. News & World Report.* Thus, even though the number of TV and radio stations and daily newspapers reporting news in the United States is enormous, and local coverage varies greatly from place to place, the number of sources of national news is actually quite small—one wire service, four broadcast networks, public radio and TV, two elite newspapers, three news magazines, and a scattering of other sources such as the national correspondents of a few large local papers, and the small independent radio networks. Beginning in the late 1980s, Cable News Network (CNN) became another major news source. The importance of CNN increased dramatically after its spectacular coverage of the Persian Gulf War. At one point, CNN was able to provide live coverage of American bombing raids on Baghdad, Iraq, after the major networks' correspondents had been forced to flee to bomb shelters.

Even the availability of new electronic media on the Internet has failed to expand news sources. Most national news available on the World Wide Web, for example, consists of electronic versions of the conventional print media.

## Nationalization of the News

In general, the national news media cover more or less the same sets of events, present similar information, and emphasize similar issues and problems. Indeed, the national news services watch one another quite carefully. It is unlikely that a major story carried by one will not soon find its way into the pages or programming of the others. As a result, we have developed in the United States a rather centralized national news through which a relatively similar picture of events, issues, and problems is presented to the entire nation.[5] The nationalization of the news was accelerated by the development of radio networks in the 1920s and 1930s and was brought to a peak by the creation of the television networks after the 1950s. This nationalization of news content has very important consequences for American politics.

Nationalization of the news has contributed greatly to the nationalization of politics and of political perspectives in the United States. Prior to the development of the national media and the nationalization of news coverage, the news traveled very slowly. Every region and city saw national issues and problems mainly through its own local lens. Concerns and perspectives varied greatly from region to region, city to city, and village to village. Today, in large measure as a result of the nationalization of the media, residents of all parts of the country share similar ideas and perspectives.[6] They may not agree on everything, but they at least see the world in similar ways.

**AMERICAN POLITICAL DEVELOPMENT**

Nationalization of the news began well before the turn of the century. A study of Cleveland newspapers printed between 1820 and 1876 found an emphasis on news coverage of national elections, issues, and institutions.

SOURCE: Samuel Kernell, "The Early Nationalization of Political News in America," *Studies in American Political Development* 1 (1986), pp. 255–78.

## Regulation of the Broadcast and Electronic Media

In some countries, the government controls media content. In other countries, the government owns the broadcast media (e.g., the BBC in Britain), but it does not tell the media what to say. In the United States, the government neither owns nor controls the communications networks, but it does regulate the broadcast media.

American radio and television are regulated by the Federal Communications Commission (FCC), an independent regulatory agency established in 1934. Radio and TV stations must have FCC licenses that must be renewed every five years. The basic rationale for licensing is that there must be some mechanism to allocate radio and TV frequencies to prevent broadcasts from interfering with

[5]See Leo Bogart, "Newspapers in Transition," *Wilson Quarterly,* special issue, 1982; and Richard Harwood, "The Golden Age of Press Diversity," *Washington Post,* 22 July 1994, p. A23.

[6]See Benjamin Ginsberg, *The Captive Public* (New York: Basic Books, 1986).

## *The Global Impact of American Media?*

Technological advances have made it easier for people in one country to stay informed about events in others. Just one hundred years ago, it could take weeks for people to learn about important events outside their own country. Moreover, they had to rely mostly on newspaper reports to get the full story. This situation gave the press enormous influence. A good example of the power of the press concerns the outbreak of the Spanish-American War. Although it was never proved that a Spanish mine caused the USS *Maine* to sink in Havana's harbor in 1898, the so-called yellow press, led by the publishing magnate William Randolph Hearst, spearheaded such a successful campaign to convince Americans of Spanish complicity that the United States ultimately declared war on Spain.

Today the lag time between an event and when people know about it is much shorter. Reporters can file stories almost instantaneously, through e-mail, faxes, or the telephone. Moreover, the advent of television coverage potentially reduces the power of the press to set the national tone on a given issue. Television allows Americans to view events in foreign lands, sometimes as they happen. The Vietnam War was the first televised conflict, and the evening news brought the horrors of war into people's living rooms. Some people argue that this unfiltered news coverage was one reason why national opinion changed on American presence in Vietnam. More recently, Americans could watch live the bombing of Baghdad during the Gulf War. In that case, live coverage may have strengthened Ameri-

$50,000 REWARD.—WHO DESTROYED THE MAINE?—$50,000 REWARD.

EDITION FOR GREATER NEW YORK

NEW YORK JOURNAL

AND ADVERTISER.

DESTRUCTION OF THE WAR SHIP MAINE WAS THE WORK OF AN ENEMY

$50,000!

$50,000 REWARD!

For the Detection of the Perpetrator of the Maine Outrage!

Assistant Secretary Roosevelt Convinced the Explosion of the War Ship Was Not an Accident.

The Journal Offers $50,000 Reward for the Conviction of the Criminals Who Sent 258 American Sailors to Their Death. Naval Officers Unanimous That the Ship Was Destroyed on Purpose.

$50,000!

$50,000 REWARD!

For the Detection of the Perpetrator of the Maine Outrage!

NAVAL OFFICERS THINK THE MAINE WAS DESTROYED BY A SPANISH MINE.

can resolve, at least in the short run, to fight the war.

Nontraditional sources of news located on the Internet have made it easier for individuals to learn about foreign events. Most major international newspapers now have an internet edition, and translators built into internet search engines allow you to read sources originally printed in another language. It is no longer necessary to rely on one government's official press statement or one newspaper's coverage of a given issue. Indeed, one out of five Americans reports that at least once a week he or she uses the Internet to read the news.[1]

In principle, these changes are good for American democracy: It means that citizens are more informed about the decisions politicians make. Yet paradoxically, fewer Americans are taking advantage of these changes to learn about international issues. The drop in interest among young Americans has been especially acute—the percentage of young Americans who stated that they followed foreign affairs dropped from 80 percent in the 1980s to 20 percent in 1997.[2] A cause or symptom (or both) of this decline may be the coverage of foreign news by the American press. A recent study indicates that press coverage of foreign events has decreased since the end of the cold war—that the number of minutes aired on the three American networks reporting from foreign bureaus declined 51 percent from 1988 to 1996. This decline in America's knowledge about other countries comes at a time when the need for that knowledge has never been greater—communities across the United States depend increasingly upon decisions made overseas for their economic well-being.

Because of these paradoxes, the press continues to play a strong role in the education of Americans on foreign topics. Indeed, even if the television networks broadcast certain events live, reporters (and sometimes governments) still choose *which* stories will be covered live and which will not. Few people have the time to go on-line, to get both sides of a given story. Indeed, today there may be too much information available for the average citizen to process, and many people rely on traditional news to tell them what is important and what is not. There has not been as much change in the role of the press on international issues over the last one hundred years as one might at first think.

[1]The Pew Research Center, "Internet News Takes Off," 8 June 1998 (available at http://www.peoplepress.org/med98rpt.htm).
[2]*New York Times,* 28 December 1997.

## AMERICAN POLITICAL DEVELOPMENT

Prior to the creation of the Federal Communications Commission in 1934, regulation of broadcast media was the responsibility of the Commerce Department and then the Federal Radio Commission, established in 1927. At its inception, the FCC was designed to regulate only radio, telephone, and telegraph communications, and its purpose was largely operational (and welcomed by the industry). With advances in technology, the FCC's purview expanded, and it began using its licensing and regulatory functions to control content as well as provide technical coordination.

SOURCE: Barry Cole and Mal Oettinger, *Reluctant Regulators: The FCC and the Broadcast Audience* (Reading, MA: Addison-Wesley, 1978), pp. 4–5.

and garbling one another. License renewals are almost always granted automatically by the FCC. Indeed, renewal requests are now filed by postcard.

For more than sixty years, the broadcast media was subject to the control of the FCC, but in 1996 Congress passed the Telecommunications Act, a broad effort to do away with regulations in effect since 1934. The act loosened restrictions on media ownership and allowed for telephone companies, cable television providers, and broadcasters to compete with one another for telecommunication services. Following the passage of the act, several mergers occurred between telephone and cable companies and between different segments of the entertainment media, creating an even greater concentration of media ownership. This development has led some to question whether there will be enough competition among the broadcast media to produce a diverse set of views on political matters.

The Telecommunications Act of 1996 also included an attempt to regulate the content of material transmitted over the Internet. This law, known as the Communications Decency Act, made it illegal to make "indecent" sexual material on the Internet accessible to those under eighteen years of age. The act was immediately denounced by civil libertarians and brought to court as an infringement of free speech. The case reached the Supreme Court in 1997 and the act was ruled an unconstitutional infringement of the First Amendment's right to freedom of speech.

While the government's ability to regulate the content of the electronic media on the Internet has been questioned, the federal government has used its licensing power to impose several regulations that can affect the political content of radio and TV broadcasts. The first of these is the ***equal time rule.*** Under federal regulations, broadcasters must provide candidates for the same political office equal opportunities to communicate their messages to the public. If, for example, a television station sells commercial time to a state's Republican gubernatorial candidate, it may not refuse to sell time to the Democratic candidate for the same position.

The second FCC regulation affecting the content of broadcasts is the ***right of rebuttal.*** This means that individuals must be given the opportunity to respond to personal attacks. In the 1969 case of *Red Lion Broadcasting Company v. FCC,* for example, the U.S. Supreme Court upheld the FCC's determination that a television station was required to provide a liberal author with an opportunity to respond to an attack from a conservative commentator that the station had aired.[7]

For many years, a third important federal regulation was the ***fairness doctrine.*** Under this doctrine, broadcasters who aired programs on controversial issues were required to provide time for opposing views. In 1985, the FCC stopped en-

[7]Red Lion Broadcasting Company v. FCC, 395 U.S. 367 (1969).

forcing the fairness doctrine on the grounds that there were so many radio and television stations—to say nothing of newspapers and news magazines—that in all likelihood many different viewpoints were already being presented without having to require each station to try to present all sides of an argument. Critics of this FCC decision charge that in many media markets the number of competing viewpoints is small. Nevertheless, a congressional effort to require the FCC to enforce the fairness doctrine was blocked by the Reagan administration in 1987.

## Freedom of the Press

Unlike the broadcast media, the print media are not subject to federal regulation. Indeed, the great principle underlying the federal government's relationship with the press is the doctrine against ***prior restraint.*** Beginning with the landmark 1931 case of *Near v. Minnesota,* the U.S. Supreme Court has held that, except under the most extraordinary circumstances, the First Amendment of the U.S. Constitution prohibits government agencies from seeking to prevent newspapers or magazines from publishing whatever they wish.[8] Indeed, in the case of *New York Times v. U.S.,* the so-called *Pentagon Papers* case, the Supreme Court ruled that the government could not even block publication of secret Defense Department documents furnished to the *New York Times* by a liberal opponent of the Vietnam War who had obtained the documents illegally.[9] In a 1990 case, however, the Supreme Court upheld a lower-court order restraining Cable Network News (CNN) from broadcasting tapes of conversations between former Panamanian leader Manuel Noriega and his lawyer, supposedly recorded by the U.S. government. By a vote of 7 to 2, the Court held that CNN could be restrained from broadcasting the tapes until the trial court in the Noriega case had listened to the tapes and had decided whether their broadcast would violate Noriega's right to a fair trial. This case would seem to weaken the "no prior restraint" doctrine. But whether the same standard will apply to the print media has yet to be tested in the courts. In 1994, the Supreme Court ruled that cable television systems were entitled to essentially the same First Amendment protections as the print media.[10]

Even though newspapers may not be restrained from publishing whatever they want, they may be subject to sanctions after the fact. Historically, newspapers were subject to the law of libel, which provided that newspapers that printed false and malicious stories could be compelled to pay damages to those they defamed. In recent years, however, American courts have greatly narrowed the meaning of libel and made it extremely difficult, particularly for politicians or other public figures, to win a libel case against a newspaper. The most important case on this topic is the 1964 U.S. Supreme Court case of *New York Times v. Sullivan,* in which the Court held that to be deemed libelous a story about a public official not only had to be untrue, but had to result from "actual malice" or "reckless disregard" for the truth.[11]

[8]Near v. Minnesota, 283 U.S. 697 (1931).

[9]New York Times v. U.S., 403 U.S. 731 (1971).

[10]Cable News Network v. Noriega, 111 S.Ct. 451 (1990); Turner Broadcasting System, Inc. v. Federal Communications Commission, 93-44 (1994).

[11]New York Times v. Sullivan, 376 U.S. 254 (1964).

In other words, the newspaper had to deliberately print false and malicious material. In practice, it is nearly impossible to prove that a paper deliberately printed false and damaging information and, as conservatives discovered in the 1980s, it is very difficult for a politician or other public figure to win a libel case. Libel suits against CBS News by General William Westmoreland and against *Time* magazine by General Ariel Sharon of Israel, both financed by conservative legal foundations who hoped to embarrass the media, were both defeated in court because they failed to show "actual malice." In the 1991 case of *Masson v. New Yorker Magazine,* this tradition was again affirmed when the Court held that fabricated quotations attributed to a public figure were libelous only if the fabricated account "materially changed" the meaning of what the person actually said.[12] For all intents and purposes, the print media can publish anything they want about a public figure.

## News Coverage

Because of the important role the media can play in national politics, it is vitally important to understand the factors that affect media coverage.[13] What accounts for the media's agenda of issues and topics? What explains the character of coverage—why does a politician receive good or bad press? What factors determine the interpretation or "spin" that a particular story will receive? Although a host of minor factors play a role, there are three major factors: (1) the journalists or producers of the news; (2) the sources or topics of the news; and (3) the audience for the news.

### Journalists

First, media content and news coverage are inevitably affected by the views, ideals, and interests of those who seek out, write, and produce news and other stories. At one time, newspaper publishers exercised a great deal of influence over their papers' news content. Publishers such as William Randolph Hearst and Joseph Pulitzer became political powers through their manipulation of news coverage. Hearst, for example, almost singlehandedly pushed the United States into war with Spain in 1898 through his newspapers' relentless coverage of the alleged brutality employed by Spain in its efforts to suppress a rebellion in Cuba, then a Spanish colony. The sinking of the American battleship *Maine* in Havana Harbor under mysterious circumstances gave Hearst the ammunition he needed to force a reluctant President McKinley to lead the nation into war. Today, few publishers have that kind of power. Most publishers are more concerned with the business end of the paper than its editorial content, although a few continue to impose their interests and tastes on the news.

[12]Masson v. New Yorker Magazine, 111 S.Ct. 2419 (1991).

[13]See the discussions in Gary Paul Gates, *Air Time* (New York: Harper & Row, 1978); Edward Jay Epstein, *News from Nowhere* (New York: Random House, 1973); Michael Parenti, *Inventing Reality* (New York: St. Martin's Press, 1986); Herbert Gans, *Deciding What's News* (New York: Vintage, 1980); and W. Lance Bennett, *News: The Politics of Illusion* (New York: Longman, 1986).

More important than publishers, for the most part, are the reporters. Those who cover the news for the national media generally have a good deal of discretion or freedom to interpret stories and, as a result, have an opportunity to interject their views and ideals into news stories. For example, the personal friendship and respect that some reporters felt for Franklin Roosevelt and John Kennedy helped to generate more favorable news coverage for these presidents. On the other hand, the dislike and distrust felt by many reporters for Richard Nixon was also communicated to the public. In the case of Ronald Reagan, the disdain that many journalists felt for the president was communicated in stories suggesting that he was often asleep or inattentive when important decisions were made. One of the major reasons that Republican presidential candidate Bob Dole chose Jack Kemp as his running mate in 1996 was Kemp's popularity with the Washington press corps. Though Dole and Kemp had long disagreed on many substantive issues, Dole strategists calculated that Kemp's presence on the ticket would result in more positive media coverage. Conservatives have long charged that the liberal biases of reporters and journalists result in distorted news coverage. In a 1996 op-ed essay in the *Wall Street Journal*, CBS news correspondent Bernard Goldberg agreed with conservative critics. According to Goldberg, "The old argument that the networks and other media elites have a liberal bias is so blatantly true, it's hardly worth discussing anymore." Goldberg's comments were criticized by CBS news anchor Dan Rather and by Jeff Fager, executive producer of the CBS Evening News. ABC correspondent David Brinkley, however, called Goldberg's assertion "probably true."[14]

A 1996 survey of Washington newspaper bureau chiefs and correspondents seems to support Goldberg's assertion.[15] The study, conducted by the Roper Center and the Freedom Forum, a conservative foundation, found that 61 percent of the bureau chiefs and correspondents polled called themselves "liberal" or "liberal to moderate." Only 9 percent called themselves "conservative" or "conservative to moderate." In a similar vein, 89 percent said they had voted for Bill Clinton in 1992, while only 7 percent indicated that they had voted for George Bush. Fifty percent said they were Democrats, and only 4 percent claimed to be Republicans.[16] Another survey has indicated that even among the radio talk-show hosts lambasted by President Clinton, Democrats outnumber Republicans by a wide margin: Of 112 hosts surveyed, 39 percent had voted for Clinton in 1992, and only 23 percent had supported George Bush.[17]

The linkage between substantial segments of the media and liberal interest groups is by no means absolute. Indeed, over the past several years a conservative media complex has emerged in opposition to the liberal media. This complex includes two major newspapers, the *Wall Street Journal* and the *Washington Times*,

[14]Rowan Scarborough, "TV News Too Liberal, Says CBS Reporter," *Washington Times*, 15 February 1996, p. 1.

[15]See Edith Efron, *The News Twisters* (Los Angeles: Nash Publishing, 1971).

[16]Rowan Scarborough, "Leftist Press? Reporters Working in Washington Acknowledge Liberal Leanings in Poll," *Washington Times*, 18 April 1996, p. 1.

[17]Michael Kinsley, "Bias and Baloney," *Washington Post*, 26 November 1992, p. A29; and Fund, "Why Clinton Shouldn't Be Steamed at Talk Radio," p. A12.

several magazines such as the *American Spectator,* and a host of conservative radio and television talk programs. These radio programs, in particular, helped Republicans win races in the 1994 and 1996 congressional elections. Conservative religious leaders like Rev. Jerry Falwell and Pat Robertson, founder of the Christian Coalition, have used their television shows to attack President Clinton's programs and to mount biting personal attacks on both Clinton and his wife. Other conservative groups not associated with the religious Right have also launched sharp assaults against the president. Nationally syndicated talk show host Rush Limbaugh, for example, is a constant critic of the administration.

The emergence of this conservative media complex has meant that liberal policies and politicians are virtually certain to come under attack even when the "liberal media" are sympathetic to them. For example, charges that President Clinton and his wife were involved in financial improprieties as partners in the Whitewater Development Corporation, as well as allegations that, while governor, Clinton had sexually harassed an Arkansas state employee, Paula Jones, were first publicized by the conservative press. Only after these stories had received a good deal of coverage in the *Washington Times* and the *American Spectator* did the mainstream "liberal" media begin to highlight them. Of course, once the stories broke, the *Washington Post,* the *New York Times,* and the major television networks devoted substantial investigative resources and time to them. In due course, the "liberal" media probably gave the Whitewater and Jones charges just as much play as the "conservative" media, often with just as little regard for evidence.[18]

Clinton's opponents later were able to gather evidence suggesting that the president had an affair with White House intern Monica Lewinsky. Once again, the "liberal" media gave the story enormous play. Interestingly, however, liberal news organizations made certain to point out that the story originated with Clinton's right-wing foes. For example, in its front-page coverage on January 24, 1998, the *Washington Post* revealed that the initial effort to gather evidence against Clinton had been the brainchild of a conservative activist and ardent foe of the president.[19] In this way, the *Post* appeared to be deflecting attention away from the allegations and toward the tactics of Clinton's enemies. Most journalists, however, deny that their political outlooks result in biased reporting.[20]

Probably more important than ideological bias is a selection bias in favor of news that the media view as having a great deal of audience appeal because of its dramatic or entertainment value. In practice, this bias often results in news coverage that focuses on crimes and scandals, especially those involving prominent individuals, despite the fact that the public obviously looks to the media for information about important political debates.[21] For example, even though most journalists may be Democrats, this partisan predisposition did not prevent an enormous media frenzy in January 1998 when reports surfaced that President Clinton may

[18]Howard Kurtz, "The Media and the Fiske Report," *Washington Post,* 3 July 1994, p. A4.

[19]David Streitfeld and Howard Kurtz, "Literary Agent Was Behind Secret Tapes," *Washington Post,* 24 January 1988, p. 1.

[20]Michael Kinsley, "Bias and Baloney," *Washington Post,* 26 November 1992, p. A29.

[21]See Kathleen Hall Jamieson and Joseph N. Cappella, *The Spiral of Cynicism: The Press and the Public Good* (New York: Oxford University Press, 1997).

have had an affair with Lewinsky. Once a hint of blood appeared in the water, partisanship and ideology were swept away by the piranhalike instincts often manifested by journalists.



## Sources of the News

News coverage is also influenced by the individuals or groups who are subjects of the news or whose interests and activities are actual or potential news topics. All politicians, for example, seek to shape or manipulate their media images by cultivating good relations with reporters as well as through news leaks and staged news events. For example, during the lengthy investigation of President Clinton, which was conducted by Special Counsel Kenneth Starr, both the Office of the Special Counsel and the White House frequently leaked information designed to bolster their respective positions in the struggle. Starr admitted speaking to reporters on a not-for-attribution basis about aspects of his investigation of the president. One journalist, Steven Brill, accused a number of prominent reporters of serving as "lap dogs" for the Special Counsel, recording as fact the information fed to them by Starr.[22]

**AMERICAN POLITICAL DEVELOPMENT**

Information about official government personnel tends to dominate news sources. Whereas issues about the presidency dominate today's politics, news about the Congress was more prominent in the nineteenth century.

SOURCE: Samuel Kernell and Gary C. Jacobson, "Congress and the Presidency as News in the Nineteenth Century," *Journal of Politics* 49 (November 1987), pp. 1016–35.

As we saw in Chapters 10 and 12, by using media consultants and "issues managers," many social, economic, and political groups vigorously promote their ideas and interests through speeches, articles, books, news releases, research reports, and other mechanisms designed to attract favorable media coverage. Typically, competing forces seek to present—and to persuade the media to present—their own interests as more general or "public" interests. In recent years, for example, liberals have been very successful in inducing the media to present their environmental, consumer, and political reform proposals as matters of the public interest. Indeed, the advocates of these goals are organized in "public interest" groups. Seldom do the national media ever question a public interest group's equation of its goals with the general interest of all.

Occasionally, a clever ploy may allow a group to shape the news completely. In September 1996, for example, opponents of California's ballot Proposition 209, which would ban all gender and race preferences from state government and universities, were able to create a story that, for a time, completely discredited the proposition's supporters. Student opponents of the proposition at California State University at Northridge invited David Duke, a former Louisiana legislator and Ku Klux Klan leader, to speak in favor of ending racial and gender preferences at a campus forum. As his hosts had anticipated, Duke's presence on the Cal State campus sparked a riot that produced statewide news coverage linking the Klansman to Proposition 209. Duke's apparent association with the proposal

[22]David Firestone, "Steven Brill Strikes a Nerve in News Media," *New York Times,* 20 June 1998, p. 4.

had the effect of silencing many of its legitimate supporters who feared being tainted by any connection to David Duke.[23]

The capacity of news sources and subjects to influence the news is hardly unlimited. Media consultants and issues managers may shape the news for a time, but it is generally not difficult for the media to penetrate the smoke screens thrown up by the news sources if they have a reason to do so. That reason is sometimes supplied by the third and most important factor influencing news content—the audience.

## The Power of Consumers

The print and broadcast media are businesses that, in general, seek to show a profit. This means that like any other business, they must cater to the preferences of consumers. This has very important consequences for the content and character of the news media.

**Catering to the Upscale Audience** In general, and especially in the political realm, the print and broadcast media and the publishing industry are not only responsive to the interests of consumers generally, but they are particularly responsive to the interests and views of the more "upscale" segments of the audience. The preferences of these audience segments have a profound effect upon the content and orientation of the press, of radio and television programming, and of books, especially in the areas of news and public affairs.[24] The influence of the upscale audience is a function of the economics of publishing and broadcasting. Books, especially books dealing with academic or intellectual issues, are purchased almost exclusively by affluent and well-educated consumers. As a result, the publishing industry caters to the tastes of this segment of the market.

For their part, newspapers, magazines, and the broadcast media depend primarily upon advertising revenues for their profits. These revenues, in turn, depend upon the character and size of the audience that they are able to provide advertisers for their product displays and promotional efforts. From the perspective of most advertisers and especially those whose products are relatively expensive, the most desirable audiences for their ads and commercials consist of younger, upscale consumers. What makes these individuals an especially desirable consumer audience is, of course, their affluence and their spending habits. Although they represent only a small percentage of the population, individuals under the age of fifty whose family income is in the 80th percentile or better account for nearly 50 percent of the retail dollars spent on consumer goods in the United States. To reach this audience, advertisers are particularly anxious to promote their products in the periodicals and newspapers and on the radio and television broadcasts that are known or believed to attract upscale patronage.

[23] "Quota of Lies," *The Detroit News*, 28 September 1996, p. C6.

[24] See Tom Burnes, "The Organization of Public Opinion," in *Mass Communication and Society*, ed. James Curran (Beverly Hills, CA: Sage, 1979), pp. 44–230. See also David Altheide, *Creating Reality* (Beverly Hills, CA: Sage, 1976).

Thus, advertisers flock to magazines like the *New Yorker, Fortune, Forbes, Architectural Digest,* and *Time*. Similarly, the pages of elite newspapers like the *New York Times* and the *Washington Post* are usually packed with advertisements for clothing, autos, computer equipment, stereo equipment, furs, jewelry, resorts and vacations, and the entire range of products and services that are such integral parts of the lifestyle of the well-to-do business and professional strata.

Although affluent consumers do watch television programs and read periodicals whose contents are designed simply to amuse or entertain, the one area that most directly appeals to the upscale audience is that of news and public affairs. The affluent—who are also typically well-educated—are the core audience of news magazines, journals of opinion, books dealing with public affairs, serious newspapers like the *New York Times* and the *Washington Post,* and broadcast news and weekend and evening public affairs programming. While other segments of the public also read newspapers and watch the television news, their level of interest in world events, national political issues, and the like is closely related to their level of education. As a result, upscale Americans are over-represented in the news and public affairs audience. The concentration of these strata in the audience makes news, politics, and public affairs potentially very attractive topics to advertisers, publishers, radio broadcasters, and television executives.

To attract audiences to their news and public affairs offerings, the media and publishing industries employ polls and other market research techniques, including the famous Nielsen and Arbitron rating services, analyses of sales, as well as a good deal of intuition to identify their audience's political interests, tastes, perspectives, and biases. The results of this research—and guesswork—affect the character, style, and content of the programming presented by the networks, as well as the topics of the books published by major houses and the stories and reports presented by the various periodicals. The media seeks to present material consistent with the interests or biases of important segments of the audience, and in a way that appeals to, or is at least not offensive to, the tastes or sensitivities of that audience.

Not surprisingly, given their general market power, it is the upper- and middle-class segments of the audience whose interests and tastes especially influence the media's news, public affairs, and political coverage. This is evident from the topics covered, the style of coverage, and in the case of network television, the types of reporters and newscasters who appear on the screen. First, the political and social topics given most extensive attention by the national media are mainly, albeit not exclusively, topics that appeal to the interests of well-educated profes-

**AMERICAN POLITICAL DEVELOPMENT**

Consumers became important to the press when changes in organizational demands on newspapers from the 1830s to the 1870s placed a premium on advertising and circulation as the newspapers' primary source of income. Prior to the rise of the "penny press"—papers that sold for one cent—most newspapers were funded and controlled by political parties. These party newspapers—which were particularly costly at six cents per copy and were sold primarily by subscription—provided partisan- and elite-oriented news. The penny press democratized and popularized news. Although this democratization created a wider distribution of information and promoted greater efforts at newsgathering, it also led to charges that the press was becoming too sensational.

SOURCE: Michael Schudson, *Discovering the News: A Social History of American Newspapers* (New York: Basic Books, 1978), pp. 12–60.

sionals, executives, and intellectuals. In recent years, these topics have included the nuclear arms race, ecological and environmental matters, budgetary and fiscal questions, regulation of business and the economy, political changes in Russia, Eastern Europe, and South Africa, attacks on Americans and American interests by terrorists, and, of course, the fluctuations of the stock market, interest rates, the value of the dollar, the price of precious metals, and the cost of real estate. While many of these topics may, indeed, be of general importance and concern, most are of more interest to the upscale segments of the audience than to the lower-middle- or working-class groups.

While these matters of concern to the upscale audience receive extensive media coverage, there are entire categories of events, issues, and phenomena of interest to lower-middle- and working-class Americans that receive scant attention from the national print and broadcast media. For example, trade union news and events are discussed only in the context of major strikes or revelations of corruption. No network or national periodical routinely covers labor organizations. Religious and church affairs receive little coverage. The activities of veterans', fraternal, ethnic, and patriotic organizations are also generally ignored. Certainly, interpretations of economic events tend to reveal a class bias. For example, an increase in airline fares—a cost borne mainly by upper-income travelers—is usually presented as a negative development. Higher prices for commodities heavily used by the poor such as alcohol and cigarettes, on the other hand, are generally presented as morally justified.

The upscale character of the national media's coverage stands in sharp contrast to the topics discussed by radio and television talk shows and the small number of news tabloids and major daily newspapers that seek to reach a blue-collar audience. These periodicals and programs feature some of the same events described by the national media. But from the perspective of these outlets and their viewers and readers, "public affairs" includes healthy doses of celebrity gossip, crime news, discussions of the occult, and sightings of UFOs. Also featured are ethnic, fraternal, patriotic, and religious affairs, and even demolition derbies. Executives, intellectuals, and professionals, as well as the journalists and writers who serve them, may sneer at this blue-collar version of the news, but after all, are the stories of UFOs presented by the decidedly downscale *New York Post* any more peculiar than the stories of the U.N. told by the imperious *New York Times*?

**The Media and Protest** While the media respond most to the upscale audience, groups who cannot afford the services of media consultants and issues managers can publicize their views and interests through protest. Frequently, the media are accused of encouraging protest and even violence as a result of the fact that they are instantly available to cover it, providing protesters with the publicity they crave. Clearly, protest and even violence can be important vehicles for attracting the attention and interest of the media, and thus may provide an opportunity for media attention to groups otherwise lacking the financial or organizational resources to broadcast their views. During the 1960s, for example, the media coverage given to civil rights demonstrators and particularly to the violence that Southern law enforcement officers in cities such as Selma and Birmingham directed against peaceful black demonstrators at least temporarily increased white sympathy for the civil rights cause. This was, of course, one of the chief aims of Dr. Martin Luther King's strategy of nonviolence.[25] In subsequent years, the media turned their attention to antiwar demonstrations and, more recently, to anti-abortion demonstrations, antinuclear demonstrations, and even to acts of international terrorism designed specifically to induce the Western media to publicize the terrorists' causes. But while protest, disorder, and even terrorism can succeed in drawing media attention, these methods ultimately do not allow groups from the bottom of the social ladder to compete effectively in the media.

The chief problem with protest as a media technique is that, in general, the media upon which the protesters depend have considerable discretion in reporting and interpreting the events they cover. For example, should a particular group of protesters be identified as "freedom fighters" or "terrorists"? If a demonstration leads to violence, was this the fault of the protesters or the authorities? The answers to these questions are typically determined by the media, not by the protesters. This means that media interpretation of protest activities is more a reflection of the views of the groups and forces to which the media are responsive—as we have seen, usually segments of the upper-middle class—than it is a function of the wishes of the protesters themselves. It is worth noting that civil rights protesters received their most favorable media coverage when a segment of the white upper-middle class saw blacks as potential political allies in the Democratic party.

Thus, the effectiveness of protest as a media strategy depends, in large measure, on the character of national political alignments and coalitions. If protesters are aligned with or potentially useful to more powerful forces, then protest can be an effective mechanism for the communication of the ideas and interests of the lower classes. If, on the other hand, the social forces to which the media are most responsive are not sympathetic to the protesters or their views, then protest is likely to be defined by the print and broadcast media as mindless and purposeless violence.

Occasionally, of course, segments of the upper social strata themselves engage in protest activities. Typically, upper-class protesters—student demonstrators and the like—have little difficulty securing favorable publicity for themselves and their causes. Witness the sympathetic coverage given anti-apartheid protests and antiwar protests, and the benign treatment afforded even upper-middle-class fringe groups like the "animal liberationists." Upper-class protesters are often more skilled than their lower-class counterparts in the techniques of media manipulation. That is, they typically have a better sense—often as a result of formal courses on the subject—of how to package messages for media consumption. For example, it is important to know what time of day a protest should occur if it is to be carried on the evening news. Similarly, the setting, definition of the issues, and character of the rhetoric used, and so on, all help to determine whether a protest will receive favorable media coverage, unfavorable coverage, or no coverage at all. Moreover, upper-middle-class protesters can often produce their own media coverage through "underground" newspapers, college papers, student radio and tele-

[25]David Garrow, *Protest at Selma* (New Haven: Yale University Press, 1978).

vision stations, and, now, the Internet. The same resources and skills that generally allow upper-middle-class people to publicize their ideas are usually not left behind when segments of this class choose to engage in disruptive forms of political action.

## Media Power in American Politics

The content and character of news and public affairs programming—what the media choose to present and how they present it—can have the most far-reaching political consequences. Media disclosures can greatly enhance—or fatally damage—the careers of public officials. Media coverage can rally support for—or intensify opposition to—national policies. The media can shape and modify, if not fully form, public perceptions of events, issues, and institutions.

### Shaping Events

In recent American political history, the media have played a central role in at least three major events. First, the media were critically important factors in the civil rights movement of the 1950s and 1960s. Television photos showing peaceful civil rights marchers attacked by club-swinging police helped to generate sympathy among Northern whites for the civil rights struggle and greatly increased the pressure on Congress to bring an end to segregation.[26] Second, the media were instrumental in compelling the Nixon administration to negotiate an end to the Vietnam War. Beginning in 1967, the national media portrayed the war as misguided and unwinnable and, as a result, helped to turn popular sentiment against continued American involvement.[27] So strong was the effect of the media, in fact, that when Walter Cronkite told television news viewers that the war was unwinnable, Johnson himself was reported to have said, "If I've lost Walter, then it's over. I've lost Mr. Average Citizen."[28]

Finally, the media were central actors in the Watergate affair, which ultimately forced President Richard Nixon, landslide victor in the 1972 presidential election, to resign from office in disgrace. It was the relentless series of investigations launched by the *Washington Post,* the *New York Times,* and the television networks that led to the disclosures of the various abuses of which Nixon was guilty and ultimately forced Nixon to choose between resignation and almost certain impeachment.

[26]Ibid.

[27]See Todd Gitlin, *The Whole World Is Watching* (Berkeley: University of California Press, 1980). See also William Hammond, *Reporting Vietnam: Media and Military at War* (Lawrence: University Press of Kansas, 1999).

[28]Quoted in George Brown Tindall, *America: A Narrative History,* 5th ed. (New York: W. W. Norton, 1996), p. 1541.

## The Sources of Media Power

**Agenda Setting** The power of the media stems from several sources. The first is ***agenda setting,*** which means the media help to set the agenda for political discussion. Groups and forces that wish to bring their ideas before the public in order to generate support for policy proposals or political candidacies must somehow secure media coverage. If the media are persuaded that an idea is newsworthy, then they may declare it an "issue" that must be resolved or a "problem" to be solved, thus clearing the first hurdle in the policy-making process. On the other hand, if an idea lacks or loses media appeal, its chance of resulting in new programs or policies is diminished. Some ideas seem to surface, gain media support for a time, lose media appeal, and then resurface.

In most instances, the media serve as conduits for agenda-setting efforts by competing groups and forces. Occasionally, however, journalists themselves play an important role in setting the agenda of political discussion. For example, whereas many of the scandals and investigations surrounding President Clinton were initiated by his political opponents, the Watergate scandal that destroyed Nixon's presidency was in some measure initiated and driven by the *Washington Post* and the national television networks.

**Framing** A second source of the media's power, known as ***framing,*** is their power to decide how political events and results are interpreted by the American people. For example, during the 1995–1996 struggle between President Clinton and congressional Republicans over the nation's budget—a struggle that led to several partial shutdowns of the federal government—the media's interpretation of events forced the Republicans to back down and agree to a budget on Clinton's terms. At the beginning of the crisis, congressional Republicans, led by then-House Speaker Newt Gingrich, were confident that they could compel Clinton to accept their budget, which called for substantial cuts in domestic social programs. Republicans calculated that Clinton would fear being blamed for lengthy government shutdowns and would quickly accede to their demands, and that once Americans saw that life went on with government agencies closed, they would support the Republicans in asserting that the United States could get along with less government.

For the most part, however, the media did not cooperate with the GOP's plans. Media coverage of the several government shutdowns during this period emphasized the hardships imposed upon federal workers who were being furloughed in the weeks before Christmas. Indeed, Speaker Gingrich, who was generally portrayed as the villain who caused the crisis, came to be called the "Gin*grinch*" who stole Christmas from the children of hundreds of thousands of federal workers. Rather than suggest that the shutdown demonstrated that America could carry on with less government, media accounts focused on the difficulties encountered by Washington tourists unable to visit the capital's monuments, museums, and galleries. The woes of American travelers whose passports were delayed were given considerable attention. This sort of coverage eventually convinced most Americans

ANALYZING AMERICAN POLITICS

## *What is the Political Impact of Television News Media?*

In addition to the many changes in political institutions that have occurred in the twentieth century, the changing nature of mass media and especially the increasing ubiquity of television have dramatically altered the political landscape. Exactly how the media affects politics is a point of some debate. Though a great deal of research has relied on public opinion surveys to gauge the impact of media and television in particular, our understanding of media and politics has been greatly advanced by the innovation of methodological experiments in media studies. These experiments involve randomly dividing subjects into two or more groups and manipulating certain conditions for one group but not the other(s). For example, Group A may be exposed to a particular broadcast news story, while Group B is not. These experiments assume that because members of the groups have been randomly assigned and the only condition that is different between the groups is the news story, any differences between the groups in, for example, their political opinions (after exposure) must be due to the news story itself. By manipulating experimental conditions, researchers can learn a great deal about the effects of particular types of media exposure. One drawback of studies that employ experiments is that, unlike public opinion surveys, they lack generalizability. One way to overcome this problem is to use a mixture of experimental and nonexperimental methodologies and data.

Two important works have used this combination with great success: Shanto Iyengar and Donald Kinder's *News That Matters* and Shanto Iyengar's *Is Anyone Responsible?*[1] Iyengar and Kinder examine

[1]Shanto Iyengar and Donald Kinder, *News That Matters: Television and American Opinion* (Chicago: University of Chicago Press, 1987); Shanto Iyengar, *Is Anyone Responsible? How Television Frames Political Issues* (Chicago: University of Chicago Press, 1991).

that the government shutdown was bad for the country. In the end, Gingrich and the congressional Republicans were forced to surrender and to accept a new budget reflecting many of Clinton's priorities. The Republicans' defeat in the budget showdown contributed to the unraveling of the GOP's legislative program and, ultimately, to the Republicans' poor showing in the 1996 presidential elections. The character of media coverage of an event thus had enormous repercussions of how Americans interpreted it.

**Media Coverage of Elections and Government** The media's agenda-setting and framing powers may often determine how people perceive an elec-

the *agenda-setting* and *priming* effects of television news media. Agenda setting involves changing the political issues that people think about, while priming involves changing the standards that people use to evaluate political actors and public policy. To test for agenda-setting effects, Iyengar and Kinder showed various groups identical news broadcasts—except for one story that was different. For example, Group A might have a story about unemployment inserted into their broadcast, while Group B might have a story about national defense. The researchers found that how the individuals reacted to the story depended on whether it was the lead story, whether the individuals were directly affected by the problem, and whether individuals were politically attentive and active. Iyengar and Kinder checked their experimental results against nonexperimental data by examining the relationship between the number of news stories on various issues and how this affected what problems people thought were most important. This analysis largely confirmed the experimental results on agenda setting.

Kinder and Iyengar also found strong support for a priming effect—that individuals evaluated a president's performance much more favorably on issues that they had already been exposed to in news broadcasts. This effect extended to evaluations of a president's overall performance, his character, and his general level of responsibility to the people. News broadcasts also prime the way voters evaluate and choose candidates. Individuals who were exposed to broadcasts that emphasized economic conditions and economic policies weighed the economy more heavily in their vote choices. If individuals were exposed to broadcasts that emphasized the personal characteristics, qualifications, and positions of the candidates for office, then their vote decisions were much more candidate-centered.

In *Is Anyone Responsible?* Shanto Iyengar extends his earlier work with Kinder by examining how television news media frames the news in order to assign political responsibility and accountability. News stories are typically presented in either *episodic* or *thematic* frames. Episodic frames present stories as specific events of particular cases, while thematic frames present stories in a general context. Using experiments similar to those described above, Iyengar finds that attributing individualistic or societal causes to an event is a direct result of how that piece of news is framed. One of the key conclusions Iyengar draws is that the tendency of television news to use episodic frames and not to focus on problems in a political and societal context (thematic framing), steers citizens away from assigning responsibility to political officials. Television news thus attenuates an accountability link that is crucial for a healthy democracy.

tion's outcome. In 1968, despite the growing strength of the opposition to his Vietnam War policies, incumbent Lyndon Johnson won two-thirds of the votes cast in New Hampshire's Democratic presidential primary. His rival, Senator Eugene McCarthy, received less than one-third. The broadcast media, however, declared the outcome to have been a great victory for McCarthy, who was said to have done much better than "expected" (or at least expected by the media). His "defeat" in New Hampshire was one of the factors that persuaded Johnson to withdraw from the 1968 presidential race.

The media also have a good deal of power to shape popular perceptions of politicians and political leaders. Most citizens will never meet Bill Clinton or Al Gore. Popular perceptions and evaluations of these individuals are based upon their media images. Obviously, through public relations and other techniques, politicians seek to cultivate favorable media images. But the media have a good deal of discretion over how individuals are portrayed, or how they are allowed to portray themselves.

In the case of political candidates, the media have considerable influence over whether or not a particular individual will receive public attention, whether or not a particular individual will be taken seriously as a viable contender, and whether the public will perceive a candidate's performance favorably. Thus, if the media find a candidate interesting, they may treat him or her as a serious contender even though the facts of the matter seem to suggest otherwise

In a similar vein, the media may declare that a candidate has "momentum," a mythical property that the media confer upon candidates they admire. Momentum has no substantive meaning—it is simply a media prediction that a particular candidate will do even better in the future than in the past. Such media prophecies can become self-fulfilling as contributors and supporters jump on the bandwagon of the candidate possessing this "momentum." In 1992, when Bill Clinton's poll standings surged in the wake of the Democratic National Convention, the media determined that Clinton had enormous momentum. In fact, nothing that happened during the remainder of the race led the media to change their collective judgment. Even when George Bush's poll standing began to improve, many news stories pointed to Bush's inability to gain momentum. While there is no way to ascertain what impact this coverage had on the race, at the very least, Republican contributors and activists must have been discouraged by the constant portrayal of their candidate as lacking—and the opposition as possessing—this magical "momentum." In 1996, the national media portrayed Bob Dole's candidacy as hopeless almost from the very beginning. Coverage of the Republican convention and the October debates emphasized Clinton's "insurmountable" lead. The media's coverage of Dole's campaign became a self-fulfilling prophecy of his defeat.[29]

Media power to shape images is not absolute. Other image-makers compete with and manipulate the media by planting stories and rumors and staging news events. Some politicians are so adept at communicating with the public and shaping their own images that the media seem to have little effect upon them.

During the 1992 presidential campaign, candidates developed a number of techniques designed to take the manipulation of the image-making process away

from journalists and media executives. Among the most important of these techniques were the many town meetings and television talk and entertainment show appearances that all the major candidates made. Frequent exposure on such programs as *Larry King Live* and *Today* gave candidates an opportunity to shape and focus their own media images and to overwhelm any negative image that might be projected by the media.

[29]See Howard Kurtz, "No Debate about It: TV Analysts Say Clinton's Winner," *Washington Post,* 18 October 1996, p. D1.

Members of the national news media responded by aggressively investigating and refuting many of the candidates' claims. Each of the major television networks, for example, aired regular critical analyses of the candidates' speeches, television commercials, and talk show appearances. In 1996, the media subjected Bob Dole's tax cut proposal to intensive scrutiny, suggesting that it was based on faulty economic assumptions.

Indeed, President Bill Clinton has been one of the few politicians in recent American history who has been able to survive repeated media attacks. Clinton and his advisors crafted what the *Washington Post* called a "toolkit" for dealing with potentially damaging media revelations. This toolkit included techniques such as chiding the press, browbeating reporters, referring inquiries to lawyers who would not comment, and acting quickly to change the agenda.[30] All these techniques helped Clinton to weather repeated revelations of sexual improprieties, financial irregularities, and campaign funding illegalities. Clinton even hoped to survive impeachment, with his popularity intact.

Rigorous political coverage serves the public interest by subjecting candidates' claims to scrutiny and refuting errors and distortions. At the same time, such critical coverage serves the interests of the news media by enhancing their own control over political imagery and perceptions and, thus, the power of the media vis-à-vis other political actors and institutions in the United States. We shall examine this topic next as we consider the development and significance of adversarial journalism.

## The Rise of Adversarial Journalism

The political power of the news media has greatly increased in recent years through the growing prominence of "adversarial journalism"—a form of journalism in which the media adopt a hostile posture toward the government and public officials.

During the nineteenth century, American newspapers were completely subordinate to the political parties. Newspapers depended upon official patronage—legal notice and party subsidies—for their financial survival and were controlled by party leaders. (A vestige of that era survived into the twentieth century in such newspaper names as the *Springfield Republican* and the *St. Louis Globe-Democrat.*) At the turn of the century, with the development of commercial advertising, newspapers became financially independent. This made possible the emergence of a formally nonpartisan press.

Presidents were the first national officials to see the opportunities in this development. By communicating directly to the electorate through newspapers and magazines, Theodore Roosevelt and Woodrow Wilson established political constituencies for themselves independent of party organizations and strengthened their own power relative to Congress. President Franklin Roosevelt used the radio, most notably in his famous fireside chats, to reach out to voters throughout the nation and to make himself the center of American politics. FDR was also adept at developing close personal relationships with reporters, which enabled

[30]Howard Kurtz, "One Too Many Revelations for the Masters of Spin, *Washington Post,* 25 January 1998, p. C1.

# Are the Media Out of Touch with the Public?

*Public confidence in national institutions has dropped in recent years, and David Shaw notes that the media have not been immune. He traces the decline to a perception that members of the media—reporters, commentators, editors—are increasingly out of touch with "the everyday concerns of the average reader and viewer." National reporters have become part of the powerful elite about which they write, and the increasing distance between reporters and readers (in terms of income, education, and tastes) injects a bias into how the media interpret events. Public reaction against these phenomena is one reason, Shaw argues, for the popularity of talk radio and other alternative media.*

*Critics of the media approve of an emerging trend called either "civic journalism" or "public journalism," in which newspapers in several cities are attempting to address the problems with political coverage and respond more directly to citizens' interests. Howard Kurtz, the* Washington Post *media critic, is less convinced of the merits of this movement. In his view, public journalism puts reporters and editors in the uncomfortable position of openly taking sides in political debates, and candidates themselves tend to dislike unscripted encounters that are the hallmark of the process.*

## SHAW

By almost any reasonable measure, the mainstream news media in this country are more responsible and more ethical today than at any time in their history.

Gone—for the most part—are the days when editors and reporters accepted extravagant gifts and free meals from news sources, when reporters routinely masqueraded as police officers, doctors and others in pursuit of a story, when stories were featured or killed almost daily to accommodate the financial, political or social interests of the publisher—or his wife.

And yet public confidence in the news media is in steady decline. In a *Times* poll conducted last month, only 17% said the media, overall, are doing a "very good" job—down from 30% in 1985. Almost 70% agreed with the statement: "The news media give more coverage to stories that support their own point of view than to those that don't." Forty percent said they have less confidence in the news media today than they did when they first began paying attention to news and current events.

Why?

One explanation may be that many members of the public feel a growing disenfranchisement from the news media, as they do from the government. Increasingly, they think, the people who report, edit and broadcast the news are elitist—well-paid, well-educated sophisticates who are more interested in (and have more in common with) the movers and shakers they cover than in the everyday concerns of the average reader and viewer.

Many in the responsible, mainstream news media—especially the print media—say there's another problem. They're paying, they say, for the sins of their less responsible, sensation-minded brethren, many of them in television.[1]

As public journalism has gained momentum in the last half-dozen years, it has taken on a variety of forms. Some news organizations have merely offered free pizzas to entice readers to attend meetings or fill out questionnaires. Others have joined forces with local universities that they also must cover. Still others have stretched the boundaries of what journalists ordinarily do.

The *Akron Beacon Journal* persuaded 22,000 citizens to mail in coupons pledging to work for improved race relations. The *Charlotte Observer* held inner-city town meetings in a "Taking Back Our Neighborhoods" campaign that prompted the city to tear down dilapidated buildings and open parks and recreational facilities. The Huntington, W. Va., *Herald-Dispatch* helped solicit volunteers for a half-dozen task forces on economic development and sponsored a visit to the state legislature to lobby on the issue. . . .

But Leonard Downie Jr., *The Washington Post*'s executive editor and a leading critic of public journalism, questioned the practice of "forcing politicians to appear at a forum of our choosing and to focus only on those questions we want to ask." He said it is "beyond the pale" for news organizations to get involved in advocating solutions, or even urging people to vote.

"That is a great danger to the credibility of the newspaper . . . even when the cause is the best possible cause," Downie said, adding: "It is very seductive, particularly for the top editors involved, who become celebrities through this process."

Some journalists expressed mixed feelings. *San Francisco Chronicle* reporter John King was at the center of a "Voice of the Voter" project during last year's mayoral race. He said he was surprised by "how thoughtful a lot of people are about the city" and contrasted it with his usual reporting: "You talk to your seven or eight appointed experts and they all say funny things that you slap in the paper. The more ridiculous the charge, the more space you give it."

At the same time, King said of the paper's practice of publishing reader comments verbatim: "It was really the Voice of the Yahoo. Instead of writing a crazy letter, people would call the voice mail and we'd run a 100-word rant from someone."[2]

[1]David Shaw, "Distrustful Public Views Media as 'Them—Not Us,' " *Los Angeles Times,* 1 April 1993.

[2]Howard Kurtz, "When News Media Go to Grass Roots, Candidates Often Don't Follow," *Washington Post,* 4 June 1996.

him to obtain favorable news coverage despite the fact that in his day a majority of newspaper owners and publishers were staunch conservatives. Following Roosevelt's example, subsequent presidents have all sought to use the media to enhance their popularity and power. For example, through televised news conferences, President John F. Kennedy mobilized public support for his domestic and foreign policy initiatives.

## AMERICAN POLITICAL DEVELOPMENT

The "muckraking" reporting of the Progressive era is a precursor of contemporary adversarial journalism. As a result of its newfound independence from party sponsorship, the press turned its attention to the ills of government, business, and society, particularly during the first decade of the twentieth century.

SOURCE: Frank Luther Mott, *American Journalism: A History of Newspapers in the United States through 250 Years, 1690 to 1940* (New York: Macmillan, 1941), p. 575.

During the 1950s and early 1960s, a few members of Congress also made successful use of the media—especially television—to mobilize national support for their causes. Senator Estes Kefauver of Tennessee became a major contender for the presidency and won a place on the 1956 Democratic national ticket as a result of his dramatic televised hearings on organized crime. Senator Joseph McCarthy of Wisconsin made himself a powerful national figure through his well-publicized investigations of alleged Communist infiltration of key American institutions. These senators, however, were more exceptional than typical. Through the mid-1960s, the executive branch continued to generate the bulk of news coverage, and the media served as a cornerstone of presidential power.

The Vietnam War shattered this relationship betwee the press and the presidency. During the early stages of U.S. involvement, American officials in Vietnam who disapproved of the way the war was being conducted leaked information critical of administrative policy to reporters. Publication of this material infuriated the White House, which pressured publishers to block its release—on one occasion, President Kennedy went so far as to ask the *New York Times* to reassign its Saigon correspondent. The national print and broadcast media—the network news divisions, the national news weeklies, the *Washington Post,* and the *New York Times*—discovered, however, that there was an audience for critical coverage among segments of the public skeptical of administration policy. As the Vietnam conflict dragged on, critical media coverage fanned antiwar sentiment. Moreover, growing opposition to the war among liberals encouraged some members of Congress, most notably Senator J. William Fulbright, chair of the Senate Foreign Relations Committee, to break with the president. In turn, these shifts in popular and congressional sentiment emboldened journalists and publishers to continue to present critical news reports. Through this process, journalists developed a commitment to adversarial journalism, while a constituency emerged that would rally to the defense of the media when it came under White House attack.

This pattern, established during the Vietnam War, endured through the 1970s and into the 1990s. Political forces opposed to presidential policies, many members of Congress, and the national news media began to find that their interests often overlapped.

For their part, aggressive use of the techniques of investigation, publicity, and exposure allowed the national media to enhance their autonomy and carve out a prominent place for themselves in American government and politics. The power derived by the press from adversarial journalism is one reason the media seem to relish opportunities to attack political institutions and to publish damaging information about important public officials. Increasingly, media coverage has come to influence politicians' careers, the mobilization of political constituencies, and the fate of issues and causes.

## Media Power and Responsibility

The free media are an institution absolutely essential to democratic government. We depend upon the media to investigate wrongdoing, to publicize and explain governmental actions, to evaluate programs and politicians, and to bring to light matters that might otherwise be known only to a handful of governmental insiders. In short, without free and active media, popular government would be virtually impossible. Citizens would have few means through which to know or assess the government's actions—other than the claims or pronouncements of the government itself. Moreover, without active—indeed, aggressive—media, citizens would be hard pressed to make informed choices among competing candidates at the polls. Often enough, the media reveal discrepancies between candidates' claims and their actual records, and between the images that candidates seek to project and the underlying realities.

At the same time, the increasing decay of party organizations (see Chapter 11) has made politicians ever more dependent upon favorable media coverage. National political leaders and journalists have had symbiotic relationships, at least since FDR's presidency, but initially politicians were the senior partners. They benefited from media publicity, but they were not totally dependent upon it so long as they could still rely upon party organizations to mobilize votes. Journalists, on the other hand, depended upon their relationships with politicians for access to information, and would hesitate to report stories that might antagonize valuable sources. Newsmen feared exclusion from the flow of information in retaliation. Thus, for example, reporters did not publicize potentially embarrassing information, widely known in Washington, about the personal lives of such figures as Franklin Roosevelt and John F. Kennedy.

With the decline of party, the balance of power between politicians and journalists has been reversed. Now that politicians have become heavily dependent upon the media to reach their constituents, journalists no longer need fear that their access to information can be restricted in retaliation for negative coverage.

Freedom gives the media enormous power. The media can make or break reputations, help to launch or to destroy political careers, and build support for or rally opposition against programs and institutions.[31] Wherever there is so much power, there exists at least the potential for its abuse or overly zealous use—the problem of freedom and power in a new and unexpected form. All things considered, free media are so critically important to the maintenance of a democratic society that we must be prepared to take the risk that the media will occasionally abuse their power. The forms of governmental control that would prevent the media from misusing their power would also certainly destroy our freedom.

[31]See Martin Linsky, *Impact: How the Press Affects Federal Policymaking* (New York: W. W. Norton, 1986).

THEN AND NOW

## Changes in American Politics

The changing role of the media in American politics is subject to a number of forces, including the technological advances that affect mass media, the role of the national government in regulating those media, and institutional and political reforms in American politics in general.

- The character of political media has changed dramatically throughout American history, particularly during the twentieth century. In the nineteenth century, advances in printing-press technology and the linking of the nation by telegraph created a greater number of news sources and broadened the national scope of news. In the twentieth century, the use of radio and television by politicians and news organizations provided for immediate, nationalized connections between political elites and masses. In the late twentieth century, the proliferation of cable television channels, talk radio, and internet technologies has led to a more complicated and atomized media.
- Television evening news programs were broadcast for only fifteen minutes in the early 1960s. By the end of that decade, the news had expanded to thirty minutes and then by the early 1980s to twenty-four hours on CNN.
- The establishment of the FCC to regulate the broadcast media was intended to provide technical coordination to the broadcast industry. As the FCC developed, it took a greater role in regulating and monitoring the content of broadcast media.
- For much of the nineteenth century, political parties controlled and funded newspapers. The rise of the advertising industry and the need to fund the press through its circulation led to the creation of a nonpartisan press. Although some scholars refer to it as the "independent" press, the new system simply replaced newspapers' dependence on political parties with a new "market" dependence on advertisers and readers.
- The relationship between politicians and the government on the one hand and the press and reporters on the other has changed several times throughout American history. In the nineteenth century, the press relied on politicians and parties for patronage and therefore was largely subservient to politicians. In part as a result of its independence from party control, the press turned to a "muckraking" style of journalism in the early twentieth century, focusing on political and societal problems. At the midpoint of the twentieth century, politicians established close relationships with reporters. But by the 1970s, the press once again took a critical stance as adversarial journalism grew.

## SUMMARY

The American news media are among the world's most free. The print and broadcast media regularly present information and opinions critical of the government, political leaders, and policies.

The media help to determine the agenda or focus of political debate in the United States, to shape popular understanding of political events and results, and to influence popular judgments of politicians and leaders.

Over the past century, the media have helped to nationalize American political perspectives. Media coverage is influenced by the perspectives of journalists, the activities of news sources, and, most important, by the media's need to appeal to upscale audiences. The attention that the media give to protest and disruptive activities is also a function of audience factors.

Free media are essential ingredients of popular government.

## FOR FURTHER READING

Altheide, David. *Creating Reality.* Beverly Hills, CA: Sage, 1976.

Braestrup, Peter. *Big Story: How the American Press and Television Reported and Interpreted the Crisis of Tet 1968 in Vietnam and Washington.* Boulder, CO: Westview Press, 1977.

Cook, Timothy. *Making Laws and Making News: Media Strategies in the House of Representatives.* Washington, DC: Brookings Institution, 1989.

Epstein, Edward. *News From Nowhere.* New York: Random House, 1973.

Gans, Herbert. *Deciding What's News.* New York: Pantheon, 1979.

Graber, Doris. *Mass Media and American Politics.* Washington, DC: Congressional Quarterly Press, 1989.

Grossman, Michael B., and Martha J. Kumar. T*he Presidency and the Mass Media in the Age of Television.* Baltimore, MD: Johns Hopkins University Press, 1981.

Hallin, Daniel C. *The Uncensored War.* Berkeley and Los Angeles: University of California Press, 1986.

Hart, Roderick. *Seducing America: How Television Charms the Modern Voter.* New York: Oxford University Press, 1994.

Hess, Stephen. *Live From Capitol Hill: Studies of Congress and the Media.* Washington, DC: Brookings Institution, 1991.

Joslyn, Richard A. *Mass Media and Elections.* Reading, MA: Addison-Wesley, 1984.

Linsky, Martin. *Impact: How the Press Affects Federal Policymaking.* New York: W. W. Norton, 1986.

Nacos, Brigitte L. *The Press, Presidents and Crises.* New York: Columbia University Press, 1990.

Owen, Diana. *Media Messages in American Presidential Elections.* Westport, CT: Greenwood, 1991.

Robinson, Michael, and Margaret Sheehan. *Over the Wire and On TV: CBS and UPI in Campaign '80.* New York: Russell Sage Foundation, 1983.

Spitzer, Robert J., ed. *Media and Public Policy.* Westport, CT: Praeger, 1993.

West, Darrell. *Air Wars: Television Advertising in Election Campaigns, 1952–1992.* Washington, DC: Congressional Quarterly Press, 1993.

Winfield, Betty Houchin. *FDR and the News Media.* Urbana: University of Illinois Press, 1990.

# GOVERNANCE

# 14

# Government in Action: Public Policy and the Economy

## TIME LINE ON GOVERNMENT AND THE ECONOMY

| Events | | Institutional Developments |
|---|---|---|
| First Congress convenes (1789) | | Constitution establishes power of Congress to make fiscal and monetary policies (1789) |
| Whiskey Rebellion quashed, establishing national power to tax (1794) | | |
| | 1800 | Tariffs and promotional policies used to encourage American industry (1800s) |
| Westward expansion (1800s) | | *Gibbons v. Ogden* stipulates that states cannot pass laws that interfere with interstate commerce (1824) |
| Civil War—end of slavery and plantation economy in the South (1861–1865) | | Income tax imposed (1861) |
| | | Bureau of Internal Revenue created (1862) |
| Industrial development; large railroad companies; rise of large corporations, a large class of laborers, commercialized agriculture, and national trade associations (1860s–1890s) | | Interstate Commerce Act to control monopolistic practices of the railroads; ICC established (1887) |
| | 1890 | Sherman Antitrust Act to protect trade and commerce against monopolies (1890) |
| | | Supreme Court declares income tax unconstitutional (1895) |
| | | Sixteenth Amendment provides for income tax (1913) |
| World War I (1914–1918) | | Congress establishes Federal Reserve System (1913), Federal Trade Commission (1914) |
| Rise of motor and air transportation; spread of mass production; radio starts epoch of mass communication (1920s) | | First government mobilization of the entire economy for war (1917–1920) |
| Stock market crash (1929) | | |
| Great Depression (1929–1930s) | 1930 | |
| Franklin Roosevelt's New Deal (1930s) | | New Deal policies rescue banks, provide relief for unemployed, establish regulatory agencies to speed recovery of agriculture and business from Depression (1930s) |
| | 1940 | |
| U.S. in World War II (1941–1945) | | Price ceilings set by the Office of Price Administration; goods allocated through rationing—the first regulation of all Americans (1942); War Production Board created to oversee industrial conversion to war; Revenue Act broadens the tax base (1942); payroll deductions for income taxes introduced (1943) |
| Postwar commitment to full employment through government programs (1946) | | |

| Events | | Institutional Developments |
|---|---|---|
| Growth of government (1960s); Kennedy assassinated; Johnson assumes presidency (1963) | 1960 | Great Society programs—government spending to reduce poverty stimulates the economy (1965) |
| Vietnam War (1965–1973) | | |
| Watergate scandal (1972–1974) | | "Social Regulation"—the last great spurt of regulatory programs (1969–1974) |
| Carter and Congress move to deregulate certain industries (1978) | | Deregulation of securities (1975), railroads (1976 and 1980), airlines (1978–1981), banking (1980), motor carriers (1980) |
| Election of Ronald Reagan (1980) | 1980 | |
| | | Deregulation through management; vast tax cut; deficits mount (1980s) |
| Election of George Bush (1988) | | |
| Recession (1990–1992) | 1990 | Some re-regulation; persistent deficits induce Bush to break "no new taxes" pledge (1990) |
| Election of Bill Clinton (1992) | | Clinton's first budget calls for large tax increases and spending cuts to fight deficits (1993) |
| Republicans win control of Congress (1994) | | Republican "Contract with America" (1995) seek further shrinkage of government |
| First two-term retention of Congress by Republicans in 68 years; Democrats keep presidency (1996) | | Republican Congress wins vast devolution of AFDC and deregulation of telecommunications and agriculture. Clinton brings Democrats along |
| Longest peacetime economic growth in American history (1992–1999) | | |
| Budget surpluses (1998, 1999) | | |

Throughout this book, "freedom and power" has been more than a theme. It has been our standard and our guide, since the relationship between freedom and power is the eternal problem that every nation must solve if we hope to have global peace. But freedom and power is a moving target. It's not a puzzle that once solved, is solved once and for all. Freedom and power is a fundamental dilemma that must be resolved over and over again, any time a new public policy is adopted.

Just having a government is something of a solution. Thomas Jefferson, one of the greatest champions of freedom, was impelled to follow his listing of the "self-evident"

## CORE OF THE ARGUMENT

- Governments are essential to the creation and maintenance of a capitalist economy and a national market.
- Governments establish public order by using three techniques of control: promotional, regulatory, and redistributive policies.
- Promotional techniques bestow benefits, regulatory techniques directly control individual conduct, and redistributive techniques manipulate the entire economy.
- Government policies must be constantly adjusted to maintain the right balance between private actions and government control. What constitutes the "right balance" in such matters is itself a political decision.

and "unalienable" rights of Life, Liberty and the pursuit of Happiness with the proviso, "That to secure these rights, Governments are instituted among Men. . . ." Jefferson was not playing a political game. And neither were the drafters of the Constitution, who may have been more practical than Jefferson but who shared his love of individual freedom. They provided both levels of government—federal and state—with impressive and extensive powers, although each surrounded with limitations (as we saw in detail in Chapters 3 and 4). Because the American Revolution was fought against an absentee, monarchical system thought to be tyrannical, the limitations were advertised more prominently than the powers. But no apologies were made for the powers. As Madison put it in *The Federalist,* No. 51, "You must *first* enable the government to control the governed; and in the next place oblige it to control itself" (emphasis added). If the Constitution had contained nothing but limitations, *that* would have been a political game meant to buy the support of those states that opposed giving the national government any powers beyond the very few granted in the Articles of Confederation. A government must be useful. And utility requires capacity for action.

Government must be able to make decisions about human needs, decisions that are sensitive to popular demands, decisions that are timely, and decisions that are appropriate. Governments have a purpose, and that purpose is the pursuit of goals we call public policies.

The job of this and the succeeding two chapters is to step beyond the play of politics and governmental institutions to look at the *purposive* actions of government—the policies. In the first section of this chapter, we will discuss the basis of public policies, public order, and control. We will then assess the rationale for government's involvement in the economy. In the next section, we will look at the goals of national economic policies. These policies have been organized into three categories: (1) policies that protect public order and private property; (2) policies that control or influence markets; and (3) policies that are designed to defend or enhance the vitality of our capitalist economy. The chapter is divided accordingly, with a section on each. Then we will provide an inventory of the controls that policy makers have to choose from when they draft policies. We will call these the "techniques of control" because they are means available to any government to get people to obey. Finally, we will consider the question, "In matters of public policy, what is the proper balance between government and freedom?"

## THE CENTRAL QUESTION

"What is the role of the government in the economy?"

# The Basis of Public Policy: Public Order

Try as we may to have a system of limited government, where freedom and control are balanced, control has to be the first priority, because without a society that is predictable and relatively safe—which is all we mean by public order—our freedom would not count for much.

The most deliberate form of government control we call "public policy." ***Public policy*** can be defined simply as an officially expressed intention backed by a sanction, which can be a reward or a punishment. Thus, a public policy is a law, a rule, a statute, an edict, a regulation, an order. Today, the term "public policy" is the term of preference, probably because it conveys more of an impression of flexibility and compassion than other terms. But the citizen, especially the student of political science, should never forget that "policy" and "police" have common origins. Both derive from *polis* and *polity,* which refer to the political community. Consequently, it must be clearly understood that all public policies are coercive, even when they are motivated by the best and most beneficent of intentions. Because public policies are coercive, many people wrongly conclude that all public policies—all government—should be opposed. For us, the coercive element in public policy should instill not absolute opposition but a healthy respect for the risks as well as the good that may be inherent in any public policy.

Another alert is in order before we begin this segment of the book. Chapters 14–17 may seem a bit historical for a subject that is constantly on newspaper front pages and network news broadcasts. But most public policies of any consequence have been in effect for decades, and it often takes years for them to have any measurable impact on the society or the economy. Despite the large numbers of bills proposed in Congress every year and despite the busy policy agenda of the president, things don't change substantially from year to year in the agencies responsible for implementing policies—that is, for governing. For example, no important policies inaugurating new programs or agencies have been added to the national government's powers and responsibilities since the mid-1970s, and few have been terminated. The only significant terminations have been the Civil Aeronautics Board (CAB), the Comprehensive Employment and Training Administration (CETA), the Interstate Commerce Commission (ICC), part of the agricultural price support program, and the Aid to Families with Dependent Children program (AFDC). And even with these, termination is a bit of an exaggeration. CAB and agriculture price supports are gone in name, but some of their functions continue to be performed in other federal agencies. AFDC "as we knew it" has been devolved to the states, but many federal standards restricting state welfare administration remain. CETA was replaced in part by another job training agency, and the ICC was terminated only after over fifteen years of effort.

The difficulty of terminating programs or substantially reducing them should not be a cause of despair, any more than the difficulty of creating new programs should lead people to give up hope for help from government. Policies *should* be difficult to adopt, because policies are coercive and government coercion should be used with care. And policies ought to be difficult to terminate, because they must be stable and enduring until proven to be no longer valuable. That is what governing is all about, and that is why all policies should be taken seriously and studied carefully, even when they seem a bit old and stale. To begin our policy inquiry, we might do well to make a slight revision in President Reagan's famous comment: Government is the problem *some* of the time; and government is the *solution* some of the time. The job of enlightened policy making is to determine what time it is.

## WHY IS GOVERNMENT INVOLVED IN THE ECONOMY?

The belief in the separation of public and private spheres is central to our understanding of the American economy. Americans are raised to believe that at one time the economy was wholly unregulated and operated on its own in the private sphere. It is true that the capitalist economy is real and has a definite structure, but it is not a structure that is independent of the state. Capitalism is a political economy; that is, the state created the conditions for a market economy and facilitated people's efforts in that economy. Capitalism is inconceivable outside of the policies that have structured it.

To convey what we are referring to when discussing the *political* economy of the market system, we must first define the term "market." The dictionary defines a market as a meeting of people for the purpose of private purchase and sale. Alternately, a market is either a place or a situation in which exchanges take place. So much for the dictionary. However, this definition of a market is not the one used by economists. For an economist, a market refers to all actual or potential economically relevant transactions. An economist's market does not require buyers facing sellers. A market refers to the totality of transactions, either in all goods or in particular goods, like the market in stock or in automobiles, and these transactions occur through a system of prices.

Both definitions of a market are correct. The politically relevant question, however, is that, assuming the dictionary definition accurately describes the market historically, and the economist's definition accurately describes the modern market, how did the economy move from the one to the other?

### The Bases of the Market Economy

Certain conditions had to be met to allow the modern market economy to emerge. These conditions in effect gave participants guarantees or rules of the game that induced them to "enter the market."

Some of these conditions had to be met before even a primitive market could take place, while other conditions only became necessary in connection with the modern market. Our objective here is to examine what these conditions are and what role government plays in establishing these conditions. Thus, we are trying to determine what guarantees must be in place to induce a farmer who grows grain, for example, to leave the farm and take the goods to market.

**Law and Order** As we saw in Chapter 1, the first condition is inherent in the very idea of government. That condition is that there must be a minimal degree of predictability about the basic rules of social interaction. In other words, there must be a system of law and order. A participant in the market must be able to assume not only that he or she can get to the market safely—that they won't be robbed on the way—but also that, having arrived, the people with whom he or she is dealing will behave predictably and will be bound by some number of calculable laws.

**Rules of Property** The second condition that must be met before people will participate in the market focuses on defining and dealing with property. If the market involves exchanges of ownership, there must be clear laws about what constitutes property. Property may be many things—your labor, or your ideas, or the bed you sleep in—but the very concept of property is inconceivable without laws that define what you can call your own.

Property ownership means we can exercise dominion over something that we have declared our own, and it is defined by laws that enable us to exercise that dominion, because something is not our own unless we can be reasonably certain that someone else cannot walk away with it. Trespass laws, for example, give concrete meaning to what constitutes property: A trespass law confers upon us a legal right to keep others away from certain kinds of property. It is clear, then, that laws or rules that define property are an essential part of the political economy. Before we can enter a market and participate in an exchange, we must be able to expect not only that we can lay claim to something but that those around us will respect that claim. In this sense, private property has a public component. Certainly there is a private component to property ownership, the dimensions of which have been debated philosophically for centuries; but the probability of enjoying property would be remote indeed unless there were laws that were widely enforced and accepted.

**Contracts** A third prerequisite that must be met before a market economy can operate involves rules governing the enforcement of contracts. There are, of course, societies that do not have a recognizable concept of contract, but our Western economy is highly dependent upon contract notions.

Contracts are closely related to property, of course, since contracts are only necessary in connection with exchanges of property, broadly construed. But the principles governing the enforcement of contracts differ from the principles governing the enforcement of property rights. A contract refers to a voluntary agreement between two or more private persons that governs future conduct. And while the agreement may be private, it has a distinctively public component: A contract must be enforceable, or it is meaningless.

**Rules of Exchange** The fourth prerequisite for the emergence or creation of a market economy is closely tied to the contract requirement. A market exists only when exchanges occur, and there must be rules governing exchange itself. Laws of exchange structure how, when, and under what conditions you can sell your property. You might think that once the laws of property have defined what you own that you ought to be able to transfer it, but that transfer is surrounded by rules that govern the transfer itself.

Certain kinds of exchanges are deemed off-limits altogether. For example, you own your own body, but under what conditions can you sell it? Laws about prostitution limit the selling or renting of one's body.

**Market Standards** The fifth prerequisite for the emergence of the modern free market is related to the fourth. When people engage in exchanges where they are not face-to-face—where they can't point to a good and say "I want that tomato or that fish"—both parties must have some way of understanding what the goods are that they are bargaining over. To do that, terminology must be standardized, and one of the essential acts any government does is to establish standard weights and measures.

With modern products, the standards must go beyond weights and measures; buyers and sellers must be able to specify both quantities and qualities of goods before they enter into their contracts. These buyers and sellers must know, for example, what is meant by long and short staple cotton, and everything in between; they must know what they are getting when they order automobile tires of a particular quality. Many of these standards today are developed by private sector trade associations, of course, but those standards are often incorporated into government regulations, and so they acquire governmental status—or, more important, they are protected by governmental action through the courts. If a member of the porcelain enamel association, for example, agrees to produce a certain type of enamel according to the trade association's specifications, they can be sued if they cut corners and evade those standards.

**Public Goods** The sixth prerequisite to the operation of a market economy involves the provision of public goods. As we saw in Chapter 1, this term refers to facilities the state provides, because no single participant can afford to provide those facilities itself. The provisions of public goods may extend from supplying the physical marketplace itself—like the commons in New England towns—to the provision of an interstate highway system to stimulate the trucking industry. The provision of social goods is essential to market operation, and the manner in which the government provides those goods will affect the market's character.

**Labor Force** The seventh prerequisite to the emergence of a market economy is the creation of a labor force. Every society has provisions that force people to work. One of the best, albeit most recent, examples of these provisions is the requirement for universal compulsory education in this society: People are educated so that they can learn the skills necessary to function in the market. Long before education laws, however, we had poor houses, vagrancy laws, and other more police-oriented means of forcing people to work; these rules meant that people could starve or be punished if they failed to earn their own keep. Our welfare system today serves the same purpose: We adjust the welfare system in cycles to be sure that the support we give is uncomfortable enough that people will prefer working to retiring on the low income they will get from welfare.

**Rules for Liability** The final prerequisite is not always obvious, but it is nonetheless critical to creating the conditions for a market economy. Before this market economy can operate, there must be provisions for allocating responsibility. Although a state's system of law and order allocates responsibility for criminal behavior in some areas, there are vast numbers of risks that fall outside of the criminal system. Thus people will be reluctant to enter a market that doesn't assure them that their liability for unintended consequences of their actions will be limited. For example, what happens if you are in the marketplace showing someone your goods and your wagon wheel comes loose and injures your neighbor's cow? In a more contemporary context, would you enter the market in petroleum products if there were no limits on your liability for oil spills?

To summarize, it is difficult to understand why the modern economy has its present shape without understanding what factors regularly affected its development. That is the history of the political economy. It should be clear to you that the idea of an unregulated market is a myth, and that the structure of the capitalist economy and every other economic system is highly dependent upon a series of governmental actions that make it possible for that economy to maintain itself in one form or another.

## Managing the Economy

Until 1929, most Americans believed that the government had little role to play in managing the economy. The world was guided by Adam Smith's theory that the economy, if left to its own devices, would produce full employment and maximum production. This traditional view of the relationship between government and the economy crumbled in 1929 before the stark reality of the Great Depression of 1929–1933. Some misfortune befell nearly everyone. Around 20 percent of the work force became unemployed, and few of these individuals had any monetary resources or the old family farm to fall back upon. Banks failed, wiping out the savings of millions who had been prudent enough or fortunate enough to have any. Thousands of businesses failed, throwing middle-class Americans onto the bread lines alongside unemployed laborers and dispossessed farmers. The Great Depression had finally proven to Americans that imperfections in the economic system could exist.

Demands mounted for the federal government to take action. In Congress, some Democrats proposed that the federal government finance public works to aid the economy and put people back to work. Other members of Congress introduced legislation to provide federal grants to the states to assist them in their relief efforts.

When President Franklin D. Roosevelt took office in 1933, he energetically threw the federal government into the business of fighting the Depression. He proposed a variety of temporary measures to provide federal relief and work programs. Most of the programs he proposed were to be financed by the federal government but administered by the states. In addition to these temporary measures,

Roosevelt presided over the creation of several important federal programs designed to provide future economic security for Americans. Since that time, the government has been instrumental in ensuring that the economy will never again collapse as it did during the Depression.

Closer to our time, during the 1970s and early 1980s, inflation was one of America's most vexing problems. Everyone agreed that inflation is caused by too many dollars chasing too few goods, bidding up prices, but there was much disagreement over what to do about it—what public policies were most appropriate and effective. The first effort, beginning in 1971, was the adoption of strict controls over wages, prices, dividends, and rents—that is, authorizing an agency in the executive branch to place limits on what wage people could be paid for their work, what rent their real estate could bring, and what interest they could get on their money. After two years of effort, these particular policies were fairly well discredited, and the search resumed for one or more other policies to fight inflation. Since oil prices had become so clearly a major source of inflation in the late 1970s, President Carter experimented with the licensing of imports of oil from the Middle East, with tariffs and excise taxes on unusually large oil profits made by producers, and with sales taxes on gasoline at the pump to discourage all casual consumption of gasoline. President Carter also attempted to reduce consumer spending in general by raising income taxes, especially Social Security taxes on employees.

The continuing high rate of inflation paved the way to an entirely different approach by President Reagan in the early 1980s. In place of oil import licensing and selective tax increases, President Reagan proposed and got a general tax cut. The Reagan theory was that if tax cuts were deep enough and were guaranteed to endure, they would increase the "supply" of money, would change people's psychology from pessimism to optimism and would thereby encourage individuals and corporations to invest enough and produce enough to get us out of inflation. At the same time, President Reagan supported the continuation of the high Social Security taxes enacted during the Carter administration, which probably went further than any other method to fight inflation by discouraging consumption. As we have said, inflation is caused by too many dollars chasing too few goods, bidding up prices. Any tax will take dollars out of consumption, but since the Social Security tax hits middle and lower-middle-income people the heaviest, and since these middle-income people are the heaviest consumers, such a tax reduces consumer dollars. Another policy supported by the Reagan administration was restraining the amount of credit in the economy by pushing up interest rates.

Inflation was finally reduced from its historic highs of nearly 20 percent down toward 2 and 3 percent each year. But no one is absolutely certain which policy, if any, contributed to this reduction. After all, the two-year recession of 1981–1982 produced such significant increases in unemployment that consumption was cut, and any cut in consumption—whether from a tax policy or a loss of wages—will reduce prices. At the same time, the international price of oil dropped, independently of our policies. Consequently, we do not know exactly what policy to adopt the next time inflation becomes a problem. But rest assured, no government will stand by and permit inflation or unemployment or global economic competition to become a problem without trying to do something about it.

# Goals: Substantive Uses of Economic Policy

Let's begin with an examination of the substantive uses of economic policy by looking at how governments implement public policies and achieve their economic goals. By maintaining public order throughout the history of the United States, both the national and the state governments have fostered a market economy that has enabled individuals and companies to function and has encouraged both private ownership and government intervention. The U.S. economy is no accident; it is the result of specific policies that have sustained massive economic growth. We have organized the substantive uses of economic policies according to the goals those policies are designed to achieve: 1) maintaining public order and private property; 2) promoting markets, including encouraging specific sectors of the economy and maintaining market efficiency and equity; and 3) defending and enhancing the vitality of America's capitalist economy.

As you read this section and encounter the many ways in which government intervenes in the economy, keep in mind two important questions: "In confronting a particular economic goal, what should government do?" and "What would be different without government and its policies?" Although economic growth or low inflation are economic goals that everyone can agree on, the public policies designed to achieve these goals are open to debate. Indeed, one area of heated debate in recent years has been over whether the national government should be involved in the nation's economy at all. In response to this question, many have cited the long-held American belief that at one time the economy was unregulated and operated on its own without government support. In our view, this belief is a myth. As we will see, a capitalist economy is highly dependent on governmental actions that make it possible for an economy to develop.

## Policies for Public Order and Private Property

We begin our discussion of substantive uses of economic policy with public order policies for two reasons. First, these policies lay and maintain the foundations of the economy. Second, because so many of these policies are old and established state government policies, most people don't appreciate them as policies and go on believing that the U.S. economy was once "unregulated" by the government.

**Federalism and Public Order** Under the American federalist system, there is no national police force, there is no national criminal law, there is no national common law, there are no national property laws. The national government does have a few policies directly concerned with public order, however, most of which are mandated by the Constitution itself. These include laws against counterfeiting, against using the mails to defraud, and against crossing state lines to avoid arrest for a violation of state laws. A few other offenses against public order have simply been presumed to be interstate crimes against which federal status have been enacted, mainly in the twentieth century. Important examples include kidnapping, narcotics dealing, and political subversion. But virtually all of the multitudes of other policies dealing with public order and the foundations of the economy are left to the states and their local governments.

**Policies and Property** Another unique feature of the American approach to public order is the emphasis placed on *private property*. Private property is valued in most of the cultures of the world but not as centrally as in the United States, where it is virtually a part of public order itself. And despite their importance, most of the laws protecting and extending property are state laws. The most important examples are laws against trespass and laws protecting and defending contracts.

Not all the policies toward property are policies that regulate the conduct of people who would trespass or take property. Many policies positively encourage property ownership on the theory that property owners are better citizens and therefore more respectful of public order. One of the most important national policies in American history was ***homesteading,*** otherwise called "squatting," which permitted people to gain ownership of property by occupying public or unclaimed lands, living on the land for a specified period of time, and making certain minimal improvements on that land.

Many other policies encourage homeownership today, the most significant being that part of the tax code that permits homeowners to deduct interest paid on mortgage loans from their taxes. In addition, three large federal agencies—the Federal Housing Administration (FHA), the Farmers Home Administration (FMHA), and the Veterans Administration (VA)—encourage homeownership by making mortgage loans available at interest rates below the market rate. The Farm Credit Administration (FCA) operates the extensive Farm Credit System, whose primary function is to make long-term and short-term loans to improve farm and rural real estate, loans available only to bona fide farm operators and farm-related companies who are members of the farm credit system. Many of these agencies make direct loans at below-market rates. Some of them (in particular the FHA and the VA) also insure or guarantee loans, so that private commercial banks have less risk and can charge proportionately lower interest rates.

**AMERICAN POLITICAL DEVELOPMENT**

Nineteenth-century homesteading policies encouraged Americans to settle new lands and expand the nation by granting them ownership of the western lands they used. Contemporary "homesteading" involves "squatters' rights" by the homeless, who occupy abandoned buildings in urban areas.

## Making and Maintaining a National Market Economy

Valuable as the states have been in fostering private property, their separate boundaries, their separate laws, and their separate traditions have also been a barrier to those enterprises seeking to expand beyond local markets. In fact, the protectionism of some states against others was precisely why our first constitution, the Articles of Confederation, was ultimately considered a failure and in need of replacement. Giving Congress the powers of Article I, Section 8, enabled the national government to provide a system of roads, canals, and communications that would foster a regional and ultimately a national market. In *Gibbons v. Ogden*, one of the most important cases the Supreme Court has ever handed down, the states were told in no uncertain terms that they could not pass laws that would tend to interrupt or otherwise burden the free flow of commerce among the states.[1] In the twentieth century, one of the major reasons why Congress began to adopt national business regulatory policies was that the regulated companies themselves felt burdened by the inconsistencies among the states. These companies often preferred a single, national regulatory authority, no matter how burdensome, because they would have consistency throughout the United States and could thereby treat the nation as a single market.[2] Table 14.1 provides a historical overview of regulation in our federal system.



**Promoting the Market** During the nineteenth century, the national government was almost exclusively a promoter of markets. National roads and canals were built to tie states and regions together. National tariff policies promoted domestic markets by restricting imported goods; a tax on an import raised its price and weakened its ability to compete with similar domestic products. The national government also heavily subsidized the railroad. Until the 1840s, railroads were thought to be of limited commercial value. But between 1850 and 1872, Congress granted over 100 million acres of public domain land to railroad interests, and state and local governments pitched in an estimated $280 million in cash and credit. Before the end of the century, 35,000 miles of track existed—almost half the world's total.

**AMERICAN POLITICAL DEVELOPMENT**

One view of the American founding suggests that the protection of property and the market economy, as well as the promotion of commerce, was a principle purpose, if not *the* principle purpose, of the Constitution.

SOURCE: Charles A. Beard, *An Economic Interpretation of the Constitution of the United States* (New York: Free Press, [1913] 1986).

Railroads were not the only clients of federal support aimed at fostering the expansion of private markets. Many sectors of agriculture received federal subsidies during the nineteenth century, and some still receive these subsidies today. Despite significant cuts in the agriculture budget in the 1980s, federal subsidies still cost the government nearly $10 billion per year, including $1.4 billion for sugar and $2 billion for the agriculture market in general, through programs such as rural electrification.

In the twentieth century, traditional promotional techniques were expanded and some new ones were invented. For example, a great proportion of the promotional activities of the national government are now done indirectly through ***categorical grants-in-aid*** (see Chapter 3). The national government offers grants

[1]Gibbons v. Ogden, 9 Wheaton 1 (1824). See also Chapter 3. This case was reaffirmed sixty years later even when the states were attempting to defend their own citizens from discriminatory charges by railroads for services rendered within their own state. The Supreme Court argued that the route of an interstate railroad could not be subdivided into its separate state segments for purposes of regulation. See Wabash, St. Louis and Pacific Railway Co. v. Illinois, 118 U.S. 557 (1886).

[2]Compare with Gabriel Kolko, *The Triumph of Conservatism* (New York: Free Press, 1963), Chapter 6.

TABLE 14.1

**Federalism and the Regulation of the U.S. Economy**

| | NATIONAL GOVERNMENT AND ECONOMIC REGULATION | STATE GOVERNMENTS AND ECONOMIC REGULATION |
|---|---|---|
| **Nineteenth century** | | |
| Pre–Civil War | Fugitive slaves | Property ownership |
| Post–Civil War | Railroads | Monopolies |
| | Interstate trusts and monopolies | Price discrimination |
| | | Contracts and their enforcement |
| | | Apprenticeship |
| | | Professional licensing |
| | | Compulsory education |
| | | Public utilities |
| | | Banking |
| | | Slaves (in Southern states) |
| | | Agricultural markets |
| | | Oil and gas extraction |
| | | Coal mines |
| **Twentieth century** | | |
| Pre-1933 | Unfair trade practices | All the nineteenth-century policies (except slavery) plus |
| | National banks | |
| | Impure food and drugs | |
| Post-1933 | Stock markets | Child labor |
| | Agricultural markets | Working conditions |
| | Trade unions | Equal employment opportunity |
| | Coal mines | Equal education opportunity |
| | Telecommunications | TV cable access |
| | Natural gas transport | Local land use (zoning) |
| | Atomic energy | Land conservation |
| | Equal employment and other civil rights | Building construction standards |
| | The environment | |
| | Consumer product safety | |

to states on condition that the state (or local) government undertake a particular activity. Thus, in order to use motor transportation to improve national markets, a national highway system of 900,000 miles was built during the 1930s, based on a formula whereby the national government would pay 50 percent of the cost if the state would provide the other 50 percent. And then for over twenty years, beginning in the late 1950s, the federal government constructed over 45,000 miles of interstate highways. This was brought about through a program whereby the national government agreed to pay 90 percent of the construction costs on the condition that each state provide for 10 percent of the costs of any portion of a highway built within its boundaries.[3] There are examples of U.S. government promotional policy in each of the country's major industrial sectors.

Among the many contemporary examples of policies promoting private industry, Sematech may be the most instructive. Sematech is a nonprofit, research and development (R&D) consortium of major U.S. computer microchip manufacturers, set up to work with government and academic institutions to reestablish U.S. leadership in semiconductor manufacturing. (The United States appeared to be in danger of losing out to the Japanese in this area in the 1980s.) The results of its research are distributed among the fourteen consortium members.[4] The federal commitment to the promotion of the microchip industry through Sematech alone amounts to nearly $100 million per year. The federal government's broader Advanced Technology Program, of which Sematech is a part, deals out close to $500 million per year to promote expansion in high technology.

In fact, the entire information industry has had particularly strong support from President Clinton and Vice President Gore. They put the White House on the Internet, and they have lobbied continuously for federal aid for computer literacy and to get "every classroom in America . . . converted to the information superhighway."[5] Despite cuts in the budgets of most federal activities, newfound generosity in many modern government-funded projects has spurred private commercial development. Nevertheless, federal R&D money is still "pork barrel," or as Republicans call it, "corporate welfare."

Although Republicans have officially opposed the Sematech subsidies, most support for the high-tech industry is bipartisan, in response to arguments that development of this infant industry is in the national interest. Of course, a certain amount of promotion of "infant industries" is justified today, just as tariffs were justified in the late nineteenth century to support infant industries. But as these infants grow up, the government policies supporting them tend to continue. Congress is better at making promotional policies to meet national commercial needs than it is at terminating those policies when the needs have been met.

**Regulating the Market** As the American economy prospered throughout the nineteenth century, some companies grew so large that they were recognized as possessing "market power." This meant that they were powerful enough to eliminate competitors and to impose conditions on consumers rather than cater to consumer demand. The growth of billion-dollar corporations led to collusion among companies to control prices, much to the dismay of smaller businesses

[3]The act of 1955 officially designated the interstate highways as the National System of Interstate and Defense Highways. It was indirectly a major part of President Eisenhower's defense program. But it was just as obviously a "pork barrel" policy as any rivers and harbors legislation.

[4]The members are AMD, Compaq, Conexant, Hewlett-Packard, Hyundai, Intel, IBM, Lucent, Motorola, Philips, STMicroelectronics, Siemens, Texas Instruments, and TSMC. What the two hundred other companies in this industry do in regard to the support given to Sematech is another story.

[5]President Clinton, 1996 State of the Union address.

and ordinary consumers. Moreover, the expanding economy was more mechanized and this involved greater dangers to employees as well as to consumers.

Small businesses, laborers, farmers, and consumers all began to clamor for protective regulation. Although the states had been regulating businesses in one way or another all along, interest groups turned toward Washington as economic problems appeared to be beyond the reach of the individual state governments. If markets were national, there would have to be national regulation.[6]

The first national regulatory policy was the Interstate Commerce Act of 1887, which created the first national independent regulatory commission, the Interstate Commerce Commission (ICC), designed to control the monopolistic practices of the railroads. Two years later, the Sherman Antitrust Act extended regulatory power to cover all monopolistic practices, including "trusts" or any other agreement between companies to eliminate competition. These were strengthened in 1914 with the enactment of the Federal Trade Act (creating the Federal Trade Commission, or FTC) and the Clayton Act. The only significant addition of national regulatory policy beyond interstate regulation of trade, however, was the establishment of the Federal Reserve System in 1913, which was given powers to regulate the banking industry along with its general monetary powers.

**AMERICAN POLITICAL DEVELOPMENT**

The early economic regulatory functions of the U.S. government involved the creation of the Interstate Commerce Commission (1887) to regulate the power of railroads. Today, most sectors of the economy are regulated. In recent years, the government has sought to curb alleged monopolistic practices by computer software companies.

The modern epoch of comprehensive national regulation began in the 1930s. Most of the regulatory programs of the 1930s were established to regulate the conduct of companies within specifically designated sectors of American industry. For example, the jurisdiction of one agency was the securities industry; the jurisdiction of another was the radio (and eventually television) industry. Another was banking. Another was coal mining; still another was agriculture. When Congress turned once again toward regulatory policies in the 1970s, it became still more bold, moving beyond the effort to regulate specific sectors of industry toward regulating some aspect of the entire economy. The scope or jurisdiction of agencies such as the Occupational Safety and Health Administration (OSHA), the Consumer Product Safety Commission (CPSC), and the Environmental Protection Agency (EPA) is as broad and as wide as the entire economy, indeed the entire society.

We will be hearing a lot more about another area of modern federal economic regulation in the years to come: Maintaining open competition for access to the Internet. In October 1997, the Department of Justice brought an antitrust suit against Microsoft, accusing the company of using its near-monopoly over personal computer operating systems to eliminate competition from Netscape's Navigator browser software by requiring that computers run by Microsoft's Windows 98 operating system give users a preloaded icon for Internet Explorer.

[6]For an account of the relationship between mechanization and law, see Lawrence Friedman, *A History of American Law* (New York: Simon and Schuster, 1973), pp. 409–29.

Computer manufacturing companies were forced to comply or "lose their Windows license and thus lose their business. . . ."[7] Such a practice of forcing a vendor to take Explorer in order to carry Windows 98 constituted "product tying," a violation of antitrust law (the oldest of federal economic regulations). The Antitrust Division of the Justice Department had a very strong case against Bill Gates and Microsoft until late 1998, when Netscape sold itself to America Online (AOL) for $4.2 billion. As Microsoft put it, the Netscape/AOL deal yanks the rug out from the government's case" by proving that access to the Internet had become "more competitive than ever."[8] However, there still was a case against Microsoft for allegedly violating antitrust laws in the past, which could involve Microsoft in substantial fines if it should lose. On the other hand, Microsoft may prove that the action by the Antitrust Division against it might have been the catalyst for the merger of AOL and Netscape, providing the very competition that the case was seeking to create.[9]



**Deregulation** Today, so-called economic conservatives, as represented by former Presidents Reagan and Bush and the "moderate wing" of the Republican party, are in principle opposed to virtually any sort of government intervention in the economy.[10] As President Reagan himself put it, they see government not as part of the solution but as part of the problem. They adamantly oppose intervention by techniques of promoting commerce and are even more opposed to intervention through techniques of regulation. They believe that markets would be bigger and healthier if not regulated at all.

The ***deregulation*** movement actually began under Presidents Ford and Carter. Their accomplishments include the Securities Act Amendment of 1975, the Railroad Revitalization Act of 1976, the Airline Deregulation Act of 1978, the Staggers Rail Deregulation Act of 1980, the Depository Institution Deregulation and Monetary Control Act of 1980, and the Motor Carrier Act of 1980.

President Reagan's approach to deregulation is a good lesson in the relationship between executive management and legislative authority. Reagan almost immediately provided for an average 20 percent cut in the budgets of all the regulatory agencies. Although this cutback did not have any significant effect on the total budget of the federal government, because the regulatory agencies are not very large, it certainly required severe reductions in the agencies' staff and

[7]*Economist,* 31 January 1998, pp. 65–66. See also *Congressional Quarterly Weekly,* 16 May 1998, p. 1312.

[8]Michael Krantz, "AOL, You've Got Netscape," *Time Magazine,* 7 December 1998, pp. 58–59.

[9]For instructive speculations on this case, and for a comparison with the first great antitrust trial of the century (against Northern Securities Company) to "bust up" the railroad monopoly held by J.P. Morgan (a direct corporate ancestor of Bill Gates), see Floyd Norris, "Does the Microsoft Trial Verdict Really Matter?" *New York Times,* 1 March 1999, p. 20.

[10]Actually, this point of view is better understood as nineteenth-century liberalism, or free-market liberalism, following the theories of Adam Smith. However, after the New Deal appropriated "liberal" for their pro-government point of view, the Republican antigovernment wing got tagged with the conservative label. With Reagan, the conservative label took on more popular connotations, while "liberal" became stigmatized as the "L-word."

AMERICAN POLITICAL DEVELOPMENT

One measure of the massive growth of federal government regulation is the increased number of pages in the *Federal Register*. In 1940, the *Federal Register* had 5,307 pages. By 1967, the *Federal Register* had 21,087 pages. This number doubled by 1974 (45,422 pages) and nearly doubled again by 1980 (87,012 pages). Although the numbers have decreased in recent years, they have still been at least ten times what they were in 1940.

SOURCE: Harold W. Stanley and Richard G. Niemi, *Vital Statistics on American Politics*, 5th ed. (Washington, DC: Congressional Quarterly Press 1995), p. 253.

therefore severe reductions in the level and vigor of regulatory activity by the federal government.

Reagan's second approach to deregulation-by-management was his appointment of agency board members who were not in sympathy with the regulatory mission of the specific agency. In fact, some of the members of these commissions were genuinely hostile to the mission of their agency.[11] Another important approach President Reagan took to the task of changing the direction of regulation was "presidential oversight." One of his first actions after taking office was Executive Order 12291, issued February 17, 1981, which gave the Office of Management and Budget (OMB) the authority to review all proposals by all executive branch agencies for new regulations to be applied to companies or people within their jurisdiction. By this means, President Reagan succeeded in reducing the total number of regulations issued by federal agencies to such an extent that the number of pages in the *Federal Register* dropped from 87,000 in 1980 to 49,600 in 1987.[12] Although Presidents Bush and Clinton also favored deregulation as a principle, the number of pages crept up steadily after 1987, reaching 69,680 by 1993. This had dropped slightly to 68,101 by 1994, and by 1996 President Clinton was claiming an additional reduction of 16,000 pages of "unnecessary regulations." These might not show up as 16,000 reduced pages in the *Federal Register*, but they do amount to a substantial reduction in regulation, and they are all the more significant coming from a Democratic president who not only reduced the number of regulations but was proud of his actions.

President Clinton's proud support of deregulation, coupled with the election of Republican majorities in 1994, 1996 and 1998, suggests that the spirit of antiregulation will stay alive awhile longer. Substantial deregulation in the telecommunications industry and in agriculture, and officially supported relaxation of regulatory activity in civil rights, pollution control, protection of endangered species, and natural resources, also tend to support that expectation.

Yet as impressive as the deregulation movement has been, there is another side. First, it is extremely significant that almost no important regulatory pro-

[11]For a good evaluation of Reagan's efforts, see Kenneth J. Meier, *Regulation: Politics, Bureaucracy, and Economics* (New York: St. Martin's Press, 1985), Chapters 4, 6, and 8; and George Eads and Michael Fix, "Regulatory Policy," in *The Reagan Experiment,* ed. John L. Palmer and Isabel Sawhill (Washington, DC: Urban Institute Press, 1982), Chapter 5.

[12]The *Federal Register* is the daily publication of all official acts of Congress, the president, and the administrative agencies. A law or executive order is not legally binding until published in the *Federal Register*.

TABLE 14.2

**Attitudes toward Government Regulation**

| | 1948 | 1952 | 1962 | 1974 | 1978 | 1979 | 1980 | 1987 | 1993 | 1996 |
|---|---|---|---|---|---|---|---|---|---|---|
| Too much | 35% | 49% | 13% | 28% | 43% | 47% | 54% | 38% | 37% | 35% |
| Right amount | 27 | 29 | 27 | 38 | 23 | 23 | 19 | 32 | 30 | 38 |
| Not enough, need more | 23 | 7 | 29 | 24 | 25 | 24 | 19 | 23 | 28 | 19 |

SOURCES: Figures for 1948, 1952, 1962, 1978, 1979, and 1980 are from various national polls as reported in Seymour Martin Lipset and William Schneider, *The Confidence Gap* (New York: Free Press, 1983), pp. 222–28. Reprinted by permission. Figures for 1974 are an average of Harris polls between 1974 and 1977, during which there was "no clear trend." Figures for 1987 are based on *Wall Street Journal* polls. Figures for 1993 are based on Gallup polls. 1996 data from Princeton Survey Research Associates for Knight-Ridder Washington Bureau. Allowances should be made for different ways in which the questions were asked.

gram has been terminated. This means that virtually all of the legislative authority and administrative agencies are in place if the time should come when popular majorities and congressional majorities revive support for more regulation. And just as there are many reasons to favor deregulation, there are a number of reasons and factors favoring regulation and re-regulation.[13]

In some instances, the government is responding to public opinion. Table 14.2 gives an interesting history of American attitudes toward regulation, support for which has modestly but noticeably increased since 1980. Political opinion is particularly pronounced on specific issues. For example, one poll in mid-1992 found that more than 60 percent of those questioned supported increased regulation of guns and alcohol.[14] Another 1992 poll found that despite the country's many economic problems, Americans favored more environmental regulation even if forced to choose between environment and economic growth.[15] On certain moral issues, such as abortions, drug dealing, and pornography, Americans tend to support even higher levels of regulation, in the form of abortion laws, stiffer prison sentences for convicted drug dealers and users, and limits on free speech over the Internet for items considered obscene or pornographic. The welfare reform law of 1996 (the Personal Responsibility and Work Opportunity Act, PRA for short) imposed a number of new regulations on dependent mothers.[16] There was so much popular support for these restrictions on single mothers that even President Clinton went along and became the major supporter of PRA.

[13]For an excellent treatment of "why regulate," with a somewhat different list of reasons, see Alan Stone, *Regulation and Its Alternatives* (Washington, DC: Congressional Quarterly Press, 1982), Chapters 3 through 5.

[14]Gordon Black poll, press release, The Gordon Black Corporation, Rochester, NY, May 1992.

[15]Roper poll, in Faye Rice, "Next Steps for the Environment," *Fortune,* 19 October 1992, p. 98.

[16]For an inventory of the strict regulations imposed on dependent mothers, see Gwendolyn Mink, *Welfare's End* (Ithaca, NY: Cornell University Press, 1998), especially Chapters 3 and 4.

# *Globalization, Government, and the Economy*

Although deepening interdependence and the revolution in information technology are tearing down barriers to free trade, worries over the "competitiveness" of American corporations and industries remain a critical concern of government.[1] President Bill Clinton once observed that a country is "like a big corporation competing in the global marketplace," implying that, for example, the United States and Germany are competitors in the same way that General Motors and Ford are.[2]

In order to ensure that America remains competitive, the government devotes considerable attention to the trade balance. A significant increase in the perpetual trade deficit with a country like Japan will probably mushroom into

[1]A commission created by President Ronald Reagan defined "competitiveness" as "the degree to which a nation can, under free and fair-market competition, produce goods and services that meet the test of international markets while simultaneously expanding the real income of its citizens." Source: Report of the President's Commission on Industrial Competitiveness in *Global Competition: The New Reality*, vol. 2 (Washington, DC: U.S. Government Printing Office, 1985), p. 6.

[2]Quoted in Paul Krugman, "Competitiveness: A Dangerous Obsession," *Foreign Affairs* (March/April 1994), p. 29.

a domestic political issue. Such increases in the deficit lead to fluctuations in the value of the dollar relative to other currencies. A strong dollar damages American exports and makes foreign imports more attractive to U.S. consumers. It is recognized that the government's economic policies can have a powerful influence in determining whether or not the nation meets the test of competitiveness. As noted in this chapter, making and maintaining a national market economy in a global marketplace tends to involve cycles of regulation and deregulation. When the U.S. economy was sagging in the late 1980s and early 1990s, there were calls for stronger government economic intervention in the form of closer government-business interaction, relaxed antitrust enforcement, and policies to "target" and promote strategic industries (e.g., semiconductors).[3] More recently, "deregulation" and increased competition have become the catchwords of the government efforts to foster competitiveness.

Concerns about competitiveness dictate that the government closely monitor the trade-related activities of foreign governments and firms. Whenever foreign governments or firms are accused of unfair trading practices—for example, the European Union's agricultural subsidies or Chinese disrespect for intellectual property rights—the Office of the United States Trade Representative, an organ of the executive branch, is obliged to investigate and, if necessary, recommend retaliatory action. This concern with ensuring fair trade derives at least in part from the perception that any gains in market share on the part of foreign-owned firms somehow mean a loss of jobs for American workers. As MIT economist Lester Thurow points out, "Those who lost their jobs in autos and machine tools as American firms lost market share at home and abroad typically took a 30 to 50 percent wage reduction, if they were young. If they were over 50 years of age, they were usually permanently exiled to the periphery of the low-wage, part-time labor market."[4] At a time when the perpetual U.S. trade imbalance with Japan was becoming a hotly contested political issue, then-President Bush felt compelled to assert that the purpose of his 1992 visit to Tokyo was all about securing "jobs, jobs, jobs" for American workers. (Ironically, as it turned out, Bush's desire to portray himself as the sturdy champion of the American worker was undermined when he suddenly became ill at a state dinner and regurgitated in the lap of the Japanese prime minister.)

[3]See, for example, Jeffrey A. Hart, *Rival Capitalists: International Competitiveness in the United States, Japan, and Western Europe* (Ithaca, NY: Cornell University Press, 1992), pp. 223–79.
[4]Lester Thurow, "The Fight over Competitiveness," *Foreign Affairs* (July/August 1994), p. 191.

DEBATING THE ISSUES

# Regulation: For and Against

*In his 1996 State of the Union address, President Clinton declared that "The era of big government is over." Even so, debate continues to rage over the size, power, and scope of government regulations. Supporters argue that government regulation continues to be the only effective means of protecting the environment, the workplace, public health and safety. Foes argue that regulations impose unnecessary costs that stifle competition and profits, and that the marketplace can control many of the problems now regulated by the government. Public administration professor Susan J. Tolchin and reporter Martin Tolchin argue that sensible regulation is indispensable to modern society. Lawyer Robert B. Charles argues that democratic accountability fails to control regulation and proposes several changes.*

## TOLCHIN AND TOLCHIN

By the late 1970s, complaints of excessive regulation had become management's all-purpose cop-out. Were profits too low? Blame regulation. Were prices too high? Blame regulation. Were inadequate funds and manpower earmarked for research and development? Blame regulation for sapping both funds and manpower. Was American industry unable to compete with foreign competitors? Blame regulation.

In a highly technological society such as ours, the need for increased regulation is manifest. It is inconceivable to think of "lessening the regulatory burden," as some put it, at a time when private industry has the power to alter our genes, invade our privacy, and destroy our environment. A single industrial accident . . . is capable of taking a huge toll in human life and suffering. Only the government has the power to create and enforce the social regulations that protect citizens from the awesome consequences of technology run amuck. Only the government has the ability to raise the national debate above the "balance sheet" perspective of American industry. This is not to dismiss the many socially conscious businessmen who are concerned with the public interest, but, unfortunately, they do not represent the political leadership of the business community. After all, the "bottom line" for business is making profit, not improving the quality of the environment or the work place. Its primary obligation is to its shareholders, not to the community at large. . . .

The rush to deregulate is a return to the law of the jungle. Ultimately, it would remove protections against the industrial excesses of the past, and return us to the nineteenth century—when child labor was commonplace, the work place was a threat to life and limb, *caveat emptor* was the prevailing consumer doctrine, and the nation's waterways were becoming public sewers. . . .

Federal regulation is the connective tissue of a civilized society. As technological and scientific advances lead us into unknown worlds with unimaginable dangers, society needs more protection, not less. This means more government regulation, intelligently crafted, skillfully managed, and sensitively enforced.[1]

## CHARLES

America may rapidly be drifting from "wise and frugal" government into a tumbling current of regulatory whitewater. Today, mangroves of environmental regulation overlap, intertwine, and grow off the pages of the *Federal Register.*

The president introduces laws, Congress enacts them, and both are accountable. Regulators, on the other hand, are not. Federal regulators are powerful, unelected, essentially unaccountable and often preoccupied, not with public policy questions that generate big legislation, but with making and enforcing the narrowest of rules.

[For example, a] recent study by the American Enterprise Institute (AEI) and Harvard showed that "neither the House of Representatives nor the Senate is a key player in defining the details of many environmental policies." The study concluded that "a striking feature of many federal environmental policies is the extent to which program staff within the EPA [Environmental Protection Agency] play a central role in developing and advancing options."

. . . America must get out of this regulatory whitewater and back into the clear water of "wise and frugal government." Here are concrete measures that would go far toward that end:

—Fund all unfunded mandates, and enact no more.
—Unabashedly make a national priority of stopping rule by regulocracy.
—Make the White House (or the Office of Information Resource Management) conduct a comprehensive review of all existing regulations, identifying significant rules and consolidating, rewriting, or rescinding every rule that poses excess transaction costs with unproven benefit.
—Support existing initiatives to restore flexibility to the regulatory process. . . .
—Specifically concerning environmental regulation, offer incentives for pollution abatement, performance standard (instead of command and control), and greater cooperation with business on phase-in periods and cost estimates; and prioritize the environmental harms that must be addressed by business.

Benefits obviously derive from limited, well-crafted, and prudently enforced regulations. . . . But America is at a crossroads. The next several years will determine whether the new regulocracy can be reined in. Otherwise, the consequences could be more than anyone bargained for.[2]

[1]Susan J. Tolchin and Martin Tolchin, *Dismantling America: The Rush to Deregulate* (New York: Oxford University Press, 1983), pp. 4–5, 257, 276.
[2]Robert B. Charles, "From Democracy to Regulocracy?" *The World & I* (July 1994). [pub. by the *Washington Times*]

Other waves of government regulation are more political in origin. The president may owe to an interest group or a sector of the economy a particular debt that can best be met by adding or subtracting a regulatory policy.[17] A third reason is morality. A number of examples have already been given of federal and state regulations aimed at "criminalizing" conduct deemed immoral—taxes on alcohol and

[17]See, for example, Martha Derthick and Paul Quirk, *The Politics of Deregulation* (Washington, DC: Brookings Institution, 1985), pp. 33–34.

tobacco products, for example. Moreover, there are signs that *more* morals-based regulation may be forthcoming, because morality is perhaps the strongest motivation regarding regulations on abortion, drug sales, AIDS testing, smoking in public, labeling foods, etc. Efficiency is a fourth reason for changes in regulation of the marketplace, because competition usually forces companies to be more efficient. For example, although many Americans believe that competition happens naturally when companies are left alone, they have also historically supported "antitrust" regulation to force certain companies to be more competitive by prohibiting them from eliminating their competition by acquisition or by collusive deals to control prices. A fifth reason for regulation is pure and simple convenience. Americans are quick to say "there ought to be a law" when people, places, or things stand in their way or add to their risk of injury. Most of the time it is difficult to draw a clear line between regulations aimed at eliminating injuries and inconveniences, and regulations aimed at reducing the *risk* of such injuries and inconveniences. But these are practical matters, and regulations vary according to how many people feel a regulation will have the desired practical consequences. Finally, a sixth reason for regulation is equity, such as when a government program seeks to reduce racial discrimination in the workplace.

As a general rule, conservatives tend to favor more regulation for moral reasons; liberals tend to favor increased regulations for instrumental reasons, such as to reduce risk of injury. But both favor regulation some of the time; and with all of the reasons specified above for favoring regulation some of the time, it is quite unlikely that any president will significantly reduce the level of government regulation. Table 14.3 is a tiny suggestion of both liberal and conservative types of regulation that are creeping back into the *Federal Register.* There will be cycles of regulation and deregulation because legislatures and administrators are highly responsive to changes in attitudes and sentiments about what needs regulating and by how much. But, for our purposes, regulation has to be accepted as a normal part of the political game.

## Maintaining a Capitalist Economy

Government and capitalism are not inherent foes; they depend on each other. The study of government policies toward our capitalist economy will thus enrich our understanding of capitalism and strengthen our grasp of the relation between freedom and power.

The Constitution provides that Congress shall have the power

> To lay and collect Taxes . . . to pay the Debts and provide for the common Defense and general Welfare . . . to borrow Money . . . to coin Money and regulate the Value thereof. . . .

These clauses of Article I, Section 8, are the constitutional sources of the fiscal and monetary policies of the national government. Nothing is said, however, about *how* these powers can be used, although the way they are used shapes the economy. Most of the policies in the history of the United States have been distinctly capitalistic, that is, they have aimed at promoting investment and

TABLE 14.3

**Types of Re-Regulation: Some Regulatory Acts Signed into Law by President Clinton**

| PUBLIC LAW | ACTION |
|---|---|
| PL 103-3* | Gives workers up to twelve weeks of unpaid leave for medical emergencies and births in the family |
| PL 103-159 | Provides for a five-day waiting period for the purchase of handguns |
| PL 103-333 | Allows for use of federal money for abortions in cases of rape and incest as well as when the life of the woman is in danger |
| PL 103-259 | Makes it a crime to interfere "by force or threat of force or by physical obstruction" with anyone who is seeking or performing an abortion or other reproductive health services |
| PL 103-322 | Provides for 100,000 new police officers, expands the death penalty to cover more than fifty federal crimes, bans the sale and possession of nineteen types of assault weapons, and authorizes $6.9 billion for "crime-prevention" programs |
| PL 103-433 | Protects millions of acres of desert in California, creating the largest wilderness area outside of Alaska |
| PL 104-193 | Authorizes IRS to enforce parental child support provisions of the 1996 Welfare Reform Law |
| PL 104-65 | (Lobbying Disclosure Act) Requires lobbyists to disclose the organizations for which they work |
| PL 104-188 | Requires employers to increase minimum hourly wage from $4.25 to $5.15 |
| PL 104-191 | Protects employees from loss of health insurance coverage when they change jobs and prevents denial of coverage due to pre-existing conditions |
| PL 104-193 | (Personal Responsibility Act) Requires single mothers to engage in community service, enter work force after two years on welfare, reveal identity of child's father, etc. |
| PL 105-261 | Gives State Department authority to regulate exports of technology that may have national security interest |

*In the numbering of a public law, PL = Public Law, 103 = the Congress during which the law was enacted (in this case, the 103rd Congress, 1993–1994), and 3 = the number assigned to the particular act.

ownership by individuals and corporations in the private sector. That was true even during the first half of the nineteenth century, before anyone had a firm understanding of what capitalism was really all about.[18]

[18]The word "capitalism" did not come into common usage, according to the *Oxford English Dictionary*, until 1854. Words like "capital" and "capitalist" were around earlier, but a concept of ***capitalism*** as an economic system really came to the forefront with the writings of Karl Marx.

**Monetary Policies** With a very few exceptions cited below, banks in the United States are privately owned and locally operated. Until well into the twentieth century, banks were regulated, if at all, by state legislatures. Each bank was granted a charter, giving it permission to make loans, hold deposits, and make investments. Although more than 25,000 banks continue to be state-chartered banks, they are less important than they used to be in the overall financial picture, as the most important banks now are members of the "federal system."

But banks did not become the core of American capitalism without intense political controversy. The Federalist majority in Congress, led by Alexander Hamilton, did in fact establish a Bank of the United States in 1791, but it was vigorously opposed by agrarian interests led by Thomas Jefferson, based on the fear that the interests of urban, industrial capitalism would dominate such a bank. The Bank of the United States was terminated during the administration of Andrew Jackson, but the fear of a central, *public* bank still existed eight decades later, when Congress in 1913 established an institution—the ***Federal Reserve System***—to integrate private banks into a single system. Yet even the "Fed" was not permitted to become a central bank. The "Fed" is a banker's bank. It charters national banks and regulates them in important respects.[19] The major advantage of belonging to the federal system is that each member bank can borrow money from the Fed, using as collateral the notes on loans already made. This enables them to expand their loan operations continually, as long as there is demand for new loans. This ability of a member bank to borrow money from the Fed is a profoundly important monetary policy. The Fed charges interest, called a discount rate, on its loans to member banks.

If the Fed significantly decreases the discount rate—i.e., the interest it charges member banks when they come for new credit—that can be a very good shot in the arm of a sagging economy. If the Fed adopts a policy of higher discount rates, that will serve as a brake on the economy if it is expanding too fast, because the higher rate pushes up the interest rates charged by leading private banks to their prime customers (called the "prime rate").

The federal government also provides insurance to foster credit and encourage private capital investment. The Federal Deposit Insurance Corporation (FDIC) protects bank deposits up to $100,000. Another important promoter of investment is the federal insurance of home mortgages through the Department of Housing and Urban Development (HUD). By federally guaranteeing mortgages, the government reduces the risks that banks run in making such loans, thus allowing banks to lower their interest rates and make such loans more affordable to middle- and lower-income families. These programs have enabled millions of families who could not have otherwise afforded it to finance the purchase of a home.

These examples illustrate the influence of the national government on the private economy. Most of these monetary policies are aimed at encouraging a maximum of property ownership and a maximum of capital investment by individuals and corporations in the private sector. And all of these policies are illustrative of the interdependence of government and capitalism.

[19]Banks can choose between a state or a national charter. Under the state system, they are less stringently regulated and avoid the fees charged members of the Fed. But they also miss out on the advantages of belonging to the Federal Reserve System.

**Taxation** All taxes discriminate, leaving to public policy the question of *what kind* of discrimination is called for. The tariff—a tax on imported goods—was the most important tax of the nineteenth century, and the "tax policy" of the tariff put most of the burden of raising revenue on foreigners seeking to export their goods to America. This policy was designed to protect our "infant industries" against the more advanced foreign competitors of the day, the implicit assumption being that the tariff would disappear once our industries were no longer in their infancy.

The most important tax of the twentieth century, and indeed the most important choice Congress ever made about taxation (or about any policy, for that matter) was the decision to raise revenue by taxing personal and corporate incomes—the "income tax."[20] The second most important policy choice Congress made was that the income tax be "progressive" or "graduated," with the heaviest burden carried by those most able to pay. A tax is called ***progressive*** if the rate of taxation goes up with each higher income bracket. A tax is called ***regressive*** if people in lower income brackets pay a higher proportion of their income toward the tax than people in higher income brackets. For example, a sales tax is deemed regressive because everybody pays at the same rate, so that the proportion of total income paid in taxes goes down as the total income goes up (assuming, as is generally the case, that as total income goes up the amount spent on sales-taxable purchases increases at a lower rate). The Social Security tax is another example of a regressive tax. Current law applies a tax of 6.2 percent on the first $68,400 of income for the retirement program and an additional 1.45 percent on all income (without limit) for Medicare benefits, for a total of 7.65 percent in Social Security taxes. This means that a person earning an income of $68,400 pays $5,232.60 in Social Security taxes, a rate of 7.65 percent. But someone earning nearly twice that income, $129,000, pays a total of $5,869.50 in Social Security taxes, a rate of 4.8 percent. As income continues to rise, the amount of Social Security taxes also rises, but the *rate,* or the percentage of income that goes to taxes, declines.

**AMERICAN POLITICAL DEVELOPMENT**

The United States' adoption of a graduated federal income tax occurred after years of trying to institutionalize a redistributive tax system. Success came as a result of the continuing efforts by early twentieth-century Progressives. The "progressive tax" was, in the words of one author, "the culmination of nearly a half century of struggle to reach the vast amounts of wealth generated by the rapid and massive industrialization of the United States."

SOURCE: John D. Buenker, *The Income Tax and the Progressive Era* (New York: Garland, 1985), pp. 381–84.

The graduated income tax is a moderately progressive tax; in other words, as it collects revenue it pursues a deliberate ***policy of redistribution,*** although moderately redistributive. Table 14.4 demonstrates the success of this policy. Before genuine progressive income taxation was instituted in the 1930s, the disparity

[20]The U.S. government imposed an income tax during the Civil War that remained in effect until 1872. In 1894, Congress enacted a modest 2 percent tax upon all incomes over $4,000. This $4,000 exemption was in fact fairly high, excluding all working-class people. But in 1895, the Supreme Court declared it unconstitutional, citing the provision of Article I, Section 9, that any direct tax would have to be proportional to the population in each state. See Pollock v. Farmers' Loan and Trust Company, 158 U.S. 601 (1895). In 1913, the Sixteenth Amendment was ratified, effectively reversing the *Pollock* case.

between the lowest income bracket and the highest reached its widest stretch, almost 46 percentage points (see Table 14.4). From the 1930s through the 1970s, this gap was reduced. Beginning in the 1980s, however, the gap began to increase again, and it is no coincidence that the biggest across-the-board income tax cuts in the history of that tax were adopted in 1981 and 1986.[21]

Redistribution of wealth is not the *only* policy being pursued by the American personal and corporate income tax. Another important policy imbedded in that tax is the encouragement of the capitalist economy. When the tax law allows individuals or companies to deduct from their taxable income any money they can justify as an investment or as a "business expense," that is an incentive to individuals and companies to spend money to expand their production, their advertising, or their staff, and it reduces the income taxes they pay. These kinds of deductions are called incentives or "equity" by those who support them. For others, they might be called "loopholes." The tax laws of 1981 actually closed a number of important loopholes. But others still exist—on home mortgages, including second homes, and on business expenses, for example—and others will return, because there is a strong consensus among members of Congress that businesses often need such incentives. They may differ on which incentives are best, but there is almost universal agreement in government that some incentives are justifiable.[22]

The persistence of large annual deficits forced President Bush to raise taxes in 1990, despite his 1988 campaign promise "Read my lips: No new taxes." Taking a cue from the popular disapproval of President Bush's tax inconsistency, President Clinton campaigned in 1992 for a "middle-class tax cut." But in 1993, even before the chair of the Oval Office was warm, he was forced, like President Bush, to betray his campaign promise by increasing rather than cutting taxes. The only flexibility he had in tax policy was to impose equal sacrifice on everyone, with increased income taxes on the wealthy and taxes on Social Security retirement benefits of people who had additional income.[23] Following his 1996 reelection, with the economy stable and growing, President Clinton tried once again to get tax cuts; he knew he could depend on Republican cooperation in Congress because of their long-standing commitment to tax cuts, which had been renewed in their 1994 Contract with America. In July of 1997, the president and Congress finally got together on the Taxpayer Relief Act of 1997. It was an extremely complex package, with well over a hundred major provisions, some of which were retro-

[21]The redistributive effect of the income tax would probably have been even more marked if it had not been neutralized to an extent by other, regressive taxes, such as Social Security taxes, state sales taxes, many federal excise taxes, and tariffs.

[22]For a systematic account of the role of government in providing incentives and inducements to business, see C. E. Lindblom, *Politics and Markets* (New York: Basic Books, 1977), Chapter 13. For a detailed account of the dramatic Reagan tax cuts and reforms, see Jeffrey Birnbaum and Alan Murray, *Showdown at Gucci Gulch—Lawmakers, Lobbyists, and the Unlikely Triumph of Tax Reform* (New York: Random House, 1987).

[23]For further background, see David E. Rosenbaum, "Cutting the Deficit Overshadows Clinton's Promise to Cut Taxes," *New York Times,* 12 January 1993, p. A1; and "Clinton Weighing Freeze or New Tax on Social Security," *New York Times,* 31 January 1993, p. A1.

TABLE 14.4

**Income Distribution in the United States (1929–1997): The Proportion of Money Income Going to Each Fifth of the Population**

| FAMILY INCOME BRACKET | 1929 | 1934 | 1944 | 1950 | 1960 | 1970 | 1980 | 1990 | 1997 |
|---|---|---|---|---|---|---|---|---|---|
| Lowest fifth | 5.4 | 5.9 | 4.9 | 4.5 | 4.8 | 5.4 | 5.1 | 4.6 | 3.6 |
| Second fifth | 10.1 | 11.5 | 10.9 | 12.0 | 12.2 | 12.2 | 11.6 | 10.7 | 8.9 |
| Third fifth | 14.4 | 15.5 | 16.2 | 17.4 | 17.8 | 17.6 | 17.5 | 16.7 | 15.0 |
| Fourth fifth | 18.8 | 20.4 | 22.2 | 23.5 | 24.0 | 23.8 | 24.3 | 24.0 | 23.2 |
| Highest fifth | 51.3 | 49.7 | 45.8 | 42.6 | 41.3 | 41.4 | 41.6 | 44.3 | 49.4 |
| Gap between lowest and highest fifths | 45.9 | 43.8 | 40.9 | 38.1 | 36.5 | 35.5 | 36.5 | 39.7 | 45.8 |

Figures are not strictly comparable because of differences in calculating procedures.

SOURCES: Data for the period 1929–50 are from Allan Rosenbaum, "State Government, Political Power, and Public Policy: The Case of Illinois" (Ph.D. diss., University of Chicago, 1974), Chapters 10–11. Used by permission. Figures for 1960–97 are from U.S. Department of Commerce, Bureau of the Census, *Current Population Reports,* Series P-60 (Washington, DC: Government Printing Office), various issues, and from www.census.gov/hhes/income/income97/in97dis.html

active, some staged to begin when the bill was signed in 1997, others beginning in 1998, and several provisions effective only in 1999 and later. Since the 1997 law contained benefits for all levels of income, it is impossible to predict whether the Taxpayer Relief Act of 1997 will have any effect at all on the distribution of wealth in the country. For example, higher income people who are most likely to make investments were given a significant cut in the capital gains tax as well as a significant increase in their estate-tax exemptions. They were also given tax credits for direct investment in the computer software industry. Working families were given a boost, with a $500 tax credit for each child and a tax credit for college tuition; but these help middle- and upper-income families as well. In the final analysis, however, there is no absolutely fair way to impose taxation. The only absolute rules should be (1) that government benefits not be hidden in the tax code and (2) that all other tax policies be made explicit to the public so that tax policy is the result of a genuine public choice.

**Government Spending** Most people associate the policy of government spending with the New Deal period of the 1930s. But government spending is as old as any government policy, and older than most. As Chapter 3 demonstrated, government spending was favored by the national government from the beginning. Today's government has more money to spend, but nineteenth-century governments spent money at a relatively high degree for the economy of the times—on highways, canals, postal services, surveys, protection of settlers, and other services.

AMERICAN POLITICAL DEVELOPMENT

Federal outlays as a percentage of the Gross Domestic Product grew steadily from 1930 to 1980, from less than 5 percent of the GDP to more than 20 percent. This massive growth is a striking reminder of the growth of federal government involvement in the twentieth century. In the late nineteenth and early twentieth centuries (1869 to 1918), outlays consistently remained below 3 percent of the Gross National Product.

SOURCE: Harold W. Stanley and Richard G. Niemi, *Vital Statistics on American Politics,* 5th ed. (Washington, DC: Congressional Quarterly Press, 1995), p. 390.

The difference today is that we recognize that the *aggregate amount* of government expenditure is even more important *as policy* than are the particular purposes and projects for which the public monies are spent—a system of thinking attributed to the great English theorist John Maynard Keynes. Lord Keynes reasoned that governments had become such a significant economic force that they could use their power to compensate for the imperfections in the capitalist system. He contended that government expenditures should be used as part of a "countercyclical" policy, in which, on the one hand, spending would be significantly increased (with significant "deficit spending" where necessary) to fight the deflationary side of the business cycle. On the other hand, spending should be reduced and tax rates kept high to produce budget surpluses when the problem was to fight the inflationary side of the business cycle.[24]

At least three serious weaknesses in the Keynesian approach to fiscal policy were exposed during the 1970s. First, although public spending can supplement private spending to produce higher demand and thereby heat up the economy, there is no guarantee that the public money will be spent on things that help produce higher productivity, higher employment, and prosperity. Public expenditure can merely inflate the economy.

Second, governments may not be able to increase spending quickly enough to reverse the declining employment or the pessimistic psychology among consumers and investors. New public works take time, arriving perhaps too late to boost the economy, perhaps just in time to inflate it.

Third, a very large and growing proportion of the annual federal budget is mandatory spending or, in the words of OMB, "relatively uncontrollable." Interest payments on the national debt, for example, are determined by the actual size of the national debt and prevailing interest rates. Legislation has mandated payment rates for such programs as retirement under Social Security, retirement for federal employees, unemployment assistance, Medicare, and farm price supports. These payments go up with the cost of living; they go up as the average age of the population goes up; they go up as national and world agricultural surpluses go up.

In the early 1960s, before Medicare and Medicaid were created, mandatory spending accounted for about 26 percent of the federal budget. By 1975, mandatory spending nearly doubled. And 1975 is also the first year mandatory spending in the federal budget exceeded discretionary spending (spending that can be con-

[24]John Maynard Keynes, *The General Theory of Employment Interest and Money* (New York: Harcourt, Brace, 1936).

trolled through the budgeting process). Since then the gap between mandatory and discretionary spending has continued to widen.

For the most part, increases in mandatory spending have been driven by growth in Social Security, Medicare, and Medicaid. In 1968, those programs represented about 17 percent of the budget. By 1975, these programs consumed more than 27 percent of the federal government. In 1999, Social Security, Medicare, and Medicaid accounted for more than one-third of federal spending. Social Security spending actually stabilized between 1985 and 1997. However, Medicare and Medicaid spending have continued to rise. In 1976, spending on these programs represented 1.4 percent of the GDP. By 1997, Medicare and Medicaid spending, as a percent of the GDP, more than doubled to 3.5 percent of the GDP.

In an effort to hold down mandatory spending, Congress has directed the Bureau of Labor Statistics to adopt a series of technical changes in calculating the Consumer Price Index (CPI), on which automatic ***cost of living adjustments (COLAS)*** are based. In other words, as the CPI goes up, reflecting inflation, the law mandates increases in Social Security and other types of benefits to the same degree. As part of the 1997 budget deal between the Clinton White House and Congress, policy makers agreed to lower the CPI by .2 percent starting in 1999. Despite these changes, mandatory spending is expected to continue to grow. In 1997, mandatory spending accounted for more than 65 percent of the budget. The Office of Management and Budget predicts that by 2003, uncontrollable expenses will consume nearly 70 percent of the federal budget.[25]

The inability of presidents or Congress to cut expenditures after having drastically cut taxes in 1981 and 1986 produced unprecedented budget deficits all during the 1980s (see Figure 14.1). These deficits actually helped pull the U.S. economy out of the 1982 recession—and that is ironic, because the 1983 recovery was a classic Keynesian (deficit-spending) recovery despite the fact that the Reagan administration was officially opposed to Keynesian economics. The struggle throughout the ten years following the tax cuts and the galloping increases in deficits (Figures 14.1 and 14.2) was how to cut, or at least "cap," government spending. Though some progress was made—thanks to President Clinton's joining the Republicans in the fight against spending—the deficit problem suddenly switched to a surplus problem. Surplus? Yes. And surplus a problem? Yes. An unprecedented eight-year run of "fat years" without a recession not only reduced the annual deficits but also created a prospect for surpluses amounting to nearly $1 trillion for fiscal 2000–2004.

This unexpected turn of events did not produce an era of partisan cooperation but only a change in the terms of the struggle over government spending. In 1999, Republicans were pushing for a 10 to 15 percent across-the-board tax cut, giving it the halo title of "Tax Cuts for All Americans Act." But it could also be called a "tax expenditure" inasmuch as the cuts were estimated to cost between $600 billion and $700 billion over the horizon of the surplus years. The Democrats proposed devoting nearly 70 percent of the anticipated annual surpluses to give Social Security a new

[25]See Office of Management and Budget, *Historical Tables, Budget of the United States Government, Fiscal Year 1999* (Washington, DC: Government Printing Office, 1998), p. 18 and Tables 8.2–8.4.

FIGURE 14.1

**Annual Federal Budget Deficits and Surpluses, 1960–2003**

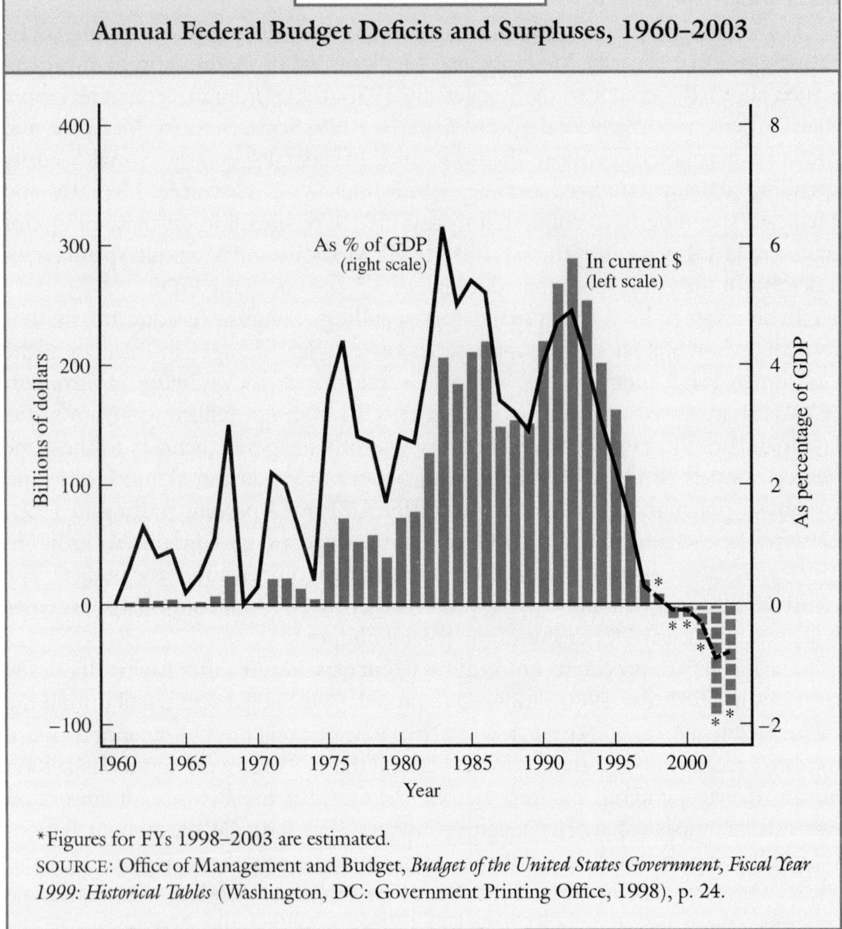


*Figures for FYs 1998–2003 are estimated.

SOURCE: Office of Management and Budget, *Budget of the United States Government, Fiscal Year 1999: Historical Tables* (Washington, DC: Government Printing Office, 1998), p. 24.

fifty-year financial security[26] and then to spend the rest of the surplus on some "targeted" tax cuts, including repairing the infrastructure (basically highways) to the tune of $200 billion, restoring President Reagan's "Star Wars" missile defense program,

[26]There are different versions of President Clinton's Social Security plan. One is to work directly on the Social Security trust fund so that it is ready to meet the demands of the "baby boom" generation when they reach retirement a few years from now. Another is to follow a more orthodox Keynesian approach by spending the money to reduce the general public debt and then to devote to Social Security all the savings on interest payments that would be derived from that reduced debt. Another issue is whether any of the new money available for Social Security should be put directly into the system, into savings accounts for each worker during his or her working years, or indeed invested *in bulk* into the private stock market. All of this may change, however, if the forecast for continued surpluses over the next fifteen years, amounting to an estimated $4.5 *trillion,* proves to be false. See David E. Rosenbaum, "Fixing Social Security, Even in the Flush Times," *New York Times,* 7 March 1999, p. 28.

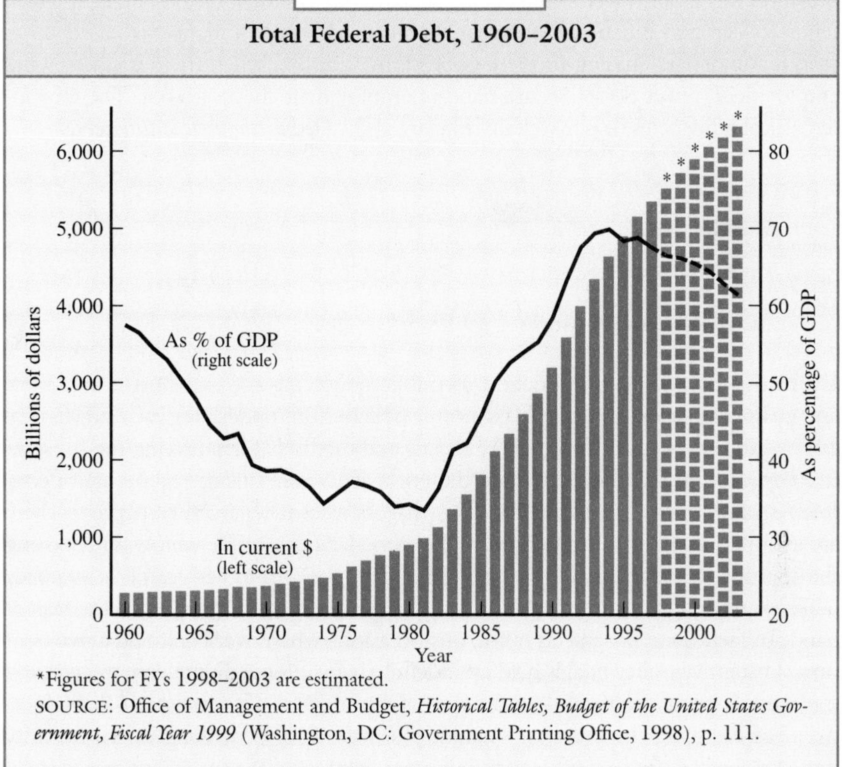


teacher hiring, and a few billion dollars on other miscellaneous items (see also Chapter 15). In other words, "caps" on spending, which had become an essential part of the effort to balance the budget, were being raised, if not erased. Even the Democrats had forgotten the second half of Keynes' system: First half, run deficits to fight deflation; second half, use the surplus during prosperous years to retire some of the national debt so that you can be ready for later deficits. In any case, it is worth repeating that a surplus is neither a blessing nor a curse but just a different kind of policy problem.

**The Welfare State** Although most of the discussion of the welfare state is reserved for the next chapter, one important aspect of it needs to be introduced here. The architects of the original Social Security system in the 1930s were probably very well aware of the fact that a large welfare system can be very good fiscal policy. When the economy is declining and more people are losing jobs or are retiring early, welfare payments go up automatically. They can go up enough to maintain consumer demand, which can help counteract a deflationary psychology, thereby also helping maintain investment. Although such payments are no cure for the down side of the business cycle, the expansion of Social Security checks almost certainly makes the down side of the business cycle shorter and shallower. Conversely, during periods of full employment and/or high levels of government spending, when inflationary pressures can mount, welfare taxes take an extra bite out of consumer dollars, which tends to dampen inflation somewhat, because, to repeat, inflation is based upon "too many dollars chasing too few goods." In addition, when there is close to full employment, fewer Social Security and unemployment checks go out. These countercyclical tendencies of our welfare state are also called ***automatic stabilizers.***

## IMPLEMENTING PUBLIC POLICIES: THE TECHNIQUES OF CONTROL

Up to this point, our introduction to public policy has focused on the substance and goals of policies, particularly economic policies. But underlying each substantive policy issue and each policy goal are means and methods for satisfying the substantive demands and for implementing the goals. These are called "techniques of control." Techniques of control are to policy makers what tools are to carpenters. There are a limited number of techniques, and experience helps guide us toward choosing the appropriate technique for the selected policy goal. Just as with carpenters, policy makers can disagree, sometimes intensely, about the best technique for the task at hand. In fact, there have been numerous occasions when overwhelming agreement on a substantive policy goal is held up indefinitely by intense disagreement regarding the most appropriate means—technique of control—of accomplishing that objective. For example, there is near unanimity on the goal of making Social Security more stable over the next fifty years, but what that technique (or techniques) should be will probably make Social Security a key issue in the 2000 presidential campaign and an important cause of continuing cleavage between the two parties in the years beyond that.

The study of techniques of control is an essential part of the study and analysis of public policy and therefore an essential part of any introduction to the study of public policy. We offer here an elementary handbook of techniques that will be useful for analyzing the policies in this and succeeding chapters. Table 14.5 lists some important techniques of control available to policy makers. They are grouped according to categories for purposes of analysis: promotional techniques, regulatory techniques, and redistributive techniques. The specifics of each will be taken up one at a time.

### Promotional Techniques

***Promotional techniques*** are the carrots of public policy. Their purpose is to encourage people to do something they might not otherwise do or to get people to do more of what they are already doing. Sometimes the purpose is merely to compensate people for something done in the past. Promotional techniques can be classified into at least three separate types—subsidies, contracts, and licenses.

**Subsidies** ***Subsidies*** are simply government grants of cash or other valuable commodities, such as land. Although subsidies are often denounced as "give-

**Table 14.5**

**Techniques of Public Control**

| TYPES OF TECHNIQUES | TECHNIQUES | DEFINITIONS AND EXAMPLES |
|---|---|---|
| Promotional techniques | Subsidies and grants of cash, land, etc. | "Patronage" is the promotion of private activity through what recipients consider "benefits" (example: in the nineteenth century the government encouraged westward settlement by granting land to those who went west) |
| | Contracting | Agreements with individuals or firms in the "private sector" to purchase goods or services |
| | Licensing | Unconditional permission to do something that is otherwise illegal (franchise, permit) |
| Regulatory techniques | Criminal penalties | Heavy fines or imprisonment, loss of citizenship |
| | Civil penalties | Less onerous fines, probation, public exposure, restitution |
| | Administrative regulation | Setting interest rates, maintaining standards of health and safety, investigating and publicizing wrongdoing |
| | Subsidies, contracting, and licensing | Regulatory techniques when certain conditions are attached (example: the government refuses to award a contract to firms that show no evidence of affirmative action in hiring) |
| | Regulatory taxation | Taxes that keep consumption or production down (liquor, gas, cigarette taxes) |
| | Expropriation | "Eminent domain"—the power to take private property for public use |
| Redistributive techniques | Fiscal use of taxes | Altering the distribution of money by changing taxes or tax rules |
| | Fiscal use of budgeting | Deficit spending to pump money into the economy when it needs a boost; creating a budget surplus through taxes to discourage consumption in inflationary times |
| | Fiscal use of credit and interest (monetary techniques) | Changing interest rates to affect both demand for money and consumption (example: the Federal Reserve Board raises interest rates to slow economic growth and ward off inflation) |

aways," they have played a fundamental role in the history of government in the United States. As we discussed at length in Chapter 3, subsidies were the dominant form of public policy of the national government and the state and local governments throughout the nineteenth century. They continue to be an important category of public policy at all levels of government. The first planning document ever written for the national government, Alexander Hamilton's *Report on Manufactures,* was based almost entirely on Hamilton's assumption that

AMERICAN POLITICAL DEVELOPMENT

During the nineteenth century, the domestic policies of the federal government "were almost entirely concerned with subsidies, bounties, and claims. Land grants were piled upon land sales at low prices, and these were piled upon still additional land grants until the frontier ran out." With such activity dominating the federal government, states were left responsible for "police powers."

SOURCE: Theodore J. Lowi, "Europeanization of America? From United States to United State," in *Nationalizing Government: Public Policies in America,* ed. Theodore J. Lowi and Alan Stone (Beverly Hills, CA: Sage, 1978), pp. 15–29.

American industry could be encouraged by federal subsidies and that these were not only desirable but constitutional.

The thrust of Hamilton's plan was not lost on later policy makers. Subsidies in the form of land grants were given to farmers and to railroad companies to encourage western settlement. Substantial cash subsidies have traditionally been given to commercial shipbuilders to help build the commercial fleet and to guarantee the use of the ships as military personnel carriers in time of war.

Subsidies have always been a technique favored by politicians because subsidies can be treated as "benefits" that can be spread widely in response to many demands that might otherwise produce profound political conflict. Subsidies can, in other words, be used to buy off the opposition. So widespread is the use of the subsidy technique in government, in fact, that it takes encyclopedias to keep track of them all. Indeed, for a number of years, one company published an annual *Encyclopedia of U.S. Government Benefits,* a thousand-page guide to benefits "for every American—from all walks of life. . . . [R]ight now, there are thousands of other American Taxpayers who are missing out on valuable Government Services, simply because they do not know about them. . . . Start your own business. . . . Take an extra vacation. . . . Here are all the opportunities your tax dollars have made possible."[27]

Another secret of the popularity of subsidies is that those who receive the benefits do not perceive the controls inherent in them. In the first place, most of the resources available for subsidies come from taxation. (In the nineteenth century, there was a lot of public land to distribute, but that is no longer the case.) Second, the effect of any subsidy has to be measured somewhat indirectly in terms of what people *would be doing* if the subsidy had not been available. For example, many thousands of people settled in lands west of the Mississippi only because land subsidies were available. Hundreds of research laboratories exist in universities and corporations only because certain types of research subsidies from the government are available. And finally, once subsidies exist, the threat of their removal becomes a very significant technique of control.

**Contracting** Like any corporation, a government agency must purchase goods and services by contract. The law requires open bidding for a substantial proportion of these contracts because government contracts are extremely valuable to businesses in the private sector and because the opportunities and incentives for

[27]Roy A. Grisham and Paul McConaughty, eds., *Encyclopedia of U.S. Government Benefits* (Union City, NJ: William H. Wise Co., 1972). The quote is taken from the dust jacket. A comparable guide published by the *New York Times* is called *Federal Aid for Cities and Towns* (New York: Quadrangle Books, 1972). It contains 1,312 pages of federal government benefits that cities and towns, rather than individuals, can apply for.

abuse are very great. But contracting is more than a method of buying goods and services. Contracting is also an important technique of policy because government agencies are often authorized to use their ***contracting power*** as a means of encouraging corporations to improve themselves, as a means of helping to build up whole sectors of the economy, and as a means of encouraging certain desirable goals or behavior, such as equal employment opportunity. For example, the infant airline industry of the 1930s was nurtured by the national government's lucrative contracts to carry airmail. A more recent example is the use of government contracting to encourage industries, universities, and other organizations to engage in research and development.

Government-by-contract has been around for a long time and has always been seen by business as a major source of economic opportunity. In the Pentagon alone, nearly $43 billion was spent in 1998 on contracts with the ten top defense companies in the United States and abroad. The top company, in terms of the value of its defense contracts, was Lockheed Martin, whose revenues from those defense contracts amounted to $12.3 billion. Boeing came in second, with nearly $11 billion in government contracts.[28]

**Licensing** A ***license*** is a privilege granted by a government to do something that it otherwise considers to be illegal. For example, state laws make practicing medicine or driving a taxi illegal without a license. The states then create a board of doctors and a "hack bureau" to grant licenses for the practice of medicine or for the operation of a cab to all persons who have met the particular qualifications specified in the statute or by the agency. Like subsidies and contracting, licensing has two sides. One is the giveaway side, making the license a desirable object of patronage. The other side of licensing is the control or regulatory side, to be dealt with below.

## Regulatory Techniques

If promotional techniques are the carrots of public policy, ***regulatory techniques*** can be considered the sticks. ***Regulation*** comes in several forms, but every regulatory technique shares a common trait: direct government control of conduct. The conduct may be regulated because people feel it is harmful to others, or threatens to be, such as drunk driving or false advertising. Or the conduct may be regulated because people think it's immoral, whether it is harming anybody or not, such as prostitution, gambling, or drinking. Because there are many forms of regulation, we have subdivided them here: (1) police regulation, through civil and criminal penalties, (2) administrative regulation, and (3) regulatory taxation.

**Police Regulation** "Police regulation" is not a technical term, but we use it for this category because these techniques come closest to the traditional exercise of ***police power***—a power traditionally reserved to the states (see Chapter 3). After a

[28]Pat Towell, "Does Security Suffer as Pentagon Shops in the Global Marketplace?" *Congressional Quarterly Weekly Report,* 13 February 1999, pp. 401–14.

person's arrest and conviction, these techniques are administered by courts and, where necessary, penal institutions. They are regulatory techniques.

***Civil penalties*** usually refer to fines or some other form of material restitution (such as public service) as a sanction for violating civil laws or such common law principles as negligence. Civil penalties can range from a $5 fine for a parking violation to a more onerous penalty for late payment of income taxes to the much more onerous penalties for violating antitrust laws against unfair competition or environmental protection laws against pollution. ***Criminal penalties*** usually refer to imprisonment but can also involve heavy fines and the loss of certain civil rights and liberties, such as the right to vote or freedom of speech.

**Administrative Regulation** Police regulation addresses conduct considered immoral. In order to eliminate such conduct, strict laws have been passed and severe sanctions enacted. But what about conduct that is not considered morally wrong but that may have harmful consequences? There is, for example, nothing morally wrong with radio or television broadcasting. But broadcasting on a particular frequency or channel is regulated by government because there would be virtual chaos if everybody could broadcast on any frequency at any time.

This kind of conduct is thought of less as *policed* conduct and more as *regulated* conduct. When conduct is said to be regulated, the purpose is rarely to eliminate the conduct but rather to influence it toward more appropriate channels, toward more appropriate locations, or toward certain qualified types of persons, all for the purpose of minimizing injuries or inconveniences. This type of regulated conduct is sometimes called ***administrative regulation*** because the controls are given over to administrative agencies rather than to the police. As we have already seen in Chapter 7, each regulatory agency has extensive powers to keep a sector of the economy under surveillance and also has powers to make rules dealing with the behavior of individual companies and people. But these administrative agencies have fewer powers of punishment than the police and the courts have, and the administrative agencies generally rely on the courts to issue orders enforcing the rules and decisions made by the agencies.

Sometimes a government will adopt administrative regulation if an economic activity is considered so important that it is not to be entrusted to competition among several companies in the private sector. This is the rationale for the regulation of local or regional power companies. A single company, traditionally called a "utility," is given an exclusive license (or franchise) to offer these services, but since the one company is made a legal ***monopoly*** and is protected from competition by other companies, the government gives an administrative agency the power to regulate the quality of the services rendered, the rates charged for those services, and the margin of profit that the company is permitted to make.

At other times, administrative regulation is the chosen technique because the legislature decides that the economy needs protection from itself—that is, it may set up a regulatory agency to protect companies from destructive or predatory competition, on the assumption that economic competition is not always its own solution. This is the rationale behind the Federal Trade Commission, which has the responsibility of watching over such practices as price discrimination or pooling agreements between two or more companies when their purpose is to eliminate competitors.

Table 14.5 listed subsidies, licensing, and contracting twice, as examples of both promotional and regulatory policies, because although these techniques can be used as strictly promotional policies, they can also be used as techniques of administrative regulation. It all depends on whether the law sets serious conditions on eligibility for the subsidy, license, or contract. To put it another way, the threat of losing a valuable subsidy, license, or contract can be used by the government to improve compliance with the goals of regulation. For example, the threat of removal of the subsidies called "federal aid to education" has had a very significant influence on the willingness of schools to cooperate in the desegregation of their student bodies and faculties. For another example, social welfare subsidies (benefits) can be lowered to encourage or force people to take low-paying jobs, or they can be increased to placate people when they are engaging in political protest.[29]

Like subsidies and licensing, government contracting can be an entirely different kind of technique of control when the contract or its denial is used as a reward or punishment to gain obedience in a regulatory program. For example, Presidents Kennedy and Johnson used their considerable power to influence the employment practices of all the corporations seeking contracts from the national government to provide goods or services. Both Kennedy and Johnson issued executive orders, administered by the Office of Federal Contract Compliance in the Department of Labor, to prohibit discrimination by firms receiving government contracts.[30] The value of these contracts to many private corporations was so great that they were quite willing to alter if not eliminate racial discrimination in employment practices if that was the only way to qualify for government contracts.

**Regulatory Taxation** Taxation is generally understood to be a fiscal technique, and it will be discussed as such below. But in many instances, the primary purpose of a tax is not to raise revenue but to discourage or eliminate an activity altogether by making it too expensive for most people. For example, since the end of Prohibition, although there has been no penalty for the production or sale of alcoholic beverages, the alcohol industry has not been free from regulation. First, all alcoholic beverages have to be licensed, allowing only those companies that are "bonded" to put their product on the market. Beyond that, federal and state taxes on alcohol are made disproportionately high, on the theory that, in addition to the revenue gained, less alcohol will be consumed.

We may be seeing a great deal more regulation by taxation in the future, for at least the following reasons. First, it is a kind of hidden regulation, acceptable to people who in principle are against regulation. Second, it permits a certain amount of choice. For example, a heavy tax on gasoline or on smokestack and chemical industries (called an "effluent tax") will encourage drivers and these companies to regulate

[29]For an evaluation of the policy of withholding subsidies to carry out desegregation laws, see Gary Orfield, *Must We Bus?* (Washington, DC: Brookings Institution, 1978). For an evaluation of the use of subsidies to encourage work or to calm political unrest, see Frances Fox Piven and Richard Cloward, *Regulating the Poor: The Functions of Public Welfare* (New York: Random House, 1971).

[30]For an evaluation of Kennedy's use of this kind of executive power, see Carl M. Brauer, *John F. Kennedy and the Second Reconstruction* (New York: Columbia University Press, 1977), especially Chapter 3.

their own activities by permitting them to decide how much pollution they can afford. Third, advocates of a ***regulatory tax*** believe it is more efficient than other forms of regulation, requiring less bureaucracy and less supervision.

**Expropriation** Seizing private property for a public use, or ***expropriation,*** is a widely used technique of control in the United States, especially in land-use regulation. Almost all public works, from highways to parks to government office buildings, involve the forceful taking of some private property in order to assemble sufficient land and the correct distribution of land for the necessary construction. The vast Interstate Highway Program required expropriation of thousands of narrow strips of private land. Urban redevelopment projects often require city governments to use the powers of seizure in the service of private developers, who actually build the urban projects on the land that would be far too expensive if purchased on the open market. Private utilities that supply electricity and gas to individual subscribers are given powers to take private property whenever a new facility or a right-of-way is needed.

We generally call the power to expropriate ***eminent domain,*** and the eminent domain power is recognized as inherent in any government. The Fifth Amendment of the U.S. Constitution surrounds this expropriation power with important safeguards against abuse, so that government agencies in the United States are not permitted to use that power except through a strict due process, and they must offer "fair market value" for the land sought.[31]

Forcing individuals to work for a public purpose is another form of expropriation. The draft of young men for the armed forces, court orders to strikers to return to work, and sentences for convicted felons to do community service are examples of the regular use of expropriation in the United States.

**AMERICAN POLITICAL DEVELOPMENT**

The large amount of public land that was available after the Louisiana purchase made expropriation of real property an unneeded policy technique. In 1803, there were ninety acres of land for every person in the United States, and by 1850, there were still fifty acres per person.

SOURCE: Robert A. Dahl, "The American Oppositions: Affirmation and Denial," in *Political Oppositions in Western Democracies,* ed. Robert A. Dahl (New Haven: Yale University Press, 1966), pp. 34–69, esp. p. 44.

## Redistributive Techniques

***Redistributive techniques*** (also called macroeconomic techniques) are usually of two types—fiscal and monetary—but they have a common purpose: to control people by manipulating the entire economy rather than by regulating people directly. (*Macroeconomic* refers to the economy as a system.) As observed earlier, regulatory techniques focus on individual conduct: "Walking on the grass is not permitted," or "Membership in a union may not be used to deny

[31]For an evaluation of the politics of eminent domain, see Theodore J. Lowi. Benjamin Ginsberg, et al., *Poliscide: Big Government, Big Science, Lilliputian Politics* (Lanham, MD: University Press of America, 1990), p. 235 and *passim,* and especially Chapters 11 and 12, written by Julia and Thomas Vitullo-Martin.

employment, nor may a worker be fired for promoting union membership." In contrast, techniques are redistributive if they seek to control conduct more indirectly by altering the conditions of conduct or manipulating the environment of conduct.



**Fiscal Techniques** Fiscal techniques of control are the government's taxing and spending powers. Personal and corporate income taxes, which raise most government revenues, are the most prominent examples. While the direct purpose of an income tax is to raise revenue, each tax has a different impact on the economy, and government can plan for that impact. For example, although the main reason favoring a significant increase in the Social Security tax (which is an income tax) under President Carter was to keep Social Security solvent, a big reason for it in the minds of many legislators was that it would reduce inflation by shrinking the amount of money people had in their hands to buy more goods and services.

Likewise, President Clinton's commitment in his 1992 campaign to a "middle-class tax cut" was motivated by the goal of encouraging economic growth through increased consumption. Soon after the election, upon learning that the deficit would be far larger than had been earlier reported to him, he confessed he would have to break his promise of such a tax cut. Nevertheless, the idea of a middle-class tax cut is an example of a fiscal policy aimed at increased consumption, because of the theory that people in middle-income brackets tend to spend a high proportion of unexpected earnings or windfalls, rather than saving or investing them.[32] This is why President Clinton returned repeatedly to the middle-class tax-cut idea. However, later in his second term, as Republicans were warming up for a 10 to 15 percent across-the-board tax cut that had served their political interests well in the past, President Clinton responded by moving from an admittedly vague reference to a "middle-class" tax cut toward a more narrowly focused (and therefore more credible) proposal for "targeted tax cuts," aimed at categories such as disabled workers, employers who provide daycare facilities for employees, families who are providing long-term care for disabled relatives, and others.[33]

**Monetary Techniques** ***Monetary techniques*** also seek to influence conduct by manipulating the entire economy through the supply or availability of money. The Federal Reserve Board (the Fed) can adopt what is called a "hard money policy" by increasing the interest rate it charges member banks (called the ***discount rate***). Another monetary policy is one of increasing or decreasing the ***reserve requirement,*** which sets the actual proportion of deposited money that a bank must

[32]For a fascinating behind-the-scenes look at how and why President Clinton abandoned his campaign commitment to tax cuts and economic stimulus, and instead accepted the fiscal conservatism advocated by the Federal Reserve and its chairman, Alan Greenspan, see Bob Woodward, *The Agenda: Inside the Clinton White House* (New York: Simon and Schuster, 1994).

[33]For a good coverage of the tax-cut issue between the two parties, see George Hager and Thomas Edsall, "Blunting the GOP Tax-Cut Wedge," *Washington Post National Weekly Edition,* 15 February 1999, p. 10.

keep "on demand" as it makes all the rest of the deposits available as new loans.[34] A third important technique used by the Fed is ***open market operations***—the buying and selling of Treasury securities to absorb excess dollars or to release more dollars into the economy.[35]

**Spending Power as Fiscal Policy** We have already discussed subsidies and contracts as examples of promotional techniques. We also took careful note of FDR's discovery and Lord Keynes' theory that the *aggregate spending power* of the national government—net deficits and net surpluses—can, when deliberately employed, be effective fiscal policy. In that case, subsidies and the use of contracts to buy goods and services are *systemic* and not merely piecemeal government actions. This is why subsidies and contracting show up on Table 14.5, as both fiscal (regulatory) and promotional techniques.

One of the most important examples of the national government's use of purchasing power as a fiscal or redistributive technique is found in a power of the Federal Reserve Board that does not involve direct manipulation of interest rates: going into the "open market" to buy and sell government bonds in order to increase or decrease the amount of money in circulation. By doing so, the Fed can raise or lower the availability of money and, through that, directly influence consumption and indirectly raise or lower interest rates. For example, when the Fed buys $1 billion government bonds, it puts $1 billion cash back in circulation and raises the price of the bonds by the added demand; then the increased price of the bond lowers the actual interest rates paid on the face value of the bond. The reverse takes place when the Fed goes out and sells a significant amount of government bonds.

Another case of the fiscal use of purchasing and contracting power is when government seeks to reach and support a sagging sector of the economy rather

**AMERICAN POLITICAL DEVELOPMENT**

Although the Federal Reserve Board was created by the Federal Reserve Act in 1913, it was not until developments in the 1930s—the Banking Act of 1933 and 1935 as well as the leadership of Marriner Eccles in 1935—that the Federal Reserve system enjoyed its current preeminence.

SOURCE: Jeffrey Worsham, *Other People's Money: Policy Change, Congress, and Bank Regulation* (Boulder, CO: Westview, 1997), pp. 21–45.

[34]In 1989, President Bush proposed to Congress a significant increase in the legal reserve requirement for savings and loan companies (S&Ls), which are simply banks by another name. This would of course have an anti-inflationary effect, but we cannot cite it as a monetary policy because it was virtually forced on President Bush as a means of preventing these banks from engaging in the reckless investment activity of the previous decade, which had forced many into bankruptcy, eventually costing the American people $300 to $500 billion. Thus, in this case, the raising of the S&L reserve requirement is more an example of a regulatory policy. On the other hand, President Clinton's 1993 plan to relax certain banking regulations to help small businesses would be considered a monetary policy.

[35]For a superb treatment of monetary policy and the U.S. government's administrative apparatus for implementing it, see Joshua C. Ramo, "The Three Marketeers," *Time Magazine,* Cover Story, 15 February 1999, pp. 34–42. This article provides a good picture of how independent our monetary policy is from the president and Congress. It also shows how monetary policy is used to further international as well as domestic policy goals. The "three marketeers" referred to in the above article were Alan Greenspan, Chairman of the Fed; Robert Rubin, Secretary of the Treasury; and Lawrence Summers, Deputy Secretary of the Treasury.

**PROCESS BOX 14.1**

## The Federal Government Dollar Fiscal Year 1996 Estimates

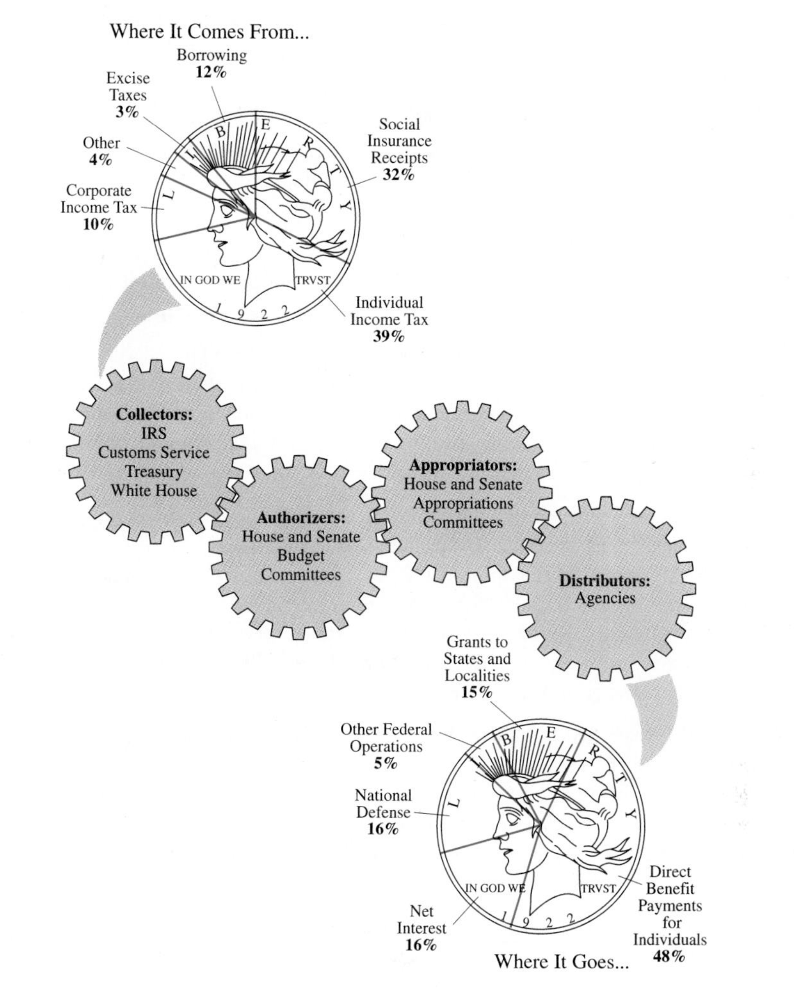


SOURCE: Office of Management and Budget, *Budget of the United States Government, Fiscal Year 1996* (Washington, DC: Government Printing Office, 1995), p. 2.

than the whole economy. For example, since the 1930s, the federal government has attempted to stabilize and sometimes to increase the prices of a number of important "surplus" commodities, such as corn or wheat, by authorizing the Department of Agriculture to buy enormous amounts of these commodities when prices on the market fall below a fixed level.

## THEN AND NOW

### Changes in American Politics

The interaction between government and economy varies as the purposes and character of government change and as the structure and performance of the economy shift.

- The role of the U.S. government in nineteenth-century economy was as a distributor of resources and benefits. In the twentieth century, the role switched more to regulating the economy and redistributing economic resources.
- Most major public policies in the United States have long histories dating back to the 1930s or earlier. Given all of the areas of government activism in contemporary politics, it is interesting to note that no important policies responsible for starting new national programs or agencies have been added since the mid-1970s.
- In the nineteenth century, the primary revenue policy of the United States was the tariff. But when additional funds were needed (particularly during the Civil War), the government turned (even prior to the Sixteenth Amendment) to some form of income tax. After the ratification of the Sixteenth Amendment in 1913, the "progressive" income tax became the primary tax policy of the U.S. government.
- The national government's administrative capacity and role in regulating the economy took hold when the government was trying to regulate the monopolistic practices of railroad barons during the nineteenth century. Government regulation of economy and business expanded significantly during the New Deal. And in the late 1960s and early 1970s, government regulation of the economy (as well as "social regulation") also increased. From the late 1970s to the present the government has largely been in a deregulatory mode.
- In the fifty years from 1930 to 1980, the national government played a much greater role in the economy than it had earlier. During those fifty years, federal outlays as a percentage of the Gross Domestic Product grew from 5 percent to 20 percent. From the late nineteenth century to the early twentieth, outlays remained consistently below 3 percent of the Gross National Product.

## Reflections on the Roles of Government

With the exception of a few radical anarchists, all the people want some policies some of the time. And there is no way to predict what policies will be adopted, expanded, de-emphasized, or terminated. But whatever happens, at least two points can be stated with some confidence.

First, nothing about public policy is natural, inherent, or divine. Policies will continue to reflect the interests of those with influence. Second, above and beyond the political realities, important moral and ethical principles are involved, because each policy decision affects the balance between citizens' freedoms and government's power.[36] All of the really important policies—including virtually all the examples in Chapters 14–16—are seen by their supporters as necessary, as a condition for their own freedom and safety. But this only confirms our assertion that *freedom depends upon control,* even as freedom is threatened by control. My freedom depends upon the restraints of all other persons who might affect my actions. Although most of society's restraints are *self*-imposed—we call that civility, without which no society can work—many restraints are governmentally imposed. What would private property be worth without governmental restraints against trespass? What would freedom of contract be worth without laws making breach of contract more expensive than observance? The study of public policies is simply one more way of exploring the shifting balance between freedom and power. Good government is not created once and for all by establishing one position for all time between popular freedom and governmental control. The requirements of freedom are not constant. Policies must be designed and redesigned to meet new challenges.

## SUMMARY

To study public policy is to understand industrial government in action, to see how government seeks to control the population through promotional and coercive techniques. Public policy is a synonym for law, and the use of public policy has become more widespread over the years, probably because it seems more reciprocal, humane, and changeable in response to demands—in a word, democratic.

The first major section of this chapter defined market economy and the conditions needed for creating a modern free market. This was followed by a discussion of the substantive goals of public policies within a market economy, that is, the objectives people seek through government. We began with the most fundamental type of policy: public order and private property. Virtually everyone supports these policies, even though people may differ on how much they want and how they want the policies implemented. We went on to another policy also widely and strongly defended in the United States: supporting and maintaining a market economy. This includes regulating the market, a restrictive approach but one motivated by the goal of making markets more stable and more competitive, not eliminating them. Deregulation is of course an aspect of regulation. All of these policies have one major objective—to maintain not only a market economy but also a sound and fiscally responsible capitalist economy.

[36]For another perspective on the political dimensions of public policy, a rational-choice analysis of the provision of public goods can be found in Kenneth A. Shepsle and Mark Bonchek, *Analyzing Politics: Rationality, Behavior, and Institutions* (New York: W. W. Norton, 1997), Chapter 10, "Public Goods, Externalities, and the Commons," pp. 260–96.

The second major section of the chapter was a handbook of the means by which policies are implemented. We called these "techniques of control" and grouped them into three historically and functionally discrete categories: promotional techniques, regulatory techniques, and redistributive techniques.

## For Further Reading

Adams, Walter, ed. *The Structure of American Industry,* 9th ed. New York: Macmillan, 1995.

Birnbaum, Jeffrey, and Alan Murray. *Showdown at Gucci Gulch.* New York: Random House, 1987.

Cochran, Clarke E., Lawrence C. Mayer, T. R. Curr, and N. Joseph Cayer. *American Public Policy—An Introduction,* 4th ed. New York: St. Martin's Press, 1993.

Derthick, Martha, and Paul Quirk. *The Politics of Deregulation.* Washington, DC: Brookings Institution, 1985.

Eisner, Marc Allan. *The State in the American Political Economy.* Englewood Cliffs, NJ: Prentice-Hall, 1995.

Greider, William. *Secrets of the Temple: How the Federal Reserve Runs the Country.* New York: Simon and Schuster, 1987.

Heilbroner, Robert. *The Nature and Logic of Capitalism.* New York: W. W. Norton, 1985.

Holmes, Stephen, and Cass R. Sunstein. *The Cost of Rights: Why Liberty Depends on Taxes.* New York: W. W. Norton, 1999.

Jansson, Bruce S. *The Reluctant Welfare State: A History of American Social Welfare Policies.* Belmont, CA: Wadsworth, 1988.

Krugman, Paul. *Peddling Prosperity: Economic Sense and Nonsense in the Age of Diminished Expectations.* New York: W. W. Norton, 1994.

Levi, Margaret. *Of Rule and Revenue.* Berkeley: University of California Press, 1988.

Levy, Frank. *The New Dollars and Dreams: American Incomes and Economic Change.* New York: The Russell Sage Foundation, 1998.

Lindblom, Charles. *Politics and Markets: The World's Political-Economic Systems.* New York: Basic Books, 1977.

Pollack, Sheldon D. *The Failure of U.S. Tax Policy: Revenue and Politics.* University Park: Pennsylvania State University Press, 1996.

Roberts, Paul C. *The Supply-Side Revolution.* Cambridge: Harvard University Press, 1984.

Sanders, M. Elizabeth. *The Regulation of Natural Gas.* Philadelphia: Temple University Press, 1981.

Sawhill, Isabel. *Challenge to Leadership: Economic and Social Issues for the Next Decade.* Washington, DC: Urban Institute Press, 1988.

Stein, Herbert. *Governing the $5 Trillion Economy.* New York: Oxford University Press, 1989.

Stone, Alan. *Wrong Number: The Breakup of AT&T.* New York: Basic Books, 1989.

Vogel, David. *Fluctuating Fortunes: The Political Power of Business in America.* New York: Basic Books, 1989.

# 15

# Government and Society

## TIME LINE ON GOVERNMENT AND SOCIETY

| Events | Institutional Developments |
|---|---|
| Federalism and the new Constitution reserve most fundamental policies to the states (1787) | Land Ordinance (1785) and Northwest Ordinance (1787) provide public land for schools |
| | U.S. Public Health Service created (1798) |
| Industrial development; powerful railroads; large corporations (1860s–1890s) | Morrill Act establishes land grant colleges and universities (1862) |
| Civil War (1861–1865) | Thirteenth Amendment abolishes slavery (1865) |
| | Freedmen's Bureau established to provide relief and educational services to newly freed blacks (1865) |
| **1900** | |
| Progressive era (1901–1917) | Pure Food and Drug Act and Meat Inspection Act to investigate and publicize abuses (1906) |
| World War I (1914–1918) | |
| Great Depression (1929–1930s) | |
| FDR proposes New Deal legislation to Congress (1930s) | National Labor Relations (Wagner) Act (1935); Social Security Act (1935); National Institutes of Health created (1937); Wagner-Steagall National Housing Act (1937); Food and Drug Administration created (1938); Fair Labor Standards Act (1938) |
| FDR's overwhelming re-election gives mandate to the New Deal (1936) | |
| U.S. enters World War II; armed forces provide first experiences with racial integration (1941–1945) | GI Bill of Rights for educational and vocational training (1944) |
| Postwar wave of strikes in key industries (1945–1946) | National School Lunch Act (1946) |
| | Housing Act provides for subsidized private housing (1949) |
| **1950** | |
| Sputnik launched by Soviet Union (1957) | National Defense Education Act (1958) |
| Civil rights movement (1950s and 1960s) | *Brown v. Board of Ed.*—Court rules against school segregation (1954) |
| Lyndon Johnson's War on Poverty (1964–1968) | Civil Rights Act establishes EEOC (1964); Food Stamp Act (1964); Elementary and Secondary Education Act (1965); Medicare and Medicaid established (1965) |

| Events | | Institutional Developments |
|---|---|---|
| "Confidence gap"; New Deal coalition collapses; Richard Nixon elected (1968) | | Voting Rights Act (1965) |
| Sustained government growth plus administrative reorganization under Nixon (1968–1974) | 1970 | Civil Rights Act (Fair Housing Act) (1968) |
| | | Indexing of welfare benefits (1972) |
| Watergate ends government growth (1974) | | Equal Employment Opportunity Act provides that suits can be brought for patterns of employment discrimination (1972) |
| Energy crisis; rise of "stagflation" (1970s) | | |
| | | CETA for job training (1973) |
| | | Supplemental Security Income (1974) |
| Ronald Reagan elected president; Republicans take control of Senate (1980) | 1980 | |
| Period of public reaction against social policies (1980s) | | Reagan cuts health and housing programs (1981–1984); Congress restores some (1985–1988) |
| | 1990 | More civil rights, education, and welfare policies relegated to states (1990) |
| Bill Clinton elected, promises reforms of welfare and health care (1992) | | Civil rights bill vetoed as a "quota bill," ultimately accepted (1992) |
| | | Family Leave Act signed (1993) |
| Congress goes Republican, with "revolutionary" agenda (1994) | | Clinton health care plan fails to win congressional passage (1994) |
| Congress stays Republican but White House remains Democratic (1996) | | Bipartisan welfare reform (1996), delegating most discretion to the states and imposing severe new restrictions on eligibility for benefits (1997) |

If there is one universally shared American ideal, it is the belief in ***equality of opportunity:*** the freedom to use whatever talents and wealth we have in order to reach our fullest potential. This ideal is enshrined in the Declaration of Independence:

> We hold these truths to be self-evident, that all men are created equal, that they are endowed by their Creator with certain unalienable Rights, that among these are Life, Liberty, and the pursuit of Happiness.

> **CORE OF THE ARGUMENT**
>
> - Social policies are primarily intended to address the material problems of both poverty and dependency.
> - The Social Security Act of 1935 distinguished between two kinds of welfare policies: contributory programs, generally called "social security," to which people must pay in order to receive benefits; and noncontributory programs, also called "welfare" or "public assistance," for which eligibility is determined by means testing.
> - Education and health policies are the most effective at breaking the circle of poverty and redistributing opportunities.

What Thomas Jefferson, the Declaration's author, meant is that all individuals have the right to pursue happiness, in fact, an *equal* right to pursue happiness—or as we put it today, an equal opportunity.

But however much we may admire it, the ideal of equal opportunity raises questions and poses problems. First, and most important, equality of opportunity inevitably means *in*equality of results or outcomes. One of the reasons for this is obviously inequalities in talent. But in the real world, talent is not the only differentiating factor. Another explanation is past inequality—the inequality of past generations visited upon the present one. This is generally called social class, or the class system. Inequality may result from poverty; lacking money for food may lead to inadequate nutrition, which may in turn explain reduced talent and reduced energies to compete. Educational opportunities also are limited by past inequalities. Since the quality of one's education and the status of one's school contribute to success, inadequate education is a tremendous disadvantage when looking for a job or a promotion. The etiquette of the work situation, which may appear to be trivial, is also essential for entry into competitive opportunities. This etiquette ranges from the elemental ability to deal with others—to get to work on time, to follow the rules—all the way to esoteric rules that are drawn into the workplace from the more exclusive schools and clubs. There are many stories of individuals with superior talents who are denied opportunities because they are "greenhorns" and unaware of the unspoken rules of the game. All of these factors make up social class, and social class shapes opportunity and success, regardless of talent.

Finally, there is prejudice pure and simple. This includes racial and religious prejudice, as well as ethnocentric bias against both genders, including traditionalist attitudes toward women. Some of these prejudices are taught as part of the culture; some come from a class structure, that, per force, separates people and breeds stereotyping.

Consequently, even in America there is a great divide between rich and poor. We discussed this in Chapter 14 vis-à-vis economic policy, and in this chapter, the great divide returns as the center of "social policy."

The distance in real income between the top 1 percent of the population and the rest of America has been growing for more than two decades, and the distance in real and family income between the richest quintile of the population and the lowest quintile has also grown, especially in the past two decades. Moreover, the income gap between the rich and the middle class has grown sharply. Inequalities in the distribution of income abound.

But there is another side to consider. First, studies on the distribution of wealth argue that inequality doesn't matter as long as *everyone* is getting better—

in other words, as long as "a rising tide lifts all boats." For example, the middle class may be falling behind the rich, but the middle class is, in absolute terms, a good deal better off than it used to be. Second, these broad inequalities in the distribution of wealth must be understood in the context of another important phenomenon in America: individual mobility. Many people who occupy the lowest brackets do not remain there for long. As George Gilder, one of the leading proponents of this point of view, puts it:

> Statistical distributions . . . can misrepresent the economy. . . . People at the bottom will move up: Six decades [after three and one-half million Jewish immigrants arrived] the mean family income of Jews was almost double the national average. Meanwhile the once supreme British Protestants (WASPs) were passed in per capita earnings . . . not only by Jews and Orientals but also by Irish, Italians, Germans, and Poles . . . and the latest generation of black West Indians.[1]

But here's the rub. Although he is correct in stating that the composition of the lowest income brackets is quite fluid in the United States, even George Gilder, the great optimist of individual opportunity and social mobility, concedes that "a free society in which the distributions are widely seen as unfair cannot long survive."[2] The fact of the matter is that people in the bottom brackets are disproportionately composed of members of groups whose opportunities are reduced precisely because of their membership in one of those groups. This is socially significant and, from the political standpoint, potential dynamite.

For example, although many African Americans have improved their economic situations over the past few decades, *as a group* African Americans remain economically deprived. In 1996, the per capita income for white Americans was $19,181, but the per capita income for blacks was more than $7,000 less, just $11,899. In 1996, 13 percent of the U.S. population—36 million people—lived in what the government defines as poverty (for a family of four, an income of less than about $16,000). Looked at according to race, the figures were strikingly different: 11.2 percent of all whites lived below the poverty level, but 28.4 percent of all African Americans lived in poverty. In the case of children, the disparities are even more glaring. More than one-fifth of all children in America, 19.8 percent, lived in poverty in 1996, but when broken down by race the numbers reveal that while one in six white children lives in poverty, 39.5 percent of black children live in officially defined poverty. These inequalities of distribution apply not only to blacks but also to Hispanic Americans. In 1996, for example, 29.4 percent of all Hispanics—and 40.3 percent of Hispanic children—lived in poverty.[3]

Even for members of minority groups who are "making it," the inequalities seem to plague them in occupations all the way up the ladder. For example, African American males in professional and technical jobs earned income on average nearly 25 percent less than whites in comparable jobs. African Americans in

[1]George Gilder, *Wealth and Poverty* (New York: Bantam, 1982), pp. 11–12.
[2]Ibid., p. 11.
[3]Bureau of the Census, *Statistical Abstract of the United States 1998* (Washington, DC: Government Printing Office, 1998), Tables 762, 759, 755, 756.

managerial, administrative, and sales positions earned only 79 percent of the incomes of white males in those same positions; and African Americans in skilled trades earned about 70 percent of what whites earned. Similar inequalities are evident between men and women in the labor force. In 1996, families headed by a single female earned an income of around 40 percent of those headed by a single male.[4] Even at the upper end of the economic ladder, inequalities persist: A 1994 study of chief executives of America's 1,000 largest publicly held corporations found that out of a total of 986 chief executives, only two were women.[5] Economic disparities between men and women at the high and low ends of the employment ladder has led to the feminist movement's demand of "equal pay for equal work."

These systematic disparities cannot go unnoticed, and when noticed they are widely seen as unfair. Let us return to the Declaration of Independence, which is quite specific on this issue. Immediately after the assertion that we all have "unalienable Rights" to "Life, Liberty, and the pursuit of Happiness," the Declaration asserts "That to secure these rights, Governments are instituted among Men. . . ." There never was any doubt about the connection between the two points: First, that all Americans share rights equally, and second, that government involvement would be necessary to ensure that enjoyment.

But when should government be called in and what should government do to help individuals secure their rights? This is what the political process is all about. The agenda for citizens' rights has varied enormously from generation to generation, beginning with the alleviation of poverty, extending beyond that to reduction of severe inequalities of wealth, to improved education and therefore opportunity, to improvement of health and safety (and again therefore opportunity), to the integration of all classes, races, nationalities, and other status groups into a single American nation. Nevertheless, the governing premise—the starting point—of all these various dissatisfactions and demands is inequality and what governments should do about it.

In brief, this chapter deals with "Who *is* poor?" and "What can government do?" Most of the public policies are called welfare policies, or cumulatively "the welfare state."

**THE CENTRAL QUESTION**

"How can government fight poverty?"

## THE WELFARE STATE

Americans do not have a long history of taking public responsibility for inequalities of opportunity. First, our faith in individualism was extremely strong. Second, this was fed by the existence of the frontier, which was so enticing that poverty was seen as a temporary condition that could be alleviated by moving westward.

[4]Ibid., Table 740.

[5]*Good for Business: Making Full Use of the Nation's Human Capital. A Fact Finding Report of the Federal Glass Ceiling Commission* (Washington, DC: Government Printing Office, 1995).

Third, Americans conceived of poverty as belonging in two separate classes, the "deserving poor" and the "undeserving poor." The deserving poor were the widows, orphans, and others rendered dependent by some misfortune beyond their control such as national disaster, injury in the course of honest labor, or effects of war. The undeserving poor were able-bodied persons unwilling to work, transients from their communities, or others of whom, for various reasons, the community did not approve. An extensive system of private charity developed during the nineteenth century on the basis of this distinction between the deserving poor and the undeserving poor. Most of this kind of welfare went through churches, related religious groups and, to an extent, ethnic and fraternal societies. This was called charity, or "Christian love," which was often coupled with a high moral sense of obligation.

Until the end of the nineteenth century, government involvement in charitable activities, or what we today call welfare, was slight, not only because of America's preference for individual endeavors and for private and voluntary approaches to charity, but also because Americans believed that all of the deserving poor would be taken care of by private efforts. Congress did enact pensions for Civil War veterans and their dependents; and for its day, this was considered a generous social policy. But these pension policies were badly undercut by a patronage-ridden administration of the benefits, thus damaging the system and depriving a large segment of American citizens of federal aid.[6] Congress also attempted to reach the lower-income groups with policies that would eliminate child labor, and a number of states joined in with attempts to eliminate the most egregiously dangerous and unsanitary working conditions. But these efforts were soon declared unconstitutional by the Supreme Court. Other efforts, such as the experiment with mothers' pensions and additional protective labor policies, were adopted by a few progressive states. But even as late as 1928, only 11.6 percent of all relief granted in fifteen of the largest cities came from public funds.[7]

**AMERICAN POLITICAL DEVELOPMENT**

Although the U.S. government did not have the capacity for a "welfare state" until the first decades of the twentieth century, there are early examples of entitlements, mostly to veterans, widows, and children. One scholar even found an example of entitlement policy in the first decades of the nineteenth century, when the government provided limited benefits for veterans of the American Revolution.

SOURCE: Laura S. Jensen, "The Early American Origins of Entitlements," *Studies in American Political Development* 10 (Fall 1996), pp. 360–404.

The traditional approach, dominated by the private sector with its severe distinction between deserving and undeserving poor, crumbled in 1929 before the stark reality of the Great Depression. During the Depression, misfortune became so widespread and private wealth shrank so drastically that private charity was out of the question and the distinction between deserving and undeserving became impossible to draw. The Great Depression proved to Americans that poverty could be a result of imperfections in the economic system rather than of

[6]See Suzanne Mettler, *Divided Citizens* (Ithaca, NY: Cornell University Press, 1998), p. 2. See also Theda Skocpol, *Protecting Soldiers and Mothers: The Political Origins of Social Policy in the United States* (Cambridge: Harvard University Press, 1992).

[7]Merle Fainsod et al., *Government and the American Economy* (New York: W. W. Norton, 1959), p. 769, based on a WPA study by Ann E. Geddes.

individual irresponsibility. Americans held to their distinction between the deserving and the undeserving poor but significantly altered their standards regarding who was deserving and who was not.

Once poverty and dependency were accepted as problems inherent in the economy, a large-scale public policy approach became practical. Indeed, there was no longer any real question about whether the national government would assume a major responsibility for poverty; from that time forward, it was a question of how generous or restrictive the government was going to be about the welfare of the poor. The national government's efforts to improve the welfare of the poor can be divided into two responses. First, it instituted policies that attempted to change the economic rules about the condition of work for those who were working and could work. Second, it set in place policies seeking to change the economic rules determining the quality of life of those who could not (and in some cases, would not) work. The first response comes under the heading of policies for labor regulation. We dealt with some of these policies in Chapter 3, showing how the Constitution itself, especially the commerce clause, had to be interpreted in a fundamentally different way in order to reach into local plants and firms to improve the conditions and rewards of work. Since the adoption of the 1935 National Labor Relations (Wagner) Act, there have been revisions (e.g., the Taft-Hartley Act of 1947 and the Landrum-Griffin Labor Management Act of 1959), but no real change of the economic rules established in 1935. These rules were designed to protect laborers so that they could organize and bargain collectively with their employers rather than (according to the older economic rules) negotiating as individuals under vastly unequal conditions.

**AMERICAN POLITICAL DEVELOPMENT**

In 1950, the federal government spent $10.5 billion on social welfare programs, and state and local governments spent $13 billion. Combined, this $23.5 billion amounted to 8.2 percent of the Gross National Product. By 1966, the federal government was spending more than state governments were—$45.2 billion to $42.6 billion—which amounted to 11.9 percent of the Gross Domestic Product. These figures doubled by 1972 and reached $676.4 billion in federal expenditures and $485.8 billion in state and local expenditures (20.5 percent of the GDP) by 1991.

SOURCE: Harold W. Stanley and Richard G. Niemi, *Vital Statistics on American Politics*, 5th ed. (Washington, DC: Congressional Quarterly Press, 1995), p. 353.

It is possible for public policies to go much further than the rules laid out under the Wagner Act, however. For example, rather than a minimum wage law, there could be a minimum annual income law. President Clinton moved in this direction when he expanded the Earned Income Tax Credit (EITC) by $21 billion in his 1993 five-year budget deal. The purpose of the EITC is to provide relief for employed parents whose earnings are close to or below the poverty line; in 1992 this group comprised 18 percent of all full-time workers. The right to sixty days' notice before closing a plant, once thought radical, was adopted by Congress in 1988. The next step could be worker participation in management decisions about closings or hiring and promotion or even ownership and investment.

The second response to welfare is the one that will most concern us in this section: policies that seek to change the economic rules regarding those who cannot work or who are, for whatever reason, outside the economic system. These policies make up the welfare state.

## Foundations of the Welfare State

The foundations of the American welfare state were established by the Social Security Act of 1935. The 1935 act provided for two separate categories of welfare—*contributory* and *noncontributory*. Table 15.1 is an outline of the key programs in each of these categories.

**Contributory Programs** ***Contributory programs*** are financed by taxation, which justifiably can be called "forced savings." These contributory programs are what most people have in mind when they refer to Social Security or social insurance. Under the original contributory program, old-age insurance, the employer and the employee were each required to pay equal amounts, which in 1937 were

TABLE 15.1

**Public Welfare Programs**

| TYPE OF PROGRAM | YEAR ENACTED | NUMBER OF RECIPIENTS IN 1998 (IN MILLIONS) | FEDERAL OUTLAYS IN 1998 (IN BILLIONS) |
|---|---|---|---|
| **Contributory (Insurance) System** | | | |
| Old Age, Survivors, and Disability Insurance | 1935 | 44.0 | $377.9 |
| Medicare | 1965 | 38.2 | $215.3 |
| Unemployment Compensation | 1935 | 7.4 | $21.5 |
| **Noncontributory (Public Assistance) System** | | | |
| Medicaid | 1965 | 33.0 | $101.0 |
| Food Stamps | 1964 | 19.8 | $22.4 |
| Supplemental Security Income (cash assistance for aged, blind, disabled) | 1974 | 6.3 | $26.1 |
| Housing Assistance to low-income families | 1937 | NA | $24.3 |
| School Lunch Program | 1946 | 31.4 | $8.8 |
| Temporary Assistance to Needy Families* | 1996 | NA | $18.2 |

NA = Not available.

*Replaced Aid to Families with Dependent Children, which was enacted in 1935.

SOURCE: Office of Management and Budget, *Budget of the United States Government, Fiscal Year 1999* (Washington, DC: Government Printing Office, 1998), pp. 291, 201.

set at 1 percent of the first $3,000 of wages, to be deducted from the paycheck of each employee and matched by the same amount from the employer. This percentage has increased over the years; the total contribution is now 7.65 percent subdivided as follows: 6.20 percent on the first $68,400 of income for Social Security benefits, plus 1.45 percent on all earnings for Medicare.[8]

Social Security is a rather conservative approach to welfare. In effect, the Social Security (FICA) tax, as a forced saving, sends a message that people cannot be trusted to save voluntarily in order to take care of their own needs. But in another sense, it is quite radical. Social Security is not real insurance; workers' contributions do not accumulate in a personal account like an annuity. Consequently, contributors do not receive benefits in proportion to their own contributions, and this means that there is a redistribution of wealth occurring. In brief, contributory Social Security mildly redistributes wealth from higher- to lower-income people, and it quite significantly redistributes wealth from younger workers to older retirees. The biggest single expansion in contributory programs after 1935 was the establishment in 1965 of ***Medicare***, which was set up to provide substantial medical services to elderly persons who were already eligible to receive old-age, survivors', and disability insurance under the original Social Security system. A further jump in Social Security growth came seven years later, in 1972, when Congress decided to end the perplexing political problem of biennial legislation to adjust Social Security benefits and costs, by establishing ***indexing***, whereby benefits paid out under contributory programs would be modified annually by ***cost of living adjustments (COLAs)*** based on changes in the Consumer Price Index, so that benefits would increase automatically as the cost of living rose (see also Chapter 14). And to pay for these automatic adjustments, Social Security taxes (contributions) also increased. This made Social Security, in the words of one observer, "a politically ideal program. It bridged partisan conflict by providing liberal benefits under conservative financial auspices."[9] In other words, conservatives could more readily yield to the demands of the well-organized and expanding constituency of elderly voters if benefit increases were guaranteed and automatic; and liberals could cement conservative support by agreeing to finance the expanded benefits through increases in the regressive Social Security tax rather than out of general revenues coming from the more progressive income tax.

**Noncontributory Programs** Programs to which beneficiaries do not have to contribute—***noncontributory programs***—are also known as ***public assistance programs,*** or, derisively, as "welfare." Until 1996, the most important noncontributory program was ***Aid to Families with Dependent Children*** (***AFDC,*** originally called Aid to Dependent Children, or ADC), which was founded in 1935 by the

[8]The figures cited are for 1998. Although on paper the employer is taxed, this is all part of "forced savings," because in reality the employer's contribution is nothing more than a mandatory wage supplement that the employee never sees or touches before it goes into the trust funds held exclusively for the contributory programs.

[9]Edward J. Harpham, "Fiscal Crisis and the Politics of Social Security Reform," in *The Attack on the Welfare State,* ed. Anthony Champagne and Edward Harpham (Prospect Heights, IL: Waveland Press, 1984), p. 13.

original Social Security Act. In 1996, Congress abolished AFDC and replaced it with the ***Temporary Assistance to Needy Families (TANF)*** block grant. Eligibility for public assistance is determined by ***means testing,*** a procedure that requires applicants to show a financial need for assistance. Between 1935 and 1965, the government created programs to provide housing assistance, school lunches, and food stamps to other needy Americans.

As with contributory programs, the noncontributory public assistance programs also made their most significant advances in the 1960s and 1970s. The largest single category of expansion was the establishment in 1965 of ***Medicaid,*** a program that provides extended medical services to all low-income persons who have already established eligibility through means testing under AFDC or TANF. Noncontributory programs underwent another major transformation in the 1970s in the level of benefits they provide. Besides being means tested, noncontributory programs are federal rather than national; grants-in-aid are provided by the national government to the states as incentives to establish the programs (see Chapter 3). Thus, from the beginning there were considerable disparities in benefits from state to state. The national government sought to rectify the disparities in levels of old-age benefits in 1974 by creating the ***Supplemental Security Income (SSI)*** program to augment benefits for the aged, the blind, and the disabled. SSI provides uniform minimum benefits across the entire nation and includes mandatory COLAs. States are allowed to be more generous if they wish, but no state is permitted to provide benefits below the minimum level set by the national government. As a result, twenty-five states increased their own SSI benefits to the mandated level.

The new TANF program is also administered by the states and, like the old-age benefits just discussed, benefit levels vary widely from state to state (see Figure 15.1). For example, although the median national "standard of need" for a family of three was $542 per month (55 percent of the poverty-line income) in 1997, the states' monthly TANF benefits varied from $120 in Mississippi to $923 in Alaska.[10]

The number of people receiving AFDC benefits expanded in the 1970s, in part because new welfare programs had been established in the mid-1960s: Medicaid (discussed earlier) and ***food stamps,*** which are coupons that can be exchanged for food at most grocery stores. These programs provide what are called ***in-kind*** benefits—noncash goods and services that would otherwise have to be paid for in cash by the beneficiary. In addition to simply adding on the cost of medical services and food to the level of benefits given to AFDC recipients, the possibility of receiving Medicaid benefits provided an incentive for many poor

**AMERICAN POLITICAL DEVELOPMENT**

The food-stamp program grew exponentially from 1964 to 1974. In 1964, the participating twenty-two states spent $28.6 million on 360,000 recipients. By 1974, all fifty states participated; there were 13,524,000 recipients and the federal cost was $2.7 billion.

SOURCE: Timothy Conlan, *New Federalism: Intergovernmental Reform from Nixon to Reagan* (Washington, DC: Brookings Institution, 1988), p. 83.

[10]Ways and Means Committee Print, WMCP:105-7, *1998 Green Book,* from U.S. GPO Online via GPO Access at http://www.access.gpo.gov/congress/wm001.html (accessed June 19, 1998).

FIGURE 15.1

Variations in State Spending on TANF Benefits

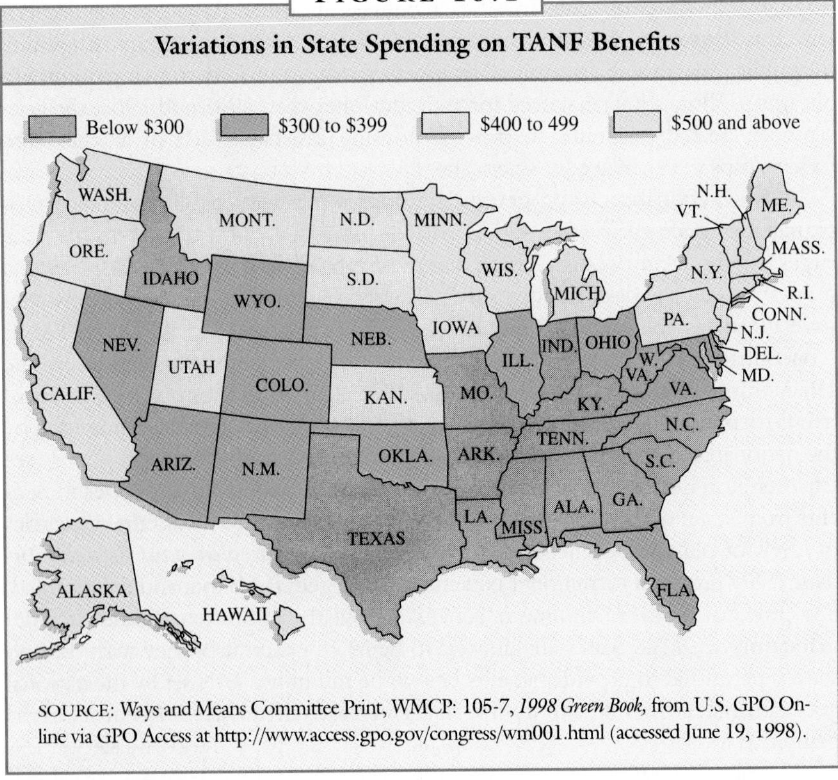


SOURCE: Ways and Means Committee Print, WMCP: 105-7, *1998 Green Book*, from U.S. GPO Online via GPO Access at http://www.access.gpo.gov/congress/wm001.html (accessed June 19, 1998).

Americans to establish their eligibility for AFDC, which would also establish their eligibility to receive Medicaid. At the same time, the government significantly expanded its publicity efforts to encourage the dependent unemployed to establish their eligibility for these various programs.

Another, more complex reason for the growth of AFDC in the 1970s was that it became more difficult for the government to terminate people's AFDC benefits for lack of eligibility. In the 1970 case of *Goldberg v. Kelly*, the Supreme Court held that the financial benefits of AFDC could not be revoked without due process—i.e., a hearing at which evidence is presented, etc.[11] This ruling inaugurated the concept of the ***entitlement,*** a class of government benefits with a status similar to that of property (which, according to the Fourteenth Amendment, cannot be taken from people "without due process of law"). *Goldberg v. Kelly* did not provide that the beneficiary had a "right" to government benefits; it provided that once a person's eligibility for AFDC was established, and as long as the program was still in effect, that person could not be denied benefits without due process. The decision left open the possibility that Congress could terminate the program and its benefits by passing a piece of legislation. If the welfare benefit were truly a property right, Congress would have no authority to deny it by a mere majority vote.

[11]Goldberg v. Kelly, 397 U.S. 254 (1970).

Thus the establishment of in-kind benefit programs and the legal obstacles involved in terminating benefits contributed to the growth of the welfare state. But it is important to note that real federal spending on AFDC itself did not rise after the mid-1970s. Unlike Social Security, AFDC was not indexed to inflation; without cost of living adjustments, the value of AFDC benefits fell by more than one-third. Moreover, the largest noncontributory welfare program, Medicaid (as shown by Table 15.1, p. 621), actually devotes less than one-third of its expenditures to poor families; the rest goes to the disabled and the elderly in nursing homes.[12] Together, these programs have significantly increased the security of the poor and the vulnerable and must be included in a genuine assessment of the redistributive influence and the cost of the welfare state today.

The expansion of the benefits and coverage of noncontributory programs during the 1970s also contributed to tremendous increases in their costs. That was already becoming a political issue, because these expenditures were coming out of the more progressive income tax revenues directly redistributing wealth from workers to nonworkers. Meanwhile, demographic changes were also contributing to the growing sense of political crisis because of the social composition of the public assistance beneficiaries, a much lower-status category of the deserted, the divorced, and unwed mothers. During the 1950s and 1960s, AFDC developed a reputation of being not only a permanent dole for unwed mothers but a program to support the permanent dependency of black women.

The actual data do not confirm this reputation. For example, between 1960 and 1974, the ratio of children to parents under AFDC did not change very much: from 77 percent children in 1960 to 72 percent children in 1974. And, more tellingly, the proportion of black beneficiaries to all beneficiaries in all means-tested programs was 35.5 percent in 1993 (the last available data) and the proportion of blacks to the total beneficiaries in AFDC alone was 16.4 percent. This is somewhat in excess of the 13 percent of the total population that is African American, but not enough to support factually the reputation of AFDC as a racial phenomenon.

Yet once such a reputation was established in the popular mind, it sustained itself and became the basis for the kinds of attacks on the entire welfare system that made it the most important "wedge issue" of the 1970s, 1980s, and 1990s.[13]

**Welfare Reform** The Republicans came to power in 1980 with welfare reform very high on the agenda of the "Reagan Revolution." But even with the apparently sincere cooperation of the Democrats, the Republicans were hardly able even to cut the "rate of increase," much less the actual annual expenditures. As shown on Figure 15.2, the increase in social welfare expenditures stayed at about the same rate as

[12]See U.S. House of Representatives, Committee on Ways and Means, *Where Your Money Goes: The 1994–95 Green Book* (Washington, DC: Brassey's, 1994), pp. 325, 802.

[13]Sources: Department of Commerce, U.S. Census Bureau, *Current Population Reports*, July 1996; *The World Almanac*, 1996, p. 382; U.S. Bureau of the Census, *Statistical Abstracts of the United States* (Washington, DC: U.S. Government Printing Office, annual issues); and James E. Anderson et al., *Public Policy and Politics in America* (North Scituate, MA: Duxbury Press, 1978), pp. 109–14.

FIGURE 15.2

**Social Welfare Expenditures under Public Programs (1970–1994)**

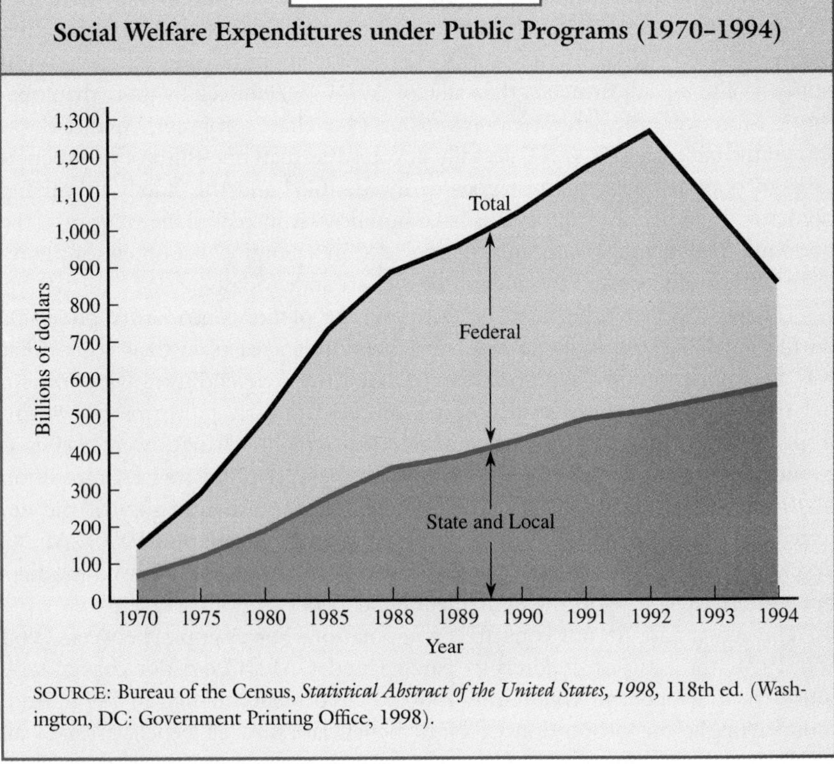


SOURCE: Bureau of the Census, *Statistical Abstract of the United States, 1998,* 118th ed. (Washington, DC: Government Printing Office, 1998).

before, and in fact continued to keep pace with the Gross Domestic Product (GDP). Moreover, no public assistance programs were terminated, despite Republican railings against all of them, AFDC in particular. And President Reagan quickly discovered how popular the Social Security (contributory) programs were in the United States and was moved to make frequent public promises not to alter what he himself called "the safety net." President Bush followed suit, not only with defense of the safety net but with a new label for it, a "kinder, gentler society."

President Clinton was elected on a platform of "putting people first," but deficit reality significantly revised the meaning of that promise. His most positive achievement was the 1994 increase in the Earned Income Tax Credit (EITC), by which working households with children can file through their income tax returns for an income supplement if their annual earned incomes fall below $20,000. Yet aside from this one, albeit important, benefit increase, Clinton's original campaign promise to "end welfare as we know it" plagued him all during 1993–1995. In 1994, Clinton in fact proposed a welfare reform plan that would have cut off benefits after two years to those who refused to work or to join job-training programs—promising to remove about 400,000 welfare recipients from the rolls by the year 2000. This represented a radical departure from traditional federal welfare policies, but Clinton was overtaken by the Republican seizure of Congress in the 1994 elections, and the ante for reduction of welfare recipients by the year 2000 went up from the Democratic promise of 400,000 to a Republican promise of 1.5 million.

Nevertheless, the stalemate over welfare was still not to be broken until the waning days of the 104th Congress and the approach of the 1996 presidential election. The Personal Responsibility and Work Opportunity Reconciliation Act (PRA) was signed into law on August 22, 1996, and it went far beyond anything the pundits could have imagined. It was made possible by unusual Republican cohesion in Congress and by the president's decision to endorse the Republican bill, based largely on his fear of public repudiation at the polls in November.

The new law replaced the sixty-one-year-old program of AFDC and its education/work training program, known as JOBS, with block grants to the states over a five-year period for Temporary Assistance to Needy Families (TANF). The act not only imposes the five-year time limit on the TANF benefits but also requires work after two years of benefits. It also requires community service after two months of benefits, unless the state administrators agree to an exemption of the rule. Many additional requirements for eligibility are spelled out in the law. The following are a few key examples of these requirements: Unwed teenage mothers are ineligible unless they live in the home of an adult relative or other adult guardian. Mothers under eighteen are also ineligible unless they have a high school diploma or are attending school. States have the option to exclude noncitizens, including legal aliens; and aliens who entered the United States after 1996 are barred from benefits for five years. Beneficiaries must prove they have never been convicted of a drug-related felony. And the states are under severe obligation to impose all these requirements on the threat of losing their TANF federal grants. (The problems of administering the new act were dealt with in Chapter 7.)[14] The two other important public assistance programs, food stamps and Medicaid, were implicated but not eliminated in the act. The food stamp program became a "simplified food stamp program," which applies many of the same TANF restrictions as outlined before. Moreover, differences in food stamp benefits from state to state are permitted to vary even more greatly than variations in cash benefits.

During the first year that this new welfare law was in effect, the number of families receiving assistance dropped by 20 percent.[15] Some observers took this as a sign that welfare reform was working; indeed, former welfare recipients have been more successful at finding and keeping jobs than many critics of the new law predicted. For example, Wisconsin became the leading state in taking people off the welfare roles and putting them to work, proudly calling it W-2, "Welfare Works." Within six months after adoption of welfare reform, Milwaukee alone cut more than 10,000 people from its welfare roles. However, states like Wisconsin were actually spending *more* money, in order to move enrollees from welfare to work. So while welfare reform can be considered a political success, it is less clear that it has been a fiscal success.

[14]For more information and an outstanding evaluation of PRA 1996, see Gwendolyn Mink, *Welfare's End* (Ithaca, NY: Cornell University Press, 1998), especially Chapter 3.

[15]Ways and Means Committee Print, WMCP:105-7, *1998 Green Book,* from U.S. GPO Online via GPO Access at http://www.access.gpo.gov/congress/wm001.html (accessed June 1998).

Other additional evidence suggests more caution in declaring welfare reform a success. Early studies show that welfare recipients are not paid enough to pull their families out of poverty and that child care and transportation continue to cause many problems for people seeking to leave welfare.[16] Moreover, two big questions remain unanswered. The first is whether welfare recipients who are still receiving aid—and whom employers are less likely to want to hire—will be able to find jobs. For example, in New York City, between 1996 and 1999, only 29 percent of welfare recipients looking for work had found jobs.[17] The second question is what will happen to former welfare recipients and other low-income workers when there is an economic downturn and fewer jobs available. Welfare reform has been implemented in time of record low unemployment levels; when employers are less desperate for workers, welfare recipients are more likely to have difficulty finding jobs. These concerns suggest that the 1996 law may not mark the end of welfare reform but may be a prelude to a round of future reforms.

**Reforming Social Security** Since its creation in 1935, the Social Security system has provided retirement, survivor, and disability benefits to millions of Americans. Up until now, the system has run "in the black"—that is, it has collected more money than it has given out. In 1995, 43 million Americans received a total of $340 billion in Social Security benefits, given to 26 million retirees, 6 million spouses and children, 7 million survivors of deceased workers, and 4 million disabled workers. Even today, more than half of all American workers do not have a private pension plan; they will have to rely solely on Social Security for their retirement. If there were no Social Security, half of all senior citizens would be living below the poverty line. Thus, Social Security guarantees a measure of equality.

Nearly all wage earners and self-employed individuals pay into Social Security. Yet many fear that the system cannot sustain itself. When the baby boomer generation—a relatively large percentage of Americans, born between 1946 and 1964—reaches retirement age, their large numbers and longer life expectancies may place too great a demand on the system, forcing today's young people to pay ever more into a system that may be bankrupt by the time they retire.

Those who argue for a major change in Social Security point out that Social Security benefits are not drawn from an interest-bearing account; rather, they are paid for from taxes collected from current workers. Therefore, current workers carry the primary financial burden for the system. When baby boomers retire, their political and economic clout will be so great that they will be able to push aside any effort to limit benefits or relieve the financial burden on a much smaller number of younger wage earners. For Social Security to continue, it may have to borrow, or draw money from the federal Treasury, leaving younger generations with a staggering debt. If no changes are made in the current system, the Social Security Trust Fund

[16] See National Conference of State Legislatures, "Tracking Recipients after They Leave Welfare," at http://www.ncsl.org/statefed/welfare/followup.htm (accessed June 1998).

[17] Jason DeParle, "What Welfare-to-Work Really Means," *New York Times Magazine,* 20 December 1998, p. 50ff.

(the account where surplus monies are held) will, according to projections, go bankrupt by 2029.

Contrary to popular impressions, Social Security benefits are not a simple repayment, plus interest, of money contributed by workers. The average retiree receives back the equivalent of all the money he or she contributed over a lifetime of work, plus interest, in the space of four to eight years. Most retirees receive far more than they put in. Why should today's student-age population provide subsidies to retirees who do not need the extra income? Several reform ideas have been suggested. One proposes an investment shift from the current low-yield, conservative, U.S. government securities to private investment in higher-yield stocks and bonds. Another proposal urges a shift to means testing, to reduce or eliminate benefits for those who already have ample income. A third proposal calls for raising the minimum retirement age. The current payroll tax for raising funds could also be altered. As of 1998, income is taxed only up to $68,400, so that a worker making a million dollars a year pays the same Social Security taxes as a worker making $69,000. If action is not taken soon, the system will likely be pushed to extinction by the burdens of the vast number of baby boomers.

Although nearly all observers favor some reform, defenders of the system argue that critics vastly overstate the problem. First, estimates of a looming Social Security crisis are based on very conservative economic projections that assume a far slower rate of growth in the nation's economy than has occurred up until now. Given the nation's history of growth, such projections are unduly pessimistic. Yet even if they are accurate, other factors will minimize the financial burden on younger workers when the baby boomers retire. In the year 2030, for example, at the height of boomer retirement, the overall workforce will be larger than during the height of the baby boom. The reasons for this surge in the twenty-first-century workforce include an increase in births and changing work patterns.

As for proposals to alter radically the distribution of benefits, system supporters point out that Social Security was created to serve several purposes. While the system provides a vital safety net to protect the elderly from poverty, it was also intended to be a universal system, entitling every worker to receive benefits from past work. It was also designed to be a progressive system by awarding greater benefits to those who earned more, and a hedge against inflation by including cost-of-living increases. Moreover, "generational sharing," whereby current workers would provide benefits for retirees, was part of the system's design. These purposes are as valid today as they were in 1935.

## The Welfare State Evaluated

**Arguments against** 1. The first is the simplest: The welfare state costs too much. This is partly inherent in the situation. It is a simple fact that because of age, education, and any number of cultural factors, a large class of people simply do not fit well into the modern industrial economic system. But part of the undue cost of the welfare state has to be attributed to bad political decisions. One of those was to spread coverage too widely and without regard to demographic factors, as outlined earlier. Another unwise decision was to index benefits without

# Welfare Reform

*In 1996, Congress passed and the president signed a sweeping welfare reform bill. Among other things, the new law cut $55 billion from federal welfare programs over six years, imposed strict work requirements on able-bodied adults, and ended federal guarantees of cash assistance to poor children. Yet debate continues to rage over such provisions as work requirements and other restrictions; even in 1996, one American child in five under the age of eighteen lived in poverty. Political scientist Lawrence M. Mead defends work requirements as a way of breaking welfare dependency, while social analysts Richard A. Cloward and Frances Fox Piven argue that such "reform" is simply another name for punishing the poor.*

## MEAD

Liberal reformers presume that welfare recipients fail to work because they face special "barriers," notably a lack of jobs, child-care, and training opportunities. If government provided more of these things, liberals assert, welfare work levels would rise. That is a misconception. Research has shown that the presumed impediments rarely keep people from working, at least in low-skilled, low-paid jobs. The main reason for nonwork, rather, is the reluctance of many recipients to take such jobs. The main task of welfare work policy is to overcome that reluctance. While this probably requires some new services, it above all requires more clear-cut *requirements* that recipients work in return for benefits. Those who favor increased benefits are seeking not so much to promote work as to advance the traditional liberal interest in social equality. . . .

The work issue has come to the fore for a good reason: Nonwork is the immediate cause of much poverty and dependency today. There is still a tendency to see the poor simply as victims entitled to government redress. That view is most plausible for the elderly and disabled poor, whom society does not expect to work. But, it is implausible for families headed by able-bodied people of working age, whom society does expect to work. . . .

It is true that most poor families have some earnings, yet remain needy. But few of these families have members working full-time. Many more people are poor for lack of work than despite work. Moreover, for the vast majority of workers, poverty is uncommon or transient. Fewer than 3 percent of able-bodied, working-age adults lived in poor households with any earnings in 1970, and only 15 percent of these—or 0.3 percent of all working-age adults—were also poor in 1980. . . .

The great question is how to get more of the employable poor to participate in the economy, in any kind of job, not how to improve those jobs. . . . For it is the *working* people that government would help by raising job quality, and who also have the greatest power to help themselves. Liberals and conservatives can dispute whether working people really need help from government. They ought to agree that dependent adults should at least become workers.[1]

## CLOWARD AND PIVEN

[Workfare] proposals reflect a rising tide of antiwelfare rhetoric, whose basic argument is that people receiving public assistance become trapped in a "cycle of dependency." . . . The national press announces that dependency has reached epidemic proportions. According to these accounts, rising unemployment, declining wage levels and disappearing fringe benefits need not concern anyone. "The old issues were economic and structural," [Lawrence] Mead says, and "the new ones are social and personal." . . .

But there is no economically and politically practical way to replace welfare with work at a time when the labor market is saturated with people looking for jobs. Unemployment averaged 4.5 percent in the 1950s, 4.7 percent in the 1960s, 6.1 percent in the 1970s and 7.2 percent in the 1980s, and job prospects look no better in the 1990s. The labor market is flooded with immigrants from Asia and Latin America, and growing numbers of women have taken up jobs to shore up family income as wages decline. Confronted with an increasingly globalized economy, corporations are shedding workers or closing domestic plants and opening new ones in Third World countries with cheap labor. Meanwhile, defense industries are making huge workforce cuts. . . .

Because most mothers who receive Aid to Families with Dependent Children are unskilled, they can command only the lowest wages and thus cannot adequately support their families, a problem that will grow worse as wages continue to decline. According to the Census Bureau, 14.4 million year-round, full-time workers 16 years of age or older (18 percent of the total) had annual earnings below the poverty level in 1990, up from 10.3 million (14.6 percent) in 1984 and 6.6 million (12.3 percent) in 1974. There is no reason to think that A.F.D.C. mothers can become "self-sufficient" when growing millions of currently employed workers cannot. In a study of the finances of welfare families, sociologists Christopher Jencks and Kathryn Edin found that "single mothers do not turn to welfare because they are pathologically dependent on handouts or unusually reluctant to work—they do so because they cannot get jobs that pay better than welfare." . . .

Despite workfare's record of failure, an aura of optimism still permeates the literature on welfare reform. . . . As sociologist Sanford Schram points out, these [workfare] initiatives serve "symbolic purposes at the expense of substantive benefits."

Politicians understand the value of this symbolism, however, and rush to divert voter discontent over rising unemployment and falling wage levels by focusing on "welfare reform," knowing that welfare mothers, a majority of whom are black and Hispanic, make convenient scapegoats.[2]

[1]Lawrence M. Mead, "Jobs for the Welfare Poor: Work Requirements Can Overcome the Barriers," *Policy Review,* Winter 1990.

[2]Richard A. Cloward and Frances Fox Piven, "Punishing the Poor, Again: The Fraud of Workfare," *The Nation,* 24 May 1993.

taking countervailing factors into account as part of the structure. One of the factors affecting benefits and coverage is lack of attention to the significantly increased life expectancy of Americans and the absence of commitment to a slow but steady stepping up of the retirement age. Another major factor contributing to cost increases is that the whole system became unnecessarily bureaucratic, especially the public assistance system. This is not an inherent feature of the welfare state or of government but of poor legislative draftsmanship. As referred to earlier in this chapter and in Chapter 7, the Social Security laws lodged far too much discretion in the state agencies where public assistance is to be administered, and the more discretion, the more administration, and of course the more staff and red tape. Another factor significantly contributing to unnecessary cost escalation was the "third-party" structure of repayment in Medicare and in Medicaid. Once the systems were set up so that doctors and patients could establish their relationship without regard to cost, which would be picked up by the government, this relieved all the parties from any concern for cost.

2. The welfare state is too paternalistic. The contributory programs are based on "forced savings," relieving all individuals to some degree of concern for their future. The noncontributory programs are also paternalistic even though it is true that people in poverty usually don't have the choice to save. There is another aspect of this that will come up under the fourth criticism.

3. The welfare state is too redistributive. The welfare state is based on taxation, but all taxes redistribute in one way or another. Although that is undeniable, the main criticism here is that the structure of the welfare state does risk class antagonism. It may be a miracle that class warfare has not happened yet. But it could, especially since the redistributive taxes are reaching lower and lower tax brackets, and lower income people are looking more angrily at the fact that some people on public assistance are making almost as much income as they are earning through hard work, while also paying taxes on those earnings.

4. The welfare state is an example of what insurance companies call *moral hazard*. Although Charles Murray does not use the term in his famous and influential critique of the welfare state, *Losing Ground*, he is probably the best known exponent of this approach to the evaluation of the welfare state.[18] Moral hazard is the danger or probability that a policy will encourage the behavior or otherwise bring about the problem that it ensures against. For example, many people whose cars are insured will take much less care to prevent their cars from being damaged or stolen. The four pieces of Murray's argument are: (a) The safety net, or what Piven and Cloward call subsistence rights, would be an example of moral hazard in the welfare state, because as observed above, some if not all of the programs weaken to some degree self-reliance and individual responsibility.[19] (b) Entitlement to benefits weakens the work incentive. In fact, even the strongest supporters of noncontributory public assistance agree that care has to be taken to keep the benefits high enough for subsistence but not so high that people will prefer to stay on the benefits rather than take a job. (c) Entitlement to child support "brings more babies" into the world. Even if child support does not "cause" the first birth, the argument goes that it increases the likelihood of a second and perhaps even a third, in order to maintain an acceptable level of subsistence. (d) By the same token, aid to the child and to the mother contributes to the breaking up

[18]Charles Murray, *Losing Ground: American Social Policy, 1950–1980* (New York: Basic Books, 10th anniversary edition, 1994).

[19]For a discussion and a defense of subsistence rights, see Frances Fox Piven and Richard Cloward, *The New Class War* (New York: Pantheon, 1982), esp. pp. 32–48.

of families by increased divorce and to the choice of the female not to marry in the first place.[20]

These critiques are not really subject to scientific proof or disproof. They are written like lawyers' briefs, summoning up the best data and logic possible in hopes that "the preponderance of the evidence" will convince the jury—that is, the public and the policy makers. It is undeniably true, for example, that single women on welfare are poor and dependent and are likely to remain so if they have children. It is also true that many of these single women have additional children while on welfare. But the conclusion that welfare is the cause of the babies and of the delinquency and crime that are attributed to these children does not logically follow. In fact, many of the most prominent opposers of welfare don't even bother trying to establish proof of this causal relationship. To Charles Murray, what matters is not the birth of babies in poverty but the *illegitimacy* of those births—in other words, the absence of marriage is the real cause. "Illegitimacy is the single most important social problem of our time—more important than crime, drugs, poverty, illiteracy, welfare or homelessness because it drives everything else."[21]

**Arguments for** 1. The welfare state is good fiscal policy. As discussed in the previous chapter, the welfare state is one of the "automatic stabilizers." When the economy is declining, welfare payments go up enough to help maintain consumer demand. In contrast, during inflationary periods, welfare taxes take an extra bite out of consumer dollars, thereby dampening inflation somewhat.

2. The welfare state is paternalistic. A vice to the critics of welfare, paternalism is a virtue to its supporters; paternalism can be good medicine, if not taken in too strong a dose. It is a notorious fact that Americans don't save enough. Welfare taxation has produced a system of universal saving, which is a safety net for employers, just as the benefits aspect of welfare constitute a safety net for employees. Social Security, unemployment compensation, disability benefits, and other features of the welfare state have cushioned employers, especially those operating on narrow margins, from many of the vicissitudes of the market. For the same reason employers quickly accepted the welfare state, American trade unions were at first ambivalent toward it because union leaders had hoped that the unions would be the channel to provide workers these services as an institutional protection against owners.

3. As a consequence of the first and second arguments, the welfare state is believed by many to be the savior of capitalism. Each and every title in the original Social Security Act creating the welfare state identified a particular imperfection

[20]These arguments, especially the latter two, have been made most forcefully by Charles Murray and were strengthened during the ten years between the two editions of his book. See Charles Murray, "Does Welfare Bring More Babies?" *Public Interest*, no. 114 (Spring 1994), pp. 17–31; these views were incorporated in the second edition of his book, op cit., esp. Chapter 9, "The Family." A good treatment of "moral hazard" will be found in a book by still another critic of the welfare state, Gilder, op. cit., Chapter 10, "The Moral Hazards of Liberalism."

[21]Charles Murray, "The Coming White Underclass," *Wall Street Journal*, 29 October 1993, p. A14.

GLOBALIZATION AND DEMOCRACY

## *How Does Globalization Affect the Welfare State?*

Today, most countries' economic health depends more on world economy than it did in the past. As trade figures show, this is true for the United States as well: The percentage of its economy engaged in exports and imports has increased from 17 percent in 1980 to 23 percent in 1998.[1]

Scholars generally agree that increased globalization affects the welfare state, but they do not agree on *how*.[2] One school of thought contends that greater openness to the world economy leads to a larger welfare state. Most economists agree that increased trade leads to higher total growth, but increased trade can also lead to more short-term fluctuations in the economy. An American example comes from the Asian financial crisis of 1997–98. Thirty years ago, a crisis in Asian economies would have had little effect on American firms because the United States did not conduct much trade in Asia. Today, however, a crisis like the one that occurred in 1997–98 can have far-reaching consequences. That crisis led airlines to cancel plane orders from Boeing, resulting in layoffs at Boeing's production plants in Seattle, Washington, and it hurt economies in states such as California that receive large numbers of tourists from Asia.

This greater insecurity can lead people to support a more developed welfare state. People living in a relatively open economy look toward government to smooth out such fluctuations. They also tend to back more government intervention in the economy, realizing that such intervention allows for more employment in the state sector where the economy is relatively closed. Even if markets outside the country collapse, at least there is some assurance that a welfare state will continue to keep many people working. In an open economy such as Denmark's, for example, where two-thirds of the national economy relies upon international trade, four out of ten

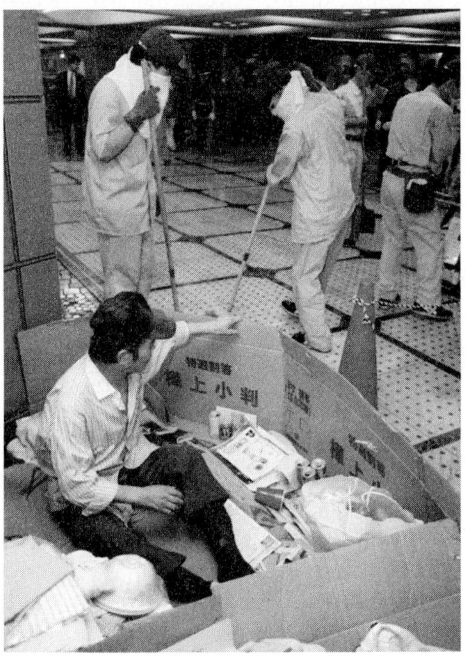

[1] *OECD Economic Outlook 59 (June 1996)* and Organization for Economic Cooperation and Development, *National Accounts* (Paris: Organization for Economic Cooperation and Development, 1998).

[2] See especially David Cameron, "The Expansion of the Public Economy," *American Political Science Review* 72 (1978), pp. 1243–61; and Peter Katzenstein, *Small States in World Markets* (Ithaca, NY: Cornell University Press, 1985).

persons work for the government or for government enterprises.[3]

People also support a more developed welfare state that can act as insurance against the vagaries of the international marketplace. Open economies are expected to have higher levels of welfare state benefits such as unemployment insurance, health insurance, and public housing. These benefits make the world markets less threatening to the average citizen.

A second school of thought argues that increased globalization will lead to a smaller welfare state. This school focuses on the potentially negative effects of a developed welfare state on the health of the economy in a globalized country. First, where the welfare state is developed, there may be fewer incentives for people to work hard if they know that the state will pay them almost as much if they were to become unemployed. Second, a developed welfare state is expensive, and people therefore pay higher taxes. One element of globalization is the increased ability of capital to move effortlessly from country to country. When faced with a choice of investing in a country with high taxes and one with low taxes, capital owners will find the low-tax country more attractive. States will feel pressure to make cuts in the welfare state in order to satisfy fickle capital.[4] The German company Allianz, for example, which is Europe's largest insurance firm, threatened in February 1999 to leave Germany for a country with lower tax rates.[5] In the American context, firms such as Levi-Strauss are increasingly locating their production plants in developing countries in order to avoid America's higher labor standards, environmental regulations, higher taxes, and higher wages. Such company threats and actual moves will lead states to compete with each other by reducing their tax levels and by cutting back the size of their welfare states. As capital becomes more mobile, such moves between countries could become commonplace, leading to the eventual degradation of welfare states around the world.

[3]The trade figure is an average for the period 1985–1994. It comes from Geoffrey Garrett, "Global Markets and National Politics: Collision Course or Virtuous Circle?" *International Organization* 52, no. 4 (Autumn 1998), p. 811. The labor force figure is for the year 1994 and comes from the Organization for Economic Cooperation and Development, *Measuring Public Employment in OECD Countries: Sources, Methods and Results* (Paris: Organization for Economic Cooperation and Development, 1997).

[4]Richard Clayton and Jonas Pontusson, "Welfare-State Retrenchment Revisited: Entitlement Cuts, Public Sector Restructuring, and Inegalitarian Trends in Advanced Capital Societies," *World Politics* 51, no. 1 (October 1998), pp. 67–98.

[5]*Financial Times,* 26 February 1999.

of capitalism and sought to cope with it: age, unemployment, widowhood, disability for injury, illness, birth defects, inadequate education/training, etc. The welfare state is not anti-capitalist. It recognizes that capitalism is neither perfect nor self-perfecting and therefore needs various deliberate, public means of dealing with its imperfections.

4. The welfare state lays most of the blame for society's woes on "the system." In other words, it removes the morality (or immorality) from poverty and also relieves employers from a large part of their traditional responsibility to take care of their own employees. This is the brighter side of the "personal responsibility" complaint covered by arguments #2 and #4 made by the critics. Welfare state proponents have to agree that there are many chiselers and abusers in the contributory as well as the noncontributory parts of the welfare state; but cheating also abounds in the private sector as well and need not discredit welfare any more than it discredits business. Roughly half the people on welfare at any one time are off it within one year. Between July and September 1997, an estimated 2.7 million adults received support from TANF, the most important remaining category of welfare. That amounts to 1.4 percent of the adult (age eighteen and over) population of the United States. Of all the TANF recipients, 36 percent were white; 35 percent were black; and 21 percent were Hispanic. The largest group of participants were between the ages of twenty and twenty-nine. Those married comprised 16 percent of recipients, while 45 percent were single and 8.3 percent were divorced. The average family on TANF consisted of two children, and of the nearly 5.5 million children receiving assistance, nearly 40 percent were black, 30 percent white, and 25 percent Hispanic.[22] If this sounds like a lot of folks taking a lot of public money, it should be noted that a large proportion of recipients of the more respectable Social Security retirement system receive far more in benefits than they contribute in taxes, especially if they live ten or more years beyond their retirement. This gives rise to an interesting question, "Which of Us Isn't Taking 'Welfare'?"[23]

5. The welfare state is politically essential. As pro-welfare state conservative George Will put the case:

> Two conservatives (Disraeli and Bismarck) pioneered the welfare state, and did so for impeccably conservative reasons: to reconcile the masses to the vicissitudes and hazards of a dynamic and hierarchical industrial economy. They acted on the principle of "economy of exertion," using government power judiciously to prevent less discriminating, more disruptive uses of power.[24]

In Bismarck's own words, in a speech to the Reichstag in 1899:

> I will consider it a great advantage when we have 700,000 small pensioners drawing their annuities from the state, especially if they belong to those classes who otherwise

[22]Statistics are from Department of Health and Human Services' National Emergency TANF Datafiles. See http://www.acf.dhh.gov/program/opre/particip/

[23]Ruth Rosen, "Which of Us Isn't Taking 'Welfare'?", *Los Angeles Times,* 27 December 1994, p. B5; sources of data: U.S. Department of Commerce; "Who Gets Assistance?" *Current Population Reports;* Household Economic Studies, July 1996.

[24]George F. Will, *Statecraft as Soulcraft* (New York: Simon and Schuster, 1983), p. 126.

TABLE 15.2

**Americans' Contradictory Attitudes toward Welfare**

| | CUT | INCREASED | OTHER |
|---|---|---|---|
| Should government spending on welfare be cut, increased, or left the same? | 48% | 13% | 39% |
| Should government spending on programs for poor children be cut, increased, or left the same? | 9 | 47 | 44 |

SOURCE: *New York Times*/CBS Poll, December 1994.

do not have much to lose by an upheaval and erroneously believe they can actually gain much by it.[25]

If this appears to be cynical, so be it. It may be difficult to sympathize in this epoch of relative prosperity and stability but the likelihood of great social and political disorder, if not revolution, was very much in the minds of the American political leaders in 1933–1935 leading up to the passage of the Social Security Act. In the spring of 1933, for example, Secretary of Labor Frances Perkins was urged by an influential friend to leave Washington for the summer if she possibly could because of expectations of widespread violence in Washington and New York.[26]

There is obviously no simple solution to the welfare state. Most critics and defenders make cogent arguments for their side, largely because they emphasize different aspects of the beast.[27] The welfare state was not a solution in the first place. It was a series of improvisations to some intractable problems that every nation faces when it tries, in George Will's words, "to reconcile the masses to the vicissitudes and hazards of a dynamic and hierarchical industrial economy," especially when those come to a head as quickly as they did in the early 1930s.[28] The welfare state is an institution of many parts, and no one approach to the whole will work. Note, for example, on Table 15.2 that the American people react quite inconsistently toward the welfare state, depending on how questions about welfare are asked. The American people are no fools. Ask a silly general question, and get

[25]Quoted in Gaston Rimlinger, *Welfare, Policy and Industrialization in Europe, America and Russia* (New York: Wiley, 1971), p. 121.

[26]Episode reported in Theodore J. Lowi, *The End of Liberalism* (New York: W. W. Norton, 1969), p. 200. For an entirely different view of the same political phenomenon, see Piven and Cloward, *The New Class War*, op cit.

[27]From the Right, the most serious academic critique is Lawrence M. Mead, *The New Politics of Poverty: The Nonworking Poor in America* (New York: Basic Books, 1992). The best academic defense of the welfare state, in our opinion, is John E. Schwarz and Thomas J. Volgy, *The Forgotten Americans: 30 Million Working Poor in the Land of Opportunity* (New York: W. W. Norton, 1992); to that must be added an outstanding evaluation of the implications of welfare reform for federalism by Demetrios Caraley, "Dismantling the Federal Safety Net: Fictions versus Realities," *Political Science Quarterly* (Summer 1996), pp. 225–58.

[28]Quote from Will, op cit.

silly general answers. One of the oldest universal laws is "if it ain't broke don't fix it." But there is an oft-forgotten corollary to that law: "If it *is* broke, just fix what's broke." If it took fifty to sixty years to reach a crisis in the welfare state, it may take a while to reform it appropriately.

## Breaking Out of the Circle of Poverty

Poverty is a circle, a vicious circle. Many individuals break out of it, but they have to overcome heavy odds. Although many policies may aim at breaking the circle and others have a beneficial effect on the redistribution of opportunities, two types of policies stand out as more effective than others: education policies and health policies.

**Education Policies** Most education of the American people is provided by the public policies of state and local governments. What may be less obvious is that these education policies—especially the policy of universal compulsory public education—are the most important single force in the distribution and redistribution of opportunity in America.

Compared to state and local efforts, the role of *national* education policy pales in comparison. With but three exceptions, the national government did not involve itself at all in education for the first century of its existence as an independent republic (see Table 15.3). The first two of these exceptions were actually prior to the Constitution—the Land Ordinance of 1785 followed by the Northwest Ordinance of 1787. These provided for a survey of all the public lands in the Northwest Territory and required that four sections of the thirty-six sections in each township be reserved for public schools and their maintenance. It was not until 1862, with adoption of the Morrill Act, that Congress took a third step, establishing the land-grant colleges and universities. Later in the nineteenth century, more federal programs were created for the education of farmers and other rural residents. But the most important national education policies have come only since World War II: the GI Bill of Rights of 1944, the National Defense Education Act (NDEA) of 1958, the Elementary and Secondary Education Act of 1965 (ESEA), and various youth and adult vocational training acts since 1958. Note, however, that since the GI Bill was aimed almost entirely at post-secondary schooling, the national government did not really enter the field of elementary education until after 1957.[29]

**AMERICAN POLITICAL DEVELOPMENT**

Although American education policy has been primarily controlled by the states, it began as a private system. In 1800, most schools were religious and private. Although the number of private schools grew throughout the nineteenth century, that growth was eclipsed by the increased number of public schools. By 1900, more than 90 percent of the nation's schools were public.

SOURCE: Eugene Eidenberg and Roy D. Morey, *An Act of Congress: The Legislative Process and the Making of Education Policy* (New York: W. W. Norton, 1969), pp. 10–11.

[29]There were a couple of minor precedents. One was the Smith-Hughes Act of 1917, which made federal funds available to the states for vocational education at the elementary and secondary levels. Second, the Lanham Act of 1940 made federal funds available to schools in "federally impacted areas," that is, areas with an unusually large number of government employees and/or where the local tax base was reduced by large amounts of government-owned property.

**TABLE 15.3**

**Growth of the Welfare State**

| | WELFARE | EDUCATION | HEALTH AND HOUSING |
|---|---|---|---|
| State Era (1789–1935) | Private and local charity<br>State child labor laws<br>State unemployment and injury compensation<br>State mothers' pensions | Northwest Ordinance of 1787 (federal)<br>Local academies<br>Local public schools<br>State compulsory education laws<br>Federal Morrill Act of 1862 for land grant colleges | Local public health ordinances |
| Federal Era (1935–present) | Federal Social Security System<br>Disability Insurance<br>VISTA, OEO*<br>Supplemental Security Income<br>Cost of Living Adjustment (indexing) | GI Bill<br>National Defense Act of 1958<br>Elementary and Secondary Education Act of 1965<br>School desegregation<br>Head Start | Public housing<br>Hospital construction<br>School lunch program<br>Food stamps<br>Medicare<br>Medicaid |

*VISTA = Volunteers in Service to America; OEO = Office of Economic Opportunity

What finally brought the national government into elementary education was embarrassment over the fact that the Soviets had beaten us into space with the launching of Sputnik. The national policy under NDEA was aimed specifically at improving education in science and mathematics. General federal aid for education did not come until ESEA in 1965, which allocated funds to school districts with substantial numbers of children from families who were unemployed or earning less than $2,000 a year. By the early 1970s, federal expenditures for elementary and secondary education were running over $4 billion per year, and rising, to a peak in 1980 at $4.8 billion.[30] Cuts by the Reagan administration of over 10 percent were substantial but not anywhere near the administration's goals. President Bush vowed, time after time, to be the "education president," and the Democratic majority in Congress was more than ready to help him. In truth, however, all of Bush's plans for improving elementary and secondary education depended on private financing or on state and local governments.

[30]Office of Management and Budget, *Budget of the United States Government, Fiscal Year 1982* (Washington, DC: Government Printing Office, 1981), p. 427.

President Clinton's education program has had a more national and public orientation, as might be expected of a Democratic president. It included more federal aid for preschool programs for needy children, national education standards coupled with teachers' incentives, and, at the post-secondary level, scholarships for minorities and an ambitious national service program available to all students to earn credit toward college tuition. Clinton's most concrete achievement in education policy was the Improving America's Schools Act of 1994, also known as Goals 2000, which aimed to reverse federal policies dating back to the 1960s that set lower academic standards for schools in poorer school districts than for those in wealthier ones. Goals 2000, in keeping with the rest of Clinton's education agenda, set uniform national standards for educational achievement from the wealthiest to the poorest school districts, and committed $400 million in federal funds to help establish these standards. But by then the sentiment in Congress had moved in the same direction for education as for welfare: devolution. In 1999, the 106th Congress overwhelmingly adopted the Education Flexibility Partnership Act, or "ed-flex", by a vote of 330 to 90 in the House and 98 to 1 in the Senate. Even though this was a "veto proof" vote, President Clinton had already endorsed the general concept of the legislation. It virtually eliminated Clinton's hope to extend national educational standards, because ed-flex, in name and spirit, was committed to freeing the states, thereby enabling them to spend the $15 billion for elementary and secondary education without having to comply with complex federal guidelines. The legislation even eliminated most of the national restrictions governing the $1.2 billion that had been provided the previous year for hiring more elementary and secondary teachers—here again, giving the states discretion on how to proceed with that highly sought-after program. The only exception in the act was that states could not waive national guidelines concerning civil rights, school safety, and special education.[31]

If Clinton had any dreams for leaving an education legacy he was going to have to look outside the Department of Education—in job training and vocational education. According to a 1995 General Accounting Office study, the federal government funded over 160 different job programs in fifteen separate agencies. Major job training programs within the Department of Education received $1.3 billion from Congress in 1998 for vocational programs, and the Labor Department received $4.1 billion for job training and employment services, which is still far below the Labor Department's original job-training program, whose appropriation in 1978 was $10 billion. In 1998, Head Start, the pre-school education program in the Department of Health and Human Services, received $3.5 billion. In 1998, Congress also moved to consolidate many job-training programs. Under pressure from critics who charged that the federal government's job-training programs duplicated services and lacked coordination, President Clinton signed the Workforce Investment Act into law on August 7, 1998. This legislation collapsed more than sixty federal employment programs

[31]Helen Dewar and Linda Perlstein, "After Partisan Debate, Education Bill Easily Passes House, Senate," *Washington Post,* 12 March 1999, p. A6.

into just three block grants to the states.[32] In its original incarnation, this legislation was intended to consolidate the federal government's fragmented workforce development programs. However, the final compromise legislation signed by Clinton placed far more emphasis on "coordination" than it did on consolidation.

**Health Policies** Until recent decades, no government in the United States—national, state, or local—concerned itself directly with individual health. But public responsibility was always accepted for *public* health. After New York City's newly created Board of Health was credited with holding down a cholera epidemic in 1867, most states followed with the creation of statewide public health agencies. Within a decade, the results were obvious. Between 1884 and 1894, for example, Massachusetts's rate of infant mortality dropped from 161.3 per 1,000 to 141.4 per 1,000.[33] Reductions in mortality rates produced by local public health programs during the late nineteenth century may be the most significant contribution ever made by government to human welfare.

The U.S. Public Health Service (USPHS) has been in existence since 1798 but was a small part of public health policy until after World War II. Created in 1937, but little noticed for twenty years, was the National Institutes of Health (NIH), an agency within USPHS created to do biomedical research. Between 1950 and 1989, NIH expenditures by the national government increased from $160 million to $7.1 billion—two-thirds of the nation's entire expenditure on health research. NIH research on the link between smoking and disease led to one of the most visible public health campaigns in American history. Today, NIH's focus has turned to cancer and acquired immunodeficiency syndrome (AIDS). As with smoking, this work on AIDS has resulted in massive public health education as well as new products and regulations.

More recent commitments to the improvement of public health are the numerous laws, now housed mainly in the Environmental Protection Agency (1970), addressing hazardous air and water pollutants along with degradation of the natural environment. The Occupational Safety and Health Administration (OSHA) was created in 1970 to make the workplace safer from air pollutants as well as threats from machinery and operations. Laws attempting to improve the health and safety of consumer products were created in 1972 and housed in the Consumer Product Safety Commission (CPSC).

But by far the most important commitments to public health were made in 1965, with the creation of Medicare and Medicaid. Medicare services are available to all persons already eligible under the Social Security Insurance Program (and it becomes automatic for retired persons when they reach the age of sixty-five). Although there are nutritional programs for the poor, particularly food stamps and the school lunch program, *Medicaid* is far and away the most important health program for this group. As referred to earlier, while Medicaid has taken some cuts, it is the one aspect of public assistance that was maintained even after AFDC and entitlements benefits were terminated in 1996. And, although the rate

[32]*Congressional Quarterly*, 1 August 1998, p. 2121.

[33]Morton Keller, *Affairs of State: Public Life in Nineteenth Century America* (Cambridge: Belknap Press of Harvard University Press, 1977), p. 500.

of increase of *Medicaid expenditures* has been cut, the budget itself has continued to increase, totaling $100 billion (estimated) for 1998 and $107.7 billion (estimated) for 1999, up from $70 billion in 1992 and $40 billion in 1990. Federal commitments to health-related research would continue to grow, albeit at a slower rate. The largest single item is the budget for the National Institutes of Health (NIH) with a budgetary commitment of $13.9 billion. Of all the health-related research efforts, AIDS is the largest and has the highest growth rate, totaling $1.7 billion in fiscal 1999. Research money also increased, even though slightly, for several other areas, including breast cancer, prevention research, gene therapy, and developmental and reproductive biology.[34]

When it comes to public health, which includes large expenditures to support medical research, defenses against epidemics, and other community-wide and nationwide campaigns such as the campaigns against tobacco or for improved nutrition, Americans seem to be unstinting in their support for "big national government." President Clinton even boosted the public health commitment by appointing an "AIDS czar" with cabinet status to coordinate and expand federal policies and activities to combat the disease. But public health is only half the health policy area. The other half is the health care system, that is, delivery of services between individual doctors and individual patients. Early in his administration, Clinton announced a plan with two key objectives: (1) to limit the rising costs of the American health care system (for example, 1991 per capita health spending in America, $2,932, was 83 percent higher than spending in twenty-one other industrialized nations)[35] and (2) to provide universal health insurance coverage for all Americans (almost 40 million Americans lacked health insurance at that time). Clinton's plan at first garnered enormous public support, and seemed likely to win congressional approval in some form. But the plan, which entailed a major expansion of federal administration of the health care system, gradually lost momentum as resistance to it took root among those who feared changes in a system that worked well for them. Though Clinton had pledged to make health care the centerpiece of his 1994 legislative agenda, no health care bill even came up for a full congressional vote in 1994. The president's failure on health care was judged by many to be one of the chief causes of the Republican landslide in the 1994 congressional elections. After that, Clinton retreated, virtually abandoning his great ambition (and that of his wife's) to transform the health

**AMERICAN POLITICAL DEVELOPMENT**

Congressional concern over health policy has been mounting steadily since 1970. At that time, House and Senate committees held fewer than ten hearings on health; by 1973, the number jumped to nearly sixty. By the late 1970s and into the mid-1980s, Congress held more than eighty hearings a year devoted to health care. The late 1980s and early 1990s saw a further increase to nearly 180 hearings in 1992.

SOURCE: Bryan D. Jones and Billy Hall, "Issue Expansion in the Early Clinton Administration: Health Care and Deficit Reduction," in *The New American Politics*, ed. Bryan D. Jones (Boulder, CO: Westview, 1995), pp. 191–211, esp. p. 203.

[34]David S. Cloud, "Special Report—Health and Medicare," *Congressional Quarterly*, 23 March 1996, p. 768; Office of Management and Budget, *Budget of the United States, Fiscal Year 1999*, Appendix, pp. 407–10.

[35]U.N. Development Program, Organization for Economic Cooperation and Development, quoted in Paul Spector, "Failure, by the Numbers," *New York Times*, 24 September 1994.

care system. But he did not grow silent in his retreat; he only expanded his rhetoric. As the rhetoric grew, the proposal shrank, with incremental steps that might prove more palatable to a Republican Congress and might also give the public an appearance of progress in health care. The most promising of these post-1994 efforts was a health care bill actually enacted in 1996 (PL 104-191) that made health insurance portable—generally guaranteeing that workers could maintain insurance coverage if they changed or lost their jobs.

President Clinton then proposed a "patient's bill of rights." It hit a responsive chord in the country, even among many Republican legislators, but it produced a bundle of smallish proposals with even smaller prospects of adoption. One proposal was to protect patient privacy by restricting the use of patient medical records to health care only. Another, sponsored by a renegade Republican in the House, would amend a twenty-year-old law so that patients could sue their health plans. A third proposal tried to improve HMO coverage for breast cancer patients by allowing doctors rather than insurers to make decisions about mastectomy surgery and post-operative hospital care.

But even as these modest proposals were going through Congress in 1998 and into 1999, a grand coalition of interest groups—namely the Health Insurance Association of America and the Health Benefits Coalition—was forming to oppose them all. The latter group, composed of manufacturers and other large employers as well as major insurance companies, spent $2 million in 1998 to block the regulatory changes sought for managed care. Americans seemed to favor improvements in health services and in health coverage but still balked at anything that intimated a return to "big national government."

**Housing Policies** Through public housing for low-income families, which originated in 1937 with the Wagner-Steagall National Housing Act, and subsidized private housing after 1950, the percent of American families living in overcrowded housing was reduced from 20 percent in 1940 to 9 percent in 1970. Housing policies made an even greater contribution to reducing "substandard" housing, defined by the Census Bureau as dilapidated houses without hot running water and without some other plumbing. In 1940, almost 50 percent of American households lived in substandard housing. By 1950, this had been reduced to 35 percent; by 1975, to 8 percent.[36] Urban redevelopment programs and rent supplement programs have helped in a small way to give low-income families access to better neighborhoods and, through that, to better schools and working conditions.

Housing programs were heavily opposed by the Reagan administration, which succeeded in reducing housing benefits by 15 percent and in cutting the number of newly assisted households from an annual average of 300,000 in the late 1970s to 100,000 by 1984.[37] President Bush reversed both, concluding his administration with a $25 billion authorization for housing programs in his 1991

[36]John E. Schwarz, *America's Hidden Success,* 2nd ed. (New York: W. W. Norton, 1988), pp. 41–42.

[37]For more details, see John L. Palmer and Isabel V. Sawhill, eds., *The Reagan Record* (Cambridge: Ballinger, 1984), Appendix C, pp. 363–79.

**AMERICAN POLITICAL DEVELOPMENT**

State capacity to address housing problems preceded the Wagner-Steagall National Housing Act by only three years. To alleviate problems of mortgage foreclosures during the Great Depression, the National Housing Act of 1934 created the Federal Housing Administration.

SOURCE: Theda Skocpol, *Social Policy in the United States: Future Possibilities in Historical Perspective* (Princeton: Princeton University Press, 1995), p. 171.

budget. Bush's secretary of Housing and Urban Development (HUD), Jack Kemp, received a great deal of credit for cleaning up a major scandal inherited from Reagan, but the most important legacy he passed on to President Clinton and his HUD secretary, Henry Cisneros, was $7 billion in unspent authorization, about $3 billion of which was earmarked for housing.[38] Since Cisneros is a former mayor (of San Antonio) and Clinton is a former governor, all the mayors and governors in the country greeted the Clinton administration with optimism about a more cooperative federalism.

Yet, despite Clinton's commitment and Cisneros earning public acclaim for his success in continuing the fight against HUD scandals, little happened on his four-year watch. (He resigned shortly after Clinton was re-elected.) In 1994, Clinton sought more housing and emergency shelter for the homeless, and through 1995 spending reached a high point of $1.7 billion. But, especially after 1994, there was mainly retreat, and that retreat continued throughout the second Clinton administration. By election year 1996, HUD virtually abandoned its long-standing rule that for every public housing unit destroyed, another had to be built. More than 23,000 public housing units were torn down in that period, with no clear record of how many were replaced. But this retreat may have saved the Department from abolition. After 1996, HUD dropped off the screen; and at one point Clinton's Office of Management and Budget proposed serving up HUD to the cut-hungry Congress. But in the end, HUD received only a severe budget cut. In 1995, HUD spent $29 billion, which fell sharply to $25.2 billion in 1996. HUD's budget rose somewhat in the late 1990s. However, even Clinton's 1999 budget proposal would hold HUD-spending essentially flat at $30 billion until 2003.[39] This level of spending is sufficient only for the management and maintenance of existing programs and for grants to state and local governments. There are no funds for new or expanded national housing policy ventures.[40]

## WHO IS POOR? WHAT CAN GOVERNMENT DO?

We saw at the beginning of this chapter that minorities, women, and children are disproportionately poor. Much of this poverty is the result of disadvantages that

[38]Guy Gugliotta, "Cisneros: Bringing a Touch of the Cities to HUD," *Washington Post National Weekly Edition,* 18–24 January 1993, pp. 11–12.

[39]Office of Management and Budget, *Historical Tables, Budget of the United States Government, Fiscal Year 1999,* pp. 68–69.

[40]Source: Jonathan Weisman, "True Impact of GOP Congress Reaches Well Beyond Bills," *Congressional Quarterly*, 7 September 1996, pp. 2515–17.

### THEN AND NOW

## Changes in American Politics

Although the national government has become more active in the economy, it has also turned its attention to playing a greater policy role in society.

- As late as 1950, state and local governments accounted for the lion's share of social welfare expenditures. By the 1970s, the federal government was spending over $200 billion more on social welfare than state and local governments were.
- Early social welfare spending in the United States was aimed at veterans, widows and children. Social spending aimed at "the poor" is largely a new development in American social policy.
- The role of the national government in promoting education grew in the twentieth century, although it still pales in comparison to the roles played by both state and local governments. In the late eighteenth century and throughout the nineteenth, the national government promoted education primarily through land grants, which set aside public land for public schools, colleges, and universities. Today, the national government has taken a wider role by providing tuition benefits, setting education goals, and establishing specific training programs.
- In many social policy areas—education, health, and housing, for example—it is clear that the administrative capacity and political willingness of the national government to address social problems has expanded since the New Deal.

stem from the position of these groups in the labor market. As we saw from the statistics in the introduction to this chapter, African Americans and Latinos tend to be economically less well off than the rest of the American population. Much of this economic inequality stems from the fact that minority workers tend to have low-wage jobs. Minorities are also more likely to become unemployed and to remain unemployed for longer periods of time than are white Americans. African Americans, for example, typically have experienced twice as much unemployment than other Americans have. The combination of low-wage jobs and unemployment often means that minorities are less likely to have jobs that give them access to the shadow welfare state. They are more likely to fall into the precarious categories of the working poor or the nonworking poor.

In the past several decades, policy analysts have begun to talk about the "feminization of poverty," or the fact that women are more likely to be poor than men are. This problem is particularly acute for single mothers, who are more than twice as likely to fall below the poverty line than the average American. When the Social Security Act was passed in 1935, the main programs for poor women were Aid to Dependent Children (ADC) and survivors' insurance for widows. The framers of the act believed that ADC would gradually disappear as more women became eligible for survivors' insurance. The social model behind the Social Security Act was that of a male breadwinner with a wife and children. Women were not expected to work, and if a woman's husband died, ADC or survivors' insurance would help her stay at home and raise her children. The framers of Social Security did not envision today's large number of single women heading families. At the same time, they did not envision that so many women with children would also be working. This combination of changes helped make AFDC (the successor program to ADC) more controversial. Many people ask, Why shouldn't welfare recipients work, if the majority of women who are not on welfare work?

Controversies over the welfare state have led to adaptations in welfare policy in recent years. Similar controversies over affirmative action policies—those that partially determine "who shall be poor"—have led to gradual changes in civil rights policies. But as we concluded in Chapter 4, although the problems of rights in America are agonizing, they can be looked at optimistically. The United States has a long way to go before it constructs a truly just, "equally protected" society. But it also has come very far in a relatively short time. Groups pressing for equality have been able to use government to change a variety of discriminatory practices. The federal government has become an active partner in ensuring civil rights and political equality. All explicit de jure barriers to minorities have been dismantled. Many de facto barriers have also been dismantled, and thousands upon thousands of new opportunities have been opened.

Madison set the tone for this chapter in *The Federalist,* No. 51, in prose that has more the character of poetry:

> Justice is the end of government.
> It is the end of civil society.
> It ever has been and ever will be pursued
> Until it be obtained,
> Or until liberty be lost in the pursuit.

His words also connect this chapter with the theme of the book, freedom and power. Equality of opportunity has produced unequal results, and the unequal results of one generation can be visited upon later generations. Considerable inequality is acceptable unless the advantages are maintained through laws and rules that favor those already in positions of power, and through prejudices that tend to develop against any group that has for a long while been on the lower rungs of society. It is in this context that the more long-standing and extreme inequalities in the United States have been perceived as unjust. Yet, efforts to reduce the inequalities or to eliminate the consequences of prejudice can produce their own injustices if government intervention is poorly planned or is too heavy-handed.

## SUMMARY

The capitalist system is the most productive type of economy on earth, but it is not perfect. Poverty amidst plenty continues. Many policies have emerged to deal with these imperfections.

The first section of this chapter discussed the welfare state and gave an account of how Americans came to recognize extremes of poverty and dependency and how Congress then attempted to reduce these extremes with policies that moderately redistribute opportunity.

Welfare state policies are subdivided into several categories. First there are the contributory programs. Virtually all employed persons are required to contribute a portion of their wages into welfare trust funds, and later on, when they retire or are disabled, they have a right, or entitlement, to draw upon those contributions. Another category of welfare is composed of noncontributory programs, also called "public assistance." These programs provide benefits and supports for people who can demonstrate need by passing a "means test." Noncontributory programs can involve either cash benefits or in-kind benefits. All of the contributory programs are implemented through cash benefits. Spending on social policies, especially Social Security and Medicare, has increased dramatically in recent decades, raising concerns about how entitlement programs will be paid for in future decades.

The second section of the chapter discussed ways of breaking out of the circle of poverty. Education, health, and housing policies are three ways to break this cycle and redistribute opportunities. The education policies of state and local governments are the most important single force in the distribution and redistribution of opportunity in America. Although states have taken the early lead in the arena of public health policy, the federal government also adopted policies in the early 1900s to protect citizens from the effects of pollution and other health hazards. Federal housing policy consists of many pork-barrel programs, but it also represents a commitment to improving the conditions and opportunities of the poor.

## For Further Reading

Bryner, Gary. *Politics and Public Morality: The Great American Welfare Reform Debate.* New York: W. W. Norton, 1998.

Bullock, Charles, III, and Charles M. Lamb. *Implementation of Civil Rights Policy.* Monterey, CA: Brooks/Cole, 1984.

Derthick, Martha. *Agency under Stress: The Social Security Administration in American Government.* Washington, DC: Brookings Institution, 1991.

Foreman, Christoper. *Signals from the Hill: Congressional Oversight and the Challenge of Social Regulation.* New Haven: Yale University Press, 1988.

Forer, Lois G. *Criminals and Victims: A Trial Judge Reflects on Crimes and Punishment.* New York: W. W. Norton, 1980.

Grofman, Bernard, and Chandler Davidson, eds. *Controversies in Minority Voting: The Voting Rights Act in Perspective.* Washington, DC: Brookings Institution, 1992.

Gutman, Amy. *Democratic Education.* Princeton: Princeton University Press, 1987.

Katz, Michael. *In the Shadow of the Poorhouse: A Social History of Welfare in America.* New York: Basic Books, 1986.

Kronenfeld, Jennie Jacobs. *Controversial Issues in Health Care Policy.* Newbury Park, CA: Sage, 1993.

Lemann, Nicholas. *The Promised Land: The Great Black Migration and How It Shaped America*. New York: Knopf, 1991.

Levy, Frank. *The New Dollars and Dreams: American Incomes and Economic Change*. New York: Russell Sage Foundation, 1998.

Marmor, Theodore R., Jerry L. Mashaw, and Phillip L. Harvey. *America's Misunderstood Welfare State*. New York: Basic Books, 1990.

Mink, Gwendolyn. *Welfare's End*. Ithaca, NY: Cornell University Press, 1998.

Murray, Charles. *Losing Ground: American Social Policy, 1950–1980*. New York: Basic Books, 1994.

Orfield, Gary, and Carole Ashkinaze. *The Closing Door: Conservative Policy and Black Opportunity*. Chicago: University of Chicago Press, 1991.

Piven, Frances Fox, and Richard A. Cloward. *Regulating the Poor*. New York: Pantheon, 1971.

Schwarz, John E. *America's Hidden Success: A Reassessment of Twenty Years of Public Policy*. New York: W. W. Norton, 1988.

Self, Peter. *Government by the Market? The Politics of Public Choice*. Boulder, CO: Westview, 1994.

Weir, Margaret, Ann Orloff, and Theda Skocpol. *The Politics of Social Policy in the United States*. Princeton: Princeton University Press, 1988.

# 16

# Foreign Policy and Democracy

## TIME LINE ON FOREIGN POLICY

| Events | | Institutional Developments |
|---|---|---|
| Treaties with Britain and Spain establish recognition of U.S. sovereignty (1795) | | U.S. attempts to steer clear of foreign alliances; pursues neutrality policy (1790s) |
| | 1800 | |
| Louisiana Purchase from France (1803) | | |
| War of 1812, despite American attempts to maintain neutrality (1812) | | Monroe Doctrine to prevent further European colonization in Western Hemisphere (1823) |
| U.S. reaches diplomatic settlement with Great Britain over Northwest Territory; Oregon Treaty sets northern U.S. border at the 49th parallel (1846) | | |
| War with Mexico, ending in Mexico's giving up claim to Texas and ceding California and New Mexico to U.S. (1846–1848) | | Manifest Destiny doctrine leads to war with Mexico (1840s); Mexican War first successful offensive war (1846–1848) |
| | 1860 | |
| Civil War (1861–1865) | | |
| U.S. purchases Alaska from Russia; Midway Islands annexed (1867) | | Unilateralism prevails (1870s–1890s) |
| First Inter-American Conference between U.S. and Latin American nations (1889–1890) | | Reciprocal agreements between U.S. and Latin American nations (1890) |
| Spanish-American War; treaty leads to U.S. annexation of Puerto Rico, Guam, Philippines; Hawaii annexed (1898) | | U.S. concern with world markets after closing of American frontier (1890s) |
| | 1900 | |
| World War I (1914–1918) | | U.S. does not join the League of Nations (1919–1920) |
| | | Rogers Act recognizes foreign service officers as part of government career system (1924) |
| U.S. in World War II (1941–1945) | | U.N. established (1945) |
| Bretton Woods conference (1944) | | Foreign Service Act creates a professional diplomatic corps (1946) |
| Soviets develop A-bomb (1949) | | Cold war and containment—Truman Doctrine (1947); Marshall Plan (1947); OAS (1947); NATO (1949); Mutual Security (1951); SEATO (1954) |
| Korean War (1950–1953) | 1950 | |
| Soviets launch Sputnik (1957); first U.S. satellite (1958) | | U.S. and Soviets race to the moon (1957–1969) |

| Events | | Institutional Developments |
|---|---|---|
| | 1960 | |
| Bay of Pigs Invasion (1961); Cuban Missile Crisis (1962) | | U.S. and Soviets face off in Cuba (1962) |
| | | Nuclear Test-Ban Treaty (1963) |
| U.S. builds up troops in Vietnam (1965–1973) | | Détente between U.S. and Soviet Union (1970s) |
| Nixon visits China (1972) | | U.S.-Soviet Trade Agreement (1972) |
| Arab oil embargo (1973–1974) | | End of U.S. military draft (1973) |
| U.S. intervenes in Chile (1974) | | Termination of Bretton Woods System (1973) |
| Camp David summit (1978) | | Panama Canal Treaty (1978) |
| U.S. formally recognizes China (1979) | | |
| Iranian hostage crisis (1979–1981) | 1980 | SALT II Agreement (1979–1981) |
| | | SALT II repudiated (1981) |
| Grenada invasion (1983) | | SDI ("Star Wars") commitment (1980s) |
| First Reagan-Gorbachev summit (1985) | | Policy of covert action in Latin America (1980s) |
| Iran-Contra affair (1986–1987) | | INF Treaty (1987) |
| Invasion of Panama by U.S.; Berlin Wall dismantled (1989) | | Soviet system collapses; NATO/Warsaw Pact withdrawals begin (1989) |
| Germany reunified (1990) | 1990 | Eastern Europe adopts capitalism (1990) |
| Iraq invades Kuwait (1990) | | 29-nation U.N. coalition conducts blockade and war against Iraq; beginning of U.S. "new world order" role (1990–1991) |
| Ethnic conflicts split Russia, Yugoslavia, and Czechoslovakia (1991–1995) | | |
| U.N.-sponsored humanitarian intervention in Somalia (1992) | | NAFTA approved (1993) |
| Crisis in Bosnia (1993–1995); Clinton favors collective approach rather than leadership role in Bosnia; acts unilaterally against Iraq (1993) | | Multilateral peace accord on Bosnia (1995) |
| Clinton-Yeltsin summit cements U.S.-Russian ties (1993) | | |
| Clinton acts unilaterally to oust military dictatorship in Haiti and to strengthen peso in Mexico (1994) | | |
| Serbian troops invade Kosovo as part of "ethnic cleansing" campaign; NATO alliance responds with bombing campaign (1999) | | |

## CORE OF THE ARGUMENT

- All foreign policies must be made and implemented in the name of the president.
- Certain values—fear of centralized power and of foreign entanglements—have traditionally shaped American foreign policy; today these values find expression in the intermingling of domestic and foreign policy institutions and the tendency toward unilateralism.
- American foreign policy is carried out through certain instruments, including diplomacy, the United Nations, the international monetary structure, economic aid, collective security, and military deterrence.
- In the conduct of foreign policy, nations can play one of several roles: the Napoleonic role, the Holy Alliance role, the balance-of-power role, and the economic expansionist role.
- The United States plays different roles in foreign affairs, depending on what it seeks to achieve in a particular situation; the Holy Alliance role seems to be the most typical American role in the post–cold war era.

Ever since George Washington, in his farewell address, warned the American people "to have . . . as little political connection as possible" with foreign nations and to "steer clear of permanent alliances," Americans have been distrustful of foreign policy. Despite this distrust, the United States has been forced to pursue its national interests in the world, even if this has meant fighting a war. As a result of its foreign entanglements, the United States emerged as a world power, but not without maintaining some misgivings about foreign policy. As Alexis de Tocqueville noted in the 1830s, democracies lack the best qualities for the successful pursuit of foreign policy goals:

> Foreign policies demand scarcely any of those qualities which are peculiar to a democracy; they require, on the contrary, the perfect use of almost all those in which it is deficient. . . . A democracy can only with great difficulty regulate the details of an important undertaking, persevere in a fixed design, and work out its execution in spite of serious obstacles. It cannot combine its measures with secrecy or await their consequences with patience.[1]

Fear and antagonism toward foreign entanglements became a revered American tradition. Only the most extraordinary affront to American sovereignty or American interest could mobilize the American people behind a sustained involvement in foreign affairs, and the mobilization, when it did occur, was usually for war, which required complete demonization of the adversary. Mere conflicts of interest between nations were rarely enough to mobilize Americans.

The cold war, which lasted from 1946 to 1989, seemed to put an end to that tradition. The term itself was coined in 1946 to distinguish America's emerging confrontation with the Soviet Union from "hot war" or "shooting war" to total mobilization for war in order to prevent war.[2] Division of the world into two antagonistic camps, each armed with enough nuclear weapons to annihilate the other, redefined (or "escalated") what had once been considered incidental threats

[1]Alexis de Tocqueville, *Democracy in America,* trans. Phillips Bradley (New York: Vintage, 1945; orig. published 1835), vol. 1, p. 243.

[2]William Safire provides a brief and informative account of the history of the term in his *Safire's Political Dictionary* (New York: Random House, 1978), pp. 127–29.

into serious challenges. Investment in total military preparedness became a race to deter the other side from any expansion, with each side attributing to the other an overriding commitment to arms' expansion.

Each of the leading nations in the cold war—the United States and the Soviet Union—developed what we call a "cold war culture." This cold war culture was built on a policy that (1) the United States must prepare for war in order to prevent war; (2) each day that war did not occur was further confirmation of America's commitment to preparedness and deterrence, because American leaders believed that the Soviet Union was aggressive and would expand communist influence wherever weaknesses were detected; and (3) the United States must continually increase its capabilities, because whatever prevented Soviet expansion today could be inadequate tomorrow, especially considering that the Soviets, like the United States, were continuing to invest in military power.

Those were simpler days. The United States's enemy was well known, and the theory about the behavior of that enemy was validated each day that war didn't break out. The cold war ended in 1989, and its culture would pass away in its wake. Today, there are many adversaries and potential adversaries to the United States. And although the world recognizes the United States as the sole superpower, it is no longer readily apparent when a threat or a challenge crosses over the threshold of genuine "American national interest." Since our national interest was the one thing that almost all Americans supported, much of today's foreign policy must be conducted without full American mobilization. Thus, although the United States is still the most powerful country in modern history, it is now forced to conduct foreign policy in much the same way that traditional powers did before the United States emerged as a Great Power. This is difficult, because Americans continue to distrust diplomacy and the secrecy that goes with it.

Even during the cold war, traditional American distrust was regularly reinforced by foreign policy actions taken in secret and only revealed after the fact. The most spectacular instance occurred in 1971, when the *New York Times* began publishing the "Pentagon Papers," excerpts from a secret Defense Department study of U.S. involvement in Vietnam. The papers revealed that U.S. officials had lied to the American public about the country's entry into the war.[3]

Two other, more recent examples also illustrate the same point: the Iran-Contra scandal from Ronald Reagan's Republican administration, and the Iran-Bosnia deal from Bill Clinton's Democratic administration. In 1986, it was discovered that the Reagan administration had furnished weapons to Iran, through Israeli intermediaries, to help free some American hostages in Lebanon and, more hopefully, to encourage moderate factions within Iran. This action was contrary to Reagan's popular promise that he would not compromise with terrorists, but more important, it was discovered that the weapons had actually been *sold* at enormous profits to Iran, in direct violation of U.S. law. These profits were then

[3]It is often forgotten that most Americans, prior to the revelations in the Pentagon Papers, actually supported the Vietnam War substantially and consistently, despite the unusually active antiwar movement and an increasingly hostile press. See Bruce Russett, "Doves, Hawks, and U.S. Public Opinion," *Political Science Quarterly* 105, no. 4 (Winter 1990–91), pp. 515–38. See also David W. Levy, *The Debate over Vietnam* (Baltimore: Johns Hopkins University Press, 1991), pp. 95–98, 111, 159.

diverted to help finance the guerilla activities of the Contras, a group fighting the socialist regime in Nicaragua. That financing was also illegal.[4]

The Iran-Bosnia deal, a product of the cold war that continued into the post–cold war epoch, was not such a full-scale scandal. In 1991, the United Nations imposed an arms embargo on the nations of the former Yugoslavia in order to stop the emerging civil war. But the embargo favored the Bosnian Serbs because they were getting weapons from Serbia and building their arsenal. President Bush had fully supported the embargo, and Bill Clinton denounced Bush in his 1992 campaign, calling for the use of "whatever it takes to stop the slaughter" in Bosnia, including the lifting of the embargo long enough to "even the playing field." Criticisms from both sides immobilized President Clinton for nearly two years, until March 1994, when he advised his ambassador to "look the other way" as Iran was moving a large flow of arms into Bosnia's Muslim government in opposition to the Serbs. Thus armed, the Croatians and the Bosnian Muslims won enough victories over the Serbs to bring all three factions to the bargaining table and to a shaky peace, for which the Clinton administration got a good deal of credit. Some may call these tactics double-dealing, while others might call it standard, traditional international conduct. Either way, it was secrecy born from fear of public judgment, which in turn contributed to public distrust.[5]

The American people possess an uncommon influence on what their government does, even in foreign policy. But people can make mistakes and bad decisions. In domestic policy situations a bad decision can be written off as one of the acceptable costs of democracy: bad decisions merely produce 20 or 30 percent cost overruns in a public project, or the collapse of a bridge, or the tearing down of public housing projects after only a decade of use. But a mistake in foreign policy can result in a war, and in modern warfare, most victories are achieved at great cost.

This chapter has no solution to the many foreign policy issues the United States confronts. Nonetheless, because the conduct of foreign policy is so complex and because there are particular problems facing a democracy such as the United States as it formulates and puts into effect particular foreign policies, a well-balanced analysis of foreign policy problems is essential. Such an analysis must treat at least five dimensions of foreign policy, which will make up the five main sections of this chapter. We will begin by asking who makes and shapes foreign policy in the United States. From there, we will cover American values: What does the United States want? What are its national interests, if any? What counts as success? In the third section, we will identify and examine the main instruments of foreign policy, such as administrative arrangements, institutions, laws, and

**THE CENTRAL QUESTION**

"What are the foreign policy roles for America today?"

[4]Robert Spitzer, *President and Congress: Executive Hegemony at the Crossroads of American Government* (New York: McGraw-Hill, 1993), p. 226; see also pp. 220–32. See also, Theodore Lowi, "Doin' the Cincinnati—Or, What Is There About the White House That Makes Its Occupants Do Bad Things?" in *National Political Science Review* 1 (1989), pp. 91–95.

[5]The best and most highly readable account of the Iran-Bosnia affair is found in Mark Danner, "Hypocrisy in Action: What's the Real Iran-Bosnia Scandal?" *New Yorker,* 13 May 1996, pp. 7–8.

programs. Finally, we will discuss how the United States behaves in world politics. Are its roles consistent with its values?



# The Players: The Makers and Shapers of Foreign Policy

Although the power of the American people over foreign policy is impossible to overestimate, "the people" should not be given all the credit or all the blame for actual policies and their outcomes. As in domestic policy, foreign policy making is a highly pluralistic arena. First there are the official players, those who comprise the "foreign policy establishment"; these players and the agencies they head can be called the actual "makers" of foreign policy. But there are other major players, less official but still influential. We call these the "shapers."

## Who Makes Foreign Policy?

**The President** Although many foreign policy decisions can be made without so much as the president's fingerprint on them, these decisions must be made and implemented in the name of the president. In Iran-Contra, much of the action took place far from the White House and was hidden from the president. But those decisions and actions were taken to further a goal that the president wanted. That all foreign policies come from the president is a necessity in making any foreign policy. All heads of state must have some confidence that each head of state has enough power and stability to negotiate, to make agreements, and to keep those agreements.

**The Bureaucracy** The major foreign policy players in the bureaucracy are the secretaries of the departments of State, Defense, and the Treasury; the Joint Chiefs of Staff (JCOS), especially the chair of the JCOS; and the director of the Central Intelligence Agency (CIA). A separate unit in the bureaucracy comprised of these people and a few others is the National Security Council (NSC), whose main purpose is to iron out the differences among the key players and to integrate their positions in order to confirm or reinforce a decision the president wants to make in foreign policy or military policy. In the Clinton administration, the secretary of commerce has also become an increasingly important foreign policy maker, with the rise and spread of economic globalization. Clinton's first secretary of commerce, Ron Brown, was not the first to be active in promoting world trade, but he may well have been the most vigorous and successful up to now.

In addition to these top cabinet-level officials, key lower-level staff members have policy-making influence as strong as that of the cabinet secretaries—some may occasionally exceed cabinet influence. These include the two or three specialized national security advisers in the White House, the staff of the NSC (headed by the national security adviser), and a few other career bureaucrats in the departments of State and Defense whose influence varies according to their specialty and to the foreign policy issue at hand.

**Congress** In foreign policy making, Congress has to be subdivided into three parts. The first part is the Senate. For most of American history, the Senate was the only important congressional foreign policy player because of its constitutional role in reviewing and approving treaties. The treaty power is still the primary entrée of the Senate into foreign policy making. But since World War II and the continual involvement of the United States in international security and foreign aid, Congress as a whole has become a major foreign policy maker because most modern foreign policies require financing, which requires both the House of Representatives and the Senate. Congress has also become increasingly involved in foreign policy making because of the increasing use by the president of ***executive agreements*** to conduct foreign policy. Executive agreements have the force of treaties but do not require prior approval by the Senate. They can, however, be revoked by action of both chambers of Congress.

The third congressional player is the foreign policy and military policy committees: in the Senate these are the Foreign Relations Committee and the Armed Services Committee; in the House, these are the International Affairs Committee and the Armed Services Committee. Usually, a few members of these committees who have spent years specializing in foreign affairs become trusted members of the foreign policy establishment and are actually makers rather than mere shapers of foreign policy. In fact, several members of Congress have left to become key foreign affairs cabinet members.[6]

## Who Shapes Foreign Policy?

The shapers of foreign policy are the nonofficial, informal players, but they are typically people or groups that have great influence in the making of foreign policy. Of course, the influence of any given group varies according to the party and the ideology that is dominant at a given moment.

**Interest Groups** Far and away the most important category of nonofficial player is the interest group—that is, the interest groups to whom one or more foreign policy issues are of long-standing and vital relevance. The type of interest group with the reputation for the most influence is the economic interest group. Yet the myths about their influence far outnumber and outweigh the realities. The actual influence of organized economic interest groups in foreign policy varies enormously from issue to issue and year to year. Most of these groups are "single-issue" groups and are therefore most active when their particular issue is on the agenda. On many of the broader and more sustained policy issues, such as the North American Free Trade Agreement (NAFTA) or the general question of American involvement in international trade, the larger interest groups, some-

[6]Under President Bush, for example, Dick Cheney left the House to become secretary of defense; under President Clinton, Senator Lloyd Bentsen and Representative Les Aspin left Congress to become the secretaries of the treasury and defense, respectively.

times called "peak associations," find it difficult to maintain tight enough control of their many members to speak with a single voice. The most systematic study of international trade policies and their interest groups concluded that the leaders of these large, economic interest groups spend more time maintaining consensus among their members than they do actually lobbying Congress or pressuring major players in the executive branch.[7] The more successful economic interest groups, in terms of influencing foreign policy, are the narrower, single-issue groups such as the tobacco industry, which over the years has successfully kept American foreign policy from putting heavy restrictions on international trade in and advertising of tobacco products, and the computer hardware and software industries, which have successfully hardened the American attitude toward Chinese piracy of intellectual property rights.

**AMERICAN POLITICAL DEVELOPMENT**

Although interest groups have always been involved in foreign policy making, their number and variety have expanded since World War II. This growth was due in part to the impact of global affairs on domestic interests, to increased congressional involvement in foreign policy, and to increased lobbying of Congress by agents of foreign governments.

SOURCE: James M. Lindsay, *Congress and the Politics of U.S. Foreign Policy* (Baltimore: Johns Hopkins University Press, 1994), pp. 28–29.

Another type of interest group with a well-founded reputation for influence in foreign policy is made up of people with strong attachments and identifications to their country of national origin. The interest group with the reputation for greatest influence is American Jews, whose family and emotional ties to Israel make them one of the most alert and potentially one of the most active interest groups in the whole field of foreign policy. But note once again how narrowly specialized that interest is—it focuses almost entirely and exclusively on policies toward Israel. Similarly, Americans of Irish heritage, despite having resided in the United States for two, three, or four generations, still maintain a vigilance about American policies toward Ireland and Northern Ireland; many even contribute to the activities of the Irish Republican Army. Many other ethnic and national interest groups wield similar influence over American foreign policy.

A third type of interest group, one with a reputation that has been growing in the past two decades, is the human rights interest group. Such groups are made up of people who, instead of having self-serving economic or ethnic interests in foreign policy, are genuinely concerned for the welfare and treatment of people throughout the world—particularly those who suffer under harsh political regimes. A relatively small but often quite influential example is Amnesty International, whose exposés of human rights abuses have altered the practices of many regimes around the world. In recent years, the Christian Right has also been a vocal advocate for the human rights of Christians who are persecuted in other parts of the world, most notably in China, for their religious beliefs. For example, the Christian Coalition joined groups like Amnesty International in lobbying Congress to cut trade with countries that permit attacks against religious believers.

[7]Raymond A. Bauer, Ithiel de Sola Pool, and Lewis Anthony Dexter, *American Business and Public Policy: The Politics of Foreign Trade*, 2nd ed. (Chicago: Aldine-Atherton, 1972).

A related type of group with a fast-growing influence is the ecological or environmental group, sometimes called the "greens." Groups of this nature often depend more on demonstrations than on the usual forms and strategies of influence in Washington—lobbying and using electoral politics, for example. Demonstrations in strategically located areas can have significant influence on American foreign policy. One good example of this is the opposition that relatively small environmental protection groups in the United States raised against American contracts to buy electrical power from the Canadian province of Quebec: The group opposed the ecological effect of the enlarged hydroelectric power dams that were going to have to be built in order to accommodate American demands.[8]

**The Media** Here again, myth may outweigh truth about media influence in foreign policy. The most important element of the policy influence of the media is the speed and scale with which the media can spread political communications. In that factor alone, the media's influence is growing—more news reaches more people faster, and people's reaction times are therefore shorter. When we combine this ability to communicate faster with the "feedback" medium of public opinion polling, it becomes clear how the media have become so influential—they enable the American people to reach the president and the other official makers of foreign policy.[9]

There is one other aspect of media influence to consider. Many unhappy politicians complain bitterly of "media bias." The complaint most often heard is that journalists have a liberal (anti-Republican) bias. Although this general complaint has never been adequately documented, one aspect of media bias has been shown. Using survey evidence, Michael Robinson demonstrated that reliance on television as a source of news gave people negative attitudes toward public policies and especially toward government and public officials.[10] Robinson called this attitude "videomalaise." A later study found, in addition, that "television news in particular has an inherent bias toward reporting negative and critical information. In other words, 'videomalaise' [is] as much a product of the medium as of the message."[11] One probable influence of the media on foreign as well as domestic policy has been to make the American people far more cynical and skeptical than they would otherwise have been. Beyond that, however, the influence of any medium of communication or any one influential journalist or news program varies from case to case.

[8]Brenda Holzinger, "Power Politics: Public Policy, Federalism, and Hydroelectric Power," unpublished Ph.D. dissertation, Cornell University, 1997.

[9]For further discussion of the vulnerability of modern presidents to the people through the media, see Theodore Lowi, *The Personal President: Power Invested, Promise Unfulfilled* (Ithaca, NY: Cornell University Press, 1985); Jeffrey K. Tulis, *The Rhetorical Presidency* (Princeton: Princeton University Press, 1987); Samuel Kernell, *Going Public: New Strategies of Presidential Leadership* (Washington, DC: Congressional Quarterly Press, 1986); Richard Rose, *The Postmodern President: The White House Meets the World* (Chatham, NJ: Chatham House, 1988); and George C. Edwards, *The Public Presidency: The Pursuit of Popular Support* (New York: St. Martin's, 1983).

[10]Michael J. Robinson, "Public Affairs Television and the Growth of Political Malaise: The Case of 'TV Selling of the Pentagon,'" *American Political Science Review* 70, no. 2 (June 1976), p. 425.

[11]Seymour Martin Lipset and William Schneider, *The Confidence Gap: Business, Labor, and Government in the Public Mind* (New York: Free Press, 1983), p. 405.

## Putting It Together

What can we say about who really makes American foreign policy? First, except for the president, the influence of players and shapers varies from case to case—this is a good reason to look with some care at each example of foreign policy in this chapter. Second, since the one constant influence is the centrality of the president in foreign policy making, it is best to evaluate other actors and factors as they interact with the president.[12] Third, the reason influence varies from case to case is that each case arises under different conditions and with vastly different time constraints: for issues that arise and are resolved quickly, the opportunity for influence is limited. Fourth, foreign policy experts will usually disagree about the level of influence any player or type of player has on policy making.

But just to get started, let's make a few tentative generalizations and then put them to the test with the substance and experience reported in the remainder of this chapter. First, when an important foreign policy decision has to be made under conditions of crisis—where "time is of the essence"—the influence of the presidency is at its strongest. Second, under those time constraints, access to the decision is limited almost exclusively to the narrowest definition of the "foreign policy establishment." The arena for participation is tiny; any discussion at all is limited to the officially and constitutionally designated players. To put this another way, in a crisis, the foreign policy establishment works as it is supposed to.[13] As time becomes less restricted, even when the decision to be made is of great importance, the arena of participation expands to include more government players and more nonofficial, informal players—the most concerned interest groups and the most important journalists. In other words, the arena becomes more pluralistic, and therefore less distinguishable from the politics of domestic policy making. Third, because there are so many other countries with power and interests on any given issue, there are severe limits on the choices the United States can make. As one author concludes, in foreign affairs, "policy takes prece-

### AMERICAN POLITICAL DEVELOPMENT

Throughout much of the twentieth century, American foreign policy relied more on executive agreements than on treaties. From the Civil War to the early decades of the twentieth century, treaties outnumbered executive agreements, but by the 1920s, there were more executive agreements than treaties. For most of the post–World War II era, the use of executive agreements has been between four and ten times as frequent as the use of treaties.

SOURCE: Gary King and Lyn Ragsdale, *The Elusive Executive: Discovering Statistical Patterns in the Presidency* (Washington, DC: Congressional Quarterly Press, 1988), pp. 131–42.

[12]A very good brief outline of the centrality of the president in foreign policy will be found in Paul E. Peterson, "The President's Dominance in Foreign Policy Making," *Political Science Quarterly* 109, no. 2 (Summer 1994), pp. 215, 234.

[13]One confirmation of this will be found in Theodore Lowi, *The End of Liberalism,* 2nd ed. (New York: W. W. Norton, 1979), pp. 127–30; another will be found in Stephen Krasner, "Are Bureaucracies Important?" *Foreign Policy* 7 (Summer 1972), pp. 159–79. However, it should be added that Krasner was writing his article in disagreement with Graham T. Allison, "Conceptual Models and the Cuban Missile Crisis," *American Political Science Review* 63, no. 3 (September 1969), pp. 689–718.

dence over politics."[14] Thus, even though foreign policy making in noncrisis situations may more closely resemble the pluralistic politics of domestic policy making, foreign policy making is still a narrower arena with fewer participants.

## The Values in American Foreign Policy

When President Washington was preparing to leave office in 1796, he crafted with great care, and with the help of Alexander Hamilton and James Madison, a farewell address that is one of the most memorable documents in American history. We have already had occasion to look at a portion of Washington's farewell address, because in it he gave some stern warnings against political parties (see Chapter 11). But Washington's greater concern was to warn the nation against foreign influence:

> History and experience prove that foreign influence is one of the most baneful foes of republican government. . . . The great rule of conduct for us in regard to foreign nations is, in extending our commercial relations to have with them as little *political* connection as possible. So far as we have already formed engagements let them be fulfilled with perfect good faith. Here let us stop. . . . There can be no greater error than to expect or calculate upon real favors from nation to nation. . . . Trust to temporary alliances for extraordinary emergencies, [but in all other instances] steer clear of permanent alliances with any portion of the foreign world. . . . Such an attachment of a small or weak toward a great and powerful nation dooms the former to be the satellite of the latter [emphasis in original].[15]

With the exception of a few leaders such as Thomas Jefferson and Thomas Paine, who were eager to take sides with the French against all others, Washington was probably expressing sentiments shared by most Americans. In fact, during most of the nineteenth century, American foreign policy was to a large extent no foreign policy. But Americans were never isolationist, if isolationism means the refusal to have any associations with the outside world. Americans were eager for trade and for treaties and contracts facilitating trade. Americans were also expansionists, but their vision of expansionism was limited to filling up the North American continent only.

Three familiar historical factors help explain why Washington's sentiments became the tradition and the source of American foreign policy values. The first was the deep anti-statist ideology shared by most Americans in the nineteenth century and into the twentieth century. Although we witness widespread anti-statism today, in the form of calls for tax cuts, deregulation, privatization, and other

[14]Peterson, "The President's Dominance in Foreign Policy," p. 232.

[15]A full version of the text of the farewell address, along with a discussion of the contribution to it made by Hamilton and Madison, will be found in Daniel J. Boorstin, ed., *An American Primer* (Chicago: University of Chicago Press, 1966), vol. 1, pp. 192–210. This editing is by Richard B. Morris.

efforts to "get the government off our backs," such sentiments were far more intense in the past, when many Americans opposed foreign entanglements, a professional military, and secret diplomacy. The second factor was federalism. The third was the position of the United States as a ***client state*** (a state that has the capacity to carry out its own foreign policy most of the time, but that still depends upon the interests of one or more of the major powers). Most nineteenth-century Americans recognized that if the United States became entangled in foreign affairs, national power would naturally grow at the expense of the states, and so would the presidency at the expense of Congress. Why? Because foreign policy meant having a professional diplomatic corps, professional armed forces with a general staff—and secrets. This meant professionalism, elitism, and remoteness from citizens. Being a client state allowed America to keep its foreign policy to a minimum. Moreover, maintaining American sovereignty was in the interest of the European powers because it prevented any one of them from gaining an advantage over the others in the Western Hemisphere.

## Legacies of the Traditional System

Two identifiable legacies flowed from the long tradition based on anti-statism, federalism, and client status. One is the intermingling of domestic and foreign policy institutions. The second is unilateralism—America's willingness to go it alone. Each of these reveals a great deal about the values behind today's conduct of foreign policy.

**Intermingling of Domestic and Foreign Policy** Because the major European powers once policed the world, American political leaders could treat foreign policy as a mere extension of domestic policy. The tariff is the best example. A tax on one category of imported goods as a favor to interests in one section of the country would directly cause friction elsewhere in the country. But the demands of those adversely affected could be met without directly compromising the original tariff, by adding a tariff to still other goods that would placate those who were complaining about the original tariff. In this manner, Congress was continually adding and adjusting tariffs on more and more classes of commodities.

An important aspect of the treatment of foreign affairs as an extension of domestic policy was amateurism. Unlike many other countries, Americans refused to develop a tradition of a separate foreign service composed of professional people who spent much of their adult lives in foreign countries, learning foreign languages, absorbing foreign cultures, and developing a sympathy for foreign points of view. Instead, Americans have tended to be highly suspicious of any American diplomat or entrepreneur who spoke

**AMERICAN POLITICAL DEVELOPMENT**

History suggests that foreign policy and domestic policy often intermingle. One example comes from the domestic politics of the 1820s, when tariffs were increased. These tariffs enhanced revenues, which in turn had a profound impact on domestic spending. Those revenues were used for internal improvements.

SOURCE: Thomas Ferguson, *Golden Rule: The Investment Theory of Party Competition and the Logic of Money-Driven Political Systems* (Chicago: University of Chicago Press), 1995, p. 56.

sympathetically of any foreign viewpoints.[16] No systematic progress was made to create a professional diplomatic corps until after the passage of the Foreign Service Act of 1946.

**Unilateralism** Unilateralism, not isolationism, was the American posture toward the world until the middle of the twentieth century. Isolationism means trying to cut off contacts with the outside, to be a self-sufficient fortress. America was never isolationist; it preferred ***unilateralism,*** or "going it alone." Americans have always been more likely to rally around the president in support of direct action rather than for a sustained, diplomatic involvement.

## The Great Leap to World Power

The traditional era of U.S. foreign policy came to an end with World War I for several important reasons. First, the "balance of power" system[17] that had kept the major European powers from world war for a hundred years had collapsed.[18] In fact, the great powers themselves had collapsed internally. The most devastating of all wars up to that time had ruined their economies, their empires, and, in most cases, their political systems. Second, the United States was no longer a client state but in fact one of the great powers. Third, as we saw in earlier chapters, the United States was soon to shed its traditional domestic system of federalism with its national government of almost pure promotional policy. Thus, virtually all the conditions that contributed to the traditional system of American foreign policy had disappeared. Yet there was no discernible change in America's approach to foreign policy in the period between World War I and World War II. After World War I, as one foreign policy analyst put it, "the United States withdrew once more into its insularity. Since America was unwilling to use its power, that power, for purposes of foreign policy, did not really exist."[19]

The Great Leap in foreign policy was finally made thirty years after conditions demanded it and only then after another world war. Following World War II, pressure for a new tradition came into direct conflict with the old. The new tradition required foreign entanglements; the old tradition feared them deeply. The new tradition required diplomacy; the old distrusted it. The new tradition required acceptance of antagonistic political systems; the old embraced democracy and was aloof from all else.

The values of the new tradition were all apparent during the cold war. Instead of unilateralism, the United States pursued ***multilateralism,*** entering into treaties

[16]E. E. Schattschneider, *Politics, Pressures, and the Tariff* (Englewood Cliffs, NJ: Prentice-Hall, 1935).

[17]"Balance of power" was the primary foreign policy role played by the major European powers during the nineteenth century, and it is a role available to the United States in contemporary foreign affairs, a role occasionally adopted but not on a world scale. This is the third of the four roles identified and discussed later in this chapter.

[18]The best analysis of what he calls the "100 years' peace" will be found in Karl Polanyi, *The Great Transformation* (New York: Rinehart, 1944; Beacon paperback ed., 1957), pp. 5ff.

[19]John G. Stoessinger, *Crusaders and Pragmatists: Movers of Modern American Foreign Policy* (New York: W. W. Norton, 1985), pp. 21, 34.

with other nations to achieve its foreign policy goals. The most notable of these treaties is that which formed the North Atlantic Treaty Organization (NATO) in 1948, which allied the United States, Canada, and most of western Europe. With its NATO allies, the United States practiced a two-pronged policy in dealing with its rival, the Soviet Union: ***containment*** and ***deterrence.*** Fearing that the Soviet Union was bent on world domination, the United States fought wars in Korea and Vietnam to "contain" Soviet power. And in order to deter a direct attack against itself or its NATO allies, the United States developed a multi-billion-dollar nuclear arsenal capable of destroying the Soviet Union many times over.

An arms race between the United States and the Soviet Union was extremely difficult if not impossible to resist because there was no way for either side to know when they had enough deterrent to continue preventing aggression by the other side. As we mentioned in the beginning of this chapter, the cold war ended abruptly in 1989, after the Soviet Union had spent itself into oblivion and allowed its empire to collapse. Many observers called the end of the cold war a victory for democracy. But more important, it was a victory for capitalism over communism, a vindication of the free market as the best way to produce the greatest wealth of nations. Furthering capitalism has long been one of the values guiding American foreign policy and this might be more true at the end of the twentieth century than at any time before.

## The Instruments of Modern American Foreign Policy

Any nation-state has at hand certain instruments, or tools, to use in implementing its foreign policy. An instrument is neutral, capable of serving many goals. There have been many instruments of American foreign policy, and we can deal here only with those instruments we deem to be most important in the modern epoch: diplomacy, the United Nations, the international monetary structure, economic aid, collective security, and military deterrence. Each of these instruments will be evaluated in this section for its utility in the conduct of American foreign policy, and each will be assessed in light of the history and development of American values.

### Diplomacy

We begin this treatment of instruments with diplomacy because it is the instrument to which all other instruments should be subordinated, although they seldom are. Diplomacy is the representation of a government to other foreign governments. Its purpose is to promote national values or interests by peaceful means. According to Hans Morgenthau, "a diplomacy that ends in war has failed in its primary objective."[20]

[20]Hans Morgenthau, *Politics among Nations,* 2nd ed. (New York: Knopf, 1956), p. 505.

AMERICAN POLITICAL DEVELOPMENT

The number of diplomatic posts has increased over the years. From 1790 to 1840, the number of posts grew from two to twenty. By 1890, the number had doubled, to forty-one, and more than doubled again to ninety-nine by 1960. Since 1970, the number has steadily increased, reaching 191 by 1994.

SOURCE: Harold W. Stanley and Richard G. Niemi, *Vital Statistics on American Politics,* 5th ed. (Washington, DC: Congressional Quarterly Press, 1995), p. 321.

The first effort to create a modern diplomatic service in the United States was made through the Rogers Act of 1924, which established the initial framework for a professional foreign service staff. But it took World War II and the Foreign Service Act of 1946 to forge the foreign service into a fully professional diplomatic corps.

Diplomacy, by its very nature, is overshadowed by spectacular international events, dramatic initiatives, and meetings among heads of state or their direct personal representatives. The traditional American distrust of diplomacy continues today, albeit in weaker form. Impatience with or downright distrust of diplomacy has been built not only into all the other instruments of foreign policy but also into the modern presidential system itself.[21] So much personal responsibility has been heaped upon the presidency that it is difficult for presidents to entrust any of their authority or responsibility in foreign policy to professional diplomats in the State Department and other bureaucracies. And the American practice of appointing political friends and campaign donors to major ambassadorial positions does not inspire trust. During his first year in office, President Bush named eighty-seven ambassadorial appointees, forty-eight of whom were important political contributors. President Clinton appointed even fewer professional diplomats to ambassadorships than either Presidents Reagan or Bush had.[22]

Electoral politics is not the only kind of politics affecting the nature and timing of ambassadorial appointments. The Republican chair of the Senate Foreign Relations Committee, Jesse Helms, blocked eighteen of President Clinton's ambassadorial nominations for most of the 1995 congressional session, demanding that Clinton agree to merge three independent foreign policy agencies with the State Department. Although Helms did not win everything he demanded from President Clinton, he did gain some important concessions in return for his approval of the ambassadors during the last days before Congress recessed in December 1995.[23]

Distrust of diplomacy has also produced a tendency among all recent presidents to turn frequently to military and civilian personnel outside the State Department to take on a special diplomatic role as direct personal representatives of the president. As discouraging as it is to those who have dedicated their careers to foreign service to have political hacks appointed over their heads, it is probably even more discouraging when they are displaced from a foreign policy issue as soon as relations with the country they are posted in begin to heat up. When a special personal representative is sent abroad to represent the president, that envoy holds a status higher than that of the local ambassador, and the embassy

[21]See Lowi, *The Personal President,* pp. 167–69.

[22]Dick Kirschten, "Life Jacket, Anyone?" *National Journal* 26 (25 June 1994), p. 1501.

[23]"Senate Slashes Agency Budgets, Confirms Eighteen Ambassadors," *Congressional Quarterly,* 16 December 1995, p. 3821.

becomes the envoy's temporary residence and base of operation. Despite the impressive professionalization of the American foreign service—with advanced training, competitive exams, language requirements, and career commitment—this practice of displacing career ambassadors with political appointees and with special personal presidential representatives continues. For instance, when President Clinton sought in 1994 to make a final diplomatic attempt to persuade Haiti's military dictator to relinquish power to the country's freely elected president before dispatching U.S. military forces to the island, he sent a team of three personal representatives—former president Jimmy Carter, Senator Sam Nunn, and former chairman of the Joint Chiefs of Staff Colin Powell.

The significance of diplomacy and its vulnerability to domestic politics may be better appreciated as we proceed to the other instruments. Diplomacy was an instrument more or less imposed on Americans as the prevailing method of dealing among nation-states in the nineteenth century. The other instruments to be identified and assessed below are instruments that Americans self-consciously crafted for themselves to take care of their own chosen place in the world affairs of the second half of the twentieth century. They are, therefore, more reflective of American culture and values than is diplomacy.

## The United Nations

The utility of the United Nations (U.N.) to the United States as an instrument of foreign policy can too easily be underestimated. During the first decade or more after its founding in 1945, the United Nations was a direct servant of American interests. The most spectacular example of the use of the United Nations as an instrument of American foreign policy was the official U.N. authorization and sponsorship of intervention in Korea with an international "peacekeeping force" in 1950. Thanks to the Soviet boycott of the United Nations at that time, which deprived the U.S.S.R. of its ability to use its veto in the Security Council of the U.N., the United States was able to conduct the Korean War under the auspices of the United Nations.

The United States provided 40 percent of the U.N. budget in 1946 (its first full year of operation) and 26 percent of the $1.2 billion U.N. budget in 1997–1998.[24] Many Americans feel that the United Nations does not give good value for the investment. But any evaluation of the United Nations must take into account the purpose for which the United States sought to create it: to achieve ***power without diplomacy.*** After World War II, when the United States could no longer remain aloof from foreign policy, the nation's leaders sought to use our power to create an international structure that could be run with a minimum of diplomatic involvement—so that Americans could return to their normal domestic pursuits. As one constitutional scholar characterized the founding of

[24]In 1997, the next five biggest contributors were Japan (16.0 percent), Germany (9 percent), France (6.7 percent), the United Kingdom (5.6 percent), and the Russian federation (4.4 percent). These figures do not include many specific U.N. operations and organizations, nor the U.S. contributions to these programs. See the *1998 Information Please Almanac* (Boston: Houghton Mifflin, 1998), pp. 348–49.

the American republic in 1787, so can we say of the effort to found the United Nations—the U.S. sought to create "a machine that would go of itself."[25]

The U.N. may have gained a new lease on life in the post–cold war era, with its performance in the 1991 Persian Gulf War. Although President Bush's immediate reaction to Iraq's invasion of Kuwait was unilateral, he quickly turned to the U.N. for sponsorship. The U.N. General Assembly initially adopted resolutions condemning the invasion and approving the full blockade of Iraq. Once the blockade was seen as having failed to achieve the unconditional withdrawal demanded by the U.N., the General Assembly adopted further resolutions authorizing the twenty-nine-nation coalition to use force if, by January 15, 1991, the resolutions were not observed. The Gulf War victory was a genuine U.N. victory. The cost of the operation was estimated at $61.1 billion. First authorized by the U.S. Congress, actual U.S. outlays were offset by pledges from the other participants—the largest shares coming from Saudi Arabia ($15.6 billion), Kuwait ($16 billion), Japan ($10 billion), and Germany ($6.5 billion). The final U.S. costs were estimated at a maximum of $8 billion.[26]

Whether or not the U.N. is able to maintain its central position in future border and trade disputes, demands for self-determination, and other provocations to war depends entirely upon the character of each dispute. The Gulf War was a special case because it was a clear instance of invasion of one country by another that also threatened the control of oil, which is of vital interest to the industrial countries of the world. But in the case of the former Yugoslavia, although the Bosnian conflict violated the world's conscience, it did not threaten vital national interests outside the country's region.

When Yugoslavia's communist regime collapsed in the early 1990s, the country broke apart into historically ethnically distinct regions. In one of these, Bosnia, a fierce war broke out between Muslims, Croatians, and Serbians. From the outset, all outside parties urged peace, and United Nations troops were deployed to create "safe havens" in several Bosnian cities and towns. Yet despite his campaign criticism of President Bush for not doing more to stop the bloodshed in Bosnia, President Clinton was also unable to muster enough support for a more active policy. Faced with resistance from NATO allies and from Russia, and with the unwillingness of the American people to risk the lives of U.S. soldiers over an issue not vital to U.S. interests, Clinton gave up his stern warnings and accepted the outcome: the international community's failure to prevent Serbs from waging a war of aggression and genocide.

Not until November 1995, after still another year of frustration and with U.N. peacekeeping troops in increasingly serious danger from both sides in the Yugoslav civil war, was President Clinton able to achieve a cease-fire and a peace agreement in Dayton, Ohio, among the heads of the warring factions. (U.N.

[25]Michael Kammen, *A Machine That Would Go of Itself: The Constitution in American Culture* (New York: Alfred A. Knopf, 1986).

[26]There was, in fact, an angry dispute over a "surplus" of at least $2.2 billion, on the basis of which Japan and others demanded a rebate. *Report of the Secretary of Defense to the President and Congress* (Washington, DC: Government Printing Office, 1992), p. 26.

peacekeepers and aid workers were again present in Kosovo immediately following the pullout of hostile Serbian troops in 1999.)

Despite the difficulty of restoring peace, the U.N. and its peacekeeping troops did an extraordinary job in the former Yugoslavia, dealing both with the intransigence of the warring parties and with the disagreement among the European powers about how to deal with a vicious and destructive civil war in their own neighborhood. This and other recent U.N. interventions show the promise and the limits of the U.N. as an instrument of foreign policy in the post–cold war era. Although the United States can no longer control U.N. decisions, as it could in the U.N.'s early days, the U.N. continues to function as a useful instrument of American foreign policy.[27]

## The International Monetary Structure

Fear of a repeat of the economic devastation that followed World War I brought the United States together with its allies (except the U.S.S.R.) to Bretton Woods, New Hampshire, in 1944 to create a new international economic structure for the postwar world. The result was two institutions: the International Bank for Reconstruction and Development (commonly called the World Bank) and the International Monetary Fund.

The World Bank was set up to finance long-term capital. Leading nations took on the obligation of contributing funds to enable the World Bank to make loans to capital-hungry countries. (The U.S. quota has been about one-third of the total.)

The International Monetary Fund (IMF) was set up to provide for the short-term flow of money. After the war, the dollar, instead of gold, was the chief means by which the currencies of one country would be "changed into" currencies of another country for purposes of making international transactions. To permit debtor countries with no international balances to make purchases and investments, the IMF was set up to lend dollars or other appropriate currencies to needy member countries to help them overcome temporary trade deficits. For many years after World War II, the IMF, along with U.S. foreign aid, in effect constituted the only international medium of exchange.

During the past decade, the IMF has returned to a position of enhanced importance through its efforts to reform some of the largest debtor nations and former communist countries and to bring them more completely into the global capitalist

**AMERICAN POLITICAL DEVELOPMENT**

In an effort to prop up both domestic and world economy in the wake of financial turmoil caused by World War II, U.S. officials called a world conference at Bretton Woods, New Hampshire, in 1944 to establish the World Bank and the International Monetary Fund (IMF). These efforts at providing economic and world order coincided with the founding of the United Nations, which was also aimed at promoting international political order.

SOURCE: Walter LaFeber, *The American Age: United States Foreign Policy at Home and Abroad since 1750* (New York: W. W. Norton, 1989), pp. 410–11.

[27]Not all American policy makers agree that the U.N. is a worthy instrument of American foreign policy. The U.N. is on the verge of bankruptcy, no thanks to the United States, which owes the U.N. nearly $1.5 billion in dues. For a review, see Barbara Crossette, "U.N., Facing Bankruptcy, Plans to Cut Payroll by Ten Percent," *New York Times,* 6 February 1996, p. A3.

economy. For example, in the early 1990s, Russia and thirteen other former Soviet republics were invited to join the IMF and the World Bank with the expectation of receiving $10.5 billion from these two agencies, primarily for a ruble-stabilization fund. Each republic was to get a permanent IMF representative, and the IMF increased its staff by at least 10 percent to provide the expertise necessary to cope with the problems of these emerging capitalist economies.[28]

These activities of the IMF indicate just how effectively it is committed to the extension of the capitalist victory over communism. The reforms imposed on poorer countries—imposed as conditions to be met before receiving IMF loans—are reforms that commit a troubled country to joining or maintaining membership in the system of global capital exchange that allows investment to seek the highest profits, without restraint. This goal can ignite a boom—as it did in South Korea, Indonesia, Singapore, and Thailand—but that boom can terminate just as abruptly, leaving the economy in question defenseless.

Two 1997–98 financial crises in East Asia are good illustrations of the role and impact of the IMF. First came the Korea crisis. Economic failure caused great national embarrassment and suffering in South Korea in the autumn of 1997, along with great fear that the newly elected president, Kim Dae Jung, who was the first in Korea's modern history to come from outside the governing oligarchy, would be in danger of a coup d'état. Yet Kim's hand was actually strengthened because Koreans heaped the shame of economic failure on the outgoing regime.

The second case is the even deeper crisis in Indonesia, which was almost entirely attributable to the monetary reforms the IMF had imposed. To keep themselves tied to the global market, Indonesia had to negotiate an international exchange rate with the IMF that moved the value of the Indonesian currency, the rupiah, from 4,000 to the U.S. dollar up to 5,000 to the dollar (a 25 percent devaluation), and then Indonesia had to allow the rupiah to reach a free-market exchange rate. Within weeks the Indonesian rupiah fell below 10,000 to the dollar, producing at Indonesian banks long lines of panicked customers seeking to withdraw their money. Recognizing this run on Indonesian banks could cause violence, the government deployed fourteen thousand additional police officers around the Indonesian capital, Jakarta. The entire society was for a while on the verge of collapse and civil war. But out of it came the removal, after a thirty-two-year reign, of the autocratic, dictatorial president, Suharto, and his replacement by a weaker but consequently less dictatorial former aide, B. J. Habibie, who immediately issued a promise of elections within a year. This kind of suffering and sacrifice may be unreasonable and unnecessary, but the IMF is playing precisely the role for which it was designed.[29]

## Economic Aid

Commitment to rebuilding war-torn countries came as early as commitment to the basic postwar international monetary structure. This is the way President

[28] "IMF: Sleeve-Rolling Time," *Economist,* 2 May 1992, pp. 98–99.

[29] For an excellent insight into the current role and influence of the IMF, coupled with a fascinating proposal on how to get the most highly indebted poor countries out of debt, see Jeffrey D. Sachs, "A Millennial Gift to Developing Nations," *New York Times,* 11 June 1999, p. 33.

Franklin Roosevelt put the case in a press conference in November 1942, less than one year after the United States entered World War II:

> Sure, we are going to rehabilitate [other nations after the war]. Why? . . . Not only from the humanitarian point of view . . . but from the viewpoint of our own pocketbooks, and our safety from future war.[30]

The particular form and timing for enacting American foreign aid was heavily influenced by Great Britain's sudden decision in 1947 that it would no longer be able to maintain its commitments to Greece and Turkey (full proof that America would now have to *have* clients rather than *be* one). Within three weeks of that announcement, President Truman recommended a $400 million direct aid program for Greece and Turkey, and by mid-May of 1947, Congress approved it. Since President Truman had placed the Greece-Turkey action within the larger context of a commitment to help rebuild and defend all countries the world over, wherever the leadership wished to develop democratic systems or to ward off communism, the Greek-Turkish aid was followed quickly by the historically unprecedented program that came to be known as the Marshall Plan, named in honor of Secretary of State (and former five-star general) George C. Marshall.[31]

The Marshall Plan—officially known as the European Recovery Program (ERP)—was essential for the rebuilding of war-torn Europe. By 1952, the United States had spent over $34 billion for the relief, reconstruction, and economic recovery of Western Europe. The emphasis was shifted in 1951, with passage of the Mutual Security Act, to building up European military capacity. Of the $48 billion appropriated between 1952 and 1961, over half went for military assistance, the rest for continuing economic aid. Over those years, the geographic emphasis of U.S. aid also shifted, toward South Korea, Taiwan, the Philippines, Vietnam, Iran, Greece, and Turkey—that is, toward the rim of communism. In the 1960s, the emphasis shifted once again, toward what became known as the Third World. From 1962 to 1975, over $100 billion was sent, mainly to Latin America for economic assistance. Other countries of Africa and Asia were also brought in.[32]

Many critics have argued that foreign aid is really aid for political and economic elites, not for the people. Although this is to a large extent true, it needs to be understood in a broader context. If a country's leaders oppose distributing food or any other form of assistance to its people, there is little the United States, or any aid organization, can do, short of terminating the assistance. Goods have to be exchanged across national borders before they can reach the people who need them. Needy people would probably be worse off if the United States cut off aid altogether. The lines of international communication must be kept open. That is why diplomacy exists, and foreign aid can facilitate

[30]Quoted in John Lewis Gaddis, *The United States and the Origins of the Cold War* (New York: Columbia University Press, 1972), p. 21.

[31]The best account of the decision and its purposes will be found in Joseph Jones, *The Fifteen Weeks* (New York: Viking, 1955).

[32]Robert A. Pastor, *Congress and the Politics of U.S. Foreign Economic Policy* (Berkeley: University of California Press, 1980), pp. 256–80.

## *Making Latin America Safe for Democracy and Markets*

The end of the cold war and an increased focus on regional trade and economic issues have shaped U.S. foreign policy and its support for democratic regimes in Latin America. Among scholars who study the region, there is considerable debate about the long-term impact of U.S. policy on democracy in Latin America.[1] What is indisputable, however, is that U.S. policies have changed over time to match changes in their interests. Globalization has created incentives for the United States to support democracy, unabashedly, in the region.

Anti-communism became the preeminent U.S. interest in Latin America from 1950 to 1989, especially after the 1959 Cuban Revolution. Democracy was a secondary interest and often received more lip service than actual support. U.S. policy called for very strong military-to-military relations and the endorsement of anti-communist dictators such as the Somozas in Nicaragua. The United States supported the military overthrow of progressive democratic leaders in Guatemala in 1954, Brazil in 1964, and Chile in 1973. It also quickly granted diplomatic recognition to dozens of military regimes that had come to power through coups, as long as they were regarded as anti-communist. Billions of dollars in military assistance flowed into the region, and military institutions became much stronger than civilian institutions. Thousands of Latin American military officers were trained in the U.S.-operated School of the Americas (SOA) in Fort Benning, Georgia, and many of the alumni later participated in military coups and were linked to massive human rights violations. According to documents released through the Freedom of Information Act, the SOA training manuals taught that executions and torture were legitimate forms of coercion against suspected leftists.[2]

[1]The most pro-American view is found in Tony Smith's *America's Mission: The United States and the Worldwide Struggle for Democracy in the Twentieth Century* (Princeton: Princeton University Press, 1994), while one critical view is found in Walter LaFeber's *Inevitable Revolutions: The United States in Central America* (New York: W. W. Norton, 1984).

[2]Dana Priest, "U.S. Instructed Latins on Executions, Torture," *Washington Post,* 21 September 1996, p. A1.

Since the fall of the Soviet Empire and the disappearance of the threat of a "second Cuba," the primary U.S. interest in Latin America has shifted from anti-communism to more material concerns. The so-called "Washington Consensus" emerged. It stated that U.S. policy and international lending institutions such as the World Bank and the International Monetary Fund should exert pressure on Latin America to create environments friendly to global investment and trade. Electoral democracy became a *sine qua non* for U.S. support, in part because Presidents Reagan, Bush, and Clinton linked economic and political liberalization, and in part because they wanted to isolate Cuba. Today, for the first time in history, every country in the Western Hemisphere except one is governed by an elected president or prime minister. Globalization and marked shifts in U.S. policy are certainly responsible for this remarkable democratic wave.

The ease of capital mobility, communications, and travel that defines globalization has also contributed to new challenges for U.S. policy in Latin America. One consequence of globalization is the ease with which drugs and drug money can flow across borders. The fight against the importation of drugs such as cocaine and marijuana poses a new foreign policy dilemma for the United States. Just as in the fight against communism in the region, Washington's drug policy centers on a military response. Some 56,000 U.S. troops served in Latin America in 1997, providing intelligence support and training host-nation militaries.[3] U.S. military helicopters now even fly drug interdiction missions in Costa Rica, a country without an army. These activities often arouse intense nationalist and anti-American sentiments, and critics argue that bulking up Latin American militaries—even to fight narcotraffickers—may threaten civilian control of military institutions in fledgling democracies.

We should not be surprised if globalization produces a host of new foreign policy challenges. The 1999 Brazilian currency crisis led Argentina and Guatemala to explore the adoption of the U.S. dollar as their official currency, a move that would require U.S. Senate approval. Most Latin American countries want to be included in an expanded NAFTA-like free-trade agreement. And immigration policy will only become more complicated as our world continues to shrink.

[3]Peter Zirnite, "Washington's Addiction to the War on Drugs," *NACLA Report on the Americas* (November/December 1998), p. 28.

diplomacy, just as diplomacy is necessary to help get foreign aid where it is most needed.

Another important criticism of U.S. foreign aid policy is that it has not been tied closely enough to U.S. diplomacy. The original Marshall Plan was set up as an independent program outside the State Department and had its own separate missions in each participating country. Essentially, "ERP became a Second State Department."[33] This did not change until the program was reorganized as the Agency for International Development (AID) in the early 1960s. Meanwhile, the Defense Department has always had principal jurisdiction over that substantial proportion of economic aid that goes to military assistance. The Department of Agriculture administers the commodity aid programs, such as Food for Peace. Each department has in effect been able to conduct its own foreign policy, leaving many foreign diplomats to ask, "Who's in charge here?"

That brings us back to the history of U.S. efforts to balance traditional values with the modern needs of world leadership. Economic assistance is an instrument of American foreign policy, but it has been less effective than it might have been because of the inability of American politics to overcome its traditional opposition to foreign entanglements and build a unified foreign policy—something that the older nation-states would call a foreign ministry. The U.S. has undoubtedly made progress, but other countries still often wonder who is in charge.

## Collective Security

In 1947, most Americans hoped that the United States could meet its world obligations through the United Nations and economic structures alone. But most foreign policy makers recognized that it was a vain hope even as they were permitting and encouraging Americans to believe it. They had anticipated the need for military entanglements at the time of drafting the original U.N. charter by insisting upon language that recognized the right of all nations to provide for their mutual defense independently of the United Nations. And almost immediately after enactment of the Marshall Plan, the White House and a parade of State and Defense Department officials followed up with an urgent request to the Senate to ratify and to Congress to finance mutual defense alliances.

At first quite reluctant to approve treaties providing for national security alliances, the Senate ultimately agreed with the executive branch. The first collective security agreement was the Rio Treaty (ratified by the Senate in September 1947), which created the Organization of American States (OAS). This was the model treaty, anticipating all succeeding collective security treaties by providing that an armed attack against any of its members "shall be considered as an attack against all the American States," including the United States. A more significant break with U.S. tradition against peacetime entanglements came with the North Atlantic Treaty (signed in April 1949), which created the North Atlantic Treaty Organization (NATO). ANZUS, a treaty tying Australia and New Zealand to the United States, was signed in September 1951. Three years later, the Southeast Asia Treaty created the Southeast Asia Treaty Organization (SEATO).

[33]Quoted in Lowi, *The End of Liberalism*, 2nd ed., p. 162.

FIGURE 16.1

**Defense Spending as a Percentage of Gross Domestic Product, 1961–1995**

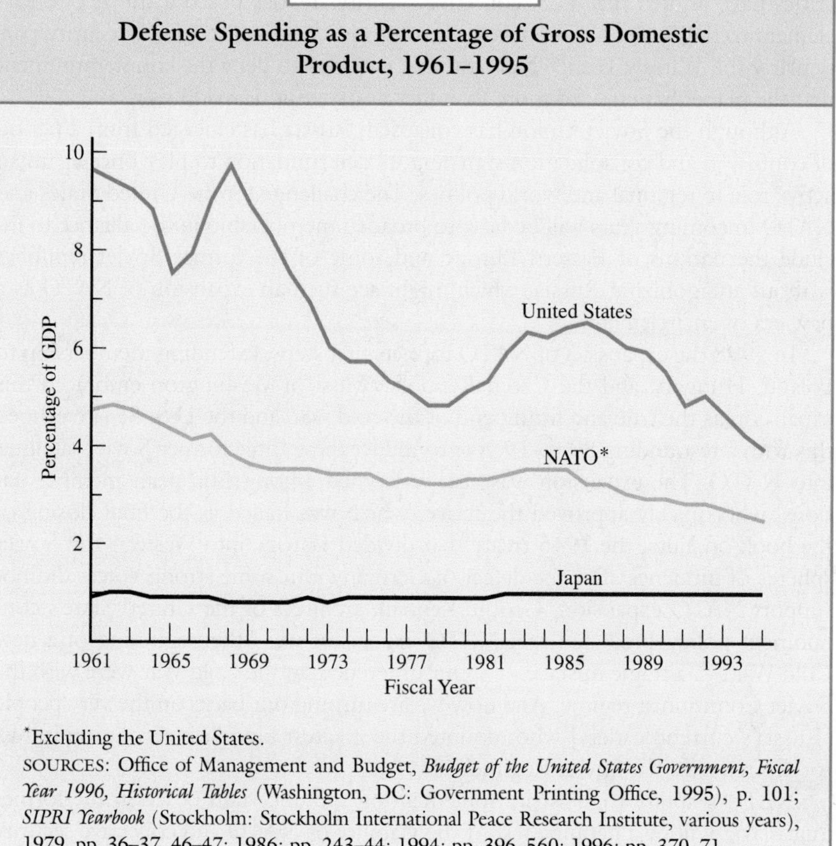


*Excluding the United States.

SOURCES: Office of Management and Budget, *Budget of the United States Government, Fiscal Year 1996, Historical Tables* (Washington, DC: Government Printing Office, 1995), p. 101; *SIPRI Yearbook* (Stockholm: Stockholm International Peace Research Institute, various years), 1979, pp. 36–37, 46–47; 1986: pp. 243–44; 1994: pp. 396, 560; 1996: pp. 370–71.

In addition to these ***multilateral treaties,*** the United States entered into a number of ***bilateral treaties***—treaties between two countries. As one author has observed, the United States has been a *producer* of security while most of its allies have been *consumers* of security.[34] Figure 16.1 demonstrates that the United States has consistently devoted a greater percentage of its gross domestic product (GDP) to defense than have its NATO allies and Japan.

This pattern has continued in the post–cold war era, and its best illustration is in the Persian Gulf War, where the United States provided the initiative, the leadership, and most of the armed forces, even though its allies were obliged to reimburse over 90 percent of the cost.

It is difficult to evaluate collective security and its treaties, because the purpose of collective security as an instrument of foreign policy is prevention, and

[34]George Quester, *The Continuing Problem of International Politics* (Hinsdale, IL: Dryden Press, 1974), p. 229.

success of this kind has to be measured according to what did *not* happen. The critics have argued that U.S. collective security treaties posed a threat of encirclement to the Soviet Union, forcing it to produce its own collective security, particularly the Warsaw Pact.[35] Nevertheless, no one can deny the counterargument that the planet has enjoyed more than fifty years without world war.

Although the Soviet Union has collapsed, Russia has emerged from a period of confusion and consolidation signaling its determination to play once again an active role in regional and world politics. The challenge for the United States and NATO in coming years will be how to broaden membership in the alliance to include the nations of Eastern Europe and some of the former Soviet republics without antagonizing Russia, which might see such an expansion of NATO as a new era of encirclement.

In 1998 the expansion of NATO took its first steps, extending membership to Poland, Hungary, and the Czech Republic. Most of Washington embraced this expansion as the true and fitting end of the cold war, and the U.S. Senate echoed this with a resounding 80-to-19 vote to induct these three former Soviet satellites into NATO. The expansion was also welcomed among European member nations, who quickly approved the move, which was hailed as the final closing of the book on Yalta, the 1945 treaty that divided Europe into Western and Soviet spheres of influence after the defeat of Germany. But some strong voices did not support NATO expansion. George Kennan, architect of the United State's containment policy, predicted that NATO expansion was "the beginning of a new Cold War . . . a tragic mistake. . . . Our differences in the Cold War were with the Soviet Communist regime. And now we are turning our backs on the very people [Russia's current leaders] who mounted the greatest bloodless revolution in history to remove that Soviet Regime."[36]

NATO's ability to assist in implementing the uncertain peace in the former Yugoslavia will be a genuine test of the viability of NATO and collective security in general, now that the cold war is over. NATO was put to the test in 1999 during its efforts to halt the "ethnic cleansing" in Kosovo by the Serbs, but after months of a relentless bombing campaign, NATO prevailed, though Kosovo's future seemed uncertain. NATO and the other mutual security organizations throughout the world are likely to survive. But these organizations are going to be less like military alliances and more like economic associations to advance technology, reduce trade barriers, and protect the world environment. Another form of collective security may well have emerged from the 1991 Persian Gulf War, with nations forming temporary coalitions under U.N. sponsorship to check a particularly aggressive nation.

[35]The Warsaw Pact was signed in 1955 by the Soviet Union, the German Democratic Republic (East Germany), Poland, Hungary, Czechoslovakia, Romania, Bulgaria, and Albania. Albania later dropped out. The Warsaw Pact was terminated in 1991.

[36]Quoted in Thomas Friedman, "NATO Expansion Starting New Cold War?" *Times-Picayune,* 5 May 1998, p. B5. See also *Baltimore Sun,* 2 May 1998, p. 12A.

## Military Deterrence

For the first century and a half of its existence as an independent republic, the United States held strongly to a "Minuteman" theory of defense: Maintain a small corps of professional officers, a few flagships, and a small contingent of marines; leave the rest of defense to the state militias. In case of war, mobilize as quickly as possible, taking advantage of the country's immense size and its separation from Europe to gain time to mobilize.

The United States applied this policy as recently as the post–World War I years and was beginning to apply it after World War II, until the new policy of preparedness won out. The cycle of demobilization-remobilization was broken, and in its place the United States adopted a new policy of constant mobilization and preparedness: *deterrence,* or the development and maintenance of military strength as a means of discouraging attack. After World War II, military deterrence against the Soviet Union became the fundamental American foreign policy objective, requiring a vast commitment of national resources. With preparedness as the goal, peacetime defense expenditures grew steadily over the course of the cold war.

The end of the cold war raised public expectations for a "peace dividend" at last, after nearly a decade of the largest peacetime defense budget increases in U.S. history. Many defense experts, liberal and conservative, feared what they called a budget "free-fall," not only because deterrence was still needed but also because severe and abrupt cuts could endanger private industry in many friendly foreign countries as well as in the United States.

The Persian Gulf War brought both points dramatically into focus. First, the Iraqi invasion of Kuwait revealed the size, strength, and advanced modern technological base not only of the Iraqi armed forces but of other countries, Arab and non-Arab, including the capability, then or soon, to make atomic weapons and other weapons of massive destructive power. Moreover, the demand for advanced weaponry was intensifying. The decisive victory of the United States and its allies in the Gulf War, far from discouraging the international arms trade, gave it fresh impetus. Following the Gulf War victory, *Newsweek* reported that "industry reps quickly realized that foreign customers would now be beating a path to their doors, seeking to buy the winning weaponry." The Soviet Union at one time led the list of major world arms sellers, and Russia and several other republics of the former Soviet Union have continued to make international arms sales, particularly since now there are "no ideological limitations" in the competition for customers.[37] The United States now leads the list of military weapons exporters, followed by Russia, France, Great Britain, and China. Thus, some shrinkage of defense expenditure has been desirable, but Democrats and Republicans alike agree that this reduction must be guided by the continuing need to maintain U.S. and allied credibility as a deterrent to post–cold war arms races.

[37] "Arms for Sale," *Newsweek,* 8 April 1991, pp. 22–27.

### PROCESS BOX 16.1

## How the F-16 Is Produced: The International Relations of Defense

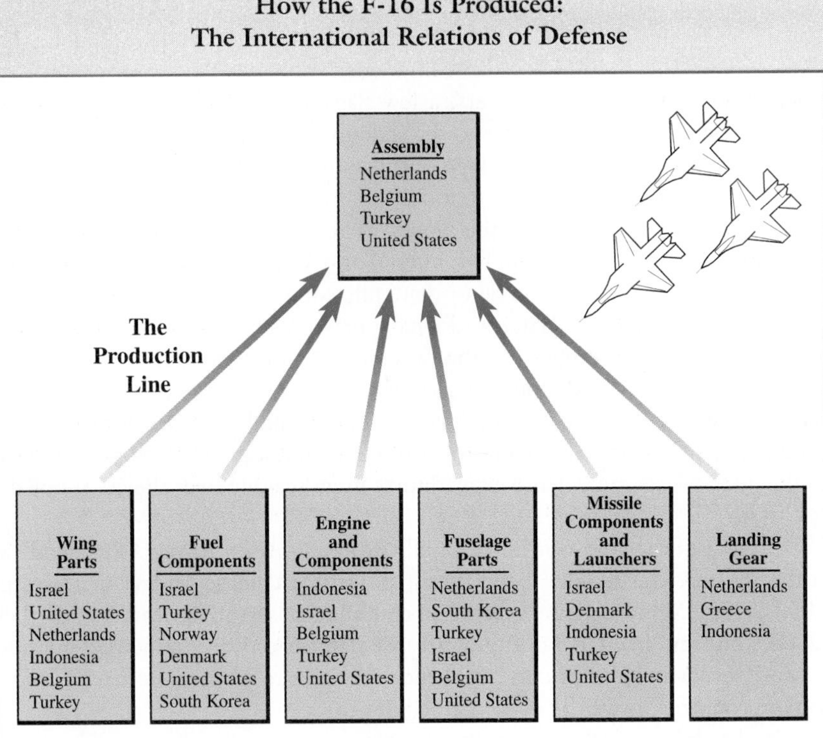


SOURCE: U.S. Congress, Office of Technology Assessment, *Arming Our Allies: Cooperation and Competition in Defense Technology,* OTA-ICS-449 (Washington, DC: Government Printing Office, May 1990), pp. 42–43, which is an extremely elaborate diagram of at least seventy-five separate parts of the F-16. The information was provided by the primary manufacturer, General Dynamics Corporation.

As to the second point, domestic pressures join international demands to fuel post–cold war defense spending. Each cut in military production and each closing of a military base or plant translates into a significant loss of jobs. Moreover, the conversion of defense industries to domestic uses is not a problem faced by the United States alone. Process Box 16.1 conveys a dramatic picture of the "international relations" of the production of one single weapons system, the F-16 fighter airplane.

Support for policies of deterrence and doubts about the applicability of cold war policies to post–cold war problems were both immensely strengthened by the sudden (because undetected) entry of two new members into the nuclear club: India and Pakistan tested nuclear devices in May and June 1998. India's initial five explosions gave it a few days of superiority, and therefore greater deterrence power, over its neighbor and rival, Pakistan. Pakistan's six blasts two weeks later immediately returned the power relationship to equality and therefore there was no long-term gain in security for either country. In fact, as the *Economist* put it, "By going first, India has if anything managed to strengthen Pakistan's security relationship with nuclear-armed China—a relationship that India used to justify breaking the nuclear taboo in the first place."[38] Economic sanctions were quickly imposed on India and Pakistan by the United States and Japan; these will inflict great harm on both countries, but particularly on Pakistan, which may move even more into the arms of China. But as the other nuclear powers were trying to decide what their policy should be toward deterring Pakistan and India from developing their nuclear capabilities further, both countries were already talking about improving their missile delivery capacities.

Just a few weeks after the Indian and Pakistan news, revelations about the sale of missile and satellite materials and technology to China by American companies with U.S. government approval raised more questions about the future of military deterrence. President Clinton asserted that such sales will help democratize China through economic engagement, but they will even more certainly feed worldwide fears that China is the pivot of a new, post–cold war arms race.

All of this suggests that the threat of the arms race and international conflicts persists. It also suggests that the United States is an important part of the problem as well as the most essential part of the solution. The only real hope for a significant reduction in the international demand for arms will come from changes in the general political and economic environment. But such changes do not happen spontaneously. On the international level, genuine reduction in the demand for arms will require diplomacy; try as we might, power without diplomacy can never be a permanent solution. And this must in turn be accompanied by economic growth, not only in the United States but everywhere.

## Roles Nations Play

Although each president has hundreds of small foreign fires to fight and can choose whichever instruments of policy best fit each particular situation, the primary foreign policy problem any president faces is choosing an overall role for the country in foreign affairs. Roles help us to define a situation in order to control the element of surprise in international relations. Surprise is in fact the most dangerous aspect of international relations, especially in a world made smaller and more fragile by advances in and the proliferation of military technology.

### Choosing a Role

The problem of choosing a role can be understood by identifying a limited number of roles played by nation-states in the past. Four such roles will be drawn from history—the Napoleonic, the Holy Alliance, the balance-of-power, and the

[38]"A Bomb in Every Backyard?" *Economist,* 6 June 1998, p. 17.

economic expansionist roles. Although the definitions given here will be exaggerations of the real world, they do capture in broad outline the basic choices available.

**The Napoleonic Role** The ***Napoleonic role*** takes its name from the role played by postrevolutionary France under Napoleon. The French at that time felt not only that their new democratic system of government was the best on earth but also that France would not be safe until democracy was adopted universally. If this meant intervention into the internal affairs of France's neighbors, and if that meant warlike reactions, then so be it. President Woodrow Wilson expressed a similar viewpoint when he supported the U.S. declaration of war in 1917 with his argument that "the world must be made safe for democracy." Obviously such a position can be adopted by any powerful nation as a rationalization for intervening at its convenience in the internal affairs of another country. But it can also be sincerely espoused, and in the United States it has from time to time enjoyed broad popular consensus. The U.S. played the Napoleonic role most recently in ousting Philippine dictator Ferdinand Marcos (February 1986), Panamanian leader Manuel Noriega (December 1989), the Sandinista government of Nicaragua (February 1990), and the military rulers of Haiti (September 1994).

**The Holy Alliance Role** The concept of the ***Holy Alliance role*** emerged out of the defeat of Napoleon and the agreement by the leaders of Great Britain, Russia, Austria, and Prussia to preserve the social order against *all* revolution, including democratic revolution, at whatever cost. (Post-Napoleonic France also joined it.) The Holy Alliance made use of every kind of political instrument available—including political suppression, espionage, sabotage, and outright military intervention—to keep existing governments in power. The Holy Alliance role is comparable to the Napoleonic role in that each operates on the assumption that intervention into the internal affairs of other countries is justified for the maintenance of peace. But Napoleonic intervention is motivated by fear of dictatorship, and it can accept and even encourage revolution. In contrast, Holy Alliance intervention is antagonistic to any form of political change, even when this means supporting an existing dictatorship.[39] Because the Holy Alliance role became more important after the cold war ended, illustrations of this role will be given later in the chapter.

**The Balance-of-Power Role** The ***balance-of-power role*** is basically an effort by the major powers to play off against each other so that no great power or combination of great and lesser powers can impose conditions on others. The most relevant example of the use of this strategy is found in the nineteenth century, especially the latter half. The feature of the balance-of-power role that is most dis-

[39]For a thorough and instructive exposition of the original Holy Alliance pattern, see Paul M. Kennedy, *The Rise and Fall of the Great Powers: Economic Change and Military Conflict from 1500 to 2000* (New York: Random House, 1987), pp. 159–60. And for a comparison of the Holy Alliance role with the balance-of-power role, to be discussed next, see Polanyi, *The Great Transformation,* pp. 5–11 and 259–62.

tinct from the two previously identified roles is that this role accepts the political system of each country, asking no questions except whether the country will join an alliance and will use its resources to ensure that each country will respect the borders and interests of all the others.[40]

**The Economic Expansionist Role** The ***economic expansionist role,*** also called the capitalist role, shares with the balance-of-power role the attitude that the political system or ideology of a country is irrelevant; the only question is whether a country has anything to buy or sell and whether its entrepreneurs, corporations, and government agencies will honor their contracts. Governments and their armies are occasionally drawn into economic expansionist relationships in order to establish, reopen, or expand trade relationships, and to keep the lines of commerce open. But the role is political, too. The point can be made that the economic expansionist role was the role consistently played by the United States in Latin and Central America, until the cold war (perhaps in the 1960s and beyond) pushed us toward the Holy Alliance role with most of those countries.

Like arms control, however, economic expansion does not happen spontaneously. In the past, economic expansion owed a great deal to military backing, because contracts do not enforce themselves, trade deficits are not paid automatically, and new regimes do not always honor the commitments made by regimes they replace. The only way to expand economic relationships is through diplomacy.

## Roles for America Today

Although "making the world safe for democracy" was used to justify the U.S. entry into World War I, it was taken more seriously after World War II, when at last the United States was willing to play a more sustained part in world affairs. The Napoleonic role was most suited to America's view of the postwar world. To create the world's ruling regimes in the American image would indeed give Americans the opportunity to return to their private pursuits, for if all or even most of the world's countries were governed by democratic constitutions, there would be no more war, since no democracy would ever attack another democracy—or so it has been assumed.[41]

**Making the World Safe for Democracy** The emergence of the Soviet Union as a superpower was the overwhelming influence on American foreign policy thinking in the post–World War II era. The distribution of power in the world was "bipolar," and Americans saw the world separated in two, with an "iron curtain" dividing the communist world from the free world. Immediately after the war, America's foreign policy goal had been "pro-democracy," a Napoleonic role dominated by the Marshall Plan and the genuine hope for a democratic world.

[40]Felix Gilbert et al., *The Norton History of Modern Europe* (New York: W. W. Norton, 1971), pp. 1222–24.

[41]For a summary of the entire literature about the "democratic peace," see Henry S. Farber and Joanne Gowa, "Politics and Peace," *International Security* 20, no. 2 (Fall 1995), pp. 123–46. See also Jack Levi, "Domestic Politics and War," *Journal of Interdisciplinary History* 18, no. 4 (Spring 1988), pp. 653–73.

This quickly shifted toward a Holy Alliance role, with "containment" as the primary foreign policy criterion.[42] Containment was fundamentally a Holy Alliance concept. According to foreign-policy expert Richard Barnet, during the 1950s and 1960s, "the United States used its military or paramilitary power on an average of once every eighteen months either to prevent a government deemed undesirable from coming to power or to overthrow a revolutionary or reformist government considered inimical to America's interests."[43] Although Barnet did not refer to Holy Alliance, his description fits the model perfectly.

During the 1970s, the United States played the Holy Alliance role less frequently, not so much because of the outcome of the Vietnam War as because of the emergence of a multipolar world. In 1972, the United States accepted (and later recognized) the communist government of the People's Republic of China and broke forever its pure bipolar, cold war view of world power distribution. Other powers became politically important as well, including Japan, the European Economic Community (now the European Union), India, and, depending on their own resolve, the countries making up the Organization of Petroleum Exporting Countries (OPEC). The United States experimented with all four of the previously identified roles, depending on which was appropriate to a specific region of the world. In the Middle East, America tended to play an almost classic balance-of-power role, by appearing sometimes cool in its relations with Israel and by playing off one Arab country against another. The United States has been able to do this despite the fact that every country in the Middle East recognizes that for cultural, domestic, and geostrategic reasons, the United States has always considered Israel its most durable and important ally in the region and has unwaveringly committed itself to Israel's survival in a very hostile environment. President Nixon introduced balance-of-power considerations in the Far East by "playing the China card." In other parts of the world, particularly in Latin America, the U.S. tended to hold to the Holy Alliance and Napoleonic roles.

This multipolar phase ended after 1989, with the collapse of the Soviet Union and the end of the cold war. Soon thereafter the Warsaw Pact collapsed too, ending armed confrontation in Europe. With almost equal suddenness, the popular demand for "self-determination" produced several new nation-states and the demand for still more. On the one hand, it was indeed good to witness the re-emergence of some twenty-five major nationalities after anywhere from forty-five to seventy-five years of suppression. On the other hand, policy makers with a sense of history are aware that this new world order bears a strong resemblance to the world of 1914. Then, the trend was known as "Balkanization." Balkanization meant nationhood and self-determination, but it also meant war. The Soviet Union after World War I and Yugoslavia after World War II kept more than twenty nationalities from making war against each other for several decades. In

[42]The original theory of containment was articulated by former ambassador and scholar George Kennan in a famous article published under the pseudonym Mr. X, "The Sources of Soviet Conduct," *Foreign Affairs* 25 (1947), p. 556.

[43]Richard Barnet, "Reflections," *New Yorker*, 9 March 1987, p. 82.

1989 and the years that followed, the world was caught unprepared for the dangers of a new disorder that the re-emergence of these nationalities produced.

It should also be emphasized that the demand for nationhood emerged with new vigor in many other parts of the world—the Middle East, South and Southeast Asia, and South Africa. Perhaps we are seeing worldwide Balkanization; we should not overlook the re-emergence of the spirit of nationhood among ethnic minorities in Canada and the United States.

**Making the World Safe for Democracy and Markets** The abrupt end of the cold war unleashed another dynamic factor, the globalization of markets; one could call it the globalization of capitalism. This is good news, but it has its problematic side because the free market can disrupt nationhood. Although the globalization of markets is enormously productive, countries like to enjoy its benefits while attempting at the same time to prevent international economic influences from affecting local jobs, local families, and established class and tribal relationships.

This struggle between capitalism and nationhood produces a new kind of bipolarity in the world. The old world order was shaped by *external bipolarity*—of West versus East. This seems to have been replaced by *internal bipolarity,* wherein each country is struggling to make its own hard policy choices to preserve its cultural uniqueness while competing effectively in the global marketplace.

Approval of the North American Free Trade Agreement (NAFTA) serves as the best example of this struggle within the United States. NAFTA was supported by a majority of Democrats and Republicans on the grounds that a freer, global market was in America's national interest. But even as NAFTA was being embraced by large bipartisan majorities in Congress, three important factions were rising to fight it. Former presidential candidate Pat Buchanan led a large segment of conservative Americans to fight NAFTA because, he argued, communities and families would be threatened by job losses and by competition from legal and illegal immigrant workers. Another large faction, led by Ross Perot, opposed NAFTA largely on the theory that American companies would move their operations to Mexico, where labor costs are lower. Organized labor also joined the fight against NAFTA.

The battle over NAFTA is just one example of the "internal bipolarity" that is coming to the fore around the world. As *New York Times* foreign affairs columnist Thomas Friedman put it, ". . . now that the free market is triumphing on a global basis, the most interesting conflicts are between the winners and losers within countries. It is these internal battles that will increasingly shape international affairs."[44]

The global market is here to stay and American values have changed enough to incorporate it, despite the toll it may take on community and family tradition. Meanwhile, many of the elements of foreign policy created during the cold war still exist because they turned out to be good adjustments to the modern era. The Marshall Plan and the various forms of international economic aid that succeeded

[44]Thomas L. Friedman, "14 Big Macs Later . . . ," *New York Times,* 31 December 1995, sec. 4, p. 9.

it continue to this day. Although appropriations for foreign aid have been shrinking, only a small minority of members of the Senate and the House favor the outright abolition of foreign aid programs. NATO and other collective security arrangements continue, as do some aspects of containment, even though there is no longer a Soviet Union, because collective security arrangements have, as we shall see, proven useful in dealing with new democracies and other nations seeking to join the global market. Even though the former Soviet Union is now more often an ally than an adversary, the United States still quite frequently uses unilateral and multilateral means of keeping civil wars contained within their own borders, so that conflict does not spread into neighboring states. America is practicing a new form of containment, but one that is based on the values and institutions of cold war containment.

The quest for a global market is more than a search for world prosperity. Economic globalization carries with it the hope that economic competition will displace armed conflict, perhaps even reducing if not eliminating the need for traditional diplomacy. But since there are too many instances in world history when economic competition actually led to war rather than avoided it, the United States has added democratization to the recipe of globalization because of the fairly well-supported hypothesis that democracies never go to war against each other. Thus democratization is a genuine and strongly committed goal of U.S. foreign policy, even if it is secondary to economic expansion. Meanwhile, we play the economic card in hopes that capitalism will contribute not only to world prosperity but also to the expansion of democratization.

One of the first indications of the post–cold war American foreign policy was President Bush's conciliatory approach to the dictatorial regime of the People's Republic of China after its brutal military suppression of the democratic student movement in Tiananman Square in June 1989. Subsequently, President Clinton also maintained friendly relations with the dictatorial regime, and both presidents continued to grant the Chinese "normal trade relations" status. Their policy was to separate China's trade status from its human rights record, arguing that economic growth provided the only effective means to bring about political reform in a country as large and as powerful as China. This ten-year policy of friendship with China was severely tested in 1999 by the discovery that during those same ten years a Chinese espionage agent had infiltrated the Los Alamos nuclear weapons laboratory and stolen the details of nuclear technologies, which greatly accelerated his country's advancement toward a modern arsenal. This security breech was undeniably serious, but every effort was made to prevent it from spoiling friendly economic relations with China. Serious and extensive measures were adopted to tighten U.S. security around the scientific and technological research installations, but underneath it all was the attitude that it was inevitable that we would be spied upon—and that we were also doing our best to spy on everyone else. America also renewed its commitment to expanding national government support for scientific research. This would put China "behind" once again, while keeping the United States on an even keel in economic intercourse.[45]

[45]For an evenhanded treatment of this espionage crisis, see the *Economist,* "How Not to Deal with China," 20 March 1999, p. 14.

**The Holy Alliance Role in the Post–Cold War Era** At first glance, it appears that America finally got what it wanted—a world that would run itself well enough without need for much U.S. foreign policy. But the U.S. has obviously been betrayed by events. U.S. foreign policy roles and priorities have not been shuffled very much, if at all. In fact, the Holy Alliance role seems to be more prominent than ever. There is, of course, one big difference—the absence of the Soviet Union and the current willingness of Russia to support rather than oppose American policies. During the cold war era, the purpose of the Holy Alliance role was to keep regimes in power as long as they did not espouse Soviet foreign policy goals. In the post–cold war world, the purpose of the Holy Alliance role is still to keep regimes in power, but only as long as they maintain general stability, keep their nationalities contained within their own borders, and encourage their economies to attain some level of participation in the global market.

We have already dealt with the first case of the Holy Alliance role in the post–cold war era, Iraq's invasion of Kuwait and our Desert Storm response to it. (It was used earlier in this chapter to illustrate the renewed importance of the U.N.) Desert Storm is in fact a very dramatic case of the Holy Alliance role. Iraq's invasion of Kuwait occurred in July 1990, and Desert Storm was not undertaken until January 1991. In the interim, President Bush was mobilizing Congress and the American people, not only in case the United States had to intervene militarily, but also in hopes that the possibility of such action might convince Saddam Hussein to withdraw voluntarily. President Bush was also putting together a worldwide alliance of twenty-nine nations—he had no intention of leading the United States into Desert Storm without this alliance, even though most of its members did not send troops but instead sent political approval plus what amounted to a monetary subscription. Bush had initially taken a Napoleonic position, urging the people of Iraq to "take matters into their own hands" and to force Hussein to "step aside." But after America withdrew its troops, and uprisings inside Iraq began to emerge, President Bush backed away, thus revealing his real intent of leaving the existing dictatorship in power, with or without Hussein. It was enough that the Iraqis stayed within their borders.

Bosnia was another clear case of America playing the Holy Alliance role. At first, the United States refused to exert leadership, and it deferred to the European nations when civil war erupted after Croatia and Bosnia-Herzegovina declared independence from Yugoslavia. When Europe failed to address the problem adequately, the United States and the United Kingdom stepped in, again to no avail. Although our surprise bombing in 1995 to drive the warring factions to the negotiating table in Dayton, Ohio, was virtually unilateral, what emerged was a new alliance of twenty-five nations acting "in concert" to separate the warring factions from one another. And, although one-third of the sixty thousand occupying troops and virtually all the navy and air force units were American, twenty-four other nations established and maintained a physical presence in the field, all in order to maintain the status quo. Almost everything about the Bosnian operation was an acting out of the traditional Holy Alliance role.

Kosovo in 1999 is the most recent and the most spectacular case of post–cold war Holy Alliance policy—although history may prove that the United States

DEBATING THE ISSUES

## American Foreign Policy: Self-Interest or Idealism?

*With the end of the cold war and the breakup of the Soviet Union, many foreign policy experts are reassessing America's role in the world community. Some argue that it is time to focus our attention and resources more directly on our own problems and needs. Others argue that this is no time for the United States to abandon its world leadership role.*

*Economist Alan Tonelson defends what he labels an "interest-based" foreign policy for America. Such a position emphasizes placing American needs first and advocates foreign interventions only when they serve our interests. Foreign-policy specialist Joshua Muravchik, on the other hand, rejects the realist view of Tonelson and others; he maintains that America has both a right and an obligation to extend democratic values around the world.*

### TONELSON

The United States cannot hope to achieve the desired level of security and prosperity by underwriting the security and prosperity of countries all over the world, and by enforcing whatever global norms of economic and political behavior this ambition requires. . . . It must therefore distinguish between what it must do that is absolutely essential for achieving this more modest set of objectives and those things it might do that are not essential. It must, in other words, begin to think in terms not of the whole world's well-being but rather of purely national interests. . . .

. . . An interest-based U.S. foreign policy would firmly subordinate international activism and the drive for world leadership to domestic concerns. Indeed, it would spring from new and more realistic ideas about what can be expected of a country's official foreign policy in the first place. . . . An interest-based approach would also reject the idea that meeting a set of global responsibilities can be the lodestar of U.S. foreign policy. . . . An interest-based foreign policy would acknowledge that the citizens of a democracy have every right to choose whatever foreign policy they please. . . .

The new foreign policy certainly would not preclude acting on principle. But it would greatly de-emphasize conforming to abstract standards of behavior. In fact, the new foreign policy would shy away from any overarching strategy of or conceptual approach to international relations. . . . Its only rule of thumb would be "whatever works" to preserve or enhance America's security and prosperity. . . . [1]

### MURAVCHIK

Although many state actions aim to defend interests, many do not. Some are motivated by altruism. The United States rushes aid to the victims of flood, famine, or other catastrophe wherever these occur for no motive other than human sympathy. Several other countries do the same. Various states offer asylum to the persecuted, provide good offices for the mediation of distant disputes, and even contribute troops to international peacekeeping forces, all for reasons that are essentially humanitarian. . . . The realists are left with the argument that it is wrong to foist our ways—that is, democracy—on others. In saying this the realists suddenly are arguing in moral terms. Their point, however, entails a logical fallacy. The reason it is wrong to impose something on others, presumably, is because it violates their will. But absent democracy, how can their will be known? Moreover, why care about violating people's will unless one begins with the democratic premise that popular will ought to be sovereign?

This argument implies that people prefer to be ruled by an indigenous dictator than to be liberated through foreign influence. The realists will have a hard time explaining this to the people of Panama who danced in the streets when U.S. invaders ousted dictator Manuel Noriega. . . .

The examples of Panama, Japan, Germany, the Dominican Republic, and Grenada notwithstanding, to foist democracy on others does not ordinarily mean to impose it by force. Nor does it mean to seek carbon copies of American institutions. . . . If individuals are obliged to abide by certain moral rules, can they be exempted from those rules when they act collectively with others in the name of the nation?[2]

[1]Alan Tonelson, "What Is the National Interest?" *The Atlantic,* July 1991, pp. 37, 39.
[2]Joshua Muravchik, *Exporting Democracy: Fulfilling America's Destiny* (Washington, DC: AEI Press, 1991), pp. 25, 34–36.

and virtually the entire Western world stumbled into this war.[46] Throughout 1998 and early 1999, ethnic cleansing was proceeding in Kosovo, but the United States would not go it alone, and the NATO nations (except for Great Britain) were not willing to intervene in Kosovo. As late as January 1999, the CIA reported to President Clinton that "[Yugoslav President Milosevic] doesn't believe NATO is going to bomb."[47] It is clear that these delays were due less to American indecision and more to America's or President Clinton's inability to forge a European, multicountry alliance. Prospects of embarrassment at the upcoming fiftieth anniversary of NATO may have forced some European leaders to reconsider an alliance—but even so, only if the United States took the lead, and then only if it promised to limit the assault to an air war only, which guaranteed a minimum of casualties, especially on the allied side.

So the United States got its alliance—and a precedent-setting one—but without any ground troops. President Clinton deserves some blame for the delays and for the artificial restrictions that allowed Milosevic to make the eventual intervention by the alliance all the more dangerous for the Kosovars, whom the United States wanted to defend and protect. The charge that Clinton's impeachment

[46]See, for example, the cover story of the *Economist,* "Stumbling into War," 27 March–2 April 1999, pp. 17, 27, 49, 50.
[47]Quoted in Elaine Sciolino and Ethan Bronner, "How a President, Distracted by Scandal, Entered Balkan War," *New York Times,* 18 April 1999, p. 12.

could not be "compartmentalized" seems to have had some basis to it.[48] But there are inherent limits to multinational coalitions, which President Clinton had to confront no matter what his domestic political distractions were at the time. NATO is simply a more formalized version of any multicountry alliance with the same fundamental problem of any such alliance: *The power of decision tends toward the weakest member.* This was undoubtedly in the mind of Admiral Leighton Smith, commander of NATO forces in southern Europe, 1994–1996, when he observed of Kosovo: "The lesson we've learned is that coalitions aren't good ways to fight a war."[49]

NATO was created as a multilateral defense treaty, which essentially states that an attack on any alliance member is an act of war against all members. And who but the most vulnerable is most likely to be the victim of an attack? The same principle applies now that NATO has become an offensive rather than a defensive alliance. Opposition within the NATO alliance to intervene in Kosovo came mostly from the weaker and more internally divided Italy and Greece than from Britain, France, or Germany. Once the alliance expanded to include Russia, America's hands were tied even more. Russia was instrumental in getting Milosevic to accept the retreat, but it also kept Milosevic in power as part of the price. As reconstruction was beginning in the summer of 1999, the European Union—essentially the political-economic wing of European NATO—voted to provide $1.5 billion for the three-year start-up of the reconstruction. But, as White House National Security Advisor Samuel Berger revealed, Russian objections had prevented the alliance from including in its policy statement that no funds would go to Serbia as long as Milosevic was in power.[50]

The Kosovo campaign validates what we have been observing throughout this chapter: Holy Alliance politics is the prevailing American role in the world today, and the United States draws virtually all its allies and potential allies into that role at one point or another. As the *Washington Post* put it in 1999:

> . . . Whatever the shortcomings, fighting in coalition arrangements appears to be an unavoidable fact of post–Cold War life. . . . "We need partners both for political legitimacy and for risk-sharing," says . . . a senior Pentagon planner earlier in the Clinton administration.[51]

The freedom-loving, free-market magazine *The Economist* goes even further:

> If the United States were indeed going to remain the world's only great power as far ahead as the eye can see, people who like this newspaper believe in the danger of mo-

[48]Note once again the title of the previously cited article, "How a President, Distracted by Scandal, Entered Balkan War."

[49]Bradley Graham and Dana Priest, "'No Way to Fight a War': The Limits of Coalitions," *Washington Post National Weekly Edition,* 14 June 1999, p. 8.

[50]Roger Cohen, "Kosovars to Get European Help for Rebuilding," *New York Times,* 20 June 1999, p. 1.

[51]Quoted in "'No Way to Fight a War': The Limits of Coalitions," op cit., p. 8.

nopoly and the need for competition would draw the necessary conclusions: Europe should provide a counterbalance to this overwhelming American power. But that is not in fact what the future really holds. . . . The one-superpower world will not last. [China, Russia, and the Muslim world will all become geopolitical competitors.] . . . This is why the alliance of the democracies needs not only new members but also a new purpose. The alliance can no longer be just a protective American arm around Europe's shoulder; it also has to be a way for Europe and America to work together in other parts of the world. . . . This must be done—if it can be done at all—in partnership with America. . . .[52]

A Holy Alliance role will never relieve the United States of the need for diplomacy, however. In fact, diplomacy becomes all the more important because despotic regimes eventually fail and in the process attempt to thrust their problems on their neighbors. The dissolution of Yugoslavia and the repeated struggles of a concert of nations to stop the genocidal ethnic struggle there testify to the limits of the Holy Alliance role. This is not to argue that war is never justifiable or that peace can always be achieved through discussions among professional diplomats or purchased by compromise or appeasement. It is only to argue that there are severe limits on how often a country like the United States can engage in Holy Alliances. When leaders in a democracy engage in unilateral or multilateral direct action, with or without military force, they must have overwhelming justification. In all instances, the political should dominate the military. That is what diplomacy is all about. In 1952, the distinguished military career of General Douglas MacArthur was abruptly terminated when President Truman dismissed him for insubordination. At issue was MacArthur's unwillingness to allow the military in Korea to be subordinated to politicians and diplomats. MacArthur's argument was "In war, there is no substitute for victory."[53] But he was overlooking the prior question and therefore missed the very point that should guide any foreign policy: Is there a substitute for war?

## SUMMARY

This chapter began by raising some dilemmas about forming foreign policy in a democracy like the United States. Skepticism about foreign entanglements and the secrecy surrounding many foreign policy issues form the basis of these dilemmas. Although we cannot provide solutions to the foreign policy issues that the United States faces, we can provide a well-balanced analysis of the problems of foreign policy. This analysis is based on the five basic dimensions of foreign policy: the players, the setting, the values, the instruments, and the roles.

The first section of this chapter looked at the players in foreign policy: the makers and shapers. The influence of institutions and groups varies from case to case, with the important exception of the president. Since the president is central

[52]Editorial, "When the Snarling's Over," *Economist,* 13 March 1999, p. 17.
[53]Address, joint meeting of Congress, 10 April 1951.

THEN AND NOW

## Changes in American Politics

As the system of international politics has changed, so too has America's role in world politics. Moreover, important changes within American domestic politics and the economy have played a role in modifying U.S. foreign policy.

- The locus of foreign policy decision-making in the executive branch has moved in post–World War II America from the Department of State to national security bureaucracies such as the National Security Council, which has further internalized foreign policy making within the White House.
- During the second half of the twentieth century, the number (and importance) of interest groups involved with foreign policy making has grown.
- Throughout the nineteenth century, the United States was considered a "client" of great powers. After World War II, the United States became a great power that had its own "clients."
- Throughout much of America's political history, the United States has resisted engaging in international alliances. Even after World War I, America seemed to back away from such unions. But World War II convinced American foreign policy makers about the value of economic alliances (such as the World Bank and the International Monetary Fund) and political alliances (such as NATO and the United Nations).
- Nineteenth-century international foreign policy was based on traditional diplomacy. But during the second half of the twentieth century, the United States turned international politics into "power without diplomacy" by creating regularized international organizations, a regularized system of economic aid, collective security agreements, and a reliance on military deterrence.

to all foreign policy, it is best to assess how other actors interact with the president. In most instances, this interaction involves only the narrowest element of the foreign policy establishment. The American people have an opportunity to influence foreign policy, but primarily through Congress or interest groups.

The next section, on values, traced the history of American values that had a particular relevance to American perspectives on the outside world. We found that the American fear of a big government applied to foreign as well as domestic governmental powers. The founders and the active public of the founding period all recognized that foreign policy was special, that the national government had special powers in its dealings with foreigners, and that presidential supremacy was justified in the conduct of foreign affairs. The only way to avoid the big national government and presidential supremacy was to avoid the foreign entanglements that made foreign policy, diplomacy, secrecy, and presidential discretion necessary. Americans held on to their "anti-statist" tradition until World War II, long after world conditions cried out for American involvement. And even as it became involved in world affairs, the United States held on tightly to the legacies of 150 years of tradition: the intermingling of domestic and foreign policy institutions, and unilateralism, the tendency to "go it alone" when confronted with foreign conflicts.

We then looked at the instruments—that is, the tools—of American foreign policy. These are the basic statutes and the institutions by which foreign policy has been conducted since World War II: diplomacy, the United Nations, the international monetary structure, economic aid, collective security, and military deterrence. Although Republicans and Democrats look at the world somewhat differently, and although each president has tried to impose a distinctive flavor on foreign policy, they have all made use of these basic instruments, and that has given foreign policies a certain continuity. When Congress created these instruments after World War II, the old tradition was still so strong that it moved Congress to try to create instruments that would do their international work with a minimum of diplomacy—a minimum of human involvement. This is what we called power without diplomacy.

The next section concentrated on the role or roles the president and Congress have sought to play in the world. To help simplify the tremendous variety of tactics and strategies that foreign policy leaders can select, we narrowed the field down to four categories of roles nations play, suggesting that there is a certain amount of consistency and stability in the conduct of a nation-state in its dealings with other nation-states. These were labeled according to actual roles that diplomatic historians have identified in the history of major Western nation-states: the Napoleonic, Holy Alliance, balance-of-power, and economic expansionist roles. We also attempted to identify and assess the role of the United States in the post–cold war era, essentially the Holy Alliance role. But whatever its advantages may be, the Holy Alliance approach will never allow the United States to conduct foreign policy without diplomacy. America is tied inextricably to the perils and ambiguities of international relationships, and diplomacy is still the monarch of all available instruments of foreign policy.

## For Further Reading

Crabb, Cecil V., and Kevin V. Mulcahy. *Presidents and Foreign Policymaking: From FDR to Reagan.* Baton Rouge: Louisiana State University Press, 1986.

Gilpin, Robert. *The Political Economy of International Relations.* Princeton: Princeton University Press, 1987.

Graubard, Stephen, ed. "The Exit from Communism." *Daedalus* 121, no. 2 (Spring 1992).

Graubard, Stephen, ed. "The Quest for World Order." *Daedalus* 124, no. 3 (Summer 1995).

Greenfield, Liah. *Nationalism: Five Roads to Modernity.* Cambridge: Harvard University Press, 1993.

Keller, William W. *Arm in Arm: The Political Economy of the Global Arms Race.* New York: Basic Books, 1995.

Kennan, George F. *Around the Cragged Hill: A Personal and Political Philosophy.* New York: W. W. Norton, 1993.

Kennedy, Paul M. *The Rise and Fall of the Great Powers: Economic Change and Military Conflict from 1500 to 2000.* New York: Random House, 1987.

LaFeber, Walter. *The American Age: United States Foreign Policy at Home and Abroad since 1750.* New York: W. W. Norton, 1989.

Smist, Frank J., Jr. *Congress Oversees the U.S. Intelligence Community, 1947–1994,* 2nd ed. Knoxville: University of Tennessee Press, 1994.

U.S. Congress. *Report of the Congressional Committees Investigating the Iran-Contra Affair.* New York: Random House, 1988.

Wirls, Daniel. *Buildup: The Politics of Defense in the Reagan Era.* Ithaca, NY: Cornell University Press, 1992.

# 17

# Can the Government Govern?

## TIME LINE ON POLITICS AND GOVERNANCE

| Events | | Institutional Developments |
|---|---|---|
| | 1960 | Decay of political party organizations (1960s) |
| | | Rise of interest-group liberalism (1960s) |
| | | Rise of activist and adversarial media (1968) |
| | 1970 | |
| Watergate hearings (1973–1974) | | Legislative limits on presidential power: War Powers Resolution (1973); Budget and Impoundment Control Act (1974); Ethics in Government Act (1978) |
| | 1980 | Reagan pledges to terminate departments of Education and Energy but fails (1980s) |
| Iran-Contra affair (1986) | | Reagan's deficits impose budgetary limits on Congress; period of intense conflict between legislative and executive branches (1980–1992) |
| | | Gramm-Rudman mandates across-the-board budget cuts (1985) |
| Clarence Thomas hearings (1990) | 1990 | |
| Health care reform fails (1993–1994) | | Democratic control of both branches ends divided government but doesn't end gridlock (1993) |
| Nannygate; Travelgate (1993); Whitewater investigation (1994–1997) | | Republicans take control of Congress (1994); divided government returns; 104th Congress passes fewer bills than any Congress since 1933 (1995–1996) |
| Temporary government shutdown (1995–1996) | | Divided government continues (1996–2000) |
| Welfare "devolution" passes (1996) | | Newt Gingrich resigns as Speaker of the House (1998) |
| Clinton and congressional Republicans agree to deficit-reduction plan, first balanced budget since the 1960s | | |
| Campaign fundraising by Democrats and Republicans investigated (1997) | | |
| Lewinsky affair investigated; Clinton impeached by House (1998) but acquitted in Senate (1999) | | |
| Republicans lose seats in midterm House elections (1998) | | |

> **CORE OF THE ARGUMENT**
>
> - Divided government has become nearly permanent, resulting in a two-party duopoly and increasingly incremental and symbolic politics.
> - Existing political forces depend on "politics by other means"—forms of conflict that neither require nor encourage citizen involvement.
> - A stronger party system is the most effective cure for America's political woes.
>
> 

Nineteen ninety-eight was a lackluster year in terms of legislative results. As we saw in Chapter 5, Congress failed to act on most of the major pieces of legislation on its agenda, including tobacco regulation, campaign finance reform, restrictions on managed-care health plans, tax cuts, fast-track trade legislation, and vouchers for children to attend public schools. Nineteen ninety-eight was noteworthy for an entirely different reason: Partisan bickering over President Clinton's personal behavior led to a protracted investigation, Clinton's impeachment in the House of Representatives, and his eventual acquittal in the Senate in early 1999. The impeachment of the president left many observers cynical about the American political process. Was 1998 an ominous sign for American democracy and its government's capacity to govern? If there is a problem with the political process, what is its source? Is divided government to blame? Or did Congress's actions in 1998 reflect the public will, which cared little for legislative initiative in a time of peace and prosperity?

Because the political focus of 1998 was on the presidency and Congress, our analysis will logically begin with those two institutions. The 105th Congress left many major legislative items unfinished, but the presidential and congressional batting averages were no lower than the last session of the 104th Congress. Congress has not displayed outstanding performances for a number of years, but this is attributable more to divided government than to the declining capacity of America's two main institutions of policy making. What needs examining is the electoral process and the two-party system, not the rules and structures of the presidency and Congress, which seem to have borne the burden of impeachment well enough.

Where the impeachment experience may have had a more corrosive effect is in the actual conduct of foreign policy. Here the signs are more ominous as we enter the twenty-first century.

The first sign bearing down on foreign policy capacity, although an ambiguous one, was renewed activity by Saddam Hussein, which tested America's resolve. In fact, Saddam consistently tested American resolve throughout 1998, and the Desert Fox attacks of December seemed to have strengthened his position. Bosnia and Kosovo were also indications of a precarious foreign policy. Yugoslav strongman Milosevic was almost certainly seeking his opportunities in Clinton's troubles. Another even more ominous sign (and a more concrete indication of weaknesses attributable to the impeachment) was Clinton's inability to reconstruct against Milosevic the "Concert of Europe," the twenty-nine nations in Desert Storm that had opposed Saddam Hussein's crossing of the Kuwait border in 1991. It took the Serb invasion of Kosovo and the near-genocidal "ethnic cleansing" of the Albanian Kosovars to bring an alliance together, under the NATO umbrella.

A final and more pointed sign of reduced capacity in America's foreign policy was the insubordination of General Anthony Zinni. General Zinni, the U.S. Marine Corps commander and highest-ranking American general in the Middle East, sharply and repeatedly criticized the Clinton administration for helping Iraqi opposition groups attempt to overthrow the Saddam Hussein regime—at the very moment when Secretary of State Albright was "criss-cross[ing] the Middle East to round up support. . . ." Zinni also denounced the Clinton administration by claiming that "a weakened, fragmented Iraq . . . is more dangerous in the long run than a contained Saddam." This opinion was given at a public congressional hearing on a plan to offer $97 million worth of military assistance to Iraqi opposition groups dedicated to the overthrow of Saddam's government. Zinni ventured a further opinion: "I don't see a lot of viability in any opposition group. . . . Do we create internal tensions there that create an Afghanistan-like situation in the end? I don't think these things have been thought out."[1] Instead of summarily firing General Zinni, as President Truman did to the insubordinate General MacArthur, the Defense Department minimized the differences between General Zinni and civilian policy makers, pointing out that Zinni was a "highly valuable officer." That left American policy toward Iraq all the more confused, and opened a large number of military and diplomatic options for Saddam Hussein and for other potential adversaries as well.[2]

President Clinton's acquittal on Friday, February 12, 1999, Lincoln's birthday, will go a long way toward restoring institutional order. The acquittals on both counts of impeachment were decisive. Although the overwhelming expectation had for months been that there were not sixty-seven votes in the Senate (two-thirds as required by the Constitution) to convict, virtually no one (except possibly a few secret Senate vote counters) was predicting that the effort to convict would collapse so completely. Article I, perjury, was defeated 55 to 45, twelve votes shy of conviction. Not even a majority (a 50-to-50 vote) could be mustered on Article II, obstruction of justice, thus depriving the Republicans of their claim to a "moral victory."

Many impediments already stood in the way of meeting important legislative goals to which both parties were committed—weak parties but deep partisan

[1]Quotes from *Congressional Quarterly Weekly,* 24 October 1998, p. 2917.

[2]For a comparable view on the subject, see A. M. Rosenthal, "Mixing American Signals," *New York Times,* 5 February 1999, p. A27. Another ominous sign was provided by former chairman of the Joint Chiefs of Staff, retired admiral Thomas H. Moorer, who said in a prepared statement for a House hearing that "The president, by his own poor choices, has created a crisis of constitutional proportions within the same armed forces he is duty-bound to lead. . . . When troops know a leader is not being held accountable for a dishonorable conduct, the corrosive effect is devastating on the good order and discipline of the Armed Forces" (*Congressional Quarterly Weekly,* 2 January 1991, p. 28). Although military officials jumped to respond, mainly insisting that military loyalty is to the institution, not the person, damage was no doubt done by statements such as Admiral Moorer's. A lengthy front-page article revealing several other instances where the president's foreign-policy conduct was compromised by the scandal is in Elaine Sciolino and Ethan Bronner's, "How a President, Distracted by Scandal, Entered Balkan War," Sunday *New York Times,* 18 April 1999, p. 1.

cleavage, increasing power of interest groups, divided government, and the rise of "politics by other means," to name a few. Whether one wants larger or smaller government, more or less generous welfare or medical benefits, more or less stringent tobacco regulation, freer or more restricted international trade, a decisive government, a capable government, is preferred over a weak or gridlocked one.

The purpose of this chapter is to look critically at the pieces of America's political process and then to consider their implications for the government's capacity to govern. We will assess the impact of divided government on the political process and how its permanent form has contributed to the rise of incremental and symbolic politics. Next, we will look at the declining importance of popular voting and the rise of new forms of conflict in the United States. Finally, we will attempt to ascertain why there are no easy solutions for America's current political problems. But a sober awareness of the problems is a healthy start. In seeking to answer the question "Can the government govern?" we hope to lead readers toward a sense of how the government's capacity to govern can be restored.

**THE CENTRAL QUESTION**

"Can the government govern?"

## Divided Government and Its Consequences

As we argued in earlier chapters, the framers of the Constitution, by setting up a system of separated powers, intended policy making to be difficult. As a result, conflict between the political forces controlling Congress and those controlling the presidency is built into the American system of government. Today, however, the separation of powers mandated by the Constitution is becoming what amounts to a system of dual sovereignty. In a separation of powers system, the power to govern is shared by disparate institutions. If government is to function, each branch must secure a measure of cooperation from the others. For example, the framers of the Constitution provided roles for both the president and Congress in the enactment of legislation. In recent decades, however, cooperation between the president and Congress has been difficult to achieve in this era of divided government. The question arises, "Is divided government the source of this lack of cooperation?" We will first look at the phenomenon of divided government. We will then examine its consequences, which we believe are detrimental to America's capacity to govern.[3]

[3]For a different perspective from ours, see Morris P. Fiorina, *Divided Government,* 2nd ed. (Needham, MA: Allyn & Bacon, 1996). Fiorina argues that divided government does not account for the problems of governance, but instead that the "perceived" failings of government reflect the lack of agreement and concern among citizens about what should be done. While we agree that the electorate is not engaged in the political process or clear about its preferences, we see that as a failure of our political institutions, as we argue later in this chapter.

## Divided Government—The Phenomenon

Between 1946 and 2000 (the end of the 106th Congress), thirty-four of the fifty-four years (almost 63 percent) were years of divided government in which one branch was controlled by the Republican party and the other branch by the Democratic party. (This includes the first six Reagan years, when Republicans controlled the presidency and the Senate but not the House of Representatives.) Of the thirty-two years between 1968 and 2000, twenty-six years—over 81 percent—were years of divided government. And in the twenty years since the election of Ronald Reagan, eighteen years—90 percent—were years of divided government.

At first, divided government didn't seem to matter very much. Presidents continued to turn out proposals, and Congress continued to pass legislation.[4] But a closer look, in particular at the past twenty years, reveals another pattern entirely, and it matters a great deal because it appears to be the culmination of virtually a new American political system with a new kind of party system. We still have essentially a two-party system, but we do not have party government in the traditional sense based on electoral competition. Party government once meant one-party government, with control of the entire government apparatus alternating between the two major parties, depending upon national and congressional electoral majorities. What we have now—and have had for long enough to consider it institutionalized—is *dual*-party government, *with each party nested in one of the branches.* This is better understood not as party government or as two-party government but as *duopoly government.*

With fully confirmed expectations (based upon a probability of over 80 percent) that each party will control one of the branches, each party operates as a *majority party.* After a while, each party begins to act like a majority party and the leaders of both parties develop a special kind of majority mentality. In fact, this is a highly anti-innovation type of mentality, comparable to the situation as it is understood in a duopolistic or oligopolistic economy.[5] With a guaranteed position, or market share, there is always a strong tendency to be risk averse. As one important economics text describes it, "the key feature of oligopoly is that sellers take one another's actions into account in making price and output decisions."[6] In other

**AMERICAN POLITICAL DEVELOPMENT**

Although unified party control of government was the norm from 1900 to 1952, the era of divided government in American politics during the second half of the twentieth century is not unique. Divided party control of government was the norm from 1840 to 1860 and from 1874 to 1896. In today's era of divided government presidential elections are as likely as midterm elections to produce divided government, but in earlier periods "divided control virtually was the result of a midterm loss of unified control achieved in the preceding presidential election."

SOURCE: Morris P. Fiorina, *Divided Government,* 2nd ed. (Boston: Allyn and Bacon, 1996), pp. 6–12.

[4]For an exhaustive coverage of most of this epoch, see David R. Mayhew, *Divided We Govern: Party Control, Lawmaking, and Investigations, 1946–1990* (New Haven: Yale University Press, 1991).

[5]An oligopoly is defined as a market situation in which there are only a few important sellers who produce all, or most, of the entire industry's output. Duopoly is a special case of oligopoly, a two-firm oligopoly.

[6]Robert H. Frank, *Microeconomics and Behavior* (New York: McGraw-Hill, 1991), p. 444.

words, "If it ain't broke, don't fix it!" "Don't quit while you're ahead." The same tendency can be observed in the political sphere, because political duopolists can easily know each other's basic interests without collusion and can cooperate without conspiracy. They can pick specialized and limited areas of competition and thereby avoid all-our competition that might harm the competitor but risks harming oneself as well. And we saw in Chapter 11 that competition from third parties is not a threat.

The following is a very telling observation by Ross Perot, a champion of competition and third parties, in his capacity as an expert on business and competition. While he served as a member of the board of directors of General Motors, he had publicly expressed his dismay at the automobile industry's oligopolistic behavior since World War II.

> . . . The entire American automobile industry had a big respite from competition. . . . [I]t got so bad that [the Big Three companies] tried to get divisions [within their own company] to compete with one another—Chevrolet compete with Pontiac, Oldsmobile with Buick, and so on. . . . I don't like that, and I say "Fellow, that's intramural sports . . . You don't even tackle there, you just touch the guy. . . . You don't even play with pads." . . . You don't understand competition.[7]

There is no reason to expect otherwise in the behavior of parties and their competition for political power. Each competitor has a vested interest in the other, and each has a vested interest in keeping additional competitors out of the political market altogether. From this perspective, we can also see that when each party has a high probability of being nested in a branch, it doesn't matter very much which branch it is, as long as the probability remains high that each party will have such a sanctuary, that each will win some power in the government.

One reaction to divided government and the decline of party competition is to see it as the absolute fulfillment of the separation of powers that was intended by the framers of the Constitution. They designed the separation of powers precisely to (1) prevent the legislative branch from dominating the executive and (2) to make it difficult for the national government to make any policy decisions at all. In other words, the framers created an "absolute separation of powers."[8]

But we also have to look at this reaction in the context of the twentieth century rather than the eighteenth, and that forces us to ask the question, "Can we live with the consequences?" since the absolute separation of powers has rendered the national government virtually incapable of governing. Let's examine some of the consequences of this state of affairs.

## Incremental, Not Innovative, Policies

Statistically, there is much to be said for David Mayhew's argument that divided government does not produce fewer acts of legislation: The flow of bills into final

[7]Quoted in Walter Adams and James Brock, eds., *The Structure of American Industry* (New York: Prentice Hall, 1995), pp. 80–81.

[8]Parts of this section are taken from Theodore Lowi, "President v. Congress: What the Two Party Duopoly Has Done to the American Separation of Powers," *Case Western Reserve Law Review* (Summer 1997), pp. 1219–36.

DEBATING THE ISSUES

## Is Divided Government a Blessing in Disguise

*The situation where one political party controls the presidency and the other party controls Congress is called "divided government." The name itself suggests that control divided between the parties invites governmental gridlock and paralysis, yet it has been the norm in recent decades—from 1968 to 2000, the United States has had a divided government for all but six years.*

*Political analyst James L. Sundquist argues that divided control erodes the ability to govern. Political scientist David R. Mayhew asserts that, at least in the post–World War II era, divided control is not an impediment to governing.*

### SUNDQUIST

Those who believe that a basic weakness of the United States government is the recurrent conflict and deadlock between the executive and legislative branches must turn, at the outset, to the problem of divided government.

When one party controls the executive branch and the opposing party has the majority in one or both houses of Congress, all of the normal difficulties of attaining harmonious and effective working relationships between the branches are multiplied manifold. For, by the nature of party competition in a democracy, the business of political parties is to oppose each other. Competition between the two major parties in the United States is a constant of political life—and it must be, as a safeguard against abuse of power and as the means of assuring the citizenry a genuine choice of leaders and of programs. In an overriding emergency, partisan competition may be set aside, but only temporarily. As soon as the crisis is surmounted, the competition must resume.

When government is divided, then, the normal and healthy partisan confrontation that occurs during debates in every democratic legislature spills over into confrontation between the branches of the government, which may render it immobile. . . . When the president sends a recommendation to the opposition-controlled Congress, the legislators are virtually compelled to reject or profoundly alter it; otherwise, they are endorsing the president's leadership as wise and sound—and, in so doing, strengthening him or his party for the next election. Conversely, if the congressional majorities initiate a measure, the president must either condemn it and use his veto or else acknowledge to the nation the prudence and creativity of his political opponents.[1]

### MAYHEW

. . . [U]nified as opposed to divided control has not made an important difference in recent times in the incidence of two particular kinds of activity. These are, first, high-publicity investigations in which congressional committees expose alleged misbehavior in the executive branch: Such extravaganzas seem to go on regardless of conditions of party control. And second, the enactment of a standard

[1]James L. Sundquist, *Constitutional Reform and Effective Government* (Washington, DC: Brookings Institution, 1986), pp. 75–76.

kind of important legislation: From the Taft-Hartley Act and Marshall Plan of 1947–48 through the Clean Air Act and $490 billion deficit-reduction package of 1990, important laws have materialized at a rate largely unrelated to conditions of party control. To see this pattern, one has to . . . look at actual enactments. There, the pattern is as stated.

. . . [I]t does not seem to make all that much difference whether party control of the American government happens to be unified or divided. One reason we assume it does is that "party government" plays a role in political science somewhere between a Platonic form and a grail. When we reach for it as a standard, we draw on abstract models, presumed European practice, and well-airbrushed American experience, but we seldom take a cold look at real American experience. We forget about Franklin Roosevelt's troubles with HUAC [the House Un-American Activities Committee] and the Rules Committee, Truman's and Kennedy's domestic policy defeats, McCarthy's square-off against Eisenhower, Johnson versus Fulbright on Vietnam, and Carter's energy program and "malaise."

Political parties can be powerful instruments, but in the United States they seem to play more of a role as "policy factions" than as, in the British case, governing instruments. A party as policy faction can often get its way even in circumstances of divided control. . . . There is the obvious structural component—separation of powers—that brings on deadlock and chronic conflict, but also nudges officials toward deliberation, compromise, and super-majority outcomes.[2]

[2]David R. Mayhew, *Divided We Govern: Party Control, Lawmaking, and Investigations, 1946–1990* (New Haven: Yale University Press, 1991), pp. 4, 198–99.

passage has in fact continued. But Mayhew's analysis extended only through 1990. The period from 1995 to 1999 reveals another pattern.

The famous Republican-controlled 104th Congress, with all its promise of revolutionary change, was a Congress of unusually low activity of any sort. The first session of the 104th Congress, 1995, adopted fewer bills into law than any Congress since 1933. Taking the two years of the 104th Congress, 1995 and 1996, only sixty-seven bills were enacted into law, compared to 210 in the 103rd Congress. The 105th Congress followed in the wake of the 104th, and its lack of legislative accomplishment led some to call it the "do-nothing Congress"—although it will probably be remembered more for its rancor and partisanship. (It was also during this period that the intense partisanship of a divided government led to the shutdown of the federal government, as we described in Chapter 5.)

More important than the number of laws, however, is the *type* of legislation Congress passed during this period. The absolute output masks the reality of

ANALYZING AMERICAN POLITICS

## *Does Divided Government in a Separation of Powers System Matter?*

The separation of powers system in the United States creates the possibility that opposing political parties will control different branches of the government. Though divided government has been a long-standing phenomenon in the United States, it has only recently garnered a significant amount of attention from political scientists. While some researchers have tried to explain why divided government occurs,[1] others have questioned whether or not we should care that different parties control different branches On the one hand, it appears that landmark legislation, such as the New Deal and the Great Society, does occur during periods of unified government. On the other hand, it is conceivable, given the relative weakness of political parties in this country, that divided party control may not have much of an impact on the way the government operates.

David Mayhew in *Divided We Govern* attempts to answer the question posed in our title by analyzing the effects of divided government on lawmaking.[2] Mayhew uses an innovative methodology to construct a data set of "significant" legislation. First, he identifies legislation included in the end-of-session wrap-up-stories in which journalists discuss the legislative accomplishments of the session. Second, he verifies the importance of the legislation identified in the first step by consulting works by policy specialists. If the specialists identified pieces of legislation not picked up in the first step, he adds these to the data set. After analyzing the conditions under which the 267 acts he identified were enacted, Mayhew found very little difference in the enactment of significant legislation under united versus divided government. Two-year segments of unified government produced an average of 12.8 acts, while two-year segments of divided government produced 11.7 acts.

When considering how much significant legislation is enacted, divided government does not seem to matter that much. Mayhew offers some speculation why this might be. One explanation is that the

[1] Morris P. Fiorina, *Divided Government,* 2nd ed. (Needham, MA: Allyn & Bacon, 1996); Alberto Alesina and Howard Rosenthal. *Partisan Politics, Divided Government, and the Economy* (Cambridge: Cambridge University Press, 1995).

[2] David R. Mayhew, *Divided We Govern: Party Control, Lawmaking, and Investigations, 1946–1990* (New Haven: Yale University Press, 1991).

substantial, substantive policy innovation. But what do we mean by *substantive policy innovation?* This means considering the *substance of a program or agency from a zero base.* Incremental or marginal decisions, on the other hand, expand or contract a program by percentage changes without taking the nature of the program or agency into account. By using this definition as a standard, we can then see

demand for important legislation does not vary with party control of the different branches. For example, members of Congress always have electoral incentives to enact legislation that will curry favor with the voters who keep them in office or help them advance to higher offices. Events exogenous to politics that create pressing national problems demanding legislative or investigative attention are equally likely to occur under unified or divided government. In the end, Mayhew's provocative book leaves us with more questions than answers, and it is inspiring much research on the topic of separation of powers and divided government.

In *Pivotal Politics,* Keith Krehbiel takes up some of the questions that Mayhew leaves unanswered.[3] Krehbiel uses a rational-choice theory of lawmaking to explain under what conditions legislative *gridlock*—the failure to enact major legislation even though it is preferred to the status quo—will or will not occur. At the center of his theory is the relationship among those whose approval is necessary to enact legislation. They include the president, the members of the House and Senate whose votes are necessary to form a two-thirds majority to override a presidential veto, and the member of the Senate whose vote is necessary to invoke cloture and stop a filibuster. Krehbiel shows how the policy preferences of these players form a "gridlock interval" where, if the status quo is inside this interval, there is no chance of enacting new legislation because one of these players will have veto power over the legislation.

Krehbiel tests his theory using Mayhew's data on significant legislation by examining the effects of the size of the gridlock interval on legislative production. He finds that an increase in the size of the gridlock interval induced by an election-based shift in preferences decreases the amount of significant legislation passed. In other words, the larger the gridlock interval is, the less likely that significant lawmaking will occur. His analysis also confirms Mayhew's finding that divided government does not matter when it comes to enacting significant legislation. Krehbiel employs a wide range of empirical tests to assess the various implications of his theory. Generally, he finds that his simple theory goes a long way toward explaining how laws are made in the United States. Still, as Krehbiel points out, there are many limitations to his study, and more research needs to be done before we can claim an understanding of all the intricacies of lawmaking under the separation of powers system of government.

[3]Keith Krehbiel, *Pivotal Politics: A Theory of U.S. Lawmaking,* (Chicago: University of Chicago Press, 1998).

that the last twenty years, at least, have been completely dominated by incremental innovations and almost completely devoid of substantive ones.

The mentality of incrementalism within the system of absolute separation of powers was actually established in 1974 with the Budget and Impoundment Control Act, which provided Congress not only with its own source of budget information through a new Congressional Budget Office (CBO) but also with the power to counterbalance the executive branch through a process called "reconciliation." This process empowered new congressional budget committees to adopt resolutions that set advance spending targets for agencies and large categories of agencies, which in turn required Congress and the executive branch to limit themselves to the "spending caps" set by Congress. Reconciliation pushed almost every policy decision into a budgetary process—to the delight of the incrementalists. From then on, the entire debate in Congress and the entire competition between the two parties in Congress took place in terms of incremental changes in budget items.

The historic tax reform laws of 1981 and 1986 can be viewed as exceptions to the rule of incrementalism, since both acts made significant reductions in the tax burden, especially in the upper brackets. But there is another side to this view as well. First, even though the increments were large, the tax reform laws were still increments and did not *rethink* the tax structure the way the Republicans had promised. Second, annual deficits mushroomed, growing at a historically large rate *because of the inability of the national government to make the substantive decisions that could reduce expenditures sufficiently to balance the revenue losses against the tax cuts.* Such expenditure cuts would have required *cutting whole domestic programs and whole agencies, whole bomber wings and whole military bases, not cutting a percentage here and a percentage there from a whole variety of agencies and programs.*

Deregulation serves as another example of the enormously strong tendency toward incrementalism. Nothing was more prominent in President Reagan's campaigns and in the commitment of his Republican party during the 1970s and the 1980s than deregulation. This was virtually the litmus test of loyalty to the Republican party. Yet *during the twelve years of Republican control of the White House and the national policy agenda under Reagan and Bush, not one single major regulatory program was eliminated, and none were sought out for elimination.* The Carter administration did better than that, eliminating the Civil Aeronautics Board (CAB). Reagan singled out one regulatory agency to eliminate, the Interstate Commerce Commission (ICC), but it wasn't abolished until President Clinton took office, after a fifteen-year effort on the part of the Republicans. Some agencies have had serious cutbacks in authority and appropriations—for example, agriculture price support programs, and telephone and cable regulation—but even here the agencies were left in place and the programs continued, perhaps available for later "upsizing."

Even the revolutionary 104th Congress, led by Newt Gingrich, the most powerful Speaker since the early part of this century, adopted very few substantial pieces of legislation, and virtually all of those disappeared in the Senate or were otherwise never heard of again. Here is the way the strongly pro-Republican British journal *The Economist* assessed the 104th Congress's Contract with America:

> So it seems like a revolution. But what are the revolutionaries actually doing? . . . They are consolidating . . . the New Deal, which they so roundly deplored. . . . By squeezing budgets without eliminating functions, the Republicans are asking the government to deliver on every promise ever made [but] with less and less money.[9]

[9] "The Evolution of a Revolution," *The Economist,* 4 November 1995, p. 25.

What an epitaph—"squeezing but not choosing"—and what an efficient definition for incrementalism.

One of the few truly substantial innovations during this entire twenty-year period was the Personal Responsibility and Work Opportunity Act (PRA) of 1996, which terminated the AFDC and devolved most means-tested public assistance programs to the states and localities. Congress basically eliminated all entitlements to the poor and dependent, especially the low- or no-income single mothers. It was indeed an exception, but an interesting one inasmuch as it was a strikingly bipartisan act in Congress. This was important to President Clinton because it proved that he had brought the entire Democratic party well to the right of the political spectrum, and that his party was no longer the party of the New Deal. It was also important to the Republicans in Congress because it gave them one of the few accomplishments they would be able to claim. In addition, the act was consistent with the Republican party mentality, especially its right wing. But this same bipartisan cooperation gave Clinton an upper hand in the 1996 presidential campaign, while at the same time depriving the Republican candidate Bob Dole of an issue he needed against Clinton. Thus it contributed to the protraction of Republican control of Congress but to the collapse of Republican chances to control the White House. Divided government continued.[10]

One final example demonstrates the strong tendency of both parties to embrace incrementalism when a big nonincremental issue is at stake. In 1994, one of the few genuinely innovative bills was placed before Congress by President Clinton, or we should say by First Lady Hillary Clinton. It was the health care reform bill that had been put together by an enormous task force of more than a hundred experts meeting for weeks under the leadership of Hillary Clinton and Ira Magaziner, one of the country's leading health care intellectuals. The bill was accurately denounced by Republicans as a return to New Deal tactics with a vengeance, and it was more or less accurately characterized by them as an effort to take over a substantial portion of the entire medical and health care industry. This health care initiative failed so badly in Congress that it never came even close to a roll-call vote in either chamber.

The Democrats continued to press for health programs after the failure of the health care initiative, and in August 1996, they came forward with an ostentatiously bipartisan bill, the Health Insurance Portability and Accountability Act. Sponsored by liberal Democrat Edward Kennedy of Massachusetts and leading moderate Republican Nancy Kassebaum of Kansas, it required insurance companies to carry over coverage for employees who lost or changed their jobs. The act was held as a major accomplishment and as a triumph of bipartisanship. And it demonstrated that despite divided government, important decisions serving the American public could be made. But a closer look revealed that it was indeed incremental and "exhibited a high ratio of hype to accomplishment."[11] It turned out that the Kennedy-Kassebaum act extended guarantees only to employees who *already* had coverage through a previous job. It also extended to them the right to

[10]Compare with Elizabeth Drew, *Whatever It Takes: The Real Struggle for Political Power in America* (New York: Viking, 1997).

[11]Theda Skocpol, *Boomerang: Health Care Reform and the Turn against Government* (New York: W. W. Norton, 1997), pp. 194–95.

buy some kind of continuing coverage only if they switched jobs or lost their employment. But that did not stop insurance companies from charging higher prices for coverage that was inferior to their old employer plan. Thus many people who thought they might be helped by the act found out that they would have to pay substantially higher amounts for maintaining coverage that would likely be of marginal quality. The act did nothing to help laid-off employees pay for continuing health coverage and did nothing to extend coverage to those who lacked insurance. Moreover, it did not prevent employers from charging more for continuing coverage or from deciding to discontinue health benefits altogether.[12]

## Symbolic Politics—A Variation on Incrementalism

When you are living a politics of incrementalism, you still have to give an impression of substance. In other words, the politics of incrementalism involves the politics of public relations, and that means "symbolic politics." Symbolic politics, like all PR, is not actually a matter of lying. Although some of that is necessary, the purpose of symbolic politics is to inflate a smaller truth into a larger one.

**The President and the "Bully Pulpit"** Although the bully pulpit concept was coined by Theodore Roosevelt, presidents before as well as after him have engaged in it, and recent presidents seem to be employing it all the time.[13] This concept is considered part of the "permanent campaign," which we mentioned in Chapter 6. The word pulpit, of course, refers to the preaching profession where a representative of the religious faith expands upon a moral lesson or conveys an uplifting message. This is almost precisely what President Theodore Roosevelt had in mind, and he used it to good effect. Playing the bully pulpit role today means presenting (at the highest possible rhetorical level) hopelessly unrealistic proposals that convey the impression of immediate effectiveness. And the nice thing is that they do not require action by that "other" branch of government.

Symbolic politics is not intended to make people cynical or more cynical than they already are. It merely recognizes a natural inclination—exaggeration through rhetoric when confronting a large audience. The tendency to exaggerate becomes even greater when the possibility of getting any real action is remote.

President Clinton has always been considered one of the most effective users of pulpit rhetoric, and he has had good precedents. President Bush, not noted for high rhetoric, reached great heights of eloquence with "a thousand points of light," preaching that all Americans unleash their energies of volunteerism on the illiterate, the delinquent, the dependent, and the homeless. He even inspired military hero Colin Powell to abandon his presidential ambitions for a new career in organized volunteerism. President Clinton was quick to move from mere gubernatorial to high presidential rhetoric, and it intensified once he lost control of Congress in 1994.

[12]Ibid.

[13]See, for example, Jeffrey K. Tulis, *The Rhetorical Presidency* (Princeton: Princeton University Press, 1987); Samuel Kernell, *Going Public: New Strategies of Presidential Leadership* (Washington, DC: Congressional Quarterly Inc., 1986); and Theodore Lowi, *The Personal President: Power Invested, Promise Unfulfilled* (Ithaca, NY: Cornell University Press, 1985).

As we mentioned, national rhetoric is boosted to even higher levels when action is considered slight. Since education is traditionally and inherently a matter of local and state power, it is difficult for the president alone or even for a unified national government to take any action, even in this era of educational crisis. Consequently, one of Clinton's most famous pronouncements was his commitment to putting school children in uniform, followed by his national goal to grade local-school and teacher effectiveness. He proposed computerizing all classrooms and organizing a "citizen army of one million volunteer tutors to make sure every child can read independently by the end of the third grade."[14] A million volunteers obviously tops a thousand points of light.

Clinton's presidency was rife with other examples of symbolic politics linked to rhetoric. Ordering federal agencies to recruit and hire welfare recipients in order to get them off welfare became one of Clinton's campaigns even as the civil service was being "downsized." This symbolic move was called "reinventing the government." In another arena, Clinton offered a tax cut of $500 a family to fulfill his "middle-class Bill of Rights."

President Clinton's "race initiative," encouraging public dialogues and town meetings so that ordinary people would come forward to discuss these "hot button" issues, was lauded by all, but poorly attended by racial liberals. It proved irksome to many conservatives who felt that their views, especially on affirmative action, were being shortchanged. It is not a coincidence, however, that Clinton's race initiative was generated in the wake of his bipartisan adoption of the only significant initiative of this epoch, the Republican/conservative welfare reform law (PRA) of 1996. This occurred at the same time the 1996 presidential election was heating up.

Finally, there are the symbolic aspects of the impeachment crisis of 1998–1999. It is our view that the primary factor behind President Clinton's high 1998 presidential performance ratings was the "rallying effect," which, in this case, was comparable to any other international event that has tended to boost the ratings of all modern presidents (see Chapter 6). When in trouble, all modern presidents have tried to find a "foreign policy fix." President Nixon's name was on everyone's lips during the heat of the Watergate crisis, and although it did not keep his performance ratings high enough to prevent resignation, it made him quite popular, in particular among the Chinese and the Europeans. President Clinton's name was also in the air a lot during 1998—and when it wasn't, his bombers and missiles were, in the Balkans, in Iraq, even in Afghanistan and the Sudan. The latter two attacks are the best examples of symbolic uses of foreign action, since the targets were insignificant and the attacks themselves were brief, superficial, and timid. As one former Army intelligence officer put it, "This was a media event, not policy. Isolated attacks on broken states that cannot retaliate do not constitute a war, despite the power of the Clinton administration's rhetoric."[15] Peace was also helpful to Clinton during the impeachment crisis when he and his representatives brokered important agreements in

[14]William J. Clinton, 1997 State of the Union address, http://www.whitehouse.gov/WH/SOU97

[15]Ralph Peters, "Smart Bombs Can't Blast Away Beliefs," *Washington Post National Weekly Edition*, 7 September 1998, p. 22.

Ireland, the Middle East, and Bosnia. He might well have shared in the Nobel Peace Prize for his role and that of his representative George Mitchell in the Northern Ireland settlement. The latter point suggests that there is always at least some substance behind even the most symbolic events.

**Congress Can Also Play the Game** Although senators have a much larger pulpit than members of the House—which is certainly why so many senators and so few members of the House are talked about as presidential contenders—the House has made great strides in recent years, with Newt Gingrich as its leader. The Contract with America was a marvelously successful bundle of symbols that played a fundamental part in the historic winning of the entire Congress by Republicans in 1994. Some of the promises in the Contract with America seemed, on the face of it, to be substantial, such as the proposal for the Personal Responsibility Act, which eventually attracted President Clinton and became the enormously important welfare reform law (PRA) of 1996, as already noted. There were also promises to pursue three amendments to the Constitution, one for a balanced budget requirement, another for giving the president line-item veto power, and the third for a term-limits amendment of twelve years maximum for members of the House and Senate. The amendment proposals, having been offered before the Contract and requiring a two-thirds vote, sounded substantial but were largely symbolic because leaders of both parties already knew there was no consensus. All the other matters were wholly symbolic, as indicated by the rhetoric of their titles: the "Taking Back Our Streets Act," adding death penalty provisions, prison construction funding, and other proposals that had already turned up in the 1994 Crime Bill; the "Family Reinforcement Act," the "American Dream Restoration Act," and the "Senior Citizens Fairness Act," all of which were high-sounding proposals simply to make some minor cuts in the taxes that each category of citizen would be required to pay. Another lovely piece of rhetoric was "the Common Sense Legal Reform Act," which would actually have been an "unfunded (state) mandate" to set ceilings on the amount of damage that can be gained in suits under product liability laws and other tort laws. Whether Gingrich was following past-presidential rhetoric or was inventing rhetoric of his own, the items in the Contract with America were certainly of the same vacuous poetry as the presidential bully pulpit rhetoric.

**AMERICAN POLITICAL DEVELOPMENT**

Over the last two decades congressional party leaders, like presidents, have become much more active in media politics, appearing more frequently on the nightly news and Sunday-morning talk shows as well as hiring press secretaries and communications' directors. Although Speaker Gingrich is considered the star in this type of public, media-oriented congressional leadership, it had its roots in the changing roles and functions of congressional parties and dates back to the speakership of Tip O'Neill.

SOURCE: Douglas B. Harris, "The Rise of the Public Speakership," *Political Science Quarterly* 113 (1998), pp. 193–212.

In many respects, the impeachment of the president was the most symbolic of all the events and actions of this era. Here again, there was substance in back of the impeachment drama, but one important fact reduced the substance to little more than the platform on which the symbolic performance took place: From the start of Act I of the impeachment drama, it was clear that getting sixty-seven votes in the Senate to convict the president would be close to impossible. They couldn't convict Andrew Johnson in 1868, an unelected president who succeeded Lincoln. To boot, Johnson was a renegade Democrat who was dedicated to terminating Reconstruction, had favored restoring a racial regime in the South, and had deliberately broken an act of Congress. How on earth could Congress hope to convict a recently re-elected president whose conduct was legally suspect and morally ambiguous but patently not weighty enough in matters of state to constitute a fully impeachable offense? During the autumn of 1998, it became increasingly clear that "Step 1," impeachment in the House, was only possible because virtually all the House Republicans, who held a majority, would vote for impeachment. But it quickly became clear during the Senate trial that the thirteen House managers who were arguing the case would not be able to expand the fifty-five Republican senators to the sixty-seven votes needed to convict. After that, everything about the impeachment process became symbolic—essentially a set of messages to Americans to raise the bar on the moral qualifications of all politicians. Gary Hart, former Democratic senator and victim of a minor sex scandal that killed his presidential candidacy in 1988, made an accurate and well-earned observation following President Clinton's acquittal:

> . . . It is premature to hope the nightmare is over. . . . The intense focus on private morality comes at the expense of focusing on public morality. Sex is more intriguing, more attractable, more commercially rewarding than an issue like hungry children or homeless youths or inadequate health care for the elderly or global warming—or any other symptoms of our warped social priorities.[16]

The bully pulpit was available throughout the thirteen-month ordeal, no matter what its ramifications.

As we have seen, symbolic politics is an end in itself and also a means to cover up the "smallness" of the incremental decisions that are actually being made. Another purpose of symbolic politics is to prevent action altogether, whether substantial or incremental. The most dependable weapon in this arena is of course the filibuster. The Senate has long prided itself in the rules protecting speech on the Senate floor. Filibusters declined after their use to block civil rights was discredited. But the filibuster has risen again, and today it is so usual and expected that the mere threat of a filibuster is so effective that Senate leaders would be loathe to bring up a bill for a vote unless they were fairly certain they had sixty votes, enough to overcome a filibuster. The problem is that even the most important and popular bills are likely to get reduced to mere skeletons while leaders try to obtain and maintain those sixty votes. Thus symbolism is not only a cover for incrementalism, it can also be a cause of incrementalism.

Finally, our discussion on symbolic politics goes a long way toward explaining why there have been so many serious and important constitutional amendments *proposed* (but only one passed) in the past two decades—for school prayer, against abortions, to require a balanced budget, to require three-fifths vote in Congress for all tax increases and all substantial increases in the deficit, for the line-item

[16]Gary Hart, "The Real Nightmare Remains," *New York Times,* 14 February 1999, section 4, p. 13.

veto, and for term limits on representatives and senators. The constitutional requirement of two-thirds vote in both chambers of Congress prior to sending constitutional proposals for ratification by three-fourths of the states means that virtually none would be adopted, or that each would be so watered down as to be meaningless. This way the leadership of both parties can offer what appears to be substantial innovations that will please the radical wings of their parties while still knowing that they'll never have to live with the reality of passage and adoption. The peculiar thing is that so many savvy politicians in both parties and in the organized groups endorsing them continue to support their party on symbolic efforts alone.

## "Politics by Other Means"

For most of U.S. history, elections were the main arenas of political combat. In recent years, however, elections have become less effective as ways of resolving political conflicts in the United States. Today's political struggles are frequently waged elsewhere, and crucial policy choices tend to be made outside the electoral realm. Unable to win decisively through elections, contending political forces rely on such weapons of institutional combat as congressional investigations, media revelations, and judicial proceedings. In contemporary America, even electoral success fails to confer the capacity to govern, and political forces, even if they lose at the polls or do not even compete in the electoral arena, have been able to exercise considerable power.

### Politics outside the Electoral Arena

Over the past thirty years competition in the electoral arena has failed to produce decisive governing majorities, and politicians have perfected alternative weapons of political combat. These weapons, deployed outside the electoral arena, have allowed opposing forces to compete for power without exposing them to the uncertainties of full-scale voter mobilization.

**President and Congress** To begin with, both parties have sought to make maximum political use of the elective institutions they controlled to undermine and disrupt institutions controlled by their rivals. In the 1970s and 1980s, Republicans responded to their inability to win control of Congress by seeking to enhance the powers of the White House relative to the legislative branch. Thus, President Nixon impounded billions of dollars appropriated by Congress and sought, through various reorganization schemes, to bring executive agencies under closer White House control while severing their ties to the House and Senate. Presidents Reagan and Bush tolerated budget deficits of unprecedented magnitude in part because these precluded new congressional spending; they also sought to increase presidential authority over executive agencies and diminish the authority of Congress by centralizing control over administrative rule-making in the Office of Management and Budget (OMB). In addition, Reagan undertook to circumvent the legislative restrictions on presidential conduct embodied in the War Powers Act. Finally, Reagan and his successor, George Bush, also sought to secure a line-item veto power to strengthen the president's hand in the legislative process. Ironically, by the time this power was secured, the presidency was in Democratic hands and Democrat Bill Clinton became the first U.S. president with the power to excise portions of spending bills. Subsequently, the Supreme Court in a 1998 decision declared the line-item veto unconstitutional.

During the same period, the Democrats responded to the Republican presidential advantage by seeking to strengthen the Congress while reducing the powers and prerogatives of the presidency, a sharp contrast with Democratic behavior from the 1930s to the 1960s, when that party enjoyed an advantage in presidential elections. In the 1970s, Congress greatly expanded the size of its committee and subcommittee staffs, thus enabling the House and Senate to monitor and supervise closely the activities of executive agencies. Through the 1974 Budget and Impoundment Act, Congress sought to increase its control over fiscal policy. Congress also enacted a number of statutory restrictions on presidential authority in the realm of foreign policy, including the Foreign Commitments Resolution and the Arms Export Control Act.

Finally, of course, when they controlled the Congress, Democrats launched a number of major legislative investigations aimed at embarrassing or discrediting Republican presidents and other officials of the executive branch. The Watergate and Iran-Contra investigations discussed below were, of course, the most important. After the GOP won control of Congress in 1994, the investigative tables were turned. Republicans used their control over congressional investigative committees to launch inquiries into allegations that the Clinton administration had sought to use confidential FBI files for political purposes. Following the 1996 national elections, Congress launched a major probe of the Clinton campaign's fund-raising practices in an effort to demonstrate that Clinton and Vice President Al Gore had committed numerous violations of campaign finance laws, including accepting money from foreign business interests and money that originated with Chinese government intelligence agencies. Republicans promised to use their investigative powers to harass Clinton for the remainder of his presidency. "Clinton will be debilitated," predicted one Republican official.[17] Republicans initially had little or no interest in actually impeaching Clinton. At least at the beginning, the GOP leadership saw the never-ending investigative process as a means of harassing Clinton and preventing him from pursuing any serious legislative agenda. This tactic proved extremely successful.[18] Later, of course, Clinton was impeached.

Institutional struggle of the sort that has characterized American politics in recent years is most likely to occur when the major branches of government are controlled by hostile political forces. This condition is neither exclusively nor is it necessarily associated with divided partisan control of Congress and the

[17]Owen Ulmann, "What Clinton Has to Fear from a Landslide," *Business Week,* 11 November 1996, p. 51.

[18]Paul Gigot, "Scandal's Price: GOP Chops Up Bill's Agenda," *Wall Street Journal,* 1 May 1998, p. A14.

presidency.[19] On the one hand, during periods of unified partisan control, institutional combat can occur when hostile factions of the same party are entrenched in different branches of government. For example, right-wing Republicans led by Joseph McCarthy in the early 1950s and antiwar Democrats led by J. William Fulbright in the mid-1960s used legislative investigations to attack presidents belonging to their own parties. On the other hand, divided control is not likely to result in intense institutional struggles in the absence of deep cleavages between the two parties. For instance, in the mid- and late 1950s, when moderates and internationalists controlled both the Democratic and Republican parties, relations between the Eisenhower White House and the Rayburn-Johnson Congress were reasonably amicable. However, when divided partisan control of government does coincide with sharp cleavages between the two parties, the importance of institutional conflict relative to electoral competition is likely to increase. This state of affairs has characterized American politics since the Vietnam and Watergate eras.

Contending political forces have sought to use not only Congress and the presidency but also the federal judiciary and the mass media as instruments of political combat. These institutions in turn have been able to ally with such forces and to bolster their own autonomy and power. Through this process, institutions that are not directly subject to the control of the electorate have become increasingly significant players in contemporary American politics.

**The Judiciary** One important substitute for electoral mobilization in contemporary politics is the growing political use of a powerful nonelectoral weapon—the criminal justice system. Between the early 1970s and 1996 there was more than a tenfold increase in the number of indictments brought by federal prosecutors against national, state, and local officials. The data given in Figure 17.1 actually understate the extent to which public officials have been subjected to criminal proceedings in recent years because they do not include those political figures (such as Ronald Reagan's attorney general Edwin Meese and former Democratic House Speaker Jim Wright) who were targets of investigations that did not result in indictments.

Many of the individuals indicted have been lower-level civil servants, but large numbers have been prominent political figures—among them more than a dozen members of Congress, several federal judges, and numerous state and local officials. Some of these indictments were initiated by Republican administrations, and their targets were primarily Democrats. At the same time, a substantial number of high-ranking Republicans in the executive branch—including former defense secretary Caspar Weinberger, former assistant secretary of state Elliott Abrams, presidential aides Michael Deaver and Lyn Nofziger, and, of course, national security official Oliver North—were the targets of criminal prosecutions stemming from allegations or investigations initiated by Democrats. Weinberger

[19]David R. Mayhew, "Does It Make a Difference Whether Party Control of American National Government Is Unified or Divided?" Paper presented at the annual meeting of the American Political Science Association, Atlanta, Georgia, 1989.

**FIGURE 17.1**

**Federal Indictments and Convictions of Public Officials, 1970–1996***

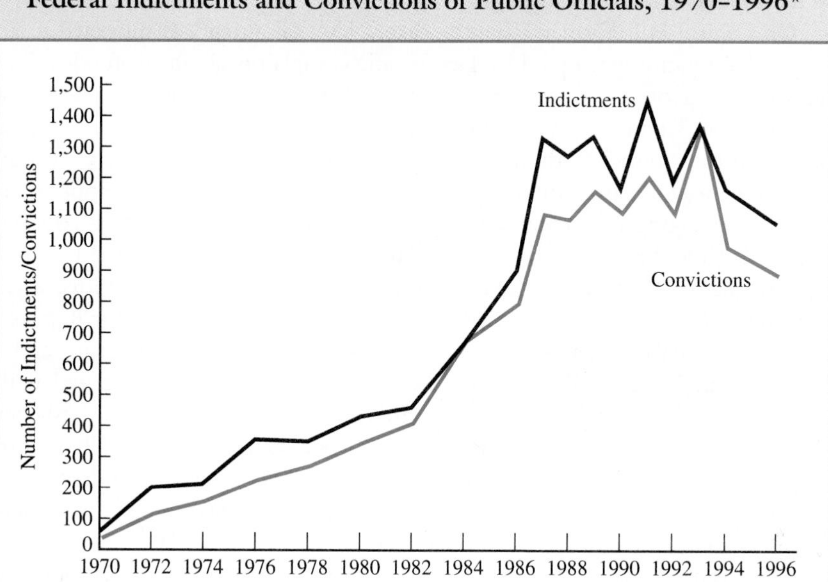


*Reporting procedures for these statistics were modified in 1983, so pre- and post-1983 data are not strictly comparable.

SOURCES: Annual reports of the U.S. Department of Justice, Public Integrity Section, 1971–1988; *Statistical Abstract of the United States* (Washington, D.C.: Government Printing Office, 1994, 1996, 1997).

and Abrams, along with several other figures in the Iran-Contra case, were pardoned by President George Bush in December 1992, just before he left office. In justifying the pardons, Bush charged that Democrats were attempting to criminalize policy differences.

During the first two years of the Clinton administration, the powerful chair of the House Ways and Means Committee, Dan Rostenkowski (D-Ill.), was forced to give up his post after being indicted on corruption charges. In 1994 and 1995, charges of improper conduct were leveled at Agriculture Secretary Mike Espy, Transportation Secretary Henry Cisneros, and Commerce Secretary Ron Brown, among others. Espy and Cisneros were forced to resign and were ultimately indicted on fraud and corruption charges. Brown died tragically in an airplane crash before the investigation into his conduct was completed. During the same period, President Clinton himself became the target of an intensive probe that led to the jailing of several of his closest associates on charges including fraud and conspiracy. This investigation is discussed in more detail below. While this investigation continued, Attorney General Janet Reno requested in February 1998 the appointment of still another independent counsel to look into the charges that

Interior Secretary Bruce Babbitt had lied to Congress about his decision to award an Indian gambling casino license to a group that had made major contributions to the 1996 Democratic campaign.

On Capitol Hill, former House Speaker Newt Gingrich was subjected to an ethics investigation prompted by Democratic complaints about his fund-raising tactics. Acting on a formal complaint from Democratic House members, the House Ethics Committee began in 1994 to investigate whether a college course organized by Gingrich with tax-deductible contributions was actually a partisan political endeavor. This would violate federal laws prohibiting tax-exempt charities from engaging in partisan efforts. In 1996, the committee and its counsel, James M. Cole, broadened the scope of their investigation to examine the relationship between the course and GOPAC, a political action committee once headed by Gingrich. GOPAC raised an enormous amount of money for Republican congressional candidates. The House Ethics Committee was also looking at the Progress and Freedom Foundation, a conservative think tank associated with Gingrich. At issue were whether the tax-exempt foundation was actually a shelter for partisan efforts and whether Gingrich's college courses were actually tied to GOPAC.[20] Gingrich was eventually forced to pay a fine of several hundred thousand dollars. More important, the investigation undermined Gingrich's leadership of the House and helped derail the GOP's legislative agenda.

There is no particular reason to believe that the level of political corruption or abuse of power in America actually increased tenfold over the past two decades, as Figure 17.1 would seem to indicate. It could be argued, however, that this sharp rise reflects a heightened level of public concern about governmental misconduct. However, as we shall see, both the issue of government ethics and the growing use of criminal sanctions against public officials have been closely linked to struggles for political power in the United States. In the aftermath of Watergate, institutions such as the Office of the Independent Counsel were established and processes to investigate allegations of unethical conduct on the part of public figures were created. Since then political forces have increasingly sought to make use of these mechanisms to discredit their opponents. When scores of investigators, accountants, and lawyers are deployed to scrutinize the conduct of a Bill Clinton or a Newt Gingrich, it is all but certain that something questionable will be found. The creation of these investigative processes, more than changes in the public's tolerance for government misconduct, explains why public officials are increasingly being charged with ethical and criminal violations.

The growing use of criminal indictments as a partisan weapon has helped enhance the political importance of the judiciary. The prominence of the courts has been heightened by the sharp increase in the number of major policy issues that have been fought and decided in the judicial realm rather than in the arena of electoral politics.[21] The federal judiciary has become the main institution for resolving struggles over such issues as race relations and abortion, and it has also

[20] R. H. Melton, "Ethics Probe Reaching Critical Stage for Frustrated Gingrich," *Washington Post*, 4 November 1996, p. A17.

[21] Jeremy Rabkin, *Judicial Compulsions* (New York: Basic Books, 1989).

come to play a more significant role in deciding questions of social welfare and economic policy.[22] The number of suits brought by civil rights, environmental, feminist, and other liberal groups seeking to advance their policy goals increased dramatically during the 1970s and 1980s, reflecting the willingness and ability of these groups to fight their battles in the judicial arena. For example, the number of civil rights cases brought in federal courts doubled during this period. After the emergence of a conservative majority on the Supreme Court in 1989, forces from the political right began to use litigation to implement their own policy agenda. In recent years a number of conservative legal foundations have pursued aggressive strategies of litigation against their opponents on the left. For example, the Paula Jones suit against Bill Clinton was partly financed by the Rutherford Institute, a foundation that champions conservative causes through the courts. The growing importance of the federal judiciary explains why judicial confirmation battles have sometimes been so bitterly fought in recent years.

**The Independent Counsel** The political importance of the federal judiciary was further enhanced by the 1978 Ethics in Government Act, which created the Office of the Special Prosecutor. This official, unlike the attorney general or other prosecutors, is independent of the executive branch and, though in principle subject to presidential removal, could only be fired at enormous political cost to the president. The idea of the independent counsel was Congress's response to Richard Nixon's dismissal of the Watergate counsel Archibald Cox in the infamous Saturday Night Massacre. Under the terms of the independent counsel provision, which is subject to renewal every five years (it was renewed in 1994 but allowed to lapse in 1999), Congress may initiate a request for the appointment of a special counsel if its own investigations have given it reason to believe that the president or some other high-ranking executive branch official may have committed some illegal act. The independent counsel provision does not apply to Congress itself. Congress created the independent counsel to undertake investigations of the executive branch; it had no interest in subjecting itself to similar investigations by government prosecutors.

Under the special counsel law, Congress or another interested party asks the attorney general to go before a statutory three-judge panel to request the appointment of a special counsel to ascertain whether or not a crime has indeed been committed by an executive official. The attorney general has some discretion and may assert that there is insufficient evidence of criminal action to warrant going further. For example, in 1997 and 1998, Attorney General Janet Reno refused to request the appointment of an independent counsel to look into allegations that the 1996 Clinton-Gore campaign violated federal election finance laws. Usually, however, the attorney general has no desire to become the target of the firestorm of criticism from Congress and the media likely to ensue if he or she fails to accede to Congress's wishes. As a result, Congress is generally able to have its way when it requests the appointment of an independent counsel.

[22]Martin Shapiro, "The Supreme Court's 'Return' to Economic Regulation," *Studies in American Political Development,* 1 (1986), pp. 91–142.

Once appointed, the independent counsel can be a powerful figure, exercising far more prosecutorial discretion than other federal or state prosecutors. First, the independent counsel is not appointed to investigate a specific crime that has already taken place. Instead he or she is assigned to determine if a crime has been committed. This vague mandate allows the independent counsel to look into a variety of events that seem suspicious without having to worry much about their relationship to the matters that triggered congressional concern in the first place.

Second, the independent counsel is often far more generously funded than other prosecutors. Unlike routine inquiries, the independent counsel's investigation is funded directly by Congress. Since, almost by definition, special counsels are conducting investigations that Congress eagerly sought, the legislative branch has every reason to provide them with ample resources. For example, Congress gave Whitewater independent counsels Robert Fiske and Kenneth Starr nearly forty million dollars over a four-year period to seek evidence of wrongdoing on the part of President Clinton and his associates. Such generous levels of funding give special counsels the ability to follow even the most unlikely leads, interview numerous witnesses, collect huge quantities of evidence, and prosecute several cases simultaneously. The independent counsel's resources are likely to overwhelm those of all but the most powerful defendant.

Finally, the independent counsel has extremely broad leeway to expand the scope of his or her investigation from its initial focus to seemingly unrelated matters. Ordinary federal prosecutors, by contrast, normally must confine themselves to the initial subject matter of an investigation. They are not free to pursue leads into unrelated areas.

In 1994, a special counsel was appointed by the Justice Department to investigate charges that President Clinton and his wife had engaged in illegal activities growing out of their partnership in the Whitewater Development Corporation while Clinton was governor of Arkansas. The same special counsel, Robert Fiske, also investigated the activities of a number of Clinton aides accused of making illegal contacts with the Treasury Department on behalf of the White House. In August 1994, Fiske was replaced by former federal prosecutor Kenneth Starr. Fiske had been appointed by Attorney General Janet Reno before Congress had restored the lapsed independent counsel provision of the Ethics in Government Act. Once this portion of the act was restored by Congress, a three-judge federal panel ruled that because Fiske had been appointed to investigate Clinton by a member of Clinton's own cabinet, there was a potential for conflict of interest.

Starr, a Republican who often had been critical of the Clinton administration, expanded his jurisdiction several times and was, by 1998, investigating charges that Clinton had had an affair with a White House intern, Monica Lewinsky, in 1996 and had subsequently pressed Lewinsky to perjure herself. An ordinary federal prosecutor would probably have been laughed out of court if he or she sought to convince a judge that an alleged Washington affair in 1996 had any relevance to real estate dealings in Arkansas in the 1980s. Starr, however, had no difficulty persuading the attorney general and the three-judge panel supervising his investigation to allow him to expand the scope of his probe. Reno was not willing to endure another storm of protest on the heels of congressional outrage at her refusal to appoint an independent counsel to investigate Clinton's fund-raising activities. For its part, the three-judge panel was simply following precedent. The leading precedent in this matter is the 1996 case of *United States v. Tucker,* in which the Eighth Circuit Court of Appeals held that independent counsels should be given broad latitude to expand the scope of an ongoing investigation.[23] The Supreme Court declined to review this decision.

Taken together, its broad mandate, generous funding, and easily expanded investigative purview made the Office of the Special Counsel a powerful instrument. In effect, when the independent counsel launched an investigation of a president or other high government official, his or her office had the resources and latitude to investigate almost any aspect of that individual's life and career. Unlike most judicial inquiries, which are aimed at specific acts, the independent counsel's mission was to identify and prosecute evidence of *any* wrongdoing on the part of the individual under investigation. In the case of executive branch officials other than the president, the special counsel could secure a grand jury criminal indictment if he or she believed that the facts warranted such action. In the case of presidential misconduct, the special counsel was limited to providing Congress with information for a possible impeachment proceeding.

When the office was initially established in 1978, congressional Democrats viewed what was then called the special prosecutor as an important weapon in their struggle with the executive branch. Until 1994, Democratic members of Congress were the office's chief defenders, while Republicans typically railed against it. In 1994, of course, the GOP won control of both houses of Congress, and the two parties changed their respective tunes. Now Democrats called for reining in Starr and the other independent counsels. Republicans, on the other hand, defended Starr and the other independent counsels probing former Clinton administration officials Henry Cisneros and Mike Espy. So long as they control the Congress, Republicans have little interest in attacking an office that the former Reagan administration official Terry Eastland once called "a loaded gun pointed at the executive branch."[24]

**The Media** Another institution whose power has risen dramatically over the past three decades is the news media. The political power of the media has increased through the growing prominence of adversarial journalism, a form of journalism in which the media adopt a hostile posture toward the government and public officials.

The national media has enhanced their autonomy and political power by aggressively investigating, publicizing, and exposing instances of official misconduct.[25] Conservative forces during the Nixon and Reagan years responded to media criticism by denouncing the press as biased and seeking to curb it. However, members of Congress and certain groups opposed to conservative presidential

[23]78 F. 3rd 1313 (8th Circuit) 1996.

[24]Quoted in John Harwood and Edward Felsenthall, "Independent Counsels Range Far Afield," *Wall Street Journal,* 29 January 1998, p. 1.

[25]Samuel P. Huntington, *American Politics: The Promise of Disharmony* (Cambridge: Harvard University Press, 1981), pp. 203–10.

policies benefited from the growing influence of the press and have been prepared to defend it when it comes under attack.

Providing the media with information is an enormous set of ancillary institutions, including conservative and liberal "think tanks," various consulting firms specializing in developing damaging information on their clients' enemies (a tactic known as opposition research), and public relations firms. These enterprises, located mainly in Washington and New York, serve up an endless supply of press releases. Conservative institutions provide damaging information about liberal politicians, while liberal entities provide damaging information about conservative politicians. The press hardly needs to engage in any investigative work of its own. It can choose the most tempting tidbits from the torrent of rumors, innuendos, accusations, and occasional facts conveniently delivered to newsrooms via fax on a daily basis.[26] Lately, *Hustler Magazine* publisher Larry Flynt has become a news source. Flynt has offered cash for damaging information about the sex lives of Republican politicians. Information acquired by Flynt forced the resignation of Republican congressman Bob Livingston, who was slated to succeed Newt Gingrich as Speaker, in December 1998.

## Revelation, Investigation, Prosecution

Taken together, the expanded political roles of the national news media and the federal judiciary have given rise to a major new weapon of political combat: revelation, investigation, and prosecution. The acronym for this, RIP, forms a fitting political epitaph for the public officials who have become its targets. The RIP weaponry was initially forged by opponents of the Nixon administration in their struggles with the White House, and through the Reagan years it was used primarily by congressional Democrats to attack their foes in the executive branch. Beginning in the 1980s, however, Republicans began to wield the RIP weapon against Democrats.

In 1972, after his re-election, President Nixon undertook to expand executive power at the expense of Congress by impounding funds appropriated for domestic programs and reorganizing executive agencies without legislative authorization. In addition, the White House established the so-called plumbers squad of former intelligence agents and mercenaries to plug leaks of information to Congress and the press, and (its opponents claimed) it sought to undermine the legitimacy of the federal judiciary by appointing unqualified justices to the Supreme Court. The administration's adversaries also charged that it tried to limit Congress's influence over foreign policy by keeping vital information from it, notably the "secret bombing" of Cambodia from 1969 to 1973.

At the same time Nixon sought to curtail the influence of the national news media. His administration brought suit against the *New York Times* in an effort to block publication of the *Pentagon Papers* and threatened, using the pretext of promoting ideological diversity, to compel the national television networks to sell the

[26]Jill Abramson, "Washington's Culture of Scandal Is Turning Inquiry into an Industry," *New York Times*, 26 April 1998, p. 1.

local stations they owned. The president's opponents denounced the administration's actions as abuses of power—which they surely were—and launched a full-scale assault upon Richard Nixon in the Watergate controversy.

The Watergate attack began with a series of revelations in the *Washington Post* linking the White House to a break-in at the Watergate Hotel headquarters of the Democratic National Committee. The *Post*'s reporters were quickly joined by scores of investigative journalists from the *New York Times, Newsweek, Time,* and the television networks.

As revelations of misdeeds by the Nixon White House proliferated, the administration's opponents in Congress demanded a full legislative investigation. In response, the Senate created a special committee, chaired by Sam Ervin, to investigate White House misconduct in the 1972 presidential election. Investigators for the Ervin committee uncovered numerous questionable activities on the part of Nixon's aides, and these were revealed to the public during a series of dramatic, nationally televised hearings.

Evidence of criminal activity unearthed by the Ervin committee led to congressional pressure for the appointment of a special prosecutor. Ultimately a large number of high-ranking administration officials were indicted, convicted, and imprisoned. Impeachment proceedings were initiated against President Nixon, and when evidence linking him directly to the cover-up of the Watergate burglary was found, he was forced to resign from office. Thus, with the help of the RIP weaponry, the Nixon administration's antagonists achieved a total victory in their conflict with the president. Although no subsequent president has been driven from office, opponents of presidential administrations have since used the RIP process to attack and weaken their foes in the executive branch.

The RIP process became institutionalized when Congress adopted the 1978 Ethics in Government Act, which established procedures for the appointment of independent counsels (initially called special prosecutors) to investigate allegations of wrongdoing in the executive branch. The act also defined as criminal several forms of influence peddling in which executive officials had traditionally engaged, such as lobbying former associates after leaving office. (Such activities are also traditional on Capitol Hill, but Congress chose not to impose the restrictions embodied in the act upon its own members and staff.) Basically Congress created new crimes that executive branch officials could be charged with. The independent counsel provision of the act lapsed during the Bush administration but was restored by Congress in 1994 and then lapsed again in 1999.

The extent to which the RIP process had come to be a routine feature of American politics became evident during the Iran-Contra conflict, when Democrats charged that the Reagan administration had covertly sold arms to Iran and used the proceeds to provide illegal funding for Nicaraguan Contra forces, in violation of the Boland amendments, which prohibit such help. After the diversion of funds to the Contras was revealed, it was universally assumed that Congress should conduct televised hearings and the judiciary should appoint an independent counsel to investigate the officials involved in the episode. Yet this procedure is really quite remarkable. Officials who in other democracies would merely be compelled to resign from office are now threatened with criminal prosecution in the United States.

The institutionalization of the RIP process became even more clear during the Clinton administration. RIP began with the Whitewater probe, in which the president's critics charged that he and his wife had been guilty of a variety of conflicts of interest and financial improprieties while involved in a partnership with a shady Arkansas banker and real estate developer. An independent counsel was appointed to look into the charges, and Republicans demanded that congressional hearings on the issue be scheduled. Democrats opposed hearings, arguing that the Republicans merely sought to embarrass the administration prior to major congressional votes and the 1994 congressional elections. Finally, hearings were scheduled, but under very limited conditions that Democrats hoped would protect the president from potentially embarrassing disclosures.

The president's critics also questioned the circumstances under which Hillary Clinton had been able to earn a profit of more than a hundred thousand dollars in a short time, through a series of highly risky and speculative commodities trades. Critics noted that the First Lady, who had no experience in the commodities market, had been guided by an attorney for Tyson Foods, Inc., a huge Arkansas-based poultry producer that stood to gain from the friendship of then-governor Clinton. Although the White House denied any wrongdoing on her part, the charges produced at least the appearance of impropriety.

After the GOP took control of both houses of Congress in 1994, new investigations were launched by the House and Senate banking committees and the House Oversight Committee. In 1995, as he investigated the Clintons' involvement in the Whitewater matter, special counsel Kenneth Starr indicted Governor Jim Guy Tucker of Arkansas and former Clinton Whitewater partners James and Susan McDougal for bank fraud and conspiracy. All three were convicted, but Starr was not immediately able to wrest incriminating testimony about the president from them. Another Clinton associate had already been sent to prison as a result of evidence turned up during the various investigations of the Clintons' business dealings in Arkansas. Former Hillary Clinton law partner and Associate U.S. Attorney General Webster Hubbell began serving a prison term in 1994 for scheming to defraud his Rose law firm partners of $482,000.

In March 1996, the scope of Starr's investigation was broadened to include the so-called Travelgate affair, in which the administration is alleged to have sought to cover up the details surrounding the firing of members of the White House travel office. In June 1996, the scope of Starr's investigation was expanded again to include Filegate, allegations that the White House had improperly obtained FBI files on some nine hundred individuals.

As noted above, in 1998 Starr once again expanded the scope of his investigation to probe charges that Clinton had been sexually intimate with a young White House intern, Monica Lewinsky, and then sought to induce Lewinsky to perjure herself by denying the story in a deposition. Lewinsky had been deposed by attorneys for Paula Jones, who was bringing a civil suit against Clinton for an alleged act of sexual harassment when he was governor of Arkansas and she was a state employee. Jones's attorneys were seeking to show that Clinton made a practice of seeking sexual favors from employees. They had learned about Lewinsky from a former White House employee, Linda Tripp, who brought Lewinsky's name to the attention of both Jones's lawyers and Starr's office. Starr offered to grant limited immunity from prosecution in exchange for her testimony against the president and his close friend and adviser Vernon Jordan. Starr believed that Clinton and Jordan had sought to persuade Lewinsky to perjure herself in the Jones civil suit and that Jordan offered to find her a job as a form of "hush money." Jordan admitted to helping Lewinsky find a position in New York but said he acted simply to be helpful to the young intern. Clinton vehemently denied all the allegations and launched a vigorous campaign to discredit Starr's investigation as nothing more than a right-wing smear campaign.

In August 1998, Clinton was forced to appear before Starr's grand jury and acknowledge the affair with Lewinsky. The president claimed that technically he had not perjured himself when denying sexual contact with Lewinsky in his deposition in the Jones case, but admitted engaging in improper behavior. Clinton delivered an extraordinary televised address to the nation, acknowledging the relationship with Lewinsky, but also attacking Starr and his other political opponents. In the ensuing weeks, Clinton was compelled to travel the country repeating humiliating apologies and requests for forgiveness. In September, the House Judiciary Committee began an impeachment inquiry to ascertain whether Clinton's offenses constituted "high crimes and misdemeanors" stipulated by the Constitution as grounds for removing a president from office. To further humiliate Clinton, the committee released a complete tape of his testimony before the Starr grand jury. The entire four-hour tape was aired on national television and viewed by millions of Americans.

Subsequently, Clinton became the second president in American history to be impeached by the House of Representatives and tried by the Senate. The House vote to impeach Clinton was almost a straight, party-line vote, reinforcing the president's contention that the entire process was little more than a partisan witch hunt. The president's opponents knew they had no chance to win the two-thirds vote that would have been needed to convict Clinton in the Senate, but proceeded with a trial mainly to humiliate the president and destroy his administration. As expected, Clinton was acquitted, with most senators casting party-line votes. Though the president claimed that he had been vindicated, his administration was temporarily in shambles. For months, the White House had been compelled to ignore foreign and domestic policy issues, and the president was now faced with a crisis in the former Yugoslavia that would eventually lead to an American-directed military campaign against Serbia. The president's domestic policy agenda had virtually evaporated, though in 1999 the White House introduced a relatively minor health care initiative—a pale shadow of Clinton's original conception.

## Politics and Governance

Alas, there is no specific set of reforms we can propose to change a situation where the parties have become virtual obstructions to democracy. What we can do is to end on a note of warning, warning about what harm American political leaders are doing, coupled with a note of optimism that those leaders have the

## *Has Globalization Eroded the Government's Ability to Govern?*

Does globalization so restrict the ability of the U.S. government to act that the government can no longer effectively govern? Several writers increasingly answer "yes" to this question. They usually look to the three economic components of globalization mentioned in the first chapter's essay (see pages 20–21).

Increasing levels of trade mean that decisions taken abroad can undermine the government's policies. Such trade flows, for example, make governments and businesses alike much more sensitive to world market prices for goods. As Jeffry A. Frieden and Ronald Rogowski write, this situation "leads to the 'import' of global economic trends into domestic politics."[1]

Greater capital market integration means that markets can punish the government by "exiting" for other countries if investors believe that America's economic policy is counter to their interests. Globalization may restrict the types of taxes a government can impose. A higher capital gains tax on profits from stocks, for example, may lead investors to flee the country for lower taxes elsewhere. Indeed, capital market integration potentially affects America's ability to execute certain policies even in non-economic areas. If China were to be angered by U.S. foreign policy towards Taiwan, for example, it could sell its large amounts of dollar-denominated Treasury bonds for euro securities. This sell-off would force a sudden depreciation of the dollar, leading to higher inflation in the United States and a possible reconsideration of American security policy in Asia.[2]

Finally, the increased presence of truly multinational firms restricts the ability of states to impose a range of policies. A firm like DaimlerChrysler, for example, could tell both the German and the U.S. government that it will locate future investment only in a country that has environmental and tax policies that are most friendly to the company's bottom line. Policy makers then have a choice of complying with the firm's wishes or with watching hundreds of thousands of jobs leave the country.

[1]Jeffry A. Frieden and Ronald Rogowski, "The Impact of the International Economy on National Policies: An Analytical Overview," in *Internationalization and Domestic Politics,* ed. Helen V. Milner and Robert O. Koehane, (Cambridge: Cambridge University Press, 1996), p. 31.

[2]Jeffrey Garten, "Euro Neurosis," *New York Times Magazine,* 19 January 1999.

Not all observers consider this erosion of the national government's power a bad thing. Conservative newspapers like the *Wall Street Journal* argue consistently that world markets effectively "discipline" countries that try to introduce "bad" policies such as higher taxes, protective tariffs on goods, and high budget deficits. Kenichi Ohmae welcomes the erosion of nation-states worldwide. He predicts greater peace and prosperity as individuals and firms worry more about making money than about national pride.[3]

To others, however, the effects of globalization are ominous. Benjamin Barber writes that greater globalization is inherently bad for democracy. It leads to a marketplace imperative to harmonize culture and to stamp out diversity.[4] William Greider focuses on the winners and losers from globalization. He sees globalization increasing the divide between the rich and poor in America and in the rest of the world.[5]

To date, it is still relatively unclear just how "globalized" the United States has become. By most measures the U.S. economy, while gradually becoming more open to the rest of the world, is second only to Japan in having the most closed economy among developed countries.[6] The United States may still be relatively insulated from the effects of globalization. As the scholars cited above have noticed, the United States is becoming increasingly exposed to globalization. Coupled with some of the domestic difficulties to effective governance mentioned in this chapter, such as divided government and interest-group liberalism, an increase in globalization could undermine further the ability of the U.S. government to govern in the years to come.

[3]Kenichi Ohmae, *The End of the Nation State: The Rise of Regional Economies* (New York: Free Press, 1995).
[4]Benjamin Barber, *Jihad versus McWorld* (New York: Times Books, 1995).
[5]William Greider, *One World, Ready or Not: The Manic Logic of Global Capitalism* (New York: Simon and Schuster, 1997).
[6]See especially Geoffrey Garrett, "Global Markets and National Politics: Collision Course or Virtuous Circle?" *International Organization,* vol. 52, no. 4 (Autumn 1998), p. 811.

power of genuine democratic reform in their own hands, which they are more likely to use if they are made aware of the harm inherent in their present course. We do indeed feel that the only solution to complex political problems is awareness of the nature of the problems.

Contemporary American politics undermines governance in four ways. First, elections today fail to accomplish what must be the primary task of any leadership selection process: they fail to determine *who will govern.* An election should award the winners with the power to govern. Only in this way can popular consent be linked to effective governance. Under the fragmented system bequeathed to us by the Constitution's framers, seldom at any point in American history have all the levers of power been grasped by a unified and disciplined party or group.

Today, however, with the decay of America's political party organizations, this fragmentation has increased sharply. There are many victorious cliques and factions with little unity among them. During the Bush presidency, fragmentation and division led to a pattern of "gridlock" in which little or nothing could be accomplished in Washington. Deep factional divisions within the Democratic party, as we have seen, posed severe problems for the Clinton administration in its first two years, and a Republican majority in Congress since 1995 has continued the paralysis begun during the Bush years.

In addition to factional opposition, Clinton's efforts were hampered by the fact that many congressional Democrats have become "soloists," willing to give the administration their support only in exchange for some set of tangible benefits for themselves and the interests they represent. In the absence of party organizations and mechanisms for enforcing party discipline, there is little to prevent legislators from demanding what amounts to immediate political payoffs in exchange for their support on important pieces of legislation. The result is that all legislation effectively becomes special-interest legislation filled with loopholes and special benefits. For example, the 1993 budget contained provisions requiring that cigarettes manufactured in the United States contain 75 percent domestically grown tobacco. This provision was inserted at the behest of Senator Wendell Ford of Kentucky for the benefit of his state's tobacco farmers. Similarly, Democratic Representative James Bilbray of Nevada agreed to support the budget only after securing a tax credit designed to offset the Social Security taxes paid on employees' tips by restaurant owners—an important constituency group in his district. Texas Democrat Solomon Ortiz traded his support of the president's budget for an enlarged share of defense conversion funds for his district. The list goes on and on.[27] No wonder columnist David Broder called the resulting budget a "pastiche of conflicting goals.[28] One Clinton administration official conceded that because the budget was "driven by politics not policy," it was "not the greatest package ever."[29]

The second problem with contemporary politics is that modern governments are weak and unstable. Elected officials subjected to RIP attacks often find that

[27]David Rogers and John Harwood, "No Reasonable Offer Refused as Administration Bargained to Nail Down Deficit Package in House," *Wall Street Journal,* 6 August 1993, p. A12.

[28]David Broder, "Some Victory," *Washington Post,* 10 August 1993, p. A15.

[29]Hobart Rowan, "It's Not Much of a Budget," *Washington Post,* 12 August 1993, p. A27.

their poll standing (today's substitute for an organized popular base) can evaporate overnight and their capacity to govern disappear with it. Thus, the Nixon administration was paralyzed for three years by the Watergate affair, the Reagan White House for two years by the Iran-Contra affair, and the Clinton White House was distracted first by Whitewater and then by the impeachment crisis in 1998 and early 1999. This is hardly a recipe for a strong government to solve America's problems.

Third, because they lack a firm popular base, politicians seldom have the capacity to confront entrenched economic or political interest groups even when the public interest seems clear. For example, after his election in 1992, President Clinton felt compelled to reassure the nation's business community and powerful banking and financial interests that his administration would be receptive to their needs. This was a major reason that Clinton—who had campaigned as a staunch opponent of business-as-usual in Washington—named Democratic National Committee chair Ron Brown to be his secretary of commerce and Texas Democratic senator Lloyd Bentsen to the post of secretary of the treasury. Brown was a veteran Washington corporate lobbyist well known to the business community. Bentsen, as chair of the Senate Finance Committee, was noted for his close and cordial relationship with banking, finance, insurance, and real estate interests.[30] President Clinton was no more eager than his predecessor to confront these interests. Later, to secure the enactment of his tax proposals, Clinton felt compelled to give major tax concessions to a variety of interests, including aluminum producers, real estate developers, multinational corporations, and the energy industry.[31] Such moves did not always guarantee him support, however; even after Clinton made significant concessions to a variety of lobby groups, a coalition of powerful interests was able to scuttle his plan for reform of America's health care system.[32]

Finally, the enhanced political power of nonelectoral institutions means that the question of who will *not* govern is unlikely to be resolved in the electoral arena. The most important function of an election is to determine who will govern. At the same time, elections must also deprive the losing party of the power to prevent the winning party from governing effectively. Today, elections not only fail to determine who will govern but also do not definitively determine *who will not exercise power.* Given the political potency of nonelectoral modes of political struggle, electoral defeat does not deprive the losing party of the power to undermine the programs and policies of the winner. Indeed, as we have seen, electoral verdicts can now be reversed outside the electoral arena.

As a result, then, even as the "winners" in the American electoral process do not

[30]Jill Abramson and John Harwood, "Some Say Likely Choice of Bentsen, the Insider, for Treasury Post Could Send the Wrong Signals," *Wall Street Journal,* 9 December 1992, p. A26.

[31]David Hilzenrath, "Bentsen Signals White House's Willingness to Deal," *Washington Post,* 17 May 1993, p. A4.

[32]A lively and enlightening account of the compromising relationships between Washington political leaders and corporate interests is by maverick Republican Kevin Phillips, *Arrogant Capital: Washington, Wall Street, and the Frustration of American Politics* (Boston: Little, Brown, 1995).

acquire firm control of the government, so the "losers" are not deprived of power. Instead, "winners" and "losers" typically engage in a continuing struggle, which often distracts them from real national problems. For example, even before he was forced to resign in 1998, former House Speaker Newt Gingrich was diverted from his efforts to lead a Republican "revolution" by a barrage of ethics complaints levied against him by the Democrats.

More important, however, this struggle compels politicians to pay greater heed to the implications of policies for their domestic political battles than for collective national purposes. The Reagan and Bush administrations' tolerance of enormous budget deficits and their program of deregulation provide examples of this phenomenon. One important reason why Republican administrations were prepared to accept the economic risks of unprecedented deficits is the constraint these deficits imposed on congressional power. Similarly, the Republicans pressed for deregulation in part because the constellations of interests surrounding many regulatory policies are important Democratic bastions. This sort of political gamesmanship caused these administrations to overlook potential costs and risks of their policies. The relaxation of regulatory restraints on financial institutions permitted many S&Ls to shift from their traditional role as home mortgage lenders into potentially more lucrative but dangerously speculative areas. We all now know the results.

Concern for their institutional and political advantage can also affect the way officials respond to the initiatives of their opponents. For example, congressional Democrats regularly voted for lower levels of military spending than the two Republican administrations proposed, not because they were less committed to the nation's defense, but because the defense establishment has been an important institutional bastion of the Republicans. This reason also played a part in Democratic opposition to the 1991 Persian Gulf War.

## Restoring the Government's Capacity to Govern

The relationship between political patterns and governmental effectiveness is a complex one. Practices that severely undermine governmental capacities in some settings may not in others; witness the ability of Japan to thrive for many decades despite widespread political corruption. But in the United States and elsewhere political patterns that have seriously inhibited governments from pursuing collective purposes have at times emerged. For example, in Israel during the late 1980s electoral stalemate between the Labor and Likud parties paralyzed the government. The stalemate prevented the government from responding effectively to uprisings in the occupied territories and to diplomatic initiatives by the Palestine Liberation Organization, thereby threatening the relationship with the United States, which is a necessary condition for Israel's very survival.

Similar examples may be found in American history. In the United States during the early 1930s prevailing political patterns led the government to pursue policies that exacerbated rather than ameliorated the Depression. A particularly notable example is the Smoot-Hawley Tariff of 1930. The logrolling practices that at the time characterized the formulation of trade policy in the U.S. Congress led to the adoption of the highest tariffs in American history. This precipitated foreign retaliation and a virtual collapse of international trade, and it helped

THEN AND NOW

## Changes in American Politics

Historical perspective can shed important light on the challenges that face contemporary American politics.

- The decline of party organizations in the twentieth century has led to a system of candidate-centered politics in which mass media and individual campaigns play an unprecedented role. These media-driven, capital-intensive campaigns have heightened the costs of campaigning and thus increased the role and influence of money in politics.
- The contemporary era of divided government is in sharp contrast to the politics of the first half of the twentieth century, although the nineteenth century had its share of divided government as well.
- Not only do mass media and symbolic politics play an increasingly important role in today's political campaigns, but presidents and now congressional leaders use the media to engage in symbolic politics for governing as well as for campaigning. In the nineteenth century, presidents did not have a significant public role. And it wasn't until the late 1970s that congressional leaders began to engage in symbolic, media leadership.
- The expanded power and political support for courts has led to more litigious politics in which independent counsels and indictments have replaced elections and voting as primary arenas for elite conflict.

turn what could have been an ordinary cyclical downturn into the most severe economic crisis of the modern era. Even more striking than the events of the early 1930s were those preceding the Civil War. Political paralysis during the Buchanan administration prevented the government from responding to its own dismemberment as Southern states seceded from the Union.

The problems facing the United States in the 1990s are not as acute as those that the nation confronted on the eve of the Civil War or in the aftermath of the 1929 stock market crash. Nevertheless, America's political processes impede governmental responses adequate to the challenges that the nation faces, including the maintenance of prosperity and American security in the post–cold war era.

Were one of the parties to mobilize and forge organizational links to new voters, it might put itself in a position to gain control of all the major institutions of government. At the same time mobilization could provide the party with a political base enabling it to prevail over entrenched interests and powerful social forces for the sake of achieving collective national purposes. Under such circumstances, the most debilitating features of the contemporary American policy-making process might be contained.

## For Further Reading

Brady, David W., and Craig Volden. *Revolving Gridlock: Politics and Policy from Carter to Clinton*. Boulder, CO: Westview Press, 1998.

Dionne, E. J., Jr. *Why Americans Hate Politics*. New York: Simon and Schuster, 1991.

Drew, Elizabeth. *On the Edge: The Clinton Presidency*. New York: Simon and Schuster, 1994.

Greider, William. *Who Will Tell the People: The Betrayal of American Democracy*. New York: Simon and Schuster, 1992.

Lowi, Theodore. *The End of Liberalism*, 2nd ed. New York: W. W. Norton, 1979.

Lowi, Theodore. *The End of the Republican Era*. Norman: University of Oklahoma Press, 1995.

Phillips, Kevin. *Boiling Point: Democrats, Republicans, and the Decline of Middle-Class Prosperity*. New York: Random House, 1993.

Rosenstone, Steven, and John Mark Hansen. *Mobilization, Participation and Democracy in America*. New York: Macmillan, 1993.

Skocpol, Theda. *Boomerang: Health Care Reform and the Turn against Government*. New York: W. W. Norton, 1997.

Stein, Robert M., and Kenneth Bickers. *Perpetuating the Pork Barrel: Policy Subsystems and American Democracy*. New York: Cambridge University Press, 1995.

Sundquist, James L. *Constitutional Reform and Effective Government*. Washington, DC: Brookings Institution, 1992 rev. ed.

Woodward, Bob. *The Agenda: Inside the Clinton White House*. New York: Simon and Schuster, 1994.

# Epilogue: America the Beacon?

In the autumn of 1989, the world began to change dramatically, beginning with the collapse of the Soviet empire. As the Berlin Wall tumbled down, the Iron Curtain was raised, revealing the Soviet military in retreat and the Soviet Union's Eastern European satellites drifting out of orbit. The "victory" for capitalism was now on a global scale, since the collapse of the Soviet empire removed one of the two remaining holdouts against open and international exchange of goods, services, technology, and ideas. The last holdout today is China, which, despite its own misgivings, is far more penetrable and permeable than ever before. China's new openness has been inspired by the miraculous economic growth of its surrounding Asian nations. And the "meltdowns" of a number of new, independent, and industrializing nations, coupled with their rapid recovery, can be taken as evidence of victory for "our side."[1]

When communism began crumbling, numerous states within the former Soviet Union were given a chance to achieve independence. The people from these newly independent countries expressed the hopes and desires that define for Americans "the pursuit of happiness." New constitutions were written, new governments were formed, and everywhere dramatic signs of economic freedom emerged. In other parts of the world, countries in Africa and Asia were also witnessing a wave of democratization. By the end of 1998, 66 percent of the world's nations relied on elections to select their political leader. And throughout the world, these fledgling democracies looked to the United States for their economic and political models. Clearly one model that was immediately emulated by these new states was *free-market capitalism.*

[1]For strategic reasons, the United States has actually erected barriers to exchange against a few countries whose leaders would be very happy to join the global club if America would let them. These include Iraq, Libya, Serbia, Iran, and Cuba (although the United States is weakening toward the last two). And there will be others against whom America will from time to time use trade sanctions and embargoes as instruments of foreign policy just short of war. But efforts by the United States toward a more "open" China, despite its human rights abuses, indicate that restrictions and barriers to international exchange are employed only in extreme cases.

# The Globalization of Capitalism

The globalization of the world's economy first became obvious in the 1970s, when the United States discovered, thanks to the "oil crisis," that even the most powerful nation-state in the world is not immune to the forces of the market. Since then, the process of globalization has created an integrated system of capital accumulation and exchange, with stock markets, commodity markets, and other markets for capital transfer open twenty-four hours a day, seven days a week. Globalization also created an integrated system of production, with most large corporations operating in an international economic context where goods and services are bought and sold in a global marketplace. By 1993, the percentage of total U.S. manufactured output that was tied to international markets was 18.9 percent, up from 5.5 percent thirty years earlier. The economy of Great Britain is tied even more to the global market, with 42.9 percent of its manufactured output involved as of 1993, compared to 17.8 percent in 1963. For West Germany, the international tie was at 41.1 percent in 1991 (the last full year before integration of East Germany), compared to 21.2 percent in 1963. Impressive as these figures are, globalization of economic life has a long way to go before the market is integrated worldwide.[2] And because of America's place in the global economy, some important questions now need to be asked: What is the United States' role in expanding and integrating the global economy? Should the United States embrace or be wary of that role? Most important, what are the implications of the global economy for democracy in America and elsewhere?

## America and the Free Market

America is viewed as a model of economic organization, a paragon of modern corporate capitalism. But capitalism is not an American invention. Neither is democracy or freedom. America has simply taken capitalism and all its attributes further than any other country, putting more of its own principles to the test, even though the United States consistently claims to be merely a follower of Adam Smith, the great eighteenth-century economist and educator.

Any country seeking to join the globalizing process needs to sacrifice and compromise a great deal if it truly wants to realize some of the benefits of economic expansion. To join, each country must reduce or eliminate its numerous barriers to trade. Often, these changes involve drastic transformations in policies and practices that are considered essential to that country's way of life. Some

[2]Many economic historians will argue that "the world was more closely integrated before 1914 than it is now, in some cases much more so." Clive Crook, "The World Economy," *The Economist,* 20 September 1997, p. 37; see also Nicholas Kristof, "At This Rate, We'll Be Global in Another Hundred Years," *New York Times,* 23 May 1999, sec. 4, p. 5.

countries have policies protecting local industrial and agricultural products from international competition because they fear that without these protections the communities and their traditions would be destroyed. Nevertheless, these trade restrictions must be eliminated. These and other countries also have policies protecting jobs, leases, rental agreements, and even traditional specialties such as lace making or wood carving. These protections also must be eliminated. Some countries have little or no history of protecting intellectual properties such as inventions, writing, or music. These kinds of protections must be added. In other words, economic expansion means penetrating traditional practices, values, and social linkages by foreign, modern "universalistic" values of contract, competition, profit, and specialization. This dynamic is why capitalism has shared with democracy a reputation as being the world's most revolutionary force—at least during the past two hundred years.

Karl Marx recognized this and assumed that a "bourgeois capitalist" revolution would (and would have to) precede the final proletarian revolution. He was far from alone in this point of view. Here is Alexis de Tocqueville twenty years before Marx:

> Can it be believed that the democracy which has overthrown the feudal system and vanquished kings will retreat before tradesman and capitalist? Will it stop now that it has grown so strong and its adversaries so weak?[3]

Tocqueville was not the enemy of "tradesmen and capitalists." He was only concerned that economic power might be democracy's undoing, which is a profound comment on today's prevailing assumption that capitalism and democracy are always on the same side. They are always on the same side in the sense that two competing producers within the context of a larger system are. According to most economic theorists since Adam Smith, vigorous competition increases output while it lowers prices, until some sort of equilibrium is reached. In a similar fashion, competition between capitalism and democracy increases the output of both. But economic competition can also lead to destructive excesses such as sweatshops and environmental degradation; this should teach us that destructive competition is also possible between capitalism and democracy, which is detrimental to both. Competition is no substitute for wisdom, reason, and deliberation—*and* enlightened public policy.

Tocqueville was concerned about whether democracy could ever enlighten itself enough to compete constructively with capitalism. To that end, Tocqueville gave what might be the only personal appeal in his classic, two-volume work, *Democracy in America:*

> The first of the duties that are at this time imposed upon those who direct our affairs is to educate democracy . . . to substitute a knowledge of statecraft for its inexperience, and an awareness of its true interest for its blind instincts, to adapt its government to

[3]Alexis de Tocqueville, *Democracy in America,* author's introduction (New York: Vintage Books, 1945), p. 5. Tocqueville considered this passage so important that he quoted it in his preface to the 12th ed., 1848.

time and place, and to modify it according to men and to conditions. *A new science of politics is needed for a new world.*[4]

In 1997, just before the frightening meltdown of the economies in many of the countries that comprised the "Asian miracle," the distinguished journalist William Greider published a book with the significant title of *One World, Ready or Not: The Manic Logic of Global Capitalism.*[5] The meltdown, which began later that year, serves as a warning—we'd better get ready to create a better functioning democracy than we already have. Other nations might want to pay heed, too.

## THE GLOBALIZATION OF DEMOCRACY

Because so many of the world's nations have sought to emulate the success of America's free-market economy, we need to ask what other models have been worthy of emulation. What about the political model of *democracy?* Can it be easily imitated? The verdict is still out. For a long time there has been a widespread assumption among observers in already industrialized nations that the transition to democracy in any country requires strongly favorable economic conditions; but no one can possibly doubt that democracy can get very far in any country with a history of grinding poverty and vast inequalities of wealth. As a consequence, intellectuals in the liberal-capitalist Western democracies are just as disposed as orthodox Marxists to look to economic conditions for the explanation of democracy.[6] But can we really say that economics *causes* democracy?

Some revisions in our theories about the economic conditions of democracy have appeared in recent years and been encapsulated by T. J. Pempel, one of America's foremost experts on the Japanese political system, who writes:

> . . . A strong linear relationship between [Gross Domestic Product, GDP] and democracy has most typically been interpreted to imply that as nation-states reach some particular level of economic development social structures become more complex and the country can no longer be run through simple dictatorship or authoritarianism. Hence, domestic pressures reach irresistible levels and increased democratization emerges as a by-product of economic development. . . . Yet . . . the transition to democracy involves

[4]Ibid., p. 7.

[5]William Greider, *One World, Ready or Not: The Manic Logic of Global Capitalism* (New York: Simon and Schuster, 1997).

[6]See, for example, Seymour Martin Lipset, "Some Social Requisites of Democracy: Economic Development and Political Legitimacy," *APSR* (March 1959), pp. 69–105; and Lipset, "The Social Requisites of Democracy Revisited," *American Sociological Review* (February 1994), pp. 1–22. A more sophisticated use of social as well as economic conditions of democracy is found in Samuel P. Huntington, *The Third Wave: Democratization in the Late Twentieth Century* (Norman: University of Oklahoma Press, 1991).

an explicitly political process more complex than anything implied by notions of democracy as the foreordained derivation of economic improvement.[7]

This is not to deny the importance of favorable economic conditions. Economic growth is important, but economic stability may be even more so. Positive social and cultural values are also important, but we don't know which social and cultural values are necessary and sufficient for democracy. The de-legitimation of previous authoritarian regimes can be considered a major factor in the history of many democracies; but losing a war may explain even more. The point is that although many uncountable conditions can be considered favorable for democracy, general conditions don't necessarily produce particular or expected outcomes.

Consequently, we are better off setting aside the idea that democracy is something caused. Democracy is far too complex to be treated as a single, definable phenomenon that comes with its own universal explanation. *Democracy has to be constructed.* Democracy as a universal abstraction can be defined as a freedom (or the absence of restraint) where all individuals are equal in their freedom. But democracy *as a form of government* is particular to each country and requires the institutionalization of freedom in each one. As we have argued elsewhere in this book, democratic government must have an architecture within which a kind of bounded freedom can take place. Call it a constitution. A constitution is a construction made from freedom and power, a harmonizing of competing and contradictory forces.

A wise observer once referred to this architecture or constitution as "that delicate balance."[8] We call it "that *in*delicate balance." There is no universal architecture of democratic government, as many eighteenth-century state makers believed. Every good government must be constructed in a manner consistent with that nation's own social/cultural values and traditions. At the same time, if it is to remain legitimate, a government must permit its culture and tradition to be expressed as a majority, through proper use of government power, while still protecting dissenters whose aim may be to change that very culture and tradition. This indeed is a most indelicate balance.

Elaborate and systematic studies of post-communist regimes in central and eastern Europe document definitively that what their citizens want most is a democratic government capable of performance. As Hans-Dieter Klingemann and associates put it,

> If the demonstrators on the streets of Prague or Leipzig in 1989 or Vilnius or Moscow in 1991 had been asked what they were seeking, few would have responded in terms of

[7]T. J. Pempel, "Democratization and Globalization: A Comparative Study of Japan, South Korea, and Taiwan," prepared for panel on Democratization and Globalization, International Political Science Association Congress, Seoul, Korea, August 1997. For an excellent treatment of *political* compromises between labor and capital that can help produce and maintain democratic as well as social democratic and democratic socialist regimes, see Adam Przeworski and Michael Wallerstein, "The Structure of Class Conflict in Democratic Society," APSR (June 1982), pp. 215–38.

[8]Fred W. Friendly and Martha Elliott, *The Constitution: That Delicate Balance* (New York: Random House, 1984).

> economics or consumer goods. . . . If asked why they were engaging in such risky behavior, the demonstrators would have answered, more often than not, for *freedom,* not for a stereo, fresh broccoli, or a new car. And they would have meant it.[9]

On the basis of their multicountry surveys, the European scholars conclude with confidence that

> virtually all of the European post-communist countries put in place at least parts of a package of political reforms . . . well before implementation of most economic reforms could even be seriously started. . . . thus . . . *political* outcomes and their effects on democratic legitimacy . . . proceeded more rapidly than . . . *economic* reforms. . . .[10]

But political reforms are only starters. When citizens in newly independent countries espouse democracy and democratic government, they also commit themselves to criticizing that government and its performance. Expectations run high at the start, and expectations increase so much as time goes by that newly democratic governments must maintain their legitimacy by observing proper procedures in the enactment of legislation, by respecting freedom of speech from both citizens and a vigorous press, and by respecting human rights in general. Consequently, there is always a large "credibility gap," also called a satisfaction or performance gap. For example, in the mid-1990s, a multicountry survey asked the following question: "On the whole, are you very satisfied, fairly satisfied, not very satisfied, or not at all satisfied with the way democracy is developing in [your country]?" The average response was that about one-third were *very* or *fairly* satisfied with the way democracy was working in 1995. Two-thirds of the respondents said they were not satisfied. The responses ranged from a 61-percent citizen satisfaction with democratic performance in Albania, to a mere 10-percent satisfaction in Russia.[11]

Many people believe that a wide credibility gap, such as the low satisfaction expressed by 90 percent of Russians in 1995, is dangerous and can bring a country close to a return to authoritarian forms of rule. We think otherwise—that a large credibility gap and a large bundle of dissatisfaction in a society is healthy for a democracy. It is, to us, what Thomas Jefferson meant by vigilance, which was deemed the price of liberty.[12]

[9]Hans-Dieter Klingemann and Richard Hofferbert, "Remembering the Bad Old Days: Human Rights, Economic Conditions, and Democratic Performance in Transitional Regimes," co-published by School of Social Sciences, University of California/Irvine, and Institutions and Social Change, Wissenschaftszentrum für Sozialforschung Berlin (WZB), Discussion Paper FS III 98–203, p. 2. These observations were based on sample surveys conducted in Berlin before, during, and after the 1948–1949 blockade and air lift. German social scientists in particular have been studying democratic values in Germany and elsewhere in Europe since that time. Emphasis in original.

[10]Ibid., p. 5. Emphasis in original.

[11]These findings and the sources of the surveys are in Klingemann, op cit., pp. 9–11. For a full history of the "credibility gap," see Seymour Martin Lipset and William Schneider, *The Confidence Gap* (New York: Free Press, 1987).

[12]The full quote attributed to Jefferson is, "Eternal vigilance is the price of liberty."

## America and Democratic Principles

In the late 1980s, a book entitled *The Rise and Fall of the Great Powers* explained why a decline of American influence in the world was all but inevitable. Within five years, however, not only had America re-emerged as the world's preeminent military power but, perhaps more than ever, American democracy had become an example—a beacon—to the new nations of the world.

Despite America's many problems, there is much about the American democratic system that *is* worthy of emulation. Americans have not always been outstanding theorists of democracy, but, for two hundred years, they have been among its foremost practitioners and have developed noteworthy ideas, institutions, and practices.

Foremost among these is the idea of *constitutionalism*. There are many good constitutions but only one principle of constitutionalism: to choose among instruments of government and then to set those choices slightly above majority rule and outside the immediate control of the people who are in power at a given moment in time. By this means, a people can set limits on the power of government and at the same time set limits on themselves.

Another American governmental institution worthy of emulation is our system of *competing political parties*. This is absolutely necessary for the American political system and for every system that wishes to maintain democracy. A *two*-party system is not sacred.[13] What is necessary is some kind of competitive party system, one in which the parties enjoy control over the nomination and election process, and one in which the parties have the resources to mobilize voters without (and despite) government sponsorship. This is the best way to ensure democratic accountability and popular participation. If only we could strengthen our party system![14]

Yet another feature carefully studied and often emulated is *presidentialism*. Few countries have considered imitating the American presidential system in all of its facets. But elites and intellectuals in many countries have been inspired by it and have adapted it to their own ends. France is perhaps the most notable example, having adopted a unique variant of the American presidential system in their Fifth Republic constitution in 1958. There is good reason to believe that their variant—with an independently elected president as head of state and an independently designated premier as head of government—is in large part responsible for the Fifth Republic lasting over forty years, the longest single regime in the two-hundred-year history of postrevolutionary France. More recently, parliamentary systems such as Israel's and Italy's have looked to a separate national election of

[13]See, for example, Lowi, "Toward a Responsible Three-Party System: Prospects and Obstacles," in Theodore Lowi and Joseph Romance, *A Republic of Parties?—Debating the Two-Party System* (Boulder, CO: Rowman & Littlefield, 1998).

[14]The classic statements on the indispensable role of party competition are E. E. Schattschneider, *Party Government* (New York: Holt, Rinehart, and Winston, 1942); and Joseph Schumpeter, *Capitalism, Socialism and Democracy* (London: Allen and Unwin, 1943).

their premier as head of government as a way to move toward a presidential system that would overcome traditional political fragmentation. Many countries in Latin America and Asia have also adopted variations of the presidential system. But in most of these instances, the flirtation with presidentialism is coupled with considerable fear that a presidential system might quickly fall back into dictatorship or, as it is called in Latin America, *caudillismo.*[15] These latter instances serve as a good warning: Copy with care.

American federalism has also been watched closely, even though there have been other federal (and confederal) experiments in the past few centuries, most notably Switzerland (admired by Rousseau in the late eighteenth century), Germany, Australia, and Canada. More recently two instructive cases have emerged, the former Soviet Union and Yugoslavia. We tend to forget that U.S.S.R. meant Union of Socialist Soviet Republics, a carefully, constitutionally designed federal system. For a while, Yugoslavia was even more admired as a successful post–World War II federal system. But these latter two cases, the U.S.S.R. and Yugoslavia, also serve as a warning that federalism imposed by military necessity will most likely fall apart as soon as the military factor is withdrawn (as in the U.S.S.R.) or is significantly weakened (as in Yugoslavia). Canada also serves as a kind of warning, inasmuch as the national government is unable (short of military imposition) to keep a dissident unit of the federation (the province of Québec) from behaving so differently from the others that it amounts to succession—and in fact wishes to secede. Here again the warning: Copy with care.

Finally, the part of the American model most likely to be studied for emulation are our provisions in the Constitution for *civil liberties* and *civil rights.* But in this instance, many countries have been more inspired by the French approach to "human rights" and have gone much further than the United States in the guarantees of rights. It is here that others would be well advised to favor the American model because of its recognition that a mere listing of liberties and rights—"parchment guarantees"—is not enough. Americans are not as generous in the extension of rights, largely because they recognize that for every right there has to be a remedy. Many countries, in their enthusiasm for extending rights to all citizens, have established a distinction between "political rights" (closest to our notion of civil liberties) and "social rights," defined as "the whole range from the right to a modicum of economic welfare and security to the right to share the full social heritage and to live the life of a civilized being according to the standards prevailing in the society."[16] An appreciation of this distinction between political and social rights has led many critics to say, quite accurately, that America is a "liberal democracy," but far more liberal (stressing equality of opportunity) than democratic (stressing equality of outcome). It may be on this point that America

[15]An excellent treatment of this and many other American attributes will be found in Klaus von Beyme, *America as a Model: The Impact of American Democracy in the World* (Aldershot, Germany: Gower, 1987). Von Beyme's table of contents is a virtual menu of American features that have been studied carefully for purposes of imitation or adaptation: the presidential system of government; federalism; judicial review; and institutions of representation and participation.

[16]T. H. Marshall, *Class, Citizenship, and Social Development* (Westport, CT: Greenwood Press, 1964), pp. 71–72. See also Reinhard Bendix, *Nation-Building and Citizenship: Studies of Our Changing Social Order,* 2nd ed. (Berkeley: University of California Press, 1964), Chapter 3.

should be careful in emulating the older and more statist countries of Europe and elsewhere. The warning here, however, is to all sides, America and elsewhere: Beware of putting promises in your constitution that you cannot keep. Rights are causes of action that must be accompanied with enforceable remedies. No government is good government without rights. But no government can be good if it provides rights without remedies.

## The Basis for Democracy: Liberty

Virtually everywhere in the world democratic controls seem to be associated with political liberty. Generally speaking, the same nations that possess democratic political institutions are also the most likely to respect basic civil liberties. The history of the relationship between liberty and democratic practices suggests that democratic institutions are usually the result of rather than the cause of freedom. The citizens of the democracies are not free because they possess democratic controls; rather, they exercise democratic controls because they are free. A measure of liberty is a necessary precondition for the functioning of democratic processes. Governmental interference with speech, assembly, association, and the press precludes open and competitive policies.[17]

More fundamentally, democratic institutions are most likely to emerge and flourish where the public already possesses some freedom from governmental control. As we saw earlier, democratic elections are often introduced when governments are unable to compel the people's acquiescence. In a sense, elections are inaugurated in order to persuade a reluctant populace to surrender at least some of its freedom and allow itself to be governed. Thus, in the United States, the introduction of democratic institutions, as well as the adoption of formal constitutional guarantees of civil liberties, was in part prompted by the fact that the citizenry was free—born free, as Tocqueville observed—and had the desire to remain so. Even several of the framers of the Constitution who were hostile to the principle of democracy nevertheless urged the adoption of democratic governmental forms on the grounds that the populace would otherwise refuse to accept the new government. John Dickinson, a prominent and well-to-do delegate from Delaware, asserted that limited monarchy was superior to any republican form of government. Unfortunately, however, limited monarchy was out of the question because of the "spirit of the times."[18] Similarly, senior Virginia delegate George Mason concluded that "notwithstanding the oppression and injustice experienced among us from democracy, the genius of the people is in favor of it, and the genius of the people must be consulted."[19] Subsequently, as we saw, the Constitution's proponents agreed to add the formal guarantees of civil liberties embodied in the Bill of Rights only when it appeared that the Constitution might otherwise

[17]See Madison's discussion in Clinton Rossiter, ed., *The Federalist Papers,* No. 10 (New York: New American Library, 1961). See also Carl Cohen, *Democracy* (Athens: University of Georgia Press, 1971), Chapter 10.

[18]Max Farrand, ed., *The Records of the Federal Convention of 1787,* 4 vols., rev. ed. (New Haven: Yale University Press, 1966), vol. 1, p. 86.

[19]Ibid., p. 101.

not be ratified. In effect, the public had to be persuaded to permit itself to be governed because it was, in fact, free to choose otherwise. Given the absence of a national military force and the virtually universal distribution of firearms and training in their use, the populace could not easily have been compelled to accept a government it did not desire.

In general, democratic political practices are most likely to emerge and prosper in "free societies"—societies in which politically relevant resources are distributed outside the control of the central government. The importance of the distribution of military force is clear. When at some critical historical juncture rulers lacked the necessary force to govern, they tended to become much more concerned with citizens' rights.

Other resources are probably of even greater importance to the maintenance of freedom. An active private press coupled with a literate population, as in America, can, with information about government activities, stimulate resistance to those in power.[20] Broadly distributed reservoirs of private financial resources often help the formation of opposition. We are fortunate in the United States to possess a democratic form of government, but it is not a substitute for—and could not exist for long without—a significant measure of popular freedom.

In the United States, constitutionally mandated controls on government offer some measure of protection for civil liberties and civil rights. The availability of governmental controls, however, if based on democratic processes, tends eventually to persuade citizens that they may enjoy the benefits of the state's power without risk to their freedom. Why, after all, should it be necessary to limit a servant's capacity to serve?

Unfortunately, despite democratic processes controlling government, individual freedom and governmental power inevitably conflict. This conflict does not necessarily mean deliberate and overt governmental efforts to abridge liberties. Typically, the erosion of citizens' liberties in the democracies is a more subtle, insidious, and often unforeseen result of routine administrative processes. As we saw earlier, federal agencies such as the Interstate Commerce Commission, the Civil Aeronautics Board, and the Federal Trade Commission have considerable control over who may enter the occupations and businesses that they regulate. The Food and Drug Administration has a good deal to say about what we may eat. The Federal Communications Commission has a measure of influence over what Americans see and hear over the airwaves. The Internal Revenue Service, in the mundane course of collecting taxes, makes decisions about what is and is not a religion, what is or is not political activity, whether given forms of education are or are not socially desirable, what types of philanthropy serve the public interest, and what sorts of information it should acquire about every citizen. The administration of tax policy is among the most intrusive activities of the federal government. Thus, congressional tax legislation and IRS regulations can have a critical effect upon every individual's business decisions, marital plans, childbirth and child-rearing decisions, vacation plans, and medical care. And housing policies, educational policies, and some welfare programs, which are often directed by

[20]See Richard Hofstadter, *The Idea of a Party System* (Berkeley: University of California Press, 1969), Chapter 3.

agencies given broad, discretionary mandates by Congress, affect the most minute details of citizens' lives.

Despite the availability of democratic institutions, Americans cannot expect to use the government's power without surrendering at least some of their freedom. This is the darkside of government. A government capable of solving our problems and maintaining America's place in the world is also a government capable of threatening our cherished liberties.

More than 150 years ago, Alexis de Tocqueville prophesied that Americans would someday become so convinced that they controlled the government that they would be willing to surrender their liberty to it. This would leave them, he warned, holding the ends of their own chains. For now, we possess both the blessing of freedom and the service of government. Let us hope we can keep them.

# APPENDIX

# The Declaration of Independence

*In Congress, July 4, 1776*

When in the course of human events, it becomes necessary for one people to dissolve the political bands which have connected them with another, and to assume among the Powers of the earth, the separate and equal station to which the Laws of Nature and of Nature's God entitle them, a decent respect to the opinions of mankind requires that they should declare the causes which impel them to the separation.

We hold these truths to be self-evident, that all men are created equal, that they are endowed by their Creator with certain unalienable rights, that among these are Life, Liberty, and the pursuit of Happiness. That to secure these rights, Governments are instituted among Men, deriving their just powers from the consent of the governed. That whenever any Form of Government becomes destructive of these ends, it is the Right of the People to alter or to abolish it, and to institute new Government, laying its foundation on such principles and organizing its powers in such form, as to them shall seem most likely to effect their Safety and Happiness. Prudence, indeed, will dictate that Governments long established should not be changed for light and transient causes; and accordingly all experience hath shown, that mankind are more disposed to suffer, while evils are sufferable, than to right themselves by abolishing the forms to which they are accustomed. But when a long train of abuses and usurpations, pursuing invariably the same Object evinces a design to reduce them under absolute Despotism, it is their right, it is their duty, to throw off such Government, and to provide new Guards for their future security.—Such has been the patient sufferance of these Colonies; and such is now the necessity which constrains them to alter their former Systems of Government. The history of the present King of Great Britain is a history of repeated injuries and usurpations, all having in direct object the establishment of an absolute Tyranny over these States. To prove this, let Facts be submitted to a candid world.

He has refused his Assent to Laws, the most wholesome and necessary for the public good.

He has forbidden his Governors to pass Laws of immediate and pressing importance, unless suspended in their operation till his Assent should be obtained; and when so suspended, he has utterly neglected to attend to them.

He has refused to pass other Laws for the accommodation of large districts of people, unless those people would relinquish the right of Representation in the Legislature, a right inestimable to them and formidable to tyrants only.

He has called together legislative bodies at places unusual, uncomfortable, and distant from the depository of their public Records, for the sole purpose of fatiguing them into compliance with his measures.

He has dissolved Representative Houses repeatedly, for opposing with manly firmness his invasions on the rights of the people.

He has refused for a long time, after such dissolutions, to cause others to be elected; whereby the Legislative powers, incapable of Annihilation, have returned to the People at large for their exercise; the State remaining in the mean time exposed to all dangers of invasion from without, and convulsions within.

He has endeavored to prevent the population of these States; for that purpose obstructing the Laws of Naturalization of Foreigners; refusing to pass others to encourage their migrations hither, and raising the conditions of new Appropriations of Lands.

He has obstructed the Administration of Justice, by refusing his Assent to Laws for establishing Judiciary powers.

He has made Judges dependent on his Will alone, for the tenure of their offices, and the amount and payment of their salaries.

He has erected a multitude of New Offices, and sent hither swarms of Officers to harass our People, and eat out their substance.

He has kept among us, in times of peace, Standing Armies without the Consent of our legislature.

He has affected to render the Military independent of and superior to the Civil Power.

He has combined with others to subject us to a jurisdiction foreign to our constitution, and unacknowledged by our laws; giving his Assent to their Acts of pretended Legislation:

For quartering large bodies of armed troops among us:

For protecting them, by a mock Trial, from Punishment for any Murders which they should commit on the Inhabitants of these States:

For cutting off our Trade with all parts of the world:

For imposing taxes on us without our Consent:

For depriving us in many cases, of the benefits of Trial by jury:

For transporting us beyond Seas to be tried for pretended offences:

For abolishing the free System of English Laws in a neighboring Province, establishing therein an Arbitrary government, and enlarging its Boundaries so as to render it at once an example and fit instrument for introducing the same absolute rule into these Colonies:

For taking away our Charters, abolishing our most valuable Laws, and altering fundamentally the Forms of our Governments:

For suspending our own Legislatures, and declaring themselves invested with Power to legislate for us in all cases whatsoever.

He has abdicated Government here, by declaring us out of his Protection and waging War against us.

He has plundered our seas, ravaged our Coasts, burnt our towns, and destroyed the lives of our people.

He is at this time transporting large armies of foreign mercenaries to compleat the works of death, desolation, and tyranny, already begun with circumstances of Cruelty & perfidy scarcely paralleled in the most barbarous ages, and totally unworthy the Head of a civilized nation.

He has constrained our fellow Citizens taken Captive on the high Seas to bear Arms against their Country, to become the executioners of their friends and Brethren, or to fall themselves by their Hands.

He has excited domestic insurrections amongst us, and has endeavored to bring on the inhabitants of our frontiers, the merciless Indian Savages, whose known rule of warfare, is an undistinguished destruction of all ages, sexes, and conditions.

In every stage of these Oppressions We have Petitioned for Redress in the most humble terms: Our repeated Petitions have been answered only by repeated injury. A Prince, whose character is thus marked by every act which may define a Tyrant, is unfit to be the ruler of a free people.

Nor have We been wanting in attention to our British brethren. We have warned them from time to time of attempts by their legislature to extend an unwarrantable jurisdiction over us. We have reminded them of the circumstances of our emigration and settlement here. We have appealed to their native justice and magnanimity, and we have conjured them by the ties of our common kindred to disavow these usurpations, which, would inevitably interrupt our connections and correspondence. They too must have been deaf to the voice of justice and of consanguinity. We must, therefore, acquiesce in the necessity, which denounces our Separation, and hold them, as we hold the rest of mankind, Enemies in War, in Peace Friends.

WE, THEREFORE, the Representatives of the UNITED STATES OF AMERICA, in General Congress, Assembled, appealing to the Supreme Judge of the world for the rectitude of our intentions, do, in the Name, and by Authority of the good People of these Colonies, solemnly publish and declare, That these United Colonies are, and of Right ought to be FREE AND INDEPENDENT STATES; that they are Absolved from all Allegiance to the British Crown, and that all political connection between them and the State of Great Britain, is and ought to be totally dissolved; and that as Free and Independent States, they have full Power to levy War, conclude Peace, contract Alliances, establish Commerce, and to do all other Acts and Things which Independent States may of right do. And for the support of this Declaration, with a firm reliance on the Protection of Divine Providence, we mutually pledge to each other our Lives, our Fortunes, and our sacred Honor.

The foregoing Declaration was, by order of Congress, engrossed, and signed by the following members:

*John Hancock*

NEW HAMPSHIRE
*Josiah Bartlett*
*William Whipple*
*Matthew Thornton*

MASSACHUSETTS BAY
*Samuel Adams*
*John Adams*
*Robert Treat Paine*
*Elbridge Gerry*

RHODE ISLAND
*Stephen Hopkins*
*William Ellery*

CONNECTICUT
*Roger Sherman*
*Samuel Huntington*
*William Williams*
*Oliver Wolcott*

NEW YORK
*William Floyd*
*Philip Livingston*
*Francis Lewis*
*Lewis Morris*

NEW JERSEY
*Richard Stockton*
*John Witherspoon*
*Francis Hopkinson*
*John Hart*
*Abraham Clark*

PENNSYLVANIA
*Robert Morris*
*Benjamin Rush*
*Benjamin Franklin*
*John Morton*
*George Clymer*
*James Smith*
*George Taylor*
*James Wilson*
*George Ross*

DELAWARE
*Caesar Rodney*
*George Read*
*Thomas M'Kean*

MARYLAND
*Samuel Chase*
*William Paca*
*Thomas Stone*
*Charles Carroll, of Carrollton*

VIRGINIA
*George Wythe*
*Richard Henry Lee*
*Thomas Jefferson*
*Benjamin Harrison*
*Thomas Nelson, Jr.*
*Francis Lightfoot Lee*
*Carter Braxton*

NORTH CAROLINA
*William Hooper*
*Joseph Hewes*
*John Penn*

SOUTH CAROLINA
*Edward Rutledge*
*Thomas Heyward, Jr.*
*Thomas Lynch, Jr.*
*Arthur Middleton*

GEORGIA
*Button Gwinnett*
*Lyman Hall*
*George Walton*

*Resolved,* That copies of the Declaration be sent to the several assemblies, conventions, and committees, or councils of safety, and to the several commanding officers of the continental troops; that it be proclaimed in each of the United States, at the head of the army.

# The Articles of Confederation

*Agreed to by Congress November 15, 1777;*
*ratified and in force March 1, 1781*

To all whom these Presents shall come, we the undersigned Delegates of the States affixed to our Names send greeting. Whereas the Delegates of the United States of America in Congress assembled did on the fifteenth day of November in the Year of our Lord One Thousand Seven Hundred and Seventy seven, and in the Second Year of the Independence of America agree to certain articles of Confederation and perpetual Union between the States of Newhampshire, Massachusetts-bay, Rhodeisland and Providence Plantations, Connecticut, New-York, New-Jersey, Pennsylvania, Delaware, Maryland, Virginia, North-Carolina, South-Carolina and Georgia in the Words following, viz. "Articles of Confederation and perpetual Union between the states of Newhampshire, Massachusetts-bay, Rhodeisland and Providence Plantations, Connecticut, New-York, New-Jersey, Pennsylvania, Delaware, Maryland, Virginia, North-Carolina, South-Carolina and Georgia.

Art. I. The Stile of this confederacy shall be "The United States of America."

Art. II. Each state retains its sovereignty, freedom and independence, and every Power, Jurisdiction and right, which is not by this confederation expressly delegated to the United States, in Congress assembled.

Art. III. The said states hereby severally enter into a firm league of friendship with each other, for their common defence, the security of their Liberties, and their mutual and general welfare, binding themselves to assist each other, against all force offered to, or attacks made upon them, or any of them, on account of religion, sovereignty, trade, or any other pretence whatever.

Art. IV. The better to secure and perpetuate mutual friendship and intercourse among the people of the different states in this union, the free inhabitants of each of these states, paupers, vagabonds and fugitives from Justice excepted, shall be entitled to all privileges and immunities of free citizens in the several states; and the people of each state shall have free ingress and regress to and from any other state, and shall enjoy therein all the privileges of trade and commerce, subject to the same duties, impositions and restrictions as the inhabitants thereof respectively, provided that such restriction shall not extend so far as to prevent the removal of property imported into any state, to any other state of which the Owner is an inhabitant; provided also that no imposition, duties or restriction shall be laid by any state, on the property of the united states, or either of them.

If any Person guilty of, or charged with treason, felony, or other high misdemeanor in any state, shall flee from Justice, and be found in any of the united states, he shall upon demand of the Governor or executive power, of the state from which he fled, be delivered up and removed to the state having jurisdiction of his offence.

Full faith and credit shall be given in each of these states to the records, acts and judicial proceedings of the courts and magistrates of every other state.

Art. V. For the more convenient management of the general interests of the united states, delegates shall be annually appointed in such manner as the legislature of each state shall direct, to meet in Congress on the first Monday in November, in every year, with a power reserved to each state, to recall its delegates, or any of them, at any time within the year, and to send others in their stead, for the remainder of the Year.

No state shall be represented in Congress by less than two, nor by more than seven Members; and no person shall be capable of being a delegate for more than three years in any term of six years; nor shall any person, being a delegate, be capable of holding any office under the united states, for which he, or another for his benefit receives any salary, fees or emolument of any kind.

Each state shall maintain its own delegates in a meeting of the states, and while they act as members of the committee of the states.

In determining questions in the united states, in Congress assembled, each state shall have one vote.

Freedom of speech and debate in Congress shall not be impeached or questioned in any Court, or place out of Congress, and the members of congress shall be protected in their persons from arrests and imprisonments, during the time of their going to and from, and attendance on congress, except for treason, felony, or breach of the peace.

Art. VI. No state without the Consent of the united states in congress assembled, shall send any embassy to, or receive any embassy from, or enter into any conference, agreement, or alliance or treaty with any King, prince or state; nor shall any person holding any office or profit or trust under the united states, or any of them, accept of any present, emolument, office or title of any kind whatever from any king, prince or foreign state; nor shall the united states in congress assembled, or any of them, grant any title of nobility.

No two or more states shall enter into any treaty, confederation or alliance whatever between them, without the consent of the united states in congress assembled, specifying accurately the purposes for which the same is to be entered into, and how long it shall continue.

No state shall lay any imposts or duties, which may interfere with any stipulations in treaties, entered into by the united states in congress assembled, with any king, prince or state, in pursuance of any treaties already proposed by congress, to the courts of France and Spain.

No vessels of war shall be kept up in time of peace by any state, except such number only, as shall be deemed necessary by the united states in congress assembled, for the defence of such state, or its trade; nor shall any body of forces be kept up by any state, in time of peace, except such number only, as in the judgment of the united states, in congress assembled, shall be deemed requisite to garrison the forts necessary for the defence of such state; but every state shall always keep up a well regulated and disciplined militia, sufficiently armed and accoutred, and shall provide and constantly have ready for use, in public stores, a due number of field pieces and tents, and a proper quantity of arms, ammunition and camp equipage.

No state shall engage in any war without the consent of the united states in congress assembled, unless such state be actually invaded by enemies, or shall have received certain advice of a resolution being formed by some nation of Indians to invade such state, and the danger is so imminent as not to admit of a delay, till the united states in congress asssembled can be consulted; nor shall any state grant commissions to any ships or vessels of war, nor letters of marque or reprisal, except it be after a declaration of war by the united states in congress assembled, and then only against the kingdom or state and the subjects thereof, against which war has been so declared, and under such regulations as shall be established by the united states in congress assembled, unless such state be infested by pirates; in which case vessels of war may be fitted out for that occasion, and kept so long as the danger shall continue, or until the united states in congress assembled shall determine otherwise.

Art. VII. When land-forces are raised by any state for the common defence, all officers of or under the rank of colonel, shall be appointed by the legislature of each state respectively by whom such forces shall be raised, or in such manner as such state shall direct, and all vacancies shall be filled up by the state which first made the appointment.

Art. VIII. All charges of war, and all other expences that shall be incurred for the common defence or general welfare, and allowed by the united states in congress assembled, shall be defrayed out of a common treasury, which shall be supplied by the several states, in proportion to the value of all land within each state, granted to or surveyed for any Person, as such land and the buildings and improvements thereon shall be estimated according to such mode as the united states in congress assembled, shall from time to time direct and appoint. The taxes for paying that proportion shall be laid and levied by the authority and direction of the legislatures of the several states within the time agreed upon by the united states in congress assembled.

Art. IX. The united states in congress assembled, shall have the sole and exclusive right and power of determining on peace and war, except in the cases mentioned in the sixth article—of sending and receiving ambassadors—entering into treaties and alliances, provided that no treaty of commerce shall be made whereby the legislative power of the respective states shall be restrained from imposing such imposts and duties on foreigners, as their own people are subjected to, or from prohibiting the exportation of any species of goods or commodities whatsoever—of establishing rules for deciding in all cases, what captures on land or water shall be legal, and in what manner prizes taken by land or naval forces in the service of the united states shall be divided or appropriated—of granting letters of marque and reprisal in times of peace—appointing courts for the trial of piracies and felonies committed on the high seas and establishing courts for receiving and determining finally appeals in all cases of captures, provided that no member of congress shall be appointed a judge of any of the said courts.

The united states in congress assembled shall also be the last resort on appeal in all disputes and differences now subsisting or that hereafter may arise between two or more states concerning boundary, jurisdiction or any other cause whatever; which authority shall always be exercised in the manner following. Whenever the legislative or executive authority or lawful agent of any state in controversy with another shall present a petition to congress stating the matter in question and praying for a hearing, notice thereof shall be given by order of congress to the legislative or executive authority of the other state in controversy, and a day assigned for the appearance of the parties by their lawful agents, who shall then be directed to appoint by joint consent, commissioners or judges to constitute a court for hearing and determining the matter in question: but if they cannot agree, congress shall name three persons out of each of the united states, and from the list of such persons each party shall alternately strike out one, the petitioners beginning, until the number shall be reduced to thirteen; and from that number not less than seven, nor more than nine names as congress shall direct, shall in the presence of congress be drawn out by lot, and the persons whose names shall be so drawn or any five of them, shall be commissioners or judges, to hear and finally determine the controversy, so always as a major part of the judges who shall hear the cause shall agree in the determination: and if either party shall neglect to attend at the day appointed, without shewing reasons, which congress shall judge sufficient, or being present shall refuse to strike, the congress shall proceed to nominate three persons out of each state, and the secretary of congress shall strike in behalf of such party absent or refusing; and the judgment and sentence of the court to be appointed, in the manner before prescribed, shall be final and conclusive; and if any of the parties shall refuse to submit to the authority of such court, or to appear to defend their claim or cause, the court shall nevertheless proceed to pronounce sentence, or judgment, which shall in like manner be final and decisive, the judgment or sentence and other proceedings being in either case transmitted to congress, and lodged among the acts of congress for the security of the parties concerned: provided that every commissioner, before he sits in judgment, shall take an oath to be administered by one of the judges of the supreme or superior court of the state, where the cause shall be tried, "well and truly to hear and determine the matter in question, according to the best of his judgment, without favour, affection or hope of reward:" provided also that no state shall be deprived of territory for the benefit of the united states.

All controversies concerning the private right of soil claimed under different grants of two or more states, whose jurisdictions as they may respect such lands, and the states which passed such grants are adjusted, the said grants or either of them being at the same time claimed to have originated antecedent to such settlement of jurisdiction, shall on the petition of either party to the congress of the united states, be finally determined as near as may be in the same manner as is before prescribed for deciding disputes respecting territorial jurisdiction between different states.

The united states in congress assembled shall also have the sole and exclusive right and power of regulating the alloy and value of coin struck by their own authority, or by that of the respective states—fixing the standard of weights and measures throughout the united states—regulating the trade and managing all affairs with the Indians, not members of any of the states, provided that the legislative right of any state within its own limits be not infringed or violated—establishing and regulating post-offices from one state to another, throughout all the united states, and exacting such postage on the papers passing thro' the same as may be requisite to defray the expences of the said office—appointing all officers of the land forces, in the service of the united states, except regimental officers—appointing all the officers of the united states—making rules for the government and regulation of the said land and naval forces, and directing their operations.

The united states in congress assembled shall have the authority to appoint a committee, to sit in the recess of congress, to be denominated "A Committee of the States," and to consist of one delegate from each state; and to appoint such other committees and civil officers as may be necessary for managing the general affairs of the united states under their direction—to appoint one of their number to preside, provided that no person be allowed to serve in the office of president more than one year in any term of three years; to ascertain the necessary sums of Money to be raised for the service of the united states, and to appropriate and apply the same for defraying the public expences—to borrow money, or emit bills on the credit of the united states, transmitting every half year to the respective states an account of the sums of money so borrowed or emitted,—to build and equip a navy—to agree upon the number of land forces, and to make requisitions from each state for its quota, in proportion to the number of white inhabitants in such state; which requisition shall be binding, and thereupon the legislature of each state shall appoint the regimental officers, raise the men and cloath, arm and equip then in a soldier like manner, at the expence of the united states, and the officers and men so cloathed, armed and equipped shall march to the place appointed, and within the time agreed on by the united states in congress assembled: But if the united states in congress assembled shall, on consideration of circumstances judge proper that any state should not raise men, or should raise a smaller number than its quota, and that any other state should raise a greater number of men than the quota thereof, such extra number shall be raised, officered, cloathed, armed and equipped in the same manner as the quota of such state, unless the legislature of such state shall judge that such extra number cannot be safely spared out of the same, in which case they shall raise officer, cloath, arm and equip as many of such extra number as they judge can be safely spared. And the officers and men so cloathed, armed and equipped, shall march to the place appointed, and within the time agreed on by the united states in congress assembled.

The united states in congress assembled shall never engage in a war, nor grant letters of marque and reprisal in time of peace, nor enter into any treaties or alliances, nor coin money, nor regulate the value thereof, nor ascertain the sums and expences necessary for the defence and welfare of the united states, or any of them, nor emit bills, nor borrow money on the credit of the united states, nor appropriate money, nor agree upon the number of vessels of war, to be built or purchased, or the number of land or sea forces to be raised, nor appoint a commander in chief of the army or navy, unless nine states assent to the same: nor shall a question on any other point, except for adjourning from day to day be determined, unless by the votes of a majority of the united states in congress assembled.

The congress of the united states shall have power to adjourn to any time within the year, and to any place within the united states, so that no period of adjournment be for a longer duration than the space of six Months, and shall publish the Journal of their proceedings monthly, except such parts thereof relating to treaties, alliances or military operations as in their judgment require secresy; and the yeas and nays of the delegates of each state on any question shall be entered on the Journal, when it is desired by any delegate; and the delegates of a state, or any of them, at his or their request shall be furnished with a transcript of the said Journal, except such parts as are above excepted to lay before the legislatures of the several states.

Art. X. The committee of the states, or any nine of them, shall be authorised to execute, in the recess of congress, such of the powers of congress as the united states in congress assembled, by the consent of nine states, shall from time to time think expedient to vest them with; provided that no power be delegated to the said committee, for the exercise of which, by the articles of confederation, the voice of nine states in the congress of the united states assembled is requisite.

Art. XI. Canada acceding to this confederation, and joining in the measures of the united states, shall be admitted into, and entitled to all the advantages of this union: but no other colony shall be admitted into the same, unless such admission be agreed to by nine states.

Art. XII. All bills of credit emitted, monies borrowed and debts contracted by, or under the authority of congress, before the assembling of the united states, in pursuance of the present confederation, shall be deemed and considered as a charge against the united states, for payment and satisfaction whereof the said united states and the public faith are hereby solemnly pledged.

Art. XIII. Every state shall abide by the determinations of the united states in congress assembled, on all questions which by this confederation are submitted to them. And the Articles of this confederation shall be inviolably observed by every state, and the union shall be perpetual; nor shall any alteration at any time hereafter be made in any of them; unless such alteration be agreed to in a congress of the united states, and be afterwards confirmed by the legislatures of every state.

AND WHEREAS it hath pleased the Great Governor of the World to incline the hearts of the legislatures we respectively represent in congress, to approve of, and to authorize us to ratify the said articles of confederation and perpetual union. KNOW YE that we the undersigned delegates, by virtue of the power and authority to us given for that purpose, do by these presents, in the name and in behalf of our respective constituents, fully and entirely ratify and confirm each and every of the said articles of confederation and perpetual union, and all and singular the matters and things therein contained: And we do further solemnly plight and engage the faith of our respective constituents, that they shall abide by the determination of the united states in congress assembled, on all questions, which by the said confederation are submitted to them. And that the articles thereof shall be inviolably observed by the states we respectively represent, and that the union shall be perpetual. In Witness whereof we have hereunto set our hands in Congress. Done at Philadelphia in the state of Pennsylvania the ninth Day of July in the Year of our Lord one Thousand seven Hundred and Seventy-eight and in the third year of the independence of America.

# The Constitution of the United States of America

*Annotated with references to the* Federalist Papers

*Federalist Paper* Number and Author

[PREAMBLE]

We the People of the United States, in Order to form a more perfect Union, estab-
84 (Hamilton) lish Justice, insure domestic Tranquility, provide for the common defence, promote
the general Welfare, and secure the Blessings of Liberty to ourselves and our Pos-
terity, do ordain and establish this Constitution for the United States of America.

## ARTICLE I

*Section 1*

[LEGISLATIVE POWERS]

10, 45 (Madison) All legislative Powers herein granted shall be vested in a Congress of the
United States, which shall consist of a Senate and House of Representatives.

*Section 2*

[HOUSE OF REPRESENTATIVES, HOW CONSTITUTED, POWER OF IMPEACHMENT]

39 (Madison) The House of Representatives shall be composed of Members chosen every
45 (Madison) second Year by the People of the several States, and the Electors in each State shall
52–53, 57 (Madison) have the Qualifications requisite for Electors of the most numerous Branch of the
State Legislature.

52 (Madison) No Person shall be a Representative who shall not have attained to the Age of
60 (Hamilton) twenty-five Years, and been seven Years a Citizen of the United States, and who
shall not, when elected, be an inhabitant of that State in which he shall be chosen.

54 (Madison) Representatives and *direct Taxes*[1] shall be apportioned among the several States
which may be included within this Union, according to their respective Numbers,
*which shall be determined by adding to the whole Number of free Persons, including those*
54 (Madison) *bound to Service for a Term of Years,* and excluding Indians not taxed, *three-fifths of all*
*other Persons.*[2] The actual Enumeration shall be made within three Years after the
58 (Madison) first Meeting of the Congress of the United States, and within every subsequent
Term of ten Years, in such Manner as they shall by Law direct. The Number of
Representatives shall not exceed one for every thirty Thousand, but each State shall
55–56 (Madison) have at Least one Representative; *and until such enumeration shall be made, the State*
*of New Hampshire shall be entitled to chuse three, Massachusetts eight, Rhode-Island and*

[1]Modified by Sixteenth Amendment.
[2]Modified by Fourteenth Amendment.

*Providence Plantations one, Connecticut five, New-York six, New Jersey four, Pennsylvania eight, Delaware one, Maryland six, Virginia ten, North Carolina five, South Carolina five, and Georgia three.*[3]

When vacancies happen in the Representation from any State, the Executive Authority thereof shall issue Writs of Election to fill such Vacancies.

79 (Hamilton) The House of Representatives shall chuse their Speaker and other Officers; and shall have the sole Power of Impeachment.

*Section 3*

[THE SENATE, HOW CONSTITUTED, IMPEACHMENT TRIALS]

39, 45 (Madison) 60 (Hamilton) The Senate of the United States shall be composed of two Senators from each State, *chosen by the Legislature thereof,*[4] for six Years; and each Senator shall have one Vote.

62–63 (Madison) 59 (Hamilton) Immediately after they shall be assembled in Consequence of the first Election, they shall be divided as equally as may be into three Classes. The Seats of the Senators of the first Class shall be vacated at the Expiration of the second Year, of the second Class at the Expiration of the fourth Year, and of the third Class at the Expiration of the sixth Year, so that one third may be chosen every second Year:
68 (Hamilton) *and if vacancies happen by Resignation, or otherwise, during the Recess of the Legislature of any State, the Executive thereof may make temporary Appointments until the next Meeting of the Legislature, which shall then fill such Vacancies.*[5]

62 (Madison) 64 (Jay) No person shall be a Senator who shall not have attained to the Age of thirty Years, and been nine Years a Citizen of the United States, and who shall not, when elected, be an Inhabitant of that State for which he shall be chosen.

The Vice-President of the United States shall be President of the Senate, but shall have no Vote, unless they be equally divided.

The Senate shall chuse their other Officers, and also a President pro tempore, in the Absence of the Vice-President, or when he shall exercise the Office of President of the United States.

39 (Madison) 65–67, 79 (Hamilton) 65 (Hamilton) The Senate shall have the sole Power to try all Impeachments. When sitting for that Purpose, they shall be on Oath or Affirmation. When the President of the United States is tried, the Chief Justice shall preside: And no Person shall be convicted without the Concurrence of two-thirds of the Members present.

84 (Hamilton) Judgment in Cases of Impeachment shall not extend further than to removal from Office, and disqualification to hold and enjoy any Office of honor, Trust or Profit under the United States: but the Party convicted shall nevertheless be liable and subject to Indictment, Trial, Judgment and Punishment, according to Law.

*Section 4*

[ELECTION OF SENATORS AND REPRESENTATIVES]

59–61 (Hamilton) The Times, Places and Manner of holding Elections for Senators and Representatives, shall be prescribed in each State by the Legislature thereof; but the Congress may at any time by Law make or alter such Regulations, except as to the Places of chusing Senators.

*The Congress shall assemble at least once in every Year, and such Meeting shall be on the first Monday in December, unless they shall by Law appoint a different Day.*[6]

[3]Temporary provision.

[4]Modified by Seventeenth Amendment.

[5]Modified by Seventeenth Amendment.

[6]Modified by Twentieth Amendment.

*Section 5*

[QUORUM, JOURNALS, MEETINGS, ADJOURNMENTS]

Each House shall be the Judge of the Elections, Returns and Qualifications of its own Members, and a Majority of each shall constitute a Quorum to do Business; but a smaller Number may adjourn from day to day, and may be authorized to compel the Attendance of absent Members, in such Manner, and under the Penalties as each House may provide.

Each House may determine the Rules of its Proceedings, punish its Members for disorderly Behavior, and, with the Concurrence of two-thirds, expel a Member.

Each House shall keep a Journal of its Proceedings, and from time to time publish the same, excepting such Parts as may in their Judgment require Secrecy; and the Yeas and Nays of the Members of either House on any questions shall, at the Desire of one-fifth of the present, be entered on the Journal.

Neither House, during the Session of Congress, shall, without the Consent of the other, adjourn for more than three days, nor to any other Place than that in which the two Houses shall be sitting.

*Section 6*

[COMPENSATION, PRIVILEGES, DISABILITIES]

The Senators and Representatives shall receive a Compensation for their Services, to be ascertained by Law, and paid out of the Treasury of the United States. They shall in all Cases, except Treason, Felony and Breach of the Peace, be privileged from Arrest during their Attendance at the Session of their respective Houses, and in going to and returning from the same; and for any Speech or Debate in either House, they shall not be questioned in any other Place.

55 (Madison) 76 (Hamilton) No Senator or Representative shall, during the time for which he was elected, be appointed to any civil Office under the authority of the United States, which shall have been created, or the Emoluments whereof shall have been encreased during such time; and no Person holding any Office under the United States, shall be a Member of either House during his Continuance in Office.

*Section 7*

[PROCEDURE IN PASSING BILLS AND RESOLUTIONS]

66 (Hamilton) All Bills for raising Revenue shall originate in the House of Representatives; but the Senate may propose or concur with Amendments as on other Bills.

69, 73 (Hamilton) Every Bill which shall have passed the House of Representatives and the Senate, shall, before it become a Law, be presented to the President of the United States; if he approve he shall sign it, but if not he shall return it, with his Objections to that House in which it shall have originated, who shall enter the Objections at large on their Journal, and proceed to reconsider it. If after such Reconsideration two-thirds of that House shall agree to pass the Bill, it shall be sent, together with the Objections, to the other House, by which it shall likewise be reconsidered, and if approved by two-thirds of that House it shall become a Law. But in all such Cases the Votes of both Houses shall be determined by Yeas and Nays, and the Names of the Persons voting for and against the Bill shall be entered on the Journal of each House respectively. If any Bill shall not be returned by the President within ten Days (Sundays excepted) after it shall have been presented to him, the Same shall be a Law, in like Manner as if he had signed it, unless the Congress by their Adjournment prevent its Return, in which Case it shall not be a Law.

69, 73 (Hamilton) Every Order, Resolution, or Vote to which the Concurrence of the Senate and House of Representatives may be necessary (except on a question of Adjournment) shall be presented to the President of the United States; and before the Same shall take Effect, shall be approved by him, or being disapproved by him, shall be repassed by two-thirds of the Senate and House of Representatives, according to the Rules and Limitations prescribed in the Case of a Bill.

*Section 8*

[POWERS OF CONGRESS]

The Congress shall have Power

30–36 (Hamilton) 41 (Madison) To lay and collect Taxes, Duties, Imposts and Excises, to pay the Debts and provide for the common Defence and general Welfare of the United States; but all Duties, Imposts and excises shall be uniform throughout the United States;

56 (Madison) To borrow Money on the Credit of the United States;

42, 45, 56 (Madison) To regulate Commerce with foreign Nations, and among the several States, and with the Indian Tribes;

32 (Hamilton) 42 (Madison) To establish an uniform Rule of Naturalization, and uniform Laws on the subject of Bankruptcies throughout the United States;

42 (Madison) To coin Money, regulate the Value thereof, and of foreign Coin, and fix the Standard of Weights and Measures;

42 (Madison) To provide for the Punishment of counterfeiting the Securities and current Coin of the United States;

42 (Madison) To establish Post Offices and post Roads;

42 (Madison) 43 (Madison) To promote the Progress of Science and useful Arts, by securing for limited Times to Authors and Inventors the exclusive Right to their respective Writings and Discoveries;

81 (Hamilton) To constitute Tribunals inferior to the supreme Court;

42 (Madison) To define and Punish Piracies and Felonies committed on the high Seas, and Offences against the Law of Nations;

41 (Madison) To declare War, grant Letters of Marque and Reprisal, and make Rules concerning Captures on Land and Water;

23, 24, 26 (Hamilton) To raise and support Armies, but no Appropriation of Money to that Use shall be for a longer Term than two Years;

41 (Madison) To provide and maintain a Navy;

To make Rules for the Government and Regulation of the land and naval forces;

29 (Hamilton) To provide for calling for the Militia to execute the Laws of the Union, suppress Insurrections and repel Invasions;

29 (Hamilton) 56 (Madison) To provide for organizing, arming, and disciplining, the Militia, and for governing such Part of them as may be employed in the Service of the United States, reserving to the States respectively, the Appointment of the Officers, and the Authority of training the Militia according to the discipline prescribed by Congress;

32 (Hamilton) 43 (Madison) To exercise exclusive Legislation in all Cases whatsoever, over such District (not exceeding ten Miles square) as may, by Cession of particular States, and the Acceptance of Congress, become the Seat of the Government of the United States, and 43 (Madison) to exercise like Authority over all Places purchased by the Consent of the Legislature of the State in which the Same shall be, for the Erection of Forts, Magazines, Arsenals, dock-Yards, and other needful Buildings;—And

29, 33 (Hamilton) 44 (Madison) To make all Laws which shall be necessary and proper for carrying into Execution the foregoing Powers, and all other Powers vested by this Constitution in the Government of the United States, or in any Department or Officer thereof.

*Section 9*

[SOME RESTRICTIONS ON FEDERAL POWER]

42 (Madison) *The Migration or Importation of such Persons as any of the States now existing shall think proper to admit, shall not be prohibited by the Congress prior to the Year one thousand eight hundred and eight, but a Tax or Duty may be imposed on such Importation, not exceeding ten dollars for each Person.*[7]

83, 84 (Hamilton) The privilege of the Writ of *Habeas Corpus* shall not be suspended, unless when in Cases of Rebellion or Invasion the public Safety may require it.

84 (Hamilton) No Bill of Attainder or ex post facto Law shall be passed.

*No Capitation, or other direct, Tax shall be laid, unless in Proportion to the Census or Enumeration herein before directed to be taken.*[8]

No Tax or Duty shall be laid on Articles exported from any State.

32 (Hamilton) No Preference shall be given by any Regulation of Commerce or Revenue to the Ports of one State over those of another; nor shall vessels bound to, or from, one State, be obliged to enter, clear, or pay Duties in another.

No Money shall be drawn from the Treasury, but in Consequence of Appropriations made by Law; and a regular Statement and Account of the Receipts and Expenditures of all public Money shall be published from time to time.

39 (Madison) 84 (Hamilton) No Title of Nobility shall be granted by the United States: And no Person holding any Office of Profit or Trust under them, shall, without the Consent of the Congress, accept of any present, Emolument, Office or Title, of any kind whatever, from any King, Prince, or foreign State.

*Section 10*

[RESTRICTIONS UPON POWERS OF STATES]

33 (Hamilton) 44 (Madison) No State shall enter into any Treaty, Alliance, or Confederation; grant Letters of Marque and Reprisal; coin Money; emit Bills of Credit; make any Thing but gold and silver Coin a Tender in Payment of Debts; pass any Bill of Attainder, ex post facto Law, or Law impairing the Obligation of Contracts, or grant any Title of Nobility.

32 (Hamilton) 44 (Madison) No State shall, without the Consent of the Congress, lay any Imposts or Duties on Imports or Exports, except what may be absolutely necessary for executing its inspection Laws: and the net Produce of all Duties and Imposts, laid by any State on Imports or Exports, shall be for the Use of the Treasury of the United States; and all such Laws shall be subject to the Revision and Control of the Congress.

No State shall, without the Consent of Congress, lay any Duty of Tonnage, keep Troops, or Ships of War in time of Peace, enter into any Agreement or Compact with another State, or with a foreign Power, or engage in War, unless actually invaded, or in such imminent Danger as will not admit of Delay.

## ARTICLE II

*Section 1*

[EXECUTIVE POWER, ELECTION, QUALIFICATIONS OF THE PRESIDENT]

39 (Madison) 70, 71, 84 (Hamilton) The executive Power shall be vested in a President of the United States of America. *He shall hold his Office during the Term of four years and, together with the Vice-President, chosen for the same Term, be elected, as follows:*[9]

[7]Temporary provision.

[8]Modified by Sixteenth Amendment.

[9]Number of terms limited to two by Twenty-second Amendment.

69, 71 (Hamilton) 39, 45 (Madison) 68, 77 (Hamilton) Each State shall appoint, in such Manner as the Legislature thereof may direct, a Number of Electors, equal to the whole Number of Senators and Representatives to which the State may be entitled in the Congress: but no Senator or Representative, or Person holding an Office of Trust or Profit under the United States, shall be appointed an Elector.

*The electors shall meet in their respective States, and vote by ballot for two Persons, of whom one at least shall not be an Inhabitant of the same State with themselves. And they shall make a List of all the Persons voted for, and of the Number of Votes for each; which List they shall sign and certify, and transmit sealed to the Seat of the Government of the United States, directed to the President of the Senate. The President of the Senate shall,*
66 (Hamilton) *in the Presence of the Senate and House of Representatives, open all the Certificates, and the Votes shall then be counted. The Person having the greatest Number of Votes shall be the President, if such Number be a Majority of the whole Number of Electors appointed; and if there be more than one who have such Majority and have an equal Number of Votes, then the House of Representatives shall immediately chuse by Ballot one of them for President; and if no person have a Majority, then from the five highest on the List the said House shall in like Manner chuse the President. But in chusing the President, the Votes shall be taken by States, the Representation from each State having one Vote; A quorum for this Purpose shall consist of a Member or Members from two-thirds of the States, and a Majority of all the States shall be necessary to a Choice. In every Case, after the Choice of the President, the person having the greatest Number of Votes of the Electors shall be the Vice-President. But if there should remain two or more who have equal vote, the Senate shall chuse from them by Ballot the Vice-President.*[10]

The Congress may determine the Time of chusing the Electors, and the Day on which they shall give their Votes; which Day shall be the same throughout the United States.

No Person except a natural born Citizen, or a Citizen of the United States, at the time of the Adoption of this Constitution, shall be eligible to the Office of President; neither shall any Person be eligible to that Office who shall not have attained
64 (Jay) to the Age of thirty-five Years, and been fourteen Years a Resident within the United States.

In Case of the Removal of the President from Office, or his Death, Resignation, or Inability to discharge the Powers and Duties of the said Office, the same shall devolve on the Vice-President, and the Congress may by Law provide for the Case of Removal, Death, Resignation, or Inability, both of the President and Vice-President, declaring what Officer shall then act as President, and such Officer shall act accordingly, until the Disability be removed, or a President shall be elected.

73, 79 (Hamilton) The President shall, at stated Times, receive for his Services, a Compensation, which shall neither be encreased nor diminished during the Period for which he shall have been elected, and he shall not receive within that Period any other Emolument from the United States, or any of them.

Before he enter on the Execution of his Office, he shall take the following Oath or Affirmation:—"I do solemnly swear (or affirm) that I will faithfully execute the Office of President of the United States, and will to the best of my Ability, preserve, protect and defend the Constitution of the United States."

### *Section 2*

[POWERS OF THE PRESIDENT]

69, 74 (Hamilton) The President shall be Commander in Chief of the Army and Navy of the United States, and of the Militia of the several States, when called into the ac-

[10]Modified by Twelfth and Twentieth Amendments.

tual Service of the United States; he may require the Opinion, in writing, of the
74 (Hamilton) principal Officer in each of the executive Departments, upon any Subject relating
69 (Hamilton) to the Duties of their respective Offices, and he shall have Power to grant Reprieves and Pardons for Offences against the United States, except in Cases of
74 (Hamilton) Impeachment.

42 (Madison) He shall have Power, by and with the Advice and Consent of the Senate, to
64 (Jay) make Treaties, provided two-thirds of the Senators present concur; and he shall
66 (Hamilton) nominate, and by and with the Advice and Consent of the Senate, shall appoint
42 (Madison) Ambassadors, other public Ministers and Consuls, Judges of the Supreme Court,
66, 69, 76, 77 (Hamilton) and all other Officers of the United States, whose Appointments are not herein
otherwise provided for, and which shall be established by Law: but the Congress
may by Law vest the Appointment of such inferior Officers, as they think proper,
in the President alone, in the Courts of Law, or in the Heads of Departments.

67, 76 (Hamilton) The President shall have Power to fill up all Vacancies that may happen during
the Recess of the Senate, by granting Commissions which shall expire at the End
of their next Session.

*Section 3*

[POWERS AND DUTIES OF THE PRESIDENT]

77 (Hamilton) He shall from time to time give to the Congress Information of the State of the
69, 77 (Hamilton) Union, and recommend to their Consideration such Measures as he shall judge
necessary and expedient; he may, on extraordinary Occasions, convene both
77 (Hamilton) Houses, or either of them, and in Case of Disagreement between them, with Re-
69, 77 (Hamilton) spect to the Time of Adjournment, he may adjourn them to such Time as he shall
42 (Madison) think proper; he shall receive Ambassadors and other public Ministers; he shall
69, 77 (Hamilton) take Care that the Laws be faithfully executed, and shall Commission all the Officers of the United States.
78 (Hamilton)

*Section 4*

[IMPEACHMENT]

39 (Madison) The President, Vice-President and all civil Officers of the United States shall be
69 (Hamilton) removed from Office on Impeachment for, and Conviction of, Treason, Bribery, or
other high Crimes and Misdemeanors.

## ARTICLE III

*Section 1*

[JUDICIAL POWER, TENURE OF OFFICE]

81, 82 (Hamilton) The judicial Power of the United States, shall be vested in one supreme Court,
65 (Hamilton) and in such inferior Courts as the Congress may from time to time ordain and establish. The Judges, both of the supreme and inferior Courts, shall hold their Of-
78, 79 (Hamilton) fices during good Behavior, and shall, at stated Times, receive for their Services, a
Compensation, which shall not be diminished during their Continuance in Office.

*Section 2*

[JURISDICTION]

80 (Hamilton) The judicial Power shall extend to all Cases, in Law and Equity, arising under
this Constitution, the Laws of the United States, and Treaties made, or which shall
be made, under their Authority;—to all Cases affecting Ambassadors, other public
Ministers and Consuls;—to all Cases of admiralty and maritime Jurisdiction;—to

Controversies to which the United States shall be a party;—to Controversies between two or more States;*—between a State and Citizens of another State;*—between Citizens of different States,—between Citizens of the same State claiming Lands under Grants of different States, *and between a State,* or the Citizens thereof, *and foreign States, Citizens or Subjects.*[11]

81 (Hamilton) In all Cases affecting Ambassadors, other public Ministers and Consuls, and those in which a State shall be Party, the supreme Court shall have original Jurisdiction. In all the other Cases before mentioned, the supreme Court shall have appellate Jurisdiction, both as to Law and Fact, with such Exceptions, and under such Regulations as Congress shall make.

83, 84 (Hamilton) The Trial of all Crimes, except in Cases of Impeachment, shall be by Jury; and such Trial shall be held in the State where the said Crimes shall have been committed; but when not committed within any State, the Trial shall be at such Place or Places as the Congress may by Law have directed.

### *Section 3*

[TREASON, PROOF, AND PUNISHMENT]

43 (Madison) 84 (Hamilton) Treason against the United States, shall consist only in levying War against them, or in adhering to their Enemies, giving them Aid and Comfort. No Person shall be convicted of Treason unless on the Testimony of two Witnesses to the same overt Act, or on Confession in open Court.

43 (Madison) 84 (Hamilton) The Congress shall have Power to declare the Punishment of Treason, but no Attainder of Treason shall work Corruption of Blood, or Forfeiture except during the Life of the Person attained.

## ARTICLE IV

### *Section 1*

[FAITH AND CREDIT AMONG STATES]

42 (Madison) Full Faith and Credit shall be given in each State to the public Acts, Records, and judicial Proceedings of every other State. And the Congress may by general Laws prescribe the Manner in which such Acts, Records and Proceedings shall be proved, and the Effect thereof.

### *Section 2*

[PRIVILEGES AND IMMUNITIES, FUGITIVES]

80 (Hamilton) The Citizens of each State shall be entitled to all Privileges and Immunities of Citizens in the several States.

A person charged in any State with Treason, Felony or other Crime, who shall flee from Justice, and be found in another State, shall on Demand of the executive Authority of the State from which he fled, be delivered up to be removed to the State having Jurisdiction of the Crime.

*No person held to Service or Labour in one State, under the Laws thereof, escaping into another, shall, in Consequence of any Law or Regulation therein, be discharged from such Service or Labour, but shall be delivered up on Claim of the Party to whom such Service or Labour may be due.*[12]

[11]Modified by Eleventh Amendment.

[12]Repealed by the Thirteenth Amendment.

*Section 3*

[ADMISSION OF NEW STATES]

43 (Madison) New States may be admitted by the Congress into this Union; but no new State shall be formed or erected within the Jurisdiction of any other State; nor any State be formed by the Junction of two or more States, or Parts of States, without the Consent of the Legislatures of the States concerned as well as of the Congress.

43 (Madison) The Congress shall have Power to dispose of and make all needful Rules and Regulations respecting the Territory or other Property belonging to the United States; and nothing in this Constitution shall be so construed as to Prejudice any Claims of the United States, or of any particular State.

*Section 4*

[GUARANTEE OF REPUBLICAN GOVERNMENT]

39, 43 (Madison) The United States shall guarantee to every State in this Union a Republican Form of Government, and shall protect each of them against Invasion; and on Application of the Legislature, or of the Executive (when the Legislature cannot be convened) against domestic Violence.

## ARTICLE V

[AMENDMENT OF THE CONSTITUTION]

39, 43 (Madison) 85 (Hamilton) The Congress, whenever two-thirds of both Houses shall deem it necessary, shall propose Amendments to this Constitution, or, on the Application of the Legislatures of two-thirds of the several States, shall call a Convention for proposing Amendments, which, in either Case, shall be valid to all Intents and Purposes, as Part of this Constitution, when ratified by the Legislatures of three-fourths of the several States, or by Conventions in three-fourths thereof, as the one or the other Mode of Ratification may be proposed by the Congress; *Provided that no Amendment which may be made prior to the Year One thousand eight hundred and eight shall in any Manner affect the first and fourth Clauses in the Ninth Section of the first Article;*[13]
43 (Madison) and that no State, without its Consent, shall be deprived of its equal Suffrage in the Senate.

## ARTICLE VI

[DEBTS, SUPREMACY, OATH]

43 (Madison) All Debts contracted and Engagements entered into, before the Adoption of this Constitution, shall be as valid against the United States under this Constitution, as under the Confederation.

27, 33 (Hamilton) 39, 44 (Madison) This Constitution, and the Laws of the United States which shall be made in Pursuance thereof; and all Treaties made, or which shall be made, under the Authority of the United States, shall be the supreme Law of the Land; and the Judges in every State shall be bound thereby, any Thing in the Constitution or Laws of any State to the Contrary notwithstanding.

27 (Hamilton) 44 (Madison) The Senators and Representatives before mentioned, and the Members of the several State Legislatures, and all executive and judicial Officers, both of the United States and of the several States, shall be bound by Oath or Affirmation, to

[13]Temporary provision.

support this Constitution; but no religious Test shall be required as a Qualification to any Office or public Trust under the United States.

## ARTICLE VII

[RATIFICATION AND ESTABLISHMENT]

39, 40, 43 (Madison) The Ratification of the Conventions of nine States, shall be sufficient for the Establishment of this Constitution between the States so ratifying the Same.[14]

Done in Convention by the Unanimous Consent of the States present the Seventeenth Day of September in the Year of our Lord one thousand seven hundred and Eighty seven and of the Independence of the United States of America the Twelfth. *In Witness* whereof We have hereunto subscribed our Names,

G:o WASHINGTON—
*Presidt, and Deputy*
*from Virginia*

| | | | |
|---|---|---|---|
| New Hampshire | JOHN LANGDON<br>NICHOLAS GILMAN | Delaware | GEO READ<br>GUNNING BEDFOR JUN<br>JOHN DICKINSON<br>RICHARD BASSETT<br>JACO: BROOM |
| Massachusetts | NATHANIEL GORHAM<br>RUFUS KING | | |
| Connecticut | WM SAML JOHNSON<br>ROGER SHERMAN | Maryland | JAMES MCHENRY<br>DAN OF ST THOS. JENIFER<br>DANL CARROLL |
| New York | ALEXANDER HAMILTON | | |
| New Jersey | WIL: LIVINGSTON<br>DAVID BREARLEY<br>WM PATERSON<br>JONA: DAYTON | Virginia | JOHN BLAIR—<br>JAMES MADISON JR. |
| | | North Carolina | WM BLOUNT<br>RICHD DOBBS SPAIGHT<br>HU WILLIAMSON |
| Pennsylvania | B FRANKLIN<br>THOMAS MIFFLIN<br>ROBT MORRIS<br>GEO. CLYMER<br>THOS. FITZSIMONS<br>JARED INGERSOLL<br>JAMES WILSON<br>GOUV MORRIS | South Carolina | J. RUTLEDGE<br>CHARLES COTESWORTH PINCKNEY<br>CHARLES PINCKNEY<br>PIERCE BUTLER |
| | | Georgia | WILLIAM FEW<br>ABR BALDWIN |

[14]The Constitution was submitted on September 17, 1787, by the Constitutional Convention, was ratified by the conventions of several states at various dates up to May 29, 1790, and became effective on March 4, 1789.

# Amendments to the Constitution

*Proposed by Congress and Ratified by the Legislatures of the Several States, Pursuant to Article V of the Original Constitution.*

*Amendments I-X, known as the Bill of Rights, were proposed by Congress on September 25, 1789, and ratified on December 15, 1791.* Federalist Papers *comments, mainly in opposition to a Bill of Rights, can be found in #84 (Hamilton).*

## AMENDMENT I

[FREEDOM OF RELIGION, OF SPEECH, AND OF THE PRESS]

Congress shall make no law respecting an establishment of religion, or prohibiting the free exercise thereof; or abridging the freedom of speech, or of the press; or the right of the people peaceably to assemble, and to petition the Government for a redress of grievances.

## AMENDMENT II

[RIGHT TO KEEP AND BEAR ARMS]

A well regulated Militia, being necessary to the security of a free State, the right of the people to keep and bear Arms, shall not be infringed.

## AMENDMENT III

[QUARTERING OF SOLDIERS]

No Soldier shall, in time of peace be quartered in any house, without the consent of the Owner, nor in time of war, but in a manner to be prescribed by law.

## AMENDMENT IV

[SECURITY FROM UNWARRANTABLE SEARCH AND SEIZURE]

The right of the people to be secure in their persons, houses, papers, and effects, against unreasonable searches and seizures, shall not be violated, and no Warrants shall issue, but upon probable cause, supported by Oath or affirmation, and particularly describing the place to be searched, and the persons or things to be seized.

## AMENDMENT V

[RIGHTS OF ACCUSED PERSONS IN CRIMINAL PROCEEDINGS]

No person shall be held to answer for a capital, or otherwise infamous crime, unless on a presentment or indictment of a Grand Jury, except in cases arising in the land or naval forces, or in the Militia, when in actual service in time of War or in public danger; nor shall any person be subject for the same offence to be twice put in jeopardy of life or limb; nor shall be compelled in any Criminal Case to be a witness against himself, nor be deprived of life, liberty, or property, without due process of law; nor shall private property be taken for public use, without just compensation.

## Amendment VI

[RIGHT TO SPEEDY TRIAL, WITNESSES, ETC.]

In all criminal prosecutions, the accused shall enjoy the right to a speedy and public trial, by an impartial jury of the State and district wherein the crime shall have been committed, which district shall have been previously ascertained by law, and to be informed of the nature and cause of the accusation; to be confronted with the witnesses against him; to have compulsory process for obtaining Witnesses in his favor, and to have the Assistance of Counsel for his defence.

## Amendment VII

[TRIAL BY JURY IN CIVIL CASES]

In suits at common law, where the value in controversy shall exceed twenty dollars, the right of trial by jury shall be preserved, and no fact tried by a jury shall be otherwise re-examined in any Court of the United States, than according to the rules of the common law.

## Amendment VIII

[BAILS, FINES, PUNISHMENTS]

Excessive bail shall not be required, nor excessive fines imposed, nor cruel and unusual punishments inflicted.

## Amendment IX

[RESERVATION OF RIGHTS OF PEOPLE]

The enumeration in the Constitution, of certain rights, shall not be construed to deny or disparage others retained by the people.

## Amendment X

[POWERS RESERVED TO STATES OR PEOPLE]

The powers not delegated to the United States by the Constitution, nor prohibited by it to the States, are reserved to the States respectively, or to the people.

## Amendment XI

*[Proposed by Congress on March 4, 1794; declared ratified on January 8, 1798.]*

[RESTRICTION OF JUDICIAL POWER]

The Judicial power of the United States shall not be construed to extend to any suit in law or equity, commenced or prosecuted against one of the United States by Citizens of another State, or by Citizens or Subjects of any Foreign State.

## Amendment XII

*[Proposed by Congress on December 9, 1803; declared ratified on September 25, 1804.]*

[ELECTION OF PRESIDENT AND VICE-PRESIDENT]

The Electors shall meet in their respective states, and vote by ballot for President and Vice-President, one of whom, at least, shall not be an inhabitant of the same state with themselves; they shall name in their ballots the person voted for as President, and in distinct ballots the person voted for as Vice-President, and they shall make distinct lists of all persons voted for as President, and of all persons voted for as Vice-President, and of the number of votes for each, which lists they shall sign and certify, and transmit sealed to the seat of the government of the United States, directed to the President of the Senate;—The President of the Senate shall, in presence of the Senate and House of Representatives, open all the certificates and the votes shall then be counted;—The person having the greatest number of votes for President, shall be the President, if such number be a majority of the whole number of Electors appointed; and if no person have such majority, then from the persons having the highest numbers not exceeding three on the list of those voted for as President, the House of Representatives shall choose immediately, by ballot, the President. But in choosing the President, the votes shall be taken by states, the representation from each state having one vote; a quorum for this purpose shall consist of a member or members from two-thirds of the states, and a majority of all states shall be necessary to a choice. And if the House of Representatives shall not choose a President whenever the right of choice shall devolve upon them, before the fourth day of March next following, then the Vice-President, shall act as President, as in the case of the death or other constitutional disability of the President. The person having the greatest number of votes as Vice-President, shall be the Vice-President, if such a number be a majority of the whole number of Electors appointed, and if no person have a majority, then from the two highest numbers on the list, the Senate shall choose the Vice-President; a quorum for the purpose shall consist of two-thirds of the whole number of Senators, and a majority of the whole number shall be necessary to a choice. But no person constitutionally ineligible to the office of President shall be eligible to that of Vice-President of the United States.

## Amendment XIII

*[Proposed by Congress on January 31, 1865; declared ratified on December 18, 1865.]*

*Section 1*

[ABOLITION OF SLAVERY]

Neither slavery nor involuntary servitude, except as a punishment for crime whereof the party shall have been duly convicted, shall exist within the United States, or any place subject to their jurisdiction.

*Section 2*

[POWER TO ENFORCE THIS ARTICLE]

Congress shall have power to enforce this article by appropriate legislation.

## Amendment XIV

*[Proposed by Congress on June 13, 1866, declared ratified on July 28, 1868.]*

*Section 1*

[CITIZENSHIP RIGHTS NOT TO BE ABRIDGED BY STATES]

All persons born or naturalized in the United States, and subject to the jurisdiction thereof, are citizens of the United States and of the State wherein they reside. No state shall make or enforce any law which shall abridge the privileges or immunities of citizens of the United States; nor shall any State deprive any person of life, liberty, or property, without due process of law; nor deny to any person within its jurisdiction the equal protection of the laws.

*Section 2*

[APPORTIONMENT OF REPRESENTATIVES IN CONGRESS]

Representatives shall be apportioned among the several States according to their respective numbers, counting the whole number of persons in each State, excluding Indians not taxed. But when the right to vote at any election for the choice of electors for President and Vice-President of the United States, Representatives in Congress, the Executive and Judicial officers of a State, or the members of the Legislature thereof, is denied to any of the male inhabitants of such State, being twenty-one years of age, and citizens of the United States, or in any way abridged, except for participation in rebellion, or other crime, the basis of representation therein shall be reduced in the proportion which the number of such male citizens shall bear to the whole number of male citizens twenty-one years of age in such State.

*Section 3*

[PERSONS DISQUALIFIED FROM HOLDING OFFICE]

No person shall be a Senator or Representative in Congress, or elector of President and Vice-President, or hold any office, civil or military, under the United States, or under any State, who, having previously taken an oath, as a member of Congress, or as an officer of the United States, or as a member of any State legislature, or as an executive or judicial officer of any State, to support the Constitution of the United States, shall have engaged in insurrection or rebellion against the same, or given aid or comfort to the enemies thereof. But Congress may by a vote of two-thirds of each House, remove such disability.

*Section 4*

[WHAT PUBLIC DEBTS ARE VALID]

The validity of the public debt of the United States, authorized by law, including debts incurred for payment of pensions and bounties for services in suppressing insurrection or rebellion, shall not be questioned. But neither the United States nor any State shall assume or pay any debt or obligation incurred in aid of insurrection or rebellion against the United States, or any claim for the loss or emancipation of any slave; but all such debts, obligations and claims shall be held illegal and void.

*Section 5*

[POWER TO ENFORCE THIS ARTICLE]

The Congress shall have power to enforce, by appropriate legislation, the provisions of this article.

## AMENDMENT XV

*[Proposed by Congress on February 26, 1869; declared ratified on March 30, 1870.]*

*Section 1*

[NEGRO SUFFRAGE]

The right of citizens of the United States to vote shall not be denied or abridged by the United States or by any State on account of race, color, or previous condition of servitude.

*Section 2*

[POWER TO ENFORCE THIS ARTICLE]

The Congress shall have power to enforce this article by appropriate legislation.

## AMENDMENT XVI

*[Proposed by Congress on July 12, 1909; declared ratified on February 25, 1913.]*

[AUTHORIZING INCOME TAXES]

The Congress shall have power to lay and collect taxes on incomes, from whatever source derived, without apportionment among the several States, and without regard to any census or enumeration.

## AMENDMENT XVII

*[Proposed by Congress on May 13, 1912; declared ratified on May 31, 1913.]*

[POPULAR ELECTION OF SENATORS]

The Senate of the United States shall be composed of two Senators from each State, elected by the people thereof, for six years; and each Senator shall have one vote. The electors in each State shall have the qualifications requisite for electors of the most numerous branch of the State Legislature.

When vacancies happen in the representation of any State in the Senate, the executive authority of such State shall issue writs of election to fill such vacancies: Provided, That the Legislature of any State may empower the executive thereof to make temporary appointment until the people fill the vacancies by election as the Legislature may direct.

This amendment shall not be so construed as to affect the election or term of any Senator chosen before it becomes valid as part of the Constitution.

## AMENDMENT XVIII

*[Proposed by Congress December 18, 1917; declared ratified on January 29, 1919.]*

*Section 1*

[NATIONAL LIQUOR PROHIBITION]

*After one year from the ratification of this article the manufacture, sale, or transportation of intoxicating liquors within, the importation thereof into, or the exportation thereof from the United States and all territory subject to the jurisdiction thereof for beverage purposes is hereby prohibited.*

*Section 2*

[POWER TO ENFORCE THIS ARTICLE]

*The Congress and the several states shall have concurrent power to enforce this article by appropriate legislation.*

*Section 3*

[RATIFICATION WITHIN SEVEN YEARS]

*This article shall be inoperative unless it shall have been ratified as an amendment to the Constitution by the legislatures of the several states, as provided in the Constitution, within seven years from the date of the submission hereof to the states by the Congress.*[15]

[15]Repealed by the Twenty-first Amendment

## Amendment XIX

*[Proposed by Congress on June 4, 1919; declared ratified on August 26, 1920.]*

[WOMAN SUFFRAGE]

The right of the citizens of the United States to vote shall not be denied or abridged by the United States or by any state on account of sex.

Congress shall have power, by appropriate legislation, to enforce this article by appropriate legislation.

## Amendment XX

*[Proposed by Congress on March 2, 1932; declared ratified on February 6, 1933.]*

### *Section 1*

[TERMS OF OFFICE]

The terms of the President and Vice-President shall end at noon on the 20th day of January, and the terms of the Senators and Representatives at noon on the 3rd day of January, of the years in which such terms would have ended if this article had not been ratified; and the terms of their successors shall then begin.

### *Section 2*

[TIME OF CONVENING CONGRESS]

The Congress shall assemble at least once in every year, and such meeting shall begin at noon on the 3rd day of January, unless they shall by law appoint a different day.

### *Section 3*

[DEATH OF PRESIDENT-ELECT]

If, at the time fixed for the beginning of the term of the President, the President-elect shall have died, the Vice-President-elect shall become President. If a President shall not have been chosen before the time fixed for the beginning of his term, or if the President-elect shall have failed to qualify, then the Vice-President-elect shall act as President until a President shall have qualified; and the Congress may by law provide for the case wherein neither a President-elect nor a Vice-President-elect shall have qualified, declaring who shall then act as President, or the manner in which one who is to act shall be selected, and such person shall act accordingly until a President or Vice President shall have qualified.

### *Section 4*

[ELECTION OF THE PRESIDENT]

The Congress may by law provide for the case of the death of any of the persons from whom the House of Representatives may choose a President whenever the right of choice shall have devolved upon them, and for the case of the death of any of the persons from whom the Senate may choose a Vice-President whenever the right of choice shall have devolved upon them.

### *Section 5*

[AMENDMENT TAKES EFFECT]

Sections 1 and 2 shall take effect on the 15th day of October following ratification of this article.

*Section 6*

[RATIFICATION WITHIN SEVEN YEARS]

This article shall be inoperative unless it shall have been ratified as an amendment to the Constitution by the legislatures of three-fourths of the several States within seven years from the date of its submission.

## AMENDMENT XXI

*[Proposed by Congress on February 20, 1933; declared ratified on December 5, 1933.]*

*Section 1*

[NATIONAL LIQUOR PROHIBITION REPEALED]

The eighteenth article of amendment to the Constitution of the United States is hereby repealed.

*Section 2*

[TRANSPORTATION OF LIQUOR INTO "DRY" STATES]

The transportation or importation into any State, Territory, or Possession of the United States for delivery or use therein of intoxicating liquors, in violation of the laws thereof, is hereby prohibited.

*Section 3*

[RATIFICATION WITHIN SEVEN YEARS]

This article shall be inoperative unless it shall have been ratified as an amendment to the Constitution by conventions in the several States, as provided in the Constitution, within seven years from the date of the submission hereof to the States by the Congress.

## AMENDMENT XXII

*[Proposed by Congress on March 21, 1947; declared ratified on February 26, 1951.]*

*Section 1*

[TENURE OF PRESIDENT LIMITED]

No person shall be elected to the office of President more than twice, and no person who has held the office of President or acted as President for more than two years of a term to which some other person was elected President shall be elected to the Office of the President more than once. But this Article shall not apply to any person holding the office of President when this Article was proposed by the Congress, and shall not prevent any person who may be holding the office of President, or acting as President, during the term within which this Article becomes operative from holding the office of President or acting as President during the remainder of such term.

*Section 2*

[RATIFICATION WITHIN SEVEN YEARS]

This Article shall be inoperative unless it shall have been ratified as an amendment to the Constitution by the legislatures of three-fourths of the several states within seven years from the date of its submission to the States by the Congress.

## Amendment XXIII

*[Proposed by Congress on June 21, 1960; declared ratified on March 29, 1961.]*

*Section 1*

[ELECTORAL COLLEGE VOTES FOR THE DISTRICT OF COLUMBIA]

The District constituting the seat of Government of the United States shall appoint in such manner as the Congress may direct:

A number of electors of President and Vice-President equal to the whole number of Senators and Representatives in Congress to which the District would be entitled if it were a State, but in no event more than the least populous State; they shall be in addition to those appointed by the States, but they shall be considered, for the purposes of the election of President and Vice-President, to be electors appointed by a State; and they shall meet in the District and perform such duties as provided by the twelfth article of amendment.

*Section 2*

[POWER TO ENFORCE THIS ARTICLE]

The Congress shall have power to enforce this article by appropriate legislation.

## Amendment XXIV

*[Proposed by Congress on August 27, 1963; declared ratified on January 23, 1964.]*

*Section 1*

[ANTI-POLL TAX]

The right of citizens of the United States to vote in any primary or other election for President or Vice-President, for electors for President or Vice-President, or for Senator or Representative of Congress, shall not be denied or abridged by the United States or any State by reasons of failure to pay any poll tax or other tax.

*Section 2*

[POWER TO ENFORCE THIS ARTICLE]

The Congress shall have power to enforce this article by appropriate legislation.

## Amendment XXV

*[Proposed by Congress on July 7, 1965; declared ratified on February 10, 1967.]*

*Section 1*

[VICE-PRESIDENT TO BECOME PRESIDENT]

In case of the removal of the President from office or his death or resignation, the Vice-President shall become President.

*Section 2*

[CHOICE OF A NEW VICE-PRESIDENT]

Whenever there is a vacancy in the office of the Vice-President, the President shall nominate a Vice-President who shall take the office upon confirmation by a majority vote of both houses of Congress.

*Section 3*

[PRESIDENT MAY DECLARE OWN DISABILITY]

Whenever the President transmits to the President pro tempore of the Senate and the Speaker of the House of Representatives his written declaration that he is unable to discharge the powers and duties of his office, and until he transmits to them a written declaration to the contrary, such powers and duties shall be discharged by the Vice-President as Acting President.

*Section 4*

[ALTERNATE PROCEDURES TO DECLARE AND TO END PRESIDENTIAL DISABILITY]

Whenever the Vice-President and a majority of either the principal officers of the executive departments, or of such other body as Congress may by law provide, transmit to the President pro tempore of the Senate and the Speaker of the House of Representatives their written declaration that the President is unable to discharge the powers and duties of his office, the Vice-President shall immediately assume the powers and duties of the office as Acting President.

Thereafter, when the President transmits to the President pro tempore of the Senate and the Speaker of the House of Representatives his written declaration that no inability exists, he shall resume the powers and duties of his office unless the Vice-President and a majority of either the principal officers of the executive departments, or of such other body as Congress may by law provide, transmit within four days to the President pro tempore of the Senate and the Speaker of the House of Representatives their written declaration that the President is unable to discharge the powers and duties of his office. Thereupon Congress shall decide the issue, assembling within 48 hours for that purpose if not in session. If the Congress, within 21 days after receipt of the latter written declaration, or, if Congress is not in session, within 21 days after Congress is required to assemble, determines by two-thirds vote of both houses that the President is unable to discharge the powers and duties of his office, the Vice-President shall continue to discharge the same as Acting President; otherwise, the President shall resume the powers and duties of his office.

## AMENDMENT XXVI

*[Proposed by Congress on March 23, 1971; declared ratified on June 30, 1971.]*

*Section 1*

[EIGHTEEN-YEAR-OLD VOTE]

The right of citizens of the United States, who are eighteen years of age or older, to vote shall not be denied or abridged by the United States or by any State on account of age.

*Section 2*

[POWER TO ENFORCE THIS ARTICLE]

The Congress shall have power to enforce this article by appropriate legislation.

## AMENDMENT XXVII

*[Proposed by Congress on September 25, 1789; ratified on May 7, 1992.]*

No law varying the compensation for the services of the Senators and Representatives shall take effect until an election of Representatives shall have intervened.

# The Federalist Papers

## No 10: Madison

Among the numerous advantages promised by a well-constructed Union, none deserves to be more accurately developed than its tendency to break and control the violence of faction. The friend of popular governments never finds himself so much alarmed for their character and fate as when he contemplates their propensity to this dangerous vice. He will not fail, therefore, to set a due value on any plan which, without violating the principles to which he is attached, provides a proper cure for it. The instability, injustice, and confusion introduced into the public councils have, in truth, been the mortal diseases under which popular governments have everywhere perished, as they continue to be the favorite and fruitful topics from which the adversaries to liberty derive their most specious declamations. The valuable improvements made by the American constitutions on the popular models, both ancient and modern, cannot certainly be too much admired; but it would be an unwarrantable partiality to contend that they have as effectually obviated the danger on this side, as was wished and expected. Complaints are everywhere heard from our most considerate and virtuous citizens, equally the friends of public and private faith and of public and personal liberty, that our governments are too unstable, that the public good is disregarded in the conflicts of rival parties, and that measures are too often decided, not according to the rules of justice and the rights of the minor party, but by the superior force of an interested and overbearing majority. However anxiously we may wish that these complaints had no foundation, the evidence of known facts will not permit us to deny that they are in some degree true. It will be found, indeed, on a candid review of our situation, that some of the distresses under which we labor have been erroneously charged on the operation of our governments; but it will be found, at the same time, that other causes will not alone account for many of our heaviest misfortunes; and, particularly, for that prevailing and increasing distrust of public engagements and alarm for private rights which are echoed from one end of the continent to the other. These must be chiefly, if not wholly, effects of the unsteadiness and injustice with which a factious spirit has tainted our public administration.

By a faction I understand a number of citizens, whether amounting to a majority or minority of the whole, who are united and actuated by some common impulse of passion, or of interest, adverse to the rights of other citizens, or to the permanent and aggregate interests of the community.

There are two methods of curing the mischiefs of faction: the one, by removing its causes; the other, by controlling its effects.

There are again two methods of removing the causes of faction: the one, by destroying the liberty which is essential to its existence; the other, by giving to every citizen the same opinions, the same passions, and the same interests.

It could never be more truly said than of the first remedy that it was worse than the disease. Liberty is to faction what air is to fire, an aliment without which it instantly expires. But it could not be a less folly to abolish liberty, which is essential to political life, because it nourishes faction than it would be to wish the annihilation of air, which is essential to animal life, because it imparts to fire its destructive agency.

The second expedient is as impracticable as the first would be unwise. As long as the reason of man continues fallible, and he is at liberty to exercise it, different opinions will be formed. As long as the connection subsists between his reason and his self-love, his opinions and his passions will have a reciprocal influence on each other; and the former will be objects to which the latter will attach themselves. The diversity in the faculties of men, from which the rights of property originate, is not less an insuperable obstacle to a uniformity of interests. The protection of these faculties is the first object of government. From the protection of different and unequal faculties of acquiring property, the possession of different degrees and kinds of property immediately results; and from the influence of these on the sentiments and views of the respective proprietors ensues a division of the society into different interests and parties.

The latent causes of faction are thus sown in the nature of man; and we see them everywhere brought into different degrees of activity, according to the different circumstances of civil society. A zeal for different opinions concerning religion, concerning government, and many other points, as well of speculation as of practice; an attachment to different leaders ambitiously contending for pre-eminence and power; or to persons of other descriptions whose fortunes have been interesting to the human passions, have, in turn, divided mankind into parties, inflamed them with mutual animosity, and rendered them much more disposed to vex and oppress each other than to co-operate for their common good. So strong is this propensity of mankind to fall into mutual animosities that where no substantial occasion presents itself the most frivolous and fanciful distinctions have been sufficient to kindle their unfriendly passions and excite their most violent conflicts. But the most common and durable source of factions has been the various and unequal distribution of property. Those who hold and those who are without property have ever formed distinct interests in society. Those who are creditors, and those who are debtors, fall under a like discrimination. A landed interest, a manufacturing interest, a mercantile interest, a moneyed interest, with many lesser interests, grow up of necessity in civilized nations, and divide them into different classes, actuated by different sentiments and views. The regulation of these various and interfering interests forms the principal task of modern legislation and involves the spirit of party and faction in the necessary and ordinary operations of government.

No man is allowed to be judge in his own cause, because his interest would certainly bias his judgment and, not improbably, corrupt his integrity. With equal, nay with greater reason, a body of men are unfit to be both judges and parties at the same time; yet what are many of the most important acts of legislation but so many judicial determinations, not indeed concerning the rights of single persons, but concerning the rights of large bodies of citizens? And what are the different classes of legislators but advocates and parties to the causes which they determine? Is a law proposed concerning private debts? It is a question to which the creditors are parties on one side and the debtors on the other. Justice ought to hold the balance between them. Yet the parties are, and must be, themselves the judges; and the most numerous party, or in other words, the most powerful faction must be expected to prevail. Shall domestic manufacturers be encouraged, and in what degree, by restrictions on foreign manufacturers? are questions which would be differently decided by the landed and the manufacturing classes, and probably by neither with a sole regard to justice and the public good. The apportionment of taxes on the various descriptions of property is an act which seems to require the most exact impartiality; yet there is, perhaps, no legislative act in which greater opportunity and temptation are given to a predominant party to trample on the rules of justice. Every shilling with which they overburden the inferior number is a shilling saved to their own pockets.

It is in vain to say that enlightened statesmen will be able to adjust these clashing interests and render them all subservient to the public good. Enlightened statesmen will not always be at the helm. Nor, in many cases, can such an adjustment be made at all without taking into view indirect and remote considerations, which will rarely prevail over the immediate interest which one party may find in disregarding the rights of another or the good of the whole.

The inference to which we are brought is that the *causes* of faction cannot be removed and that relief is only to be sought in the means of controlling its *effects*.

If a faction consists of less than a majority, relief is supplied by the republican principle, which enables the majority to defeat its sinister views by regular vote. It may clog the administration, it may convulse the society; but it will be unable to execute and mask its violence under the forms of the Constitution. When a majority is included in a faction, the form of popular government, on the other hand, enables it to sacrifice to its ruling passion or interest both the public good and the rights of other citizens. To secure the public good and private rights against the danger of such a faction, and at the same time to preserve the spirit and the form of popular government, is then the great object to which our inquiries are directed. Let me add that it is the great desideratum by which alone this form of government can be rescued from the opprobrium under which it has so long labored and be recommended to the esteem and adoption of mankind.

By what means is this object attainable? Evidently by one of two only. Either the existence of the same passion or interest in a majority at the same time must be prevented, or the majority, having such coexistent passion or interest, must be rendered, by their number and local situation, unable to concert and carry into effect schemes of oppression. If the impulse and the opportunity be suffered to coincide, we well know that neither moral nor religious motives can be relied on as an adequate control. They are not found to be such on the injustice and violence of individuals, and lose their efficacy in proportion to the number combined together, that is, in proportion as their efficacy becomes needful.

From this view of the subject it may be concluded that a pure democracy, by which I mean a society consisting of a small number of citizens, who assemble and administer the government in person, can admit of no cure for the mischiefs of faction. A common passion or interest will, in almost every case, be felt by a majority of the whole; a communication and concert results from the form of government itself; and there is nothing to check the inducements to sacrifice the weaker party or an obnoxious individual. Hence it is that such democracies have ever been spectacles of turbulence and contention; have ever been found incompatible with personal security or the rights of property; and have in general been as short in their lives as they have been violent in their deaths. Theoretic politicians, who have patronized this species of government, have erroneously supposed that by reducing mankind to a perfect equality in their political rights, they would at the same time be perfectly equalized and assimilated in their possessions, their opinions, and their passions.

A republic, by which I mean a government in which the scheme of representation takes place, opens a different prospect and promises the cure for which we are seeking. Let us examine the points in which it varies from pure democracy, and we shall comprehend both the nature of the cure and the efficacy which it must derive from the Union.

The two great points of difference between a democracy and a republic are: first, the delegation of the government, in the latter, to a small number of citizens elected by the rest; secondly, the greater number of citizens and greater sphere of country over which the latter may be extended.

The effect of the first difference is, on the one hand, to refine and enlarge the public views by passing them through the medium of a chosen body of citizens, whose wisdom may best discern the true interest of their country and whose patriotism and love of justice will be least likely to sacrifice it to temporary or partial considerations. Under such a regulation it may well happen that the public voice, pronounced by the representatives of the people, will be more consonant to the public good than if pronounced by the people themselves, convened for the purpose. On the other hand, the effect may be inverted. Men of factious tempers, of local prejudices, or of sinister designs, may, by intrigue, by corruption, or by other means, first obtain the suffrages, and then betray the interests of the people. The question resulting is, whether small or extensive republics are most favorable to the election of proper guardians of the public weal; and it is clearly decided in favor of the latter by two obvious considerations.

In the first place it is to be remarked that however small the republic may be the representatives must be raised to a certain number in order to guard against the cabals of a few; and that however large it may be they must be limited to a certain number in order to guard against the confusion of a multitude. Hence, the number of representatives in the two cases not being in proportion to that of the constituents, and being proportionally greatest in the small republic, it follows that if the proportion of fit characters be not less in the large than in the small republic, the former will present a greater option, and consequently a greater probability of a fit choice.

In the next place, as each representative will be chosen by a greater number of citizens in the large than in the small republic, it will be more difficult for unworthy candidates to practise with success the vicious arts by which elections are too often carried; and the suffrages of the people being more free, will be more likely to center on men who possess the most attractive merit and the most diffusive and established characters.

It must be confessed that in this, as in most other cases, there is a mean, on both sides of which inconveniencies will be found to lie. By enlarging too much the number of electors, you render the representative too little acquainted with all their local circumstances and lesser interests; as by reducing it too much, you render him unduly attached to these, and too little fit to comprehend and pursue great and national objects. The federal Constitution forms a happy combination in this respect; the great and aggregate interests being referred to the national, the local and particular to the State legislatures.

The other point of difference is the greater number of citizens and extent of territory which may be brought within the compass of republican than of democratic government; and it is this circumstance principally which renders factious combinations less to be dreaded in the former than in the latter. The smaller the society, the fewer probably will be the distinct parties and interests composing it; the fewer the distinct parties and interests, the more frequently will a majority be found of the same party; and the smaller the number of individuals composing a majority, and the smaller the compass within which they are placed, the more easily will they concert and execute their plans of oppression. Extend the sphere and you take in a greater variety of parties and interests; you make it less probable that a majority of the whole will have a common motive to invade the rights of other citizens; or if such a common motive exists, it will be more difficult for all who feel it to discover their own strength and to act in unison with each other. Besides other impediments, it may be remarked that, where there is a consciousness of unjust or dishonorable purposes, communication is always checked by distrust in proportion to the number whose concurrence is necessary.

Hence, it clearly appears that the same advantage which a republic has over a democracy in controlling the effects of faction is enjoyed by a large over a small republic—is enjoyed by the Union over the States composing it. Does this advantage consist in the substitution of representatives whose enlightened views and virtuous sentiments render them superior to local prejudices and to schemes of injustice? It will not be denied that the representation of the Union will be most likely to possess these requisite endowments. Does it consist in the greater security afforded by a greater variety of parties, against the event of any one party being able to outnumber and oppress the rest? In an equal degree does the increased variety of parties comprised within the Union increase this security? Does it, in fine, consist in the greater obstacles opposed to the concert and accomplishment of the secret wishes of an unjust and interested majority? Here again the extent of the Union gives it the most palpable advantage.

The influence of factious leaders may kindle a flame within their particular States but will be unable to spread a general conflagration through the other States. A religious sect may degenerate into a political faction in a part of the Confederacy; but the variety of sects dispersed over the entire face of it must secure the national councils against any danger from that source. A rage for paper money, for an abolition of debts, for an equal division of property, or for any other improper or wicked project, will be less apt to pervade the whole body of the

Union than a particular member of it, in the same proportion as such a malady is more likely to taint a particular county or district than an entire State.

In the extent and proper structure of the Union, therefore, we behold a republican remedy for the diseases most incident to republican government. And according to the degree of pleasure and pride we feel in being republicans ought to be our zeal in cherishing the spirit and supporting the character of federalist.

PUBLIUS

## NO. 51: MADISON

To what expedient, then, shall we finally resort, for maintaining in practice the necessary partition of power among the several departments as laid down in the Constitution? The only answer that can be given is that as all these exterior provisions are found to be inadequate the defect must be supplied, by so contriving the interior structure of the government as that its several constituent parts may, by their mutual relations, be the means of keeping each other in their proper places. Without presuming to undertake a full development of this important idea I will hazard a few general observations which may perhaps place it in a clearer light, and enable us to form a more correct judgment of the principles and structure of the government planned by the convention.

In order to lay a due foundation for that separate and distinct exercise of the different powers of government, which to a certain extent is admitted on all hands to be essential to the preservation of liberty, it is evident that each department should have a will of its own; and consequently should be so constituted that the members of each should have as little agency as possible in the appointment of the members of the others. Were this principle rigorously adhered to, it would require that all the appointments for the supreme executive, legislative, and judiciary magistracies should be drawn from the same fountain of authority, the people, through channels having no communication whatever with one another. Perhaps such a plan of constructing the several departments would be less difficult in practice than it may in contemplation appear. Some difficulties, however, and some additional expense would attend the execution of it. Some deviations, therefore, from the principle must be admitted. In the constitution of the judiciary department in particular, it might be inexpedient to insist rigorously on the principle: first, because peculiar qualifications being essential in the members, the primary consideration ought to be to select that mode of choice which best secures these qualifications; second, because the permanent tenure by which the appointments are held in that department must soon destroy all sense of dependence on the authority conferring them.

It is equally evident that the members of each department should be as little dependent as possible on those of the others for the emoluments annexed to their offices. Were the executive magistrate, or the judges, not independent of the legislature in this particular, their independence in every other would be merely nominal.

But the great security against a gradual concentration of the several powers in the same department consists in giving to those who administer each department the necessary constitutional means and personal motives to resist encroachments of the others. The provision for defense must in this, as in all other cases, be made commensurate to the danger of attack. Ambition must be made to counteract ambition. The interest of the man must be connected with the constitutional rights of the place. It may be a reflection on human nature that such devices should be necessary to control the abuses of government. But what is government itself but the greatest of all reflections on human nature? If men were angels, no government would be necessary. If angels were to govern men, neither external nor internal controls on government would be necessary. In framing a government which is to be administered by men over men, the great difficulty lies in this: you must first enable the government to control the governed; and in the next place oblige it to control itself. A dependence on the people is, no doubt, the primary control on the government; but experience has taught mankind the necessity of auxiliary precautions.

This policy of supplying, by opposite and rival interests, the defect of better motives, might be traced through the whole system of human affairs, private as well as public. We see it particularly displayed in all the subordinate distributions of power, where the constant aim is to divide and arrange the several offices in such a manner as that each may be a check on the other—that the private interest of every individual may be a sentinel over the public rights. These inventions of prudence cannot be less requisite in the distribution of the supreme powers of the State.

But it is not possible to give to each department an equal power of self-defense. In republican government, the legislative authority necessarily predominates. The remedy for this inconveniency is to divide the legislature into different branches; and to render them, by different modes of election and different principles of action, as little connected with each other as the nature of their common functions and their common dependence on the society will admit. It may even be necessary to guard against dangerous encroachments by still further precautions. As the weight of the legislative authority requires that it should be thus divided, the weakness of the executive may require, on the other hand, that it should be fortified. An absolute negative on the legislature appears, at first view, to be the natural defense with which the executive magistrate should be armed. But perhaps it would be neither altogether safe nor alone sufficient. On ordinary occasions it might not be exerted with the requisite firmness, and on extraordinary occasions it might be perfidiously abused. May not this defect of an absolute negative be supplied by some qualified connection between this weaker branch of the stronger department, by which the latter may be led to support the constitutional rights of the former, without being too much detached from the rights of its own department?

If the principles on which these observations are founded be just, as I persuade myself they are, and they be applied as a criterion to the several State constitutions, and to the federal Constitution, it will be found that if the latter does not perfectly correspond with them, the former are infinitely less able to bear such a test.

There are, moreover, two considerations particularly applicable to the federal system of America, which place that system in a very interesting point of view.

*First.* In a single republic, all the power surrendered by the people is submitted to the administration of a single government; and the usurpations are guarded against by a division of the government into distinct and separate departments. In the compound republic of America, the power surrendered by the people is first divided between two distinct governments, and then the portion allotted to each subdivided among distinct and separate departments. Hence a double security arises to the rights of the people. The different governments will control each other, at the same time that each will be controlled by itself.

*Second.* It is of great importance in a republic not only to guard the society against the oppression of its rulers, but to guard one part of the society against the injustice of the other part. Different interests necessarily exist in different classes of citizens. If a majority be united by a common interest, the rights of the minority will be insecure. There are but two methods of providing against this evil: the one by creating a will in the community independent of the majority—that is, of the society itself; the other, by comprehending in the society so many separate descriptions of citizens as will render an unjust combination of a majority of the whole very improbable, if not impracticable. The first method prevails in all governments possessing an hereditary or self-appointed authority. This, at best, is but a precarious security; because a power independent of the society may as well espouse the unjust views of the major as the rightful interests of the minor party, and may possibly be turned against both parties. The second method will be exemplified in the federal republic of the United States.

Whilst all authority in it will be derived from and dependent on the society, the society itself will be broken into so many parts, interests and classes of citizens, that the rights of individuals, or of the minority, will be in little danger from interested combinations of the majority. In a free government the security for civil rights must be the same as that for religious rights. It consists in the one case in the multiplicity of interests, and in the other in the multiplicity of sects. The degree of security in both cases will depend on the number of interests and sects; and this may be presumed to depend on the extent of country and number of people comprehended under the same government. This view of the subject must particularly recommend a proper federal system to all the sincere and considerate friends of republican government, since it shows that in exact proportion as the territory of the Union may be formed into more circumscribed Confederacies, or States, oppressive combinations of a majority will be facilitated; the best security, under the republican forms, for the rights of every class of citizen, will be diminished; and consequently the stability and independence of some member of the government, the only other security, must be proportionally increased. Justice is the end of government. It is the end of civil society. It ever has been and ever will be pursued until it be obtained, or until liberty be lost in the pursuit. In a society under the forms of which the stronger faction can readily unite and oppress the weaker, anarchy may as truly be said to reign as in a state of nature, where the weaker individual is not secured against the violence of the stronger; and as, in the latter state, even the stronger individuals are prompted, by the uncertainty of their condition, to submit to a government which may protect the weak as well as themselves; so, in the former state, will the more powerful factions or parties be gradually induced, by a like motive, to wish for a government which will protect all parties, the weaker as well as the more powerful. It can be little doubted that if the State of Rhode Island was separated from the Confederacy and left to itself, the insecurity of rights under the popular form of government within such narrow limits would be displayed by such reiterated oppressions of factious majorities that some power altogether independent of the people would soon be called for by the voice of the very factions whose misrule had proved the necessity of it. In the extended republic of the United States, and among the great variety of interests, parties, and sects which it embraces, a coalition of a majority of the whole society could seldom take place on any other principles than those of justice and the general good; whilst there being thus less danger to a minor from the will of a major party, there must be less pretext, also, to provide for the security of the former, by introducing into the government a will not dependent on the latter, or, in other words, a will independent of the society itself. It is no less certain than it is important, notwithstanding the contrary opinions which have been entertained, that the larger the society, provided it lie within a practicable sphere, the more duly capable it will be of self-government. And happily for the *republican cause,* the practicable sphere may be carried to a very great extent by a judicious modification and mixture of the *federal principle.*

PUBLIUS

# Glossary of Terms

**absolute majority** Fifty percent plus one of all those eligible to vote. Absolute rather than simple majorities are required for some types of congressional votes.

**administrative adjudication** Applying rules and precedents to specific cases to settle disputes with regulated parties.

**administrative regulation** Rules made by **regulatory agencies** and commissions.

**affirmative action** A policy or program designed to redress historic injustices committed against specified groups by making special efforts to provide members of these groups with access to educational and employment opportunities.

**agency representation** The type of representation by which representatives are held accountable to their constituents if they fail to represent them properly; that is, constituents have the power to hire and fire their representatives. This is the incentive for good representation when the personal backgrounds, views, and interests of the representatives differ from their constituents'.

**Aid to Families with Dependent Children (AFDC)** Federal funds, administered by the states, for children living with parents or relatives who fall below state standards of need. The largest federal cash transfer program (as distinguished from assistance in kind). In 1996, Congress abolished AFDC and replaced it with the **Temporary Assistance to Needy Families (TANF)** block grant.

***amicus curiae*** "Friend of the court"; individuals or groups who are not parties to a lawsuit but who seek to assist the court in reaching a decision by presenting additional briefs.

**appellate court** A court that hears the appeals of trial court decisions.

**appropriations** The amounts approved by Congress in statutes (bills) that each unit or agency of government can spend.

**area sampling** A polling technique used for large cities, states, or the whole nation, when a high level of accuracy is desired. The population is broken down into small, homogeneous units, such as counties; then several units are randomly selected to serve as the sample.

**Articles of Confederation and Perpetual Union** America's first written constitution. Adopted by the Continental Congress in 1777, the Articles of Confederation and Perpetual Union was the formal basis for America's national government until 1789, when it was supplanted by the Constitution.

**attitude (or opinions)** A specific preference on a specific issue.

**Australian ballot** An electoral format that presents the names of all the candidates for any given office on the same ballot. Introduced at the turn of the century, the Australian ballot replaced the partisan ballot and facilitated **split-ticket voting.**

**authoritarian government** A system of rule in which the government recognizes no formal limits but may nevertheless be restrained by the power of other social institutions.

**authorization** The process by which Congress enacts or rejects proposed statutes (bills) embodying the positive laws of government.

**autocracy** A form of government in which a single individual—a king, queen, or dictator—rules.

**automatic stabilizers** A category of public policy, largely fiscal and monetary, that automatically works against inflationary and deflationary tendencies in the economy.

**balance of power** A system of political alignments by which stability can be achieved.

**balance-of-power role** The strategy whereby many countries form alliances with one or more other countries in order to counterbalance the behavior of other, usually more powerful, nation-states.

**bandwagon effect** A situation wherein reports of voter or delegate opinion can influence the actual outcome of an election or a nominating convention.

**bellwether district** A town or district that is a microcosm of the whole population or that has been found to be a good predictor of electoral outcomes.

**bicameral legislature** A legislative assembly composed of two chambers or houses; opposite of unicameral legislature.

**bilateral treaty** Treaty made between two nations; contrast with **multilateral treaty.**

**Bill of Rights** The first ten amendments to the U.S. Constitution, ratified in 1791. They ensure certain rights and liberties to the people.

**binding primary** Primary election in which the candidates for election as delegates to a presidential nominating convention pledge themselves to a certain candidate and are bound to vote for that person until released from the obligation.

**bipartisan foreign policy** Based on the assumption that "politics stops at the water's edge," this is a strategy pursued by most presidents since World War II to coopt the opposition party leaders in order to minimize the amount of public criticism and the leakage of confidential information for political purposes.

**bipartisanship** Close cooperation between two parties; usually an effort by the two major parties in Congress to cooperate with the president in making foreign policy.

**block grants** Federal funds given to state governments to pay for goods, services, or programs, with relatively few restrictions on how the funds may be spent.

**bureaucracy** The complex structure of offices, tasks, rules, and principles of organization that are employed by all large-scale institutions to coordinate the work of their personnel.

**cabinet** The secretaries, or chief administrators, of the major departments of the federal government. Cabinet secretaries are appointed by the president with the consent of the Senate.

**capitalism** An economic system in which most of the means of production and distribution are privately owned and operated for profit.

**categorical grants-in-aid** Funds given by Congress to states and localities, earmarked by law for specific categories such as education or crime prevention.

**caucus** A normally closed meeting of a political or legislative group to select candidates, plan strategy, or make decisions regarding legislative matters.

**checks and balances** Mechanisms through which each branch of government is able to participate in and influence the activities of the other branches. Major examples include the presidential veto power over congressional legislation, the power of the Senate to approve presidential appointments, and judicial review of congressional enactments.

**chief justice** Justice on the Supreme Court who presides over the Court's public sessions.

**citizenship** The duties, rights, and privileges of being a citizen of a political unit.

**civil disobedience** A form of **direct action politics** that involves the refusal to obey civil laws considered unjust. This is usually a nonviolent or passive resistance.

**civil law** A system of jurisprudence, including private law and governmental actions, to settle disputes that do not involve criminal penalties.

**civil liberties** Areas of personal freedom with which governments are constrained from interfering.

**civil penalties** Regulatory techniques in which fines or another form of material restitution is imposed for violating civil laws or common law principles, such as negligence.

**civil rights** Legal or moral claims that citizens are entitled to make upon the government.

**class action suit** A lawsuit in which large numbers of persons with common interests join together under a representative party to bring or defend a lawsuit, such as hundreds of workers joining together to sue a company.

**clientele agencies** Departments or bureaus of government whose mission is to promote, serve, or represent a particular interest.

**client state** A **nation-state** whose foreign policy is subordinated to that of another nation.

**closed primary** A primary election in which voters can participate in the nomination of candidates, but only of the party in which they are enrolled for a period of time prior to primary day. Contrast with **open primary.**

**closed rule** Provision by the House Rules Committee limiting or prohibiting the introduction of amendments during debate.

**cloture** Rule allowing a majority of two-thirds or three-fifths of the members in a legislative body to set a time limit on debate over a given bill.

**coattail effect** Result of voters casting their ballot for president or governor and "automatically" voting for the remainder of the party's ticket.

**commerce power** Power of Congress to regulate trade among the states and with foreign countries.

**conscription** Compulsory military service, usually for a prescribed period or for the duration of a war; "the draft."

**conservative** Today this term refers to those who generally support the social and economic status quo and are suspicious of efforts to introduce new political formulae and economic arrangements. Many conservatives also believe that a large and powerful government poses a threat to citizens' freedoms.

**constituency** The district comprising the area from which an official is elected.

**constitutional government** A system of rule in which formal and effective limits are placed on the powers of the government.

**constitutionalism** An approach to legitimacy in which the rulers give up a certain amount of power in return for their right to utilize the remaining powers.

**containment** The primary cold war foreign policy of the United States during the 1950s and 1960s, whereby the U.S. used its political, economic, and military power to prevent the spread of communism to developing or unstable countries.

**contracting power** The power of government to set conditions on companies seeking to sell goods or services to government agencies.

**contract model** A theory asserting that governments originate from general agreements among members of the public about the necessity of dealing with common problems.

**contributory programs** Social programs financed in whole or in part by taxation or other mandatory contributions by their present or future recipients. The most important example is **Social Security,** which is financed by a payroll tax.

**cooperative federalism** A type of federalism existing since the New Deal era in which **grants-in-aid** have been used strategically to encourage states and localities (without commanding them) to pursue nationally defined goals. Also known as intergovernmental cooperation.

**cost of living adjustments (COLAs)** See **indexing.**

**criminal law** The branch of law that deals with disputes or actions involving criminal penalties (as opposed to civil law). It regulates the conduct of individuals, defines crimes, and provides punishment for criminal acts.

criminal penalties Regulatory techniques in which imprisonment or heavy fines and the loss of certain civil rights and liberties are imposed.

critical electoral realignment The point in history when a new party supplants the ruling party, becoming in turn the dominant political force. In the United States, this has tended to occur roughly every thirty years.

debt The cumulative total amount of money owed due to yearly operating **deficits.**

debt limit Ceiling established by Congress upon the total amount of debt the government can accumulate. Can be changed by Congress as need requires.

debt service Interest paid on the public debt; an "uncontrollable" budget item because the amount is determined by general interest rates.

de facto segregation Racial segregation that is not a direct result of law or government policy but is, instead, a reflection of residential patterns, income distributions, or other social factors.

defendant The individual or organization charged with a complaint in court.

deficit An annual debt incurred when the government spends more than it collects. Each yearly deficit adds to the nation's total **debt.**

deficit financing Usually refers to deficits that are deliberately incurred as part of an effort to fight off a deflationary phase of the business cycle. Deficits are financed by borrowing.

de jure segregation Racial segregation that is a direct result of law or official policy.

delegated powers Constitutional powers assigned to one governmental agency that are exercised by another agency with the express permission of the first.

democracy A system of rule that permits citizens to play a significant part in the governmental process, usually through the selection of key public officials.

deregulation A policy of reducing or eliminating regulatory restraints on the conduct of individuals or private institutions.

deterrence The development and maintenance of military strength for the purpose of discouraging attack.

devolution A policy to remove a program from one level of government by deregulating it or passing it down to a lower level of government, such as from the national government to the state and local governments.

direct action politics A form of politics, such as violent politics or civil disobedience, that uses informal channels to attempt to force rulers into a new course of action.

discount rate The interest rate charged by the **Federal Reserve** when commercial banks borrow in order to expand their lending operations. An effective tool of monetary policy.

divided government The condition in American government wherein the presidency is controlled by one party while the opposing party controls one or both houses of Congress.

double jeopardy Trial more than once for the same crime. The Constitution guarantees that no one shall be subjected to double jeopardy.

dual federalism The system of government that prevailed in the United States from 1789 to 1937 in which most fundamental governmental powers were shared between the federal and state governments. Compare with **cooperative federalism.**

due process The right of every citizen against arbitrary action by national or state governments.

economic expansionist role The strategy often pursued by capitalist countries to adopt foreign policies that will maximize the success of domestic corporations in their dealings with other countries.

elastic clause See **necessary and proper clause.**

**electoral college** The presidential electors from each state who meet in their respective state capitals after the popular election to cast ballots for president and vice president.

**electoral realignment** The point in history when a new party supplants the ruling party, becoming in turn the dominant political force. In the United States, this has tended to occur roughly every thirty years.

**electorate** All of the eligible voters in a legally designated area.

**eminent domain** The right of government to take private property for public use, with reasonable compensation awarded for the property.

**entitlement** Eligibility for benefits by virtue of a category of benefits defined by law. Category can only be changed by legislation. Deprivation of individual benefits can be determined only through **due process** in court.

**environmental impact statement** Since 1969, all federal agencies must file this statement demonstrating that a new program or project will not have a net negative impact on the human or physical environment.

**equality of opportunity** A universally shared American ideal that all have the freedom to use whatever talents and wealth they have to reach their fullest potential.

**equal time rule** A Federal Communications Commission requirement that broadcasters provide candidates for the same political office an equal opportunity to communicate their messages to the public.

**exclusive power** Power belonging exclusively to and exercised only by the national or state government.

**executive agreement** An agreement between the president and another country which has the force of a treaty but does not require the Senate's "advice and consent."

**executive privilege** The claim that confidential communications between a president and close advisers should not be revealed without the consent of the president.

**ex post facto law** "After the fact" law; law that is retroactive and that has an adverse effect on someone accused of a crime. Under Article I, Sections 9 and 10, of the Constitution, neither the state nor the national government can enact such laws; this provision does not apply, however, to civil laws.

**expressed power** The notion that the Constitution grants to the federal government only those powers specifically named in its text.

**expropriation** Confiscation of property with or without compensation.

**extraction-coercion cycle** A process of state-building in which governments use military force to extract money and other resources from the populace. These resources are then used to enhance the government's military power, which is used to extract more resources, and so on.

**faction** Group of people with common interests, usually in opposition to the aims or principles of a larger group or the public.

**fairness doctrine** A Federal Communications Commission requirement for broadcasters who air programs on controversial issues to provide time for opposing views.

**federalism** System of government in which power is divided by a constitution between a central government and regional governments.

**Federal Reserve Board** Seven-member governing board of the **Federal Reserve System.**

**Federal Reserve System (Fed)** Consisting of twelve Federal Reserve Banks, the Fed facilitates exchanges of cash, checks, and credit; it regulates member banks; and it uses monetary policies to fight inflation and deflation.

**filibuster** A tactic used by members of the Senate to prevent action on legislation they oppose by continuously holding the floor and speaking until the majority backs down. Once given the floor, Senators have unlimited time to speak, and it requires a **cloture** vote of three-fifths of the Senate to end the filibuster.

**fiscal year** The yearly accounting period, which for the national government is October 1–September 30. The actual fiscal year is designated by the year in which it ends.

**food stamps** The largest **in-kind benefits** program, administered by the Department of Agriculture, providing coupons to individuals and families who satisfy a "needs test"; the food stamps can be exchanged for food at most grocery stores.

**formula grants** **Grants-in-aid** in which a formula is used to determine the amount of federal funds a state or local government will receive.

**framing** The power of the media to influence how events and issues are interpreted.

**franchise** The right to vote; see **license, suffrage.**

**full faith and credit clause** Article IV, Section 1, of the Constitution, which provides that each state must accord the same respect to the laws and judicial decisions of other states that it accords to its own.

**gender gap** A distinctive pattern of voting behavior reflecting the differences in views between men and women.

**gerrymandering** Apportionment of voters in districts in such a way as to give unfair advantage to one political party.

**government** Institutions and procedures through which a territory and its people are ruled.

**government corporation** A government agency that performs a service nominally provided by the public sector.

**grants-in-aid** A general term for funds given by Congress to state and local governments. See also **categorical grants-in-aid.**

**grass roots** Local communities and home-town political constituencies.

**Great Compromise** Agreement reached at the Constitutional Convention of 1787 that gave each state an equal number of senators regardless of its population, but linked representation in the House of Representatives to population.

**Gross Domestic Product (GDP)** An index of the total output of goods and services. A very imperfect measure of prosperity, productivity, inflation, deflation; its regular publication both reflects and influences business conditions.

**haphazard sampling** A type of sampling of public opinion that is an unsystematic choice of respondents.

**Holy Alliance role** A strategy pursued by a superpower to prevent any change in the existing distribution of power among nation-states, even if this requires intervention into the internal affairs of the country in order to keep an authoritarian ruler from being overturned.

**homesteading** A national policy that permits people to gain ownership of property by occupying public or unclaimed lands, living on the land for a specified period of time, and making certain minimal improvements on that land. Also known as squatting.

**home rule** Power delegated by the state to a local unit of government to manage its own affairs.

**ideology** The combined doctrines, assertions, and intentions of a social or political group that justify its behavior.

**illusion of central tendency** The assumption that opinions are "normally distributed"—that responses to opinion questions are heavily distributed toward the center, as in a bell-shaped curve.

**illusion of saliency** Impression conveyed by polls that something is important to the public when actually it is not.

**impeachment** To charge a governmental official (president or otherwise) with "Treason, Bribery, or other high Crimes and Misdemeanors" and bring him or her before Congress to determine guilt.

**impoundment** Efforts by presidents to thwart congressional programs that they cannot otherwise defeat by refusing to spend the funds that Congress has appropriated for them. Congress placed limits on impoundment in the Budget and Impoundment Control Act of 1974.

**independent agencies** Agencies set up by Congress to be independent of direct presidential authority. Congress usually accomplishes this by providing the head or heads of the agency with a set term of office rather than allowing their removal at the pleasure of the president.

**independent counsel** An official appointed under the terms of the Ethics in Government Act to investigate criminal misconduct by members of the executive branch.

**indexing** Periodic adjustments of welfare payments, wages, or taxes, tied to the cost of living. Also known as cost of living adjustments, or COLAs.

**indirect election** Provision for election of an official where the voters first select the delegates or "electors," who are in turn charged with making the final choice. The presidential election is an indirect election.

**inherent powers** Powers claimed by a president that are not expressed in the Constitution, but are inferred from it.

**in-kind benefits** Goods and services provided to needy individuals and families by the federal government, as contrasted with cash benefits. The largest in-kind federal welfare program is **food stamps.**

**interest groups** A group of individuals and organizations that share a common set of goals and have joined together in an effort to persuade the government to adopt policies that will help them.

**interest-group liberalism** The theory of governance that in principle all claims on government resources and action are equally valid, and that all interests are equally entitled to participation in and benefits from government.

**iron triangle** Name assigned by political scientists to the stable and cooperative relationships that often develop between a congressional committee or subcommittee, an administrative agency, and one or more supportive interest groups. Not all of these relationships are triangular, but the iron triangle formulation is perhaps the most typical.

**issue network** A loose network of elected leaders, public officials, activists, and interest groups drawn together by a specific policy issue.

**judicial review** Power of the courts to declare actions of the legislative and executive branches invalid or unconstitutional. The Supreme Court asserted this power in *Marbury v. Madison.*

**jurisdiction** The sphere of a court's power and authority.

**Kitchen Cabinet** An informal group of advisers to whom the president turns for counsel and guidance. Members of the official **cabinet** may or may not also be members of the Kitchen Cabinet.

**laissez-faire** An economic theory first advanced by Adam Smith, it calls for a "hands off" policy by government toward the economy, in an effort to leave business enterprises free to act in their own self-interest.

**legislative clearance** The power given to the president to require all agencies of the executive branch to submit through the budget director all requests for new legislation along with estimates of their budgetary needs.

**legislative intent** The supposed real meaning of a statute as it can be interpreted from the legislative history of the bill.

**legislative supremacy** The preeminent position assigned to the Congress by the Constitution.

**legislative veto** A provision in a statute permitting Congress (or a congressional committee) to review and approve actions undertaken by the executive under authority of the statute. Although the U.S. Supreme Court held the legislative veto unconstitutional in the 1983 case of *Immigration and Naturalization Service v. Chadha,* Congress continues to enact legislation incorporating such a veto.

**legitimacy** Popular acceptance of a government and its decisions.

**liberal** A liberal today generally supports political and social reform; extensive governmental intervention in the economy; the expansion of federal social services; more vigorous efforts on behalf of the poor, minorities, and women; and greater concern for consumers and the environment.

**license** Permission to engage in some activity that is otherwise illegal, such as hunting or practicing medicine. Synonymous with franchise, permit, certificate of convenience and necessity.

**line agency** Department, bureau, or other unit of administration whose primary mission requires it to deal directly with the public; contrast with **staff agency.**

**line-item veto** The power to veto specific provisions (lines) of a bill. Although most state governors possess this power to some degree, at this time the president of the United States does not, and must accept or veto a bill in its entirety. See also **veto.**

**lobbying** Strategy by which organized interests seek to influence the passage of legislation by exerting direct pressure on members of the legislature.

**logrolling** A legislative practice wherein reciprocal agreements are made between legislators, usually in voting for or against a bill. In contrast to bargaining, logrolling unites parties that have nothing in common but their desire to exchange support.

**majority leader** The elected leader of the party holding a majority of the seats in the House of Representatives or in the Senate. In the House, the majority leader is subordinate in the party hierarchy to the **Speaker.**

**majority rule** Rule by at least one vote more than half (50 percent plus 1) of those voting.

**majority system** A type of electoral system in which, to win a seat in the parliament or other representative body, a candidate must receive a majority (50 percent plus 1) of all the votes cast in the relevant district.

**mandate (electoral)** A claim made by a victorious candidate that the electorate has given him or her special authority to carry out campaign promises.

**marketplace of ideas** The public forum in which beliefs and ideas are exchanged and compete.

**means testing** Procedure by which a potential beneficiary of an assistance program must show a need for assistance and an inability to provide for it. Means testing determines eligibility for government public assistance programs.

**Medicaid** A federally financed, state-operated program for medical services to low-income people. Eligibility tied largely to **AFDC.**

**Medicare** National health insurance for the elderly and for the disabled.

**minority leader** The elected leader of the party holding less than a majority of the seats in the House or Senate.

**Miranda rule** Principles developed by the Supreme Court in the 1966 case of *Miranda v. Arizona* requiring that persons under arrest be informed of their legal rights, including their right to counsel, prior to police interrogation.

**monetary techniques** Efforts to regulate the economy through manipulation of the supply of money and credit. America's most powerful institution in the area of monetary policy is the **Federal Reserve Board.**

**monopoly** The existence of a single firm in a market that divides all the goods and services of that market. Absence of competition.

**mootness** A criterion used by courts to screen cases that no longer require resolution.

**multilateral treaty** A treaty among more than two nations.

**multilateralism** A foreign policy that seeks to encourage the involvement of several nation-states in coordinated action, usually in relation to a common adversary, with terms and conditions usually specified in a multi-country treaty, such as NATO.

**multiple-member constituency** Electorate that selects all candidates at large from the whole district; each voter is given the number of votes equivalent to the number of seats to be filled.

**multiple-member district** See **multiple-member constituency.**

**Napoleonic role** Strategy pursued by a powerful nation to prevent aggressive actions against themselves by improving the internal state of affairs of a particular country, even if this means encouraging revolution in that country. Based on the assumption that countries with comparable political systems will never go to war against each other.

**nationalism** The widely held belief that the people who occupy the same territory have something in common, that the nation is a single community.

**national supremacy** A principle that asserts that national law is superior to all other law. See **supremacy clause.**

**nation-state** A political entity consisting of a people with some common cultural experience (nation) who also share a common political authority (state) recognized by other sovereignties (nation-states).

**necessary and proper clause** Article I, Section 8, of the Constitution, which enumerates the powers of Congress and provides Congress with the authority to make all laws "necessary and proper" to carry them out; also referred to as the "elastic clause."

**nomination** The process through which political parties select their candidates for election to public office.

**noncontributory programs** Social programs that provide assistance to people based on demonstrated need rather than any contribution they have made.

**oligarchy** A form of government in which a small group of landowners, military officers, or wealthy merchants controls most of the governing decisions.

**oligopoly** The existence of two or more competing firms in a given market, where price competition is usually avoided because they know that they would all lose from such competition. Rather, competition is usually through other forms, such as advertising, innovation, and obsolescence.

**open market operations** Process whereby the Open Market Committee of the **Federal Reserve** buys and sells government securities, etc., to help finance government operations and to loosen or tighten the total amount of credit circulating in the economy.

**open primary** A primary election in which the voter can wait until the day of the primary to choose which party to enroll in to select candidates for the general election. Contrast with **closed primary.**

**ordinance** The legislative act of a local legislature or municipal commission. Puts the force of law under city charter but is a lower order of law than a statute of the national or state legislature.

**overhead agency** A department, bureau, or other unit of administration whose primary mission is to regulate the activities of other agencies; it generally has no direct authority over the public. Contrast with **line agency.**

**oversight** The effort by Congress, through hearings, investigations and other techniques, to exercise control over the activities of executive agencies.

**partisanship** Loyalty to a particular political party.

**party identification** An individual voter's psychological ties to one party or another.

**party vote** A **roll-call vote** in the House or Senate in which at least 90 percent of the members of one party take a particular position and are opposed by at least 90 percent of the members of the other party. Party votes are rare today, although they were fairly common in the nineteenth century.

**patriotism** Love of one's country; loyalty to one's country.

**patronage** The resources available to higher officials, usually opportunities to make partisan appointments to offices and to confer grants, licenses, or special favors to supporters.

***per curiam*** Decision by an appellate court, without a written opinion, that refuses to review the decision of a lower court; amounts to a reaffirmation of the lower court's opinion.

**petition** Right granted by the First Amendment to citizens to inform representatives of their opinions and to make pleas before government agencies.

**plaintiff** The individual or organization who brings a complaint in court.

**plea bargains** Negotiated agreements in criminal cases in which a defendant agrees to plead guilty in return for the state's agreement to reduce the severity of the criminal charge the defendant is facing.

**plebiscite** A direct vote by the electorate on an issue presented to it by a government.

**pluralism** The theory that all interests are and should be free to compete for influence in the government. The outcome of this competition is compromise and moderation.

**pluralist politics** Politics in which political elites actively compete for leadership, voters choose from among these elites, and new elites can emerge in quest of leadership.

**plurality system** A type of electoral system in which victory goes to the individual who gets the most votes in an election, not necessarily a majority of votes cast.

**pocket veto** Method by which the president vetoes a bill by taking no action on it when Congress has adjourned. See also **veto.**

**police power** Power reserved to the state to regulate the health, safety, and morals of its citizens.

**policy of redistribution** An objective of the graduated income tax—to raise revenue in such a way as to reduce the disparities of wealth between the lowest and the highest income brackets.

**political action committe (PAC)** A private group that raises and distributes funds for use in election campaigns.

**political ideology** A cohesive set of beliefs that form a general philosophy about the role of government.

**poll tax** A state-imposed tax upon the voters as a prerequisite to registration. It was rendered unconstitutional in national elections by the Twenty-fourth Amendment and in state elections by the Supreme Court in 1966.

**pork-barrel legislation** Appropriations made by legislative bodies for local projects that are often not needed but that are created so that local representatives can carry their home district in the next election.

**power without diplomacy** Post–World War II foreign policy in which the goal was to use American power to create an international structure that could be run with a minimum of regular diplomatic involvement.

**precedents** Prior cases whose principles are used by judges as the bases for their decisions in present cases.

**prior restraint** An effort by a governmental agency to block the publication of material it deems libelous or harmful in some other way; censorship. In the United States, the courts forbid prior restraint except under the most extraordinary circumstances.

**private bill** A proposal in Congress to provide a specific person with some kind of relief, such as a special exemption from immigration quotas.

**privileges and immunities clause** Article IV of the Constitution, which provides that the citizens of any one state are guaranteed the "privileges and immunities" of every other state, as though they were citizens of that state.

**probability sampling** A method used by pollsters to select a sample in which every individual in the population has a known (usually equal) probability of being selected as a respondent so that the correct weight can be given to all segments of the population.

**procedural due process** The Supreme Court's efforts to forbid any procedure that shocks the conscience or that makes impossible a fair judicial system. See also **due process.**

**progressive/regressive taxes** A judgment made by students of taxation about whether a particular tax hits the upper brackets more heavily (progressive) or the lower brackets (regressive) more heavily.

**project grants** Grant programs in which state and local governments submit proposals to federal agencies and for which funding is provided on a competitive basis.

**promotional techniques** A technique of control that encourages people to do something they might not otherwise do, or continue an action or behavior. There are three types; subsidies, contracts, and licenses.

**proportional representation** A multiple-member district system that allows each political party representation in proportion to its percentage of the vote.

**prospective voting** Voting based on the imagined future performance of a candidate.

**protective tariff** A tariff intended to give an advantage to a domestic manufacturer's product by increasing the cost of a competing imported product.

**public assistance program** A noncontributory social program providing assistance for the aged, poor, or disabled. Major examples include **Aid to Families with Dependent Children** (AFDC) and **Supplemental Security Income** (SSI).

**public law** Cases in private law, civil law, or criminal law in which one party to the dispute argues that a license is unfair, a law is inequitable or unconstitutional, or an agency has acted unfairly, violated a procedure, or gone beyond its jurisdiction.

**public opinion** Citizens' attitudes about political issues, leaders, institutions, and events.

**public policy** A governmental law, rule, statute, or edict that expresses the government's goals and provides for rewards and punishments to promote their attainment.

**push polling** Polling technique that is designed to shape the respondent's opinion. For example, "If you knew that Candidate X was an adulterer, would you support his election?"

**quota sampling** A type of sampling of public opinion that is used by most commercial polls. Respondents are selected whose characteristics closely match those of the general population along several significant dimensions, such as geographic region, sex, age, and race.

**rallying effect** The generally favorable reaction of the public to presidential actions taken in foreign policy, or more precisely, to decisions made during international crises.

**random sampling** Polls in which respondents are chosen mathematically, at random, with every effort made to avoid bias in the construction of the sample.

**reapportionment** The redrawing of election districts and the redistribution of legislative representatives due to shifts in population.

**redistributive techniques** Economic policies designed to control the economy through taxing and spending (fiscal policy) and manipulation of the supply of money and credit (monetary policy).

**referendum** The practice of referring a measure proposed or passed by a legislature to the vote of the electorate for approval or rejection.

**regulation** A particular use of government power, a "technique of control" in which the government adopts rules imposing restrictions on the conduct of private citizens.

**regulatory agencies** Departments, bureaus, or independent agencies whose primary mission is to eliminate or restrict certain behaviors defined as being evil in themselves or evil in their consequences.

**regulatory tax** A tax whose primary purpose is not to raise revenue but to influence conduct—e.g., a heavy tax on gasoline to discourage recreational driving.

**regulatory techniques** Techniques that government uses to control the conduct of the people.

**representative democracy** A system of government that provides the populace with the opportunity to make the government responsive to its views through the selection of representatives, who, in turn, play a significant role in governmental decision making.

**reserve requirement** The amount of liquid assets and ready cash that the Federal Reserve requires banks to hold to meet depositors' demands for their money. Ratio revolves above or below 20 percent of all deposits, with the rest being available for new loans.

**retrospective voting** Voting based on the past performance of a candidate.

**revolutionary politics** A form of politics that rejects the existing system of government entirely and attempts to replace it with a different organizational structure and a different ruling group.

**right of rebuttal** A Federal Communications Commission regulation giving individuals the right to have the opportunity to respond to personal attacks made on a radio or TV broadcast.

**roll-call vote** Vote in which each legislator's yes or no vote is recorded as the clerk calls the names of the members alphabetically.

A quasi-legislative administrative process that produces regulations by government agencies.

**selective polling** A sample drawn deliberately to reconstruct meaningful distributions of an entire constituency; not a random sample.

**seniority** Priority or status ranking given to an individual on the basis of length of continuous service in an organization.

**seperate but equal rule** Doctrine that public accommodations could be segregated by race but still be equal.

**separation of powers** The division of governmental power among several institutions that must cooperate in decision making.

**service agencies** Departments or other bureaus whose primary mission is to promote the interests of dependent persons or to deal with their problems.

**single-member constituency** An electorate that is allowed to elect only one representative from each district; the normal method of representation in the United States.

**single-member district** See **single-member constituency.**

**Social Security** A contributory welfare program into which working Americans contribute a percentage of their wages, and from which they receive cash benefits after retirement.

**sociological representation** A type of representation in which representatives have the same racial, ethnic, religious, or educational backgrounds as their constituents. It is based on the principle that if two individuals are similar in background, character, interests, and perspectives, then one could correctly represent the other's views.

**soft money** Money contributed directly to political parties for voter registration and organization.

**sovereignty** Supreme and independent political authority.

**Speaker of the House** The chief presiding officer of the House of Representatives. The Speaker is elected at the beginning of every Congress on a straight **party vote.** The Speaker is the most important party and House leader, and can influence the legislative agenda, the fate of individual pieces of legislation, and members' positions within the House.

**split-ticket voting** The practice of casting ballots for the candidates of at least two different political parties in the same election. Voters who support only one party's candidates are said to vote a straight party ticket.

**staff agency** An agency responsible for maintaining the bureaucracy, with responsibilities such as purchasing, budgeting, personnel management, planning.

**standing** The right of an individual or organization to initiate a court case.

**standing committee** A regular legislative committee that considers legislation within its designated subject area; the basic unit of deliberation in the House and Senate.

***stare decisis*** Literally "let the decision stand." A previous decision by a court applies as a precedent in similar cases until that decision is overruled.

**state** A community that claims the monopoly of legitimate use of physical force within a given territory; the ultimate political authority; sovereign.

**states' rights** The principle that states should oppose increasing authority of the national government. The period was most popular before the Civil War.

**statute** A law enacted by a state legislature or by Congress.

**subsidies** Governmental grants of cash or other valuable commodities such as land to individuals or organizations. Subsidies can be used to promote activities desired by the government, to reward political support, or to buy off political opposition.

**substantive due process** A judicial doctrine used by the appellate courts, primarily before 1937, to strike down economic legislation the courts felt was arbitrary or unreasonable.

**suffrage** The right to vote; see also **franchise.**

**Supplemental Security Income (SSI)** A program providing a minimum monthly income to people who pass a "needs test" and who are sixty-five years or older, blind, or disabled. Financed from general revenues rather than from Social Security contributions.

**supremacy clause** Article VI of the Constitution, which states that all laws passed by the national government and all treaties are the supreme laws of the land and superior to all laws adopted by any state or any subdivision.

**supreme court** The highest court in a particular state or in the United States. This court primarily serves an appellate function.

**systematic sampling** A method used in probability sampling to ensure that every individual in the population has a known probability of being chosen as a respondent. For example, by choosing every ninth name from a list.

**Temporary Assistance to Needy Families (TANF)** See **Aid to Families with Dependent Children (AFDC).**

**third parties** Parties that organize to compete against the two major American political parties.

**Three-fifths Compromise** Agreement reached at the Constitutional Convention of 1787 which stipulated that for purposes of the apportionment of congressional seats, every slave would be counted as three-fifths of a person.

**ticket balancing** Strategy of party leaders to nominate candidates from each of the major ethnic, racial, and religious affiliations.

**ticket splitting** The practice of voting for candidates of different parties on the same ballot.

**totalitarian government** A system of rule in which the government recognizes no formal limits on its power and seeks to absorb or eliminate other social institutions that might challenge it.

**treaty** A formal agreement between sovereign nations to create or restrict rights and responsibilities. In the U.S. all treaties must be approved by a two-thirds vote in the Senate. See also **executive agreement.**

**trial court** The first court to hear a criminal or civil case.

**turnout** The percentage of eligible individuals who actually vote.

**tyranny** Oppressive and unjust government that employs cruel and unjust use of power and authority.

**unfunded mandates** Regulations or conditions for receiving grants that impose costs on state and local governments for which they are not reimbursed by the federal government.

**Uniform Commercial Code** Code used in many states in the area of contract law to reduce interstate differences in judicial decisions.

**unilateralism** A foreign policy that seeks to avoid international alliances, entanglements, and permanent commitments in favor of independence, neutrality, and freedom of action.

**values (or beliefs)** Basic principles that shape a person's opinions about political issues and events.

**vested interests** Fixed or established interests; interests not varying with changing conditions; privileges respected or accepted by others.

**veto** The president's constitutional power to turn down acts of Congress. A presidential veto may be overridden by a two-thirds vote of each house of Congress. See also **line-item veto.**

**whip system** Primarily a communications network in each house of Congress, whips take polls of the membership in order to learn their intentions on specific legislative issues and to assist the majority and minority leaders in various tasks.

**writ of *certiorari*** A decision concurred in by at least four of the nine Supreme Court justices to review a decision of a lower court; from the Latin "to make more certain."

**writ of *habeas corpus*** A court order demanding that an individual in custody be brought into court and shown the cause for detention. *Habeas corpus* is guaranteed by the Constitution and can be suspended only in cases of rebellion or invasion.

# Glossary of Court Cases

*Abrams v. United States* (1919) The Supreme Court upheld the convictions of five Bolshevik sympathizers under the Espionage Act, which made it an offense to intend interference in the war with Germany. Although the defendants actually opposed American intervention in the Russian Revolution, the Court imputed to them the knowledge that their actions would necessarily impede the war effort against Germany. [See also page 308.]

*Adarand Constructors, Inc. v. Pena* (1995) In this case, Adarand Constructors claimed that its equal protection rights had been violated when a firm with a federal Department of Transportation contract selected a minority-owned company for a subcontract, despite Adarand's submission of a lower bid for the project. With its decision in favor of Adarand, the Court prompted a review of federal affirmative action programs that classify people and organizations on the basis of race. [See also pages 148, 325, and 333.]

*Agostini v. Felton* (1997) By a 5-to-4 decision, the Court ordered a federal district court in New York to lift an injunction established in 1985 that forbade public school teachers from entering on parochial school grounds to provide remedial education. [See also page 125.]

*Arizona v. Fulminante* (1991) A bare majority of the Rehnquist Court held that coerced confessions may be used at trial if it could be shown that other evidence was also used to support a guilty verdict. But the Court also held that in this case, the admission of a coerced confession was not "harmless error" and remanded the case for a new trial. [See also page 330.]

*Baker v. Carr* (1962) The Court held that the issue of malapportionment of election districts raised a justiciable claim under the Equal Protection Clause of the Fourteenth Amendment. The effect of the case was to force the reapportionment of nearly all federal, state, and local election districts nationwide. [See also page 323.]

*Barron v. Baltimore* (1833) This was one of the most significant cases ever handed down by the Court. Chief Justice John Marshall confirmed the concept of "dual citizenship," wherein each American is separately a citizen of the national government and of the state government. This meant that the Bill of Rights applied only nationally, and not at the state or local level. The consequences of this ruling were felt well into the twentieth century. [See also pages 115–16, 118, 119, 126, 156, and 157.]

*Benton v. Maryland* (1969) The Court ruled that double jeopardy was a right incorporated in the Fourteenth Amendment as a restriction on the states. [See also page 120.]

*Board of Education of Oklahoma City v. Dowell* (1991) This case, which restricted the use of court-ordered busing to achieve school integration, gave an early indication of the attitude of the new Bush Court. [See also pages 138 and 329.]

*Bolling v. Sharpe* (1954) This case, which did not directly involve the Fourteenth Amendment because the District of Columbia is not a state, confronted the Court on the grounds that segregation is inherently unequal. Its victory in effect was "incorporation in reverse," with equal protection moving from the Fourteenth Amendment to become part of the Bill of Rights. [See also page 130.]

*Bowsher v. Synar* (1986) This was the second of two cases since 1937 in which the Court invalidated an act of Congress on constitutional grounds. In this case, the Court struck down the Gramm-Rudman Act mandating a balanced federal budget, ruling that it was unconstitutional to grant the comptroller general "executive" powers. [See also pages 103, 225, and 238.]

*Bragdon v. Abbott* (1998) The Court ruled that the American Disabilities Act of 1990 applied to persons with human immunodeficiency virus (HIV). [See also page 339.]

*Brandenburg v. Ohio* (1969) The Court overturned an Ohio statute forbidding any person from urging criminal acts as a means of inducing political reform or from joining any association that advocated such activities, on the grounds that the statute punished "mere advocacy" and therefore violated the free speech provisions of the federal Constitution. [See also page 321.]

*Brown v. Board of Education of Topeka, Kansas* (1954) The Supreme Court struck down the "separate but equal" doctrine as fundamentally unequal. This case eliminated state power to use race as a criterion of discrimination in law and provided the national government with the power to intervene by exercising strict regulatory policies against discriminatory actions. [See also pages 120, 129, 130, 131–32, 134, 138, 156, 321, 323, and 517.]

*Brown v. Board of Education of Topeka, Kansas (Brown II)* (1955) One year after *Brown*, the Court issued a mandate for state and local school boards to proceed "with all deliberate speed" to desegregate schools. [See also page 131.]

*Buckley v. American Constitutional Law Foundation* (1999) The Court ruled that Colorado's restrictions on the initiative-petition process was unconstitutional as an infringement of the First Amendment right to free speech. [See also page 126.]

*Buckley v. Valeo* (1976) The Supreme Court limited congressional attempts to regulate campaign financing by declaring unconstitutional any absolute limits on the freedom of individuals to spend their own money on campaigns. [See also pages 431 and 434.]

*Burlington Industries, Inc. v. Ellerth* (1998) The Court ruled that employers are liable for sexual harassment arising from a hostile environment unless the employers show reasonable care to prevent or correct sexual harassment and show that the sexually harassed employee failed to utilize procedures offered by the employer to remedy the grievance.

*Cable News Network v. Noriega* (1990) The doctrine of "no prior restraint" was weakened when the Supreme Court held that Cable News Network (CNN) could be restrained from broadcasting supposedly illegally obtained tapes of conversations between former Panamanian leader Manuel Noriega and his lawyer until the trial court had listened to the tapes and had determined whether such a broadcast would violate Noriega's right to a fair trial. [See also page 543.]

*Chicago, Burlington, and Quincy Railway Company v. Chicago* (1897) This case effectively overruled *Barron* by affirming that the due process clause of the Fourteenth Amendment did prohibit states from taking property for a public use without just compensation. [See also page 118.]

*Citizens to Preserve Overton Park, Inc. v. Volpe* (1971) Beginning with the Supreme Court's decision in this case, the federal courts allowed countless challenges to federal agency actions, under the National Environmental Policy Act (NEPA), brought by public interest groups asserting that the agencies had failed to consider the adverse effects of their actions upon the environment as required by NEPA. [See also page 343.]

*City of Boerne v. Flores* (1997) In this decision the Court supported a Texas federal district court's ruling that the Religious Freedom Restoration Act of 1993 is unconstitutional as a violation of the separation of powers. [See also pages 81 and 104.]

*The Civil Rights Cases* (1883) The Court struck down the Civil Rights Act of 1875, which attempted to protect blacks from discriminatory treatment by proprietors of public facilities. It ruled that the Fourteenth Amendment applied only to discriminatory actions by state officials and did not apply to discrimination against blacks by private individuals. [See also page 117.]

*Clinton v. City of New York* (1998) The Court struck down the Line-Item Veto Act of 1996, ruling that the line-item veto power violated Article I of the Constitution. [See also pages 195 and 334.]

*Clinton v. Jones* (1997) The Court unanimously rejected President Clinton's claim of immunity from a civil suit while in office. [See also pages 104 and 334.]

*Colegrove v. Green* (1946) Despite evidence that the state of Illinois had not redrawn electoral district lines since 1901, the Court upheld that reapportionment was not a justiciable issue but must be decided by state legislatures and Congress. [See page 323.]

*Colorado Republican Federal Campaign Committee v. (Jones) FEC* (1996) The Court held that the Federal Election Campaign Act of 1971 does not violate First Amendment rights by imposing spending limits on independent campaign expenditures by political parties. [See also pages 455 and 525.]

*Cooper v. Aaron* (1958) In this historic case, the Supreme Court required that Little Rock, Arkansas, desegregate its public schools by immediately complying with a lower court's order, and warned that it is "emphatically the province and duty of the judicial department to say what the law is." [See also page 134.]

*Craig v. Boren* (1976) In this decision, the Court made it easier for plaintiffs to file and win suits on the basis of gender discrimination. [See also page 139.]

*Doe v. Bolton* (1973) Decided along with Roe, this case extended the decision in *Roe* by striking down state requirements that abortions be performed in licensed hospitals; that abortions be approved beforehand by a hospital committee; and that two physicians concur in the abortion decision. [See also page 118.]

*Dolan v. City of Tigard* (1994) This case overturned an Oregon building permit law that required a portion of property being developed to be set aside for public use. The Court established stricter guidelines to be followed in order for state and local governments to avoid violating the Fifth Amendment by taking property "without just compensation." [See also page 125.]

*Dred Scott v. Sandford* (1857) The Court ruled against Scott, who was trying to establish that he was a free man because he lived for a time in free territory in the North, holding that he had no standing to sue because he was not and could not be a citizen since he was a Negro and a slave. The Court went on to declare the anti-slavery provision of the Missouri Compromise of 1820 unconstitutional. [See also pages 68, 110, and 308.]

*Duke Power Co. v. Carolina Environmental Study Group* (1978) The Supreme Court dealt anti-nuclear power activists a significant blow by upholding a federal statute limiting liability for damages accruing from accidents at nuclear power plants. [See also pages 517 and 518.]

*Duncan v. Louisiana* (1968) The Court established the right to trial by jury in state criminal cases where the accused faces a serious charge and sentencing. [See also page 120.]

*Eisenstadt v. Baird* (1972) The Court struck down state laws prohibiting the use of contraceptives by unmarried persons. [See also pages 121 and 516.]

*Engel v. Vitale* (1962) In interpreting the separation of church and state doctrine, the Court ruled that organized prayer in the public schools was unconstitutional. [See also pages 123 and 323.]

*Escobedo v. Illinois* (1964) The Supreme Court expanded the rights of the accused in this case by giving suspects the right to remain silent and the right to have counsel present during questioning. [See also page 323.]

***Faragher v. City of Boca Raton* (1998)** As in *Burlington*, the Court ruled that employers are liable for sexual harassment arising from a hostile environment unless the employers show reasonable care to prevent or correct sexual harassment and show that the sexually harassed employee failed to utilize procedures offered by the employer to remedy the grievance. The Court also held that even if the employee did not suffer the loss of promotion or employment, the employer is liable if the sexual harassment was severe or pervasive.

***Felker v. Turpin* (1996)** The Court unanimously upheld provisions of the Anti-Terrorism and Effective Death Penalty Act of 1996, which imposes tight time limits on appeals and restrictions on federal courts' review of death sentences, among other things. [See also page 124.]

***Flast v. Cohen* (1968)** The Court ruled that a taxpayer has standing to file suit in federal court if alleging that Congress has breached restrictions placed on its taxing and spending powers by the Constitution. [See also page 309.]

***Freeman v. Pitts* (1992)** The Court unanimously overruled a decision of a court of appeals regarding judicial supervision of a school district's desegregation efforts. The Court held that federal courts have the authority to end their supervision and control of school districts in stages, even if full compliance has not been reached in every area of operations. [See also page 138.]

***Frontiero v. Richardson* (1973)** The Court rendered an important decision relating to the economic status of women when it held that the armed services could not deny married women fringe benefits, such as housing allowances and health care, that were automatically granted to married men. [See also page 139.]

***Garcia v. San Antonio Metropolitan Transit Authority* (1985)** The question of whether the national government had the right to regulate state and local businesses was again raised in this case. The Court ruled that the national government had the right to apply minimum-wage and overtime standards to state and local government employees. This case overturned *National League of Cities v. Usery* (1976). [See also page 238.]

***Gibbons v. Ogden* (1824)** An early, major case establishing the supremacy of the national government in all matters affecting interstate commerce, in which John Marshall broadly defined what Article I, Section 8, meant by "commerce among the several states." He affirmed that the federal government alone could regulate trade, travel, and navigation between the states. [See also pages 76–78 and 579.]

***Gideon v. Wainwright* (1963)** The Warren Court overruled an earlier case (*Betts* [1942]) and established that "any person haled into court, who is too poor to hire a lawyer, cannot be assured a fair trial unless counsel is provided for him." [See also pages 121, 322, and 323.]

***Gitlow v. New York* (1925)** The Court ruled that the freedom of speech is "among the fundamental personal rights and 'liberties' protected by the due process clause of the Fourteenth Amendment from impairment by the states." [See also page 119.]

***Goldberg v. Kelly* (1970)** The Court ruled that recipients of Aid to Families with Dependent Children were entitled to a trial-type hearing prior to the termination of their benefits. [See also page 624.]

***Griffin v. Prince Edward County School Board* (1964)** The Supreme Court forced all the schools in Prince Edward County, Virginia, to reopen after they had been closed for five years to avoid desegregation. [See also page 134.]

***Griggs v. Duke Power Company* (1971)** The Court held that although the statistical evidence did not prove intentional discrimination, and although an employer's hiring requirements were race-neutral in appearance, their effects were sufficient to shift the burden of justification to the employer to show that the requirements were a "business necessity" that bore "a demonstrable relationship to successful performance." [See also pages 139 and 147.]

*Griswold v. Connecticut* (1965) The Court ruled that the right to privacy included the right to marital privacy and struck down state laws restricting married persons' use of contraceptives and the circulation of birth control information. [See also pages 121, 321, and 516.]

*Hague v. Committee for Industrial Organization (CIO)* (1939) The Court extended the concept of a public forum to include public streets and meeting halls and incorporated the freedom of assembly into the list of rights held to be fundamental and therefore binding on the states as well as on the national government. [See also page 118.]

*Heart of Atlanta Motel v. United States* (1964) With this ruling, the Court upheld the Civil Rights Act of 1964, which banned racial discrimination or segregation in public accommodations. [See also page 79.]

*Hicklin v. Orbeck* (1978) The Court overturned the "Alaska Hire" statute, which had stipulated that oil and gas companies with leases from the state of Alaska were required to hire qualified residents of Alaska over nonresidents. The Court held that the Alaska statute violated the "privileges and immunitites" clause of the Constitution. [See also page 86.]

*Hodgson v. Minnesota* (1990) In this case the Supreme Court upheld a Minnesota statute requiring parental notification before an abortion could be performed on a woman under the age of eighteen. [See also page 329.]

*Hopwood v. State of Texas* (1996) The federal court of appeals decision—which applied only in Texas, Louisiana, and Mississippi—ruled that race could never be considered in granting admissions and scholarships at state colleges and universities. [See also pages 148–49 and 150.]

*Humphrey's Executor v. United States* (1935) The Court in this case made a distinction between "purely executive" officials—whom the president could remove at his discretion—and officials with "quasi-judicial and quasi-legislative" duties—who could be removed only for reasons specified by Congress. This decision limited the president's removal powers. [See also page 225.]

*Hustler Magazine v. Falwell* (1988) The Court ruled that televangelist Jerry Falwell was not libelled by a cartoon parody of him, which appeared in *Hustler*, and thus could not recover damages for emotional distress. This 9-to-0 vote was an indication of the Court's broad interpretation of freedom of speech. [See also page 140.]

*Immigration and Naturalization Service (INS) v. Chadha* (1983) This was the first of two cases since 1937 in which the Court invalidated an act of Congress on constitutional grounds. In this case the Court declared the legislative veto unconstitutional. [See also pages 103 amd 303.]

*In re Agent Orange Product Liability Litigation* (1983) In this case, a federal judge in New York certified Vietnam War veterans as a class with standing to sue a manufacturer of herbicides for damages allegedly incurred from exposure to the defendants' product while they were in Vietnam. [See also page 343.]

*In re Neagle* (1890) The Supreme Court held that the protection of a federal judge was a reasonable extension of the president's constitutional power to "take care that the laws be faithfully executed." [See also page 221.]

*In re Oliver* (1948) The Court incorporated the right to a public trial in the Fourteenth Amendment as a restriction on the states. [See also page 120.]

*Jacobellis v. Ohio* (1964) This case is famous for Justice Stewart's quip about how to determine if a form of speech is pornographic: "I know it when I see it." [See also page 141.]

*Katzenbach v. McClung* (1964) The Court gave an extremely broad definition to "interstate commerce" so as to allow Congress the constitutional authority to cover discrimination by virtually any local employer. Although the Court agreed that this case involved a strictly intrastate restaurant, they found a sufficient connection to interstate commerce resulting from the restaurant's acquisition of food and supplies so as to hold that racial discrimination at such an establishment would "impose commercial burdens of national magnitude upon interstate commerce." [See also pages 79 and 138.]

*Korematsu v. United States* (1944) The Court held that it was not unconstitutional to impose legal restrictions on a single racial group, in this case wartime measures prohibiting persons of Japanese ancestry from living in certain areas. [See also page 308.]

*Lochner v. New York* (1905) Seeking to protect business from government regulation, the Court invalidated a New York state law regulating the sanitary conditions and hours of labor of bakers on the grounds that the law interfered with liberty of contract. [See also page 79.]

*Loving v. Virginia* (1967) The Court invalidated a Virginia statute prohibiting interracial marriages, on the grounds that the statute violated guarantees of due process and equal protection contained in the Fourteenth Amendment of the Constitution. [See also page 321.]

*Lucas v. South Carolina Coastal Council* (1992) The Court remanded this case to the state courts to determine whether the owner of a beachfront property had suffered economic loss by a zoning restriction aimed at preserving the beach and sand dunes. The Court's ruling recognized that a property owner is entitled to just compensation when a government's regulations diminish the value of private property, just as in an eminent domain proceeding. [See also page 330.]

*Lujan v. Defenders of Wildlife* (1992) The Court restricted the concept of standing by requiring that a party bringing suit against a government policy show that the policy is likely to cause them direct and imminent injury. [See also pages 346–47 and 518.]

*McCleskey v. Zant* (1991) This ruling redefined the "abuse of writ" doctrine, thereby limiting the number of writs of *habeas corpus* appeals a death-row inmate can make. [See also page 124.]

*McCulloch v. Maryland* (1819) This was the first and most important case favoring national control of the economy over state control. In his ruling, John Marshall established the "implied powers" doctrine enabling Congress to use the "necessary and proper" clause of Article I, Section 8, to interpret its delegated powers. This case also concluded that, when state law and federal law were in conflict, national law took precedence. [See also pages 71, 76, and 78.]

*Mack v. United States* (1997) Filed with *Printz v. United States.*

*Madsen v. Women's Health Center* (1994) The Court upheld the decision of a Florida judge to enjoin (issue an order prohibiting) peaceful picketing by protesters outside abortion clinics, ruling that such injunctions do not necessarily constitute "prior restraint" in violation of the First Amendment. [See also page 123.]

*Malloy v. Hogan* (1964) The Court ruled that the right of a person to remain silent and avoid self-incrimination applied to the states as well as to the federal government. This decision incorporated the Fifth Amendment into the Fourteenth Amendment. [See also page 118.]

*Mapp v. Ohio* (1961) The Court held that evidence obtained in violation of the Fourth Amendment ban on unreasonable searches and seizures would be excluded from trial. [See also page 121.]

*Marbury v. Madison* (1803) This was the landmark case in which Chief Justice Marshall established that the Court had the right to rule on the constitutionality of federal and state laws, although judicial review was not explicity granted by the Constitution. [See also pages 64, 103, 319, 320, and 347.]

*Martin v. Hunter's Lessee* (1816) In this case, the Supreme Court confirmed its congressionally conferred power to review and reverse state constitutions and laws whenever they are clearly in conflict with the U.S. Constitution, federal laws, or treaties. [See also page 320.]

*Martin v. Wilks* (1989) The Supreme Court further eased the way for employers to prefer white males when it held that any affirmative action program already approved by federal courts could be subsequently challenged by white males who alleged that the program discriminated against them. [See also page 148.]

*Masson v. New Yorker Magazine* (1991) The Supreme Court held that a successful libel claim must prove that an allegedly libelous author and/or publisher acted with requisite knowledge of falsity or reckless disregard as to truth or falsity in publishing the allegedly libelous material. [See also pages 140 and 544.]

*Miller v. Johnson* (1995) This decision struck down a congressional redistricting plan in the state of Georgia that had purposely created black-majority electoral districts. The Court found that the creation of electoral districts solely or predominantly on the basis of race violated the equal protection rights of non-black voters in those districts. [See also pages 176, 325, and 418.]

*Milliken v. Bradley* (1974) The Supreme Court severely restricted the *Swann* ruling when it determined in this case that only cities found guilty of deliberate and *de jure* segregation (segregation in law) would have to desegregate their schools. This ruling exempted most Northern states and cities from busing because school segregation in Northern cities is generally *de facto* segregation (segregation in fact) that follows from segregated housing and other forms of private discrimination. [See also pages 135–37.]

*Miranda v. Arizona* (1966) The Warren Court ruled that anyone placed under arrest must be informed of the right to remain silent and to have counsel present during interrogation. [See also pages 121 and 323.]

*Missouri ex rel. Gaines v. Canada* (1938) Rather than question the "separate but equal" doctrine, the Court in this case ruled that Missouri had violated the equal protection clause of the Fourteenth Amendment by not providing a law school for blacks. The ruling reiterated that states must furnish "equal facilities in separate schools." [See also page 128.]

*Missouri v. Holland* (1920) The Court recognized that a treaty could enlarge federal power at the expense of the states, under the "supremacy clause" in Article VI. [See also page 128.]

*Missouri v. Jenkins* (1990) The Court upheld the authority of a federal judge to order the Kansas City, Missouri, school board to raise taxes to pay for a school plan to achieve racial integration. [See also pages 138, 325, and 334.]

*Missouri v. Jenkins* (1995) In this decision, part of an ongoing lower-court involvement in the desegregation efforts of the Kansas City, Missouri, school district, the Court found that a federal district court had exceeded its remedial powers in its efforts to eliminate the vestiges of past discrimination. While it did not overturn its previous decision in *Missouri v. Jenkins* (1990), the Court's opinion encouraged lower courts to withdraw from supervision of school districts when the requirements of the Constitution have been met. [See also page 138.]

*Moran v. McDonough* (1976) In an effort to retain jurisdiction of the case until the court's mandated school-desegregation plan had been satisfactorily implemented, District Court Judge Arthur Garrity issued fourteen decisions relating to different aspects of the Boston school plan that had been developed under his authority and put into effect under his supervision. [See also page 345.]

*Myers v. United States* (1926) The Court upheld a broad interpretation of the president's power to remove executive officers whom he had appointed, despite restrictions imposed by Congress. (Later limited by *Humphrey's* [1935].) [See also page 225.]

*NAACP v. Alabama* (1958) The Court recognized the right to "privacy in one's association" in its ruling protecting the NAACP from the state of Alabama using its membership list. [See also page 121.]

*National Labor Relations Board v. Jones & Laughlin Steel Corporation* (1937) In a case involving New Deal legislation, the Court reversed its earlier rulings on "interstate commerce" and redefined it to permit the national government to regulate local economic and social conditions. [See also pages 72, 79, 120, and 237–38.]

*National League of Cities v. Usery* (1976) Although in this case the Court invalidated a congressional act applying wage and hour regulations to state and local governments, it reversed its decision nine years later in *Garcia v. San Antonio Metropolitan Transit Authority* (1985). [See also page 238.]

*Near v. Minnesota* (1931) In this landmark case, which established the doctrine of "no prior restraint," the Court held that, except under extraordinary circumstances, the First Amendment prohibits government agencies from seeking to prevent newspapers or magazines from printing whatever they wish. [See also pages 119 and 543.]

*New State Ice Co. v. Liebmann* (1932) This case is most notable for Justice Brandeis's dictum that "one of the happy incidents of the federal system is that a single courageous state may, if its citizens choose, serve as a laboratory of democracy." [See also page 98.]

*New York Times v. Sullivan* (1964) In this case, the Supreme Court held that to be deemed libelous, a story about a public official not only had to be untrue, but had to result from "actual malice" or "reckless disregard" for the truth. In practice, this standard of proof is nearly impossible to reach. [See also pages 140 and 543.]

*New York Times v. United States* (1971) In this case, the so-called *Pentagon Papers* case, the Supreme Court ruled that the government could not block publication of secret Defense Department documents that had been furnished to the *New York Times* by a liberal opponent of the Vietnam War who had obtained the documents illegally. [See also page 543.]

*Office of the President v. Office of Independent Counsel* (1998) The Court denied President Clinton's petition claiming that conversations with his lawyers were subject to executive privelege and thus were not admissible as evidence in the independent counsel's investigation of the president.

*Ohio v. Akron Center for Reproductive Health* (1990) The Supreme Court upheld a state law requiring parental notification before an abortion could be performed on a woman under the age of eighteen. [See also page 329.]

*Oncale v. Sundowner Offshore Services* (1998) The Court ruled unanimously that sexual harassment laws apply to same-sex harassment.

*Palko v. Connecticut* (1937) The Court decided that double jeopardy was not a provision of the Bill of Rights protected at the state level. This was not reversed until 1969 in *Benton v. Maryland.* [See also pages 119, 120, and 121.]

*Panama Refining Company v. Ryan* (1935) The Court ruled against a section of the National Industrial Recovery Act, a New Deal statute, as being an invalid delegation of legislative power to the executive branch. [See also pages 103 and 239.]

*Penry v. Lynaugh* (1989) In this case the Supreme Court eased restrictions on the use of capital punishment by allowing states to execute mentally retarded murderers. [See also page 329.]

*Planned Parenthood of Southeastern Pennsylvania v. Casey* (1992) Abandoning *Roe*'s assertion of a woman's "fundamental right" to choose abortion, a bare majority of the Court redefined it as a "limited or qualified" right subject to regulation by the states, so long as the states do not impose an "undue burden" on women. Specifically, the Court upheld portions of Pennsylvania's strict abortion law that included the requirement of parental notification for minors and a twenty-four-hour waiting period. [See also pages 125 and 331.]

*Plessy v. Ferguson* (1896) The Court, in this famous case, held that the Fourteenth Amendment's "equal protection of the laws" was not violated by racial distinction as long as the "separate" facilities were "equal." [See also pages 120, 127–28, 129, 130, and 132.]

*Plyler v. Doe* (1982) The Supreme Court invalidated on equal-protection grounds a Texas statute that withheld state funds from local school districts for the education of children who were illegal aliens and that further authorized the local school districts to deny enrollment to such children. [See also page 340.]

*Pollock v. Farmers' Loan and Trust Company* (1895) In this case involving the unconstitutionality of an income tax of 2 percent on all incomes over $4,000, the Supreme Court declared that any direct tax as such must be apportioned in order to be valid. [See also page 593.]

*Printz v. United States* (1997) With this ruling, the Court struck down the provision of the Brady Handgun Violence Prevention Act of 1993 that required state and local law enforcement officials to run background checks on gun purchasers. The Court found that it was unconstitutional for Congress to require state and local officials to enforce a federal law. [See also pages 80 and 104.]

*Red Lion Broadcasting Co. v. FCC* (1969) In upholding the fairness doctrine in this case, the Court differentiated between the broadcast media and the print media with regard to the First Amendment. The Court ruled that "a license permits broadcasting, but the licensee has no constitutional right to be the one who holds the license or to monopolize a radio frequency to the exclusion of his fellow citizens." [See also page 542.]

*Regents of the University of California v. Bakke* (1978) This case addressed the issue of qualification versus minority preference. The Court held that universities could continue to take minority status into consideration because a "diverse student body" contributing to a "robust exchange of ideas" is a "constitutionally permissible goal" on which a race-conscious university admissions program may be predicated. [See also pages 145–47 and 148.]

*Reno v. A.C.L.U.* (1997) With this ruling, the Court repealed parts of the Communications Decency Act of 1996, extending First Amendment free speech principles to the internet. [See also page 126.]

*Roe v. Wade* (1973) This is the famous case that rendered unconstitutional all state laws making abortion a crime, ruling that the states could not interfere in a woman's "right to privacy" and her right to choose to terminate a pregnancy. [See also pages 122, 125, 126, 325, 329, 332, and 516–17.]

*Romer v. Evans* (1996) The Court upheld the ruling of the Colorado State Supreme Court, which invalidated an amendment to the Colorado state constitution that forbid the enactment of ordinances outlawing discrimination against homosexuals. [See also page 144.]

*Rosenberger v. University of Virginia* (1995) This case was brought by a group of students who published a Christian newspaper but who were refused funding for their publication by the University of Virginia's Student Activities Fund. The university argued that it excludes funding for religious activities because such funding would violate the principle of separation between church and state. A bare majority of the Court found that the university's policy violated the First Amendment guarantees of free speech and religious exercise and was not in itself a violation of the First Amendment's establishment clause. [See also pages 125 and 325.]

*Roth v. United States* (1957) An important obscenity case where a constitutional test for obscenity was proposed: "whether to the average person, applying contemporary community standards, the dominant theme of the material taken as a whole appeals to the prurient interests." [See also page 140.]

*Rubin v. United States* (1998) The Court denied a petition claiming that presidential conversations or actions overheard or witnessed by Secret Service agents were subject to executive privelege. [See also page 334.]

*Rust v. Sullivan* (1991) In this case, the Court upheld regulations of the Department of Health and Human Services that prohibited the use of Title X family planning funds for abortion counseling, referral, or activities advocating abortion as a method of family planning. [See also pages 329 and 330.]

*St. Mary's Honor Center v. Hicks* (1993) Hicks accused his former employer (St. Mary's Honor Center) of discharging him for racially motivated reasons, but ultimately failed to prove, as the law requires in such cases, that the adverse actions were racially motivated. A court of appeals then held that Hicks was entitled to judgment as a matter of law because he was able to prove that all of St. Mary's proffered reasons for firing him were pretextual. The Supreme Court reversed the decision, arguing that a court may not so rule in favor of judgment for the plaintiff just because it has rejected the employer's explanation of its actions. [See also page 148.]

*Schechter Poultry Co. v. United States* (1935) The Court declared the National Industrial Recovery Act of 1933 unconstitutional on the grounds that Congress had delegated legislative power to the executive branch without sufficient standards or guidelines for presidential discretion. [See also pages 103 and 239.]

*Seminole Tribe of Florida v. Florida* (1996) This decision repealed a provision of the Indian Gaming Regulatory Act of 1988 that authorized Native American nations to bring suit in federal court against a state that does not in good faith negotiate a compact allowing the nation to conduct certain gaming activities. The Court found that this provision of the Act infringed on the states' sovereign immunity. [See also page 80.]

*Shaw v. Hunt* (1996) The Court reversed the ruling of the federal district court in North Carolina, finding that the creation of a majority black electoral district in the state was unconstitutional. Race was the primary factor considered in creating the district, which was not acceptable in this case under a proper reading of the Voting Rights Act. [See also page 418.]

*Shaw v. Reno* (1993) The Court ruled that a North Carolina congressional district was so irregular in its shape and clearly drawn to ensure the election of a minority representative that it violated the Fourteenth Amendment rights of white voters. [See also pages 330 and 418.]

*Shelley v. Kraemer* (1948) In this case, the Supreme Court ruled against the widespread practice of "restrictive covenants," declaring that although private persons could sign such covenants, they could not be judicially enforced, since the Fourteenth Amendment prohibits any organ of the state, including the courts, from denying equal protection of its laws. [See also pages 128, 129, and 322.]

*Shuttlesworth v. Birmingham Board of Education* (1958) This decision upheld a "pupil placement" plan purporting to assign pupils on various bases, with no mention of race. This case interpreted *Brown v. Board of Education* to mean that school districts must stop explicit racial discrimination but were under no obligation to take positive steps to desegregate. [See also page 134.]

*The Slaughter-House Cases* (1873) The Court ruled that the federal government was under no obligation to protect the "privileges and immunities" of citizens of a particular state against arbitrary action by that state's government. This was similar to the *Barron* case, except it was thought that the Fourteenth Amendment would now incorporate the Bill of Rights, applying it to the states. The Court, however, ruled that the Fourteenth Amendment was meant to "protect Negroes as a class" and had nothing to do with individual liberties. [See also page 117.]

*Smith v. Allwright* (1944) The Supreme Court struck down the Southern practice of "white primaries," which legally excluded blacks from participation in the nominating process. The Court recognized that primaries could no longer be regarded as the private affairs of parties because parties were an integral aspect of the electoral process, and thus became an "agency of the State" prohibited from discriminating against blacks within the meaning of the Fifteenth Amendment. [See also pages 129, 335, and 472.]

*Stanford v. Kentucky* (1989) The Supreme Court again eased restrictions on capital punishment by allowing states to execute murderers who were as young as sixteen at the time of the crime. [See also page 329.]

*Steel Seizure Case* See *Youngstown Sheet and Tube Co. v. Sawyer.*

*Steward Machine Co. v. Davis* (1937) A case, resulting from New Deal legislation, in which the Court upheld the Social Security Act of 1935. [See also page 79.]

*Swann v. Charlotte-Mecklenberg Board of Education* (1971) This case involved the most important judicial extension of civil rights in education after 1954. The Court held that state-imposed desegregation could be brought about by "busing," and under certain limited circumstances even racial quotas could be used as the "starting point in shaping a remedy to correct past constitutional violations." [See also pages 135–37.]

*Sweatt v. Painter* (1950) The Court ruled in favor of a black student who refused to go to the Texas law school for blacks, arguing that it was inferior to the state school for whites. Although the Court still did not confront the "separate but equal" rule in this case, it did question whether any segregated facility could be equal. [See also page 129.]

*Turner Broadcasting, Inc. v. FCC* (1994) The Court upheld the 1992 Cable Television Act's "must carry" provision, which requires cable television systems to carry some local commercial and public broadcast stations, on the grounds that the act was not a violation of the First Amendment. [See also page 543.]

*United States v. Curtiss-Wright Export Co.* (1936) In this case the Court held that Congress may delegate a degree of discretion to the president in foreign affairs that might violate the separation of powers if it were in a domestic arena. [See also page 223.]

*United States v. Darby Lumber Company* (1941) This case upheld the constitutionality of the Fair Labor Standards Act of 1938, which made it unlawful to ship interstate commerce goods produced in violation of employment standards set by the law. [See also page 80.]

*United States v. Lopez* (1995) In this 5-to-4 decision, the Court struck down a federal law banning the possession of a gun near a school. This was the first limitation in almost sixty years on Congress's "interstate commerce" authority. [See also pages 80, 81, and 103.]

*United States v. Nixon* (1974) The Court declared unconstitutional President Nixon's refusal to surrender subpoenaed tapes as evidence in a criminal prosecution. The Court argued that executive privilege did not extend to data in presidential files or tapes bearing upon criminal prosecution. [See also page 104.]

*United States v. Pink* (1942) The Court ruled that executive agreements have the same legal status as treaties, despite the fact that they do not require the "advice and consent" of the Senate. [See also pages 205 and 223.]

*United Steelworkers v. Weber* (1979) In rejecting the claim of a white employee who had been denied a place in a training program in which half the spots were reserved for black employees, the Supreme Court claimed that Title VII of the Civil Rights Act of 1964 did not apply to affirmative action programs voluntarily established by private companies. [See also page 147.]

*Wabash, St. Louis and Pacific Railway Company v. Illinois* (1886) The Supreme Court struck down a state law prohibiting rate discrimination by a railroad, arguing that the route of an interstate railroad could not be subdivided into its separate state segments for purposes of regulation. In response to the need for some form of regulation, Congress passed the Interstate Commerce Act of 1887, creating the Interstate Commerce Commission (ICC), the first federal administrative agency. [See also pages 78 and 579.]

*Wards Cove Packing, Inc. v. Atonio* (1989) The Court held that the burden of proof of unlawful discrimination should be shifted from the defendant (the employer) to the plaintiff (the person claiming to be the victim of discrimination). [See also pages 147, 148, and 329.]

*Webster v. Reproductive Health Services* (1989) In upholding a Missouri law that restricted the use of public medical facilities for abortion, the Court opened the way for states to again limit the availability of abortions. [See also pages 125, 329, and 517.]

*Wickard v. Filburn* (1942) In this case, the Supreme Court established the "cumulative effect" principle. The Court held that Congress could control a farmer's production of wheat for home consumption because the cumulative effect of home consumption of wheat by many farmers might reasonably be thought to alter the supply-and-demand relationships of the interstate commodity market. [See also page 239.]

*Wiener v. United States* (1958) Pursuant to *Humphrey's Executor*, the Court ruled that the president did not have unrestrained power to remove an executive official from office. [See also page 225.]

*Worcester v. Georgia* (1832) The Court ruled that states could not pass laws affecting federally recognized Indian nations, and therefore, Georgia had no right to trespass on Cherokee lands without their assent. To which President Andrew Jackson is reported to have replied, "John Marshall has made his decision, now let him enforce it." [See also page 341.]

*Youngstown Sheet and Tube Co. v. Sawyer* (1952) This case is also known as the *Steel Seizure* case. During the Korean War, when the United Steelworkers threatened to go on strike, President Truman seized the mills and placed them under military operation. He argued he had inherent power to prevent a strike that would interfere with the war. The Court ruled against him, however, saying that presidential powers must be authorized by statute and did not come from anything inherent in the presidency. [See also page 104.]

# Acknowledgments


## Chapter 1

**Page 3** New York City Police Department Photo Unit; **page 20** Corbis/Keren Su; **page 21** © Rob Nelson/Black Star/PNI.

## Chapter 2

**Page 27** Corbis-Bettmann; **page 50** AP/Wide World Photos; **pages 51** AP/Wide World Photos.

## Chapter 3

**Page 67** Architect of the Capitol; **page 82** AP/Wide World Photos; **page 83** AP/Wide World Photos.

## Chapter 4

**Page 109** © 1985 Flip Schulke/Black Star; **page 142** AP/Wide World Photos; **page 143** AP/Wide World Photos.

## Chapter 5

**Page 161** Courtesy of U.S. Capitol Historical Society; **page 208** AP/Wide World Photos; **page 209** AP/Wide World Photos.

## Chapter 6

**Page 215** AP/Wide World Photos; **page 248** AP/Wide World Photos; **page 249** AP/Wide World Photos.

## Chapter 7

**Page 263** AP/Wide World Photos; **pages 290** AP/Wide World Photos; **page 291** AP/Wide World Photos.

## Chapter 8

**Page 307** Collection of the Supreme Court of the United States; **page 314** AP/Wide World Photos; **page 315** AP/Wide World Photos.

## Chapter 9

**Page 353** Mark Antman, Image Works; **page 364** AP/Wide World Photos; **page 365** AP/Wide World Photos.

## Chapter 10

**Page 399** Corbis/Robert Maass; **page 432** AP/Wide World Photos; **page 433** AP/Wide World Photos.

## Chapter 11

**Page 447** AP/Wide World Photos; **page 484** AP/Wide World Photos; **page 485** AP/Wide World Photos.

## Chapter 12

**Page 491** Corbis-Bettmann; **page 508** AP/Wide World Photos; **page 509** AP/Wide World Photos.

## Chapter 13

**Page 531** AP/Wide World Photos; **page 540** The Warder Collection; **page 541** AP/Wide World Photos.

## Chapter 14

**Page 567** Paul Hosefros/NYT Pictures; **page 586** AP/Wide World Photos; **page 587** AP/Wide World Photos.

## Chapter 15

**Page 613** Corbis-Bettmann; **page 634** AP/Wide World Photos; **page 635** AP/Wide World Photos.

## Chapter 16

**Page 649** Joseph Sohm/Chromo Sohm Inc./Corbis; **page 670** AP/Wide World Photos; **page 671** AP/Wide World Photos.

## Chapter 17

**Page 691** © Smithsonian Institution; **page 720** AP/Wide World Photos; **page 721** © Charles E. Rotkin/Corbis.

# INDEX